PRESENTS

THE COMPLETE BOOK OF
MAJOR U.S. SHOW BUSINESS AWARDS

Garland Reference Library
of the Humanities
(Volume 572)

PRESENTS

THE COMPLETE BOOK OF
MAJOR U.S. SHOW BUSINESS AWARDS

Mike Kaplan
Editor

Garland Publishing, Inc.
New York & London
1985

Library of Congress Cataloging in Publication Data
Main entry under title:

Variety presents the complete book of major U.S. show
business awards.

(Garland reference library of the humanities;
v. 572)
Rev. ed of: Variety major U.S. showbusiness awards.
1982.
Includes index.
1. Performing arts—United States—Awards.
I. Kaplan, Mike, 1918–   . II. Daily variety.
III. Variety major U.S. showbusiness awards.
IV. Title: Complete book of major U.S. show business
awards. V. Series.
PN2270.A93V37 1985   790.2'079   84-18734
ISBN 0-8240-8919-7

Manufactured in the United States of America

CONTENTS

PREFACE

When the Pulitzer Prizes were established in 1917, under the terms of the will of newspaper publisher Joseph Pulitzer, the inclusion of an award for the best play by an American writer suddenly gave U.S. show business a new stature. A decade later, when the Academy of Motion Picture Arts and Sciences began its annual Oscar awards for achievement in films, the idea that the popular arts were worthy of serious recognition was firmly implanted.

In the intervening half century, there has been a proliferation of awards in show business, some by groups representing a particular branch of the business, others by various groups of critics, and still others by individuals and companies seeking to enhance their own prestige by attaching themselves to an honors list which would receive widespread attention.

Yet over that long period of time, only three other show business awards have achieved lasting recognition: the Tonys, which were inaugurated in 1947 to honor outstanding work in the Broadway Theatre; the Emmys, which started the following year, to salute achievements in Television; and the Grammys, first awarded in 1958, in the field of Recording.

Each, like the Oscars, is based on voting by individuals directly involved in the particular area of show business, the Emmys and Grammys by members of the respective Academies and the Tonys by a committee composed of members of the governing boards of key theatrical organizations together with persons whose names appear on the first and second night press lists for Broadway openings.

No complete compilation of all winners and nominees for all of these awards had been undertaken until the list was included in the VARIETY INTERNATIONAL SHOWBUSINESS REFERENCE (Garland Publishing, 1981), where it appeared solely for the record. This current volume—devoted solely to the awards—covers each of the five major awards and every individual category within those awards, from inception through honors, presented in December 1983.

Except for the Pulitzer Prizes, the structure of the awards sometimes leads to confusion about actual winners. It is not uncommon for someone to boast of having an award when in fact the individual was only one of many who participated in a particular award-winning achievement. Winners indicated in this volume are those who actually received a trophy.

For assistance in clearing through this confusion and pinpointing the actual winners who have been honored over the years in more than 4,000 categories, the editor is grateful to the staff of the Margaret Herrick Library of the Academy of Motion Pictures Arts and Sciences, which awards the Oscars; Claudia Rossetti of the Academy of Television Arts and Sciences and Judith Feinstein and Trudy Wilson of the National Academy of Television Arts and Sciences, which respectively award the Primetime and Daytime Emmys; Sid Garfield of the American Theatre Wing, bestower of the Antoinette Perry "Tony®" Award; and Shelly Wright of N.A.R.A.S.® The Grammy® portion of this publication was printed by permission of the National Academy of Recording Arts and Sciences®.

Mike Kaplan
Editor

NOTE TO USERS

This compilation covers the five major U.S. show business awards—Oscars, Emmys, Tonys, Grammys, and Pulitzer Prize Plays. A separate section is devoted to each of these awards. Except for Pulitzer Prize Plays, which has no subdivisions, categories within each of the awards are listed in chronological order from inception through December 31, 1983. All winners are listed in bold-face type.

A fully alphabetized master index lists all winners and nominees, both individuals and titles, for all of the awards. To facilitate locating individual achievements, index numbers have been assigned to each category within an individual award. The numbers are preceded by an alphabetic designation: O for Oscar Awards; E for Emmy Awards; T for Tony Awards; G for Grammy Awards; and P for Pulitzer Prize Plays. The Pulitzer numbers indicate the year of the award.

Thus, the first entry under the Oscar text, for example, is

1927/28
BEST PICTURE (O–01).

This number is automatically applied to the nominees within the category and will be found next to their alphabetic listing in the index.

Nominations in the various award branches have been merged in the alphabetic index. The listing for Julie Harris, for example, immediately provides the index numbers to all of her Oscar, Emmy, Tony, and Grammy nominations.

In looking up individual nominations in the index, it should be noted that they follow the credit used by the individual for the particular nominated achievement. These sometimes vary. The index, for example, lists both "Cummings, Bob" and "Cummings, Robert" to reflect actual billing in a specific nomination; similarly, actresses may be indexed under more than one surname, e.g., Patty Duke Astin is indexed under both Duke and Astin. The discrepancies are particularly evident in Emmy technical awards where nominees are sometimes listed by full names and sometimes by nicknames or initials.

DISTRIBUTOR CODE

These abbreviations refer to the distributor designation
of Oscar-nominated films.

AA Allied Artists

ABP Associated British Pathe

AFD Associated Film Distributing Corp.

AFT American Film Theatre

AIP American-International

ALT Altura

API API-Janus

ARK Artkino (USSR)

ART Artixo

ASR Astor

ATL Atlantic

ATO Athos

AVE Avco Embassy

BCP Bing Crosby Productions

BEC Beckman Film Corp.

BOR Borde

BRA Brandon

BV Buena Vista

BYN Burstyn

C5 Cinema 5

CLR Claridge

CME Commercial Pictures

COL Columbia

CON Continental

CRC Cinerama Releasing Corp.

CUE Commonwealth United

CVC Cavalcade

DCA Distributors Corp. of America

DNY Disney

DRH De Rochemont

EAG Eagle-Lion

EBP Embassy Pictures

EDH Edward Harrison

EDU Educational

ELC Eagle-Lion Classics

EX Excelsior

FA Favorite

FIZ Films, Inc.

FN First National

FOX 20th Century-Fox

FRP Film Representations, Inc.

GAU Gaumont

GBD GBD Films

GN Grand National (U.S.)

GOL Goldstone Film Enterprises

HD Harrison and Davidson

IFE Italian Film Export

INT Interwest

JAN Janus

KGU Kingsley-Union

KGY Kingsley International Pictures

KYM Kingsley-MJP Enterprises

LIO Lion International

LIP Lippert

LOP Lopert

MAB Mayer-Burstyn

MAK Mayer-Kingsley

MAN Manson

MGM Metro-Goldwyn-Mayer

MKD Mayer-Kingsley-Distinguished

MNA Magna

MNG Monogram

MNV Minerva

MOT March of Time

NFC National Film Board (Canada)

NGP National General Pictures

NTH Northal Film Distributors

NW New World Pictures

PAR Paramount

PC Pathe Contemporary

PRA Praesens (Switzerland)

PRC Producers Releasing Corp.

PRE Premier

PRM Prominent

RBF Rembrandt-Film Representations

REP Republic

RGY Regency

RIZ Rizzoli (Italy)

RKO RKO

RNK Rank

RYI Royal Films Int'l (France)

SCH Schoenfeld

SEN Seneca International

SRO Selznick Releasing Org.

SZI Selznick International

TIM Times

TL Trans-Lux

U Universal

UA United Artists

UI Universal-International

UMP United Motion Picture Org.

UPA United Productions of America

VAU Vaudeo

WB Warner Bros.

WBO Warner Bros.-Orion

WBS Warner Bros.-Seven Arts

WRC Walter Reade-Continental

WSC Walter Reade-Sterling-Continental

ZEN Zenith

OSCARS

1927/28

BEST PICTURE (O-01)
WINGS, PAR.
THE LAST COMMAND, PAR.
THE RACKET, Caddo, PAR.
SEVENTH HEAVEN, FOX.
THE WAY OF ALL FLESH, PAR.

ACTOR (O-02)
EMIL JANNINGS, The Last Command.
EMIL JANNINGS, The Way Of All Flesh.
RICHARD BARTHELMESS, *The Noose,* FN.
RICHARD BARTHELMESS, *The Patent Leather Kid,* FN.
CHARLES CHAPLIN, *The Circus,* Chaplin, UA.

ACTRESS (O-03)
JANET GAYNOR, Seventh Heaven.
JANET GAYNOR, Street Angel, FOX.
JANET GAYNOR, Sunrise, FOX.
LOUISE DRESSER, *A Ship Comes In,* Pathe-RKO.
GLORIA SWANSON, *Sadie Thompson,* UA.

DIRECTING (O-04)
FRANK BORZAGE, Seventh Heaven.
HERBERT BRENON, *Sorrell And Son,* UA.
KING VIDOR, *The Crowd,* MGM.
(COMEDY Direction)
LEWIS MILESTONE, Two Arabian Knights, UA.
CHARLES CHAPLIN, *The Circus.*
TED WILDE, *Speedy,* PAR.

WRITING (O-05)
(Adaptation)
SEVENTH HEAVEN. Benjamin Glazer.
GLORIOUS BETSY, WB. Anthony Coldeway.
THE JAZZ SINGER, WB. Alfred Cohn.
(Original Story)
UNDERWORLD, PAR. Ben Hecht.
THE LAST COMMAND, PAR. Lajos Biro.
THE PATENT LEATHER KID. Rupert Hughes.
(Title Writing)
THE FAIR CO-ED, MGM. Joseph Farnham.
LAUGH, CLOWN, LAUGH, MGM. Joseph Farnham.
TELLING THE WORLD, MGM. Joseph Farnham.
THE PRIVATE LIFE OF HELEN OF TROY, FN. Gerald Duffy.
OH KAY!, FN. George Marion, Jr.
(Award discontinued after this year.)

CINEMATOGRAPHY (O-06)
SUNRISE. Charles Rosher and Karl Struss.
DEVIL DANCER, UA. George Barnes.
DRUMS OF LOVE, UA. Karl Struss.
MAGIC FLAME, UA. George Barnes.
MY BEST GIRL, Pickford, UA. Charles Rosher.
SADIE THOMPSON. George Barnes.
THE TEMPEST, UA. Charles Rosher.

ART DIRECTION - SET DECORATION (O-07)
THE DOVE, UA. William Cameron Menzies.
THE TEMPEST. William Cameron Menzies.
SEVENTH HEAVEN. Harry Oliver.
SUNRISE. Rochus Gliese.

HONORARY AND OTHER (O-08)
(Other)

WB for producing The Jazz Singer, the pioneer outstanding talking picture, which has revolutionized the industry.
CHARLES CHAPLIN for versatility and genius in writing, acting, directing and producing The Circus.

ARTISTIC QUALITY OF PRODUCTION (O-09)
SUNRISE.
CHANG, PAR.
THE CROWD.
(Award discontinued after this year.)

ENGINEERING EFFECTS (O-10)
WINGS. Roy Pomeroy.
THE JAZZ SINGER. Nugent Slaughter.
THE PRIVATE LIFE OF HELEN OF TROY. Ralph Hammeras.
(Award discontinued after this year.)

1928/29

BEST PICTURE (O-11)
BROADWAY MELODY, MGM.
ALIBI, Feature Prod., UA.
HOLLYWOOD REVUE, MGM.
IN OLD ARIZONA, FOX.
THE PATRIOT, PAR.

ACTOR (O-12)
WARNER BAXTER, In Old Arizona.
GEORGE BANCROFT, *Thunderbolt,* PAR.
CHESTER MORRIS, *Alibi.*
PAUL MUNI, *The Valiant,* FOX.
LEWIS STONE, *The Patriot.*

ACTRESS (O-13)
MARY PICKFORD, Coquette, Pickford, UA.
RUTH CHATTERTON, *Madame X,* MGM.
BETTY COMPSON, *The Barker,* FN.
JEANNE EAGELS, *The Letter,* PAR.
BESSIE LOVE, *Broadway Melody.*

DIRECTING (O-14)
FRANK LLOYD, The Divine Lady, FN.
LIONEL BARRYMORE, *Madame X.*
HARRY BEAUMONT, *Broadway Melody.*
IRVING CUMMINGS, *In Old Arizona.*
FRANK LLOYD, *Weary River,* FN.
FRANK LLOYD, *Drag,* FN.
ERNST LUBITSCH, *The Patriot.*

WRITING (O-15)
(Achievement)
THE PATRIOT. Hans Kraly.
IN OLD ARIZONA. Tom Barry.
THE LEATHERNECK, Pathe, Elliott Clawson.
OUR DANCING DAUGHTERS, MGM. Josephine Lovett.
THE VALIANT. Tom Barry.
WONDER OF WOMEN, MGM. Bess Meredyth.

CINEMATOGRAPHY (O-16)
WHITE SHADOWS IN THE SOUTH SEAS, MGM. Clyde De Vinna.
THE DIVINE LADY. John Seitz.
FOUR DEVILS, FOX. Ernest Palmer.
IN OLD ARIZONA. Arthur Edeson.
OUR DANCING DAUGHTERS. George Barnes.
STREET ANGEL, FOX. Ernest Palmer.

ART DIRECTION - SET DECORATION (O-17)

THE BRIDGE OF SAN LUIS REY, MGM. Cedric Gibbons.
DYNAMITE, Pathe. Mitchell Leisen.
HOLLYWOOD REVUE. Cedric Gibbons.
THE IRON MASK, UA. William Cameron Menzies.
THE PATRIOT. Hans Dreier.
STREET ANGEL. Harry Oliver.

1929/30

BEST PICTURE (O-18)

ALL QUIET ON THE WESTERN FRONT, U.
THE BIG HOUSE, MGM.
DISRAELI, WB.
THE DIVORCEE, MGM.
THE LOVE PARADE, PAR.

ACTOR (O-19)

GEORGE ARLISS, Disraeli.
GEORGE ARLISS, *The Green Goddess*, WB.
WALLACE BEERY, *The Big House.*
MAURICE CHEVALIER, *The Love Parade.*
MAURICE CHEVALIER, *The Big Pond*, PAR.
RONALD COLMAN, *Bulldog Drummond*, Goldwyn, UA.
RONALD COLMAN, *Condemned*, Goldwyn, UA.
LAWRENCE TIBBETT, *The Rogue Song*, MGM.

ACTRESS (O-20)

NORMA SHEARER, The Divorcee.
NANCY CARROLL, *The Devil's Holiday*, PAR.
RUTH CHATTERTON, *Sarah And Son*, PAR.
GRETA GARBO, *Anna Christie*, MGM.
GRETA GARBO, *Romance*, MGM.
NORMA SHEARER, *Their Own Desire*, MGM.
GLORIA SWANSON, *The Trespasser*, Kennedy, UA.

DIRECTING (O-21)

LEWIS MILESTONE, All Quiet On The Western Front.
CLARENCE BROWN, *Anna Christie.*
CLARENCE BROWN, *Romance.*
ROBERT LEONARD, *The Divorcee.*
ERNST LUBITSCH, *The Love Parade.*
KING VIDOR, *Hallelujah*, MGM.

WRITING (O-22)

(Achievement)
THE BIG HOUSE. Frances Marion.
ALL QUIET ON THE WESTERN FRONT. George Abbott, Maxwell Anderson and Dell Andrews.
DISRAELI. Julian Josephson.
THE DIVORCEE. John Meehan.
STREET OF CHANCE, PAR. Howard Estabrook.
(Award discontinued after this year.)

CINEMATOGRAPHY (O-23)

WITH BYRD AT THE SOUTH POLE, PAR. Joseph T. Rucker and Willard Van Der Veer.
ALL QUIET ON THE WESTERN FRONT. Arthur Edeson.
ANNA CHRISTIE. William Daniels.
HELL'S ANGELS, UA. Gaetano Gaudio and Harry Perry.
THE LOVE PARADE. Victor Milner.

ART DIRECTION - SET DECORATION (O-24)

KING OF JAZZ, U. Herman Rosse.
BULLDOG DRUMMOND. William Cameron Menzies.
THE LOVE PARADE. Hans Dreier.
SALLY, FN. Jack Okey.
THE VAGABOND KING, PAR. Hans Dreier.

SOUND (O-25)

THE BIG HOUSE. Douglas Shearer.
THE CASE OF SERGEANT GRISCHA, RKO. John Tribby.
THE LOVE PARADE. Franklin Hansen.
RAFFLES, Goldwyn, UA. Oscar Lagerstrom.
SONG OF THE FLAME, FN. George Groves.

1930/31

BEST PICTURE (O-26)

CIMARRON, RKO.
EAST LYNNE, FOX.
THE FRONT PAGE, Caddo, UA.
SKIPPY, PAR.
TRADER HORN, MGM.

ACTOR (O-27)

LIONEL BARRYMORE, A Free Soul, MGM.
JACKIE COOPER, *Skippy.*
RICHARD DIX, *Cimarron.*
FREDRIC MARCH, *The Royal Family of Broadway*, PAR.
ADOLPHE MENJOU, *The Front Page.*

ACTRESS (O-28)

MARIE DRESSLER, Min And Bill, MGM.
MARLENE DIETRICH, *Morocco*, PAR.
IRENE DUNNE, *Cimarron.*
ANN HARDING, *Holiday*, RKO Pathe.
NORMA SHEARER, *A Free Soul.*

DIRECTING (O-29)

NORMAN TAUROG, Skippy.
CLARENCE BROWN, *A Free Soul.*
LEWIS MILESTONE, *The Front Page.*
WESLEY RUGGLES, *Cimarron.*
JOSEF VON STERNBERG, *Morocco.*

WRITING (O-30)

(Adaptation)
CIMARRON. Howard Estabrook.
THE CRIMINAL CODE, COL. Seton Miller and Fred Niblo, Jr.
HOLIDAY. Horace Jackson.
THE LITTLE CAESAR, WB. Francis Faragoh and Robert N. Lee.
SKIPPY. Joseph Mankiewicz and Sam Mintz.
(Original Story)
THE DAWN PATROL, WB.-FN. John Monk Saunders.
DOORWAY TO HELL, WB.-FN. Rowland Brown.
LAUGHTER, PAR. Harry d'Abbadie d'Arrast, Douglas Doty and Donald Ogden Stewart.
THE PUBLIC ENEMY, WB.-FN. John Bright and Kubec Glasmon.
SMART MONEY, WB.-FN. Lucien Hubbard and Joseph Jackson.

CINEMATOGRAPHY (O-31)

TABU, PAR. Floyd Crosby.
CIMARRON. Edward Cronjager.
MOROCCO. Lee Garmes.
THE RIGHT TO LOVE, PAR. Charles Lang.
SVENGALI, WB-FN. Barney "Chick" McGill.

ART DIRECTION - SET DECORATION (O-32)

CIMARRON. Max Ree.
JUST IMAGINE, FOX. Stephen Goosson and Ralph Hammeras.
MOROCCO. Hans Dreier.
SVENGALI. Anton Grot.
WHOOPEE, Goldwyn, UA. Richard Day.

SOUND (O-33)

PAR STUDIO SOUND DEPARTMENT.
MGM STUDIO SOUND DEPARTMENT.
RKO STUDIO SOUND DEPARTMENT.
SAMUEL GOLDWYN SOUND DEPARTMENT.

SCIENTIFIC OR TECHNICAL (O-34)

(Class I)

ELECTRICAL RESEARCH PRODUCTS, INC., RCA-PHOTOPHONE, INC., and RKO PICTURES, INC., for noise reduction recording equipment.
DuPONT FILM MANUFACTURING CORP. and EASTMAN KODAK CO. for super-sensitive panchromatic film.
(Class II)
FOX FILM CORP. for effective use of synchro-projection composite photography.
(Class III)
ELECTRICAL RESEARCH PRODUCTS, INC., for moving coil microphone transmitters.
RKO PICTURES, INC., for reflex type microphone concentrators.
RCA-PHOTOPHONE, INC., for ribbon microphone transmitters.

1931/32

BEST PICTURE (O-35)

GRAND HOTEL, MGM.
ARROWSMITH, Goldwyn, UA.
BAD GIRL, FOX.
THE CHAMP, MGM.
FIVE STAR FINAL, FN.
ONE HOUR WITH YOU, PAR.
SHANGHAI EXPRESS, PAR.
SMILING LIEUTENANT, PAR.

ACTOR (O-36)

WALLACE BEERY, The Champ.
FREDRIC MARCH, Dr. Jekyll And Mr. Hyde, PAR.
ALFRED LUNT, *The Guardsman*, MGM.

ACTRESS (O-37)

HELEN HAYES, The Sin Of Madelon Claudet, MGM.
MARIE DRESSLER, *Emma*, MGM.
LYNN FONTANNE, *The Guardsman*.

DIRECTING (O-38)

FRANK BORZAGE, Bad Girl.
KING VIDOR, *The Champ*.
JOSEF VON STERNBERG, *Shanghai Express*.

WRITING (O-39)

(Adaptation)
BAD GIRL. Edwin Burke.
ARROWSMITH. Sidney Howard.
DR. JEKYLL AND MR. HYDE. Percy Heath and Samuel Hoffenstein.
(Original Story)
THE CHAMP. Frances Marion.
LADY AND GENT, PAR. Grover Jones and William Slavens McNutt.
STAR WITNESS. Lucien Hubbard.
WHAT PRICE HOLLYWOOD, RKO. Adela Rogers St. John.

CINEMATOGRAPHY (O-40)

SHANGHAI EXPRESS. Lee Garmes.
ARROWSMITH. Ray June.
DR. JEKYLL AND MR. HYDE. Karl Struss.

ART DIRECTION - SET DECORATION (O-41)

TRANSATLANTIC, FOX. Gordon Wiles.
A NOUS LA LIBERTE, (French). Lazare Meerson.
ARROWSMITH. Richard Day.

SOUND (O-42)

PAR STUDIO SOUND DEPARTMENT.

SHORT FILMS (O-43)

(Cartoons)
FLOWERS AND TREES, Walt Disney, UA.
MICKEY'S ORPHANS, Walt Disney, COL.
IT'S GOT ME AGAIN, Leon Schlesinger, WB.
(Comedy)
THE MUSIC BOX, Hal Roach, MGM. (Laurel & Hardy)
THE LOUD MOUTH, Mack Sennett. EDU.
STOUT HEARTS AND WILLING HANDS, RKO. (Masquers Comedies)
(Novelty)
WRESTLING SWORDFISH, Mack Sennett, EDU. (Cannibals of The Deep)
SCREEN SOUVENIRS, PAR.
SWING HIGH, MGM. (Sport Champion)

HONORARY AND OTHER (O-44)

(Other)
WALT DISNEY for the creation of Mickey Mouse.

SCIENTIFIC OR TECHNICAL (O-45)

(Class II)
TECHNICOLOR MOTION PICTURE CORP. for their color cartoon process.
(Class III)
EASTMAN KODAK CO. for the Type II-B Sensitometer.

1932/33

BEST PICTURE (O-46)

CAVALCADE, FOX.
A FAREWELL TO ARMS, PAR.
FORTY-SECOND STREET, WB.
I AM A FUGITIVE FROM A CHAIN GANG, WB.
LADY FOR A DAY, COL.
LITTLE WOMEN, RKO.
THE PRIVATE LIFE OF HENRY VIII, London Films, UA (British).
SHE DONE HIM WRONG, PAR.
SMILIN' THRU, MGM.
STATE FAIR, FOX.

ACTOR (O-47)

CHARLES LAUGHTON, The Private Life Of Henry VIII.
LESLIE HOWARD, *Berkeley Square*, FOX.
PAUL MUNI, *I Am A Fugitive From A Chain Gang*.

ACTRESS (O-48)

KATHARINE HEPBURN, Morning Glory, RKO.
MAY ROBSON, *Lady For A Day*.
DIANA WYNYARD, *Calvalcade*.

DIRECTING (O-49)

FRANK LLOYD, Cavalcade.

FRANK CAPRA, *Lady For A Day.*
GEORGE CUKOR, *Little Women.*

WRITING (O-50)
(Adaptation)
LITTLE WOMEN. Victor Heerman and Sarah Y. Mason.
LADY FOR A DAY. Robert Riskin.
STATE FAIR. Paul Green and Sonya Levien.
(Original Story)
ONE WAY PASSAGE, WB. Robert Lord.
THE PRIZEFIGHTER AND THE LADY, MGM. Frances Marion.
RASPUTIN AND THE EMPRESS, MGM. Charles MacArthur.

CINEMATOGRAPHY (O-51)
A FAREWELL TO ARMS. Charles Bryant Lang, Jr.
REUNION IN VIENNA, MGM. George J. Folsey, Jr.
SIGN OF THE CROSS, PAR. Karl Struss.

ART DIRECTION - SET DECORATION (O-52)
CAVALCADE. William S. Darling.
A FAREWELL TO ARMS. Hans Dreier and Roland Anderson.
WHEN LADIES MEET, MGM. Cedric Gibbons.

SOUND (O-53)
A FAREWELL TO ARMS. Harold C. Lewis.
FORTY-SECOND STREET. Nathan Levinson.
GOLDDIGGERS of 1933. Nathan Levinson.
I AM A FUGITIVE FROM A CHAIN GANG. Nathan Levinson.

SHORT FILMS (O-54)
(Cartoons)
THE THREE LITTLE PIGS, Walt Disney, UA.
BUILDING A BUILDING, Walt Disney, UA.
THE MERRY OLD SOUL, Walter Lantz, U.
(Comedy)
SO THIS IS HARRIS, RKO. (Special)
MISTER MUGG, U. (Comedies)
PREFERRED LIST, RKO. (Headliner Series #5)
(Novelty)
KRAKATOA, EDU. (Three-reel Special)
MENU, Pete Smith, MGM. (Oddities)
THE SEA, EDU. (Battle For Life)

SCIENTIFIC OR TECHNICAL (O-55)
(Class II)
ELECTRICAL RESEARCH PRODUCTS, INC., for their wide range recording and reproducing system.
RCA-VICTOR CO., INC., for their high-fidelity recording and reproducing system.
(Class III)
FOX FILM CORP., FRED JACKMAN and WB PICTURES, INC., and SIDNEY SANDERS of RKO Studios, Inc., for their development and effective use of the translucent cellulose screen in composite photography.

ASSISTANT DIRECTOR (O-56)
CHARLES BARTON, PAR.
SCOTT BEAL, U.
CHARLES DORIAN, MGM.
FRED FOX, UA.
GORDON HOLLINGSHEAD, WB.
DEWEY STARKEY, RKO.
WILLIAM TUMMEL, FOX.
(Multiple award given this year only.)

1934

BEST PICTURE (O-57)
IT HAPPENED ONE NIGHT, COL.
THE BARRETTS OF WIMPOLE STREET, MGM.
CLEOPATRA, PAR.
FLIRTATION WALK, FN.
THE GAY DIVORCEE, RKO.
HERE COMES THE NAVY, WB.
THE HOUSE OF ROTHSCHILD, 20th Cent., UA.
IMITATION OF LIFE, U.
ONE NIGHT OF LOVE, COL.
THE THIN MAN, MGM.
VIVA VILLA, MGM.
THE WHITE PARADE, FOX.

ACTOR (O-58)
CLARK GABLE, It Happened One Night.
FRANK MORGAN, *Affairs Of Cellini,* FOX, UA.
WILLIAM POWELL, *The Thin Man.*

ACTRESS (O-59)
CLAUDETTE COLBERT, It Happened One Night.
GRACE MOORE, *One Night Of Love.*
NORMA SHEARER, *The Barretts Of Wimpole Street.*

DIRECTING (O-60)
FRANK CAPRA, It Happened One Night.
VICTOR SCHERTZINGER, *One Night Of Love.*
W. S. VAN DYKE, *The Thin Man.*

WRITING (O-61)
(Adaptation)
IT HAPPENED ONE NIGHT. Robert Riskin.
THE THIN MAN. Frances Goodrich and Albert Hackett.
VIVA VILLA. Ben Hecht.
(Original Story)
MANHATTAN MELODRAMA, MGM. Arthur Caesar.
HIDE-OUT, MGM. Mauri Grashin.
THE RICHEST GIRL IN THE WORLD, RKO. Norman Krasna.

CINEMATOGRAPHY (O-62)
CLEOPATRA. Victor Milner.
THE AFFAIRS OF CELLINI. Charles Rosher.
OPERATION 13, MGM. George Folsey.

ART DIRECTION - SET DECORATION (O-63)
THE MERRY WIDOW, MGM. Cedric Gibbons and Frederic Hope.
AFFAIRS OF CELLINI. Richard Day.
THE GAY DIVORCEE. Van Nest Polglase and Carroll Clark.

FILM EDITING (O-64)
ESKIMO, MGM. Conrad Nervig.
CLEOPATRA. Anne Bauchens.
ONE NIGHT OF LOVE. Gene Milford.

MUSIC - SCORING (O-65)
(Best Score)
ONE NIGHT OF LOVE. Columbia Music Dept., Louis Silvers, Head. Thematic music by Victor Schertzinger and Gus Kahn.
THE GAY DIVORCEE, RKO Music Dept. Max Steiner, Head. Score by Kenneth Webb and Samuel Hoffenstein.
THE LOST PATROL, RKO Music Dept. Max Steiner, Head. Score by Max Steiner.

MUSIC - BEST SONG (O-66)

THE CONTINENTAL, The Gay Divorcee, RKO. Music, Con Conrad. Lyrics, Herb Magidson.
CARIOCA, *Flying Down To Rio*, RKO. Music, Vincent Youmans. Lyrics, Edward Eliscu and Gus Kahn.
LOVE IN BLOOM, *She Loves Me Not*, PAR. Music, Ralph Rainger. Lyrics, Leo Robin.

SOUND (O-67)

ONE NIGHT OF LOVE. Paul Neal.
AFFAIRS OF CELLINI. Thomas T. Moulton.
CLEOPATRA. Franklin Hansen.
FLIRTATION WALK. Nathan Levinson.
THE GAY DIVORCEE. Carl Dreher.
IMITATION OF LIFE. Gilbert Kurland.
VIVA VILLA. Douglas Shearer.

SHORT FILMS (O-68)

(Cartoons)
THE TORTOISE AND THE HARE, Walt Disney.
HOLIDAY LAND, Charles Mintz, COL.
JOLLY LITTLE ELVES, U.
(Comedy)
LA CUCARACHA, RKO. (Special)
MEN IN BLACK, COL. (Broadway Comedies)
WHAT, NO MEN!, WB. (Broadway Brevities)
(Novelty)
CITY OF WAX, EDU. (Battle For Life)
BOSOM FRIENDS, EDU. (Treasure Chest)
STRIKES AND SPARES, MGM. (Oddities)

HONORARY AND OTHER (O-69)

(Other)
SHIRLEY TEMPLE, in grateful recognition of her outstanding contribution to screen entertainment during the year 1934.

SCIENTIFIC OR TECHNICAL (O-70)

(Class II)
ELECTRICAL RESEARCH PRODUCTS, INC., for their development of the vertical cut disc method of recording sound for motion pictures (hill and dale recording).
(Class III)
COL PICTURES CORP. for their application of the vertical cut disc method (hill and dale recording) to actual studio production, with their recording of the sound on the picture "One Night of Love".
BELL AND HOWELL CO. for their development of the Bell and Howell fully automatic sound and picture printer.

ASSISTANT DIRECTOR (O-71)

JOHN WATERS, Viva Villa.
SCOTT BEAL, *Imitation Of Life.*
CULLEN TATE, *Cleopatra.*

1935

BEST PICTURE (O-72)

MUTINY ON THE BOUNTY, MGM.
ALICE ADAMS, RKO.
BROADWAY MELODY OF 1936, MGM.
CAPTAIN BLOOD, WB.-Cosmopolitan.
DAVID COPPERFIELD, MGM.
THE INFORMER, RKO.
LES MISERABLES, 20th Cent., UA.
LIVES OF A BENGAL LANCER, PAR.
A MIDSUMMER NIGHT'S DREAM, WB.
NAUGHTY MARIETTA, MGM.
RUGGLES OF RED GAP, PAR.
TOP HAT, RKO.

ACTOR (O-73)

VICTOR McLAGLEN, The Informer.
CLARK GABLE, *Mutiny On The Bounty.*
CHARLES LAUGHTON, *Mutiny On The Bounty.*
FRANCHOT TONE, *Mutiny On The Bounty.*

ACTRESS (O-74)

BETTE DAVIS, Dangerous, WB.
ELISABETH BERGNER, *Escape Me Never*, British & Dominions, UA. (British)
CLAUDETTE COLBERT, *Private Worlds*, PAR.
KATHARINE HEPBURN, *Alice Adams.*
MIRIAM HOPKINS, *Becky Sharp*, Pioneer, RKO.
MERLE OBERON, *The Dark Angel*, Goldwyn, UA.

DIRECTING (O-75)

JOHN FORD, The Informer.
HENRY HATHAWAY, *Lives Of A Bengal Lancer.*
FRANK LLOYD, *Mutiny On The Bounty.*

WRITING (O-76)

(Original Story)
THE SCOUNDREL, PAR. Ben Hecht and Charles MacArthur.
BROADWAY MELODY OF 1936. Moss Hart.
THE GAY DECEPTION, Lasky, FOX. Don Hartman and Stephen Avery.
(Screenplay)
THE INFORMER. Dudley Nichols.
LIVES OF A BENGAL LANCER. Achmed Abdullah, John L. Balderston, Grover Jones, William Slavens McNutt and Waldemar Young.
MUTINY ON THE BOUNTY. Jules Furthman, Talbot Jennings and Carey Wilson.

CINEMATOGRAPHY (O-77)

A MIDSUMMER NIGHT'S DREAM. Hal Mohr.
BARBARY COAST, Goldwyn, UA. Ray June.
THE CRUSADES, PAR. Victor Milner.
LES MISERABLES. Gregg Toland.

ART DIRECTION - SET DECORATON (O-78)

THE DARK ANGEL. Richard Day.
LIVES OF A BENGAL LANCER. Hans Dreier and Roland Anderson.
TOP HAT. Carroll Clark and Van Nest Polglase.

FILM EDITING (O-79)

A MIDSUMMER NIGHT'S DREAM. Ralph Dawson.
DAVID COPPERFIELD. Robert J. Kern.
THE INFORMER. George Hively.
LES MISERABLES. Barbara McLean.
LIVES OF A BENGAL LANCER. Ellsworth Hoagland.
MUTINY ON THE BOUNTY. Margaret Booth.

MUSIC - SCORING (O-80)

(Best Score)
THE INFORMER, RKO Music Dept. Max Steiner, Head. Score by Max Steiner.
MUTINY ON THE BOUNTY, MGM Music Dept. Nat W. Finston, Head. Score by Herbert Stothart.
PETER IBBETSON, PAR Music Dept. Irvin Talbot, Head. Score by Ernst Toch.

MUSIC - BEST SONG (O-81)

LULLABY OF BROADWAY, Gold Diggers of 1935, WB. Music, Harry Warren. Lyrics, Al Dubin.
CHEEK TO CHEEK, *Top Hat.* Music and Lyrics by Irving Berlin.
LOVELY TO LOOK AT, *Roberta*, RKO. Music, Jerome Kern. Lyrics, Dorothy Fields and Jimmy McHugh.

SOUND (O-82)

NAUGHTY MARIETTA. Douglas Shearer.
THE BRIDE OF FRANKENSTEIN, U. Gilbert Kurland.
CAPTAIN BLOOD. Nathan Levinson.
THE DARK ANGEL. Goldwyn Sound Department. Thomas T. Moulton.
I DREAM TOO MUCH, RKO. Carl Dreher.
LIVES OF A BENGAL LANCER. Franklin Hansen.
LOVE ME FOREVER, COL. John Livadary.
ONE THOUSAND DOLLARS A MINUTE, REP. Republic Sound Department.
THANKS A MILLION, FOX. E. H. Hansen.

SHORT FILMS (O-83)

(Cartoons)
THREE ORPHAN KITTENS, Walt Disney, UA.
THE CALICO DRAGON, Harman-Ising, MGM.
WHO KILLED COCK ROBIN?, Walt Disney, UA.
(Comedy)
HOW TO SLEEP, MGM. (Miniature)
OH, MY NERVES, COL. (Broadway Comedies)
TIT FOR TAT, Hal Roach, MGM. (Laurel & Hardy)
(Novelty)
WINGS OVER MT. EVEREST, EDU. (Special)
AUDIOSCOPIKS, MGM. (Special)
CAMERA THRILLS, U. (Special)

HONORARY AND OTHER (O-84)

(Other)
DAVID WARK GRIFFITH, for his distinguished creative achievements as director and producer and his invaluable initiative and lasting contributions to the progress of the motion picture arts.

SCIENTIFIC OR TECHNICAL (O-85)

(Class II)
AGFA ANSCO CORP. for their development of the Agfa infra-red film.
EASTMAN KODAK CO. for their development of the Eastman Pola-Screen.
(Class III)
MGM STUDIO for the development of anti-directional negative and positive development by means of jet turbulation, and the application of the method to all negative and print processing of the entire product of a major producing company.
WILLIAM A. MUELLER of WB-FN Studio Sound Department for his method of dubbing, in which the level of the dialogue automatically controls the level of the accompanying music and sound effects.
MOLE-RICHARDSON CO. for their development of the "Solar-spot" spot lamps.
DOUGLAS SHEARER and MGM STUDIO SOUND DEPARTMENT for their automatic control system for cameras and sound recording machines and auxiliary stage equipment.
ELECTRICAL RESEARCH PRODUCTS, INC., for their study and development of equipment to analyze and measure flutter resulting from the travel of the film through the mechanisms used in the recording and reproduction of sound.
PARAMOUNT PRODUCTIONS, INC., for the design and construction of the PARAMOUNT transparency air turbine developing machine.
NATHAN LEVINSON, Director of Sound Recording for WB.-FN Studio, for the method of intercutting variable density and variable area sound tracks to secure an increase in the effective volume range of sound recorded for motion pictures.

ASSISTANT DIRECTOR (O-86)

CLEM BEAUCHAMP, Lives Of A Bengal Lancer.
PAUL WING, Lives Of A Bengal Lancer.
ERIC STACEY, Les Miserables.
JOSEPH NEWMAN, David Copperfield.

DANCE DIRECTION (O-87)

DAVE GOULD, "I've Got A Feeling You're Fooling" number, Broadway Melody Of 1936. "Straw Hat" number, Folies Bergere, 20th Cent, UA.
BUSBY BERKELEY, "Lullaby Of Broadway" number, and "The Words Are In My Heart" number, Gold Diggers Of 1935, WB.
BOBBY CONNOLLY, "Latin From Manhattan" number, Go Into Your Dance, WB. "Playboy From Paree" number, Broadway Hostess, WB.
SAMMY LEE, "Lovely Lady" number, and "Too Good To Be True" number, King Of Burlesque, FOX.
HERMES PAN for "Piccolino" number, and "Top Hat" number, Top Hat.
LEROY PRINZ, "Elephant Number -- It's The Animal In Me", Big Broadcast Of 1936, PAR. "Viennese Waltz" number, All The King's Horses, PAR.
B. ZEMACH, "Hall Of Kings" number, She, RKO.

1936

BEST PICTURE (O-88)

THE GREAT ZIEGFELD, MGM.
ANTHONY ADVERSE, WB.
DODSWORTH, Goldwyn, UA.
LIBELED LADY, MGM.
MR. DEEDS GOES TO TOWN, COL.
ROMEO AND JULIET, MGM.
SAN FRANCISCO, MGM.
THE STORY OF LOUIS PASTEUR, WB.
A TALE OF TWO CITIES, MGM.
THREE SMART GIRLS, U.

ACTOR (O-89)

PAUL MUNI, The Story Of Louis Pasteur.
GARY COOPER, Mr. Deeds Goes To Town.
WALTER HUSTON, Dodsworth.
WILLIAM POWELL, My Man Godfrey, U.
SPENCER TRACY, San Francisco.

ACTRESS (O-90)

LUISE RAINER, The Great Ziegfeld.
IRENE DUNNE, Theodora Goes Wild, COL.
GLADYS GEORGE, Valiant Is The Word For Carrie, PAR.
CAROLE LOMBARD, My Man Godfrey.
NORMA SHEARER, Romeo And Juliet.

SUPPORTING ACTOR (O-91)

WALTER BRENNAN, Come And Get It, Goldwyn, UA.
MISCHA AUER, My Man Godfrey.
STUART ERWIN, Pigskin Parade, FOX.
BASIL RATHBONE, Romeo And Juliet.
AKIM TAMIROFF, The General Died At Dawn, PAR.

SUPPORTING ACTRESS (O-92)

GALE SONDERGAARD, Anthony Adverse.
BEULAH BONDI, The Gorgeous Hussy, MGM.
ALICE BRADY, My Man Godfrey.
BONITA GRANVILLE, These Three, Goldwyn, UA.
MARIA OUSPENSKAYA, Dodsworth.

DIRECTING (O-93)

FRANK CAPRA, Mr. Deeds Goes To Town.
GREGORY LACAVA, My Man Godfrey.
ROBERT Z. LEONARD, The Great Ziegfeld.
W. S. VAN DYKE, San Francisco.
WILLIAM WYLER, Dodsworth.

WRITING (O-94)

(Original Story)

THE STORY OF LOUIS PASTEUR. Pierre Collings and Sheridan Gibney.
FURY, MGM. Norman Krasna.
THE GREAT ZIEGFELD. William Anthony McGuire.
SAN FRANCISCO. Robert Hopkins.
THREE SMART GIRLS. Adele Commandini.

(Screenplay)

THE STORY OF LOUIS PASTEUR. Pierre Collings and Sheridan Gibney.
AFTER THE THIN MAN, MGM. Frances Goodrich and Albert Hackett.
DODSWORTH. Sidney Howard.
MR. DEEDS GOES TO TOWN. Robert Riskin.
MY MAN GODFREY. Eric Hatch and Morris Ryskind.

CINEMATOGRAPHY (O-95)

ANTHONY ADVERSE. Gaetano Gaudio.
THE GENERAL DIED AT DAWN, PAR. Victor Milner.
THE GORGEOUS HUSSEY. George Folsey.

ART DIRECTION - SET DECORATION (O-96)

DODSWORTH. Richard Day.
ANTHONY ADVERSE. Anton Grot.
THE GREAT ZIEGFELD. Cedric Gibbons, Eddie Imazu and Edwin B. Willis.
LLOYDS OF LONDON, FOX. William S. Darling.
THE MAGNIFICENT BRUTE, U. Albert S. D'Agostino and Jack Otterson.
ROMEO AND JULIET. Cedric Gibbons, Frederic Hope and Edwin B. Willis.
WINTERSET, RKO. Perry Ferguson.

FILM EDITING (O-97)

ANTHONY ADVERSE. Ralph Dawson.
COME AND GET IT. Edward Curtiss.
THE GREAT ZIEGFELD. William S. Gray.
LLOYDS OF LONDON. Barbara McLean.
A TALE OF TWO CITIES. Conrad A. Nervig.
THEODORA GOES WILD. Otto Meyer.

MUSIC - SCORING (O-98)

(Best Score)

ANTHONY ADVERSE, WB Music Dept. Leo Forbstein, Head. Score by Erich Wolfgang Korngold.
THE CHARGE OF THE LIGHT BRIGADE, WB Music Dept. Leo Forbstein, Head. Score by Max Steiner.
THE GARDEN OF ALLAH, Selznick Int'l Pictures Music Dept. Max Steiner, Head. Score by Max Steiner.
THE GENERAL DIED AT DAWN, PAR Music Dept. Boris Morros, Head. Score by Werner Janssen.
WINTERSET, RKO Music Dept. Nathaniel Shilkret, Head. Score by Nathaniel Shilkret.

MUSIC - BEST SONG (O-99)

THE WAY YOU LOOK TONIGHT, Swing Time, RKO. Music, Jerome Kern. Lyrics, Dorothy Fields.
DID I REMEMBER, *Suzy*, MGM. Music, Walter Donaldson. Lyrics, Harold Adamson.
I'VE GOT YOU UNDER MY SKIN, *Born To Dance*, MGM. Music and Lyrics by Cole Porter.
A MELODY FROM THE SKY, *Trail of The Lonesome Pine*, PAR. Music, Louis Alter. Lyrics, Sidney Mitchell.
PENNIES FROM HEAVEN, *Pennies From Heaven*, COL. Music, Arthur Johnston. Lyrics, Johnny Burke.
WHEN DID YOU LEAVE HEAVEN, *Sing Baby Sing*, FOX. Music, Richard A. Whiting. Lyrics, Walter Bullock.

SOUND (O-100)

SAN FRANCISCO. Douglas Shearer.
BANJO ON MY KNEE, FOX. E. H. Hansen.
THE CHARGE OF THE LIGHT BRIGADE. Nathan Levinson.
DODSWORTH. Oscar Lagerstrom.
GENERAL SPANKY, Roach, MGM. Elmer A. Raguse.
MR. DEEDS GOES TO TOWN. John Livadary.
THE TEXAS RANGERS, PAR. Franklin Hansen.
THAT GIRL FROM PARIS, RKO. J. O. Aalberg.
THREE SMART GIRLS. Homer G. Tasker.

SHORT FILMS (O-101)

(Cartoons)

COUNTRY COUSIN, Walt Disney, UA.
OLD MILL POND, Harman-Ising, MGM.
SINBAD THE SAILOR, PAR.

(One-reel)

BORED OF EDUCATION, Hal Roach, MGM. (Our Gang)
MOSCOW MOODS, PAR. (Headliners)
WANTED, A MASTER, Pete Smith, MGM (Pete Smith Specialties)

(Two-reel)

THE PUBLIC PAYS, MGM. (Crime Doesn't Pay)
DOUBLE OR NOTHING, WB. (Broadway Brevities)
DUMMY ACHE, RKO. (Edgar Kennedy Comedies)

(Color)

GIVE ME LIBERTY, WB. (Broadway Brevities)
LA FIESTA DE SANTA BARBARA, MGM. (Musical Revues)
POPULAR SCIENCE J-6-2, PAR.

HONORARY AND OTHER (O-102)

(Other)

MARCH OF TIME for its significance to motion pictures and for having revolutionized one of the most important branches of the industry - the newsreel.
W. HOWARD GREENE and HAROLD ROSSON for the color cinematography of the Selznick Int'l Production, The Garden Of Allah.

SCIENTIFIC OR TECHNICAL (O-103)

(Class I)

DOUGLAS SHEARER and the MGM STUDIO SOUND DEPARTMENT for the development of a practical two-way horn system and a biased Class A push-pull recording system.

(Class II)

E. C. WENTE and the BELL TELEPHONE LABORATORIES for their multi-cellular high-frequency horn and receiver.
RCA MANUFACTURING CO., INC., for their rotary stabilizer sound head.

(Class III)

RCA MANUFACTURING CO., INC., for their development of a method of recording and printing sound records utilizing a restricted spectrum (known as ultra-violet light recording).
ELECTRICAL RESEARCH PRODUCTS, INC., for the ERPI "Type Q" portable recording channel.
RCA MANUFACTURING CO., INC., for furnishing a practical design and specifications for a non-slip printer.
UA STUDIO CORP. for the development of a practical, efficient and quiet wind machine.

ASSISTANT DIRECTOR (O-104)

JACK SULLIVAN, The Charge Of The Light Brigade.
CLEM BEAUCHAMP, *Last Of The Mohicans*, Reliance, UA.
WILLIAM CANNON, *Anthony Adverse*.
JOSEPH NEWMAN, *San Francisco*.
ERIC G. STACEY, *Garden Of Allah*.

DANCE DIRECTION (O-105)

SEYMOUR FELIX, "A Pretty Girl Is Like A Melody" number The Great Ziegfeld.
BUSBY BERKELEY, "Love And War" number, *Gold Diggers Of 1937,*

WB.
BOBBY CONNOLLY, "1000 Love Songs" number, *Cain And Mabel*, WB.
DAVE GOULD, "Swingin' The Jinx" number, *Born To Dance*.
JACK HASKELL, "Skating Ensemble" number, *One In A Million*, FOX.
RUSSELL LEWIS, "The Finale" number, *Dancing Pirate*, RKO.
HERMES PAN, "Bo Jangles" number, *Swing Time*.

1937

BEST PICTURE (O-106)
THE LIFE OF EMILE ZOLA, WB.
THE AWFUL TRUTH, COL.
CAPTAINS COURAGEOUS, MGM.
DEAD END, Goldwyn, UA.
THE GOOD EARTH, MGM.
IN OLD CHICAGO, FOX.
LOST HORIZON, COL.
100 MEN AND A GIRL, U.
STAGE DOOR, RKO.
A STAR IS BORN, Selznick Int'l, UA.

ACTOR (O-107)
SPENCER TRACY, Captains Courageous.
CHARLES BOYER, *Conquest*, MGM.
FREDRIC MARCH, *A Star Is Born*.
ROBERT MONTGOMERY, *Night Must Fall*, MGM.
PAUL MUNI, *The Life Of Emile Zola*.

ACTRESS (O-108)
LUISE RAINER, The Good Earth.
IRENE DUNNE, *The Awful Truth*.
GRETA GARBO, *Camille*, MGM.
JANET GAYNOR, *A Star Is Born*.
BARBARA STANWYCK, *Stella Dallas*, Goldwyn, UA.

SUPPORTING ACTOR (O-109)
JOSEPH SCHILDKRAUT, The Life Of Emile Zola.
RALPH BELLAMY, *The Awful Truth*.
THOMAS MITCHELL, *Hurricane*, Goldwyn, UA.
H. B. WARNER, *Lost Horizon*.
ROLAND YOUNG, *Topper*, Roach, MGM.

SUPPORTING ACTRESS (O-110)
ALICE BRADY, In Old Chicago.
ANDREA LEEDS, *Stage Door*.
ANNE SHIRLEY, *Stella Dallas*.
CLAIRE TREVOR, *Dead End*.
DAME MAY WHITTY, *Night Must Fall*.

DIRECTING (O-111)
LEO McCAREY, The Awful Truth.
WILLIAM DIETERLE, *The Life Of Emile Zola*.
SIDNEY FRANKLIN, *The Good Earth*.
GREGORY LACAVA, *Stage Door*.
WILLIAM WELLMAN, *A Star Is Born*.

WRITING (O-112)
(Original Story)
A STAR IS BORN. William A. Wellman and Robert Carson.
BLACK LEGION, WB. Robert Lord.
IN OLD CHICAGO. Niven Busch.
THE LIFE OF EMILE ZOLA. Heinz Herald and Geza Herczeg.
100 MEN AND A GIRL. Hans Kraly.
(Screenplay)
THE LIFE OF EMILE ZOLA. Heinz Herald, Geza Herczeg and Norman Reilly Raine.
THE AWFUL TRUTH. Vina Delmar.

CAPTAINS COURAGEOUS. Marc Connolly, John Lee Mahin and Dale Van Every.
STAGE DOOR. Morris Ryskind and Anthony Veiller.
A STAR IS BORN. Alan Campbell, Robert Carson and Dorothy Parker.

CINEMATOGRAPHY (O-113)
THE GOOD EARTH. Karl Freund.
DEAD END. Gregg Toland.
WINGS OVER HONOLULU, U. Joseph Valentine.

ART DIRECTION - SET DECORATION (O-114)
LOST HORIZON. Stephen Goosson.
CONQUEST. Cedric Gibbons and William Horning.
A DAMSEL IN DISTRESS, RKO. Carroll Clark.
DEAD END. Richard Day.
EVERY DAY'S A HOLIDAY, Major Prods., PAR. Wiard Ihnen.
THE LIFE OF EMILE ZOLA. Anton Grot.
MANHATTAN MERRY-GO-ROUND, REP. John Victor Mackay.
THE PRISONER OF ZENDA, Selznick, UA. Lyle Wheeler.
SOULS AT SEA, PAR. Hans Dreier and Roland Anderson.
VOGUES OF 1938, Wanger. UA. Alexander Toluboff.
WEE WILLIE WINKIE, FOX. William S. Darling and David Hall.
YOU'RE A SWEETHEART, U. Jack Otterson.

FILM EDITING (O-115)
LOST HORIZON. Gene Havlick and Gene Milford.
THE AWFUL TRUTH. Al Clark.
CAPTAINS COURAGEOUS. Elmo Vernon.
THE GOOD EARTH. Basil Wrangell.
100 MEN AND A GIRL. Bernard W. Burton.

MUSIC - SCORING (O-116)
(Best Score)
100 MEN AND A GIRL, U Music Dept. Charles Previn, Head. No composer credit.
HURRICANE, Samuel Goldwyn Music Dept. Alfred Newman, Head. Score by Alfred Newman.
IN OLD CHICAGO, FOX Music Dept. Louis Silvers, Head. No composer credit.
THE LIFE OF EMILE ZOLA, WB. Music Dept. Leo Forbstein, Head. Score by Max Steiner.
LOST HORIZON, COL Music Dept. Morris Stoloff, Head. Score by Dimitri Tiomkin.
MAKE A WISH, Principal Productions. Dr. Hugo Riesenfeld, Musical Director. Score by Dr. Hugo Riesenfeld.
MAYTIME, MGM Music Dept. Nat W. Finston, Head. Score by Herbert Stothart.
PORTIA ON TRIAL, REP Music Dept. Alberto Colombo, Head. Score by Alberto Colombo.
THE PRISONER OF ZENDA, Selznick Int'l Pictures Music Dept. Alfred Newman, Musical Director. Score by Alfred Newman.
QUALITY STREET, RKO Music Dept. Roy Webb, Musical Director. Score by Roy Webb.
SNOW WHITE AND THE SEVEN DWARFS, Walt Disney Music Dept. Leigh Harline, Head. Score by Frank Churchill, Leigh Harline and Paul J. Smith.
SOMETHING TO SING ABOUT, GN Music Dept. C. Bakaleinikoff, Musical Director. Score by Victor Schertzinger.
SOULS AT SEA, PAR Music Dept. Boris Morros, Head. Score by W. Franke Harling and Milan Roder.
WAY OUT WEST, Hal Roach Music Dept. Marvin Hatley, Head. Score by Marvin Hatley.
(through 1937, this was a Music Achievement Award and presented to department head
instead of to the composer).

MUSIC - BEST SONG (O-117)
SWEET LEILANI, Waikiki Wedding, PAR. Music and Lyrics by Harry Owens.
REMEMBER ME, *Mr. Dodd Takes The Air*, WB. Music, Harry Warren. Lyrics, Al Dubin.

1927/28—Frank Borzage (Best Director) and Janet Gaynor (Best Actress)

1930/31—Marie Dressler (Best Actress) and Lionel Barrymore (Best Actor)

1934—Irvin S. Cobb presents Shirley Temple with her Special Award

1935—Victor McLaglen (Best Actor), Bette Davis (Best Actress), and D.W. Griffith (Special Award)

1940—Ginger Rogers (Best Actress) and Bob Hope (Special Award)

1939—Hattie McDaniel (Best Supporting Actress)

1941—Gary Cooper (Best Actor), Joan Fontaine (Best Actress), Wendell Willkie (presenter), Mary Astor (Best Supporting Actress), and Donald Crisp (Best Supporting Actor).

1939—Judy Garland being presented with her Special Award by Mickey Rooney

THAT OLD FEELING, *Vogues Of 1938*. Music, Sammy Fain. Lyrics, Lew Brown.
THEY CAN'T TAKE THAT AWAY FROM ME, *Shall We Dance*, RKO. Music, George Gershwin. Lyrics, Ira Gershwin.
WHISPERS IN THE DARK, *Artists and Models*, PAR. Music, Frederick Hollander. Lyrics, Leo Robin.

SOUND (O-118)

THE HURRICANE. Thomas Moulton.
THE GIRL SAID NO, GN. A. E. Kaye.
HITTING A NEW HIGH, RKO. John Aalberg.
IN OLD CHICAGO. E. H. Hansen.
THE LIFE OF EMILE ZOLA. Nathan Levinson.
LOST HORIZON. John Livadary.
MAYTIME, MGM. Douglas Shearer.
100 MEN AND A GIRL. Homer Tasker.
TOPPER. Elmer Raguse.
WELLS FARGO, PAR. L. L. Ryder.

SHORT FILMS (O-119)

(Cartoons)
THE OLD MILL, Walt Disney, RKO.
EDUCATED FISH, PAR.
THE LITTLE MATCH GIRL, Charles Mintz, COL.
(One-reel)
PRIVATE LIFE OF THE GANNETS, EDU.
A NIGHT AT THE MOVIES, MGM. (Robert Benchley)
ROMANCE OF RADIUM, Pete Smith, MGM. (Pete Smith Specialties)
(Two-reels)
TORTURE MONEY, MGM. (Crime Doesn't Pay)
DEEP SOUTH, RKO. (Radio Musical Comedies)
SHOULD WIVES WORK, RKO. (Leon Errol Comedies)
(Color)
PENNY WISDOM, Pete Smith, MGM. (Pete Smith Specialties)
THE MAN WITHOUT A COUNTRY, WB. (Broadway Brevities)
POPULAR SCIENCE J-7-1, PAR.

HONORARY AND OTHER (O-120)

(Irving G. Thalberg Memorial Award)
Darryl F. Zanuck
(Other)
MACK SENNETT, "for his lasting contribution to the comedy technique of the screen, the basic principles of which are as important today as when they were first put into practice, the Academy presents a Special Award to that master of fun, discoverer of stars, sympathetic, kindly, understanding comedy genius - Mack Sennett."
EDGAR BERGEN for his outstanding comedy creation, Charlie McCarthy.
THE MUSEUM OF MODERN ART FILM LIBRARY for its significant work in collecting films dating from 1895 to the present and for the first time making available to the public the means of studying the historical and aesthetic development of the motion picture as one of the major arts.
W. HOWARD GREENE for the color photography of A Star Is Born. (This Award was recommended by a committee of leading cinematographers after viewing all the color pictures made during the year.)

SCIENTIFIC OR TECHNICAL (O-121)

(Class I)
AGFA ANSCO CORP. for Agfa Supreme and Agfa Ultra Speed pan motion picture negatives.
(Class II)
WALT DISNEY PRODS., LTD., for the design and application to production of the Multi-Plane Camera.
EASTMAN KODAK CO. for two fine-grain duplicating film stocks.
FARCIOT EDOUART and PARAMOUNT PICTURES, INC., for the development of the PARAMOUNT dual screen transparency camera setup.
DOUGLAS SHEARER and the MGM STUDIO SOUND DEPARTMENT

for a method of varying the scanning width of variable density sound tracks (squeeze tracks) for the purpose of obtaining an increased amount of noise reduction.
(Class III)
JOHN ARNOLD and the MGM STUDIO CAMERA DEPARTMENT for their improvement of the semi-automatic follow focus device and its application to all of the cameras used by the MGM Studio.
JOHN LIVADARY, Director of Sound Recording for Columbia Pictures Corp. for the application of the bi-planar light valve to motion picture sound recording.
THOMAS T. MOULTON and the UNITED ARTISTS STUDIO SOUND DEPARTMENT for the application to motion picture sound recording of volume indicators which have peak reading response and linear decibel scales.
RCA MANUFACTURING CO., INC., for the introduction of the modulated high-frequency method of determining optimum photographic processing conditions for variable width sound tracks.
JOSEPH E. ROBBINS and PARAMOUNT PICTURES, INC., for an exceptional application of acoustic principles to the sound proofing of gasoline generators and water pumps.
DOUGLAS SHEARER and the MGM STUDIO SOUND DEPARTMENT for the design of the film drive mechanism as incorporated in the ERPI 1010 reproducer.

ASSISTANT DIRECTOR (O-122)

ROBERT WEBB, In Old Chicago.
C. C. COLEMAN, JR., *Lost Horizon.*
RUSS SAUNDERS, *The Life Of Emile Zola.*
ERIC STACEY, *A Star Is Born.*
HAL WALKER, *Souls At Sea.*
(Award discontinued after this year.)

DANCE DIRECTION (O-123)

HERMES PAN, "Fun House" number, Damsel In Distress.
BUSBY BERKELEY, "The Finale" number, *Varsity Show*, WB.
BOBBY CONNOLLY, "Too Marvelous For Words" number, *Ready, Willing And Able*, WB.
DAVE GOULD, "All God's Children Got Rhythm" number, *A Day At The Races*, MGM.
SAMMY LEE, "Swing Is Here To Stay" number, *Ali Baba Goes To Town*, FOX.
HARRY LOSEE, "Prince Igor Suite" number, *Thin Ice*, FOX.
LEROY PRINZ, "Luau" number, *Waikiki Wedding*.
(Award discontinued after this year).

1938

BEST PICTURE (O-124)

YOU CAN'T TAKE IT WITH YOU, COL.
THE ADVENTURES OF ROBIN HOOD, WB.
ALEXANDER'S RAGTIME BAND, FOX.
BOYS TOWN, MGM.
THE CITADEL, MGM (British).
FOUR DAUGHTERS, WB.-FN.
GRAND ILLUSION, R.A.O., World Pictures (French).
JEZEBEL, WB.
PYGMALION, MGM. (British)
TEST PILOT, MGM.

ACTOR (O-125)

SPENCER TRACY, Boys Town.
CHARLES BOYER, *Algiers*, Wanger, UA.
JAMES CAGNEY, *Angels With Dirty Faces*, WB.
ROBERT DONAT, *The Citadel.*
LESLIE HOWARD, *Pygmalion.*

ACTRESS (O-126)

BETTE DAVIS, Jezebel.
FAY BAINTER, *White Banners*, WB.

WENDY HILLER, *Pygmalion*.
NORMA SHEARER, *Marie Antoinette*, MGM.
MARGARET SULLAVAN, *Three Comrades*, MGM.

SUPPORTING ACTOR (O-127)

WALTER BRENNAN, Kentucky, FOX.
JOHN GARFIELD, *Four Daughters*.
GENE LOCKHART, *Algiers*.
ROBERT MORLEY, *Marie Antoinette*.
BASIL RATHBONE, *If I Were King*, PAR.

SUPPORTING ACTRESS (O-128)

FAY BAINTER, Jezebel.
BEULAH BONDI, *Of Human Hearts*, MGM.
BILLIE BURKE, *Merrily We Live*, Roach, MGM.
SPRING BYINGTON, *You Can't Take It With You*.
MILIZA KORJUS, *The Great Waltz*, MGM.

DIRECTING (O-129)

FRANK CAPRA, You Can't Take It With You.
MICHAEL CURTIZ, *Angels With Dirty Faces*.
MICHAEL CURTIZ, *Four Daughters*.
NORMAN TAUROG, *Boys Town*.
KING VIDOR, *The Citadel*.

WRITING (O-130)

(Adaptation)
PYGMALION. Ian Dalrymple, Cecil Lewis and W. P. Lipscomb.
(Original Story)
BOYS TOWN. Eleanore Griffin and Dore Schary.
ALEXANDER'S RAGTIME BAND, FOX. Irving Berlin.
ANGELS WITH DIRTY FACES. Rowland Brown.
BLOCKADE, Wanger, UA. John Howard Lawson.
MAD ABOUT MUSIC, U. Marcella Burke and Frederick Kohner.
TEST PILOT. Frank Wead.
(Screenplay)
PYGMALION. George Bernard Shaw.
BOYS TOWN. John Meehan and Dore Schary.
THE CITADEL. Ian Dalrymple, Elizabeth Hill and Frank Wead.
FOUR DAUGHTERS. Lenore Coffee and Julius J. Epstein.
YOU CAN'T TAKE IT WITH YOU. Robert Riskin.

CINEMATOGRAPHY (O-131)

THE GREAT WALTZ. Joseph Ruttenberg.
ALGIERS. James Wong Howe.
ARMY GIRL, REP. Ernest Miller and Harry Wild.
THE BUCCANEER, PAR. Victor Milner.
JEZEBEL. Ernest Haller.
MAD ABOUT MUSIC. Joseph Valentine.
MERRILY WE LIVE. Norbert Brodine.
SUEZ, FOX. Peverell Marley.
VIVACIOUS LADY, RKO. Robert de Grasse.
YOU CAN'T TAKE IT WITH YOU. Joseph Walker.
THE YOUNG IN HEART, Selznick, UA. Leon Shamroy.

ART DIRECTION - SET DECORATION (O-132)

ADVENTURES OF ROBIN HOOD. Carl J. Weyl.
ADVENTURES OF TOM SAWYER, Selznick, UA. Lyle Wheeler.
ALEXANDER'S RAGTIME BAND. Bernard Herzbrun and Boris Leven.
ALGIERS. Alexander Toluboff.
CAREFREE, RKO. Van Nest Polglase.
HOLIDAY, COL. Stephen Goosson and Lionel Banks.
IF I WERE KING. Hans Dreier and John Goodman.
MAD ABOUT MUSIC. Jack Otterson.
MARIE ANTOINETTE. Cedric Gibbons.
MERRILY WE LIVE. Charles D. Hall.

FILM EDITING (O-133)

THE ADVENTURES OF ROBIN HOOD. Ralph Dawson.
ALEXANDER'S RAGTIME BAND. Barbara McLean.
THE GREAT WALTZ. Tom Held.
TEST PILOT. Tom Held.
YOU CAN'T TAKE IT WITH YOU. Gene Havlick.

MUSIC - SCORING (O-134)

(Best Score)
ALEXANDER'S RAGTIME BAND. Alfred Newman.
CAREFREE, Victor Baravalle.
GIRLS SCHOOL, COL. Morris Stoloff and Gregory Stone.
GOLDWYN FOLLIES, Goldwyn, UA. Alfred Newman.
JEZEBEL. Max Steiner.
MAD ABOUT MUSIC. Charles Previn and Frank Skinner.
STORM OVER BENGAL, REP. Cy Feuer.
SWEETHEARTS, MGM. Herbert Stothart.
THERE GOES MY HEART, Hal Roach, UA. Marvin Hatley.
TROPIC HOLIDAY, PAR. Boris Morros.
THE YOUNG IN HEART. Franz Waxman.
(Original Score)
THE ADVENTURES OF ROBIN HOOD. Erich Wolfgang Korngold.
ARMY GIRL. Victor Young.
BLOCKADE. Werner Janssen.
BLOCKHEADS, Hal Roach, UA. Marvin Hatley.
BREAKING THE ICE, RKO. Victor Young.
THE COWBOY AND THE LADY, Goldwyn, UA. Alfred Newman.
IF I WERE KING. Richard Hageman.
MARIE ANTOINETTE. Herbert Stothart.
PACIFIC LINER, RKO. Russell Bennett.
SUEZ. Louis Silvers.
THE YOUNG IN HEART. Franz Waxman.

MUSIC - BEST SONG (O-135)

THANKS FOR THE MEMORY, Big Broadcast Of 1938, PAR. Music, Ralph Rainger. Lyrics, Leo Robin.
ALWAYS AND ALWAYS, *Mannequin*, MGM. Music, Edward Ward. Lyrics, Chet Forrest and Bob Wright.
CHANGE PARTNERS AND DANCE WITH ME, *Carefree*. Music and Lyrics by Irving Berlin.
COWBOY AND THE LADY, *The Cowboy And The Lady*. Music, Lionel Newman. Lyrics, Arthur Quenzer.
DUST, *Under Western Stars*, REP. Music and Lyrics by Johnny Marvin.
JEEPERS CREEPERS, *Going Places*, WB. Music, Harry Warren. Lyrics, Johnny Mercer.
MERRILY WE LIVE, *Merrily We Live*. Music, Phil Craig. Lyrics, Arthur Quenzer.
A MIST OVER THE MOON, *The Lady Objects*, COL. Music, Ben Oakland. Lyrics, Oscar Hammerstein II.
MY OWN, *That Certain Age*, U. Music, Jimmy McHugh. Lyrics, Harold Adamson.
NOW IT CAN BE TOLD, *Alexander's Ragtime Band*. Music and Lyrics by Irving Berlin.

SOUND (O-136)

THE COWBOY AND THE LADY. Thomas Moulton.
ARMY GIRL. Charles Lootens.
FOUR DAUGHTERS. Nathan Levinson.
IF I WERE KING. L. L. Ryder.
MERRILY WE LIVE. Elmer Raguse.
SWEETHEARTS. Douglas Shearer.
SUEZ. Edmund Hansen.
THAT CERTAIN AGE, U. Bernard B. Brown.
VIVACIOUS LADY. James Wilkinson.
YOU CAN'T TAKE IT WITH YOU. John Livadary.

SHORT FILMS (O-137)

(Cartoons)
FERDINAND THE BULL, Walt Disney, RKO.
BRAVE LITTLE TAILOR, Walt Disney, RKO.
MOTHER GOOSE GOES HOLLYWOOD, Walt Disney, RKO.

GOOD SCOUTS, Walt Disney, RKO.
HUNKY AND SPUNKY, PAR.
(One-reel)
THAT MOTHERS MIGHT LIVE, MGM (Miniature)
THE GREAT HEART, MGM. (Miniature)
TIMBER TOPPERS, FOX. (Ed Thorgensen-Sports)
(Two-reel)
DECLARATION OF INDEPENDENCE, WB. (Historical Featurette)
SWINGTIME IN THE MOVIES, WB. (Broadway Brevities)
THEY'RE ALWAYS CAUGHT, MGM. (Crime Doesn't Pay)

HONORARY AND OTHER (O-138)

(Irving G. Thalberg Memorial Award)

Hal B. Wallis
(Other)
DEANNA DURBIN and MICKEY ROONEY for their significant contribution in bringing to the screen the spirit and personification of youth, and as juvenile players setting a high standard of ability and achievement.
HARRY M. WARNER in recognition of patriotic service in the production of historical short subjects presenting significant episodes in the early struggle of the American people for liberty.
WALT DISNEY, Snow White And The Seven Dwarfs, recognized as a significant screen innovation which has charmed millions and pioneered a great new entertainment field for the motion picture cartoon.
OLIVER MARSH and ALLEN DAVEY for the color cinematography of the MGM production, Sweethearts. (plaques)
For outstanding achievement in creating Special Photographic and Sound Effects in the PAR production, Spawn Of The North. Special Effects by GORDON JENNINGS, assisted by JAN DOMELA, DEV JENNINGS, IRMIN ROBERTS and ART SMITH. Transparencies by FARCIOT EDOUART, assisted by LOYAL GRIGGS. Sound Effects by LOREN RYDER, assisted by HARRY MILLS, LOUIS H. MESENKOP and WALTER OBERST.
J. ARTHUR BALL for his outstanding contributions to the advancement of color in Motion Picture Photography.

SCIENTIFIC OR TECHNICAL (O-139)

(Class III)

JOHN AALBERG and the RKO STUDIO SOUND DEPARTMENT for the application of compression to variable area recording in motion picture production.
BYRON HASKIN and the SPECIAL EFFECTS DEPARTMENT of WB STUDIO for pioneering the development and for the first practical application to motion picture production of the triple head background projector.

1939

BEST PICTURE (O-140)

GONE WITH THE WIND, Selznick, MGM.
DARK VICTORY, WB.
GOODBYE, MR. CHIPS, MGM (British).
LOVE AFFAIR, RKO.
MR. SMITH GOES TO WASHINGTON, COL.
NINOTCHKA, MGM.
OF MICE AND MEN, Roach, UA.
STAGECOACH, Wanger, UA.
WIZARD OF OZ, MGM.
WUTHERING HEIGHTS, Goldwyn, UA.

ACTOR (O-141)

ROBERT DONAT, Goodbye, Mr. Chips.
CLARK GABLE, *Gone With The Wind.*
LAURENCE OLIVIER, *Wuthering Heights.*
MICKEY ROONEY, *Babes In Arms,* MGM.
JAMES STEWART, *Mr. Smith Goes To Washington.*

ACTRESS (O-142)

VIVIEN LEIGH, Gone With The Wind.
BETTE DAVIS, *Dark Victory.*
IRENE DUNNE, *Love Affair.*
GRETA GARBO, *Ninotchka.*
GREER GARSON, *Goodbye, Mr. Chips.*

SUPPORTING ACTOR (O-143)

THOMAS MITCHELL, Stagecoach.
BRIAN AHERNE, *Juarez,* WB.
HARRY CAREY, *Mr. Smith Goes To Washington.*
BRIAN DONLEVY, *Beau Geste,* PAR.
CLAUDE RAINS, *Mr. Smith Goes To Washington.*

SUPPORTING ACTRESS (O-144)

HATTIE McDANIEL, Gone With The Wind.
OLIVIA DE HAVILLAND, *Gone With The Wind.*
GERALDINE FITZGERALD, *Wuthering Heights.*
EDNA MAY OLIVER, *Drums Along The Mohawk,* FOX.
MARIA OUSPENSKAYA, *Love Affair.*

DIRECTING (O-145)

VICTOR FLEMING, Gone With The Wind.
FRANK CAPRA, *Mr. Smith Goes To Washington.*
JOHN FORD, *Stagecoach.*
SAM WOOD, *Goodbye, Mr. Chips.*
WILLIAM WYLER, *Wuthering Heights.*

WRITING (O-146)

(Original Story)
MR. SMITH GOES TO WASHINGTON. Lewis R. Foster.
BACHELOR MOTHER, RKO. Felix Jackson.
LOVE AFFAIR. Mildred Cram and Leo McCarey.
NINOTCHKA. Melchior Lengyel.
YOUNG MR. LINCOLN, FOX. Lamar Trotti.
(Screenplay)
GONE WITH THE WIND. Sidney Howard.
GOODBYE, MR. CHIPS. Eric Maschwitz, R.C. Sherriff and Claudine West.
MR. SMITH GOES TO WASHINGTON. Sidney Buchman.
NINOTCHKA. Charles Brackett, Walter Reisch and Billy Wilder.
WUTHERING HEIGHTS. Ben Hecht and Charles MacArthur.

CINEMATOGRAPHY (O-147)

(Black-and-White)
WUTHERING HEIGHTS. Gregg Toland.
STAGECOACH. Bert Glennon.
(Color)
GONE WITH THE WIND. Ernest Haller and Ray Rennahan.
THE PRIVATE LIVES OF ELIZABETH AND ESSEX, WB. Sol Polito and W. Howard Greene.

ART DIRECTION - SET DECORATION (O-148)

GONE WITH THE WIND. Lyle Wheeler.
BEAU GESTE. Hans Dreier and Robert Odell.
CAPTAIN FURY, Roach, UA. Charles D. Hall.
FIRST LOVE, U. Jack Otterson and Martin Obzina.
LOVE AFFAIR. Van Nest Polglase and Al Herman.
MAN OF CONQUEST, REP. John Victor Mackay.
MR. SMITH GOES TO WASHINGTON. Lionel Banks.
THE PRIVATE LIVES OF ELIZABETH AND ESSEX. Anton Grot.
THE RAINS CAME, FOX. William Darling and George Dudley.
STAGECOACH. Alexander Toluboff.
THE WIZARD OF OZ. Cedric Gibbons and William A. Horning.
WUTHERING HEIGHTS. James Basevi.

FILM EDITING (O-149)
GONE WITH THE WIND. Hal C. Kern and James E. Newcom.
GOODBYE, MR. CHIPS. Charles Frend.
MR. SMITH GOES TO WASHINGTON. Gene Havlick and Al Clark.
THE RAINS CAME. Barbara McLean.
STAGECOACH. Otho Lovering and Dorothy Spencer.

MUSIC - SCORING (O-150)
(Best Score)
STAGECOACH. Richard Hageman, Frank Harling, John Leipold and Leo Shuken.
BABES IN ARMS. Roger Edens and George E. Stoll.
FIRST LOVE. Charles Previn.
THE GREAT VICTOR HERBERT, PAR. Phil Boutelje and Arthur Lange.
THE HUNCHBACK OF NOTRE DAME, RKO. Alfred Newman.
INTERMEZZO, Selznick, UA. Lou Forbes.
MR. SMITH GOES TO WASHINGTON. Dimitri Tiomkin.
OF MICE AND MEN, Roach, UA. Aaron Copland.
THE PRIVATE LIVES OF ELIZABETH AND ESSEX. Erich Wolfgang Korngold.
SHE MARRIED A COP, REP. Cy Feuer.
SWANEE RIVER, FOX. Louis Silvers.
THEY SHALL HAVE MUSIC, Goldwyn, UA. Alfred Newman.
WAY DOWN SOUTH, Lesser, RKO. Victor Young.
(Original Score)
THE WIZARD OF OZ. Herbert Stothart.
DARK VICTORY. Max Steiner.
ETERNALLY YOURS, Walter Wanger, UA. Werner Janssen.
GOLDEN BOY, COL. Victor Young.
GONE WITH THE WIND. Max Steiner.
GULLIVER'S TRAVELS, PAR. Victor Young.
THE MAN IN THE IRON MASK, Small, UA. Lud Gluskin and Lucien Moraweck.
MAN OF CONQUEST. Victor Young.
NURSE EDITH CAVELL, RKO. Anthony Collins.
OF MICE AND MEN. Aaron Copland.
THE RAINS CAME. Alfred Newman.
WUTHERING HEIGHTS. Alfred Newman.

MUSIC - BEST SONG (O-151)
OVER THE RAINBOW, The Wizard Of Oz. Music, Harold Arlen. Lyrics, E. Y. Harburg.
FAITHFUL FOREVER from *Gulliver's Travels.* Music, Ralph Rainger. Lyrics, Leo Robin.
I POURED MY HEART INTO A SONG, *Second Fiddle,* FOX. Music and Lyrics by Irving Berlin.
WISHING, *Love Affair.* Music and Lyrics by Buddy de Sylva.

SOUND (O-152)
WHEN TOMORROW COMES, U. Bernard B. Brown.
BALALAIKA, MGM. Douglas Shearer.
GONE WITH THE WIND. Thomas T. Moulton.
GOODBYE, MR. CHIPS. A. W. Watkins.
THE GREAT VICTOR HERBERT. Loren Ryder.
THE HUNCHBACK OF NOTRE DAME. John Aalberg.
MAN OF CONQUEST. C. L. Lootens.
MR. SMITH GOES TO WASHINGTON. John Livadary.
OF MICE AND MEN. Elmer Raguse.
THE PRIVATE LIVES OF ELIZABETH AND ESSEX. Nathan Levinson.
THE RAINS CAME. E. H. Hansen.

SHORT FILMS (O-153)
(Cartoons)
THE UGLY DUCKLING, Walt Disney, RKO.
DETOURING AMERICA, WB.
PEACE ON EARTH, MGM.
THE POINTER, Walt Disney, RKO.
(One-reel)
BUSY LITTLE BEARS, PAR. (Paragraphics)
INFORMATION PLEASE, RKO.
PROPHET WITHOUT HONOR, MGM. (Miniature)

SWORD FISHING, WB. (Vitaphone Varieties)
(Two-reel)
SONS OF LIBERTY, WB. (Historical Featurette)
DRUNK DRIVING, MGM. (Crime Doesn't Pay)
FIVE TIMES FIVE, RKO. (Special)

SPECIAL EFFECTS (O-154)
THE RAINS CAME. E. H. Hansen and Fred Sersen.
GONE WITH THE WIND. John R. Cosgrove, Fred Albin and Arthur Johns.
ONLY ANGELS HAVE WINGS, COL. Roy Davidson and Edwin C. Hahn.
PRIVATE LIVES OF ELIZABETH AND ESSEX. Byron Haskin and Nathan Levinson.
TOPPER TAKES A TRIP, Roach, UA. Roy Seawright.
UNION PACIFIC, PAR. Farciot Edouart, Gordon Jennings and Loren Ryder.
THE WIZARD OF OZ. A. Arnold Gillespie and Douglas Shearer.

HONORARY AND OTHER (O-155)
(Irving G. Thalberg Memorial Award)
David O. Selznick
(Other)
DOUGLAS FAIRBANKS (Commemorative Award) - recognizing the unique and outstanding contribution of Douglas Fairbanks, first President of the Academy, to the international development of the motion picture.
MOTION PICTURE RELIEF FUND - acknowledging the outstanding services to the industry during the past year of the Motion Picture Relief Fund and its progressive leadership. Presented to JEAN HERSHOLT, President; RALPH MORGAN, Chairman of the Executive Committee; RALPH BLOCK, First Vice-President; CONRAD NAGEL.
(plaques)
JUDY GARLAND for her outstanding performance as a screen juvenile during the past year.
WILLIAM CAMERON MENZIES for outstanding achievement in the use of color for the enhancement of dramatic mood in the production of Gone With The Wind.
TECHNICOLOR COMPANY for its contributions in successfully bringing three-color feature production to the screen.

SCIENTIFIC OR TECHNICAL (O-156)
(Class III)
GEORGE ANDERSON of WB Studio for an improved positive head for sun arcs.
JOHN ARNOLD of MGM Studio for the MGM mobile camera crane.
THOMAS T. MOULTON, FRED ALBIN and the SOUND DEPARTMENT of the SAMUEL GOLDWYN STUDIO for the origination and application of the Delta db test to sound recording in motion pictures.
FARCIOT EDOUART, JOSEPH E. ROBBINS, WILLIAM RUDOLPH and PARAMOUNT PICTURES, INC., for the design and construction of a quiet portable treadmill.
EMERY HUSE and RALPH B. ATKINSON of Eastman Kodak Co. for their specifications for chemical analysis of photographic developers and fixing baths.
HAROLD NYE of WB Studio for a miniature incandescent spot lamp.
A. J. TONDREAU of WB Studio for the design and manufacture of an improved sound track printer.
Multiple Award for important contributions in cooperative development of new improved Process Projection Equipment:
F. R. ABBOTT, HALLER BELT, ALAN COOK and BAUSCH & LOMB OPTICAL CO. for faster projection lenses.
MITCHELL CAMERA CO. for a new type process projection head.
MOLE-RICHARDSON CO. for a new type automatically controlled projection arc lamp.
CHARLES HANDLEY, DAVID JOY and NATIONAL CARBON CO. for improved and more stable high intensity carbons.
WINTON HOCH and TECHNICOLOR MOTION PICTURE CORP. for an auxiliary optical system.
DON MUSGRAVE and SELZNICK INTERNATIONAL PICTURES, INC., for pioneering in the use of coordinated equipment in the production, Gone With The Wind.

1940

BEST PICTURE (O-157)
REBECCA, Selznick Int'l, UA.
ALL THIS, AND HEAVEN TOO, WB.
FOREIGN CORRESPONDENT, Wanger, UA.
THE GRAPES OF WRATH, FOX.
THE GREAT DICTATOR, Chaplin, UA.
KITTY FOYLE, RKO.
THE LETTER, WB.
THE LONG VOYAGE HOME, Argosy-Wanger, UA.
OUR TOWN, Lesser, UA.
THE PHILADELPHIA STORY, MGM.

ACTOR (O-158)
JAMES STEWART, The Philadelphia Story.
CHARLES CHAPLIN, *The Great Dictator.*
HENRY FONDA, *The Grapes Of Wrath.*
RAYMOND MASSEY, *Abe Lincoln In Illinois*, RKO.
LAURENCE OLIVIER, *Rebecca.*

ACTRESS (O-159)
GINGER ROGERS, Kitty Foyle.
BETTE DAVIS, *The Letter.*
JOAN FONTAINE, *Rebecca.*
KATHARINE HEPBURN, *The Philadelphia Story.*
MARTHA SCOTT, *Our Town.*

SUPPORTING ACTOR (O-160)
WALTER BRENNAN, The Westerner.
ALBERT BASSERMANN, *Foreign Correspondent.*
WILLIAM GARGAN, *They Knew What They Wanted.*
JACK OAKIE, *The Great Dictator.*
JAMES STEPHENSON, *The Letter.*

SUPPORTING ACTRESS (O-161)
JANE DARWELL, The Grapes Of Wrath.
JUDITH ANDERSON, *Rebecca.*
RUTH HUSSEY, *The Philadelphia Story.*
BARBARA O'NEIL, *All This, And Heaven Too.*
MARJORIE RAMBEAU, *Primrose Path*, RKO.

DIRECTING (O-162)
JOHN FORD, The Grapes Of Wrath.
GEORGE CUKOR, *The Philadelphia Story.*
ALFRED HITCHCOCK, *Rebecca.*
SAM WOOD, *Kitty Foyle.*
WILLIAM WYLER, *The Letter.*

WRITING (O-163)
(Original Story)
ARISE, MY LOVE, PAR. Benjamin Glazer and John S. Toldy.
COMRADE X, MGM. Walter Reisch.
EDISON THE MAN, MGM. Hugo Butler and Dore Schary.
MY FAVORITE WIFE, RKO. Leo McCarey, Bella Spewack & Samuel Spewack.
THE WESTERNER. Stuart N. Lake.
(Original Screenplay)
THE GREAT McGINTY, PAR. Preston Sturges.
ANGELS OVER BROADWAY, COL. Ben Hecht.
DR. EHRLICH'S MAGIC BULLET, WB. Norman Burnside, Heinz Herald and John Huston.
FOREIGN CORRESPONDENT. Charles Bennett and Joan Harrison.
THE GREAT DICTATOR. Charles Chaplin.
(Screenplay)
THE PHILADELPHIA STORY. Donald Ogden Stewart.
THE GRAPES OF WRATH. Nunnally Johnson.
KITTY FOYLE. Dalton Trumbo.

THE LONG VOYAGE HOME. Dudley Nichols.
REBECCA. Robert E. Sherwood and Joan Harrison.

CINEMATOGRAPHY (O-164)
(Black-and-White)
REBECCA. George Barnes.
ABE LINCOLN IN ILLINOIS. James Wong Howe.
ALL THIS, AND HEAVEN TOO. Ernest Haller.
ARISE, MY LOVE. Charles B. Lang, Jr.
BOOM TOWN, MGM. Harold Rosson.
FOREIGN CORRESPONDENT. Rudolph Mate.
THE LETTER. Gaetano Gaudio.
THE LONG VOYAGE HOME. Gregg Toland.
SPRING PARADE, U. Joseph Valentine.
WATERLOO BRIDGE, MGM. Joseph Ruttenberg.
(Color)
THIEF OF BAGDAD, Korda, UA (British). George Perinal.
BITTER SWEET, MGM. Oliver T. Marsh and Allen Davey.
THE BLUE BIRD, FOX. Arthur Miller and Ray Rennahan.
DOWN ARGENTINE WAY, FOX. Leon Shamroy and Ray Rennahan.
NORTH WEST MOUNTED POLICE, PAR. Victor Milner and W. Howard Greene.
NORTHWEST PASSAGE, MGM. Sidney Wagner and William V. Skall.

ART DIRECTION - SET DECORATION (O-165)
(Black-and-White)
PRIDE AND PREJUDICE, MGM. Cedric Gibbons and Paul Groesse.
ARISE, MY LOVE. Hans Dreier and Robert Usher.
ARIZONA, COL. Lionel Banks and Robert Peterson.
THE BOYS FROM SYRACUSE, U. John Otterson.
DARK COMMAND, REP. John Victor Mackay.
FOREIGN CORRESPONDENT. Alexander Golitzen.
LILLIAN RUSSELL, FOX. Richard Day and Joseph C. Wright.
MY FAVORITE WIFE. Van Nest Polglase and Mark-Lee Kirk.
MY SON, MY SON, Small, UA. John DuCasse Schulze.
OUR TOWN. Lewis J. Rachmil.
REBECCA. Lyle Wheeler.
SEA HAWK, WB. Anton Grot.
THE WESTERNER. James Basevi.
(Color)
THIEF OF BAGDAD. Vincent Korda.
BITTER SWEET. Cedric Gibbons and John S. Detlie.
DOWN ARGENTINE WAY. Richard Day and Joseph C. Wright.
NORTH WEST MOUNTED POLICE. Hans Dreier and Roland Anderson.

FILM EDITING (O-166)
NORTH WEST MOUNTED POLICE. Anne Bauchens.
THE GRAPES OF WRATH. Robert E. Simpson.
THE LETTER. Warren Low.
THE LONG VOYAGE HOME. Sherman Todd.
REBECCA. Hal C. Kern.

MUSIC - SCORING (O-167)
(Best Score)
TIN PAN ALLEY, FOX. Alfred Newman.
ARISE, MY LOVE. Victor Young.
HIT PARADE OF 1941, REP. Cy Feuer.
IRENE, Imperadio, RKO. Anthony Collins.
OUR TOWN, Sol Lesser. Aaron Copland.
THE SEA HAWK. Erich Wolfgang Korngold.
SECOND CHORUS, PAR. Artie Shaw.
SPRING PARADE. Charles Previn.
STRIKE UP THE BAND, MGM. Georgie Stoll and Roger Edens.
(Original Score)
PINOCCHIO, Disney, RKO. Leigh Harline, Paul J. Smith and Ned Washington.
ARIZONA. Victor Young.
THE DARK COMMAND. Victor Young.
THE FIGHT FOR LIFE, U.S. Government-COL. Louis Gruenberg.
THE GREAT DICTATOR. Meredith Willson.

THE HOUSE OF SEVEN GABLES, U. Frank Skinner.
THE HOWARDS OF VIRGINIA, COL. Richard Hageman.
THE LETTER. Max Steiner.
THE LONG VOYAGE HOME. Richard Hageman.
THE MARK OF ZORRO, FOX. Alfred Newman.
MY FAVORITE WIFE. Roy Webb.
NORTH WEST MOUNTED POLICE. Victor Young.
ONE MILLION B. C., Hal Roach, UA. Werner Heymann.
OUR TOWN. Aaron Copland.
REBECCA. Franz Waxman.
THE THIEF OF BAGDAD. Miklos Rozsa.
WATERLOO BRIDGE. Herbert Stothart.

MUSIC - BEST SONG (O-168)

WHEN YOU WISH UPON A STAR, Pinocchio. Music, Leigh Harline. Lyrics, Ned Washington.
DOWN ARGENTINE WAY, *Down Argentine Way.* Music, Harry Warren. Lyrics, Mack Gordon.
I'D KNOW YOU ANYWHERE, *You'll Find Out,* RKO. Music, Jimmy McHugh. Lyrics, Johnny Mercer.
IT'S A BLUE WORLD, *Music In My Heart,* COL. Music and Lyrics by Chet Forrest and Bob Wright.
LOVE OF MY LIFE, *Second Chorus.* Music, Artie Shaw. Lyrics, Johnny Mercer.
ONLY FOREVER, *Rhythm On The River,* PAR. Music, James Monaco. Lyrics, John Burke.
OUR LOVE AFFAIR, *Strike Up The Band.* Music and Lyrics by Roger Edens and Georgie Stoll.
WALTZING IN THE CLOUDS, *Spring Parade.* Music, Robert Stolz. Lyrics, Gus Kahn.
WHO AM I?, *Hit Parade Of 1941.* Music, Jule Styne. Lyrics, Walter Bullock.

SOUND (O-169)

STRIKE UP THE BAND. Douglas Shearer.
BEHIND THE NEWS, REP. Charles Lootens.
CAPTAIN CAUTION, Roach, UA. Elmer Raguse.
THE GRAPES OF WRATH. E. H. Hansen.
THE HOWARDS OF VIRGINIA. Jack Whitney, General Service.
KITTY FOYLE. John Aalberg.
NORTH WEST MOUNTED POLICE. Loren Ryder.
OUR TOWN. Thomas Moulton.
THE SEA HAWK. Nathan Levinson.
SPRING PARADE. Bernard B. Brown.
TOO MANY HUSBANDS, COL. John Livadary.

SHORT FILMS (O-170)

(Cartoons)
MILKY WAY, MGM. (Rudolph Ising Series)
PUSS GETS THE BOOT, MGM. (Cat and Mouse Series)
A WILD HARE, Leon Schlesinger, WB.
(One-reel)
QUICKER 'N A WINK, Pete Smith, MGM.
LONDON CAN TAKE IT, WB. (Vitaphone Varieties)
MORE ABOUT NOSTRADAMUS, MGM.
SIEGE, RKO. (Reelism)
(Two-reel)
TEDDY, THE ROUGH RIDER, WB. (Historical Featurette)
EYES OF THE NAVY, MGM. (Crime Doesn't Pay)
SERVICE WITH THE COLORS, WB. (National Defense Series)

SPECIAL EFFECTS (O-171)

THE THIEF OF BAGDAD. Photographic: Lawrence Butler. Sound: Jack Whitney.
THE BLUE BIRD. Photographic: Fred Sersen. Sound: E. H. Hansen.
BOOM TOWN. Photographic: A. Arnold Gillespie. Sound: Douglas Shearer.
THE BOYS FROM SYRACUSE. Photographic: John P. Fulton. Sound: Bernard B. Brown and Joseph Lapis.
DR. CYCLOPS, PAR. Photographic: Farciot Edouart and Gordon Jennings. Sound: No credit listed.
FOREIGN CORRESPONDENT. Photographic: Paul Eagler. Sound:

Thomas T. Moulton.
THE INVISIBLE MAN RETURNS, U. Photographic: John P. Fulton. Sound: Bernard B. Brown and William Hedgecock.
THE LONG VOYAGE HOME. Photographic: R. T. Layton and R. O. Binger. Sound: Thomas T. Moulton.
ONE MILLION B. C. Photographic: Roy Seawright. Sound: Elmer Raguse.
REBECCA. Photographic: Jack Cosgrove. Sound: Arthur Johns.
THE SEA HAWK. Photographic: Byron Haskin. Sound: Nathan Levinson.
SWISS FAMILY ROBINSON, RKO. Photographic: Vernon L. Walker. Sound. John O. Aalberg.
TYPHOON, PAR. Photographic: Farciot Edouart and Gordon Jennings. Sound: Loren Ryder.
WOMEN IN WAR, REP. Photographic: Howard J. Lydecker, William Bradford and Ellis J. Thackery. Sound: Herbert Norsch.

HONORARY AND OTHER (O-172)

(Other)
BOB HOPE, in recognition of his unselfish services to the Motion Picture Industry.
COLONEL NATHAN LEVINSON for his outstanding service to the industry and the Army during the past nine years, which has made possible the present efficient mobilization of the motion picture industry facilities for the production of Army Training Films.

SCIENTIFIC OR TECHNICAL (O-173)

(Class I)
20TH CENTURY-FOX FILM CORP. for the design and construction of the 20th Century Silenced Camera, developed by DANIEL CLARK, GROVER LAUBE, CHARLES MILLER and ROBERT W. STEVENS.
(Class III)
WB STUDIO ART DEPARTMENT and ANTON GROT for the design and perfection of the WB water ripple and wave illusion machine.

1941

BEST PICTURE (O-174)

HOW GREEN WAS MY VALLEY, FOX.
BLOSSOMS IN THE DUST, MGM.
CITIZEN KANE, Mercury, RKO.
HERE COMES MR. JORDAN, COL.
HOLD BACK THE DAWN, PAR.
THE LITTLE FOXES, Goldwyn, RKO.
THE MALTESE FALCON, WB.
ONE FOOT IN HEAVEN, WB.
SERGEANT YORK, WB.
SUSPICION, RKO.

ACTOR (O-175)

GARY COOPER, Sergeant York.
CARY GRANT, *Penny Serenade,* COL.
WALTER HUSTON, *All That Money Can Buy,* RKO.
ROBERT MONTGOMERY, *Here Comes Mr. Jordan.*
ORSON WELLES, *Citizen Kane.*

ACTRESS (O-176)

JOAN FONTAINE, Suspicion.
BETTE DAVIS, *The Little Foxes.*
OLIVIA DE HAVILLAND, *Hold Back The Dawn.*
GREER GARSON, *Blossoms In The Dust.*
BARBARA STANWYCK, *Ball Of Fire,* Goldwyn, RKO.

SUPPORTING ACTOR (O-177)

DONALD CRISP, How Green Was My Valley.
WALTER BRENNAN, *Sergeant York.*
CHARLES COBURN, *The Devil And Miss Jones,* RKO.

JAMES GLEASON, *Here Comes Mr. Jordan.*
SYDNEY GREENSTREET, *The Maltese Falcon*, WB.

SUPPORTING ACTRESS (O-178)

MARY ASTOR, The Great Lie, WB.
SARA ALLGOOD, *How Green Was My Valley.*
PATRICIA COLLINGE, *The Little Foxes.*
TERESA WRIGHT, *The Little Foxes.*
MARGARET WYCHERLY, *Sergeant York.*

DIRECTING (O-179)

JOHN FORD, How Green Was My Valley.
ALEXANDER HALL, *Here Comes Mr. Jordan.*
HOWARD HAWKS, *Sergeant York.*
ORSON WELLES, *Citizen Kane.*
WILLIAM WYLER, *The Little Foxes.*

WRITING (O-180)

(Original Story)

HERE COMES MR. JORDAN. Harry Segall.
BALL OF FIRE. Thomas Monroe and Billy Wilder.
THE LADY EVE, PAR. Monckton Hoffe.
MEET JOHN DOE, WB. Richard Connell and Robert Presnell.
NIGHT TRAIN, FOX. Gordon Wellesley.

(Original Screenplay)

CITIZEN KANE. Herman J. Mankiewicz and Orson Welles.
THE DEVIL AND MISS JONES. Norman Krasna.
SERGEANT YORK. Harry Chandlee, Abem Finkel, John Huston and Howard Koch.
TALL, DARK AND HANDSOME, FOX. Karl Tunberg and Darrell Ware.
TOM, DICK AND HARRY, RKO. Paul Jarrico.

(Screenplay)

HERE COMES MR. JORDAN. Sidney Buchman and Seton I. Miller.
HOLD BACK THE DAWN. Charles Brackett and Billy Wilder.
HOW GREEN WAS MY VALLEY. Philip Dunne.
THE LITTLE FOXES. Lillian Hellman.
THE MALTESE FALCON. John Huston.

CINEMATOGRAPHY (O-181)

(Black-and-White)

HOW GREEN WAS MY VALLEY. Arthur Miller.
THE CHOCOLATE SOLDIER, MGM. Karl Freund.
CITIZEN KANE. Gregg Toland.
DR. JEKYLL AND MR. HYDE, MGM. Joseph Ruttenberg.
HERE COMES MR. JORDAN. Joseph Walker.
HOLD BACK THE DAWN. Leo Tover.
SERGEANT YORK. Sol Polito.
SUN VALLEY SERENADE, FOX. Edward Cronjager.
SUNDOWN, Wanger, UA. Charles Lang.
THAT HAMILTON WOMAN, Korda, UA. Rudolph Mate.

(Color)

BLOOD AND SAND, FOX. Ernest Palmer and Ray Rennahan.
ALOMA OF THE SOUTH SEAS, PAR. Wilfred M. Cline, Karl Struss and William Snyder.
BILLY THE KID, MGM. William V. Skall and Leonard Smith.
BLOSSOMS IN THE DUST. Karl Freund and W. Howard Greene.
DIVE BOMBER, WB. Bert Glennon.
LOUISIANA PURCHASE, PAR. Harry Hallenberger and Ray Rennahan.

ART DIRECTION - SET DECORATION (O-182)

(Black-and-White)

HOW GREEN WAS MY VALLEY. Richard Day and Nathan Juran. Interior Decoration: Thomas Little.
CITIZEN KANE. Perry Ferguson and Van Nest Polglase. Interior Decoration: Al Fields and Darrell Silvera.
FLAME OF NEW ORLEANS, U. Martin Obzina and Jack Otterson. Interior Decoration: Russell A. Gausman.
HOLD BACK THE DAWN. Hans Dreier and Robert Usher. Interior Decoration: Sam Comer.
LADIES IN RETIREMENT, COL. Lionel Banks. Interior Decoration: George Montgomery.
THE LITTLE FOXES. Stephen Goosson. Interior Decoration: Howard Bristol.
SERGEANT YORK. John Hughes. Interior Decoration: Fred MacLean.
SON OF MONTE CRISTO, Small, UA. John DuCasse Schulze. Interior Decoration: Edward G. Boyle.
SUNDOWN. Alexander Golitzen. Interior Decoration: Richard Irvine.
THAT HAMILTON WOMAN. Vincent Korda. Interior Decoration: Julia Heron.
WHEN LADIES MEET, MGM. Cedric Gibbons and Randall Duell. Interior Decoration: Edwin B. Willis.

(Color)

BLOSSOMS IN THE DUST. Cedric Gibbons and Urie McCleary. Interior Decoration: Edwin B. Willis.
BLOOD AND SAND. Richard Day and Joseph C. Wright. Interior Decoration: Thomas Little.
LOUISIANA PURCHASE. Raoul Pene du Bois. Interior Decoration: Stephen A. Seymour.

FILM EDITING (O-183)

SERGEANT YORK. William Holmes.
CITIZEN KANE. Robert Wise.
DR. JEKYLL AND MR. HYDE. Harold F. Kress.
HOW GREEN WAS MY VALLEY. James B. Clark.
THE LITTLE FOXES. Daniel Mandell.

MUSIC - SCORING (O-184)

(Scoring of a Dramatic Picture)

ALL THAT MONEY CAN BUY. Bernard Herrmann.
BACK STREET, U. Frank Skinner.
BALL OF FIRE. Alfred Newman.
CHEERS OF MISS BISHOP, Rowland, UA. Edward Ward.
CITIZEN KANE. Bernard Herrmann.
DR. JEKYLL AND MR. HYDE. Franz Waxman.
HOLD BACK THE DAWN. Victor Young.
HOW GREEN WAS MY VALLEY. Alfred Newman.
KING OF THE ZOMBIES, MNG. Edward Kay.
LADIES IN RETIREMENT. Morris Stoloff and Ernst Toch.
THE LITTLE FOXES. Meredith Willson.
LYDIA, Korda, UA. Miklos Rozsa.
MERCY ISLAND, REP. Cy Feuer and Walter Scharf.
SERGEANT YORK. Max Steiner.
SO ENDS OUR NIGHT, Loew-Lewin, UA. Louis Gruenberg.
SUNDOWN. Miklos Rozsa.
SUSPICION. Franz Waxman.
TANKS A MILLION, Roach, UA. Edward Ward.
THAT UNCERTAIN FEELING, Lubitsch, UA. Werner Heymann.
THIS WOMAN IS MINE, U. Richard Hageman.

(Scoring of a Musical Picture)

DUMBO, Disney, RKO. Frank Churchill and Oliver Wallace.
ALL AMERICAN CO-ED, Roach, UA. Edward Ward.
BIRTH OF THE BLUES, PAR. Robert Emmett Dolan.
BUCK PRIVATES, U. Charles Previn.
THE CHOCOLATE SOLDIER. Herbert Stothart and Bronislau Kaper.
ICE-CAPADES, REP. Cy Feuer.
THE STRAWBERRY BLONDE, WB. Heinz Roemheld.
SUN VALLEY SERENADE. Emil Newman.
SUNNY, RKO. Anthony Collins.
YOU'LL NEVER GET RICH, COL. Morris Stoloff.

MUSIC - BEST SONG (O-185)

THE LAST TIME I SAW PARIS, Lady Be Good, MGM. Music, Jerome Kern. Lyrics, Oscar Hammerstein II.
BABY MINE, *Dumbo.* Music, Frank Churchill. Lyrics, Ned Washington.
BE HONEST WITH ME, *Ridin' On A Rainbow*, REP. Music and Lyrics by Gene Autry and Fred Rose.
BLUES IN THE NIGHT, *Blues In The Night*, WB. Music, Harold Arlen. Lyrics, Johnny Mercer.
BOOGIE WOOGIE BUGLE BOY OF COMPANY B, *Buck Privates.* Hugh Prince. Lyrics, Don Raye.
CHATTANOOGA CHOO CHOO, *Sun Valley Serenade.* Music, Harry Warren. Lyrics, Mack Gordon.

DOLORES, *Las Vegas Nights*, PAR. Music, Lou Alter. Lyrics, Frank Loesser.
OUT OF THE SILENCE, *All American Co-Ed*. Music and Lyrics by Lloyd B. Norlind.
SINCE I KISSED MY BABY GOODBYE, *You'll Never Get Rich*. Music and Lyrics by Cole Porter.

SOUND (O-186)

THAT HAMILTON WOMAN. Jack Whitney, General Service.
APPOINTMENT FOR LOVE, U. Bernard B. Brown.
BALL OF FIRE. Thomas Moulton.
THE CHOCOLATE SOLDIER. Douglas Shearer.
CITIZEN KANE. John Aalberg.
THE DEVIL PAYS OFF, REP, Charles Lootens.
HOW GREEN WAS MY VALLEY. E. H. Hansen.
THE MEN IN HER LIFE, COL. John Livadary.
SERGEANT YORK. Nathan Levinson.
SKYLARK, PAR. Loren Ryder.
TOPPER RETURNS, Roach, UA. Elmer Raguse.

SHORT FILMS (O-187)

(Cartoons)

LEND A PAW, Walt Disney, RKO.
BOOGIE WOOGIE BUGLE BOY OF COMPANY B, Walter Lantz, U.
HIAWATHA'S RABBIT HUNT, Leon Schlesinger, WB.
HOW WAR CAME, COL. (Raymond Gram Swing Series)
THE NIGHT BEFORE CHRISTMAS, MGM. (Tom and Jerry Series)
RHAPSODY IN RIVETS, Leon Schlesinger, WB.
THE ROOKIE BEAR, MGM. (Bear Series)
RHYTHM IN THE RANKS, PAR. (George Pal Puppetoon Series)
SUPERMAN NO. 1, PAR.
TRUANT OFFICER DONALD, Walt Disney, RKO.

(One-reel)

OF PUPS AND PUZZLES, MGM. (Passing Parade Series)
ARMY CHAMPIONS, Pete Smith, MGM. (Pete Smith Specialties)
BEAUTY AND THE BEACH, PAR. (Headliner Series)
DOWN ON THE FARM, PAR. (Speaking of Animals)
FORTY BOYS AND A SONG, WB. (Melody Master Series)
KINGS OF THE TURF, WB. (Color Parade Series)
SAGEBRUSH AND SILVER, FOX. (Magic Carpet Series)

(Two-reel)

MAIN STREET ON THE MARCH, MGM. (Two-reel Special)
ALIVE IN THE DEEP, Woodard Productions, Inc.
FORBIDDEN PASSAGE, MGM. (Crime Doesn't Pay)
THE GAY PARISIAN, WB. (Miniature Featurette Series)
THE TANKS ARE COMING, WB. (National Defense Series)

DOCUMENTARY (O-188)

CHURCHILL'S ISLAND, NFC, UA.
ADVENTURES IN THE BRONX, Film Assocs.
BOMBER, U.S. Office for Emergency Management Film Unit.
CHRISTMAS UNDER FIRE, British Ministry of Information, WB.
LETTER FROM HOME, British Ministry of Information.
LIFE OF A THOROUGHBRED, FOX.
NORWAY IN REVOLT, MOT, RKO.
SOLDIERS OF THE SKY, FOX.
WAR CLOUDS IN THE PACIFIC, NFC.

SPECIAL EFFECTS (O-189)

I WANTED WINGS, PAR. Photographic: Farciot Edouart and Gordon Jennings. Sound: Louis Mesenkop.
ALOMA OF THE SOUTH SEAS. Photographic: Farciot Edouart and Gordon Jennings. Sound: Louis Mesenkop.
FLIGHT COMMAND, MGM. Photographic: A. Arnold Gillespie. Sound: Douglas Shearer.
THE INVISIBLE WOMAN, U. Photographic: John Fulton. Sound: John Hall.
THE SEA WOLF, WB. Photographic: Byron Haskin. Sound: Nathan Levinson.
THAT HAMILTON WOMAN. Photographic: Lawrence Butler. Sound: William H. Wilmarth.
TOPPER RETURNS. Photographic: Roy Seawright. Sound: Elmer Raguse.
A YANK IN THE R.A.F., FOX. Photographic: Fred Sersen. Sound: E. H. Hansen.

HONORARY AND OTHER (O-190)

(Irving G. Thalberg Memorial Award)

Walt Disney

(Other)

REY SCOTT for his extraordinary achievement in producing Kukan, the film record of China's struggle, including its photography with a 16mm camera under the most difficult and dangerous conditions.
THE BRITISH MINISTRY OF INFORMATION for its vivid and dramatic presentation of the heroism of the RAF in the documentary film, Target For Tonight.
LEOPOLD STOKOWSKI and his associates for their unique achievement in the creation of a new form of visualized music in Walt Disney's production Fantasia, thereby widening the scope of the motion picture as entertainment and as an art form.
WALT DISNEY, WILLIAM GARITY, JOHN N. A. HAWKINS and the RCA MANUFACTURING COMPANY, for their outstanding contribution to the advancement of the use of sound in motion pictures through the production of Fantasia.

SCIENTIFIC OR TECHNICAL (O-191)

(Class II)

ELECTRICAL RESEARCH PRODUCTS DIVISION OF WESTERN ELECTRIC CO., INC., for the development of the precision integrating sphere densitometer.
RCA MANUFACTURING CO. for the design and development of the MI-3043 Uni-directional microphone.

(Class III)

RAY WILKINSON and the PARAMOUNT STUDIO LABORATORY for pioneering in the use of and for the first practical application to release printing of fine grain positive stock.
CHARLES LOOTENS and the REPUBLIC STUDIO SOUND DEPARTMENT for pioneering the use of and for the first practical application to motion picture production of CLASS B push-pull variable area recording.
WILBUR SILVERTOOTH and the PARAMOUNT STUDIO ENGINEERING DEPARTMENT for the design and computation of a relay condenser system applicable to transparency process projection, delivering considerably more usable light.
PARAMOUNT PICTURES, INC., and 20TH CENTURY-FOX FILM CORP. for the development and first practical application to motion picture production of an automatic scene slating device.
DOUGLAS SHEARER and the MGM STUDIO SOUND DEPARTMENT, and to LOREN RYDER and the PARAMOUNT STUDIO SOUND DEPARTMENT for pioneering the development of fine grain emulsions for variable density original sound recording in studio production.

1942

BEST PICTURE (O-192)

MRS. MINIVER, MGM.
THE INVADERS, Ortus, COL (British).
KINGS ROW, WB.
THE MAGNIFICENT AMBERSONS, Mercury, RKO.
THE PIED PIPER, FOX.
THE PRIDE OF THE YANKEES, Goldwyn, RKO.
RANDOM HARVEST, MGM.
THE TALK OF THE TOWN, COL.
WAKE ISLAND, PAR.
YANKEE DOODLE DANDY, WB.

ACTOR (O-193)

JAMES CAGNEY, Yankee Doodle Dandy.
RONALD COLMAN, *Random Harvest.*
GARY COOPER, *The Pride Of The Yankees.*
WALTER PIDGEON, *Mrs. Miniver.*

MONTY WOOLLEY, *The Pied Piper.*

ACTRESS (O-194)
GREER GARSON, Mrs. Miniver.
BETTE DAVIS, *Now, Voyager,* WB.
KATHARINE HEPBURN, *Woman Of the Year,* MGM.
ROSALIND RUSSELL, *My Sister Eileen,* COL.
TERESA WRIGHT, *The Pride Of The Yankees.*

SUPPORTING ACTOR (O-195)
VAN HEFLIN, Johnny Eager, MGM.
WILLIAM BENDIX, *Wake Island,* PAR.
WALTER HUSTON, *Yankee Doodle Dandy.*
FRANK MORGAN, *Tortilla Flat,* MGM.
HENRY TRAVERS, *Mrs. Miniver.*

SUPPORTING ACTRESS (O-196)
TERESA WRIGHT, Mrs. Miniver.
GLADYS COOPER, *Now, Voyager.*
AGNES MOOREHEAD, *The Magnificent Ambersons.*
SUSAN PETERS, *Random Harvest.*
DAME MAY WHITTY, *Mrs. Miniver.*

DIRECTING (O-197)
WILLIAM WYLER, Mrs. Miniver.
MICHAEL CURTIZ, *Yankee Doodle Dandy.*
JOHN FARROW, *Wake Island.*
MERVYN LEROY, *Random Harvest.*
SAM WOOD, *Kings Row.*

WRITING (O-198)
(Original Story)
THE INVADERS, Ortus, COL (British). Emeric Pressburger.
HOLIDAY INN, PAR. Irving Berlin.
THE PRIDE OF THE YANKEES. Paul Gallico.
THE TALK OF THE TOWN. Sidney Harmon.
YANKEE DOODLE DANDY. Robert Buckner.
(Original Screenplay)
WOMAN OF THE YEAR. Michael Kanin & Ring Lardner, Jr.
ONE OF OUR AIRCRAFT IS MISSING, Powell, UA (British). Michael Powell and Emeric Pressburger.
THE ROAD TO MOROCCO, PAR. Frank Butler and Don Hartman.
WAKE ISLAND. W. R. Burnett and Frank Butler.
THE WAR AGAINST MRS. HADLEY, MGM. George Oppenheimer.
(Screenplay)
MRS. MINIVER. George Froeschel, James Hilton, Claudine West and Arthur Wimperis.
THE INVADERS. Rodney Ackland and Emeric Pressburger.
THE PRIDE OF THE YANKEES. Herman J. Mankiewicz and Jo Swerling.
RANDOM HARVEST. George Froeschel, Claudine West and Arthur Wimperis.
THE TALK OF THE TOWN. Sidney Buchman and Irwin Shaw.

CINEMATOGRAPHY (O-199)
(Black-and-White)
MRS. MINIVER. Joseph Ruttenberg.
KINGS ROW. James Wong Howe.
THE MAGNIFICENT AMBERSONS. Stanley Cortez.
MOONTIDE, FOX. Charles Clarke.
THE PIED PIPER. Edward Cronjager.
THE PRIDE OF THE YANKEES. Rudolph Mate.
TAKE A LETTER, DARLING, PAR. John Mescall.
THE TALK OF THE TOWN. Ted Tetzlaff.
TEN GENTLEMEN FROM WEST POINT, FOX. Leon Shamroy.
THIS ABOVE ALL, FOX. Arthur Miller.
(Color)
THE BLACK SWAN, FOX. Leon Shamroy.
ARABIAN NIGHTS, Wanger, U. Milton Krasner, William V. Skall and W. Howard Greene.
CAPTAINS OF THE CLOUDS, WB. Sol Polito.
JUNGLE BOOK, Korda, UA. W. Howard Greene.
REAP THE WILD WIND, PAR. Victor Milner and William V. Skall.
TO THE SHORES OF TRIPOLI, FOX. Edward Cronjager and William V. Skall.

ART DIRECTION - SET DECORATION (O-200)
(Black-and-White)
THIS ABOVE ALL. Richard Day and Joseph Wright. Interior Decoration: Thomas Little.
GEORGE WASHINGTON SLEPT HERE, WB. Max Parker and Mark-Lee Kirk. Interior Decoration: Casey Roberts.
THE MAGNIFICENT AMBERSONS. Albert S. D'Agostino. Interior Decoration: Al Fields and Darrell Silvera.
THE PRIDE OF THE YANKEES. Perry Ferguson. Interior Decoration: Howard Bristol.
RANDOM HARVEST. Cedric Gibbons and Randall Duell. Interior Decoration: Edwin B. Willis and Jack Moore.
THE SHANGHAI GESTURE, Arnold, UA. Boris Leven. Interior Decoration: Boris Leven.
SILVER QUEEN, Sherman, UA. Ralph Berger. Interior Decoration: Emile Kuri.
THE SPOILERS, U. John B. Goodman and Jack Otterson. Interior Decoration: Russell A. Gausman and Edward R. Robinson.
TAKE A LETTER, DARLING. Hans Dreier and Roland Anderson. Interior Decoration: Sam Comer.
THE TALK OF THE TOWN. Lionel Banks and Rudolph Sternad. Interior Decoration: Fay Babcock.
(Color)
MY GAL SAL, FOX. Richard Day and Joseph Wright. Interior Decoration: Thomas Little.
ARABIAN NIGHTS. Alexander Golitzen and Jack Otterson. Interior Decoration: Russell A. Gausman and Ira S. Webb.
CAPTAINS OF THE CLOUDS. Ted Smith. Interior Decoration: Casey Roberts.
JUNGLE BOOK. Vincent Korda. Interior Decoration: Julia Heron.
REAP THE WILD WIND. Hans Dreier and Roland Anderson. Interior Decoration: George Sawley.

FILM EDITING (O-201)
THE PRIDE OF THE YANKEES. Daniel Mandell.
MRS. MINIVER. Harold F. Kress.
THE TALK OF THE TOWN. Otto Meyer.
THIS ABOVE ALL. Walter Thompson.
YANKEE DOODLE DANDY. George Amy.

MUSIC - SCORING (O-202)
(Scoring of a Dramatic or Comedy Picture)
NOW, VOYAGER. Max Steiner.
ARABIAN NIGHTS. Frank Skinner.
BAMBI, Disney, RKO. Frank Churchill and Edward Plumb.
THE BLACK SWAN. Alfred Newman.
THE CORSICAN BROTHERS, Small, UA. Dimitri Tiomkin.
FLYING TIGERS, REP. Victor Young.
THE GOLD RUSH, Chaplin, UA. Max Terr.
I MARRIED A WITCH, Cinema Guild, UA. Roy Webb.
JOAN OF PARIS, RKO. Roy Webb.
JUNGLE BOOK. Miklos Rozsa.
KLONDIKE FURY, MNG. Edward Kay.
THE PRIDE OF THE YANKEES. Leigh Harline.
RANDOM HARVEST. Herbert Stothart.
THE SHANGHAI GESTURE. Richard Hageman.
SILVER QUEEN. Victor Young.
TAKE A LETTER, DARLING. Victor Young.
THE TALK OF THE TOWN. Frederick Hollander and Morris Stoloff.
TO BE OR NOT TO BE, Lubitsch, UA. Werner Heymann.
(Scoring of a Musical Picture)
YANKEE DOODLE DANDY. Ray Heindorf and Heinz Roemheld.
FLYING WITH MUSIC, Roach, UA. Edward Ward.
FOR ME AND MY GAL, MGM. Roger Edens and Georgie Stoll.
HOLIDAY INN. Robert Emmett Dolan.

IT STARTED WITH EVE, U. Charles Previn and Hans Salter.
JOHNNY DOUGHBOY, REP. Walter Scharf.
MY GAL SAL. Alfred Newman.
YOU WERE NEVER LOVELIER, COL. Leigh Harline.

MUSIC - BEST SONG (O-203)

WHITE CHRISTMAS, Holiday Inn. Music and Lyrics by Irving Berlin.
ALWAYS IN MY HEART, *Always In My Heart*, WB. Music, Ernesto Lecuona. Lyrics, Kim Gannon.
DEARLY BELOVED, *You Were Never Lovelier*. Music, Jerome Kern. Lyrics, Johnny Mercer.
HOW ABOUT YOU? from *Babes On Broadway*, MGM. Music, Burton Lane. Lyrics, Ralph Freed.
IT SEEMS I HEARD THAT SONG BEFORE, *Youth On Parade*, REP. Music, Jule Styne. Lyrics, Sammy Cahn.
I'VE GOT A GAL IN KALAMAZOO, *Orchestra Wives*, FOX. Music, Harry Warren. Lyrics, Mack Gordon.
LOVE IS A SONG, *Bambi*. Music, Frank Churchill. Lyrics, Larry Morey.
PENNIES FOR PEPPINO, *Flying With Music*. Music, Edward Ward. Lyrics, Chet Forrest and Bob Wright.
PIG FOOT PETE, *Hellzapoppin*, U. Music, Gene de Paul. Lyrics, Don Raye.
THERE'S A BREEZE ON LAKE LOUISE, *The Mayor Of 44th Street*, RKO. Music, Harry Revel. Lyrics, Mort Greene.

SOUND (O-204)

YANKEE DOODLE DANDY. Nathan Levinson.
ARABIAN NIGHTS. Bernard Brown.
BAMBI. Sam Slyfield.
FLYING TIGERS. Daniel Bloomberg.
FRIENDLY ENEMIES, Small, UA. Jack Whitney, Sound Service, Inc.
THE GOLD RUSH. James Fields, RCA Sound.
MRS. MINIVER. Douglas Shearer.
ONCE UPON A HONEYMOON, RKO. Steve Dunn.
THE PRIDE OF THE YANKEES. Thomas Moulton.
ROAD TO MOROCCO. Loren Ryder.
THIS ABOVE ALL. E. H. Hansen.
YOU WERE NEVER LOVELIER. John Livadary.

SHORT FILMS (O-205)

(Cartoons)

DER FUEHRER'S FACE, Walt Disney, RKO.
ALL OUT FOR V, FOX.
THE BLITZ WOLF, MGM.
JUKE BOX JAMBOREE, Walt Lantz, U.
PIGS IN A POLKA, Leon Schlesinger, WB.
TULIPS SHALL GROW, PAR. (George Pal Puppetoon)

(One-reel)

SPEAKING OF ANIMALS AND THEIR FAMILIES. PAR. (Speaking Of Animals)
DESERT WONDERLAND, FOX. (Magic Carpet Series)
MARINES IN THE MAKING, MGM. (Pete Smith Specialties)
UNITED STATES MARINE BAND, WB. (Melody Master Bands)

(Two-reel)

BEYOND THE LINE OF DUTY, WB. (Broadway Brevities)
DON'T TALK, MGM. (Two-reel Special)
PRIVATE SMITH OF THE U.S.A., RKO. (This Is America Series)

DOCUMENTARY (O-206)

BATTLE OF MIDWAY, U.S. Navy, FOX.
KOKODA FRONT LINE, Australian News Information Bureau.
MOSCOW STRIKES BACK, ARK (Russian).
PRELUDE TO WAR, U.S. Army Special Services.
A SHIP IS BORN, U.S. Merchant Marine, WB.
AFRICA, PRELUDE TO VICTORY, MOT, FOX.
COMBAT REPORT, U.S. Army Signal Corps.
CONQUER BY THE CLOCK, Office of War Information, RKO. Frederic Ullman, Jr.
THE GRAIN THAT BUILT A HEMISPHERE, Coordinator's Office, Motion Picture Society for the Americas. DNY.

HENRY BROWNE, FARMER, U.S. Department of Agriculture, REP.
HIGH OVER THE BORDERS, NFC.
HIGH STAKES IN THE EAST, Netherlands Information Bureau.
INSIDE FIGHTING CHINA, NFC.
IT'S EVERYBODY'S WAR, Office of War Information, FOX.
LISTEN TO BRITAIN, British Ministry of Informaton.
LITTLE BELGIUM, Belgian Ministry of Information.
LITTLE ISLES OF FREEDOM, Victor Stoloff and Edgar Loew. WB.
MR. BLABBERMOUTH, Office of War Information, MGM.
MR. GARDENIA JONES, Office of War Information, MGM.
NEW SPIRIT, U.S. Treasury Department. DNY.
THE PRICE OF VICTORY, Office of War Information, PAR. Pine-Thomas.
TWENTY-ONE MILES, British Ministry of Information.
WE REFUSE TO DIE, Office of War Information, PAR. William C. Thomas.
WHITE EAGLE, Cocanen Films.
WINNING YOUR WINGS, U.S. Army Air Force, WB.

SPECIAL EFFECTS (O-207)

REAP THE WILD WIND. Photographic: Farciot Edouart, Gordon Jennings and William L. Pereira. Sound: Louis Mesenkop.
THE BLACK SWAN. Photographic: Fred Sersen. Sound: Roger Heman and George Leverett.
DESPERATE JOURNEY, WB. Photographic: Byron Haskin. Sound: Nathan Levinson.
FLYING TIGERS. Photographic: Howard Lydecker. Sound: Daniel J. Bloomberg.
INVISIBLE AGENT, U. Photographic: John Fulton. Sound: Bernard B. Brown.
JUNGLE BOOK. Photographic: Lawrence Butler. Sound: William H. Wilmarth.
MRS. MINIVER. Photographic: A. Arnold Gillespie and Warren Newcombe. Sound: Douglas Shearer.
THE NAVY COMES THROUGH, RKO. Photographic: Vernon L. Walker. Sound: James G. Stewart.
ONE OF OUR AIRCRAFT IS MISSING. Photographic: Ronald Neame. Sound: C. C. Stevens.
PRIDE OF THE YANKEES. Photographic: Jack Cosgrove and Ray Binger. Sound: Thomas T. Moulton.

HONORARY AND OTHER (O-208)

(Irving G. Thalberg Memorial Award)

Sidney Franklin

(Other)

CHARLES BOYER for his progressive cultural achievement in establishing the French Research Foundation in Los Angeles as a source of reference for the Hollywood Motion Picture Industry.
NOEL COWARD for his outstanding production achievement in In Which We Serve.
MGM STUDIO for its achievement in representing the American Way of Life in the production of the Andy Hardy series of films.

SCIENTIFIC OR TECHNICAL (O-209)

(Class II)

CARROLL CLARK, F. THOMAS THOMPSON and the RKO STUDIO ART and MINIATURE DEPARTMENTS for the design and construction of a moving cloud and horizon machine.
DANIEL B. CLARK and the 20TH CENTURY-FOX FILM CORP. for the development of a lens calibration system and the application of this system to exposure control in cinematography.

(Class III)

ROBERT HENDERSON and the PARAMOUNT STUDIO ENGINEERING and TRANSPARENCY DEPARTMENTS for the design and construction of adjustable light bridges and screen frames for transparency process photography.
DANIEL J. BLOOMBERG and the REPUBLIC STUDIO SOUND DEPARTMENT for the design and application to motion picture production of a device for marking action negative for pre-selection purposes.

1943

BEST PICTURE (O-210)
CASABLANCA, WB.
FOR WHOM THE BELL TOLLS, PAR.
HEAVEN CAN WAIT, FOX.
THE HUMAN COMEDY, MGM.
IN WHICH WE SERVE, Two Cities, UA (British).
MADAME CURIE, MGM.
THE MORE THE MERRIER, COL.
THE OX-BOW INCIDENT, FOX.
THE SONG OF BERNADETTE, FOX.
WATCH ON THE RHINE, WB.

ACTOR (O-211)
PAUL LUKAS, Watch On The Rhine.
HUMPHREY BOGART, *Casablanca.*
GARY COOPER, *For Whom The Bell Tolls.*
WALTER PIDGEON, *Madame Curie.*
MICKEY ROONEY, *The Human Comedy.*

ACTRESS (O-212)
JENNIFER JONES, The Song Of Bernadette.
JEAN ARTHUR, *The More The Merrier.*
INGRID BERGMAN, *For Whom The Bell Tolls.*
JOAN FONTAINE, *The Constant Nymph,* WB.
GREER GARSON, *Madame Curie.*

SUPPORTING ACTOR (O-213)
CHARLES COBURN, The More The Merrier.
CHARLES BICKFORD, *The Song Of Bernadette.*
J. CARROL NAISH, *Sahara,* COL.
CLAUDE RAINS, *Casablanca.*
AKIM TAMIROFF, *For Whom The Bell Tolls.*

SUPPORTING ACTRESS (O-214)
KATINA PAXINOU, For Whom The Bell Tolls.
GLADYS COOPER, *The Song Of Bernadette.*
PAULETTE GODDARD, *So Proudly We Hail,* PAR.
ANNE REVERE, *The Song Of Bernadette.*
LUCILE WATSON, *Watch On The Rhine.*

DIRECTING (O-215)
MICHAEL CURTIZ, Casablanca.
CLARENCE BROWN, *The Human Comedy.*
HENRY KING, *The Song Of Bernadette.*
ERNST LUBITSCH, *Heaven Can Wait.*
GEORGE STEVENS, *The More The Merrier.*

WRITING (O-216)
(Original Story)
ACTION IN THE NORTH ATLANTIC, WB. Guy Gilpatric.
THE HUMAN COMEDY. William Saroyan.
DESTINATION TOKYO, WB. Steve Fisher.
THE MORE THE MERRIER. Frank Ross and Robert Russell.
SHADOW OF A DOUBT, U. Gordon McDonell.
(Original Screenplay)
PRINCESS O'ROURKE, WB. Norman Krasna.
AIR FORCE, WB. Dudley Nichols.
IN WHICH WE SERVE. Noel Coward.
THE NORTH STAR, Goldwyn, RKO. Lillian Hellman.
SO PROUDLY WE HAIL. Allan Scott.
(Screenplay)
CASABLANCA. Julius J. Epstein, Philip G. Epstein and Howard Koch.
HOLY MATRIMONY, FOX. Nunnally Johnson.
THE MORE THE MERRIER. Richard Flournoy, Lewis R. Foster, Frank Ross and Robert Russell.

THE SONG OF BERNADETTE. George Seaton.
WATCH ON THE RHINE. Dashiell Hammett.

CINEMATOGRAPHY (O-217)
(Black-and-White)
THE SONG OF BERNADETTE. Arthur Miller.
AIR FORCE. James Wong Howe, Elmer Dyer and Charles Marshall.
CASABLANCA. Arthur Edeson.
CORVETTE K-225, U. Tony Gaudio.
FIVE GRAVES TO CAIRO, PAR. John Seitz.
THE HUMAN COMEDY. Harry Stradling.
MADAME CURIE. Joseph Ruttenberg.
THE NORTH STAR. James Wong Howe.
SAHARA. Rudolph Mate.
SO PROUDLY WE HAIL. Charles Lang.
(Color)
PHANTOM OF THE OPERA, U. Hal Mohr and W. Howard Greene.
FOR WHOM THE BELL TOLLS. Ray Rennahan.
HEAVEN CAN WAIT. Edward Cronjager.
HELLO, FRISCO, HELLO, FOX. Charles G. Clarke and Allen Davey.
LASSIE COME HOME, MGM. Leonard Smith.
THOUSANDS CHEER, MGM. George Folsey.

ART DIRECTION - SET DECORATION (O-218)
(Black-and-White)
THE SONG OF BERNADETTE. James Basevi and William Darling. Interior Decoration: Thomas Little.
FIVE GRAVES TO CAIRO. Hans Dreier and Ernst Fegte. Interior Decoration: Bertram Granger.
FLIGHT FOR FREEDOM, RKO. Albert S. D'Agostino and Carroll Clark. Interior Decoration: Darrell Silvera and Harley Miller.
MADAME CURIE. Cedric Gibbons and Paul Groesse. Interior Decoration: Edwin B. Willis and Hugh Hunt.
MISSION TO MOSCOW, WB. Carl Weyl. Interior Decoration: George J. Hopkins.
THE NORTH STAR. Perry Ferguson. Interior Decoration: Howard Bristol.
(Color)
PHANTOM OF THE OPERA. Alexander Golitzen and John B. Goodman. Interior Decoration: Russell A. Gausman and Ira S. Webb.
FOR WHOM THE BELL TOLLS. Hans Dreier and Haldane Douglas. Interior Decoration: Bertram Granger.
THE GANG'S ALL HERE, FOX. James Basevi and Joseph C. Wright. Interior Decoration: Thomas Little.
THIS IS THE ARMY, WB. John Hughes and Lt. John Koenig. Interior Decoration: George J. Hopkins.
THOUSANDS CHEER. Cedric Gibbons and Daniel Cathcart. Interior Decoration: Edwin B. Willis and Jacques Mersereau.

FILM EDITING (O-219)
AIR FORCE. George Amy.
CASABLANCA. Owen Marks.
FIVE GRAVES TO CAIRO. Doane Harrison.
FOR WHOM THE BELL TOLLS. Sherman Todd and John Link.
THE SONG OF BERNADETTE. Barbara McLean.

MUSIC - SCORING (O-220)
(Scoring of a Dramatic or Comedy Picture)
THE SONG OF BERNADETTE. Alfred Newman.
THE AMAZING MRS. HOLLIDAY, U. Hans J. Salter and Frank Skinner.
CASABLANCA. Max Steiner.
THE COMMANDOS STRIKE AT DAWN, COL. Louis Gruenberg and Morris Stoloff.
THE FALLEN SPARROW, RKO. C Bakaleinikoff and Roy Webb.
FOR WHOM THE BELL TOLLS. Victor Young.
HANGMEN ALSO DIE, Arnold, UA. Hanns Eisler.
HI DIDDLE DIDDLE, Stone, UA. Phil Boutelje.
IN OLD OKLAHOMA, REP. Walter Scharf.
JOHNNY COME LATELY, Cagney, UA. Leigh Harline.
THE KANSAN, Sherman, UA. Gerard Carbonara.
LADY OF BURLESQUE, Stromberg, UA. Arthur Lange.
MADAME CURIE. Herbert Stothart.

THE MOON AND SIXPENCE, Loew-Lewin, UA. Dimitri Tiomkin.
THE NORTH STAR. Aaron Copland.
VICTORY THROUGH AIR POWER, Disney, UA. Edward H. Plumb, Paul J. Smith and Oliver G. Wallace.

(Scoring of a Musical Picture)

THIS IS THE ARMY. Ray Heindorf.
CONEY ISLAND, FOX. Alfred Newman.
HIT PARADE OF 1943, REP. Walter Scharf.
THE PHANTOM OF THE OPERA. Edward Ward.
SALUDOS AMIGOS, Disney, RKO. Edward H. Plumb, Paul J. Smith and Charles Wolcott.
THE SKY'S THE LIMIT, RKO. Leigh Harline.
SOMETHING TO SHOUT ABOUT, COL. Morris Stoloff.
STAGE DOOR CANTEEN, Lesser, UA. Frederic E. Rich.
STAR SPANGLED RHYTHM, PAR. Robert Emmett Dolan.
THOUSANDS CHEER. Herbert Stothart.

MUSIC - BEST SONG (O-221)

YOU'LL NEVER KNOW, Hello, Frisco, Hello. Music, Harry Warren. Lyrics, Mack Gordon.
BLACK MAGIC, *Star Spangled Rhythm*. Music, Harold Arlen. Lyrics, Johnny Mercer.
CHANGE OF HEART, *Hit Parade Of 1943*. Music, Jule Styne. Lyrics, Harold Adamson.
HAPPINESS IS A THING CALLED JOE, *Cabin In The Sky*, MGM. Music, Harold Arlen. Lyrics, E. Y. Harburg.
MY SHINING HOUR, *The Sky's The Limit*. Music, Harold Arlen. Lyrics, Johnny Mercer.
SALUDOS AMIGOS, *Saludos Amigos*. Music, Charles Wolcott. Lyrics, Ned Washington.
SAY A PRAYER FOR THE BOYS OVER THERE, *Her's To Hold*, U. Music, Jimmy McHugh. Lyrics, Herb Magidson.
THEY'RE EITHER TOO YOUNG OR TOO OLD, *Thank Your Lucky Stars*, WB. Music, Arthur Schwartz. Lyrics, Frank Loesser.
WE MUSTN'T SAY GOOD BYE, *Stage Door Canteen*. Music, James Monaco. Lyrics, Al Dubin.
YOU'D BE SO NICE TO COME HOME TO, *Something To Shout About*. Music and Lyrics by Cole Porter.

SOUND (O-222)

THIS LAND IS MINE, RKO. Stephen Dunn.
HANGMEN ALSO DIE. Jack Whitney, Sound Service, Inc.
IN OLD OKLAHOMA. Daniel J. Bloomberg.
MADAME CURIE. Douglas Shearer.
THE NORTH STAR. Thomas Moulton.
THE PHANTOM OF THE OPERA. Bernard B. Brown.
RIDING HIGH, PAR. Loren L. Ryder.
SAHARA. John Livadary.
SALUDOS AMIGOS. C. O. Slyfield.
SO THIS IS WASHINGTON, Votion, RKO. J. L. Fields, RCA Sound.
THE SONG OF BERNADETTE. E. H. Hansen.
THIS IS THE ARMY. Nathan Levinson.

SHORT FILMS (O-223)

(Cartoons)

YANKEE DOODLE MOUSE, MGM. Frederick Quimby, Prod.
THE DIZZY ACROBAT, Walter Lantz, U. Walter Lantz, Prod.
THE FIVE HUNDRED HATS OF BARTHOLOMEW CUBBINS, PAR. (George Pal Puppetoon)
GREETINGS, BAIT, WB. Leon Schlesinger, Prod.
IMAGINATION, COL. Dave Fleischer, Prod.
REASON AND EMOTION, Walt Disney, RKO. Walt Disney, Prod.

(One-reel)

AMPHIBIOUS FIGHTERS, PAR. Grantland Rice, Prod.
CAVALCADE OF THE DANCE WITH VELOZ AND YOLANDA, WB. (Melody Master Bands) Gordon Hollingshead, Prod.
CHAMPIONS CARRY ON, FOX. (Sports Reviews) Edmund Reek, Prod.
HOLLYWOOD IN UNIFORM, COL. (Screen Snapshots #1, Series 22) Ralph Staub, Prod.
SEEING HANDS, MGM. (Pete Smith Specialty)

(Two-reel)

HEAVENLY MUSIC, MGM. Jerry Bresler and Sam Coslow, Prods.

LETTER TO A HERO, RKO. (This Is America) Fred Ullman, Prod.
MARDI GRAS, PAR. (Musical Parade) Walter MacEwen, Prod.
WOMEN AT WAR, WB. (Technicolor Special) Gordon Hollingshead, Prod.

DOCUMENTARY (O-224)

(Short Subjects)

DECEMBER 7TH, U.S. Navy, Field Photographic Branch, Office of Strategic Services.
CHILDREN OF MARS, This is America Series, RKO.
PLAN FOR DESTRUCTION, MGM.
SWEDES IN AMERICA, Office of War Information, Overseas Motion Picture Bureau.
TO THE PEOPLE OF THE UNITED STATES, U.S. Public Health Service, Walter Wanger Prods.
TOMORROW WE FLY, U.S. Navy, Bureau of Aeronautics.
YOUTH IN CRISIS, MOT, FOX.

(Features)

DESERT VICTORY, British Ministry of Information.
BATTLE OF RUSSIA, Special Service Division of the War Department.
BAPTISM OF FIRE, U.S. Army, Fighting Men Series.
REPORT FROM THE ALEUTIANS, U.S. Army Pictorial Service, Combat Film Series.
WAR DEPARTMENT REPORT, Field Photographic Branch, Office of Strategic Services.

SPECIAL EFFECTS (O-225)

CRASH DIVE, FOX. Photographic: Fred Sersen. Sound: Roger Heman.
AIR FORCE. Photographic: Hans Koenekamp and Rex Wimpy. Sound: Nathan Levinson.
BOMBARDIER, RKO. Photographic: Vernon L. Walker. Sound: James G. Stewart and Roy Granville.
THE NORTH STAR. Photographic: Clarence Slifer and R. O. Binger. Sound: Thomas T. Moulton.
SO PROUDLY WE HAIL. Photographic: Farciot Edouart and Gordon Jennings. Sound: George Dutton.
STAND BY FOR ACTION, MGM. Photographic: A. Arnold Gillespie and Donald Jahraus. Sound: Michael Steinore.

HONORARY AND OTHER (O-226)

(Irving G. Thalberg Memorial Award)

Hal B. Wallis

(Other)

GEORGE PAL for the development of novel methods and techniques in the production of short subjects known as Puppetoons. (plaque)

SCIENTIFIC OR TECHNICAL (O-227)

(Class II)

FARCIOT EDOUART, EARLE MORGAN, BARTON THOMPSON and the PARAMOUNT STUDIO ENGINEERING and TRANSPARENCY DEPARTMENTS for the development and practical application to motion picture production of a method of duplicating and enlarging natural color photographs, transferring the image emulsions to glass plates and projecting these slides by especially designed stereopticon equipment.
PHOTO PRODUCTS DEPARTMENT, E. I. duPONT de NEMOURS AND CO., INC., for the development of fine-grain motion picture films.

(Class III)

DANIEL J. BLOOMBERG and the REPUBLIC STUDIO SOUND DEPARTMENT for the design and development of an inexpensive method of converting Moviolas to Class B push-pull reproduction.
CHARLES GALLOWAY CLARKE and the 20TH CENTURY-FOX STUDIO CAMERA DEPARTMENT for the development and practical application of a device for composing artificial clouds into motion picture scenes during production photography.
FARCIOT EDOUART and the PARAMOUNT STUDIO TRANSPARENCY DEPARTMENT for an automatic electric transparency cueing timer.

WILLARD H. TURNER and the RKO STUDIO SOUND DEPARTMENT for the design and construction of the phono-cue starter.

1944

BEST PICTURE (O-228)
GOING MY WAY, PAR.
DOUBLE INDEMNITY, PAR.
GASLIGHT, MGM.
SINCE YOU WENT AWAY, Selznick Int'l, UA.
WILSON, FOX.

ACTOR (O-229)
BING CROSBY, Going My Way.
CHARLES BOYER, *Gaslight.*
BARRY FITZGERALD, *Going My Way.*
CARY GRANT, *None But The Lonely Heart*, RKO.
ALEXANDER KNOX, *Wilson.*

ACTRESS (O-230)
INGRID BERGMAN, Gaslight.
CLAUDETTE COLBERT, *Since You Went Away.*
BETTE DAVIS, *Mr. Skeffington*, WB.
GREER GARSON, *Mrs. Parkington*, MGM.
BARBARA STANWYCK, *Double Indemnity.*

SUPPORTING ACTOR (O-231)
BARRY FITZGERALD, Going My Way.
HUME CRONYN, *The Seventh Cross*, MGM.
CLAUDE RAINS, *Mr. Skeffington.*
CLIFTON WEBB, *Laura*, FOX.
MONTY WOOLLEY, *Since You Went Away.*

SUPPORTING ACTRESS (O-232)
ETHEL BARRYMORE, None But The Lonely Heart.
JENNIFER JONES, *Since You Went Away.*
ANGELA LANSBURY, *Gaslight.*
ALINE MacMAHON, *Dragon Seed*, MGM.
AGNES MOOREHEAD, *Mrs. Parkington.*

DIRECTING (O-233)
LEO McCAREY, Going My Way.
ALFRED HITCHCOCK, *Lifeboat*, FOX.
HENRY KING, *Wilson.*
OTTO PREMINGER, *Laura.*
BILLY WILDER, *Double Indemnity.*

WRITING (O-234)
(Original Story)
GOING MY WAY. Leo McCarey.
A GUY NAMED JOE, MGM. David Boehm and Chandler Sprague.
LIFEBOAT. John Steinbeck.
NONE SHALL ESCAPE, COL. Alfred Neumann and Joseph Than.
THE SULLIVANS, FOX. Edward Doherty and Jules Schermer.
(Original Screenplay)
WILSON. Lamar Trotti.
HAIL THE CONQUERING HERO, PAR. Preston Sturges.
THE MIRACLE OF MORGAN'S CREEK, PAR. Preston Sturges.
TWO GIRLS AND A SAILOR, MGM. Richard Connell and Gladys Lehman.
WING AND A PRAYER, FOX. Jerome Cady.
(Screenplay)
GOING MY WAY. Frank Butler and Frank Cavett.
DOUBLE INDEMNITY. Raymond Chandler and Billy Wilder.
GASLIGHT. John L. Balderston, Walter Reisch and John Van Druten.
LAURA. Jay Dratler, Samuel Hoffenstein and Betty Reinhardt.
MEET ME IN ST. LOUIS, MGM. Irving Brecher and Fred F. Finkelhoffe.

CINEMATOGRAPHY (O-235)
(Black-and-White)
LAURA. Joseph LaShelle.
DOUBLE INDEMNITY. John Seitz.
DRAGON SEED. Sidney Wagner.
GASLIGHT. Joseph Ruttenberg.
GOING MY WAY. Lionel Lindon.
LIFEBOAT. Glen MacWilliams.
SINCE YOU WENT AWAY. Stanley Cortez and Lee Garmes.
THIRTY SECONDS OVER TOKYO, MGM. Robert Surtees and Harold Rosson.
THE UNINVITED, PAR. Charles Lang.
THE WHITE CLIFFS OF DOVER, MGM. George Folsey.
(Color)
WILSON. Leon Shamroy.
COVER GIRL, COL. Rudy Mate and Allen M. Davey.
HOME IN INDIANA, FOX. Edward Cronjager.
KISMET, MGM. Charles Rosher.
LADY IN THE DARK, PAR. Ray Rennahan.
MEET ME IN ST. LOUIS. George Folsey.

ART DIRECTION - SET DECORATION (O-236)
(Black-and-White)
GASLIGHT. Cedric Gibbons and William Ferrari. Interior Decoration: Edwin B. Willis and Paul Huldschinsky.
ADDRESS UNKNOWN, COL. Lionel Banks and Walter Holscher. Interior Decoration: Joseph Kish.
THE ADVENTURES OF MARK TWAIN, WB. John J. Hughes. Interior Decoration: Fred MacLean.
CASANOVA BROWN, Int'l, RKO. Perry Ferguson. Interior Decoration: Julia Heron.
LAURA. Lyle Wheeler and Leland Fuller. Interior Decoration: Thomas Little.
NO TIME FOR LOVE, PAR. Hans Dreier and Robert Usher. Interior Decoration: Sam Comer.
SINCE YOU WENT AWAY. Mark-Lee Kirk. Interior Decoration: Victor A. Gangelin.
STEP LIVELY, RKO. Albert S. D'Agostino and Carroll Clark. Interior Decoration: Darrell Silvera and Claude Carpenter.
(Color)
WILSON. Wiard Ihnen. Interior Decoration: Thomas Little.
THE CLIMAX, U. John B. Goodman and Alexander Golitzen. Interior Decoration: Russell A. Gausman and Ira S. Webb.
COVER GIRL. Lionel Banks and Cary Odell. Interior Decoration: Fay Babcock.
THE DESERT SONG, WB. Charles Novi. Interior Decoration: Jack McConaghy.
KISMET. Cedric Gibbons and Daniel B. Cathcart. Interior Decoration: Edwin B. Willis and Richard Pefferle.
LADY IN THE DARK. Hans Dreier and Raoul Pene du Bois. Interior Decoration: Ray Moyer.
THE PRINCESS AND THE PIRATE, Goldwyn, RKO. Ernst Fegte. Interior Decoration: Howard Bristol.

FILM EDITING (O-237)
WILSON. Barbara McLean.
GOING MY WAY. Leroy Stone.
JANIE, WB. Owen Marks.
NONE BUT THE LONELY HEART. Roland Gross.
SINCE YOU WENT AWAY. Hal C. Kern and James E. Newcom.

MUSIC - SCORING (O-238)
(Scoring of a Dramatic or Comedy Picture)
SINCE YOU WENT AWAY. Max Steiner.
ADDRESS UNKNOWN, COL. Morris Stoloff and Ernst Toch.
THE ADVENTURES OF MARK TWAIN. Max Steiner.
THE BRIDGE OF SAN LUIS REY, Bogeaus, UA. Dimitri Tiomkin.
CASANOVA BROWN. Arthur Lange.
CHRISTMAS HOLIDAY, U. H. J. Salter.
DOUBLE INDEMNITY. Miklos Rozsa.
THE FIGHTING SEABEES, REP. Walter Scharf and Roy Webb.

THE HAIRY APE, Levey, UA. Michel Michelet and Edward Paul.
IT HAPPENED TOMORROW, Arnold, UA. Robert Stolz.
JACK LONDON, Bronston, UA. Frederic E. Rich.
KISMET. Herbert Stothart.
NONE BUT THE LONELY HEART. C. Bakaleinikoff and Hanns Eisler.
THE PRINCESS AND THE PIRATE. David Rose.
SUMMER STORM, Angelus, UA. Karl Hajos.
THREE RUSSIAN GIRLS, R & F Prods., UA. Franke Harling.
UP IN MABEL'S ROOM, Small, UA. Edward Paul.
VOICE IN THE WIND, Ripley-Monter, UA. Michel Michelet.
WILSON. Alfred Newman.
WOMAN OF THE TOWN, Sherman, UA. Miklos Rozsa.

(Scoring of a Musical Picture)

COVER GIRL. Carmen Dragon and Morris Stoloff.
BRAZIL, REP. Walter Scharf.
HIGHER AND HIGHER, RKO. C. Bakaleinikoff.
HOLLYWOOD CANTEEN, WB. Ray Heindorf.
IRISH EYES ARE SMILING, FOX. Alfred Newman.
KNICKERBOCKER HOLIDAY, RCA, UA. Werner R. Heymann and Kurt Weill.
LADY IN THE DARK. Robert Emmett Dolan.
LADY LET'S DANCE, MNG. Edward Kay.
MEET ME IN ST. LOUIS. Georgie Stoll.
THE MERRY MONAHANS, U, H. J. Salter.
MINSTREL MAN, PRC. Leo Erdody and Ferdie Grofe.
SENSATIONS OF 1945, Stone, UA. Mahlon Merrick.
SONG OF THE OPEN ROAD, Rogers, UA. Charles Previn.
UP IN ARMS, Avalon, RKO. Louis Forbes and Ray Heindorf.

MUSIC - BEST SONG (O-239)

SWINGING ON A STAR, Going My Way. Music, James Van Heusen. Lyrics, Johnny Burke.
I COULDN'T SLEEP A WINK LAST NIGHT, *Higher And Higher.* Music, Jimmy McHugh. Lyrics, Harold Adamson.
I'LL WALK ALONE, *Follow The Boys,* U. Music, Jule Styne. Lyrics, Sammy Cahn.
I'M MAKING BELIEVE, *Sweet And Lowdown,* FOX. Music, James V. Monaco. Lyrics, Mack Gordon.
LONG AGO AND FAR AWAY, *Cover Girl.* Music, Jerome Kern. Lyrics, Ira Gershwin.
NOW I KNOW, *Up In Arms.* Music, Harold Arlen. Lyrics, Ted Koehler.
REMEMBER ME TO CAROLINA, *Minstrel Man.* Music, Harry Revel. Lyrics, Paul Webster.
RIO DE JANEIRO, *Brazil.* Music, Ary Barroso. Lyrics, Ned Washington.
SILVER SHADOWS AND GOLDEN DREAMS, *Lady Let's Dance.* Music, Lew Pollack. Lyrics, Charles Newman.
SWEET DREAMS SWEETHEART, *Hollywood Canteen.* Music, M. K. Jerome. Lyrics, Ted Koehler.
TOO MUCH IN LOVE, *Song Of The Open Road.* Music, Walter Kent. Lyrics, Kim Gannon.
THE TROLLEY SONG, *Meet Me In St. Louis.* Music and Lyrics by Ralph Blane and Hugh Martin.

SOUND (O-240)

WILSON. E. H. Hansen.
BRAZIL. Daniel J. Bloomberg.
CASANOVA BROWN. Thomas T. Moulton, Goldwyn Sound Department.
COVER GIRL. John Livadary.
DOUBLE INDEMNITY. Loren Ryder.
HIS BUTLER'S SISTER, U. Bernard B. Brown.
HOLLYWOOD CANTEEN. Nathan Levinson.
IT HAPPENED TOMORROW, Arnold, UA. Jack Whitney, Sound Service, Inc.
KISMET. Douglas Shearer.
MUSIC IN MANHATTAN, RKO. Stephen Dunn.
VOICE IN THE WIND. W. M. Dalgleish, RCA Sound.

SHORT FILMS (O-241)

(Cartoons)

MOUSE TROUBLE, MGM. Frederick C. Quimby, Prod.

AND TO THINK I SAW IT ON MULBERRY STREET, PAR. (George Pal Puppetoon)
THE DOG, CAT AND CANARY, COL. (Screen Gems)
FISH FRY, U. Walter Lantz, Prod.
HOW TO PLAY FOOTBALL, Walt Disney, RKO. Walt Disney, Prod.
MY BOY, JOHNNY, FOX. Paul Terry, Prod.
SWOONER CROONER, WB.

(One-reel)

WHO'S WHO IN ANIMAL LAND, PAR. (Speaking of Animals) Jerry Fairbanks, Prod.
BLUE GRASS GENTLEMEN, FOX. (Sports Review) Edmund Reek, Prod.
JAMMIN' THE BLUES, WB. (Melody Master Bands) Gordon Hollingshead, Prod.
MOVIE PESTS, MGM. (Pete Smith Specialty)
50TH ANNIVERSARY OF MOTION PICTURES, COL. (Screen Snapshots #9, Series 23) Ralph Staub, Prod.

(Two-reel)

I WON'T PLAY, WB. (Featurette) Gordon Hollingshead, Prod.
BOMBALERA, PAR. (Muscial Parade) Louis Harris, Prod.
MAIN STREET TODAY, MGM. (Two-reel Special) Jerry Bresler, Prod.

DOCUMENTARY (O-242)

(Short Subjects)

WITH THE MARINES AT TARAWA, U.S. Marine Corps.
ARTURO TOSCANINI, Motion Picture Bureau, Overseas Branch, Office of War Information.
NEW AMERICANS, This is America Series, RKO.

(Features)

THE FIGHTING LADY, FOX and U.S. Navy.
RESISTING ENEMY INTERROGATION, U.S. Army Air Force.

SPECIAL EFFECTS (O-243)

THIRTY SECONDS OVER TOKYO. Photographic: A. Arnold Gillespie, Donald Jahraus and Warren Newcombe. Sound: Douglas Shearer.
THE ADVENTURES OF MARK TWAIN. Photographic: Paul Detlefsen and John Crouse. Sound: Nathan Levinson.
DAYS OF GLORY, RKO. Photographic: Vernon L. Walker. Sound: James G. Stewart and Roy Granville.
SECRET COMMAND, COL. Photographic: David Allen, Ray Cory and Robert Wright. Sound: Russell Malmgren and Harry Kusnick.
SINCE YOU WENT AWAY. Photographic: John R. Cosgrove. Sound: Arthur Johns.
THE STORY OF DR. WASSELL, PAR. Photographic: Farciot Edouart and Gordon Jennings. Sound: George Dutton.
WILSON. Photographic: Fred Sersen. Sound: Roger Heman.

HONORARY AND OTHER (O-244)

(Irving G. Thalberg Memorial Award)

Darryl F. Zanuck

(Other)

MARGARET O'BRIEN, outstanding child actress of 1944.
BOB HOPE, for his many services to the Academy, a Life Membership in the Academy of Motion Picture Arts and Sciences.

SCIENTIFIC OR TECHNICAL (O-245)

(Class II Plaque)

STEPHEN DUNN and the RKO STUDIO SOUND DEPARTMENT and RADIO CORPORATION OF AMERICA for the design and development of the electronic compressor-limiter.

(Class III)

LINWOOD DUNN, CECIL LOVE and ACME TOOL MANUFACTURING CO. for the design and construction of the Acme-Dunn Optical Printer.
GROVER LAUBE and the 20TH CENTURY-FOX STUDIO CAMERA DEPARTMENT for the development of a continuous loop projection

device.

WESTERN ELECTRIC CO. for the design and construction of the 1126A Limiting Amplifier for variable density sound recording.
RUSSELL BROWN, RAY HINSDALE and **JOSEPH E. ROBBINS** for the development and production use of the Paramount floating hydraulic boat rocker.
GORDON JENNINGS for the design and construction of the Paramount nodal point tripod.
RADIO CORPORATION OF AMERICA and the **RKO STUDIO SOUND DEPARTMENT** for the design and construction of the RKO reverberation chamber.
DANIEL J. BLOOMBERG and the **REPUBLIC STUDIO SOUND DEPARTMENT** for the design and development of a multi-interlock selector switch.
BERNARD B. BROWN and **JOHN P. LIVADARY** for the design and engineering of a separate soloist and chorus recording room.
PAUL ZEFF, S. J. TWINING and **GEORGE SEID** of the Columbia Studio Laboratory for the formula and application to production of a simplified variable area sound negative developer.
PAUL LERPAE for the design and construction of the Paramount traveling matte projection and photographing device.

1945

BEST PICTURE (O-246)

THE LOST WEEKEND, PAR.
ANCHORS AWEIGH, MGM.
THE BELLS OF ST. MARY'S, Rainbow, RKO.
MILDRED PIERCE, WB.
SPELLBOUND, Selznick Int'l, UA.

ACTOR (O-247)

RAY MILLAND, The Lost Weekend.
BING CROSBY, *The Bells Of St. Mary's.*
GENE KELLY, *Anchors Aweigh.*
GREGORY PECK, *The Keys Of The Kingdom,* FOX.
CORNEL WILDE, *A Song To Remember,* COL.

ACTRESS (O-248)

JOAN CRAWFORD, Mildred Pierce.
INGRID BERGMAN, *The Bells Of St. Mary's.*
GREER GARSON, *The Valley Of Decision,* MGM.
JENNIFER JONES, *Love Letters,* Wallis, PAR.
GENE TIERNEY, *Leave Her To Heaven,* FOX.

SUPPORTING ACTOR (O-249)

JAMES DUNN, A Tree Grows In Brooklyn, FOX.
MICHAEL CHEKHOV, *Spellbound.*
JOHN DALL, *The Corn Is Green,* WB.
ROBERT MITCHUM, *G. I. Joe,* Cowan, UA.
J. CARROL NAISH, *A Medal For Benny,* PAR.

SUPPORTING ACTRESS (O-250)

ANNE REVERE, National Velvet, MGM.
EVE ARDEN, *Mildred Pierce.*
ANN BLYTH, *Mildred Pierce.*
ANGELA LANSBURY, *The Picture Of Dorian Gray,* MGM.
JOAN LORRING, *The Corn Is Green.*

DIRECTING (O-251)

BILLY WILDER, The Lost Weekend.
CLARENCE BROWN, *National Velvet.*
ALFRED HITCHCOCK, *Spellbound.*

LEO McCAREY, *The Bells Of St. Mary's.*
JEAN RENOIR, *The Southerner,* Loew-Hakim, UA.

WRITING (O-252)

(Original Story)
THE HOUSE ON 92ND STREET, FOX. Charles G. Booth.
THE AFFAIRS OF SUSAN, Wallis, PAR. Laszlo Gorog and Thomas Monroe.
A MEDAL FOR BENNY. John Steinbeck and Jack Wagner.
OBJECTIVE-BURMA, WB. Alvah Bessie.
A SONG TO REMEMBER. Ernst Marischka.
(Original Screenplay)
MARIE-LOUISE, PRA (Swiss). Richard Schweizer.
DILLINGER, MNG. Philip Yordan.
MUSIC FOR MILLIONS, MGM. Myles Connolly.
SALTY O'ROURKE, PAR. Milton Holmes.
WHAT NEXT, CORPORAL HARGROVE?, MGM. Harry Kurnitz.
(Screenplay)
THE LOST WEEKEND. Charles Brackett and Billy Wilder.
G. I. JOE. Leopold Atlas, Guy Endore and Philip Stevenson.
MILDRED PIERCE. Ranald MacDougall.
PRIDE OF THE MARINES, WB. Albert Maltz.
A TREE GROWS IN BROOKLYN. Frank Davis and Tess Slesinger.

CINEMATOGRAPHY (O-253)

(Black-and-White)
THE PICTURE OF DORIAN GRAY. Harry Stradling.
THE KEYS OF THE KINGDOM. Arthur Miller.
THE LOST WEEKEND. John F. Seitz.
MILDRED PIERCE. Ernest Haller.
SPELLBOUND. George Barnes.
(Color)
LEAVE HER TO HEAVEN. Leon Shamroy.
ANCHORS AWEIGH. Robert Planck and Charles Boyle.
NATIONAL VELVET. Leonard Smith.
A SONG TO REMEMBER. Tony Gaudio and Allen M. Davey.
THE SPANISH MAIN, RKO. George Barnes.

ART DIRECTION - SET DECORATION (O-254)

(Black-and-White)
BLOOD ON THE SUN, Cagney, UA. Wiard Ihnen. Interior Decoration: A. Roland Fields.
EXPERIMENT PERILOUS, RKO. Albert S. D'Agostino and Jack Okey. Interior Decoration: Darrell Silvera and Claude Carpenter.
THE KEYS OF THE KINGDOM. James Basevi and William Darling. Interior Decoration: Thomas Little and Frank E. Hughes.
LOVE LETTERS, Hal Wallis, PAR. Hans Dreier and Roland Anderson. Interior Decoration: Sam Comer and Ray Moyer.
THE PICTURE OF DORIAN GRAY. Cedric Gibbons and Hans Peters. Interior Decoration: Edwin B. Willis, John Bonar and Hugh Hunt.
(Color)
FRENCHMAN'S CREEK, PAR. Hans Dreier and Ernst Fegte. Interior Decoration: Sam Comer.
LEAVE HER TO HEAVEN. Lyle Wheeler and Maurice Ransford. Interior Decoration: Thomas Little.
NATIONAL VELVET. Cedric Gibbons and Urie McCleary. Interior Decoration: Edwin B. Willis and Mildred Griffiths.
SAN ANTONIO, WB. Ted Smith. Interior Decoration: Jack McConaghy.
A THOUSAND AND ONE NIGHTS, COL. Stephen Goosson and Rudolph Sternad. Interior Decoration: Frank Tuttle.

FILM EDITING (O-255)

NATIONAL VELVET. Robert J. Kern.
THE BELLS OF ST. MARY'S. Harry Marker.
THE LOST WEEKEND. Doane Harrison.
OBJECTIVE-BURMA. George Amy.
A SONG TO REMEMBER. Charles Nelson.

MUSIC - SCORING (O-256)
(Scoring of a Dramatic or Comedy Picture)
SPELLBOUND. Miklos Rozsa.
THE BELLS OF ST. MARY'S. Robert Emmett Dolan.
BREWSTER'S MILLIONS, Small, UA. Lou Forbes.
CAPTAIN KIDD, Bogeaus, UA. Werner Janssen.
ENCHANTED COTTAGE, RKO. Roy Webb.
FLAME OF THE BARBARY COAST, REP. Dale Butts and Morton Scott.
G. I. HONEYMOON, MNG. Edward J. Kay.
G. I. Joe. Louis Applebaum and Ann Ronell.
GUEST IN THE HOUSE, Guest in The House, Inc., UA. Werner Janssen.
GUEST WIFE, Greentree Prods., UA. Daniele Amfitheatrof.
THE KEYS OF THE KINGDOM. Alfred Newman.
THE LOST WEEKEND. Miklos Rozsa.
LOVE LETTERS. Victor Young.
MAN WHO WALKED ALONE, PRC. Karl Hajos.
OBJECTIVE-BURMA. Franz Waxman.
PARIS-UNDERGROUND, Bennett, UA. Alexander Tansman.
A SONG TO REMEMBER. Miklos Rozsa and Morris Stoloff.
THE SOUTHERNER. Werner Janssen.
THIS LOVE OF OURS, U. H. J. Salter.
VALLEY OF DECISION. Herbert Stothart.
WOMAN IN THE WINDOW, Int'l, RKO. Hugo Friedhofer and Arthur Lange.

(Scoring of a Musical Picture)
ANCHORS AWEIGH. Georgie Stoll.
BELLE OF THE YUKON, Int'l, RKO. Arthur Lange.
CAN'T HELP SINGING, U. Jerome Kern and H. J. Salter.
HITCHHIKE TO HAPPINESS, REP. Morton Scott.
INCENDIARY BLONDE, PAR. Robert Emmett Dolan.
RHAPSODY IN BLUE, WB. Ray Heindorf and Max Steiner.
STATE FAIR, FOX. Charles Henderson and Alfred Newman.
SUNBONNET SUE, MNG. Edward J. Kay.
THE THREE CABALLEROS, Disney-RKO. Edward Plumb, Paul J. Smith and Charles Wolcott.
TONIGHT AND EVERY NIGHT, COL. Marlin Skiles and Morris Stoloff.
WHY GIRLS LEAVE HOME, PRC. Walter Greene.
WONDER MAN, Beverly, RKO. Lou Forbes and Ray Heindorf.

MUSIC - BEST SONG (O-257)
IT MIGHT AS WELL BE SPRING, State Fair. Music, Richard Rodgers. Lyrics, Oscar Hammerstein II.
ACCENTUATE THE POSITIVE, *Here Come The Waves*, PAR. Music, Harold Arlen. Lyrics, Johnny Mercer.
ANYWHERE, *Tonight And Every Night*. Music, Jule Styne. Lyrics, Sammy Cahn.
AREN'T YOU GLAD YOU'RE YOU, *The Bells Of St. Mary's*. Music, James Van Heusen. Lyrics, Johnny Burke.
THE CAT AND THE CANARY, *Why Girls Leave Home*. Music, Jay Livingston. Lyrics, Ray Evans.
ENDLESSLY, *Earl Carroll Vanities*, REP. Music, Walter Kent. Lyrics, Kim Gannon.
I FALL IN LOVE TOO EASILY, *Anchors Aweigh*. Music, Jule Styne. Lyrics, Sammy Cahn.
I'LL BUY THAT DREAM, *Sing Your Way Home*, RKO. Music, Allie Wrubel. Lyrics, Herb Magidson.
LINDA, *G. I. Joe*. Music and Lyrics by Ann Ronell.
LOVE LETTERS, *Love Letters*. Music, Victor Young. Lyrics, Edward Heyman.
MORE AND MORE, *Can't Help Singing*, U. Music, Jerome Kern. Lyrics, E. Y. Harburg.
SLEIGHRIDE IN JULY, *Belle Of The Yukon*. Music, James Van Heusen. Lyrics, Johnny Burke.
SO IN LOVE, *Wonder Man*. Music, David Rose. Lyrics, Leo Robin.
SOME SUNDAY MORNING, *San Antonio*. Music, Ray Heindorf and M. K. Jerome. Lyrics, Ted Koehler.

SOUND (O-258)
THE BELLS OF ST. MARY'S. Stephen Dunn.
THE FLAME OF THE BARBARY COAST. Daniel J. Bloomberg.
LADY ON A TRAIN, U. Bernard B. Brown.
LEAVE HER TO HEAVEN. Thomas T. Moulton.
RHAPSODY IN BLUE, WB. Nathan Levinson.

A SONG TO REMEMBER. John Livadary.
THE SOUTHERNER. Jack Whitney, General Service.
THEY WERE EXPENDABLE, MGM. Douglas Shearer.
THE THREE CABALLEROS. C. O. Slyfield.
THREE IS A FAMILY, Master Productions, UA. W. V. Wolfe, RCA Sound.
THE UNSEEN, PAR. Loren L. Ryder.
WONDER MAN. Gordon Sawyer.

SHORT FILMS (O-259)
(Cartoons)
QUIET PLEASE, MGM. (Tom & Jerry Series) Frederick Quimby, Prod.
DONALD'S CRIME, Walt Disney, RKO. (Donald Duck) Walt Disney, Prod.
JASPER AND THE BEANSTALK, PAR. (Pal Puppetoon-Jasper Series) George Pal, Prod.
LIFE WITH FEATHERS, WB. (Merrie Melodies) Eddie Selzer, Prod.
MIGHTY MOUSE IN GYPSY LIFE, FOX. (Terrytoon) Paul Terry, Prod.
POET AND PEASANT, U. (Lantz Technicolor Cartune) Walter Lantz, Prod.
RIPPLING ROMANCE, COL. (Color Rhapsodies)

(One-reel)
STAIRWAY TO LIGHT, MGM. (John Nesbitt Passing Parade) Herbert Moulton, Prod.
ALONG THE RAINBOW TRAIL, FOX. (Movietone Adventure) Edmund Reek, Prod.
SCREEN SNAPSHOTS 25TH ANNIVERSARY, COL. (Screen Snapshots) Ralph Staub, Prod.
STORY OF A DOG, WB. (Vitaphone Varieties) Gordon Hollingshead, Prod.
WHITE RHAPSODY, PAR. (Sportlights) Grantland Rice, Prod.
YOUR NATIONAL GALLERY, U. (Variety Views) Joseph O'Brien and Thomas Mead, Prods.

(Two-reel)
STAR IN THE NIGHT, WB. (Broadway Brevities) Gordon Hollingshead, Prod.
A GUN IN HIS HAND, MGM. (Crime Does Not Pay) Chester Franklin, Prod.
THE JURY GOES ROUND 'N' ROUND, COL. (All Star Comedies) Jules White, Prod.
THE LITTLE WITCH, PAR. (Musical Parade) George Templeton, Prod.

DOCUMENTARY (O-260)
(Short Subjects)
HITLER LIVES?, WB.
LIBRARY OF CONGRESS, Overseas Motion Picture Bureau, Office of War Information.
TO THE SHORES OF IWO JIMA, U.S. Marine Corps.

(Features)
THE TRUE GLORY, Governments of Great Britain and USA.
THE LAST BOMB, U.S. Army Air Force.

SPECIAL EFFECTS (O-261)
WONDER MAN. Photographic: John Fulton. Sound: A. W. Johns.
CAPTAIN EDDIE, FOX. Photographic: Fred Sersen and Sol Halprin. Sound: Roger Heman and Harry Leonard.
SPELLBOUND. Photographic: Jack Cosgrove. Sound: No credits listed.
THEY WERE EXPENDABLE. Photographic: A. Arnold Gillespie, Donald Jahraus and R. A. MacDonald. Sound: Michael Steinore.
A THOUSAND AND ONE NIGHTS. Photographic: L. W. Butler. Sound: Ray Bomba.

HONORARY AND OTHER (O-262)
(Other)
WALTER WANGER for his six years service as President of the Academy of Motion Picture Arts and Sciences.
PEGGY ANN GARNER, outstanding child actress of 1945.
THE HOUSE I LIVE IN, tolerance short subject; produced by Frank Ross and Mervyn LeRoy; directed by Mervyn LeRoy; screenplay by

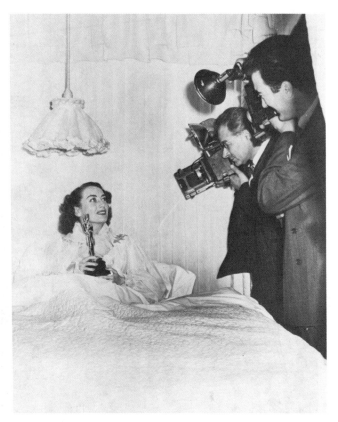

1945—Too ill to attend the ceremony, Joan Crawford (Best Actress) received her Oscar in her bedroom

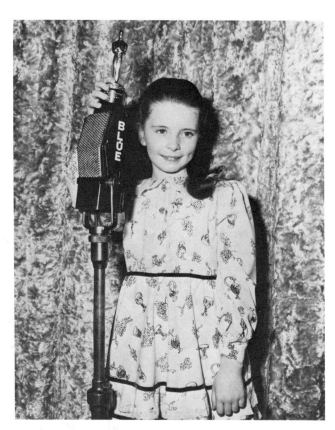

1944—Margaret O'Brien (Special Award)

1942—Van Heflin (Best Supporting Actor), Greer Garson (Best Actress), James Cagney (Best Actor), and Teresa Wright (Best Supporting Actress)

1943—Paul Lukas (Best Actor), Jennifer Jones (Best Actress), Katina Paxinou (Best Supporting Actress), and Charles Coburn (Best Supporting Actor)

1947—Ronald Colman (Best Actor) and Loretta Young (Best Actress) being interviewed

1949—James Cagney (presenter), Mercedes McCambridge (Best Supporting Actress), Jane Wyman (presenter), Broderick Crawford (Best Actor), and Olivia de Haviland (Best Actress)

1946—Anne Baxter (Best Supporting Actress), Sam Goldwyn (recipient of the Irving G. Thalberg Memorial Award and producer, Best Picture), Olivia de Haviland (Best Actress), and Harold Russell (Best Supporting Actor and Special Award)

1952—Cecil B. DeMille (producer, Best Picture and recipient of the Irving G. Thalberg Memorial Award) with presenters Mary Pickford and Darryl F. Zanuck

Albert Maltz; song "The House I Live In," music by Earl Robinson, lyrics by Lewis Allen; starring Frank Sinatra; released by RKO.
REPUBLIC STUDIO, DANIEL J. BLOOMBERG and the REPUBLIC SOUND DEPARTMENT for the building of an outstanding musical scoring auditorium which provides optimum recording conditions and combines all elements of acoustic and engineering design.

SCIENTIFIC OR TECHNICAL (O-263)

(Class III)

LOREN L. RYDER, CHARLES R. DAILY and the PARAMOUNT STUDIO SOUND DEPARTMENT for the design, construction and use of the first dial controlled step-by-step sound channel line-up and test circuit.
MICHAEL S. LESHING, BENJAMIN C. ROBINSON, ARTHUR B. CHATELAIN and ROBERT C. STEVENS of 20th Century-Fox Studio and JOHN G. CAPSTAFF of Eastman Kodak Co. for the 20th Century-Fox film processing machine.

1946

BEST PICTURE (O-264)

THE BEST YEARS OF OUR LIVES, Goldwyn, RKO.
HENRY V, Rank-Two Cities, UA (British).
IT'S A WONDERFUL LIFE, Liberty, RKO.
THE RAZOR'S EDGE, FOX.
THE YEARLING, MGM.

ACTOR (O-265)

FREDRIC MARCH, The Best Years Of Our Lives.
LAURENCE OLIVIER, Henry V.
LARRY PARKS, The Jolson Story, COL.
GREGORY PECK, The Yearling.
JAMES STEWART, It's A Wonderful Life.

ACTRESS (O-266)

OLIVIA DE HAVILLAND, To Each His Own, PAR.
CELIA JOHNSON, Brief Encounter, Rank, UI. (British)
JENNIFER JONES, Duel In The Sun, SZI.
ROSALIND RUSSELL, Sister Kenny, RKO.
JANE WYMAN, The Yearling.

SUPPORTING ACTOR (O-267)

HAROLD RUSSELL, The Best Years Of Our Lives.
CHARLES COBURN, The Green Years, MGM.
WILLIAM DEMAREST, The Jolson Story.
CLAUDE RAINS, Notorious, RKO.
CLIFTON WEBB, The Razor's Edge.

SUPPORTING ACTRESS (O-268)

ANNE BAXTER, The Razor's Edge.
ETHEL BARRYMORE, The Spiral Staircase, RKO.
LILLIAN GISH, Duel In The Sun.
FLORA ROBSON, Saratoga Trunk, WB.
GALE SONDERGAARD, Anna And The King Of Siam, FOX.

DIRECTING (O-269)

WILLIAM WYLER, The Best Years Of Our Lives.
CLARENCE BROWN, The Yearling.
FRANK CAPRA, It's A Wonderful Life.
DAVID LEAN, Brief Encounter.
ROBERT SIODMAK, The Killers, Hellinger, U.

WRITING (O-270)

(Original Story)

VACATION FROM MARRIAGE, London Films, MGM (British). Clemence Dane.
THE DARK MIRROR, UI. Vladimir Pozner.
THE STRANGE LOVE OF MARTHA IVERS, Wallis, PAR. Jack Patrick.

THE STRANGER, Int'l, RKO. Victor Trivas.
TO EACH HIS OWN, PAR. Charles Brackett.

(Original Screenplay)

THE SEVENTH VEIL, Rank, U (British). Muriel Box and Sydney Box.
THE BLUE DAHLIA, PAR. Raymond Chandler.
CHILDREN OF PARADISE, Pathe-Cinema, Tricolore (French). Jacques Prevert.
NOTORIOUS. Ben Hecht.
THE ROAD TO UTOPIA, PAR. Norman Panama and Melvin Frank.

(Screenplay)

THE BEST YEARS OF OUR LIVES. Robert E. Sherwood.
ANNA AND THE KING OF SIAM. Sally Benson and Talbot Jennings.
BRIEF ENCOUNTER. Anthony Havelock-Allan, David Lean and Ronald Neame.
THE KILLERS. Anthony Veiller.
OPEN CITY, MNV (Italian). Sergio Amidei and F. Fellini.

CINEMATOGRAPHY (O-271)

(Black-and-White)

ANNA AND THE KING OF SIAM. Arthur Miller.
THE GREEN YEARS, MGM. George Folsey.

(Color)

THE YEARLING. Charles Rosher, Leonard Smith and Arthur Arling.
THE JOLSON STORY. Joseph Walker.

ART DIRECTION - SET DECORATION (O-272)

(Black-and-White)

ANNA AND THE KING OF SIAM. Lyle Wheeler and William Darling. Interior Decoration: Thomas Little and Frank E. Hughes.
KITTY, PAR. Hans Dreier and Walter Tyler. Interior Decoration: Sam Comer and Ray Moyer.
THE RAZOR'S EDGE. Richard Day and Nathan Juran. Interior Decoration: Thomas Little and Paul S. Fox.

(Color)

THE YEARLING. Cedric Gibbons and Paul Groesse. Interior Decoration: Edwin B. Willis.
CAESAR AND CLEOPATRA, Rank, UA (British). John Bryan. Interior Decoration: No credits listed.
HENRY V. Paul Sheriff and Carmen Dillon. Interior Decoration: No credits listed.

FILM EDITING (O-273)

THE BEST YEARS OF OUR LIVES. Daniel Mandell.
IT'S A WONDERFUL LIFE. William Hornbeck.
THE JOLSON STORY. William Lyon.
THE KILLERS. Arthur Hilton.
THE YEARLING. Harold Kress.

MUSIC - SCORING (O-274)

(Scoring of a Dramatic or Comedy Picture)

THE BEST YEARS OF OUR LIVES. Hugo Friedhofer.
ANNA AND THE KING OF SIAM. Bernard Herrmann.
HENRY V. William Walton.
HUMORESQUE, WB. Franz Waxman.
THE KILLERS. Miklos Rozsa.

(Scoring of a Musical Picture)

THE JOLSON STORY, COL. Morris Stoloff.
BLUE SKIES, PAR. Robert Emmett Dolan.
CENTENNIAL SUMMER, FOX. Alfred Newman.
THE HARVEY GIRLS, MGM. Lennie Hayton.
NIGHT AND DAY, WB. Ray Heindorf and Max Steiner.

MUSIC - BEST SONG (O-275)

ON THE ATCHISON, TOPEKA AND SANTA FE, Harvey Girls. Music, Harry Warren. Lyrics, Johnny Mercer.
ALL THROUGH THE DAY, Centennial Summer. Music, Jerome Kern. Lyrics, Oscar Hammerstein II.
I CAN'T BEGIN TO TELL YOU, The Dolly Sisters, FOX. Music, James Monaco. Lyrics, Mack Gordon.

OLE BUTTERMILK SKY, *Canyon Passage,* Wanger, U. Music, Hoagy Carmichael. Lyrics, Jack Brooks.
YOU KEEP COMING BACK LIKE A SONG, *Blue Skies.* Music and Lyrics by Irving Berlin.

SOUND (O-276)

THE JOLSON STORY. John Livadary.
THE BEST YEARS OF OUR LIVES. Gordon Sawyer.
IT'S A WONDERFUL LIFE. John Aalberg.

SHORT FILMS (O-277)

(Cartoons)

THE CAT CONCERTO, MGM. (Tom & Jerry) Frederick Quimby, Prod.
CHOPIN'S MUSICAL MOMENTS, U. (Musical Miniatures) Walter Lantz, Prod.
JOHN HENRY AND THE INKY POO, PAR. (Puppetoon) George Pal, Prod.
SQUATTER'S RIGHTS, Disney-RKO. (Mickey Mouse) Walt Disney, Prod.
WALKY TALKY HAWKY, WB. (Merrie Melodies) Edward Selzer, Prod.

(One-reel)

FACING YOUR DANGER, WB. (Sports Parade) Gordon Hollingshead, Prod.
DIVE-HI CHAMPS, PAR. (Sportlights) Jack Eaton, Prod.
GOLDEN HORSES, FOX. (Movietone Sports Review) Edmund Reek, Prod.
SMART AS A FOX, WB. (Varieties) Gordon Hollingshead, Prod.
SURE CURES, MGM. (Pete Smith Specialty) Pete Smith, Prod.

(Two-reel)

A BOY AND HIS DOG, WB. (Featurettes) Gordon Hollingshead, Prod.
COLLEGE QUEEN, PAR. (Musical Parade) George Templeton, Prod.
HISS AND YELL, COL. (All Star Comedies) Jules White, Prod.
THE LUCKIEST GUY IN THE WORLD, MGM. (Two-reel Special) Jerry Bresler, Prod.

DOCUMENTARY (O-278)

(Short Subjects)

SEEDS OF DESTINY, U.S. War Department.
ATOMIC POWER, FOX.
LIFE AT THE ZOO, ARK.
PARAMOUNT NEWS ISSUE #37, PAR.
TRAFFIC WITH THE DEVIL, MGM.

SPECIAL EFFECTS (O-279)

BLITHE SPIRIT, Rank UA (British). Visual: Thomas Howard. Audible: No credit.
A STOLEN LIFE, WB. Visual: William McGann. Audible: Nathan Levinson.

HONORARY AND OTHER (O-280)

(Irving G. Thalberg Memorial Award)

Samuel Goldwyn

(Other)

LAURENCE OLIVIER for his outstanding achievement as actor, producer and director in bringing Henry V to the screen. (statuette)
HAROLD RUSSELL for bringing hope and courage to his fellow veterans through his appearance in The Best Years Of Our Lives.
ERNST LUBITSCH for his distinguished contributions to the art of the motion picture.
CLAUDE JARMAN, JR., outstanding child actor of 1946.

SCIENTIFIC OR TECHNICAL (O-281)

(Class III)

HARLAN L. BAUMBACH and the PARAMOUNT WEST COAST LABORATORY for an improved method for the quantitative determination of hydroquinone and metol in photographic developing baths.
HERBERT E. BRITT for the development and application of formulas

and equipment for producing cloud and smoke effects.
BURTON F. MILLER and the WB STUDIO SOUND and ELECTRICAL DEPARTMENTS for the design and construction of a motion picture arc lighting generator filter.
CARL FAULKNER of the 20th Century-Fox Studio Sound Department for the reversed bias method, including a double bias method for light valve and galvonometer density recording.
MOLE-RICHARDSON CO. for the Type 450 super high intensity carbon arc lamp.
ARTHUR F. BLINN, ROBERT O. COOK, C. O. SLYFIELD and the WALT DISNEY STUDIO SOUND DEPARTMENT for the design and development of an audio finder and track viewer for checking and locating noise in sound tracks.
BURTON F. MILLER and the WB STUDIO SOUND DEPARTMENT for the design and application of an equalizer to eliminate relative spectral energy distortion in electronic compressors.
MARTY MARTIN and HAL ADKINS of the RKO Studio Miniature Department for the design and construction of equipment providing visual bullet effects.
HAROLD NYE and the WB STUDIO ELECTRICAL DEPARTMENT for the development of the electronically controlled fire and gaslight effect.

1947

BEST PICTURE (O-282)

GENTLEMAN'S AGREEMENT, FOX.
THE BISHOP'S WIFE, Goldwyn, RKO.
CROSSFIRE, RKO.
GREAT EXPECTATIONS, Rank-Cineguild, U (British).
MIRACLE ON 34TH STREET, FOX.

ACTOR (O-283)

RONALD COLMAN, A Double Life, Kanin, U.
JOHN GARFIELD, *Body And Soul,* Enterprise, UA.
GREGORY PECK, *Gentleman's Agreement.*
WILLIAM POWELL, *Life With Father,* WB.
MICHAEL REDGRAVE, *Mourning Becomes Electra,* RKO.

ACTRESS (O-284)

LORETTA YOUNG, The Farmer's Daughter, RKO.
JOAN CRAWFORD, *Possessed,* WB.
SUSAN HAYWARD, *Smash Up - The Story Of A Woman,* Wanger, U.
DOROTHY McGUIRE, *Gentleman's Agreement.*
ROSALIND RUSSELL, *Mourning Becomes Electra.*

SUPPORTING ACTOR (O-285)

EDMUND GWENN, Miracle On 34th Street.
CHARLES BICKFORD, *The Farmer's Daughter.*
THOMAS GOMEZ, *Ride The Pink Horse,* U.
ROBERT RYAN, *Crossfire.*
RICHARD WIDMARK, *Kiss Of Death,* FOX.

SUPPORTING ACTRESS (O-286)

CELESTE HOLM, Gentleman's Agreement.
ETHEL BARRYMORE, *The Paradine Case,* SRO.
GLORIA GRAHAME, *Crossfire.*
MARJORIE MAIN, *The Egg And I,* U.
ANNE REVERE, *Gentleman's Agreement.*

DIRECTING (O-287)

ELIA KAZAN, Gentleman's Agreement.
GEORGE CUKOR, *A Double Life.*
EDWARD DMYTRYK, *Crossfire.*
HENRY KOSTER, *The Bishop's Wife.*
DAVID LEAN, *Great Expectations.*

WRITING (O-288)

(Original Story)

MIRACLE ON 34TH STREET. Valentine Davies.
A CAGE OF NIGHTINGALES, GAU-LOP (French). Georges Chaperot and Rene Wheeler.
IT HAPPENED ON FIFTH AVENUE, Roy Del Ruth, AA. Herbert Clyde Lewis and Frederick Stephani.
KISS OF DEATH. Eleazar Lipsky.
SMASH-UP - THE STORY OF A WOMAN. Dorothy Parker and Frank Cavett.

(Original Screenplay)

THE BACHELOR AND THE BOBBY-SOXER, RKO. Sidney Sheldon.
BODY AND SOUL. Abraham Polonsky.
A DOUBLE LIFE. Ruth Gordon & Garson Kanin.
MONSIEUR VERDOUX, Chaplin, UA. Charles Chaplin.
SHOE-SHINE, LOP (Italian). Sergio Amidei, Adolfo Franci, C. G. Viola and Cesare Zavattini.

(Screenplay)

MIRACLE ON 34TH STREET. George Seaton.
BOOMERANG!, FOX. Richard Murphy.
CROSSFIRE. John Paxton.
GENTLEMAN'S AGREEMENT. Moss Hart.
GREAT EXPECTATIONS. David Lean, Ronald Neame and Anthony Havelock-Allan.

CINEMATOGRAPHY (O-289)

(Black-and-White)

GREAT EXPECTATIONS. Guy Green.
THE GHOST AND MRS. MUIR, FOX. Charles Lang, Jr.
GREEN DOLPHIN STREET, MGM. George Folsey.

(Color)

BLACK NARCISSUS. Rank-Archers, U (British). Jack Cardiff.
LIFE WITH FATHER. Peverell Marley and William V. Skall.
MOTHER WORE TIGHTS, FOX. Harry Jackson.

ART DIRECTION - SET DECORATION (O-290)

(Black-and-White)

GREAT EXPECTATIONS. John Bryan. Set Decoration: Wilfred Shingleton.
THE FOXES OF HARROW, FOX. Lyle Wheeler and Maurice Ransford. Set Decoration: Thomas Little and Paul S. Fox.

(Color)

BLACK NARCISSUS. Alfred Junge. Set Decoration: Alfred Junge.
LIFE WITH FATHER. Robert M. Haas. Set Decoration: George James Hopkins.

FILM EDITING (O-291)

BODY AND SOUL. Francis Lyon and Robert Parrish.
THE BISHOP'S WIFE. Monica Collingwood.
GENTLEMAN'S AGREEMENT. Harmon Jones.
GREEN DOLPHIN STREET. George White.
ODD MAN OUT, Rank-Two Cities, U (British). Fergus McDonnell.

MUSIC - SCORING (O-292)

(Scoring of a Dramatic or Comedy Picture)

A DOUBLE LIFE. Miklos Rozsa.
THE BISHOP'S WIFE. Hugo Friedhofer.
CAPTAIN FROM CASTILE, FOX. Alfred Newman.
FOREVER AMBER, FOX. David Raksin.
LIFE WITH FATHER. Max Steiner.

(Scoring of a Musical Picture)

MOTHER WORE TIGHTS. Alfred Newman.
FIESTA, MGM. Johnny Green.
MY WILD IRISH ROSE, WB. Ray Heindorf and Max Steiner.
ROAD TO RIO, Hope-Crosby, PAR. Robert Emmett Dolan.
SONG OF THE SOUTH, Disney, RKO. Daniele Amfitheatrof, Paul J. Smith and Charles Wolcott.

MUSIC - BEST SONG (O-293)

ZIP-A-DEE-DOO-DAH, Song Of The South. Music, Allie Wrubel. Lyrics, Ray Gilbert.
A GAL IN CALICO, *The Time, Place And The Girl*, WB. Music, Arthur Schwartz. Lyrics, Leo Robin.
I WISH I DIDN'T LOVE YOU SO, *The Perils Of Pauline*, PAR. Music and Lyrics by Frank Loesser.
PASS THAT PEACE PIPE, *Good News*, MGM. Music and Lyrics by Ralph Blane, Hugh Martin and Roger Edens.
YOU DO, *Mother Wore Tights*. Music, Josef Myrow. Lyrics, Mack Gordon.

SOUND (O-294)

THE BISHOP'S WIFE. Goldwyn Sound Department.
GREEN DOLPHIN STREET. MGM Sound Department.
T-MEN, Reliance Pictures, EAG, Sound Services. Inc.

SHORT FILMS (O-295)

(Cartoons)

TWEETIE PIE, WB. (Merrie Melodies) Edward Selzer, Prod.
CHIP AN' DALE, Walt Disney, RKO. (Donald Duck) Walt Disney, Prod.
DR. JEKYLL AND MR. MOUSE, MGM. (Tom & Jerry) Frederick Quimby, Prod.
PLUTO'S BLUE NOTE, Walt Disney, RKO. (Pluto) Walt Disney, Prod.
TUBBY THE TUBA, PAR. (George Pal Puppetoon) George Pal, Prod.

(One-reel)

GOODBYE MISS TURLOCK, MGM. (John Nesbitt Passing Parade) Herbert Moulton, Prod.
BROOKLYN, U.S.A., U. (Variety Series) Thomas Mead, Prod.
MOON ROCKETS, PAR. (Popular Science) Jerry Fairbanks, Prod.
NOW YOU SEE IT, MGM. Pete Smith, Prod.
SO YOU WANT TO BE IN PICTURES, WB. (Joe McDoakes) Gordon Hollingshead, Prod.

(Two-reel)

CLIMBING THE MATTERHORN, MNG. (Color) Irving Allen, Prod.
CHAMPAGNE FOR TWO, PAR, (Musical Parade Featurette) Harry Grey, Prod.
FLIGHT OF THE WILD STALLIONS, U. (Special) Thomas Mead, Prod.
GIVE US THE EARTH, MGM. (Special) Herbert Morgan, Prod.
A VOICE IS BORN, COL. (Musical Featurette) Ben Blake, Prod.

DOCUMENTARY (O-296)

(Short Subjects)

FIRST STEPS, United Nations Division of Films and Visual Education.
PASSPORT TO NOWHERE, RKO (This Is America Series). Frederic Ullman, Jr., Prod.
SCHOOL IN THE MAILBOX, Australian News and Information Bureau.

(Features)

DESIGN FOR DEATH, RKO. Sid Rogell, Ex Prod; Theron Warth and Richard O. Fleischer, Prods.
JOURNEY INTO MEDICINE, U.S. Dept. of State, Office of Information and Educational Exhange.
THE WORLD IS RICH, British Information Services. Paul Rotha, Prod.

SPECIAL EFFECTS (O-297)

GREEN DOLPHIN STREET. Visual: A. Arnold Gillespie and Warren Newcombe. Audible: Douglas Shearer and Michael Steinore.
UNCONQUERED, PAR. Visual: Farciot Edouart, Devereux Jennings, Gordon Jennings, Wallace Kelley and Paul Lerpae. Audible: George Dutton.

HONORARY AND OTHER (O-298)

(Other)

**JAMES BASKETTE for his able and heart-warming characterization of Uncle Remus, friend and story teller to the children of the world.
BILL AND COO, in which artistry and patience blended in a novel and entertaining use of the medium of motion pictures.
SHOE-SHINE - the high quality of this motion picture, brought to**

eloquent life in a country scarred by war, is proof to the world that the creative spirit can triumph over adversity.

COLONEL WILLIAM N. SELIG, ALBERT E. SMITH, THOMAS ARMAT and GEORGE K. SPOOR (one of) the small group of pioneers whose belief in a new medium, and whose contributions to its development, blazed the trail along which the motion picture has progressed, in their lifetime, from obscurity to world-wide acclaim.

SCIENTIFIC OR TECHNICAL (O-299)

(Class II Plaque)

C. C. DAVIS and ELECTRICAL RESEARCH PRODUCTS, DIVISION OF WESTERN ELECTRIC CO., for the development and application of an improved film drive filter mechanism.

C. R. DAILY and the PAR STUDIO FILM LABORATORY, STILL and ENGINEERING DEPARTMENTS for the development and first practical application to motion picture and still photography of a method of increasing film speed as first suggested to the industry by E. I. duPont de Nemours & Co.

(Class III)

NATHAN LEVINSON and the WB STUDIO SOUND DEPARTMENT for the design and construction of a constant-speed sound editing machine.

FARCIOT EDOUART, C. R. DAILY, HAL CORL, H. G. CARTWRIGHT and the PARAMOUNT STUDIO TRANSPARENCY and ENGINEERING DEPARTMENTS for the first application of a special anti-solarizing glass to high intensity background and spot arc projectors.

FRED PONEDEL of WB Studio for pioneering the fabrication and practical application to motion picture color photography of large translucent photographic backgrounds.

KURT SINGER and the RCA-VICTOR DIVISION of the RADIO CORPORATION OF AMERICA for the design and development of a continuously variable band elimination filter.

JAMES GIBBONS of WB Studio for the development and production of large dyed plastic filters for motion picture photography.

1948

BEST PICTURE (O-300)

HAMLET, Rank-Two Cities, U (British).
JOHNNY BELINDA, WB.
THE RED SHOES, Rank-Archers, EAG. (British)
THE SNAKE PIT, FOX.
TREASURE OF SIERRA MADRE, WB.

ACTOR (O-301)

LAURENCE OLIVIER, Hamlet.
LEW AYRES, Johnny Belinda.
MONTGOMERY CLIFT, The Search, Praesens Films, MGM. (Swiss)
DAN DAILEY, When My Baby Smiles At Me, FOX.
CLIFTON WEBB, Sitting Pretty, FOX.

ACTRESS (O-302)

JANE WYMAN, Johnny Belinda.
INGRID BERGMAN, Joan Of Arc, Sierra, RKO.
OLIVIA DE HAVILLAND, The Snake Pit.
IRENE DUNNE, I Remember Mama, RKO.
BARBARA STANWYCK, Sorry, Wrong Number, Wallis, PAR.

SUPPORTING ACTOR (O-303)

WALTER HUSTON, Treasure Of Sierra Madre.
CHARLES BICKFORD, Johnny Belinda.
JOSE FERRER, Joan Of Arc.
OSCAR HOMOLKA, I Remember Mama.
CECIL KELLAWAY, The Luck Of The Irish, FOX.

SUPPORTING ACTRESS (O-304)

CLAIRE TREVOR, Key Largo, WB.
BARBARA BEL GEDDES, I Remember Mama.
ELLEN CORBY, I Remember Mama.
AGNES MOOREHEAD, Johnny Belinda.
JEAN SIMMONS, Hamlet.

DIRECTING (O-305)

JOHN HUSTON, Treasure Of Sierra Madre.
ANATOLE LITVAK, The Snake Pit.
JEAN NEGULESCO, Johnny Belinda.
LAURENCE OLIVIER, Hamlet.
FRED ZINNEMANN, The Search.

WRITING (O-306)

(Motion Picture Story)

THE SEARCH. Richard Schweizer and David Wechsler.
THE LOUISIANA STORY, Robert Flaherty, LOP. Frances Flaherty and Robert Flaherty.
THE NAKED CITY, Hellinger, U. Malvin Wald.
RED RIVER, Monterey Productions, UA. Borden Chase.
THE RED SHOES. Emeric Pressburger.

(Screenplay)

TREASURE OF SIERRA MADRE. John Huston.
A FOREIGN AFFAIR, PAR. Charles Brackett, Billy Wilder and Richard L. Breen.
JOHNNY BELINDA. Irmgard Von Cube and Allen Vincent.
THE SEARCH. Richard Schweizer and David Wechsler.
THE SNAKE PIT. Frank Partos and Millen Brand.

CINEMATOGRAPHY (O-307)

(Black-and-White)

THE NAKED CITY. William Daniels.
A FOREIGN AFFAIR. Charles B. Lang, Jr.
I REMEMBER MAMA. Nicholas Musuraca.
JOHNNY BELINDA. Ted McCord.
PORTRAIT OF JENNIE, SRO. Joseph August.

(Color)

JOAN OF ARC. Joseph Valentine, William V. Skall and Winton Hoch.
GREEN GRASS OF WYOMING, FOX. Charles G. Clarke.
THE LOVES OF CARMEN, Beckworth Corp, COL. William Snyder.
THE THREE MUSKETEERS, MGM. Robert Planck.

COSTUME DESIGN (O-308)

(Black-and-White)

HAMLET. Roger K. Furse.
B. F.'S DAUGHTER, MGM. Irene.

(Color)

JOAN OF ARC. Dorothy Jeakins and Karinska.
THE EMPEROR WALTZ, PAR. Edith Head and Gile Steele.

ART DIRECTION - SET DECORATION (O-309)

(Black-and-White)

HAMLET. Roger K. Furse. Set Decoration: Carmen Dillon.
JOHNNY BELINDA. Robert Haas. Set Decoration: William Wallace.

(Color)

THE RED SHOES. Hein Heckroth. Set Decoration: Arthur Lawson.
JOAN OF ARC. Richard Day. Set Decoration: Edwin Casey Roberts and Joseph Kish.

FILM EDITING (O-310)

THE NAKED CITY. Paul Weatherwax.
JOAN OF ARC. Frank Sullivan.
JOHNNY BELINDA. David Weisbart.
RED RIVER. Christian Nyby.
THE RED SHOES. Reginald Mills.

MUSIC - SCORING (O-311)

(Scoring of a Dramatic or Comedy Picture)

THE RED SHOES. Brian Easdale.
HAMLET. William Walton.
JOAN OF ARC. Hugo Friedhofer.
JOHNNY BELINDA. Max Steiner.
THE SNAKE PIT. Alfred Newman.

(Scoring of a Musical Picture)

EASTER PARADE, MGM. Johnny Green and Roger Edens.
THE EMPEROR WALTZ. Victor Young.
THE PIRATE, MGM. Lennie Hayton.
ROMANCE OF THE HIGH SEAS, Curtiz, WB. Ray Heindorf.
WHEN MY BABY SMILES AT ME. Alfred Newman.

MUSIC - BEST SONG (O-312)

BUTTONS AND BOWS, The Paleface, PAR. Music and Lyrics by Jay Livingston and Ray Evans.
FOR EVERY MAN THERE'S A WOMAN, *Casbah*, Marston Pictures, UI. Music, Harold Arlen. Lyrics, Leo Robin.
IT'S MAGIC, *Romance On The High Seas*. Music, Jule Styne. Lyrics, Sammy Cahn.
THIS IS THE MOMENT, *That Lady In Ermine*, FOX. Music, Frederick Hollander. Lyrics, Leo Robin.
THE WOODY WOODPECKER SONG, *Wet Blanket Policy*, Walter Lantz, UA (Cartoon). Music and Lyrics by Ramey Idriss and George Tibbles.

SOUND (O-313)

THE SNAKE PIT. FOX Sound Department.
JOHNNY BELINDA. WB Sound Department.
MOONRISE, Marshall Grant Prods., REP. REP Sound Department.

SHORT FILMS (O-314)

(Cartoons)

THE LITTLE ORPHAN, MGM. (Tom & Jerry) Fred Quimby, Prod.
MICKEY AND THE SEAL, Walt Disney, RKO. (Pluto) Walt Disney, Prod.
MOUSE WRECKERS, WB. (Looney Tunes) Edward Selzer, Prod.
ROBIN HOODLUM, United Productions Of America, COL. (Fox & Crow)
TEA FOR TWO HUNDRED, Walt Disney, RKO. (Donald Duck) Walt Disney, Prod.

(One-reel)

SYMPHONY OF A CITY, FOX. (Movietone Specialty) Edmund H. Reek, Prod.
ANNIE WAS A WONDER, MGM. (John Nesbitt Passing Parade) Herbert Moulton, Prod.
CINDERELLA HORSE, WB. (Sports Parade) Gordon Hollingshead, Prod.
SO YOU WANT TO BE ON THE RADIO, WB. (Joe McDoakes) Gordon Hollingshead, Prod.
YOU CAN'T WIN, MGM. (Pete Smith Specialty) Pete Smith, Prod.

(Two-reel)

SEAL ISLAND, Walt Disney, RKO. (True Life Adventure Series) Walt Disney, Prod.
CALGARY STAMPEDE, WB. (Technicolor Special) Gordon Hollingshead, Prod.
GOING TO BLAZES, MGM. (Special) Herbert Morgan, Prod.
SAMBA-MANIA, PAR. (Musical Parade) Harry Grey, Prod.
SNOW CAPERS, UI. (Special Series) Thomas Mead, Prod.

DOCUMENTARY (O-315)

(Short Subjects)

TOWARD INDEPENDENCE, U.S. Army.
HEART TO HEART, Fact Film Organization. Herbert Morgan, Prod.
OPERATION VITTLES, U.S. Army Air Force.

(Features)

THE SECRET LAND, U.S. Navy, MGM. O.O. Dull, Prod.
THE QUIET ONE, MAB. Janice Loeb, Prod.

SPECIAL EFFECTS (O-316)

PORTRAIT OF JENNIE. Visual: Paul Eagler, J. McMillan Johnson, Russell Shearman and Clarence Slifer. Audible: Charles Freeman and James G. Stewart.
DEEP WATERS, FOX. Visual: Ralph Hammeras, Fred Sersen and Edward Snyder. Audible: Roger Heman.

HONORARY AND OTHER (O-317)

(Irving G. Thalberg Memorial Award)

Jerry Wald

(Other)

MONSIEUR VINCENT (French) - voted by the Academy Board of Governors as the most outstanding foreign language film released in the United States during 1948.
IVAN JANDL, for the outstanding juvenile performance of 1948, The Search.
SID GRAUMAN, master showman, who raised the standard of exhibition of motion pictures.
ADOLPH ZUKOR, a man who has been called the father of the feature film in America, for his services to the industry over a period of forty years.
WALTER WANGER for distinguished service to the industry in adding to its moral stature in the world community by his production of the picture Joan Of Arc.

SCIENTIFIC OR TECHNICAL (O-318)

(Class II)

VICTOR CACCIALANZA, MAURICE AYERS and the **PARAMOUNT STUDIO SET CONSTRUCTION DEPARTMENT** for the development and application of "Paralite," a new lightweight plaster process for set construction.
NICK KALTEN, LOUIS J. WITTI and the **20TH CENTURY-FOX STUDIO MECHANICAL EFFECTS DEPARTMENT** for a process of preserving and flame-proofing foliage.

(Class III)

MARTY MARTIN, JACK LANNON, RUSSELL SHEARMAN and the **RKO STUDIO SPECIAL EFFECTS DEPARTMENT** for the development of a new method of simulating falling snow on motion picture sets.
A. J. MORAN and the **WB STUDIO ELECTRICAL DEPARTMENT** for a method of remote control for shutters on motion picture arc lighting equipment.

1949

BEST PICTURE (O-319)

ALL THE KING'S MEN, Rossen, COL.
BATTLEGROUND, MGM.
THE HEIRESS, PAR.
A LETTER TO THREE WIVES, FOX.
TWELVE O'CLOCK HIGH, FOX.

ACTOR (O-320)

BRODERICK CRAWFORD, All The King's Men.
KIRK DOUGLAS, *Champion*, Screen Plays Corp., UA.
GREGORY PECK, *Twelve O'Clock High.*
RICHARD TODD, *The Hasty Heart*, WB.
JOHN WAYNE, *Sands Of Iwo Jima*, REP.

ACTRESS (O-321)

OLIVIA DE HAVILLAND, The Heiress.
JEANNE CRAIN, *Pinky*, FOX.
SUSAN HAYWARD, *My Foolish Heart*, Goldwyn, RKO.
DEBORAH KERR, *Edward, My Son*, MGM.
LORETTA YOUNG, *Come To The Stable*, FOX.

SUPPORTING ACTOR (O-322)
DEAN JAGGER, Twelve O'Clock High.
JOHN IRELAND, *All The King's Men.*
ARTHUR KENNEDY, *Champion.*
RALPH RICHARDSON, *The Heiress.*
JAMES WHITMORE, *Battleground.*

SUPPORTING ACTRESS (O-323)
MERCEDES McCAMBRIDGE, All The King's Men.
ETHEL BARRYMORE, *Pinky.*
CELESTE HOLM, *Come To The Stable.*
ELSA LANCHESTER, *Come To The Stable.*
ETHEL WATERS, *Pinky.*

DIRECTING (O-324)
JOSEPH L. MANKIEWICZ, A Letter To Three Wives.
CAROL REED, *The Fallen Idol,* London Films, SRO (British).
ROBERT ROSSEN, *All The King's Men.*
WILLIAM A. WELLMAN, *Battleground.*
WILLIAM WYLER, *The Heiress.*

WRITING (O-325)
(Motion Picture Story)
THE STRATTON STORY, MGM. Douglas Morrow.
COME TO THE STABLE. Clare Boothe Luce.
IT HAPPENS EVERY SPRING, FOX. Shirley W. Smith and Valentine Davies.
SANDS OF IWO JIMA. Harry Brown.
WHITE HEAT. Virginia Kellogg.
(Screenplay)
A LETTER TO THREE WIVES. Joseph L. Mankiewicz.
ALL THE KING'S MEN. Robert Rossen.
THE BICYCLE THIEF, De Sica, MAB (Italian). Cesare Zavattini.
CHAMPION. Carl Foreman.
THE FALLEN IDOL. Graham Greene.
(Story and Screenplay)
BATTLEGROUND. Robert Pirosh.
JOLSON SINGS AGAIN, COL. Sidney Buchman.
PAISAN, Roberto Rossellini, MAB (Italian). Alfred Hayes, Federico Fellini, Sergio Amidei, Marcello Pagliero and Roberto Rossellini.
PASSPORT TO PIMLICO, Rank-Ealing, EAG (British). T.E.B. Clarke.
THE QUIET ONE, Film Documents, MAB. Helen Levitt, Janice Loeb and Sidney Meyers.

CINEMATOGRAPHY (O-326)
(Black-and-White)
BATTLEGROUND. Paul C. Vogel.
CHAMPION. Frank Planer.
COME TO THE STABLE. Joseph LaShelle.
THE HEIRESS. Leo Tover.
PRINCE OF FOXES, FOX. Leon Shamroy.
(Color)
SHE WORE A YELLOW RIBBON, Argosy, RKO. Winton Hoch.
THE BARKLEYS OF BROADWAY, MGM. Harry Stradling.
JOLSON SINGS AGAIN. William Snyder.
LITTLE WOMEN, MGM. Robert Planck and Charles Schoenbaum.
SAND, FOX. Charles G. Clarke.

COSTUME DESIGN (O-327)
(Black-and-White)
THE HEIRESS. Edith Head and Gile Steele.
PRINCE OF FOXES. Vittorio Nino Novarese.
(Color)
ADVENTURES OF DON JUAN, WB. Leah Rhodes, Travilla and Marjorie Best.
MOTHER IS A FRESHMAN, FOX. Kay Nelson.

ART DIRECTION - SET DECORATION (O-328)
(Black-and-White)
THE HEIRESS. John Meehan and Harry Horner. Set Decoration: Emile Kuri.
COME TO THE STABLE. Lyle Wheeler and Joseph C. Wright. Set Decoration: Thomas Little and Paul S. Fox.
MADAME BOVARY, MGM. Cedric Gibbons and Jack Martin Smith. Set Decoration: Edwin B. Willis and Richard A. Pefferle.
(Color)
LITTLE WOMEN. Cedric Gibbons and Paul Groesse. Set Decoration: Edwin B. Willis and Jack D. Moore.
ADVENTURES OF DON JUAN. Edward Carrere. Set Decoration: Lyle Reifsnider.
SARABAND, Rank-Ealing, EAG (British). Jim Morahan, William Kellner and Michael Relph. Set Decoration: No credits listed.

FILM EDITING (O-329)
CHAMPION. Harry Gerstad.
ALL THE KING'S MEN. Robert Parrish and Al Clark.
BATTLEGROUND. John Dunning.
SANDS OF IWO JIMA. Richard L. Van Enger.
THE WINDOW, RKO. Frederic Knudtson.

MUSIC - SCORING (O-330)
(Scoring of a Dramatic or Comedy Picture)
THE HEIRESS. Aaron Copland.
BEYOND THE FOREST, WB. Max Steiner.
CHAMPION. Dimitri Tiomkin.
(Scoring of a Musical Picture)
ON THE TOWN, MGM. Roger Edens and Lennie Hayton.
JOLSON SINGS AGAIN. Morris Stoloff and George Duning.
LOOK FOR THE SILVER LINING, WB. Ray Heindorf.

MUSIC - BEST SONG (O-331)
BABY, IT'S COLD OUTSIDE, Neptune's Daughter, MGM. Music and Lyrics by Frank Loesser.
IT'S A GREAT FEELING, *It's A Great Feeling,* WB. Music, Jule Styne. Lyrics, Sammy Cahn.
LAVENDER BLUE, *So Dear To My Heart,* Disney-RKO. Music, Eliot Daniel. Lyrics, Larry Morey.
MY FOOLISH HEART, *My Foolish Heart,* Goldwyn-RKO. Music, Victor Young. Lyrics, Ned Washington.
THROUGH A LONG AND SLEEPLESS NIGHT, *Come To The Stable.* Music, Alfred Newman. Lyrics, Mack Gordon.

SOUND (O-332)
TWELVE O'CLOCK HIGH. FOX Sound Department.
ONCE MORE, MY DARLING, Neptune Films, U. U Sound Department.
SANDS OF IWO JIMA. REP Sound Department.

SHORT FILMS (O-333)
(Cartoons)
FOR SCENT-IMENTAL REASONS, WB. (Looney Tunes) Edward Selzer, Prod.
HATCH UP YOUR TROUBLES, MGM. (Tom & Jerry) Fred Quimby, Prod.
MAGIC FLUKE, United Productions Of America, COL. (Fox & Crow) Stephen Bosustow, Prod.
TOY TINKERS, Walt Disney, RKO. Walt Disney, Prod.
(One-reel)
AQUATIC HOUSE-PARTY, PAR. (Grantland Rice Sportlights) Jack Eaton, Prod.
ROLLER DERBY GIRL, PAR. (Pacemaker) Justin Herman, Prod.
SO YOU THINK YOU'RE NOT GUILTY, WB. (Joe McDoakes) Gordon Hollingshead, Prod.
SPILLS AND CHILLS, WB. (Black-and-White Sports Review) Walton C. Ament, Prod.
WATER TRIX, MGM. (Pete Smith Specialty) Pete Smith, Prod.
(Two-reel)

VAN GOGH, Canton-Weiner. Gaston Diehl and Robert Haessens, Prods.
BOY AND THE EAGLE, RKO. William Lasky, Prod.
CHASE OF DEATH, Irving Allen Productions. (Color Series) Irving Allen, Prod.
THE GRASS IS ALWAYS GREENER, WB. (Black-and-White) Gordon Hollingshead, Prod.
SNOW CARNIVAL, WB. (Technicolor) Gordon Hollingshead, Prod.

DOCUMENTARY (O-334)
(Short Subjects)

A CHANCE TO LIVE, MOT, FOX. Richard de Rochemont, Prod.
SO MUCH FOR SO LITTLE, WB. Cartoons, Inc. Edward Selzer, Prod.
1848, A.F. Films, Inc. French Cinema General Cooperative, Prod.
THE RISING TIDE, NFC. St. Francis-Xavier University (Nova Scotia), Prod.

(Features)

DAYBREAK IN UDI, British Information Services. Crown Film Unit, Prod.
KENJI COMES HOME, A Protestant Film Commission Prod. Paul F. Heard, Prod.

SPECIAL EFFECTS (O-335)

MIGHTY JOE YOUNG, ARKO, RKO.
TULSA, Walter Wanger Pictures, EAG.

HONORARY AND OTHER (O-336)
(Other)

THE BICYCLE THIEF - voted by the Academy Board of Governors as the most outstanding foreign language film released in the United States during 1949.
BOBBY DRISCOLL, as the outstanding juvenile actor of 1949.
FRED ASTAIRE for his unique artistry and his contributions to the technique of musical pictures.
CECIL B. DEMILLE, distinguished motion picture pioneer, for 37 years of brilliant showmanship.
JEAN HERSHOLT, for distinguished service to the motion picture industry.

SCIENTIFIC OR TECHNICAL (O-337)
(Class I)

EASTMAN KODAK CO. for the development and introduction of an improved safety base motion picture film.

(Class III)

LOREN L. RYDER, BRUCE H. DENNEY, ROBERT CARR and the PARAMOUNT STUDIO SOUND DEPARTMENT for the development and application of the supersonic playback and public address system.
M. B. PAUL for the first successful large-area seamless translucent backgrounds.
HERBERT BRITT for the development and application of formulas and equipment producing artificial snow and ice for dressing motion picture sets.
ANDRE COUTANT and JACQUES MATHOT for the design of the Eclair Camerette.
CHARLES R. DAILY, STEVE CSILLAG and the PARAMOUNT STUDIO ENGINEERING, EDITORIAL and MUSIC DEPARTMENTS for a new precision method of computing variable tempo-click tracks.
INTERNATIONAL PROJECTOR CORP. for a simplified and self-adjusting take-up device for projection machines.
ALEXANDER VELCOFF for the application to production of the infra-red photographic evaluator.

1950

BEST PICTURE (O-338)

ALL ABOUT EVE, FOX.
BORN YESTERDAY, COL.
FATHER OF THE BRIDE, MGM.
KING SOLOMON'S MINES, MGM.
SUNSET BOULEVARD, PAR.

ACTOR (O-339)

JOSE FERRER, Cyrano De Bergerac, Stanley Kramer, UA.
LOUIS CALHERN, *The Magnificent Yankee*, MGM.
WILLIAM HOLDEN, *Sunset Boulevard*.
JAMES STEWART, *Harvey*, U.
SPENCER TRACY, *Father Of The Bride*.

ACTRESS (O-340)

JUDY HOLLIDAY, Born Yesterday.
ANNE BAXTER, *All About Eve*.
BETTE DAVIS, *All About Eve*.
ELEANOR PARKER, *Caged*, WB.
GLORIA SWANSON, *Sunset Boulevard*.

SUPPORTING ACTOR (O-341)

GEORGE SANDERS, All About Eve.
JEFF CHANDLER, *Broken Arrow*, FOX.
EDMUND GWENN, *Mister 880*, FOX.
SAM JAFFE, *The Asphalt Jungle*, MGM.
ERICH VON STROHEIM, *Sunset Boulevard*.

SUPPORTING ACTRESS (O-342)

JOSEPHINE HULL, Harvey.
HOPE EMERSON, *Caged*.
CELESTE HOLM, *All About Eve*.
NANCY OLSON, *Sunset Boulevard*.
THELMA RITTER, *All About Eve*.

DIRECTING (O-343)

JOSEPH L. MANKIEWICZ, All About Eve.
GEORGE CUKOR, *Born Yesterday*.
JOHN HUSTON, *The Asphalt Jungle*.
CAROL REED, *The Third Man*, Selznick-London Films, SRO (British).
BILLY WILDER, *Sunset Boulevard*.

WRITING (O-344)
(Motion Picture Story)

PANIC IN THE STREETS, FOX. Edna Anhalt and Edward Anhalt.
BITTER RICE, LUX (Italian). Giuseppe De Santis and Carlo Lizzani.
THE GUNFIGHTER, FOX. William Bowers and Andre de Toth.
MYSTERY STREET, MGM. Leonard Spigelgass.
WHEN WILLIE COMES MARCHING HOME, FOX. Sy Gomberg.

(Screenplay)

ALL ABOUT EVE. Joseph L. Mankiewicz.
THE ASPHALT JUNGLE. Ben Maddow and John Huston.
BORN YESTERDAY. Albert Mannheimer.
BROKEN ARROW. Michael Blankfort.
FATHER OF THE BRIDE. Frances Goodrich and Albert Hackett.

(Story and Screenplay)

SUNSET BOULEVARD. Charles Brackett, Billy Wilder and D. M. Marshman, Jr.
ADAM'S RIB, MGM. Ruth Gordon and Garson Kanin.
CAGED. Virginia Kellogg and Bernard C. Schoenfeld.
THE MEN, Kramer, UA. Carl Foreman.
NO WAY OUT, FOX. Joseph L. Mankiewicz and Lesser Samuels.

CINEMATOGRAPHY (O-345)
(Black-and-White)

THE THIRD MAN. Robert Krasker.
ALL ABOUT EVE. Milton Krasner.
THE ASPHALT JUNGLE. Harold Rosson.
THE FURIES, Wallis, PAR. Victor Milner.
SUNSET BOULEVARD. John F. Seitz.

(Color)

KING SOLOMON'S MINES. Robert Surtees.
ANNIE GET YOUR GUN, MGM. Charles Rosher.

BROKEN ARROW. Ernest Palmer.
THE FLAME AND THE ARROW, Norma-F.R., WB. Ernest Haller.
SAMSON AND DELILAH, DeMille, PAR. George Barnes.

COSTUME DESIGN (O-346)

(Black-and-White)

ALL ABOUT EVE. Edith Head and Charles LeMaire.
BORN YESTERDAY. Jean Louis.
THE MAGNIFICENT YANKEE. Walter Plunkett.

(Color)

SAMSON AND DELILAH. Edith Head, Dorothy Jeakins, Elois Jenssen, Gile Steele and Gwen Wakeling.
THE BLACK ROSE, FOX. Michael Whittaker.
THAT FORSYTE WOMAN, MGM. Walter Plunkett and Valles.

ART DIRECTION - SET DECORATION (O-347)

(Black-and-White)

SUNSET BOULEVARD. Hans Dreier and John Meehan. Set Decoration: Sam Comer and Ray Moyer.
ALL ABOUT EVE. Lyle Wheeler and George Davis. Set Decoration: Thomas Little and Walter M. Scott.
THE RED DANUBE, MGM. Cedric Gibbons and Hans Peters. Set Decoration: Edwin B. Willis and Hugh Hunt.

(Color)

SAMSON AND DELILAH. Hans Dreier and Walter Tyler. Set Decoration: Sam Comer and Ray Moyer.
ANNIE GET YOUR GUN. Cedric Gibbons and Paul Groesse. Set Decoration: Edwin B. Willis and Richard A. Pefferle.
DESTINATION MOON, George Pal, ELC. Ernst Fegte. Set Decoration: George Sawley.

FILM EDITING (O-348)

KING SOLOMON'S MINES. Ralph E. Winters and Conrad A. Nervig.
ALL ABOUT EVE. Barbara McLean.
ANNIE GET YOUR GUN. James E. Newcom.
SUNSET BOULEVARD. Arthur Schmidt and Doane Harrison.
THE THIRD MAN. Oswald Hafenrichter.

MUSIC - SCORING (O-349)

(Scoring of a Musical Picture)

SUNSET BOULEVARD. Franz Waxman.
ALL ABOUT EVE. Alfred Newman.
THE FLAME AND THE ARROW. Max Steiner.
NO SAD SONGS FOR ME, COL. George Duning.
SAMSON AND DELILAH. Victor Young.

(Scoring of a Dramatic or Comedy Picture)

ANNIE GET YOUR GUN. Adolph Deutsch and Roger Edens.
CINDERELLA, Disney, RKO. Oliver Wallace and Paul J. Smith.
I'LL GET BY, FOX. Lionel Newman.
THREE LITTLE WORDS, MGM. Andre Previn.
THE WEST POINT STORY, WB. Ray Heindorf.

MUSIC - BEST SONG (O-350)

MONA LISA, Captain Carey, USA, PAR. Music and Lyrics by Ray Evans and Jay Livingston.
BE MY LOVE, *The Toast Of New Orleans*, MGM. Music, Nicholas Brodszky. Lyrics, Sammy Cahn.
BIBBIDY-BOBBIDI-BOO, *Cinderella*. Music and Lyrics by Mack David, Al Hoffman and Jerry Livingston.
MULE TRAIN, *Singing Guns*, Polomar Pictures, REP. Music and Lyrics by Fred Glickman, Hy Heath and Johnny Lange.
WILHELMINA, *Wabash Avenue*, FOX. Music, Josef Myrow. Lyrics, Mack Gordon.

SOUND (O-351)

ALL ABOUT EVE. FOX Sound Department.
CINDERELLA. Disney Sound Department.

LOUISA, U. U Sound Department.
OUR VERY OWN, Goldwyn, RKO. Goldwyn Sound Department.
TRIO, Rank-Sydney Box, PAR (British).

SHORT FILMS (O-352)

(Cartoons)

GERALD MCBOING-BOING, United Productions Of America, COL. (Jolly Frolics Series) Stephen Bosustow, Ex Prod.
JERRY'S COUSIN, MGM. (Tom & Jerry) Fred Quimby, Prod.
TROUBLE INDEMNITY, United Productions Of America, COL. (Mr. Magoo Series) Stephen Bosustow, Ex Prod.

(One-reel)

GRANDAD OF RACES, WB. (Sports Parade) Gordon Hollingshead, Prod.
BLAZE BUSTERS, WB. (Vitaphone Novelties) Robert Youngson, Prod.
WRONG WAY BUTCH, MGM. Pete Smith, Prod.

(Two-reel)

IN BEAVER VALLEY, Walt Disney, RKO. (True-Life Adventure) Walt Disney, Prod.
GRANDMA MOSES, Falcon Films, Inc., A.F. Films. Falcon Films, Inc., Prod.
MY COUNTRY 'TIS OF THEE, WB. (Featurette Series) Gordon Hollingshead, Prod.

DOCUMENTARY (O-353)

(Short Subjects)

WHY KOREA?, FOX Movietone. Edmund Reek, Prod.
THE FIGHT: SCIENCE AGAINST CANCER, NFC in cooperation with the Medical Film Institute of the Association of American Medical Colleges.
THE STAIRS, Film Documents, Inc.

(Features)

THE TITAN: STORY OF MICHELANGELO, Michelangelo Co., Classics Pictures, Inc. Robert Snyder, Prod.
WITH THESE HANDS, Promotional Films Co., Inc. Jack Arnold and Lee Goodman, Prods.

SPECIAL EFFECTS (O-354)

DESTINATION MOON.
SAMSON AND DELILAH.

HONORARY AND OTHER (O-355)

(Irving G. Thalberg Memorial Award)

Darryl F. Zanuck

(Other)

GEORGE MURPHY for his services in interpreting the film industry to the country at large.
LOUIS B. MAYER for distinguished service to the motion picture industry.
THE WALLS OF MALAPAGA (Franco-Italian) - voted by the Board of Governors as the most outstanding foreign language film released in the United States in 1950.

SCIENTIFIC OR TECHNICAL (O-356)

(Class II)

JAMES B. GORDON and the 20TH CENTURY-FOX STUDIO CAMERA DEPARTMENT for the design and development of a multiple image film viewer.
JOHN PAUL LIVADARY, FLOYD CAMPBELL, L. W. RUSSELL and the COLUMBIA STUDIO SOUND DEPARTMENT for the development of a multi-track magnetic re-recording system.
LOREN L. RYDER and the PARAMOUNT STUDIO SOUND DEPARTMENT for the first studio-wide application of magnetic sound recording to motion picture production.

1951

BEST PICTURE (O-357)

AN AMERICAN IN PARIS, MGM. Arthur Freed, Prod.
DECISION BEFORE DAWN, FOX. Anatole Litvak & Frank McCarthy, Prods.
A PLACE IN THE SUN, PAR. George Stevens, Prod.
QUO VADIS, MGM. Sam Zimbalist, Prod.
A STREETCAR NAMED DESIRE, Charles K. Feldman Group Prods., WB. Charles K. Feldman, Prod.

ACTOR (O-358)

HUMPHREY BOGART, The African Queen, Horizon, UA.
MARLON BRANDO, *A Streetcar Named Desire.*
MONTGOMERY CLIFT, *A Place In The Sun.*
ARTHUR KENNEDY, *Bright Victory,* U.
FREDRIC MARCH, *Death Of A Salesman,* Stanley Kramer, COL.

ACTRESS (O-359)

VIVIEN LEIGH, A Streetcar Named Desire.
KATHARINE HEPBURN, *The African Queen.*
ELEANOR PARKER, *Detective Story,* PAR.
SHELLEY WINTERS, *A Place In The Sun.*
JANE WYMAN, *The Blue Veil,* Wald-Krasna, RKO.

SUPPORTING ACTOR (O-360)

KARL MALDEN, A Streetcar Named Desire.
LEO GENN, *Quo Vadis.*
KEVIN McCARTHY, *Death Of A Salesman.*
PETER USTINOV, *Quo Vadis.*
GIG YOUNG, *Come Fill The Cup,* WB.

SUPPORTING ACTRESS (O-361)

KIM HUNTER, A Streetcar Named Desire.
JOAN BLONDELL, *The Blue Veil.*
MILDRED DUNNOCK, *Death Of A Salesman.*
LEE GRANT, *Detective Story.*
THELMA RITTER, *The Mating Season,* PAR.

DIRECTING (O-362)

GEORGE STEVENS, A Place In The Sun.
JOHN HUSTON, *The African Queen.*
ELIA KAZAN, *A Streetcar Named Desire.*
VINCENTE MINNELLI, *An American In Paris.*
WILLIAM WYLER, *Detective Story.*

WRITING (O-363)

(Motion Picture Story)
SEVEN DAYS TO NOON, Boulting Bros., MKD (British). Paul Dehn and James Bernard.
BULLFIGHTER AND THE LADY, REP. Budd Boetticher and Ray Nazarro.
THE FROGMEN, FOX. Oscar Millard.
HERE COMES THE GROOM, PAR. Robert Riskin and Liam O'Brien.
TERESA, MGM. Alfred Hayes and Stewart Stern.
(Screenplay)
A PLACE IN THE SUN. Michael Wilson and Harry Brown.
THE AFRICAN QUEEN. James Agee and John Huston.
DETECTIVE STORY. Philip Yordan and Robert Wyler.
LA RONDE, Sacha Gordine, CME (French). Jacques Natanson and Max Ophuls.
A STREETCAR NAMED DESIRE. Tennessee Williams.
(Story and Screenplay)
AN AMERICAN IN PARIS. Alan Jay Lerner.
THE BIG CARNIVAL, PAR. Billy Wilder, Lesser Samuels and Walter

Newman.
DAVID AND BATHSHEBA, FOX. Philip Dunne.
GO FOR BROKE!, MGM. Robert Pirosh.
THE WELL, Popkin, UA. Clarence Greene and Russell Rouse.

CINEMATOGRAPHY (O-364)

(Black-and-White)
A PLACE IN THE SUN. William C. Mellor.
DEATH OF A SALESMAN. Franz Planer.
THE FROGMEN. Norbert Brodine.
STRANGERS ON A TRAIN, WB. Robert Burks.
A STREETCAR NAMED DESIRE. Harry Stradling.
(Color)
AN AMERICAN IN PARIS. Alfred Gilks; Ballet photographed by John Alton.
DAVID AND BATHSHEBA. Leon Shamroy.
QUO VADIS. Robert Surtees and William V. Skall.
SHOW BOAT, MGM. Charles Rosher.
WHEN WORLDS COLLIDE, PAR. John F. Seitz and W. Howard Greene.

COSTUME DESIGN (O-365)

(Black-and-White)
A PLACE IN THE SUN. Edith Head.
KIND LADY, MGM. Walter Plunkett and Gile Steele.
THE MODEL AND THE MARRIAGE BROKER, FOX. Charles LeMaire and Renie.
THE MUDLARK, FOX. Edward Stevenson and Margaret Furse.
A STREETCAR NAMED DESIRE. Lucinda Ballard.
(Color)
AN AMERICAN IN PARIS. Orry-Kelly, Walter Plunkett and Irene Sharaff.
DAVID AND BATHSHEBA. Charles LeMaire and Edward Stevenson.
THE GREAT CARUSO, MGM. Helen Rose and Gile Steele.
QUO VADIS. Herschel McCoy.
TALES OF HOFFMANN, Powell-Pressburger, LOP (British). Hein Heckroth.

ART DIRECTION - SET DECORATION (O-366)

(Black-and-White)
A STREETCAR NAMED DESIRE. Richard Day. Set Decoration: George James Hopkins.
FOURTEEN HOURS, FOX. Lyle Wheeler and Leland Fuller. Set Decoration: Thomas Little and Fred J. Rode.
HOUSE ON TELEGRAPH HILL, FOX. Lyle Wheeler and John DeCrui. Set Decoration: Thomas Little and Paul S. Fox.
LA RONDE. D'Eaubonne. Set Decoration: No credits listed.
TOO YOUNG TO KISS, MGM. Cedric Gibbons and Paul Groesse. Set Decoration: Edwin B. Willis and Jack D. Moore.
(Color)
AN AMERICAN IN PARIS. Cedric Gibbons and Preston Ames. Set Decoration: Edwin B. Willis and Keogh Gleason.
DAVID AND BATHSHEBA. Lyle Wheeler and George Davis. Set Decoration: Thomas Little and Paul S. Fox.
ON THE RIVIERA, FOX. Lyle Wheeler and Leland Fuller. Musical Settings: Joseph C. Wright. Set Decoration: Thomas Little and Walter M. Scott.
QUO VADIS. William A. Horning, Cedric Gibbons and Edward Carfagno. Set Decoration: Hugh Hunt.
TALES OF HOFFMANN. Hein Heckroth. Set Decoration: No credits listed.

FILM EDITING (O-367)

A PLACE IN THE SUN. William Hornbeck.
AN AMERICAN IN PARIS. Adrienne Fazan.
DECISION BEFORE DAWN. Dorothy Spencer.
QUO VADIS. Ralph E. Winters.
THE WELL. Chester Schaeffer.

MUSIC - SCORING (O-368)

(Scoring of a Dramatic or Comedy Picture)

A PLACE IN THE SUN. Franz Waxman.
DAVID AND BATHSHEBA. Alfred Newman.
DEATH OF A SALESMAN. Alex North.
QUO VADIS. Miklos Rozsa.
A STREETCAR NAMED DESIRE. Alex North.

(Scoring of a Musical Picture)

AN AMERICAN IN PARIS. Johnny Green and Saul Chaplin.
ALICE IN WONDERLAND, Disney, RKO. Oliver Wallace.
THE GREAT CARUSO. Peter Herman Adler and Johnny Green.
ON THE RIVIERA. Alfred Newman.
SHOW BOAT. Adolph Deutsch and Conrad Salinger.

MUSIC - BEST SONG (O-369)

**IN THE COOL, COOL, COOL OF THE EVENING, Here Comes The
Groom. Music, Hoagy Carmichael. Lyrics, Johnny Mercer.**
A KISS TO BUILD A DREAM ON, *The Strip*, MGM. Music and Lyrics
by Bert Kalmar, Harry Ruby and Oscar Hammerstein II.
NEVER, *Golden Girl*, FOX. Music, Lionel Newman. Lyrics, Eliot Daniel.
TOO LATE NOW, *Royal Wedding*, MGM. Music, Burton Lane. Lyrics,
Alan Jay Lerner.
WONDER WHY, *Rich, Young And Pretty*, MGM. Music, Nicholas
Brodszky. Lyrics, Sammy Cahn.

SOUND (O-370)

THE GREAT CARUSO. Douglas Shearer, Sound Director.
BRIGHT VICTORY. Leslie I. Carey, Sound Director.
I WANT YOU, Samuel Goldwyn Prods., Inc., RKO. Gordon Sawyer,
Sound Director.
A STREETCAR NAMED DESIRE. Col. Nathan Levinson, Sound Director.
TWO TICKETS TO BROADWAY, RKO. John O. Aalberg, Sound Director.

SHORT FILMS (O-371)

(Cartoons)

TWO MOUSEKETEERS, MGM. (Tom & Jerry) Fred Quimby, Prod.
LAMBERT, THE SHEEPISH LION, Walt Disney, RKO. (Special) Walt
Disney, Prod.
ROOTY TOOT TOOT, United Productions Of America, COL. (Jolly
Frolics) Stephen Bosustow, Ex Prod.

(One-reel)

**WORLD OF KIDS, WB. (Vitaphone Novelties) Robert Youngson,
Prod.**
RIDIN' THE RAILS, PAR. (Sportlights) Jack Eaton, Prod.
THE STORY OF TIME, A Signal Films Production by Robert G. Leffing-
well, Cornell Film Co (British).

(Two-reel)

**NATURE'S HALF ACRE, Walt Disney, RKO. (True-Life Adventure)
Walt Disney, Prod.**
BALZAC, Les Films Du Compass, A.F. Films, Inc. (French). Les Films
Du Compass, Prod.
DANGER UNDER THE SEA, UI. Tom Mead, Prod.

DOCUMENTARY (O-372)

(Short Subjects)

**BENJY, Made by Fred Zinnemann with the cooperation of Para-
mount for the Los Angeles Orthopaedic Hospital.**
ONE WHO CAME BACK, Owen Crump, Prod. (Film sponsored by the
Disabled American Veterans, in cooperation with the United States
Department of Defense and the Association of Motion Picture Prods.)
THE SEEING EYE, WB. Gordon Hollingshead, Prod.

(Features)

KON-TIKI, An Artfilm Prod., RKO (Norwegian). Olle Nordemar, Prod.
I WAS A COMMUNIST FOR THE F.B.I., WB. Bryan Foy, Prod.

SPECIAL EFFECTS (O-373)

WHEN WORLDS COLLIDE.

HONORARY AND OTHER (O-374)

(Irving G. Thalberg Memorial Award)

Arthur Freed

(Other)

GENE KELLY in appreciation of his versatility as an actor, singer,
director and dancer, and specifically for his brilliant achievements
in the art of choreography on film.
RASHOMON (Japanese) - voted by the Board of Governors as the
most outstanding foreign language film released in the United
States during 1951.

SCIENTIFIC OR TECHNICAL (O-375)

(Class II)

GORDON JENNINGS, S. L. STANCLIFFE and the Paramount STUDIO
SPECIAL PHOTOGRAPHIC and ENGINEERING DEPARTMENTS for
the design, construction and application of a servo-operated recording and repeating device.
OLIN L. DUPY of MGM Studio for the design, construction and
application of a motion picture reproducing system.
RADIO CORPORATION OF AMERICA, VICTOR DIVISION, for pioneering direct positive recording with anticipatory noise reduction.

(Class III)

RICHARD M. HAFF, FRANK P. HERRNFELD, GARLAND C. MISENER
and the ANSCO FILM DIVISION OF GENERAL ANILINE AND FILM
CORP. for the development of the Ansco color scene tester.
FRED PONEDEL, RALPH AYRES and **GEORGE BROWN** of WB Studio
for an air-driven water motor to provide flow, wake and white water
for marine sequences in motion pictures.
GLEN ROBINSON and the MGM STUDIO CONSTRUCTION DEPART-
MENT for the development of a new music wire and cable cutter.
JACK GAYLORD and the MGM STUDIO CONSTRUCTION DEPART-
MENT for the development of balsa falling snow.
CARLOS RIVAS of MGM Studio for the development of an automatic
magnetic film splicer.

1952

BEST PICTURE (O-376)

**THE GREATEST SHOW ON EARTH, Cecil B. DeMille, PAR. Cecil B.
DeMille, Prod.**
HIGH NOON, Stanley Kramer Prods., UA. Stanley Kramer, Prod.
IVANHOE, MGM. Pandro S. Berman, Prod.
MOULIN ROUGE, Romulus Films, UA.
THE QUIET MAN, Argosy Pictures Corp., REP. John Ford and Merian
C. Cooper, Prods.

ACTOR (O-377)

GARY COOPER, High Noon.
MARLON BRANDO, *Viva Zapata!*, FOX.
KIRK DOUGLAS, *The Bad And The Beautiful*, MGM.
JOSE FERRER, *Moulin Rouge.*
ALEC GUINNESS, *The Lavender Hill Mob*, J. Arthur Rank Presentation-
Ealing Studios, U. (British)

ACTRESS (O-378)

SHIRLEY BOOTH, Come Back, Little Sheba, Hal Wallis, PAR.
JOAN CRAWFORD, *Sudden Fear*, Joseph Kaufman Prods., RKO.
BETTE DAVIS, *The Star*, Bert E. Friedlob, FOX.
JULIE HARRIS, *The Member Of The Wedding*, Stanley Kramer, COL.
SUSAN HAYWARD, *With A Song In My Heart*, FOX.

SUPPORTING ACTOR (O-379)

ANTHONY QUINN, Viva Zapata!
RICHARD BURTON, *My Cousin Rachel*, FOX.
ARTHUR HUNNICUTT, *The Big Sky*, Winchester, RKO.

VICTOR McLAGLEN, *The Quiet Man.*
JACK PALANCE, *Sudden Fear.*

SUPPORTING ACTRESS (O-380)

GLORIA GRAHAME, The Bad And The Beautiful.
JEAN HAGEN, *Singin' In The Rain*, MGM.
COLETTE MARCHAND, *Moulin Rouge.*
TERRY MOORE, *Come Back, Little Sheba.*
THELMA RITTER, *With A Song In My Heart.*

DIRECTING (O-381)

JOHN FORD, The Quiet Man.
CECIL B. DEMILLE, *The Greatest Show On Earth.*
JOHN HUSTON, *Moulin Rouge.*
JOSEPH L. MANKIEWICZ, *Five Fingers*, FOX.
FRED ZINNEMANN, *High Noon.*

WRITING (O-382)

(Motion Picture Story)

THE GREATEST SHOW ON EARTH. Frederic M. Frank, Theodore St. John and Frank Cavett.
MY SON JOHN, Rainbow, PAR. Leo McCarey.
THE NARROW MARGIN, RKO. Martin Goldsmith and Jack Leonard.
THE PRIDE OF ST. LOUIS, FOX. Guy Trosper.
THE SNIPER, Kramer, COL. Edna Anhalt and Edward Anhalt.

(Screenplay)

THE BAD AND THE BEAUTIFUL. Charles Schnee.
FIVE FINGERS. Michael Wilson.
HIGH NOON. Carl Foreman.
THE MAN IN THE WHITE SUIT, Rank-Ealing, U (British). Roger Mac-Dougall, John Dighton and Alexander Mackendrick.
THE QUIET MAN. Frank S. Nugent.

(Story and Screenplay)

THE LAVENDER HILL MOB. T.E.B. Clarke.
THE ATOMIC CITY, PAR. Sydney Boehm.
BREAKING THE SOUND BARRIER, London Films, UA (British). Terence Rattigan.
PAT AND MIKE, MGM. Ruth Gordon and Garson Kanin.
VIVA ZAPATA! John Steinbeck.

CINEMATOGRAPHY (O-383)

(Black-and-White)

THE BAD AND THE BEAUTIFUL. Robert Surtees.
THE BIG SKY. Russell Harlan.
MY COUSIN RACHEL. Joseph LaShelle.
NAVAJO, Bartlett-Foster, LIP. Virgil E. Miller.
SUDDEN FEAR. Charles B. Lang, Jr.

(Color)

THE QUIET MAN. Winton C. Hoch and Archie Stout.
HANS CHRISTIAN ANDERSEN, Goldwyn, RKO. Harry Stradling.
IVANHOE. F. A. Young.
MILLION DOLLAR MERMAID, MGM. George J. Folsey.
THE SNOWS OF KILIMANJARO, FOX. Leon Shamroy.

COSTUME DESIGN (O-384)

(Black-and-White)

THE BAD AND THE BEAUTIFUL. Helen Rose.
AFFAIR IN TRINIDAD, Beckworth, COL. Jean Louis.
CARRIE, PAR. Edith Head.
MY COUSIN RACHEL. Charles LeMaire and Dorothy Jeakins.
SUDDEN FEAR. Sheila O'Brien.

(Color)

MOULIN ROUGE. Marcel Vertes.
THE GREATEST SHOW ON EARTH. Edith Head, Dorothy Jeakins and Miles White.
HANS CHRISTIAN ANDERSEN. Clave, Mary Wills and Madame Karinska.
THE MERRY WIDOW, MGM. Helen Rose and Gile Steele.
WITH A SONG IN MY HEART. Charles LeMaire.

ART DIRECTION - SET DECORATION (O-385)

(Black-and-White)

THE BAD AND THE BEAUTIFUL. Cedric Gibbons and Edward Carfagno. Set Decoration: Edwin B. Willis and Keogh Gleason.
CARRIE. Hal Pereira and Roland Anderson. Set Decoration: Emile Kuri.
MY COUSIN RACHEL. Lyle Wheeler and John DeCuir. Set Decoration: Walter M. Scott.
RASHO-MON, Daiei, RKO (Japanese). Matsuyama. Set Decoration: H. Motsumoto.
VIVA ZAPATA! Lyle Wheeler and Leland Fuller. Set Decoration: Thomas Little and Claude Carpenter.

(Color)

MOULIN ROUGE. Paul Sheriff. Set Decoration: Marcel Vertes.
HANS CHRISTIAN ANDERSEN. Richard Day and Clave. Set Decoration: Howard Bristol.
THE MERRY WIDOW. Cedric Gibbons and Paul Groesse. Set Decoration: Edwin B. Willis and Arthur Krams.
THE QUIET MAN. Frank Hotaling. Set Decoration: John McCarthy, Jr. and Charles Thompson.
THE SNOWS OF KILIMANJARO. Lyle Wheeler and John DeCuir. Set Decoration: Thomas Little and Paul S. Fox.

FILM EDITING (O-386)

HIGH NOON. Elmo Williams and Harry Gerstad.
COME BACK, LITTLE SHEBA. Warren Low.
FLAT TOP, MNG. William Austin.
THE GREATEST SHOW ON EARTH. Anne Bauchens.
MOULIN ROUGE. Ralph Kemplen.

MUSIC - SCORING (O-387)

(Scoring of a Dramatic or Comedy Picture)

HIGH NOON. Dimitri Tiomkin.
IVANHOE. Miklos Rozsa.
MIRACLE OF FATIMA, WB. Max Steiner.
THE THIEF, Fran Prods., UA. Herschel Burke Gilbert.
VIVA ZAPATA! Alex North.

(Scoring of a Musical Picture)

WITH A SONG IN MY HEART. Alfred Newman.
HANS CHRISTIAN ANDERSEN. Walter Scharf.
THE JAZZ SINGER, WB. Ray Heindorf and Max Steiner.
THE MEDIUM, Transfilm-Lopert (Italian). Gian-Carlo Menotti.
SINGIN' IN THE RAIN. Lennie Hayton.

MUSIC - BEST SONG (O-388)

HIGH NOON (DO NOT FORSAKE ME, OH MY DARLIN'), High Noon. Music, Dimitri Tiomkin. Lyrics, Ned Washington.
AM I IN LOVE, *Son Of Paleface*, PAR. Music and Lyrics by Jack Brooks.
BECAUSE YOU'RE MINE, *Because You're Mine*, MGM. Music, Nicholas Brodszky. Lyrics, Sammy Cahn.
THUMBELINA, *Hans Christian Andersen*. Music and Lyrics by Frank Loesser.
ZING A LITTLE ZONG, *Just For You*, PAR. Music, Harry Warren. Lyrics, Leo Robin.

SOUND (O-389)

BREAKING THE SOUND BARRIER. London Film Sound Department.
HANS CHRISTIAN ANDERSEN. Goldwyn Sound Department. Gordon Sawyer, Sound Director.
THE PROMOTER, Rank, Ronald Neame, UI (British). Pinewood Studios Sound Department.
THE QUIET MAN. Republic Sound Department. Daniel J. Bloomberg, Sound Director.
WITH A SONG IN MY HEART. FOX Sound Department. Thomas T. Moulton, Sound Director.

SHORT FILMS (O-390)

(Cartoons)

JOHANN MOUSE, MGM. (Tom & Jerry) Fred Quimby, Prod.
LITTLE JOHNNY JET, MGM. (MGM Series) Fred Quimby, Prod.
MADELINE, UPA, COL. (Jolly Frolics) Stephen Bosustow, Ex Prod.

PINK AND BLUE BLUES, UPA, COL. (Mister Magoo) Stephen Bosustow, Ex Prod.
ROMANCE OF TRANSPORTATION, NFC (Canadian). Tom Daly, Prod.

(One-reel)

LIGHT IN THE WINDOW, Art Films Prods., FOX. (Art Series) Boris Vermont, Prod.
ATHLETES OF THE SADDLE, PAR. (Sportlights Series) Jack Eaton, Prod.
DESERT KILLER, WB. (Sports Parade) Gordon Hollingshead, Prod.
NEIGHBOURS, NFC (Canadian). Norman McLaren, Prod.
ROYAL SCOTLAND, Crown Film Unit, British Information Services (British).

(Two-reel)

WATER BIRDS, Walt Disney, RKO. (True-Life Adventure) Walt Disney, Prod.
BRIDGE OF TIME, A London Film Prod., British Information Services (British).
DEVIL TAKE US, A Theatre Of Life Prod. (Theatre Of Life Series) Herbert Morgan, Prod.
THAR SHE BLOWS!, WB. (Technicolor Special) Gordon Hollingshead, Prod.

DOCUMENTARY (O-391)

(Short Subjects)

NEIGHBOURS, NFC, MAK (Canadian). Norman McLaren, Prod.
DEVIL TAKE US, Theatre of Life Prod. Herbert Morgan, Prod.
THE GARDEN SPIDER (EPEIRA DIADEMA), Cristallo Films, IFE. (Italian). Alberto Ancilotto, Prod.
MAN ALIVE!, Made by United Productions of America for the American Cancer Society. Stephen Bosustow, Ex Prod.

(Features)

THE SEA AROUND US, RKO. Irwin Allen, Prod.
THE HOAXTERS, MGM. Dore Schary, Prod.
NAVAJO, LIP. Hall Bartlett, Prod.

SPECIAL EFFECTS (O-392)

PLYMOUTH ADVENTURE, MGM.

HONORARY AND OTHER (O-393)

(Irving G. Thalberg Memorial Award)

Cecil B. DeMille

(Other)

GEORGE ALFRED MITCHELL for the design and development of the camera which bears his name and for his continued and dominant presence in the field of cinematography.
JOSEPH M. SCHENCK for long and distinguished service to the motion picture industry.
MERIAN C. COOPER for his many innovations and contributions to the art of motion pictures.
HAROLD LLOYD, master comedian and good citizen.
BOB HOPE for his contribution to the laughter of the world, his service to the motion picture industry, and his devotion to the American premise.
FORBIDDEN GAMES (French) - Best Foreign Language Film first released in the United States during 1952.

SCIENTIFIC OR TECHNICAL (O-394)

(Class I)

EASTMAN KODAK CO. for the introduction of Eastman color negative and Eastman color print film.
ANSCO DIVISION, GENERAL ANILINE AND FILM CORP., for the introduction of Ansco color negative and Ansco color print film.

(Class II)

TECHNICOLOR MOTION PICTURE CORP. for an improved method of color motion picture photography under incandescent light.

(Class III)

PROJECTION, STILL PHOTOGRAPHIC and DEVELOPMENT ENGINEERING DEPARTMENTS of MGM STUDIO for an improved method of projecting photographic backgrounds.
JOHN G. FRAYNE and **R. R. SCOVILLE** and **WESTREX CORP.** for a method of measuring distortion in sound reproduction.
PHOTO RESEARCH CORP. for creating the Spectra color temperature meter.
GUSTAV JIROUCH for the design of the Robot automatic film splicer.
CARLOS RIVAS of MGM Studio for the development of a sound reproducer for magnetic film.

1953

BEST PICTURE (O-395)

FROM HERE TO ETERNITY, COL. Buddy Adler, Prod.
JULIUS CAESAR, MGM. John Houseman, Prod.
THE ROBE, FOX. Frank Ross, Prod.
ROMAN HOLIDAY, PAR. William Wyler, Prod.
SHANE, PAR. George Stevens, Prod.

ACTOR (O-396)

WILLIAM HOLDEN, Stalag 17, PAR.
MARLON BRANDO, *Julius Caesar.*
RICHARD BURTON, *The Robe.*
MONTGOMERY CLIFT, *From Here To Eternity.*
BURT LANCASTER, *From Here To Eternity.*

ACTRESS (O-397)

AUDREY HEPBURN, Roman Holiday.
LESLIE CARON, *Lili,* MGM.
AVA GARDNER, *Mogambo,* MGM.
DEBORAH KERR, *From Here To Eternity.*
MAGGIE McNAMARA, *The Moon Is Blue,* Preminger-Herbert, UA.

SUPPORTING ACTOR (O-398)

FRANK SINATRA, From Here To Eternity.
EDDIE ALBERT, *Roman Holiday.*
BRANDON DE WILDE, *Shane.*
JACK PALANCE, *Shane.*
ROBERT STRAUSS, *Stalag 17.*

SUPPORTING ACTRESS (O-399)

DONNA REED, From Here To Eternity.
GRACE KELLY, *Mogambo.*
GERALDINE PAGE, *Hondo.*
MARJORIE RAMBEAU, *Torch Song,* MGM.
THELMA RITTER, *Pickup On South Street,* FOX.

DIRECTING (O-400)

FRED ZINNEMANN, From Here To Eternity.
GEORGE STEVENS, *Shane.*
CHARLES WALTERS, *Lili.*
BILLY WILDER, *Stalag 17.*
WILLIAM WYLER, *Roman Holiday.*

WRITING (O-401)

(Motion Picture Story)

ROMAN HOLIDAY. Ian McLellan Hunter.
ABOVE AND BEYOND, MGM. Beirne Lay, Jr.
THE CAPTAIN'S PARADISE, London Films, Lopert-UA (British). Alec Coppel.
LITTLE FUGITIVE, Little Fugitive Prod. Co., BYN. Ray Ashley, Morris Engel and Ruth Orkin.

(Screenplay)

FROM HERE TO ETERNITY. Daniel Taradash.
THE CRUEL SEA, Rank-Ealing, UI (British). Eric Ambler.
LILI. Helen Deutsch.
ROMAN HOLIDAY. Ian McLellan Hunter and John Dighton.

SHANE. A. B. Guthrie, Jr.
(Story and Screenplay)
TITANIC, FOX. Charles Brackett, Walter Reisch and Richard Breen.
THE BAND WAGON, MGM. Betty Comden and Adolph Green.
THE DESERT RATS, FOX. Richard Murphy.
THE NAKED SPUR, MGM. Sam Rolfe and Harold Jack Bloom.
TAKE THE HIGH GROUND, MGM. Millard Kaufman.

CINEMATOGRAPHY (O-402)
(Black-and-White)
FROM HERE TO ETERNITY. Burnett Guffey.
THE FOUR POSTER, Kramer, COL. Hal Mohr.
JULIUS CAESAR. Joseph Ruttenberg.
MARTIN LUTHER, DRH. Joseph C. Brun.
ROMAN HOLIDAY. Franz Planer and Henry Alekan.
(Color)
SHANE. Loyal Griggs.
ALL THE BROTHERS WERE VALIANT, MGM. George Folsey.
BENEATH THE TWELVE-MILE REEF, FOX. Edward Cronjager.
LILI. Robert Planck.
THE ROBE. Leon Shamroy.

COSTUME DESIGN (O-403)
(Black-and-White)
ROMAN HOLIDAY. Edith Head.
THE ACTRESS, MGM. Walter Plunkett.
DREAM WIFE, MGM. Helen Rose and Herschel McCoy.
FROM HERE TO ETERNITY. Jean Louis.
THE PRESIDENT'S LADY, FOX. Charles LeMaire and Renie.
(Color)
THE ROBE. Charles LeMaire and Emile Santiago.
THE BAND WAGON. Mary Ann Nyberg.
CALL ME MADAM, FOX. Irene Sharaff.
HOW TO MARRY A MILLIONAIRE, FOX. Charles LeMaire and Travilla.
YOUNG BESS, MGM. Walter Plunkett.

ART DIRECTION - SET DECORATION (O-404)
(Black-and-White)
JULIUS CAESAR. Cedric Gibbons and Edward Carfagno. Set Decoration: Edwin B. Willis and Hugh Hunt.
MARTIN LUTHER. Fritz Maurischat and Paul Markwitz. Set Decoration: No credits listed.
THE PRESIDENT'S LADY. Lyle Wheeler and Leland Fuller. Set Decoration: Paul S. Fox.
ROMAN HOLIDAY. Hal Pereira and Walter Tyler. Set Decoration: No credits listed.
TITANIC. Lyle Wheeler and Maurice Ransford. Set Decoration: Stuart Reiss.
(Color)
THE ROBE. Lyle Wheeler and George W. Davis. Set Decoration: Walter M. Scott and Paul S. Fox.
KNIGHTS OF THE ROUND TABLE, MGM. Alfred Junge and Hans Peters. Set Decoration: John Jarvis.
LILI. Cedric Gibbons and Paul Groesse. Set Decoration: Edwin B. Willis and Arthur Krams.
THE STORY OF THREE LOVES, MGM. Cedric Gibbons, Preston Ames, Edward Carfagno and Gabriel Scognamillo. Set Decoration: Edwin B. Willis, Keogh Gleason, Arthur Krams and Jack D. Moore.
YOUNG BESS. Cedric Gibbons and Urie McCleary. Set Decoration: Edwin B. Willis and Jack D. Moore.

FILM EDITING (O-405)
FROM HERE TO ETERNITY. William Lyon.
CRAZYLEGS, Bartlett, REP. Irvine (Cotton) Warburton.
THE MOON IS BLUE. Otto Ludwig.
ROMAN HOLIDAY. Robert Swink.
WAR OF THE WORLDS, PAR. Everett Douglas.

MUSIC - SCORING (O-406)
(Scoring of a Dramatic or Comedy Picture)
LILI. Bronislau Kaper.
ABOVE AND BEYOND. Hugo Friedhofer.
FROM HERE TO ETERNITY. Morris Stoloff and George Duning.
JULIUS CAESAR. Miklos Rozsa.
THIS IS CINERAMA, CRC. Louis Forbes.
(Scoring of a Musical Picture)
CALL ME MADAM. Alfred Newman.
THE BAND WAGON. Adolph Deutsch.
CALAMITY JANE, WB. Ray Heindorf.
5,000 FINGERS OF DR. T., Kramer-COL. Frederick Hollander and Morris Stoloff.
KISS ME KATE, MGM. Andre Previn and Saul Chaplin.

MUSIC - BEST SONG (O-407)
SECRET LOVE, Calamity Jane. Music, Sammy Fain. Lyrics, Paul Francis Webster.
THE MOON IS BLUE, *The Moon Is Blue.* Music, Herschel Burke Gilbert. Lyrics, Sylvia Fine.
MY FLAMING HEART, *Small Town Girl,* MGM. Music, Nicholas Brodszky. Lyrics, Leo Robin.
SADIE THOMPSON'S SONG (BLUE PACIFIC BLUES), *Miss Sadie Thompson,* Beckworth, COL. Music, Lester Lee. Lyrics, Ned Washington.
THAT'S AMORE, *The Caddy,* York Pictures, PAR. Music, Harry Warren. Lyrics, Jack Brooks.

SOUND (O-408)
FROM HERE TO ETERNITY. COL Sound Department. John P. Livadary, Sound Director.
CALAMITY JANE. WB Sound Department. William A. Mueller, Sound Director.
KNIGHTS OF THE ROUND TABLE, MGM. A. W. Watkins, Sound Director.
THE MISSISSIPPI GAMBLER, U. U Sound Department. Leslie I. Carey, Sound Director.
THE WAR OF THE WORLDS. PAR Sound Department. Loren L. Ryder, Sound Director.

SHORT FILMS (O-409)
(Cartoons)
TOOT, WHISTLE, PLUNK AND BOOM, Walt Disney, BV. (Special Music Series) Walt Disney, Prod.
CHRISTOPHER CRUMPET, UPA, COL. (Jolly Frolics) Stephen Bosustow, Prod.
FROM A TO Z-Z-Z-Z, WB. (Looney Tunes) Edward Selzer, Prod.
RUGGED BEAR, Walt Disney, RKO. (Donald Duck) Walt Disney, Prod.
THE TELL TALE HEART, UPA, COL. (UPA Cartoon Special) Stephen Bosustow, Prod.
(One-reel)
THE MERRY WIVES OF WINDSOR OVERTURE, MGM. (Overture Series) Johnny Green, Prod.
CHRIST AMONG THE PRIMITIVES, IFE (Italian). Vincenzo Lucci-Chiarissi, Prod.
HERRING HUNT, (NFC), RKO (Canadian). (Canada Carries On Series)
JOY OF LIVING, Art Film Prods., FOX. (Art Film Series) Boris Vermont, Prod.
WEE WATER WONDERS, PAR. (Grantland Rice Sportlights Series) Jack Eaton, Prod.
(Two-reel)
BEAR COUNTRY, Walt Disney, RKO. (True-Life Adventure) Walt Disney, Prod.
BEN AND ME, Walt Disney, BV. (Cartoon Special Series) Walt Disney, Prod.
RETURN TO GLENNASCAUL, Dublin Gate Theatre Prod., MAK.
VESUVIUS EXPRESS, FOX. (CinemaScope Shorts Series) Otto Lang, Prod.
WINTER PARADISE, WB. (Technicolor Special) Cedric Francis, Prod.

DOCUMENTARY (O-410)

(Short Subjects)

THE ALASKAN ESKIMO, Walt Disney Prods., RKO. Walt Disney, Prod.
THE LIVING CITY, Encyclopaedia Britannica Films, Inc. John Barnes, Prod.
OPERATION BLUE JAY, U.S. Army Signal Corps.
THEY PLANTED A STONE, World Wide Pictures, British Information Services (British). James Carr, Prod.
THE WORD, FOX. John Healy and John Adams, Prods.

(Features)

THE LIVING DESERT, Walt Disney Prods., BV. Walt Disney, Prod.
THE CONQUEST OF EVEREST, Countryman Films, Ltd. & Group 3 Ltd., UA (British) John Taylor, Leon Clore and Grahame Tharp, Prods.
A QUEEN IS CROWNED, J. Arthur Rank Organization, Ltd., UI (British). Castleton Knight, Prod.

SPECIAL EFFECTS (O-411)

THE WAR OF THE WORLDS.

HONORARY AND OTHER (O-412)

(Irving G. Thalberg Memorial Award)

George Stevens

(Other)

PETE SMITH for his witty and pungent observations on the American scene in his series of Pete Smith Specialties.
20TH CENTURY-FOX FILM CORPORATION in recognition of their imagination, showmanship and foresight in introducing the revolutionary process known as CinemaScope.
JOSEPH I. BREEN for his conscientious, open-minded and dignified management of the Motion Picture Production Code.
BELL AND HOWELL COMPANY for their pioneering and basic achievements in the advancement of the motion picture industry.

SCIENTIFIC OR TECHNICAL (O-413)

(Class I)

PROFESSOR HENRI CHRETIEN and EARL SPONABLE, SOL HALPRIN, LORIN GRIGNON, HERBERT BRAGG and CARL FAULKNER of 20th Century Fox Studios for creating, developing and engineering the equipment, processes and techniques known as CinemaScope.
FRED WALLER for designing and developing the multiple photographic and projection systems which culminated in Cinerama.

(Class II)

REEVES SOUNDCRAFT CORP. for their development of a process of applying stripes of magnetic oxide to motion picture film for sound recording and reproduction.

(Class III)

WESTREX CORP. for the design and construction of a new film editing machine.

1954

BEST PICTURE (O-414)

ON THE WATERFRONT, Horizon-American Corp., COL. Sam Spiegel, Prod.
THE CAINE MUTINY, A Stanley Kramer Prod., COL. Stanley Kramer, Prod.
THE COUNTRY GIRL, Perlberg-Seaton, PAR. William Perlberg, Prod.
SEVEN BRIDES FOR SEVEN BROTHERS, MGM. Jack Cummings, Prod.
THREE COINS IN THE FOUNTAIN, FOX. Sol C. Siegel, Prod.

ACTOR (O-415)

MARLON BRANDO, On The Waterfront.
HUMPHREY BOGART, *The Caine Mutiny.*
BING CROSBY, *The Country Girl.*
JAMES MASON, *A Star Is Born,* Transcona, WB.

DAN O'HERLIHY, *Adventures Of Robinson Crusoe,* Dancigers-Ehrlich, UA.

ACTRESS (O-416)

GRACE KELLY, The Country Girl.
DOROTHY DANDRIDGE, *Carmen Jones,* Otto Preminger, FOX.
JUDY GARLAND, *A Star Is Born.*
AUDREY HEPBURN, *Sabrina,* PAR.
JANE WYMAN, *The Magnificent Obsession,* U.

SUPPORTING ACTOR (O-417)

EDMOND O'BRIEN, The Barefoot Contessa, Figaro, UA.
LEE J. COBB, *On The Waterfront.*
KARL MALDEN, *On The Waterfront.*
ROD STEIGER, *On The Waterfront.*
TOM TULLY, *The Caine Mutiny.*

SUPPORTING ACTRESS (O-418)

EVA MARIE SAINT, On The Waterfront.
NINA FOCH, *Executive Suite,* MGM.
KATY JURADO, *Broken Lance,* FOX.
JAN STERLING, *The High And The Mighty,* Wayne-Fellows, WB.
CLAIRE TREVOR, *The High And The Mighty.*

DIRECTING (O-419)

ELIA KAZAN, On The Waterfront.
ALFRED HITCHCOCK, *Rear Window,* Patron, Inc., PAR.
GEORGE SEATON, *The Country Girl.*
WILLIAM WELLMAN, *The High And The Mighty.*
BILLY WILDER, *Sabrina.*

WRITING (O-420)

(Motion Picture Story)

BROKEN LANCE. Philip Yordan.
BREAD, LOVE AND DREAMS, Titanus, IFE (Italian). Ettore Margadonna.
FORBIDDEN GAMES, Silver Films, TIM. (French). Francois Boyer.
NIGHT PEOPLE, FOX. Jed Harris and Tom Reed.
THERE'S NO BUSINESS LIKE SHOW BUSINESS, FOX. Lamar Trotti.

(Screenplay)

THE COUNTRY GIRL. George Seaton.
THE CAINE MUTINY. Stanley Roberts.
REAR WINDOW. John Michael Hayes.
SABRINA. Billy Wilder, Samuel Taylor and Ernest Lehman.
SEVEN BRIDES FOR SEVEN BROTHERS. Albert Hackett, Frances Goodrich and Dorothy Kingsley.

(Story and Screenplay)

ON THE WATERFRONT. Budd Schulberg.
THE BAREFOOT CONTESSA. Joseph Mankiewicz.
GENEVIEVE, A J. Arthur Rank Presentation-Sirius Prods., Ltd., UI (British). William Rose.
THE GLENN MILLER STORY, U. Valentine Davies and Oscar Brodney.
KNOCK ON WOOD, Dena Prods., PAR. Norman Panama and Melvin Frank.

CINEMATOGRAPHY (O-421)

(Black-and-White)

ON THE WATERFRONT. Boris Kaufman.
THE COUNTRY GIRL. John F. Warren.
EXECUTIVE SUITE. George Folsey.
ROGUE COP, MGM. John Seitz.
SABRINA. Charles Lang, Jr.

(Color)

THREE COINS IN THE FOUNTAIN. Milton Krasner.
THE EGYPTIAN, FOX. Leon Shamroy.
REAR WINDOW. Robert Burks.
SEVEN BRIDES FOR SEVEN BROTHERS. George Folsey.
THE SILVER CHALICE, A Victor Saville Prod., WB. William V. Skall.

COSTUME DESIGN (O-422)

(Black-and-White)

SABRINA. Edith Head.
THE EARRINGS OF MADAME DE. . ., Franco-London Prods., Arlan Pictures (French). Georges Annenkov and Rosine Delamare.
EXECUTIVE SUITE. Helen Rose.
INDISCRETION OF AN AMERICAN WIFE, A Vittorio DeSica Prod., COL. Christian Dior.
IT SHOULD HAPPEN TO YOU, COL. Jean Louis.

(Color)

GATE OF HELL, A Daiei Prod., EDH (Japanese). Sanzo Wada.
BRIGADOON, MGM. Irene Sharaff.
DESIREE, FOX. Charles LeMaire and Rene Hubert.
A STAR IS BORN. Jean Louis, Mary Ann Nyberg and Irene Sharaff.
THERE'S NO BUSINESS LIKE SHOW BUSINESS. Charles LeMaire, Travilla and Miles White.

ART DIRECTION - SET DECORATION (O-423)

(Black-and-White)

ON THE WATERFRONT. Richard Day. Set Decoration: No credits listed.
THE COUNTRY GIRL. Hal Pereira and Roland Anderson. Set Decoration: Sam Comer and Grace Gregory.
EXECUTIVE SUITE. Cedric Gibbons and Edward Carfagno. Set Decoration: Edwin B. Willis and Emile Kuri.
LE PLAISIR, Stera Film-CCFC Prod., MAK (French). Max Ophuls. Set Decoration: No credits listed.
SABRINA. Hal Pereira and Walter Tyler. Set Decoration: Sam Comer and Ray Moyer.

(Color)

20,000 LEAGUES UNDER THE SEA, Walt Disney Prods., BV. John Meehan. Set Decoration: Emile Kuri.
BRIGADOON. Cedric Gibbons and Preston Ames. Set Decoration: Edwin B. Willis and Keogh Gleason.
DESIREE. Lyle Wheeler and Leland Fuller. Set Decoration: Walter M. Scott and Paul S. Fox.
RED GARTERS, PAR. Hal Pereira and Roland Anderson. Set Decoration: Sam Comer and Ray Moyer.
A STAR IS BORN. Malcolm Bert, Gene Allen and Irene Sharaff. Set Decoration: George James Hopkins.

FILM EDITING (O-424)

ON THE WATERFRONT. Gene Milford.
THE CAINE MUTINY. William A. Lyon and Henry Batista.
THE HIGH AND THE MIGHTY. Ralph Dawson.
SEVEN BRIDES FOR SEVEN BROTHERS. Ralph E. Winters.
20,000 LEAGUES UNDER THE SEA. Elmo Williams.

MUSIC - SCORING (O-425)

(Scoring of a Dramatic or Comedy Picture)

THE HIGH AND THE MIGHTY. Dimitri Tiomkin.
THE CAINE MUTINY. Max Steiner.
GENEVIEVE. Muir Mathieson.
ON THE WATERFRONT. Leonard Bernstein.
THE SILVER CHALICE. Franz Waxman.

(Scoring of a Musical Picture)

SEVEN BRIDES FOR SEVEN BROTHERS. Adolph Deutsch and Saul Chaplin.
CARMEN JONES. Herschel Burke Gilbert.
THE GLENN MILLER STORY. Joseph Gershenson and Henry Mancini.
A STAR IS BORN. Ray Heindorf.
THERE'S NO BUSINESS LIKE SHOW BUSINESS. Alfred Newman and Lionel Newman.

MUSIC - BEST SONG (O-426)

THREE COINS IN THE FOUNTAIN, Three Coins In The Fountain. Music, Jule Styne. Lyrics, Sammy Cahn.
COUNT YOUR BLESSINGS INSTEAD OF SHEEP, *White Christmas*, PAR. Music and Lyrics, Irving Berlin.
THE HIGH AND THE MIGHTY, *The High And The Mighty*. Music, Dimitri Tiomkin. Lyrics, Ned Washington.
HOLD MY HAND, *Susan Slept Here*, RKO. Music and Lyrics by Jack Lawrence and Richard Myers.
THE MAN THAT GOT AWAY, *A Star Is Born*. Music, Harold Arlen. Lyrics, Ira Gershwin.

SOUND (O-427)

THE GLENN MILLER STORY. Leslie I. Carey, Sound Director.
BRIGADOON. Wesley C. Miller, Sound Director.
THE CAINE MUTINY. John P. Livadary, Sound Director.
REAR WINDOW. Loren L. Ryder, Sound Director.
SUSAN SLEPT HERE. John O. Aalberg, Sound Director.

SHORT FILMS (O-428)

(Cartoons)

WHEN MAGOO FLEW, UPA, COL. Stephen Bosustow, Prod.
CRAZY MIXED UP PUP, Walter Lantz Prods., U. Walter Lantz, Prod.
PIGS IS PIGS, Walt Disney Prods., RKO. Walt Disney, Prod.
SANDY CLAWS, WB. Cartoons, Inc. Edward Selzer, Prod.
TOUCHE, PUSSY CAT, MGM. Fred Quimby, Prod.

(One-reel)

THIS MECHANICAL AGE, WB. Robert Youngson, Prod.
THE FIRST PIANO QUARTETTE, FOX. Otto Lang, Prod.
THE STRAUSS FANTASY, MGM. Johnny Green, Prod.

(Two-reel)

A TIME OUT OF WAR, Carnival Prods., Denis and Terry Sanders, Prods.
BEAUTY AND THE BULL, WB. Cedric Francis, Prod.
JET CARRIER, FOX. Otto Lang, Prod.
SIAM, Walt Disney Prods., BV. Walt Disney, Prod.

DOCUMENTARY (O-429)

(Short Subjects)

THURSDAY'S CHILDREN, British Information Services (British). World Wide Pictures and Morse Films, Prods.
JET CARRIER, FOX. Otto Lang, Prod.
REMBRANDT: A SELF-PORTRAIT, DCA. Morrie Roizman, Prod.

(Features)

THE VANISHING PRAIRIE, Walt Disney Prods., BV. Walt Disney, Prod.
THE STRATFORD ADVENTURE, NFC, CON. (Canadian). Guy Glover, Prod.

SPECIAL EFFECTS (O-430)

20,000 LEAGUES UNDER THE SEA.
HELL AND HIGH WATER, FOX.
THEM!, WB.

HONORARY AND OTHER (O-431)

(Other)

BAUSCH & LOMB OPTICAL COMPANY for their contributions to the advancement of the motion picture industry.
KEMP R. NIVER for the development of the Renovare Process which has made possible the restoration of the Library of Congress Paper Film Collection.
GRETA GARBO for her unforgettable screen performances.
DANNY KAYE for his unique talents, his service to the Academy, the motion picture industry, and the American people.
JON WHITELEY for his outstanding juvenile performance in The Little Kidnappers.
VINCENT WINTER for his outstanding juvenile performance in The Little Kidnappers.
GATE OF HELL - Best Foreign Language Film first released in the United States during 1954.

SCIENTIFIC OR TECHNICAL (O-432)

(Class I)

PARAMOUNT PICTURES, INC., LOREN L. RYDER, JOHN R. BISHOP and all the members of the technical and engineering staff for

developing a method of producing and exhibiting motion pictures known as VistaVision.

(Class III)

DAVID S. HORSLEY and the UI STUDIO SPECIAL PHOTOGRAPHIC DEPARTMENT for a portable remote control device for process projectors.

KARL FREUND and FRANK CRANDELL of Photo Research Corp. for the design and development of a direct reading brightness meter.

WESLEY C. MILLER, J. W. STAFFORD, K. M. FRIERSON and the MGM STUDIO SOUND DEPARTMENT for an electronic sound printing comparison device.

JOHN P. LIVADARY, LLOYD RUSSELL and the COLUMBIA STUDIO SOUND DEPARTMENT for an improved limiting amplifier as applied to sound level comparison devices.

ROLAND MILLER and MAX GOEPPINGER of Magnascope Corp. for the design and development of a cathode ray magnetic sound track viewer.

CARLOS RIVAS, G. M. SPRAGUE and the MGM STUDIO SOUND DEPARTMENT for the design of a magnetic sound editing machine.

FRED WILSON of the Samuel Goldwyn Studio Sound Department for the design of a variable multiple-band equalizer.

P. C. YOUNG of the MGM Studio Projection Department for the practical application of a variable focal length attachment to motion picture projector lenses.

FRED KNOTH and ORIEN ERNEST of the UI Studio Technical Department for the development of a hand portable, electric, dry oil-fog machine.

1955

BEST PICTURE (O-433)

MARTY, Hecht & Lancaster's Steven Prods., UA. Harold Hecht, Prod.
LOVE IS A MANY-SPLENDORED THING, FOX. Buddy Adler, Prod.
MISTER ROBERTS, An Orange Prod., WB. Leland Hayward, Prod.
PICNIC, COL. Fred Kohlmar, Prod.
THE ROSE TATTOO, Hal Wallis, PAR. Hal B. Wallis, Prod.

ACTOR (O-434)

ERNEST BORGNINE, Marty.
JAMES CAGNEY, Love Me Or Leave Me, MGM.
JAMES DEAN, East Of Eden, WB.
FRANK SINATRA, The Man With The Golden Arm, Preminger, UA.
SPENCER TRACY, Bad Day At Black Rock, MGM.

ACTRESS (O-435)

ANNA MAGNANI, The Rose Tattoo.
SUSAN HAYWARD, I'll Cry Tomorrow, MGM.
KATHARINE HEPBURN, Summertime, Ilya Lopert-David Lean, UA. (Anglo-American)
JENNIFER JONES, Love Is A Many-Splendored Thing.
ELEANOR PARKER, Interrupted Melody, MGM.

SUPPORTING ACTOR (O-436)

JACK LEMMON, Mister Roberts.
ARTHUR KENNEDY, Trial, MGM.
JOE MANTELL, Marty.
SAL MINEO, Rebel Without A Cause, WB.
ARTHUR O'CONNELL, Picnic.

SUPPORTING ACTRESS (O-437)

JO VAN FLEET, East Of Eden.
BETSY BLAIR, Marty.
PEGGY LEE, Pete Kelly's Blues, A Mark VII Ltd. Prod., WB.

MARISA PAVAN, The Rose Tattoo.
NATALIE WOOD, Rebel Without A Cause.

DIRECTING (O-438)

DELBERT MANN, Marty.
ELIA KAZAN, East Of Eden.
DAVID LEAN, Summertime.
JOSHUA LOGAN, Picnic.
JOHN STURGES, Bad Day At Black Rock.

WRITING (O-439)

(Motion Picture Story)

LOVE ME OR LEAVE ME. Daniel Fuchs.
THE PRIVATE WAR OF MAJOR BENSON, U. Joe Connelly and Bob Mosher.
REBEL WITHOUT A CAUSE. Nicholas Ray.
THE SHEEP HAS 5 LEGS, Raoul Ploquin, UMP (French). Jean Marsan, Henry Troyat, Jacques Perret, Henri Verneuil and Raoul Ploquin.
STRATEGIC AIR COMMAND, PAR. Beirne Lay, Jr.

(Best Screenplay)

MARTY. Paddy Chayefsky.
BAD DAY AT BLACK ROCK. Millard Kaufman.
BLACKBOARD JUNGLE, MGM. Richard Brooks.
EAST OF EDEN. Paul Osborn.
LOVE ME OR LEAVE ME. Daniel Fuchs and Isobel Lennart.

(Story and Screenplay)

INTERRUPTED MELODY, MGM. William Ludwig and Sonya Levien.
THE COURT-MARTIAL OF BILLY MITCHELL, A United States Pictures Prod., WB. Milton Sperling and Emmet Lavery.
IT'S ALWAYS FAIR WEATHER, MGM. Betty Comden and Adolph Green.
MR. HULOT'S HOLIDAY, Fred Orain Prod., GBD. (French). Jacques Tati and Henri Marquet.
THE SEVEN LITTLE FOYS, Hope Enterprises, Inc. and Scribe Prods. Melville Shavelson and Jack Rose.

CINEMATOGRAPHY (O-440)

(Black-and-White)

THE ROSE TATTOO. James Wong Howe.
BLACKBOARD JUNGLE. Russell Harlan.
I'LL CRY TOMORROW. Arthur E. Arling.
MARTY. Joseph LaShelle.
QUEEN BEE, COL. Charles Lang.

(Color)

TO CATCH A THIEF, PAR. Robert Burks.
GUYS AND DOLLS, Samuel Goldwyn Prods., Inc. MGM. Harry Stradling.
LOVE IS A MANY-SPLENDORED THING. Leon Shamroy.
A MAN CALLED PETER, FOX. Harold Lipstein.
OKLAHOMA!, Rodgers & Hammerstein Pictures, Inc., MNA. Robert Surtees.

COSTUME DESIGN (O-441)

(Black-and-White)

I'LL CRY TOMORROW. Helen Rose.
THE PICKWICK PAPERS, Renown Prod., KGY (British). Beatrice Dawson.
QUEEN BEE. Jean Louis.
THE ROSE TATTOO. Edith Head.
UGETSU, Daiei Motion Picture Co., EDH (Japanese). Tadaoto Kainoscho.

(Color)

LOVE IS A MANY-SPLENDORED THING. Charles LeMaire.
GUYS AND DOLLS. Irene Sharaff.
INTERRUPTED MELODY. Helen Rose.
TO CATCH A THIEF. Edith Head.
THE VIRGIN QUEEN, FOX. Charles LeMaire and Mary Wills.

ART DIRECTION - SET DECORATION (O-442)

(Black-and-White)

THE ROSE TATTOO. Hal Pereira and Tambi Larsen. Set Decoration: Sam Comer and Arthur Krams.
BLACKBOARD JUNGLE. Cedric Gibbons and Randall Duell. Set Decoration: Edwin B. Willis and Henry Grace.
I'LL CRY TOMORROW. Cedric Gibbons and Malcolm Brown. Set Decoration: Edwin B. Willis and Hugh B. Hunt.
THE MAN WITH THE GOLDEN ARM. Joseph C. Wright. Set Decoration: Darrell Silvera.
MARTY. Edward S. Haworth and Walter Simonds. Set Decoration: Robert Priestley.

(Color)

PICNIC. William Flannery and Jo Mielziner. Set Decoration: Robert Priestley.
DADDY LONG LEGS, FOX. Lyle Wheeler and John DeCuir. Set Decoration: Walter M. Scott and Paul S. Fox.
GUYS AND DOLLS. Oliver Smith and Joseph C. Wright. Set Decoration: Howard Bristol.
LOVE IS A MANY-SPLENDORED THING. Lyle Wheeler and George W. Davis. Set Decoration: Walter M. Scott and Jack Stubbs.
TO CATCH A THIEF. Hal Pereira and Joseph McMillan Johnson. Set Decoration: Sam Comer and Arthur Krams.

FILM EDITING (O-443)

PICNIC. Charles Nelson and William A. Lyon.
BLACKBOARD JUNGLE. Ferris Webster.
THE BRIDGES AT TOKO-RI, Perlberg-Seaton, PAR. Alma Macrorie.
OKLAHOMA! Gene Ruggiero and George Boemler.
THE ROSE TATTOO. Warren Low.

MUSIC - SCORING (O-444)

(Scoring of a Dramatic or Comedy Picture)

LOVE IS A MANY-SPLENDORED THING. Alfred Newman.
BATTLE CRY, WB. Max Steiner.
THE MAN WITH THE GOLDEN ARM. Elmer Bernstein.
PICNIC. George Duning.
THE ROSE TATTOO. Alex North.

(Scoring of a Musical Picture)

OKLAHOMA! Robert Russell Bennett, Jay Blackton and Adolph Deutsch.
DADDY LONG LEGS. Alfred Newman.
GUYS AND DOLLS. Jay Blackton and Cyril J. Mockridge.
IT'S ALWAYS FAIR WEATHER, MGM. Andre Previn.
LOVE ME OR LEAVE ME. Percy Faith and George Stoll.

MUSIC - BEST SONG (O-445)

LOVE IS A MANY-SPLENDORED THING, Love Is A Many-Splendored Thing. Music, Sammy Fain. Lyrics, Paul Francis Webster.
I'LL NEVER STOP LOVING YOU, *Love Me Or Leave Me.* Music, Nicholas Brodszky. Lyrics, Sammy Cahn.
SOMETHING'S GOTTA GIVE, *Daddy Long Legs.* Music and Lyrics by Johnny Mercer.
(LOVE IS) THE TENDER TRAP, *The Tender Trap,* MGM. Music, James Van Heusen. Lyrics, Sammy Cahn.
UNCHAINED MELODY, *Unchained,* Hall Bartlett Prods., Inc., WB. Music, Alex North. Lyrics, Hy Zaret.

SOUND (O-446)

OKLAHOMA!, Todd-AO Sound Department, Fred Hynes, Sound Director.
LOVE IS A MANY-SPLENDORED THING, FOX Studio Sound Department. Carl W. Faulkner, Sound Director.
LOVE ME OR LEAVE ME, MGM Studio Sound Department. Wesley C. Miller, Sound Director.
MISTER ROBERTS, WB. Studio Sound Department. William A. Mueller, Sound Director.
NOT AS A STRANGER, Radio Corp of America Sound Department. Watson Jones, Sound Director.

SHORT FILMS (O-447)

(Cartoons)

SPEEDY GONZALES, WB. Cartoons, Inc. Edward Selzer, Prod.
GOOD WILL TO MEN, MGM. Fred Quimby, William Hanna and Joseph Barbera, Prods.
THE LEGEND OF ROCK-A-BYE-POINT, Walter Lantz Prods., UI. Walter Lantz, Prod.
NO HUNTING, Walt Disney Prods., RKO. Walt Disney, Prod.

(One-reel)

SURVIVAL CITY, FOX. Edmund Reek, Prod.
GADGETS GALORE, WB. Robert Youngson, Prod.
3RD AVE. EL, Carson Davidson Prods., Ardee Films. Carson Davidson, Prod.
THREE KISSES, PAR. Justin Herman, Prod.

(Two-reel)

THE FACE OF LINCOLN, University Of Southern California Presentation, Cavalcade Pictures, Inc. Wilbur T. Blume, Prod.
THE BATTLE OF GETTYSBURG, MGM. Dore Schary, Prod.
ON THE TWELFTH DAY. . ., Go Pictures, Inc., George Brest & Assocs. George K. Arthur, Prod.
SWITZERLAND, Walt Disney Prods., BV. Walt Disney, Prod.
24 HOUR ALERT, WB. Cedric Francis, Prod.

DOCUMENTARY (O-448)

(Short Subjects)

MEN AGAINST THE ARCTIC, Walt Disney Prods., BV. Walt Disney, Prod.
THE BATTLE OF GETTYSBURG, MGM. Dore Schary, Prod.
THE FACE OF LINCOLN, University of Southern California Presentation, CVC. Wilbur T. Blume, Prod.

(Features)

HELEN KELLER IN HER STORY, Nancy Hamilton Presentation. Nancy Hamilton, Prod.
HEARTBREAK RIDGE, Rene Risacher Prod., Tudor Pictures (French). Rene Risacher, Prod.

SPECIAL EFFECTS (O-449)

THE BRIDGES AT TOKO-RI.
THE DAM BUSTERS, ABR. (British).
THE RAINS OF RANCHIPUR, FOX.

HONORARY AND OTHER (O-450)

(Other)

SAMURAI, The Legend of Musashi (Japanese) - Best Foreign Language Film first released in the United States during 1955.

SCIENTIFIC OR TECHNICAL (O-451)

(Class I)

NATIONAL CARBON CO. for the development and production of a high efficiency yellow flame carbon for motion picture color photography.

(Class II)

EASTMAN KODAK CO. for Eastman Tri-X panchromatic negative film.
FARCIOT EDOUART, HAL CORL and the PARAMOUNT STUDIO TRANSPARENCY DEPARTMENT for the engineering and development of a double-frame, triple-head background projector.

(Class III)

20TH CENTURY-FOX STUDIO and BAUSCH & LOMB CO. for the new combination lenses for CinemaScope photography.
WALTER JOLLEY, MAURICE LARSON and R. H. SPIES of 20th Century-Fox Studio for a spraying process which creates simulated metallic surfaces.
STEVE KRILANOVICH for an improved camera dolly incorporating multi-directional steering.
DAVE ANDERSON of 20th Century-Fox Studio for an improved spotlight capable of maintaining a fixed circle of light at constant intensity over varied distances.
LOREN L. RYDER, CHARLES WEST, HENRY FRACKER and PARA-

MOUNT STUDIO for a projection film index to establish proper framing for various aspect ratios.

FARCIOT EDOUART, HAL CORL and the PARAMOUNT STUDIO TRANSPARENCY DEPARTMENT for an improved dual stereopticon background projector.

1956

BEST PICTURE (O-452)

AROUND THE WORLD IN 80 DAYS, The Michael Todd Co., Inc., UA. Michael Todd, Prod.
FRIENDLY PERSUASION, AA. William Wyler, Prod.
GIANT, Giant Prod., WB. George Stevens & Henry Ginsberg, Prods.
THE KING AND I, FOX. Charles Brackett, Prod.
THE TEN COMMANDMENTS, Motion Picture Assocs., Inc., PAR. Cecil B. DeMille, Prod.

ACTOR (O-453)

YUL BRYNNER, The King And I.
JAMES DEAN, *Giant.*
KIRK DOUGLAS, *Lust For Life,* MGM.
ROCK HUDSON, *Giant.*
SIR LAURENCE OLIVIER, *Richard III,* Laurence Olivier Prod., Lopert Films Dist. Corp. (British)

ACTRESS (O-454)

INGRID BERGMAN, Anastasia, FOX.
CARROLL BAKER, *Baby Doll,* A Newtown Prod., WB.
KATHARINE HEPBURN, *The Rainmaker,* Hal Wallis Prods., PAR.
NANCY KELLY, *The Bad Seed,* WB.
DEBORAH KERR, *The King And I.*

SUPPORTING ACTOR (O-455)

ANTHONY QUINN, Lust For Life.
DON MURRAY, *Bus Stop,* FOX.
ANTHONY PERKINS, *Friendly Persuasion.*
MICKEY ROONEY, *The Bold And The Brave,* Filmakers Releasing Org., RKO.
ROBERT STACK, *Written On The Wind,* U.

SUPPORTING ACTRESS (O-456)

DOROTHY MALONE, Written On The Wind.
MILDRED DUNNOCK, *Baby Doll.*
EILEEN HECKART, *The Bad Seed.*
MERCEDES McCAMBRIDGE, *Giant.*
PATTY McCORMACK, *The Bad Seed.*

DIRECTING (O-457)

GEORGE STEVENS, Giant.
MICHAEL ANDERSON, *Around The World In 80 Days.*
WALTER LANG, *The King And I.*
KING VIDOR, *War And Peace,* A Ponti-DeLaurentiis Prod., PAR (Italo-American).
WILLIAM WYLER, *Friendly Persuasion.*

WRITING (O-458)

(Motion Picture Story)

THE BRAVE ONE, King Bros. Prods., Inc., RKO. Dalton Trumbo aka Robert Rich.
THE EDDY DUCHIN STORY, COL. Leo Katcher.
HIGH SOCIETY, AA. Edward Bernds and Elwood Ullman. (Withdrawn from final ballot)
THE PROUD AND THE BEAUTIFUL, La Compagnie Industrielle Commerciale Cinematographique, KGY (French). Jean Paul Sartre.
UMBERTO D., Rizzoli-De Sica-Amato Prod., HD (Italian). Cesare Zavattini.

(Best Screenplay adapted)

AROUND THE WORLD IN 80 DAYS. James Poe, John Farrow and S. J. Perelman.
BABY DOLL. Tennessee Williams.
GIANT. Fred Guiol and Ivan Moffat.
LUST FOR LIFE. Norman Corwin.
FRIENDLY PERSUASION. (Writer ineligible for nomination under Academy By-Laws.)

(Best Screenplay original)

THE RED BALLOON, Films Montsouris, LOP. (French). Albert Lamorisse.
THE BOLD AND THE BRAVE. Robert Lewin.
JULIE, Arwin Prods., MGM. Andrew L. Stone.
LA STRADA, Ponti-De Laurentiis Prod., TL. (Italian). Federico Fellini and Tullio Pinelli.
THE LADY KILLERS, Ealing Studios Ltd., CON. (British). William Rose.

CINEMATOGRAPHY (O-459)

(Black-and-White)

SOMEBODY UP THERE LIKES ME, MGM. Joseph Ruttenberg.
BABY DOLL. Boris Kaufman.
THE BAD SEED. Hal Rosson.
THE HARDER THEY FALL, COL. Burnett Guffey.
STAGECOACH TO FURY, Regal Films, Inc. Prod., FOX. Walter Strenge.

(Color)

AROUND THE WORLD IN 80 DAYS. Lionel Lindon.
THE EDDY DUCHIN STORY. Harry Stradling.
THE KING AND I. Leon Shamroy.
THE TEN COMMANDMENTS. Loyal Griggs.
WAR AND PEACE. Jack Cardiff.

COSTUME DESIGN (O-460)

(Black-and-White)

THE SOLID GOLD CADILLAC, COL. Jean Louis.
THE MAGNIFICENT SEVEN, A Toho Prod., KGY (Japanese). Kohei Ezaki.
THE POWER AND THE PRIZE, MGM. Helen Rose.
THE PROUD AND THE PROFANE, The Perlberg-Seaton Prod., PAR. Edith Head.
TEENAGE REBEL, FOX. Charles LeMaire and Mary Wills.

(Color)

THE KING AND I. Irene Sharaff.
AROUND THE WORLD IN 80 DAYS. Miles White.
GIANT. Moss Mabry and Marjorie Best.
THE TEN COMMANDMENTS. Edith Head, Ralph Jester, John Jensen, Dorothy Jeakins and Arnold Friberg.
WAR AND PEACE. Marie De Matteis.

ART DIRECTION - SET DECORATION (O-461)

(Black-and-White)

SOMEBODY UP THERE LIKES ME. Cedric Gibbons and Malcolm F. Brown. Set Decoration: Edwin B. Willis and F. Keogh Gleason.
THE MAGNIFICENT SEVEN, A Toho Prod., KGY (Japanese). Takashi Matsuyama. Set Decoration: No credits listed.
THE PROUD AND THE PROFANE. Hal Pereira and A. Earl Hedrick. Set Decoration: Samuel M. Comer and Frank R. McKelvy.
THE SOLID GOLD CADILLAC. Ross Bellah. Set Decoration: William R. Kiernan and Louis Diage.
TEENAGE REBEL. Lyle R. Wheeler and Jack Martin Smith. Set Decoration: Walter M. Scott and Stuart A. Reiss.

(Color)

THE KING AND I. Lyle R. Wheeler and John DeCuir. Set Decoration: Walter M. Scott and Paul S. Fox.
AROUND THE WORLD IN 80 DAYS. James W. Sullivan and Ken Adams. Set Decoration: Ross J. Dowd.
GIANT. Boris Leven. Set Decoration: Ralph S. Hurst.
LUST FOR LIFE. Cedric Gibbons, Hans Peters and Preston Ames. Set Decoration: Edwin B. Willis and F. Keogh Gleason.
THE TEN COMMANDMENTS. Hal Pereira, Walter H. Tyler and Albert Nozaki. Set Decoration: Sam M. Comer and Ray Moyer.

FILM EDITING (O-462)

AROUND THE WORLD IN 80 DAYS. Gene Ruggiero and Paul Weatherwax.
THE BRAVE ONE. Merrill G. White.
GIANT. William Hornbeck, Philip W. Anderson and Fred Bohanan.
SOMEBODY UP THERE LIKES ME. Albert Akst.
THE TEN COMMANDMENTS. Anne Bauchens.

FOREIGN LANGUAGE FILM (O-463)

LA STRADA. Dino De Laurentiis and Carlo Ponti, Prods.
THE CAPTAIN OF KOPENICK, Real-Film (Germany). Gyula Trebitsch and Walter Koppel, Prods.
GERVAISE, Agnes Delahaie Productions Cinematographiques & Silver Film (France). Annie Dorfmann, Prod.
HARP OF BURMA, Nikkatsu Corp (Japan). Masayuki Takagi, Prod.
QIVITOQ, A/S Nordisk Films Kompagni (Denmark). O. Dalsgaard-Olsen, Prod.

MUSIC - SCORING (O-464)

(Scoring of a Dramatic or Comedy Picture)
AROUND THE WORLD IN 80 DAYS. Victor Young.
ANASTASIA. Alfred Newman.
BETWEEN HEAVEN AND HELL, FOX. Hugo Friedhofer.
GIANT. Dimitri Tiomkin.
THE RAINMAKER. Alex North.
(Scoring of a Musical Picture)
THE KING AND I. Alfred Newman and Ken Darby.
THE BEST THINGS IN LIFE ARE FREE, FOX. Lionel Newman.
THE EDDY DUCHIN STORY. Morris Stoloff and George Duning.
HIGH SOCIETY. Johnny Green and Saul Chaplin.
MEET ME IN LAS VEGAS, MGM. George Stoll and Johnny Green.

MUSIC - BEST SONG (O-465)

WHATEVER WILL BE, WILL BE (QUE SERA, SERA), The Man Who Knew Too Much, Filwite Prods., Inc., PAR. Music and Lyrics by Jay Livingston and Ray Evans.
FRIENDLY PERSUASION (THEE I LOVE), *Friendly Persuasion.* Music, Dimitri Tiomkin. Lyrics, Paul Francis Webster.
JULIE, *Julie.* Music, Leith Stevens. Lyrics, Tom Adair.
TRUE LOVE, *High Society.* Music and Lyrics by Cole Porter.
WRITTEN ON THE WIND, *Written On The Wind.* Music, Victor Young. Lyrics, Sammy Cahn.

SOUND (O-466)

THE KING AND I, FOX Studio Sound Department. Carl Faulkner, Sound Director.
THE BRAVE ONE. John Myers, Sound Director.
THE EDDY DUCHIN STORY, COL Studio Sound Department. John Livadary, Sound Director.
FRIENDLY PERSUASION. Westrex Sound Services, Inc., Gordon R. Glennan, Sound Director; and Samuel Goldwyn Studio Sound Department. Gordon Sawyer, Sound Director.
THE TEN COMMANDMENTS, PAR Studio Sound Department. Loren L. Ryder, Sound Director.

SHORT FILMS (O-467)

(Cartoons)
MISTER MAGOO'S PUDDLE JUMPER, UPA Pictures, COL. Stephen Bosustow, Prod.
GERALD MCBOING-BOING ON PLANET MOO, UPA Pictures, COL. Stephen Bosustow, Prod.
THE JAYWALKER, UPA Pictures, COL. Stephen Bosustow, Prod.
(One-reel)
CRASHING THE WATER BARRIER, WB. Konstantin Kalser, Prod.
I NEVER FORGET A FACE, WB. Robert Youngson, Prod.
TIME STOOD STILL, WB. Cedric Francis, Prod.
(Two-reel)
THE BESPOKE OVERCOAT, George K. Arthur. Romulus Films, Prod.
COW DOG, Walt Disney Prods., BV. Larry Lansburgh, Prod.
THE DARK WAVE, FOX. John Healy, Prod.

SAMOA, Walt Disney Prods., BV. Walt Disney, Prod.

DOCUMENTARY (O-468)

(Short Subjects)
THE TRUE STORY OF THE CIVIL WAR, Camera Eye Pictures, Inc. Louis Clyde Stoumen, Prod.
A CITY DECIDES, Charles Guggenheim & Assocs., Inc. Prod.
THE DARK WAVE, FOX. John Healy, Prod.
THE HOUSE WITHOUT A NAME, U. Valentine Davies, Prod.
MAN IN SPACE, Walt Disney Prods., BV. Ward Kimball, Prod.
(Features)
THE SILENT WORLD, A Filmad-F.S.J.Y.C. Prod., COL (French). Jacques-Yves Cousteau, Prod.
THE NAKED EYE, Camera Eye Pictures, Inc. Louis Clyde Stoumen, Prod.
WHERE MOUNTAINS FLOAT, BRA. (Danish). The Government Film Committee of Denmark, Prod.

SPECIAL EFFECTS (O-469)

THE TEN COMMANDMENTS. John Fulton.
FORBIDDEN PLANET, MGM. A. Arnold Gillespie, Irving Ries and Wesley C. Miller.

HONORARY AND OTHER (O-470)

(Irving G. Thalberg Memorial Award)
Buddy Adler
(Jean Hersholt Humanitarian Award)
Y. Frank Freeman
(Other)
EDDIE CANTOR for distinguished service to the film industry.

SCIENTIFIC OR TECHNICAL (O-471)

(Class III)
RICHARD H. RANGER of Rangertone, Inc., for the development of a synchronous recording and reproducing system for quarter-inch magnetic tape.
TED HIRSCH, CARL HAUGE and **EDWARD REICHARD** of Consolidated Film Industries for an automatic scene counter for laboratory projection rooms.
THE TECHNICAL DEPARTMENTS of PARAMOUNT PICTURES CORP. for the engineering and development of the Paramount lightweight horizontal-movement VistaVision camera.
ROY C. STEWART AND SONS of Stewart-Trans Lux Corp., **DR. C. R. DAILY** and the TRANSPARENCY DEPARTMENT of PARAMOUNT PICTURES CORP. for the engineering and development of the Hi-Trans and Para-HiTrans rear projection screens.
THE CONSTRUCTION DEPARTMENT of MGM STUDIO for a new hand-portable fog machine.
DANIEL J. BLOOMBERG, JOHN POND, WILLIAM WADE and the ENGINEERING and CAMERA DEPARTMENTS of REPUBLIC STUDIO for the Naturama adaptation to the Mitchell camera.

1957

BEST PICTURE (O-472)

THE BRIDGE ON THE RIVER KWAI, A Horizon Picture, COL. Sam Spiegel, Prod.
PEYTON PLACE, Jerry Wald Prods., Inc., FOX. Jerry Wald, Prod.
SAYONARA, William Goetz, Prod., WB. William Goetz, Prod.
12 ANGRY MEN, Orion-Nova Prod., UA. Henry Fonda & Reginald Rose, Prods.
WITNESS FOR THE PROSECUTION, Edward Small-Arthur Hornblow Prod., UA. Arthur Hornblow, Jr., Prod.

ACTOR (O-473)

ALEC GUINNESS, The Bridge On The River Kwai.
MARLON BRANDO, *Sayonara.*

ANTHONY FRANCIOSA, *A Hatful Of Rain,* FOX.
CHARLES LAUGHTON, *Witness For The Prosecution.*
ANTHONY QUINN, *Wild Is The Wind,* A Hal Wallis Prod., PAR.

ACTRESS (O-474)
JOANNE WOODWARD, The Three Faces Of Eve, FOX.
DEBORAH KERR, *Heaven Knows, Mr. Allison,* FOX.
ANNA MAGNANI, *Wild Is The Wind.*
ELIZABETH TAYLOR, *Raintree County,* MGM.
LANA TURNER, *Peyton Place.*

SUPPORTING ACTOR (O-475)
RED BUTTONS, Sayonara.
VITTORIO DE SICA, *A Farewell To Arms,* The Selznick Co., Inc., FOX.
SESSUE HAYAKAWA, *The Bridge On The River Kwai.*
ARTHUR KENNEDY, *Peyton Place.*
RUSS TAMBLYN, *Peyton Place.*

SUPPORTING ACTRESS (O-476)
MIYOSHI UMEKI, Sayonara.
CAROLYN JONES, *The Bachelor Party,* Norma Prod., UA.
ELSA LANCHESTER, *Witness For The Prosecution.*
HOPE LANGE, *Peyton Place.*
DIANE VARSI, *Peyton Place.*

DIRECTING (O-477)
DAVID LEAN, The Bridge On The River Kwai.
JOSHUA LOGAN, *Sayonara.*
SIDNEY LUMET, *12 Angry Men.*
MARK ROBSON, *Peyton Place.*
BILLY WILDER, *Witness For The Prosecution.*

WRITING (O-478)
(Best Story and Screenplay written directly for the screen)
DESIGNING WOMAN, MGM. George Wells.
FUNNY FACE, PAR. Leonard Gershe.
MAN OF A THOUSAND FACES. U. Story by Ralph Wheelright. Screenplay by R. Wright Campbell, Ivan Goff and Ben Roberts.
THE TIN STAR, The Perlberg-Seaton Prod., PAR. Story by Barney Slater and Joel Kane. Screenplay by Dudley Nichols.
VITELLONI, Peg Films/Cite Films, API (Italian). Story by Federico Fellini, Ennio Flaiano and Tullio Pinelli. Screenplay by Federico Fellini and Ennio Flaiano.

(Best Screenplay based on material from another medium)
THE BRIDGE ON THE RIVER KWAI. Pierre Boulle.
HEAVEN KNOWS, MR. ALLISON. John Lee Mahin and John Huston.
PEYTON PLACE. John Michael Hayes.
SAYONARA. Paul Osborn.
12 ANGRY MEN. Reginald Rose.

CINEMATOGRAPHY (O-479)
THE BRIDGE ON THE RIVER KWAI. Jack Hildyard.
AN AFFAIR TO REMEMBER. Jerry Wald Prods., Inc., FOX. Milton Krasner.
FUNNY FACE, PAR. Ray June.
PEYTON PLACE. William Mellor.
SAYONARA. Ellsworth Fredericks.

COSTUME DESIGN (O-480)
LES GIRLS, Sol C. Siegel Prods., Inc., MGM. Orry-Kelly.
AN AFFAIR TO REMEMBER. Charles LeMaire.
FUNNY FACE. Edith Head and Hubert de Givenchy.
PAL JOEY, Essex-George Sidney Prod., COL. Jean Louis.
RAINTREE COUNTY. Walter Plunkett.

ART DIRECTION - SET DECORATION (O-481)
SAYONARA. Ted Haworth. Set Decoration: Robert Priestley.
FUNNY FACE. Hal Pereira and George W. Davis. Set Decoration: Sam Comer and Ray Moyer.
LES GIRLS. William A. Horning and Gene Allen. Set Decoration: Edwin B. Willis and Richard Pefferle.
PAL JOEY. Walter Holscher. Set Decoration: William Kiernan and Louis Diage.
RAINTREE COUNTY. William A. Horning and Urie McCleary. Set Decoration: Edwin B. Willis and Hugh Hunt.

FILM EDITING (O-482)
THE BRIDGE ON THE RIVER KWAI. Peter Taylor.
GUNFIGHT AT THE O.K. CORRAL, A Hal Wallis Prod., PAR. Warren Low.
PAL JOEY. Viola Lawrence and Jerome Thoms.
SAYONARA. Arthur P. Schmidt and Philip W. Anderson.
WITNESS FOR THE PROSECUTION. Daniel Mandell.

FOREIGN LANUAGE FILM (O-483)
THE NIGHTS OF CABIRIA, Dino De Laurentiis Production (Italy).
THE DEVIL CAME AT NIGHT, Gloria Film (Germany).
GATES OF PARIS, Filmsonor S.A. Production (France).
MOTHER INDIA, Mehboob Productions (India).
NINE LIVES, Nordsjofilm (Norway).

MUSIC - SCORING (O-484)
THE BRIDGE ON THE RIVER KWAI, (Dramatic or Comedy). Malcolm Arnold.
AN AFFAIR TO REMEMBER, (Dramatic or Comedy). Hugo Friedhofer.
BOY ON A DOLPHIN, (Dramatic or Comedy), FOX. Hugo Friedhofer.
PERRI, (Dramatic or Comedy), Walt Disney Prods., BV. Paul Smith.
RAINTREE COUNTY, (Dramatic or Comedy). Johnny Green.

MUSIC - BEST SONG (O-485)
ALL THE WAY, The Joker Is Wild A.M.B.L. Prod., PAR. Music, James Van Heusen. Lyrics, Sammy Cahn.
AN AFFAIR TO REMEMBER, *An Affair To Remember.* Music, Harry Warren. Lyrics, Harold Adamson and Leo McCarey.
APRIL LOVE, *April Love,* FOX. Music, Sammy Fain. Lyrics, Paul Francis Webster.
TAMMY, *Tammy And The Bachelor,* U. Music and Lyrics by Ray Evans and Jay Livingston.
WILD IS THE WIND, *Wild Is The Wind.* Music, Dimitri Tiomkin. Lyrics, Ned Washington.

SOUND (O-486)
SAYONARA, WB Studio Sound Department. George Groves, Sound Director.
GUNFIGHT AT THE O.K. CORRAL, PAR Studio Sound Department. George Dutton, Sound Director.
LES GIRLS, MGM Studio Sound Department. Dr. Wesley C. Miller, Sound Director.
PAL JOEY, COL Studio Sound Department. John P. Livadary, Sound Director.
WITNESS FOR THE PROSECUTION, Samuel Goldwyn Studio Sound Department. Gordon Sawyer, Sound Director.

SHORT FILMS (O-487)
(Cartoons)
BIRDS ANONYMOUS, WB. Edward Selzer, Prod.
ONE DROOPY KNIGHT, MGM. William Hanna and Joseph Barbera, Prods.
TABASCO ROAD, WB. Edward Selzer, Prod.
TREES AND JAMAICA DADDY, UPA Pictures, COL. Stephen Bosustow, Prod.
THE TRUTH ABOUT MOTHER GOOSE, Walt Disney Prods., BV. Walt Disney, Prod.
(Live Action Subjects)
THE WETBACK HOUND, Walt Disney Prods., BV. Larry Lansburgh,

1954—Grace Kelly (Best Actress) and Marlon Brando (Best Actor)

1959—William Wyler (Best Director), Mrs. Sam Zimbalist (accepting for her husband, producer, Best Picture), and Charlton Heston (Best Actor)

1955—Marisa Pavan (accepting for Anna Magnani, Best Actress), Jack Lemmon (Best Supporting Actor), Jo Van Fleet (Best Supporting Actress), Ernest Borgnine (Best Supporting Actor), Audrey Hepburn (presenter), and Harold Hecht (producer, Best Picture)

1953—Fred Zinnemann (Best Director), Donna Reed (Best Supporting Actress), Buddy Adler (producer, Best Picture), and Daniel Taradash (Best Writing—Screenplay)

1960—Peter Ustinov (Best Supporting Actor), Shirley Jones (Best Supporting Actress), Burt Lancaster (Best Actor), Elizabeth Taylor (Best Actress), and Billy Wilder (Best Picture, Best Writing, and Best Direction)

1961—George Chakiris (Best Supporting Actor), Jerome Robbins (Best Director), Robert Wise (Best Director), and Rita Moreno (Best Supporting Actress)

1963—Sidney Poitier (Best Actor) with presenter Anne Bancroft

1962—Gregory Peck (Best Actor), Patty Duke (Best Supporting Actress), Joan Crawford (accepting for Anne Bancroft, Best Actress), and Ed Begley (Best Supporting Actor)

Prod.
A CHAIRY TALE, NFC, KGY. Norman McLaren, Prod.
CITY OF GOLD, NFC, KGY. Tom Daly, Prod.
FOOTHOLD ON ANTARCTICA, World Wide Pictures, SCH. James Carr, Prod.
PORTUGAL, Walt Disney Prods., BV. Ben Sharpsteen, Prod.

DOCUMENTARY (O-488)

(Features)

ALBERT SCHWEITZER, Hill and Anderson Prod., DRH. Jerome Hill, Prod.
ON THE BOWERY, Lionel Rogosin Prods., FRP. Lionel Rogosin, Prod.
TORERO!, PBP, COL (Mexican). Manuel Barbachano Ponce, Prod.

SPECIAL EFFECTS (O-489)

THE ENEMY BELOW, FOX. Audible: Walter Rossi.
THE SPIRIT OF ST. LOUIS, Leland Hayward-Billy Wilder, WB. Visual: Louis Lichtenfield.

HONORARY AND OTHER (O-490)

(Jean Hersholt Humanitarian Award)

Samuel Goldwyn

(Other)

CHARLES BRACKETT for outstanding service to the Academy.
B. B. KAHANE for distinguished service to the motion picture industry.
GILBERT M. (Broncho Billy) ANDERSON, motion picture pioneer, for his contributions to the development of motion pictures as entertainment.
THE SOCIETY OF MOTION PICTURE AND TELEVISION ENGINEERS for their contributions to the advancement of the motion picture industry.

SCIENTIFIC OR TECHNICAL (O-491)

(Class I)

TODD-AO CORP. and WESTREX CORP. for developing a method of producing and exhibiting wide-film motion pictures known as the Todd-AO System.
MOTION PICTURE RESEARCH COUNCIL for the design and development of a high efficiency projection screen for drive-in theatres.
(Class II)
SOCIETE D'OPTIQUE ET DE MECANIQUE DE HAUTE PRECISION for the development of a high speed vari-focal photographic lens.
HARLAN L. BAUMBACH, LORAND WARGO, HOWARD M. LITTLE and the UNICORN ENGINEERING CORP. for the development of an automatic printer light selector.
(Class III)
CHARLES E. SUTTER, WILLIAM B. SMITH, PARAMOUNT PICTURES CORP. and GENERAL CABLE CORP. for the engineering and application to studio use of aluminum lightweight electrical cable and connectors.

1958

BEST PICTURE (O-492)

GIGI, Arthur Freed Prods., Inc., MGM. Arthur Freed, Prod.
AUNTIE MAME, WB.
CAT ON A HOT TIN ROOF, Avon Prods., Inc. MGM, Lawrence Weingarten, Prod.
THE DEFIANT ONES, Stanley Kramer, UA. Stanley Kramer, Prod.
SEPARATE TABLES, Clifton Prods., Inc., UA. Harold Hecht, Prod.

ACTOR (O-493)

DAVID NIVEN, Separate Tables.
TONY CURTIS, *The Defiant Ones.*
PAUL NEWMAN, *Cat On A Hot Tin Roof.*
SIDNEY POITIER, *The Defiant Ones.*
SPENCER TRACY, *The Old Man And The Sea,* Leland Hayward, WB.

ACTRESS (O-494)

SUSAN HAYWARD, I Want To Live!, Figaro, Inc., UA.
DEBORAH KERR, *Separate Tables.*
SHIRLEY MACLAINE, *Some Came Running,* Sol C. Siegel Prods., Inc., MGM.
ROSALIND RUSSELL, *Auntie Mame.*
ELIZABETH TAYLOR, *Cat On A Hot Tin Roof.*

SUPPORTING ACTOR (O-495)

BURL IVES, The Big Country, Anthony-Worldwide Prods., UA.
THEODORE BIKEL, *The Defiant Ones.*
LEE J. COBB, *The Brothers Karamazov,* Avon Prods., Inc., MGM.
ARTHUR KENNEDY, *Some Came Running.*
GIG YOUNG, *Teacher's Pet,* Perlberg-Seaton, PAR.

SUPPORTING ACTRESS (O-496)

WENDY HILLER, Separate Tables.
PEGGY CASS, *Auntie Mame.*
MARTHA HYER, *Some Came Running.*
MAUREEN STAPLETON, *Lonelyhearts,* Schary Prods., Inc., UA.
CARA WILLIAMS, *The Defiant Ones.*

DIRECTING (O-497)

VINCENTE MINNELLI, Gigi.
RICHARD BROOKS, *Cat On A Hot Tin Roof.*
STANLEY KRAMER, *The Defiant Ones.*
MARK ROBSON, *The Inn Of The Sixth Happiness,* FOX.
ROBERT WISE, *I Want To Live!*

WRITING (O-498)

(Best Story and Screenplay written directly for the screen)

THE DEFIANT ONES. Nathan E. Douglas and Harold Jacob Smith.
THE GODDESS, Carnegie Prods., Inc., COL. Paddy Chayefsky.
HOUSEBOAT, PAR and Scribe, PAR. Melville Shavelson and Jack Rose.
THE SHEEPMAN, MGM. Story by James Edward Grant. Screenplay by William Bowers and James Edward Grant.
TEACHER'S PET. Fay and Michael Kanin.

(Best Screenplay based on material from another medium)

GIGI. Alan Jay Lerner.
CAT ON A HOT TIN ROOF. Richard Brooks and James Poe.
THE HORSE'S MOUTH, Knightsbridge, UA (British). Alec Guinness.
I WANT TO LIVE! Nelson Gidding and Don Mankiewicz.
SEPARATE TABLES. Terence Rattigan and John Gay.

CINEMATOGRAPHY (O-499)

(Black-and-White)

THE DEFIANT ONES. Sam Leavitt.
DESIRE UNDER THE ELMS, Don Hartman, PAR. Daniel L. Fapp.
I WANT TO LIVE! Lionel Lindon.
SEPARATE TABLES. Charles Lang, Jr.
THE YOUNG LIONS, FOX. Joe MacDonald.
(Color)
GIGI. Joseph Ruttenberg.
AUNTIE MAME. Harry Stradling, Sr.
CAT ON A HOT TIN ROOF. William Daniels.
THE OLD MAN AND THE SEA. James Wong Howe.
SOUTH PACIFIC, South Pacific Enterprises, Inc., MNA. Leon Shamroy.

COSTUME DESIGN (O-500)

GIGI. Cecil Beaton.
BELL, BOOK AND CANDLE, Phoenix Prods., Inc., COL. Jean Louis.
THE BUCCANEER, Cecil B. DeMille, PAR. Ralph Jester, Edith Head and John Jensen.
A CERTAIN SMILE, FOX. Charles LeMaire and Mary Wills.
SOME CAME RUNNING. Walter Plunkett.

ART DIRECTION - SET DECORATION (O-501)

GIGI. William A. Horning and Preston Ames. Set Decoration: Henry Grace and Keogh Gleason.
AUNTIE MAME. Malcolm Bert. Set Decoration: George James Hopkins.
BELL, BOOK AND CANDLE. Cary Odell. Set Decoration: Louis Diage.
A CERTAIN SMILE. Lyle R. Wheeler and John DeCuir. Set Decoration: Walter M. Scott and Paul S. Fox.
VERTIGO, Alfred J. Hitchcock Prods., Inc., PAR. Hal Pereira and Henry Bumstead. Set Decoration: Sam Comer and Frank McKelvy.

FILM EDITING (O-502)

GIGI. Adrienne Fazan.
AUNTIE MAME. William Ziegler.
COWBOY, Phoenix Pictures, COL. William A. Lyon and Al Clark.
THE DEFIANT ONES. Frederic Knudtson.
I WANT TO LIVE! William Hornbeck.

FOREIGN LANGUAGE FILM (O-503)

MY UNCLE, Specta-Gray-Alter Films in association with Films del Centaure (France).
ARMS AND THE MAN, H. R. Sokal-P. Goldbaum Production, Bavaria Filmkunst A.G. (Germany).
LA VENGANZA, Guion Producciones Cinematograficas (Spain).
THE ROAD A YEAR LONG, Jadran Film (Yugoslavia).
THE USUAL UNIDENTIFIED THIEVES, Lux-Vides-Cinecitta (Italy).

MUSIC - SCORING (O-504)

(Scoring of a Dramatic or Comedy Picture)
THE OLD MAN AND THE SEA. Dimitri Tiomkin.
THE BIG COUNTRY. Jerome Moross.
SEPARATE TABLES. David Raksin.
WHITE WILDERNESS, Walt Disney Prods., BV. Oliver Wallace.
THE YOUNG LIONS, FOX. Hugo Friedhofer.

(Scoring of a Musical Picture)
GIGI. Andre Previn.
THE BOLSHOI BALLET, A Rank Organization Presentation-Harmony Film, RNK (British). Yuri Faier and G. Rozhdestvensky.
DAMN YANKEES, WB. Ray Heindorf.
MARDI GRAS, Jerry Wald Prods., Inc., FOX. Lionel Newman.
SOUTH PACIFIC. Alfred Newman and Ken Darby.

MUSIC - BEST SONG (O-505)

GIGI, Gigi. Music, Frederick Loewe. Lyrics, Alan Jay Lerner.
ALMOST IN YOUR ARMS (Love Song from "Houseboat"), *Houseboat*, PAR and Scribe, PAR. Music and Lyrics by Jay Livingston and Ray Evans.
A CERTAIN SMILE, *A Certain Smile*. Music, Sammy Fain. Lyrics, Paul Francis Webster.
TO LOVE AND BE LOVED, *Some Came Running*. Music, James Van Heusen. Lyrics, Sammy Cahn.
A VERY PRECIOUS LOVE, *Marjorie Morningstar*, Beachwold Pictures, WB. Music, Sammy Fain. Lyrics, Paul Francis Webster.

SOUND (O-506)

SOUTH PACIFIC, Todd-AO Sound Department. Fred Hynes, Sound Director.
I WANT TO LIVE!, Samuel Goldwyn Studio Sound Department. Gordon E. Sawyer. Sound Director.
A TIME TO LOVE AND A TIME TO DIE, U Studio Sound Department. Leslie I. Carey, Sound Director.
VERTIGO, PAR Studio Sound Department. George Dutton, Sound Director.
THE YOUNG LIONS, FOX Studio Sound Department. Carl Faulkner, Sound Director.

SHORT FILMS (O-507)

(Cartoons)
KNIGHTY KNIGHT BUGS, WB. John W. Burton, Prod.
PAUL BUNYAN, Walt Disney Prods., BV Film Distribution Co., Inc. Walt Disney, Prod.
SIDNEY'S FAMILY TREE, Terrytoons, FOX. William M. Weiss, Prod.
(Live Action Subjects)
GRAND CANYON, Walt Disney Prods., BV. Walt Disney, Prod.
JOURNEY INTO SPRING, British Transport Films, SCH. Ian Ferguson, Prod.
THE KISS, Cohay Prods., CON. John Patrick Hayes, Prod.
SNOWS OF AORANGI, New Zealand Screen Board, George Brest Associates.
T IS FOR TUMBLEWEED, CON. James A Lebenthal, Prod.

DOCUMENTARY (O-508)

(Short Subjects)
AMA GIRLS, Walt Disney Prods., BV. Inc. Ben Sharpsteen, Prod.
EMPLOYEES ONLY, Hughes Aircraft Co. Kenneth G. Brown, Prod.
JOURNEY INTO SPRING, British Transport Films, SCH. Ian Ferguson, Prod.
THE LIVING STONE, NFC. Tom Daly, Prod.
OVERTURE, United Nations Film Service. Thorold Dickinson, Prod.
(Features)
WHITE WILDERNESS, Walt Disney Prods., BV. Ben Sharpsteen, Prod.
ANTARCTIC CROSSING, World Wide Pictures, SCH. James Carr, Prod.
THE HIDDEN WORLD, Small World Co. Robert Snyder, Prod.
PSYCHIATRIC NURSING, Dynamic Films, Inc. Nathan Zucker, Prod.

SPECIAL EFFECTS (O-509)

tom thumb, Galaxy Pictures, MGM. Visual: Tom Howard.
TORPEDO RUN, MGM. Visual: A. Arnold Gillespie. Audible: Harold Humbrock.

HONORARY AND OTHER (O-510)

(Irving G. Thalberg Memorial Award)
Jack L. Warner
(Other)
MAURICE CHEVALIER for his contributions to the world of entertainment for more than half a century.

SCIENTIFIC OR TECHNICAL (O-511)

(Class II)
DON W. PRIDEAUX, LEROY G. LEIGHTON and the LAMP DIVISION of GENERAL ELECTRIC CO. for the development and production of an improved 10 kilowatt lamp for motion picture set lighting.
PANAVISION, INC., for the design and development of the Auto Panatar anamorphic photographic lens for 35mm CinemaScope photography.
(Class III)
WILLY BORBERG of the General Precision Laboratory, Inc., for the development of a high speed intermittent movement for 35mm motion picture theatre projection equipment.
FRED PONEDEL, GEORGE BROWN and CONRAD BOYE of the WB Special Effects Department for the design and fabrication of a new rapid fire marble gun.

1959

BEST PICTURE (O-512)

BEN-HUR, MGM. Sam Zimbalist, Prod.
ANATOMY OF A MURDER, Otto Preminger, COL. Otto Preminger, Prod.
THE DIARY OF ANNE FRANK, FOX. George Stevens, Prod.
THE NUN'S STORY, WB. Henry Blanke, Prod.

ROOM AT THE TOP, Romulus Films, Ltd., Continental Distr., Inc., (British). John & James Woolf, Prods.

ACTOR (O-513)

CHARLTON HESTON, Ben-Hur.
LAURENCE HARVEY, *Room At The Top.*
JACK LEMMON, *Some Like It Hot,* Ashton Prods. & The Mirisch Co., UA.
PAUL MUNI, *The Last Angry Man,* Fred Kohlmar Prods., COL.
JAMES STEWART, *Anatomy Of A Murder.*

ACTRESS (O-514)

SIMONE SIGNORET, Room At The Top.
DORIS DAY, *Pillow Talk,* Arwin Prods., Inc., U.
AUDREY HEPBURN, *The Nun's Story.*
KATHARINE HEPBURN, *Suddenly, Last Summer,* Horizon Prod., COL.
ELIZABETH TAYLOR, *Suddenly, Last Summer.*

SUPPORTING ACTOR (O-515)

HUGH GRIFFITH, Ben-Hur.
ARTHUR O'CONNELL, *Anatomy Of A Murder.*
GEORGE C. SCOTT, *Anatomy Of A Murder.*
ROBERT VAUGHN, *The Young Philadelphians,* WB.
ED WYNN, *The Diary Of Anne Frank.*

SUPPORTING ACTRESS (O-516)

SHELLEY WINTERS, The Diary Of Anne Frank.
HERMIONE BADDELEY, *Room At The Top.*
SUSAN KOHNER, *Imitation Of Life,* U.
JUANITA MOORE, *Imitation Of Life.*
THELMA RITTER, *Pillow Talk.*

DIRECTING (O-517)

WILLIAM WYLER, Ben-Hur.
JACK CLAYTON, *Room At The Top.*
GEORGE STEVENS, *The Diary Of Anne Frank.*
BILLY WILDER, *Some Like It Hot.*
FRED ZINNEMANN, *The Nun's Story.*

WRITING (O-518)

(Best Story and Screenplay written directly for the screen)
PILLOW TALK. Story by Russell Rouse and Clarence Greene. Screenplay by Stanley Shapiro and Maurice Richlin.
THE 400 BLOWS, Les Films du Carrosse & SEDIF, ZEN (French). Francois Truffaut and Marcel Moussy.
NORTH BY NORTHWEST, MGM. Ernest Lehman.
OPERATION PETTICOAT, Granart Co., U. Story by Paul King and Joseph Stone. Screenplay by Stanley Shapiro and Maurice Richlin.
WILD STRAWBERRIES, Svensk Filmindustri, JAN (Swedish). Ingmar Bergman.

(Best Screenplay based on material from another medium)
ROOM AT THE TOP. Neil Paterson.
ANATOMY OF A MURDER. Wendell Mayes.
BEN-HUR. Karl Tunberg.
THE NUN'S STORY. Robert Anderson.
SOME LIKE IT HOT. Billy Wilder and I.A.L. Diamond.

CINEMATOGRAPHY (O-519)

(Black-and-White)
THE DIARY OF ANNE FRANK. William C. Mellor.
ANATOMY OF A MURDER. Sam Leavitt.
CAREER, Hal Wallis Prods., PAR. Joseph LaShelle.
SOME LIKE IT HOT. Charles Lang, Jr.
THE YOUNG PHILADELPHIANS. Harry Stradling, Sr.
(Color)

BEN-HUR. Robert L. Surtees.
THE BIG FISHERMAN, Rowland V. Lee Prods., BV. Lee Garmes.
THE FIVE PENNIES, Dena Prod., PAR. Daniel L. Fapp.
THE NUN'S STORY. Franz Planer.
PORGY AND BESS, Samuel Goldwyn Prods., COL. Leon Shamroy.

COSTUME DESIGN (O-520)

(Black-and-White)
SOME LIKE IT HOT. Orry-Kelly.
CAREER. Edith Head.
THE DIARY OF ANNE FRANK. Charles LeMaire and Mary Wills.
THE GAZEBO, Avon Prod., MGM. Helen Rose.
THE YOUNG PHILADELPHIANS. Howard Shoup.
(Color)
BEN-HUR. Elizabeth Haffenden.
THE BEST OF EVERYTHING, Co of Artists, Inc., FOX. Adele Palmer.
THE BIG FISHERMAN. Renie.
THE FIVE PENNIES. Edith Head.
PORGY AND BESS. Irene Sharaff.

ART DIRECTION - SET DECORATION (O-521)

(Black-and-White)
THE DIARY OF ANNE FRANK. Lyle R. Wheeler and George W. Davis. Set Decoration: Walter M. Scott and Stuart A. Reiss.
CAREER. Hal Pereira and Walter Tyler. Set Decoration: Sam Comer and Arthur Krams.
THE LAST ANGRY MAN. Carl Anderson. Set Decoration: William Kiernan.
SOME LIKE IT HOT. Ted Haworth. Set Decoration: Edward G. Boyle.
SUDDENLY, LAST SUMMER. Oliver Messel and William Kellner. Set Decoration: Scot Slimon.
(Color)
BEN-HUR. William A. Horning and Edward Carfagno. Set Decoration: Hugh Hunt.
THE BIG FISHERMAN. John DeCuir. Set Decoration: Julia Heron.
JOURNEY TO THE CENTER OF THE EARTH, Joseph M. Schenck Enterprises, Inc. & Cooga Mooga Film Prods., Inc., FOX. Lyle R. Wheeler, Franz Bachelin and Herman A. Blumenthal. Set Decoration: Walter M. Scott and Joseph Kish.
NORTH BY NORTHWEST. William A. Horning, Robert Boyle and Merrill Pye. Set Decoration: Henry Grace and Frank McKelvy.
PILLOW TALK. Richard H. Riedel. Set Decoration: Russell A. Gausman and Ruby R. Levitt.

FILM EDITING (O-522)

BEN-HUR. Ralph E. Winters and John D. Dunning.
ANATOMY OF A MURDER. Louis R. Loeffler.
NORTH BY NORTHWEST. George Tomasini.
THE NUN'S STORY. Walter Thompson.
ON THE BEACH, Lomitas Prods., UA. Frederic Knudtson.

FOREIGN LANGUAGE FILM (O-523)

BLACK ORPHEUS, Dispatfilm & Gemma Cinematografica (France).
THE BRIDGE, Fono Film (Germany).
THE GREAT WAR, Dino De Laurentiis Cinematografica (Italy).
PAW, Laterna Film (Denmark).
THE VILLAGE ON THE RIVER, N. V. Nationale Filmproductie Maatschappij (The Netherlands).

MUSIC - SCORING (O-524)

(Scoring of a Dramatic or Comedy Picture)
BEN-HUR. Miklos Rozsa.
THE DIARY OF ANNE FRANK. Alfred Newman.
THE NUN'S STORY. Franz Waxman.
ON THE BEACH. Ernest Gold.
PILLOW TALK. Frank DeVol.
(Scoring of a Musical Picture)
PORGY AND BESS. Andre Previn and Ken Darby.
THE FIVE PENNIES. Leith Stevens.

LI'L ABNER, Panama and Frank, PAR. Nelson Riddle and Joseph J. Lilley.
SAY ONE FOR ME, Bing Crosby Prods., FOX. Lionel Newman.
SLEEPING BEAUTY, Walt Disney Prods., BV. George Bruns.

MUSIC - BEST SONG (O-525)

HIGH HOPES, A Hole In The Head, Sincap Prods., UA. Music, James Van Heusen. Lyrics, Sammy Cahn.
THE BEST OF EVERYTHING, *The Best Of Everything.* Music, Alfred Newman. Lyrics, Sammy Cahn.
THE FIVE PENNIES, *The Five Pennies.* Music and Lyrics by Sylvia Fine.
THE HANGING TREE, *The Hanging Tree,* Baroda Prods., Inc., WB. Music, Jerry Livingston. Lyrics, Mack David.
STRANGE ARE THE WAYS OF LOVE from *The Young Land,* C. V. Whitney Pictures, Inc., COL. Music, Dimitri Tiomkin. Lyrics, Ned Washington.

SOUND (O-526)

BEN-HUR, MGM Studio Sound Department. Franklin E. Milton, Sound Director.
JOURNEY TO THE CENTER OF THE EARTH, FOX Studio Sound Department. Carl Faulkner, Sound Director.
LIBEL!, MGM London Sound Department (British). A. W. Watkins, Sound Director.
THE NUN'S STORY, WB Studio Sound Department. George R. Groves, Sound Director.
PORGY AND BESS, Samuel Goldwyn Studio Sound Department. Gordon E. Sawyer, Sound Director; and Todd-AO Sound Department. Fred Hynes, Sound Director.

SHORT FILMS (O-527)

(Cartoons)

MOONBIRD, Storyboard, Inc., EDH, John Hubley, Prod.
MEXICALI SHMOES, WB. John W. Burton, Prod.
NOAH'S ARK, Walt Disney Prods., BV. Walt Disney, Prod.
THE VIOLINIST, Pintoff Prods., Inc., KGY. Ernest Pintoff, Prod.

(Live Action Subjects)

THE GOLDEN FISH, Les Requins Associes, COL (French). Jacques-Yves Cousteau, Prod.
BETWEEN THE TIDES, British Transport Films, SCH (British). Ian Ferguson, Prod.
MYSTERIES OF THE DEEP, Walt Disney Prods., BV. Walt Disney, Prod.
THE RUNNING, JUMPING AND STANDING-STILL FILM, Lion Int'l Films Ltd., KGU (British). Peter Sellers, Prod.
SKYSCRAPER, BYN. Shirley Clarke, Willard Van Dyke and Irving Jacoby, Prods.

DOCUMENTARY (O-528)

(Short Subjects)

GLASS, Netherlands Government, George K. Arthur-Go Pictures, Inc. (The Netherlands) Bert Haanstra, Prod.
DONALD IN MATHMAGIC LAND, Walt Disney Prods., BV. Walt Disney, Prod.
FROM GENERATION TO GENERATION, Cullen Assocs., Maternity Center Assoc. Edward F. Cullen, Prod.

(Features)

SERENGETI SHALL NOT DIE, Okapia-Film Prod., Transocean Film (German). Bernhard Grzimek, Prod.
THE RACE FOR SPACE, Wolper, Inc. David L. Wolper, Prod.

SPECIAL EFFECTS (O-529)

BEN-HUR. Visual: A. Arnold Gillespie and Robert MacDonald. Audible: Milo Lory.
JOURNEY TO THE CENTER OF THE EARTH. Visual: L. B. Abbott and James B. Gordon. Audible: Carl Faulkner.

HONORARY AND OTHER (O-530)

(Jean Hersholt Humanitarian Award)

Bob Hope

(Other)

LEE DE FOREST for his pioneering inventions which brought sound to the motion picture.
BUSTER KEATON for his unique talents which brought immortal comedies to the screen.

SCIENTIFIC OR TECHNICAL (O-531)

(Class II)

DOUGLAS G. SHEARER of MGM, Inc., and ROBERT E. GOTTSCHALK and JOHN R. MOORE of Panavision, Inc., for the development of a system of producing and exhibiting wide-film motion pictures known as Camera 65.
WADSWORTH E. POHL, WILLIAM EVANS, WERNER HOPF, S. E. HOWSE, THOMAS P. DIXON, STANFORD RESEARCH INSTITUTE and TECHNICOLOR CORP. for the design and development of the Technicolor electronic printing timer.
WADSWORTH E. POHL, JACK ALFORD, HENRY IMUS, JOSEPH SCHMIT, PAUL FASSNACHT, AL LOFQUIST and TECHNICOLOR CORP. for the development and practical application of equipment for wet printing.
DR. HOWARD S. COLEMAN, DR. A. FRANCIS TURNER, HAROLD H. SCHROEDER, JAMES R. BENFORD and HAROLD E. ROSENBERGER of the Bausch & Lomb Optical Co. for the design and development of the Balcold projection mirror.
ROBERT P. GUTTERMAN of General Kinetics, Inc., and the LIPSNER-SMITH CORP. for the design and development of the CF-2 Ultrasonic Film Cleaner.

(Class III)

UB IWERKS of Walt Disney Prods. for the design of an improved optical printer for special effects and matte shots.
E. L. STONES, GLEN ROBINSON, WINFIELD HUBBARD and LUTHER NEWMAN of the MGM Studio Construction Department for the design of a multiple cable remote controlled winch.

1960

BEST PICTURE (O-532)

THE APARTMENT, The Mirisch Co., Inc., UA. Billy Wilder, Prod.
THE ALAMO, Batjac Prod., UA. John Wayne, Prod.
ELMER GANTRY, Burt Lancaster-Richard Brooks Prod., UA. Bernard Smith, Prod.
SONS AND LOVERS, Co of Artists, Inc., FOX. Jerry Wald, Prod.
THE SUNDOWNERS, WB. Fred Zinnemann, Prod.

ACTOR (O-533)

BURT LANCASTER, Elmer Gantry.
TREVOR HOWARD, *Sons And Lovers.*
JACK LEMMON, *The Apartment.*
LAURENCE OLIVIER, *The Entertainer,* Woodfall Prod., Continental Dist., Inc. (British)
SPENCER TRACY, *Inherit The Wind,* Stanley Kramer, UA.

ACTRESS (O-534)

ELIZABETH TAYLOR, Butterfield 8, Afton-Linebrook Prod., MGM.
GREER GARSON, *Sunrise At Campobello,* Schary Prod., WB.
DEBORAH KERR, *The Sundowners.*
SHIRLEY MACLAINE, *The Apartment.*
MELINA MERCOURI, *Never On Sunday,* Melinafilm Prod., LOP. (Greek)

SUPPORTING ACTOR (O-535)

PETER USTINOV, Spartacus, Bryna Prods., Inc., UI.
PETER FALK, *Murder, Inc.,* FOX.
JACK KRUSCHEN, *The Apartment.*

SAL MINEO, *Exodus*, Carlyle-Alpina S.A. Prod., UA.
CHILL WILLS, *The Alamo*.

SUPPORTING ACTRESS (O-536)

SHIRLEY JONES, Elmer Gantry.
GLYNIS JOHNS, *The Sundowners*.
SHIRLEY KNIGHT, *The Dark At The Top Of The Stairs*, WB.
JANET LEIGH, *Psycho*, Alfred J. Hitchcock Prods., PAR.
MARY URE, *Sons And Lovers*.

DIRECTING (O-537)

BILLY WILDER, The Apartment.
JACK CARDIFF, *Sons And Lovers*.
JULES DASSIN, *Never On Sunday*.
ALFRED HITCHCOCK, *Psycho*.
FRED ZINNEMANN, *The Sundowners*.

WRITING (O-538)

(Best Story and Screenplay written directly for the screen)

THE APARTMENT. Billy Wilder and I.A.L. Diamond.
THE ANGRY SILENCE, Beaver Films Ltd Prod., Joseph Harris-Sig Shore (British). Story by Richard Gregson and Michael Craig. Screenplay by Bryan Forbes.
THE FACTS OF LIFE, Panama & Frank Prod., UA. Norman Panama and Melvin Frank.
HIROSHIMA, MON AMOUR, Argos Films-Como Films-Daiei Pictures, Ltd.-Pathe Overseas Prod., ZEN. (French-Japanese). Marguerite Duras.
NEVER ON SUNDAY. Jules Dassin.

(Best Screenplay based on material from another medium)

ELMER GANTRY. Richard Brooks.
INHERIT THE WIND. Nathan E. Douglas and Harold Jacob Smith.
SONS AND LOVERS. Gavin Lambert and T.E.B. Clarke.
THE SUNDOWNERS. Isobel Lennart.
TUNES OF GLORY, H. M. Films Ltd Prod., LOP. (British). James Kennaway.

CINEMATOGRAPHY (O-539)

(Black-and-White)

SONS AND LOVERS. Freddie Francis.
THE APARTMENT. Joseph LaShelle.
THE FACTS OF LIFE. Charles B. Lang, Jr.
INHERIT THE WIND. Ernest Laszlo.
PSYCHO. John L. Russell.

(Color)

SPARTACUS. Russell Metty.
THE ALAMO. William H. Clothier.
BUTTERFIELD 8. Joseph Ruttenberg and Charles Harten.
EXODUS. Sam Leavitt.
PEPE, G. S.-Posa Films International Prod., COL. Joe MacDonald.

COSTUME DESIGN (O-540)

(Black-and-White)

THE FACTS OF LIFE. Edith Head and Edward Stevenson.
NEVER ON SUNDAY. Denny Vachlioti.
THE RISE AND FALL OF LEGS DIAMOND, United States Prod., WB. Howard Shoup.
SEVEN THIEVES, FOX. Bill Thomas.
THE VIRGIN SPRING, Svensk Filmindustri Prod., JAN. (Swedish). Marik Vos.

(Color)

SPARTACUS. Valles and Bill Thomas.
CAN-CAN, Suffolk-Cummings Prods., FOX. Irene Sharaff.
MIDNIGHT LACE, Ross Hunter-Arwin Prod., U. Irene.
PEPE. Edith Head.
SUNRISE AT CAMPOBELLO. Marjorie Best.

ART DIRECTION - SET DECORATION (O-541)

(Black-and-White)

THE APARTMENT. Alexander Trauner. Set Decoration: Edward G. Boyle.
THE FACTS OF LIFE. Joseph McMillan Johnson and Kenneth A. Reid. Set Decoration: Ross Dowd.
PSYCHO. Joseph Hurley and Robert Clatworthy. Set Decoration: George Milo.
SONS AND LOVERS. Tom Morahan. Set Decoration: Lionel Couch.
VISIT TO A SMALL PLANET, Hall Wallis Prods., PAR. Hal Pereira and Walter Tyler. Set Decoration: Sam Comer and Arthur Krams.

(Color)

SPARTACUS. Alexander Golitzen and Eric Orbom. Set Decoration: Russell A. Gausman and Julia Heron.
CIMARRON, MGM. George W. Davis and Addison Hehr. Set Decoration: Henry Grace, Hugh Hunt and Otto Siegel.
IT STARTED IN NAPLES, PAR and Capri Prod., PAR. Hal Pereira and Roland Anderson. Set Decoration: Sam Comer and Arrigo Breschi.
PEPE. Ted Haworth. Set Decoration: William Kiernan.
SUNRISE AT CAMPOBELLO. Edward Carrere. Set Decoration: George James Hopkins.

FILM EDITING (O-542)

THE APARTMENT. Daniel Mandell.
THE ALAMO. Stuart Gilmore.
INHERIT THE WIND. Frederic Knudtson.
PEPE. Viola Lawrence and Al Clark.
SPARTACUS. Robert Lawrence.

FOREIGN LANGUAGE FILM (O-543)

THE VIRGIN SPRING.
KAPO, Vides-Zebrafilm-Cineriz (Italy).
LA VERITE, Han Productions (France).
MACARIO, Clasa Films Mundiales, S.A. (Mexico).
THE NINTH CIRCLE, Jadran Film Production (Yugoslavia).

MUSIC - SCORING (O-544)

(Scoring of a Dramatic or Comedy Picture)

EXODUS. Ernest Gold.
THE ALAMO. Dimitri Tiomkin.
ELMER GANTRY. Andre Previn.
THE MAGNIFICENT SEVEN, Mirisch-Alpha Prod., UA. Elmer Bernstein.
SPARTACUS. Alex North.

(Scoring of a Musical Picture)

SONG WITHOUT END (The Story Of Franz Liszt), Goetz-Vidor Pictures Prod., COL. Morris Stoloff and Harry Sukman.
BELLS ARE RINGING, Arthur Freed Prod., MGM. Andre Previn.
CAN-CAN. Nelson Riddle.
LET'S MAKE LOVE, Co of Artists, Inc., FOX. Lionel Newman and Earle H. Hagen.
PEPE. Johnny Green.

MUSIC - BEST SONG (O-545)

NEVER ON SUNDAY, Never On Sunday. Music and Lyrics by Manos Hadjidakis.
THE FACTS OF LIFE, *The Facts Of Life*. Music and Lyrics by Johnny Mercer.
FARAWAY PART OF TOWN, *Pepe*. Music, Andre Previn. Lyrics, Dory Langdon.
THE GREEN LEAVES OF SUMMER, *The Alamo*. Music, Dimitri Tiomkin. Lyrics, Paul Francis Webster.
THE SECOND TIME AROUND, *High Time*, Bing Crosby Prods., FOX. Music, James Van Heusen. Lyrics, Sammy Cahn.

SOUND (O-546)

THE ALAMO, Samuel Goldwyn Studio Sound Department, Gordon E. Sawyer, Sound Director; and Todd-AO Sound Department, Fred Hynes, Sound Director.
THE APARTMENT, Samuel Goldwyn Studio Sound Department. Gordon E. Sawyer, Sound Director.

CIMARRON, MGM Studio Sound Department. Franklin E. Milton, Sound Director.
PEPE, COL Studio Sound Department. Charles Rice, Sound Director.
SUNRISE AT CAMPOBELLO, WB. Studio Sound Department. George R. Groves, Sound Director.

SHORT FILMS (O-547)

(Cartoons)

MUNRO, Rembrandt Films, FRP. William L. Snyder, Prod.
GOLIATH II, Walt Disney Prods., BV. Walt Disney, Prod.
HIGH NOTE, WB.
MOUSE AND GARDEN, WB.
A PLACE IN THE SUN, George K. Arthur-Go Pictures, Inc. (Czechoslovakian). Frantisek Vystrecil, Prod.

(Live Action Subjects)

DAY OF THE PAINTER, Little Movies, KGU. Ezra R. Baker, Prod.
THE CREATION OF WOMAN, Trident Films, Inc., SWD. (Indian). Charles F. Schwep and Ismail Merchant, Prods.
ISLANDS OF THE SEA, Walt Disney Prods., BV. Walt Disney, Prod.
A SPORT IS BORN, PAR. Leslie Winik, Prod.

DOCUMENTARY (O-548)

(Short Subjects)

GIUSEPPINA, James Hill Prod., SCH (British). James Hill, Prod.
BEYOND SILENCE, United States Information Agency.
A CITY CALLED COPENHAGEN, Statens Filmcentral, Danish Government Film Office (Danish).
GEORGE GROSZ' INTERREGNUM, Educational Communications Corp. Charles and Altina Carey, Prods.
UNIVERSE, NFC, SCH (Canadian). Colin Low, Prod.

(Features)

THE HORSE WITH THE FLYING TAIL, Walt Disney Prods., BV. Larry Lansburgh, Prod.
REBEL IN PARADISE, Tiare Co. Robert D. Fraser, Prod.

SPECIAL EFFECTS (O-549)

THE TIME MACHINE, Galaxy Films Prod., MGM. Visual: Gene Warren and Tim Baar.
THE LAST VOYAGE, Andrew and Virginia Stone Prod., MGM. Visual: A. J. Lohman.

HONORARY AND OTHER (O-550)

(Jean Hersholt Humanitarian Award)

Sol Lesser

(Other)

GARY COOPER for his many memorable screen performances and the international recognition he, as an individual, has gained for the motion picture industry.
STAN LAUREL for his creative pioneering in the field of cinema comedy.
HAYLEY MILLS for Pollyanna, the most outstanding juvenile performance during 1960.

SCIENTIFIC OR TECHNICAL (O-551)

(Class II)

AMPEX PROFESSIONAL PRODUCTS CO. for the production of a well-engineered multi-purpose sound system combining high standards of quality with convenience of control, dependable operation and simplified emergency provisions.

(Class III)

ARTHUR HOLCOMB, PETRO VLAHOS and COLUMBIA STUDIO CAMERA DEPARTMENT for a camera flicker indicating device.
ANTHONY PAGLIA and the 20TH CENTURY-FOX STUDIO MECHANICAL EFFECTS DEPARTMENT for the design and construction of a miniature flak gun and ammunition.
CARL HAUGE, ROBERT GRUBEL and EDWARD REICHARD of Consolidated Film Industries for the development of an automatic developer replenisher system.

1961

BEST PICTURE (O-552)

WEST SIDE STORY, Mirisch Pictures, Inc. and B and P Enterprises, Inc., UA. Robert Wise, Prod.
FANNY, Mansfield Prod., WB. Joshua Logan, Prod.
THE GUNS OF NAVARONE, Carl Foreman Prod., COL. Carl Foreman, Prod.
THE HUSTLER, Robert Rossen Prod., FOX. Robert Rossen, Prod.
JUDGMENT AT NUREMBERG, Stanley Kramer Prod., UA. Stanley Kramer, Prod.

ACTOR (O-553)

MAXIMILIAN SCHELL, Judgment At Nuremberg.
CHARLES BOYER, *Fanny.*
PAUL NEWMAN, *The Hustler.*
SPENCER TRACY, *Judgment At Nuremberg.*
STUART WHITMAN, *The Mark,* Raymond Stross-Sidney Buchman Prod., Continental Dist., Inc. (British)

ACTRESS (O-554)

SOPHIA LOREN, Two Women, Champion-Les Films Marceau-Cocinor and Societe Generale De Cinematographie Prod., EBP. (Italo-French)
AUDREY HEPBURN, *Breakfast At Tiffany's,* Jurow-Shepherd Prod., PAR.
PIPER LAURIE, *The Hustler.*
GERALDINE PAGE, *Summer And Smoke,* Hal Wallis Prod., PAR.
NATALIE WOOD, *Splendor In The Grass,* NBI Prod., WB.

SUPPORTING ACTOR (O-555)

GEORGE CHAKIRIS, West Side Story.
MONTGOMERY CLIFT, *Judgment At Nuremberg.*
PETER FALK, *Pocketful Of Miracles,* Franton Prod., UA.
JACKIE GLEASON, *The Hustler.*
GEORGE C. SCOTT, *The Hustler.*

SUPPORTING ACTRESS (O-556)

RITA MORENO, West Side Story.
FAY BAINTER, *The Children's Hour,* Mirisch-Worldwide Prod., UA.
JUDY GARLAND, *Judgment At Nuremberg.*
LOTTE LENYA, *The Roman Spring Of Mrs. Stone,* Seven Arts Presentation, WB.
UNA MERKEL, *Summer And Smoke.*

DIRECTING (O-557)

JEROME ROBBINS, West Side Story.
ROBERT WISE, West Side Story.
FEDERICO FELLINI, *La Dolce Vita,* Riama Film Prod., ASR. (Italian).
STANLEY KRAMER, *Judgment At Nuremberg.*
ROBERT ROSSEN, *The Hustler.*
J. LEE THOMPSON, *The Guns Of Navarone.*

WRITING (O-558)

(Best Story and Screenplay written directly for the screen)

SPLENDOR IN THE GRASS. William Inge.
BALLAD OF A SOLDIER, Mosfilm Studio Prod., KYM. (Russian). Valentin Yoshov and Grigori Chukhrai.
GENERAL DELLA ROVERE, Zebra & S.N.E. Gaumont Prod., CON. (Italian). Sergio Amidei, Diego Fabbri and Indro Montanelli.
LA DOLCE VITA. Federico Fellini, Tullio Pinelli, Ennio Flaiano and Brunello Rondi.
LOVER COME BACK, U-The 7 Pictures Corp., Nob Hill Prods., Inc., Arwin Prods., Inc., UI. Stanley Shapiro and Paul Henning.

(Best Screenplay based on material from another medium)

JUDGMENT AT NUREMBERG. Abby Mann.

BREAKFAST AT TIFFANY'S. George Axelrod.
THE GUNS OF NAVARONE. Carl Foreman.
THE HUSTLER. Sidney Carroll and Robert Rossen.
WEST SIDE STORY. Ernest Lehman.

CINEMATOGRAPHY (O-559)
(Black-and-White)
THE HUSTLER. Eugen Shuftan.
THE ABSENT MINDED PROFESSOR, Walt Disney Prods., BV. Edward Colman.
THE CHILDREN'S HOUR. Franz F. Planer.
JUDGMENT AT NUREMBERG. Ernest Laszlo.
ONE, TWO, THREE, Mirisch Co, Inc. in association with Pyramid Prods., A. G., UA. Daniel L. Fapp.
(Color)
WEST SIDE STORY. Daniel L. Fapp.
FANNY. Jack Cardiff.
FLOWER DRUM SONG, U-Ross Hunter Prod. in association with Joseph Fields, U. Russell Metty.
A MAJORITY OF ONE, WB. Harry Stradling, Sr.
ONE-EYED JACKS, Pennebaker Prod., PAR. Charles Lang, Jr.

COSTUME DESIGN (O-560)
(Black-and-White)
LA DOLCE VITA. Piero Gherardi.
THE CHILDREN'S HOUR. Dorothy Jeakins.
CLAUDELLE INGLISH, WB. Howard Shoup.
JUDGMENT AT NUREMBERG. Jean Louis.
YOJIMBO, TOH. & Kurosawa Prod., Toho Co, Ltd. (Japanese). Yoshiro Muraki.
(Color)
WEST SIDE STORY. Irene Sharaff.
BABES IN TOYLAND, Walt Disney Prods., BV. Bill Thomas.
BACK STREET, U-Ross Hunter Prods., Inc.-Carrollton, Inc., U. Jean Louis.
FLOWER DRUM SONG. Irene Sharaff.
POCKETFUL OF MIRACLES. Edith Head and Walter Plunkett.

ART DIRECTION - SET DECORATION (O-561)
(Black-and-White)
THE HUSTLER. Harry Horner. Set Decoration: Gene Callahan.
THE ABSENT MINDED PROFESSOR. Carroll Clark. Set Decoration: Emile Kuri and Hal Gausman.
THE CHILDREN'S HOUR. Fernando Carrere. Set Decoration: Edward G. Boyle.
JUDGMENT AT NUREMBERG. Rudolph Sternad. Set Decoration: George Milo.
LA DOLCE VITA. Piero Gherardi.
(Color)
WEST SIDE STORY. Boris Leven. Set Decoration: Victor A. Gangelin.
BREAKFAST AT TIFFANY'S. Hal Pereira and Roland Anderson. Set Decoration: Sam Comer and Ray Moyer.
EL CID, Samuel Bronston Prod., in association with Dear Film Prod., AA. Veniero Colasanti and John Moore.
FLOWER DRUM SONG. Alexander Golitzen and Joseph Wright. Set Decoration: Howard Bristol.
SUMMER AND SMOKE. Hal Pereira and Walter Tyler. Set Decoration: Sam Comer and Arthur Krams.

FILM EDITING (O-562)
WEST SIDE STORY. Thomas Stanford.
FANNY. William H. Reynolds.
THE GUNS OF NAVARONE. Alan Osbiston.
JUDGMENT AT NUREMBERG. Frederic Knudtson.
THE PARENT TRAP, Walt Disney Prods., BV. Philip W. Anderson.

FOREIGN LANGUAGE FILM (O-563)
THROUGH A GLASS DARKLY, A. B. Svensk Filmindustri (Sweden).
HARRY AND THE BUTLER, Bent Christensen Production (Denmark).
IMMORTAL LOVE, Shochiku Co., Ltd. (Japan).

THE IMPORTANT MAN, Peliculas Rodriguez, S.A. (Mexico).
PLACIDO, Jet Films (Spain).

MUSIC - SCORING (O-564)
(Scoring of a Dramatic or Comedy Picture)
BREAKFAST AT TIFFANY'S. Henry Mancini.
EL CID. Miklos Rozsa.
FANNY. Morris Stoloff and Harry Sukman.
THE GUNS OF NAVARONE. Dimitri Tiomkin.
SUMMER AND SMOKE. Elmer Bernstein.
(Scoring of a Musical Picture)
WEST SIDE STORY. Saul Chaplin, Johnny Green, Sid Ramin and Irwin Kostal.
BABES IN TOYLAND. George Bruns.
FLOWER DRUM SONG. Alfred Newman and Ken Darby.
KHOVANSHCHINA, Mosfilm Studios, ARK (Russian). Dimitri Shostakovich.
PARIS BLUES, Pennebaker, Inc., UA. Duke Ellington.

MUSIC - BEST SONG (O-565)
MOON RIVER, Breakfast At Tiffany's. Music, Henry Mancini. Lyrics, Johnny Mercer.
BACHELOR IN PARADISE, *Bachelor In Paradise,* Ted Richmond Prod., MGM. Music, Henry Mancini. Lyrics, Mack David.
LOVE THEME FROM EL CID (The Falcon And The Dove), *El Cid.* Music, Miklos Rozsa. Lyrics, Paul Francis Webster.
POCKETFUL OF MIRACLES, *Pocketful Of Miracles.* Music, James Van Heusen. Lyrics, Sammy Cahn.
TOWN WITHOUT PITY, *Town Without Pity,* Mirisch Co in association with Gloria Films, UA. Music, Dimitri Tiomkin. Lyrics, Ned Washington.

SOUND (O-566)
WEST SIDE STORY, Todd-AO Sound Department, Fred Hynes, Sound Director; and Samuel Goldwyn Studio Sound Department, Gordon E. Sawyer, Sound Director.
THE CHILDREN'S HOUR, Samuel Goldwyn Studio Sound Department. Gordon E. Sawyer, Sound Director.
FLOWER DRUM SONG, Revue Studio Sound Department. Waldon O. Watson, Sound Director.
THE GUNS OF NAVARONE, Shepperton Studio Sound Department. John Cox, Sound Director.
THE PARENT TRAP, Walt Disney Studio Sound Department. Robert O. Cook, Sound Director.

SHORT FILMS (O-567)
(Cartoons)
ERSATZ (The Substitute), Zagreb Film, HLI.
AQUAMANIA, Walt Disney Prods., BV. Walt Disney, Prod.
BEEP PREPARED, WB. Chuck Jones, Prod.
NELLY'S FOLLY, WB. Chuck Jones, Prod.
PIED PIPER OF GUADALUPE, WB. Friz Freleng, Prod.
(Live Action Subjects)
SEAWARDS THE GREAT SHIPS, Templar Film Studios, SCH.
BALLON VOLE (Play Ball!), Cine-Documents, KGY.
THE FACE OF JESUS, Dr. John D. Jennings, Harry Stern, Inc. Dr. John D. Jennings, Prod.
ROOFTOPS OF NEW YORK, McCarty-Rush Prod. in association with Robert Gaffney, COL.
VERY NICE, VERY NICE, NFC, KGY.

DOCUMENTARY (O-568)
(Short Subjects)
PROJECT HOPE, MacManus, John & Adams, Inc., Ex-Cell-O Corp. A Klaeger Film Production. Frank P. Bibas, Prod.
BREAKING THE LANGUAGE BARRIER, United States Air Force.
CRADLE OF GENIUS, Plough Prods., An Irving M. Lesser Film Presentation (Irish). Jim O'Connor and Tom Hayes, Prods.
KAHL, Dido-Film-GmbH., AEG-Filmdienst (German).
L'UOMO IN GRIGIO (The Man In Gray), (Italian). Benedetto Benedetti, Prod.

(Features)

LE CIEL ET LA BOUE (Sky Above And Mud Beneath), Ardennes Films and Michael Arthur Film Prods., RNK. (French). Arthur Cohn and Rene Lafuite, Prods.
LA GRANDE OLIMPIADE (Olympic Games 1960), dell Istituto Nazionale Luce, Comitato Organizzatore Del Giochi Della XVII Olimpiade. CNZ (Italian).

SPECIAL EFFECTS (O-569)

THE GUNS OF NAVARONE. Visual: Bill Warrington. Audible: Vivian C. Greenham.
THE ABSENT MINDED PROFESSOR. Visual: Robert A. Mattey and Eustace Lycett.

HONORARY AND OTHER (O-570)

(Irving G. Thalberg Memorial Award)

Stanley Kramer

(Jean Hersholt Humanitarian Award)

George Seaton

(Other)

WILLIAM L. HENDRICKS for his outstanding patriotic service in the conception, writing and production of the Marine Corps film, A Force In Readiness, which has brought honor to the Academy and the motion picture industry.
FRED L. METZLER for his dedication and outstanding service to the Academy of Motion Picture Arts and Sciences.
JEROME ROBBINS for his brilliant achievements in the art of choreography on film.

SCIENTIFIC OR TECHNICAL (O-571)

(Class II)

SYLVANIA ELECTRIC PRODUCTS, INC., for the development of a hand held high-power photographic lighting unit known as the Sun Gun Professional.
JAMES DALE, S. WILSON, H. E. RICE, JOHN RUDE, LAURIE ATKIN, WADSWORTH E. POHL, H. PEASGOOD and TECHNICOLOR CORP. for a process of automatic selective printing.
20TH CENTURY-FOX RESEARCH DEPARTMENT, under the direction of E. I. SPONABLE and HERBERT E. BRAGG, and DELUXE LABORATORIES, INC., with the assistance of F. D. LESLIE, R. D. WHITMORE, A. A. ALDEN, ENDEL POOL and JAMES B. GORDON for a system of decompressing and recomposing CinemaScope pictures for conventional aspect ratios.

(Class III)

HURLETRON, INC., ELECTRIC EYE EQUIPMENT DIVISION, for an automatic light changing system for motion picture printers.
WADSWORTH E. POHL and TECHNICOLOR CORP. for an integrated sound and picture transfer process.

1962

BEST PICTURE (O-572)

LAWRENCE OF ARABIA, Horizon Pictures (G.B.), Ltd.-Sam Spiegel-David Lean Prod., COL. Sam Spiegel, Prod.
THE LONGEST DAY, Darryl F. Zanuck Prod., FOX. Darryl F. Zanuck, Prod.
Meredith Willson's THE MUSIC MAN, WB. Morton Da Costa, Prod.
MUTINY ON THE BOUNTY, Arcola Prod., MGM. Aaron Rosenberg, Prod.
TO KILL A MOCKINGBIRD, U-Pakula-Mulligan-Brentwood Prod., U. Alan J. Pakula, Prod.

ACTOR (O-573)

GREGORY PECK, To Kill A Mockingbird.
BURT LANCASTER, *Bird Man Of Alcatraz*, Harold Hecht Prod., UA.
JACK LEMMON, *Days Of Wine And Roses*, Martin Manulis-Jalem Prod., WB.
MARCELLO MASTROIANNI, *Divorce - Italian Style*, Lux-Vides-Galatea

Film Prod., EBP.
PETER O'TOOLE, *Lawrence Of Arabia.*

ACTRESS (O-574)

ANNE BANCROFT, The Miracle Worker, Playfilms Prod., UA.
BETTE DAVIS, *What Ever Happened To Baby Jane?*, Seven Arts-Associates & Aldrich Co. Prod., WB.
KATHARINE HEPBURN, *Long Day's Journey Into Night*, Ely Landau Prods., EBP.
GERALDINE PAGE, *Sweet Bird Of Youth*, Roxbury Prod., MGM.
LEE REMICK, *Days Of Wine And Roses.*

SUPPORTING ACTOR (O-575)

ED BEGLEY, Sweet Bird Of Youth.
VICTOR BUONO, *What Ever Happened To Baby Jane?*
TELLY SAVALAS, *Bird Man Of Alcatraz.*
OMAR SHARIF, *Lawrence Of Arabia.*
TERENCE STAMP, *Billy Budd*, Harvest Prods., AA.

SUPPORTING ACTRESS (O-576)

PATTY DUKE, The Miracle Worker.
MARY BADHAM, *To Kill A Mockingbird.*
SHIRLEY KNIGHT, *Sweet Bird Of Youth.*
ANGELA LANSBURY, *The Manchurian Candidate*, M. C. Prod., UA.
THELMA RITTER, *Bird Man Of Alcatraz.*

DIRECTING (O-577)

DAVID LEAN, Lawrence Of Arabia.
PIETRO GERMI, *Divorce - Italian Style.*
ROBERT MULLIGAN, *To Kill A Mockingbird.*
ARTHUR PENN, *The Miracle Worker.*
FRANK PERRY, *David And Lisa*, Heller-Perry Prods., CON.

WRITING (O-578)

(Best Story and Screenplay written directly for the screen)

DIVORCE - ITALIAN STYLE. Ennio de Concini, Alfredo Giannetti and Pietro Germi.
FREUD, U-John Huston Prod., U. Story by Charles Kaufman. Screenplay by Charles Kaufman and Wolfgang Reinhardt.
LAST YEAR AT MARIENBAD, Preceitel-Terra Film Prod., ASR. Alain Robbe-Grillet.
THAT TOUCH OF MINK, U-Granley-Arwin-Nob Hill Prod., U. Stanley Shapiro and Nate Monaster.
THROUGH A GLASS DARKLY. Ingmar Bergman.

(Best Screenplay based on material from another medium)

TO KILL A MOCKINGBIRD. Horton Foote.
DAVID AND LISA. Eleanor Perry.
LAWRENCE OF ARABIA. Robert Bolt.
LOLITA, Seven Arts Prods., MGM. Vladimir Nabokov.
THE MIRACLE WORKER. William Gibson.

CINEMATOGRAPHY (O-579)

(Black-and-White)

THE LONGEST DAY. Jean Bourgoin and Walter Wottitz.
BIRD MAN OF ALCATRAZ. Burnett Guffey.
TO KILL A MOCKINGBIRD. Russell Harlan.
TWO FOR THE SEESAW, Mirisch-Argyle-Talbot Prod. in association with Seven Arts Prods., UA. Ted McCord.
WHAT EVER HAPPENED TO BABY JANE? Ernest Haller.

(Color)

LAWRENCE OF ARABIA. Fred A. Young.
GYPSY, WB. Harry Stradling, Sr.
HATARI!, Malabar Prods., PAR. Russell Harlan.
MUTINY ON THE BOUNTY, Arcola Prod., MGM. Robert L. Surtees.
THE WONDERFUL WORLD OF THE BROTHERS GRIMM, MGM & CRC. Paul C. Vogel.

COSTUME DESIGN (O-580)

(Black-and-White)

WHAT EVER HAPPENED TO BABY JANE? Norma Koch.
DAYS OF WINE AND ROSES. Don Feld.
THE MAN WHO SHOT LIBERTY VALANCE, John Ford Prod., PAR. Edith Head.
THE MIRACLE WORKER. Ruth Morley.
PHAEDRA, Jules Dassin-Melinafilm Prod., LOP. Denny Vachlioti.

(Color)

THE WONDERFUL WORLD OF THE BROTHERS GRIMM. Mary Wills.
BON VOYAGE, Walt Disney Prod., BV. Bill Thomas.
GYPSY. Orry-Kelly.
Meredith Willson's THE MUSIC MAN. Dorothy Jeakins.
MY GEISHA, Sachiko Prod., PAR. Edith Head.

ART DIRECTION - SET DECORATION (O-581)

(Black-and-White)

TO KILL A MOCKINGBIRD. Alexander Golitzen and Henry Bumstead. Set Decoration: Oliver Emert.
DAYS OF WINE AND ROSES. Joseph Wright. Set Decoration: George James Hopkins.
THE LONGEST DAY. Ted Haworth, Leon Barsacq and Vincent Korda. Set Decoration: Gabriel Bechir.
PERIOD OF ADJUSTMENT, Marten Prod., MGM. George W. Davis and Edward Carfagno. Set Decoration: Henry Grace and Dick Pefferle.
THE PIGEON THAT TOOK ROME, Llenroc Prods., PAR, Hal Pereira and Roland Anderson. Set Decoration: Sam Comer and Frank R. McKelvy.

(Color)

LAWRENCE OF ARABIA. John Box and John Stoll. Set Decoration: Dario Simoni.
Meredith Willson's THE MUSIC MAN. Paul Groesse. Set Decoration: George James Hopkins.
MUTINY ON THE BOUNTY. George W. Davis and J. McMillan Johnson. Set Decoration: Henry Grace and Hugh Hunt.
THAT TOUCH OF MINK. Alexander Golitzen and Robert Clatworthy. Set Decoration: George Milo.
THE WONDERFUL WORLD OF THE BROTHERS GRIMM. George W. Davis and Edward Carfagno. Set Decoration: Henry Grace and Dick Pefferle.

FILM EDITING (O-582)

LAWRENCE OF ARABIA. Anne Coates.
THE LONGEST DAY. Samuel E. Beetley.
THE MANCHURIAN CANDIDATE. Ferris Webster.
Meredith Willson's THE MUSIC MAN. William Ziegler.
MUTINY ON THE BOUNTY. John McSweeney, Jr.

FOREIGN LANGUAGE FILM (O-583)

SUNDAYS AND CYBELE, Terra-Fides-Orsay-Trocadero Films (France.)
ELECTRA, A Michael Cacoyannis Production (Greece).
THE FOUR DAYS OF NAPLES, Titanus-Metro (Italy).
KEEPER OF PROMISES (The Given Word), Cinedistri (Brazil).
TLAYUCAN, Producciones Matouk, S.A. (Mexico).

MUSIC - SCORING (O-584)

(Music Score-substantially original)

LAWRENCE OF ARABIA. Maurice Jarre.
FREUD. Jerry Goldsmith.
MUTINY ON THE BOUNTY. Bronislau Kaper.
TARAS BULBA, Harold Hecht Prod., UA. Franz Waxman.
TO KILL A MOCKINGBIRD. Elmer Bernstein.

(Scoring of Music-adaptation or treatment)

Meredith Willson's THE MUSIC MAN. Ray Heindorf.
Billy Rose's JUMBO, Euterpe-Arwin Prod., MGM. George Stoll.
GIGOT, Seven Arts Prods., FOX. Michel Magne.
GYPSY. Frank Perkins.
THE WONDERFUL WORLD OF THE BROTHERS GRIMM. Leigh Harline.

MUSIC - BEST SONG (O-585)

DAYS OF WINE AND ROSES, Days Of Wine And Roses. Music, Henry Mancini. Lyrics, Johnny Mercer.
LOVE SONG FROM MUTINY ON THE BOUNTY (Follow Me), *Mutiny On The Bounty*. Music, Bronislau Kaper. Lyrics, Paul Francis Webster.
SONG FROM TWO FOR THE SEESAW (Second Chance), *Two For The Seesaw*. Music, Andre Previn. Lyrics, Dory Langdon.
TENDER IS THE NIGHT, *Tender Is The Night,* FOX. Music, Sammy Fain. Lyrics, Paul Francis Webster.
WALK ON THE WILD SIDE, *Walk On The Wild Side,* Famous Artists Prods., COL. Music, Elmer Bernstein. Lyrics, Mack David.

SOUND (O-586)

LAWRENCE OF ARABIA, Shepperton Studio Sound Department. John Cox, Sound Director.
BON VOYAGE, Walt Disney Studio Sound Department. Robert O. Cook, Sound Director.
Meredith Willson's THE MUSIC MAN. WB Studio Sound Department. George R. Groves, Sound Director.
THAT TOUCH OF MINK, U Studio Sound Department. Waldon O. Watson, Sound Director.
WHAT EVER HAPPENED TO BABY JANE?, Glen Glenn Sound Department. Joseph Kelly, Sound Director.

SHORT FILMS (O-587)

(Cartoons)

THE HOLE, Storyboard Inc., BRA. John and Faith Hubley, Prods.
ICARUS MONTGOLFIER WRIGHT, Format Films, UA. Jules Engel, Prod.
NOW HEAR THIS, WB.
SELF DEFENSE---FOR COWARDS, Rembrandt Films, FRP. William L. Snyder, Prod.
SYMPOSIUM ON POPULAR SONGS, Walt Disney Prods., BV. Walt Disney, Prod.

(Live Action Subjects)

HEUREUX ANNIVERSAIRE (Happy Anniversary), CAPAC Prods., ATL. Pierre Etaix and J. C. Carriere, Prods.
BIG CITY BLUES, MFR. Martina and Charles Huguenot van der Linden, Prods.
THE CADILLAC, United Prods Releasing Org. Robert Clouse, Prod.
THE CLIFF DWELLERS (formerly titled *One Plus One*), Group II Film Prods., SCH. Hayward Anderson, Prod.
PAN, MFR. Herman van der horst, Prod.

DOCUMENTARY (O-588)

(Short Subjects)

DYLAN THOMAS, TWW Ltd., JAN (Welsh). Jack Howells, Prod.
THE JOHN GLENN STORY, Department of the Navy, WB. William L. Hendricks, Prod.
THE ROAD TO THE WALL, CBS Films, Inc., Department of Defense. Robert Saudek, Prod.

(Features)

BLACK FOX, Image Prods., Inc., Heritage Films, Inc. Louis Clyde Stoumen, Prod.
ALVORADA (Brazil's Changing Face), MW Filmproduktion (German). Hugo Niebeling, Prod.

SPECIAL EFFECTS (O-589)

THE LONGEST DAY. Visual: Robert MacDonald. Audible: Jacques Maumont.
MUTINY ON THE BOUNTY. Visual: A. Arnold Gillespie. Audible: Milo Lory.

HONORARY AND OTHER (O-590)

(Jean Hersholt Humanitarian Award)

Steve Broidy

SCIENTIFIC OR TECHNICAL (O-591)

(Class II)

RALPH CHAPMAN for the design and development of an advanced motion picture camera crane.
ALBERT S. PRATT, JAMES L. WASSELL and HANS C. WOHLRAB of the Professional Division, Bell & Howell Co., for the design and development of a new and improved automatic motion picture additive color printer.
NORTH AMERICAN PHILIPS CO., INC., for the design and engineering of the Norelco Universal 70/35mm motion picture projector.
CHARLES E. SUTTER, WILLIAM BRYSON SMITH and LOUIS C. KENNELL of Paramount Pictures Corp. for the engineering and application to motion picture production of a new system of electric power distribution.

(Class III)

ELECTRO-VOICE, INC., for a highly directional dynamic line microphone.
LOUIS G. MACKENZIE for a selective sound effects repeater.

1963

BEST PICTURE (O-592)

TOM JONES, Woodfall Prod., UA-Lopert Pictures. Tony Richardson, Prod.
AMERICA AMERICA, Athena Enterprises Prod., WB. Elia Kazan, Prod.
CLEOPATRA, FOX Ltd.-MCL Films S.A.-WALWA Films S.A. Prod., FOX. Walter Wanger, Prod.
HOW THE WEST WAS WON, MGM & CRC. Bernard Smith, Prod.
LILIES OF THE FIELD, Rainbow Prod., UA. Ralph Nelson, Prod.

ACTOR (O-593)

SIDNEY POITIER, Lilies Of The Field.
ALBERT FINNEY, *Tom Jones.*
RICHARD HARRIS, *This Sporting Life,* Julian Wintle-Leslie Parkyn Prod., WRS-CON.
REX HARRISON, *Cleopatra.*
PAUL NEWMAN, *Hud,* Salem-Dover Prod., PAR.

ACTRESS (O-594)

PATRICIA NEAL, Hud.
LESLIE CARON, *The L-Shaped Room,* Romulus Prods., Ltd., COL.
SHIRLEY MACLAINE, *Irma La Douce,* Mirisch-Phalanx Prod., UA.
RACHEL ROBERTS, *This Sporting Life.*
NATALIE WOOD, *Love With The Proper Stranger,* Boardwalk-Rona Prod., PAR.

SUPPORTING ACTOR (O-595)

MELVYN DOUGLAS, Hud.
NICK ADAMS, *Twilight Of Honor,* Perlberg-Seaton Prod., MGM.
BOBBY DARIN, *Captain Newman, M.D.,* U-Brentwood-Reynard Prod., U.
HUGH GRIFFITH, *Tom Jones.*
JOHN HUSTON, *The Cardinal,* Gamma Prod., COL.

SUPPORTING ACTRESS (O-596)

MARGARET RUTHERFORD, The V.I.P.s, MGM.
DIANE CILENTO, *Tom Jones.*
DAME EDITH EVANS, *Tom Jones.*
JOYCE REDMAN, *Tom Jones.*
LILIA SKALA, *Lilies Of The Field.*

DIRECTING (O-597)

TONY RICHARDSON, Tom Jones.
FEDERICO FELLINI, *Federico Fellini's 8 1/2,* Cineriz Prod., EBP.
ELIA KAZAN, *America America.*
OTTO PREMINGER, *The Cardinal.*
MARTIN RITT, *Hud.*

WRITING (O-598)

(Best Story and Screenplay written directly for the screen)

HOW THE WEST WAS WON. James R. Webb.
AMERICA AMERICA. Elia Kazan.
FEDERICO FELLINI'S 8 1/2. Federico Fellini, Ennio Flaiano, Tullio Pinelli and Brunello Rondi.
THE FOUR DAYS OF NAPLES, Titanus Prod., MGM. Story by Pasquale Feste Campanile, Massimo Franciosa, Nanni Loy and Vasco Pratolini. Screenplay by Carlo Bernari, Pasquale Festa Campanile, Massimo Franciosa and Nanni Loy.
LOVE WITH THE PROPER STRANGER. Arnold Schulman.

(Best Screenplay based on material from another medium)

TOM JONES. John Osborne.
CAPTAIN NEWMAN, M.D. Richard L. Breen, Phoebe and Henry Ephron.
HUD. Irving Ravetch and Harriet Frank, Jr.
LILIES OF THE FIELD. James Poe.
SUNDAYS AND CYBELE, Terra-Fides-Orsay-Films Trocadero Prods., COL. Serge Bourguignon and Antoine Tudal.

CINEMATOGRAPHY (O-599)

(Black-and-White)

HUD. James Wong Howe.
THE BALCONY, Walter Reade-Sterling-Allen-Hodgdon Prod., George Folsey.
THE CARETAKERS, Hall Bartlett Prod., UA. Lucien Ballard.
LILIES OF THE FIELD. Ernest Haller.
LOVE WITH THE PROPER STRANGER. Milton Krasner.

(Color)

CLEOPATRA. Leon Shamroy.
THE CARDINAL. Leon Shamroy.
HOW THE WEST WAS WON. William H. Daniels, Milton Krasner, Charles Lang, Jr. and Joseph LaShelle.
IRMA LA DOUCE. Joseph LaShelle.
IT'S A MAD, MAD, MAD, MAD WORLD, Casey Prod., UA. Ernest Laszlo.

COSTUME DESIGN (O-600)

(Black-and-White)

FEDERICO FELLINI'S 8 1/2. Piero Gherardi.
LOVE WITH THE PROPER STRANGER. Edith Head.
THE STRIPPER, Jerry Wald Prods., FOX. Travilla.
TOYS IN THE ATTIC, Mirisch-Claude Prod., UA. Bill Thomas.
WIVES AND LOVERS, Hal Wallis Prod., PAR. Edith Head.

(Color)

CLEOPATRA. Irene Sharaff, Vittorio Nino Novarese and Renie.
THE CARDINAL. Donald Brooks.
HOW THE WEST WAS WON. Walter Plunkett.
THE LEOPARD, Titanus Prod., FOX. Piero Tosi.
A NEW KIND OF LOVE, Llenroc Prods., PAR. Edith Head.

ART DIRECTION - SET DECORATION (O-601)

(Black-and-White)

AMERICA AMERICA. Gene Callahan.
FEDERICO FELLINI'S 8 1/2. Piero Gherardi.
HUD. Hal Pereira and Tambi Larsen. Set Decoration: Sam Comer and Robert Benton.
LOVE WITH THE PROPER STRANGER. Hal Pereira and Roland Anderson. Set Decoration: Sam Comer and Grace Gregory.
TWILIGHT OF HONOR. George W. Davis and Paul Groesse. Set Decoration: Henry Grace and Hugh Hunt.

(Color)

CLEOPATRA. John DeCuir, Jack Martin Smith, Hilyard Brown, Herman Blumenthal, Elven Webb, Maurice Pelling and Boris Juraga. Set Decoration: Walter M. Scott, Paul S. Fox and Ray Moyer.
THE CARDINAL. Lyle Wheeler. Set Decoration: Gene Callahan.
COME BLOW YOUR HORN, Essex-Tandem Enterprises Prod., PAR. Hal Pereira and Roland Anderson. Set Decoration: Sam Comer and

James Payne.
HOW THE WEST WAS WON. George W. Davis, William Ferrari and Addison Hehr. Set Decoration: Henry Grace, Don Greenwood, Jr. and Jack Mills.
TOM JONES. Ralph Brinton, Ted Marshall and Jocelyn Herbert. Set Decoration: Josie MacAvin.

FILM EDITING (O-602)

HOW THE WEST WAS WON. Harold F. Kress.
THE CARDINAL. Louis R. Loeffler.
CLEOPATRA. Dorothy Spencer.
THE GREAT ESCAPE, Mirisch-Alpha Picture Prod., UA. Ferris Webster.
IT'S A MAD, MAD, MAD, MAD WORLD. Frederic Knudtson, Robert C. Jones and Gene Fowler, Jr.

FOREIGN LANGUAGE FILM (O-603)

FEDERICO FELLINI'S 8 1/2.
KNIFE IN THE WATER, A Kamera Unit of Film Polski Production (Poland).
LOS TARANTOS, Tecisa-Films R.B. (Spain).
THE RED LANTERNS, Th. Damaskinos & V. Michaelides A.E. (Greece).
TWIN SISTERS OF KYOTO, Shochiku Co., Ltd. (Japan).

MUSIC - SCORING (O-604)

(Music Score-substantially original)

TOM JONES. John Addison.
CLEOPATRA. Alex North.
55 DAYS AT PEKING, Samuel Bronston Prod., AA. Dimitri Tiomkin.
HOW THE WEST WAS WON. Alfred Newman and Ken Darby.
IT'S A MAD, MAD, MAD, MAD WORLD. Ernest Gold.

(Scoring of Music-adaptation or treatment)

IRMA LA DOUCE. Andre Previn.
BYE BYE BIRDIE, Kohlmar-Sidney Prod., COL. John Green.
A NEW KIND OF LOVE. Leith Stevens.
SUNDAYS AND CYBELE. Maurice Jarre.
THE SWORD IN THE STONE, Walt Disney Prods., BV. George Bruns.

MUSIC - BEST SONG (O-605)

CALL ME IRRESPONSIBLE, Papa's Delicate Condition, Amro Prods., PAR. Music, James Van Heusen. Lyrics, Sammy Cahn.
CHARADE, *Charade*, U-Stanley Donen Prod., U. Music, Henry Mancini. Lyrics, Johnny Mercer.
IT'S A MAD, MAD, MAD, MAD WORLD, *It's A Mad, Mad, Mad, Mad World.* Music, Ernest Gold. Lyrics, Mack David.
MORE, *Mondo Cane*, Cineriz Prod., TIM. Music, Riz Ortolani and Nino Oliviero. Lyrics, Norman Newell.
SO LITTLE TIME, *55 Days At Peking.* Music, Dimitri Tiomkin. Lyrics, Paul Francis Webster.

SOUND (O-606)

HOW THE WEST WAS WON, MGM Studio Sound Department. Franklin E. Milton, Sound Director.
BYE BYE BIRDIE, COL Studio Sound Department. Charles Rice, Sound Director.
CAPTAIN NEWMAN, M.D., U Studio Sound Department. Waldon O. Watson, Sound Director.
CLEOPATRA, FOX Studio Sound Department, James P. Corcoran, Sound Director; and Todd-AO Sound Department, Fred Hynes, Sound Director.
IT'S A MAD, MAD, MAD, MAD WORLD, Samuel Goldwyn Studio Sound Department. Gordon E. Sawyer, Sound Director.

SHORT FILMS (O-607)

(Cartoons)

THE CRITIC, Pintoff-Crossbow Prods., COL. Ernest Pintoff, Prod.
AUTOMANIA 2000, Halas and Batchelor Prod., PC. John Halas, Prod.
THE GAME (Igra), Zagreb Film, RBF. Dusan Vukotic, Prod.
MY FINANCIAL CAREER, NFC, WSC Distributing. Colin Low and Tom Daly, Prods.

PIANISSIMO, Cinema 16. Carmen D'Avino, Prod.

(Live Action Subjects)

AN OCCURRENCE AT OWL CREEK BRIDGE, Films Du Centaure-Filmartic, Cappagariff-Janus Films. Paul de Roubaix and Marcel Ichac, Prods.
THE CONCERT, James A. King Corp., George K. Arthur-Go Pictures. Ezra Baker, Prod.
HOME-MADE CAR, BP (North America) Ltd., SCH. James Hill, Prod.
SIX-SIDED TRIANGLE, Milesian Film Prod. Ltd., LIO. Christopher Miles, Prod.
THAT'S ME, Stuart Prods., PC. Walker Stuart, Prod.

DOCUMENTARY (O-608)

(Short Subjects)

CHAGALL, Auerbach Film Enterprises, Ltd.-Flag Films. Simon Schiffrin, Prod.
THE FIVE CITIES OF JUNE, United States Information Agency. George Stevens, Jr., Prod.
THE SPIRIT OF AMERICA, Spotlite News. Algernon G. Walker, Prod.
THIRTY MILLION LETTERS, British Transport Films. Edgar Anstey, Prod.
TO LIVE AGAIN, Wilding Inc. Mel London, Prod.

(Features)

ROBERT FROST: A LOVER'S QUARREL WITH THE WORLD, WGBH Educational Foundation. Robert Hughes, Prod.
LE MAILLON ET LA CHAINE (The Link And The Chain), Films Du Centaure-Filmartic. Paul de Roubaix, Prod.
THE YANKS ARE COMING, David L. Wolper Prods., Marshall Flaum, Prod.

VISUAL EFFECTS (O-609)

CLEOPATRA. Emil Kosa, Jr.
THE BIRDS, Alfred J. Hitchcock Prod., U. Ub Iwerks.

SOUND EFFECTS (O-610)

IT'S A MAD, MAD, MAD, MAD WORLD. Walter G. Elliott.
A GATHERING OF EAGLES, U. Robert L. Bratton.

HONORARY AND OTHER (O-611)

(Irving G. Thalberg Memorial Award)

Sam Spiegel

SCIENTIFIC OR TECHNICAL (O-612)

(Class III)

DOUGLAS G. SHEARER and A. ARNOLD GILLESPIE of MGM Studios for the engineering of an improved Background Process Projection System.

1964

BEST PICTURE (O-613)

MY FAIR LADY, WB. Jack L. Warner, Prod.
BECKET, Hal Wallis Prod., PAR. Hal B. Wallis, Prod.
DR. STRANGELOVE OR: HOW I LEARNED TO STOP WORRYING AND LOVE THE BOMB, Hawk Films, Ltd. Prod., COL. Stanley Kubrick, Prod.
MARY POPPINS, Walt Disney Prods. BV. Walt Disney and Bill Walsh, Prods.
ZORBA THE GREEK, Rochley, Ltd. Prod., Int'l Classics. Michael Cacoyannis, Prod.

ACTOR (O-614)

REX HARRISON, My Fair Lady.
RICHARD BURTON, *Becket.*
PETER O'TOOLE, *Becket.*
ANTHONY QUINN, *Zorba The Greek.*
PETER SELLERS, *Dr. Strangelove Or: How I Learned To Stop Worrying And Love The Bomb.*

ACTRESS (O-615)

JULIE ANDREWS, Mary Poppins.
ANNE BANCROFT, *The Pumpkin Eater,* Romulus Films, Ltd. Prod., RYI.
SOPHIA LOREN, *Marriage Italian Style,* Champion-Concordia Prod., EBP.
DEBBIE REYNOLDS, *The Unsinkable Molly Brown,* Marten Prod., MGM.
KIM STANLEY, *Seance On A Wet Afternoon,* Richard Attenborough-Bryan Forbes Prod., ART.

SUPPORTING ACTOR (O-616)

PETER USTINOV, Topkapi, Filmways Prod., UA.
JOHN GIELGUD, *Becket.*
STANLEY HOLLOWAY, *My Fair Lady.*
EDMOND O'BRIEN, *Seven Days In May,* Joel Prods., PAR.
LEE TRACY, *The Best Man,* Millar-Turman Prod., UA.

SUPPORTING ACTRESS (O-617)

LILA KEDROVA, Zorba The Greek.
GLADYS COOPER, *My Fair Lady.*
DAME EDITH EVANS, *The Chalk Garden,* Quota Rentals, Ltd.-Ross Hunter Prod., U.
GRAYSON HALL, *The Night Of The Iguana,* Seven Arts Prod., MGM.
AGNES MOOREHEAD, *Hush. . .Hush, Sweet Charlotte,* Associates & Aldrich Co. Prod., FOX.

DIRECTING (O-618)

GEORGE CUKOR, My Fair Lady.
MICHAEL CACOYANNIS, *Zorba The Greek.*
PETER GLENVILLE, *Becket.*
STANLEY KUBRICK, *Dr. Stangelove Or: How I Learned To Stop Worrying And Love The Bomb.*
ROBERT STEVENSON, *Mary Poppins.*

WRITING (O-619)

(Best Story and Screenplay written directly for the screen)

FATHER GOOSE, U-Granox Prod., U. Story by S. H. Barnett. Screenplay by Peter Stone and Frank Tarloff.
A HARD DAY'S NIGHT, Walter Shenson Prod., UA. Alun Owen.
ONE POTATO, TWO POTATO, Bawalco Picture Prod., C5. Story by Orville H. Hampton. Screenplay by Raphael Hayes and Orville H. Hampton.
THE ORGANIZER, Lux-Vides-Mediterranee Cinema Prod., WRC. Age, Scarpelli and Mario Monicelli.
THAT MAN FROM RIO, Ariane-Les Artistes Prod., LOP. Jean-Paul Rappeneau, Ariane Mnouchkine, Daniel Boulanger and Philippe De Broca.

(Best Screenplay based on material from another medium)

BECKET. Edward Anhalt.
DR. STRANGELOVE OR: HOW I LEARNED TO STOP WORRYING AND LOVE THE BOMB. Stanley Kubrick, Peter George and Terry Southern.
MARY POPPINS. Bill Walsh and Don DaGradi.
MY FAIR LADY. Alan Jay Lerner.
ZORBA THE GREEK. Michael Cacoyannis.

CINEMATOGRAPHY (O-620)

(Black-and-White)

ZORBA THE GREEK. Walter Lassally.
THE AMERICANIZATION OF EMILY, Martin Ransohoff Prod., MGM. Philip H. Lathrop.
FATE IS THE HUNTER, Arcola Pictures Prod., FOX. Milton Krasner.
HUSH. . .HUSH, SWEET CHARLOTTE. Joseph Biroc.
THE NIGHT OF THE IGUANA. Gabriel Figueroa.

(Color)

MY FAIR LADY. Harry Stradling.
BECKET. Geoffrey Unsworth.

CHEYENNE AUTUMN, John Ford-Bernard Smith Prod., WB. William H. Clothier.
MARY POPPINS. Edward Colman.
THE UNSINKABLE MOLLY BROWN. Daniel L. Fapp.

COSTUME DESIGN (O-621)

(Black-and-White)

THE NIGHT OF THE IGUANA. Dorothy Jeakins.
A HOUSE IS NOT A HOME, Clarence Greene-Russell Rouse Prod., EBP. Edith Head.
HUSH. . .HUSH, SWEET CHARLOTTE. Norma Koch.
KISSES FOR MY PRESIDENT, Pearlayne Prod., WB. Howard Shoup.
THE VISIT, Cinecitta-Dear Film-Les Films du Siecle-P.E.C.S. Prod., FOX. Rene Hubert.

(Color)

MY FAIR LADY. Cecil Beaton.
BECKET. Margaret Furse.
MARY POPPINS. Tony Walton.
THE UNSINKABLE MOLLY BROWN. Morton Haack.
WHAT A WAY TO GO, Apjac-Orchard Prod., FOX. Edith Head and Moss Mabry.

ART DIRECTION - SET DECORATION (O-622)

(Black-and-White)

ZORBA THE GREEK. Vassilis Fotopoulos.
THE AMERICANIZATION OF EMILY. George W. Davis, Hans Peters and Elliot Scott. Set Decoration: Henry Grace and Robert R. Benton.
HUSH. . .HUSH, SWEET CHARLOTTE. William Glasgow. Set Decoration: Raphael Bretton.
THE NIGHT OF THE IGUANA. Stephen Grimes.
SEVEN DAYS IN MAY. Cary Odell. Set Decoration: Edward G. Boyle.

(Color)

MY FAIR LADY. Gene Allen and Cecil Beaton. Set Decoration: George James Hopkins.
BECKET. John Bryan and Maurice Carter. Set Decoration: Patrick McLoughlin and Robert Cartwright.
MARY POPPINS. Carroll Clark and William H. Tuntke. Set Decoration: Emile Kuri and Hal Gausman.
THE UNSINKABLE MOLLY BROWN. George W. Davis and Preston Ames. Set Decoration: Henry Grace and Hugh Hunt.
WHAT A WAY TO GO. Jack Martin Smith and Ted Haworth. Set Decoration: Walter M. Scott and Stuart A. Reiss.

FILM EDITING (O-623)

MARY POPPINS. Cotton Warburton.
BECKET. Anne Coates.
FATHER GOOSE. Ted J. Kent.
HUSH. . .HUSH, SWEET CHARLOTTE. Michael Luciano.
MY FAIR LADY. William Ziegler.

FOREIGN LANGUAGE FILM (O-624)

YESTERDAY, TODAY AND TOMORROW, A Champion-Concordia Production (Italy).
RAVEN'S END, AB Europa Film (Sweden).
SALLAH, A Sallah Film Ltd. Production (Israel).
THE UMBRELLAS OF CHERBOURG, A Parc-Madeleine-Beta Films Production (France).
WOMAN IN THE DUNES, A Teshigahara Production (Japan).

MUSIC - SCORING (O-625)

(Music Score—substantially original)

MARY POPPINS. Richard M. Sherman and Robert B. Sherman.
THE FALL OF THE ROMAN EMPIRE, Bronston-Roma Prod., PAR. Dimitri Tiomkin.
HUSH. . .HUSH, SWEET CHARLOTTE. Frank DeVol.
THE PINK PANTHER, Mirisch-G-E Prod., UA. Henry Mancini.

(Scoring of Music-adaptation or treatment)

MY FAIR LADY. Andre Previn.
A HARD DAY'S NIGHT. George Martin.
MARY POPPINS. Irwin Kostal.

ROBIN AND THE 7 HOODS, P-C Prod., WB. Nelson Riddle.
THE UNSINKABLE MOLLY BROWN. Robert Armbruster, Leo Arnaud, Jack Elliott, Jack Hayes, Calvin Jackson and Leo Shuken.

MUSIC - BEST SONG (O-626)

CHIM CHIM CHER-EE, Mary Poppins. Music and Lyrics by Richard M. Sherman & Robert B. Sherman.
DEAR HEART, *Dear Heart*, W.B.-Out-Of-Towners Prod., WB. Music, Henry Mancini. Lyrics, Jay Livingston and Ray Evans.
HUSH. . .HUSH, SWEET CHARLOTTE, *Hush. . .Hush, Sweet Charlotte*. Music, Frank DeVol. Lyrics, Mack David.
MY KIND OF TOWN, *Robin And The 7 Hoods*. Music, James Van Heusen. Lyrics, Sammy Cahn.
WHERE LOVE HAS GONE, *Where Love Has Gone*, PAR-Embassy Pictures Prod., PAR. Music, James Van Heusen. Lyrics, Sammy Cahn.

SOUND (O-627)

MY FAIR LADY, WB. Studio Sound Department. George R. Groves, Sound Director.
BECKET, Shepperton Studio Sound Department. John Cox, Sound Director.
FATHER GOOSE, U Studio Sound Department. Waldon O. Watson, Sound Director.
MARY POPPINS, Walt Disney Studio Sound Department, Robert O. Cook, Sound Director.
THE UNSINKABLE MOLLY BROWN, MGM Studio Sound Department. Franklin E. Milton, Sound Director.

SHORT FILMS (O-628)

(Cartoons)

THE PINK PHINK, Mirisch-Geoffrey Prods., UA. David H. DePatie and Friz Freleng, Prods.
CHRISTMAS CRACKER, NFC, FA.
HOW TO AVOID FRIENDSHIP, RBF. William L. Snyder, Prod.
NUDNIK #2, RBF. William L. Snyder, Prod.

(Live Action Subjects)

CASALS CONDUCTS: 1964, Thalia Films, BEC. Edward Schreiber, Prod.
HELP! MY SNOWMAN'S BURNING DOWN, Carson Davidson Prods., PC. Carson Davidson, Prod.
THE LEGEND OF JIMMY BLUE EYES, Robert Clouse Associates, Topaz Film Corp. Robert Clouse, Prod.

DOCUMENTARY (O-629)

(Short Subjects)

NINE FROM LITTLE ROCK, United States Information Agency, Guggenheim Productions.
BREAKING THE HABIT, American Cancer Society, Modern Talking Picture Service. Henry Jacobs and John Korty, Prods.
CHILDREN WITHOUT, National Education Association, Guggenheim Productions.
KENOJUAK, NFC.
140 DAYS UNDER THE WORLD, New Zealand National Film Unit, RNK (New Zealand). Geoffrey Scott and Oxley Hughan, Prods.

(Features)

Jacques-Yves Cousteau's WORLD WITHOUT SUN, Filmad-Les Requins Associes-Orsay-CEIAP, COL. Jacques-Yves Cousteau, Prod.
THE FINEST HOURS, Le Vien Films, Ltd., COL. Jack Le Vien, Prod.
FOUR DAYS IN NOVEMBER, David L. Wolper Prods., UA. Mel Stuart, Prod.
THE HUMAN DUTCH, Haanstra Filmproductie. Bert Haanstra, Prod.
OVER THERE, 1914-18, Zodiac Prods., PC. Jean Aurel, Prod.

VISUAL EFFECTS (O-630)

MARY POPPINS. Peter Ellenshaw, Hamilton Luske and Eustace Lycett.
7 FACES OF DR. LAO, Galaxy-Scarus Prod., MGM. Jim Danforth.

SOUND EFFECTS (O-631)

GOLDFINGER, Eon Prod., UA. Norman Wanstall.
THE LIVELY SET, U. Robert L. Bratton.

HONORARY AND OTHER (O-632)

(Other)

WILLIAM TUTTLE for his outstanding make-up achievement for 7 Faces Of Dr. Lao.

SCIENTIFIC OR TECHNICAL (O-633)

(Class I)

PETRO VLAHOS, WADSWORTH E. POHL and **UB IWERKS** for the conception and perfection of techniques for Color Traveling Matte Composite Cinematography.

(Class II)

SIDNEY P. SOLOW, EDWARD H. REICHARD, CARL W. HAUGE and **JOB SANDERSON** of Consolidated Film Industries for the design and development of a versatile Automatic 35mm Composite Color Printer.
PIERRE ANGENIEUX for the development of a ten-to-one Zoom Lens for cinematography.

(Class III)

MILTON FORMAN, RICHARD B. GLICKMAN and **DANIEL J. PEARLMAN** of ColorTran Industries for advancements in the design and application to motion picture photography of lighting units using quartz iodine lamps.
STEWART FILMSCREEN CORPORATION for a seamless translucent Blue Screen for Traveling Matte Color Cinematography.
ANTHONY PAGLIA and the **20TH CENTURY-FOX STUDIO MECHANICAL EFFECTS DEPARTMENT** for an improved method of producing Explosion Flash Effects for motion pictures.
EDWARD H. REICHARD and **CARL W. HAUGE** of Consolidated Film Industries for the design of a Proximity Cue Detector and its application to motion picture printers.
EDWARD H. REICHARD, LEONARD L. SOKOLOW and **CARL W. HAUGE** of Consolidated Film Industries for the design and application to motion picture laboratory practice of a Stroboscopic Scene Tester for color and black-and-white film.
NELSON TYLER for the design and construction of an improved Helicopter Camera System.

1965

BEST PICTURE (O-634)

THE SOUND OF MUSIC, Argyle Enterprises Prod., FOX. Robert Wise, Prod.
DARLING, Anglo-Amalgamated, Ltd. Prod., Embassy. Joseph Janni, Prod.
DOCTOR ZHIVAGO, Sostar S.A.-MGM British Studios, Ltd. Prod., MGM. Carlo Ponti, Prod.
SHIP OF FOOLS, COL. Stanley Kramer, Prod.
A THOUSAND CLOWNS, Harrell Prod., UA. Fred Coe, Prod.

ACTOR (O-635)

LEE MARVIN, Cat Ballou, Harold Hecht Prod., COL.
RICHARD BURTON, *The Spy Who Came In From The Cold*, Salem Films, Ltd. Prod., PAR.
LAURENCE OLIVIER, *Othello*, B.H.E. Prod., WB.
ROD STEIGER, *The Pawnbroker*, Ely Landau Prod., AIP.
OSKAR WERNER. *Ship Of Fools*.

ACTRESS (O-636)

JULIE CHRISTIE, Darling.
JULIE ANDREWS, *The Sound Of Music*.
SAMANTHA EGGAR, *The Collector*, The Collector Co, COL.
ELIZABETH HARTMAN, *A Patch Of Blue*, Pandro S. Berman-Guy Green Prod., MGM.
SIMONE SIGNORET, *Ship Of Fools*.

SUPPORTING ACTOR (O-637)

MARTIN BALSAM, A Thousand Clowns.
IAN BANNEN, *The Flight Of The Phoenix,* Associates & Aldrich Co Prod., FOX.
TOM COURTENAY, *Doctor Zhivago.*
MICHAEL DUNN, *Ship Of Fools.*
FRANK FINLAY, *Othello.*

SUPPORTING ACTRESS (O-638)

SHELLEY WINTERS, A Patch Of Blue.
RUTH GORDON, *Inside Daisy Clover,* Park Place Prod., WB.
JOYCE REDMAN, *Othello.*
MAGGIE SMITH, *Othello.*
PEGGY WOOD, *The Sound Of Music.*

DIRECTING (O-639)

ROBERT WISE, The Sound Of Music.
DAVID LEAN, *Doctor Zhivago.*
JOHN SCHLESINGER, *Darling.*
HIROSHI TESHIGAHARA, *Woman In The Dunes,* Teshigahara Prod., PC.
WILLIAM WYLER, *The Collector.*

WRITING (O-640)

(Best Story and Screenplay written directly for the screen)

DARLING. Frederic Raphael.
CASANOVA '70, C.C. Champion-Les Films Concordia Prod., EBP. Age, Scarpelli, Mario Monicelli, Tonino Guerra, Giorgio Salvioni and Suso Cecchi D'Amico.
THOSE MAGNIFICENT MEN IN THEIR FLYING MACHINES, FOX, Ltd. Prod., FOX. Jack Davies and Ken Annakin.
THE TRAIN, Les Prods. Artistes Associes, UA. Franklin Coen and Frank Davis.
THE UMBRELLAS OF CHERBOURG, Parc-Madeleine Films Prod., American Int'l. Jacques Demy.

(Best Screenplay based on material from another medium)

DOCTOR ZHIVAGO. Robert Bolt.
CAT BALLOU. Walter Newman and Frank R. Pierson.
THE COLLECTOR. Stanley Mann and John Kohn.
SHIP OF FOOLS. Abby Mann.
A THOUSAND CLOWNS. Herb Gardner.

CINEMATOGRAPHY (O-641)

(Black-and-White)

SHIP OF FOOLS. Ernest Laszlo.
IN HARM'S WAY, Sigma Prods., PAR. Loyal Griggs.
KING RAT, Coleytown Prod., COL. Burnett Guffey.
MORITURI, Arcola-Colony Prod., FOX. Conrad Hall.
A PATCH OF BLUE. Robert Burks.

(Color)

DOCTOR ZHIVAGO. Freddie Young.
THE AGONY AND THE ECSTASY, Int'l Classics Prod., FOX. Leon Shamroy.
THE GREAT RACE, Patricia-Jalem-Reynard Prod., WB. Russell Harlan.
THE GREATEST STORY EVER TOLD, George Stevens Prod., UA. William C. Mellor & Loyal Griggs.
THE SOUND OF MUSIC. Ted McCord.

COSTUME DESIGN (O-642)

(Black-and-White)

DARLING. Julie Harris.
MORITURI. Moss Mabry.
A RAGE TO LIVE, Mirisch Corp. of Delaware-Araho Prod., UA. Howard Shoup.
SHIP OF FOOLS. Bill Thomas and Jean Louis.
THE SLENDER THREAD, PAR. Edith Head.

(Color)

DOCTOR ZHIVAGO. Phyllis Dalton.
THE AGONY AND THE ECSTASY. Vittorio Nino Novarese.
THE GREATEST STORY EVER TOLD. Vittorio Nino Novarese and Marjorie Best.
INSIDE DAISY CLOVER. Edith Head and Bill Thomas.
THE SOUND OF MUSIC. Dorothy Jeakins.

ART DIRECTION - SET DECORATION (O-643)

(Black-and-White)

SHIP OF FOOLS. Robert Clatworthy. Set Decoration: Joseph Kish.
KING RAT. Robert Emmet Smith. Set Decoration: Frank Tuttle.
A PATCH OF BLUE. George W. Davis and Urie McCleary. Set Decoration: Henry Grace and Charles S. Thompson.
THE SLENDER THREAD. Hal Pereira and Jack Poplin. Set Decoration: Robert Benton and Joseph Kish.
THE SPY WHO CAME IN FROM THE COLD. Hal Pereira, Tambi Larsen and Edward Marshall. Set Decoration: Josie MacAvin.

(Color)

DOCTOR ZHIVAGO. John Box and Terry Marsh. Set Decoration: Dario Simoni.
THE AGONY AND THE ECSTASY. John DeCuir and and Jack Martin Smith. Set Decoration: Dario Simoni.
THE GREATEST STORY EVER TOLD. Richard Day, William Creber and David Hall. Set Decoration: Ray Moyer, Fred MacLean and Norman Rockett.
INSIDE DAISY CLOVER. Robert Clatworthy. Set Decoration: George James Hopkins.
THE SOUND OF MUSIC. Boris Leven. Set Decoration: Walter M. Scott and Ruby Levitt.

FILM EDITING (O-644)

THE SOUND OF MUSIC. William Reynolds.
CAT BALLOU. Charles Nelson.
DOCTOR ZHIVAGO. Norman Savage.
THE FLIGHT OF THE PHOENIX. Michael Luciano.
THE GREAT RACE. Ralph E. Winters.

FOREIGN LANGUAGE FILM (O-645)

THE SHOP ON MAIN STREET, A Ceskoslovensky Film Production (Czechoslovakia).
BLOOD ON THE LAND, Th. Damaskinos & V. Michaelides, A.E.-Finos Film (Greece).
DEAR JOHN, A.B. Sandrew-Ateljeerna (Sweden).
KWAIDAN, A Toho Co, Ltd. Production (Japan).
MARRIAGE ITALIAN STYLE, A Champion-Concordia Production (Italy).

MUSIC - SCORING (O-646)

(Music Score-substantially original)

DOCTOR ZHIVAGO. Maurice Jarre.
THE AGONY AND THE ECSTASY. Alex North.
THE GREATEST STORY EVERY TOLD. Alfred Newman.
A PATCH OF BLUE. Jerry Goldsmith.
THE UMBRELLAS OF CHERBOURG. Michel Legrand and Jacques Demy.

(Scoring of Music-adaptation or treatment)

THE SOUND OF MUSIC. Irwin Kostal.
CAT BALLOU. DeVol.
THE PLEASURE SEEKERS, FOX. Lionel Newman and Alexander Courage.
A THOUSAND CLOWNS. Don Walker.
THE UMBRELLAS OF CHERBOURG. Michel Legrand.

MUSIC - BEST SONG (O-647)

THE SHADOW OF YOUR SMILE, The Sandpiper, Filmways-Venice Prod., MGM. Music, Johnny Mandel. Lyrics, Paul Francis Webster.
THE BALLAD OF CAT BALLOU, *Cat Ballou.* Music, Jerry Livingston. Lyrics, Mack David.

1964—"My Fair Lady" Winners: Jack L. Warner (producer, Best Picture), Audrey Hepburn, Rex Harrison (Best Actor), George Cukor (Best Director)

1965—Lee Marvin (Best Actor), Julie Christie (Best Actress), Shelley Winters (Best Supporting Actress), Martin Balsam (Best Supporting Actor)

1968—Barbra Streisand (Best Actress)

1967—Rod Steiger (Best Actor), Estelle Parsons (Best Supporting Actress), George Kennedy (Best Supporting Actor), George Cukor (accepting for Katharine Hepburn, Best Actress)

1971—Charles Chaplin (Honorary Award) with Jack Lemmon (Master of Ceremonies)

1971—Philip D'Antoni (producer, Best Picture), Gene Hackman (Best Actor), Jane Fonda (Best Actress), William Friedkin (Best Director)

1969—John Wayne (Best Actor) and Barbra Streisand (presenter)

1970—Lillian Gish (Honorary Award) and Melvyn Douglas (presenter)

I WILL WAIT FOR YOU, *The Umbrellas Of Cherbourg*. Music, Michel Legrand. Lyrics, Jacques Demy.

THE SWEETHEART TREE, *The Great Race*. Music, Henry Mancini. Lyrics, Johnny Mercer.

WHAT'S NEW PUSSYCAT?, *What's New Pussycat?*, Famous Artists-Famartists Prod., UA. Music, Burt Bacharach. Lyrics, Hal David.

SOUND (O-648)

THE SOUND OF MUSIC, FOX Studio Sound Department, James P. Corcoran, Sound Director; and Todd-AO Sound Department, Fred Hynes, Sound Director.

THE AGONY AND THE ECSTASY, FOX Studio Sound Department. James P. Corcoran, Sound Director.

DOCTOR ZHIVAGO, MGM British Studio Sound Department, A. W. Watkins, Sound Director; and MGM Studio Sound Department. Franklin E. Milton, Sound Director.

THE GREAT RACE, WB. Studio Sound Department. George R. Groves, Sound Director.

SHENANDOAH, U Studio Sound Department. Waldon O. Watson, Sound Director.

SHORT FILMS (O-649)

(Cartoons)

THE DOT AND THE LINE, MGM. Chuck Jones and Les Goldman, Prods.

CLAY OR THE ORIGIN OF SPECIES, Harvard University, PC. Eliot Noyes, Jr., Prod.

THE THIEVING MAGPIE (La Gazza Ladra), Giulio Gianini-Emanuele Luzzati, AA. Emanuele Luzzati, Prod.

(Live Action Subjects)

THE CHICKEN (Le Poulet), Renn Prods., PC. Claude Berri, Prod.

FORTRESS OF PEACE, Lothar Wolff Prods. for Farner-Looser Films, CRC. Lothar Wolff, Prod.

SKATERDATER, Byway Prods., UA. Marshal Backlar and Noel Black, Prods.

SNOW, British Transport Films in association with Geoffrey Jones (Films) Ltd., MAN. Edgar Anstey, Prod.

TIME PIECE, Muppets, Inc., PC. Jim Henson, Prod.

DOCUMENTARY (O-650)

(Short Subjects)

TO BE ALIVE!, Johnson Wax. Francis Thompson, Inc., Prod.

MURAL ON OUR STREET, Henry Street Settlement, PC. Kirk Smallman, Prod.

OUVERTURE, Mafilm Prods., Hungarofilm-Pathe Contemporary Films.

POINT OF VIEW, Vision Associates Prod., National Tuberculosis Assoc.

YEATS COUNTRY, Aengus Films Ltd. for the Dept. of External Affairs of Ireland. Patrick Carey and Joe Mendoza, Prods.

(Features)

THE ELEANOR ROOSEVELT STORY, Sidney Glazier Prod., AIP. Sidney Glazier, Prod.

THE BATTLE OF THE BULGE. . .THE BRAVE RIFLES, Mascott Prods. Laurence E. Mascott, Prod.

THE FORTH ROAD BRIDGE, Random Film Prods., Ltd., Shell-Mex and B.P. Film Library. Peter Mills, Prod.

LET MY PEOPLE GO, Wolper Prods. Marshall Flaum, Prod.

TO DIE IN MADRID, Ancinex Prods., ALT. Frederic Rossif, Prod.

VISUAL EFFECTS (O-651)

THUNDERBALL, Broccoli-Saltzman-McClory Prod., UA. John Stears.

THE GREATEST STORY EVERY TOLD. J. McMillan Johnson.

SOUND EFFECTS (O-652)

THE GREAT RACE. Tregoweth Brown.

VON RYAN'S EXPRESS, P-R Prods., FOX. Walter A. Rossi.

HONORARY AND OTHER (O-653)

(Irving G. Thalberg Memorial Award)

William Wyler

(Jean Hersholt Humanitarian Award)

Edmond L. DePatie

(Other)

BOB HOPE for unique and distinguished service to our industry and the Academy.

SCIENTIFIC OR TECHNICAL (O-654)

(Class II)

ARTHUR J. HATCH of The Strong Electric Corp, subsidiary of General Precision Equipment Corp, for the design and development of an Air Blown Carbon Arc Projection Lamp.

STEFAN KUDELSKI for the design and development of the Nagra portable 1/4' tape recording system for motion picture sound recording.

1966

BEST PICTURE (O-655)

A MAN FOR ALL SEASONS, Highland Films, Ltd. Prod., COL. Fred Zinnemann, Prod.

ALFIE, Sheldrake Films, Ltd. Prod., PAR. Lewis Gilbert, Prod.

THE RUSSIANS ARE COMING, THE RUSSIANS ARE COMING, Mirisch Corp. of Delaware Prod., U.A. Norman Jewison, Prod.

THE SAND PEBBLES, Argyle-Solar Prod., FOX. Robert Wise, Prod.

WHO'S AFRAID OF VIRGINIA WOOLF?, Chenault Prod., WB. Ernest Lehman, Prod.

ACTOR (O-656)

PAUL SCOFIELD, A Man For All Seasons.

ALAN ARKIN, *The Russians Are Coming, The Russians Are Coming.*

RICHARD BURTON, *Who's Afraid Of Virginia Woolf?*

MICHAEL CAINE, *Alfie.*

STEVE MC QUEEN, *The Sand Pebbles.*

ACTRESS (O-657)

ELIZABETH TAYLOR, Who's Afraid Of Virginia Woolf?

ANOUK AIMEE, *A Man And A Woman*, Les Films 13 Prod., AA.

IDA KAMINSKA, *The Shop On Main Street*, Ceskoslovensky Film Co Prod., PRM.

LYNN REDGRAVE, *Georgy Girl*, Everglades Prods., Ltd., COL.

VANESSA REDGRAVE, *Morgan!*, Quintra Films, Ltd. Prod., C5.

SUPPORTING ACTOR (O-658)

WALTER MATTHAU, The Fortune Cookie, Phalanx-Jalem-Mirisch Corp. of Delaware Prod., UA.

MAKO, *The Sand Pebbles.*

JAMES MASON, *Georgy Girl.*

GEORGE SEGAL, *Who's Afraid Of Virginia Woolf?*

ROBERT SHAW, *A Man For All Seasons.*

SUPPORTING ACTRESS (O-659)

SANDY DENNIS, Who's Afraid Of Virginia Woolf?

WENDY HILLER, *A Man For All Seasons.*

JOCELYNE LAGARDE, *Hawaii*, Mirisch Corp. of Delaware Prod., UA.

VIVIEN MERCHANT, *Alfie.*

GERALDINE PAGE, *You're A Big Boy Now*, Seven Arts.

DIRECTING (O-660)

FRED ZINNEMANN, A Man For All Seasons.

MICHELANGELO ANTONIONI, *Blow-Up*, Carlo Ponti Prod., PRE.

RICHARD BROOKS, *The Professionals*, Pax Enterprises Prod., COL.

CLAUDE LELOUCH, *A Man And A Woman.*

MIKE NICHOLS, *Who's Afraid Of Virginia Woolf?*

WRITING (O-661)

(Best Story and Screenplay written directly for the screen)

A MAN AND A WOMAN. Story by Claude Lelouch. Screenplay by Pierre Uytterhoeven and Claude Lelouch.
BLOW-UP. Story by Michelangelo Antonioni. Screenplay by Michelangelo Antonioni, Tonino Guerra and Edward Bond.
THE FORTUNE COOKIE. Billy Wilder and I.A.L. Diamond.
KHARTOUM, Julian Blaustein Prod., UA. Robert Ardrey.
THE NAKED PREY, Theodora Prod., PAR. Clint Johnston and Don Peters.

(Best Screenplay based on material from antoher medium)

A MAN FOR ALL SEASONS. Robert Bolt.
ALFIE. Bill Naughton.
THE PROFESSIONALS. Richard Brooks.
THE RUSSIANS ARE COMING, THE RUSSIANS ARE COMING. William Rose.
WHO'S AFRAID OF VIRGINIA WOOLF? Ernest Lehman.

CINEMATOGRAPHY (O-662)

(Black-and-White)

WHO'S AFRAID OF VIRGINIA WOOLF? Haskell Wexler.
THE FORTUNE COOKIE. Joseph LaShelle.
GEORGY GIRL. Ken Higgins.
IS PARIS BURNING?, Transcontinental Films-Marianne Prod., PAR. Marcel Grignon.
SECONDS, The Seconds Co, PAR. James Wong Howe.

(Color)

A MAN FOR ALL SEASONS. Ted Moore.
FANTASTIC VOYAGE, FOX. Ernest Laszlo.
HAWAII. Russell Harlan.
THE PROFESSIONALS. Conrad Hall.
THE SAND PEBBLES. Joseph MacDonald.

COSTUME DESIGN (O-663)

(Black-and-White)

WHO'S AFRAID OF VIRGINIA WOOLF?. Irene Sharaff.
THE GOSPEL ACCORDING TO ST. MATTHEW, Arco-Lux Cie Cinematografique de France Prod., WRC. Danilo Donati.
MANDRAGOLA, Europix-Consolidated. Danilo Donati.
MISTER BUDDWING, DDD-Cherokee Prod., MGM. Helen Rose.
MORGAN! Jocelyn Rickards.

(Color)

A MAN FOR ALL SEASONS. Elizabeth Haffenden and Joan Bridge.
GAMBIT, U. Jean Louis.
HAWAII. Dorothy Jeakins.
JULIET OF THE SPIRITS, RIZ. S.P.A. Prod., Rizzoli Films. Piero Gherardi.
THE OSCAR, Greene-Rouse Prod., EBP. Edith Head.

ART DIRECTION - SET DECORATION (O-664)

(Black-and-White)

WHO'S AFRAID OF VIRGINIA WOOLF? Richard Sylbert. Set Decoration: George James Hopkins.
THE FORTUNE COOKIE. Robert Luthardt. Set Decoration: Edward G. Boyle.
THE GOSPEL ACCORDING TO ST. MATTHEW. Luigi Scaccianoce.
IS PARIS BURNING? Willy Holt. Set Decoration: Marc Frederix and Pierre Guffroy.
MISTER BUDDWING. George W. Davis and Paul Groesse. Set Decoration: Henry Grace and Hugh Hunt.

(Color)

FANTASTIC VOYAGE. Jack Martin Smith and Dale Hennesy. Set Decoration: Walter M. Scott and Stuart A. Reiss.
GAMBIT. Alexander Golitzen and George C. Webb. Set Decoration: John McCarthy and John Austin.
JULIET OF THE SPIRITS. Piero Gherardi.
THE OSCAR. Hal Pereira and Arthur Lonergan. Set Decoration: Robert Benton and James Payne.
THE SAND PEBBLES. Boris Leven. Set Decoration: Walter M. Scott, John Sturtevant and William Kiernan.

FILM EDITING (O-665)

GRAND PRIX, Douglas-Lewis-John Frankenheimer-Cherokee Prod., MGM. Fredric Steinkamp, Henry Berman, Stewart Linder and Frank Santillo.
FANTASTIC VOYAGE. William B. Murphy.
THE RUSSIANS ARE COMING, THE RUSSIANS ARE COMING. Hal Ashby and J. Terry Williams.
THE SAND PEBBLES. William Reynolds.
WHO'S AFRAID OF VIRGINIA WOOLF? Sam O'Steen.

FOREIGN LANGUAGE FILM (O-666)

A MAN AND A WOMAN.
THE BATTLE OF ALGIERS, Igor Film-Casbah Film Production (Italy).
LOVES OF A BLONDE, Barrandov Film Production (Czechoslovakia).
PHARAOH, Kadr Film Unit Production (Poland).
THREE, Avala Film Production (Yugoslavia).

MUSIC - SCORING (O-667)

(Original Music Score)

BORN FREE, Open Road Films, Ltd.-Atlas Films, Ltd. Prod., COL. John Barry.
THE BIBLE, Thalia-A.G. Prod., FOX. Toshiro Mayuzumi.
HAWAII. Elmer Bernstein.
THE SAND PEBBLES. Jerry Goldsmith.
WHO'S AFRAID OF VIRGINIA WOOLF? Alex North.

(Scoring of Music-adaptation or treatment)

A FUNNY THING HAPPENED ON THE WAY TO THE FORUM, Melvin Frank Prod., UA. Ken Thorne.
THE GOSPEL ACCORDING TO ST. MATTHEW. Luis Enrique Bacalov.
RETURN OF THE SEVEN, Mirisch Prods., UA. Elmer Bernstein.
THE SINGING NUN, MGM. Harry Sukman.
STOP THE WORLD--I WANT TO GET OFF, WB. Prods., Ltd., WB. Al Ham.

MUSIC - BEST SONG (O-668)

BORN FREE, Born Free. Music, John Barry. Lyrics, Don Black.
ALFIE, *Alfie*. Music, Burt Bacharach. Lyrics, Hal David.
GEORGY GIRL, *Georgy Girl*. Music, Tom Springfield. Lyrics, Jim Dale.
MY WISHING DOLL, *Hawaii*. Music, Elmer Bernstein. Lyrics, Mack David.
A TIME FOR LOVE, *An American Dream*, WB. Music, Johnny Mandel. Lyrics, Paul Francis Webster.

SOUND (O-669)

GRAND PRIX, MGM Studio Sound Department. Franklin E. Milton, Sound Director.
GAMBIT, U Studio Sound Department. Waldon O. Watson, Sound Director.
HAWAII, Samuel Goldwyn Studio Sound Department. Gordon E. Sawyer, Sound Director.
THE SAND PEBBLES, FOX Studio Sound Deparment. James P. Corcoran, Sound Director.
WHO'S AFRAID OF VIRGINIA WOOLF?, WB. Studio Sound Department. George R. Groves, Sound Director.

SHORT FILMS (O-670)

(Cartoons)

HERB ALPERT AND THE TIJUANA BRASS DOUBLE FEATURE, Hubley Studio, PAR. John and Faith Hubley, Prods.
THE DRAG, NFC, FA. Wolf Koenig and Robert Verrall, Prods.
THE PINK BLUEPRINT, Mirisch-Geoffrey-DePatie-Freleng, UA. David H. DePatie and Friz Freleng, Prods.

(Live Action Subjects)

WILD WINGS, British Transport Films, MAN. Edgar Anstey, Prod.
TURKEY THE BRIDGE, Samaritan Prods., SCH. Derek Williams, Prod.
THE WINNING STRAIN, Winik Films, PAR. Leslie Winik, Prod.

DOCUMENTARY (O-671)

(Short Subjects)

A YEAR TOWARD TOMORROW, Sun Dial Films, Inc. Prod. for Office of Economic Opportunity. Edmond A. Levy, Prod.
ADOLESCENCE, M.K. Prods. Marin Karmitz and Vladimir Forgency, Prods.
COWBOY, United States Information Agency. Michael Ahnemann and Gary Schlosser, Prods.
THE ODDS AGAINST, Vision Associates Prod. for The American Foundation Institute of Corrections. Lee R. Bobker and Helen Kristt Radin, Prods.
SAINT MATTHEW PASSION, Mafilm Studio, HU.

(Features)

THE WAR GAME, BBC Prod. for the British Film Institute, PC. Peter Watkins, Prod.
THE FACE OF GENIUS, WBZ-TV, Group W, Boston. Alfred R. Kelman, Prod.
HELICOPTER CANADA, Centennial Commission, NFC. Peter Jones and Tom Daly, Prods.
LE VOLCAN INTERDIT (The Forbidden Volcano), Cine Documents Tazieff, ATO. Haroun Tazieff, Prod.
THE REALLY BIG FAMILY, David L. Wolper Prod. Alex Grasshoff, Prod.

VISUAL EFFECTS (O-672)

FANTASTIC VOYAGE. Art Cruickshank.
HAWAII. Linwood G. Dunn.

SOUND EFFECTS (O-673)

GRAND PRIX. Gordon Daniel.
FANTASTIC VOYAGE. Walter Rossi.

HONORARY AND OTHER (O-674)

(Irving G. Thalberg Memorial Award)

Robert Wise

(Jean Hersholt Humanitarian Award)

George Bagnall

(Other)

Y. FRANK FREEMAN for unusual and outstanding service to the Academy during his thirty years in Hollywood.
YAKIMA CANUTT for achievements as a stunt man and for developing safety devices to protect stunt men everywhere.

SCIENTIFIC OR TECHNICAL (O-675)

(Class II)

MITCHELL CAMERA CORPORATION for the design and development of the Mitchell Mark II 35mm Portable Motion Picture Reflex Camera.
ARNOLD & RICHTER KG for the design and development of the Arriflex 35mm Portable Motion Picture Reflex Camera.

(Class III)

PANAVISION INCORPORATED for the design of the Panatron Power Inverter and its application to motion picture camera operation.
CARROLL KNUDSON for the production of a Composers Manual for Motion Picture Music Synchronization.
RUBY RAKSIN for the production of a Composers Manual for Motion Picture Music Synchronization.

1967

BEST PICTURE (O-676)

IN THE HEAT OF THE NIGHT, Mirisch Corp. Prod., UA. Walter Mirisch, Prod.
BONNIE AND CLYDE, Tatira-Hiller Prod., WB.-Seven Arts. Warren Beatty, Prod.
DOCTOR DOLITTLE, Apjac Prods., FOX. Arthur P. Jacobs, Prod.
THE GRADUATE, Mike Nichols-Lawrence Turman Prod., EBP. Lawrence Turman, Prod.
GUESS WHO'S COMING TO DINNER, COL. Stanley Kramer, Prod.

ACTOR (O-677)

ROD STEIGER, In The Heat Of The Night.
WARREN BEATTY, *Bonnie And Clyde.*
DUSTIN HOFFMAN in *The Graduate.*
PAUL NEWMAN, *Cool Hand Luke,* Jalem Prod., WBS.
SPENCER TRACY, *Guess Who's Coming To Dinner.*

ACTRESS (O-678)

KATHARINE HEPBURN, Guess Who's Coming To Dinner.
ANNE BANCROFT, *The Graduate.*
FAYE DUNAWAY, *Bonnie And Clyde.*
DAME EDITH EVANS, *The Whisperers,* Seven Pines Prods., Ltd., UA.
AUDREY HEPBURN, *Wait Until Dark,* WBS.

SUPPORTING ACTOR (O-679)

GEORGE KENNEDY, Cool Hand Luke.
JOHN CASSAVETES, *The Dirty Dozen,* MKH Prods., Ltd., MGM.
GENE HACKMAN, *Bonnie And Clyde.*
CECIL KELLAWAY, *Guess Who's Coming To Dinner.*
MICHAEL J. POLLARD, *Bonnie And Clyde.*

SUPPORTING ACTRESS (O-680)

ESTELLE PARSONS, Bonnie And Clyde.
CAROL CHANNING, *Thoroughly Modern Millie,* Ross Hunter-U Prod., U.
MILDRED NATWICK, *Barefoot In The Park,* Hal Wallis Prod., PAR.
BEAH RICHARDS, *Guess Who's Coming To Dinner.*
KATHARINE ROSS, *The Graduate.*

DIRECTING (O-681)

MIKE NICHOLS, The Graduate.
RICHARD BROOKS, *In Cold Blood,* Pax Enterprises Prod., COL.
NORMAN JEWISON, *In The Heat Of The Night.*
STANLEY KRAMER, *Guess Who's Coming To Dinner.*
ARTHUR PENN, *Bonnie And Clyde.*

WRITING (O-682)

(Best Story and Screenplay written directly for the screen)

GUESS WHO'S COMING TO DINNER. William Rose.
BONNIE AND CLYDE. David Newman and Robert Benton.
DIVORCE AMERICAN STYLE, Tandem Prods. for NGP, COL. Story by Robert Kaufman. Screenplay by Norman Lear.
LA GUERRE EST FINIE, Sofracima and Europa-Film Prod., BRA. Jorge Semprun.
TWO FOR THE ROAD, Stanley Donen Films Prod., FOX. Frederic Raphael.

(Best Screenplay based on material from another medium)

IN THE HEAT OF THE NIGHT. Stirling Silliphant.
COOL HAND LUKE. Donn Pearce and Frank R. Pierson.
THE GRADUATE. Calder Willingham and Buck Henry.
IN COLD BLOOD. Richard Brooks.
ULYSSES, Walter Reade, Jr.-Joseph Strick Prod., WRC. Joseph Strick and Fred Haines.

CINEMATOGRAPHY (O-683)

BONNIE AND CLYDE. Burnett Guffey.
CAMELOT, WBS. Richard H. Kline.
DOCTOR DOLITTLE. Robert Surtees.
THE GRADUATE. Robert Surtees.
IN COLD BLOOD. Conrad Hall.

COSTUME DESIGN (O-684)

CAMELOT. John Truscott.
BONNIE AND CLYDE. Theadora Van Runkle.
THE HAPPIEST MILLIONAIRE, Walt Disney Prods., BV. Bill Thomas.
THE TAMING OF THE SHREW, Royal Films Int'l-Films Artistici Interna-

zionali S.r.L. Prod., COL. Irene Sharaff and Danilo Donati. THOROUGHLY MODERN MILLIE. Jean Louis.

ART DIRECTION - SET DECORATION (O-685)

CAMELOT. John Truscott and Edward Carrere. Set Decoration: John W. Brown.
DOCTOR DOLITTLE. Mario Chiari, Jack Martin Smith and Ed Graves. Set Decoration: Walter M. Scott and Stuart A. Reiss.
GUESS WHO'S COMING TO DINNER. Robert Clatworthy. Set Decoration: Frank Tuttle.
THE TAMING OF THE SHREW. Renzo Mongiardino, John DeCuir, Elven Webb and Giuseppe Mariani. Set Decoration: Dario Simoni and Luigi Gervasi.
THOROUGHLY MODERN MILLIE. Alexander Golitzen and George C. Webb. Set Decoration: Howard Bristol.

FILM EDITING (O-686)

IN THE HEAT OF THE NIGHT. Hal Ashby.
BEACH RED, Theodora Prods., UA. Frank P. Keller.
THE DIRTY DOZEN. Michael Luciano.
DOCTOR DOLITTLE. Samuel E. Beetley and Marjorie Fowler.
GUESS WHO'S COMING TO DINNER. Robert C. Jones.

FOREIGN LANGUAGE FILM (O-687)

CLOSELY WATCHED TRAINS, Barrandov Film Studio Production (Czechoslovakia).
EL AMOR BRUJO, Films R.B., S.A. Production (Spain).
I EVEN MET HAPPY GYPSIES, Avala Film Production (Yugoslavia).
LIVE FOR LIFE, Les Films Ariane-Les Productions Artistes Associes-Vides Films Production (France).
PORTRAIT OF CHIEKO, Shochiku Co., Ltd. Production (Japan).

MUSIC - SCORING (O-688)

(Original Music Score)
THOROUGHLY MODERN MILLIE. Elmer Bernstein.
COOL HAND LUKE. Lalo Schifrin.
DOCTOR DOLITTLE. Leslie Bricusse.
FAR FROM THE MADDING CROWD, Appia Films, Ltd. Prod., MGM. Richard Rodney Bennett.
IN COLD BLOOD. Quincy Jones.
(Scoring of Music-adaptation or treatment)
CAMELOT. Alfred Newman and Ken Darby.
DOCTOR DOLITTLE. Lionel Newman and Alexander Courage.
GUESS WHO'S COMING TO DINNER. DeVol.
THROUGHLY MODERN MILLIE. Andre Previn and Joseph Gershenson.
VALLEY OF THE DOLLS, Red Lion Prods., FOX. John Williams.

MUSIC - BEST SONG (O-689)

TALK TO THE ANIMALS, Doctor Dolittle. Music and lyrics by Leslie Bricusse.
THE BARE NECESSITIES, *The Jungle Book,* Walt Disney Prods., BV. Music and Lyrics by Terry Gilkyson.
THE EYES OF LOVE, *Banning,* U. Music, Quincy Jones. Lyrics, Bob Russell.
THE LOOK OF LOVE, *Casino Royale,* Famous Artists Prods., Ltd., COL. Music, Burt Bacharach. Lyrics, Hal David.
THOROUGHLY MODERN MILLIE, *Thoroughly Modern Millie.* Music and lyrics by James Van Heusen and Sammy Cahn.

SOUND (O-690)

IN THE HEAT OF THE NIGHT, Samuel Goldwyn Studio Sound Department.
CAMELOT, WBS Sound Department.
THE DIRTY DOZEN, MGM Studio Sound Department.
DOCTOR DOLITTLE, FOX Studio Sound Department.
THOROUGLY MODERN MILLIE, U Studio Sound Department.

SHORT FILMS (O-691)

(Cartoons)
THE BOX, Murakami-Wolf Films, BRA. Fred Wolf, Prod.
HYPOTHESE BETA, Films Orzeaux, PC. Jean-Charles Meunier, Prod.
WHAT ON EARTH!, NFC, COL. Robert Verrall and Wolf Koenig, Prods.
(Live Action Subjects)
A PLACE TO STAND, T.D.F. Prod. for the Ontario Department of Economics and Development, COL. Christopher Chapman, Prod.
PADDLE TO THE SEA, NFC, FA. Julian Biggs, Prod.
SKY OVER HOLLAND, John Ferno Prod. for The Netherlands, SEN. John Ferno, Prod.
STOP, LOOK AND LISTEN, MGM. Len Janson and Chuck Menville, Prods.

DOCUMENTARY (O-692)

(Short Subjects)
THE REDWOODS, King Screen Prods. Mark Harris and Trevor Greenwood, Prods.
MONUMENT TO THE DREAM, Guggenheim Prods. Charles E. Guggenheim, Prod.
A PLACE TO STAND, T.D.F. Prod. for The Ontario Dept. of Economics and Development. Christopher Chapman, Prod.
SEE YOU AT THE PILLAR, ABP. Robert Fitchett, Prod.
WHILE I RUN THIS RACE, Sun Dial Films for VISTA, An Economic Opportunity Program. Carl V. Ragsdale, Prod.
(Features)
THE ANDERSON PLATOON, French Broadcasting System. Pierre Schoendoerffer, Prod.
FESTIVAL, Patchke Prods. Murray Lerner, Prod.
HARVEST, United States Information Agency. Carroll Ballard, Prod.
A KING'S STORY, Jack Le Vien Prod. Jack Le Vien, Prod.
A TIME FOR BURNING, Quest Prods. for Lutheran Film Associates. William C. Jersey, Prod.

VISUAL EFFECTS (O-693)

DOCTOR DOLITTLE. L. B. Abbott.
TOBRUK, Gibraltar Prods.-Corman Co-U Prod., U. Howard A. Anderson, Jr. and Albert Whitlock.

SOUND EFFECTS (O-694)

THE DIRTY DOZEN. John Poyner.
IN THE HEAT OF THE NIGHT. James A. Richard.

HONORARY AND OTHER (O-695)

(Irving G. Thalberg Memorial Award)
Alfred Hitchcock
(Jean Hersholt Humanitarian Award)
Gregory Peck
(Other)
ARTHUR FREED for distinguished service to the Academy and the production of six top-rated Awards telecasts.

SCIENTIFIC OR TECHNICAL (O-696)

(Class III)
ELECTRO-OPTICAL DIVISION of the KOLLMORGEN CORPORATION for the design and development of a series of Motion Picture Projection Lenses.
PANAVISION INCORPORATED for a Variable Speed Motor for Motion Picture Cameras.
FRED R. WILSON of the SAMUEL GOLDWYN STUDIO SOUND DEPARTMENT for an Audio Level Clamper.
WALDON O. WATSON and the UNIVERSAL CITY STUDIO SOUND DEPARTMENT for new concepts in the design of a Music Scoring Stage.

1968

BEST PICTURE (O-697)

OLIVER!, Romulus Films, COL, John Woolf, Prod.
The Franco Zeffirelli Prodn of ROMEO & JULIET, B.H.E. Film-Verona Prod.-Dino De Laurentiis Cinematografica Prod., PAR. Anthony Havelock-Allan and John Brabourne, Prods.
FUNNY GIRL, Rastar Prods., COL. Ray Stark, Prod.
THE LION IN WINTER, Haworth Prods., AVE. Martin Poll, Prod.
RACHEL, RACHEL, Kayos Prod., WB.-Seven Arts. Paul Newman, Prod.

ACTOR (O-698)

CLIFF ROBERTSON, Charly, American Broadcasting Companies-Selmur Pictures Prod., CRC.
ALAN ARKIN, *The Heart Is A Lonely Hunter*, WBS.
ALAN BATES, *The Fixer*, John Frankenheimer-Edward Lewis Prods., MGM.
RON MOODY, *Oliver!*
PETER O'TOOLE, *The Lion In Winter*.

ACTRESS (O-699)

KATHARINE HEPBURN, The Lion In Winter.
BARBRA STREISAND, Funny Girl.
PATRICIA NEAL, *The Subject Was Roses*, MGM.
VANESSA REDGRAVE, *Isadora*, Robert and Raymond Hakim-U, Ltd. Prod., U.
JOANNE WOODWARD, *Rachel, Rachel*.

SUPPORTING ACTOR (O-700)

JACK ALBERTSON, The Subject Was Roses.
SEYMOUR CASSEL, *Faces*, John Cassavetes Prod., WRC.
DANIEL MASSEY, *Star!*, Robert Wise Prod., FOX.
JACK WILD, *Oliver!*
GENE WILDER, *The Prods*, Sidney Glazier Prod., AVE.

SUPPORTING ACTRESS (O-701)

RUTH GORDON, Rosemary's Baby, William Castle Enterprises Prod., PAR.
LYNN CARLIN, *Faces*.
SONDRA LOCKE, *The Heart Is A Lonely Hunter*.
KAY MEDFORD, *Funny Girl*.
ESTELLE PARSONS, *Rachel, Rachel*.

DIRECTING (O-702)

CAROL REED, Oliver!
ANTHONY HARVEY, *The Lion In Winter*.
STANLEY KUBRICK, *2001: A Space Odyssey*, Polaris Prod., MGM.
GILLO PONTECORVO, *The Battle Of Algiers*, Igor-Casbah Film Prod., AA.
FRANCO ZEFFIRELLI, *The Franco Zeffirelli prodn of ROMEO & JULIET*.

WRITING (O-703)

(Best Story and Screenplay written directly for the screen)
THE PRODUCERS. Mel Brooks.
THE BATTLE OF ALGIERS. Franco Solinas and Gillo Pontecorvo.
FACES. John Cassavetes.
HOT MILLIONS, Mildred Freed Alberg Prod., MGM. Ira Wallach and Peter Ustinov.
2001: A SPACE ODYSSEY. Stanley Kubrick and Arthur C. Clarke.

(Best Screenplay based on material from another medium)
THE LION IN WINTER. James Goldman.
THE ODD COUPLE, Howard W. Koch Prod., PAR. Neil Simon.
OLIVER! Vernon Harris.
RACHEL, RACHEL. Stewart Stern.
ROSEMARY'S BABY. Roman Polanski.

CINEMATOGRAPHY (O-704)

The Franco Zeffirelli prodn of ROMEO & JULIET. Pasqualino De Santis.
FUNNY GIRL. Harry Stradling.
ICE STATION ZEBRA, Filmways Prod., MGM. Daniel L. Fapp.
OLIVER! Oswald Morris.
STAR! Ernest Laszlo.

COSTUME DESIGN (O-705)

The Franco Zeffirelli prodn of ROMEO & JULIET. Danilo Donati.
THE LION IN WINTER. Margaret Furse.
OLIVER! Phyllis Dalton.
PLANET OF THE APES, APJAC Prods., FOX. Morton Haack.
STAR! Donald Brooks.

ART DIRECTION - SET DECORATION (O-706)

OLIVER! John Box and Terence Marsh. Set Decoration: Vernon Dixon and Ken Muggleston.
THE SHOES OF THE FISHERMAN, George Englund Prod., MGM. George W. Davis and Edward Carfagno.
STAR! Boris Leven. Set Decoration: Walter M. Scott and Howard Bristol.
2001: A SPACE ODYSSEY. Tony Masters, Harry Lange and Ernie Archer.
WAR AND PEACE, Mosfilm Prod., WRC. Mikhail Bogdanov and Gennady Myasnikov. Set Decoration: G. Koshelev and V. Uvarov.

FILM EDITING (O-707)

BULLITT, Solar Prod., WBS. Frank P. Keller.
FUNNY GIRL. Robert Swink, Maury Winetrobe and William Sands.
THE ODD COUPLE. Frank Bracht.
OLIVER!. Ralph Kemplen.
WILD IN THE STREETS, AIP. Fred Feitshans and Eve Newman.

FOREIGN LANGUAGE FILM (O-708)

WAR AND PEACE, Mosfilm Production (U.S.S.R.).
THE BOYS OF PAUL STREET, Bohgros Films-Mafilm Studio I Production (Hungary).
THE FIREMEN'S BALL, Barrandov Film Studio Production (Czechoslovakia).
THE GIRL WITH THE PISTOL, Documento Film Production (Italy).
STOLEN KISSES, Les Films du Carrosse-Les Productions Artistes Associes Production (France).

MUSIC - SCORING (O-709)

(Best Original Score for a Motion Picture-not a musical)
THE LION IN WINTER. John Barry.
THE FOX, Raymond Stross-Motion Pictures Int'l Prod., CLR. Lalo Schifrin.
PLANET OF THE APES. Jerry Goldsmith.
THE SHOES OF THE FISHERMAN. Alex North.
THE THOMAS CROWN AFFAIR, Mirisch-Simkoe-Solar Prod., UA. Michel Legrand.

(Best Score of a Musical Picture—original or adaptation)
OLIVER! Adapted by John Green.
FINIAN'S RAINBOW, WBS. Adapted by Ray Heindorf.
FUNNY GIRL. Adapted by Walter Scharf.
STAR! Adapted by Lennie Hayton.
THE YOUNG GIRLS OF ROCHEFORT, Mag Bodard-Gilbert de Goldschmidt-Parc Film-Madeleine Films Prod., WBS. Michel Legrand and Jacques Demy.

MUSIC - BEST SONG (O-710)

THE WINDMILLS OF YOUR MIND, The Thomas Crown Affair. Music, Michel Legrand. Lyrics, Alan and Marilyn Bergman.
CHITTY CHITTY BANG BANG, *Chitty Chitty Bang Bang*, Warfield Prods., UA. Music and lyrics by Richard M. Sherman and Robert B. Sherman.

FOR LOVE OF IVY, *For Love Of Ivy*, American Broadcasting Companies-Palomar Pictures Int'l Prod., CRC. Music, Quincy Jones. Lyrics, Bob Russell.
FUNNY GIRL, *Funny Girl*. Music, Jule Styne. Lyrics, Bob Merrill.
STAR! *Star!* Music, Jimmy Van Heusen. Lyrics, Sammy Cahn.

SOUND (O-711)

OLIVER! Shepperton Studio Sound Department.
BULLITT, WBS.-Seven Arts Studio Sound Department.
FINIAN'S RAINBOW, WBS.-Seven Arts Studio Sound Department.
FUNNY GIRL, COL Studio Sound Department.
STAR! FOX Studio Sound Department.

SHORT FILMS (O-712)

(Cartoons)
WINNIE THE POOH AND THE BLUSTERY DAY, Walt Disney Prods., BV. Walt Disney, Prod.
THE HOUSE THAT JACK BUILT, COL. Wolf Koenig and Jim MacKay, Prods.
THE MAGIC PEAR TREE, Murakami-Wolf Prods., BCP. Jimmy Murakami, Prod.
WINDY DAY, Hubley Studios, PAR. John and Faith Hubley, Prods.

(Live Action Subjects)
ROBERT KENNEDY REMEMBERED, Guggenheim Prods., NGP. Charles Guggenheim, Prod.
THE DOVE, Coe-Davis, SCH. George Coe, Sidney Davis and Anthony Lover, Prods.
DUO, NFC, COL.
PRELUDE, Prelude Co, EX. John Astin, Prod.

DOCUMENTARY (O-713)

(Short Subjects)
WHY MAN CREATES, Saul Bass & Associates. Saul Bass, Prod.
THE HOUSE THAT ANANDA BUILT, Films Division, Government of India. Fali Bilimoria, Prod.
THE REVOLVING DOOR, Vision Associates for the American Foundation Institute of Corrections. Lee R. Bobker, Prod.
A SPACE TO GROW, Office of Economic Opportunity for Project Upward Bound. Thomas P. Kelly, Jr., Prod.
A WAY OUT OF THE WILDERNESS, John Sutherland Prods. Dan E. Weisburd, Prod.

(Features)
JOURNEY INTO SELF, Western Behavioral Sciences Institute. Bill McGaw, Prod.
A FEW NOTES ON OUR FOOD PROBLEM, United States Information Agency. James Blue, Prod.
THE LEGENDARY CHAMPIONS, Turn Of The Century Fights. William Cayton, Prod.
OTHER VOICES, DHS Films. David H. Sawyer, Prod.
YOUNG AMERICANS, The Young Americans Prod. Robert Cohn and Alex Grasshoff, Prods. (Declared ineligible May 7, 1969 because first released during 1967.)

VISUAL EFFECTS (O-714)

2001: A SPACE ODYSSEY. Stanley Kubrick.
ICE STATION ZEBRA. Hal Millar and J. McMillan Johnson.

HONORARY AND OTHER (O-715)

(Jean Hersholt Humanitarian Award)
Martha Raye
(Other)
JOHN CHAMBERS for his outstanding make-up achievement for Planet Of The Apes.
ONNA WHITE for her outstanding choreography achievement for Oliver!.

SCIENTIFIC OR TECHNICAL (O-716)

(Class I)
PHILIP V. PALMQUIST of MINNESOTA MINING AND MANUFACTURING CO., DR. HERBERT MEYER of the MOTION PICTURE AND TELEVISION RESEARCH CENTER, and CHARLES D. STAFFELL of the RANK ORGANISATION for the development of a successful embodiment of the reflex background projection system for composite cinematography.
EASTMAN KODAK COMPANY for the development and introduction of a color reversal intermediate film for motion pictures.

(Class II)
DONALD W. NORWOOD for the design and development of the Norwood Photographic Exposure Meters.
EASTMAN KODAK COMPANY and PRODUCERS SERVICE COMPANY for the development of a new high-speed step-optical reduction printer.
EDMUND M. DiGIIULIO, NIELS G. PETERSEN and NORMAN S. HUGHES of the CINEMA PRODUCT DEVELOPMENT COMPANY for the design and application of a conversion which makes available the reflex viewing system for motion picture cameras.
OPTICAL COATING LABORATORIES, INC., for the development of an improved anti-reflection coating for photographic and projection lens systems.
EASTMAN KODAK COMPANY for the introduction of a new high speed motion picture color negative film.
PANAVISION INCORPORATED for the conception, design and introduction of a 65mm hand-held motion picture camera.
TODD-AO COMPANY and the MITCHELL CAMERA COMPANY for the design and engineering of the Todd-AO hand-held motion picture camera.

(Class III)
CARL W. HAUGE and EDWARD H. REICHARD of CONSOLIDATED FILM INDUSTRIES and E. MICHAEL MEAHL and ROY J. RIDENOUR of RAMTRONICS for engineering an automatic exposure control for printing-machine lamps.
EASTMAN KODAK COMPANY for a new direct positive film and **CONSOLIDATED FILM INDUSTRIES** for the application of this film to the making of post-production work prints.

1969

BEST PICTURE (O-717)

MIDNIGHT COWBOY, Jerome Hellman-John Schlesinger Production. UA. Jerome Hellman, Prod.
ANNE OF THE THOUSAND DAYS, Hal B. Wallis-U Pictures, Ltd. Production, U. Hal B. Wallis, Prod.
BUTCH CASSIDY AND THE SUNDANCE KID, George Roy Hill-Paul Monash Prod., FOX. John Foreman, Prod.
HELLO, DOLLY!, Chenault Production, FOX. Ernest Lehman, Prod.
Z, Reggane Films-O.N.C.I.C. Production, Cinema V. Jacques Perrin and Hamed Rachedi, Prods.

ACTOR (O-718)

JOHN WAYNE, True Grit, Hal Wallis Prod., PAR.
RICHARD BURTON, *Anne Of The Thousand Days.*
DUSTIN HOFFMAN, *Midnight Cowboy.*
PETER O'TOOLE, *Goodbye, Mr. Chips,* APJAC Prod., MGM.
JON VOIGHT, *Midnight Cowboy.*

ACTRESS (O-719)

MAGGIE SMITH, The Prime Of Miss Jean Brodie, FOX Prods, Ltd., FOX.
GENEVIEVE BUJOLD, *Anne Of The Thousand Days.*
JANE FONDA, *They Shoot Horses, Don't They?,* Chartoff-Winkler-Pollack Prod., ABC Pictures Presentation, CRC.
LIZA MINNELLI, *The Sterile Cuckoo,* Boardwalk Prods., PAR.
JEAN SIMMONS, *The Happy Ending,* Pax Films Prod., UA.

SUPPORTING ACTOR (O-720)
GIG YOUNG, They Shoot Horses, Don't They?
RUPERT CROSSE, *The Reivers,* Irving Ravetch-Arthur Kramer-Solar Prods., Cinema Center Films Presentation, NGP.
ELLIOTT GOULD, *Bob & Carol & Ted & Alice,* Frankovich Prods., COL.
JACK NICHOLSON, *Easy Rider,* Pando-Raybert Prods., COL.
ANTHONY QUAYLE, *Anne Of The Thousand Days.*

SUPPORTING ACTRESS (O-721)
GOLDIE HAWN, Cactus Flower, Frankovich Prods., COL.
CATHERINE BURNS, *Last Summer,* Frank Perry-Alsid Prod., AA.
DYAN CANNON, *Bob & Carol & Ted & Alice.*
SYLVIA MILES, *Midnight Cowboy.*
SUSANNAH YORK, *They Shoot Horses, Don't They?*

DIRECTING (O-722)
JOHN SCHLESINGER, Midnight Cowboy.
COSTA-GAVRAS, *Z.*
GEORGE ROY HILL, *Butch Cassidy And The Sundance Kid.*
ARTHUR PENN, *Alice's Restaurant,* Florin Prod., UA.
SYDNEY POLLACK, *They Shoot Horses, Don't They?*

WRITING (O-723)
(Best Story and Screenplay based on material not previously published or produced)
BUTCH CASSIDY AND THE SUNDANCE KID. William Goldman.
BOB & CAROL & TED & ALICE. Paul Mazursky and Larry Tucker.
THE DAMNED, Pegaso-Praesidens Film Prod., WB. Story by Nicola Badalucco. Screenplay by Nicola Badalucco, Enrico Medioli and Luchino Visconti.
EASY RIDER. Peter Fonda, Dennis Hopper and Terry Southern.
THE WILD BUNCH, Phil Feldman Prod., WB. Story by Walon Green and Roy N. Sickner. Screenplay by Walon Green and Sam Peckinpah.
(Best Screenplay based on material from another medium)
MIDNIGHT COWBOY. Waldo Salt.
ANNE OF THE THOUSAND DAYS. John Hale and Bridget Boland. Adaptation by Richard Sokolove.
GOODBYE, COLUMBUS, Willow Tree Prods., PAR. Arnold Schulman.
THEY SHOOT HORSES, DON'T THEY? James Poe and Robert E. Thompson.
Z. Jorge Semprun and Costa-Gavras.

CINEMATOGRAPHY (O-724)
BUTCH CASSIDY AND THE SUNDANCE KID. Conrad Hall.
ANNE OF THE THOUSAND DAYS. Arthur Ibbetson.
BOB & CAROL & TED & ALICE. Charles B. Lang.
HELLO, DOLLY! Harry Stradling.
MAROONED, Frankovich-Sturges Prod., COL. Daniel Fapp.

COSTUME DESIGN (O-725)
ANNE OF THE THOUSAND DAYS. Margaret Furse.
GAILY, GAILY, Mirisch-Cartier Prod., UA. Ray Aghayan.
HELLO, DOLLY! Irene Sharaff.
SWEET CHARITY, U. Edith Head.
THEY SHOOT HORSES, DON'T THEY? Donfeld.

ART DIRECTION - SET DECORATION (O-726)
HELLO, DOLLY! John DeCuir, Jack Martin Smith and Herman Blumenthal. Set Decoration: Walter M. Scott, George Hopkins and Raphael Bretton.
ANNE OF THE THOUSAND DAYS. Maurice Carter and Lionel Couch. Set Decoration: Patrick McLoughlin.
GAILY, GAILY. Robert Boyle and George B. Chan. Set Decoration: Edward Boyle and Carl Biddiscombe.
SWEET CHARITY. Alexander Golitzen and George C. Webb. Set Decoration: Jack D. Moore.
THEY SHOOT HORSES, DON'T THEY? Harry Horner. Set Decoration: Frank McKelvey.

FILM EDITING (O-727)
Z. Francoise Bonnot.
HELLO, DOLLY! William Reynolds.
MIDNIGHT COWBOY. Hugh A. Robertson.
THE SECRET OF SANTA VITTORIA, Stanley Kramer Co Prod., UA. William Lyon and Earle Herdan.
THEY SHOOT HORSES, DON'T THEY? Fredric Steinkamp.

FOREIGN LANGUAGE FILM (O-728)
Z.
ADALEN '31, AB Svensk Filmindustri Production (Sweden).
THE BATTLE OF NERETVA, United Film Prods-Igor Film-Eichberg Film-Commonwealth United Production (Yugoslavia).
THE BROTHERS KARAMAZOV, Mosfilm Production (U.S.S.R.)
MY NIGHT WITH MAUD, Films du Losange-F.F.P.-Films du Carrosse-Films des Deux Mondes- Films de la Pleiade-Gueville-Renn-Simar Films Production (France).

MUSIC - SCORING (O-729)
(Best Original Score for a Motion Picture-not a musical)
BUTCH CASSIDY AND THE SUNDANCE KID. Burt Bacharach.
ANNE OF THE THOUSAND DAYS. Georges Delerue.
THE REIVERS. John Williams.
THE SECRET OF SANTA VITTORIA. Ernest Gold.
THE WILD BUNCH. Jerry Fielding.
(Best Score of a Musical Picture-original or adaptation)
HELLO, DOLLY! Adapted by Lennie Hayton and Lionel Newman.
GOODBYE, MR. CHIPS. Musics and lyric by Leslie Bricusse. Adapted by John Williams.
PAINT YOUR WAGON, Alan Jay Lerner Prod., PAR. Adapted by Nelson Riddle.
SWEET CHARITY. Adapted by Cy Coleman.
THEY SHOOT HORSES, DON'T THEY? Adapted by John Green and Albert Woodbury.

MUSIC - BEST SONG (O-730)
RAINDROPS KEEP FALLIN' ON MY HEAD, Butch Cassidy And The Sundance Kid. Music, Burt Bacharach. Lyrics, Hal David.
COME SATURDAY MORNING, *The Sterile Cuckoo.* Music, Fred Karlin. Lyrics, Dory Previn.
JEAN, *The Prime Of Miss Jean Brodie.* Music and lyrics by Rod McKuen.
TRUE GRIT, *True Grit.* Music, Elmer Bernstein. Lyrics, Don Black. Lyrics, Don Black.
WHAT ARE YOU DOING THE REST OF YOUR LIFE, *The Happy Ending.* Music, Michel Legrand. Lyrics, Alan and Marilyn Bergman.

SOUND (O-731)
HELLO DOLLY! Jack Solomon and Murray Spivack.
ANNE OF THE THOUSAND DAYS. John Aldred.
BUTCH CASSIDY AND THE SUNDANCE KID. William Edmundson and David Dockendorf.
GAILY, GAILY. Robert Martin and Clem Portman.
MAROONED. Les Fresholtz and Arthur Piantadosi.

SHORT FILMS (O-732)
(Cartoons)
IT'S TOUGH TO BE A BIRD, Walt Disney Prods., BV. Ward Kimball, Prod.
OF MEN AND DEMONS, Hubley Studios, PAR. John and Faith Hubley, Prods.
WALKING, NFC, COL. Ryan Larkin, Prod.
(Live Action Subjects)
THE MAGIC MACHINES, Fly-By-Night Prods., MAN. Joan Keller Stern, Prod.
BLAKE, NFC, VAU. Doug Jackson, Prod.
PEOPLE SOUP, Pangloss Prods., COL. Marc Merson, Prod.

DOCUMENTARY (O-733)

(Short Subjects)

CZECHOSLOVAKIA 1968, Sanders-Fresco Film Makers for United States Information Agency. Denis Sanders and Robert M. Fresco, Prods.
AN IMPRESSION OF JOHN STEINBECK: WRITER, Donald Wrye Prods. for United States Information Agency. Donald Wrye, Prod.
JENNY IS A GOOD THING, A.C.I. Prod. for Project Head Start. Joan Horvath, Prod.
LEO BEUERMAN, Centron Prod. Arthur H. Wolf and Russell A. Mosser, Prods.
THE MAGIC MACHINES, Fly-By-Night Prods. Joan Keller Stern, Prod.

(Features)

ARTHUR RUBINSTEIN - THE LOVE OF LIFE, Midem Prod. Bernard Chevry, Prod.
BEFORE THE MOUNTAIN WAS MOVED, Robert K. Sharpe Prods. for The Office of Economic Opportunity. Robert K. Sharpe, Prod.
IN THE YEAR OF THE PIG, Emile de Antonio Prod. Emile de Antonio, Prod.
THE OLYMPICS IN MEXICO, Film Section of the Organizing Committee for the XIX Olympic Games.
THE WOLF MEN, MGM Documentary. Irwin Rosten, Prod.

VISUAL EFFECTS (O-734)

MAROONED. Robbie Robertson.
KRAKATOA, EAST OF JAVA, American Broadcasting Companies-CRC Prod., Cinerama. Eugene Lourie and Alex Weldon.

HONORARY AND OTHER (O-735)

(Jean Hersholt Humanitarian Award)

George Jessel

(Other)

CARY GRANT for his unique mastery of the art of screen acting with the respect and affection of his colleagues.

SCIENTIFIC OR TECHNICAL (O-736)

(Class II)

HAZELTINE CORPORATION for the design and development of the Hazeltine Color Film Analyzer.
FOUAD SAID for the design and introduction of the Cinemobile series of equipment trucks for location motion picture production.
JUAN DE LA CIERVA and DYNASCIENCES CORPORATION for the design and development of the Dynalens optical image motion compensator.

(Class III)

OTTO POPELKA of Magna-Tech Electronics Co., Inc., for the development of an Electronically Controlled Looping System.
FENTON HAMILTON of MGM Studios for the concept and engineering of a mobile battery power unit for location lighting.
PANAVISION INCORPORATED for the design and development of the Panaspeed Motion Picture Camera Motor.
ROBERT M. FLYNN and RUSSELL HESSY of Universal City Studios, Inc. for a machine-gun modification for motion picture photography.

1970

BEST PICTURE (O-737)

PATTON, FOX. Frank McCarthy, Prod.
AIRPORT, Ross Hunter-U Prod., U. Ross Hunter, Prod.
FIVE EASY PIECES, BBS Prods., COL. Bob Rafelson and Richard Wechsler, Prods.
LOVE STORY, The Love Story Co Prod., PAR. Howard G. Minsky, Prod.
M*A*S*H, Aspen Prods., FOX. Ingo Preminger, Prod.

ACTOR (O-738)

GEORGE C. SCOTT, Patton.
MELVYN DOUGLAS, *I Never Sang For My Father*, Jamel Prods., COL.
JAMES EARL JONES, *The Great White Hope*, Lawrence Turman Films Prod., FOX.
JACK NICHOLSON, *Five Easy Pieces.*
RYAN O'NEAL, *Love Story.*

ACTRESS (O-739)

GLENDA JACKSON, Women In Love, Larry Kramer-Martin Rosen Prod., UA.
JANE ALEXANDER, *The Great White Hope.*
ALI MacGRAW, *Love Story.*
SARAH MILES, *Ryan's Daughter*, Faraway Prods, MGM.
CARRIE SNODGRESS, *Diary Of A Mad Housewife*, Frank Perry Films Prod., U.

SUPPORTING ACTOR (O-740)

JOHN MILLS, Ryan's Daughter.
RICHARD CASTELLANO, *Lovers And Other Strangers*, ABC Pictures Prod., CRC.
CHIEF DAN GEORGE, *Little Big Man*, Hiller Prods., Ltd.-Stockbridge Prods., Cinema Center Films Presentation, NGP.
GENE HACKMAN, *I Never Sang For My Father.*
JOHN MARLEY, *Love Story.*

SUPPORTING ACTRESS (O-741)

HELEN HAYES, Airport.
KAREN BLACK, *Five Easy Pieces.*
LEE GRANT, *The Landlord*, A Mirisch-Cartier II Prod., UA.
SALLY KELLERMAN, *M*A*S*H.*
MAUREEN STAPLETON, *Airport.*

DIRECTING (O-742)

FRANKLIN J. SCHAFFNER, Patton.
ROBERT ALTMAN, *M*A*S*H.*
FEDERICO FELLINI, *Fellini Satyricon*, Alberto Grimaldi Prod., UA.
ARTHUR HILLER, *Love Story.*
KEN RUSSELL, *Women In Love.*

WRITING (O-743)

(Best Story and Screenplay based on factual material or material not previously published or produced)

PATTON. Francis Ford Coppola and Edmund H. North.
FIVE EASY PIECES. Story by Bob Rafelson and Adrien Joyce. Screenplay by Adrien Joyce.
JOE, Cannon Group Prod., Cannon Releasing. Norman Wexler.
LOVE STORY. Erich Segal.
MY NIGHT AT MAUD'S, Films du Losange-Carrosse-Renn-Deux Mondes-La Gueville-Simar-La Pleiade-F.F.P. Prod., PC. Eric Rohmer.

(Best Screenplay based on material from another medium)

M*A*S*H. Ring Lardner, Jr.
AIRPORT. George Seaton.
I NEVER SANG FOR MY FATHER. Robert Anderson.
LOVERS AND OTHER STRANGERS. Renee Taylor, Joseph Bologna and David Zelag Goodman.
WOMEN IN LOVE. Larry Kramer.

CINEMATOGRAPHY (O-744)

RYAN'S DAUGHTER. Freddie Young.
AIRPORT. Ernest Laszlo.
PATTON. Fred Koenekamp.
TORA! TORA! TORA!, FOX. Charles F. Wheeler, Osami Furuya, Sinsaku Himeda & Masamichi Satoh.
WOMEN IN LOVE. Billy Williams.

COSTUME DESIGN (O-745)

CROMWELL, Irving Allen, Ltd. Prod., COL. Nino Novarese.
AIRPORT. Edith Head.
DARLING LILI, Geoffrey Prods., PAR. Donald Brooks and Jack Bear.
THE HAWAIIANS, Mirisch Prods., UA. Bill Thomas.
SCROOGE, Waterbury Films, Ltd. Prod., Cinema Center Films Presentation, NGP. Margaret Furse.

ART DIRECTION - SET DECORATION (O-746)

PATTON. Urie McCleary and Gil Parrondo. Set Decoration: Antonio Mateos and Pierre-Louis Thevenet.
AIRPORT. Alexander Golitzen and E. Preston Ames. Set Decoration: Jack D. Moore and Mickey S. Michaels.
THE MOLLY MAGUIRES, Tamm Prods., PAR. Tambi Larsen. Set Decoration: Darrell Silvera.
SCROOGE. Terry Marsh and Bob Cartwright. Set Decoration: Pamela Cornell.
TORA! TORA! TORA! Jack Martin Smith, Yoshiro Muraki, Richard Day and Taizoh Kawashima. Set Decoration: Walter M. Scott, Norman Rockett and Carl Biddiscombe.

FILM EDITING (O-747)

PATTON. Hugh S. Fowler.
AIRPORT. Stuart Gilmore.
M*A*S*H. Danford B. Greene.
TORA! TORA! TORA! James E. Newcom, Pembroke J. Herring and Inoue Chikaya.
WOODSTOCK, Wadleigh-Maurice, Ltd. Prod., WB. Thelma Schoonmaker.

FOREIGN LANGUAGE FILM (O-748)

INVESTIGATION OF A CITIZEN ABOVE SUSPICION, Vera Films Prod. (Italy).
FIRST LOVE, Alfa Prods.-Seitz Film Prod. (Switzerland).
HOA-BINH, Madeleine-Parc-La Gueville-C.A.P.A.C. Prod. (France).
PAIX SUR LES CHAMPS, Philippe Collette-E.G.C. Prod. (Belgium).
TRISTANA, Forbes Films, Ltd.-United Cineworld-Epoca Films- Talia Film-Les Films Corona-Selenia Cinematografica Prod. (Spain).

MUSIC - SCORING (O-749)

(Best Original Score)
LOVE STORY. Francis Lai.
AIRPORT. Alfred Newman.
CROMWELL. Frank Cordell.
PATTON. Jerry Goldsmith.
SUNFLOWER, Sostar Prod., AVE. Henry Mancini.

(Best Original Song Score)
LET IT BE, Beatles-Apple Prod., UA. Music and lyrics by The Beatles.
THE BABY MAKER, Robert Wise Prod., NGP. Music, Fred Karlin. Lyrics, Tylwyth Kymry.
A BOY NAMED CHARLIE BROWN, Lee Mendelson-Melendez Features Prod., Cinema Center Films Presentation, NGP. Music by Rod McKuen and John Scott Trotter. Lyrics by Rod McKuen, Bill Melendez and Al Shean. Adapted by Vince Guaraldi.
DARLING LILI. Music, Henry Mancini. Lyrics, Johnny Mercer.
SCROOGE. Music and lyrics by Leslie Bricusse. Adapted, Ian Fraser and Herbert W. Spencer.

MUSIC - BEST SONG (O-750)

FOR ALL WE KNOW, Lovers And Other Strangers. Music, Fred Karlin. Lyrics, Robb Royer and James Griffin aka Robb Wilson and Arthur James.
PIECES OF DREAMS, *Pieces Of Dreams*, RFB Enterprises Prod., UA. Music, Michel Legrand. Lyrics, Alan and Marilyn Bergman.
THANK YOU VERY MUCH, *Scrooge*. Music and lyrics by Leslie Bricusse.
TILL LOVE TOUCHES YOUR LIFE, *Madron*, Edric-Isracine-Zev Braun Prods., 4SX. Music, Riz Ortolani. Lyrics, Arthur Hamilton.
WHISTLING AWAY THE DARK, *Darling Lili*. Music, Henri Mancini. Lyrics, Johnny Mercer.

SOUND (O-751)

PATTON. Douglas Williams and Don Bassman.
AIRPORT. Ronald Pierce and David Moriarty.
RYAN'S DAUGHTER. Gordon K. McCallum and John Bramall.
TORA! TORA! TORA! Murray Spivack and Herman Lewis.
WOODSTOCK. Dan Wallin and Larry Johnson.

SHORT FILMS (O-752)

(Cartoons)
IS IT ALWAYS RIGHT TO BE RIGHT?, Stephen Bosustow Prods., SCH. Nick Bosustow, Prod.
THE FURTHER ADVENTURES OF UNCLE SAM: PART TWO, The Haboush Co, GOL. Robert Mitchell and Dale Case, Prods.
THE SHEPHERD, Cameron Guess and Associates, BRA. Cameron Guess, Prod.

(Live Action Subjects)
THE RESURRECTION OF BRONCHO BILLY, University of Southern California, Dept. of Cinema, U. John Longenecker, Prod.
SHUT UP. . .I'M CRYING, Robert Siegler Prods., SCH. Robert Siegler, Prod.
STICKY MY FINGERS. . .FLEET MY FEET, The American Film Institute, SCH. John Hancock, Prod.

DOCUMENTARY (O-753)

(Short Subjects)
INTERVIEWS WITH MY LAI VETERANS, Laser Film Corp. Joseph Strick, Prod.
THE GIFTS, Richter-McBride Prods. for the Water Quality Office of the Environmental Protection Agency. Robert McBride, Prod.
A LONG WAY FROM NOWHERE, Robert Aller Prods. Bob Aller, Prod.
OISIN, An Aengus Film. Vivien and Patrick Carey, Prods.
TIME IS RUNNING OUT, Gesellschaft fur bildende Filme. Horst Dallmayr and Robert Menegoz, Prods.

(Features)
WOODSTOCK. Bob Maurice, Prod.
CHARIOTS OF THE GODS, Terra-Filmkunst GmbH. Dr. Harald Reinl, Prod.
JACK JOHNSON, The Big Fights. Jim Jacobs, Prod.
KING: A FILMED RECORD. . .MONTGOMERY TO MEMPHIS. CUE. Ely Landau, Prod.
SAY GOODBYE, A Wolper Prod. David H. Vowell., Prod.

VISUAL EFFECTS (O-754)

TORA! TORA! TORA! A. D. Flowers and L. B. Abbott.
PATTON. Alex Weldon.

HONORARY AND OTHER (O-755)

(Irving G. Thalberg Memorial Award)
Ingmar Bergman
(Jean Hersholt Humanitarian Award)
Frank Sinatra
(Other)
LILLIAN GISH for superlative artistry and for distinguished contribution to the progress of motion pictures.
ORSON WELLES for superlative artistry and versatility in the creation of motion pictures.

SCIENTIFIC OR TECHNICAL (O-756)

(Class II)
LEONARD SOKOLOW and EDWARD H. REICHARD of Consolidated Film Industries for the concept and engineering of the Color Proofing Printer for motion pictures.
(Class III)
SYLVANIA ELECTRIC PRODUCTS INC. for the development and introduction of a series of compact tungsten halogen lamps for motion picture production.
B. J. LOSMANDY for the concept, design and application of microminiature solid state amplifier modules used in motion picture re-

cording equipment.
EASTMAN KODAK COMPANY and PHOTO ELECTRONICS CORPORATION for the design and engineering of an improved video color analyzer for motion picture laboratories.
ELECTRO SOUND INCORPORATED for the design and introduction of the Series 8000 Sound System for motion picture theatres.

1971

BEST PICTURE (O-757)

THE FRENCH CONNECTION, A Philip D'Antoni Prod. in association with Schine-Moore Prods., FOX. Philip D'Antoni, Prod.
A CLOCKWORK ORANGE, A Hawks Films, Ltd. Prod., WB. Stanley Kubrick, Prod.
FIDDLER ON THE ROOF, Mirisch-Cartier Prods., UA. Norman Jewison, Prod.
THE LAST PICTURE SHOW, BBS Prods., COL. Stephen J. Friedman, Prod.
NICHOLAS AND ALEXANDRA, A Horizon Pictures Prod., COL. Sam Spiegel, Prod.

ACTOR (O-758)

GENE HACKMAN, The French Connection.
PETER FINCH, Sunday Bloody Sunday, A Joseph Janni Prod., UA.
WALTER MATTHAU, Kotch, A Kotch Company Prod., ABC Pictures Presentation, CRC.
GEORGE C. SCOTT, The Hospital, A Howard Gottfried-Paddy Chayefsky Prod. in association with Arthur Hiller, UA.
TOPOL, Fiddler On The Roof, A Mirisch-Cartier Prods., UA.

ACTRESS (O-759)

JANE FONDA, Klute, A Gus Prod., WB.
JULIE CHRISTIE, McCabe & Mrs. Miller, A Robert Altman-David Foster Prod., WB.
GLENDA JACKSON, Sunday Bloody Sunday.
VANESSA REDGRAVE, Mary, Queen Of Scots, A Hal Wallis-U Pictures, Ltd. Prod., U.
JANET SUZMAN, Nicholas And Alexandra.

SUPPORTING ACTOR (O-760)

BEN JOHNSON, The Last Picture Show.
JEFF BRIDGES, The Last Picture Show.
LEONARD FREY, Fiddler On The Roof.
RICHARD JAECKEL, Sometimes A Great Notion, A U-Newman-Foreman Co Prod., U.
ROY SCHEIDER, The French Connection.

SUPPORTING ACTRESS (O-761)

CLORIS LEACHMAN, The Last Picture Show.
ELLEN BURSTYN, The Last Picture Show.
BARBARA HARRIS, Who Is Harry Kellerman, And Why Is He Saying Those Terrible Things About Me?, A Who Is Harry Kellerman Co Prod., Cinema Center Films Presentation, NGP.
MARGARET LEIGHTON, The Go-Between, A World Film Services, Ltd. Prod., COL.
ANN-MARGRET, Carnal Knowledge, Icarus Prods., AVE.

DIRECTING (O-762)

WILLIAM FRIEDKIN, The French Connection.
PETER BOGDANOVICH, The Last Picture Show.
NORMAN JEWISON, Fiddler On The Roof.
STANLEY KUBRICK, A Clockwork Orange.
JOHN SCHLESINGER, Sunday Bloody Sunday.

WRITING (O-763)

(Best Story and Screenplay based on factual material or material not previously published or produced)
THE HOSPITAL. Paddy Chayefsky.
INVESTIGATION OF A CITIZEN ABOVE SUSPICION, A Vera Films, S.P.A. Prod., COL. Elio Petri and Ugo Pirro.
KLUTE. Andy and Dave Lewis.
SUMMER OF '42, A Robert Mulligan-Richard Alan Roth Prod., WB. Herman Raucher.
SUNDAY BLOODY SUNDAY. Penelope Gilliatt.
(Best Screenplay based on material from another medium)
THE FRENCH CONNECTION. Ernest Tidyman.
A CLOCKWORK ORANGE. Stanley Kubrick.
THE CONFORMIST, Mars Film Produzione, S.P.A.-Marianne prods., PAR. Bernardo Bertolucci.
THE GARDEN OF THE FINZI-CONTINIS, A Gianni Hecht Lucari-Arthur Cohn Prod., C5. Ugo Pirro and Vittorio Bonicelli.
THE LAST PICTURE SHOW. Larry McMurtry and Peter Bogdanovich.

CINEMATOGRAPHY (O-764)

FIDDLER ON THE ROOF. Oswald Morris.
THE FRENCH CONNECTION. Owen Roizman.
THE LAST PICTURE SHOW. Robert Surtees.
NICHOLAS AND ALEXANDRA. Freddie Young.
SUMMER OF '42. Robert Surtees.

COSTUME DESIGN (O-765)

NICHOLAS AND ALEXANDRA. Yvonne Blake and Antonio Castillo.
BEDKNOBS AND BROOMSTICKS, Walt Disney Prods., BV. Bill Thomas.
DEATH IN VENICE, An Alfa Cinematografica-P.E.C.F. Prod., WB. Piero Tosi.
MARY, QUEEN OF SCOTS. Margaret Furse.
WHAT'S THE MATTER WITH HELEN?, A Filmways-Raymax Prod., UA. Morton Haack.

ART DIRECTION - SET DECORATION (O-766)

NICHOLAS AND ALEXANDRA. John Box, Ernest Archer, Jack Maxsted and Gil Parrondo. Set Decoration: Vernon Dixon.
THE ANDROMEDA STRAIN, A U-Robert Wise Prod., U. Boris Leven and William Tuntke. Set Decoration: Ruby Levitt.
BEDKNOBS AND BROOMSTICKS. John B. Mansbridge and Peter Ellenshaw. Set Decoration: Emile Kuri and Hal Gausman.
FIDDLER ON THE ROOF. Robert Boyle and Michael Stringer. Set Decoration: Peter Lamont.
MARY, QUEEN OF SCOTS. Terence Marsh and Robert Cartwright. Set Decorations: Peter Howitt.

FILM EDITING (O-767)

THE FRENCH CONNECTION. Jerry Greenberg.
THE ANDROMEDA STRAIN. Stuart Gilmore and John W. Holmes.
A CLOCKWORK ORANGE. Bill Butler.
KOTCH. Ralph E. Winters.
SUMMER OF '42. Folmar Blangsted.

FOREIGN LANGUAGE FILM (O-768)

THE GARDEN OF THE FINZI-CONTINIS.
DODES'KA-DEN, A Toho Co, Ltd.-Yonki no Kai Prod. (Japan).
THE EMIGRANTS, A Svensk Filmindustri Prod. (Sweden).
THE POLICEMAN, An Ephi-Israeli Motion Picture Studios Prod. (Israel)
TCHAIKOVSKY, A Dimitri Tiomkin-Mosfilm Studios Prod. (U.S.S.R.)

MUSIC - SCORING (O-769)

(Best Original Dramatic Score)
SUMMER OF '42. Michel Legrand.
MARY, QUEEN OF SCOTS. John Barry.
NICHOLAS AND ALEXANDRA. Richard Rodney Bennett.
SHAFT, Shaft Prods., Ltd., MGM. Isaac Hayes.

STRAW DOGS, A Talent Associates, Ltd.-Amerbroco Films, Ltd. Prod., ABC Pictures Presentation, CRC. Jerry Fielding.

(Best Scoring-Adaptation and Original Song Score)
FIDDLER ON THE ROOF. Adapted by John Williams.
BEDKNOBS AND BROOMSTICKS. Song Score by Richard M. Sherman and Robert B. Sherman. Adapted by Irwin Kostal.
THE BOY FRIEND, A Russflix, Ltd. Prod., MGM. Adapted by Peter Maxwell Davies and Peter Greenwell.
TCHAIKOVSKY. Adapted by Dimitri Tiomkin.
WILLY WONKA AND THE CHOCOLATE FACTORY, A Wolper Pictures, Ltd. Prod., PAR. Song Score by Leslie Bricusse and Anthony Newley. Adapted by Walter Scharf.

MUSIC - BEST SONG (O-770)
THEME FROM SHAFT, Shaft. Music and lyrics by Isaac Hayes.
THE AGE OF NOT BELIEVING, *Bedknobs And Broomsticks.* Music and lyrics by Richard M. Sherman and Robert B. Sherman.
ALL HIS CHILDREN, *Sometimes A Great Notion.* Music, Henry Mancini. Lyrics, Alan and Marilyn Bergman.
BLESS THE BEASTS & CHILDREN, *Bless The Beasts & Children,* COL. Music and lyrics by Barry DeVorzon and Perry Botkin, Jr.
LIFE IS WHAT YOU MAKE IT, *Kotch.* Music, Marvin Hamlisch. Lyrics, Johnny Mercer.

SOUND (O-771)
FIDDLER ON THE ROOF. Gordon K. McCallum and David Hildyard.
DIAMONDS ARE FOREVER, An Albert R. Broccoli-Harry Saltzman Prod., UA. Gordon K. McCallum, John Mitchell and Alfred J. Overton.
THE FRENCH CONNECTION. Theodore Soderberg and Christopher Newman.
KOTCH. Richard Portman and Jack Solomon.
MARY, QUEEN OF SCOTS. Bob Jones and John Aldred.

SHORT FILMS (O-772)
(Animated)
THE CRUNCH BIRD, Maxwell-Petok-Petrovich Prods., RGY. Ted Petok, Prod.
EVOLUTION, NFC, COL. Michael Mills, Prod.
THE SELFISH GIANT, Potterton Prods., Pyramid Films. Peter Sander and Murray Shostak, Prods.

(Live Action)
SENTINELS OF SILENCE, Producciones Concord, PAR. Manuel Arango and Robert Amram, Prods.
GOOD MORNING, E/G Films, BOR. Denny Evans and Ken Greenwald, Prods.
THE REHEARSAL, A Cinema Verona Prod., SCH. Stephen F. Verona, Prod.

DOCUMENTARY (O-773)
(Short Subjects)
SENTINELS OF SILENCE, Producciones Concord, PAR. Manuel Arango and Robert Amram, Prods.
ADVENTURES IN PERCEPTION, Han van Gelder Filmproduktie for Netherlands Information Service. Han van Gelder, Prod.
ART IS. . ., Henry Strauss Associates for Sears Roebuck Foundation. Julian Krainin and DeWitt L. Sage, Jr., Prods.
THE NUMBERS START WITH THE RIVER, A WH Picture for United States Information Agency. Donald Wrye, Prod.
SOMEBODY WAITING, Snider Prods. for University of California Medical Film Library. Hal Riney, Dick Snider and Sherwood Omens, Prods.

(Features)
THE HELLSTROM CHRONICLE, David L. Wolper Prods. C5. Walon Green, Prod.
ALASKA WILDERNESS LAKE, Alan Landsburg Prods. Alan Landsburg, Prod.
ON ANY SUNDAY, Bruce Brown Films-Solar Prods., C5. Bruce Brown, Prod.
THE RA EXPEDITIONS, Swedish Broadcasting Co, INT. Lennart Ehrenborg and Thor Heyerdahl, Prods.
THE SORROW AND THE PITY, Television Rencontre-Norddeutscher Rundfunk-Television Swiss Romande, C5. Marcel Ophuls, Prod.

VISUAL EFFECTS (O-774)
BEDKNOBS AND BROOMSTICKS. Alan Maley, Eustace Lycett and Danny Lee.
WHEN DINOSAURS RULED THE EARTH, A Hammer Film Prod., WB. Jim Danforth and Roger Dicken.

HONORARY AND OTHER (O-775)
(Other)
CHARLES CHAPLIN for the incalculable effect he has had in making motion pictures the art form of this century.

SCIENTIFIC OR TECHNICAL (O-776)
(Class II)
JOHN N. WILKINSON of Optical Radiation Corp for the development and engineering of a system of xenon arc lamphouses for motion picture projection.
(Class III)
THOMAS JEFFERSON HUTCHINSON, JAMES R. ROCHESTER and FENTON HAMILTON for the development and introduction of the Sunbrute system of xenon arc lamps for location lighting in motion picture production.
PHOTO RESEARCH, a Division of Kollmorgen Corp, for the development and introduction of the film-lens balanced Three Color Meter.
ROBERT D. AUGUSTE and CINEMA PRODUCTS CO. for the development and introduction of a new crystal controlled lightweight motor for the 35mm motion picture Arriflex camera.
PRODUCERS SERVICE CORPORATION and CONSOLIDATED FILM INDUSTRIES; and CINEMA RESEARCH CORPORATION and RESEARCH PRODUCTS, INC. for the engineering and implementation of fully automated blow-up motion picture printing systems.
CINEMA PRODUCTS CO. for a control motor to actuate zoom lenses on motion picture cameras.

1972

BEST PICTURE (O-777)
THE GODFATHER, An Albert S. Ruddy Production, PAR. Albert S. Ruddy, Prod.
CABARET, An ABC Pictures Production, AA. Cy Feuer, Prod.
DELIVERANCE, WB. John Boorman, Prod.
THE EMIGRANTS, A Svensk Filmindustri Production, WB. Bengt Forslund, Prod.
SOUNDER, Radnitz/Mattel Productions, FOX. Robert B. Radnitz, Prod.

ACTOR (O-778)
MARLON BRANDO, The Godfather.
MICHAEL CAINE, *Sleuth,* A Palomar Pictures Int'l Production, FOX.
LAURENCE OLIVIER, *Sleuth.*
PETER O'TOOLE, *The Ruling Class,* A Keep Films, Ltd. Production, AVE.
PAUL WINFIELD, *Sounder.*

ACTRESS (O-779)
LIZA MINNELLI, Cabaret.
DIANA ROSS, *Lady Sings The Blues,* A Motown-Weston-Furie Production, PAR.
MAGGIE SMITH, *Travels With My Aunt,* Robert Fryer Productions, MGM.
CICELY TYSON, *Sounder.*
LIV ULLMANN, *The Emigrants.*

SUPPORTING ACTOR (O-780)
JOEL GREY, Cabaret.
EDDIE ALBERT, *The Heartbreak Kid,* A Palomar Pictures Int'l Production, FOX.
JAMES CAAN, *The Godfather.*
ROBERT DUVALL, *The Godfather.*
AL PACINO, *The Godfather.*

SUPPORTING ACTRESS (O-781)

EILEEN HECKART, Butterflies Are Free, Frankovich Productions, COL.
JEANNIE BERLIN, *The Heartbreak Kid.*
GERALDINE PAGE, *Pete 'N' Tillie,* A U-Martin Ritt-Julius J. Epstein Production, U.
SUSAN TYRRELL, *Fat City,* Rastar Productions, COL.
SHELLEY WINTERS, *The Poseidon Adventure,* An Irwin Allen Production, FOX.

DIRECTING (O-782)

BOB FOSSE, Cabaret.
JOHN BOORMAN, *Deliverance.*
FRANCIS FORD COPPOLA, *The Godfather.*
JOSEPH L. MANKIEWICZ, *Sleuth.*
JAN TROELL, *The Emigrants.*

WRITING (O-783)

(Best Story and Screenplay based on factual material or material not previously published or produced)
THE CANDIDATE, A Redford-Ritchie Prod., WB. Jeremy Larner.
THE DISCREET CHARM OF THE BOURGEOISIE, A Serge Silberman Prod., FOX. Luis Bunuel in collaboration with Jean-Claude Carriere.
LADY SINGS THE BLUES. Terence McCloy, Chris Clark and Suzanne de Passe.
MURMUR OF THE HEART, A Nouvelles Editions De Films-Marianne Productions-Vides Cinematografica-Franz Seitz Filmproduktion, CON. Louis Malle.
YOUNG WINSTON, An Open Road Films, Ltd. Prod., COL. Carl Foreman.

(Best Screenplay based on material from another medium)
THE GODFATHER. Mario Puzo and Francis Ford Coppola.
CABARET. Jay Allen.
THE EMIGRANTS. Jan Troell and Bengt Forslund.
PETE N' TILLIE. Julius J. Epstein.
SOUNDER. Lonne Elder, III.

CINEMATOGRAPHY (O-784)

CABARET. Geoffrey Unsworth.
BUTTERFLIES ARE FREE. Charles B. Lang.
THE POSEIDON ADVENTURE. Harold E. Stine.
1776, A Jack L. Warner Production, COL. Harry Stradling, Jr.
TRAVELS WITH MY AUNT. Douglas Slocombe.

COSTUME DESIGN (O-785)

TRAVELS WITH MY AUNT. Anthony Powell.
THE GODFATHER. Anna Hill Johnstone.
LADY SINGS THE BLUES. Bob Mackie, Ray Aghayan and Norma Koch.
THE POSEIDON ADVENTURE. Paul Zastupnevich.
YOUNG WINSTON. Anthony Mendleson.

ART DIRECTION - SET DECORATION (O-786)

CABARET. Rolf Zehetbauer and Jurgen Kiebach. Set Decoration: Herbert Strabel.
LADY SINGS THE BLUES. Carl Anderson. Set Decoration: Reg Allen.
THE POSEIDON ADVENTURE. William Creber. Set Decoration: Raphael Bretton.
TRAVELS WITH MY AUNT. John Box, Gil Parrondo and Robert W. Laing.
YOUNG WINSTON. Don Ashton, Geoffrey Drake, John Graysmark and William Hutchinson. Set Decoration: Peter James.

FILM EDITING (O-787)

CABARET. David Bretherton.
DELIVERANCE. Tom Priestley.
THE GODFATHER. William Reynolds and Peter Zinner.
THE HOT ROCK, A Landers-Roberts Production, FOX. Frank P. Keller and Fred W. Berger.
THE POSEIDON ADVENTURE. Harold F. Kress.

FOREIGN LANGUAGE FILM (O-788)

THE DISCREET CHARM OF THE BOURGEOISIE. A Serge Silberman Prod.
THE DAWNS HERE ARE QUIET, A Gorky Film Studios Prod. (U.S.S.R.).
I LOVE YOU ROSA, A Noah Films Ltd. Prod. (Israel).
MY DEAREST SENORITA, An El Iman Prod. (Spain).
THE NEW LAND, A Svensk Filmindustri Prod. (Sweden).

MUSIC - SCORING (O-789)

(Best Original Dramatic Score)
LIMELIGHT, A Charles Chaplin Prod., COL. Charles Chaplin, Raymond Rasch and Larry Russell.
IMAGES, A Hemdale Group, Ltd.-Lion's Gate Films Prod., COL. John Williams.
NAPOLEON AND SAMANTHA, A Walt Disney Prods., BV. Buddy Baker.
THE POSEIDON ADVENTURE. John Williams.
SLEUTH. John Addison.

(Best Scoring-Adaptation and Original Song Score)
CABARET. Adapted by Ralph Burns.
LADY SINGS THE BLUES. Adapted by Gil Askey.
MAN OF LA MANCHA, A PEA Produzioni Europee Associate Prod., UA. Adapted by Laurence Rosenthal.

MUSIC - BEST SONG (O-790)

THE MORNING AFTER, The Poseidon Adventure. Music and lyrics by Al Kasha and Joel Hirschhorn.
BEN, *Ben,* BCP Productions, CRC. Music, Walter Scharf. Lyrics, Don Black.
COME FOLLOW, FOLLOW ME, *The Little Ark,* Robert Radnitz Productions, Ltd., Cinema Center Films Presentation, NGP. Music, Fred Karlin. Lyrics, Marsha Karlin.
MARMALADE, MOLASSES & HONEY, *The Life And Times Of Judge Roy Bean,* A First Artists Production Co, Ltd. Production, NGP. Music, Maurice Jarre. Lyrics, Marilyn and Alan Bergman.
STRANGE ARE THE WAYS OF LOVE, *The Stepmother,* Magic Eye of Hollywood Productions, Crown Int'l. Music, Sammy Fain. Lyrics, Paul Francis Webster.

SOUND (O-791)

CABARET. Robert Knudson and David Hildyard.
BUTTERFLIES ARE FREE. Arthur Piantadosi and Charles Knight.
THE CANDIDATE. Richard Portman and Gene Cantamessa.
THE GODFATHER. Bud Grenzbach, Richard Portman and Christopher Newman.
THE POSEIDON ADVENTURE. Theodore Soderberg and Herman Lewis.

SHORT FILMS (O-792)

(Animated)
A CHRISTMAS CAROL, A Richard Williams Production, American Broadcasting Co Film Serivces. Richard Williams, Prod.
KAMA SUTRA RIDES AGAIN, Bob Godfrey Films, Ltd., LIO. Bob Godfrey, Prod.
TUP TUP, A Zagreb Film-Corona Cinematografica Production, MAN. Nedeljko Dragic, Prod.

(Live Action)
NORMAN ROCKWELL'S WORLD. . .AN AMERICAN DREAM, A Concepts Unlimited Production, COL. Richard Barclay, Prod.
FROG STORY, Gidron Productions, SCH. Ron Satlof and Ray Gideon,

Prods.
SOLO, Pyramid Films, UA. David Adams, Prod.

DOCUMENTARY (O-793)

(Short Subjects)

THIS TINY WORLD, A Charles Huguenot van der Linden Production. Charles and Martina Huguenot van der Linden, Prods.
HUNDERTWASSER'S RAINY DAY, An Argos Films-Peter Schamoni Film Prod. Peter Schamoni, Prod.
K-Z, A Nexus Film Production. Giorgio Treves, Prod.
SELLING OUT, A Unit Productions Film. Tadeusz Jaworski, Prod.
THE TIDE OF TRAFFIC, A BP-Greenpark Production. Humphrey Swingler, Prod.

(Features)

MARJOE, A Cinema X Production, C5. Howard Smith and Sarah Kernochan, Prods.
APE AND SUPER-APE, A Bert Haanstra Film Production, Netherlands Ministry of Culture, Recreation and Social Welfare. Bert Haanstra, Prod.
MALCOLM X, A Marvin Worth Production, WB. Marvin Worth and Arnold Perl, Prods.
MANSON, Robert Hendrickson and Laurence Merrick, Prods.
THE SILENT REVOLUTION, A Leonaris Film Production. Eckehard Munck, Prod.

HONORARY AND OTHER (O-794)

(Jean Hersholt Humanitarian Award)

Rosalind Russell

(Special Achievement)

L.B. ABBOTT and A.D. FLOWERS for Visual Effects for The Poseidon Adventure.

(Other)

CHARLES S. BOREN, Leader for 38 years of the industry's enlightened labor relations and architect of its policy of non-discrimination. With the respect and affection of all who work in films.
EDWARD G. ROBINSON, who achieved greatness as a player, a patron of the arts and a dedicated citizen. . .in sum, a Renaissance man. From his friends in the industry he loves.

SCIENTIFIC OR TECHNICAL (O-795)

(Class II)

JOSEPH E. BLUTH for research and development in the field of electronic photography and transfer of video tape to motion picture film.
EDWARD H. REICHARD and HOWARD T. LA ZARE of Consolidated Film Industries, and EDWARD EFRON of IBM for the engineering of a computerized light valve monitoring system for motion picture printing.
PANAVISION INCORPORATED for the development and engineering of the Panaflex motion picture camera.

(Class III)

PHOTO RESEARCH, a Division of Kollmorgen Corp, and PSC TECHNOLOGY INC., Acme Products Division, for the Spectra Film Gate Photometer for motion picture printers.
CARTER EQUIPMENT COMPANY, INC. and RAMTRONICS for the RAMtronics light-valve photometer for motion picture printers.
DAVID DEGENKOLB, HARRY LARSON, MANFRED MICHELSON and FRED SCOBEY of DeLuxe General Inc for the development of a computerized motion picture printer and process control system.
JIRO MUKAI and RYUSHO HIROSE of Canon, Inc. and WILTON R. HOLM of the AMPTP Motion Picture and Television Research Center for development of the Canon Macro Zoom Lens for motion picture photography.
PHILIP V. PALMQUIST and LEONARD L. OLSON of the 3M Co, and FRANK P. CLARK of the AMPTP Motion Picture and Television Research Center for development of the Nextel simulated blood for motion picture color photography.
E. H. GEISSLER and G. M. BERGGREN of Wil-Kin Inc. for engineering of the Ultra-Vision Motion Picture Theater Projection System.

1973

BEST PICTURE (O-796)

THE STING, A U-Bill/Phillips-George Roy Hill Film Prod., Zanuck/Brown Presentation, U. Tony Bill, Michael and Julia Phillips, Prods.
AMERICAN GRAFFITI, A U-Lucasfilm, Ltd.-Coppola Co Prod., U. Francis Ford Coppola, Prod. Gary Kurtz, Co-Prod.
CRIES AND WHISPERS, A Svenska Filminstitutet-Cinematograph AB Prod., NW. Ingmar Bergman, Prod.
THE EXORCIST, Hoya Prods., WB. William Peter Blatty, Prod.
A TOUCH OF CLASS, Brut Prods., AVE. Melvin Frank, Prod.

ACTOR (O-797)

JACK LEMMON, Save The Tiger, Filmways-Jalem-Cirandinha Prods., PAR.
MARLON BRANDO, *Last Tango In Paris*, A PEA Produzioni Europee Associate S.A.S.-Les Productions Artistes Associes S.A. Prod., UA.
JACK NICHOLSON, *The Last Detail*, An Acrobat Films Prod., COL.
AL PACINO, *Serpico*.
ROBERT REDFORD, *The Sting*.

ACTRESS (O-798)

GLENDA JACKSON, A Touch Of Class.
ELLEN BURSTYN, *The Exorcist*.
MARSHA MASON, *Cinderella Liberty*, A Sanford Prod., FOX.
BARBRA STREISAND, *The Way We Were*, Rastar Prods., COL.
JOANNE WOODWARD, *Summer Wishes, Winter Dreams*, A Rastar Pictures Prod., COL.

SUPPORTING ACTOR (O-799)

JOHN HOUSEMAN, The Paper Chase, Thompson-Paul Productions, FOX.
VINCENT GARDENIA, *Bang The Drum Slowly*, A Rosenfield Production, PAR.
JACK GILFORD, *Save The Tiger*.
JASON MILLER, *The Exorcist*.
RANDY QUAID, *The Last Detail*.

SUPPORTING ACTRESS (O-800)

TATUM O'NEAL, Paper Moon, A Directors Co Prod., PAR.
LINDA BLAIR, *The Exorcist*.
CANDY CLARK, *American Graffiti*.
MADELINE KAHN, *Paper Moon*.
SYLVIA SIDNEY, *Summer Wishes, Winter Dreams*.

DIRECTING (O-801)

GEORGE ROY HILL, The Sting.
INGMAR BERGMAN, *Cries And Whispers*.
BERNARDO BERTOLUCCI, *Last Tango In Paris*.
WILLIAM FRIEDKIN, *The Exorcist*.
GEORGE LUCAS, *American Graffiti*.

WRITING (O-802)

(Best Story and Screenplay based on factual material or material not previously published or produced)

THE STING. David S. Ward.
AMERICAN GRAFFITI. George Lucas, Gloria Katz and Willard Huyck.
CRIES AND WHISPERS. Ingmar Bergman.
SAVE THE TIGER. Steve Shagan.
A TOUCH OF CLASS. Melvin Frank and Jack Rose.

(Best Screenplay based on material from another medium)

THE EXORCIST. William Peter Blatty.
THE LAST DETAIL. Robert Towne.
THE PAPER CHASE. James Bridges.
PAPER MOON. Alvin Sargent.
SERPICO, A Produzioni De Laurentiis Int'l Manufacturing Co S.p.A. Prod., PAR. Waldo Salt and Norman Wexler.

CINEMATOGRAPHY (O-803)

CRIES AND WHISPERS. Sven Nykvist.
THE EXORCIST. Owen Roizman.
JONATHAN LIVINGSTON SEAGULL, A JLS Ltd Partnership Prod., PAR. Jack Couffer.
THE STING. Robert Surtees.
THE WAY WE WERE. Harry Stradling, Jr.

COSTUME DESIGN (O-804)

THE STING. Edith Head.
CRIES AND WHISPERS. Marik Vos.
LUDWIG, A Mega Film S.p.A. Prod., MGM. Piero Tosi.
TOM SAWYER, An Arthur P. Jacobs Prod., Reader's Digest Presentation, UA. Donfeld.
THE WAY WE WERE. Dorothy Jeakins and Moss Mabry.

ART DIRECTION - SET DECORATION (O-805)

THE STING. Henry Bumstead. Set Decoration: James Payne.
BROTHER SUN SISTER MOON, Euro Int'l Films-Vic Film (Prods.), Ltd., PAR. Lorenzo Mongiardino and Gianni Quaranta. Set Decoration: Carmelo Patrono.
THE EXORCIST. Bill Malley. Set Decoration: Jerry Wunderlich.
TOM SAWYER. Philip Jefferies. Set Decoration: Robert de Vestel.
THE WAY WE WERE. Stephen Grimes. Set Decoration: William Kiernan.

FILM EDITING (O-806)

THE STING. William Reynolds.
AMERICAN GRAFFITI. Verna Fields and Marcia Lucas.
THE DAY OF THE JACKAL, Warwick Film Prods., Ltd.-U Prods., France S.A., U. Ralph Kemplen.
THE EXORCIST. Jordan Leondopoulos, Bud Smith, Evan Lottman and Norman Gay.
JONATHAN LIVINGSTON SEAGULL. Frank P. Keller and James Galloway.

FOREIGN LANGUAGE FILM (O-807)

DAY FOR NIGHT, A Les Films Du Carrosse-P.E.C.F. (Paris)-P.I.C. (Rome) Prod. (France).
THE HOUSE ON CHELOUCHE STREET, A Noah Films Prod. (Israel).
L'INVITATION, A Groupe 5 Geneve-Television Suisse Romande-Citel Films-Planfilm (Paris) Prod. (Switzerland).
THE PEDESTRIAN, An ALFA Glarus-MFG-Seitz-Zev Braun Prod. (Federal Republic of West Germany).
TURKISH DELIGHT, A Rob Houwer Film Prod. (The Netherlands).

MUSIC - SCORING (O-808)

(Best Original Dramatic Score)
THE WAY WE WERE. Marvin Hamlisch.
CINDERELLA LIBERTY. John Williams.
THE DAY OF THE DOLPHIN, Icarus Prods., AVE. Georges Delerue.
PAPILLON, A Corona-General Production Co Prod., AA. Jerry Goldsmith.
A TOUCH OF CLASS. John Cameron.

(Best Scoring-Original Song Score and/or Adaptation)
THE STING. Adapted by Marvin Hamlisch.
JESUS CHRIST SUPERSTAR, A U-Norman Jewison-Robert Stigwood Prod., U. Adapted by Andre Previn, Herbert Spencer and Andrew Lloyd Webber.
TOM SAWYER. Song Score by Richard M. Sherman and Robert B. Sherman. Adapted by John Williams.

MUSIC - BEST SONG (O-809)

THE WAY WE WERE, The Way We Were. Music, Marvin Hamlisch. Lyrics, Alan and Marilyn Bergman.
ALL THAT LOVE WENT TO WASTE, *A Touch Of Class.* Music, George Barrie. Lyrics, Sammy Cahn.
LIVE AND LET DIE, *Live And Let Die,* Eon Prods., UA. Music and lyrics by Paul and Linda McCartney.
LOVE, *Robin Hood,* Walt Disney Prods., BV. Music, George Bruns.

Lyrics, Floyd Huddleston.
NICE TO BE AROUND, *Cinderella Liberty.* Music, John Williams. Lyrics, Paul Williams.

SOUND (O-810)

THE EXORCIST. Robert Knudson and Chris Newman.
THE DAY OF THE DOLPHIN. Richard Portman and Lawrence O. Jost.
THE PAPER CHASE. Donald O. Mitchell and Lawrence O. Jost.
PAPER MOON. Richard Portman and Les Fresholtz.
THE STING. Ronald K. Pierce and Robert Bertrand.

SHORT FILMS (O-811)

(Animated)
FRANK FILM, A Frank Mouris Production. Frank Mouris, Prod.
THE LEGEND OF JOHN HENRY, A Stephen Bosustow-Pyramid Films Prod. Nick Bosustow and David Adams, Prods.
PULCINELLA, A Luzzati-Gianini Prod. Emanuele Luzzati and Guilio Gianini, Prods.

(Live Action)
THE BOLERO, An Allan Miller Production. Allan Miller and William Fertik, Prods.
CLOCKMAKER, James Street Prods. Ltd. Richard Gayer, Prod.
LIFE TIMES NINE, Insight Prods. Pen Densham and John Watson, Prods.

DOCUMENTARY (O-812)

(Short Subjects)
PRINCETON: A SEARCH FOR ANSWERS, Krainin-Sage Prods. Julian Krainin and DeWitt L. Sage, Jr., Prods.
BACKGROUND, D'Avino and Fucci-Stone Prods. Carmen D'Avino, Prod.
CHILDREN AT WORK, (Paisti Ag Obair), Gael-Linn Films. Louis Marcus, Prod.
CHRISTO'S VALLEY CURTAIN, A Maysles Films Prod. Albert and David Maysles, Prods.
FOUR STONES FOR KANEMITSU, A Tamarind Prod. (Prod credit in controversy)

(Features)
THE GREAT AMERICAN COWBOY, Kieth Merrill Associates-Rodeo Film Prods. Kieth Merrill, Prod.
ALWAYS A NEW BEGINNING, Goodell Motion Pictures. John D. Goodell, Prod.
BATTLE OF BERLIN, Chronos Film. Bengt von zur Muehlen, Prod.
JOURNEY TO THE OUTER LIMITS, The National Geographic Society and Wolper Prods. Alex Grasshoff, Prod.
WALLS OF FIRE, Mentor Prods. Gertrude Ross Marks and Edmund F. Penney, Prods.

HONORARY AND OTHER (O-813)

(Irving G. Thalberg Memorial Award)

Lawrence Weingarten

(Jean Hersholt Humanitarian Award)

Lew Wasserman

(Other)
**HENRI LANGLOIS for his devotion to the art of film, his massive contributions in preserving its past and his unswerving faith in its future.
GROUCHO MARX in recognition of his brilliant creativity and for the unequalled achievements of the Marx Brothers in the art of motion picture comedy.**

SCIENTIFIC OR TECHNICAL (O-814)

(Class II)
**JOACHIM GERB and ERICH KASTNER of The Arnold and Richter Co for the development and engineering of the Arriflex 35BL motion-picture camera.
MAGNA-TECH ELECTRONIC CO., INC. for the engineering and development of a high-speed re-recording system for motion-picture production.**

WILLIAM W. VALLIANT of PSC Technology Inc., HOWARD F. OTT of Eastman Kodak Co, and GERRY DIEBOLD of The Richmark Camera Service Inc. for the development of a liquid-gate system for motion-picture printers.
HAROLD A. SCHEIB, CLIFFORD H. ELLIS and ROGER W. BANKS of Research Products Inc for the concept and engineering of the Model 2101 optical printer for motion-picture optical effects.
(Class III)
ROSCO LABORATORIES, INC. for the technical advances and the development of a complete system of light-control materials for motion-picture photography.
RICHARD H. VETTER of the Todd-AO Corp for the design of an improved anamorphic focusing system for motion-picture photography.

1974

BEST PICTURE (O-815)

THE GODFATHER PART II, A Coppola Co Production, PAR. Francis Ford Coppola, Prod. Gray Frederickson and Fred Roos, Co-Prods.
CHINATOWN, A Robert Evans Production, PAR. Robert Evans, Prod.
THE CONVERSATION, A Directors Co Production, PAR. Francis Ford Coppola, Prod. Fred Roos, Co-Prod.
LENNY, A Marvin Worth Production, UA. Marvin Worth, Prod.
THE TOWERING INFERNO, An Irwin Allen Production, FOX/WB. Irwin Allen, Prod.

ACTOR (O-816)

ART CARNEY, Harry And Tonto, FOX.
ALBERT FINNEY, *Murder On The Orient Express,* A G.W. Films, Ltd. Production, PAR.
DUSTIN HOFFMAN, *Lenny.*
JACK NICHOLSON, *Chinatown.*
AL PACINO, *The Godfather Part II.*

ACTRESS (O-817)

ELLEN BURSTYN, Alice Doesn't Live Here Anymore, WB.
DIAHANN CARROLL, *Claudine,* Third World Cinema Productions in association with Joyce Selznick and Tina Pine, FOX.
FAYE DUNAWAY, *Chinatown.*
VALERIE PERRINE, *Lenny.*
GENA ROWLANDS, *A Woman Under The Influence,* A Faces Int'l Films Production.

SUPPORTING ACTOR (O-818)

ROBERT DE NIRO, The Godfather Part II.
FRED ASTAIRE, *The Towering Inferno.*
JEFF BRIDGES, *Thunderbolt And Lightfoot,* A Malpaso Co Film Production, UA.
MICHAEL V. GAZZO, *The Godfather Part II.*
LEE STRASBERG, *The Godfather Part II.*

SUPPORTING ACTRESS (O-819)

INGRID BERGMAN, Murder On The Orient Express.
VALENTINA CORTESE, *Day For Night,* A Les Films Du Carrosse and P.E.C.F., Paris; P.I.C., Rome Prod., WB.
MADELINE KAHN, *Blazing Saddles,* WB.
DIANE LADD, *Alice Doesn't Live Here Anymore.*
TALIA SHIRE, *The Godfather Part II.*

DIRECTING (O-820)

FRANCIS FORD COPPOLA, The Godfather Part II.
JOHN CASSAVETES, *A Woman Under The Influence.*
BOB FOSSE, *Lenny.*
ROMAN POLANSKI, *Chinatown.*
FRANCOIS TRUFFAUT, *Day For Night.*

WRITING (O-821)

(Best Original Screenplay)
CHINATOWN. Robert Towne.
ALICE DOESN'T LIVE HERE ANYMORE. Robert Getchell.
THE CONVERSATION. Francis Ford Coppola.
DAY FOR NIGHT. Francois Truffaut, Jean-Louis Richard, and Suanne Schiffman.
HARRY AND TONTO. Paul Mazursky and Josh Greenfeld.
(Best Screenplay adapted from other medium)
THE GODFATHER PART II. Screenplay by Francis Ford Coppola and Mario Puzo.
THE APPRENTICESHIP OF DUDDY KRAVITZ, An Int'l Cinemedia Centre, Ltd. Prod., PAR. Screenplay by Mordecai Richler. Adaptation by Lionel Chetwynd.
LENNY. Screenplay by Julian Barry.
MURDER ON THE ORIENT EXPRESS. Screenplay by Paul Dehn.
YOUNG FRANKENSTEIN, A Gruskoff/Venture Films-Crossbow Prods.,-Jouer, Ltd. Production, FOX. Screenplay by Gene Wilder and Mel Brooks.

CINEMATOGRAPHY (O-822)

THE TOWERING INFERNO. Fred Koenekamp & Joseph Biroc.
CHINATOWN. John A. Alonzo.
EARTHQUAKE, A U-Mark Robson-Filmakers Group Prod., U. Philip Lathrop.
LENNY. Bruce Surtees.
MURDER ON THE ORIENT EXPRESS, A G.W. Films, Ltd. Prod., PAR. Geoffrey Unsworth.

COSTUME DESIGN (O-823)

THE GREAT GATSBY, A David Merrick Prod., PAR. Theoni V. Aldredge.
CHINATOWN, A Robert Evans Prod., PAR. Anthea Sylbert.
DAISY MILLER, A Directors Co Prod., PAR. John Furness.
THE GODFATHER PART II, A Coppola Co Prod., PAR. Theadora Van Runkle.
MURDER ON THE ORIENT EXPRESS, A G.W. Films, Ltd. Prod., PAR. Tony Walton.

ART DIRECTION - SET DECORATION (O-824)

THE GODFATHER PART II. Dean Tavoularis and Angelo Graham. Set Decoration: George R. Nelson.
CHINATOWN. Richard Sylbert and W. Stewart Campbell. Set Decoration: Ruby Levitt.
EARTHQUAKE, A U-Mark Robson-Filmakers Group Prod., U. Alexander Golitzen and E. Preston Ames. Set Decoration: Frank McKelvy.
THE ISLAND AT THE TOP OF THE WORLD, Walt Disney Prods., BV. Peter Ellenshaw, John B. Mansbridge, Walter Tyler and Al Roelofs. Set Decoration: Hal Gausman.
THE TOWERING INFERNO, An Irwin Allen Prod., FOX/WB. William Creber and Ward Preston. Set Decoration: Raphael Bretton.

FILM EDITING (O-825)

THE TOWERING INFERNO. Harold F. Kress and Carl Kress.
BLAZING SADDLES, WB. John C. Howard and Danford Greene.
CHINATOWN. Sam O'Steen.
EARTHQUAKE. Dorothy Spencer.
THE LONGEST YARD, An Albert S. Ruddy Prod., PAR. Michael Luciano.

FOREIGN LANGUAGE FILM (O-826)

AMARCORD, An F.C. (Rome)-P.E.C.F. (Paris) Prod. (Italy).
CATSPLAY, A Hunnia Studio Prod. (Hungary).
THE DELUGE, A Film Polski Prod. (Poland).
LACOMBE, LUCIEN, An NEF-UPF (Paris)-Vides Film (Rome)-Hallelujah Film (Munich) Prod. (France).
THE TRUCE, A Tamames-Zemborain Prod. (Argentina).

MUSIC - SCORING (O-827)

(Best Original Dramatic Score)

THE GODFATHER PART II. Nino Rota and Carmine Coppola.
CHINATOWN. Jerry Goldsmith.
MURDER ON THE ORIENT EXPRESS. Richard Rodney Bennett.
SHANKS, William Castle Prods., PAR. Alex North.
THE TOWERING INFERNO. John Williams.

(Best Scoring-Original Song Score and/or Adaptation)

THE GREAT GATSBY, A David Merrick Prod., PAR. Adapted by Nelson Riddle.
THE LITTLE PRINCE, A Stanley Donen Enterprises, Ltd. Prod., PAR. Song Score by Alan Jay Lerner and Frederick Loewe. Adapted by Angela Morley and Douglas Gamley.
PHANTOM OF THE PARADISE, Harbor Prods., FOX. Song score by Paul Williams. Adapted by Paul Williams and George Aliceson Tipton.

MUSIC - BEST SONG (O-828)

WE MAY NEVER LOVE LIKE THIS AGAIN, The Towering Inferno. Music and lyrics by Al Kasha and Joel Hirschhorn.
BENJI'S THEME (I FEEL LOVE), *Benji,* Mulberry Square. Music, Euel Box. Lyrics, Betty Box.
BLAZING SADDLES, *Blazing Saddles.* Music, John Morris. Lyrics, Mel Brooks.
LITTLE PRINCE, *The Little Prince.* Music, Frederick Loewe. Lyrics, Alan Jay Lerner.
WHEREVER LOVE TAKES ME, *Gold,* Avton Film Productions, Ltd. AA. Music, Elmer Bernstein. Lyrics, Don Black.

SOUND (O-829)

EARTHQUAKE. Ronald Pierce and Melvin Metcalfe, Sr.
CHINATOWN. Bud Grenzbach and Larry Jost.
THE CONVERSATION, A Directors Co Production, PAR. Walter Murch and Arthur Rochester.
THE TOWERING INFERNO. Theodore Soderberg and Herman Lewis.
YOUNG FRANKENSTEIN, A Gruskoff/Venture Films-Crossbow Prods.-Jouer, Ltd. Production, FOX. Richard Portman and Gene Cantamessa.

SHORT FILMS (O-830)

(Animated)

CLOSED MONDAYS, Lighthouse Productions. Will Vinton and Bob Gardiner, Prods.
THE FAMILY THAT DWELT APART, NFC. Yvon Mallette and Robert Verrall, Prods.
HUNGER, NFC. Peter Foldes and Rene Jodoin, Prods.
VOYAGE TO NEXT, The Hubley Studio. Faith and John Hubley, Prods.
WINNIE THE POOH AND TIGGER TOO, Walt Disney Productions. Wolfgang Reitherman, Prod.

(Live Action)

ONE-EYED MEN ARE KINGS, C.A.P.A.C. Productions (Paris). Paul Claudon and Edmond Sechan, Prods.
CLIMB, Dewitt Jones Productions. Dewitt Jones, Prod.
THE CONCERT, The Black And White Colour Film Co, Ltd. Julian and Claude Chagrin, Prods.
PLANET OCEAN, Graphic Films. George V. Casey, Prod.
THE VIOLIN, A Sincinkin, Ltd. Production. Andrew Welsh and George Pastic, Prods.

DOCUMENTARY (O-831)

(Short Subjects)

DON'T, R. A. Films. Robin Lehman, Prod.
CITY OUT OF WILDERNESS, Francis Thompson Inc. Francis Thompson, Prod.
EXPLORATORIUM, A Jon Boorstin Prod. Jon Boorstin, Prod.
JOHN MUIR'S HIGH SIERRA, Dewitt Jones Prods. Dewitt Jones and Lesley Foster, Prods.
NAKED YOGA, A Filmshop Prod. Ronald S. Kass and Mervyn Lloyd, Prods.

(Features)

HEARTS AND MINDS, A Touchstone-Audjeff-BBS Prod., Howard

Zucker/Henry Jaglom-Rainbow Pictures Presentation. Peter Davis and Bert Schneider, Prods.
ANTONIA: A PORTRAIT OF THE WOMAN, Rocky Mountain Prods. Judy Collins and Jill Godmilow, Prods.
THE CHALLENGE. . .A TRIBUTE TO MODERN ART, A World View Prod. Herbert Kline, Prod.
THE 81ST BLOW, A Film by Ghetto Fighters House. Jacquot Ehrlich, David Bergman and Haim Gouri, Prods.
THE WILD AND THE BRAVE, E.S.J. Prods. in association with Tomorrow Entertainment Inc. & Jones/Howard Ltd. Natalie R. Jones and Eugene S. Jones, Prods.

HONORARY AND OTHER (O-832)

(Jean Hersholt Humanitarian Award)

Arthur B. Krim

(Special Achievement)

FRANK BRENDEL, GLEN ROBINSON and ALBERT WHITLOCK for Visual Effects, Earthquake.

(Other)

HOWARD HAWKS - A master American filmmaker whose creative efforts hold a distinguished place in world cinema.
JEAN RENOIR - a genius who, with grace, responsibility and enviable devotion through silent film, sound film, feature, documentary and television, has won the world's admiration.

SCIENTIFIC OR TECHNICAL (O-833)

(Class II)

JOSEPH D. KELLY of Glen Glenn Sound for the design of new audio control consoles which have advanced the state of the art of sound recording and rerecording for motion picture production.
THE BURBANK STUDIOS SOUND DEPARTMENT for the design of new audio control consoles engineered and constructed by the Quad-Eight Sound Corp.
SAMUEL GOLDWYN STUDIOS SOUND DEPARTMENT for the design of a new audio control console engineered and constructed by the Quad-Eight Sound Corp.
QUAD-EIGHT SOUND CORPORATION for the engineering and construction of new audio control consoles designed by The Burbank Studios Sound Department and by the Samuel Goldwyn Studios Sound Department.
WALDON O. WATSON, RICHARD J. STUMPF, ROBERT J. LEONARD and the UNIVERSAL CITY STUDIOS SOUND DEPARTMENT for the development and engineering of the Sensurround System for motion picture presentation.

(Class III)

ELEMACK COMPANY, Rome, Italy, for the design and development of their Spyder camera dolly.
LOUIS AMI of the Universal City Studios for the design and construction of a reciprocating camera platform used when photographing special visual effects for motion pictures.

1975

BEST PICTURE (O-834)

ONE FLEW OVER THE CUCKOO'S NEST, A Fantasy Films Production, UA. Saul Zaentz and Michael Douglas, Prods.
BARRY LYNDON, A Hawk Films, Ltd. Production, WB. Stanley Kubrick Prod.
DOG DAY AFTERNOON, WB. Martin Bregman and Martin Elfand, Prods.
JAWS, A U-Zanuck/Brown Production, U. Richard D. Zanuck and David Brown, Prods.
NASHVILLE, An ABC Entertainment-Jerry Weintraub-Robert Altman Production, PAR. Robert Altman, Prod.

ACTOR (O-835)

JACK NICHOLSON, One Flew Over The Cuckoo's Nest.
WALTER MATTHAU, *The Sunshine Boys,* A Ray Stark Production, MGM.

1972—Albert S. Ruddy (producer, Best Picture), Liza Minnelli (Best Actress), and Joel Gray (Best Actor)

1975—"One Flew Over the Cuckoo's Nest" Winners: Michael Douglas (producer, Best Picture), Milos Forman (Best Director), Louise Fletcher (Best Actress), Jack Nicholson (Best Actor), and Saul Zaentz (producer, Best Picture)

1976—"Rocky" Winners: John Avildsen (Best Director), Robert Chartoff (producer, Best Picture), Jack Nicholson (presenter), Sylvester Stallone, and Irwin Winkler (producer, Best Picture)

1974—Carmine Coppola (Best Score) and Francis Ford Coppola (Best Director)

1976—Mrs. Peter Finch (accepting the Best Actor award for her husband) and Faye Dunaway (Best Actress)

1977—Richard Dreyfuss (Best Actor), Jack Rollins (producer, Best Picture), Diane Keaton (Best Actress), presenter Jack Nicholson, and Charles H. Joffe (producer, Best Picture)

1978—Cary Grant (presenter) and Laurence Olivier (Honorary Award)

1978—John Voigt (Best Actor), Jane Fonda (Best Actress), and Michael Cimino (Best Director)

AL PACINO, *Dog Day Afternoon.*
MAXIMILIAN SCHELL, *The Man In The Glass Booth,* An Ely Landau Organization Production, AFT.
JAMES WHITMORE, *Give 'em Hell, Harry!,* A Theatrovision Production, AVE.

ACTRESS (O-836)

LOUISE FLETCHER, One Flew Over The Cuckoo's Nest.
ISABELLE ADJANI, *The Story Of Adele H.,* A Les Films du Carrosse-Les Productions Artistes Associes Production, NW.
ANN-MARGRET, *Tommy,* A Robert Stigwood Organisation, Ltd. Production, COL.
GLENDA JACKSON, *Hedda,* A Royal Shakespeare-Brut Productions-George Barrie/Robert Enders Film Production, Brut Productions.
CAROL KANE, *Hester Street,* Midwest Film Productions.

SUPPORTING ACTOR (O-837)

GEORGE BURNS, The Sunshine Boys.
BRAD DOURIF, *One Flew Over The Cuckoo's Nest.*
BURGESS MEREDITH, *The Day Of The Locust,* A Jerome Hellman Production, PAR.
CHRIS SARANDON, *Dog Day Afternoon.*
JACK WARDEN, *Shampoo,* Rubeeker Productions, COL.

SUPPORTING ACTRESS (O-838)

LEE GRANT, Shampoo.
RONEE BLAKELY, *Nashville.*
SYLVIA MILES, *Farewell, My Lovely,* An Elliott Kastner-ITC Production, AVE.
LILY TOMLIN, *Nashville,*
BRENDA VACCARO in Jacqueline Susann's *Once Is Not Enough,* A Howard W. Koch Production, PAR.

DIRECTING (O-839)

MILOS FORMAN, One Flew Over The Cuckoo's Nest.
ROBERT ALTMAN, *Nashville.*
FEDERICO FELLINI, *Amarcord,* An F.C. Productions-P.E.C.F. Production, NW.
STANLEY KUBRICK, *Barry Lyndon.*
SIDNEY LUMET, *Dog Day Afternoon.*

WRITING (O-840)

(Best Original Screenplay)
DOG DAY AFTERNOON. Frank Pierson.
AMARCORD. Federico Fellini and Tonino Guerra.
AND NOW MY LOVE, A Rizzoli Film-Les Films 13 Production, AVE. Claude Lelouch and Pierre Uytterhoeven.
LIES MY FATHER TOLD ME, Pentimento Productions, Ltd.-Pentacle VIII Productions, Ltd., COL. Ted Allan.
SHAMPOO. Robert Towne and Warren Beatty.

(Best Screenplay adapted from other material)
ONE FLEW OVER THE CUCKOO'S NEST. Screenplay by Lawrence Hauben and Bo Goldman.
BARRY LYNDON. Screenplay by Stanley Kubrick.
THE MAN WHO WOULD BE KING, An AA-COL Pictures Production, AA. Screenplay by John Huston and Gladys Hill.
SCENT OF A WOMAN, A Dean Film Production, FOX. Screenplay by Ruggero Maccari and Dino Risi.
THE SUNSHINE BOYS. Screenplay by Neil Simon.

CINEMATOGRAPHY (O-841)

BARRY LYNDON. John Alcott.
THE DAY OF THE LOCUST. Conrad Hall.
FUNNY LADY, A Rastar Pictures Production, COL. James Wong Howe.
THE HINDENBURG, A Robert Wise-Filmakers Group-U Production, U. Robert Surtees.
ONE FLEW OVER THE CUCKOO'S NEST. Haskell Wexler and Bill Butler.

COSTUME DESIGN (O-842)

BARRY LYNDON. Ulla-Britt Soderlund and Milena Canonero.
THE FOUR MUSKETEERS, A Film Trust S.A. Production, FOX. Yvonne Blake and Ron Talsky.
FUNNY LADY, A Rastar Pictures Production, COL. Ray Aghayan and Bob Mackie.
THE MAGIC FLUTE, A Sveriges Radio A.B. Production, Surrogate Releasing. Henny Noremark and Karin Erskine.
THE MAN WHO WOULD BE KING. Edith Head.

ART DIRECTION - SET DECORATION (O-843)

BARRY LYNDON. Ken Adam and Roy Walker. Set Decoration: Vernon Dixon.
THE HINDENBURG. Edward Carfagno. Set Decoration: Frank McKelvy.
THE MAN WHO WOULD BE KING. Alexander Trauner and Tony Inglis. Set Decoration: Peter James.
SHAMPOO. Richard Sylbert and W. Stewart Campbell. Set Decoration: George Gaines.
THE SUNSHINE BOYS. Albert Brenner. Set Decoration: Marvin March.

FILM EDITING (O-844)

JAWS. Verna Fields.
DOG DAY AFTERNOON. Dede Allen.
THE MAN WHO WOULD BE KING. Russell Lloyd.
ONE FLEW OVER THE CUCKOO'S NEST. Richard Chew, Lynzee Klingman and Sheldon Kahn.
THREE DAYS OF THE CONDOR, A Dino De Laurentiis Production, PAR. Frederic Steinkamp and Don Guidice.

FOREIGN LANGUAGE FILM (O-845)

DERSU UZALA, A Mosfilms Studios Production (U.S.S.R.).
LAND OF PROMISE, A Film Polski Production (Poland).
LETTERS FROM MARUSIA, A Conacine Production (Mexico).
SANDAKAN NO. 8, A Toho-Haiyuza Production (Japan).
SCENT OF A WOMAN. A Dean Film. (Italy).

MUSIC - SCORING (O-846)

(Best Original Score)
JAWS. John Williams.
BIRDS DO IT, BEES DO IT, A Wolper Pictures Production, COL. Gerald Fried.
BITE THE BULLET, A Pax Enterprises Production, COL. Alex North.
ONE FLEW OVER THE CUCKOO'S NEST. Jack Nitzsche.
THE WIND AND THE LION, A Herb Jaffe Production, MGM. Jerry Goldsmith.

(Best Scoring-Original Song Score and/or Adaptation)
BARRY LYNDON. Adapted by Leonard Rosenman.
FUNNY LADY. Adapted by Peter Matz.
TOMMY. Adapted by Peter Townshend.

MUSIC - BEST SONG (O-847)

I'M EASY, Nashville. Music and lyrics by Keith Carradine.
HOW LUCKY CAN YOU GET, *Funny Lady.* Music and lyrics by Fred Ebb and John Kander.
NOW THAT WE'RE IN LOVE, *Whiffs,* Brut Productions, FOX. Music, George Barrie. Lyrics, Sammy Cahn.
RICHARD'S WINDOW, *The Other Side Of The Mountain,* A Filmways-Larry Peerce-U Production, U. Music, Charles Fox. Lyrics, Norman Gimbel.
THEME FROM MAHOGANY (DO YOU KNOW WHERE YOU'RE GOING TO), *Mahogany,* A Jobete Film Production, PAR. Music, Michael Masser. Lyrics, Gerry Goffin.

SOUND (O-848)

JAWS. Robert L. Hoyt, Roger Heman, Earl Madery and John Carter.
BITE THE BULLET. Arthur Piantadosi, Les Fresholtz, Richard Tyler and Al Overton, Jr.
FUNNY LADY. Richard Portman, Don MacDougall, Curly Thirlwell and Jack Solomon.
THE HINDENBERG. Leonard Peterson, John A. Bolger, Jr., John Mack

and Don K. Sharpless.
THE WIND AND THE LION. Harry W. Tetrick, Aaron Rochin, William McCaughey and Roy Charman.

SHORT FILMS (O-849)

(Animated)

GREAT, Grantstern Ltd. and British Lion Films Ltd. Bob Godfrey, Prod.
KICK ME, Robert Swarthe Productions. Robert Swarthe Prod.
MONSIEUR POINTU, NFC. Rene Jodoin, Bernard Longpre and Andre Leduc, Prods.
SISYPHUS, Hungarofilms. Marcell Jankovics, Prod.

(Live Action)

ANGEL AND BIG JOE, Bert Salzman Productions. Bert Salzman, Prod.
CONQUEST OF LIGHT, Louis Marcus Films Ltd. Louis Marcus, Prod.
DAWN FLIGHT, Lawrence M. Lansburgh Productions. Lawrence M. Lansburgh and Brian Lansburgh, Prods.
A DAY IN THE LIFE OF BONNIE CONSOLO, Barr Films. Barry Spinello, Prod.
DOUBLETALK, Beattie Productions. Alan Beattie, Prod.

DOCUMENTARY (O-850)

(Short Subjects)

THE END OF THE GAME, Opus Films Ltd. Claire Wilbur and Robin Lehman, Prods.
ARTHUR AND LILLIE, Department of Communication, Stanford University. Jon Else, Steven Kovacs and Kristine Samuelson, Prods.
MILLIONS OF YEARS AHEAD OF MAN, BASF. Manfred Baier, Prod.
PROBES IN SPACE, Graphic Films. George V. Casey, Prod.
WHISTLING SMITH, NFC. Barrie Howells and Michael Scott, Prods.

(Features)

THE MAN WHO SKIED DOWN EVEREST, A Crawley Films Presentation. F.R. Crawley, James Hager and Dale Hartleben, Prods.
THE CALIFORNIA REICH, Yasny Talking Pictures. Walter F. Parkes and Keith F. Critchlow, Prods.
FIGHTING FOR OUR LIVES, A Farm Worker Film. Glen Pearcy, Prod.
THE INCREDIBLE MACHINE, The National Geographic Society and Wolper Prods. Irwin Rosten, Prod.
THE OTHER HALF OF THE SKY: A CHINA MEMOIR, MacLaine Productions. Shirley MacLaine, Prod.

HONORARY AND OTHER (O-851)

(Irving G. Thalberg Memorial Award)

Mervyn LeRoy

(Jean Hersholt Humanitarian Award)

Jules C. Stein

(Special Achievement)

PETER BERKOS for Sound Effects, The Hindenburg.
ALBERT WHITLOCK and GLEN ROBINSON for Visual Effects, The Hindenburg.

(Other)

MARY PICKFORD in recognition of her unique contributions to the film industry and the development of film as an artistic medium.

SCIENTIFIC OR TECHNICAL (O-852)

(Class II)

CHADWELL O'CONNOR of the O'Connor Engineering Laboratories for the concept and engineering of a fluid-damped camerahead for motion-picture photography.
WILLIAM F. MINER of Universal City Studios, Inc. and the WESTINGHOUSE ELECTRIC CORPORATION for the development and engineering of a solid-state, 500 kilowatt, direct-current static rectifier for motion-picture lighting.

(Class III)

LAWRENCE W. BUTLER and ROGER BANKS for the concept of applying low inertia and stepping electric motors to film transport systems and optical printers for motion-picture production.
DAVID J. DEGENKOLB and FRED SCOBEY of Deluxe General Inc and

JOHN C. DOLAN and RICHARD DUBOIS of the Akwaklame Co for the development of a technique for silver recovery from photographic wash-waters by ion exchange.
JOSEPH WESTHEIMER for the development of a device to obtain shadowed titles on motion-picture films.
CARTER EQUIPMENT CO., INC. and RAMTRONICS for the engineering and manufacture of a computerized tape punching system for programming laboratory printing machines.
THE HOLLYWOOD FILM COMPANY for the engineering and manufacture of a computerized tape punching system for programming laboratory printing machines.
BELL & HOWELL for the engineering and manufacture of a computerized tape punching system for programming laboratory printing machines.
FREDRIK SCHLYTER for the engineering and manufacture of a computerized tape punching system for programming laboratory printing machines.

1976

BEST PICTURE (O-853)

ROCKY, A Robert Chartoff-Irwin Winkler Production, UA. Irwin Winkler and Robert Chartoff, Prods.
ALL THE PRESIDENT'S MEN, A Wildwood Enterprises Production, WB. Walter Coblenz, Prod.
BOUND FOR GLORY, The Bound For Glory Co Production, UA. Robert F. Blumofe and Harold Leventhal, Prods.
NETWORK, A Howard Gottfried/Paddy Chayefsky Production, MGM/UA. Howard Gottfried, Prod.
TAXI DRIVER, A Bill/Phillips Production of a Martin Scorsese Film, COL. Michael Phillips and Julia Phillips, Prods.

ACTOR (O-854)

PETER FINCH, Network.
ROBERT DE NIRO, *Taxi Driver.*
GIANCARLO GIANNINI, *Seven Beauties,* A Medusa Distribuzione Production, C5.
WILLIAM HOLDEN, *Network.*
SYLVESTER STALLONE, *Rocky.*

ACTRESS (O-855)

FAYE DUNAWAY, Network.
MARIE-CHRISTINE BARRAULT, *Cousin, Cousine,* Les Films Pomereu-Gaumont Production, NTH.
TALIA SHIRE, *Rocky.*
SISSY SPACEK, *Carrie,* A Redbank Films Production, UA.
LIV ULLMANN, *Face To Face,* A Cinematograph A.B. Production, PAR.

SUPPORTING ACTOR (O-856)

JASON ROBARDS, All The President's Men.
NED BEATTY, *Network.*
BURGESS MEREDITH, *Rocky.*
LAURENCE OLIVIER, *Marathon Man,* A Robert Evans-Sidney Beckerman Production, PAR.
BURT YOUNG, *Rocky.*

SUPPORTING ACTRESS (O-857)

BEATRICE STRAIGHT, Network.
JANE ALEXANDER, *All The President's Men.*
JODIE FOSTER, *Taxi Driver.*
LEE GRANT, *Voyage Of The Damned,* An ITC Entertainment Production, AVE.
PIPER LAURIE, *Carrie.*

DIRECTING (O-858)

JOHN G. AVILDSEN, Rocky.
INGMAR BERGMAN, *Face To Face.*
SIDNEY LUMET, *Network.*

ALAN J. PAKULA, *All The President's Men.*
LINA WERTMULLER, *Seven Beauties.*

WRITING (O-859)

(Best Screenplay written directly for the screen)
NETWORK. Story and Screenplay by Paddy Chayefsky.
COUSIN, COUSINE. Story and Screenplay by Jean-Charles Tacchella. Adaptation by Daniele Thompson.
THE FRONT, COL Pictures. Story and Screenplay by Walter Bernstein.
ROCKY. Story and Screenplay by Sylvester Stallone.
SEVEN BEAUTIES. Story and Screenplay by Lina Wertmuller.

(Best Screenplay based on material from another medium)
ALL THE PRESIDENT'S MEN. Screenplay by William Goldman.
BOUND FOR GLORY. Screenplay by Robert Getchell.
FELLINI'S CASANOVA, A P.E.A.-Produzioni Europee Associate S.p.A. Production, U. Screenplay by Federico Fellini and Bernadino Zapponi.
THE SEVEN-PER-CENT SOLUTION, A Herbert Ross Film/Winitsky-Sellers Production, A U Release. Screenplay by Nicholas Meyer.
VOYAGE OF THE DAMNED. Screenplay by Steve Shagan and David Butler.

CINEMATOGRAPHY (O-860)

BOUND FOR GLORY. Haskell Wexler.
KING KONG, A Dino De Laurentiis Production, PAR. Richard H. Kline.
LOGAN'S RUN, A Saul David Production, MGM. Ernest Laszlo.
NETWORK. Owen Roizman.
A STAR IS BORN, A Barwood/Jon Peters Production, First Artists Presentation, WB. Robert Surtees.

COSTUME DESIGN (O-861)

FELLINI'S CASANOVA. Danilo Donati.
BOUND FOR GLORY. William Theiss.
THE INCREDIBLE SARAH, A Helen M. Strauss-Reader's Digest Films, Ltd. Production, BOR. Anthony Mendleson.
THE PASSOVER PLOT, Coast Industries-Golan-Globus Productions, Ltd., ATF. Mary Wills.
THE SEVEN-PER-CENT SOLUTION. Alan Barrett.

ART DIRECTION - SET DECORATION (O-862)

ALL THE PRESIDENT'S MEN. George Jenkins. Set Decoration: George Gaines.
THE INCREDIBLE SARAH. Elliot Scott and Norman Reynolds.
THE LAST TYCOON, A Sam Spiegel-Elia Kazan Film Production, PAR. Gene Callahan and Jack Collis. Set Decoration: Jerry Wunderlich.
LOGAN'S RUN. Dale Hennesy. Set Decoration: Robert de Vestel.
THE SHOOTIST, A Frankovich/Self Production, Dino De Laurentiis Presentation, PAR. Robert F. Boyle. Set Decoration: Arthur Jeph Parker.

FILM EDITING (O-863)

ROCKY. Richard Halsey and Scott Conrad.
ALL THE PRESIDENT'S MEN. Robert L. Wolfe.
BOUND FOR GLORY. Robert Jones and Pembroke J. Herring.
NETWORK. Alan Heim.
TWO-MINUTE WARNING, A Filmways/Larry Peerce-Edward S. Feldman Film Production, U. Eve Newman and Walter Hannemann.

FOREIGN LANGUAGE FILM (O-864)

BLACK AND WHITE IN COLOR, An Arthur Cohn Production/Societe Ivoirienne De Cinema (Ivory Coast).
COUSIN, COUSINE. (France).
JACOB, THE LIAR, A VEB/DEFA Production (German Democratic Republic).
NIGHTS AND DAYS, A Polish Corp for Film-"KADR" Film Unit Production (Poland).
SEVEN BEAUTIES. Medusa Distribuzione Production (Italy).

MUSIC - SCORING (O-865)

(Best Original Score)
THE OMEN, FOX Productions, Ltd., FOX, Jerry Goldsmith.
OBSESSION, George Litto Productions, COL. Bernard Herrmann.
THE OUTLAW JOSEY WALES, A Malpaso Co Production, WB. Jerry Fielding.
TAXI DRIVER. Bernard Herrmann.
VOYAGE OF THE DAMNED. Lalo Schifrin.

(Best Original Song Score and Its Adaptation or Best Adaptation Score)
BOUND FOR GLORY. Adapted by Leonard Rosenman.
BUGSY MALONE, A Goodtimes Enterprises, Ltd. Production, PAR. Song score and Its Adaptation by Paul Williams.
A STAR IS BORN. Adapted by Roger Kellaway.

MUSIC - BEST SONG (O-866)

EVERGREEN (Love Theme From A STAR IS BORN), A Star Is Born. Music, Barbra Streisand. Lyrics, Paul Williams.
AVE SATANI, *The Omen.* Music and lyrics by Jerry Goldsmith.
COME TO ME, *The Pink Panther Strikes Again,* Amjo Productions, Ltd., UA. Music, Henri Mancini. Lyrics, Don Black.
GONNA FLY NOW, *ROCKY.* Music, Bill Conti. Lyrics, Carol Connors and Ayn Robbins.
A WORLD THAT NEVER WAS, *Half A House,* Lenro Productions, First American Films. Music, Sammy Fain. Lyrics, Paul Francis Webster.

SOUND (O-867)

ALL THE PRESIDENT'S MEN. Arthur Piantadosi, Les Fresholtz, Dick Alexander and Jim Webb.
KING KONG. Harry Warren Tetrick, William McCaughey, Aaron Rochin and Jack Solomon.
ROCKY. Harry Warren Tetrick, William McCaughey, Lyle Burbridge and Bud Alper.
SILVER STREAK, A Frank Yablans Presentations Production, FOX. Donald Mitchell, Douglas Williams, Richard Tyler and Hal Etherington.
A STAR IS BORN. Robert Knudson, Dan Wallin, Robert Glass and Tom Overton.

SHORT FILMS (O-868)

(Animated)
LEISURE, A Film Australia Production. Suzanne Baker, Prod.
DEDALO, A Cineteam Realizzazioni Production. Manfredo Manfredi, Prod.
THE STREET, NFC. Caroline Leaf and Guy Glover, Prods.

(Live Action)
IN THE REGION OF ICE, An American Film Institute Production. Andre Guttfreund and Peter Werner, Prods.
KUDZU, A Short Production. Marjorie Anne Short, Prod.
THE MORNING SPIDER, The Black and White Colour Film Co. Julian Chagrin and Claude Chagrin, Prods.
NIGHTLIFE, Opus Films, Ltd. Claire Wilbur and Robin Lehman, Prods.
NUMBER ONE, Number One Productions. Dyan Cannon and Vince Cannon, Prods.

DOCUMENTARY (O-869)

(Short Subjects)
NUMBER OUR DAYS, Community Television of Southern California. Lynne Littman, Prod.
AMERICAN SHOESHINE, Titan Films. Sparky Greene, Prod.
BLACKWOOD, NFC. Tony Ianzelo and Andy Thompson, Prods.
THE END OF THE ROAD, Pelican Films. John Armstrong, Prod.
UNIVERSE, Graphic Films Corp. for NASA. Lester Novros, Prod.

(Features)
HARLAN COUNTY, U.S.A., Cabin Creek Films. Barbara Kopple, Prod.
HOLLYWOOD ON TRIAL, October Films/Cinema Associates Production. James Gutman and David Helpern, Jr., Prods.
OFF THE EDGE, Pentacle Films. Michael Firth, Prod.
PEOPLE OF THE WIND, Elizabeth E. Rogers Productions. Anthony

Howarth and David Koff, Prods.
VOLCANO: An Inquiry Into The Life And Death Of Malcolm Lowry, NFC. Donald Brittain and Robert Duncan, Prods.

HONORARY AND OTHER (O-870)
(Irving G. Thalberg Memorial Award)

Pandro S. Berman
(Special Achievement)
CARLO RAMBALDI, GLEN ROBINSON and FRANK VAN DER VEER for Visual Effects, King Kong.
L.B. ABBOTT, GLEN ROBINSON and MATTHEW YURICICH for Visual Effects, Logan's Run.

SCIENTIFIC OR TECHNICAL (O-871)
(Class II)

CONSOLIDATED FILM INDUSTRIES and the **BARNEBEY-CHENEY COMPANY** for the development of a system for the recovery of film-cleaning solvent vapors in a motion-picture laboratory.
WILLIAM L. GRAHAM, MANFRED G. MICHELSON, GEOFFREY F. NORMAN and **SIEGFRIED SEIBERT** of Technicolor for the development and engineering of a Continuous, High-Speed, Color Motion-Picture Printing System.

(Class III)

FRED BARTSCHER of the Kollmorgen Corp and **GLENN BERGGREN** of the Schneider Corp for the design and development of a single-lens magnifier for motion-picture projection lenses.
PANAVISION INCORPORATED for the design and development of super-speed lenses for motion-picture photography.
HIROSHI SUZUKAWA of Canon and **WILTON R. HOLM** of AMPTP MotionPicture and Television Research Center for the design and development of super-speed lenses for motion-picture photography.
CARL ZEISS COMPANY for the design and development of super-speed lenses for motion-picture photography.
PHOTO RESEARCH DIVISION of the **KOLLMORGEN CORPORATION** for the engineering and manufacture of the spectra TriColor Meter.

1977

BEST PICTURE (O-872)

ANNIE HALL, Jack Rollins-Charles H. Joffe Productions, UA. Charles H. Joffe, Prod.
THE GOODBYE GIRL, A Ray Stark Production, MGM/WB. Ray Stark, Prod.
JULIA, FOX. Richard Roth, Prod.
STAR WARS, A Lucasfilm Ltd. Prodn., FOX. Gary Kurtz, Prod.
THE TURNING POINT, Hera Productions, FOX. Herbert Ross and Arthur Laurents, Prods.

ACTOR (O-873)

RICHARD DREYFUSS, The Goodbye Girl.
WOODY ALLEN, *Annie Hall.*
RICHARD BURTON, *Equus,* A Winkast Co, Ltd./P.B., Ltd. Production, UA.
MARCELLO MASTROIANNI, *A Special Day,* A Canafox Films Production, C5.
JOHN TRAVOLTA, *Saturday Night Fever,* A Robert Stigwood Production, PAR.

ACTRESS (O-874)

DIANE KEATON, Annie Hall.
ANNE BANCROFT, *The Turning Point.*
JANE FONDA, *Julia.*
SHIRLEY MACLAINE, *The Turning Point.*
MARSHA MASON, *The Goodbye Girl.*

SUPPORTING ACTOR (O-875)

JASON ROBARDS, Julia.
MIKHAIL BARYSHNIKOV, *The Turning Point.*
PETER FIRTH, *Equus.*
ALEC GUINNESS, *Star Wars.*
MAXIMILIAN SCHELL, *Julia.*

SUPPORTING ACTRESS (O-876)

VANESSA REDGRAVE, Julia.
LESLIE BROWNE, *The Turning Point.*
QUINN CUMMINGS, *The Goodbye Girl.*
MELINDA DILLON, *Close Encounters Of The Third Kind,* A Julia Phillips/Michael Phillips-Steven Spielberg Film Prodn., COL.
TUESDAY WELD, *Looking For Mr. Goodbar,* A Freddie Fields Production, PAR.

DIRECTING (O-877)

WOODY ALLEN, Annie Hall.
GEORGE LUCAS, *Star Wars.*
HERBERT ROSS, *The Turning Point.*
STEVEN SPIELBERG, *Close Encounters Of The Third Kind.*
FRED ZINNEMANN, *Julia.*

WRITING (O-878)
(Best Screenplay written directly for the screen)

ANNIE HALL. Story and screenplay by Woody Allen and Marshall Brickman.
THE GOODBYE GIRL. Story and screenplay by Neil Simon.
THE LATE SHOW, A Lion's Gate Film Production, WB. Story and screenplay by Robert Benton.
STAR WARS. Story and screenplay by George Lucas.
THE TURNING POINT. Story and screenplay by Arthur Laurents.

(Best Screenplay based on material from another medium)

JULIA. Screenplay by Alvin Sargent.
EQUUS. Screenplay by Peter Shaffer.
I NEVER PROMISED YOU A ROSE GARDEN, A Scherick/Blatt Production, NW. Screenplay by Gavin Lambert and Lewis John Carlino.
OH, GOD!, WB. Screenplay by Larry Gelbart.
THAT OBSCURE OBJECT OF DESIRE, A Greenwich-Les Films Galaxie-Incine Compania Industrial, S.A. Production, First Artists. Screenplay by Luis Bunuel and Jean-Claude Carriere.

CINEMATOGRAPHY (O-879)

CLOSE ENCOUNTERS OF THE THIRD KIND. Vilmos Zsigmond.
ISLANDS IN THE STREAM, A Peter Bart/Max Palevsky Production, PAR. Fred J. Koenekamp.
JULIA. Douglas Slocombe.
LOOKING FOR MR. GOODBAR. William A. Fraker.
THE TURNING POINT. Robert Surtees.

COSTUME DESIGN (O-880)

STAR WARS, A Lucasfilm Ltd. Prodn, FOX. John Mollo.
AIRPORT '77. Edith Head and Burton Miller.
JULIA. Anthea Sylbert.
A LITTLE NIGHT MUSIC, A Sascha-Wien Film Production in association with Elliott Kastner, NW. Florence Klotz.
THE OTHER SIDE OF MIDNIGHT, A Frank Yablans Presentations Production, FOX. Irene Sharaff.

ART DIRECTION - SET DECORATION (O-881)

STAR WARS. John Barry, Norman Reynolds and Leslie Dilley. Set Decoration: Roger Christian.
AIRPORT '77. George C. Webb. Set Decoration: Mickey S. Michaels.
CLOSE ENCOUNTERS OF THE THIRD KIND. Joe Alves and Dan Lomino. Set Decoration: Phil Abramson.
THE SPY WHO LOVED ME, Eon Productions, UA. Ken Adam and Peter Lamont. Set Decoration: Hugh Scaife.
SET TURNING POINT. Albert Brenner. Set Decoration: Marvin March.

FILM EDITING (O-882)

STAR WARS. Paul Hirsch, Marcia Lucas and Richard Chew.
CLOSE ENCOUNTERS OF THE THIRD KIND. Michael Kahn.
JULIA. Walter Murch.
SMOKEY AND THE BANDIT, A U/Rastar Production, U. Walter Hannemann and Angelo Ross.
THE TURNING POINT. William Reynolds.

FOREIGN LANGUAGE FILM (O-883)

MADAME ROSA, A Lira Films Production (France).
IPHIGENIA, A Greek Film Centre Production (Greece).
OPERATION THUNDERBOLT, A Golan-Globus Production (Israel).
A SPECIAL DAY, A Canafox Films Production (Italy).
THAT OBSCURE OBJECT OF DESIRE. (Spain).

MUSIC - SCORING (O-884)

(Best Original Score)
STAR WARS. John Williams.
CLOSE ENCOUNTERS OF THE THIRD KIND. John Williams.
JULIA. Georges Delerue.
MOHAMMAD-MESSENGER OF GOD, A Filmco Int'l Production, Irwin Yablans Co. Maurice Jarre.
THE SPY WHO LOVED ME. Marvin Hamlisch.

(Best Original Song Score and Its Adaptation or Best Adaptation Score)
A LITTLE NIGHT MUSIC. Adapted by Jonathan Tunick.
PETE'S DRAGON, Walt Disney Productions, BV. Song Score by Al Kasha and Joel Hirschhorn. Adapted by Irwin Kostal.
THE SLIPPER AND THE ROSE - THE STORY OF CINDERELLA, Paradine Co-Productions, Ltd., U. Song Score by Richard M. Sherman and Robert B. Sherman. Adapted by Angela Morley.

MUSIC - BEST SONG (O-885)

YOU LIGHT UP MY LIFE, You Light Up My Life, The Session Co Production, COL. Music and lyrics by Joseph Brooks.
CANDLE ON THE WATER, *Pete's Dragon.* Music and lyrics by Al Kasha and Joel Hirschhorn.
NOBODY DOES IT BETTER, *The Spy Who Loved Me.* Music, Marvin Hamlisch. Lyrics, Carole Bayer Sager.
THE SLIPPER AND THE ROSE WALTZ (He Danced With Me/She Danced With Me), *The Slipper And The Rose* - The Story Of Cinderella. Music and lyrics, Richard M. Sherman and Robert B. Sherman.
SOMEONE'S WAITING FOR YOU, *The Rescuers,* Walt Disney Productions, BV. Music, Sammy Fain. Lyrics, Carol Connors and Ayn Robbins.

SOUND (O-886)

STAR WARS. Don MacDougall, Ray West, Bob Minkler and Derek Ball.
CLOSE ENCOUNTERS OF THE THIRD KIND. Robert Knudson, Robert J. Glass, Don MacDougall and Gene S. Cantamessa.
THE DEEP, A Casablanca Filmworks Production, COL. Walter Goss, Dick Alexander, Tom Beckert and Robin Gregory.
SORCERER, A William Friedkin Film Production, PAR-U. Robert Knudson, Robert J. Glass, Richard Tyler and Jean-Louis Ducarme.
THE TURNING POINT. Theodore Soderberg, Paul Wells, Douglas O. Williams and Jerry Jost.

SHORT FILMS (O-887)

(Animated)
SAND CASTLE, NFC. Co Hoedeman, Prod.
THE BEAD GAME, NFC. Ishu Patel, Prod.
THE DOONESBURY SPECIAL, The Hubley Studio. John and Faith Hubley and Garry Trudeau, Prods.
JIMMY THE C, A Motionpicker Production. Jimmy Picker, Robert Grossman and Craig Whittaker, Prods.

(Live Action)
I'LL FIND A WAY, NFC. Beverly Shaffer and Yuki Yoshida, Prods.
THE ABSENT-MINDED WAITER, The Aspen Film Society. William E. McEuen, Prod.

FLOATING FREE, A Trans World Int'l Production. Jerry Butts, Prod.
NOTES ON THE POPULAR ARTS, Saul Bass Films. Saul Bass, Prod.
SPACEBORNE, A Lawrence Hall of Science Production for the Regents of the University of California with the cooperation of NASA. Philip Dauber, Prod.

DOCUMENTARY (O-888)

(Short Subjects)
GRAVITY IS MY ENEMY, A John Joseph Production. John Joseph and Jan Stussy, Prods.
AGUEDA MARTINEZ: OUR PEOPLE, OUR COUNTRY, A Moctesuma Esparza Production. Moctesuma Esparza, Prod.
FIRST EDITION, D. L. Sage Productions. Helen Whitney and DeWitt L. Sage, Jr., Prods.
OF TIME, TOMBS AND TREASURE, A Charlie/Papa Production. James R. Messenger and Paul N. Raimondi, Prods.
THE SHETLAND EXPERIENCE, Balfour Films. Douglas Gordon, Prod.

(Features)
WHO ARE THE DEBOLTS? AND WHERE DID THEY GET NINETEEN KIDS?, Korty Films and Charles M. Schulz Creative Associates in association with Sanrio Films. John Korty, Dan McCann and Warren L. Lockhart, Prods.
THE CHILDREN OF THEATRE STREET, Mack-Vaganova Co. Robert Dornhelm and Earle Mack, Prods.
HIGH GRASS CIRCUS, NFC. Bill Brind, Torben Schioler and Tony Ianzelo, Prods.
HOMAGE TO CHAGALL--THE COLOURS OF LOVE, A CBC Production. Harry Rasky, Prod.
UNION MAIDS, A Klein, Reichert, Mogulescu Production. James Klein, Julia Reichert and Miles Mogulescu, Prods.

SPECIAL VISUAL EFFECTS (O-889)

STAR WARS. John Stears, John Dykstra, Richard Edlund, Grant McCune and Robert Blalack.
CLOSE ENCOUNTERS OF THE THIRD KIND. Roy Arbogast, Douglas Trumbull, Matthew Yuricich, Gregory Jein and Richard Yuricich.

HONORARY AND OTHER (O-890)

(Irving G. Thalberg Memorial Award)
Walter Mirisch
(Jean Hersholt Humanitarian Award)
Charlton Heston
(Special Achievement)
BENJAMIN BURTT, JR. for the creation of the alien, creature and robot voices featured in "Star Wars".
Sound Effects Editing: FRANK E. WARNER for "Close Encounters Of The Third Kind".
(Other)
MARGARET BOOTH for her exceptional contribution to the art of film editing in the motion picture industry.
GORDON E. SAWYER in appreciation for outstanding service and dedication in upholding the high standards of the Academy of Motion Picture Arts and Sciences.
SIDNEY PAUL SOLOW in appreciation for outstanding service and dedication in upholding the high standards of the Academy of Motion Picture Arts and Sciences.

SCIENTIFIC OR TECHNICAL (O-891)

(Class I)
GARRETT BROWN and the CINEMA PRODUCTS CORP. engineering staff under the supervision of JOHN JURGENS, for the invention and development of Steadicam.
(Class II)
JOSEPH D. KELLY, EMORY M. COHEN, BARRY K. HENLEY, HAMMOND H. HOLT and JOHN AGALSOFF of Glen Glenn Sound for the concept and development of a Post-production Audio Processing System for Motion Picture Films.
PANAVISION INC., for the concept and engineering of the improvements incorporated in the Panaflex Motion Picture Camera.
N. PAUL KENWORTHY JR. and WILLIAM R. LATADY, for the inven-

tion and development of the Kenworthy Snorkel Camera System for motion picture photography.

JOHN C. DYKSTRA, for the development of a facility uniquely oriented toward visual effects photography, and to ALVAH J. MILLER and JERRY JEFFRESS, for the engineering of the Electronic Motion Control System used in concert for multiple exposure visual effects motion picture photography.

EASTMAN KODAK COMPANY, for the development and introduction of a new duplicating film for motion pictures.

STEFAN KUDELSKI of Nagra Magentic Recorders Inc., for the engineering of the improvements incorporated in the Nagra 4.2L sound recorder for motion picture production.

(Class III)

ERNST NETTMANN of the Astrovision Division of Continental Camera Systems Inc., for the engineering of its Periscope Aerial Camera System.

EECO (Electronic Engineering Co of California), for developing a method for interlocking non-sprocketed film and tape media used in motion picture production.

DR. BERNHARD KUHL and WERNER BLOCK of OSRAM, GmbH, for the development of the HMI high-efficiency discharge lamp for motion picture lighting.

PANAVISION INC., for the design of Panalite, a camera-mounted controllable light for motion picture photography.

PANAVISION INC., for the engineering of the Panahead gearhead for motion picture cameras. (Panavision rejected the three awards because its Panaflex camera was voted a Class Two instead of a Class One award.)

PICLEAR INC., for originating and developing an attachment to motion picture projectors to improve screen image quality.

1978

BEST PICTURE (O-892)

THE DEER HUNTER, An EMI Films/Michael Cimino Film Prod., U. Barry Spikings, Michael Deeley, Michael Cimino and John Peverall, Prods.
COMING HOME. A Jerome Hellman Enterprises Prods, UA. Jerome Hellman, Prod.
HEAVEN CAN WAIT. Dogwood Productions, PAR. Warren Beatty, Prod.
MIDNIGHT EXPRESS, A Casablanca Filmworks Prod., COL. Alan Marshall and David Puttnam, Prods.
AN UNMARRIED WOMAN, A FOX Prod., FOX. Paul Mazursky and Tony Ray, Prods.

ACTOR (O-893)

JON VOIGHT, Coming Home.
WARREN BEATTY, Heaven Can Wait.
GARY BUSEY, The Buddy Holly Story, An Innovisions-ECA Prod., COL.
ROBERT DE NIRO, The Deer Hunter.
LAURENCE OLIVIER, The Boys From Brazil, An ITC Entertainment Prod., FOX.

ACTRESS (O-894)

JANE FONDA, Coming Home.
INGRID BERGMAN, Autumn Sonata, A Personafilm GmbH Prod., Sir Lew Grade-Martin Starger-ITC Entertainment Presentation, NW.
ELLEN BURSTYN, Same Time, Next Year, A Walter Mirisch-Robert Mulligan Prod., Mirisch Corporation/U Pictures Presentation, U.
JILL CLAYBURGH, An Unmarried Woman.
GERALDINE PAGE, Interiors, A Jack Rollins-Charles H Joffe Prod., UA.

SUPPORTING ACTOR (O-895)

CHRISTOPHER WALKEN, The Deer Hunter.
BRUCE DERN, Coming Home.
RICHARD FARNSWORTH, Comes a Horseman, A Robert Chartoff-Irwin Winkler Prod., UA.
JOHN HURT, Midnight Express.
JACK WARDEN, Heaven Can Wait.

SUPPORTING ACTRESS (O-896)

MAGGIE SMITH, California Suite, A Ray Stark Prod., COL.
DYAN CANNON, Heaven Can Wait.
PENELOPE MILFORD, Coming Home.
MAUREEN STAPLETON, Interiors.
MERYL STREEP, The Deer Hunter.

DIRECTING (O-897)

MICHAEL CIMINO, The Deer Hunter.
WOODY ALLEN, Interiors.
HAL ASHBY, Coming Home.
WARREN BEATTY, Heaven Can Wait.
BUCK HENRY, Heaven Can Wait.
ALAN PARKER, Midnight Express.

WRITING (O-898)

(Best Screenplay Written Directly For The Screen)

COMING HOME. Story by Nancy Dowd. Screenplay by Waldo Salt and Robert C Jones.
AUTUMN SONATA. Story and screenplay by Ingmar Bergman.
THE DEER HUNTER. Story by Michael Cimino, Deric Washburn, Louis Garfinkle and Quinn K Redeker. Screenplay by Deric Washburn.
INTERIORS. Story and screenplay by Woody Allen.
AN UNMARRIED WOMAN. Story and screenplay by Paul Mazursky.

(Best Screenplay Based On Material From Another Medium)

MIDNIGHT EXPRESS. Screenplay by Oliver Stone.
BLOODBROTHERS, A WB Prod., WB. Screenplay by Walter Newman.
CALIFORNIA SUITE. Screenplay by Neil Simon.
HEAVEN CAN WAIT. Screenplay by Elaine May and Warren Beatty.
SAME TIME, NEXT YEAR. Screenplay by Bernard Slade.

CINEMATOGRAPHY (O-899)

DAYS OF HEAVEN, An OP Prod., PAR. Nestor Almendros.
THE DEER HUNTER. Vilmos Zsigmond.
HEAVEN CAN WAIT. William A Fraker.
SAME TIME, NEXT YEAR. Robert Surtees.
THE WIZ, A Motown/U Pictures Prod., U. Oswald Morris.

COSTUME DESIGN (O-900)

DEATH ON THE NILE, A John Brabourne-Richard Goodwin Prod., PAR. Anthony Powell.
CARAVANS, An Ibex Films-F.I.D.C.I. Prod., U. Renie Conley.
DAYS OF HEAVEN. Patricia Norris.
THE SWARM, A WB Prod., WB. Paul Zastupnevich.
THE WIZ. Tony Walton.

ART DIRECTION - SET DECORATION (O-901)

HEAVEN CAN WAIT. Paul Sylbert and Edwin O'Donovan. Set Decoration: George Gaines.
THE BRINK'S JOB, A William Friedkin Film/U Prod., Dino De Laurentiis Presentation, U. Dean Tavoularis and Angelo Graham. Set Decoration: George R Nelson and Bruce Kay.
CALIFORNIA SUITE. Albert Brenner. Set Decoration: Marvin March.
INTERIORS. Mel Bourne. Set Decoration: Daniel Robert.
THE WIZ. Tony Walton and Philip Rosenberg. Set Decoration: Edward Stewart and Robert Drumheller.

FILM EDITING (O-902)

THE DEER HUNTER. Peter Zinner.
THE BOYS FROM BRAZIL. Robert E Swink.
COMING HOME. Don Zimmerman.
MIDNIGHT EXPRESS. Gerry Hambling.
SUPERMAN, A Dovemead Ltd Prod., Alexander Salkind Presentation, WB. Stuart Baird.

FOREIGN LANGUAGE FILM (O-903)

GET OUT YOUR HANDKERCHIEFS, A Les Films Ariane - C.A.P.A.C. Prod. (France).
THE GLASS CELL, A Roxy Film Prod. (German Federal Republic).
HUNGARIANS, A Dialog Studio Prod. (Hungary).
VIVA ITALIA!, A Dean Film Prod. (Italy).
WHITE BIM BLACK EAR, A Central Studio of Films for Children and Youth Prod. (U.S.S.R.).

MUSIC - SCORING (O-904)

(Best Original Score)

MIDNIGHT EXPRESS. Giorgio Moroder.
THE BOYS FROM BRAZIL. Jerry Goldsmith.
DAYS OF HEAVEN. Ennio Morricone.
HEAVEN CAN WAIT. Dave Grusin.
SUPERMAN. John Williams.

(Best Adaptation Score)

THE BUDDY HOLLY STORY. Adaptation score by Joe Renzetti.
PRETTY BABY, A Louis Malle Film Prod., PAR. Adaptation score by Jerry Wexler.
THE WIZ. Adaptation score by Quincy Jones.

MUSIC - BEST SONG (O-905)

LAST DANCE, Thank God It's Friday, A Casablanca-Motown Prod., COL. Music and lyrics by Paul Jabara.
HOPELESSLY DEVOTED TO YOU, *Grease*, A Robert Stigwood/Allan Carr Prod., PAR. Music and lyrics by John Farrar.
THE LAST TIME I FELT LIKE THIS, *Same Time, Next Year*. Music by Marvin Hamlisch. Lyrics by Alan and Marilyn Bergman.
READY TO TAKE A CHANCE AGAIN, *Foul Play*, A Miller-Milkis/Colin Higgins Picture Prod., PAR. Music by Charles Fox. Lyrics by Norman Gimbel.
WHEN YOU'RE LOVED, *The Magic of Lassie*, Lassie Prods., The Int'l Picture Show Co. Music and lyrics by Richard M Sherman and Robert B Sherman.

SOUND (O-906)

THE DEER HUNTER. Richard Portman, William McCaughey, Aaron Rochin and Darrin Knight.
THE BUDDY HOLLY STORY. Tex Rudloff, Joel Fein, Curly Thirlwell and Willie Burton.
DAYS OF HEAVEN. John K Wilkinson, Robert W Glass, Jr, John T Reitz and Barry Thomas.
HOOPER, A WB Prod., WB. Robert Knudson, Robert J Glass, Don MacDougall and Jack Solomon.
SUPERMAN. Gordon K McCallum, Graham Hartstone, Nicolas Le Mesurier and Roy Charman.

SHORT FILMS (O-907)

(Animated)

SPECIAL DELIVERY, National Film Board of Canada. Eunice Macaulay and John Weldon, Prods.
OH MY DARLING, Nico Crama Prods. Nico Crama, Prod.
RIP VAN WINKLE, A Will Vinton/Billy Budd Film, Will Vinton, Prod.

(Live Action)

TEENAGE FATHER, New Visions Inc. for the Children's Home Society of California. Taylor Hackford, Prod.
A DIFFERENT APPROACH, A Jim Belcher/Brookfield Prod. Jim Belcher and Fern Field, Prods.
MANDY'S GRANDMOTHER, Illumination Films. Andrew Sugerman, Prod.
STRANGE FRUIT, The America Film Institute. Seth Pinsker, Prod.

DOCUMENTARY (O-908)

(Short Subjects)

THE FLIGHT OF THE GOSSAMER CONDOR, A Shedd Prod. Jacqueline Phillips Shedd, Ben Shedd, Prods.
THE DIVIDED TRAIL: A Native American Odyssey, A Jerry Aronson Prod. Jerry Aronson, Prod.
AN ENCOUNTER WITH FACES, Films Division, Government of India.

K K Kapil, Prod.
GOODNIGHT MISS ANN, An August Cinquegrana Films Prod. August Cinquegrana, Prod.
SQUIRES OF SAN QUENTIN, The J Gary Mitchell Film Co. J Gary Mitchell, Prod.

(Features)

SCARED STRAIGHT!, A Golden West Television Prod. Arnold Shapiro, Prod.
THE LOVERS' WIND, Ministry of Culture & Arts of Iran. Albert Lamorisse, Prod.
MYSTERIOUS CASTLES OF CLAY, A Survival Anglia Ltd Prod. Alan Root, Prod.
RAONI, A Franco-Brazilian Prod. Jean-Pierre Dutilleux, Barry Williams and Michel Gast, Prods.
WITH BABIES AND BANNERS: STORY OF THE WOMEN'S EMERGENCY BRIGADE, A Women's Labor History Film Project Prod. Anne Bohlen, Lyn Goldfarb and Lorraine Gray, Prods.

HONORARY AND OTHER (O-909)

(Jean Hersholt Humanitarian Award):

Leo Jaffe.

(Special Achievement Awards):

Visual Effects: LES BOWIE, COLIN CHILVERS, DENYS COOP, ROY FELD, DEREK MEDDINGS and ZORAN PERISIC, Superman.

(Other)

WALTER LANTZ for bringing joy and laughter to every part of the world through his unique animated motion pictures.
THE MUSEUM OF MODERN ART, DEPARTMENT OF FILM for the contribution it has made to the public's perception of movies as an art form.
LAURENCE OLIVIER for the full body of his work, for the unique achievements of his entire career and his lifetime of contribution to the art of film.
KING VIDOR for his incomparable achievements as a cinematic creator and innovator.

(Medals Of Commendation)

LINWOOD G DUNN, LOREN L RYDER and WALDON O WATSON in appreciation for outstanding service and dedication in upholding the high standards of the Academy of Motion Picture Arts and Sciences.

SCIENTIFIC OR TECHNICAL (O-910)

(Academy Award of Merit)

EASTMAN KODAK COMPANY, for the research and development of a Duplicating Color Film for Motion Pictures.
STEFAN KUDELSKI of Nagra Magnetic Recorders, Inc., for the continuing research, design and development of the Nagra Production Sound Recorder for Motion Pictures.
PANAVISION, INC., and its engineering staff under the direction of ROBERT E GOTTSCHALK, for the concept, design and continuous development of the Panaflex Motion Picture Camera System.

(Scientific and Engineering Award)

RAY M DOLBY, IOAN R ALLEN, DAVID P ROBINSON, STEPHEN M KATZ and PHILIP S J BOOLE of Dolby Laboratories, Inc., for the development and implementation of an improved Sound Recording and Reproducing System for Motion Picture Prod. and Exhibition.

(Technical Achievement Award)

KARL MACHER and GLENN M BERGGREN of Isco Optische Werke for the development and introduction of the Cinelux-ULTRA Lens for 35mm Motion Picture Projection.
DAVID J DEGENKOLB, ARTHUR L FORD and FRED J SCOBEY of DeLuxe General, Inc., for the development of a method to Recycle Motion Picture Laboratory Photographic Wash Waters by Ion Exchange.
KIICHI SEKIGUCHI of Cine-Fi International for the development of the CINE-FI Auto Radio Sound System for Drive-in Theaters.
LEONARD CHAPMAN of Leonard Equipment Co., for the design and manufacture of a small, mobile, motion picture camera platform known as the Chapman Hustler Dolly.
JAMES L FISHER of J L Fisher, Inc., for the design and manufacture of a small, mobile, motion picture camera platform known as the

Fisher Model Ten Dolly.
ROBERT STINDT of Production Grip Equipment Co., for the design and manufacture of a small, mobile, motion picture camera platform known as the Stindt Dolly.

1979

BEST PICTURE (O-911)

KRAMER VS. KRAMER, Stanley Jaffe Productions, Col. Stanley R Jaffe Prod.
ALL THAT JAZZ, A Columbia/Twentieth Century-Fox Production, Fox. Robert Alan Aurthur, Prod.
APOCALYPSE NOW, An Omni Zoetrope Production, UA. Francis Coppola, Prod. Fred Roos, Gray Frederickson and Tom Sternberg, Co-Prods.
BREAKING AWAY, Fox. Peter Yates, Prod.
NORMA RAE, Fox. Tamara Asseyev and Alex Rose, Prods.

ACTOR (O-912)

DUSTIN HOFFMAN, Kramer vs. Kramer.
JACK LEMMON, *The China Syndrome*, A Michael Douglas/IPC Films Production, Col.
AL PACINO, . . .*And Justice For All*, A Malton Films Limited Production, Col.
ROY SCHEIDER, *All That Jazz*.
PETER SELLERS, *Being There*, A Lorimar Film-Und Fernsehproduktion GmbH Production, UA.

ACTRESS (O-913)

SALLY FIELD, Norma Rae.
JILL CLAYBURGH, *Starting Over*, An Alan J Pakula/James L Brooks Production, Par.
JANE FONDA, *China Syndrome*.
MARSHA MASON, *Chapter Two*, A Ray Stark Production, Col.
BETTE MIDLER, *The Rose*, Fox.

SUPPORTING ACTOR (O-914)

MELVYN DOUGLAS, Being There.
ROBERT DUVALL, *Apocalypse Now*.
FREDERIC FORREST, *The Rose*.
JUSTIN HENRY, *Kramer vs. Kramer*.
MICKEY ROONEY, *The Black Stallion*, An Omni Zoetrope Production, UA.

SUPPORTING ACTRESS (O-915)

MERYL STREEP, Kramer vs. Kramer.
JANE ALEXANDER, *Kramer vs. Kramer*.
BARBARA BARRIE, *Breaking Away*.
CANDICE BERGEN, *Starting Over*.
MARIEL HEMINGWAY, *Manhattan*, A Jack Rollins-Charles H Joffe Production, UA.

DIRECTING (O-916)

ROBERT BENTON, Kramer vs. Kramer.
BOB FOSSE, *All That Jazz*.
FRANCIS COPPOLA, *Apocalypse Now*.
PETER YATES, *Breaking Away*.
EDOUARD MOLINARO, *La Cage Aux Folles*, A Les Productions Artistes Associes Da Ma Produzione SPA Production, UA.

WRITING (O-917)

(Best Screenplay Written Directly For The Screen)
BREAKING AWAY. Story and screenplay by Steve Tesich.
ALL THAT JAZZ. Story and screenplay by Robert Alan Aurthur and Bob Fosse.
. . .AND JUSTICE FOR ALL. Story and screenplay by Valerie Curtin and Barry Levinson.
THE CHINA SYNDROME. Story and screenplay by Mike Gray, T S Cook and James Bridges.

MANHATTAN. Story and screenplay by Woody Allen and Marshall Brickman.

(Best Screenplay Based On Material From Another Medium)
KRAMER VS. KRAMER. Screenplay by Robert Benton.
APOCALYPSE NOW. Screenplay by John Milius and Francis Coppola.
LA CAGE AUX FOLLES. Screenplay and adaptation by Francis Veber, Edouard Molinaro, Marcello Danon and Jean Poiret.
A LITTLE ROMANCE, A Pan Arts Associates Production, Orion Pictures Company. Screenplay by Allan Burns.
NORMA RAE. Screenplay by Irving Ravetch and Harriet Frank, Jr.

CINEMATOGRAPHY (O-918)

APOCALYPSE NOW. Vittorio Storaro.
ALL THAT JAZZ. Giuseppe Rotunno.
THE BLACK HOLE, Walt Disney Productions, Frank Phillips.
KRAMER VS. KRAMER. Nestor Almendros.
1941, An A-Team/Steven Spielberg Film Production, Universal-Columbia Presentation, U. William A Fraker.

COSTUME DESIGN (O-919)

ALL THAT JAZZ. FOX. Albert Wolsky.
AGATHA, A Sweetwall Production in association with Casablanca Filmworks, First Artists Presentation. WB. Shirley Russell.
BUTCH AND SUNDANCE: THE EARLY DAYS. FOX. William Ware Theiss.
THE EUROPEANS, Merchant Ivory Productins, Levitt-Pickman. Judy Moorcroft.
LA CAGE AUX FOLLES, UA Piero Tosi and Ambra Danon.

ART DIRECTION - SET DECORATION (O-920)

ALL THAT JAZZ. Philip Rosenberg and Tony Walton. Set Decoration: Edward Stewart and Gary Brink.
ALIEN. Michael Seymour, Les Dilley and Roger Christian. Set Decoration: Ian Whittaker.
APOCALYPSE NOW. Dean Tavoularis and Angelo Graham. Set Decoration: George R Nelson.
THE CHINA SYNDROME. George Jenkins. Set Decoration: Arthur Jeph Parker.
STAR TREK - THE MOTION PICTURE, A Century Associates Production, PAR. Harold Michelson, Joe Jennings, Leon Harris and John Vallone. Set Decoration: Linda DeScenna.

FILM EDITING (O-921)

ALL THAT JAZZ. Alan Heim.
APOCALYPSE NOW. Richard Marks, Walter Murch, Gerald B Greenberg and Lisa Fruchtman.
THE BLACK STALLION. Robert Dalva.
KRAMER VS. KRAMER. Jerry Greenberg.
THE ROSE. Robert L Wolfe and C Timothy O'Meara.

FOREIGN LANGUAGE FILM (O-922)

THE TIN DRUM, A Franz Seitz Film/Bioskop Film/Artemis Film/ Hallelujah Film/ GGB 14.KG/Argos Films Production (Federal Republic of Germany).
THE MAIDS OF WILKO, A Polish Corporation for Film Production (Poland).
MAMA TURNS A HUNDRED, Elias Querejeta P C Production (Spain).
A SIMPLE STORY, A Renn Productions/Sara Films/F R 3/Rialto Films Production, Quartet Films (France).
TO FORGET VENICE, A Rizzoli Film/Action Film Production, Quartet Films (Italy).

MUSIC - SCORING (O-923)

(Best Original Score)
A LITTLE ROMANCE. WB. Georges Delerue.
THE AMITYVILLE HORROR, An American International/Professional Films Production. AIP. Lalo Schifrin.
THE CHAMP. MGM Dave Grusin.
STAR TREK - THE MOTION PICTURE. Jerry Goldsmith.

10, Geoffrey Productions, Orion Pictures Company. WB. Henry Mancini.

(Best Original Song Score and Its Adaptation or Best Adaptation Score)

ALL THAT JAZZ. Adaptation Score by Ralph Burns.
BREAKING AWAY. Adaptation Score by Patrick Williams.
THE MUPPET MOVIE, A Jim Henson Production. Lord Grade/Martin Starger Presentation. AFD. Original Song Score by Paul Williams and Kenny Ascher. Adapted by Paul Williams.

MUSIC - BEST SONG (O-924)

IT GOES LIKE IT GOES, Norma Rae. Music by David Shire. Lyric by Norman Gimbel.
THE RAINBOW CONNECTION, *The Muppet Movie.* Music and lyric by Paul Williams and Kenny Ascher.
IT'S EASY TO SAY, *10.* Music by Henry Mancini. Lyric by Robert Wells.
THROUGH THE EYES OF LOVE, *Ice Castles,* An International Cinemedia Center Production, Col. Music by Marvin Hamlisch. Lyric by Carole Bayer Sager.
I'LL NEVER SAY "GOODBYE", *The Promise,* A Fred Weintraub-Paul Heller Present/Universal Production, U. Music by David Shire. Lyric by Alan and Marilyn Bergman.

SOUND (O-925)

APOCALYPSE NOW. Walter Murch, Mark Berger, Richard Beggs and Nat Boxer.
THE ELECTRIC HORSEMAN. Arthur Piantadosi, Les Fresholtz, Michael Minkler and Al Overton.
METEOR, Meteor Productions, AIP. William McCaughey, Aaron Rochin, Michael J Kohut and Jack Solomon.
1941. Robert Knudson, Robert J Glass, Don MacDougall and Gene S Cantamessa.
THE ROSE. Theodore Soderberg, Douglas Williams, Paul Wells and Jim Webb.

SHORT FILMS (O-926)

(Animated)

EVERY CHILD, National Film Board of Canada. Derek Lamb, Prod.
DREAM DOLL, Bob Godfrey Films/Zagreb Films/Halas and Batchelor, Filmwright. Bob Godfrey and Zlatko Grgic, Prods.
IT'S SO NICE TO HAVE A WOLF AROUND THE HOUSE, AR&T Productions for Learning Corporation of America. Paul Fierlinger, Prod.

(Live Action)

BOARD AND CARE, Ron Ellis Films. Sarah Pillsbury and Ron Ellis, Prods.
BRAVERY IN THE FIELD, National Film Board of Canada. Roman Kroitor and Stefan Wodoslawsky, Prods.
OH BROTHER, MY BROTHER, Ross Lowell Productions, Pyramid Films, Inc. Carol and Ross Lowell, Prods.
THE SOLAR FILM, Wildwood Enterprises Inc. Saul Bass and Michael Britton, Prods.
SOLLY'S DINER, Mathias/Zukerman/Hankin Productions. Harry Mathias, Jay Zukerman and Larry Hankin, Prods.

DOCUMENTARY (O-927)

(Short Subjects)

PAUL ROBESON: TRIBUTE TO AN ARTIST, Janus Films, Inc. Saul J Turell, Prod.
DAE, Vardar Film/Skopje. Risto Teofilovski, Prod.
KORYO CELADON, Charlie/Papa Productions, Inc. Donald A Connolly and James R Messenger, Prods.
NAILS, National Film Board of Canada. Phillip Borsos, Prod.
REMEMBER ME, Dick Young Productions, Ltd. Dick Young, Prod.

(Features)

BEST BOY, Only Child Motion Pictures, Inc. Ira Wohl, Prod.
GENERATION ON THE WIND, More Than One Medium. David A Vassar, Prod.
GOING THE DISTANCE, National Film Board of Canada. Paul Cowan and Jacques Bobet, Prods.
THE KILLING GROUND, ABC News Closeup Unit. Steve Singer and Tom Priestley, Prods.
THE WAR AT HOME, Catalyst Films/Madison Film Production Co. Glenn Silber and Barry Alexander Brown, Prods.

VISUAL EFFECTS (O-928)

ALIEN. H R Giger, Carlo Rambaldi, Brian Johnson, Nick Allder and Denys Ayling.
THE BLACK HOLE. Peter Ellenshaw, Art Cruickshank, Eustace Lycett, Danny Lee, Harrison Ellenshaw and Joe Hale.
MOONRAKER, Eon Productions Ltd, UA. Derek Meddings, Paul Wilson and John Evans.
1941. William A Fraker, A D Flowers and Gregory Jein.
STAR TREK - THE MOTION PICTURE. Douglas Trumbull, John Dykstra, Richard Yuricich, Robert Swarthe, Dave Stewart and Grant McCune.

HONORARY AND OTHER (O-929)

(Irving G. Thalberg Memorial Award)

RAY STARK.

(Jean Hersholt Humanitarian Award)

ROBERT BENJAMIN.

(Special Achievement) (Sound Editing)

ALAN SPLET, The Black Stallion.

(Other)

HAL ELIAS for his dedication and distinguished service to the Academy of Motion Picture Arts and Sciences.
ALEC GUINNESS for advancing the art of screen acting through a host of memorable and distinguished performances.

(Medals Of Commendation)

JOHN O AALBERG, CHARLES G CLARKE and JOHN G FRAYNE in appreciation for outstanding service and dedication in upholding the high standards of the Academy of Motion Picture Arts and Sciences.

SCIENTIFIC OR TECHNICAL (O-930)

(Academy Award of Merit)

MARK SERRURIER for the progressive development of the Moviola from the 1924 invention of his father, Iwan Serrurier, to the present Series 20 sophisticated film editing equipment.

(Scientific and Engineering Award)

NEIMAN-TILLAR ASSOCIATES for the creative development, and to Mini-Micro Systems, Inc., for the design and engineering of an Automated Computer Controlled Editing Sound System (ACCESS) for motion picture post-production.

(Technical Achievement Award)

MICHAEL V CHEWEY, WALTER G EGGERS and ALLEN HECHT of M-G-M Laboratories for the development of a Computer-controlled Paper Tape Programmer System and its applications in the motion picture laboratory.
IRWIN YOUNG, PAUL KAUFMAN and FREDRIK SCHLYTER of Du Art Film Laboratories, Inc., for the development of a Computer-controlled Paper Tape Programmer System and its applications in the motion picture laboratory.
JAMES S STANFIELD and PAUL W TRESTER for the development and manufacture or a device for the repair or protection of sprocket holes in motion picture film.
ZORAN PERISIC of Courier Films, Limited, for the Zoptic Special Optical Effects Device for motion picture photography.
A D FLOWERS and LOGAN R FRAZEE for the development of a device to control flight patterns of miniature airplanes during motion picture photography.
THE PHOTO RESEARCH DIVISION OF KOLLMORGEN CORP. for the development of the Spectra Series II Cine Special Exposure Meter for motion picture photography.
BRUCE LYON and JOHN LAMB for the development of a Video Animation System for testing motion picture animation sequences.
ROSS LOWELL of Lowel-Light Manufacturing, Inc., for the development of compact lighting equipment for motion picture photography.

1980

PICTURE: (O-931)

ORDINARY PEOPLE, Wildwood Enterprises Production, PAR. Ronald L. Schwary, Prod.
COAL MINER'S DAUGHTER, Bernard Schwartz-Universal Pictures Production, U. Bernard Schwartz, Prod.
THE ELEPHANT MAN, Brooksfilms Ltd. Production, PAR. Jonathan Sanger, Prod.
RAGING BULL, Robert Chartoff-Irwin Winkler Production, UA. Irwin Winkler, Robert Chartoff, Prods.
TESS, Renn-Burrill Coproduction with the participation of the Societe Francaise de Production, COL. Claude Berri, Prod, Timothy Burrill, Coprod.

ACTOR: (O-932)

ROBERT DE NIRO, Raging Bull.
ROBERT DUVALL, *The Great Santini,* Orion Pictures-Bing Crosby Production, WBO.
JOHN HURT, *The Elephant Man.*
JACK LEMMON, *Tribute,* Lawrence Turman-David Foster presentation of a Joel B. Michaels-Garth H. Drabinsky Production, FOX.
PETER O'TOOLE, *The Stunt Man,* Melvin Simon Prods, FOX.

ACTRESS: (O-933)

SISSY SPACEK, Coal Miner's Daughter.
ELLEN BURSTYN, *Resurrection,* Universal Production, U.
GOLDIE HAWN, *Private Benjamin,* Warner Bros. Production, WB.
MARY TYLER MOORE, *Ordinary People.*
GENA ROWLANDS, *Gloria,* Columbia Pictures Production, COL.

SUPPORTING ACTOR: (O-934)

TIMOTHY HUTTON, Ordinary People.
JUDD HIRSCH, *Ordinary People.*
MICHAEL O'KEEFE, *The Great Santini.*
JOE PESCI, *Raging Bull.*
JASON ROBARDS, *Melvin And Howard,* Linson/Phillips/Demme- Universal Pictures Production, U.

SUPPORTING ACTRESS: (O-935)

MARY STEENBURGEN, Melvin And Howard.
EILEEN BRENNAN, *Private Benjamin.*
EVA LE GALLIENNE, *Resurrection.*
CATHY MORIARTY, *Raging Bull.*
DIANA SCARWID, *Inside Moves,* Goodmark Production, AFD.

DIRECTING: (O-936)

ROBERT REDFORD, Ordinary People.
DAVID LYNCH, *The Elephant Man.*
MARTIN SCORSESE, *Raging Bull.*
RICHARD RUSH, *The Stunt Man.*
ROMAN POLANSKI, *Tess.*

WRITING: (O-937)

(Best Original Screenplay)

MELVIN AND HOWARD. Screenplay by Bo Goldman.
BRUBAKER, Twentieth Century-Fox Production, FOX. Screenplay by W.D. Richter. Story by Richter, Arthur Ross.
FAME. Screenplay by Christopher Gore.
MON ONCLE D'AMERIQUE, Philippe Dussart-Andrea Films - T.F. 1 Production, NW. Screenplay by Jean Gruault.
PRIVATE BENJAMIN. Screenplay by Nancy Meyers, Charles Shyer, Harvey Miller.

(Screenplay Adaptation)

ORDINARY PEOPLE. Alvin Sargent.
BREAKER MORANT, produced in association with the Australian Film Commission, the South Australian Film Corp. and the Seven Network and Pact Prods., NW/ART/FIZ. Screenplay adaptation by Jonathan Hardy, David Stevens, Bruce Beresford.

COAL MINER'S DAUGHTER. Tom Rickman.
THE ELEPHANT MAN. Christopher DeVore, Eric Bergren, David Lynch.
THE STUNT MAN. Screenplay by Lawrence B. Marcus. Adaptation by Richard Rush.

CINEMATOGRAPHY: (O-938)

TESS. Geoffrey Unsworth and Ghislain Cloquet.
THE BLUE LAGOON, Columbia Pictures Production, COL. Nestor Almendros.
COAL MINER'S DAUGHTER. Ralf D. Bode.
THE FORMULA, Metro-Goldwyn-Mayer Production, MGM. James Crabe.
RAGING BULL. Michael Chapman.

COSTUME DESIGN: (O-939)

TESS, Anthony Powell.
THE ELEPHANT MAN, Patricia Norris.
MY BRILLIANT CAREER, Margaret Fink Films Pty Ltd production, ANY. Anna Senior.
SOMEWHERE IN TIME, Rastar-Stephen Deutsch-Universal Pictures production, U. Jean-Pierre Dorleac.
WHEN TIME RAN OUT, Warner Bros production, WB. Paul Zastupnevich.

ART DIRECTION - SET DECORATION: (O-940)

TESS. Art Direction: Pierre Guffroy, Jack Stevens.
COAL MINER'S DAUGHTER. Art Direction: John W Corso. Set Decoration: John M Dwyer.
THE ELEPHANT MAN. Art Direction: Stuart Craig, Bob Cartwright. Set Decoration: Hugh Scaife.
THE EMPIRE STRIKES BACK, Lucasfilm Ltd production. FOX. Art Direction: Norman Reynolds, Leslie Dilley, Harry Lange, Alan Tomkins. Set Decoration: Michael Ford.
KAGEMUSHA (The Shadow Warrior), Toho Co Ltd-Kurosawa Prods Ltd Coproduction (Japan). Art Direction: Yoshiro Muraki.

FILM EDITING: (O-941)

RAGING BULL. Thelma Schoonmaker.
COAL MINER'S DAUGHTER. Arthur Schmidt.
THE COMPETITION, Rastar Films Production, COL. David Blewitt.
THE ELEPHANT MAN. Anne V. Coates.
FAME. Gerry Hambling.

FOREIGN-LANGUAGE FILM: (O-942)

MOSCOW DOES NOT BELIEVE IN TEARS, Mosfilm Studio Production (U.S.S.R.).
CONFIDENCE, Mafilm Studios Production (Hungary).
KAGEMUSHA (The Shadow Warrior).
THE LAST METRO, Les Films du Carrosse Production (France).
THE NEST, A. Punto E.L. S.A. Production (Spain).

MUSIC - SCORING: (O-943)

(Best Original Score)

FAME, Metro-Goldwyn-Mayer Presentation. UA. Michael Gore.
ALTERED STATES, Warner Bros production, WB. John Corigliano.
THE ELEPHANT MAN, John Morris.
THE EMPIRE STRIKES BACK. John Williams.
TESS, Philippe Sarde.

MUSIC - BEST SONG: (O-944)

FAME, Fame. Music by Michael Gore. Lyric by Dean Pitchford.
NINE TO FIVE, *Nine To Five.* Twentieth Century-Fox production, FOX. Music and lyric by Dolly Parton.
ON THE ROAD AGAIN, *Honeysuckle Rose.* Warner Bros production, WB. Music and lyric by Willie Nelson.
OUT HERE ON MY OWN, *Fame.* Music by Michael Gore. Lyric by Lesley Gore.
PEOPLE ALONE, *The Competition.* Music by Lalo Schifrin. Lyric by Wilbur Jennings.

1979—Dustin Hoffman (Best Actor) and Alec Guinness (Honorary Award)

1980—Robert De Niro (Best Actor), Sissy Spacek (Best Actress), Robert L. Schwary (producer, Best Picture), and Robert Redford (Best Director)

1981—John Travolta (presenter) and Barbara Stanwyck (Honorary Award)

1981—Warren Beatty (Best Director)

1982—Meryl Streep (Best Actress)

1982—Richard Attenborough (producer, Best Picture and Best Director)
and Ben Kingsley (Best Actor)

SOUND: (O-945)

THE EMPIRE STRIKES BACK, Bill Varney, Steve Maslow, Gregg Landaker, Peter Sutton.
ALTERED STATES, Arthur Piantadosi, Les Fresholtz, Michael Minkler, Willie D. Burton.
COAL MINER'S DAUGHTER, Richard Portman, Roger Heman, Jim Alexander.
FAME, Michael J Kohut, Aaron Rochin, Jay M Harding, Chris Newman.
RAGING BULL, Donald O Mitchell, Bill Nicholson, David J Kimball, Les Lazarowitz.

SHORT FILMS: (O-946)

(Animated)

THE FLY, Pannonia Film, Budapest. Ferenc Rofusz, producer.
ALL NOTHING, Radio Canada. Frederic Back, producer.
HISTORY OF THE WORLD IN THREE MINUTES FLAT, Michael Mills productions Ltd. Michael Mills, producer.

(Live Action)

THE DOLLAR BOTTOM, Rocking Horse Films Ltd, PAR. Lloyd Phillips, producer.
FALL LINE, Sports Imagery Inc Bob Carmichael, Greg Lowe, producers.
A JURY OF HER PEERS, Sally Heckel Prods. Sally Heckel, producer.

DOCUMENTARY: (O-947)

(Short Subjects)

KARL HESS: TOWARD LIBERTY, Halle/Ladue Inc. Peter W Ladue, Roland Halle, producers.
DON'T MESS WITH BILL, John Watson and Pen Densham's Insight Prods Inc. John Watson, Pen Densham, producers.
THE ERUPTION OF MOUNT ST HELENS, Graphic Films Corp. George Casey, producer.
IT'S THE SAME WORLD, Dick Young Prods Ltd. Dick Young, producer.
LUTHER METKE AT 94, UCLA Ethnographic Film Program. Richard Hawkins, Jorge Preloran, producers.

(Features)

FROM MAO TO MOZART: ISAAC STERN IN CHINA, Hopewell Foundation. Murray Lerner, producer.
AGEE, James Agee Film Project. Ross Spears, producer.
THE DAY AFTER TRINITY, Jon Else Prods. Jon Else, producer.
FRONT LINE, David Bradbury Prods. David Bradbury, producer.
THE YELLOW STAR - THE PERSECUTION OF EUROPEAN JEWS 1933-45, Chronos Films. Bengt von zur Muehlen, producer.

HONORARY AND OTHER AWARDS: (O-948)

HENRY FONDA, the consummate actor, in recognition of his brilliant accomplishments and enduring contribution to the art of motion pictures.

(Special Achievement) (Visual Effects)

THE EMPIRE STRIKES BACK, Brian Johnson, Richard Edlund, Dennis Muren, Bruce Nicholson.

(Medal of Commendation)

FRED HYNES

SCIENTIFIC OR TECHNICAL AWARDS: (O-949)

(Academy Award of Merit)

LINWOOD G. DUNN, CECIL D. LOVE, EDWARD FURER and ACME TOOL & MANUFACTURING CO., for concept, engineering and development of Acme-Dunn Optical Printer for motion picture special effects.

(Scientific and Engineering Award)

JEAN-MARIE LAVALOU, ALAIN MASSERON and DAVID SAMUELSON of Samuelson Alga Cinema S.A. and Samuelson Film Service Ltd., for engineering and development of the Louma Camera Crane and remote-control system for motion picture production.
EDWARD B. KRAUSE of Filmline Corp., for the engineering and manufacture of the microdemand drive for continuous motion picture film processors.
ROSS TAYLOR, for concept and development of a system of air guns for propelling objects used in special effects motion picture production.
DR. BERNHARD KUHL and DR. WERNER BLOCK of OSRAM GmbH, for progressive engineering and manufacture of the OSRAM HMI light source for motion picture color photography.
DAVID A. GRAFTON, for optical design and engineering of a telecentric anamorphic lens for motion picture optical effects printers.

(Technical Achievement Award)

CARTER EQUIPMENT CO., for development of a continuous contact, total immersion, additive color motion picture printer.
HOLLYWOOD FILM CO., for development of a continuous contact, total immersion, additive color motion picture printer.
ANDRE DeBRIE S.A., for development of a continuous contact, total immersion, additive color motion picture printer.
CHARLES VAUGHN and EUGENE NOTTINGHAM of Cinetron Computer Systems Inc., for development of a versatile general purpose computer system for animation and optical effects motion picture photography.
JOHN W. LANG, WALTER HRASTNIK and CHARLES J. WATSON of Bell & Howell Co., for development and manufacture of a modular continuous contact motion picture film printer.
WORTH BAIRD of LaVezzi Machine Works Inc., for the advanced design and manufacture of a film sprocket for motion picture projectors.
PETER A. REGLA and DAN SLATER of Elicon, for development of a follow focus system for motion picture optical printers and animation stands.

1981

PICTURE: (O-950)

CHARIOTS OF FIRE, Enigma Productions Ltd., The Ladd Company/Warner Bros. David Puttnam, Producer.
ATLANTIC CITY, International Cinema Corp. production, Par; Denis Heroux, Producer.
ON GOLDEN POND, ITC Films/IPC Films Production, U; Bruce Gilbert, Producer.
RAIDERS OF THE LOST ARK, Lucasfilm Production, Par; Frank Marshall, Producer.
REDS, J.R.S. Production, Par; Warren Beatty, Producer.

ACTOR: (O-951)

HENRY FONDA, On Golden Pond.
WARREN BEATTY, *Reds.*
BURT LANCASTER, *Atlantic City.*
DUDLEY MOORE, *Arthur,* Rollins, Joffe, Morra and Brezner Production, Orion.
PAUL NEWMAN, *Absence Of Malice,* Mirage Enterprises Production, Col.

ACTRESS: (O-952)

KATHARINE HEPBURN, On Golden Pond.
DIANE KEATON, *Reds.*
MARSHA MASON, *Only When I Laugh,* Columbia Pictures Production, Col.
SUSAN SARANDON, *Atlantic City.*
MERYL STREEP, *The French Lieutenant's Woman,* Parlon Production, UA.

SUPPORTING ACTOR: (O-953)

JOHN GIELGUD, Arthur.
JAMES COCO, *Only When I Laugh.*
IAN HOLM, *Chariots Of Fire.*
JACK NICHOLSON, *Reds.*
HOWARD E ROLLINS JR, *Ragtime,* Ragtime Production, Par.

SUPPORTING ACTRESS: (O-954)

MAUREEN STAPLETON, Reds.
MELINDA DILLON, *Absence Of Malice.*
JANE FONDA, *On Golden Pond.*
JOAN HACKETT, *Only When I Laugh.*
ELIZABETH MCGOVERN, *Ragtime.*

DIRECTING: (O-955)

WARREN BEATTY, Reds.
LOUIS MALLE, *Atlantic City.*
HUGH HUDSON, *Chariots Of Fire.*
MARK RYDELL, *On Golden Pond.*
STEVEN SPIELBERG, *Raiders Of The Lost Ark.*

WRITING: (O-956)

(Original Screenplay)

COLIN WELLAND, Chariots Of Fire.
KURT LUEDTKE, *Absence Of Malice.*
STEVE GORDON, *Arthur.*
JOHN GUARE, *Atlantic City.*
WARREN BEATTY, TREVOR GRIFFITHS, *Reds.*

(Screenplay Adaptation)

ERNEST THOMPSON, On Golden Pond.
HAROLD PINTER, *The French Lieutenant's Woman.*
DENNIS POTTER, *Pennies From Heaven,* Metro-Goldwyn-Mayer/Herbert Ross/Hera Production, MGM.
JAY PRESSON ALLEN, SIDNEY LUMET, *Prince Of The City,* Orion Pictures/Warner Bros. Production; Orion/Warner Bros.
MICHAEL WELLER, *Ragtime.*

CINEMATOGRAPHY: (O-957)

VITTORIO STORARO, Reds.
ALEX THOMSON, *Excalibur,* Orion Pictures Production, Orion.
BILLY WILLIAMS, *On Golden Pond.*
MIROSLAV ONDRICEK, *Ragtime.*
DOUGLAS SLOCOMBE, *Raiders Of The Lost Ark.*

COSTUME DESIGN: (O-958)

MILENA CANONERO, Chariots Of Fire.
TOM RAND, *The French Lieutenant's Woman.*
BOB MACKIE, *Pennies From Heaven.*
ANNA HILL JOHNSTONE, *Ragtime.*
SHIRLEY RUSSELL, *Reds.*

ART DIRECTION: (O-959)

NORMAN REYNOLDS, LESLIE DILLEY, Art Direction; MICHAEL FORD, Set Decoration; Raiders Of The Lost Ark.
ASSHETON GORTON, Art Direction; ANN MOLLO, Set Decoration; *The French Lieutenant's Woman.*
TAMBI LARSEN, Art Direction; JIM BERKEY, Set Decoration; *Heaven's Gate,* Partisan Production Ltd., UA.
JOHN GRAYSMARK, PATRIZIA VON BRANDENSTEIN, ANTHONY READING, Art Direction; GEORGE de TITTA SR., GEORGE de TITTA JR., PETER HOWITT, Set Decoration; *Ragtime.*
RICHARD SYLBERT, Art Direction; MICHAEL SEIRTON, Set Decoration; *Reds.*

FILM EDITING: (O-960)

MICHAEL KAHN, Raiders Of The Lost Ark.
TERRY RAWLINGS, *Chariots Of Fire.*
JOHN BLOOM, *The French Lieutenant's Woman.*
ROBERT L WOLFE, *On Golden Pond.*
DEDE ALLEN, CRAIG MCKAY, *Reds.*

FOREIGN-LANGUAGE FILM: (O-961)

MEPHISTO, Mafilm-Objektiv Studio and Manfred Durniok Production (Hungary).
THE BOAT IS FULL, Limbo Film AG Production (Switzerland).
MAN OF IRON, Polish Corporation for Film, Unit *X* Production (Poland).
MUDDY RIVER, Kimura Production (Japan).
THREE BROTHERS, Iter Film (Rome)/Gaumont (Paris) Production (Italy).

MUSIC-SCORING: (O-962)

VANGELIS, Chariots Of Fire.
ALEX NORTH, *Dragonslayer.* Barwood/Robbins Production, Par.
DAVE GRUSIN, *On Golden Pond.*
RANDY NEWMAN, *Ragtime.*
JOHN WILLIAMS, *Raiders Of The Lost Ark.*

MUSIC–SONG: (O-963)

ARTHUR'S THEME (BEST THAT YOU CAN DO), Arthur. Music and lyric by Burt Bacharach, Carole Bayer Sager, Christopher Cross and Peter Allen.
ENDLESS LOVE, *Endless Love,* Polygram/Universal Pictures/Keith Barish/Dyson Lovell production, U; Music and lyric by Lionel Richie.
THE FIRST TIME IT HAPPENS, *The Great Muppet Caper,* Jim Henson/ITC Film Entertainment Ltd. production, U; Music and lyric by Joe Raposo.
FOR YOUR EYES ONLY, *For Your Eyes Only,* EON Production, UA. Music by Bill Conti. Lyric by Mick Leeson.
ONE MORE HOUR, *Ragtime.* Music and lyric by Randy Newman.

SOUND: (O-964)

BILLY VARNEY, STEVE MASLOW, GREGG LANDAKER, ROY CHARMAN, Raiders Of The Lost Ark.
RICHARD PORTMAN, DAVID RONNE, *On Golden Pond.*
JOHN K. WILKINSON, ROBERT W. GLASS JR., ROBERT M. THIRLWELL, ROBIN GREGORY, *Outland,* Ladd Company production, The Ladd Company.
MICHAEL J. KOHUT, JAY M. HARDING, RICHARD TYLER, AL OVERTON, *Pennies From Heaven.*
DICK VORISEK, TOM FLEISCHMAN, SIMON KAYE, *Reds.*

MAKEUP: (O-965)

RICK BAKER, An American Werewolf In London, Lycanthrope/Polygram/Universal Pictures production, U.
STAN WINSTON, *Heartbeeps,* Michael Phillips/Universal Pictures production, U.

SHORT FILMS: (O-966)

(Animated)

CRAC, Societe Radio-Canada. Frederic Back, producer.
THE CREATION, Will Vinton Prods. Will Vinton, producer.
THE TENDER TALE OF CINDERELLA PENGUIN, National Film Board of Canada. Janet Perlman, producer.

(Live Action)

VIOLET, The American Film Institute. Paul Kemp, Shelley Levinson, producers.
COUPLES AND ROBBERS, Flamingo Pictures Ltd. Christine Oestreicher, producer.
FIRST WINTER, National Film Board of Canada. John N. Smith, producer.

DOCUMENTARY: (O-967)

(Features)

GENOCIDE, Arnold Schwartzman Productions Inc. Arnold Schwartzman, Rabbi Marvin Hier, producers.
AGAINST WIND AND TIDE: A CUBAN ODYSSEY, Seven League Productions Inc. Susanne Bauman, Paul Neshamkin, producers.
BROOKLYN BRIDGE, Florentine Films. Ken Burns, producer.
EIGHT MINUTES TO MIDNIGHT: A PORTRAIT OF DR. HELEN CALDICOTT, The Caldicott Project. Mary Benjamin, Susanne Simpson, Boyd Estus, producers.
EL SALVADOR: ANOTHER VIETNAM, Catalyst Media Prods. Glenn Silver, Tete Vasconcellos, producers.

(Short Subjects)

CLOSE HARMONY, Noble Enterprise. Nigel Noble, producer.
AMERICAS IN TRANSITION, Americas in Transition Inc. Obie Benz, producer.
JOURNEY FOR SURVIVAL, Dick Young Productions Inc. Dick Young, producer.
SEE WHAT I SAY, Michigan Women Filmmakers Prods. Linda Chapman, Pam LeBlanc, Freddi Stevens, producers.
URGE TO BUILD, Roland Halle Productions Inc. Roland Halle and John Hoover, producers.

VISUAL EFFECTS: (O-968)
RICHARD EDLUND, KIT WEST, BRUCE NICHOLSON, JOE JOHNSTON, Raiders of the Lost Ark.

HONORARY AND OTHER: (O-969)
(Irving G. Thalberg Memorial Award)
ALBERT R. (CUBBY) BROCCOLI
(Jean Hersholt Humanitarian Award)
DANNY KAYE
(Other)
BARBARA STANWYCK, "An artist of impeccable grace and beauty, a dedicated artist, and one of the great ladies of Hollywood."

SCIENTIFIC OR TECHNICAL: (O-970)
(Gordon E. Sawyer Award)
JOSEPH B. WALKER
(Academy Award Of Merit)
FUJI PHOTO FILM CO., LTD.
(Special Achievement Award)
RICHARD L. ANDERSON and BENJAMIN P. BURTT JR., for sound effects editing, Raiders of the Lost Ark.
(Scientific and Engineering Award)
LEONARD SOKOLOW, for the concept and design, and HOWARD LAZARE, for development, of the Consolidated Film Industries' Stroboscan Motion Picture Viewer
RICHARD EDLUND and INDUSTRIAL LIGHT and MAGIC for concept and engineering of a beam-splitter optical composite motion picture printer.
RICHARD EDLUND and INDUSTRIAL LIGHT and MAGIC for engineering of the Empire Motion Picture Camera System.
EDWARD J. BLASKO and DR. RODERICK T. RYAN, EASTMAN KODAK CO., for application of the Prostar Microfilm Processor for motion picture title and special optical effects production.
NELSON TYLER, for progressive development and improvement of the Tyler Helicopter motion picture camera platform.
(Technical Achievement Award)
HAL LANDAKER, for concept, and ALAN D. LANDAKER for engineering of the Burbank Studio's Production Sound Dept. 24-frame color video system.
BILL HOGAN of Ruxton Ltd., and RICHARD J. STUMPF and DANIEL R. BREWER of Universal City Studios' Production Sound Dept. for engineering of a 24-frame color video system.
ERNST F. NETTMAN CONTINENTAL CAMERA SYSTEMS INC., for development of a pitching lens for motion picture photography.
BILL TAYLOR, Universal Studios, for concept and specifications for a Two Format, Rotating Head, Aerial Image Optical Printer.
PETER D. PARKS, Oxford Scientific Films, for development of the OSF Microscopic Photography.
DR. LOUIS STANKIEWICZ and H.L. BLACHFORD for development of Baryfol sound barrier materials.
DENNIS MUREN and STUART ZIFF, Industrial Light & Magic Inc., for development of a Motion Picture Figure Mover for animation photography.

1982

BEST PICTURE: (O-971)
GANDHI, Indo-British Films production, Columbia. Richard Attenborough, producer.
E.T. - THE EXTRATERRESTRIAL, Universal Pictures production, Universal. Steven Spielberg, Kathleen Kennedy, producers.
MISSING, Universal Pictures/Polygram Pictures presentation of an Edward Lewis production, Universal. Edward Lewis, Mildred Lewis, producers.
TOOTSIE, Mirage/Punch production, Columbia. Sydney Pollack, Dick Richards, producers.
THE VERDICT, Fox-Zanuck/Brown production, Twentieth Century-Fox. Richard D Zanuck, David Brown, producers.

ACTOR: (O-972)
BEN KINGSLEY, Gandhi.
DUSTIN HOFFMAN, Tootsie.
JACK LEMMON, Missing.
PAUL NEWMAN, The Verdict.
PETER O'TOOLE, My Favorite Year, MGM/Brooksfilm/Michael Gruskoff production, MGM/UA.

ACTRESS: (O-973)
MERYL STREEP, Sophie's Choice, ITC Entertainment presentation of a Pakula-Barish production, Universal/AFD.
JULIE ANDREWS, Victor/Victoria, MGM production, MGM/UA.
JESSICA LANGE, Frances, Brooksfilm/EMI production, Universal/AFD.
SISSY SPACEK, Missing.
DEBRA WINGER, An Officer And A Gentleman, Lorimar production in association with Martin Elfand, Paramount.

SUPPORTING ACTOR: (O-974)
LOUIS GOSSETT JR, An Officer And A Gentleman.
CHARLES DURNING, The Best Little Whorehouse In Texas, Universal and RKO Pictures presentation of a Miller-Milkis-Boyett production, Universal.
JOHN LITHGOW, The World According to Garp, Warner Bros. production, Warner Bros.
JAMES MASON, The Verdict.
ROBERT PRESTON, Victor/Victoria.

SUPPORTING ACTRESS: (O-975)
JESSICA LANGE, Tootsie.
GLENN CLOSE, The World According To Garp.
TERI GARR, Tootsie.
KIM STANLEY, Frances.
LESLEY ANN WARREN, Victor/Victoria.

DIRECTING: (O-976)
RICHARD ATTENBOROUGH, Gandhi.
WOLFGANG PETERSEN, Das Boot, Bavaria Atelier GmbH production, Columbia.
STEVEN SPIELBERG, E.T. - The ExtraTerrestrial.
SYDNEY POLLACK, Tootsie.
SIDNEY LUMET, The Verdict.

WRITING: (O-977)
(Best Original Screenplay)
JOHN BRILEY, Gandhi.
BARRY LEVINSON, Diner, Jerry Weintraub production, MGM/UA.
MELISSA MATHISON, E.T. - The ExtraTerrestrial.
DOUGLAS DAY STEWART, An Officer And A Gentleman.
LARRY GELBART, MURRAY SCHISGAL, Tootsie, story by Don McGuire, Larry Gelbart.
(Best Screenplay Adaptation)
COSTA-GAVRAS, DONALD STEWART, Missing.
WOLFGANG PETERSEN, Das Boot.

ALAN J PAKULA, *Sophie's Choice.*
DAVID MAMET, *The Verdict.*
BLAKE EDWARDS, *Victor/Victoria.*

CINEMATOGRAPHY: (O-978)

BILLY WILLIAMS, RONNIE TAYLOR, Gandhi.
JOST VACANO, *Das Boot.*
ALLEN DAVIAU, *E.T. - The ExtraTerrestrial.*
NESTOR ALMENDROS, *Sophie's Choice.*
OWEN ROIZMAN, *Tootsie.*

COSTUME DESIGN: (O-979)

JOHN MOLLO, BHANU ATHALYA, Gandhi.
PIERO TOSI, *La Traviata.*
ALBERT WOLSKY, *Sophie's Choice.*
ELOIS JENSSEN, ROSANNA NORTON, *Tron,* Walt Disney production, Buena Vista Distribution.
PATRICIA NORRIS, *Victor/Victoria.*

ART DIRECTION: (O-980)

STUART CRAIG, BOB LAING, Art Direction; MICHAEL SEIRTON, Set Decoration; Gandhi.
DALE HENNESY, Art Direction; MARVIN MARCH, Set Decoration; *Annie.*
LAWRENCE G PAULL, DAVID SNYDER, Art Direction; LINDA De-SCENNA, Set Decoration; *Blade Runner,* Michael Deeley-Ridley Scott production, The Ladd Company/Sir Run Run Shaw.
FRANCO ZEFFIRELLI, Art Direction; GIANNI QUARANTA, Set Decoration; *La Traviata,* Accent Films BV production in association with RAI-Radiotelevisione Italiana, Producers Sales Organization.
RODGER MAUS, TIM HUTCHINSON, WILLIAM CRAIG SMITH, Art Direction; HARRY CORDWELL, Set Decoration; *Victor/Victoria.*

FILM EDITING: (O-981)

JOHN BLOOM, Gandhi.
HANNES NIKEL, *Das Boot.*
CAROL LITTLETON, *E.T. - The ExtraTerrestrial.*
PETER ZINNER, *An Officer And A Gentleman.*
FREDRIC STEINKAMP, WILLIAM STEINKAMP, *Tootsie.*

FOREIGN LANGUAGE FILM: (O-982)

VOLVER A EMPEZAR (TO BEGIN AGAIN), Nickel Odeon, SA production (Spain).
ALSINO AND THE CONDOR, Nicaraguan Film Institute production (Nicaragua).
COUP DE TORCHON (CLEAN SLATE), Films de la Tour production (France).
THE FLIGHT OF THE EAGLE, Bold Productions for The Swedish Film Institute, The Swedish Television SVT2, Svensk Filmindustri and Norsk Film A/S production (Sweden).
PRIVATE LIFE, Mosfilm Studio production (USSR).

MUSIC - ORIGINAL SCORE: (O-983)

JOHN WILLIAMS, E.T. - The ExtraTerrestrial.
RAVI SHANKAR, GEORGE FENTON, *Gandhi.*
JACK NITZSCHE, *An Officer And A Gentleman.*
JERRY GOLDSMITH, *Poltergeist,* MGM/Steven Spielberg production, MGM/UA.
MARVIN HAMLISCH, *Sophie's Choice.*

MUSIC - ORIGINAL SONG SCORE: (O-984)

HENRY MANCINI, LESLIE BRICUSSE; adapted by Henry Mancini; Victor/Victoria.
RALPH BURNS, *Annie,* Rastar Films production, Columbia.
TOM WAITS, *One From The Heart,* Zoetrope Studios production, Columbia.

MUSIC - ORIGINAL SONG: (O-985)

UP WHERE WE BELONG, An Officer And A Gentleman. Music by Jack Nitzsche and Buffy Sainte-Marie. Lyric by Will Jennings.
EYE OF THE TIGER, *Rocky III,* Robert Chartoff-Irwin Winkler/United Artists production, MGM/UA. Music and lyric by Jim Peterik and Frankie Sullivan III.
HOW DO YOU KEEP THE MUSIC PLAYING? *Best Friends,* Timberlane Films production, Warner Bros. Music by Michel Legrand. Lyric by Alan and Marilyn Bergman.
IF WE WERE IN LOVE, *Yes, Giorgio,* Metro-Goldwyn-Mayer production, MGM/UA. Music by John Williams. Lyric by Alan and Marilyn Bergman.
IT MIGHT BE YOU, *Tootsie.* Music by Dave Grusin. Lyric by Alan and Marilyn Bergman.

SOUND: (O-986)

BUZZ KNUDSON, ROBERT GLASS, DON DIGIROLAMO, GENE CANTAMESSA, E.T. - The ExtraTerrestrial.
MILAN BOR, TREVOR PYKE, MIKE Le-MARE, *Das Boot.*
GERRY HUMPHREYS, ROBIN O'DONOGHUE, JONATHAN BATES, SIMON KAYE, *Gandhi.*
ARTHUR PIANTADOSI, LES FRESHOLTZ, DICK ALEXANDER, LES LAZAROWITZ, *Tootsie.*
MICHAEL MINKLER, BOB MINKLER, LEE MINKLER, JIM La RUE, *Tron.*

SOUND EDITING: (O-987)

STEPHEN HUNTER FLICK, RICHARD L ANDERSON, Poltergeist.
MIKE Le-MARE, *Das Boot.*
CHARLES L CAMPBELL, BEN BURTT, *E.T. - The ExtraTerrestrial.*

MAKE-UP: (O-988)

QUEST FOR FIRE, International Cinema Corporation production, 20th Century-Fox. Credits in controversy.
TOM SMITH, *Gandhi.*

SHORT FILMS: (O-989)

(Animated)
TANGO, Film Polski. Zbigniew Rybczynski, producer.
THE GREAT COGNITO, Will Vinton Productions. Will Vinton, producer.
THE SNOWMAN, Snowman Enterprises Ltd. John Coates, producer.
(Live Action)
A SHOCKING ACCIDENT, Flamingo Pictures Ltd. Christine Oestreicher, producer.
BALLET ROBOTIQUE, Bob Rogers and Company. Bob Rogers, producer.
THE SILENCE, The American Film Institute. Michael Toshiyuki Uno, Joseph Benson, producers.
SPLIT CHERRY TREE, Learning Corporation of America. Jan Saunders, producer.
SRENDI VASHTAR, Laurentic Film Productions Ltd. Andrew Birkin, producer.

DOCUMENTARIES: (O-990)

(Features)
JUST ANOTHER MISSING KID, Canadian Broadcasting Corporation. John Zaritsky, producer.
AFTER THE AXE, National Film Board of Canada. Sturla Gunnarsson, Steve Lucas, producers.
BEN'S MILL, Public Broadcasting Associates - Odyssey. John Karol, Michel Chalufour, producers.
IN OUR WATER, Foresight Films production. Meg Switzgable, producer.
A PORTRAIT OF GISELLE, Wishupon Productions. Joseph Wishy, producer.
(Short Subjects)
IF YOU LOVE THIS PLANET, National Film Board of Canada. Edward Le Lorrain, producer.
GODS OF METAL, Richter Productions, Robert Richter, producer.
THE KLAN: A LEGACY OF HATE IN AMERICA, Guggenheim Productions Inc. Charles Guggenheim, Werner Schumann, producers.

TO LIVE OR LET DIE, American Film Foundation. Freida Lee Mock, producer.
TRAVELING HOPEFULLY, Arnuthfonyus Films Inc. John G Avildsen, producer.

VISUAL EFFECTS: (O-991)

CARLO RAMBALDI, DENNIS MURREN, KENNETH F SMITH, E.T. - The ExtraTerrestrial.
DOUGLAS TRUMBULL, RICHARD YURICICH, DAVID DRYER, *Blade Runner*.
RICHARD EDLUND, MICHAEL WOOD, BRUCE NICHOLSON, *Poltergeist*.

HONORARY AND OTHER: (O-992)

(Jean Hersholt Humanitarian Award)

WALTER MIRISCH

(Other)

MICKEY ROONEY for "50 years of versatility in a variety of memorable film performances."

SCIENTIFIC OR TECHNICAL: (O-993)

(Gordon E Sawyer Award)

JOHN O AALBERG for his technological contributions to the motion picture industry.

(Academy Award of Merit)

AUGUST ARNOLD and ERICH KAESTNER, for the concept and engineering of the first operational 35m, hand-held, spinning-mirror reflex motion picture camera.

(Scientific and Engineering Award)

COLIN F MOSSMAN and the RESEARCH & DEVELOPMENT GROUP of RANK FILM LABORATORIES, LONDON, for the engineering and implementation of a 4000-meter printing system for motion picture laboratories.
SANTEE ZELLI and SALVATORE ZELLI of ELEMACK ITALIA S.R.L., ROME, ITALY, for the continuing engineering design and development that has resulted in the Elemack Camera Dolly Systems for motion picture production.
LEONARD CHAPMAN, for the engineering design, development and manufacture of the PeeWee Camera Dolly for motion picture production.
DR MOHAMMAD S NOZARI of MINNESOTA MINING & MANUFACTURING COMPANY, for the research and development of the 3M Photogard protective coating for motion picture film.
BRIANNE MURPHY and DONALD SCHISLER of MITCHELL INSERT SYSTEMS INC., for the concept, design and manufacture of the MSI Camera Insert Car and Process Trailer.
JACOBUS L DIMMERS, for the engineering and manufacture of the Teccon Enterprises' magnetic transducer for motion picture sound recording and playback.

(Technical Achievement Award)

RICHARD W DEATS, for the design and manufacture of the "Little Big Crane" for motion picture production.
CONSTANT TRESFON and ADRIAAN DeROOY of EGRIPMENT, and ED PHILLIPS and CARLOS DeMATTOS of MATTHEWS STUDIO EQUIPMENT INC., for the design and manufacture of the "Tulip Crane" for motion picture production.
BRAN FERREN of ASSOCIATES & FERREN, for the design and development of a computerized lightning-effect system for motion picture photography.
CHRISTIE ELECTRIC CORP and LaVEZZI MACHINE WORKS INC., for the design and manufacture of the Ultramittent film transport for Christie motion picture projectors.

EMMYS

1948

OUTSTANDING PERSONALITY (E-01)

SHIRLEY DINSDALE and her puppet Judy Splinters (KTLA)
RITA LeROY (KTLA)
PATRICIA MORRISON
MIKE STOKEY (KTLA)
BILL WELSH (KTLA)

MOST POPULAR PROGRAM (E-02)

PANTOMIME QUIZ TIME (Mike Stokey) (KTLA)
ARMCHAIR DETECTIVE (KTLA)
DON LEE MUSIC HALL (KTSL)
FELIX DE COLA SHOW (KTLA)
JUDY SPLINTERS (KTLA)
MABEL'S FABLES (KTLA)
MASKED SPOONER (KTSL)
TREASURE OF LITERATURE (KFI-TV)
TUESDAY VARIETIES (KTLA)
WHAT'S THE NAME OF THAT SONG (KTSL)

FILM MADE FOR TELEVISION (E-03)

THE NECKLACE Marshall Grant-Realm Productions (Your Show Time Series)
CHRISTOPHER COLUMBUS Emerson Film Corp.
HOLLYWOOD BREVITIES Tele-features
IT COULD HAPPEN TO YOU Vallee Video
TELL TALE HEART Telepak
TIME SIGNAL Centaur Productions

STATION AWARD (E-04)

KTLA For outstanding overall achievement in 1948

TECHNICAL AWARD (E-05)

CHARLES MESAK Don Lee Television for "PHASEFADER" in recognition of an outstanding advancement in the video field.

SPECIAL AWARD (E-06)

LOUIS McMANUS For his original design of the Emmy

1949

LIVE SHOW (E-07)

ED WYNN (KTTV)
PANTOMIME QUIZ (KTTV)
YOUR WITNESS (KECA-TV)

KINESCOPE SHOW (E-08)

TEXACO STAR THEATRE (KNBH, NBC)
FRED WARING (KTTV, CBS)
THE GOLDBERGS (KTTV, CBS)
STUDIO ONE (KTTV, CBS)

CHILDREN'S SHOW (E-09)

TIME FOR BEANY (KTLA)
CYCLONE MALONE (KNBH)
KUKLA, FRAN and OLLIE (KNBH)

OUTSTANDING LIVE PERSONALITY (E-10)

ED WYNN (KTTV)
TOM HARMON (KFI-TV, KECA-TV, KTTV)
MIKE STOKEY (KTTV, KTLA)
BILL WELSH (KFI-TV, KTLA)

FILM MADE FOR TELEVISION (E-11)

LIFE OF RILEY (KNBH)
GUIDING STAR (KTTV)
LONE RANGER (KECA-TV)
TIME BOMB (KNBH)
VAIN GLORY (KNBH)
YOUR SHOWTIME

OUTSTANDING KINESCOPED PERSONALITY (E-12)

MILTON BERLE (KNBH, NBC)
FRAN ALLISON (KNBH, NBC)
ARTHUR GODFREY (KTTV, CBS)

PUBLIC SERVICE, CULTURAL OR EDUCATIONAL PROGRAM (E-13)

CRUSADE IN EUROPE (KECA-TV & KTTV)
FORD NEWS & WEATHER (KNBH)
KATHY FISCUS RESCUE (KTLA)
MAN'S BEST FRIEND (KTLA)
NUREMBERG TRIALS (KTSL)
TELEFORUM (KTLA)

SPORTS COVERAGE (E-14)

WRESTLING (KTLA)
AMATEUR BOXING (KTLA)
BASEBALL (KLAC)
COLLEGE BASKETBALL (KTTV)
ICE HOCKEY (KTLA)
USC-UCLA FOOTBALL (KECA)

STATION ACHIEVEMENT (E-15)

KTLA For outstanding overall achievement in 1949
Honorable mention to KECA-TV

COMMERCIAL MADE FOR TELEVISION (E-16)

LUCKY STRIKE N W Ayer & Son, Inc, for the American Tobacco Company

TECHNICAL AWARD (E-17)

HAROLD W. JURY OF KTSL, LOS ANGELES For the synchronizing co-ordinator which allows superimposition from more than one location.

1950

ACTOR (E-18)

ALAN YOUNG (KTTV, CBS)
SID CAESAR (KNBH, NBC)
JOSE FERRER
STAN FREBERG as CECIL THE SEA SERPENT (KTLA)
CHARLES RUGGLES (KCEA-TV)

ACTRESS (E-19)

GERTRUDE BERG (KTTV, CBS)
JUDITH ANDERSON
IMOGENE COCA (KNBH, NBC)
HELEN HAYES (KECA-TV)
BETTY WHITE (KLAC)

OUTSTANDING PERSONALITY (E-20)

GROUCHO MARX (KNBH, NBC)
SID CAESAR (KNBH, NBC)
FAYE EMERSON (KTTV, KECA-TV)
DICK LANE (KTLA)
ALAN YOUNG (KTTV, CBS)

PUBLIC SERVICE (E-21)

CITY AT NIGHT (KTLA)
CLASSIFIED COLUMN (KTTV)
COMMUNITY CHEST KICKOFF
IN OUR TIME (KTTV)
MARSHALL PLAN (KECA-TV)
TELEFORUM (KTLA)

CULTURAL SHOW (E-22)

CAMPUS CHORUS AND ORCHESTRA (KTSL)
DESIGNED FOR WOMEN (KNBH)
SUNSET SERVICE (KNBH)
VIENNA PHILHARMONIC (KTTV)
THE WOMAN'S VOICE (KTTV)

SPECIAL EVENTS (E-23)

DEPARTURE OF MARINES FOR KOREA (KFMB-TV San Diego & KTLA)
ARRIVAL OF CRUISER FROM KOREA (KTLA)
COMMISSIONING OF HOSPITAL SHIP HAVEN
ELECTION COVERAGE (KECA-TV)
TOURNAMENT OF ROSES (KECA-TV)

SPORTS PROGRAM (E-24)

RAMS FOOTBALL (KNBH)
COLLEGE BASKETBALL GAMES (KTTV, CBS)
COLLEGE FOOTBALL GAMES (KTTV, CBS)
HOLLYWOOD BASEBALL (KLAC)
LOS ANGELES BASEBALL (KFI-TV)

VARIETY SHOW (E-25)

THE ALAN YOUNG SHOW (KTTV, CBS)
FOUR STAR REVUE (KNBH, NBC)
KEN MURRAY (KTTV, CBS)
SHOW OF SHOWS (KNBH, NBC)
TEXACO STAR THEATRE (KNBH, NBC)

EDUCATIONAL SHOW (E-26)

KFI-TV UNIVERSITY (KFI-TV)
KIERAN'S KALEIDOSCOPE (KECA-TV)
KNOW YOUR SCHOOLS (KFI-TV)
MAGAZINE OF THE WEEK (KTLA)
ZOO PARADE (KNBH)

CHILDREN'S SHOW (E-27)

TIME FOR BEANY (KTLA)
CISCO KID (KNBH)
JUMP JUMP (KTTV)
KUKLA, FRAN AND OLLIE (KNBH, NBC)
LONE RANGER (KTLA)

DRAMATIC SHOW (E-28)

PULITZER PRIZE PLAYHOUSE (KECA-TV)
FIRESIDE THEATER (KTLA)
I REMEMBER MAMA (KTTV, CBS)
PHILCO TV PLAYHOUSE (KNBH, NBC)
STUDIO ONE (KTTV, CBS)

NEWS PROGRAM (E-29)

KTLA NEWSREEL
CLETE ROBERTS (KLAC)
FLEETWOOD LAWTON (KTSL)
FORD NEWS AND WEATHER (KNBH)

GAMES AND AUDIENCE PARTICIPATION SHOW (E-30)

TRUTH OR CONSEQUENCES (KTTV, CBS)
KAY KYSER COLLEGE OF MUSICAL KNOWLEDGE (KNBH, NBC)
LIFE WITH LINKLETTER (KECA-TV)
PANTOMIME QUIZ (KTTV, CBS)
YOU BET YOUR LIFE (KNBH, NBC)

STATION ACHIEVEMENT (E-31)

KTLA

TECHNICAL ACHIEVEMENT (E-32)

ORTHOGRAM TV AMPLIFIER BY KNBH-NBC.

1951

DRAMATIC SHOW (E-33)

STUDIO ONE (CBS)
CELANESE THEATRE (ABC)
PHILCO-GOODYEAR TV PLAYHOUSE (NBC)
PULITZER PRIZE PLAYHOUSE (NBC)
ROBERT MONTGOMERY PRESENTS (NBC)

COMEDY SHOW (E-34)

RED SKELTON SHOW (NBC)
BURNS AND ALLEN (CBS)
GROUCHO MARX (NBC)
HERB SHRINER SHOW (ABC)
I LOVE LUCY (CBS)

VARIETY SHOW (E-35)

YOUR SHOW OF SHOWS (NBC)
ALL STAR REVUE (NBC)
COMEDY HOUR (NBC)
FRED WARING (CBS)
TOAST OF THE TOWN (CBS)

ACTOR (E-36)

SID CAESAR
WALTER HAMPDEN
CHARLTON HESTON
ROBERT MONTGOMERY
THOMAS MITCHELL
VAUGHN TAYLOR

ACTRESS (E-37)

IMOGENE COCA
HELEN HAYES
MARIA RIVA
MARY SINCLAIR
MARGARET SULLAVAN

COMEDIAN OR COMEDIENNE (E-38)

RED SKELTON (NBC)
LUCILLE BALL (CBS)
SID CAESAR (NBC)
IMOGENE COCA (NBC)
JIMMY DURANTE (NBC)
MARTIN AND LEWIS (NBC)
HERB SHRINER (ABC)

SPECIAL ACHIEVEMENT AWARDS (E-39)

U. S. SENATOR ESTES KEFAUVER For outstanding Public Service on Television
AMERICAN TELEPHONE & TELEGRAPH CO. For the transcontinental Micro-Wave Relay System

JACK BURRELL OF STATION KNBH, LOS ANGELES For the development of an independent TV transmission Mobile Unit.

1952

DRAMATIC PROGRAM (E-40)
ROBERT MONTGOMERY PRESENTS (NBC)
CELANESE THEATRE (ABC)
KRAFT TV THEARE (NBC)
PHILCO-GOODYEAR TV PLAYHOUSE (NBC)
STUDIO ONE (CBS)

VARIETY PROGRAM (E-41)
YOUR SHOW OF SHOWS (NBC)
ARTHUR GODFREY AND HIS FRIENDS (CBS)
COLGATE COMEDY HOUR (NBC)
THE JACKIE GLEASON SHOW (CBS)
TOAST OF THE TOWN (CBS)

PUBLIC AFFAIRS PROGRAM (E-42)
SEE IT NOW (CBS)
BISHOP FULTON J. SHEEN (Syndicated)
CAMEL NEWS CARAVAN (NBC)
MEET THE PRESS (NBC)
VICTORY AT SEA (NBC)

MYSTERY, ACTION OR ADVENTURE PROGRAM (E-43)
DRAGNET (NBC)
BIG STORY (NBC)
FOREIGN INTRIGUE (Syndicated)
MARTIN KANE (NBC)
RACKET SQUAD (CBS)

SITUATION COMEDY (E-44)
I LOVE LUCY (CBS)
AMOS 'N' ANDY (CBS)
BURNS & ALLEN (CBS)
MR. PEEPERS (NBC)
OUR MISS BROOKS (CBS)
OZZIE AND HARRIET (ABC)

AUDIENCE PARTICIPATION, QUIZ OR PANEL PROGRAM (E-45)
WHAT'S MY LINE? (CBS)
DOWN YOU GO
THIS IS YOUR LIFE (NBC)
TWO FOR THE MONEY (CBS)
YOU BET YOUR LIFE (NBC)

CHILDREN'S PROGRAM (E-46)
TIME FOR BEANY (KTLA)
BIG TOP (CBS)
GABBY HAYES
HOWDY DOODY (NBC)
KUKLA, FRAN AND OLLIE (NBC)
SUPER CIRCUS (NBC)
ZOO PARADE (NBC)

ACTOR (E-47)
THOMAS MITCHELL
JOHN FORSYTHE
CHARLTON HESTON
JOHN NEWLAND
VAUGHN TAYLOR
JACK WEBB

ACTRESS (E-48)
HELEN HAYES
SARAH CHURCHILL
JUNE LOCKHART
MARIA RIVA
PEGGY WOOD

COMEDIAN (E-49)
JIMMY DURANTE (NBC)
SID CAESAR (NBC)
WALLY COX (NBC)
JACKIE GLEASON (CBS)
HERB SHRINER (ABC)

COMEDIENNE (E-50)
LUCILLE BALL (CBS)
EVE ARDEN (CBS)
IMOGENE COCA (NBC)
JOAN DAVIS (NBC)
MARTHA RAYE (NBC)

OUTSTANDING PERSONALITY (E-51)
BISHOP FULTON J. SHEEN (DUMONT)
LUCILLE BALL (CBS)
ARTHUR GODFREY (CBS)
JIMMY DURANTE (NBC)
EDWARD R. MURROW (CBS)
DONALD O'CONNOR (NBC)
ADLAI STEVENSON (NBC)

1953

DRAMATIC PROGRAM (E-52)
U.S. STEEL HOUR (ABC)
KRAFT TELEVISION THEATRE (NBC)
PHILCO-GOODYEAR TV PLAYHOUSE (NBC)
ROBERT MONTGOMERY PRESENTS (NBC)
STUDIO ONE (CBS)

SITUATION COMEDY (E-53)
I LOVE LUCY (CBS)
BURNS & ALLEN (CBS)
MR. PEEPERS (NBC)
OUR MISS BROOKS (CBS)
TOPPER (CBS)

VARIETY PROGRAM (E-54)
OMNIBUS (CBS)
COLGATE COMEDY HOUR (NBC)
JACKIE GLEASON SHOW (CBS)
YOUR SHOW OF SHOWS (NBC)
TOAST OF THE TOWN (CBS)

NEWS OR SPORTS PROGRAM (E-55)
SEE IT NOW (CBS)
CAMEL NEWS CARAVAN (NBC)
GILLETTE CAVALCADE OF SPORTS (NBC)
NCAA FOOTBALL GAMES (NBC)
PABST FIGHT (CBS)
PROFESSIONAL FOOTBALL (DUMONT)

PUBLIC AFFAIRS PROGRAM (E-56)
VICTORY AT SEA (NBC)
ADVENTURE AT SEA (NBC)
BISHOP FULTON J. SHEEN (Syndicated)
MEET THE PRESS (NBC)
PERSON TO PERSON (CBS)

CHILDREN'S PROGRAM (E-57)

KUKLA, FRAN AND OLLIE (NBC)
BIG TOP (CBS)
DING DONG SCHOOL (NBC)
SUPER CIRCUS (NBC)
ZOO PARADE (NBC)

NEW PROGRAM (E-58)

MAKE ROOM FOR DADDY (ABC)
U.S. STEEL HOUR (ABC)
ADVENTURE (NBC)
DING DONG SCHOOL (NBC)
LETTER TO LORETTA (NBC)
PERSON TO PERSON (CBS)

ACTOR - REGULAR SERIES (E-59)

DONALD O'CONNOR (Colgate Comedy Hour) (NBC)
SID CAESAR (Your Show of Shows) (NBC)
WALLY COX (Mr. Peepers) (NBC)
JACKIE GLEASON (Jackie Gleason Show) (CBS)
JACK WEBB (Dragnet) (NBC)

ACTRESS - REGULAR SERIES (E-60)

EVE ARDEN (Our Miss Brooks) (CBS)
LUCILLE BALL (I Love Lucy) (CBS)
IMOGENE COCA (Your Show of Shows) (NBC)
DINAH SHORE (Dinah Shore Show) (NBC)
LORETTA YOUNG (Letter to Loretta) (NBC)

SERIES SUPPORTING ACTOR (E-61)

ART CARNEY (Jackie Gleason Show) (CBS)
BEN ALEXANDER (Dragnet) (NBC)
WILLIAM FRAWLEY (I Love Lucy) (CBS)
TONY RANDALL (Mr. Peepers) (NBC)
CARL REINER (Your Show of Shows) (NBC)

SERIES SUPPORTING ACTRESS (E-62)

VIVIAN VANCE (I Love Lucy) (CBS)
BEA BENEDARET (Burns & Allen) (CBS)
RUTH GILBERT (Milton Berle Show) (NBC)
MARION LORNE (Mr. Peepers) (NBC)
AUDREY MEADOWS (Jackie Gleason Show) (CBS)

MYSTERY, ACTION OR ADVENTURE PROGRAM (E-63)

DRAGNET (NBC)
FOREIGN INTRIGUE (NBC)
I LED THREE LIVES
SUSPENSE (CBS)
THE WEB (CBS)

AUDIENCE PARTICIPATION, QUIZ OR PANEL PROGRAM (E-64)

THIS IS YOUR LIFE (NBC)
WHAT'S MY LINE? (CBS)
I'VE GOT A SECRET (CBS)
TWO FOR THE MONEY (CBS)
YOU BET YOUR LIFE (NBC)

OUTSTANDING PERSONALITY (E-65)

EDWARD R. MURROW (CBS)
ARTHUR GODFREY (NBC)
MARTHA RAYE (NBC)
BISHOP FULTON J. SHEEN (Syndicated)
JACK WEBB (NBC).

1954

OUTSTANDING NEW PERSONALITY (E-66)

GEORGE GOBEL (NBC)
RICHARD BOONE (NBC)
WALT DISNEY (ABC)
TENNESSEE ERNIE FORD (CBS)
PRESTON FOSTER (Syndicated)
MICHAEL O'SHEA (NBC)
FESS PARKER (ABC)

CULTURAL, RELIGIOUS OR EDUCATIONAL PROGRAM (E-67)

OMNIBUS (CBS)
LIFE IS WORTH LIVING (DUMONT)
MEET THE PRESS (NBC)
PERSON TO PERSON (CBS)
SEE IT NOW (CBS)

SPORTS PROGRAM (E-68)

GILLETTE CAVALCADE OF SPORTS (NBC)
BLUE RIBBON BOUTS (CBS)
FOREST HILLS TENNIS MATCHES (NBC)
GREATEST MOMENTS IN SPORTS (NBC)
NCAA FOOTBALL (ABC)
PROFESSIONAL FOOTBALL (DUMONT)

CHILDREN'S PROGRAM (E-69)

LASSIE (CBS)
ART LINKLETTER AND THE KIDS (Syndicated)
DING DONG SCHOOL (NBC)
KUKLA, FRAN AND OLLIE (ABC)
TIME FOR BEANY (Syndicated)
ZOO PARADE (NBC)

DAYTIME PROGRAM (E-70)

ART LINKLETTER'S HOUSE PARTY (CBS)
BETTY WHITE SHOW (NBC)
BOB CROSBY SHOW (CBS)
GARRY MOORE SHOW (CBS)
ROBERT Q. LEWIS (CBS)

WESTERN OR ADVENTURE SERIES (E-71)

STORIES OF THE CENTURY (Syndicated)
ANNIE OAKLEY (Syndicated)
DEATH VALLEY DAYS (CBS)
ROY ROGERS SHOW (NBC)
WILD BILL HICKOK (Syndicated)

NEWS REPORTER OR COMMENTATOR (E-72)

JOHN DALY (ABC)
DOUGLAS EDWARDS (CBS)
CLETE ROBERTS (Syndicated)
ERIC SEVAREID (CBS)
JOHN CAMERON SWAYZE (NBC)

AUDIENCE, GUEST PARTICIPATION OR PANEL PROGRAM (E-73)

THIS IS YOUR LIFE (NBC)
MASQUERADE PARTY (ABC)
PEOPLE ARE FUNNY (NBC)
WHAT'S MY LINE? (CBS)
YOU BET YOUR LIFE (NBC)

ACTOR - SINGLE PERFORMANCE (E-74)
ROBERT CUMMINGS Twelve Angry Men (Studio One) (CBS)
FRANK LOVEJOY Double Indemnity (Lux Video Theatre) (CBS)
FREDRIC MARCH Christmas Carol (Shower of Stars) (CBS)
FREDRIC MARCH Royal Family (Best of Broadway) (CBS)
THOMAS MITCHELL Good Of His Soul (Ford Theatre) (NBC)
DAVID NIVEN The Answer (Four Star Playhouse) (CBS)

ACTRESS - SINGLE PERFORMANCE (E-75)
JUDITH ANDERSON Macbeth (Hallmark Hall of Fame) (NBC)
ETHEL BARRYMORE The 13th Chair (Climax) (CBS)
BEVERLY GARLAND White Is The Color (Medic) (NBC)
RUTH HUSSEY Craig's Wife (Lux Video Theatre) (NBC)
DOROTHY McGUIRE The Giaconda Smile (Climax) (CBS)
EVA MARIE SAINT Middle Of The Night (Philco TV Playhouse) (NBC)
CLAIRE TREVOR Ladies In Retirement (Lux Video Theatre) (NBC)

MALE SINGER (E-76)
PERRY COMO (CBS)
EDDIE FISHER (NBC)
FRANKIE LAINE (Syndicated)
TONY MARTIN (NBC)
GORDON MAC RAE (NBC)

FEMALE SINGER (E-77)
DINAH SHORE (NBC)
JANE FROMAN (CBS)
PEGGY KING (NBC)
GISELE MAC KENZIE (NBC)
JO STAFFORD (CBS)

SUPPORTING ACTOR - REGULAR SERIES (E-78)
ART CARNEY (Jackie Gleason Show) (CBS)
BEN ALEXANDER (Dragnet) (NBC)
DON DEFORE (The Adventures of Ozzie and Harriet) (ABC)
BILL FRAWLEY (I Love Lucy) (CBS)
GALE GORDON (Our Miss Brooks) (CBS)

SUPPORTING ACTRESS - REGULAR SERIES (E-79)
AUDREY MEADOWS (Jackie Gleason Show) (CBS)
BEA BENEDARET (Burns & Allen Show) (CBS)
JEAN HAGEN (Make Room For Daddy) (ABC)
MARION LORNE (Mr. Peepers) (NBC)
VIVIAN VANCE (I Love Lucy) (CBS)

ACTOR - REGULAR SERIES (E-80)
DANNY THOMAS (Make Room For Daddy) (ABC)
RICHARD BOONE (Medic) (NBC)
ROBERT CUMMINGS (My Hero) (Syndicated)
JACKIE GLEASON (Jackie Gleason Show) (CBS)
JACK WEBB (Dragnet) (NBC)

ACTRESS - REGULAR SERIES (E-81)
LORETTA YOUNG (Loretta Young Show) (NBC)
EVE ARDEN (Our Miss Brooks) (CBS)
GRACIE ALLEN (Burns & Allen Show) (CBS)
LUCILLE BALL (I Love Lucy) (CBS)
ANN SOTHERN (Private Secretary) (CBS)

MYSTERY OR INTRIGUE SERIES (E-82)
DRAGNET (NBC)
FOREIGN INTRIGUE (NBC)
I LED THREE LIVES (Syndicated)
RACKET SQUAD (Syndicated)
WATERFRONT (Syndicated)

VARIETY SERIES INCLUDING MUSICAL VARIETIES (E-83)
DISNEYLAND (ABC)
GEORGE GOBEL SHOW (NBC)
JACK BENNY SHOW (CBS)
JACKIE GLEASON SHOW (CBS)
TOAST OF THE TOWN (CBS)
YOUR HIT PARADE (NBC)

SITUATION COMEDY SERIES (E-84)
MAKE ROOM FOR DADDY (ABC)
BURNS & ALLEN (CBS)
I LOVE LUCY (CBS)
MR. PEEPERS (NBC)
OUR MISS BROOKS (CBS)
PRIVATE SECRETARY (CBS)

DRAMATIC SERIES (E-85)
UNITED STATES STEEL HOUR (ABC)
FOUR STAR PLAYHOUSE (CBS)
MEDIC (NBC)
PHILCO TELEVISION PLAYHOUSE (NBC)
STUDIO ONE (CBS)

PROGRAM OF THE YEAR (E-86)
OPERATION UNDERSEA (Disneyland) (ABC)
DIAMOND JUBILEE OF LIGHT (4 networks)
WHITE IS THE COLOR (Medic) (NBC)
A CHRISTMAS CAROL (Shower Of Stars) (CBS)
TWELVE ANGRY MEN (Studio One) (CBS)

ART DIRECTION - LIVE SHOW (E-87)
BOB MARKELL Mallory's Tragedy On Mt. Everest (You Are There) (CBS)
ROBERT TYLER LEE (Shower Of Stars) (CBS)
CARL MACAULEY (Space Patrol) (ABC)
WILLIAM T. MARTIN (Dinah Shore Show) (NBC)
JAMES VANCE (Climax) (CBS)

ART DIRECTION - FILMED SHOW (E-88)
RALPH BERGER and ALBERT PYKE A Christmas Carol (Shower Of Stars) (CBS)
DUNCAN CRAMER (Four Star Playhouse) (CBS)
FRANK DURLAUF (Ozzie and Harriet Show) (ABC)
CLAUDIO GUZMAN (Ray Bolger Show) (ABC)
SERGE KRIZMAN The Roman And The Renegade (Schlitz Playhouse Of Stars) (CBS)

DIRECTION OF PHOTOGRAPHY (E-89)
LESTER SHORR I Climb The Stairs (Medic) (NBC)
NORBERT BRODINE The Clara Schumann Story (Loretta Young Show) (NBC)
GEORGE T. CLEMENS The Roman And The Renegade (Schlitz Playhouse Of Stars) (CBS)
EDWARD COLMAN The Big Bible (Dragnet) (NBC)
HAROLD E. STINE Night Call (Cavalcade Of America) (Syndicated)
WALTER STRENGE (My Little Margie) (NBC)

WRITTEN DRAMATIC MATERIAL (E-90)
REGINALD ROSE Twelve Angry Men (Studio One) (CBS)
PADDY CHAYEFSKY (Philco Television Playhouse) (NBC)
DAVID DORTORT An Error In Chemistry (Climax) (CBS)
LEONARD FREEMAN The Answer (Four Star Playhouse) (CBS)
JAMES MOSER White Is The Color (Medic) (NBC)

WRITTEN COMEDY MATERIAL (E-91)
JAMES ALLARDICE, JACK DOUGLAS, HAL KANTER, HARRY WINKLER (George Gobel Show) (NBC)
GEORGE BALZER, MILT JOSEFSBERG, SAM PERRIN and JOHN

TACKABERRY (Jack Benny Show) (CBS)
JAMES FRITZELL and EVERETT GREENBAUM (Mr. Peepers) (NBC)
JACKIE GLEASON and STAFF WRITERS (Jackie Gleason Show) (CBS)
JESS OPPENHEIMER, ROBERT G. CARROLL and MADELYN PUGH (I Love Lucy) (CBS)
DANNY THOMAS and STAFF WRITERS (Make Room For Daddy) (ABC)

TECHNICAL ACHIEVEMENT (E-92)
NBC, Color TV Policy and Burbank Color - JOHN WEST
CBS, West Coast Color TV Facilities - L.H. BOWMAN
Ozzie and Harriet Productions facilities - GEORGE E. H. HANSON.

ENGINEERING EFFECTS (E-93)
FOUR QUADRANT SCREEN - NBC - 1954 National Election Coverage - ROBERT SHELBY
ELECTRONIC EDITING "Background" (NBC) - JOHN GOETZ, WALTER O'MEARS and DANIEL ZAMPINO
JACKIE GLEASON SHOW - (CBS) - Jackie Gleason Enterprises
SPACE PATROL - ABC - CAMERON PIERCE

SOUND EDITING (E-94)
GEORGE NICHOLSON (Dragnet) (NBC)
CATHEY BURROW (Waterfront) (CBS)
JOHNNY BUSHELMAN (Ramar Of The Jungle) (Syndicated)
STANLEY CALLAHAN (Rin-Tin-Tin) (ABC)
JOSEF VON STROHEIM Red Christmas (Medic) (NBC)

FILM EDITING (E-95)
GRANT SMITH and LYNN HARRISON Operation Undersea (Disneyland) (ABC)
GEORGE AMY The Roman And The Renegade (Schlitz Playhouse Of Stars) (ABC)
SAMUEL E. BEETLEY The Answer (Four Star Playhouse) (CBS)
JODIE COPELAN White Is The Color (Medic) (NBC)
CHESTER W. SCHAEFFER Davy Crockett - Indian Fighter (Disneyland) (ABC)

DIRECTION (E-96)
FRANKLIN SCHAFFNER Twelve Angry Men (Studio One) (CBS)
ROBERT FLOREY The Clara Schumann Story (Loretta Young Show) (NBC)
CLARK JONES (Your Hit Parade) (NBC)
ROY KELLINO The Answer (Four Star Playhouse) (CBS)
TED POST Christmas On The Waterfront (Waterfront) (CBS)
ALEX SEGAL (U.S. Steel Hour) (ABC)

ORIGINAL MUSIC (E-97)
WALTER SCHUMANN (Dragnet) (NBC)
BERNARD HERRMAN A Christmas Carol (Shower of Stars) (NBC)
GIAN CARLO MENOTTI Amahl and the Night Visitors (Hallmark Hall of Fame) (NBC)
VICTOR YOUNG Diamond Jubilee of Light (4 networks)
VICTOR YOUNG (Medic) (NBC)

SCORING OF A DRAMATIC OR VARIETY PROGRAM (E-98)
VICTOR YOUNG Diamond Jubilee of Light (4 networks)
BUDDY BREGMAN Anything Goes (Colgate Comedy Hour) (NBC)
GORDON JENKINS Shower of Stars (first show) (CBS)
NELSON RIDDLE Satins and Spurs
WALTER SCHARF Here Comes Donald (Texaco Star Theatre) starring Donald O'Connor (NBC)

CHOREOGRAPHER (E-99)
JUNE TAYLOR (Jackie Gleason Show) (CBS)
ROD ALEXANDER (Max Liebman Spectaculars) (NBC)
TONY CHARMOLI and BOB HERGET (Your Hit Parade) (NBC)

LOUIS DA PRON Here Comes Donald (Texaco Star Theatre) starring Donald O'Connor (NBC)

1955

CHILDREN'S SERIES (E-100)
LASSIE (CBS)
DING DONG SCHOOL (NBC)
HOWDY DOODY (NBC)
KUKLA, FRAN and OLLIE (ABC)
MICKEY MOUSE CLUB (ABC)
THE PINKY LEE SHOW (NBC)

DAYTIME PROGRAMMING (E-101)
MATINEE THEATRE (NBC)
THE BOB CROSBY SHOW (CBS)
THE GARRY MOORE SHOW (CBS)
HOME - ARLENE FRANCIS (NBC)
TODAY - DAVE GARROWAY (NBC)

SPECIAL EVENT OR NEWS PROGRAM (E-102)
A-BOMB COVERAGE (CBS)
ACADEMY OF MOTION PICTURE ARTS & SCIENCES AWARDS (NBC)
ACADEMY OF TELEVISION ARTS & SCIENCES AWARDS (NBC)
FOOTBALL - ROSE BOWL - (NBC)
BASEBALL - WORLD SERIES - (NBC)

DOCUMENTARY PROGRAM (E-103)
(Religious, Informational, Educational Or Interview)
OMNIBUS (CBS)
MEET THE PRESS (NBC)
PERSON TO PERSON (CBS)
SEE IT NOW (CBS)
WIDE WIDE WORLD (NBC)

AUDIENCE PARTICIPATION SERIES (QUIZ, PANEL, ETC.) (E-104)
THE $64,000 QUESTION (CBS)
I'VE GOT A SECRET (CBS)
PEOPLE ARE FUNNY (NBC)
WHAT'S MY LINE? (CBS)
YOU BET YOUR LIFE (NBC)

ACTION OR ADVENTURE SERIES (E-105)
DISNEYLAND (Davy Crockett Series, etc.) (ABC)
ALFRED HITCHCOCK PRESENTS (CBS)
DRAGNET (NBC)
GUNSMOKE (CBS)
LINE-UP (CBS)

COMEDY SERIES (E-106)
PHIL SILVERS (You'll Never Get Rich) (CBS)
JACK BENNY SHOW (CBS)
BOB CUMMINGS SHOW (CBS)
CAESAR'S HOUR (NBC)
GEORGE GOBEL SHOW (NBC)
MAKE ROOM FOR DADDY (ABC)

VARIETY SERIES (E-107)
ED SULLIVAN SHOW (CBS)
DINAH SHORE SHOW (NBC)
FORD STAR JUBILEE (CBS)
PERRY COMO SHOW (NBC)
SHOWER OF STARS (CBS)

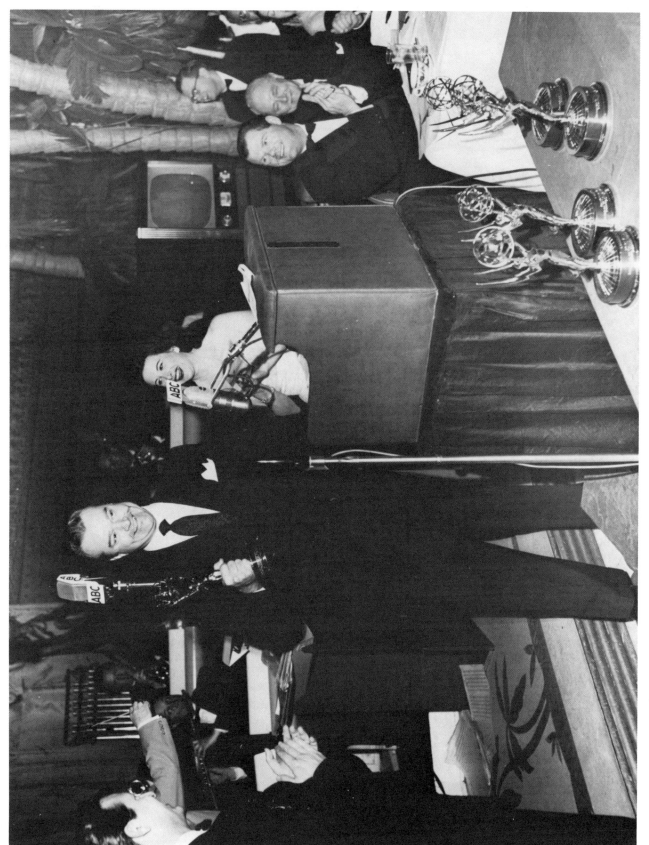

1951—Red Skelton (Best Comedian)

1957—Peter Ustinov (Best Actor—Single Performance) and Polly Bergen (Best Actress—Single Performance)

MUSIC SERIES (E-108)
YOUR HIT PARADE (NBC)
COKE TIME - EDDIE FISHER (NBC)
DINAH SHORE SHOW (NBC)
PERRY COMO SHOW (NBC)
VOICE OF FIRESTONE (CBS)

DRAMATIC SERIES (E-109)
PRODUCERS' SHOWCASE (NBC)
ALCOA-GOODYEAR TV PLAYHOUSE (NBC)
CLIMAX (CBS)
STUDIO ONE (CBS)
U. S. STEEL HOUR (CBS)

PROGRAM OF THE YEAR (E-110)
PETER PAN Mary Martin (Producers' Showcase) (NBC)
THE AMERICAN WEST (Wide Wide World) (NBC)
CAINE MUTINY COURT MARTIAL (Ford Star Jubilee) (CBS)
DAVY CROCKETT AND RIVER PIRATES (Disneyland) (ABC)
NO TIME FOR SERGEANTS (U. S. Steel Hour) (ABC)
PETER PAN MEETS RUSTY WILLIAMS (Make Room For Daddy) (ABC)
THE SLEEPING BEAUTY (Producers' Showcase) (NBC)

ACTOR - SINGLE PERFORMANCE (E-111)
LLOYD NOLAN as CAPT. QUEEG Caine Mutiny Court Martial (Ford Star Jubilee) (CBS)
RALPH BELLAMY as FATHER Fearful Decision (U. S. Steel Hour) (CBS)
JOSE FERRER as CYRANO Cyrano de Bergerac (Producers' Showcase) (NBC)
EVERETT SLOANE as PRESIDENT Patterns (Kraft Theatre) (NBC)
BARRY SULLIVAN as DEFENSE ATTORNEY GREENWALD Caine Mutiny Court Martial (Ford Star Jubilee) (CBS)

ACTRESS - SINGLE PERFORMANCE (E-112)
MARY MARTIN as PETER Peter Pan (Producers' Showcase) (NBC)
JULIE HARRIS as SHEVAWN Wind from the South (U. S. Steel Hour) (CBS)
EVA MARIE SAINT as EMILY Our Town (Producers' Showcase) (NBC)
JESSICA TANDY as WIFE The Fourposter (Producers' Showcase) (NBC)
LORETTA YOUNG as SADIE Christmas Stopover (Loretta Young Show) (NBC)

ACTOR - CONTINUING PERFORMANCE (E-113)
PHIL SILVERS as SERGEANT BILKO (Phil Silvers Show, You'll Never Get Rich) (CBS)
BOB CUMMINGS as BOB COLLINS (Bob Cummings Show) (CBS)
JACKIE GLEASON as RALPH KRAMDEN (Honeymooners) (CBS)
DANNY THOMAS as DANNY WILLIAMS (Make Room for Daddy) (ABC)
ROBERT YOUNG as FATHER (Father Knows Best) (CBS)

ACTRESS - CONTINUING PERFORMANCE (E-114)
LUCILLE BALL as LUCY RICARDO (I Love Lucy) (CBS)
GRACIE ALLEN as GRACIE (Burns & Allen) (CBS)
EVE ARDEN as CONNIE BROOKS (Our Miss Brooks) (CBS)
JEAN HAGEN as MARGARET WILLIAMS (Make Room for Daddy) (ABC)
ANN SOTHERN as SUSIE MAC NAMARA (Private Secretary) (CBS)

SUPPORTING ACTOR (E-115)
ART CARNEY as ED NORTON (Honeymooners) (CBS)
ED BEGLEY as ANDY SLOANE Patterns (Kraft Theatre) (NBC)
WILLIAM FRAWLEY as FRED MERTZ (I Love Lucy) (CBS)
CARL REINER in various roles (Caesar's Hour) (NBC)
CYRIL RITCHARD as Mr. DARLING and CAPT. HOOK Peter Pan (Producers' Showcase) (NBC)

SUPPORTING ACTRESS (E-116)
NANETTE FABRAY in various roles (Caesar's Hour) (NBC)
ANN B. DAVIS as SCHULTZY Schultzy's Dream World (Bob Cummings Show) (CBS)
JEAN HAGEN as MARGARET WILLIAMS (Make Room for Daddy) (ABC)
AUDREY MEADOWS as Mrs. KRAMDEN (Honeymooners) (CBS)
THELMA RITTER as THE MOTHER A Catered Affair (Alcoa-Goodyear Playhouse) (NBC)

COMEDIAN (E-117)
PHIL SILVERS (CBS)
JACK BENNY (CBS)
SID CAESAR (NBC)
ART CARNEY (CBS)
GEORGE GOBEL (CBS)

COMEDIENNE (E-118)
NANETTE FABRAY (NBC)
GRACIE ALLEN (CBS)
EVE ARDEN (CBS)
LUCILLE BALL (CBS)
ANN SOTHERN (CBS)

MALE SINGER (E-119)
PERRY COMO (NBC)
HARRY BELAFONTE
EDDIE FISHER (NBC)
GORDON MAC RAE (NBC)
FRANK SINATRA (NBC)

FEMALE SINGER (E-120)
DINAH SHORE (NBC)
ROSEMARY CLOONEY (Syndicated)
JUDY GARLAND (CBS)
PEGGY LEE
GISELE MAC KENZIE (NBC)

M.C. OR PROGRAM HOST - MALE OR FEMALE (E-121)
PERRY COMO (NBC)
ALISTAIR COOKE (CBS)
JOHN DALY (CBS)
DAVE GARROWAY (NBC)
ALFRED HITCHCOCK (NBC)

NEWS COMMENTATOR OR REPORTER (E-122)
EDWARD R. MURROW (CBS)
JOHN DALY (ABC)
DOUGLAS EDWARDS (CBS)
CLETE ROBERTS (CBS)
JOHN CAMERON SWAYZE (NBC)

SPECIALTY ACT - SINGLE OR GROUP (E-123)
MARCEL MARCEAU (NBC)
HARRY BELAFONTE
VICTOR BORGE
SAMMY DAVIS, JR.
DONALD O'CONNOR (NBC)

ORIGINAL TELEPLAY WRITING (E-124)
ROD SERLING Patterns (Kraft TV Theatre) (NBC)
DAVID DAVIDSON Thunder Over Washington (Alcoa-Goodyear Playhouse) (NBC)
ROBERT ALAN AURTHUR A Man Is Ten Feet Tall (Philco Playhouse) (NBC)
PADDY CHAYEFSKY A Catered Affair (Alcoa-Goodyear Playhouse) (NBC)

CYRIL HUME & RICHARD MAIBAUM Fearful Decision (U. S. Steel Hour) (CBS)

COMEDY WRITING (E-125)

NAT HIKEN, BARRY BLITSER, ARNOLD AUERBACH, HARVEY ORKIN, VINCENT BOGERT, ARNOLD ROSEN, COLEMAN JACOBY, TONY WEBSTER & TERRY RYAN (Phil Silvers Show, You'll Never Get Rich) (CBS)
HAL KANTER, HOWARD LEEDS, EVERETT GREENBAUM & HARRY WINKLER (George Gobel Show) (NBC)
JESS OPPENHEIMER, MADELYN PUGH, BOB CARROLL, JR., BOB SCHILLER & BOB WEISKOPF L. A. At Last (I Love Lucy) (CBS)
SAM PERRIN, GEORGE BALZER, HAL GOLDMAN & AL GORDON (Jack Benny Show) (CBS)
MEL TOLKIN, SELMA DIAMOND, LARRY GELBART, MEL BROOKS & SHELDON KELLER (Caesar's Hour) (NBC)

TELEVISION ADAPTATION (E-126)

PAUL GREGORY & FRANKLIN SCHAFFNER Caine Mutiny Court Martial by Herman Wouk (Ford Star Jubilee) (CBS)
DAVID DORTORT The Ox-Bow Incident by Walter Van Tilberg Clark (20th Century Fox Hour) (CBS)
JOHN MONKS, JR. Miracle On 34th St. by Valentine Davies (20th Century Fox Hour) (CBS)
ROD SERLING The Champion by Ring Lardner (Climax) (CBS)
DAVID SHAW Our Town by Thornton Wilder (Producers' Showcase) (NBC)

MUSICAL CONTRIBUTION (E-127)

A Song from "Our Town" "Love and Marriage" by Sammy Cahn and James Van Heusen (Producers' Showcase) (NBC)
The Arranging of CAMARATA for "Together with Music" (Ford Star Jubilee) (Mary Martin & Noel Coward) (CBS)
The Score of "Our Town" by Sammy Cahn and James Van Heusen (Producers' Showcase) (NBC)
The Arranging of NELSON RIDDLE for "Our Town" (Producers' Showcase) (NBC)
The Series Scoring by DAVID BROEKMAN (Wide Wide World) (NBC)

PRODUCER - LIVE SERIES (E-128)

FRED COE (Producers' Showcase) (NBC)
HERBERT BRODKIN (Alcoa-Goodyear Playhouse) (NBC)
HAL KANTER (George Gobel Show) (NBC)
MARTIN MANULIS (Climax) (CBS)
THE THEATRE GUILD (U. S. Steel Hour) (CBS)
BARRY WOOD (Wide Wide World) (NBC)

PRODUCER - FILM SERIES (E-129)

WALT DISNEY (Disneyland) (ABC)
JAMES D. FONDA (You Are There) (CBS)
PAUL HENNING (Bob Cummings Show) (CBS)
NAT HIKEN (Phil Silver Show, You'll Never Get Rich) (CBS)
FRANK LA TOURETTE (Medic) (NBC)

DIRECTOR - LIVE SERIES (E-130)

FRANKLIN SCHAFFNER Caine Mutiny Court Martial (Ford Star Jubilee) (CBS)
JOHN FRANKENHEIMER Portrait in Celluloid (Climax) (CBS)
CLARK JONES Peter Pan (Producers' Showcase) (NBC)
DELBERT MANN Our Town (Producers' Showcase) (NBC)
ALEX SEGAL No Time for Sergeants (U. S. Steel Hour) (CBS)

DIRECTOR - FILM SERIES (E-131)

NAT HIKEN (Phil Silvers Show, You'll Never Get Rich) (CBS)
ROD AMATEAU Return of the Wolf (Bob Cummings Show) (CBS)
BERNARD GIRARD Grant & Lee at Appomatox (You Are There) (CBS)
ALFRED HITCHCOCK The Case of Mr. Pelham (Alfred Hitchcock Presents) (CBS)
SHELDON LEONARD (Make Room for Daddy) (ABC)
JACK WEBB Christmas Story (Dragnet) (NBC)

ART DIRECTION - LIVE SERIES (E-132)

OTIS RIGGS (Playwrights '56 and Producers' Showcase) (NBC)
CARL KENT (U. S. Steel Hour) (CBS)
JAN SCOTT (Hallmark Hall of Fame) (NBC)
DON SHIRLEY (Perry Como Show) (NBC)
WILLIAM CRAIG SMITH (Lux Video Theatre) (NBC)
JAMES D. VANCE (Climax) (CBS)

ART DIRECTION - FILM SERIES (E-133)

WILLIAM FERRARI (You Are There) (CBS)
DUNCAN CRAMER (Four Star Playhouse) (CBS)
ERNST FEGTE (Medic) (NBC)
SERGE KRIZMAN (Schlitz Playhouse)
PETER PROUD (Robin Hood)

CINEMATOGRAPHY (E-134)

WILLIAM SCIKNER Black Friday (Medic) (NBC)
NORBERT BRODINE I Remember The Rani (Loretta Young Show) (NBC)
EDWARD COLMAN (Dragnet) (NBC)
GEORGE DISKANT The Collar (Four-Star Playhouse) (CBS)
ROBERT PITTACK (Private Secretary) (CBS)

CAMERA WORK - LIVE SHOW (E-135)

T. MILLER (Studio One) (CBS)
A. J. CUNNINGHAM (Climax) (CBS)
JOE STRAUSS (Lux Video Theatre) (NBC)
LES VAUGHT (Art Linkletter's House Party) (CBS)

FILM EDITING (E-136)

EDWARD W. WILLIAMS Breakdown (Alfred Hitchcock Presents) (CBS)
SAMUEL E. BEETLEY The Collar (Four Star Playhouse) (CBS)
JASON H. BERNIE Operation 3 in 1 (Navy Log) (CBS)
STANLEY FRAZEN & GUY SCARPITTA Miss Coffee Break (Bob Cummings Show) (CBS)
DANIEL NATHAN Little Guy (Fireside Theatre, Jane Wyman) (NBC)

CHOREOGRAPHER (E-137)

TONY CHARMOLI Show Biz (Your Hit Parade) (NBC)
ROD ALEXANDER (Max Liebman Spectaculars) (NBC)
JEROME ROBBINS Peter Pan (Producers Showcase) (NBC)
JAMES STARBUCK (Max Liebman Presents) and (Shower of Stars with Ethel Merman) (NBC & CBS)
JUNE TAYLOR (Jackie Gleason Show) (CBS)

ENGINEERING TECHNICAL ACHIEVEMENT (E-138)

RCA TRICOLOR PICTURE TUBE which made the commercial color receiver practical
AUTOMATIC IRIS CONTROL for NBC pick-up of complete atom blast at Yucca Flats
COLOR WIPE AMPLIFIER developed by CBS Engineering
DUMONT ELECTRONICAM
ELECTRONIC EDITING MACHINE developed at the Disney Studios
ULTRA-VIOLET KINESCOPE RECORDING OF RCA which improved the quality of television recording

COMMERCIAL CAMPAIGN (E-139)

FORD
BANK OF AMERICA
CHRYSLER
HAMM'S BEER
PIEL'S BEER

GOVERNOR'S AWARD (E-140)

(The first Presidential size Emmy to be awarded)
PRESIDENT DWIGHT D. EISENHOWER For his use and encouragement of television

1956

PROGRAM OF THE YEAR (E-141)

REQUIEM FOR A HEAVYWEIGHT (Playhouse 90) (CBS)
A NIGHT TO REMEMBER Titanic (Kraft Television Theatre) (NBC)
LEONARD BERNSTEIN (Omnibus) (CBS)
SECRET LIFE OF DANNY KAYE (See It Now) (CBS)
VICTOR BORGE SHOW

NEW PROGRAM SERIES (E-142)

PLAYHOUSE 90 (CBS)
AIR POWER (CBS)
THE CHEVY SHOW Dinah Shore (NBC)
ERNIE KOVACS SHOW (NBC)
STEVE ALLEN SUNDAY SHOW (NBC)

SERIES - HALF HOUR OR LESS (E-143)

PHIL SILVERS SHOW (CBS)
ALFRED HITCHCOCK PRESENTS (CBS)
FATHER KNOWS BEST (NBC)
JACK BENNY SHOW (CBS)
PERSON TO PERSON (CBS)

SERIES - ONE HOUR OR MORE (E-144)

CAESAR'S HOUR (NBC)
CLIMAX (CBS)
ED SULLIVAN SHOW (CBS)
OMNIBUS (CBS)
PERRY COMO SHOW (NBC)

PUBLIC SERVICE SERIES (E-145)

SEE IT NOW (CBS)
MEET THE PRESS (NBC)
NBC OPERA (NBC)
WIDE WIDE WORLD (NBC)
YOU ARE THERE (CBS)

COVERAGE OF A NEWSWORTHY EVENT (E-146)

"YEARS OF CRISIS," Year-end report, Murrow and correspondents (CBS)
ANDREA DORIA SINKING, Live and Film (CBS)
ANDREA DORIA SURVIVORS ARRIVE IN NEW YORK (NBC)
NATIONAL POLITICAL CONVENTIONS (ABC)
NATIONAL POLITICAL CONVENTIONS (NBC)

ACTOR - CONTINUING PERFORMANCE - DRAMATIC SERIES (E-147)

ROBERT YOUNG (Father Knows Best) (NBC)
JAMES ARNESS (Gunsmoke) (CBS)
CHARLES BOYER (Four Star Playhouse) (CBS)
DAVID NIVEN (Four Star Playhouse) (CBS)
HUGH O'BRIAN Wyatt Earp (Life and Legend of) (ABC)

ACTRESS - CONTINUING PERFORMANCE - DRAMATIC SERIES (E-148)

LORETTA YOUNG (Loretta Young Show) (NBC)
JAN CLAYTON (Lassie) (CBS)
IDA LUPINO (Four Star Playhouse) (CBS)
PEGGY WOOD (I Remember Mama) (CBS)
JANE WYMAN (Jane Wyman Theatre) (NBC)

COMEDIAN - CONTINUING PERFORMANCE (E-149)

SID CAESAR (Caesar's Hour) (NBC)
JACK BENNY (Jack Benny Show) (CBS)
BOB CUMMINGS (Bob Cummings Show) (CBS)
ERNIE KOVACS (Ernie Kovacs Show) (NBC)
PHIL SILVERS (Phil Silvers Show) (CBS)

COMEDIENNE - CONTINUING PERFORMANCE (E-150)

NANETTE FABRAY (Caesar's Hour) (NBC)
EDIE ADAMS (Ernie Kovacs Show) (NBC)
GRACIE ALLEN (Burns & Allen) (CBS)
LUCILLE BALL (I Love Lucy) (CBS)
ANN SOTHERN (Private Secretary) (CBS)

ACTOR - SINGLE PERFORMANCE (E-151)

JACK PALANCE as PRIZEFIGHTER Requiem for a Heavyweight (Playhouse 90) (CBS)
LLOYD BRIDGES as ALEC BEGGS Tragedy in a Temporary Town (Alcoa Hour-Goodyear Playhouse) (NBC)
FREDRIC MARCH as DODSWORTH Dodsworth (Producers' Showcase) (NBC)
SAL MINEO as DINO Dino (Studio One) (CBS)
RED SKELTON as BUDDY MC COY The Big Slide (Playhouse 90) (CBS)

ACTRESS - SINGLE PERFORMANCE (E-152)

CLAIRE TREVOR as Mrs. DODSWORTH Dodsworth (Producers' Showcase) (NBC)
EDNA BEST as WIFE This Happy Breed (Ford Star Jubilee) (CBS)
GRACIE FIELDS as OLD LADY Old Lady Shows Her Medals (U.S. Steel Hour) (CBS)
NANCY KELLY as NUN The Pilot (Studio One) (CBS)
EVELYN RUDIE as ELOISE Eloise (Playhouse 90) (CBS)

SUPPORTING ACTOR (E-153)

CARL REINER Various Roles (Caesar's Hour) (NBC)
ART CARNEY as NORTON (Jackie Gleason Show) (CBS)
PAUL FORD as COLONEL (Phil Silvers Show) (CBS)
WILLIAM FRAWLEY as FRED MERTZ (I Love Lucy) (CBS)
ED WYNN as TRAINER Requiem for a Heavyweight (Playhouse 90) (CBS)

SUPPORTING ACTRESS (E-154)

PAT CARROLL Various Roles (Caesar's Hour) (NBC)
ANN B. DAVIS as SCHULTZY (Bob Cummings Show) (CBS)
AUDREY MEADOWS as ALICE KRAMDEN (Jackie Gleason Show) (CBS)
MILDRED NATWICK as MEDIUM Blithe Spirit (Ford Star Jubilee) (CBS)
VIVIAN VANCE as ETHEL MERTZ (I Love Lucy) (CBS)

MALE PERSONALITY - CONTINUING PERFORMANCE (E-155)

PERRY COMO (NBC)
STEVE ALLEN (NBC)
LEONARD BERNSTEIN (CBS)
TENNESSEE ERNIE FORD (NBC)
ALFRED HITCHCOCK (CBS)
BISHOP FULTON J. SHEEN (DUMONT)

FEMALE PERSONALITY - CONTINUING PERFORMANCE (E-156)

DINAH SHORE (NBC)
ROSEMARY CLOONEY (Syndicated)
FAYE EMERSON (CBS)
ARLENE FRANCIS (NBC)
GISELE MAC KENZIE (NBC)

NEWS COMMENTATOR (E-157)

EDWARD R. MURROW (CBS)
WALTER CRONKITE (CBS)
JOHN DALY (ABC)
DOUGLAS EDWARDS (CBS)
CHET HUNTLEY (NBC)

TELEPLAY WRITING - HALF-HOUR OR LESS (E-158)

JAMES P. CAVANAUGH Fog Closing In (Alfred Hitchcock Presents) (CBS)
MORTON FINE and DAVID FRIEDKIN Patrol (Frontier) (NBC)
RICHARD MORRIS The Pearl (Loretta Young Show) (NBC)
JOHN NESBITT Man with the Beard (Telephone Time) (ABC)
DAN ULLMAN The Buntline (Wyatt Earp) (ABC)

TELEPLAY WRITING - ONE HOUR OR MORE (E-159)

ROD SERLING Requiem for a Heavyweight (Playhouse 90) (CBS)
LOUIS PETERSON Joey (Alcoa Hour-Goodyear Playhouse) (NBC)
GEORGE ROY HILL and JOHN WHEDON A Night To Remember (Kraft Television Theatre) (NBC)
ELICK MOLL Sizeman and Son (Playhouse 90) (CBS)
REGINALD ROSE Tragedy in a Temporary Town (Alcoa Hour-Goodyear Playhouse) (NBC)

WRITING - VARIETY OR SITUATION COMEDY (E-160)

NAT HIKEN, BILLY FRIEDBERG, TONY WEBSTER, LEONARD STERN, ARNOLD ROSEN, COLEMAN JACOBY (Phil Silvers Show) (CBS)
GOODMAN ACE, JAY BURTON, MORT GREEN, GEORGE FOSTER (Perry Como Show) (NBC)
ERNIE KOVACS, LOUIS M. HEYWARD, REX LARDNER, MIKE MARMER (Ernie Kovacs Show) (NBC)
SAM PERRIN, GEORGE BALZER, HAL GOLDMAN, AL GORDON (Jack Benny Show) (CBS)
MEL TOLKIN, GARY BELKIN, MEL BROOKS, SHELDON KELLER, NEIL SIMON, LARRY GELBART and MIKE STEWART (Caesar's Hour) (NBC)

DIRECTION - HALF HOUR OR LESS (E-161)

SHELDON LEONARD Danny's Comeback (Danny Thomas Show) (ABC)
GEORGE ARCHAINBAUD The Traitor (77th Bengal Lancers) (NBC)
HERSCHEL DAUGHERTY The Road That Led Afar (G. E. Theatre) (CBS)
WILLIAM RUSSELL First Moscow Purge Trail (You Are There) (CBS)
CLAY YURDIN As I Lay Dying (Camera Three) (CBS)

DIRECTION - ONE HOUR OR MORE (E-162)

RALPH NELSON Requiem for a Heavyweight (Playhouse 90) (CBS)
LEWIS ALLEN Child of the Regiment (20th Century-Fox Hour) (CBS)
BOB BANNER October 5 with Sinatra (Chevy Show - Dinah Shore) (NBC)
KIRK BROWNING La Boheme (NBC Opera Theatre) (NBC)
JOHN FRANKENHEIMER Forbidden Area (Playhouse 90) (CBS)
GEORGE ROY HILL A Night to Remember (Kraft Television Theatre) (NBC)

ART DIRECTION - HALF HOUR OR LESS (E-163)

PAUL BARNES (Your Hit Parade) (NBC)
WARREN CLYMER (Frontiers of Faith) (NBC)
GROVER COLE (Adventure) (CBS)
MARTIN OBZINA, JOHN ROBERT LLOYD, JOHN J. LLOYD, JOHN MEEHAN and GEORGE PATRICK (G. E. Theatre) (CBS)
FRANKLIN SWIG (Dinah Shore Show) (NBC)

ART DIRECTION - ONE HOUR OR MORE (E-164)

ALBERT HESCHONG Requiem for a Heavyweight (Playhouse 90) (CBS)
HENRY MAY (Omnibus) (CBS)
DUANE MC KINNEY (Kraft Television Theatre) (NBC)
JAN SCOTT (Kaiser Aluminum Hour) (NBC)
DON SHIRLEY (Perry Como Show) (NBC)

CINEMATOGRAPHY (E-165)

NORBERT BRODINE The Pearl (Loretta Young Show) (NBC)
LLOYD AHERN Stranger in the Night (20th Century-Fox Hour) (CBS)
GEORGE E. DISKANT Tunnel of Fear (Four Star Playhouse) (CBS)
ROBERT W. PITTACK The Glorious Gift of Molly Malloy (G. E. Theatre) (CBS)
JOHN L. RUSSELL The Night Goes On (G. E. Theatre) (CBS)

FILM EDITING (E-166)

FRANK KELLER Our Mr. Sun (A.T.&T. Science Series) (CBS)
SAMUEL E. BEETLEY Tunnel of Fear (Four Star Playhouse) (CBS)
RICHARD FANTL Betty's Birthday (Father Knows Best) (NBC)
DANIEL A. NATHAN Between Jobs (Jane Wyman Theatre) (NBC)
ROBERT WATTS Bounty Killers (Cheyenne) (ABC)

MUSICAL CONTRIBUTION (E-167)

LEONARD BERNSTEIN Composing Conducting (Omnibus) (CBS)
SIDNEY FINE Orchestrations of Victor Young's Music (Medic) (NBC)
NELSON RIDDLE Arrangement of Musical Score (Rosemary Clooney Show) (Syndicated)
WALTER SCHUMANN Vocal Arrangements (Tennessee Ernie Ford Show) (NBC)
OLIVER WALLACE Composing of Score (Disneyland TV Show) (ABC)

LIVE CAMERA WORK (E-168)

A NIGHT TO REMEMBER (Kraft Television Theatre) (NBC)
AN AMERICAN SUNDAY (Wide Wide World) (NBC)
JACK AND THE BEANSTALK (Producers' Showcase) (NBC)
REPUBLICAN CONVENTION (ABC-CBS-NBC Pool)
REQUIEM FOR A HEAVYWEIGHT (Playhouse 90) (CBS)

ENGINEERING OR TECHNICAL ACHIEVEMENT (E-169)

DEVELOPMENT OF VIDEO TAPE BY AMPEX and FURTHER DEVELOPMENT AND PRACTICAL APPLICATIONS BY CBS - DUAL ENTRY
APPLICATION OF LENTICULAR FILM TO RECORDING PROCESS FOR COLOR DELAYED RELEASE (NBC)
DEVELOPMENT OF THE TRULY PORTABLE "CREEPIE PEEPIE" FOR TELEVISION PICK-UP BY RCA
TELESCOPIC LENS WITH 100' FOCAL LENGTH ("BIG JAKE") DEVELOPED AND USED BY ABC
"WIDE WIDE WORLD," LIVE PICK-UP FROM HAVANA, CUBA (NBC)

1957

PROGRAM OF THE YEAR (E-170)

May be either one of a series or an individual presentation, either entertainment, public service or coverage of a newsworthy event.

THE COMEDIAN (Playhouse 90) (CBS)
EDSEL SHOW (CBS)
GREEN PASTURES (Hallmark Hall of Fame) (NBC)
HELEN MORGAN STORY (Playhouse 90) (CBS)

NEW PROGRAM SERIES OF THE YEAR (E-171)

The most outstanding series of programs of any format presented originally in 1957.

SEVEN LIVELY ARTS (CBS)
LEAVE IT TO BEAVER (CBS)
MAVERICK (ABC)
TONIGHT - JACK PAAR (NBC)
WAGON TRAIN (NBC)

DRAMATIC ANTHOLOGY SERIES (E-172)

The most outstanding group of dramatic programs presented on a regular basis which employs individual stories and characters for each presentation, except comedy series which have a separate category.

PLAYHOUSE 90 (CBS)
ALFRED HITCHCOCK PRESENTS (CBS)
CLIMAX (CBS)
HALLMARK HALL OF FAME (NBC)
STUDIO ONE (CBS)

DRAMATIC SERIES WITH CONTINUING CHARACTERS (E-173)

The most outstanding group of dramatic programs presented multi-weekly, weekly, or from time to time on a regular basis and employing the same continuing characters; but excludes all comedy series which have a separate category.

GUNSMOKE (CBS)
LASSIE (CBS)
MAVERICK (ABC)
PERRY MASON (CBS)
WAGON TRAIN (NBC)

COMEDY SERIES (E-174)

The most outstanding group of comedy programs presented multi-weekly, weekly, or from time to time on a regular basis.

PHIL SILVERS SHOW (CBS)
BOB CUMMINGS SHOW (CBS & NBC)
CAESAR'S HOUR (NBC)
FATHER KNOWS BEST (NBC)
JACK BENNY SHOW (CBS)

MUSICAL, VARIETY, AUDIENCE PARTICIPATION OR QUIZ SERIES (E-175)

The most outstanding group of programs, not in the area of drama or comedy, presented multi-weekly, weekly, or from time to time on a regular basis.

DINAH SHORE - CHEVY SHOW (NBC)
ED SULLIVAN SHOW (CBS)
PERRY COMO SHOW (NBC)
STEVE ALLEN SHOW (NBC)
TONIGHT - JACK PAAR (NBC)

PUBLIC SERVICE PROGRAM OR SERIES (E-176)

OMNIBUS (ABC & NBC)
BELL TELEPHONE SCIENCE SERIES (NBC)
PERSON TO PERSON (CBS)
SEE IT NOW (CBS)
WIDE WIDE WORLD (NBC)

COVERAGE OF AN UNSCHEDULED NEWSWORTHY EVENT (E-177)

COVERAGE OF THE RIKERS ISLAND NEW YORK PLANE CRASH as presented on "World News Roundup" (CBS)
FOUR NEWSMEN INTERVIEW GOVERNOR ORVAL FAUBUS OF ARKANSAS IN LITTLE ROCK (ABC)
NEWS COVERAGE OF THE INTEGRATION STORY IN LITTLE ROCK AND OTHER SOUTHERN CITIES (NBC)
COVERAGE OF THE LITTLE ROCK SCHOOL RIOT, as presented on "Little Rock, 1957" (CBS)

NEWS COVERAGE OF FIRST RUSSIAN SPUTNIK, THE U.S. SATELLITE LAUNCHING EFFORTS AND VANGUARD FAILURE ON DEC. 6 (NBC)

ACTOR - CONTINUING PERFORMANCE - DRAMATIC OR COMEDY SERIES (E-178)

ROBERT YOUNG as JIM ANDERSON (Father Knows Best) (NBC)
JAMES ARNESS as MATT DILLON (Gunsmoke) (CBS)
BOB CUMMINGS as BOB COLLINS (Bob Cummings Show) (CBS & NBC)
PHIL SILVERS as BILKO (Phil Silvers Show) (CBS)
DANNY THOMAS as DANNY WILLIAMS (Danny Thomas Show) (ABC & CBS)

ACTRESS - CONTINUING PERFORMANCE - DRAMATIC OR COMEDY SERIES (E-179)

JANE WYATT as MARGARET ANDERSON (Father Knows Best) (NBC)
EVE ARDEN as LIZA HAMMOND (Eve Arden Show) (CBS)
SPRING BYINGTON as LILY RUSKIN (December Bride) (CBS)
JAN CLAYTON as AUNT ELLEN (Lassie) (CBS)
IDA LUPINO as EVE DRAKE (Mr. Adam and Eve) (CBS)

SERIES PERFORMANCE BY A COMEDIAN, SINGER, HOST, DANCER, M.C., ANNOUNCER, NARRATOR, PANELIST, OR ANY PERSON WHO ESSENTIALLY PLAYS HIMSELF (E-180)

JACK BENNY (Jack Benny Show) (CBS)
STEVE ALLEN (Steve Allen Show) (NBC)
SID CAESAR (Caesar's Hour) (NBC)
PERRY COMO (Perry Como Show) (NBC)
JACK PAAR (Tonight - Jack Paar) (NBC)

SERIES PERFORMANCE BY A COMEDIENNE, SINGER, HOSTESS, DANCER, M.C., ANNOUNCER, NARRATOR, PANELIST, OR ANY PERSON WHO ESSENTIALLY PLAYS HERSELF (E-181)

DINAH SHORE (Dinah Shore Chevy Show) (NBC)
GRACIE ALLEN (Burns and Allen Show) (CBS)
LUCILLE BALL (I Love Lucy) (CBS)
DODY GOODMAN (Tonight - Jack Paar) (NBC)
LORETTA YOUNG (Loretta Young Show) (NBC)

ACTOR - SINGLE PERFORMANCE - LEAD OR SUPPORT (E-182)

PETER USTINOV as SAMUEL JOHNSON The Life of Samuel Johnson (Omnibus) (NBC)
LEE J. COBB as PATHOLOGIST - DR. PEARSON No Deadly Medicine (Studio One) (CBS)
MICKEY ROONEY as SAMMY HOGARTH The Comedian (Playhouse 90) (CBS)
DAVID WAYNE as MENICK Heartbeat (Suspicion) (NBC)
ED WYNN as GRAMPS On Borrowed Time (Hallmark Hall of Fame) (NBC)

ACTRESS - SINGLE PERFORMANCE - LEAD OR SUPPORT (E-183)

POLLY BERGEN as HELEN MORGAN Helen Morgan Story (Playhouse 90) (CBS)
JULIE ANDREWS as CINDERELLA Cinderella (CBS)
HELEN HAYES as MRS. GILLING Mrs. Gilling and the Skyscraper (Alcoa Hour) (NBC)
PIPER LAURIE as RUTH CORNELIUS The Deaf Heart (Studio One) (CBS)
TERESA WRIGHT as ANNIE SULLIVAN The Miracle Worker (Playhouse 90) (CBS)

SUPPORTING ACTOR - DRAMATIC OR COMEDY SERIES (E-184)

CARL REINER Various Roles (Caesar's Hour) (NBC)
PAUL FORD as COLONEL HALL (Phil Silvers Show) (CBS)
BILL FRAWLEY as FRED MERTZ (I Love Lucy) (CBS)
LOUIS NYE as GORDON HATHAWAY (Steve Allen Show) (NBC)
DENNIS WEAVER as CHESTER (Gunsmoke) (CBS)

SUPPORTING ACTRESS - DRAMATIC OR COMEDY SERIES (E-185)

ANN B. DAVIS as SCHULTZY (Bob Cummings Show) (CBS & NBC)
PAT CARROLL Various Roles (Caesar's Hour) (NBC)
VERNA FELTON as HILDA CROCKER (December Bride) (CBS)
MARION LORNE as MRS. MABEL BANFORD (Sally) (NBC)
VIVIAN VANCE as ETHEL MERTZ (I Love Lucy) (CBS)

NEWS COMMENTARY (E-186)

EDWARD R. MURROW (See It Now) (CBS)
JOHN DALY News (ABC)
DOUGLAS EDWARDS News (CBS)
CHET HUNTLEY and DAVID BRINKLEY News (NBC)
ERIC SEVAREID World News Roundup (CBS)

TELEPLAY WRITING - HALF HOUR OR LESS (E-187)

PAUL MONASH The Lonely Wizard (Schlitz Playhouse of Stars) (CBS)
JOE CONNELLY and BOB MOSHER Beaver Gets Spelled (Leave it to Beaver) (CBS)
JOHN MESTON Born to Hang (Gunsmoke) (CBS)
ROSWELL ROGERS Margaret Hires a Gardener (Father Knows Best) (NBC)
MORTON WISHENGRAD A Chassidic Tale (Frontiers of Faith) (NBC)

TELEPLAY WRITING - ONE HOUR OR MORE (E-188)

ROD SERLING The Comedian (Playhouse 90) (CBS)
MARC CONNELLY Green Pastures (Hallmark Hall of Fame) (NBC)
WILLIAM GIBSON The Miracle Worker (Playhouse 90) (CBS)
ARTHUR HAILEY No Deadly Medicine (Studio One) (CBS)
JAMES LEE Life of Samuel Johnson (Omnibus) (NBC)

COMEDY WRITING (E-189)

NAT HIKEN, BILLY FRIEDBERG, PHIL SHARP, TERRY RYAN, COLEMAN JACOBY, ARNOLD ROSEN, SIDNEY ZELINKA, A.J. RUSSELL and TONY WEBSTER (Phil Silvers Show) (CBS)
ERNIE KOVACS No Dialogue Show (Ernie Kovacs Show) (NBC)
SAM PERRIN, GEORGE BALZER, AL GORDON, HAL GOLDMAN (Jack Benny Show) (CBS)
MEL TOLKIN, LARRY GELBART, MEL BROOKS, NEIL SIMON, SHELDON KELLER, MIKE STEWART, GARY BELKIN (Caesar's Hour) (NBC)
ROSWELL ROGERS and PAUL WEST (Father Knows Best) (NBC)

DIRECTION - HALF HOUR OR LESS (E-190)

ROBERT STEVENS The Glass Eye (Alfred Hitchcock Presents) (CBS)
BILL HOBIN (Your Hit Parade) (NBC)
CLARK JONES (Patrice Munsel Show) (ABC)
SHELDON LEONARD (Danny Thomas Show) (ABC & CBS)
PETER TEWKSBURY (Father Knows Best) (NBC)

DIRECTION - ONE HOUR OR MORE (E-191)

BOB BANNER Entire Series (Dinah Shore Chevy Show) (NBC)
JOHN FRANKENHEIMER The Comedian (Playhouse 90) (CBS)
GEORGE ROY HILL Helen Morgan Story (Playhouse 90) (CBS)
ARTHUR PENN The Miracle Worker (Playhouse 90) (CBS)
GEORGE SCHAEFER Green Pastures (Hallmark Hall of Fame) (NBC)

ART DIRECTION (E-192)

ROUBEN TER-ARUTUNIAN Twelfth Night (Hallmark Hall of Fame) (NBC)
BEULAH FRANKEL Don't Ever Come Back (Climax) (CBS)
HOWARD E. JOHNSON (Wagon Train) (NBC)
ROBERT KELLY (George Gobel Show) (NBC)
DON SHIRLEY (Perry Como Show) (NBC)

CINEMATOGRAPHY (E-193)

HAROLD E. WELLMAN Hemo The Magnificent (Bell Telephone Science Series) (CBS)
NORBERT BRODINE Miss Ashley's Demon (Loretta Young Show) (NBC)
ROBERT DE GRASSE Entire Series (Danny Thomas Show) (ABC & CBS)
GEORGE E. DISKANT Voices in the Fog (Goodyear Theatre) (NBC)
WILLIAM MARGULIES Outlaw (Have Gun--Will Travel) (CBS)

LIVE CAMERA WORK (E-194)

PLAYHOUSE 90 (CBS)
ANNIE GET YOUR GUN (NBC)
CINDERELLA (CBS)
GENERAL MOTORS 50th ANNIVERSARY SHOW (NBC)
WIDE WIDE WORLD (NBC)

FILM EDITING (E-195)

Eligible in this category are motion pictures made primarily for television release, rather than theatrical pictures edited or adapted for use on television.

MIKE POZEN How to Kill a Woman (Gunsmoke) (CBS)
SAMUEL E. BEETLEY The Tinhorn (Goodyear Theatre) (NBC)
DANNY LANDRES Lonely Wizard (Schlitz Playhouse of Stars) (CBS)
MICHAEL R. MC ADAM Trail to Christmas (G. E. Theatre) (CBS)
ROBERT SPARR The Quick and the Dead (Maverick) (ABC)

MUSICAL CONTRIBUTION (E-196)

LEONARD BERNSTEIN Conducting and Analyzing Music of Johann Sebastian Bach (Omnibus) (ABC)
MITCHELL AYRES Music Direction (Perry Como Show) (NBC)
ROBERT RUSSELL BENNETT Arranging and Conducting - The Innocent Years on Project 20 (NBC)
NELSON RIDDLE Arranging and Conducting (Frank Sinatra Show) (ABC)
RICHARD RODGERS Music Score Cinderella (CBS)

ENGINEERING OR TECHNICAL ACHIEVEMENT (E-197)

ENGINEERING AND CAMERA TECHNIQUES ON WIDE WIDE WORLD (NBC)
CHROMA KEY SYSTEM as developed by Frank Gaskins, Milt Altman, and Associates at NBC
COLOR MATTING AMPLIFIER (CBS)
DAGE VIDICON CAMERA adapted as a portable TV camera - Thompson Products Co.
LIVE PICK-UP FROM HAVANA OVER THE HORIZON (NBC)

TRUSTEES AWARD (E-198)

JACK BENNY For his significant contributions to the television industry as a showman. For the high standard, for all to emulate, set by his personal skill and excellence as a performer. For the consistency, quality and good taste of his programs through may years and many media.

1958/59

PROGRAM OF THE YEAR (E-199)

AN EVENING WITH FRED ASTAIRE (NBC)
CHILD OF OUR TIME (Playhouse 90) (CBS)
LITTLE MOON OF ALBAN (Hallmark Hall of Fame) (NBC)
THE OLD MAN (Playhouse 90) (CBS)

DRAMATIC SERIES - ONE HOUR OR LONGER (E-200)

PLAYHOUSE 90 (CBS)
U.S. STEEL HOUR (CBS)

DRAMATIC SERIES - LESS THAN ONE HOUR (E-201)

ALCOA-GOODYEAR THEATRE (NBC)
ALFRED HITCHCOCK PRESENTS (CBS)
GENERAL ELECTRIC THEATRE (CBS)
LORETTA YOUNG SHOW (NBC)
THE NAKED CITY (ABC)
PETER GUNN (NBC)

COMEDY SERIES (E-202)

JACK BENNY SHOW (CBS)
BOB CUMMINGS SHOW (NBC)
DANNY THOMAS SHOW (CBS)
FATHER KNOWS BEST (CBS & NBC)
PHIL SILVERS SHOW (CBS)
RED SKELTON SHOW (CBS)

MUSICAL OR VARIETY SERIES (E-203)

DINAH SHORE-CHEVY SHOW (NBC)
PERRY COMO SHOW (NBC)
STEVE ALLEN SHOW (NBC)

WESTERN SERIES (E-204)

MAVERICK (ABC)
GUNSMOKE (CBS)
HAVE GUN, WILL TRAVEL (CBS)
THE RIFLEMAN (ABC)
WAGON TRAIN (NBC)

PUBLIC SERVICE PROGRAM OR SERIES (E-205)

OMNIBUS (NBC)
BOLD JOURNEY (ABC)
MEET THE PRESS (NBC)
SMALL WORLD (CBS)
THE TWENTIETH CENTURY (CBS)
YOUNG PEOPLE'S CONCERTS - N.Y. PHILHARMONIC (CBS)

NEWS REPORTING SERIES (E-206)

HUNTLEY-BRINKLEY REPORT (NBC)
DOUGLAS EDWARDS WITH THE NEWS (CBS)
JOHN DALY AND THE NEWS (ABC)

PANEL, QUIZ, OR AUDIENCE PARTICIPATION SERIES (E-207)

WHAT'S MY LINE? (CBS)
I'VE GOT A SECRET (CBS)
KEEP TALKING (CBS)
THE PRICE IS RIGHT (NBC)
THIS IS YOUR LIFE (NBC)
YOU BET YOUR LIFE (NBC)

SPECIAL DRAMATIC PROGRAM - ONE HOUR OR LONGER (E-208)

LITTLE MOON OF ALBAN (Hallmark Hall of Fame) (NBC)
THE BRIDGE OF SAN LUIS REY (Du Pont Show of the Month) (CBS)
HAMLET (Du Pont Show of the Month) (CBS)
THE HASTY HEART (Du Pont Show of the Month) (CBS)
JOHNNY BELINDA (Hallmark Hall of Fame) (NBC)

SPECIAL MUSICAL OR VARIETY PROGRAM - ONE HOUR OR LONGER (E-209)

AN EVENING WITH FRED ASTAIRE (NBC)
ART CARNEY MEETS "PETER AND THE WOLF" (ABC)

SPECIAL NEWS PROGRAM (E-210)

FACE OF RED CHINA (CBS)
AMERICAN GI'S IN LEBANON (Outlook) (NBC)
ELECTION NIGHT RETURNS (CBS)
PROJECTION '59 (NBC)
THE STORY OF ATLAS 10B (Chet Huntley Reporting) (NBC)
WHERE WE STAND II (CBS)
YEARS OF CRISIS (CBS)

ACTOR - CONTINUING PERFORMANCE - DRAMATIC SERIES (E-211)

RAYMOND BURR as PERRY MASON (Perry Mason) (CBS)
JAMES ARNESS as MATT DILLON (Gunsmoke) (CBS)
RICHARD BOONE as PALADIN (Have Gun, Will Travel) (CBS)
JAMES GARNER as BRET MAVERICK (Maverick) (ABC)
CRAIG STEVENS as PETER GUNN (Peter Gunn) (NBC)
EFREM ZIMBALIST, JR. as STUART BAILEY (77 Sunset Strip) (ABC)

ACTRESS - CONTINUING PERFORMANCE - DRAMATIC SERIES (E-212)

LORETTA YOUNG as HOSTESS (Loretta Young Show) (NBC)
PHYLLIS KIRK as NORA CHARLES (The Thin Man) (NBC)
JUNE LOCKHART as MOTHER (Lassie) (CBS)
JANE WYMAN as HOSTESS (Jane Wyman Show) (NBC)

ACTOR - CONTINUING CHARACTER - COMEDY SERIES (E-213)

JACK BENNY as HIMSELF (Jack Benny Show) (CBS)
WALTER BRENNAN as "GRAMPA" (The Real McCoys) (ABC)
BOB CUMMINGS as BOB COLLINS (Bob Cummings Show) (NBC)
PHIL SILVERS as SGT. BILKO (Phil Silvers Show) (CBS)
DANNY THOMAS as DANNY WILLIAMS (Danny Thomas Show) (CBS)
ROBERT YOUNG as JIM ANDERSON (Father Knows Best) (CBS & NBC)

ACTRESS - CONTINUING CHARACTER - COMEDY SERIES (E-214)

JANE WYATT as MARGARET ANDERSON (Father Knows Best) (CBS & NBC)
GRACIE ALLEN as HERSELF (Burns & Allen) (CBS)
SPRING BYINGTON as LILY RUSKIN (December Bride) (CBS)
IDA LUPINO as EVE DRAKE (Mr. Adams and Eve) (CBS)
DONNA REED as DONNA STONE (Donna Reed Show) (ABC)
ANN SOTHERN as KATIE O'CONNOR (Ann Sothern Show) (CBS)

SUPPORTING ACTOR - DRAMATIC SERIES (E-215)

DENNIS WEAVER as CHESTER (Gunsmoke) (CBS)
HERSCHEL BERNARDI as LT. JACOBY (Peter Gunn) (NBC)
JOHNNY CRAWFORD as MARK MC CAIN (The Rifleman) (ABC)
WILLIAM HOPPER as PAUL DRAKE (Perry Mason) (CBS)

SUPPORTING ACTRESS - DRAMATIC SERIES (E-216)

BARBARA HALE as DELLA STREET (Perry Mason) (CBS)
LOLA ALBRIGHT as EDIE HART (Peter Gunn) (NBC)
AMANDA BLAKE as KITTY (Gunsmoke) (CBS)
HOPE EMERSON as MOTHER (Peter Gunn) (NBC)

SUPPORTING ACTOR - COMEDY SERIES (E-217)

TOM POSTON as MAN IN THE STREET, OTHERS (Steve Allen Show) (NBC)
RICHARD CRENNA as LUKE MC COY (The Real McCoys) (ABC)
PAUL FORD as COLONEL HALL (Phil Silvers Show) (CBS)
MAURICE GOSFIELD as PVT. DOBERMAN (Phil Silvers Show) (CBS)
BILLY GRAY as BUD ANDERSON (Father Knows Best) (CBS & NBC)
HARRY MORGAN as PETE (December Bride) (CBS)

SUPPORTING ACTRESS - COMEDY SERIES (E-218)

ANN B. DAVIS as SCHULTZY (Bob Cummings Show) (NBC)
ROSEMARY DE CAMP as MARGARET COLLINS (Bob Cummings Show) (NBC)
ELINOR DONAHUE as BETTY ANDERSON (Father Knows Best) (CBS & NBC)
VERNA FELTON as HILDA (December Bride) (CBS)
KATHY NOLAN as KATE MC COY (The Real McCoys) (ABC)
ZA SU PITTS as MISS NUGENT (Oh Susanna) (CBS)

ACTOR - MUSICAL OR VARIETY SERIES (E-219)

PERRY COMO (Perry Como Show) (NBC)
STEVE ALLEN (Steve Allen Show) (NBC)
JACK PAAR (Jack Paar Show) (NBC)

ACTRESS - MUSICAL OR VARIETY SERIES (E-220)

DINAH SHORE (Dinah Shore Chevy Show) (NBC)
PATTI PAGE (Patti Page Show) (ABC)

SINGLE PERFORMANCE BY AN ACTOR (E-221)

Any type or length program, live or film

FRED ASTAIRE as FRED ASTAIRE (An Evening with Fred Astaire) (NBC)
ROBERT CRAWFORD as TANGUY Child of our Time (Playhouse 90) (CBS)
PAUL MUNI as SAM ARLEN Last Clear Chance (Playhouse 90) (CBS)
CHRISTOPHER PLUMMER as KENNETH BOYD Little Moon of Alban (Hallmark Hall of Fame) (NBC)
MICKEY ROONEY as EDDIE Eddie (Alcoa-Goodyear Theatre) (NBC)
ROD STEIGER as HARVEY DENTON A Town Has Turned to Dust (Playhouse 90) (CBS)

SINGLE PERFORMANCE BY AN ACTRESS (E-222)

Any type or length program, live or film

JULIE HARRIS as BRIGID MARY Little Moon of Alban (Hallmark Hall of Fame) (NBC)
JUDITH ANDERSON as MARQUESA DE MONTEMAYOR Bridge of San Luis Rey (Du Pont Show of the Month) (CBS)
HELEN HAYES as MOTHER SERAPHIM One Red Rose for Christmas (U.S. Steel Hour) (CBS)
PIPER LAURIE as KIRSTEN CLAY Days of Wine and Roses (Playhouse 90) (CBS)
GERALDINE PAGE as THE YOUNG WOMAN The Old Man (Playhouse 90) (CBS)
MAUREEN STAPLETON as SADIE BURKE All the Kings Men (Kraft Theatre) (NBC)

NEWS COMMENTATOR OR ANALYST (E-223)

EDWARD R. MURROW (CBS)
JOHN DALY (ABC)
CHET HUNTLEY (NBC)

DIRECTION - SINGLE PROGRAM OF A DRAMATIC SERIES - LESS THAN ONE HOUR (E-224)

JACK SMIGHT Eddie (Alcoa-Goodyear Theatre) (NBC)
HERSCHEL DAUGHERTY One is a Wanderer (General Electric Theatre) (CBS)
BLAKE EDWARDS The Kill (Peter Gunn) (NBC)
ALFRED HITCHCOCK Lamb to the Slaughter (Alfred Hitchcock Presents) (CBS)
JAMES NEILSON Kid at the Stick (General Electric Theatre) (CBS)

DIRECTION - SINGLE DRAMATIC PROGRAM - ONE HOUR OR LONGER (E-225)

GEORGE SCHAEFER Little Moon of Alban (Hallmark Hall of Fame) (NBC)
JOHN FRANKENHEIMER A Town has Turned to Dust (Playhouse 90) (CBS)
GEORGE ROY HILL Child of our Time (Playhouse 90) (CBS)

DIRECTION - SINGLE PROGRAM, COMEDY SERIES (E-226)

PETER TEWKSBURY Medal for Margaret (Father Knows Best) (CBS)
HY AVERBACK Kate's Career (The Real McCoys) (ABC)
SEYMOUR BERNS Jack Benny Show with Gary Cooper (Jack Benny Show) (CBS)
RICHARD KINON The Interview (Mr. Adams and Eve) (CBS)
SHELDON LEONARD Pardon My Accent (Danny Thomas Show) (CBS)

DIRECTION - SINGLE MUSICAL OR VARIETY PROGRAM (E-227)

BUD YORKIN (An Evening with Fred Astaire) (NBC)
CLARK JONES Perry Como Show with Maureen O'Hara, Robert Preston (Perry Como Show) (NBC)
GOWER CHAMPION, JOE CATES Accent on Love (Pontiac Star Parade) (NBC)

WRITING - SINGLE PROGRAM OF A DRAMATIC SERIES - LESS THAN ONE HOUR (E-228)

ALFRED BRENNER, KEN HUGHES Eddie (Alcoa-Goodyear Theatre) (NBC)
ROALD DAHL Lamb to the Slaughter (Alfred Hitchcock Presents) (CBS)
BLAKE EDWARDS The Kill (Peter Gunn) (NBC)
CHRISTOPHER KNOPF The Loudmouth (Alcoa-Goodyear Theatre) (NBC)
SAMUEL TAYLOR One is a Wanderer (From story by James Thurber) (General Electric Theatre) (CBS)

WRITING - SINGLE DRAMATIC PROGRAM - ONE HOUR OR LONGER (E-229)

JAMES COSTIGAN Little Moon of Alban (Hallmark Hall of Fame) (NBC)
HORTON FOOTE The Old Man (From story by William Faulkner) (Playhouse 90) (CBS)
J.P. MILLER Days of Wine and Roses (Playhouse 90) (CBS)
IRVING GAYNOR NEIMAN Child of Our Time (From novel by Michael De Castillo) (Playhouse 90) (CBS)
ROD SERLING A Town Has Turned to Dust (Playhouse 90) (CBS)

WRITING - SINGLE PROGRAM, COMEDY SERIES (E-230)

SAM PERRIN, GEORGE BALZER, HAL GOLDMAN, AL GORDON Jack Benny Show with Ernie Kovacs (Jack Benny Show) (CBS)
BILLY FRIEDBERG, ARNIE ROSEN, COLEMAN JACOBY Bilko's Vampire (Phil Silvers Show) (CBS)
PAUL HENNING, DICK WESSON Grampa Clobbers the Air Force (Bob Cummings Show) (NBC)
BILL MANHOFF Once There Was a Traveling Salesman (The Real

1958/59—Fred Astaire (Best Single Performance by an Actor), Bud Yorkin (Best Writing—Single Musical or Variety Program), and David Rose (Best Musical Contribution)

1959/60—Outstanding Directorial Achievement in Comedy: Bud Yorkin and Jack Benny (accepting for Ralph Levy)

1961/62—Franklin Schaffner (Outstanding Directorial Achievement in Drama), with Jack Webb and Barbara Stanwyck (presenters)

McCoys) (ABC)
ROSWELL ROGERS Medal for Margaret (Father Knows Best) (CBS)

WRITING - SINGLE MUSICAL OR VARIETY PROGRAM (E-231)

BUD YORKIN, HERBERT BAKER (An Evening with Fred Astaire) (NBC)
GOODMAN ACE, MORT GREEN, GEORGE FOSTER, JAY BURTON (Perry Como Show with Pier Angeli, Andy Griffith, Helen O'Connell) (NBC)
LARRY GELBART, WOODY ALLEN (Sid Caesar's Chevy Show with Shirley MacLaine, Art Carney, Jo Stafford (NBC)
A.J. RUSSELL Art Carney Meets "Peter and the Wolf" (ABC)
LEONARD STERN, STAN BURNS, HERB SARGENT, BILL DANA, DON HINKLEY, HAL GOODMAN, LARRY KLEIN (Steve Allen Show with Peter Ustinov, Louis Armstrong, Van Cliburn) (NBC)

CINEMATOGRAPHY (E-232)

ELLIS W. CARTER Alphabet Conspiracy (Bell Telephone Special) (NBC)
FRED JACKMAN, JR. Corporal Hardy (Alcoa-Goodyear Theatre) (NBC)
WILLIAM MARGULIES Ella West (Have Gun, Will Travel) (CBS)
MACK STENGLER Day of Glory (Jane Wyman Show) (NBC)
HAROLD STINE Shady Deal at Sunny Acres (Maverick) (ABC)
RALPH WOOLSEY Diamond in the Rough (Maverick) (ABC)

LIVE CAMERA WORK (E-233)

Any type or length program

AN EVENING WITH FRED ASTAIRE (NBC)
BRIDGE OF SAN LUIS REY (DuPont Show of the Month) (CBS)
CHILD OF OUR TIME (Playhouse 90) (CBS)
THE OLD MAN (Playhouse 90) (CBS)
A TOWN HAS TURNED TO DUST (Playhouse 90) (CBS)

ART DIRECTION - FILM (E-234)

Any type or length program

CLAUDIO GUZMAN Bernadette (Westinghouse Desilu Playhouse) (CBS)
RALPH BERGER, CHARLES F. PYKE The Duchess of Denver (The Texan) (CBS)
JOHN MC CORMACK Corporal Hardy (Alcoa-Goodyear Theatre) (NBC)
ALBERT M. PYKE Man From Paris (The Californians) (NBC)
FRANK SYLOS Most Honorable Day (Loretta Young Show) (NBC)

ART DIRECTION - LIVE PROGRAM (E-235)

Any type or length

EDWARD STEPHENSON (An Evening with Fred Astaire) (NBC)
WARREN CLYMER Little Moon of Alban (Hallmark Hall of Fame) (NBC)
WALTER SCOTT HERNDON The Old Man (Playhouse 90) (CBS)
BOB MARKELL Hamlet (Du Pont Show of the Month) (CBS)
JAN SCOTT Hans Brinker or The Silver Skates (Hallmark Hall of Fame) (NBC)
ROBERT WADE Count of Monte Cristo (Du Pont Show of the Month) (CBS)

FILM EDITING (E-236)

Any type or length

SILVIO D'ALISERA Meet Mr. Lincoln (Project 20) (NBC)
ROBERT CRAWFORD Grandpa Clobbers the Air Force (Bob Cummings Show) (NBC)
RICHARD FANTL Eddie (Alcoa-Goodyear Theatre) (NBC)
DANNY B. LANDRES Long Distance (Schlitz Playhouse) (CBS)
ROBERT T. SPARR Rope of Cards (Maverick) (ABC)
RICHARD VAN ENGER Two Graves for Swan Valley (Bat Masterson) (NBC)
ROBERT WATTS Saga of Waco Williams (Maverick)

MUSICAL CONTRIBUTION (E-237)

Regular or special, any length, live or film

DAVID ROSE Musical direction of An Evening with Fred Astaire (NBC)
FRANK DE VOL Musical direction of Lux Show starring Rosemary Clooney (NBC)
BERNARD GREEN Musical direction of Johnny Belinda on Hallmark Hall of Fame (NBC)
HENRY MANCINI Composing Peter Gunn theme (NBC)
EDDY MANSON Composing and conducting music for Harvey on Du Pont Show of the Month (CBS)
PAUL WESTON Composing and conducting music for Art Carney Meets "Peter and the Wolf" (ABC)

CHOREOGRAPHY (E-238)

Any type or length program, live or film

HERMES PAN An Evening with Fred Astaire (NBC)
GENE KELLY Dancing is a Man's Game (Omnibus) (NBC)

ENGINEERING OR TECHNICAL ACHIEVEMENT (E-239)

Industry-wide improvement of editing of Video Tape as exemplified by ABC-CBS-NBC
Practical application of automation to TV program switching (NBC) Washington, D.C.
RCA Development of Color Video Tape

ON-THE-SPOT COVERAGE OF A NEWS EVENT - ANY LENGTH, LIVE OR FILM (E-240)

CBS Cuban Revolution. Live interview with new president. Jack Fern, Film Director; Correspondents, Stuart Novins and Richard Bate; Frank Donghi, Coordinator; Cameramen, Paul Rubenstein, Ralph Santos, Larry Smith.
CBS Lebanon Civil War Street Battle - Beirut. Frank Kearns, Correspondent; Paul Bruck, Cameraman.
NBC First Air Force attempt to probe the moon. Frank McGee of NBC News Washington, Roy Neal of NBC News Los Angeles; Producer Chet Hagen, NBC New York; Director, Jim Kitchell, NBC New York.
ABC Election of Pope John XXIII. John Secondari; Director, Marshall Diskin.
CBS Chicago Fire at Our Lady of Angels Parochial School. George Faber, Producer; Reporters, Joe Sauris, Hugh Hill, Frank Reynolds; Cameramen, Maury Bleckman, John Richardson, Irv Heberg, Wesley Marks.
CBS Crash of American Airlines Electra off LaGuardia into Flushing Bay. Paul Levitan, Producer; Don Hewitt, Director; Tom Costigan, Correspondent; Reporters Phil Scheffler, Charles Kuralt, Sam Jaffe, Bob Schakne; Cameramen, Arthur Kingham, George Snyder, Larry Racies, Lou Hutt, Mike Evdokimoff, Irving Heitzner.

TRUSTEES AWARD (E-241)

BOB HOPE - Presented with appreciation and admiration for bringing the great gift of laughter to all peoples of all nations; for selflessly entertaining American troops throughout the world over many years; and for making television finer by these deeds and by the consistently high quality of his television programs through the years.

1959/60

PROGRAM ACHIEVEMENT - HUMOR (E-242)

A regular program, a special program, or a series, any length, live, tape or film

ART CARNEY SPECIAL (NBC)
DANNY THOMAS SHOW (CBS)
FATHER KNOWS BEST (CBS)
JACK BENNY SHOW (CBS)
RED SKELTON SHOW (CBS)

PROGRAM ACHIEVEMENT - DRAMA (E-243)

A regular program, a special program, or a series, any length, live, tape or film

PLAYHOUSE 90 (CBS)
ETHAN FROME (Du Pont Show of the Month) (CBS)
THE MOON AND SIXPENCE (NBC)
THE TURN OF THE SCREW (Ford Startime) (NBC)
THE UNTOUCHABLES (ABC)

PROGRAM ACHIEVEMENT - VARIETY (E-244)

A regular program, a special program, or a series, any length, live, tape or film

FABULOUS FIFTIES (CBS)
ANOTHER EVENING WITH FRED ASTAIRE (NBC)
DINAH SHORE CHEVY SHOW (NBC)
GARRY MOORE SHOW (CBS)
TONIGHT WITH BELAFONTE (Revlon Revue) (CBS)

PROGRAM ACHIEVEMENT - NEWS (E-245)

A regular program, a special program, or a series, any length, live, tape or film

HUNTLEY-BRINKLEY REPORT (NBC)
CHET HUNTLEY REPORTING (NBC)
DOUGLAS EDWARDS WITH THE NEWS (CBS)
JOURNEY TO UNDERSTANDING (NBC)
KHRUSHCHEV'S ARRIVAL, APPEARANCE AT NATIONAL PRESS CLUB, SPEECH TO THE NATION (Pool Coverage by NBC)

PROGRAM ACHIEVEMENT - PUBLIC AFFAIRS AND EDUCATION (E-246)

A regular program, a special program, or a series, any length, live, tape or film

TWENTIETH CENTURY (CBS)
MEET THE PRESS, (NBC)
THE POPULATION EXPLOSION (CBS Reports) (CBS)
SMALL WORLD (CBS)
WINTER OLYMPICS (CBS)

PROGRAM ACHIEVEMENT - CHILDREN'S PROGRAMMING (E-247)

A regular program, a special program, or a series, any length, live, tape or film

HUCKLEBERRY HOUND (Syndicated)
CAPTAIN KANGAROO (CBS)
LASSIE (CBS)
QUICK DRAW MC GRAW (Syndicated)
WATCH MR. WIZARD (NBC)

PROGRAM ACHIEVEMENT - MUSIC (E-248)

A regular program, a special program or a series, any length, live, tape or film, composing, arranging, conducting, etc.

LEONARD BERNSTEIN AND THE NEW YORK PHILHARMONIC (CBS)
BELL TELEPHONE HOUR (NBC)
GREEN PASTURES (Hallmark Hall of Fame) (NBC)
MUSIC OF GERSHWIN (Bell Telephone Hour) (NBC)
YOUNG PEOPLE'S CONCERTS Leonard Bernstein (CBS)

ACTOR - SINGLE PERFORMANCE - LEAD OR SUPPORT (E-249)

Single performance only, any length, live, tape or film

LAURENCE OLIVIER The Moon and Sixpence (NBC)
LEE J COBB Project Immortality (Playhouse 90) (CBS)

ALEC GUINNESS The Wicked Scheme of Jebal Deeks (Ford Startime) (NBC)

ACTRESS - SINGLE PERFORMANCE - LEAD OR SUPPORT (E-250)

Single performance only, any length, live, tape or film

INGRID BERGMAN The Turn of the Screw (Ford Startime) (NBC)
JULIE HARRIS Ethan Frome (Du Pont Show of the Month) (CBS)
TERESA WRIGHT Margaret Bourke-White Story (Breck Sunday Showcase) (NBC)

ACTOR - SERIES - LEAD OR SUPPORT (E-251)

Continued performance only, any length, live, tape or film

ROBERT STACK (The Untouchables) (ABC)
RICHARD BOONE (Have Gun, Will Travel) (CBS)
RAYMOND BURR (Perry Mason) (CBS)

ACTRESS - SERIES - LEAD OR SUPPORT (E-252)

Continued performance only, any length, live, tape, or film

JANE WYATT (Father Knows Best) (CBS)
DONNA REED (Donna Reed Show) (ABC)
LORETTA YOUNG (Loretta Young Show) (NBC)

PERFORMANCE IN A VARIETY OR MUSICAL PROGRAM OR SERIES (E-253)

Regular or special, any length, live, tape or film

HARRY BELAFONTE Tonight with Belafonte (Revlon Revue) (CBS)
FRED ASTAIRE Another Evening with Fred Astaire (NBC)
DINAH SHORE (Dinah Shore Chevy Show) (NBC)

WRITING ACHIEVEMENT - DRAMA (E-254)

Regular or special, any length, live, tape or film

ROD SERLING Various Episodes (Twilight Zone) (CBS)
JAMES COSTIGAN The Turn of the Screw (Ford Startime) (NBC)
LORI MANDEL Project Immortality (Plahouse 90) (CBS)

WRITING ACHIEVEMENT - COMEDY (E-255)

Regular or special, any length, live, tape or film

SAM PERRIN, GEORGE BALZER, AL GORDON, HAL GOLDMAN (Jack Benny Show) (CBS)
DOROTHY COOPER, ROSWELL ROGERS Various Episodes (Father Knows Best) (CBS)
NAT HIKEN Ballad of Louie The Louse (CBS)

WRITING ACHIEVEMENT - DOCUMENTARY (E-256)

Regular or special, any length, live, tape or film

HOWARD K. SMITH, AV WESTIN The Population Explosion (CBS)
JAMES BENJAMIN From Kaiser to Fuehrer (Twentieth Century) (CBS)
RICHARD F. HANSER Life in the Thirties (Project 20) (NBC)

DIRECTORIAL ACHIEVEMENT - DRAMA (E-257)

Regular or special, any length, live, tape or film

ROBERT MULLIGAN The Moon and Sixpence (NBC)
JOHN FRANKENHEIMER The Turn of the Screw (Ford Startime) (NBC)
PHIL KARLSON The Untouchables (Westinghouse-Desilu Playhouse) (CBS)

DIRECTORIAL ACHIEVEMENT - COMEDY (E-258)

Regular or special, any length, live, tape or film

RALPH LEVY, BUD YORKIN, (Jack Benny Hour Specials) (CBS)
SEYMOUR BERNS, (Red Skelton Show) (CBS)
SHELDON LEONARD (Danny Thomas Show) (CBS)

ART DIRECTION AND SCENIC DESIGN (E-259)

Any type or length program or series

RALPH BERGER and FRANK SMITH The Untouchables (Westinghouse-Desilu Playhouse) (CBS)
CHARLES LISANBY (Garry Moore Show) (CBS)
JOHN J. LLOYD Various Episodes (Alfred Hitchcock Presents) (CBS)

CINEMATOGRAPHY (E-260)

Any type or length filmed program or series

CHARLES STRAUMER The Untouchables (Westinghouse-Desilu Playhouse) (CBS)
WILLIAM MARGULIES The Morrison Story (The Lawless Years) (NBC)
RALPH WOOLSEY Secret Island (77 Sunset Strip) (ABC)

ELECTRONIC CAMERA WORK (E-261)

Any type or length program or series

WINTER OLYMPICS (CBS)
PLAYHOUSE 90 (CBS)
THE TURN OF THE SCREW (Ford Startime) (NBC)

ENGINEERING OR TECHNICAL ACHIEVEMENT (E-262)

In picture, in sound, in development of technical equipment, etc.

THE NEW GENERAL ELECTRIC SUPERSENSITIVE CAMERA TUBE permitting colorcasting in no more light than is needed for black and white.
THE BRITISH BROADCASTING CORPORATION and THE NATIONAL BROADCASTING COMPANY for the development of the cable-film process speeding the transmission of overseas events.

FILM EDITING (E-263)

Any type or length filmed program

BEN H. RAY, ROBERT L. SWANSON (The Untouchables) (ABC)
DAN LANDRES The Patsy (General Electric Theatre) (CBS)
EDWARD WILLIAMS Man from the South (Alfred Hitchcock Presents) (CBS)

TRUSTEES AWARD (E-264)

DR. FRANK STANTON, President, The Columbia Broadcasting System, Inc. by forthright and courageous action, has advanced immeasurably the freedom of television as an arm of the free press and in so doing has strengthened the total freedom of television.

TRUSTEES CITATION (E-265)

THE AMPEX CORPORATION, THE RADIO CORPORATION OF AMERICA, MICHAEL R. GARGIULO, RICHARD GILLASPY In recognition of the cooperative effort of all phases of television production - For capturing on Videotape the Nixon-Khrushchev debate of July 25, 1959 in Moscow.

1960/61

PROGRAM ACHIEVEMENT - HUMOR (E-266)

A regular program, a special program, or a series, any length, live, tape or film

JACK BENNY SHOW (CBS)
ANDY GRIFFITH SHOW (CBS)
BOB HOPE BUICK SHOW (NBC)
CANDID CAMERA (CBS)
FLINTSTONES (ABC)

PROGRAM ACHIEVEMENT - DRAMA (E-267)

A regular program, a special program, or a series, any length, live, tape or film

MACBETH (Hallmark Hall of Fame) (NBC)
NAKED CITY (ABC)
SACCO-VANZETTI (NBC)
TWILIGHT ZONE (CBS)
THE UNTOUCHABLES (ABC)

PROGRAM ACHIEVEMENT - VARIETY (E-268)

A regular program, a special program, or a series, any length, live, tape or film

ASTAIRE TIME (NBC)
BELAFONTE, N.Y. 19 (CBS)
GARRY MOORE SHOW (CBS)
AN HOUR WITH DANNY KAYE (CBS)
JACK PAAR SHOW (NBC)

PROGRAM ACHIEVEMENT - NEWS (E-269)

A regular program, a special program, or a series, any length, live, tape or film

HUNTLEY-BRINKLEY REPORT (NBC)
CONVENTION COVERAGE (NBC)
DOUGLAS EDWARDS WITH THE NEWS (CBS)
EYEWITNESS TO HISTORY (CBS)
PRESIDENT KENNEDY'S LIVE NEWS CONFERENCES (ABC-CBS-NBC)

PROGRAM ACHIEVEMENT - PUBLIC AFFAIRS AND EDUCATION (E-270)

A regular program, a special program, or a series, any length, live, tape or film

THE TWENTIETH CENTURY (CBS)
CBS REPORTS (CBS)
PROJECT TWENTY (NBC)
THE U-2 AFFAIR (NBC White Paper) (NBC)
WINSTON CHURCHILL, THE VALIANT YEARS (ABC)

PROGRAM ACHIEVEMENT - CHILDREN'S PROGRAMMING (E-271)

A regular program, a special program, or a series, any length, live, tape or film

YOUNG PEOPLE'S CONCERT Aaron Copland's Birthday Party (CBS)
CAPTAIN KANGAROO (CBS)
HUCKLEBERRY HOUND (Syndicated)
SHARI LEWIS SHOW (NBC)
SHIRLEY TEMPLE SHOW (NBC)

ACTOR - SINGLE PERFORMANCE (E-272)

Single performance only, any length, live, tape or film

MAURICE EVANS Macbeth (Hallmark Hall of Fame) (NBC)
CLIFF ROBERTSON The Two Worlds of Charlie Gordon (U.S. Steel Hour) (CBS)
ED WYNN The Man in the Funny Suit (Westinghouse-Desilu Playhouse) (CBS)

ACTRESS - SINGLE PERFORMANCE (E-273)

Single performance only, any length, live, tape or film

JUDITH ANDERSON Macbeth (Hallmark Hall of Fame) (NBC)
INGRID BERGMAN 24 Hours in a Woman's Life (CBS)
ELIZABETH MONTGOMERY The Rusty Heller Story (The Untouchables) (ABC)

ACTOR - SERIES (E-274)

Continued performance only, any length, live, tape or film

RAYMOND BURR (Perry Mason) (CBS)
JACKIE COOPER (Hennesey) (CBS)
ROBERT STACK (The Untouchables) (ABC)

ACTRESS - SERIES (E-275)

Continued performance only, any length, live, tape or film

BARBARA STANWYCK (Barbara Stanwyck Show) (NBC)
DONNA REED (Donna Reed Show) (ABC)
LORETTA YOUNG (Loretta Young Show) (NBC)

SUPPORTING ACTOR OR ACTRESS - SINGLE PROGRAM (E-276)

Regular or special, any length, live tape or film

RODDY MC DOWALL Not Without Honor (Equitable's American Heritage) (NBC)
CHARLES BRONSON Memory in White (GE Theatre) (CBS)
PETER FALK Cold Turkey (The Law and Mr. Jones) (ABC)

SUPPORTING ACTOR OR ACTRESS - SERIES (E-277)

Continued performance only, any length, live, tape or film

DON KNOTTS as DEPUTY SHERIFF (Andy Griffith Show) (CBS)
ABBY DALTON as THE NURSE (Hennesey) (CBS)
BARBARA HALE as DELLA STREET (Perry Mason) (CBS)

PERFORMANCE IN A VARIETY OR MUSICAL PROGRAM OR SERIES (E-278)

Regular or special, any length, live, tape or film

FRED ASTAIRE Astaire Time (NBC)
HARRY BELAFONTE Belafonte, N.Y. 19 (CBS)
DINAH SHORE (Dinah Shore Chevy Show) (NBC)

PROGRAM OF THE YEAR (E-279)

That program, created originally or fully adapted for televison, which is considered to be the most outstanding presentation during the awards period. Such a program may be either one of a series or an individual presentation, either entertainment, public service or coverage of a newsworthy event, but may not include a duplicate or an approximate duplication of a presentation previously used in another medium.

MACBETH (Hallmark Hall of Fame) (NBC)
ASTAIRE TIME (NBC)
CONVENTION COVERAGE (NBC)
AN HOUR WITH DANNY KAYE (CBS)
SACCO-VANZETTI (NBC)

ACHIEVEMENT IN MUSIC (E-280)

Composing, arranging, conducting, etc, or a regular program, a special program, or a series any length, live, tape or film

LEONARD BERNSTEIN for (Leonard Bernstein and the New York Philharmonic) (CBS)
ANDRE PREVIN for the Donald O'Connor Show (NBC)
PETE RUGOLO, JERRY GOLDSMITH for The Thriller (NBC)

WRITING ACHIEVEMENT - DRAMA (E-281)

Regular or special, any length, live tape or film

ROD SERLING Various Episodes (The Twilight Zone) (CBS)
REGINALD ROSE Sacco-Vanzetti (NBC)
DALE WASSERMAN The Lincoln Murder Case (Du Pont of the Month) (CBS)

WRITING ACHIEVEMENT - COMEDY (E-282)

Regular or special, any length, live, tape or film

SHERWOOD SCHWARTZ, DAVE O'BRIEN, AL SCHWARTZ, MARTIN RAGAWAY, RED SKELTON Various Episodes (Red Skelton Show) (CBS)
RICHARD BAER Various Episodes (Hennesey) (CBS)
CHARLES STEWART, JACK ELINSON Various Episodes (The Danny Thomas Show) (CBS)

WRITING ACHIEVEMENT - DOCUMENTARY (E-283)

Regular or special, any length, live, tape or film

VICTOR WOLFSON Various Episodes (Winston Churchill, The Valiant Years) (ABC)
ARTHUR BARRON, AL WASSERMAN The U-2 Affair (NBC White Paper) (NBC)
FRED FRIENDLY, DAVID LOWE, EDWARD R. MURROW Harvest of Shame (CBS Reports) (CBS)

DIRECTORIAL ACHIEVEMENT - DRAMA (E-284)

Regular or special, any length, live, tape or film

GEORGE SCHAEFER Macbeth (Hallmark Hall of Fame) (NBC)
SIDNEY LUMET Sacco-Vanzetti (NBC)
RALPH NELSON The Man in the Funny Suit (Westinghouse-Desilu Playhouse) (CBS)

DIRECTORIAL ACHIEVEMENT - COMEDY (E-285)

Regular or special, any length, live, tape or film

SHELDON LEONARD (The Danny Thomas Show) (CBS)
JACK SHEA, RICHARD McDONOUGH (Bob Hope Buick Show) (NBC)
PETER TEWKSBURY (My Three Sons) (ABC)

ART DIRECTION AND SCENIC DESIGN (E-286)

Regular or special, any length, live, tape or film

JOHN J. LLOYD Various Episodes (Checkmate) (CBS)
GARY SMITH Various Episodes (Perry Como's Kraft Music Hall) (NBC)
JAC VENZA 24 Hours in a Woman's Life (CBS)

CINEMATOGRAPHY (E-287)

Any type or length filmed program or series

GEORGE CLEMENS Various Episodes (Twilight Zone) (CBS)
WILLIAM MARGULIES Outrage at Pawnee Bend (Outlaws) (NBC)
WALTER STRENGE Sam Elder Story (Wagon Train) (NBC)

ELECTRONIC CAMERA WORK (E-288)

Any type or length program or series

SOUNDS OF AMERICA (Bell Telephone Hour) (RED-EO-TAPE Mobile Unit for NBC)
DINAH SHORE CHEVY SHOW (NBC)
JOURNEY TO THE DAY (Playhouse 90) (CBS)
WRANGLER (KTLA-Hollywood Camera Crew for NBC)

FILM EDITING (E-289)

Any type or length filmed program or series

HARRY COSWICK, AARON NIBLEY, MILTON SHIFMAN Various Episodes (Naked City) (ABC)
RICHARD H. CAHOON, JOHN FAURE Various Episodes (Perry Mason) (CBS)
EDWARD W. WILLIAMS Incident in a Small Jail (Alfred Hitchcock Presents) (NBC)

ENGINEERING OR TECHNICAL ACHIEVEMENT (E-290)

RADIO CORPORATION OF AMERICA and MARCONI'S WIRELESS TELEGRAPH COMPANY, LTD. - ENGLISH ELECTRIC VALVE COMPANY, LTD. for the independent development of the 4 1/2 inch image orthicon tube and cameras.

TRUSTEES' AWARD (E-291)

NATIONAL EDUCATIONAL TELEVISION AND RADIO CENTER AND ITS AFFILIATED STATIONS - For its foresight and perseverence in promoting the development of Educational Television in the United States; and for its stimulation and transmission of the imaginative educational programs produced by the individual Educational Television Stations.

MR. JOYCE C. HALL, PRESIDENT OF HALLMARK CARDS, INC. - For his personal interest in uplifting the standards of television through complete sponsorship over a ten-year period of Hallmark Hall of Fame, which has brought many enriching hours of entertainment to the viewing public; and or furthering the interests of young playwrights by establishing the Hallmark Teleplay-Writing Competition.

1961/62

PROGRAM ACHIEVEMENT - HUMOR (E-292)

A regular program, a special program, or a series, any length, live, tape or film

BOB NEWHART SHOW (NBC)
ANDY GRIFFITH SHOW (CBS)
CAR 54, WHERE ARE YOU? (NBC)
HAZEL (NBC)
RED SKELTON SHOW (CBS)

PROGRAM ACHIEVEMENT - DRAMA (E-293)

A regular program, a special program, or a series, any length, live, tape or film

THE DEFENDERS (CBS)
BEN CASEY (ABC)
DICK POWELL SHOW (NBC)
NAKED CITY (ABC)
PEOPLE NEED PEOPLE (Alcoa Premiere) (ABC)
VICTORIA REGINA (Hallmark Hall of Fame) (NBC)

PROGRAM ACHIEVEMENT - VARIETY (E-294)

A regular program, a special program, or a series, any length, live, tape or film

GARRY MOORE SHOW (CBS)
HERE'S EDIE (ABC)
JUDY GARLAND SHOW (CBS)
PERRY COMO'S KRAFT MUSIC HALL (NBC)
WALT DISNEY'S WONDERFUL WORLD OF COLOR (NBC)

PROGRAM ACHIEVEMENT - MUSIC (E-295)

A regular program, a special program, or a series, any length, live, tape or film

LEONARD BERNSTEIN AND THE NEW YORK PHILHARMONIC IN JAPAN (CBS)
BELL TELEPHONE HOUR (NBC)
NBC OPERA (NBC)
THE THIEF AND THE HANGMAN (ABC)

PROGRAM ACHIEVEMENT - NEWS (E-296)

A regular program, a special program, or a series, any length, live, tape or film

HUNTLEY-BRINKLEY REPORT (NBC)
CAPITAL CITIES BROADCASTING FOR THE EICHMANN TRIAL (Syndicated)
DOUGLAS EDWARDS WITH THE NEWS (CBS)
EYEWITNESS (with Walter Cronkite) (CBS)
NBC-TV GULF INSTANT NEWS SPECIALS (NBC)

PROGRAM ACHIEVEMENT - EDUCATIONAL AND PUBLIC AFFAIRS PROGRAMMING (E-297)

A regular program, a special program, or a series, any length, live, tape or film

DAVID BRINKLEY'S JOURNAL (NBC)
ABC'S WIDE WORLD OF SPORTS (ABC)
BELL AND HOWELL CLOSE-UP (ABC)
CBS REPORTS (CBS)
HOWARD K. SMITH-NEWS AND COMMENT (ABC)
NBC WHITE PAPER (NBC)

PROGRAM ACHIEVEMENT - CHILDREN'S PROGRAMMING (E-298)

A regular program, a special program, or a series, any length, live, tape or film

NEW YORK PHILHARMONIC YOUNG PEOPLE'S CONCERTS WITH LEONARD BERNSTEIN (CBS)
CAPTAIN KANGAROO (CBS)
1, 2, 3, GO! (NBC)
SHARI LEWIS SHOW (NBC)
UPDATE (NBC)
WALT DISNEY'S WONDERFUL WORLD OF COLOR (NBC)

ACTOR - SINGLE PERFORMANCE (E-299)

Single performance only, any length, live, tape or film

PETER FALK as TRUCK DRIVER The Price of Tomatoes (Dick Powell Show) (NBC)
MILTON BERLE as DOYLE Doyle Against the House (Dick Powell Show) (NBC)
JAMES DONALD as PRINCE ALBERT Victoria Regina (Hallmark Hall of Fame) (NBC)
LEE MARVIN as SERGEANT HUGHES People Need People (Alcoa Premiere) (ABC)
MICKEY ROONEY as AUGIE MILLER Somebody's Waiting (Dick Powell Show) (NBC)

ACTRESS - SINGLE PERFORMANACE (E-300)

Single performance only, any length, live or film

JULIE HARRIS as VICTORIA Victoria Regina (Hallmark Hall of Fame) (NBC)
GERALDINE BROOKS as KATHERINE BARNES Call Back Yesterday (Bus Stop) (ABC)
SUZANNE PLESHETTE as JULIE LAWLER Shining Image (Dr. Kildare) (NBC)
INGER STEVENS as ANNA The Price of Tomatoes (Dick Powell Show)(NBC)
ETHEL WATERS as JENNY HENDERSON Goodnight Sweet Blues (Route 66) (CBS)

ACTOR - SERIES (E-301)

Continued performance only, any length, live, tape or film

E. G. MARSHALL as LAWRENCE PRESTON (The Defenders) (CBS)
PAUL BURKE as ADAM FLINT (Naked City) (ABC)
JACKIE COOPER as CHICK (Hennesey) (CBS)
VINCENT EDWARDS as DR. BEN CASEY (Ben Casey) (ABC)
GEORGE MAHARIS as BUZ (Route 66) (CBS)

ACTRESS - SERIES (E-302)

Continued performance only, any length, live tape or film

SHIRLEY BOOTH as HAZEL (Hazel) (NBC)
GERTRUDE BERG as MRS. G. (Gertrude Berg Show) (CBS)
DONNA REED as DONNA STONE (Donna Reed Show) (ABC)
MARY STUART as JOANNE TATE (Search For Tomorrow) (CBS)
CARA WILLIAMS as GLADYS (Pete and Gladys) (CBS)

SUPPORTING ACTOR (E-303)

Regular or special any length, live, tape or film

DON KNOTTS as DEPUTY BARNEY FIFE (Andy Griffith Show) (CBS)
SAM JAFFE as DR. ZORBA (Ben Casey) (ABC)
BARRY JONES as DEAN Victoria Regina (Hallmark Hall of Fame) (NBC)
HORACE McMAHON as PARKER (Naked City) (ABC)
GEORGE C. SCOTT as KARL ANDERS I Remember a Lemon Tree (Ben Casey) (ABC)

SUPPORTING ACTRESS (E-304)

Regular or special any length, live, tape or film

PAMELA BROWN as DUCHESS OF KENT Victoria Regina (Hallmark Hall of Fame) (NBC)
JEANNE COOPER as LINDA But Linda Only Smiled (Ben Casey) (ABC)
COLLEEN DEWHURST as GERTRUDE HART Focus (NBC)
JOAN HACKETT as ELLEN PARKER A Certain Time, A Certain Darkness (Ben Casey) (ABC)
MARY WICKES as MAXFIELD (Gertrude Berg Show) (CBS)

PERFORMANCE IN A VARIETY OR MUSICAL PROGRAM OR SERIES (E-305)

Regular or special any length, live, tape or film

CAROL BURNETT (Garry Moore Show) (CBS)
EDIE ADAMS Here's Edie (ABC)
PERRY COMO (Perry Como's Kraft Music Hall) (NBC)
JUDY GARLAND Judy Garland Show (CBS)
YVES MONTAND Yves Montand On Broadway (ABC)

DAYTIME PROGRAM (PROGRAM SPECIFICALLY CREATED FOR DAYTIME TELEVISION) (E-306)

Regular or special any length, live, tape or film

PUREX SPECIALS FOR WOMEN (NBC)
ART LINKLETTER'S HOUSE PARTY (CBS)
CALENDAR (CBS)
TODAY (NBC)
VERDICT IS YOURS (CBS)

PROGRAM OF THE YEAR (E-307)

That program, created originally or fully adapted for television, which is considered to be the most outstanding presentation during the awards period. Such a program may be either one of a series or an individual presentation, either entertainment, public service or coverage of a newsworthy event, but may not include a duplicate or an approximate duplication of a presentation previously used in another medium

VICTORIA REGINA (Hallmark Hall of Fame) (NBC)
BIOGRAPHY OF A BOOKIE JOINT (CBS Reports) (CBS)
JUDY GARLAND SHOW (CBS)
VINCENT VAN GOGH: A SELF PORTRAIT (NBC)
WALK IN MY SHOES (Bell and Howell Close-Up) (ABC)

ORIGINAL MUSIC FOR TELEVISION (E-308)

A regular program, a special program, or a series, any lenght, live tape, or film

RICHARD RODGERS (Winston Churchill-The Valiant Years) (ABC)
JACQUES BELASCO Vincent Van Gogh: A Self Portrait (NBC)
ROBERT RUSSELL BENNETT (Project 20) (NBC)
LEITH STEVENS The Price of Tomatoes (Dick Powell Show) (NBC)
JOHN WILLIAMS (Alcoa Premiere) (ABC)

WRITING ACHIEVEMENT - DRAMA (E-309)

A regular program, a special program, a series, or a single program of a series, any length, live, tape or film

REGINALD ROSE Various Episodes (The Defenders) (CBS)
HENRY F. GREENBERG People Need People (Alcoa Premiere) (ABC)
JACK LAIRD I Remember a Lemon Tree (Ben Casey) (ABC)
ROD SERLING Various Episodes (Twilight Zone) (CBS)
RICHARD ALAN SIMMONS The Price of Tomatoes (Dick Powell Show) (NBC)

WRITING ACHIEVEMENT - COMEDY (E-310)

A regular program, a special program, a series, or a single program of a series, any length, live, tape or film

CARL REINER (Dick Van Dyke Show) (CBS)
STAN FREBERG Chunking Chow Mein Hour (ABC)
NAT HIKEN, TONY WEBSTER, TERRY RYAN (Car 54, Where Are You?) (NBC)
ROLAND KIBBEE, BOB NEWHART, DON HINKLEY, MILT ROSEN, ERNIE CHAMBERS, DEAN HARGROVE, ROBERT KAUFMAN, NORM LIEBMAN, CHARLES SHERMAN, HOWARD SNYDER, LARRY SIEGEL (Bob Newhart Show) (NBC)
ED SIMMONS, DAVID O'BRIEN, MARTY RAGAWAY, ARTHUR PHILLIPS, AL SCHWARTZ, SHERWOOD SCHWARTZ, RED SKELTON (Red Skelton Show) (CBS)

WRITING ACHIEVEMENT - DOCUMENTARY (E-311)

A regular program, a special program, a series, or a single program of a series, any length, live, tape or film

LOU HAZAM Vincent Van Gogh; A Self Portrait (NBC)
ARTHUR HOLCH Walk In My Shoes (Bell and Howell Close-Up) (ABC)
GEORGE LEFFERTS (Purex Specials for Women) (NBC)
JAY McMULLEN Biography of a Bookie Joint (CBS Reports) (CBS)
AL WASSERMAN, ARTHUR ZEGART Battle for Newburgh (NBC White Paper) (NBC)

DIRECTORIAL ACHIEVEMENT - DRAMA (E-312)

A regular program, a special program, a series, or a single program of a series, any length, live, tape or film

FRANKLIN SCHAFFNER Various Episodes (The Defenders) (CBS)
ARTHUR HILLER Various Episodes (Naked City) (ABC)
BUZZ KULIK Shining Image (Dr. Kildare) (NBC)
GEORGE SCHAEFER Victoria Regina (Hallmark Hall of Fame) (NBC)
ALEX SEGAL People Need People (Alcoa Premiere) (ABC)
JACK SMIGHT Come Again to Carthage (Westinghouse Presents) (CBS)

DIRECTORIAL ACHIEVEMENT IN COMEDY (E-313)

A regular program, a special program, a series, or a single program of a series, any length, live, tape or film

NAT HIKEN (Car 54, Where Are You?) (NBC)
SEYMOUR BERNS (Red Skelton Show) (CBS)
DAVE GEISEL (Garry Moore Show) (CBS)

JOHN RICH (Dick Van Dyke Show) (CBS)
BUD YORKIN Henry Fonda and the Family (CBS)

ART DIRECTION AND SCENIC DESIGN (E-314)

A regular program, a special program, a series, or a single program of a series, any length, live, tape or film

GARY SMITH (Perry Como's Kraft Music Hall) (NBC)
PHILIP BARBER (Twilight Zone) (CBS)
CHARLES LISANBY (Garry Moore Show) (CBS)
JAN SCOTT (Theatre '62) (NBC)
BURR SMIDT The Power and the Glory (CBS)

CINEMATOGRAPHY (E-315)

Any type or length filmed program or series

JOHN S. PRIESTLEY (Naked City) (ABC)
GUY BLANCHARD Vincent Van Gogh: A Self Portrait (NBC)
WALTER CASTLE, HASKELL BOGGS (Bonanza) (NBC)
GEORGE CLEMENS (Twilight Zone) (CBS)
WALTER STRENGE (Wagon Train) (NBC)
TED VOIGTLANDER (Ben Casey) (ABC)

ELECTRONIC CAMERA WORK (E-316)

Any type or length program or series, live or taped

ERNIE KOVACS Ernie Kovacs Shows (ABC)
LOU ONOFRIO Judy Garland Show (CBS)
HEINO RIPPE (Perry Como's Kraft Music Hall) (NBC)
O. TAMBURRI Victoria Regina (Hallmark Hall of Fame) (NBC)

FILM EDITING (E-317)

Any type or length filmed program or series

HUGH CHALOUPKA, AARON NIBLEY, CHARLES L. FREEMAN (Naked City) (ABC)
ARAM BOYAJIAN, ROBERT COLLINSON, BERNARD FRIEND, LORA HAYS, WALTER KATZ, LAWRENCE SILK, HAROLD SILVER, LEO ZOCHLING (Twentieth Century) (CBS)
MARSTON FAY, GENE PALMER (Wagon Train) (NBC)
CONSTANTINE GOCHIS U.S. #1: American Profile (NBC)
RICHARD L. VAN ENGER, A.C.E. (Bus Stop) (ABC)

ENGINEERING OR TECHNICAL ACHIEVEMENT (E-318)

ABC VIDEO TAPE EXPANDER, or VTX-slow motion tape developed by ABC-Mr. Albert Malang, chief engineer, Video Facilities, ABC
AMTEC-device to correct timing faults on tape playbacks
INTERLEAVED SOUND-an NBC development which provides an emergency circuit available whenever there is a failure of the regular network television sound
SLOW MOTION KINESCOPE-as developed by CBS

TRUSTEES AWARD (E-319)

CBS NEWS FOR THE SPECIAL PROGRAM-A TOUR OF THE WHITE HOUSE
MRS. JACQUELINE KENNEDY A Tour of the White House.
THE HEADS OF THE NEWS DEPARTMENTS OF ABC, CBS AND NBC
John Glenn and Friendship VII space mission.
BRIGADIER GENERAL DAVID SARNOFF For his many years of vision and accomplishment.

1962/63

PROGRAM OF THE YEAR (E-320)

That program, created originally or fully adapted for television, which is considered to be the most outstanding presentation during the awards period. Such a program may be either one of a series or an individual presentation, either entertainment, public service or coverage of a newsworthy event, but may not include a duplicate or an approximate duplication of a presentation previously used in another medium.

THE TUNNEL (NBC)
THE DANNY KAYE SHOW WITH LUCILLE BALL (NBC)
THE MADMAN (The Defenders) (CBS)
THE VOICE OF CHARLIE PONT (Premiere Presented by Fred Astaire) (ABC)

PROGRAM ACHIEVEMENT - HUMOR (E-321)

A regular program, a special program, or a series - any length; live, tape or film

THE DICK VAN DYKE SHOW (CBS)
THE BEVERLY HILLBILLIES (CBS)
THE DANNY KAYE SHOW WITH LUCILLE BALL (NBC)
MCHALE'S NAVY (ABC)

PROGRAM ACHIEVEMENT - DRAMA (E-322)

A regular program, a special program, or a series - any length; live, tape or film

THE DEFENDERS (CBS)
ALCOA PREMIERE/PREMIERE, PRESENTED BY FRED ASTAIRE (ABC)
THE DICK POWELL THEATRE (NBC)
THE ELEVENTH HOUR (NBC)
NAKED CITY (ABC)

PROGRAM ACHIEVEMENT - MUSIC (E-323)

A regular program, a special program, or a series - any length; live, tape or film

JULIE AND CAROL AT CARNEGIE HALL (CBS)
BELL TELEPHONE HOUR (NBC)
JUDY GARLAND AND HER GUESTS PHIL SILVERS AND ROBERT GOULET (CBS)
THE LIVELY ONES (NBC)
NBC OPERA (NBC)

PROGRAM ACHIEVEMENT - VARIETY (E-324)

A regular program, a special program, or a series - any length; live, tape or film

THE ANDY WILLIAMS SHOW (NBC)
CAROL AND COMPANY (CBS)
THE GARRY MOORE SHOW (CBS)
HERE'S EDIE (ABC)
THE RED SKELTON HOUR (CBS)

PROGRAM ACHIEVEMENT - PANEL, QUIZ, OR AUDIENCE PARTICIPATION (E-325)

A regular program, a special program, or a series - any length; live, tape or film

G-E COLLEGE BOWL (CBS)
PASSWORD (CBS)
TO TELL THE TRUTH (CBS)

PROGRAM ACHIEVEMENT - CHILDREN'S PROGRAMMING (E-326)

A regular program, a special program, or a series - any length; live, tape or film

WALT DISNEY'S WONDERFUL WORLD OF COLOR (NBC)
CAPTAIN KANGAROO (CBS)
DISCOVERY '62-'63 (ABC)
THE SHARI LEWIS SHOW (NBC)
UPDATE WITH ROBERT ABERNATHY (NBC)
WATCH MR. WIZARD (NBC)

PROGRAM ACHIEVEMENT - DOCUMENTARY (E-327)

THE TUNNEL Produced by Reuven Frank (NBC)
EMERGENCY WARD (Du Pont Show of the Week) Produced by Irving Gitlin and Frank De Felitta; Written and Directed by Frank De Felitta (NBC)
HE IS RISEN (Project 20) Produced and Directed by Donald B Hyatt; Written by Richard Hanser (NBC)
THE RIVER NILE Produced and Written by Lou Hazam (NBC)
SHAKESPEARE: SOUL OF AN AGE Produced and Written by Lou Hazam (NBC)

PROGRAM ACHIEVEMENT - NEWS (E-328)

A regular program, a special program, or a series - any length; live, tape or film

HUNTLEY-BRINKLEY REPORT (NBC)
CBS NEWS EVENING REPORT WITH WALTER CRONKITE (CBS)
EYEWITNESS (CBS)
NBC SPECIAL NEWS REPORTS, GULF OIL CORPORATION (NBC)

PROGRAM ACHIEVEMENT - NEWS COMMENTARY OR PUBLIC AFFAIRS (E-329)

A regular program, a special program, or a series - any length; live, tape or film

DAVID BRINKLEY'S JOURNAL (NBC)
BELL & HOWELL CLOSE-UP! (ABC)
CBS REPORTS (CBS)
HOWARD K. SMITH, NEWS AND COMMENT (ABC)
TWENTIETH CENTURY (CBS)

ACHIEVEMENT IN INTERNATIONAL REPORTING OR COMMENTARY (E-330)

Overseas Origination - Person or Program

PIERS ANDERTON, BERLIN CORRESPONDENT, NBC for The Tunnel, (NBC)
GERMANY: FATHERS AND SONS with John Rich, Produced by George A. Vicas (NBC)
MARVIN KALB, MOSCOW CORRESPONDENT, CBS for general reporting (CBS)
JAMES ROBINSON, SOUTHEAST ASIA, NBC for general reporting (NBC)
JOHN SECONDARI for The Vatican, Produced by Helen Jean Rogers (Bell & Howell Close-Up!) (ABC)

ACTOR - SINGLE PERFORMANCE (E-331)

Single performance only - any length; live, tape or film

TREVOR HOWARD as DISRAELI The Invincible Mr. Disraeli (Hallmark Hall of Fame) (NBC)
BRADFORD DILLMAN as CHARLIE PONT The Voice of Charlie Pont (Premiere, Presented by Fred Astaire) (ABC)
DON GORDON as JOEY TASSILI The Madman (The Defenders) (CBS)
WALTER MATTHAU as MEREDITH Big Deal in Laredo (Du Pont Show of the Week) (NBC)
JOSEPH SCHILDKRAUT as RABBI GOTTLIEB Hear the Mellow Wedding Bells (Sam Benedict) (NBC)

ACTRESS - SINGLE PERFORMANCE (E-332)

Single performance only - any length; live, tape or film

KIM STANLEY as FAITH PARSONS A Cardinal Act of Mercy (Ben Casey) (ABC)
DIAHANN CARROLL as RUBY JAY A Horse Has a Big Head, Let Him Worry (Naked City) (ABC)
DIANA HYLAND as LIZA LAURENTS The Voice of Charlie Pont (Premiere, Presented by Fred Astaire) (ABC)
ELEANOR PARKER as CONNIE FOLSOM Why Am I Grown So Cold? (The Eleventh Hour) (NBC)
SYLVIA SIDNEY as ADELA The Madman (The Defenders) (CBS)

ACTOR - SERIES (E-333)

Continued performance only - any length; live, tape or film

E. G. MARSHALL as LAWRENCE PRESTON (The Defenders) (CBS)
ERNEST BORGNINE as LT. COMDR. QUINTON McHALE (McHale's Navy) (ABC)
PAUL BURKE as ADAM FLINT (Naked City) (ABC)
VIC MORROW as SGT. CHIP SAUNDERS (Combat) (ABC)
DICK VAN DYKE as ROB PETRIE (The Dick Van Dyke Show) (CBS)

ACTRESS - SERIES (E-334)

Continued performance only - any length; live, tape or film

SHIRLEY BOOTH as HAZEL (Hazel) (NBC)
LUCILLE BALL as LUCY CARMICHAEL (The Lucille Ball Show) (CBS)
SHIRL CONWAY as LIZ THORPE (The Nurses) (CBS)
MARY TYLER MOORE as LAURA PETRIE (The Dick Van Dyke Show) (CBS)
IRENE RYAN as GRANNY (The Beverly Hillbillies) (CBS)

SUPPORTING ACTOR (E-335)

A regular program, a special program, or a series - any length; live, tape or film

DON KNOTTS as DEPUTY BARNEY FIFE (The Andy Griffith Show) (CBS)
TIM CONWAY as ENSIGN CHARLES PARKER (McHale's Navy) (ABC)
PAUL FORD as COLONEL PURDY Teahouse of the August Moon (Hallmark Hall of Fame) (NBC)
HURD HATFIELD as ROTHSCHILD The Invincible Mr. Disraeli (Hallmark Hall of Fame) (NBC)
ROBERT REDFORD as GEORGE LAURENTS The Voice of Charlie Pont (Premiere, Presented by Fred Astaire) (ABC)

SUPPORTING ACTRESS (E-336)

A regular program, a special program, or a series - any length; live, tape or film

GLENDA FARRELL as MARTHA MORRISON A Cardinal Act of Mercy (Ben Casey) (ABC)
DAVEY DAVISON as LAURA HUNTER Of Roses and Nightingales and Other Lovely Things (The Eleventh Hour) (NBC)
NANCY MALONE as LIBBY (Naked City) (ABC)
ROSE MARIE as SALLY ROGERS (The Dick Van Dyke Show) (CBS)
KATE REID as QUEEN VICTORIA The Invincible Mr. Disraeli (Hallmark Hall of Fame) April 4, 1963 (NBC)

PERFORMANCE IN A VARIETY OR MUSICAL PROGRAM OR SERIES (E-337)

A regular program, a special program, or a series - any length; live, tape or film

CAROL BURNETT Julie and Carol at Carniege Hall (CBS) and Carol and Company (CBS)
EDIE ADAMS (Here's Edie) (ABC)
MERV GRIFFIN (The Merv Griffin Show) (NBC)
DANNY KAYE The Danny Kaye Show with Lucille Ball (NBC)
ANDY WILLIAMS (The Andy Williams Show) (NBC)

ORIGINAL MUSIC (E-338)

A regular program, a special program, or a series - any length; live, tape or film

ROBERT RUSSELL BENNETT He Is Risen (Project 20) (NBC)
EDDY MANSON The River Nile (NBC)
GIAN CARLO MENOTTI Labyrinth (NBC Opera) (NBC)
JOSEPH MULLENDORE (The Dick Powell Theatre) (NBC)
JOHNNY WILLIAMS (Alcoa Premiere/Premiere, Presented by Fred Astaire) (ABC)

ART DIRECTION AND SCENIC DESIGN (E-339)

A regular program, a special program, or a series - any length; live, tape or film

CARROLL CLARK, MARVIN AUBREY DAVIS (Walt Disney's Wonderful World of Color) (NBC)
WARREN CLYMER (Hallmark Hall of Fame) (NBC)
WILLARD LEVITAS (The Defenders) (CBS)
HAL PEREIRA, EARL HENDRICK (Bonanza) (NBC)
GEORGE W. DAVIS, MERRILL PYE (The Eleventh Hour) (NBC)
JAN SCOTT various episodes (Du Pont Show of the Week) (NBC)

WRITING ACHIEVEMENT - DRAMA (E-340)

A regular program, a special program, or a series - any length; live, tape or film

ROBERT THOM, REGINALD ROSE The Madman (The Defenders) (CBS)
SIDNEY CARROLL Big Deal in Laredo (Du Pont Show of the Week) (NBC)
NORMAN KATKOV A Cardinal Act of Mercy (Ben Casey) (ABC)
JAMES LEE The Invincible Mr. Disraeli (Hallmark Hall of Fame) (NBC)
HALSTED WELLES The Voice of Charlie Pont (Premiere, Presented by Fred Astaire) (ABC)

WRITING ACHIEVEMENT - COMEDY (E-341)

A regular program, a special program, or a series - any length; live, tape or film

CARL REINER (The Dick Van Dyke Show) (CBS)
SAM PERRIN, GEORGE BALZER, HAL GOLDMAN, AL GORDON (The Jack Benny Program) (CBS)
PAUL HENNING (The Beverly Hillbillies) (CBS)
NAT HIKEN (Car 54, Where Are You?) (NBC)
ED SIMMONS, DAVE O'BRIEN, MARTIN A. RAGAWAY, ARTHUR PHILLIPS, LARRY RHINE, MORT GREENE, HUGH WEDLOCK, RED SKELTON, BRUCE HOWARD, RICK MITTLEMAN (The Red Skelton Hour) (CBS)

DIRECTORIAL ACHIEVEMENT - DRAMA (E-342)

A regular program, a special program, or a series - any length; live, tape or film

STUART ROSENBERG The Madman (The Defenders) (CBS)
FIELDER COOK Big Deal in Laredo (Du Pont Show of the Week) (NBC)
ROBERT ELLIS MILLER The Voice of Charlie Pont (Premiere, Presented by Fred Astaire) (ABC)
SYDNEY POLLACK A Cardinal Act of Mercy (Ben Casey) (ABC)
GEORGE SCHAEFER The Invincible Mr. Disraeli (Hallmark Hall of Fame) (NBC)

DIRECTORIAL ACHIEVEMENT - COMEDY (E-343)

A regular program, a special program, or a series - any length; live, tape or film

JOHN RICH (The Dick Van Dyke Show) (CBS)
SEYMOUR BURNS (The Red Skelton Hour) (CBS)
FREDERICK de CORDOVA (The Jack Benny Program) (CBS)
DAVID GEISEL (The Garry Moore Show) (CBS)
RICHARD WHORF (The Beverly Hillbillies) (CBS)

CINEMATOGRAPHY (E-344)

Any type or length filmed program or series

JOHN S. PRIESTLEY (Naked City) (ABC)
GUY BLANCHARD Shakespeare: Soul of An Age, and The River Nile (NBC)
GEORGE T. CLEMENS, ROBERT W. PITTACK (Twilight Zone) (CBS)
ROBERT HAUSER (Combat) (ABC)
JOE VADALA Comedian Backstage (Du Pont Show of the Week) (NBC)
WILLIAM HARTIGAN, EDMONDO RICCI The Vatican (Bell & Howell Close-Up!) (ABC)

ELECTRONIC CAMERA WORK (E-345)

Any type or length program or series; live or tape

THE INVINCIBLE MR. DISRAELI (Hallmark Hall of Fame) (NBC)
HERE'S EDIE (ABC)
THE LIVELY ONES (NBC)
ABC'S WIDE WORLD OF SPORTS (ABC)

FILM EDITING (E-346)

Any type or length filmed program or series

SID KATZ (The Defenders) (CBS)
JAMES BALLAS, GEORGE BOEMLER, AL CLARK, MIKE POZEN, AARON STELL (Ben Casey) (ABC)
DAVID E.ROLAND Comedian Backstage (Du Pont Show of the Week) (NBC)
HUGH CHALOUPKA, AARON NIBLEY, CHARLES FREEMAN, HARRY COSWICK, JACK GLEASON (Naked City) (ABC)
HOWARD EPSTEIN, RICHARD BELDING, TONY MARTINELLI (Alcoa Premiere/Premiere, Presented by Fred Astaire) (ABC)

ELECTRONIC ENGINEERING ACHIEVEMENT (E-347)

No Nominations

THE INTERNATIONAL AWARD (E-348)

Judging by Special Committee of Former Emmy Award Winners of entries from countries throughout the world

WAR AND PEACE (Granada TV Network Ltd. of England)
THE BIRD (Steptoe and Son) (British Broadcasting Corporation)
CAESARIAN SECTION (Your Life in Their Hands) (British Broadcasting Corporation)
THE OFFSHORE ISLAND (Canadian Broadcasting Corporation)
TAKAJOH (English Title: YOUNG HAWK, OLD HAWK) (Nippon Television Network Corporation) Japan

THE STATION AWARD (E-349)

Regional Winners judged by Committees at National Academy Chapters; Final Judging by Special Committee

SUPERFLUOUS PEOPLE (WCBS-TV, New York)
THE DARK CORNER (WBAL-TV, Baltimore)
SUSPECT (KING-TV, Seattle)
TIME'S MAN-(WKY-TV, Oklahoma City)
THE WASTED YEARS (WBBM-TV, Chicago)
OPERATION SOS (KMTV, Omaha)
BURDEN OF SHAME (KNXT, Los Angeles)
CONFORMITY (WCAU-TV, Philadelphia)

TRUSTEES AWARD (E-350)

AMERICAN TELEPHONE AND TELEGRAPH COMPANY For conceiving and developing Telstar #1 and Telstar #2.
DICK POWELL In grateful memory of his conspicuous contributions to and reflections of credit upon the industry as an actor, director, producer and executive; and for his consistent and unselfish cooperation with and support of the Academy.

TRUSTEES CITATION (E-351)

This citation is presented to the PRESIDENT OF THE UNITED STATES. . .JOHN F. KENNEDY. For making News Conferences available to television and participating in the program "Conversation with the President".

1963/64

PROGRAM OF THE YEAR (E-352)

That program, created originally or fully adapted for television, which is considered to be the most outstanding presentation during the awards period. Such a program may be either one of a series or an individual presentation, either entertainment, public service or coverage of a newsworthy event.

THE MAKING OF THE PRESIDENT 1960 (ABC)
AMERICAN REVOLUTION OF '63 (NBC)
BLACKLIST (The Defenders) (CBS)
THE KREMLIN (NBC)
TOWN MEETING OF THE WORLD (CBS)

PROGRAM ACHIEVEMENT - COMEDY (E-353)

A special program, one of a series, or a series - any length; live, tape or film

THE DICK VAN DYKE SHOW (CBS)
THE BILL DANA SHOW (NBC)
THE FARMER'S DAUGHTER (ABC)
McHALE'S NAVY (ABC)
THAT WAS THE WEEK THAT WAS (NBC)

PROGRAM ACHIEVEMENT - DRAMA (E-354)

A special program, one of a series, or a series - any length; live, tape or film

THE DEFENDERS (CBS)
BOB HOPE PRESENTS THE CHRYSLER THEATRE (NBC)
EAST SIDE/WEST SIDE (CBS)
MR. NOVAK (NBC)
THE RICHARD BOONE SHOW (NBC)

PROGRAM ACHIEVEMENT - MUSIC (E-355)

A special program, one of a series, or a series - any length; live, tape or film

BELL TELEPHONE HOUR (NBC)
THE LIVELY ONES (NBC)
NEW YORK PHILHARMONIC YOUNG PEOPLE'S CONCERTS WITH LEONARD BERNSTEIN (CBS)

PROGRAM ACHIEVEMENT - VARIETY (E-356)

A special program, one of a series, or a series - any length; live, tape or film

THE DANNY KAYE SHOW (CBS)
THE ANDY WILLIAMS SHOW (NBC)
THE GARRY MOORE SHOW (CBS)
THE JUDY GARLAND SHOW (CBS)
THE TONIGHT SHOW STARRING JOHNNY CARSON (NBC)

PROGRAM ACHIEVEMENT - CHILDREN'S PROGRAMMING (E-357)

A special program, one of a series, or a series - any length; live, tape or film

DISCOVERY '63-'64 (ABC)
EXPLORING (NBC)

NBC CHILDREN'S THEATRE (NBC)
SCIENCE ALL STARS (ABC)
WILD KINGDOM (NBC)

PROGRAM ACHIEVEMENT - DOCUMENTARY (E-358)

A special program, one of a series, or a series - any length; live, tape or film

THE MAKING OF THE PRESIDENT 1960 Produced by David L. Wolper and Mel Stuart; Written by Theodore H. White (ABC)
GREECE: THE GOLDEN AGE Produced and Written by Lou Hazam (NBC)
THE KREMLIN Produced by George Vicas; Written by Norman Borisoff, George Vicas, Aram Boyajian (NBC)
MANHATTAN BATTLEGROUND (DuPont Show of the Week) Produced and Written by William Jersey (NBC)
SAGA OF WESTERN MAN Produced by John H. Secondari and Helen Jean Rogers; Written by John H. Secondari (ABC)
THE TWENTIETH CENTURY Produced by Isaac Kleinerman (CBS)

PROGRAM ACHIEVEMENT - NEWS REPORTS (E-359)

A special program, one of a series, or a series - any length; live, tape or film

HUNTLEY-BRINKLEY REPORT (NBC)
CBS EVENING NEWS WITH WALTER CRONKITE (CBS)
NBC SPECIAL NEWS REPORTS (NBC)
RON COCHRAN WITH THE NEWS (ABC)

PROGRAM ACHIEVEMENT - NEWS COMMENTARY OR PUBLIC AFFAIRS (E-360)

A special program, one of a series, or a series - any length; live, tape or film

CUBA: PARTS I & II-THE BAY OF PIGS; THE MISSILE CRISIS (NBC White Paper) (NBC)
AMERICAN REVOLUTION OF '63 (NBC)
CBS REPORTS (CBS)
CHRONICLE (CBS)
TOWN MEETING OF THE WORLD (CBS)

ACTOR - SINGLE PERFORMANCE (E-361)

Single performance only - any length; live, tape or film

JACK KLUGMAN as JOE LARCH Blacklist (The Defenders) (CBS)
JAMES EARL JONES as JOE Who Do You Kill? (EastSide/WestSide) (CBS)
RODDY McDOWALL as PAUL LeDOUX Journey Into Darkness (Arrest and Trial) (ABC)
JASON ROBARDS, JR. as ABE LINCOLN Abe Lincoln In Illinois (Hallmark Hall of Fame) (NBC)
ROD STEIGER as MIKE KIRSCH A Slow Fade To Black (Bob Hope Presents The Chrysler Theatre) (NBC)
HAROLD J. STONE as ELIHU KAMINSKY Nurse Is A Feminine Noun (The Nurses) (CBS)

ACTRESS - SINGLE PERFORMANCE (E-362)

Single performance only - any length; live, tape or film

SHELLEY WINTERS as JENNY DWORAK Two Is The Number (Bob Hope Presents The Chrysler Theatre) (NBC)
RUBY DEE as JENNY BISHOP Express Stop from Lenox Avenue (The Nurses) (CBS)
BETHEL LESLIE as ELLEN DUDLEY Statement of Fact (The Richard Boone Show) (NBC)
JEANETTE NOLAN as JESSIE McCOONY Vote No On 11! (The Richard Boone Show) (NBC)
DIANA SANDS as RUTH Who Do You Kill? (East Side/West Side) (CBS)

ACTOR - SERIES (E-363)

Continued performance only - any length; live, tape or film

DICK VAN DYKE as ROB PETRIE (The Dick Van Dyke Show) (CBS)
RICHARD BOONE in various roles (The Richard Boone Show) (NBC)
DEAN JAGGER as ALBERT VANE (Mr. Novak) (NBC)
DAVID JANSSEN as DR RICHARD KIMBLE (The Fugitive) (ABC)
GEORGE C. SCOTT as NEIL BROCK (East Side/West Side) (CBS)

ACTRESS - SERIES (E-364)

Continued performance only - any length; live, tape or film

MARY TYLER MOORE as LAURA PETRIE (The Dick Van Dyke Show) (CBS)
SHIRLEY BOOTH as HAZEL (Hazel) (NBC)
PATTY DUKE as PATTY LANE and CATHY LANE (The Patty Duke Show) (ABC)
IRENE RYAN as GRANNY (The Beverly Hillbillies) (CBS)
INGER STEVENS as KATIE HOLSTRUM (The Farmer's Daughter) (ABC)

SUPPORTING ACTOR (E-365)

A special program, one of a series, or a series - any length; live, tape or film

ALBERT PAULSEN as LIEUTENANT VOLKOVOI One Day In the Life of Ivan Denisovich (Bob Hope Presents the Chrysler Theatre) (NBC)
SORRELL BOOKE as JULIUS ORLOFF What's God to Julius? (Dr. Kildare) (NBC)
CONLAN CARTER as DOC The Hostages (Combat) (ABC)
CARL LEE as LONNIE HILL Express Stop From Lenox Avenue (The Nurses) (CBS)

SUPPORTING ACTRESS (E-366)

A special program, one of a series, or a series - any length; live, tape or film

RUTH WHITE as MRS. MANGAN Little Moon of Alban (Hallmark Hall of Fame) (NBC)
MARTINE BARTLETT as MIRANDA Journey Into Darkness (Arrest and Trial) (ABC)
ANJANETTE COMER as ANNABELLE Journey Into Darkness (Arrest and Trial) (ABC)
ROSE MARIE as SALLY ROGERS (The Dick Van Dyke Show) (CBS)
CLAUDIA McNEIL as MRS. HILL Express Stop From Lenox Avenue (The Nurses) (CBS)

PERFORMANCE IN A VARIETY OR MUSICAL PROGRAM OR SERIS (E-367)

A special program, one of a series, or a series - any length; live, tape or film

DANNY KAYE (The Danny Kaye Show) (CBS)
JUDY GARLAND (The Judy Garland Show) (CBS)
BARBRA STREISAND (The Judy Garland Show) (CBS)
BURR TILLSTROM (That Was the Week That Was) various episodes (NBC)
ANDY WILLIAMS (The Andy Williams Show) (NBC)

ORIGINAL MUSIC (E-368)

A special program, one of a series, or a series - any length; live, tape or film

ELMER BERNSTEIN The Making of the President 1960 (ABC)
GEORGES AURIC The Kremlin (NBC)
JOHN BARRY Elizabeth Taylor in London (CBS)
KENYON HOPKINS (East Side/West Side) (CBS)
GEORGE KLEINSINGER Greece: The Golden Age (NBC)
ULPIO MINUCCI, JOE MOON, RAYBURN WRIGHT Saga of Western Man (ABC)

ART DIRECTION AND SCENIC DESIGN (E-369)

A special program, one of a series, or a series - any length; live, tape or film

WARREN CLYMER (Hallmark Hall of Fame) (NBC)
ROBERT KELLY, GARY SMITH (The Judy Garland Show) (CBS)
JACK POPLIN (The Outer Limits) (ABC)
EDWARD STEPHENSON (The Danny Kaye Show) (CBS)

WRITING - DRAMA - ORIGINAL (E-370)

A special program or one of a series - any length; live, tape or film

ERNEST KINOY Blacklist (The Defenders) (CBS)
ARNOLD PERL Who Do You Kill? (East Side/West Side) (CBS)
DAVID RAYFIEL Something About Lee Wiley (Bob Hope Presents The Chrysler Theatre) (NBC)
ALLAN SLOANE And James Was A Very Small Snail (Breaking Point) (ABC)
ADRIAN SPIES What's God To Julius? (Dr. Kildare) (NBC)

WRITING - DRAMA - ADAPTATION (E-371)

A special program or one of a series - any length; live, tape or film

ROD SERLING It's Mental Work (Bob Hope Presents The Chrysler Theatre) From the story by John O'Hara (NBC)
JAMES BRIDGES The Jar (The Alfred Hitchcock Hour) From a short story by Ray Bradbury (CBS)
ROBERT HARTUNG The Patriots (Hallmark Hall of Fame) From the play by Sidney Kingsley (NBC)
WALTER BROWN NEWMAN The Hooligan (The Richard Boone Show) From a play by Anton Chekov (NBC)

WRITING - COMEDY OR VARIETY (E-372)

A special program, one of a series, or a series - any length; live, tape or film

CARL REINER, SAM DENOFF, BILL PERSKY (The Dick Van Dyke Show) various episodes (CBS)
HERBERT BAKER, MEL TOLKIN, ERNEST CHAMBERS, SAUL ILSON, SHELDON KELLER, PAUL MAZURSKY, LARRY TUCKER, GARY BELKIN, LARRY GELBART (The Danny Kaye Show) (CBS)
ROBERT EMMETT, GERALD GARDNER, SAUL TURTLETAUB, DAVID PANICH, TONY WEBSTER, THOMAS MEEHAN, ED SHERMAN (That Was the Week That Was) (NBC)
STEVEN GETHERS, JERRY DAVIS and LEE LOEB, JOHN McGREEVEY (The Farmer's Daughter) various episodes (ABC)

DIRECTORIAL ACHIEVEMENT - DRAMA (E-373)

A special program or one of a series - any length; live, tape or film

TOM GRIES Who Do You Kill? (East Side/West Side) (CBS)
PAUL BOGART Moment of Truth (The Defenders) (CBS)
SYDNEY POLLACK Something About Lee Wiley (Bob Hope Presents The Chrysler Theatre) (NBC)
STUART ROSENBERG Blacklist (The Defenders) (CBS)
GEORGE SCHAEFER The Patriots (Hallmark Hall of Fame) (NBC)

DIRECTORIAL ACHIEVEMENT - COMEDY (E-374)

A special program, one of a series, or a series - any length; live, tape or film

JERRY PARIS (The Dick Van Dyke Show) (CBS)
SIDNEY LANFIELD (McHale's Navy) (ABC)
PAUL NICKELL, WILLIAM RUSSELL, DON TAYLOR (The Farmer's Daughter) various episodes (ABC)
RICHARD WHORF (The Beverly Hillbillies) (CBS)

DIRECTORIAL ACHIEVEMENT - VARIETY OR MUSIC (E-375)

A special program, one of a series, or a series - any length; live, tape or film

ROBERT SCHEERER (The Danny Kaye Show) (CBS)
ROGER ENGLANDER A Tribute To Teachers (New York Philharmonic Young People's Concerts With Leonard Bernstein) (CBS)
BOB HENRY (The Andy Williams Show) (NBC)
MARSHALL JAMISON (That Was the Week That Was) (NBC)
CLARK JONES, SID SMITH (Bell Telephone Hour) various programs (NBC)

CINEMATOGRAPHY (E-376)

Any type or length filmed program or series

J. BAXTER PETERS The Kremlin (NBC)
JOHN S. PRIESTLEY (East Side/West Side) (CBS)
BRADFORD KRESS Greece: The Golden Age (NBC)
ELLIS F. THACKERY Once Upon a Savage Night (Kraft Suspense Theatre) (NBC)

ELECTRONIC PHOTOGRAPHY (E-377)

Any type or length program or series, live or taped

THE DANNY KAYE SHOW (CBS)
BELL TELEPHONE HOUR (NBC)
THE LIVELY ONES (NBC)
RIDE WITH TERROR (DuPont Show of the Week (NBC)

FILM EDITING (E-378)

Any type or length filmed program or series

WILLIAM T. CARTWRIGHT The Making of the President 1960 (ABC)
JAMES ALGIE, SAMUEL COHEN, HANS DUDELHEIM, WALTER ESSENFELD, ALEXANDER HAMILTON, EDWARD LEMPA, WALTER MORAN, NILS RASMUSSEN, JOHN ROBERTS, ROBERT SANDBO, EDWARD SHEA Saga of Western Man (ABC)
ARAM BOYAJIAN The Kremlin (NBC)
CONSTANTINE S. GOCHIS Greece: The Golden Age (NBC)
DANNY LANDRES, MILTON SHIFMAN, RICHARD WRAY Arrest and Trial (ABC)

THE INTERNATIONAL AWARD (E-379)

Judged by Special Committee of former Emmy Award Winners of entries from countries throughout the world

LES RAISINS VERTS (Radiodiffusion Television Francais)
BUNRAKU DOLLS (NHK, Japan Broadcasting Corporation)
PALE HORSE, PALE RIDER (Canadian Broadcasting Corporation)

THE STATION AWARD (E-380)

Regional Winners judged by Committees at National Academy Chapters; final judging by Special Committee

OPERATION CHALLENGE - A STUDY IN HOPE (KSD-TV, St. Louis)
THE CASE FOR THE LIMITED CHILD (KPIX San Francisco)
CHILD BEATING (WMAL-TV, Washington, D.C.)
DATE LINE: CHICAGO COMPOSITE (WNBQ, Chicago)
THE LAST PROM (WLW-TV, Cincinnati)
THE NEXT REVOLUTION (WCBS-TV, New York)
POISON IN THE AIR (KNXT, Los Angeles)
WEDNESDAY'S CHILD (KGW-TV, Portland, Oregon)
WITHOUT VIOLENCE (WBRZ-TV, Baton Rouge)

1964/65

PROGRAM ACHIEVEMENTS IN ENTERTAINMENT (E-381)

THE DICK VAN DYKE SHOW (CBS) Carl Reiner, Producer
THE MAGNIFICENT YANKEE (Hallmark Hall of Fame) (NBC) George Schaefer, Producer
MY NAME IS BARBRA (CBS) Richard Lewine, Producer
WHAT IS SONATA FORM? (New York Philharmonic Young People's Concerts with Leonard Bernstein) (CBS) Roger Englander, Producer
THE ANDY WILLIAMS SHOW (NBC) Bob Finkel, Producer
BOB HOPE PRESENTS THE CHRYSLER THEATRE (NBC) Dick Berg, Executive Producer
THE DEFENDERS (CBS) Bob Markell, Producer
HALLMARK HALL OF FAME (NBC) George Schaefer, Producer
THE MAN FROM U.N.C.L.E. (NBC) Sam Rolfe, Producer
MR. NOVAK (NBC) Leonard Freeman, Producer
PROFILES IN COURAGE (NBC) Robert Saudek, Executive Producer
WALT DISNEY'S WONDERFUL WORLD OF COLOR (NBC) Walt Disney, Executive Producer
THE WONDERFUL WORLD OF BURLESQUE (NBC) George Schlatter, Producer
XEROX SPECIALS (Based on the activities of the United Nations) "Carol For Another Christmas" (ABC)Joseph L. Mankiewicz, Producer; "Who Has Seen The Wind?" (ABC) George Sidney, Producer

INDIVIDUAL ACHIEVEMENTS IN ENTERTAINMENT

ACTORS AND PERFORMERS (E-382)

LEONARD BERNSTEIN (New York Philharmonic Young People's Concerts with Leonard Bernstein) (CBS)
LYNN FONTANNE as FANNY DIXWELL HOLMES The Magnificent Yankee (Hallmark Hall of Fame) (NBC)
ALFRED LUNT as OLIVER WENDELL HOLMES The Magnificent Yankee (Hallmark Hall of Fame) (NBC)
BARBRA STREISAND My Name is Barbra (CBS)
DICK VAN DYKE as ROB PETRIE (The Dick Van Dyke Show) (CBS)
JULIE ANDREWS (The Andy Williams Show) (NBC)
JOHNNY CARSON (The Tonight Show Starring Johnny Carson) (NBC)
GLADYS COOPER as AUNT MARGARET (The Rogues) (NBC)
ROBERT COOTE as TIMMY ST. CLAIR (The Rogues) (NBC)
RICHARD CRENNA as SLATTERY (Slattery's People) (CBS)
JULIE HARRIS as FLORENCE NIGHTINGALE The Holy Terror (Hallmark Hall of Fame) (NBC)
BOB HOPE (Chrysler Presents A Bob Hope Comedy Special) (NBC)
DEAN JAGGER as ALBERT VANE (Mr. Novak) (NBC)
DANNY KAYE (The Danny Kaye Show) (CBS)
DAVID McCALLUM as ILLYA KURYAKIN (The Man From U.N.C.L.E.) (NBC)
RED SKELTON (The Red Skelton Hour) (CBS)

WRITERS (E-383)

DAVID KARP The 700 Year Old Gang (The Defenders) (CBS)
WILLIAM BOARDMAN, DEE CARUSO, ROBERT EMMETT, DAVID FROST, GERALD GARDNER, BUCK HENRY, JOSEPH HURLEY, TOM MEEHAN, HERB SARGENT, LARRY SIEGEL, GLORIA STEINEM, JIM STEVENSON, CALVIN TRILLIN, SAUL TURTLETAUB (That Was The Week That Was) (NBC)
ROBERT HARTUNG Adaption of Emmet Lavery's "The Magnificent Yankee" (Hallmark Hall of Fame) (NBC)
COLEMAN JACOBY, ARNEY ROSEN The Wonderful World of Burlesque (NBC)
CARL REINER Never Bathe On Saturday (The Dick Van Dyke Show) (CBS)

DIRECTORS (E-384)

PAUL BOGART The 700 Year Old Gang (The Defenders) (CBS)
DWIGHT HEMION My Name is Barbra (CBS)
GEORGE SCHAEFER The Magnificent Yankee (Hallmark Hall of Fame) (NBC)

CONCEPTION, CHOREOGRAPHY AND STAGING (E-385)

JOE LAYTON My Name is Barbra (CBS)

ART DIRECTORS AND SET DECORATORS (E-386)

WARREN CLYMER The Holy Terror (Hallmark Hall of Fame) (NBC)
TOM JOHN, Art Director; BILL HARP, Set Decorator, My Name is Barbra (CBS)
GENE CALLAHAN, Art Director; JACK WRIGHT JR, Set Decorator, Carol For Another Christmas (Xerox Special) (ABC)
WARREN CLYMER The Magnificent Yankee (Hallmark Hall of Fame) (NBC)

COSTUME DESIGNER (E-387)

NOEL TAYLOR The Magnificent Yankee (Hallmark Hall of Fame) (NBC)

MAKE-UP ARTIST (E-388)

ROBERT O'BRADOVICH The Magnificent Yankee (Hallmark Hall of Fame) (NBC)

MUSICIANS (E-389)

PETER MATZ, Music Director, My Name is Barbra (CBS)
HERBERT GROSSMAN, Music Director, The Fantasticks (Hallmark Hall of Fame) (NBC)

CINEMATOGRAPHERS (E-390)

WILLIAM SPENCER (Twelve O'Clock High) (ABC)
HASKELL BOGGS, WILLIAM WHITLEY (Bonanza) (NBC)
FRED KOENEKAMP (The Man From U.N.C.L.E.) (NBC)

FILM EDITORS (E-391)

HENRY BERMAN, JOSEPH DERVIN, WILL GULICK (The Man From U.N.C.L.E.) (NBC)

LIGHTING DIRECTOR (E-392)

PHIL HYMES The Magnificent Yankee (Hallmark Hall of Fame) (NBC)

SPECIAL PHOTOGRAPHIC EFFECTS (E-393)

L. B. ABBOTT (Voyage to the Bottom of the Sea) (ABC)

USE OF SPECIAL EFFECTS (E-394)

PRODUCTION TEAM EFFORT (The Man from U.N.C.L.E.) (NBC)

COLOR CONSULTANT (E-395)

EDWARD ANCONA (Bonanza) (NBC)

TECHNICAL DIRECTOR (E-396)

CLAIR McCOY The Wonderful World of Burlesque (NBC)

PROGRAM ACHIEVEMENTS IN NEWS, DOCUMENTARIES, INFORMATION AND SPORTS (E-397)

I, LEONARDO DA VINCI (Saga of Western Man) (ABC) John H. Secondari, Helen Jean Rogers, Producers
THE LOUVRE (NBC) Lucy Jarvis, Producer, John J. Sughrue, Co-Producer
NBC CONVENTION COVERAGE (NBC) Reuven Frank, Producer
THE DECISION TO DROP THE BOMB (NBC White Paper) (NBC) Fred Freed, Producer

INDIVIDUAL ACHIEVEMENTS IN NEWS, DOCUMENTARIES, INFORMATION AND SPORTS

NARRATORS (E-398)

RICHARD BASEHART Let My People Go (Syndicated)
CHARLES BOYER The Louvre (NBC)

DIRECTORS (E-399)

JOHN J. SUGHRUE The Louvre (NBC)
FRANK DE FELITTA Battle of the Bulge (NBC)
TOM PRIESTLEY John F. Kennedy Remembered (NBC)
HELEN JEAN ROGERS I, Leonardo da Vinci (Saga of Western Man) (ABC)

WRITERS (E-400)

SIDNEY CARROLL The Louvre (NBC)
JOHN H. SECONDARI I, Leonardo da Vinci (Saga of Western Man) (ABC)

FILM EDITORS (E-401)

ARAM BOYAJIAN The Louvre (NBC)
WALTER ESSENFELD, NILS RASMUSSEN I, Leonardo da Vinci (Saga of Western Man) (ABC)
ANGELO FARINA, BEN SCHILLER Battle of the Bulge (NBC)

CINEMATOGRAPHERS (E-402)

TOM PRIESTLEY The Louvre (NBC)
DEXTER ALLEY, RICHARD NORLING The Journals of Lewis & Clark (NBC)
WILLIAM B. HARTIGAN I, Leonardo da Vinci (Saga of Western Man) (ABC)

MUSICIANS (E-403)

NORMAN DELLO JOIO, Composer-Conductor, The Louvre (NBC)
ULPIO MINUCCI, Composer; RAYBURN WRIGHT, Conductor, I, Leonardo da Vinci (Saga of Western Man) (ABC)

THE INTERNATIONAL AWARD (E-404)

Judged by Special Committee of former Emmy Award Winners of entries from countries throughout the world
LE BARBIER DE SEVILLE (Canadian Broadcasting Corporation, Canada)
ANTONIO E CLEOPATRA (RAI-Radiotelevisione Italiana, Italy)
BILDER AUS DER SOWJET-UNION: SIBIRIEN-TRAUM UND WIRKLICH-KEIT (Norddeutscher Rundfunk, West Germany)
ISLAND YEARBOOK (Sveriges Radio, Sweden)
SEVEN-UP (Granada Television Limited, England)
SHOW BECAUD (Office de Radiodiffusion-Television Francaise, France)

THE STATION AWARD (E-405)

Regional Winners judged by Committees at National Academy Chapters; Final judging by Special Committee
KU KLUX KLAN (WDSU-TV, New Orleans, La)
CONVERSATIONS WITH JAMES EMORY BOND (WBAL-TV, Baltimore, Md)
KOREAN LEGACY (KTLA, Los Angeles, Calif)
MY CHILDHOOD (WNEW-TV, New York, NY)
NO ROOM AT THE BOTTOM (KSD-TV, St. Louis, Mo)
THE OUTSIDERS (WOW-TV, Omaha, Neb)
ROSES HAVE THORNS (WOOD-TV, Grand Rapids, Mich)
STRANGERS IN THE SHADOWS (WBNS-TV, Columbus, Ohio)

1965/66

COMEDY SERIES (E-406)

THE DICK VAN DYKE SHOW (CBS) Carl Reiner, Producer
BATMAN (ABC) Howie Horwitz, Producer
BEWITCHED (ABC) Jerry Davis, Producer
GET SMART! (NBC) Leonard Stern, Executive Producer
HOGAN'S HEROES (CBS) Edward H. Feldman, Producer

VARIETY SERIES (E-407)

Awards to Producer and Star

THE ANDY WILLIAMS SHOW (NBC) Bob Finkel, Producer
THE DANNY KAYE SHOW (CBS) Bob Scheerer, Producer
THE HOLLYWOOD PALACE (ABC) William O. Harback and Nick Van-off, Producers
THE RED SKELTON HOUR (CBS) Seymour Berns, Producer
THE TONIGHT SHOW STARRING JOHNNY CARSON (NBC) Art Stark, Producer

VARIETY SPECIAL (E-408)

Awards to Producer and Star

CHRYSLER PRESENTS THE BOB HOPE CHRISTMAS SPECIAL (NBC) Bob Hope, Executive Producer
AN EVENING WITH CAROL CHANNING (CBS) Bud Yorkin, Producer
JIMMY DURANTE MEETS THE LIVELY ARTS (ABC) Alan Handley and Bob Wynn, Producers
THE JULIE ANDREWS SHOW (NBC) Alan Handley, Producer
THE SWINGING WORLD OF SAMMY DAVIS, JR. (Syndicated) Stan Greene, Producer

DRAMATIC SERIES (E-409)

THE FUGITIVE (ABC) Alan Armer, Producer
BONANZA (NBC) David Dortort, Producer
I SPY (NBC) David Friedkin and Mort Fine, Producers
THE MAN FROM U.N.C.L.E. (NBC) Norman Felton, Executive Producer
SLATTERY'S PEOPLE (CBS) Irving Elman, Producer

DRAMATIC PROGRAM (E-410)

A single program

AGES OF MAN (CBS) David Suskind and Daniel Melnick, Producers
EAGLE IN A CAGE (Hallmark Hall of Fame) (NBC) George Schaefer, Producer
INHERIT THE WIND (Hallmark Hall of Fame) (NBC) George Schaefer, Producer
RALLY 'ROUND YOUR OWN FLAG, MISTER (Slattery's People) (CBS) Irving Elman, Producer

MUSICAL PROGRAM (E-411)

A special program, one of a series, or a series - Awards to Producer and Star

FRANK SINATRA: A MAN AND HIS MUSIC (NBC) Dwight Hemion, Producer
BELL TELEPHONE HOUR (NBC) Barry Wood, Executive Producer
THE BOLSHOI BALLET (Syndicated) Ted Mills, Producer
COLOR ME BARBRA (CBS) Joe Layton and Dwight Hemion, Producers
NEW YORK PHILHARMONIC YOUNG PEOPLE'S CONCERTS WITH LEONARD BERNSTEIN (CBS) Roger Englander, Producer

CHILDREN'S PROGRAM (E-412)

A special program, one of a series, or a series

A CHARLIE BROWN CHRISTMAS (CBS) Lee Mendelson and Bill Melendez, Producers
CAPTAIN KANGAROO (CBS) Al Hyslop, Producer
DISCOVERY (ABC) Jules Power, Executive Producer
FURTHER ADVENTURES OF GALLEGHER (Walt Disney's Wonderful World of Color) (NBC) Walt Disney and Ron Miller, Producers

THE WORLD OF STUART LITTLE (NBC Children's Theatre) (NBC) George A. Heinemann, Producer

ACTOR - SINGLE PERFORMANCE - DRAMA (E-413)

CLIFF ROBERTSON as QUINCEY PARKER The Game (Bob Hope Presents the Chrysler Theatre) (NBC)
ED BEGLEY as MATTHEW HARRISON BRADY Inherit The Wind (Hallmark Hall of Fame) (NBC)
MELVYN DOUGLAS as HENRY DRUMMOND Inherit The Wind (Hallmark Hall of Fame) (NBC)
TREVOR HOWARD as NAPOLEON Eagle In A Cage (Hallmark Hall of Fame) (NBC)
CHRISTOPHER PLUMMER as HAMLET Hamlet (Syndicated)

ACTRESS - SINGLE PERFORMANCE - DRAMA (E-414)

SIMONE SIGNORET as SARA LESCAUT A Small Rebellion (Bob Hope Presents The Chrysler Theatre) (NBC)
EARTHA KITT as ANGEL The Loser (I Spy) (NBC)
MARGARET LEIGHTON as CHRIS BECKER Behold The Great Man; A Life For A Life; Web of Hate; Horizontal Hero (Dr. Kildare) (NBC)
SHELLEY WINTERS as EDITH Back to Back (Bob Hope Presents the Chrysler Theatre) (NBC)

ACTOR - DRAMATIC SERIES (E-415)

BILL COSBY as ALEXANDER SCOTT (I Spy) (NBC)
RICHARD CRENNA as SLATTERY (Slattery's People) (CBS)
ROBERT CULP as KELLY ROBINSON (I Spy) (NBC)
DAVID JANSSEN as DR. RICHARD KIMBLE (The Fugitive) (ABC)
DAVID McCALLUM as ILLYA KURYAKIN (The Man From U.N.C.L.E.) (NBC)

ACTRESS - DRAMATIC SERIES (E-416)

BARBARA STANWYCK as VICTORIA BARKLEY (The Big Valley) (ABC)
ANNE FRANCIS as HONEY WEST (Honey West) (ABC)
BARBARA PARKINS as BETTY ANDERSON (Peyton Place) (ABC)

ACTOR - COMEDY SERIES (E-417)

DICK VAN DYKE as ROB PETRIE (The Dick Van Dyke Show) (CBS)
DON ADAMS as MAXWELL SMART (Get Smart!) (NBC)
BOB CRANE as COL. ROBERT HOGAN (Hogan's Heroes) (CBS)

ACTRESS - COMEDY SERIES (E-418)

MARY TYLER MOORE as LAURA PETRIE (The Dick Van Dyke Show) (CBS)
LUCILLE BALL as LUCY CARMICHAEL (The Lucy Show) (CBS)
ELIZABETH MONTGOMERY as SAMANTHA STEPHENS (Betwitched) (ABC)

SUPPORTING ACTOR - DRAMA (E-419)

A single program or series

JAMES DALY as DR. O'MEARA Eagle In A Cage (Hallmark Hall of Fame) (NBC)
DAVID BURNS as GREAT McGONIGLE (Trials Of O'Brien) (CBS)
LEO G. CARROLL as ALEXANDER WAVERLY (The Man From U.N.C.L.E.) (NBC)

SUPPORTING ACTRESS - DRAMA (E-420)

A single program or series

LEE GRANT as STELLA CHERNAK (Peyton Place) (ABC)
DIANE BAKER as RACHEL BROWN Inherit The Wind (Hallmark Hall of Fame) (NBC)
PAMELA FRANKLIN as BETSY BALCOMBE Eagle In A Cage (Hallmark Hall Of Fame) (NBC)
JEANETTE NOLAN as MAUDE MURDOCK The Conquest Of Maude Murdock (I Spy) (NBC)

Montage of Emmy Winners: (Clockwise from top left) comedian Sid Caesar, NBC News Documentary producer Lucy Jarvis, singer Perry Como, singer Dinah Shore, comedians Jack Benny and Bob Hope, and actress Loretta Young

SUPPORTING ACTOR - COMEDY (E-421)

A single program or series

DON KNOTTS as BARNEY FIFE The Return Of Barney Fife (The Andy Griffith Show) (CBS)
MOREY AMSTERDAM as BUDDY SORRELL (The Dick Van Dyke Show) (CBS)
FRANK GORSHIN as THE RIDDLER Hi Diddle Riddle (Batman) (ABC)
WERNER KLEMPERER as COL. WILHELM KLINK (Hogan's Heroes) (CBS)

SUPPORTING ACTRESS - COMEDY (E-422)

A single program or series

ALICE PEARCE as GLADYS KRAVITZ (Bewitched) (ABC)
AGNES MOOREHEAD as ENDORA (Bewitched) (ABC)
ROSEMARIE as SALLY ROGERS (The Dick Van Dyke Show) (CBS)

WRITING ACHIEVEMENT - DRAMA (E-423)

A special program or one of a series

MILLARD LAMPELL Eagle In A Cage (Hallmark Hall Of Fame) (NBC)
MORTON FINE, DAVID FRIEDKIN A Cup Of Kindness (I Spy) (NBC)
S. LEE POGOSTIN The Game (Bob Hope Presents The Chrysler Theatre) (NBC)

WRITING ACHIEVEMENT - COMEDY (E-424)

A special program, one of a series, or a series

BILL PERSKY, SAM DENOFF Coast To Coast Big Mouth (The Dick Van Dyke Show) (CBS)
MEL BROOKS, BUCK HENRY Mr. Big (Get Smart!) (NBC)
BILL PERSKY, SAM DENOFF The Ugliest Dog In The World (The Dick Van Dyke Show) (CBS)

WRITING ACHIEVEMENT - VARIETY (E-425)

A special program, one of a series, or a series

AL GORDON, HAL GOLDMAN, SHELDON KELLER An Evening With Carol Channing (CBS)
ERNEST CHAMBERS, PAT McCORMICK, RON FRIEDMAN, LARRY TUCKER, PAUL MAZURSKY, BILLIE BARNES, BERNARD ROTHMAN, NORMAN BARASCH, CARROL MOORE The Danny Kaye Show (CBS)
BILL PERSKY, SAM DENOFF The Julie Andrews Show (NBC)

DIRECTORIAL ACHIEVEMENT - DRAMA (E-426)

A special program or one of a series

SIDNEY POLLACK The Game (Bob Hope Presents The Chrysler Theatre) (NBC)
SHELDON LEONARD Hong Kong portions of: So Long, Patrick Henry; A Cup of Kindness; Carry Me Back To Old Tsing-Tao (I Spy) (NBC)
GEORGE SCHAEFER Eagle In A Cage (Hallmark Hall Of Fame) (NBC)
GEORGE SCHAEFER Inherit The Wind (Hallmark Hall Of Fame) (NBC)

DIRECTORIAL ACHIEVEMENT - COMEDY (E-427)

A special program, one of a series, or a series

WILLIAM ASHER Bewitched (ABC)
PAUL BOGART Diplomat's Daughter (Get Smart!) (NBC)
JERRY PARIS The Dick Van Dyke Show (CBS)

DIRECTORIAL ACHIEVEMENT - VARIETY OR MUSIC (E-428)

A special program, one of a series, or a series

ALAN HANDLEY The Julie Andrews Show (NBC)
GREG GARRISON The Dean Martin Show (NBC)
DWIGHT HEMION Frank Sinatra: A Man And His Music (NBC)
DWIGHT HEMION Color Me Barbra (CBS)
BOB HENRY The Andy Williams Show (NBC)

THE CRAFT AND PROGRAMMING AREAS

(Possibility of Multiple Awards)

ACHIEVEMENTS IN NEWS AND DOCUMENTARIES (E-429)

PROGRAMS (E-430)

AMERICAN WHITE PAPER: UNITED STATES FOREIGN POLICY (NBC) Fred Freed, Producer
KKK - THE INVISIBLE EMPIRE (CBS Reports) (CBS) David Lowe, Producer
SENATE HEARINGS ON VIETNAM (NBC) Chet Hagan, Producer
CBS REPORTS (CBS) Palmer Williams, Executive Producer
COVERAGE OF THE PAPAL VISIT (NBC) Chet Hagan, Producer
KTLA COVERAGE OF WATTS RIOTS (ABC, CBS and NBC) KTLA News Department
HUNTLEY-BRINKLEY REPORT (NBC) Robert Northshield, Executive Producer
THE MAKING OF THE PRESIDENT 1964 (CBS) David L. Wolper and Mel Stuart, Producers
MICHELANGELO: THE LAST GIANT (NBC) Louis Hazam, Producer
NATIONAL DRIVERS TEST (CBS) Warren V. Bush, Producer
TWENTIETH CENTURY (CBS) Isaac Kleinerman, Producer

INDIVIDUALS (E-431)

WILLIAM BOARDMAN, LISA COMMAGER, DIANA FETTER, ROBERT RICKNER Researchers on Beethoven: Ordeal and Triumph (Saga Of Western Man) (ABC)
WALTER CRONKITE Commentator on CBS Evening News With Walter Cronkite (CBS)
LOU HAZAM Writer of Michelangelo: The Last Giant (NBC)
CHET HUNTLEY AND DAVID BRINKLEY Commentators on Huntley-Brinkley Report (NBC)
DAVID LOWE Writer of KKK - The Invisible Empire (CBS Reports) (CBS)
FRANK McGEE Commentator on The Frank McGee Report (NBC)
FRANK McGEE Commentator on The Papal Visit (NBC)
TOM PRIESTLEY Director of Michelangelo: The Last Giant (NBC)
HARRY REASONER Narrator of The Great Love Affair (CBS)
RICHARD SCHNEIDER Director of Papal Mass (ABC, CBS and NBC)
ERIC SEVAREID Commentator on CBS Evening News With Walter Cronkite (CBS)
HOWARD K. SMITH Commentator on United States Policy on Vietnam (Issues and Answers) (ABC)
MEL STUART Director of The Making Of The President 1964 (CBS)
PETER USTINOV Voice of Michelangelo on Michelangelo: The Last Giant (NBC)
THEODORE H. WHITE Writer of The Making Of the President 1964 (CBS)

DAYTIME PROGRAMS (E-432)

CAMERA THREE (CBS) Dan Gallagher, Producer
MUTUAL OF OMAHA'S WILD KINGDOM (NBC) Don Meier, Producer
A TRIBUTE TO STEVENSON (Today) (NBC) Al Morgan, Producer

ACHIEVEMENTS IN SPORTS

PROGRAMS (E-433)

ABC WIDE WORLD OF SPORTS (ABC) Roone Arledge, Executive Producer
CBS GOLF CLASSIC (CBS) Frank Chirkinian, Producer
SHELL'S WONDERFUL WORLD OF GOLF (NBC) Fred Raphael, Producer
NFL GAME OF THE WEEK (CBS) William C. Fitts III, Executive Producer
U.S.-RUSSIAN TRACK MEET (ABC) Chuck Howard, Producer

INDIVIDUAL (E-434)

VIN SCULLY Sports Announcer on The World Series (NBC)

ACHIEVEMENTS IN EDUCATIONAL TELEVISION

PROGRAMS (E-435)
AMERICA'S CRISIS: TROUBLE IN THE FAMILY (NET) Harold Mayer, Producer
AN HOUR WITH JOAN SUTHERLAND (NET) Curtis W. Davis, Producer
A ROOMFUL OF MUSIC (Festival Of Arts) (NET) David Sloss, Producer
BALDWIN VS. BUCKLEY (NET) Paul Bonner, Producer
HISTORY OF THE NEGRO PEOPLE (NET) Arthur Rabin, Producer
POLAND (Changing World) (NET) Richard Moore and Irving Saraf, Producers
THE DANCE THEATRE OF JOSE LIMON (Festival Of Arts) (NET) Jac Venza, Producer

INDIVIDUALS (E-436)
JULIA CHILD Instructor and Hostess on The French Chef (NET)
KARL GENUS Writer and Director of Sibelius, A Symphony For Finland (NET)
LANE SLATE Director of The Creative Person - Robert Osborn (NET)
TOM WICKER, MAX FRANKEL, LESTER MARKEL Commentators on News In Perspective (NET)

INDIVIDUAL ACHIEVEMENTS IN MUSIC

COMPOSITION (E-437)
LAURENCE ROSENTHAL Michelangelo: The Last Giant (NBC)
JERRY GOLDSMITH For original theme music on The Man From U.N.C.L.E. (NBC)
EARLE HAGEN I Spy (NBC)
DAVID ROSE Bonanza (NBC)
PETE RUGOLO Run For Your Life (NBC)
LALO SCHIFRIN The Making Of The President 1964 (CBS)
MORTON STEVENS Seven Hours To Dawn (Gunsmoke) (CBS)

CONDUCTING (E-438)
MITCHELL AYRES The Hollywood Palace (ABC)
IRWIN KOSTAL The Julie Andrews Show (NBC)
GORDON JENKINS, NELSON RIDDLE Frank Sinatra: A Man And His Music (NBC)
ERICH LEINSDORF Beethoven: Ordeal And Triumph (Saga Of Western Man) (ABC)
LAURENCE ROSENTHAL Michelangelo: The Last Giant (NBC)
DONALD VOORHEES Bell Telephone Hour (NBC)

ARRANGING (E-439)
JOE LIPMAN The Hollywood Palace (ABC)
MARTY PAICH Alice In Wonderland or What's A Nice Kid Like You Doing In A Place Like This? (ABC)

SPECIAL (E-440)
RAY CHARLES Special vocal material for The Julie Andrews Show (NBC)
CLAUDE FRANK Pianist on Beethoven: Ordeal And Triumph (Saga Of Western Man) (ABC)

INDIVIDUAL ACHIEVEMENTS IN ART DIRECTION AND ALLIED CRAFTS

ART DIRECTION (E-441)
JAMES TRITTIPO The Hollywood Palace (ABC)
CARROLL CLARK, WILLIAM TUNTKE Further Adventures of Gallegher (Walt Disney's Wonderful World Of Color) (NBC)
WILLIAM J. CREBER Voyage To The Bottom Of The Sea (ABC)
GEORGE DAVIS, MERRILL PYE, JAMES SULLIVAN The Man From U.N.C.L.E. (NBC)
TOM JOHN Color Me Barbra (CBS)
EDWARD STEPHENSON The Andy Williams Show (NBC)

SET DECORATION (E-442)
HENRY GRACE, FRANCISCO LOMBARDO, JACK MILLS, CHARLES THOMPSON The Man From U.N.C.L.E. (NBC)
BILL HARP Color Me Barbra (CBS)
NORMAN ROCKETT Voyage to The Bottom Of The Sea (ABC)

COSTUME DESIGN (E-443)
RAY AGHAYAN, BOB MACKIE Wonderful World of Burlesque II - Danny Thomas Special (NBC)

WARDROBE (E-444)
ED SMITH The Hollywood Palace (ABC)

MAKE-UP (E-445)
BOB O'BRADOVICH Inherit The Wind (Hallmark Hall Of Fame) (NBC)

SPECIAL (E-446)
ARNOLD GOODE, BILL GRAHAM, BOB MURDOCK For creating the unusual props for The Man From U.N.C.L.E. (NBC)
ROBERT TAIT For the mechanical effects on Voyage to The Bottom Of The Sea (ABC)

INDIVIDUAL ACHIEVEMENTS IN CINEMATOGRAPHY

CINEMATOGRAPHY (E-447)
WINTON C. HOCH Voyage to The Bottom Of the Sea (ABC)
HASKELL BOGGS, WILLIAM F. WHITLEY Bonanza (NBC)
FRED KOENEKAMP The Man From U.N.C.L.E. (NBC)
LIONEL LINDON The Cold, Cold War Of Paul Bryan (Run For Your Life) (NBC)
MEREDITH M. NICHOLSON The Fugitive (ABC)
TOM PRIESTLEY Michelangelo: The Last Giant (NBC)
TED VOIGTLANDER The Wild, Wild West (CBS)

SPECIAL (E-448)
L. B. ABBOTT, HOWARD LYDECKER For photographic effects on Voyage To The Bottom Of The Sea (ABC)
L. B. ABBOTT, HOWARD LYDECKER For photographic effects on Lost In Space (CBS)
EDWARD ANCONA Color Co-ordinator on Bonanza (NBC)

FILM EDITING (E-449)
DAVID BLEWITT, WILLIAM T. CARTWRIGHT The Making Of The President 1964 (CBS)
MARVIN COIL, EVERETT DOUGLAS, ELLSWORTH HOAGLAND Bonanza (NBC)
JAMES BAIOTTO, ROBERT BELCHER, RICHARD WORMELL Voyage to The Bottom Of The Sea (ABC)
HENRY BERMAN, JOSEPH DERVIN, WILLIAM GULICK The Man From U.N.C.L.E. (NBC)
LOFTUS McDONOUGH Michelangelo: The Last Giant (NBC)

SOUND EDITING (E-450)
JAMES BOURGEOIS Mutual Of Omaha's Wild Kingdom (NBC)
ROBERT CORNETT, DON HALL, JR., DONALD HIGGINS, ELWELL JACKSON Voyage To The Bottom Of The Sea (ABC)
RICHARD LEGRAND, ROSS TAYLOR, HAROLD WOOLEY, RALPH HICKEY Batman (ABC)
JOHN J. LIPOW, WILLIAM RIVAL The Man From U.N.C.L.E. (NBC)

INDIVIDUAL ACHIEVEMENTS IN ELECTRONIC PRODUCTION

AUDIO ENGINEERING (E-451)
LAURENCE SCHNEIDER Seventh Annual Young Performers Program (New York Philharmonic Young People's Concerts With Leonard Bernstein) (CBS)

WILLIAM COLE The Andy Williams Show (NBC)
HERMAN LEWIS Perry Mason (CBS)

VIDEO TAPE EDITING (E-452)
CRAIG CURTIS, ART SCHNEIDER The Julie Andrews Show (NBC)
STAN CHLEBEK, CRAIG CURTIS, ART SCHNEIDER Lorne Greene's
American West (NBC)

VIDEO CONTROL (E-453)
ARNOLD DICK Bell Telephone Hour (NBC)

LIGHTING (E-454)
LON STUCKY Frank Sinatra: A Man And His Music (NBC)
ROBERT BARRY Color Me Barbra (CBS)
JOHN FRESCHI The Andy Williams Show (NBC)
PHIL HYMES Bell Telephone Hour (NBC)

TECHNICAL DIRECTORS (E-455)
O. TAMBURRI Inherit The Wind (Hallmark Hall Of Fame) (NBC)
KARL MESSERSCHMIDT The Dean Martin Show (NBC)

ELECTRONIC CAMERAMEN (E-456)
MIKE ENGLISH, EMIL HUSNI, AL LORETO, JOHN LINCOLN The Strollin' 20's (CBS)

SPECIAL ELECTRONIC EFFECTS (E-457)
MILT ALTMAN the Julie Andrews Show (NBC)

INDIVIDUAL ACHIEVEMENTS IN ENGINEERING DEVELOPMENT (E-458)
Because of the unique nature of engineering developments all possible achievements in this awards year were considered by the Blue Ribbon Panel.
STOP ACTION PLAYBACK MVR Corporation and CBS
EARLY BIRD SATELLITE Hughes Aircraft Company and Communications Satellite Corporation

SPECIAL CLASSIFICATIONS OF INDIVIDUAL ACHIEVEMENTS (E-459)
BURR TILLSTROM For his "Berlin Wall" hand ballet on That Was The Week That Was (NBC)
ART CARNEY For his performance as ED NORTON on The Adoption (The Jackie Gleason Show) (CBS)
NICK CASTLE Choreographer of The Andy Williams Show (NBC)
TONY CHARMOLI Choreograher of The Danny Kaye Show (CBS)
TONY CHARMOLI Choreographer of The Julie Andrews Show (NBC)
ROBERT HARTUNG For the adaption of Inherit The Wind (Hallmark Hall Of Fame) (NBC)
GENE KELLY For his performance on The Julie Andrews Show (NBC)
CARL REINER For the voices on Linus The Lionhearted (CBS)
CHARLES SCHULZ Writer of A Charlie Brown Christmas (CBS)

INTERNATIONAL NON-FICTION AWARD (E-460)
WYVERN AT WAR - NO. 2 "BREAKOUT" (Westward Television Limited, Plymouth, England)
THE HOUSE ON THE BEACH (Rediffusion Television Limited, London, England)
MOZART IN PRAGUE (Osterreichischer Rundfunk/Fernsehen, Vienna, Austria)

INTERNATIONAL FICTION AWARD (E-461)
STASERA RITA (RAI-Radiotelevisione Italiana, Rome, Italy)
THE SUCCESSOR (Anglia-Television Limited, Norwich, England)
THE TALE OF GENJI (Mainichi Broadcasting System, Inc., Osaka, Japan)

THE STATION AWARD (E-462)
I SEE CHICAGO (WBBM-TV, Chicago, Illinois)
AS THEY LIKE IT (KGW-TV, Portland, Oregon)
THE CORNER (KTVI, St. Louis, Missouri)
GOVERNMENT BY GASLIGHT (WJXT-TV, Jacksonville, Florida)
GUNS ARE FOR KILLING (KPRC-TV, Houston, Texas)
MAKE A JOYFUL SOUND (WCBS-TV, New York, New York)
THE MINER'S STORY (WCAU-TV, Philadelphia, Pennsylvania)
NO DEPOSIT - NO RETURN (KRON-TV, San Francisco, California)
VIET NAM '65: A DISTANT CHRISTMAS (WWL-TV, New Orleans, Louisiana)

TRUSTEES AWARD (E-463)
EDWARD R. MURROW Who brought together the highest qualities of broadcasting and journalism so that he became a symbol to colleagues and the public alike of the complete broadcast journalist.
XEROX CORPORATION
For its presentation of some of the finest art, news and historical documentaries.

1966/67

COMEDY SERIES (E-464)
THE MONKEES (NBC) Bert Schneider and Bob Rafelson, Producers
BEWITCHED (ABC) William Froug, Producer
GET SMART! (NBC) Arnie Rosen, Producer
THE ANDY GRIFFITH SHOW (CBS) Bob Ross, Producer
HOGAN'S HEROES (CBS) Edward H. Feldman, Producer

VARIETY SERIES (E-465)
Awards to Producer and Star
THE ANDY WILLIAMS SHOW (NBC) Edward Stephenson and Bob Finkel, Producers
THE DEAN MARTIN SHOW (NBC) Greg Garrison, Producer
THE JACKIE GLEASON SHOW (CBS) Ronald Wayne, Producer
HOLLYWOOD PALACE (ABC) Nick Vanoff and William O. Harbach, Producers
THE SMOTHERS BROTHERS COMEDY HOUR STARRING TOM AND DICK SMOTHERS (CBS) Saul Ilson and Ernest Chambers, Producers
THE TONIGHT SHOW STARRING JOHNNY CARSON (NBC) Art Stark, Producer

VARIETY SPECIAL (E-466)
Awards to Producer and Star
THE SID CAESAR, IMOGENE COCA, CARL REINER, HOWARD MORRIS SPECIAL (CBS) Jack Arnold, Producer
CHRYSLER PRESENTS THE BOB HOPE CHRISTMAS SPECIAL (NBC) Bob Hope, Executive Producer
A TIME FOR LAUGHTER: A LOOK AT NEGRO HUMOR IN AMERICA (ABC Stage 67) Phil Stein, Producer
DICK VAN DYKE (CBS) Byron Paul and Jack Donohue, Producers

DRAMATIC SERIES (E-467)
MISSION: IMPOSSIBLE (CBS) Joseph Gantman and Bruce Geller, Producers
THE AVENGERS (ABC) Julian Wintle, Executive Producer
I SPY (NBC) David Friedkin and Mort Fine, Producers
RUN FOR YOUR LIFE (NBC) Jo Swerling, Jr. Producer
STAR TREK (NBC) Gene Coon and Eugene Roddenberry, Producers

DRAMATIC PROGRAM (E-468)
A single program or a series
DEATH OF A SALESMAN (CBS) David Susskind and Daniel Melnick, Producers
A CHRISTMAS MEMORY (ABC Stage 67) (ABC) Frank Perry, Producer

THE FINAL WAR OF OLLY WINTER (CBS Playhouse) (CBS) Fred Coe, Producer

THE GLASS MENAGERIE (CBS Playhouse) (CBS) Davis Susskind, Producer

THE LOVE SONG OF BARNEY KEMPINSKI (ABC Stage 67) (ABC) Marc Merson, Producer

MARK TWAIN TONIGHT! (CBS) David Susskind, Producer

MUSICAL PROGRAM (E-469)

A special program, one of a series or a series - Awards to Producer and Star

BRIGADOON (ABC) Fielder Cook, Producer
FRANK SINATRA: A MAN AND HIS MUSIC PART II (CBS) Dwight Hemion, Producer
TOSCANINI: THE MAESTRO REVISTED (Bell Telephone Hour) (NBC) Gerald Green, Producer

CHILDREN'S PROGRAM (E-470)

A special program, one of a series or a series

JACK AND THE BEANSTALK (NBC) Gene Kelly, Producer
CHARLIE BROWN'S ALL STARS (CBS) Lee Mendelson and Bill Melendez, Producers
DISCOVERY '66-'67 (ABC) Jules Power, Executive Producer
IT'S THE GREAT PUMPKIN, CHARLIE BROWN (CBS) Lee Mendelson and Bill Melendez, Producers

ACTOR - SINGLE PERFORMANCE - DRAMA (E-471)

PETER USTINOV as SOCRATES Barefoot in Athens (Hallmark Hall of Fame) (NBC)
ALAN ARKIN as BARNEY KEMPINSKI The Love Song of Barney Kempinski (ABC Stage 67) (ABC)
LEE J. COBB as WILLY LOMAN Death Of A Salesman (CBS)
IVAN DIXON as OLLY WINTER The Final War of Olly Winter (CBS Playhouse) (CBS)
HAL HOLBROOK as MARK TWAIN Mark Twain Tonight! (CBS)

ACTRESS - SINGLE PERFORMANCE - DRAMA (E-472)

GERALDINE PAGE as SOOKIE A Christmas Memory (ABC Stage 67) (ABC)
SHIRLEY BOOTH as AMANDA The Glass Menagerie (CBS Playhouse) (CBS)
MILDRED DUNNOCK as LINDA LOMAN Death Of A Salesman (CBS)
LYNN FONTANNE as DOWAGER EMPRESS Anastasia (Hallmark Hall of Fame) (NBC)
JULIE HARRIS as ANASTASIA Anastasia (Hallmark Hall of Fame) (NBC)

ACTOR - DRAMATIC SERIES (E-473)

BILL COSBY as ALEXANDER SCOTT (I Spy) (NBC)
ROBERT CULP as KELLY ROBINSON (I Spy) (NBC)
BEN GAZZARA as PAUL BRYAN (Run For Your Life) (NBC)
DAVID JANSSEN as DR. RICHARD KIMBLE (The Fugitive) (ABC)
MARTIN LANDAU as ROLLIN HAND (Mission: Impossible) (CBS)

ACTRESS - DRAMATIC SERIES (E-474)

BARBARA BAIN as CINNAMON CARTER (Mission: Impossible) (CBS)
DIANA RIGG as MRS. EMMA PEEL (The Avengers) (ABC)
BARBARA STANWYCK as VICTORIA BARKLEY (The Big Valley) (ABC)

ACTOR - COMEDY SERIES (E-475)

DON ADAMS as MAXWELL SMART (Get Smart!) (NBC)
BOB CRANE as COL. ROBERT HOGAN (Hogan's Heroes) (CBS)
BRIAN KEITH as BILL DAVIS (Family Affair) (CBS)
LARRY STORCH as CORPORAL AGARN (F Troop) (ABC)

ACTRESS - COMEDY SERIES (E-476)

LUCILLE BALL as LUCY CARMICHAEL (The Lucy Show) (CBS)
ELIZABETH MONTGOMERY as SAMANTHA STEVENS (Bewitched) (ABC)
AGNES MOOREHEAD as ENDORA (Bewitched) (ABC)
MARLO THOMAS as ANN MARIE (That Girl) (ABC)

SUPPORTING ACTOR - DRAMA (E-477)

A single program or a series

ELI WALLACH as LOCARNO The Poppy Is Also A Flower (Xerox Special) (ABC)
LEO G. CARROLL as ALEXANDER WAVERLY (The Man From U.N.C.L.E.) (NBC)
LEONARD NIMOY as MR. SPOCK (Star Trek) (NBC)

SUPPORTING ACTRESS - DRAMA (E-478)

A single program or a series

AGNES MOOREHEAD as EMMA VALENTINE Night of the Vicious Valentine (The Wild, Wild West) (CBS)
TINA CHEN as VIETMANESE GIRL The Final War of Olly Winter (CBS Playhouse) (CBS)
RUTH WARRICK as HANNAH CORD (Peyton Place) (ABC)

SUPPORTING ACTOR - COMEDY (E-479)

A single program or a series

DON KNOTTS as BARNEY FIFE Barney Comes to Mayberry (The Andy Griffith Show) (CBS)
GALE GORDON as THEODORE MOONEY (The Lucy Show) (CBS)
WERNER KLEMPERER as COL. WILHELM KLINK (Hogan's Heroes) (CBS)

SUPPORTING ACTRESS - COMEDY (E-480)

A single program or a series

FRANCES BAVIER as AUNT BEE (The Andy Griffith Show) (CBS)
NANCY KULP as JANE HATHAWAY (The Beverly Hillbillies) (CBS)
MARION LORNE as AUNT CLARA (Bewitched) (ABC)

WRITING ACHIEVEMENT - DRAMA (E-481)

A special program or one of a series

BRUCE GELLER (Mission: Impossible) (CBS)
ROBERT CULP The Warlord (I Spy) (NBC)
RONALD RIBMAN The Final War of Olly Winter (CBS Playhouse) (CBS)

WRITING ACHIEVEMENT - COMEDY (E-482)

A special program, one of a series or a series

BUCK HENRY, LEONARD STERN Ship of Spies (2 parts) (Get Smart!) (NBC)
EDMUND HARTMANN Buffy (Family Affair) (CBS)
SIDNEY SHELDON (I Dream of Jeannie) (NBC)

WRITING ACHIEVEMENT - VARIETY (E-483)

A special program, one of a series or a series

MEL BROOKS, SAM DENOFF, BILL PERSKY, CARL REINER, MEL TOLKIN The Sid Caesar, Imogene Coca, Carl Reiner, Howard Morris Special (CBS)
HARRY CRANE, RICH EUSTIS, LEE HALE, PAUL KEYES, AL ROGERS The Dean Martin Show (NBC)
MARVIN MARX, WALTER STONE, ROD PARKER The Jackie Gleason Show (CBS)

DIRECTOR - DRAMA (E-484)

A special program, one of a series or a series

ALEX SEGAL Death Of A Salesman (CBS)
PAUL BOGART The Final War of Olly Winter (CBS Playhouse) (CBS)
PAUL BOGART Mark Twain Tonight! (CBS)
GEORGE SCHAEFER Anastasia (Hallmark Hall of Fame) (NBC)

DIRECTOR - COMEDY (E-485)

A special program, one of a series or a series

JAMES FRAWLEY Royal Flush (The Monkees) (NBC)
WILLIAM ASHER (Bewitched)(ABC)
EARL BELLAMY One Of Our Bombs Is Missing (I Spy) (NBC)
WILLIAM RUSSELL (Family Affair) (CBS)
MAURY THOMPSON (The Lucy Show) (CBS)

DIRECTOR - VARIETY OR MUSIC (E-486)

A special program, one of a series or a series

FIELDER COOK Brigadoon (ABC)
GREG GARRISON The Dean Martin Show (NBC)
DWIGHT HEMION Frank Sinatra: A Man And His Music Part II (CBS)
BOB HENRY The Andy Williams Show (NBC)
BILL HOBIN The Sid Caesar, Imogene Coca, Carl Reiner, Howard Morris Special (CBS)

THE CRAFT AND PROGRAMMING AREAS
(Possibility of Multiple Awards)

ACHIEVEMENTS IN NEWS AND DOCUMENTARIES

PROGRAMS (E-487)

CHINA: THE ROOTS OF MADNESS (Syndicated) Mel Stuart, Producer
HALL OF KINGS (ABC) Harry Rasky, Producer
THE ITALIANS (CBS) Bernard Birnbaum, Producer
THE ANGRY VOICES OF WATTS (NBC) Stuart Schulberg, Producer
CBS REPORTS (CBS) Palmer Williams, Executive Producer
THE HOMOSEXUALS (CBS Reports) (CBS) Harry Morgan, Producer
IF IT'S TUESDAY, THIS MUST BE BELGIUM (CBS) J. C. Sheers, Producer
ORGANIZED CRIME IN AMERICA (American White Paper) (NBC) Fred Freed, Executive Producer

INDIVIDUALS (E-488)

THEODORE H. WHITE Writer of China: The Roots of Madness (Syndicated)
LUIGI BARZINI Narrator of The Italians (CBS)
LUIGI BARZINI AND PERRY WOLFF Writers of The Italians (CBS)
WALTER CRONKITE Commentator on CBS Evening News With Walter Cronkite (CBS)
CHET HUNTLEY AND DAVID BRINKLEY Commentators on Huntley-Brinkley Report (NBC)
JAMES MASON Narrator of Hall of Kings (ABC)
FRANK McGEE Commentator on The Frank McGee Report (NBC)
BUDD SCHULBERG Writer of The Angry Voices of Watts (NBC)
ERIC SEVAREID Commentator on CBS Evening News With Walter Cronkite (CBS)
HOWARD K. SMITH Commentator on Elections '66 (ABC)

INDIVIDUAL ACHIEVEMENTS IN ART DIRECTION AND ALLIED CRAFTS

ART DIRECTION (E-489)

EARL G. CARLSON Set Decorator for Death Of A Salesman (CBS)
TOM JOHN Art Director for Death Of A Salesman (CBS)

COSTUME DESIGN (E-490)

RAY AGHAYAN AND BOB MACKIE Alice Through The Looking Glass (NBC)

MAKE-UP (E-491)

DICK SMITH Mark Twain Tonight! (CBS)
CLAUDE THOMPSON Alice Through The Looking Glass (NBC)

MECHANICAL SPECIAL EFFECTS (E-492)

JIM RUGG Star Trek (NBC)
ROBERT TAIT Voyage To The Bottom Of The Sea (ABC)

INDIVIDUAL ACHIEVEMENTS IN CINEMATOGRAPHY

CINEMATOGRAPHY (E-493)

HASKELL BOGGS, WILLIAM F. WHITELY Bonanza (NBC)

PHOTOGRAPHIC SPECIAL EFFECTS (E-494)

L. B. ABBOTT The Time Tunnel (ABC)
L. B. ABBOTT Voyage To The Bottom Of The Sea (ABC)
DARRELL ANDERSON, LINWOOD G. DUNN, JOSEPH WESTHEIMER Star Trek (NBC)

FILM AND SOUND EDITING (E-495)

PAUL KRASNY, ROBERT WATTS For Film Editing on Mission: Impossible (CBS)
DON HALL, DICK LEGRAND, DANIEL MANDELL, JOHN MILLS For Sound Editing on Voyage To The Bottom Of The Sea (ABC)
DOUGLAS H. GRINDSTAFF For Sound Editing on Star Trek (NBC)

INDIVIDUAL ACHIEVEMENTS IN ELECTRONIC PRODUCTION

TECHNICAL DIRECTORS (E-496)

A. J. CUNNINGHAM Brigadoon (ABC)
A. J. CUNNINGHAM Death Of A Salesman (CBS)
KARL MESSERSCHMIDT The Dean Martin Show (NBC)
JOSEPH STRAUSS Frank Sinatra: A Man And His Music Part II (CBS)
O. TAMBURRI Damn Yankees (NBC)

LIGHTING DIRECTORS (E-497)

LEARD DAVIS Brigadoon (ABC)
LEARD DAVIS Death Of A Salesman (CBS)
JOHN FRESCHI The Andy Williams Show (NBC)
LON STUCKY Frank Sinatra: A Man And His Music Part II (CBS)

VIDEO TAPE EDITING (E-498)

JAMES E. BRADY Death Of A Salesman (CBS)
JAMES E. BRADY Brigadoon (ABC)
LEWIS W. SMITH The Red Skelton Hour (CBS)

AUDIO ENGINEERING (E-499)

BILL COLE Frank Sinatra: A Man And His Music Part II (CBS)
RAY KEMPER Brigadoon (ABC)

SOUND RECORDING (E-500)

FRED BOSCH The Cleveland Orchestra: One Man's Triumph (Bell Telephone Hour) (NBC)

ELECTRONIC CAMERAMEN (E-501)

ROBERT DUNN, GORM ERICKSON, BEN WOLF, NICK DEMOS Brigadoon (ABC)
ROBERT DUNN, GORM ERICKSON, FRED GOUGH, JACK JENNINGS, DICK NELSON Death Of A Salesman (CBS)

INDIVIDUAL ACHIEVEMENTS IN ENGINEERING DEVELOPMENT (E-502)

Because of the unique nature of engineering developments all possible achievements in this awards year were considered by the Blue Ribbon Panel.

PLUMBICON TUBE N. V. Philips Gloeilampenfabrieken
HIGH-BAND VIDEO TAPE RECORDER Ampex Company

SPECIAL CLASSIFICATIONS OF INDIVIDUAL ACHIEVEMENTS (E-503)

ART CARNEY The Jackie Gleason Show (CBS)
TRUMAN CAPOTE AND ELEANOR PERRY For the adaption of A Christmas Memory (ABC Stage 67) (ABC)
ARTHUR MILLER For the adaption of Death Of a Salesman (CBS)
PETER GENNARO Choreographer of Brigadoon (ABC)
SHELDON KELLER AND GLENN WHEATON Writers of Frank Sinatra: A Man And His Music Part II (CBS)
BILL MELENDEZ Director of children's special It's The Great Pumpkin, Charlie Brown (CBS)
CHARLES SCHULZ Writer of children's special It's The Great Pumpkin, Charlie Brown (CBS)
CHARLES SCHULZ Writer of children's special Charlie Brown's All Stars (CBS)
BURR TILLSTROM Puppeteer on Perry Como's Kraft Music Hall (NBC)

DAYTIME PROGRAMMING

PROGRAMS (E-504)

MUTUAL OF OMAHA'S WILD KINGDOM (NBC) Don Meier, Producer
G. E. COLLEGE BOWL (NBC) John Cleary, Producer
THE MIKE DOUGLAS SHOW (Syndicated) Larry Rosen, Producer

INDIVIDUALS (E-505)

MIKE DOUGLAS Master of Ceremonies on The Mike Douglas Show (Syndicated)
TOM KENNEDY Master of Ceremonies on You Don't Say (NBC)
GENE RAYBURN Master of Ceremonies on The Match Game (NBC)

ACHIEVEMENTS IN SPORTS

PROGRAMS (E-506)

ABC'S WIDE WORLD OF SPORTS (ABC) Roone Arledge, Executive Producer
PORTRAIT OF WILLIE MAYS (ABC) Robert Riger, Producer
SHELL'S WONDERFUL WORLD OF GOLF (NBC) Fred Raphael, Producer

INDIVIDUALS (E-507)

JIM McKAY Sports Commentator on Fifth Anniversary Program (ABC's Wide World of Sports) (ABC)
CHRIS SCHENKEL Sports Commentator on Portrait of a Team (ABC)
CHRIS SCHENKEL Sports Commentator on NBA Basketball (ABC)

ACHIEVEMENTS IN MUSIC

COMPOSITION (E-508)

AARON COPLAND Thematic Music on CBS Playhouse (CBS)
EARLE HAGEN I Spy (NBC)
PETE RUGOLO Run For Your Life (NBC)
LALO SCHIFRIN Mission: Impossible (CBS)

CONDUCTORS (E-509)

GORDON JENKINS AND NELSON RIDDLE Frank Sinatra: A Man And His Music Part II (CBS)

ARRANGERS (E-510)

RAY ELLIS AND LENNIE HAYTON Lena (Syndicated)
GORDON JENKINS AND NELSON RIDDLE Frank Sinatra: A Man And His Music Part II (CBS)

MUSICAL ROUTINES AND CHORAL DIRECTION (E-511)

TICKER FREEMAN AND GEORGE WYLE The Andy Williams Show
(NBC)
Finalists judged by Special Committee of former Emmy Award Winners from countries throughout the world

INTERNATIONAL DOCUMENTARY AWARD (E-512)

BIG DEAL AT GOTHENBURG (Tyne Tees Television Limited, Newcastle-upon-Tyne, England)
DARWIN - "THE GALAPAGOS" (Canadian Broadcasting Corporation, Ottawa, Canada)
FAMILY OF MAN (RODZINA CZLOWIECZA) (Film Polski, Warsaw, Poland)

INTERNATIONAL ENTERTAINMENT AWARD (E-513)

THE CARETAKER (Rediffusion Television Limited, London, England)
D.H. LAWRENCE - "THE BLIND MAN" (Granada Television Network Limited, London, England)
PHEDRE (Office de Radiodiffusion Television Francaise, O.R.T.F., Paris, France)
BERNARD SHOW (Societe Suisse de Radiodiffusion et Television, Swiss Television, Zurich, Switzerland)

THE STATION AWARD (E-514)

Regional Winners judged by Committees at National Academy Chapters; Final judging by Special Committee

THE ROAD TO NOWHERE (KLZ-TV, Denver, Colorado)
ASSIGNMENT: 1747 RANDOLPH STREET (WFIL-TV, Philadelphia, Pennsylvania)
A BABY IS A WONDERFUL THING (WBAL-TV, Baltimore, Maryland)
THE FACE OF GENIUS (WBZ-TV Boston, Massachusetts)
FIVE CIVILIZED TRIBES: AN UNFINISHED JOURNEY (KTUL-TV, Tulsa, Oklahoma)
THE GOLDEN CALF (KGW-TV, Portland, Oregon)
I SEE CHICAGO: THE ILLINOIS VOTER'S TEST (WBBM-TV, Chicago, Illinois)
THE LENGTHENING SHADOW (KSD-TV, St. Louis, Missouri)
MEDAL OF VALOR (KTTV, Hollywood, California)

TRUSTEES AWARD (E-515)

SYLVESTER L. "PAT" WEAVER, JR.
"For his constant conviction that the American public deserves better than it gets on the television screen; for introducing the "special" to television, thus breathing new life into the weekly schedule; for providing us with TODAY and TONIGHT; but finally and most importantly, for the imagination, leadership, courage and integrity which he has brought to our medium during the eighteen years he has been a part of it."

1967/68

NEWS AND DOCUMENTARY PROGRAM AND INDIVIDUAL ACHIEVEMENTS

(Possibility of one Award, more than one Award, or no Award)

ACHIEVEMENT WITHIN REGULARLY SCHEDULED NEWS PROGRAMS

PROGRAMS (E-516)

CRISIS IN THE CITIES (Public Broadcast Laboratory) (NET) Av Westin, Executive Producer
COVERAGE OF THE MILWAUKEE OPEN HOUSING CRISIS, FATHER GROPPI, DEMONSTRATIONS, RIOTS (The Huntley/Brinkley Report) (NBC) Robert J. Northshield, Executive Producer
IMMEDIATE AND ON-THE-SPOT COVERAGE OF THE TET ATTACKS

(The Huntley/Brinkley Report) (NBC) Ron Steiman, Chief of NBC News' Saigon Bureau
POLICE CHIEF EXECUTING VC DURING TET ATTACK (The Huntley/Brinkley Report) (NBC) Robert J. Northshield, Executive Producer
SGT. SIMPSON: VIETNAM (Peter Jennings With The News) (ABC) Ken Gale and Sandy Goodman, Producers

INDIVIDUALS (E-517)

JOHN LAURENCE AND KEITH KAY CBS News Correspondent and CBS News Cameraman, Respectively, For "1st Cavalry," "Con Thien" And Other Segments (CBS Evening News With Walter Cronkite) (CBS)
DEAN BRELIS For Coverage of Attack on Hills 882 and 875 (The Huntley/Brinkley Report) (NBC)
KIRK BROWNING For Direction of "Crisis In The Cities" (Public Broadcast Laboratory) (NET)
WINSTON BURDETT CBS News Correspondent, For Middle East Coverage (CBS Evening News With Walter Cronkite and CBS News Special Reports) (CBS)
WALTER CRONKITE CBS News Correspondent, For Vietnam Coverage (CBS Evening News With Walter Cronkite and Report From Vietnam by Walter Cronkite) (CBS)
DAVID DOUGLAS DUNCAN For Still Photo Essays on the Marines Under Bombardment at Con Thien and Khesanh (ABC Evening News With Bob Young) (ABC)
DON FARMER Correspondent, For Reports On The Black And White Communities Preparing For Another Apparently Long Hot Summer (ABC Evening News With Bob Young) (ABC)
PETER JENNINGS For Dramatic Report on Fred Esherick, a 15 Year-Old Boy Facing Death For Killing His Father (ABC Evening News With Bob Young) (ABC)
CHARLES KURALT AND JAMES WILSON CBS News Correspondent and CBS News Cameraman, Respectively, For "On The Road" (CBS Evening News With Walter Cronkite) (CBS)
WALTER LIPPMAN For Walter Lippman On Vietnam And Politics (Public Broadcast Laboratory)(NET)
EDWARD P. MORGAN Program Commentator, for Public Broadcast Laboratory (Series) And Particularly "A Conversation With Dean Acheson" (Public Broadcast Laboratory) (NET)
ERIC SEVAREID CBS News National Correspondent (CBS Evening News With Walter Cronkite) (CBS)
HOWARD K. SMITH, JOHN SCALI, WILLIAM H. LAWRENCE, JOSEPH C. HARSCH For Their Commentaries On Vietnam, Politics and Various Domestic Issues (Evening News) (ABC)
HOWARD TUCKNER For Reporting While Wounded in Vietnam (The Huntley/Brinkley Report) (NBC)
AV WESTIN Executive Producer For Public Broadcast Laboratory (Series) And Particularly "George Wallace's America" (Public Broadcast Laboratory) (NET)

ACHIEVEMENT IN COVERAGE OF SPECIAL EVENTS

PROGRAMS (E-518)

NEWS ANALYSIS (State of the Union/68) (NET) Jim Karayn, Producer
CBS NEWS CONTINUOUS COVERAGE OF WAR IN MIDDLE EAST (CBS News Special Reports and Special Broadcasts) (CBS) Harold Haley, Ernest Leiser, Phillip Lewis, and Robert Wussler, Producers
CBS NEWS SPECIAL REPORT: VIETNAM PERSPECTIVE: THE ORDEAL OF CON THIEN (CBS) Burton Benjamin, Producer
COMPLETE LIVE COVERAGE OF THE UNITED NATIONS DURING THE MIDDLE EAST CRISIS (NBC) James Kitchell, Producer
COVERAGE OF THE MIDDLE EAST WAR AND OTHER SPECIALS FROM THE U.N. (War In The Middle East) (ABC) Walter Pfister, Jr., Executive Producer
SATELLITE COVERAGE OF ADENAUER'S FUNERAL (NBC) James Kitchell, Producer
SATELLITE COVERAGE OF POPE'S VISIT TO FATIMA (NBC) James Kitchell, Producer

INDIVIDUALS (E-519)

FRANK McGEE For His Commentary on Satellite Coverage of Ade-

nauer's Funeral (NBC)
WALTER CRONKITE CBS News Correspondent, For His Coverage of Apollo 4 (Saturn V) (CBS News Special Report: The Flight of Apollo 4) (CBS)

ACHIEVEMENT IN NEWS DOCUMENTARIES

PROGRAMS (E-520)

AFRICA (ABC) James Fleming, Executive Producer
SUMMER '67: WHAT WE LEARNED (NBC) Fred Freed, Producer
ABC SCOPE: THE VIETNAM WAR Series (ABC) Arthur Holch, Executive Producer
CBS NEWS INQUIRY: THE WARREN REPORT (CBS News Hour) (CBS) Leslie Midgley, Producer
CBS NEWS SPECIAL: DESTINATION: NORTH POLE (CBS) Palmer Williams, Producer
CBS NEWS SPECIAL: VIET CONG (CBS News Hour) (CBS) James B. Faichney, Producer
CBS NEWS SPECIAL REPORT: MORLEY SAFER'S RED CHINA DIARY (CBS News Hour) (CBS) Morley Safer, Producer
CBS REPORTS: WHAT ABOUT RONALD REAGAN? (CBS News Hour) (CBS) Gene De Poris, Producer
ISRAEL: VICTORY OR ELSE (NBC) George Murray, Producer
KHRUSHCHEV IN EXILE (NBC) Lucy Jarvis, Producer
ON FACE VALUE (Your Dollar's Worth) (NET) Ofra Bikel, Producer
THE POOR PAY MORE (NET Journal) (NET) Morton Silverstein, Producer
SAME MUD, SAME BLOOD (NBC) Eliot Frankel, Producer
SOUTHERN ACCENTS, NORTHERN GHETTOS (ABC) William Peters, Producer
SOVIETS IN SPACE (NBC) George Vicas, Producer
WAR IN THE SKIES (ABC) Lester Cooper, Producer
THE WAY IT IS (NET Journal) (NET) Harold Mayer, Producer
WHAT HARVEST FOR THE REAPER? (NET Journal) (NET) Morton Silverstein, Producer
WHERE IS PREJUDICE? (NET Journal) (NET) Richard McCutchen, Producer
WHO IN '68? (ABC) Paul Altmeyer, Producer

INDIVIDUALS (E-521)

HARRY REASONER Writer of CBS Reports: What About Ronald Reagan? (CBS)
VO HUYNH Cameraman on Same Mud, Same Blood (NBC)
ETHEL HUBER For Music Supervision on CBS News Special: Road Signs On a Merry-Go-Round (CBS)
JOHN LAURENCE Correspondent on CBS News Special Report: Vietnam Perspective: The Ordeal Of Con Thien (CBS)
PETER McINTYRE Soundman on Same Mud, Same Blood (NBC)
MASAAKI SHIHARA Soundman on Same Mud, Same Blood (NBC)
JERI SOPANEN Cameraman on The Way It is (NET Journal) (NET)

ACHIEVEMENT IN CULTURAL DOCUMENTARIES

PROGRAMS (E-522)

CBS NEWS SPECIAL: ERIC HOFFER: THE PASSIONATE STATE OF MIND (CBS News Hour) (CBS) Harry Morgan, Producer
CBS NEWS SPECIAL: GAUGUIN IN TAHITI: THE SEARCH FOR PARADISE (CBS News Hour) (CBS) Martin Carr, Producer
JOHN STEINBECK'S "AMERICA AND AMERICANS" (NBC) Lee Mendelson, Producer
DYLAN THOMAS: THE WORLD I BREATHE (NET Festival) (NET) Perry Miller Adato, Producer
AMERICAN PROFILE: MUSIC FROM THE LAND (American Profile) (NBC) Chet Hagan, Producer
AMERICAN PROFILE: THE NATIONAL GALLERY OF ART (American Profile) (NBC) Louis J. Hazam, Producer
AN EVENING AT TANGLEWOOD (NBC) George A. Heinemann, Producer
CAN YOU HEAR ME? (ABC) Lester Cooper, Producer
CBS NEWS SPECIAL: GALILEO GALILEI (CBS) Pamela Ilott, Producer

CBS NEWS SPECIAL: ROAD SIGNS ON A MERRY-GO-ROUND (CBS) Joseph Clement, Producer

DIALOGUE: MARTIN BUBER AND ISRAEL (NET) Michael Roemer and Robert Young, Producers

DUKE ELLINGTON: LOVE YOU MADLY (NET) Richard Moore and Ralph S. Gleason, Producers

EVERETT DIRKSEN'S WASHINGTON (ABC) James Benjamin, Producer

LIFE AND TIMES OF JOHN HUSTON, ESQUIRE (NET) Tom Slevin, Producer

MR. DICKENS OF LONDON (ABC) Daniel E. Wilson, Producer

ROBERT SCOTT AND THE RACE FOR THE SOUTH POLE (ABC) John H. Secondari and Helen Jean Rogers, Producers

THE LAW AND THE PROPHETS (Project 20) (NBC) Donald B. Hyatt, Producer

THE PURSUIT OF EXCELLENCE - THE VIENNA CHOIR BOYS (ABC) Ernest Pendrell, Producer

THE RISE AND FALL OF THE THIRD REICH (ABC) Mel Stuart, Executive Producer; Jack Kaufman, Producer

THE WYETH PHENOMENON ON "WHO, WHAT, WHEN, WHERE, WHY WITH HARRY REASONER" (CBS News Hour) (CBS) Harry Morgan, Producer

INDIVIDUALS (E-523)

NATHANIEL DORSKY For His Art Photography For CBS News Special: "Gauguin In Tahiti: The Search For Paradise" (CBS News Hour) (CBS)

HARRY MORGAN Writer For the Wyeth Phenomenon On "Who, What, When, Where, Why With Harry Reasoner" (CBS News Hour) (CBS)

THOMAS A. PRIESTLEY AND ROBERT LOWEREE Director of Photography And Film Editor, Respectively, For John Steinbeck's "America and Americans" (NBC)

MARTIN CARR Writer For CBS News Special: "Gauguin In Tahiti: The Search For Paradise" (CBS News Hour) (CBS)

GERALD FRIED Composer For CBS News Special: 'Gauguin In Tahiti: The Search For Paradise" (CBS News Hour) (CBS)

WILLIAM B. HARTIGAN Director Of Photography For Robert Scott And The Race For The South Pole (ABC)

LOUIS J. HAZAM Writer For American Profile: The National Gallery Of Art (American Profile) (NBC)

PETER MOSELEY Film Editor For Life And Times Of John Huston, Esquire (NET)

ERIC SEVAREID Interviewer For CBS News Special: "Eric Hoffer: The Passionate State Of Mind" (CBS News Hour) (CBS)

JOHN WILCOX Cinematographer For CBS News Special: "Gauguin In Tahiti: The Search For Paradise" (CBS News Hour) (CBS)

ROBERT YOUNG Cinematographer For Dialogue: Martin Buber And Israel (NET)

OTHER NEWS AND DOCUMENTARY ACHIEVEMENTS

PROGRAMS (E-524)

THE 21ST CENTURY (CBS) Isaac Kleinerman, Producer
SCIENCE AND RELIGION: WHO WILL PLAY GOD? (CBS News Special) (CBS) Ben Flynn, Producer
ANIMAL SECRETS Series (NBC) Edward Stanley, Producer
A CONVERSATION WITH SVETLANA ALLILUYEVA (NET Journal) (NET) Henry Morgenthau III, Producer
BOSTON POPS CONCERT FOR YOUNGSTERS (NBC) George A. Heinemann, Producer
DIRECTIONS Series (ABC) Wiley F. Hance, Executive Producer
DISCOVERY '68 Series (ABC) Jules Power, Executive Producer
THE LEARNING PROCESS (NBC) Craig Fisher, Producer
NEW MORALITY: CHALLENGE OF THE STUDENT GENERATION (CBS News Special) (CBS) Chalmers Dale, Producer
OUR WORLD (Global Telecast) (NET) Robert D. Squier, Executive Producer
THE SHEPARDES PLAYE (ABC) Wiley F. Hance, Producer

INDIVIDUAL (E-525)

GEORGES DELERUE Composer For Our World (Global Telecast) (NET)

ENTERTAINMENT PROGRAM AND INDIVIDUAL ACHIEVEMENTS
(One Award only in each of the remaining Categories)

COMEDY SERIES (E-526)

GET SMART (NBC) Burt Nodella, Producer
BEWITCHED (ABC) William Asher, Producer
FAMILY AFFAIR (CBS) Edmund Hartmann, Producer
HOGAN'S HEROES (CBS) Edward H. Feldman, Producer
THE LUCY SHOW (CBS) Tommy Thompson, Producer

DRAMATIC SERIES (E-527)

MISSION: IMPOSSIBLE (CBS) Joseph E. Gantman, Producer
THE AVENGERS (ABC) Albert Fennell and Brian Clemens, Producers
I SPY (NBC) Morton Fine and David Friedkin, Producers
NET PLAYHOUSE (NET) Curtis Davis, Executive Producer
RUN FOR YOUR LIFE (NBC) Roy Huggins, Executive Producer
STAR TREK (NBC) Gene Roddenberry, Executive Producer

DRAMATIC PROGRAM (E-528)

A single program of a series or a special program

ELIZABETH THE QUEEN (Hallmark Hall of Fame) (NBC) George Schaefer, Producer
DO NOT GO GENTLE INTO THAT GOOD NIGHT (CBS Playhouse) (CBS) George Schaefer, Producer
DEAR FRIENDS (CBS Playhouse) (CBS) Herbert Brodkin, Producer
THE STRANGE CASE OF DR. JEKYLL AND MR. HYDE (ABC) Dan Curtis, Producer
UNCLE VANYA (NET Playhouse) (NET) Sir Laurence Olivier, Producer
LUTHER (Xerox Special) (ABC) Michael Style and Trevor Wallace, Producers

MUSICAL OR VARIETY SERIES (E-529)

Awards to producer and star (if applicable)

ROWAN AND MARTIN'S LAUGH-IN (NBC) George Schlatter, Producer
BELL TELEPHONE HOUR (NBC) Henry Jaffe, Executive Producer; Robert Drew, Michael Jackson and Mel Stuart, Producers
THE CAROL BURNETT SHOW (CBS) Joseph Hamilton, Producer
THE DEAN MARTIN SHOW (NBC) Greg Garrison, Producer
THE SMOTHERS BROTHERS COMEDY HOUR (CBS) Saul Ilson and Ernest Chambers, Producers

MUSICAL OR VARIETY PROGRAM (E-530)

A special program or one of a series Awards to producer and star (if applicable)

ROWAN AND MARTIN'S LAUGH-IN SPECIAL (NBC) George Schlatter, Producer
A MAN AND HIS MUSIC ▪ ELLA ▪ JOBIM (NBC) Robert Sheerer, Producer
CHRYSLER PRESENTS THE BOB HOPE CHRISTMAS SPECIAL (Chrysler Presents the Bob Hope Show) (NBC) Bob Hope, Executive Producer
FIVE BALLETS OF THE FIVE SENSES (Lincoln Center/Stage 5 - Syndicated) (NET) Jac Venza, Producer
THE FRED ASTAIRE SHOW (NBC) Fred Astaire and Gil Rodin, Producers
HERB ALPERT AND THE TIJUANA BRASS (CBS) Gary Smith and Dwight Hemion, Producers

ACTOR - SINGLE PERFORMANCE - DRAMA (E-531)

MELVYN DOUGLAS as PETER SCHERMAN Do Not Go Gentle Into

That Good Night (CBS Playhouse) (CBS)
RAYMOND BURR as CHIEF IRONSIDE Ironside, World Premiere (NBC)
VAN HEFLIN as ROBERT SLOAN A Case of Libel (ABC)
GEORGE C. SCOTT as JOHN PROCTOR The Crucible (CBS)
ELI WALLACH as DOUG LAMBERT Dear Friends (CBS Playhouse) (CBS)

ACTRESS - SINGLE PERFORMANCE - DRAMA (E-532)

MAUREEN STAPLETON as MARY O'MEAGHAN Among The Paths to Eden (Xerox Special) (ABC)
DAME JUDITH ANDERSON as ELIZABETH Elizabeth The Queen (Hallmark Hall of Fame) (NBC)
GENEVIEVE BUJOLD as JOAN Saint Joan (Hallmark Hall of Fame) (NBC)
COLLEEN DEWHURST as ELIZABETH PROCTOR The Crucible (CBS)
ANNE JACKSON as VIVIAN SPEARS Dear Friends (CBS Playhouse) (CBS)

ACTOR - DRAMATIC SERIES (E-533)

BILL COSBY as ALEXANDER SCOTT (I Spy) (NBC)
ROBERT CULP as KELLY ROBINSON (I Spy) (NBC)
RAYMOND BURR as CHIEF IRONSIDE (Ironside) (NBC)
BEN GAZZARA as PAUL BRYAN (Run For Your Life) (NBC)
MARTIN LANDAU as ROLLIN HAND (Mission: Impossible) (CBS)

ACTRESS - DRAMATIC SERIES (E-534)

BARBARA BAIN as CINNAMON CARTER (Mission: Impossible) (CBS)
DIANA RIGG as MRS. EMMA PEEL (The Avengers) (ABC)
BARBARA STANWYCK as VICTORIA BARKLEY (The Big Valley) (ABC)

ACTOR - COMEDY SERIES (E-535)

DON ADAMS as MAXWELL SMART (Get Smart) (NBC)
RICHARD BENJAMIN as DICK HOLLISTER (He and She) (CBS)
SEBASTIAN CABOT as FRENCH (Family Affair) (CBS)
BRIAN KEITH as BILL DAVIS (Family Affair) (CBS)
DICK YORK as DARRIN STEVENS (Bewitched) (ABC)

ACTRESS - COMEDY SERIES (E-536)

LUCILLE BALL as LUCY (The Lucy Show) (CBS)
BARBARA FELDON as AGENT '99' (Get Smart) (NBC)
ELIZABETH MONTGOMERY as SAMANTHA STEVENS (Bewitched) (ABC)
PAULA PRENTISS as PAULA HOLLISTER (He and She) (CBS)
MARLO THOMAS as ANN MARIE (That Girl) (ABC)

SUPPORTING ACTOR - DRAMA (E-537)

A single program of a series, a special program or a series

MILBURN STONE as DOC (Gunsmoke) (CBS)
JOSEPH CAMPANELLA as LEW WICKERSHAM (Mannix) (CBS)
LAWRENCE DOBKIN as GETTLINGER Do Not Go Gentle Into That Good Night (CBS Playhouse) (CBS)
LEONARD NIMOY as MR. SPOCK (Star Trek) (NBC)

SUPPORTING ACTRESS - DRAMA (E-538)

A single program of a series, a special program or a series

BARBARA ANDERSON as OFFICER EVE WHITFIELD (Ironside) (NBC)
LINDA CRISTAL as VICTORIA CANNON (The High Chaparral) (NBC)
TESSIE O'SHEA as TESSIE O'TOOLE The Strange Case of Dr. Jekyll and Mr. Hyde (ABC)

SUPPORTING ACTOR - COMEDY (E-539)

A single program of a series, a special program or a series

WERNER KLEMPERER as COL. WILHELM KLINK (Hogan's Heroes) (CBS)
JACK CASSIDY as OSCAR NORTH (He and She) (CBS)
WILLIAM DEMAREST as UNCLE CHARLEY (My Three Sons) (CBS)
GALE GORDON as THEODORE MOONEY (The Lucy Show) (CBS)

SUPPORTING ACTRESS - COMEDY (E-540)

A single program of a series, a special program or a series

MARION LORNE as AUNT CLARA (Bewitched) (ABC)
AGNES MOOREHEAD as ENDORA (Bewitched) (ABC)
MARGE REDMOND as SISTER JACQUELINE (The Flying Nun) (ABC)
NITA TALBOT as MARYA The Hostage (Hogan's Heroes) (CBS)

WRITING - DRAMA (E-541)

A special program or one of a series

LORING MANDEL Do Not Go Gentle Into That Good Night (CBS Playhouse) (CBS)
ALLAN BALTER AND WILLIAM READ WOODFIELD The Seal (Mission: Impossible) (CBS)
DON M. MANKIEWICZ Ironside, World Premiere (NBC)
REGINALD ROSE Dear Friends (CBS Playhouse) (CBS)

WRITING - COMEDY (E-542)

A special program or one of a series

ALLAN BURNS AND CHRIS HAYWARD The Coming Out Party (He and She) (CBS)
DANNY ARNOLD AND RUTH BROOKS FLIPPEN The Mailman Cometh (That Girl) (ABC)
MILT JOSEFSBERG AND RAY SINGER Lucy Gets Jack Benny's Account (The Lucy Show) (CBS)
LEONARD STERN AND ARNE SULTAN The Old Man And The She (He and She) (CBS)

WRITING - MUSIC OR VARIETY (E-543)

A special program or one of a series

CHRIS BEARD, PHIL HAHN, JACK HANRAHAN, COSLOUGH JOHNSON, PAUL KEYES, MARC LONDON, ALLAN MANNINGS, DAVID PANICH, HUGH WEDLOCK, DIGBY WOLFE Rowan and Martin's Laugh-In (NBC)
BILL ANGELOS, STAN BURNS, DON HINKLEY, BUZ KOHAN, MIKE MARMER, GAIL PARENT, ARNIE ROSEN, KENNY SOLMS, SAUL TURTLETAUB The Carol Burnett Show (CBS)
LARRY HOVIS, PAUL W. KEYES, JIM MULLIGAN, DAVID PANICH, GEORGE SCHLATTER, DIGBY WOLFE Rowan and Martin's Laugh-In Special (NBC)
TED BERGMAN, ALLAN BLYE, SAM BOBRICK, ERNEST CHAMBERS, RON CLARK, GENE FARMER, HAL GOLDMAN, AL GORDON, SAUL ILSON, JERRY MUSIC, MASON WILLIAMS The Smothers Brothers Comedy Hour (CBS)

DIRECTOR - DRAMA (E-544)

A special program or one of a series

PAUL BOGART Dear Friends (CBS Playhouse) (CBS)
LEE H. KATZIN The Killing (Mission: Impossble) (CBS)
GEORGE SCHAEFER Do Not Go Gentle Into That Good Night (CBS Playhouse) (CBS)
ALEX SEGAL The Crucible (CBS)

DIRECTOR - COMEDY (E-545)

A special program or one of a series

BRUCE BILSON Maxwell Smart, Private Eye (Get Smart) (NBC)
DANNY ARNOLD The Apartment (That Girl) (ABC)
JAMES FRAWLEY The Devil and Peter Tork (The Monkees) (NBC)

DIRECTOR - MUSIC OR VARIETY (E-546)

A special program or one of a series

JACK HALEY, JR. Movin' With Nancy (NBC)
BILL R. FOSTER Rowan and Martin's Laugh-In Special (NBC)
GREG GARRISON The Dean Martin Show (NBC)
DWIGHT HEMION Herb Alpert and the Tijuana Brass (CBS)
GORDON W. WILES Rowan and Martin's Laugh-In, (NBC)

MUSICAL COMPOSITION (E-547)

A special program or one of a series

EARLE HAGEN Laya (I Spy) (NBC)
BERNARD GREEN My Father and My Mother (CBS Playhouse) (CBS)
PETE RUGOLO Cry Hard, Cry Fast (Run For Your Life) (NBC)
LALO SCHIFRIN The Seal (Mission: Impossible) (CBS)
MORTON STEVENS Major Glory (Gunsmoke) (CBS)
HARRY SUKMAN The Champion of the Western World (The High Chaparral) (NBC)

ART DIRECTION AND SCENIC DESIGN (E-548)

A special program or one of a series; Award to Art Director and Scenic Designer - and to Set Decorator (if applicable)

JAMES W. TRITTIPO Art Director for The Fred Astaire Show (NBC)
WARREN CLYMER Art Director for Elizabeth The Queen (Hallmark Hall Of Fame) (NBC)
ROMAIN JOHNSTON AND CHARLES KREINER Art Director and Set Decorator, Respectively, for The Smothers Brothers Comedy Hour (CBS)
WILLIAM P. ROSS Art Director for Echo Of Yesterday (Mission: Impossible) (CBS)
JAN SCOTT AND GEORGE GAINES Art Director and Set Decorator, Respectively, for Kismet (Armstrong Circle Theatre) (ABC)

CINEMATOGRAPHY (E-549)

A special program or one of a series

RALPH WOOLSEY A Thief Is A Thief Is A Thief (It Takes A Thief) (ABC)
GORDON AVIL How To Escape From A Prison Camp Without Really Leaving (Hogan's Heroes) (CBS)
WINTON C. HOCH Raiders From Outerspace (Time Tunnel) (ABC)

ELECTRONIC CAMERAWORK (E-550)

A special program or one of a series; Award to Technical Director, with Certificates to Cameramen

A. J. CUNNINGHAM, Technical Director; EDWARD CHANEY, ROBERT FONOROW, HARRY TATARIAN, BEN WOLFE, Cameramen, Do Not Go Gentle Into That Good Night (CBS Playhouse) (CBS)
CHUCK HOWARD Director of Program Productions, 10th Winter Olympic Games (ABC)
HEINO RIPP Technical Director, Herb Alpert and the Tijuana Brass (CBS)
JOE STRAUSS, Technical Director; RICHARD DURHAM, RAY FIGELSKI, ROY HOLM, ROBERT KEYS, CARL PITSCH, RON SHELDON, TONY YARLETT, Cameramen, The Fred Astaire Show (NBC)

FILM EDITING (E-551)

A special program or one of a series

PETER JOHNSON The Sounds and Sights of Chicago (Bell Telephone Hour) (NBC)
RICHARD BROCKWAY, DONN CAMBERN, JOHN C. FULLER Chrysler Presents The Bob Hope Christmas Special (NBC)
PETER V. PUNZI Four Days To Omaha (NBC Experiment in Television) (NBC)
DONALD R. RODE The Doomsday Machine (Star Trek) (NBC)
DONALD D. WAGES The Photographer (Mission: Impossible) (CBS)
ROBERT WATTS The Traitor (Mission: Impossible) (CBS)

THE AREAS

(Possibility of one Award, more than one Award, or no Award)

ACHIEVEMENT IN CHILDREN'S PROGRAMMING

PROGRAMS (CHILDREN'S) (E-552)

HE'S YOUR DOG, CHARLIE BROWN (CBS) Lee Mendelson and Bill Melendez, Producers
MISTEROGER'S NEIGHBORHOOD (NET) Fred Rogers, Producer
YOU'RE IN LOVE, CHARLIE BROWN (CBS) Lee Mendelson and Bill Melendez, Producers

INDIVIDUAL (CHILDREN'S PROGRAMS) (E-553)

FRED ROGERS Host on Misteroger's Neighborhood (NET)

ACHIEVEMENT IN DAYTIME PROGRAMMING

PROGRAMS (E-554)

TODAY (NBC) Al Morgan, Producer
CAMERA THREE (CBS) Nick Havinga and James MacAllen, Producers
THE MIKE DOUGLAS SHOW (Syndicated) Roger E. Ailes, Producer

INDIVIDUALS (E-555)

MacDONALD CAREY as DR. TOM HORTON Days of Our Lives (NBC)
JOAN BENNETT as ELIZABETH COLLINS STODDARD Dark Shadows (ABC)
CELESTE HOLM as MRS. BERN Fat Hands and a Diamond Ring (Insight) (Syndicated)

ACHIEVEMENT IN SPORTS PROGRAMMING

PROGRAMS (E-556)

ABC'S WIDE WORLD OF SPORTS (ABC) Roone P. Arledge, Executive Producer
THE AMERICAN SPORTSMAN (ABC) Lorne Hassan, Producer
THE FLYING FISHERMAN (Syndicated) Nicholas W. Russo, Executive Producer
10TH WINTER OLYMPIC GAMES (ABC) Roone P. Arledge, Executive Producer

INDIVIDUALS (E-557)

JIM McKAY Sports Commentator on ABC's Wide World of Sports (ABC)
DICK BUTTON Sports Commentator on 10th Winter Olympic Games (ABC)
CHRISTOPHER SCHENKEL Sports Commentator on NCAA Football (ABC)

SPECIAL CLASSIFICATION OF INDIVIDUAL ACHIEVEMENTS (E-558)

ART CARNEY for performances on The Jackie Gleason Show (CBS)
PAT PAULSEN for performances on The Smothers Brothers Comedy Hour (CBS)
THE WESTHEIMER COMPANY for Special Photographic Effects on Metamorphosis (Star Trek) (NBC)
JOSEPH G. SOROKIN Sound Editor of The Survivors (Mission: Impossible) (CBS)
CHARLES M. SCHULZ Writer of Children's Special, You're In Love, Charlie Brown (CBS)
BILL MELENDEZ Director of Children's Special, You're In Love, Charlie Brown (CBS)
DAVID WINTERS Choreographer of Movin' With Nancy (NBC)

INDIVIDUAL ACHIEVEMENT - MUSIC (E-559)
(Other than composer)
MITCHELL AYRES Conductor of The Hollywood Palace (ABC)
ARTHUR FIEDLER Conductor of A Boston Pops Concert for Youngsters (Children's Theatre) (NBC)
NEAL HEFTI Conductor of The Fred Astaire Show (NBC)
SAMMY CAHN Lyricist for The Legend of Robin Hood (NBC)
LEE HALE for Special Musical Material on The Dean Martin Christmas Show (The Dean Martin Show) (NBC)
ARTHUR MALVIN for Special Musical Material on A Man and His Music plus Ella plus Jobim (NBC)

INDIVIDUAL ACHIEVEMENT - VISUAL ARTS (E-560)
BERT GORDON for Graphic Design on The Strange Case of Dr. Jekyll and Mr. Hyde (ABC)
DICK SMITH for Make-Up on The Strange Case of Dr. Jekyll and Mr. Hyde (ABC)
DAN STRIEPEKE for Make-Up on The Space Destructors (Lost In Space) (CBS)

INDIVIDUAL ACHIEVEMENT - ELECTRONIC PRODUCTION (E-561)
ARTHUR SCHNEIDER Tape Editor of Rowan and Martin's Laugh-In Special (NBC)
WILLIAM M. KLAGES Lighting Director of Herb Alpert and The Tijuana Brass (CBS)
LON STUCKY Lighting Director of Carousel (Armstrong Circle Theatre) (ABC)
BILL COLE Audio Engineer of The Fred Astaire Show (NBC)
ROBERT H. GUHL Audio Engineer of Home to Judgement (I Spy) (NBC)
NICK V. GIORDANO Tape Editor of The Hollywood Palace (ABC)
JERRY SMITH for Video Control of Carousel (Armstrong Circle Theatre) (ABC)
HERB WEISS for Video Control of The Hollywood Palace (ABC)

SPECIAL AWARDS

THE TRUSTEES AWARD (E-562)
DONALD H. McGANNON, President and Chairman of the Board of Directors of Group W (Westinghouse Broadcasting Company) "For his creative leadership of one of the most dynamic groups of radio and television stations in the United States; for innovating and encouraging the development by a Station Group of public service and entertainment programs of unparalleled scope and quality; and particularly for his early recognition of broadcasting's need to train and employ individuals from minority groups."

ACHIEVEMENT IN ENGINEERING DEVELOPMENT (E-563)
BRITISH BROADCASTING CORPORATION For the "Electronic Field-Store Colour Television Standards Converter." By converting television pictures instantaneously from the 525-line/60-field NTSC system used in America and other countries to the 625-line/50-field PAL or SECAM systems used in Europe and in other parts of the world.

THE STATION AWARD (E-564)
NOW IS THE TIME (WCAU-TV, Philadelphia, Pennsylvania)
OPERATION THANKS - PARTS I AND II (KFMB-TV, San Diego, California)
ALBINA: GHETTO OF THE MIND (KGW-TV, Portland, Oregon)
OUR KIND OF WORLD - EPISODE NO. 6 (KRMA-TV, Denver, Colorado)
WHAT'S A MAN WORTH? (KSD-TV, St. Louis, Missouri)
THE DROPOUT DRUGS (KUTV, Salt Lake City, Utah)
A MATTER OF LIFE (WNBC-TV, New York City, New York)
THE GIANTS AND THE COMMON MEN (WMAQ-TV, Chicago, Illinois)
THE OTHER WASHINGTON (WRC-TV, Washington, D.C.)

SPECIAL CITATION (E-565)
THE OTHER SIDE OF THE SHADOW (WWL-TV, New Orleans, Louisiana)
THE OTHER WASHINGTON (WRC-TV, Washington, D.C.)
TONY McBRIDE (KDKA-TV, Pittsburgh, Pennsylvania)
POVERTY'S CHILDREN ARE NOT ALIKE (KLZ-TV, Denver, Colorado)
THE INVISIBLE MINORITY (KNBC-TV, Los Angeles, California)
WHAT'S A MAN WORTH? (KSD-TV, St. Louis, Missouri)
SIX DAYS IN JULY (WWJ-TV, Detroit, Michigan)

INTERNATIONAL DOCUMENTARY AWARD (E-566)
LA SECTION ANDERSON (office de Radiodiffusion Television Francaise, O.R.T.F., Paris, France)
THE ENCHANTED ISLES (Anglia Television Limited, London, England)
HIGH STREET MAYFAIR (BOND STREET) (ATV Network Limited, London, England)
THE PRICE OF A RECORD (Four Companies Productions, Border Television Limited, Cumberland, England)
CONTRACT 736 (Scottish Television Limited, Glasgow, Scotland)
THE SERVANTS (Tyne Tees Television Limited, Newcastle upon Tyne, England)

INTERNATIONAL ENTERTAINMENT AWARD (E-567)
CALL ME DADDY (Armchair Theatre) (ABC Television Limited, Middlesex, England)
SWAN LAKE (Canadian Broadcasting Corporation, Ottawa, Canada)
THE GOOD AND FAITHFUL SERVANT (Rediffusion Television Limited, London, England)
RIEDAIGLIA (Sveriges Radio, Stockholm, Sweden)
DI OFARIMS (Westdeutscher Rundfunk, Cologne, Germany)

1968/69

ACHIEVEMENT WITHIN REGULARLY SCHEDULED NEWS PROGRAMS

PROGRAMS (E-568)
COVERAGE OF HUNGER IN THE UNITED STATES (The Huntley-Brinkley Report) (NBC) Wallace Westfeldt, Executive Producer
DEBATE BETWEEN SENATOR ROBERT F. KENNEDY AND SENATOR EUGENE McCARTHY (Issues And Answers) (ABC) Peggy Whedon, Producer
RECAP OF SENATOR ROBERT F. KENNEDY FUNERAL (The ABC Weekend News) (ABC) Sid Darion, Executive Producer

INDIVIDUALS (E-569)
CHARLES KURALT, JAMES WILSON, ROBERT FUNK Correspondent, Cameraman and Soundman, Respectively, For "On The Road" (CBS Evening News With Walter Cronkite) (CBS)
JOHN LAURENCE Correspondent for "Police After Chicago" (CBS Evening News With Walter Cronkite) (CBS)
FRANK BOURGHOLTZER Reporter for "Coverage of Russian Naval Emergence in Mediterranean" (The Frank McGee Report) (NBC)
FRED BRIGGS Reporter For "Coverage of the Campaign to Obtain Black Lung Compensation" (The Huntley-Brinkley Report) (NBC)
HEYWOOD HALE BROUN Special Correspondent For "Special Sports Reporting" (CBS Evening News With Roger Mudd-Saturday) (CBS)
JOHN CHANCELLOR Reporter For "Coverage of 1968 Political Campaign" (The Huntley-Brinkley Report) (NBC)
PETER JENNINGS For "Report on Slaughter of Baby Seals" (ABC News With Frank Reynolds) (ABC)
FRANK REYNOLDS For "Commentaries" (ABC Evening News With Frank Reynolds) (ABC)

MORLEY SAFER Correspondent For Coverage of "Nigerian-Biafran War" (CBS Evening News With Walter Cronkite) (CBS)

ERIC SEVARIED Correspondent For "Analysis" (CBS Evening News With Walter Cronkite) (CBS)

HOWARD K. SMITH For "Commentaries" (ABC Evening News With Frank Reynolds) (ABC)

LIZ TROTTA Reporter For Coverage of "Vietnam War" (The Huntley-Brinkley Report) (NBC)

ACHIEVEMENT IN COVERAGE OF SPECIAL EVENTS

PROGRAMS (E-570)

COVERAGE OF MARTIN LUTHER KING ASSASSINATION AND AFTERMATH (CBS News Special Reports And Special Broadcasts) (CBS) Robert Wussler, Ernest Leiser, Burton Benjamin, Don Hewitt, Executive Producers

APOLLO: A JOURNEY TO THE MOON (FLIGHT NOS. VII, VIII AND IX) (NBC News Special) (NBC) James Kitchell, Producer

ASSASSINATION AND FUNERAL OF SENATOR ROBERT F. KENNEDY (ABC) Walter J. Pfister, Jr, Executive Producer

JULES BERGMAN AND RALPH LAPP DISCUSSIONS ON MANNED SPACE PROGRAMS-APOLLO VIII (Space '68) (ABC) Walter J. Pfister, Jr, Executive Producer

CHICAGO DEMOCRATIC CONVENTION COVERAGE (NBC News Special) George Murray, Executive Producer

COVERAGE OF THE DEMOCRATIC CONVENTION AND SURROUNDING EVENTS (CBS News Special Reports and Special Broadcasts) (CBS) Robert Wussler, Executive Producer

COVERAGE OF ROBERT F. KENNEDY ASSASSINATION AND AFTERMATH (CBS News Special Reports and Special Broadcasts) (CBS) Ernest Leiser, William Small, Robert Wussler, Don Hewitt, Executive Producers

NEWS ANALYSIS (The President's Farewell) (NET) Ned Schnurman, Executive Producer

NEWS ANALYSIS (The Nixon Administration) (NET) Jim Karayn, Executive Producer

THE INVASION OF CZECHOSLOVAKIA (NBC News Special) (NBC) Robert Shafer, Producer

UNCONVENTIONAL CONVENTION COVERAGE (The Race To The White House) (ABC) Walter J. Pfister, Jr, Executive Producer

INDIVIDUALS (E-571)

JULES BERGMAN Science Editor For Commentary "Space '68" (ABC)

WILLIAM BOYLE, DENNIS DALTON, GENE FARINET, ARTHUR LORD Writers For "Apollo: A Journey To The Moon" (Flight Nos. VII, VIII and IX) (NBC News Special) (NBC)

VERN DIAMOND Director For "Coverage Of The Democratic Convention And Surrounding Events" (CBS News Special Reports And Special Broadcasts) (CBS)

DELOS HALL Cameraman For "Coverage Of The Democratic Convention And Surrounding Events" (CBS News Special Reports And Special Broadcasts) (CBS)

CHET HUNTLEY, DAVID BRINKLEY, SANDY VANOCUR, JOHN CHANCELLOR, FRANK McGEE, EDWIN NEWMAN News Reporters For Team Coverage "Chicago Democratic Convention Coverage" (NBC News Special) (NBC)

WILLIAM H. LAWRENCE National Affairs Editor For Commentaries "Assassination And Funeral Of Senator Robert F. Kennedy" (ABC)

FRANK McGEE Reporter For "Apollo: A Journey To The Moon" (Flight Nos. VII, VII and IX) (NBC News Special) (NBC)

ANTHONY MESSURI Director For "Apollo: A Journey To The Moon" (Flight Nos. VII, VIII and IX) (NBC)

DAN RATHER Reporter For "Coverage Of The Democratic Convention And Surrounding Events" (CBS News Special Reports and Special Broadcasts) (CBS)

FRANK REYNOLDS Commentator For "Assassination And Funeral Of Senator Robert F. Kennedy" (ABC)

HOWARD K. SMITH Commmentator For "The Race To The White House" (ABC)

MIKE WALLACE Reporter For "Coverage Of The Democratic Convention And Surrounding Events" (CBS News Special Reports And Special Broadcasts) (CBS)

ACHIEVEMENT IN NEWS DOCUMENTARY PROGRAM

PROGRAMS (E-572)

CBS REPORTS: HUNGER IN AMERICA (CBS News Hour) (CBS) Martin Carr, Producer

LAW AND ORDER (Public Broadcast Laboratory) (NET) Frederick Wiseman, Producer

APPALACHIA: RICH LAND, POOR PEOPLE (NET Journal) (NET) Jack Willis, Producer

BIAS AND THE MASS MEDIA, PART I (Time For Americans) (ABC) Hubbell Robinson, Stephen Fleischman, Executive Producers

CBS REPORTS: CAMPAIGN AMERICAN STYLE (CBS News Hour) (CBS) Jay McMullen, Producer

CITIES HAVE NO LIMITS (White Paper: The Ordeal Of The American City) (NBC) Fred Freed, Executive Producer

ELEGY AND MEMORY (ABC) Thomas Wolf, Executive Producer

FREE AT LAST (MARTIN LUTHER KING) (Public Broadcast Laboratory) (NET) Greg Shuker, Producer

HANOI: A REPORT BY CHARLES COLLINGWOOD (CBS News Hour) (CBS) Charles Collingwood, Producer

HEART ATTACK! (ABC) Lester Cooper, Producer

HOME COUNTRY, USA (American Profile) (NBC) Robert Rogers, Producer

ROBERT KENNEDY REMEMBERED (Guggenheim Productions, Inc) (ABC, CBS, NBC) Charles Guggenheim, Producer

OF BLACK AMERICA (CBS News Hour) Series (CBS) Perry Wolff, Executive Producer

RUSSIA IN THE MEDITERRANEAN (NBC News Special) (NBC) George Murray, Executive Producer

STILL A BROTHER (NET Journal) (NET) William Greaves, William Branch, Producers

THE CITIES: A CITY IS TO LIVE IN, DILEMMA IN BLACK AND WHITE, TO BUILD THE FUTURE (CBS News Hour) (CBS) Ernest Leiser, Executive Producer

VIEW FROM SPACE (ABC) James Benjamin, Producer

THE WHOLE WORLD IS WATCHING (Public Broadcast Laboratory) (NET) Av Westin, Executive Producer

INDIVIDUALS (E-573)

PERRY WOLFF AND ANDY ROONEY Writers: "Black History: Lost, Stolen Or Strayed-Of Black America" (CBS News Hour) (CBS)

CHARLES AUSTIN, A.S.C. Cinematographer "Cities Have No Limits-White Paper: The Ordeal of the American City" (NBC)

MILI BONSIGNORI Film Editor "CBS Reports: Hunger In America" (CBS News Hour) (CBS)

MILI BONSIGNORI AND MORTON ROSENFELD Film Editors For 'View From Space" (ABC)

RENE'BRAS Animation For "View From Space" (ABC)

BILL BRAYNE Cameraman For "Law And Order" (Public Broadcast Laboratory) (NET)

CHARLES COLLINGWOOD Reporter For "Hanoi: A Report By Charles Collingwood" (CBS News Hour) (CBS)

DAVID CULHANE Reporter For "CBS Reports: Hunger In America" (CBS News Hour) (CBS)

JOSEPH LOUW Reporter For "Free At Last (Martin Luther King)" (Public Broadcast Laboratory) (NET)

DESMOND McELROY AND DAROLD MURRAY Film Editors "Home Country, USA-American Profile" (NBC)

DAROLD MURRAY Supervising Film Editor For "Cities Have No Limits-White Paper: The Ordeal Of The American City" (NBC)

RICHARD NORLING Cameraman For "Home Country, USA-American Profile" (NBC)

RICHARD ROY Cameraman For "Heart Attack!" (ABC)

FREDERICK WISEMAN Director "Law And Order" (Public Broadcast Laboratory) (NET)

FREDERICK WISEMAN Writer For "Law And Order" (Public Broadcast Laboratory) (NET)

1968/69—Don Adams (Outstanding Continued Performance by an Actor in a Leading Role in a Comedy Series)

1968/69—Arte Johnson (Outstanding Individual Achievement—Special Classification)

ACHIEVEMENT IN CULTURAL DOCUMENTARY AND "MAGAZINE-TYPE" PROGRAM OR SERIES

PROGRAMS (E-574)

DON'T COUNT THE CANDLES (CBS News Hour) (CBS) William K. McClure, Producer
JUSTICE BLACK AND THE BILL OF RIGHTS (CBS News Hour) (CBS) Burton Benjamin, Producer
MAN WHO DANCES: EDWARD VILLELLA (Bell Telephone Hour) (Drew Associates, Inc) (NBC) Robert Drew, Mike Jackson, Producers
THE GREAT AMERICAN NOVEL (CBS News Hour) (CBS) Arthur Barron, Producer
BIRTH AND DEATH (Public Broadcast Laboratory) (NET) Arthur and Evelyn Barron, Producers
BLACK JOURNAL NO. 1 (NET Journal) (NET) Alvin H. Perlmutter, Executive Producer
CHILDREN'S LETTERS TO GOD (Lee Mendelson Film Producers, Inc) (NBC) Lee Mendelson, Frank Buxton, Producers
COSMOPOLIS: BIG CITY, 2000 A.D. (Man And His Universe) (John H. Secondari Productions, Ltd) (ABC) John H. Secondari, Helen Jean Rogers, Producers
DOWN TO THE SEA IN SHIPS (Project XX) (NBC) Donald B. Hyatt, Producer
ECCE HOMO (The Southern Baptist Hour) (NBC) Doris Ann, Producer
FIRST TUESDAY (NBC) Eliot Frankel, Executive Producer
HEMINGWAY'S SPAIN-A LOVE AFFAIR (ABC) Lester Cooper, Producer
HOW LIFE BEGINS (ABC) Jules Power, Executive Producer
INGMAR BERGMAN INTERVIEW (Public Broadcast Laboratory) (NET) Lewis Freedman, Producer
JAZZ: THE INTIMATE ART (Bell Telephone Hour) (Drew Associates, Inc) (NBC) Robert Drew, Mike Jackson, Producers
JESSIE OWENS RETURNS TO BERLIN (Syndicated) (Cappy Productions, Inc) Bud Greenspan, Producer
JOHN STEINBECK'S TRAVELS WITH CHARLEY (Lee Mendelson Film Productions, Inc) (NBC) Lee Mendelson, Executive Producer
LOVE IN A SEXY SOCIETY (One Reach One) The Episcopal Radio-TV Foundation (Syndicated) Caroline Rakestraw, Executive Producer
MARGARET MEAD'S NEW GUINEA JOURNAL (NET Festival) (NET) Craig Gilbert, Producer
ONCE UPON A WALL--THE GREAT AGE OF FRESCO (CBS News Hour) (CBS)Peter Davis, Producer
ONE NATION INDIVISIBLE (Syndicated) (Westinghouse Broadcasting Company) Dick Hubert, Sr, Producer
ONE REACH ONE Series (Syndicated) (The Episcopal Radio-TV Foundation) Caroline Rakestraw, Executive Producer
REMBRANDT AND THE BIBLE (Directions) (ABC) Aram Boyajian, Producer
REPTILES AND AMPHIBIANS (National Geographic Special) (Metromedia Producers Corporation) (CBS) Walon Green, Producer; Robert Doyle, Executive Producer For National Geographic Society
60 MINUTES (CBS News Hour) Series (CBS) Don Hewitt, Executive Producer
SUNKEN TREASURE (The Undersea World Of Jacques Cousteau) (Metromedia Producers Corporation) (ABC) Alan Landsburg, Jacques Cousteau, Executive Producers
THE ACTOR (ABC) James Fleming, Producer
THE AMERICAN ALCOHOLIC (NBC News Special) (NBC) Len Giovannitti, Producer
THE BIG LITTLE WORLD OF ROMAN VISHNIAC (NBC News Special) (NBC) Craig Fisher, Producer
THE CONFRONTATION (ABC) Emile de Antonio, Producer
THE ENDLESS THREAD (One Reach One) The Episcopal Radio-TV Foundation (Syndicated) Caroline Rakestraw, Executive Producer
THE NEW VOICES OF WATTS (NBC Experiment In Television) (NBC) Stuart Schulberg, Producer
THE ROAD TO GETTYSBURG (The Saga Of Western Man) (John H. Secondari Productions, Ltd) (ABC) John H. Secondari, Helen Jean Rogers, Producers
THE SAVAGE HEART: A CONVERSATION WITH ERIC HOFFER (CBS News Hour) (CBS) Perry Wolff, Producer

THE SECRET OF MICHELANGELO: EVERY MAN'S DREAM (Capital Cities Broadcasting Corporation) (ABC) Milton A. Fruchtman, Producer
THE SENSE OF WONDER (ABC) Jules Power, Executive Producer
THE UNEXPECTED VOYAGE OF PEPITO AND CRISTOBAL (The Undersea World of Jacques Cousteau) (Metromedia Producers Corporation) (ABC) Warren V. Bush, Producer
WHALES (The Undersea World Of Jacques Cousteau) (Metromedia Productions Corporation) (ABC) Alan Landsburg, Jacques Cousteau, Executive Producers
WHAT COLOR IS THE WIND? (NBC Experiment In Television) (NBC) Allan Grant, Producer
WHAT MANNER OF MAN (Syndicated) (Shelby Storck and Company, Inc) Shelby Storck, Producer

INDIVIDUALS (E-575)

WALTER DOMBROW AND JERRY SIMS Cinematographers For "The Great American Novel" (CBS News Hour) (CBS)
TOM PETIT Producer For "CBW: The Secrets Of Secrecy" Segment of "First Tuesday" (NBC)
LORD SNOWDON Cinematograher For "Don't Count The Candles" (CBS News Hour) (CBS)
RALPH BELLAMY Host For "One Reach One" Series (The Episcopal Radio-TV Foundation) (Syndicated)
WARREN V. BUSH Writer "Sunken Treasure" (The Undersea World of Jacques Cousteau) (Metromedia Producers Corporation) (ABC)
PATRICK CAREY, RON HEADFORD, JAMES GODFREY, LEWIS McLEOD Cameramen For "Hemingway's Spain-A Love Affair" (ABC)
WALT DeFARIA, SHELDON FAY, JR. Directors For "John Steinbeck's Travels With Charley" (Lee Mendelson Film Productions, Inc) (NBC)
WALTER ESSENFELD, NILS RASMUSSEN, SAMUEL COHEN Film Editors For "The Road To Gettysburg" (The Saga of Western Man) (John H. Secondari Productions, Ltd) (ABC)
JOSEPH FACKOVEC, REG BROWNE, PIERRE VACHO Film Editors For "What Manner Of Man" Shelby Storck and Company, Inc. (Syndicated)
SHELDON FAY, JR. Cameraman "John Steinbeck's Travels With Charley" (Lee Mendelson Film Production, Inc) (NBC)
ARTHUR FILLMORE, LASZLO PAL Cameramen "What Manner Of Man" Shelby Storck and Company, Inc. (Syndicated)
MILTON A. FRUCHTMAN Director "The Secret Of Michelangelo: Every Man's Dream" (Capital Cities Broadcasting Corporation) (ABC)
CRAIG GILBERT Director "Margaret Mead's New Guinea Journal" NET Festival (NET)
CRAIG GILBERT Writer for "Margaret Mead's New Guinea Journal" NET Festival (NET)
LEON GLUCKMAN Director For "The Actor" (ABC)
ALLEN GRANT Cameraman For "What Color Is The Wind?" (NBC Experiment In Television) (NBC)
MARSHALL FLAUM Writer For "What Color Is The Wind?" (NBC Experiment In Television) Allen Grant (NBC)
BUD GREENSPAN Director For "Jessie Owens Returns To Berlin" Cappy Productions, Inc. (Syndicated)
BUD GREENSPAN Writer For "Jessie Owens Returns To Berlin" Cappy Productions, Inc. (Syndicated)
WILLIAM B. HARTIGAN Cameraman For "The Road To Gettysburg" (The Saga of Western Man) (John H. Secondari Productions, Ltd) (ABC)
DICK HUBERT, SR. Writer For "One Nation Indivisible" Westinghouse Broadcasting Company (Syndicated)
MIKE JACKSON Director "Man Who Dances: Edward Villella" (Bell Telephone Hour) (Drew Associates, Inc) (NBC)
NORTON JUSTER, STUART HAMPLE Writers "Children's Letters To God" (Lee Mendelson Film Productions, Inc) (NBC)
ALAN LANDSBURG, WALON GREEN Writers "Reptiles And Amphibians" (National Geographic Special) (Metromedia Producers Corporation) (CBS)
JULES LAVENTHOL Film Editor For "Don't Count The Candles" (CBS News Hour) (CBS)
RICHARD LEITERMAN Director of Photography For "Margaret Mead's New Guinea Journal" NET Festival (NET)
ABBOT MILLS Cameraman "Man Who Dances: Edward Villella" (Bell Telephone Hour) (Drew Associates, Inc) (NBC)
JOHN OETTINGER, FRANK HOST, PAUL GALAN Film Editors For

"One Nation Indivisible" Westinghouse Broadcasting Company (Syndicated)

LAURENCE D. SAVADOVE Writer For "Whales" (The Undersea World of Jacques Cousteau) (Metromedia Producer Corporation) (ABC)

JOHN H. SECONDARI Writer "Cosmopolis: Big City, 2000 A.D." (Man And His Universe) (John H. Secondari Productions, Ltd) (ABC)

JOHN H. SECONDARI Writer "The Road To Gettysburg" (The Saga of Western Man) (John H. Secondari Production, Ltd) (ABC)

JOHN SOH Film Editor For "Whales" And "Sunken Treasure" (The Undersea World of Jacques Cousteau) (Metromedia Producers Corporation) (ABC)

JOHN STEINBECK Writer "John Steinbeck's Travels With Charley" (Lee Mendelson Film Productions, Inc) (NBC)

SHELBY STORCK Narrator "What Manner Of Man" Shelby Storck and Company, Inc. (Syndicated)

SHELBY STORCK Writer For "What Manner Of Man" Shelby Storck and Company, Inc. (Syndicated)

WALKER STUART Director For "Hemingway's Spain - A Love Affair" (ABC)

JOHN TEEPLE Film Editor For "Ecce Homo" (The Southern Baptist Hour) (NBC)

THOMAS TOMIZAWA Producer For "College For The New Generation" Segment of (First Tuesday) (NBC)

KENNETH TYNAN Writer "The Actor" (ABC)

JOSEPH VADALA Photographer "Ecce Homo" (The Southern Baptist Hour) (NBC)

MIKE WALLACE, HARRY REASONER Reporters For "60 Minutes" (CBS News Hour) Series (CBS)

ENTERTAINMENT PROGRAM AND INDIVIDUAL ACHIEVEMENTS
(One Award Only in Each of the Remaining Categories)

COMEDY SERIES (E-576)
GET SMART (NBC) Burt Nodella, Producer
BEWITCHED (ABC) William Asher, Producer
FAMILY AFFAIR (CBS) Edmund Hartmann, Producer
THE GHOST AND MRS. MUIR (NBC) Stanley Rubin, Producer
JULIA (NBC) Hal Kanter, Executive Producer

DRAMATIC SERIES (E-577)
NET PLAYHOUSE (NET) Curtis Davis, Executive Producer
THE FBI (ABC) Charles Larson, Producer
IRONSIDE (NBC) Cy Chermak, Executive Producer
JUDD FOR THE DEFENSE (ABC) Harold Gast, Producer
THE NAME OF THE GAME (NBC) Richard Irving, Leslie Stevens, David Victor, Producers
MISSION: IMPOSSIBLE (CBS) Bruce Geller, Executive Producer

DRAMATIC PROGRAM (E-578)
A single program of a series or a special program
TEACHER, TEACHER (NBC) (Hallmark Hall Of Fame) (NBC) George Lefferts, Producer
THE EXECUTION (Mission: Impossible) (CBS) William Read Woodfield, Allan Balter, Producers
HEIDI (NBC) Frederick Brogger, James Franciscus, Producers
A MIDSUMMER NIGHT'S DREAM (CBS) Lord Michael Birkett, Producer
THE PEOPLE NEXT DOOR (CBS Playhouse) (CBS) Herbert Brodkin, Producer
TALKING TO A STRANGER (NET Playhouse) Four Part Presentation (NET) Michael Blakewell, Producer

VARIETY OR MUSICAL SERIES (E-579)
Award(s) To Producer and Star (If Applicable)
ROWAN AND MARTIN'S LAUGH-IN (NBC) Paul W. Keyes, Carolyn Raskin, Producers; Dan Rowan, Dick Martin, Stars
THE CAROL BURNETT SHOW (CBS) Joseph Hamilton, Producer; Carol Burnett, Star
THE DEAN MARTIN SHOW (NBC) Greg Garrison, Producer; Dean Martin, Star
THE SMOTHERS BROTHERS COMEDY HOUR (CBS) Allan Blye and George A. Sunga, Producers; Tom Smothers and Dick Smothers, Stars
THAT'S LIFE (ABC) Marvin Marx and Stan Harris, Producers; Robert Morse, Star

VARIETY OR MUSICAL PROGRAM (E-580)
A Single program of a series or a special program. Award(s) To Producer and Star (If Applicable)
THE BILL COSBY SPECIAL (NBC) Roy Silver, Executive Producer; Bill Cosby, Star
BARBRA STREISAND: A HAPPENING IN CENTRAL PARK (CBS) Robert Scheerer, Producer; Barbra Streisand, Star
DUKE ELLINGTON CONCERT OF SACRED MUSIC (NET Playhouse) (NET) Richard Moore and Ralph J. Gleason, Producers; Duke Ellington, Star
FRANCIS ALBERT SINATRA DOES HIS THING (CBS) Saul Ilson and Ernest Chambers, Producers; Frank Sinatra, Star
THE RITE OF SPRING (NET Festival) (NET) Robert Foshko, Producer: Zubin Mehta, Conductor
ROWAN AND MARTIN'S LAUGH-IN (NBC) Paul W. Keyes and Carolyn Raskin, Producers; Dan Rowan, Dick Martin and Marcel Marceau, Stars
VLADIMIR HOROWITZ: A TELEVISION CONCERT AT CARNEGIE HALL (CBS) Roger Englander, Producer; Vladimir Horowitz, Pianist

ACTOR - SINGLE PERFORMANCE (E-581)
A one-time appearance in a series or for a special program
PAUL SCOFIELD "Male Of The Species" (Prudential's On Stage) (NBC)
OSSIE DAVIS "Teacher, Teacher" (Hallmark Hall Of Fame) (NBC)
DAVID McCULLUM "Teacher, Teacher" (Hallmark Hall Of Fame) (NBC)
BILL TRAVERS "The Admirable Crichton" (Hallmark Hall Of Fame) (NBC)

ACTRESS - SINGLE PERFORMANCE (E-582)
A one-time appearance in a series or for a special program
GERALDINE PAGE "The Thanksgiving Visitor" (ABC)
ANNE BAXTER "The Bobbie Currier Story" (The Name of the Game) (NBC)
LEE GRANT "The Gates of Cerberus" (Judd for the Defense) (ABC)

ACTOR - DRAMATIC SERIES (E-583)
CARL BETZ "Judd for the Defense" (ABC)
RAYMOND BURR "Ironside" (NBC)
PETER GRAVES "Mission: Impossible" (CBS)
MARTIN LANDAU "Mission: Impossible" (CBS)
ROSS MARTIN "The Wild, Wild West" (CBS)

ACTRESS - DRAMATIC SERIES (E-584)
BARBARA BAIN "Mission: Impossible" (CBS)
JOAN BLONDELL "Here Come The Brides" (ABC)
PEGGY LIPTON "The Mod Squad" (ABC)

ACTOR - COMEDY SERIES (E-585)
DON ADAMS "Get Smart" (NBC)
BRIAN KEITH "Family Affair" (CBS)
EDWARD MULHARE "The Ghost And Mrs. Muir" (NBC)
LLOYD NOLAN "Julia" (NBC)

ACTRESS - COMEDY SERIES (E-586)

HOPE LANGE "The Ghost And Mrs. Muir" (NBC)
DIAHANN CARROLL "Julia" (NBC)
BARBARA FELDON "Get Smart" (NBC)
ELIZABETH MONTGOMERY "Bewitched" (ABC)

SUPPORTING ACTOR - SINGLE PERFORMANCE (E-587)

A one-time appearance in a series or for a special program (No Award Presented)
NED GLASS "A Little Chicken Soup Never Hurt Anybody" (Julia) (NBC)
HAL HOLBROOK "The Whole World Is Watching" (World Premiere) (NBC)
BILLY SCHULMAN "Teacher, Teacher" (Hallmark Hall Of Fame) (NBC)

SUPPORTING ACTRESS - SINGLE PERFORMANCE (E-588)

A one-time appearance in a series or for a special program
ANNA CALDER-MARSHALL "Male Of The Species" (Prudential's On Stage) (NBC)
PAMELA BROWN "The Admirable Crichton" (Hallmark Hall Of Fame) (NBC)
IRENE HERVEY "The O'Casey Scandal" (My Three Sons) (CBS)
NANCY KOVACK "The Girl Who Came In With The Tide" (Mannix) (CBS)

SUPPORTING ACTOR - SERIES (E-589)

WERNER KLEMPERER "Hogan's Heroes" (CBS)
GREG MORRIS "Mission: Impossible" (CBS)
LEONARD NIMOY "Star Trek" (NBC)

SUPPORTING ACTRESS - SERIES (E-590)

SUSAN SAINT JAMES "The Name Of The Game" (NBC)
BARBARA ANDERSON "Ironside" (NBC)
AGNES MOOREHEAD "Bewitched" (ABC)

WRITING - DRAMA (E-591)

A single program or a series or a special program
JP MILLER "The People Next Door" (CBS Playhouse) (CBS)
ALLAN E. SLOANE "Teacher, Teacher" (Hallmark Hall Of Fame) (NBC)
ELLEN M. VIOLETT "The Experiment" (CBS Playhouse) (CBS)

WRITING - COMEDY, VARIETY OR MUSIC (E-592)

A single program or a series or a special program
ALLAN BLYE, BOB EINSTEIN, MURRAY ROMAN, CARL GOTTLIEB, JERRY MUSIC, STEVE MARTIN, CECIL TUCK, PAUL WAYNE, CY HOWARD, MASON WILLIAMS "The Smothers Brothers Comedy Hour" (CBS)
PAUL W. KEYES, HUGH WEDLOCK, JR, ALLAN S. MANINGS, CHRIS BEARD, DAVID PANICH, COSLOUGH H. JOHNSON, MARC LONDON, DAVID M. COX, JIM CARLSON, JACK MENDELSOHN, JAMES MULLIGAN, LORNE D. MICHAELS, HART POMERANTZ, PHIL HAHN, JACK HANRAHAN "Rowan And Martin's Laugh-In" (NBC)
ARNIE ROSEN, STAN BURNS, MIKE MARMER, HAL GOLDMAN, AL GORDON, DON HINKLEY, KENNY SOLMS, GAIL PARENT, BILL ANGELOS, ALAN KOHAN "The Carol Burnett Show" (CBS)

DIRECTOR - DRAMA (E-593)

A single program or a series or a special program
DAVID GREEN "The People Next Door" (CBS Playhouse) (CBS)
PAUL BOGART "Secrets" (CBS Playhouse) (CBS)
FIELDER COOK "Teacher, Teacher" (Hallmark Hall Of Fame) (NBC)

DIRECTOR - COMEDY, VARIETY OR MUSIC (E-594)

A single program or a series or a special program (No Award Presented)
GREG GARRISON "The Dean Martin Show" (NBC)
BILL HOBIN "The Bill Cosby Special" (NBC)
GORDON W. WILES "Rowan And Martin's Laugh-In" (NBC)

MUSIC COMPOSITION (E-595)

A single program or a series or a special program
JOHN T. WILLIAMS "Heidi" (NBC)
JACQUES BELASCO "Hemingway's Spain-A Love Affair" (ABC)
HUGO MONTENEGRO "Take Your Lover In The Ring" (The Outcasts) (ABC)
LALO SCHIFRIN "The Heir Apparent" (Mission: Impossible) (CBS)
MORTON STEVENS "Hawaii Five-O" (CBS Friday Night At The Movies) (CBS)

ART DIRECTION AND SCENIC DESIGN (E-596)

A single program of a series or a special program. Award to Art Director and Scenic Designer, and to Set Decorator (If Applicable)
WILLIAM P. ROSS AND LOU HAFLEY Art Director and Set Decorator, Respectively, For "The Bunker" (Parts I and II), (Mission: Impossible) (CBS)
WALTER M. JEFFERIES, JR. AND JOHN DWYER Art Director and Set Decorator, Respectively, For "All Our Yesterdays" (Star Trek) (NBC)
KEN JOHNSON Art Director For "Rowan And Martin's Laugh-In" (NBC)

CINEMATOGRAPHY (E-597)

GEORGE FOLSEY "Here's Peggy Fleming" (NBC)
FRANK PHILLIPS "Up-Tight" (Hawaii Five-O) (CBS)
ROBERT RIGER "19th Summer Olympic Games Special Reports" (ABC)
HOWARD SCHWARTZ "The Crash" (Land Of The Giants) (ABC)

ELECTRONIC CAMERAWORK (E-598)

A single program of a series or a special program. Award to Technical Director, with Certificate to Cameramen
A.J. CUNNINGHAM Technical Director; NICK DeMOS, BOB FONAROW, FRED GOUGH, JACK JENNINGS, DICK NELSON, RICK TANZI, BEN WOLF Cameramen "The People Next Door"" (CBS Playhouse) (CBS)
FRANK BIONDO Cameraman "Our First Fight" (That's Life) (ABC)
KARL MESSERSCHMIDT Technical Director; ROY HOLM, BOB KEYES, WAYNE NOSTAJA, TONY YARLETT Cameramen "Petula" (NBC)

FILM EDITING (E-599)

A single program of a series or a special program
BILL MOSHER "An Elephant In A Cigar Box" (Judd For The Defense) (ABC)
JOHN C. FULLER, PATRICK KENNEDY, IGO KANTOR, FRANK McKELVEY 'Chrysler Presents The Bob Hope Christmas Special" (NBC)
SIDNEY KATZ "Teacher, Teacher" (Hallmark Hall Of Fame) (NBC)
DONALD R. RODE "Assignment: Earth" (Star Trek) (NBC)

THE AREAS
(Possibility of One Award, More Than One Award, or No Award)

ACHIEVEMENT IN CHILDREN'S PROGRAMMING

PROGRAMS (E-600)
MISTEROGER'S NEIGHBORHOOD Series (NET) Fred Rogers, Producer
WALT DISNEY'S WONDERFUL WORLD OF COLOR Series (NBC) Ron Miller, Executive Producer

INDIVIDUALS (E-601)
BOB KEESHAN ''Captain Kangaroo'' Series (CBS) (Performer)
BURR TILLSTROM ''The Reluctant Dragon'' (NBC Children's Theatre) (NBC) (Performer)

ACHIEVEMENT IN DAYTIME PROGRAMMING

PROGRAMS (E-602)
THE DICK CAVETT SHOW Series (ABC) Don Silverman, Producer
HOLLYWOOD SQUARES Series (NBC) Merrill Heatter And Robert Quigley, Executive Producers

INDIVIDUALS (E-603)
HUGH DOWNS ''Concentration'' Series (NBC) (Host)

ACHIEVEMENT IN SPORTS PROGRAMMING

PROGRAMS (E-604)
I9TH SUMMER OLYMPICS GAMES (ABC) Roone P. Arledge, Executive Producer
ABC'S WIDE WORLD OF SPORTS Series (ABC) Roone P. Arledge, Executive Producer

INDIVIDUALS (E-605)
BILL BENNINGTON, MIKE FREEDMAN, MAC MEMION, ROBERT RIGER, MARV SCHLENKER, ANDY SIDARIS, LOU VOLPICELLI, DOUG WILSON ''19th Summer Olympic Games'' (ABC) (Directors)
CHRIS SCHENKEL ''19th Summer Olympic Game'' (ABC) (Commentator)

SPECIAL CLASSIFICATION ACHIEVEMENTS

PROGRAMS (E-606)
FIRING LINE WITH WILLIAM F. BUCKLEY, JR. Series (Syndicated) Warren Steibel, Producer
MUTUAL OF OMAHA'S WILD KINGDOM Series (NBC) Don Meier, Producer
BROADWAY '68 - THE TONY AWARDS (NBC) Alexander Cohen, Producer
1969 TOURNAMENT OF ROSES PARADE (CBS) Paul Levitan, Producer

INDIVIDUALS - (VARIETY PERFORMANCES) (E-607)
ARTE JOHNSON For ''Rowan And Martin's Laugh-In'' Series (NBC)
HARVEY KORMAN For ''The Carol Burnett Show'' Series (CBS)
RUTH BUZZI For ''Rowan And Martin's Laugh-In'' Series (NBC)
GOLDIE HAWN For ''Rowan And Martin's Laugh-In'' Series (NBC)

SPECIAL PHOTOGRAPHIC EFFECTS (E-608)
VAN DER VEER PHOTO EFFECTS, HOWARD A. ANDERSON COMPANY, THE WESTHEIMER COMPANY AND CINEMA RESEARCH For ''The Tholian Web'' (Star Trek) (NBC)

INDIVIDUAL ACHIEVEMENT - MUSIC (E-609)
MORT LINDSEY Musical Director ''Barbra Streisand: A Happening In Central Park'' (CBS)
TOM ADAIR AND JOHN SCOTT TROTTER Words and Music ''Babar The Elephant'' (NBC)
HERB ALPERT Arranger and Conductor ''The Beat Of The Brass'' (CBS)
BILLY BARNES Special Material ''Rowan And Martin's Laugh-In'' (NBC)

INDIVIDUAL ACHIEVEMENT - THE VISUAL ARTS (E-610)
RAY AGHAYAN Costume Designer For ''Carol Channing And Pearl Bailey On Broadway'' (ABC)
ANGEL G. ESPARZA Graphic Designer For ''U.S.S. Pueblo Court Of Inquiry'' (The Huntley-Brinkley Report) (NBC)
BOB MACKIE Costume Designer For ''The Carol Burnett Show'' (CBS)
CLAUDE THOMPSON Make-Up Artist For ''And Debbie Makes Six'' (ABC)

INDIVIDUAL ACHIEVEMENT - ELECTRONIC PRODUCTION (E-611)
BILL COLE Audio Engineer For ''TCB'' (NBC)
JOHN FRESCHI Lighting Director For ''H. Andrew Williams Kaleidoscope Company'' (NBC)
ROBERT GUHL, JIM STEWART, LARRY JONES Audio Engineers For ''A Hint Of Darkness, A Hint Of Light'' (The Mod Squad) (ABC)
ARTHUR SCHNEIDER Video Tape Editor For ''Rowan And Martin's Laugh-In'' (NBC)
BRUCE VERRAN AND JOHN TEELE Video Tape Editors For ''Rowan And Martin's Laugh-In'' (NBC)

SPECIAL AWARDS

CITATION (E-612)
BILLY SCHULMAN For recognition of an extraordinary achievement in the television drama, ''Teacher, Teacher'' presented by Hallmark Hall of Fame.

THE TRUSTEES AWARD (E-613)
WILLIAM R. McANDREW, 1914-1968 Who shaped television news to be his permanent memorial by imposing on it early the American news tradition - honesty, bravery and public enlightment.
APOLLO VII, VIII, IX AND X SPACE MISSIONS Apollo VII Astronauts Walter Schirra, Donn Eisele, Walter Cunningham Apollo VIII Astronauts Frank Borman, James A Lovell, Jr, William A. Anders Apollo IX Astronauts James A. McDivitt, David R. Scott, Russel L. Schweickart Apollo X Astronauts Thomas B. Stafford, Eugene A. Cernan, John W. Young For sharing with the American public and the rest of the world the incredible experience of the unfolding of the mysteries of outer space and the surface of the moon via live television.

ACHIEVEMENT IN ENGINEERING DEVELOPMENT (E-614)
EASTMAN KODAK COMPANY For the ME-4 Process, making it possible to develop color film with greater speed and sharper images than ever before.

CITATION (E-615)
COLUMBIA BROADCASTING SYSTEM For the development of the Digital Control Technique used in the Minicam miniaturized television color camera, which provides a new degree of mobility by permitting control via a substantially smaller and more mobile connecting cable or, alternatively, a single wireless channel.

THE STATION AWARD (E-616)
PRETTY SOON RUNS OUT (WHA-TV, Madison, Wisconsin)
APPALACHIAN HERITAGE (WLWT, Cincinnati, Ohio)
BEGGAR AT THE GATES (WBZ-TV, Boston, Massachusetts)
COLOR ME SOMEBODY (KING-TV, Seattle, Washington)

HEAL THE HURT CHILD (KSD-TV, St. Louis, Missouri)
JOB MAN CARAVAN (SCE-TV, Columbia, South Carolina)
MISTEROGERS SPECIAL PROGRAM FOR PARENTS (WQED, Pittsburgh, Pennsylvania)
OPERATION THANKS, Part I and II (KFMB-TV, San Diego, California)
SOMETHING FOR NOTHING (WFIL-TV, Philadelphia, Pennsylvania)
WE ARE ALL POLICEMEN (WNBC-TV, New York, New York)

SPECIAL CITATION (E-617)

ASSIGNMENT: THE YOUNG GREATS (WFIL-TV, Philadelphia, Pennsylvania)
JOB MAN CARAVAN (SCE-TV, Columbia, South Carolina)
OPPORTUNITY LINE (KNXT-TV, Los Angeles, California)
PROJECT SUMMER (WMAL-TV, Washington, D.C.)
TELL IT LIKE IT IS (KPRC-TV, Houston, Texas)
THE NEW GENERATION AND THE ESTABLISHMENT (WHA-TV, Madison, Wisconsin)
THE SCHOOL THAT WOULD NOT DIE (WDSU-TV, New Orleans, Louisiana)
THE URBAN BATTLEGROUND (WIIC-TV, Pittsburg, Pennsylvania)
TO BE SOMEBODY (WTIC-TV, Hartford, Connecticut)
YA ES TIEMPO (IT'S ABOUT TIME) (WNJU-TV, Newark, New Jersey)

INTERNATIONAL DOCUMENTARY AWARD (E-618)

THE LAST CAMPAIGN OF ROBERT KENNEDY (Swiss Broadcasting and Television, Zurich, Switzerland)
AN EXPEDITION INTO THE STONE AGE (Nippon Television Network, Tokyo, Japan)
ARCHEOLOGY (Film Polski, Warsaw, Poland)
CHRISTMAS EVE IN BIAFRA (Independent Television News, London, England)
LIFE, DEATH AND JAPANESE MUSIC (Mainichi Broadcasting System, Osaka, Japan)

INTERNATIONAL ENTERTAINMENT AWARD (E-619)

A SCENT OF FLOWERS (Canadian Broadcasting Corporation, Ontario, Canada)
BLESSETH IS ONE (Hiroshima Telecasting Company, Ltd, Hiroshima City, Japan)
PAVONCELLO (Film Polski, Warsaw, Poland)
STAR QUALITY (Thames Television Limited, London, England)
THE CAESARS - CLAUDIUS (Granada Television Limited, London, England)

1969/70

NEWS AND DOCUMENTARY PROGRAM AND INDIVIDUAL ACHIEVEMENTS

(Possibility of one Award, more than one Award, or no Award)

ACHIEVEMENT WITHIN REGULARLY SCHEDULED NEWS PROGRAMS

PROGRAMS (E-620)

AN INVESTIGATION OF TEENAGE DRUG ADDICTION - ODYSSEY HOUSE (The Huntley-Brinkley Report) (NBC) Wallace Westfeldt, Executive Producer; Les Crystal, Producer
CAN THE WORLD BE SAVED? (CBS Evening News With Walter Cronkite) (CBS) Ronald Bonn, Producer
CHICAGO CONSPIRACY TRIAL (CBS Evening News With Walter Cronkite) (CBS) Stanhope Gould, Producer
COVERAGE OF HURRICANE CAMILLE (ABC Evening News With Frank Reynolds And Howard K. Smith) (ABC) Avram Westin, Executive Producer; David Buksbaum, Producer
COVERAGE OF THE NIGERIAN/BIAFRAN CONFLICT (ABC Evening

News With Frank Reynolds And Howard K. Smith) (ABC) Avram Westin, Executive Producer; David Buksbaum, Producer
THE HUNTLEY-BRINKLEY REPORT (NBC) Wallace Westfeldt, Executive Producer; Les Crystal, Producer
J. EDGAR HOOVER AND THE FBI (CBS Morning News With Joseph Benti) (CBS) Robert Markowitz, Producer
MAN AND HIS ENVIRONMENT (ABC Evening News With Frank Reynolds And Howard K. Smith) (ABC) Avram Westin, Executive Producer; David Buksbaum, Producer
MORATORIUM AND THE SILENT MAJORITY (ABC Evening News With Frank Reynolds And Howard K.Smith) (ABC) Avram Westin, Executive Producer; David Buksbaum, Producer

INDIVIDUALS (E-621)

HEYWOOD HALE BROUN Special Correspondent For "Special Sports Reporting" (CBS Evening News With Roger Mudd) (CBS)
JOHN CHANCELLOR Correspondent For "Coverage of the Poison Grain Incident" (The Huntley-Brinkley Report) (NBC)
ROBERT GORALSKI Correspondent For "Investigation of the Green Beret Case" (The Huntley-Brinkley Report) (NBC)
CHET HUNTLEY Correspondent For "Coverage of the West German Elections" (The Huntley-Brinkley Report) (NBC)
FRANK REYNOLDS AND HOWARD K. SMITH For "News Commentaries" (ABC Evening News With Frank Reynolds And Howard K. Smith) (ABC)
MIKE WALLACE Correspondent For "Interviews With Meadlo And Medina" (CBS Evening News With Walter Cronkite) (CBS)

ACHIEVEMENT IN COVERAGE OF SPECIAL EVENTS

PROGRAMS (E-622)

APOLLO: A JOURNEY TO THE MOON (APOLLO X, XI, XII) (NBC) James W. Kitchell, Executive Producer
SOLAR ECLIPSE: A DARKNESS AT NOON (NBC) Robert Northshield, Executive Producer; Walter Kravetz, Producer
COVERAGE OF THE ABM HEARINGS (NBC) Charles Jones, Producer
DWIGHT DAVID EISENHOWER: 1890-1969 (CBS) Ernest Leiser and Robert Wussler, Executive Producers
FOOTSTEPS ON THE MOON: THE FLIGHT OF APOLLO XI (ABC) Walter J. Pfister, Jr., Executive Producer; Robert Siegenthaler, Producer
MAN ON THE MOON: THE EPIC JOURNEY OF APOLLO XI (CBS) Robert Wussler, Executive Producer; Joan Richman, Clarence Cross, Producers
MR. NIXON IN ASIA (ABC) Walter J. Pfister, Jr., Executive Producer; Bob Rogow, Producer
SOLAR ECLIPSE: DARKNESS AT MIDDAY (ABC) Walter J. Pfister, Jr., Executive Producer; Robert Siegenthaler, Producer

INDIVIDUALS (E-623)

WALTER CRONKITE Reporter For "Man On The Moon: The Epic Journey Of Apollo XI" (CBS)
JOEL BANOW Director For "Man On The Moon: the Epic Journey Of Apollo XI" (CBS)
JULES BERGMAN Co-Anchorman For "Footsteps On The Moon: The Flight Of Apollo XI" (ABC)
FRANK McGEE, CHET HUNTLEY AND DAVID BRINKLEY Reporters For "Apollo: A Journey To The Moon" (Apollo X, XI, XII) (NBC)
JOHN CHANCELLOR, FRANK McGEE AND JACK PERKINS Reporters For "Solar Eclipse: A Darkness At Noon" (NBC)
GENE FARINET, DENNIS DALTON, ARTHUR LORD AND KEN DONOAHUE Writers For "Apollo: A Journey To The Moon" (Apollo X, XI, XII) (NBC)
ROBERT J. LE DONNE News Editor For "Footsteps On The Moon: The Flight Of Apollo XI" (ABC)
LARRY PICKARD News Editor For "Footsteps On The Moon: The Flight Of Apollo XI" (ABC)
FRANK REYNOLDS Co-Anchorman For "Footsteps On The Moon: The Flight Of Apollo XI" (ABC)
FRED RHEINSTEIN Director For "Solar Eclipse: A Darkness At Noon" (Miahuatlan, Mexico, Segment) (NBC)
WALTER M. SCHIRRA, JR. Commentator For "Man On The Moon: The Epic Journey Of Apollo XI" (CBS)

ACHIEVEMENT IN NEWS DOCUMENTARY PROGRAMMING

PROGRAMS (E-624)

HOSPITAL (NET Journal) (NET) Frederick Wiseman, Producer
THE MAKING OF THE PRESIDENT, 1968 (Metromedia Producers Corporation) (CBS) M.J. Rifkin, Executive Producer; Mel Stuart, Producer
ABORTION (Summer Focus) (ABC) Lester Cooper, Executive Producer; Ernest Pendrell, Producer
ADVENTURES AT THE JADE SEA (Metromedia Producers Corporation) (CBS) Harvey Bernhard, Executive Producer; David Seltzer, Producer
THE BATTLE OF EAST ST. LOUIS (CBS News Hours) (CBS) Perry Wolff, Executive Producer; Peter Davis, Producer
BLACK FIDDLER: PREJUDICE AND THE NEGRO (Summer Focus) (ABC) Stephen Fleischman, Executive Producer; Howard Enders, Producer
CBS REPORTS: A TIMETABLE FOR VIETNAM (CBS News Hour) (CBS) Ernest Leiser, Executive Producer; Bernard Birnbaum, Producer
DO YOU THINK A JOB IS THE ANSWER? (Public Broadcast Laboratory) (NET) Dave Dugan, Executive Producer; Gary Gilson, Producer
FASTEN YOUR SEATBELTS (NET Journal) (Document Associates, Inc.) (NET) Don Dixon, Executive Producer; Douglas Leiterman, Producer
FROM HERE TO THE SEVENTIES (NBC) Robert Northshield, Executive Producer; Mel Ferber, Producer
THE GREAT DOLLAR ROBBERY: CAN WE ARREST INFLATION? (ABC) Lester Cooper, Executive Producer; Herbert Dorfman, Producer
LBJ: WHY I CHOSE NOT TO RUN (CBS News Hour) (CBS) Burton Benjamin, Executive Producer; John Sharnik, Producer
THE NATURAL HISTORY OF OUR WORLD: THE TIME OF MAN (Metromedia Producers Corporation) (CBS) Marshall Flaum, Producer
THE ORDEAL OF THE AMERICAN CITY - CONFRONTATION (NBC White Paper) (NBC) Fred Freed, Executive Producer; Albert Waller, Producer
THE WAITING GAME (Lifewatch Six) Directors Group, Inc. (Syndicated) Walter King, Executive Producer; Ben Gradus, Producer
WHO INVITED US? (NET Journal) (NET) Alvin H. Perlmutter, Executive Producer; Alan M. Levin, Producer
WHO KILLED LAKE ERIE? (NBC) Fred Freed, Executive Producer
WHO SPEAKS FOR MAN? (NET Journal) (NET) Arthur Zegart, Producer
WILD RIVER (National Geographic Special) (Metromedia Producers Corporation) (CBS) Robert C. Doyle, Executive Producer For National Geographic Society; Jack Kaufman, Executive Producer For Metromedia Producers Corporation; Ed Spiegel, Producer

INDIVIDUALS (E-625)

FREDERICK WISEMAN Director For "Hospital" (NET Journal) (NET)
RICHARD BASEHART Narrator For "The Natural History Of Our World: The Time Of Man" (Metromedia Producers Corporation) (CBS)
CHARLES COLLINGWOOD Reporter For "CBS Reports: A Timetable For Vietnam" (CBS News Hour) (CBS)
WALTER CRONKITE Reporter "LBJ: Why I Chose Not To Run" (CBS News Hour) (CBS)
PETER DAVIS Writer For "The Battle Of East St. Louis" (CBS News Hour) (CBS)
MARSHALL FLAUM Writer For 'The Natural History Of Our World: The Time Of Man" (Metromedia Producers Corporation) (CBS)
GARY GILSON Reporter-Writer For "Do You Think A Job Is The Answer?" (Public Broadcast Laboratory) (NET)
DOUGLAS LEITERMAN Writer-Director For "Fasten Your Seatbelts" (Document Associates, Inc.) (NET)
FRANK McGEE Reporter For 'The Ordeal Of The American City - Confrontation" (NBC White Paper) (NBC)
FRANK McGEE Reporter For "Who Killed Lake Erie?" (NBC)
NBC NEWS TEAM Commentators For "From Here To The Seventies" (NBC)
ROBERT NORTHSHIELD Writer For "From Here To The Seventies" (NBC)
HUGHES RUDD Reporter For "The Battle Of East St. Louis" (CBS News Hour) (CBS)
LOUIS RUKEYSER Correspondent-Writer For "The Great Dollar Robbery: Can We Arrest Inflation?" (ABC)
DAVID SELTZER Writer For "Adventurers At The Jade Sea" (Metromedia Producers Corporation) (CBS)
ARTHUR ZEGART Writer-Director For "Who Speaks For Man?" (NET Journal) (NET)

ACHIEVEMENT IN MAGAZINE-TYPE PROGRAMMING

PROGRAMS (E-626)

BLACK JOURNAL (Series) (NET) William Greaves, Executive Producer
60 MINUTES (Series) (CBS) Don Hewitt, Executive Producer
60 MINUTES November 25, 1969 (CBS) Don Hewitt, Executive Producer
SOME FOOTNOTES TO 25 NUCLEAR YEARS "Segment of First Tuesday" (NBC) Eliot Frankel, Executive Producer; William B. Hill, Producer
VOICES ON THE INSIDE "Segment of First Tuesday" (NBC) Eliot Frankel, Executive Producer; Len Giovannitti, Producer

INDIVIDUALS (E-627)

TOM PETTIT Reporter-Writer For "Some Footnotes To 25 Nuclear Years" (Segment of First Tuesday) (NBC)
LEN GIOVANNITTI AND RAFAEL ABRAMOVITZ Directors For "Voices On The Inside" (Segment of First Tuesday) (NBC)
HARRY REASONER Reporter For "60 Minutes" (Series) (CBS)
MIKE WALLACE Reporter For "60 Minutes" (Series) (CBS)

ACHIEVEMENT IN CULTURAL DOCUMENTARY PROGRAMMING

PROGRAMS (E-628)

ARTHUR RUBINSTEIN (NBC) George A. Vicas, Producer
FATHERS AND SONS (CBS News Hour) (CBS) Ernest Leiser, Executive Producer; Harry Morgan, Producer
THE JAPANESE (CBS News Hour) (CBS) Perry Wolff, Executive Producer; Igor Oganesoff, Producer
THE BALLAD OF THE IRON HORSE (John H. Secondari Productions, Ltd.) (ABC) John H. Secondari and Helen Jean Rogers, Producers
CHARLIE BROWN AND CHARLES SCHULZ (Lee Mendelson Film Productions, Inc.) (CBS) Lee Mendelson and Walt DeFaria, Executive Producers; Sheldon Fay, Jr., Producer
THE DESERT WHALES (The Undersea World Of Jacques Cousteau) (Metromedia Producers Corporation) (ABC) Warren Bush and Jacques Cousteau, Executive Producers
FERMENT AND THE CATHOLIC CHURCH (Summer Focus) (ABC) Lester Cooper, Executive Producer; James Benjamin, Producer
HOLLYWOOD: THE SELZNICK YEARS (Metromedia Producers Corporation) (NBC) M.J. Rifkin and Alan Landsburg, Executive Producers; Marshall Flaum, Producer
IN SEARCH OF REMBRANDT (NET Festival) (NET) Lane Slate, Executive Producer; Richard F. Siemanowski, Producer
THE JOURNEY OF ROBERT F. KENNEDY (Wolper Productions, Inc.) (ABC) David L. Wolper, Executive Producer; David Seltzer, Producer
THE MAN HUNTERS (MGM Documentary) (NBC) Irwin Rosten, Executive Producer; Nicolas Noxon, Producer
MODERN MAN: THE LOSER (Directions) (ABC) Wiley F. Hance, Producer
THE MYSTERY OF ANIMAL BEHAVIOR (National Geographic Special) (Metromedia Producers Corporation) (CBS) Robert C. Doyle, Executive Producer For National Geographic Society; Jack Kaufman, Executive Producer For Metromedia Producers Corporation; Walon Green, Producer
SAHARA: LA CARAVANE DU SEL (NBC) Lou Hazam, Producer
SIBERIA: THE ENDLESS HORIZON (National Geographic Special) (Metromedia Producers Corporation) (CBS) Robert C. Doyle, Executive Producer For National Geographic Society; Jack Kaufman, Executive Producer For Metromedia Producers Corporation; Larry Neiman, Producer
SURVIVAL ON THE PRAIRIE (NBC) Craig Fisher, Producer
THREE YOUNG AMERICANS IN SEARCH OF SURVIVAL (ABC) Stephen Fleischmen, Executive Producer

VOLCANO: BIRTH OF AN ISLAND (CBS News Hour) (CBS) Burton Benjamin, Executive Producer; Isaac Kleinerman, Producer
THE WARREN YEARS (NET) Jim Karayn, Executive Producer

INDIVIDUALS (E-629)

EDWIN O. REISCHAUER Commentator For "The Japanese" (CBS News Hour) (CBS)
ARTHUR RUBINSTEIN Commentator For "Arthur Rubinstein" (NBC)
JAMES BENJAMIN Writer For "Ferment And The Catholic Church" (Summer Focus) (ABC)
WARREN BUSH Writer For "The Desert Whales" (The Undersea World of Jacques Cousteau) (Metromedia Producers Corporation) (ABC)
HUGH DOWNS Reporter For "Survival On The Prairie" (NBC)
MARSHALL FLAUM Writer For "Hollywood: The Selznick Years" (Metromedia Producers Corporation) (NBC)
MARSHALL FLAUM Director For "Hollywood: The Selznick Years" (Metromedia Producers Corporation) (NBC)
STEPHEN FLEISCHMAN Writer For "Three Young Americans In Search Of Survival" (ABC)
LOU HAZAM Writer For "Sahara: La Caravane Du Sel" (NBC)
JOHN HUSTON Narrator For "The Journey Of Robert F. Kennedy" (Wolper Productions, Inc.) (ABC)
CHARLES KURALT Reporter For "Volcano: Birth Of An Island" (CBS News Hour) (CBS)
JAMES MASON Host And Narrator For "In Search Of Rembrandt" (NET Festival) (NET)
HARRY MORGAN Writer For "Fathers And Sons" (CBS News Hour) (CBS)
NICOLAS NOXON Writer For "The Man Hunters" (MGM Documentary) (NBC)
NICOLAS NOXON Director For "The Man Hunters" (MGM Documentary) (NBC)
THOMAS A. PRIESTLEY Director For "Sahara: La Caravane Du Sel" (NBC)
HELEN JEAN ROGERS Director For "The Ballad Of The Iron Horse" (John H. Secondari Productions, Ltd.) (ABC)
ARTHUR SCHLESINGER, JR. Writer For "The Journey Of Robert F. Kennedy" (Wolper Productions, Inc.) (ABC)
JOHN H. SECONDARI Writer For "The Ballad Of The Iron Horse" (John H. Secondari Productions, Ltd.) (ABC)
RICHARD F. SIEMANOWSKI Writer For "In Search Of Rembrandt" (NET Festival) (NET)
MEL STUART Director For "The Journey Of Robert F. Kennedy" (Wolper Productions, Inc.) (ABC)
BUD WISER Writer For "Siberia: The Endless Horizon" (National Geographic Special) (Metromedia Producers Corporation) (CBS)
PERRY WOLFF Writer For "The Japanese" (CBS News Hour) (CBS)

ENTERTAINMENT PROGRAM AND INDIVIDUAL ACHIEVEMENTS

(One Award Only In Each of the Remaining Categories)

COMEDY SERIES (E-630)

Award(s) to Executive Producer(s) and Producer(s)
MY WORLD AND WELCOME TO IT (NBC) Sheldon Leonard, Executive Producer; Danny Arnold, Producer
THE BILL COSBY SHOW (NBC) William H. Cosby, Jr., Executive Producer; Marvin Miller, Producer
THE COURTSHIP OF EDDIE'S FATHER (ABC) James Komack, Producer
LOVE, AMERICAN STYLE (ABC) Arnold Margolin, Jim Parker, Executive Producers; Bill D' Angelo, Producer
ROOM 222 (ABC) Gene Reynolds, Producer

DRAMATIC SERIES (E-631)

Award(s) to Executive Producer(s) and Producer(s)
MARCUS WELBY, M.D. (ABC) David Victor, Executive Producer; David J. O'Connell, Producer
THE FORSYTE SAGA (NET) Donald Wilson, Producer
IRONSIDE (NBC) Cy Chermak, Executive Producer; Douglas Benton,

Winston Miller, Joel Rogosin, Albert Aley, Producers
THE MOD SQUAD (ABC) Danny Thomas, Aaron Spelling, Executive Producers; Tony Barrett, Harve Bennett, Producers
THE NAME OF THE GAME (NBC) Richard Irving, Executive Producer; George Eckstein, Dean Hargrove, Norman Lloyd, Boris Sagal, Producers
NET PLAYHOUSE (NET) Jac Venza, Executive Producer

DRAMATIC PROGRAM (E-632)

A single program of a series or a special program
Award(s) to Executive Producer(s) and Producer(s)
A STORM IN SUMMER (NBC) (Hallmark Hall Of Fame) M.J. Rifkin, Executive Producer; Alan Landsburg, Producer
DAVID COPPERFIELD (NBC) Frederick Brogger, Producer
HELLO, GOODBYE, HELLO (ABC) (Marcus Welby, M.D.) David Victor, Executive Producer; David J. O'Connell, Producer
MY SWEET CHARLIE (NBC) (World Premiere) Bob Banner, Executive Producer; Richard Levinson, William Link, Producers

VARIETY OR MUSICAL SERIES (E-633)

Award(s) to Executive Producer(s) and Producer(s) and Star (if applicable)
THE DAVID FROST SHOW (Syndicated) Peter Baker, Producer; David Frost, Star
THE CAROL BURNETT SHOW (CBS) Joe Hamilton, Producer; Carol Burnett, Star
THE DEAN MARTIN SHOW (NBC) Greg Garrison, Producer; Dean Martin, Star
THE DICK CAVETT SHOW (ABC) Jack Rollins, Executive Producer; Tony Converse, Producer; Dick Cavett, Star
ROWAN AND MARTIN'S LAUGH-IN (NBC) George Schlatter, Executive Producer; Carolyn Raskin, Paul Keyes, Producers; Dan Rowan and Dick Martin, Stars

VARIETY OR MUSICAL PROGRAM (E-634)

A single program of a series or a special program
Award(s) to Executive Producer(s) and Producer(s) and Star (if applicable) A. Variety and Popular Music
ANNIE, THE WOMEN IN THE LIFE OF A MAN (CBS) Joseph Cates, Executive Producer; Martin Charnin, Producer; Anne Bancroft, Star
THE FRIARS CLUB "ROASTS" JACK BENNY (NBC) (Kraft Music Hall) Gary Smith, Dwight Hemion, Producers; Jack Benny, Star
THE SECOND BILL COSBY SPECIAL (NBC) Roy Silver, Executive Producer; Bruce Campbell, Roy Silver, Producers; Bill Cosby, Star
SINATRA (CBS) Frank Sinatra, Executive Producer; Carolyn Raskin, Producer; Frank Sinatra, Star
THE SOUND OF BURT BACHARACH (NBC) (Kraft Music Hall) Gary Smith, Dwight Hemion, Producers; Burt Bacharach, Star
B. Classical Music
CINDERELLA (NATIONAL BALLET OF CANADA) (NET) (NET Festival) John Barnes and Curtis Davis, Executive Producers; Norman Campbell, Producer
S. HUROK PRESENTS - PART III (CBS) Jim Krayer, Executive Producer; Roger Englander, Producer
SOUNDS OF SUMMER (The Blossom Music Center with Pierre Boulez) (NET) Craig Gilbert, Executive Producer; Jack Sameth, Producer
THE SWITCHED-ON SYMPHONY (NBC) Pierre Cossette, Burt Sugarman, Executive Producers; Jack Good, Producer

NEW SERIES (E-635)

Award(s) to Executive Producer(s) and Producer(s)
ROOM 222 (ABC) Gene Reynolds, Producer
THE BILL COSBY SHOW (NBC) William H. Cosby, Jr., Executive Producer; Marvin Miller, Producer
THE FORSYTE SAGA (NET) Donald Wilson, Producer
MARCUS WELBY, M.D. (ABC) David Victor, Executive Producer; David J. O'Connell, Producer
SESAME STREET (NET) David D. Connell, Executive Producer; Sam Gibbon, Jon Stone, Lutrelle Horne, Producers

ACTOR - SINGLE PERFORMANCE (E-636)

A one-time appearance in a series or for a special program

PETER USTINOV "A Storm In Summer" (Hallmark Hall Of Fame) (NBC)
AL FREEMAN, JR. "My Sweet Charlie" (World Premiere) (NBC)
SIR LAURENCE OLIVIER "David Copperfield" (NBC)

ACTRESS - SINGLE PERFORMANCE (E-637)

A one-time appearance in a series or for a special program

PATTY DUKE "My Sweet Charlie" (World Premiere) (NBC)
DAME EDITH EVANS "David Copperfield" (NBC)
SHIRLEY JONES "Silent Night, Lonely Night" (World Premiere) (NBC)

ACTOR - DRAMATIC SERIES (E-638)

ROBERT YOUNG "Marcus Welby, M.D." (ABC)
RAYMOND BURR "Ironside" (NBC)
MIKE CONNORS "Mannix" (CBS)
ROBERT WAGNER "It Takes A Thief" (ABC)

ACTRESS - DRAMATIC SERIES (E-639)

SUSAN HAMPSHIRE "The Forsyte Saga" (NET)
JOAN BLONDELL "Here Comes The Brides" (ABC)
PEGGY LIPTON "The Mod Squad" (ABC)

ACTOR - COMEDY SERIES (E-640)

WILLIAM WINDOM "My World And Welcome To It" (NBC)
BILL COSBY "The Bill Cosby Show" (NBC)
LLOYD HAYNES "Room 222" (ABC)

ACTRESS - COMEDY SERIES (E-641)

HOPE LANGE "The Ghost And Mrs. Muir" (ABC)
ELIZABETH MONTGOMERY "Bewitched" (ABC)
MARLO THOMAS "That Girl" (ABC)

SUPPORTING ACTOR - DRAMA (E-642)

A continuing or one-time appearance in a series, or for a special program

JAMES BROLIN "Marcus Welby, M.D." (Series) (ABC)
TIGE ANDREWS "The Mod Squad" (Series) (ABC)
GREG MORRIS "Mission: Impossible" (Series) (CBS)

SUPPORTING ACTRESS - DRAMA (E-643)

A continuing or one-time appearance in a series, or for a special program

GAIL FISHER "Mannix" (Series) (CBS)
BARBARA ANDERSON "Ironside" (Series) (NBC)
SUSAN SAINT JAMES "The Name Of The Game" (Series) (NBC)

SUPPORTING ACTOR - COMEDY (E-644)

A continuing or one-time appearance in a series, or for a special program

MICHAEL CONSTANTINE "Room 222" (Series) (ABC)
WERNER KLEMPERER "Hogan's Heroes" (Series) (CBS)
CHARLES NELSON REILLY "The Ghost And Mrs. Muir" (Series) (ABC)

SUPPORTING ACTRESS - COMEDY (E-645)

A continuing or one-time appearance in a series, or for a special program

KAREN VALENTINE "Room 222" (Series) (ABC)
AGNES MOOREHEAD "Bewitched" (Series) (ABC)
LURENE TUTTLE "Julia" (Series) (NBC)

WRITING - DRAMA (E-646)

A single program of a series or a special program

RICHARD LEVINSON, WILLIAM LINK "My Sweet Charlie" (World Premiere) (NBC)
GEORGE BELLAK "Sadbird" (CBS Playhouse) (CBS)
DON M. MANKIEWICZ "Marcus Welby, M.D." (The ABC Wednesday Night Movie) (Pilot) (ABC)

WRITING - COMEDY, VARIETY OR MUSIC (E-647)

A single program of a series or a special program

GARY BELKIN, PETER BELLWOOD, HERB SARGENT, THOMAS MEEHAN, JUDITH VIORST "Annie, The Women In The Life Of A Man" (CBS)
PAUL W. KEYES, DAVID PANICH, MARC LONDON, COSLOUGH JOHNSON, JIM CARLSON, JIM MULLIGAN, JOHN CARSEY, GENE FARMER, JEREMY LLOYD, JOHN RAPPAPORT, STEPHEN SPEARS, JACK DOUGLAS, ALLAN MANNINGS "Rowan And Martin's Laugh-In" (with Buddy Hackett) (NBC)
ALLAN MANINGS, DAVID PANICH, COSLOUGH JOHNSON, JOHN CARSEY, STEPHEN SPEARS, JOHN RAPPAPORT, JIM CARLSON, MARC LONDON, CHET DOWLING, JIM ABELL, BARRY TOOK, JACK DOUGLAS, JIM MULLIGAN, GENE FARMER, JEREMY LLOYD "Rowan And Martin's Laugh-In" (with Nancy Sinatra) (NBC)

DIRECTOR - DRAMA (E-648)

A single program of a series or a special program

PAUL BOGART "Shadow Game" (CBS Playhouse) (CBS)
BUZZ KULIK "A Storm In Summer" (Hallmark Hall Of Fame) (NBC)
LAMONT JOHNSON "My Sweet Charlie" (World Premiere) (NBC)

DIRECTOR - COMEDY, VARIETY OR MUSIC (E-649)

A single program of a series or a special program

DWIGHT A. HEMION "The Sound Of Burt Bacharach" (Kraft Music Hall) (NBC)
SEYMOUR BERNS "The Second Bill Cosby Special" (NBC)
ROGER ENGLANDER "Berlioz Takes A Trip" (N.Y. Philharmonic Young People's Concerts) (CBS)

CHOREOGRAPHY (E-650)

A single program of a series or a special program

NORMAN MAEN "This Is Tom Jones" (with Mary Hopkins, Jose Feliciano, Shelley Berman) (ABC)
TOM HANSEN "The Red Skelton Show" (with Walter Brennan) (Unidentified Flying Objects) (CBS)
DAVID WINTERS "Ann Margaret - From Hollywood With Love" (CBS)

MUSIC COMPOSITION (E-651)

A. For a series or a single program of a series (in its first year only) (In the first year of original music's use only)

MORTON STEVENS "A Thousand Pardons, You're Dead" (Hawaii Five-O) (CBS)
QUINCY JONES "The Bill Cosby Show" (Series) (NBC)
FRANKLYN MARKS "Charlie, The Lonesome Cougar" (The Wonderful World of Disney) (NBC)

B. For a special program

PETE RUGOLO "The Challengers" (CBS Friday Night Movie) (CBS)
VAN ALEXANDER "Gene Kelley's Wonderful World Of Girls With 50 Girls, Count 'Em, 50" (NBC)
JACQUES BELASCO "'The Threshold" (Apollo: Journey To The Moon) (NBC)

MUSIC DIRECTION OF A VARIETY, MUSICAL OR DRAMATIC PROGRAM (E-652)

A single program of a series or a special program

PETER MATZ "The Sound Of Burt Bacharach" (Kraft Music Hall) (NBC)
MORT LINDSEY "The Merv Griffin Show" (from Las Vegas with Chuck

Connors, Joey Heatherton, Buddy Greco, Jack E. Leonard, Jerry Van Dyke) (CBS)
JOHNNIE SPENCE "This Is Tom Jones" (with Mary Hopkins, Shelley Berman, Jose Feliciano) (ABC)

MUSIC, LYRICS AND SPECIAL MATERIAL (E-653)

A series or a single program of a series or a special program written for television

ARNOLD MARGOLIN, CHARLES FOX "Love, American Style" (Series) (ABC)
CHARLES AIDMAN, NAOMI C. HIRSHHORN "Spoon River" (CBS)
BILLY BARNES "Rowan And Martin's Laugh-In" (with Carol Channing) (NBC)

ART DIRECTION OR SCENIC DESIGN (E-654)

For a dramatic program or feature length film made for television; for a series, a single program of a series or a special program

JAN SCOTT AND EARL CARLSON Art Director and Set Decorator Respectively, For "Shadow Game" (CBS Playhouse) (CBS)
GIBSON HOLLEY AND LUCIEN M. HAFLEY Art Director and Set Decorator Respectively, For "The Falcon" (3 Parts) (Mission: Impossible) (CBS)
HUGH GRAY RAISKY AND WESLEY LAWS Art Director and Set Decorator Respectively, For "Man On The Moon: The Epic Journey of Apollo XI" (CBS)
JAMES TRITTIPO Art Director For "The File On Devlin" (Hallmark Hall Of Fame) (NBC)
B. For a Musical or Variety single program of a series or a special program
E. JAY KRAUSE Art Director For "Mitzi's 2nd Special" (NBC)
PAUL BARNES AND BOB SANSOM; BILL HARP Art Directors and Set Decorator Respectively, For "The Carol Burnett Show" (with Steve Lawrence, Edward Villella) (CBS)
RENE LAGLER AND ROBERT CHECCHI Art Director and Set Decorator Respectively, For "The Glen Campbell Goodtime Hour" (with Tom Jones, Totie Fields, Jackie DeShannon) (CBS)

LIGHTING DIRECTION (E-655)

A single program of a series or a special program, produced for electronic television only

LEARD DAVIS, ED HILL (Video: RICHARD SCOVEL, CLIVE BASSETT) "Appalachian Autumn" (CBS Playhouse) (CBS)
JOHN FRESCHI "The Switched-On Symphony" (NBC)
JIM KILGORE "The Johnny Cash Show" (with Rod McKuen, The Everly Brothers, Dusty Springfield) (ABC)
WILLIAM KLAGES "Kraft Music Hall" (with Petula Clark, Anthony Newley, Lou Rawls) (NBC)

COSTUME DESIGN (E-656)

A single program of a series or a special program

BOB MACKIE "Diana Ross And The Supremes And The Temptations On Broadway" (NBC)
MICHAEL TRAVIS "Rowan And Martin's Laugh-In" (with Danny Kaye) (NBC)
GEORGE WHITTAKER "The Don Adams Special: Hooray For Hollywood" (CBS)

MAKE-UP (E-657)

A single program of a series or a special program

RAY SEBASTIAN AND LOUIS A. PHILLIPPI "The Don Adams Special: Hooray For Hollywood" (CBS)
SHIRLEY MUSLIN AND MARIE ROCHE "This Is Tom Jones" (with Mary Hopkins, Jose Feliciano, Shelley Berman) (ABC)

CINEMATOGRAPHY - ENTERTAINMENT PROGRAMMING (E-658)

A. For a series or a single program of a series

WALTER STRENGE "Hello, Goodbye, Hello" (Marcus Welby, M.D.) (ABC)
HARVEY GENKINS "N.Y.P.D." (Series) (ABC)
AL FRANCIS "The Amnesiac" (Mission: Impossible) (CBS)
B. For a special or feature length program made for television
LIONEL LINDON "Ritual Of Evil" (NBC Monday Night at the Movies) (NBC)
GENE POLITO "My Sweet Charlie" (World Premiere) (NBC)
HOWARD R. SCHWARTZ "The Immortal" (ABC Movie of the Week) (ABC)

CINEMATOGRAPHY - NEWS AND DOCUMENTARY PROGRAMMING (E-659)

A. For a series, a single program of a series, a special program, program segments or elements within a regularly scheduled News programs and coverage of Special Events

EDWARD WINKLE "Model Hippie" (The Huntley-Brinkley Report) (NBC)
CHARLES W. BOYLE "Middle Town U.S.A." (The Huntley-Brinkley Report) (NBC)
JAMES P. WATT, JR. "High School Profile" (The Huntley-Brinkley Report) (NBC)
B. Documentary, Magazine-type or Mini-documentary programs
THOMAS A. PRIESTLEY "Sahara: La Caravane due Sel" (NBC)
CHUCK AUSTIN, A.S.C. "The Ordeal of the American City - Confrontation" (NBC White Paper) (NBC)
RONALD W. VAN NOSTRAND "Hide And Go Seek" (First Tuesday) (NBC)

FILM EDITING - ENTERTAINMENT PROGRAMMING (E-660)

A. For a series or a single program of a series

BILL MOSHER "Sweet Smell Of Failure" (Bracken's World) (NBC)
ARTHUR DAVID HILTON "The Falcon" (3 Parts) (Mission: Impossible) (CBS)
AXEL R. HUBERT "The Great Power Failure" (The Ghost And Mrs. Muir) (ABC)
B. For a special or feature length program made for television
EDWARD M. ABROMS "My Sweet Charlie" (World Premiere) (NBC)
IGO KANTOR, JAMES HENRIKSON, STAN SIEGEL, TONY CARRAS, FRANK McKELVEY "Bob Hope Christmas Special" (NBC)
GENE PALMER "Marcus Welby, M.D." (ABC Wednesday Night Movie) (Pilot) (ABC)

FILM EDITING - NEWS AND DOCUMENTARY PROGRAMMING (E-661)

A. For a series, a single program of a series, a special program, program segments or elements within a regularly scheduled News programs and coverage of Special Events

MICHAEL C. SHUGRUE "The High School Profile" (The Huntley-Brinkley Report) (NBC)
RAYMOND L. ELBERFELD AND RICHARD A. HESSEL "Eisenhower Funeral" (The Huntley Brinkley Report) (NBC)
FRED FLAMENHAFT, MARTIN SHEPPARD, TOM DUNPHY, PAT MINERVA, KEN SHEA, GEORGE JOHNSON (The Huntley-Brinkley Report) (Series) (NBC)

B. Documentary, Magazine-type or Mini-documentary Programs

JOHN SOH "The Desert Whales" (The Undersea World Of Jacques Cousteau) (ABC)
PETER C. JOHNSON "The Mystery Of Animal Behavior" (CBS)
ROBERT B. LOWEREE AND HANK GRENNON "Arthur Rubinstein" (NBC)

FILM SOUND EDITING (E-662)

A single program of a series or a special program

DOUGLAS H. GRINDSTAFF, ALEX BAMATTRE, MICHAEL COLGAN, BILL LEE, JOE KAVIGAN, JOSEF E. VON STROHEIM "The Immortal" (Movie of the Week) (ABC)
RICHARD E. RADERMAN AND NORMAN KARLIN "Charlie Noon" (Gunsmoke) (CBS)
DON HALL, JR., LARRY MEEK, WILLIAM HOWARD, JOHN KLINE, ROBERT CORNETT, FRANK R. WHITE "A Small War" (Land Of the Giants) (ABC)

FILM SOUND MIXING (E-663)

A single program of a series or a special program

GORDON L. DAY AND DOMINICK GAFFEY "The Submarine" (Mission: Impossible) (CBS)
MELVIN M. METCALFE, SR., JOHN A. STRANSKY, JR., CLARENCE SELF, ROGER HEMAN "My Sweet Charlie" (World Premi re) (NBC)
ROGER GARY ANDREWS "Some Footnotes To K5 Nuclear Years" (First Tuesday) (NBC)

LIVE OR TAPE SOUND MIXING (E-664)

A single program of a series or a special program

BILL COLE AND DAVE WILLIAMS "The Switched-On Symphony" (NBC)
MAHLON H. FOX "The Sound Of Burt Bacharach" (Kraft Music Hall) (NBC)
NEAL WEINSTEIN "The Jim Nabors Hour" (with Vikki Carr) (CBS)

VIDEO TAPE EDITING (E-665)

A single program of a series or a special program

JOHN SHULTIS "The Sound Of Burt Bacharach" ("Pas de deaux" Segment and "Promises, Promises" Segment) (Kraft Music Hall) (NBC)
NICK GIORDANO "Finale" (The Hollywood Palace) (ABC)
ARMAND POITRAS "An Evening With Julie Andrews And Harry Belafonte" (NBC)

TECHNICAL DIRECTION AND ELECTRONIC CAMERAWORK (E-666)

A single program of a series or a special program

HEINO RIPP, Technical Director; Al Camoin, Gene Martin, Donald Mulvaney, Cal Shadwell, Cameramen "The Sound Of Burt Bacharach" (Kraft Music Hall) (NBC)
CHARLES FRANKLIN AND KEN LAMKIN, Technical Directors; Robert Fonarow, Nick DeMos, Ben Wolf, Cameramen "A Storm In Summer" (Hallmark Hall Of Fame) (NBC)
O.TAMBURRI, Technical Director; Gene Schwarz, Robert Keyes, Kurt Tonnessen, Ronald Sheldon, Roy Holm, Wayne Osterhout, Cameramen "An Evening With Julie Andrews And Harry Belafonte" (NBC)

THE AREAS

(Possibility of One Award, More Than One Award, or No Award)

ACHIEVEMENT IN CHILDREN'S PROGRAMMING

PROGRAMS (E-667)

SESAME STREET Series (NET) David D. Connell, Executive Producer; Sam Gibbon, Jon Stone, Lutrelle Horne, Producers

THE WONDERFUL WORLD OF DISNEY Series (NBC) Ron Miller, Executive Producer

INDIVIDUALS (E-668)

JOE RAPOSO AND JEFFREY MOSS Music and Lyrics For "This Way to Sesame Street" (NBC)
JON STONE, JEFFREY MOSS, RAY SIPHERD, JERRY JUHL, DAN WILCOX, DAVE CONNELL, BRUCE HART, CAROLE HART, VIRGINIA SCHONE Writer For "Sally Sees Sesame Street" (Sesame Street) (NET)
MICHAEL LOEWENSTEIN Scenic Design For "Kukla, Fran And Ollie" (NET)

ACHIEVEMENT IN DAYTIME PROGRAMMING

PROGRAMS (E-669)

TODAY Series (NBC) Stuart Schulberg, Producer
THE GALLOPING GOURMET Series (Syndicated) Treena Kerr, Producer; Graham Kerr, Host

INDIVIDUALS (E-670)

HUGH DOWNS "Today" Series (NBC)
JOE GARAGIOLA "Today" Series (NBC)

ACHIEVEMENT IN SPORTS PROGRAMMING

PROGRAMS (E-671)

THE NFL GAMES (CBS) William Fitts, Executive Producer
ABC'S WIDE WORLD OF SPORTS Series (ABC) Roone Arledge, Executive Producer
1969 WORLD SERIES (NBC) Lou Kusserow, Producer

INDIVIDUALS (E-672)

ROBERT R. FORTE Film Editing For "Pre-Game Program" (Pro-Bowl Game) (CBS)
ROBERT RIGER Director For "International Ski Championships Val D'Isere, France" (ABC's Wide World of Sports) (ABC)

SPECIAL CLASSIFICATION OF OUTSTANDING PROGRAM AND INDIVIDUAL ACHIEVEMENT

PROGRAMS (E-673)

MUTUAL OF OMAHA'S WILD KINGDOM Series (NBC) Don Meier, Producer
FELLINI - A DIRECTOR'S NOTEBOOK "NBC Experiment in Television" (NBC) Peter Goldfarb, Producer

INDIVIDUALS (E-674)

GOLDIE HAWN "Rowan And Martin's Laugh-In" Series (NBC)
ARTE JOHNSON "Rowan And Martin's Laugh-In" Series (NBC)

ACHIEVEMENT IN ANY AREA OF CREATIVE TECHNICAL CRAFTS (E-675)

JONNIE BURKE Special Visual Effects For "Time Bomb" (Mission: Impossible) (CBS)
HOWARD A. ANDERSON, JR., WILFRID CLINE, BILL HANSARD Special Photographic Effects For "Rally 'Round The Flag Boys" (My World And Welcome To It) (NBC)
EDIE J. PANDA Hair Styling For "The Don Adams Special - Hooray For Hollywood" (CBS)

SPECIAL AWARDS (E-676)

OUTSTANDING ACHIEVEMENT IN ENGINEERING DEVELOPMENT
APOLLO COLOR TELEVISION FROM SPACE For the conceptual aspects, an Emmy to the VIDEO COMMUNICATIONS DIVISION, NASA, and for development of the camera, an Emmy Award to the WESTINGHOUSE ELECTRIC CORPORATION.

CITATION
AMPEX CORPORATION For the development of the HS-200 Color Television Production System.

THE STATION AWARD (E-677)
THE SLOW GUILLOTINE (KNBC-TV, Los Angeles, California)
CITY IN CRISIS (WDSU-TV, New Orleans, Louisiana)
JOB MAN CARAVAN (SCE-TV, Columbia, South Carolina)
JOURNEY TO A PINE BOX (WRC-TV, Washington, D.C.)
NEW VOICES IN THE WILDERNESS (WNBC-TV, New York, New York)
THE SAVAGE ROOT (WBZ-TV, Boston, Massachusetts)
URBAN MYTHOLOGY (WGTV, Athens, Georgia)
A VISIT TO ALLENVILLE (KOOL-TV, Phoenix, Arizona)
YOUNG, BLACK AND EXPLOSIVE (KOMO-TV, Seattle, Washington)

SPECIAL CITATION (E-678)
THE OTHER AMERICANS (WJZ-TV, Baltimore, Maryland)
Honorable Mention - YOUNG, BLACK AND EXPLOSIVE (KOMO-TV, Seattle, Washington)
THE CHILDREN ARE WAITING (WBBM-TV, Chicago, Illinois)
THE FIRST STEP (WETK-TV, Winooski, Vermont)
SICKLE CELL ANEMIA (WABC-TV, New York, New York)
WHAT'S SO SPECIAL ABOUT WARRENDALE? (WIIC-TV, Pittsburgh, Pennsylvania)
WHOSE MUSEUM? (KPIX-TV, San Francisco, California)

THE TRUSTEES AWARD (E-679)
To the Presidents of the News Divisions for "safeguarding the public's right to full information, at a time when the constitutional right of freedom of the press is under its strongest attack."

The Trustee Citation to the hundreds of men comprising the staff of NASA who "made it possible for hundreds of millions of people throughout the world to witness history being made 238,000 miles away."

The Trustee Citation to the 3M Company for "having presented some of the finest art, cultural, scientific, and entertainment programs in the public interest. This company has contributed significantly to upgrading the quality of television while presenting its sales message with modesty and taste."

1970/71
NEWS AND DOCUMENTARY PROGRAM AND INDIVIDUAL ACHIEVEMENTS
(Possibility of one Award, more than one Award, or no Award)

ACHIEVEMENT WITHIN REGULARLY SCHEDULED NEWS PROGRAMS

PROGRAMS (E-680)
FIVE PART INVESTIGATION OF WELFARE (NBC Nightly News) (NBC) Wallace Westfeldt, Executive Producer; David Teitelbaum, Producer
COVERAGE OF THE INDO CHINA WAR (ABC Evening News) (ABC) Avram Westin, Executive Producer
COVERAGE OF THE PAKISTANI TIDAL WAVE DISASTER (NBC Nightly News) (NBC) Wallace Westfeldt, Executive Producer; David Teitelbaum, Producer
COVERAGE OF THE MIDDLE EAST PLANE HIJACKINGS (NBC Nightly News) (NBC) Wallace Westfeldt, Executive Producer; David Teitelbaum, Producer

INDIVIDUALS (E-681)
BRUCE MORTON Correspondent For "Reports From The Lt. Calley Trial" (CBS Evening News With Walter Cronkite) (CBS)
PHIL BRADY Correspondent For "Investigation Of GI Drug Addiction In Vietnam" (NBC Nightly News) (NBC)

ACHIEVEMENT IN COVERAGE OF SPECIAL EVENTS

PROGRAMS (E-682)
CBS NEWS SPACE COVERAGE FOR 1970-71: "Aquarius On The Moon: The Flight Of Apollo 13" and "Ten Years Later: The Flight Of Apollo 14" (CBS) Robert Wussler, Executive Producer; Joan Richman, Producer
EARTH DAY: A QUESTION OF SURVIVAL (CBS) Ernest Leiser, Executive Producer; Bernard Birnbaum, Phillip Scheffler and Paul Greenberg, Producers
NBC NEWS COVERAGE OF THE SOUTHERN CALIFORNIA EARTHQUAKE (NBC) William B. Hill, Richard Fischer, Producers

INDIVIDUALS (E-683)
WALTER CRONKITE Correspondent For "CBS News Space Coverage For 1970-71: Aquarius on the Moon: The Flight of Apollo 13" and "Ten Years Later: The Flight of Apollo 14" (CBS)
DOUGLAS KIKER Correspondent for "The War In Jordan" (NBC)

ACHIEVEMENT IN NEWS DOCUMENTARY PROGRAMMING

PROGRAMS (E-684)
THE SELLING OF THE PENTAGON (CBS News) Perry Wolff, Executive Producer; Peter Davis, Producer (CBS)
THE WORLD OF CHARLIE COMPANY (CBS News) Ernest Leiser, Executive Producer; Russ Bensley, Producer (CBS)
NBC WHITE PAPER: POLLUTION IS A MATTER OF CHOICE (NBC News) Fred Freed, Producer (NBC)

INDIVIDUALS (E-685)
JOHN LAURENCE Correspondent For "The World Of Charlie Company" (CBS News) (CBS)
FRED FREED Writer For "NBC White Paper: Pollution Is A Matter of Choice" (NBC News) (NBC)
DENIS SANDERS AND ROBERT FRESCO Directors For "Trial: The City and County of Denver vs. Lauren R. Watson" (NET Journal) (PBS)

ACHIEVEMENT IN MAGAZINE-TYPE PROGRAMMING

PROGRAMS (E-686)
GULF OF TONKIN SEGMENT "60 Minutes" Joseph Wershba, Producer (CBS)
THE GREAT AMERICAN DREAM MACHINE (Series) A. H. Perlmutter, Jack Willis, Executive Producers (PBS)
BLACK JOURNAL (Series) Tony Brown, Executive Producer; Phil Burton, Stan Lathan, Producers (PBS)

INDIVIDUALS (E-687)
MIKE WALLACE Correspondent For "60 Minutes" (Series) (CBS)
MORLEY SAFER Correspondent For "Gulf Of Tonkin Segment" (60 Minutes) (CBS)
ELINOR BUNIN Director of Animated Film "The Great American Dream Machine" (PBS)

ACHIEVEMENT IN CULTURAL DOCUMENTARY PROGRAMMING

PROGRAMS (E-688)

THE EVERGLADES (NBC News) Craig Fisher, Producer (NBC)
THE MAKING OF "BUTCH CASSIDY & THE SUNDANCE KID" (Penthouse Productions, Inc.) Ronald Preissman, Producer (NBC)
ARTHUR PENN, 1922-: THEMES AND VARIANTS (Robert Hughes Productions) Robert Hughes, Producer (PBS)
GERTRUDE STEIN: WHEN THIS YOU SEE, REMEMBER ME "Fanfare" Perry Miller Adato, Producer (PBS)
WHICH WAY, AMERICA? (KNBC Productions) John Gentri, Producer (NBC)

INDIVIDUALS (E-689)

NANA MAHOMO Narrator For "A Black View Of South Africa" (CBS News) (CBS)
ROBERT GUENETTE AND THEODORE H. STRAUSS Writers For "They've Killed President Lincoln!" (Wolper Productions, Inc.) (NBC)
ROBERT YOUNG Director For "The Eskimo: Fight for Life" (Education Development Center) (CBS)
CRAIG GILBERT Director-Writer For "The Triumph Of Christy Brown" (Realities) (PBS)
GEORGE C. SCOTT Narrator For "A Man Named Lombardi" (Simon & Flynn, Inc.) (NBC)
JERRY IZENBERG Writer For "A Man Named Lombardi" (Simon & Flynn, Inc.) (NBC)
PERRY MILLER ADATO Director For "Gertrude Stein: When This You See, Remember Me" (Fanfare) (PBS)
NATHAN KROLL Director For "Helen Hayes - Portrait Of An American Actress" (Net Playhouse) (Kroll Productions, Inc.) (PBS)

ENTERTAINMENT PROGRAM AND INDIVIDUAL ACHIEVEMENTS
(One Award Only In Each Of The Remaining Categories)

COMEDY SERIES (E-690)
Award(s) to Executive Producer(s) and Producer(s)

ALL IN THE FAMILY (CBS) Norman Lear, Producer
ARNIE (CBS) Rick Mittleman, Producer
LOVE, AMERICAN STYLE (ABC) Arnold Margolin, Jim Parker, Executive Producers; Bill Idelson, Harvey Miller, William P. D'Angelo, Producers
THE MARY TYLER MOORE SHOW (CBS) James L. Brooks, Allan Burns, Executive Producers; David Davis, Producer
THE ODD COUPLE (ABC) Jerry Belson, Gary Marshall, Executive Producers; Jerry Davis, Producer

DRAMA SERIES (E-691)
Award(s) to Executive Producer(s) and Producers(s)

THE SENATOR - THE BOLD ONES (NBC) David Levinson, Producer
THE FIRST CHURCHILLS - MASTERPIECE THEATRE (PBS) Donald Wilson, Christopher Sarson, Producers
IRONSIDE (NBC) Cy Chermak, Executive Producer; Douglas Benton, Winston Miller, Joel Rogosin, Albert Aley, Producers
NET PLAYHOUSE (PBS) Jac Venza, Executive Producer
MARCUS WELBY, M.D. (ABC) David Victor, Executive Producer; David J. O'Connell, Producer

OUTSTANDING SINGLE PROGRAM - DRAMA OR COMEDY (E-692)
A Single Program of a series or a special program Award(s) to Executive Producer(s) and Producer(s)

THE ANDERSONVILLE TRIAL (PBS) (Hollywood Television Theatre) Lewis Freedman, Producer
HAMLET (NBC) (Hallmark Hall of Fame) Cecil Clarke, Executive Producer; George LeMaire, Producer
THE PRICE (NBC) (Hallmark Hall of Fame) David Susskind, Producer

THEY'RE TEARING DOWN TIM RILEY'S BAR (NBC) (Rod Serling's Night Gallery - Four-In-One) Jack Laird, Producer
VANISHED - PARTS I & II (NBC) (World Premiere Monday & Tuesday Night At The Movies) David Victor, Executive Producer; David J. O'Connell, Producer

VARIETY SERIES - MUSICAL (E-693)
Award(s) to Executive Producer(s) and Producer(s) and Star (if applicable)

THE FLIP WILSON SHOW (NBC) Monte Kay, Executive Producer; Bob Henry, Producer; Flip Wilson, Star
THE CAROL BURNETT SHOW (CBS) Joe Hamilton, Executive Producer; Arnie Rosen, Producer; Carol Burnett, Star
ROWAN AND MARTIN'S LAUGH-IN (NBC) George Schlatter, Executive Producer; Carolyn Raskin, Producer; Dick Martin & Dan Rowan, Stars

VARIETY SERIES - TALK (E-694)
Award(s) to Executive Producer(s) and Producer(s) and Star (if applicable)

THE DAVID FROST SHOW (Syndicated) Peter Baker, Producer; David Frost, Star
THE DICK CAVETT SHOW (ABC) Jack Rollins, Executive Producer; John Gilroy, Producer; Dick Cavett, Star
THE TONIGHT SHOW STARRING JOHNNY CARSON (NBC) Fred DeCordova and Rudy Tellez, Producers; Johnny Carson, Star

OUTSTANDING SINGLE PROGRAM - VARIETY OR MUSICAL (E-695)
A single program of a series or a special program Award(s) to Executive Producer(s) and Producer(s) and Star (if applicable) A. Variety and Popular Music

SINGER PRESENTS BURT BACHARACH (CBS) Gary Smith, Dwight Hemion, Producers; Burt Bacharach, Star
ANOTHER EVENING WITH BURT BACHARACH (NBC) (Kraft Music Hall) Gary Smith, Dwight Hemion, Producers; Burt Bacharach, Star
HARRY AND LENA (ABC) Chiz Schultz, Producer; Harry Belafonte and Lena Horne, Stars
B. Classical Music

LEOPOLD STOKOWSKI (PBS) "Net Festival" Curtis W. Davis, Executive Producer; Thomas Slevin, Producer; Leopold Stokowski, Star
QUEEN OF SPADES (PBS) "Fanfare - NET Opera Theatre" Herman Adler, Producer
SWAN LAKE (PBS) "Fanfare" Curtis W. Davis, John Barnes, Executive Producers; Norman Campbell, Producer

NEW SERIES (E-696)
Award(s) to Executive Producer(s) and Producer(s)

ALL IN THE FAMILY (CBS) Norman Lear, Producer
THE FLIP WILSON SHOW (NBC) Monte Kay, Executive Producer; Bob Henry, Producer
THE MARY TYLER MOORE SHOW (CBS) James L. Brooks, Allan Burns, Executive Producers; David Davis, Producer
THE ODD COUPLE (ABC) Jerry Belson, Gary Marshall, Executive Producers; Jerry Davis, Producer
THE SENATOR - THE BOLD ONES (NBC) David Levinson, Producer

ACTOR - SINGLE PERFORMANCE (E-697)
A one-time appearance in a series or for a special program

GEORGE C. SCOTT "The Price" (Hallmark Hall of Fame) (NBC)
JACK CASSIDY "The Andersonville Trial" (Hollywood Television Theatre) (PBS)
HAL HOLBROOK 'A Clear And Present Danger" (World Premiere NBC Saturday Night At The Movies) (NBC)
RICHARD WIDMARK "Vanished, Parts I & II" (World Premiere NBC Monday & Tuesday Night At The Movies) (NBC)

GIG YOUNG "The Neon Ceiling" (World Premiere NBC Monday Night At The Movies) (NBC)

ACTRESS - SINGLE PERFORMANCE (E-698)

A one-time appearance in a series or for a special program

LEE GRANT "The Neon Ceiling" (World Premiere NBC Monday Night At The Movies) (NBC)
COLLEEN DEWHURST "The Price" (Hallmark Hall of Fame) (NBC)
LEE GRANT "Ransom For A Dead Man" (World Premiere NBC Monday Night At The Movies) (NBC)

ACTOR - DRAMATIC SERIES (E-699)

HAL HOLBROOK (The Senator: The Bold ones) (NBC)
RAYMOND BURR (Ironside) (NBC)
MIKE CONNORS (Mannix) (CBS)
ROBERT YOUNG (Marcus Welby, M.D.) (ABC)

ACTRESS - DRAMATIC SERIES (E-700)

SUSAN HAMPSHIRE (The First Churchills) (Masterpiece Theatre) (PBS)
LINDA CRISTAL (The High Chaparral) (NBC)
PEGGY LIPTON (The Mod Squad) (ABC)

ACTOR - COMEDY SERIES (E-701)

JACK KLUGMAN (The Odd Couple) (ABC)
TED BESSELL (That Girl) (ABC)
BILL BIXBY (The Courtship Of Eddie's Father) (ABC)
CARROLL O'CONNOR (All In The Family) (CBS)
TONY RANDALL (The Odd Couple) (ABC)

ACTRESS - COMEDY SERIES (E-702)

JEAN STAPLETON (All In The Family) (CBS)
MARY TYLER MOORE (The Mary Tyler Moore Show) (CBS)
MARLO THOMAS (That Girl) (ABC)

SUPPORTING ACTOR - DRAMA (E-703)

A continuing or one-time appearance in a series, or for a special program

DAVID BURNS "The Price" (Hallmark Hall of Fame) (NBC)
JAMES BROLIN (Marcus Welby, M.D.) (Series) (ABC)
ROBERT YOUNG "Vanished, Parts I & II" (World Premiere NBC Monday & Tuesday Night At The Movies) (NBC)

SUPPORTING ACTRESS - DRAMA (E-704)

A continuing or one-time appearance in a series, or for a special program

MARGARET LEIGHTON "Hamlet" (Hallmark Hall of Fame) (NBC)
GAIL FISHER (Mannix) (Series) (CBS)
SUSAN SAINT JAMES (The Name Of The Game) (Series) (NBC)
ELENA VERDUGO (Marcis Welby, M.D.) (Series) (ABC)

SUPPORTING ACTOR - COMEDY (E-705)

A continuing or one-time appearance in a series, or for a special program

EDWARD ASNER (The Mary Tyler Moore Show) (Series) (CBS)
MICHAEL CONSTANTINE (Room 222) (Series) (ABC)
GALE GORDON (Here's Lucy) (Series) (CBS)

SUPPORTNG ACTRESS - COMEDY (E-706)

A continuing or one-time appearance in a series, or for a special program

VALERIE HARPER (The Mary Tyler Moore Show) (Series) (CBS)
AGNES MOOREHEAD (Bewitched) (Series) (ABC)
KAREN VALENTINE (Room 222) (Series) (ABC)

DIRECTOR - DRAMA (E-707)

A single program of a series with continuing characters and/or theme

DARYL DUKE "The Day The Lion Died" (The Bold Ones - The Senator Segment) (NBC)
BOB SWEENEY "Over 50? Steal" (Hawaii Five-O) (CBS)
JOHN M. BADHAM "A Single Blow Of A Sword" (The Bold Ones - The Senator Segment) (NBC)

DIRECTOR - DRAMA (E-708)

A single program

FIELDER COOK "The Price" (Hallmark Hall of Fame) (NBC)
PETER WOOD "Hamlet" (Hallmark Hall of Fame) (NBC)
JOSEPH SARGENT "Tribes" (Move Of The Week On ABC) (ABC)
JAMES GOLDSTONE "A Clear And Present Danger" (World Premiere NBC Saturday Night At The Movies) (NBC)

DIRECTOR - COMEDY (E-709)

A single program of a series with continuing characters and/or theme

JAY SANDRICH "Toulouse Lautrec Is One Of My Favorite Artists" (The Mary Tyler Moore Show) (CBS)
ALAN RAFKIN "Support Your Local Mother" (The Mary Tyler Moore Show) (CBS)
JOHN RICH "Gloria's Pregnancy" (All In The Family) (CBS)

DIRECTOR - VARIETY OR MUSIC (E-710)

A single program of a series

MARK WARREN "Rowan And Martin's Laugh-In" (With Orson Welles) (NBC)
ART FISHER "Andy Williams Christmas Show" (The Andy Williams Show) (NBC)
TIM KILEY "The Flip Wilson Show" (With David Frost, James Brown and The Muppets) (NBC)

DIRECTOR - COMEDY, VARIETY OR MUSIC (E-711)

A special program

STERLING JOHNSON "Timex Presents Peggy Fleming At Sun Valley" (NBC)
WALTER C. MILLER, MARTIN CHARNIN "George M!" (Bell System Family Theatre) (NBC)
ROGER ENGLANDER "The Anatomy Of A Symphony Orchestra" (New York Philharmonic Young People's Concert) (CBS)

CHOREOGRAPHY (E-712)

A single program of a series or a special program

ERNEST O. FLATT "The Carol Burnett Show" (With Nanette Fabray and Ken Berry) (CBS)
CLAUDE CHAGRIN "Hamlet" (Hallmark Hall of Fame) (NBC)
ALAN JOHNSON 'George M!" (Bell System Family Theatre) (NBC)

WRITING - DRAMA (E-713)

A single program of a series with continuing characters and/or theme

JOEL OLIANSKY "To Taste Of Death But Once" (The Bold Ones - The Senator Segment) (NBC)
DAVID W. RINTELS "A Continual Roar Of Musketry, Parts I & II" (The Bold Ones - The Senator Segment) (NBC)
JERROLD FREEDMAN "In Death's Other Kingdom" (The Psychiatrist, Four-In-One) (NBC)

WRITING - DRAMA, ORIGINAL TELEPLAY (E-714)

A single program

TRACY KEENAN WYNN, MARVIN SCHWARTZ "Tribes" (Movie Of The Week On ABC) (ABC)
WILLIAM READ WOODFIELD, ALLAN BALTER "San Francisco Interna-

tional Airport'' (World Premiere NBC Tuesday Night At The Movies) (NBC)

DAVID KARP "The Brotherhood Of The Bell" (CBS Thursday Night Movies) (CBS)

WRITING - DRAMA, ADAPTATION (E-715)

A single program

SAUL LEVITT "The Andersonville Trial" (Hollywood Television Theatre) (PBS)

JOHN BARTON "Hamlet" (Hallmark Hall of Fame) (NBC)

DEAN RIESNER "Vanished" (World Premiere NBC Monday & Tuesday Night At The Movies) (NBC)

WRITING - COMEDY (E-716)

A single program of a series with continuing characters and/or theme

JAMES L. BROOKS, ALLAN BURNS "Support Your Local Mother" (The Mary Tyler Moore Show) (CBS)

NORMAN LEAR "Meet The Bunkers" (All In The Family) (CBS)

STANLEY RALPH ROSS "Oh, My Aching Back" (All In The Family) (CBS)

BOB CARROLL, JR., MADELYN DAVIS "Lucy Meets The Burtons" (Here's Lucy) (CBS)

WRITING - VARIETY OR MUSIC (E-717)

A single program of a series

HERBERT BAKER, HAL GOODMAN, LARRY KLEIN, BOB WEISKOPF, BOB SCHILLER, NORMAN STEINBERG, FLIP WILSON "The Flip Wilson Show" (With Lena Horne and Tony Randall) (NBC)

ARTHUR JULIAN, DON HINKLEY, JACK MENDELSOHN, STAN HART, LARRY SIEGEL, WOODY KLING, ROGER BEATTY, ARNIE ROSEN, KENNY SOLMS, GAIL PARENT "The Carol Burnett Show" (With Rita Hayworth) (CBS)

DANNY SIMON, MARTY FARRELL, NORMAN BARASCH, CARROLL MOORE, TONY WEBSTER, COLEMAN JACOBY, BOB ELLISON, "The Kopykats Kopy TV" (Kraft Music Hall) (NBC)

WRITING - COMEDY, VARIETY OR MUSIC (E-718)

A special program

BOB ELLISON, MARTY FARRELL "Singer Presents Burt Bacharach" (CBS)

HAL GOLDMAN, AL GORDON, HILLIARD MARKS, HUGH WEDLOCK, JR. "Timex Presents Jack Benny's 20th TV Anniversary Special" (NBC)

SAUL ILSON, ERNEST CHAMBERS, GARY BELKIN, ALEX BARRIS "The Doris Mary Anne Kappelhoff Special" (CBS)

MUSIC COMPOSITION (E-719)

A. For a series or a single program of a series (In the first year of music's use only)

DAVID ROSE "The Love Child" (Bonanza) (NBC)

ROBERT PRINCE, BILLY GOLDENBERG "LA 2017" (The Name Of The Game) (Gene Barry Segment) (NBC)

FRANK COMSTOCK "Elegy For A Pig" (Adam-12) (NBC)

CHARLES FOX (Love, American Style) (Series) (ABC)

B. For a special program

WALTER SCHARF "The Tragedy Of The Red Salmon" (The Undersea World Of Jacques Cousteau) (ABC)

JOHN ADDISON "Hamlet" (Hallmark Hall Of Fame) (NBC)

PETE RUGOLO "Do You Take This Stranger"(World Premiere NBC Monday Night At The Movies) (NBC)

MUSIC DIRECTION OF A VARIETY, MUSICAL OR DRAMATIC PROGRAM (E-720)

A single program of a series or a special program

DOMINIC FRONTIERE "Swing Out, Sweet Land" (NBC)

JOHN ADDISON "Hamlet" (Hallmark Hall Of Fame) (NBC)

MORT LINDSEY "Big Band Salute, Parts I & II" (The Merv Griffin Show) (CBS)

ACHIEVEMENT IN MUSIC, LYRICS AND SPECIAL MATERIAL (E-721)

A series or a single program of a series or a special program written for television

RAY CHARLES "The First Nine Months Are The Hardest" (NBC)

BILLY BARNES "Clairol Command Performance Presents. . .Pure Goldie" (NBC)

LEE HALE "The Dean Martin Show" (Series) (NBC)

WILLIAM GOLDENBERG, DAVID WILSON "All The Old Familiar Faces" (The Name of the Game) (Gene Barry Segment) (NBC)

CINEMATOGRAPHY - ENTERTAINMENT PROGRAMMING (E-722)

A. For a series or a single program of a series

JACK MARTA "Cynthia Is Alive And Living In Avalon" (The Name of The Game) (Gene Barry Segment) (NBC)

TED VOIGTLANDER, A.S.C. "The Love Child" (Bonanza) (NBC)

WALTER STRENGE, A.S.C. "A Spanish Saying I Made Up" (Marcus Welby, M.D.) (ABC)

B. For a special or feature length program made for television

LIONEL LINDON, A.S.C. "Vanished, Parts I & II" (World Premiere NBC Monday & Tuesday Night At The Movies) (NBC)

BOB COLLINS "Timex Presents Peggy Fleming At Sun Valley" (NBC)

RUSSELL L. METTY, A.S.C. "Tribes" (Movie Of The Week On ABC) (ABC)

EDWARD ROSSON "The Neon Ceiling" (World Premiere NBC Monday Night At The Movies) (NBC)

CINEMATOGRAPHY - NEWS AND DOCUMENTARY PROGRAMMING (E-723)

For a series, a single program of a series, a special program, program segment or elements within: A. Regularly scheduled News programs and coverage of Special Events

LARRY TRAVIS "Los Angeles - Earthquake" (Sylmar V.A. Hospital) (CBS Evening News With Walter Cronkite) (CBS)

JAMES WATT "Cattle Drive Parts I & II" (The Huntley-Brinkley Report) (NBC)

HOUSTON HALL "They Paved Paradise" (The Huntley-Brinkley Report) (NBC)

B. Documentary, Magazine-type or Mini-documentary programs

JACQUES RENOIR "The Tragedy Of The Red Salmon" (The Undersea World of Jacques Cousteau) (ABC)

PHILIPPE COUSTEAU "Lagoon Of Lost Ships" (The Undersea World Of Jacques Cousteau) (ABC)

MICHEL DeLOIRE, JACQUES RENOIR "The Dragons Of Galapagos" (The Undersea World of Jacques Cousteau) (ABC)

JAMES S. WILSON, GUY ADENIS, GEORGE APOSTOLIDES, JOE BARDO-YESKO, TONY COGGANS, MICHAEL DUGAN, J. BARRY HERRON, ROBERT E. THOMAS, LARRY TRAVIS "Wildfire!" (GE Monogram Series) (NBC)

ART DIRECTION OR SCENIC DESIGN (E-724)

A. For a dramatic program or feature length film; a single program of a series or a special program

PETER RODEN "Hamlet" (Hallmark Hall of Fame) (NBC)

JOHN J. LLOYD AND RUBY R. LEVITT Art Director and Set Decorator Respectively, "Vanished, Parts I & II" (World Premiere NBC Monday and Tuesday Night At The Movies) (NBC)

JAN SCOTT "Montserrat" (Hollywood Television Theatre) (PBS)

JOHN CLEMENTS "The Price" (Hallmark Hall of Fame) (NBC)

J.M. VAN TAMELEN AND FRED PRICE Art Director and Set Decorator Respectively, "The Mouse That Died" (Mannix) (CBS)

B. For a musical or variety single program of a series, or a special program

JAMES W. TRITTIPO AND GEORGE GAINES Art Director and Set Decorator Respectively, "Robert Young And The Family" (CBS)
RENE LAGLER AND ROBERT CHECCI Art Director and Set Decorator Respectively, "The Glen Campbell Goodtime Hour" (With Neil Diamond, Linda Ronstadt) (CBS)
ROMAIN JOHNSTON "The Flip Wilson Show" (With Robert Goulet and Lola Falana) (NBC)
FRED LUFF "Love Is" (Oral Roberts Valentine Special - Contact) (Syndicated)

COSTUME DESIGN (E-725)

A single program of a series or a special program

MARTIN BAUGH AND DAVID WALKER "Hamlet" (Hallmark Hall of Fame) (NBC)
ROBERT CARLTON "Bing Crosby - Cooling It" (NBC)
RET TURNER "Andy Williams Christmas Show" (The Andy Williams Show) (NBC)
PATRICIA SEGNAN "They've Killed President Lincoln!" (NBC)

MAKE-UP (E-726)

A single program of a series or a special program

ROBERT DAWN 'Catafalque" (Mission: Impossible) (CBS)
MARIE ROCHE "Hamlet" (Hallmark Hall of Fame) (NBC)
ROLF J. MILLER "Samantha's Old Man" (Bewitched) (ABC)
PERC WESTMORE AND HARRY C. BLAKE "The Third Bill Cosby Special" (NBC)

FILM EDITING - ENTERTAINMENT PROGRAMMING (E-727)

A. For a series or a single program of a series

MICHAEL ECONOMOU "A Continual Roar Of Musketry, Parts I & II" (The Bold Ones - The Senator Segment) (NBC)
ARTHUR DAVID HILTON "Over 50? Steal" (Hawaii Five-O) (CBS)
DOUGLAS STEWART "To Taste Of Death But Once" (The Bold Ones - The Senator Segment) (NBC)

B. For a special or feature length program made for television

GEORGE J. NICHOLSON "Longstreet" (Movie Of The Week On ABC) (ABC)
ROBERT F. SHUGRUE "The Neon Ceiling" (World Premier NBC Monday Night At The Movies) (NBC)
ROBERT WATTS "Vanished, Parts I & II" (World Premier NBC Monday and Tuesday Night At The Movies) (NBC)

FILM EDITING - NEWS AND DOCUMENTARY PROGRAMMING (E-728)

For a series, a single program of a series, a special program, program segments or elements within: A. Regularly scheduled news programs and coverage of special events

GEORGE L. JOHNSON "Prison, Parts I Thru IV" (NBC Nightly News) (NBC)
MICHAEL C. SHUGRUE " The Welfare Worker" (NBC Nightly News) (NBC)
LOUIS BUCHIGNANI " L.A. Earthquake!" (ABC Evening News With Howard K. Smith And Harry Reasoner) (ABC)

B. Documentary, Magazine-type or Mini-documentary programs

ROBERT B. LOWEREE AND HENRY J. GRENNON "Cry Help! An NBC White Paper On Mentally Disturbed Youth" (NBC)
DAVID E. BLEWITT "The Tragedy Of The Red Salmon" (The Undersea World of Jacques Cousteau) (ABC)

DENA LEVITT "CBS Reports: The Selling Of The Pentagon" (CBS)
JOHN F. TEEPLE "The Prado" (The Southern Baptist Hour) (NBC)

FILM SOUND EDITING (E-729)

A single program of a series or a special program

DON HALL, JR., JACK JACKSON, BOB WEATHERFORD, DICK JENSEN "Tribes" (Movie Of The Week On ABC) (ABC)
DOUGLAS H. GRINDSTAFF, FRANK R. WHITE, JOE KAVIGAN, DON CROSBY, CHUCK PERRY "The Blast" (Mission: Impossible) (CBS)
DOUGLAS H. GRINDSTAFF, EDWARD L. SANDLIN, JOSEF E. VON STROHEIM, SETH D. LARSEN, BILL RIVOL, BILLIE OWENS "Sunburst" (Mannix) (CBS)

FILM SOUND MIXING (E-730)

A single program of a series or a special program

THEODORE SODERBERG "Tribes" (Movie Of The Week On ABC) (ABC)
JOEL F. MOSS AND DON RUSH "Sunburst" (Mannix) (CBS)
RONALD K. PIERCE AND JAMES Z. FLASTER "Vanished, Parts I & II" (World Premiere NBC Monday and Tuesday Night At The Movies) (NBC)
ROGER PARISH AND ROBERT L. HOYT "San Francisco International Airport" (World Premiere NBC Tuesday Night At The Movies) (NBC)

LIGHTING DIRECTION (E-731)

A single program of a series or a special program produced for electronic television only

JOHN ROOK "Hamlet" (Hallmark Hall of Fame) (NBC)
KENNETH DETTLING "The Andersonville Trial" (Hollywood Television Theatre) (PBS)
JOHN FRESCHI "Andy Williams Christmas Show" (The Andy Williams Show) (NBC)
CARL GIBSON "Love Is" (Oral Roberts Valentine Special - Contact) (Syndicated)

LIVE OR TAPE SOUND MIXING (E-732)

A single program of a series or a special program

HENRY BIRD "Hamlet" (Hallmark Hall of Fame) (NBC)
DAVE WILLIAMS "The Flip Wilson Show" (With Lena Horne and Tony Randall) (NBC)
MARSHALL KING "Swing Out, Sweet Land" (NBC)

VIDEO TAPE EDITING (E-733)

A single program of a series or a special program

MARCO ZAPPIA "Hee-Haw" (With Roger Miller and Peggy Little) (CBS)
RAY KNIPE "Hamlet" (Hallmark Hall of Fame) (NBC)
STEVEN ORLAND AND MARTIN J. PETERS "Clairol Command Performance Presents. . .Pure Goldie" (NBC)

TECHNICAL DIRECTION AND ELECTRONIC CAMERAWORK (E-734)

A single program of a series or a special program

GORDON BAIRD; TOM ANCELL, RICK BENNEWITZ, LARRY BENTLEY, JACK READER Technical Director and Cameramen Respectively 'The Andersonville Trial" (Hollywood Television Theatre) (PBS)
LOUIS FUSARI; TONY YARLETT, RAY FIGELSKI, MARVIN AULT, JON OLSON Technical Director and Cameramen Respectively, 'Rowan And Martin's Laugh-In" (With Orson Welles) (NBC)
BILL SCHERTLE; BARNEY NEELEY, TOM McCONNELL, ALAN LATTER Technical Director and Cameramen Respectively, 'Apollo 14 Recovery Aboard The USS New Orleans" (Network Pool Coverage)

THE AREAS
(Possibility of One Award, More Than One Award, or No Award)

ACHIEVEMENT IN CHILDREN'S PROGRAMMING (E-735)

PROGRAMS (E-736)
SESAME STREET (Series) (PBS) David D. Connell, Executive Producer; Jon Stone, Lutrelle Horne, Producers
KUKLA, FRAN AND OLLIE (Series) (PBS) John J. Sommers, Richard Carter, Executive Producers

INDIVIDUALS (E-737)
BURR TILLSTROM Performer "Kukla, Fran And Ollie" (Series) (PBS)
GEORGE W. RIESENBERGER Lighting Director "Sesame Street" (Series) (PBS)

ACHIEVEMENT IN DAYTIME PROGRAMMING (E-738)

PROGRAMS (E-739)
TODAY (Series) (NBC) Stuart Schulberg, Producer
THE GALLOPING GOURMET (Series) (Syndicated) Treena Kerr, Producer; Graham Kerr, Host

INDIVIDUALS (E-740)
JAMES ANGERAME Technical Director "Love Is A Many Splendored Thing" (CBS)
VICTOR L. PAGANUZZI AND JOHN A. WENDELL Art Director and Set Decorator Respectively, "Love Is A Many Splendored Thing" (CBS)

ACHIEVEMENT IN SPORTS PROGRAMMING (E-741)

PROGRAMS (E-742)
ABC'S WIDE WORLD OF SPORTS (Series) (ABC) Roone Arledge, Executive Producer
34TH MASTERS TOURNAMENT (CBS) Frank Chirkinian, Producer
NFL MONDAY NIGHT FOOTBALL (Series) (ABC) Roone Arledge, Executive Producer; Chet Forte, Producer

INDIVIDUALS (E-743)
JIM McKAY Commentator "ABC's Wide World of Sports" (Series) (ABC)
DON MEREDITH Commentator "NFL Monday Night Football" (Series) (ABC)
WALT KUBILUS; DICK KERR, JOHN MORREALLE, MIKE REBICH, STUART GOODMAN, MORT LEVIN, SAL FOLINO, DON LANGFORD, ED PAYNE Technical Director and Cameramen Respectively, "NCAA Football" (Series) (ABC)

SPECIAL CLASSIFICATION OF OUTSTANDING PROGRAM AND INDIVIDUAL ACHIEVEMENT (E-744)

PROGRAMS (E-745)
THE WONDERFUL WORLD OF DISNEY (Series) (NBC) Ron Miller, Executive Producer

MUTUAL OF OMAHA'S WILD KINGDOM (Series) (NBC) Don Meier, Producer

INDIVIDUALS (E-746)
HARVEY KORMAN Performer "The Carol Burnett Show" (Series) (CBS)
LILY TOMLIN Performer "Rowan And Martin's Laugh-In" (Series) (NBC)
ARTE JOHNSON Performer "Rowan And Martin's Laugh-In" (Series) (NBC)

ACHIEVEMENT IN ANY AREA OF CREATIVE TECHNICAL CRAFTS (E-747)
LENWOOD B. ABBOTT, JOHN C. CALDWELL Special Photographic Effects "City Beneath The Sea" (World Premiere NBC Monday Night At The Movies) (NBC)
GENE WIDHOFF Graphic Art - Court Room Sketches 'Manson Trial" (The Huntley-Brinkley Report - NBC Nightly News) (NBC)
ALBERT J. WHITLOCK Special Photographic Effects "Vanished, Parts I & II" (World Premiere NBC Monday and Tuesday Night At The Movies) (NBC)

SPECIAL AWARDS

TRUSTEES AWARD (E-748)
ED SULLIVAN For serving as a founder of The National Academy and its first National President; for pioneering in the variety format which has become a backbone of television programming; for having the foresight and courage to provide network exposure for minority performers; for bringing to millions of Americans cultural performances from ballet to opera to legitimate drama; for introducing performers from throughout the world to audiences who would otherwise never have known them; and, finally, for his showmanship, tastes and personal commitment in entertaining a nation for 23 years.

ACHIEVEMENT IN ENGINEERING DEVELOPMENT (E-749)
THE COLUMBIA BROADCASTING SYSTEM For the development of the Color Corrector which can provide color uniformity between television picture segments and scenes shot and recorded under different conditions at different times and locations.

THE AMERICAN BROADCASTING COMPANY For the development of an "Open-Loop" Synchronizing System which enables the simultaneous synchronization of any number of color programs from remote locations.

CITATIONS (E-750)
GENERAL ELECTRIC For development of the Portable Earth Station Transmitter.
STEFAN KUDELSKI For his design of the NAGRA IV Recorder.

THE STATION AWARD (E-751)
IF YOU TURN ON (KNXT, Los Angeles, Calforia)
ARE WE KILLING THE GULF? (KPRC-TV, Houston, Texas)
FATHER MOUNTAIN'S CHRISTMAS (KOOL-TV, Phoenix, Arizona)
HEY DOC (WCAU-TV, Philadelphia, Pennsylvania)
HOMES LIKE THESE (WLBT, Jackson, Mississippi)
THE LOST - THE LONELY (WJW-TV, Cleveland, Ohio)
NINE HEROES (WGBH, Educational Station, Allston, Massachusetts)
NO PLACE TO HIDE (WBBM-TV, Chicago, Illinois)
OUR CITY'S HISTORY - BOSTON: JUNE 1970 (WNAC-TV, Boston, Massachusetts)
TIMETABLE FOR DISASTER (WMC-TV, Memphis, Tennessee)

1971/72

NEWS AND DOCUMENTARY PROGRAM AND INDIVIDUAL ACHIEVEMENTS
(Possibility of One Award, More than One Award, or No Award)

ACHIEVEMENT WITHIN REGULARLY SCHEDULED NEWS PROGRAMS (E-752)

PROGRAMS (E-753)
DEFEAT OF DACCA (NBC Nightly News) Wallace Wesfeldt, Executive Producer; Robert Mulholland and David Teitelbaum, Producers (NBC)
COVERAGE OF PRESIDENT NIXON'S VISIT TO CHINA (NBC Nightly News) Wallace Westfeldt, Executive Producer; Les Crystal, Richard Fischer, Robert Mulholland, David Teitelbaum, Producers (NBC)
HOWARD HUGHES PHONE INTERVIEW (Segment) (NBC Nightly News) Wallace Westfeldt, Executive Producer; Richard Fischer, Bruce Sloan, Roy Neal, Producers (NBC)

INDIVIDUALS (E-754)
PHIL BRADY, Reporter "Defeat of Dacca" (NBC Nightly News) (NBC)
BOB SCHIEFFER, PHIL JONES, DON WEBSTER, BILL PLANTE, Correspondents "The Air War" (CBS Evening News With Walter Cronkite) (CBS)
DAVID BRINKLEY, Correspondent "David Brinkley's Journal" (NBC Nightly News) (NBC)
JOHN CHANCELLOR, Correspondent "President Nixon's Visit to China" (NBC Nightly News) (NBC)

ACHIEVEMENT FOR REGULARLY SCHEDULED MAGAZINE-TYPE PROGRAMS (E-755)

PROGRAMS (E-756)
CHRONOLOG Eliot Frankel, Executive Producer (Series) (NBC)
THE GREAT AMERICAN DREAM MACHINE A. H. Perlmutter, Executive Producer (Series) (PBS)
60 MINUTES Don Hewitt, Executive Producer; Palmer Williams, Producer (Series) (CBS)

INDIVIDUALS (E-757)
MIKE WALLACE, Correspondent "60 Minutes" (Series) (CBS)
TOM PETTIT, Reporter "The Business of Blood" (Segment) (Chronolog) (NBC)
ANDREW A. ROONEY, Writer "An Essay on War" (The Great American Dream Machine) (PBS)
MORLEY SAFER, Correspondent "60 Minutes" (Series) (CBS)

ACHIEVEMENT IN COVERAGE OF SPECIAL EVENTS (E-758)

PROGRAMS (E-759)
THE CHINA TRIP Av Westin and Wally Pfister, Executive Producers; Bill Lord, Producer (ABC)
JUNE 30, 1971, A DAY FOR HISTORY: THE SUPREME COURT AND THE PENTAGON PAPERS Lawrence E. Spivak, Executive Producer (NBC)
A RIDE ON THE MOON: THE FLIGHT OF APOLLO 15 Robert Wussler, Executive Producer; Joan Richman, Producer (CBS)
LOUIS ARMSTRONG 1900-1971 Robert Wussler, Executive Producer; Joan Richman, Producer (CBS)
THE PRESIDENT IN CHINA Robert Wussler and Ernest Leiser, Executive Producers (CBS)

INDIVIDUALS (E-760)
JOEL BANOW, Director "Louis Armstrong 1900-1971" (CBS)
ANTHONY C. MESSURI, Director "The Flight of Apollo 15: A Journey To Hadley Rille" (NBC)

DOCUMENTARY PROGRAM ACHIEVEMENT (E-761)

PROGRAMS - CURRENT SIGNIFICANCE (E-762)
A NIGHT IN JAIL, A DAY IN COURT (CBS Reports) Burton Benjamin, Executive Producer; John Sharnik, Producer (CBS)
THIS CHILD IS RATED X: AN NBC NEWS WHITE PAPER ON JUVENILE JUSTICE Martin Carr, Producer (NBC)
JUSTICE IN AMERICA - Parts II and III (CBS Reports) Burton Benjamin, Executive Producer; John Sharnik and Harry Morgan, Producers (CBS)
SOME ARE MORE EQUAL THAN OTHERS "Justice in America" (CBS Reports) Burton Benjamin, Executive Producer; John Sharnik and Harry Morgan, Producers (CBS)
UNDER SURVEILLANCE (CBS Reports) Burton Benjamin, Executive Producer; Robert Chandler, Producer (CBS)

PROGRAMS - CULTURAL (E-763)
HOLLYWOOD: THE DREAM FACTORY "The Monday Night Special" Nicolas Noxon, Executive Producer; Irwin Rosten and Bud Friedgen, Producers (ABC)
A SOUND OF DOLPHINS "The Undersea World of Jacques Cousteau" Jacques Cousteau and Marshall Flaum, Executive Producers; Andy White, Producer (ABC)
THE UNSINKABLE SEA OTTER "The Undersea World of Jacques Cousteau" Jacques Cousteau and Marshall Flaum, Executive Producers; Andy White, Producer (ABC)
THE AMERICAN WEST OF JOHN FORD Bob Banner, Executive Producer; Tom Egan, Dan Ford and Britt Lomond, Producers (CBS)
THE FORGOTTEN MERMAIDS "The Undersea World of Jacques Cousteau" Jacques Cousteau and Marshall Flaum, Executive Producers (ABC)
PICASSO IS 90 (CBS Reports) Burton Benjamin, Executive Producer; William K. McClure, Producer (CBS)

INDIVIDUALS (E-764)
LOUIS J. HAZAM, Writer "Venice Be Damned!" (NBC)
ROBERT NORTHSHIELD, Writer "Suffer The Little Children - An NBC News White Paper on Northern Ireland" (NBC)
MARTIN CARR, Writer "This Child Is Rated X: An NBC White Paper on Juvenile Justice" (NBC)
FRED FLAMENHAFT, Director "Suffer The Little Children - An NBC News White Paper on Northern Ireland" (NBC)
ANDY WHITE, Writer "Octopus, Octopus" (The Undersea World of Jacques Cousteau) (ABC)

ENTERTAINMENT PROGRAM AND INDIVIDUAL ACHIEVEMENTS
(One Award Only In Each of the Remaining Categories)

COMEDY SERIES (E-765)
Award to Executive Producer(s) and/or Producer(s).
ALL IN THE FAMILY (CBS) Norman Lear, Producer
THE MARY TYLER MOORE SHOW (CBS) James L. Brooks and Allan Burns, Executive Producers; David Davis, Producer
THE ODD COUPLE (ABC) Jerry Belson and Garry Marshall, Executive Producers; Jerry Davis, Producer
SANFORD AND SON (NBC) Bud Yorkin, Executive Producer; Aaron Ruben, Producer

DRAMA SERIES (E-766)
Award to Executive Producer(s) and/or Producer(s).
ELIZABETH R (PBS) Masterpiece Theatre; Christopher Sarson, Executive Producer; Roderick Graham, Producer
COLUMBO (NBC) NBC Mystery Movie; Richard Levinson and William

Link, Executive Producers; Everett Chambers, Producer
MANNIX (CBS) Bruce Geller, Executive Producer; Ivan Goff and Ben Roberts, Producers
MARCUS WELBY, M.D. (ABC) David Victor, Executive Producer; David J. O'Connell, Producer
THE SIX WIVES OF HENRY VIII (CBS) Ronald Travers and Mark Shivas, Producers

OUTSTANDING SINGLE PROGRAM - DRAMA OR COMEDY (E-767)

A single program of a series or a special program - Award to Executive Producer(s) and/or Producer(s)

BRIAN'S SONG (ABC) Movie of The Week; Paul Junger Witt, Producer
JANE SEYMOUR (CBS) The Six Wives of Henry VIII; Ronald Travers and Mark Shivas, Producers
THE LION'S CUB (PBS) Elizabeth R; Masterpiece Theatre; Christopher Sarson, Executive Producer; Roderick Graham, Producer
SAMMY'S VISIT (CBS) All In The Family; Norman Lear, Producer
THE SNOW GOOSE (NBC) Hallmark Hall of Fame; Frank O'Connor, Producer

VARIETY SERIES - MUSICAL (E-768)

Award(s) to Executive Producer(s) and/or Producer(s) and Star (if applicable).

THE CAROL BURNETT SHOW (CBS) Joe Hamilton, Executive Producer; Arnie Rosen, Producer; Carol Burnett, Star
THE DEAN MARTIN SHOW (NBC) Greg Garrison, Producer; Dean Martin, Star
THE FLIP WILSON SHOW (NBC) Monte Kay, Executive Producer; Robert Henry, Producer; Flip Wilson, Star
THE SONNY & CHER COMEDY HOUR (CBS) Allan Blye and Chris Bearde, Producers; Sonny & Cher, Stars

VARIETY SERIES - TALK (E-769)

Award(s) to Executive Producer(s) and/or Producer(s) and Star.

THE DICK CAVETT SHOW (ABC) John Gilroy, Producer; Dick Cavett, Star
THE DAVID FROST SHOW (Synd) Peter Baker, Producer; David Frost, Star
THE TONIGHT SHOW STARRING JOHNNY CARSON (NBC) Fred De Cordova, Producer; Johnny Carson, Star

OUTSTANDING SINGLE PROGRAM - VARIETY OR MUSICAL (E-770)

A single program of a series or a special program - Award(s) to Executive Producer(s) and/or Producer(s) and Star (if applicable). A. Variety and Popular Music.

JACK LEMMON IN 'S WONDERFUL, 'S MARVELOUS, 'S GERSHWIN (NBC) Bell System Family Theatre; Joseph Cates, Executive Producer; Martin Charnin, Producer; Jack Lemmon, Star
THE FLIP WILSON SHOW (NBC) (with Sammy Davis Jr., Lily Tomlin and Ed McMahon) Monte Kay, Executive Producer; Robert Henry, Producer; Flip Wilson, Star
JULIE AND CAROL AT LINCOLN CENTER (CBS) Joe Hamilton, Producer; Julie Andrews and Carol Burnett, Stars
THE SONNY AND CHER COMEDY HOUR (CBS) (with Tony Randall) Allan Blye and Chris Bearde, Producers; Sonny and Cher, Stars
B. Classical Music.
BEETHOVEN'S BIRTHDAY: A CELEBRATION IN VIENNA WITH LEONARD BERNSTEIN (CBS) James Krayer, Executive Producer; Humphrey Burton, Producer; Leonard Bernstein, Star
HEIFETZ (NBC) Bell System Family Theatre; Lester Shurr, Executive Producer; Paul Louis, Producer, Jascha Heifetz, Star
THE PEKING BALLET: FIRST SPECTACULAR FROM CHINA (NBC) Lucy Jarvis, Producer
THE TRIAL OF MARY LINCOLN (PBS) NET Opera Theatre; Peter Herman Adler, Executive Producer; David Griffiths, Producer

NEW SERIES (E-771)

Award to Executive Producer(s) and/or Producer(s).

ELIZABETH R (PBS) Masterpiece Theatre; Christopher Sarson, Executive Producer; Roderick Graham, Producer
COLUMBO (NBC) NBC Mystery Movie; Richard Levinson and William Link, Executive Producers; Everett Chambers, Producer
SANFORD AND SON (NBC) Bud Yorkin, Executive Producer; Aaron Ruben, Producer
THE SIX WIVES OF HENRY VIII (CBS) Ronald Travers and Mark Shivas, Producers
THE SONNY & CHER COMEDY HOUR (CBS) Allan Blye and Chris Bearde, Producers

ACTOR - SINGLE PERFORMANCE (E-772)

A one-time appearance in a series or for a special program.

KEITH MICHELL "Catherine Howard" (The Six Wives of Henry VIII) (CBS)
JAMES CAAN "Brian's Song" (Movie of The Week) (ABC)
RICHARD HARRIS "The Snow Goose" (Hallmark Hall of Fame) (NBC)
GEORGE C. SCOTT "Jane Eyre" (Bell System Family Theatre) (NBC)
BILLY DEE WILLIAMS "Brian's Song" (Movie of The Week) (ABC)

ACTRESS - SINGLE PERFORMANCE (E-773)

A one-time appearance in a series or for a special program.

GLENDA JACKSON "Shadow In The Sun" Elizabeth R (Masterpiece Theatre) (PBS)
GLENDA JACKSON "The Lion's Cub" Elizabeth R (Masterpiece Theatre) (PBS)
HELEN HAYES "Do Not Fold, Spindle or Mutilate" (Movie of The Week) (ABC)
PATRICIA NEAL "The Homecoming - A Christmas Story" (CBS)
SUSANNAH YORK "Jane Eyre" (Bell System Family Theatre) (NBC)

ACTOR - DRAMATIC SERIES (E-774)

PETER FALK "Columbo" (NBC Mystery Movie) (NBC)
RAYMOND BURR (Ironside) (NBC)
MIKE CONNORS (Mannix) (CBS)
KEITH MICHELL (The Six Wives of Henry VIII) (CBS)
ROBERT YOUNG (Marcus Welby, M.D.) (ABC)

ACTRESS - DRAMATIC SERIES (E-775)

GLENDA JACKSON Elizabeth R (Masterpiece Theatre) (PBS)
PEGGY LIPTON (The Mod Squad) (ABC)
SUSAN SAINT JAMES McMillan & Wife (NBC Mystery Movie) (NBC)

ACTOR - COMEDY SERIES (E-776)

CARROLL O'CONNOR (All in The Family) (CBS)
REDD FOXX (Sanford and Son) (NBC)
JACK KLUGMAN (The Odd Couple) (ABC)
TONY RANDALL (The Odd Couple) (ABC)

ACTRESS - COMEDY SERIES (E-777)

JEAN STAPLETON (All In The Family) (CBS)
SANDY DUNCAN (Funny Face) (CBS)
MARY TYLER MOORE (The Mary Tyler Moore Show) (CBS)

SUPPORTING ACTOR - DRAMA (E-778)

A continuing or one-time appearance in a series, or for a special program.

JACK WARDEN (Brian's Song) (Movie of The Week) (ABC)
JAMES BROLIN (Marcus Welby, M.D.) (Series) (ABC)
GREG MORRIS (Mission: Impossible) (Series) (CBS)

SUPPORTING ACTRESS - DRAMA (E-779)

A continuing or one-time appearance in a series, or for a special program.

JENNY AGUTTER (The Snow Goose) (Hallmark Hall of Fame) (NBC)
GAIL FISHER (Mannix) (Series) (CBS)
ELENA VERDUGO (Marcus Welby, M.D.) (Series) (ABC)

SUPPORTING ACTOR - COMEDY (E-780)

A continuing or one-time appearance in a series, or for a special program.

EDWARD ASNER (The Mary Tyler Moore Show) (Series) (CBS)
TED KNIGHT (The Mary Tyler Moore Show) (Series) (CBS)
ROB REINER (All in The Family) (Series) (CBS)

SUPPORTING ACTRESS - COMEDY (E-781)

A continuing or one-time appearance in a series, or for a special program.

VALERIE HARPER (The Mary Tyler Moore Show) (Series) (CBS)
SALLY STRUTHERS (All in The Family) (Series) (CBS)
CLORIS LEACHMAN (The Mary Tyler Moore Show) (Series) (CBS)

MUSIC OR VARIETY PERFORMER (E-782)

A continuing or one-time appearance in a series, or for a special program.

HARVEY KORMAN (The Carol Burnett Show) (Series) (CBS)
RUTH BUZZI (Rowan and Martin's Laugh-In) (Series) (NBC)
LILY TOMLIN (Rowan and Martin's Laugh-In) (Series) (NBC)

DIRECTOR - DRAMA (E-783)

A single program of a series with continuing characters and/or theme.

ALEXANDER SINGER "The Invasion of Kevin Ireland" (The Bold Ones - The Lawyers) (NBC)
EDWARD M. ABROMS "Short Fuse" (Columbo) (NBC Mystery Movie) (NBC)
DANIEL PETRIE "Hands of Love" (The Man and The City) (ABC)

DIRECTOR - DRAMA - SINGLE PROGRAM (E-784)

TOM GRIES "The Glass House" (The New CBS Friday Night Movies) (CBS)
PAUL BOGART "Look Homeward, Angel" (CBS Playhouse 90) (CBS)
FIELDER COOK "The Homecoming - A Christmas Story" (CBS)
PATRICK GARLAND "The Snow Goose" (Hallmark Hall of Fame) (NBC)
BUZZ KULIK "Brian's Song" (Movie of The Week) (ABC)

DIRECTOR - COMEDY (E-785)

A single program of a series with continuing characters and/or theme.

JOHN RICH "Sammy's Visit" (All in The Family) (CBS)
PETER BALDWIN "Where There's Smoke, There's Rhoda" (The Mary Tyler Moore Show) (CBS)
JAY SANDRICH "Thoroughly Unmilitant Mary" (The Mary Tyler Moore Show) (CBS)

DIRECTOR - VARIETY OR MUSIC (E-786)

A single program of a series.

ART FISHER "The Sonny & Cher Comedy Hour" (with Tony Randall) (CBS)
TIM KILEY "The Flip Wilson Show" (with Petula Clark and Redd Foxx) (NBC)
DAVID P. POWERS "The Carol Burnett Show" (with Carol Channing and Steve Lawrence) (CBS)

DIRECTOR - COMEDY, VARIETY OR MUSIC SPECIAL PROGRAM (E-787)

WALTER C. MILLER and MARTIN CHARNIN "Jack Lemmon in 'S Wonderful, 'S Marvelous, 'S Gershwin" (Bell System Family Theatre) (NBC)
ROGER ENGLANDER "Liszt and The Devil" (New York Philharmonic Young People's Concert) (CBS)
DAVID P. POWERS "Julie and Carol at Lincoln Center" (CBS)

CHOREOGRAPHY (E-788)

A single program of a series or a special program.

ALAN JOHNSON "Jack Lemmon in 'S Wonderful, 'S Marvelous, 'S Gershwin" (Bell System Family Theatre) (NBC)
ERNEST O. FLATT "The Carol Burnett Show" (with Mel Torme and Nanette Fabray) (CBS)
TOM HANSEN "The Fabulous Fordies" (NBC)

WRITING - DRAMA (E-789)

A single program of a series with continuing characters and/or theme.

RICHARD L. LEVINSON and WILLIAM LINK "Death Lends A Hand" (Columbo) (NBC Mystery Movie) (NBC)
STEVE BOCHCO "Murder By The Book" (Columbo) (NBC Mystery Movie) (NBC)
JACKSON GILLIS "Suitable for Framing" (Columbo) (NBC Mystery Movie) (NBC)

WRITING - DRAMA, ORIGINAL TELEPLAY (E-790)

A single program.

ALLAN SLOANE "To All My Friends On Shore" (CBS)
JOHN D. F. BLACK "Thief" (Movie of The Weekend) (ABC)
JACK SHER "Goodbye, Raggedy Ann" (The New CBS Friday Night Movies) (CBS)

WRITING - DRAMA, ADAPTATION (E-791)

A single program.

WILLIAM BLINN "Brian's Song" (Movie of The Week) (ABC)
PAUL W. GALLICO "The Snow Goose" (Hallmark Hall of Fame) (NBC)
EARL HAMNER, JR. "The Homecoming - A Christmas Story" (CBS)
TRACY KEENAN WYNN "The Glass House" (The New CBS Friday Night Movies) (CBS)

WRITING - COMEDY (E-792)

A single program of a series with continuing characters and/or theme.

BURT STYLER "Edith's Problem" (All in The Family) (CBS)
BURT STYLER and NORMAN LEAR "The Saga of Cousin Oscar" (All in The Family) (CBS)
PHILIP MISHKIN and ALAN J. LEVITT "Mike's Problem" (All in The Family) (CBS)

WRITING - VARIETY OR MUSIC (E-793)

A single program of a series.

DON HINKLEY, STAN HART, LARRY SIEGEL, WOODY KLING, ROGER BEATTY, ART BAER, BEN JOELSON, STAN BURNS, MIKE MARMER and ARNIE ROSEN "The Carol Burnett Show" (with Tim Conway and Ray Charles) (CBS)
HERBERT BAKER, HAL GOODMAN, LARRY KLEIN, BOB SCHILLER, BOB WEISKOPF, SID GREEN, DICK HILLS and FLIP WILSON "The Flip Wilson Show" (with Sammy Davis, Jr., Lily Tomlin and Ed McMahon) (NBC)
PHIL HAHN, PAUL WAYNE, GEORGE BURDITT, COSLOUGH JOHNSON, BOB ARNOTT, STEVE MARTIN, BOB EINSTEIN, ALLAN BLYE and CHRIS BEARDE "The Sonny & Cher Comedy Hour" (with Carroll O'Connor) (CBS)

WRITING - COMEDY, VARIETY OR MUSIC - SPECIAL (E-794)

A special program.

ANNE HOWARD BAILEY "The Trial of Mary Lincoln" (NET Opera Theatre) (PBS)
MARTIN CHARNIN "Jack Lemmon in 'S Wonderful, 'S Marvelous, 'S Gershwin" (Bell System Family Theatre) (NBC)
BOB ELLISON, MARTY FARRELL and KEN and MITZI WELCH "Julie And Carol At Lincoln Center" (CBS)

MUSIC COMPOSITION (E-795)

A. For a series or a single program of a series.

PETE RUGOLO "In Defense of Ellen McKay" (The Bold Ones - The Lawyers) (NBC)
CHARLES FOX "Love, American Style" (Series) (ABC)
WILLIAM GOLDENBERG "Lady In Waiting" (Columbo) (NBC Mystery Movie) (NBC)

B. For a special program.

JOHN T. WILLIAMS "Jane Eyre" (Bell System Family Theatre) (NBC)
CARL DAVIS "The Snow Goose" (Hallmark Hall of Fame) (NBC)
MICHEL LEGRAND "Brian's Song" (Movie of The Week) (ABC)

MUSIC DIRECTION OF A VARIETY, MUSICAL OR DRAMATIC PROGRAM (E-796)

A single program of a series or a special program.

ELLIOT LAWRENCE "Jack Lemmon in 'S Wonderful, 'S Marvelous, 'S Gershwin" (Bell System Family Theatre) (NBC)
VAN ALEXANDER "The Golddiggers Chevrolet Show" (with Fess Parker) (Synd)
JAMES E. DALE "The Sonny & Cher Comedy Hour" (with Jean Stapleton and Mike Connors) (CBS)

MUSIC, LYRICS AND SPECIAL MATERIAL (E-797)

A series or a single program of a special program written for television.

RAY CHARLES "The Funny Side of Marriage" (The Funny Side) (NBC)
BILLY BARNES "Rowan And Martin's Laugh-In" (with Liza Minnelli) (NBC)
EARL BROWN "The Sonny and Cher Comedy Hour" (Series) (CBS)

ART DIRECTION OR SCENIC DESIGN (E-798)

A. For a dramatic program or feature length film made for television; a single program of a series or a special program.

JAN SCOTT "The Scarecrow" (Hollywood Television Theatre) (PBS)
BEN EDWARDS "Look Homeward, Angel" (CBS Playhouse 90) (CBS)
GIBSON HOLLEY, Art Director; LUCIEN HAFLEY, Set Decorator "Encore" (Mission: Impossible) (CBS)
STANLEY MORRIS "The Snow Goose" (Hallmark Hall of Fame) (NBC)

B. For a Musical or Variety single program of a series or a special program.

E. JAY KRAUSE "Diana!" (ABC)
PAUL BARNES and BOB SANSOM, Art Directors; BILL HARP, Set Decorator "The Carol Burnett Show" (with Vincent Price and Eydie Gorme) (CBS)
ROMAIN JOHNSTON "The Flip Wilson Show" (with Petula Clark and Redd Foxx) (NBC)
RENE LAGLER, Art Director; ROBERT CHECCHI, Set Decorator "The Glen Campbell Show" (with John Wayne) (CBS)

COSTUME DESIGN (E-799)

A single program of a series or a special program.

ELIZABETH WALLER "The Lion's Cub" Elizabeth R (Masterpiece Theatre) (PBS)
BOB MACKIE and RET TURNER "The Sonny & Cher Comedy Hour" (with Art Carney) (CBS)
RET TURNER "The Fabulous Fordies" (NBC)

MAKE-UP (E-800)

A single program of a series or a special program.
FRANK WESTMORE "Kung Fu" (Movie of The Week) (ABC)
HARRY C. BLAKE "Gideon" (Hallmark Hall of Fame) (NBC)
NICK MARCELLINO, LEONARD ENGELMAN and JOHN F. CHAMBERS "Pickman's Model" (Rod Serling's Night Gallery) (NBC)

CINEMATOGRAPHY - ENTERTAINMENT PROGRAMMING (E-801)

A. For a series or a single program of a series.

LLOYD AHERN, A.S.C. "Blue Print For Murder" Columbo (NBC Mystery Movie) (NBC)
CHARLES G. CLARKE "The Only Way to Go" (Arnie) (CBS)
ROBERT L. MORRISON "Hawaii Five-O" (Series) (CBS)

B. For a special or feature length program made for television.

JOSEPH BIROC "Brian's Song" (Movie of The Week) (ABC)
RAY HENMAN "The Snow Goose" (Hallmark Hall of Fame) (NBC)
JACK A. MARTA "Duel" (Movie of The Weekend) (ABC)

CINEMATOGRAPHY - NEWS AND DOCUMENTARY PROGRAMMING (E-802)

A. Regularly scheduled News programs and coverage of Special Events.

PETER McINTYRE and LIM YOUN CHOUL "Dacca" (NBC Nightly News) (NBC)
WILLIAM BRYAN "Pontiac Bussing" (NBC Nightly News) (NBC)
VO HUYNH "Beautiful Vietnam" (NBC Nightly News) (NBC)
KYUNG MO LEE "Seoul Hotel Fire" (NBC Nightly News) (NBC)
HOANG TRONG NGHIA and VO SUU "Viet Casualties" (NBC Nightly News) (NBC)
CHARLES A. RAY "West Virginia Flood" (NBC Nightly News) (NBC)
LARRY TRAVIS "Nitrogen Kills Columbia River Fish" (CBS Evening News With Walter Cronkite) (CBS)

B. Documentary, Magazine-type or Mini-documentary programs.

THOMAS PRIESTLEY "Venice Be Damned!" (NBC)
PHILIPPE COUSTEAU "Forgotten Mermaids" (The Undersea World of Jacques Cousteau) (ABC)
PHILIPPE COUSTEAU and MICHEL DELOIRE "The Unsinkable Sea Otter" (The Undersea World of Jacques Cousteau) (ABC)
MICHEL DELOIRE "Octopus, Octopus" (The Undersea World of Jacques Cousteau) (ABC)
JACQUES RENOIR "A Sound of Dolphins" (The Undersea World of Jacques Cousteau) (ABC)

FILM EDITING - ENTERTAINMENT PROGRAMMING (E-803)

A. For a series or a single program of a series.

EDWARD M. ABROMS "Death Lends A Hand" Columbo (NBC Mystery Movie) (NBC)
RICHARD BRACKEN, GLORYETTE CLARK and TERRY WILLIAMS "The Bold Ones - The Lawyers" (Series) (NBC)
JOSEPH T. DERVIN, SR. "Spell Legacy Like Death" (Longstreet) (ABC)

B. For a special or feature length program made for television.

BUD S. ISAACS "Brian's Song" (Movie of The Week) (ABC)
GENE FOWLER "The Glass House" (The New CBS Friday Night Movies) (CBS)
KEN PEARCE "The Snow Goose" (Hallmark Hall of Fame) (NBC)

FILM EDITING - NEWS AND DOCUMENTARY PROGRAMMING (E-804)

A. Regularly scheduled News programs and coverage of Special Events.

DAROLD MURRAY "War Song" (NBC Nightly News) (NBC)
GERALD C. BREESE "Native Hawaiians" (NBC Nightly News) (NBC)
GEORGE L. JOHNSON "Slaughter in East Pakistan Village of Sub-hadya" (NBC Nightly News) (NBC)

B. Documentary, Magazine-type or Mini-documentary programs.

SPENCER DAVID SAXON "Monkeys, Apes And Man" (National Geographic Society) (CBS)
SAMUEL COHEN and JAMES FLANAGAN "Earthquake!" (The Monday Night Special) (ABC)
JOHN SOH "The Forgotten Mermaids" (The Undersea World of Jacques Cousteau) (ABC)

FILM SOUND EDITING (E-805)

A single program of a series or a special program.

JERRY CHRISTIAN, JAMES TROUTMAN, RONALD LaVINE, SIDNEY LUBOW, RICHARD RADERMAN, DALE JOHNSTON, SAM CAYLOR, JOHN STACY and JACK KIRSCHNER "Duel" (Movie of The Weekend) (ABC)
COLIN C. MOUAT, CHARLES L. CAMPBELL and ROGER A. SWORD "The Forgotten Mermaids" (The Undersea World of Jacques Cousteau) (ABC)
HAROLD E. WOOLEY, PAUL LAUNE, MARVIN KOSBERG, GEORGE EMICK, RALPH HICKEY, WAYNE FURY and MONTY PEARCE "Brian's Song" (Movie of The Week) (ABC)

FILM SOUND MIXING (E-806)

A single program of a series or a special program.

THEODORE SODERBERG and RICHARD OVERTON "Fireball Forward" (The ABC Sunday Night Movie) (ABC)
WILLIAM J. MONTAGUE and ALFRED E. OVERTON "Brian's Song" (Movie of The Week) (ABC)
GEORGE PORTER, ROY GRANVILLE and ED NELSON "The Forgotten Mermaids" (The Undersea World of Jacques Cousteau) (ABC)

TECHNICAL DIRECTION AND ELECTRONIC CAMERAWORK (E-807)

A single program of a series or a special program.

HEINO RIPP, Technical Director; ALBERT CAMOIN, FRANK GAETA, GENE MARTIN and DONALD MULVANEY, Cameramen "Jack Lemmon in 'S Wonderful, 'S Marvelous, 'S Gershwin" (Bell System Family Theatre) (NBC)
LOUIS FUSARI, Technical Director; RAY FIGELSKI, RICK LOMBARDO, WAYNE OSTERHOUDT and JON OLSON, Cameramen "The Flip Wilson Show" (with Petula Clark and Redd Foxx) (NBC)
O. TAMBURRI, Technical Director; DON MULVANEY, JON OLSON and BOB KEYS, Cameramen "Gideon" (Hallmark Hall of Fame) (NBC)

LIGHTING DIRECTION (E-808)

A single program of a series or a special program, produced for electronic television only.

JOHN FRESCHI "Gideon" (Hallmark Hall of Fame) (NBC)
WILLIAM KLAGES "Good Vibrations from Central Park" (ABC)
JOHN R. NANCE "The Flip Wilson Show" (with Petula Clark and Redd Foxx) (NBC)

VIDEO TAPE EDITING (E-809)

A single program of a series or a special program.

PAT McKENNA "Hogan's Goat" (Special of The Week) (PBS)

FRANK HEROLD "Paradise Lost - Part II" (NET Playhouse on The 30's) (PBS)
MIKE WENIG "The Twentieth Century Follies" (The ABC Comedy Hour) (ABC)

LIVE OR TAPE SOUND MIXING (E-810)

A single program of a series or a special program.

NORMAN H. DEWES "The Elevator Story" (All in The Family) (CBS)
BILL COLE "Bing Crosby And His Friends" (NBC)
DAVE WILLIAMS "The Flip Wilson Show" (with Petula Clark and Redd Foxx) (NBC)

THE AREAS

(Possibility of One Award, More Than One Award, or No Award)

SPECIAL CLASSIFICATION OF OUTSTANDING PROGRAM AND INDIVIDUAL ACHIEVEMENT (E-811)

GENERAL PROGRAMMING (E-812)

THE PENTAGON PAPERS "PBS Special" David Prowitt, Executive Producer; Martin Clancy, Producer (PBS)
THE ADVOCATES Gregory G. Harney, Executive Producer; Russell Morash and Tom Burrows, Producers (Series) (PBS)
THE FRENCH CHEF Ruth Lockwood, Producer; Julia Child, Hostess (Series) (PBS)
MUTUAL OF OMAHA'S WILD KINGDOM Don Meier, Producer (Series) (Synd)
THE WONDERFUL WORLD OF DISNEY Ron Miller, Producer (Series) (NBC)

DOCU-DRAMA (E-813)

THE SEARCH FOR THE NILE - PARTS I-VI Christopher Ralling, Producer (NBC)
THE PLOT TO MURDER HITLER "Appointment With Destiny" Robert Larson and Warren Bush, Executive Producers; Robert Guenette, Producer (CBS)

INDIVIDUALS (E-814)

MICHAEL HASTINGS and DEREK MARLOW, Writers "The Search For The Nile - Parts I-VI" (NBC)
JESS PALEY, Cinematographer "The Plot to Murder Hitler" (Appointment With Destiny) (CBS)
BRIAN TUFANO and JOHN BAKER, Cinematographers "The Search For The Nile - Parts I-VI" (NBC)
GEORGE PORTER, DAVID RONNE, ROY GRANVILLE and EDWARD NELSON, Film Sound Mixers "Showdown At O.K. Corral" (Appointment With Destiny) (CBS)
WILLIAM MORRIS, Technical Director; ROBERT BERNSTEIN, PHILIP FONTANA, RICHARD KERR, JESSEL KOHN, MORTON LEVIN, JOHN MORREALE and MICHAEL REBICH, Cameramen, 25th Annual Antoinette Perry (Tony) Awards (ABC)

SPORTS PROGRAMMING (E-815)

PROGRAMS (E-816)

ABC'S WIDE WORLD OF SPORTS Roone Arledge, Executive Producer (Series) (ABC)
NFL MONDAY NIGHT FOOTBALL Roone Arledge, Executive Producer; Chet Forte and Dennis Lewin, Producers (Series) (ABC)
ROSE BOWL GAME Scotty Connal, Executive Producer; Lou Kusserow, Producer (NBC)
WORLD SERIES (Baseball) Lou Kusserow, Producer (NBC)
JACK PERKINS, Correspondent "The Perkins Piece" (XI Olympic Winter Games) (NBC)

INDIVIDUALS (E-817)

WILLIAM P. KELLEY, Technical Director; JIM CULLEY, JACK BEN-NETT, BUDDY JOSEPH, MARIO CIARLO, FRANK MANFREDI, COREY LEIBLE, GENE MARTIN, CAL SHADWELL, BILLY BARNES and RON CHARBONNEAU, Cameramen "AFC Championship Game" (NBC)

CHILDREN'S PROGRAMMING (E-818)

PROGRAMS (E-819)

SESAME STREET David D. Connell, Executive Producer; Jon Stone, Producer (Series) (PBS)
THE ELECTRIC COMPANY David D. Connell, Executive Producer; Samuel Y. Gibbon Jr., Producer (Series) (PBS)

INDIVIDUALS (E-820)

GEORGE W. RIESENBERGER, Lighting Director "Sesame Street" (Series) (PBS)
JOHN SCOTT TROTTER, Music Director "Play It Again, Charlie Brown" (CBS)

DAYTIME DRAMA (E-821)

PROGRAMS (E-822)

THE DOCTORS Allen Potter, Producer (Series) (NBC)
GENERAL HOSPITAL Jim Young, Producer (Series) (ABC)

INDIVIDUALS (E-823)

JOHN L. COFFEY, Technical Director; SELWYN REED, LOUIS GERARD and GENE MARTIN, Cameramen "Another World" (NBC)
MEL HANDELSMAN, Lighting Director "All My Children" (ABC)

OUTSTANDING ACHIEVEMENT IN DAYTIME PROGRAMMING (E-824)

PROGRAMS (E-825)

DINAH'S PLACE Henry Jaffe, Executive Producer; Fred Tatashore, Producer; Dinah Shore, Star (Series) (NBC)
THE HOLLYWOOD SQUARES Merrill Heatter and Robert Quigley, Executive Producers; Bill Armstrong and Jay Redack, Producers (Series) (NBC)

INDIVIDUALS (E-826)

PAUL LYNDE 'The Hollywood Squares" (Series) (NBC)
PETER MARSHALL "The Hollywood Squares" (Series) (NBC)

RELIGIOUS PROGRAMMING (E-827)

PROGRAMS (E-828)

INSIGHT Father Ellwood E. Kieser, Executive Producer; John Meredyth Lucas, Producer (Series) (Synd)
THIS IS THE LIFE Martin J. Neeb, Jr., Executive Producer; Stan Hersh and Melvin Hersh, Producers (Series) (Synd)

INDIVIDUALS (E-829)

ALFRED ANTONINI, Music Director "And David Wept" (CBS)
LON STUCKY, Lighting Director "A City of The King" (Contact) (Synd)

OUTSTANDING ACHIEVEMENT IN ANY AREA OF CREATIVE TECHNICAL CRAFTS (E-830)

PIERRE GOUPIL, MICHEL DELOIRE and YVES OMER, Underwater Cameramen "Secrets of the Sunken Caves" (The Undersea World of Jacques Cousteau) (ABC)

ROBERT GUENETTE, DAVID WOLPER, WARREN BUSH, NICHOLAS WEBSTER and ROBERT LARSON For re-creation of vintage film "The Plot To Murder Hitler," "The Last Days of John Dillinger," "Showdown at O.K. Corral" (Appointment With Destiny) (CBS)
EDIE PANDA, Hairstylist 'U.S.A." (Hollywood Television Theatre) (PBS)

TRUSTEES AWARDS (E-831)

BILL LAWRENCE, NATIONAL AFFAIRS EDITOR, ABC NEWS (DECEASED) For dedicating more than four decades of his life to reporting the news of the nation, the last one of which was devoted to television; ranging from international politics to international affairs and global combat; with that degree of objectivity, that devotion to truth, that professional preeminence which can only serve as a model for all television newsmen.
DR. FRANK STANTON, PRESIDENT, CBS For his selfless leadership and unwavering principle in defense of our industry under attack, his outspoken stance and courageous posture in protecting the right of the people to know, frequently in the face of potential dangers, both personal and professional, from those many forces which have attempted to abridge or even to abolish that right.

OUTSTANDING ACHIEVEMENT IN ENGINEERING DEVELOPMENT (E-832)

LEE HARRISON, III For the development of Scanimate, a unique electronic means of generating picture animation.

CITATIONS (E-833)

RICHARD E. HILL and ELECTRONIC ENGINEERING COMPANY OF CALIFORNIA For the development of a time code and equipment to facilitate the editing of magnetic video tape.
NATIONAL BROADCASTING COMPANY For the development of the Hum Bucker, which provides a practical means to correct a picture transmission defect commonly encountered on remote pickups.

THE STATION AWARD (E-834)

SICKLE CELL DISEASE: PARADOX OF NEGLECT (WZZM-TV) Grand Rapids, Michigan
ALL ABOUT WELFARE (WITF-TV) Hershey, Pennsylvania (Educational Station)
THE AWKWARD AGE (WCKT-TV) Miami, Florida
DRUG CRISES IN EAST HARLEM (WABC-TV) New York City, New York
INSIDE PARISH PRISON (WWL-TV) New Orleans, Louisiana
LOUISVILLE: OPEN CITY (WHAS) Louisville, Kentucky
MAKE NO MISTAKE ABOUT IT: THE PRESIDENT CAME TO IOWA (KDIN-TV) Des Moines, Iowa (Educational Station)
A PLACE FOR MUSIC (WHDH-TV) Boston, Massachusetts
PROBE. . .AND THROW AWAY THE KEY (WRC-TV) Washington, D.C.
. . .STILL GOT LIFE TO GO (WKY-TV) Oklahoma City, Oklahoma

1972/73

ENTERTAINMENT PROGRAM AND INDIVIDUAL ACHIEVEMENTS
(One Award Only In Each of the Following Categories)

COMEDY SERIES (E-835)

Award to Executive Producer(s) and/or Producer(s).

ALL IN THE FAMILY Norman Lear, Executive Producer, John Rich, Producer (CBS)
THE MARY TYLER MOORE SHOW James L. Brooks and Allan Burns, Executive Producers; Ed Weinberger, Producer (CBS)
M*A*S*H Gene Reynolds, Producer (CBS)
MAUDE Norman Lear, Executive Producer; Rod Parker, Producer (CBS)
SANFORD AND SON Bud Yorkin, Executive Producer; Aaron Ruben, Producer (NBC)

DRAMA SERIES - CONTINUING (E-836)
Award to Executive Producer(s) and/or Producer(s).

THE WALTONS Lee Rich, Executive Producer; Robert L. Jacks, Producer (CBS)
CANNON Quinn Martin, Executive Producer; Harold Gast and Adrian Samish, Producers (CBS)
COLUMBO, NBC Sunday Mystery Movie; Dean Hargrove, Producer (NBC)
HAWAII FIVE-O Leonard Freeman, Executive Producer; Bob Sweeney and William Finnegan, Producers (CBS)
KUNG-FU Jerry Thorpe, Producer (ABC)
MANNIX Bruce Geller, Executive Producer; Ivan Goff and Ben Roberts, Producers (CBS)

DRAMA/COMEDY - LIMITED EPISODES (E-837)
Award to Executive Producer(s) and/or Producer(s).

TOM BROWN'S SCHOOLDAYS Masterpiece Theatre: Parts I Through V; John D. McRae, Producer (PBS)
THE LAST OF THE MOHICANS Masterpiece Theatre: Parts I Through VIII; John D. McRae, Producer (PBS)
THE LIFE OF LEONARDO DA VINCI Parts I Through V; RAI Radiotelevisione Italiana, Executive Producer (CBS)

VARIETY MUSICAL SERIES (E-838)
Award(s) to Executive Producer(s) and/or Producer(s) and Star(s) (if applicable).

THE JULIE ANDREWS HOUR Nick Vanoff and William O. Harbach, Producers; Julie Andrews, Star (ABC)
THE CAROL BURNETT SHOW Joe Hamilton, Executive Producer; Bill Angelos, Buz Kohan and Arnie Rosen, Producers; Carol Burnett, Star (CBS)
THE DICK CAVETT SHOW John Gilroy, Producer; Dick Cavett, Star (ABC)
THE FLIP WILSON SHOW Monte Kay, Executive Producer; Bob Henry, Producer; Flip Wilson, Star (NBC)
THE SONNY & CHER COMEDY HOUR Allan Blye and Chris Bearde, Producers; Sonny and Cher, Stars (CBS)

OUTSTANDING SINGLE PROGRAM - DRAMA OR COMEDY (E-839)
A special program - Award to Executive Producer(s) and/or Producer(s).

A WAR OF CHILDREN The New CBS Tuesday Night Movies; Roger Gimbel, Executive Producer; George Schaefer, Producer (CBS)
LONG DAY'S JOURNEY INTO NIGHT Cecil Clarke, Executive Producer (ABC)
THE MARCUS-NELSON MURDERS The CBS Thursday Night Movies; Abby Mann, Executive Producer; Matthew Rapf, Producer (CBS)
THE RED PONY Bell System Family Theatre; Frederick W. Brogger, Producer (NBC)
THAT CERTAIN SUMMER Wednesday Movie Of The Week; Richard Levinson and William Link, Producers (ABC)

OUTSTANDING SINGLE PROGRAM - VARIETY AND POPULAR MUSIC (E-840)
A special program - Award(s) to Executive Producer(s) and/or Producer(s) and Star(s) (if applicable).

SINGER PRESENTS LIZA WITH A "Z" Bob Fosse and Fred Ebb, Producers; Liza Minnelli, Star (NBC)
APPLAUSE Alexander Cohen, Executive Producer; Joseph Kipness, Lawrence Kasha, Dick Rosenbloom, Producers (CBS)
ONCE UPON A MATTRESS Joe Hamilton, Producer (CBS)

OUTSTANDING SINGLE PROGRAM - CLASSICAL MUSIC (E-841)
A special program - Award(s) to Executive Producer(s) and/or Producer(s) and Star(s) (if applicable).

THE SLEEPING BEAUTY, J.W. Barnes and Robert Kotlowitz, Executive Producers; Norman Campbell, Producer (PBS)
BERNSTEIN IN LONDON Special Of The Week; Curtis W. Davis, Executive Producer; Mary Feldbauer and Brian Large, Producers; Leonard Bernstein, Star (PBS)
THE METROPOLITAN OPERA SALUTE TO SIR RUDOLF BING William Eliscu, Executive Producer; Charles E. Andrews, Producer (CBS)

NEW SERIES (E-842)
Award to Executive Producer(s) and/or Producer(s).

AMERICA Michael Gill, Producer (NBC)
THE JULIE ANDREWS HOUR Nick Vanoff, Producer; Julie Andrews, Star (ABC)
KUNG FU Jerry Thorpe, Producer (ABC)
M*A*S*H Gene Reynolds, Producer (CBS)
MAUDE Norman Lear, Executive Producer; Rod Parker, Producer (CBS)
THE WALTONS Lee Rich, Executive Producer; Robert L. Jacks, Producer (CBS)

PROGRAM ACHIEVEMENT IN DAYTIME DRAMA (E-843)
Award to Executive Producer(s) and/or Producer(s).

THE EDGE OF NIGHT Erwin Nicholson, Producer; Series (CBS)
DAYS OF OUR LIVES Betty Corday, Executive Producer; H. Wesley Kenney, Producer; Series (NBC)
THE DOCTORS Allen Potter, Producer; Series (NBC)
ONE LIFE TO LIVE Doris Quinlan and Agnes Nixon, Producers; Series (ABC)

PROGRAM ACHIEVEMENT IN DAYTIME (E-844)
Award to Executive Producer(s) and/or Producer(s). An Award for program achievements which do not qualify as Daytime Drama.

DINAH'S PLACE Henry Jaffe, Executive Producer; Fred Tatashore, Producer; Dinah Shore, Star; Series (NBC)
THE HOLLYWOOD SQUARES Merrill Heatter and Robert Quigley, Executive Producers; Bill Armstrong and Jay Redack, Producers; Series (NBC)
JEOPARDY Robert H. Rubin, Producer; Series (NBC)
THE MIKE DOUGLAS SHOW Barry Sand, Producer; Mike Douglas, Star; Series (SYND)
PASSWORD Frank Wayne, Executive Producer; Howard Felsher, Producer; Series (ABC)

ACTOR - SINGLE PERFORMANCE (E-845)
A single appearance in a "Continuing" or "Limited" Drama or Comedy Series; or for a special program.

LAURENCE OLIVIER Long Day's Journey Into Night (ABC)
HENRY FONDA The Red Pony; Bell System Family Theatre (NBC)
HAL HOLBROOK That Certain Summer; Wednesday Movie Of The Week (ABC)
TELLY SAVALAS The Marcus-Nelson Murders; The CBS Thursday Night Movies (CBS)

ACTRESS - SINGLE PERFORMANCE (E-846)
A single appearance in a "Continuing" or "Limited" Drama or Comedy Series; or for a special program.

CLORIS LEACHMAN A Brand New Life; Tuesday Movie Of The Week (ABC)
LAUREN BACALL Applause (CBS)
HOPE LANGE That Certain Summer; Wednesday Movie Of The Week (ABC)

ACTOR (E-847)

A. Drama Series - Continuing.

RICHARD THOMAS The Waltons (CBS)
DAVID CARRADINE Kung Fu (ABC)
MIKE CONNORS Mannix (CBS)
WILLIAM CONRAD Cannon (CBS)
PETER FALK Columbo; NBC Sunday Mystery Movie (NBC)

B. Drama/Comedy - Limited Episodes.

ANTHONY MURPHY Tom Brown's Schooldays; Masterpiece Theatre: Parts 1 Through V (PBS)
JOHN ABINERI The Last Of The Mohicans; Masterpiece Theatre: Parts I Through VIII (PBS)
PHILLIPE LeROY The Life Of Leonardo da Vinci (CBS)

ACTRESS (E-848)

A. Drama Series - Continuing

MICHAEL LEARNED The Waltons (CBS)
LINDA DAY GEORGE Mission: Impossible (CBS)
SUSAN SAINT JAMES McMillan & Wife; NBC Sunday Mystery Movie (NBC)

B. Drama/Comedy - Limited Episodes.

SUSAN HAMPSHIRE Vanity Fair; Masterpiece Theatre: Parts I Through V (PBS)
VIVIEN HEILBRON The Moonstone; Masterpiece Theatre: Parts I Through V (PBS)
MARGARET TYZACK Cousin Bette; Masterpiece Theatre: Parts I Through V (PBS)

ACTOR - COMEDY SERIES (E-849)

JACK KLUGMAN The Odd Couple (ABC)
ALAN ALDA M*A*S*H (CBS)
REDD FOXX Sanford And Son (NBC)
CARROLL O'CONNOR All In The Family (CBS)
TONY RANDALL The Odd Couple (ABC)

ACTRESS - COMEDY SERIES (E-850)

MARY TYLER MOORE The Mary Tyler Moore Show (CBS)
BEATRICE ARTHUR Maude (CBS)
JEAN STAPLETON All In The Family (CBS)

SUPPORTING ACTOR - DRAMA (E-851)

A continuing or one-time appearance in a series, or for a special program.

SCOTT JACOBY That Certain Summer; Wednesday Movie Of The Week (ABC)
WILL GEER The Waltons; Series (CBS)
JAMES BROLIN Marcus Welby, M.D.; Series (ABC)

SUPPORTING ACTRESS - DRAMA (E-852)

A continuing or one-time appearance in a series, or for a special program.

ELLEN CORBY The Waltons; Series (CBS)
GAIL FISHER Mannix; Series (CBS)
NANCY WALKER McMillan & Wife; NBC Sunday Mystery Movie; Series (NBC)

SUPPORTING ACTOR - COMEDY (E-853)

A continuing or one-time appearance in a series, or for a special program.

TED KNIGHT The Mary Tyler Moore Show; Series (CBS)
EDWARD ASNER The Mary Tyler Moore Show; Series (CBS)
GARY BURGHOFF M*A*S*H; Series (CBS)
ROB REINER All In The Family; Series (CBS)
McLEAN STEVENSON M*A*S*H; Series (CBS)

SUPPORTING ACTRESS - COMEDY (E-854)

A continuing or one-time appearance in a series, or for a special program.

VALERIE HARPER The Mary Tyler Moore Show; Series (CBS)
CLORIS LEACHMAN The Mary Tyler Moore Show; My Brother's Keeper (CBS)
SALLY STRUTHERS All In The Family; Series (CBS)

SUPPORTING PERFORMER - MUSIC OR VARIETY (E-855)

A continuing or one-time appearance in a series, or for a special program.

TIM CONWAY The Carol Burnett Show (CBS)
HARVEY KORMAN The Carol Burnett Show; Series (CBS)
LIZA MINNELLI A Royal Gala Variety Performance In the Presence Of Her Majesty The Queen (ABC)
LILY TOMLIN Rowan And Martin's Laugh-In; Series (NBC)

DIRECTOR - DRAMA (E-856)

A single program of a series with combining characters and/or theme.

JERRY THORPE An Eye For An Eye; Kung Fu (ABC)
EDWARD M. ABROMS The Most Dangerous Match; Columbo; NBC Sunday Mystery Movie (NBC)
LEE PHILIPS The Love Story; The Waltons (CBS)

DIRECTOR - DRAMA - SINGLE PROGRAM (E-857)

JOSEPH SARGENT The Marcus-Nelson Murders; The CBS Thursday Night Movies (CBS)
LAMONT JOHNSON That Certain Summer; Wednesday Movie Of The Week (ABC)
GEORGE SCHAEFER A War Of Children; The New CBS Thursday Night Movies (CBS)

DIRECTOR - COMEDY (E-858)

A single program of a series with continuing characters and/or theme.

JAY SANDRICH It's Whether You Win Or Lose; The Mary Tyler Moore Show (CBS)
GENE REYNOLDS, P-i-l-o-t; M*A*S*H (CBS)
JOHN RICH and BOB LA HENDRO The Bunkers And The Swingers; All In The Family (CBS)

DIRECTOR - VARIETY OR MUSIC (E-859)

A single program of a series.

BILL DAVIS The Julie Andrews Hour (with "Liza Doolittle" and "Mary Poppins") (ABC)
ART FISHER The Sonny & Cher Comedy Hour (with Mike Connors) (CBS)
TIM KILEY The Flip Wilson Show (with Roberta Flack and Burt Reynolds) (NBC)

DIRECTOR - COMEDY, VARIETY OR MUSIC SPECIAL PROGRAM (E-860)

BOB FOSSE Singer Presents Liza With A "Z" (NBC)
MARTIN CHARNIN and DAVE WILSON Jack Lemmon - Get Happy (NBC)
STAN HARRIS Duke Ellington. . .We Love You Madly (CBS)
WALTER C. MILLER You're A Good Man, Charlie Brown; Hallmark Hall Of Fame (NBC)
DAVE POWERS and RON FIELD Once Upon A Mattress (CBS)

WRITING - DRAMA (E-861)

A single program of a series with continuing characters and/or theme.

JOHN McGREEVEY The Scholar; The Waltons (CBS)
STEVE BOCHCO Etude In Black; Columbo; NBC Sunday Mystery Movie (NBC)
EARL HAMNER, JR. The Love Story; The Waltons (CBS)

WRITING - DRAMA, ORIGINAL TELEPLAY (E-862)

A single program.

ABBY MANN The Marcus-Nelson Murders; The CBS Thursday Night Movies (CBS)
DAVID KARP Hawkins On Murder; The New CBS Tuesday Night Movies (CBS)
RICHARD LEVINSON and WILLIAM LINK That Certain Summer; Wednesday Movie Of The Week (ABC)

WRITING - DRAMA, ADAPTATION (E-863)

A single program.

ELEANOR PERRY The House Without A Christmas Tree (CBS)
ROBERT TOTTEN and RON BISHOP The Red Pony; Bell System Family Theatre (NBC)
ELLEN M. VIOLETT Go Ask Alice; Wednesday Movie Of The Week (ABC)

WRITING - COMEDY (E-864)

A single program of a series with continuing characters and/or theme.

MICHAEL ROSS, BERNIE WEST, and LEE KALCHEIM The Bunkers And The Swingers; All In The Family (CBS)
ALLAN BURNS and JAMES L. BROOKS The Good-Time News; The Mary Tyler Moore Show (CBS)
LARRY GELBART, P-i-l-o-t; M*A*S*H (CBS)

WRITING - VARIETY OR MUSIC (E-865)

A single program of a series.

STAN HART, LARRY SIEGEL, GAIL PARENT, WOODY KLING, ROGER BEATTY, TOM PATCHETT, JAY TARSES, ROBERT HILLIARD, ARNIE KOGEN, BILL ANGELOS and BUZ KOHAN The Carol Burnett Show (with Steve Lawrence And Lily Tomlin) (CBS)
HERBERT BAKER, MIKE MARMER, STAN BURNS, DON HINKLEY, DICK HILLS, SID GREEN, PAUL McCAULEY, PETER GALLAY and FLIP WILSON The Flip Wilson Show (with Sammy Davis, Jr., Ed Sullivan and Marilyn Michaels) (NBC)
BOB ELLISON, HAL GOODMAN, LARRY KLEIN, JAY BURTON, GEORGE BLOOM, LILA GARRETT, JOHN AYLESWORTH and FRANK PEPPIATT The Julie Andrews Hour (with "Eliza Doolittle" and "Mary Poppins") (ABC)

WRITING - COMEDY, VARIETY OR MUSIC - SPECIAL PROGRAM (E-866)

RENEE TAYLOR and JOSEPH BOLOGNA Acts Of Love - And Other Comedies (ABC)
FRED EBB Singer Presents Liza with a "Z" (NBC)
ALLAN MANNINGS, ANN ELDER, KARYL GELD, RICHARD PRYOR, JOHN RAPPAPORT, JIM RUSK, LILY TOMLIN, JANE WAGNER, ROD WARREN, and GEORGE YANOK The Lily Tomlin Show (CBS)

CHOREOGRAPHY (E-867)

A single program of a series or a special program.

BOB FOSSE Singer Presents Liza With A "Z" (NBC)
TONY CHARMOLI The Julie andrews Hour (with Robert Goulet And Joel Grey) (ABC)
ERNEST O. FLATT Family Show; The Carol Burnett Show (CBS)

MUSIC COMPOSITION (E-868)

A. For a series or a single program of a series (in the first year of music's use only).

CHARLES FOX Love, American Style; Series (ABC)
ALEXANDER COURAGE Cycle Of Peril; Medical Center (CBS)
MARTY PAICH Ironside; Series (NBC)

B. For a special program.

JERRY GOLDSMITH The Red Pony; Bell System Family Theatre (NBC)
FRED EBB and JOHN KANDER Singer Presents Liza With A "Z" (NBC)
BILLY GOLDENBERG A Brand New Life; Tuesday Movie Of The Week (ABC)

MUSIC DIRECTION OF A VARIETY, MUSICAL OR DRAMATIC PROGRAM (E-869)

A single program of a series or a special program.

PETER MATZ The Carol Burnett Show (with Anthony Newley and Bernadette Peters) (CBS)
VAN ALEXANDER The Wacky World Of Jonathan Winters (with Debbie Reynolds) (SYND)
IRWIN KOSTAL, Dr. Jekyll And Mr. Hyde (NBC)

MUSIC, LYRICS AND SPECIAL MATERIAL (E-870)

A series or a single program of a series or a special program written for television.

FRED EBB and JOHN KANDER Singer Presents Liza With A "Z" (NBC)
EARL BROWN The Gloria Majestic Story; The Sonny And Cher Comedy Hour (with Jean Stapleton) (CBS)
BILLY GOLDENBERG and BOBBY RUSSELL The Marcus-Nelson Murders; The CBS Thursday Night Movies (CBS)

ART DIRECTION OR SCENIC DESIGN (E-871)

A. For a dramatic program or feature length film made for television; for a series, a single program of a series or a special program.

TOM JOHN Much Ado About Nothing (CBS)
ROBERT BOYLE and JAMES HULSEY, Art Directors; JOHN KURL, Set Decorator; The Red Pony; Bell System Family Theatre (NBC)
WILLIAM CAMPBELL Night Of Terror; Tuesday Movie Of The Week (ABC)
GIBSON HOLLY, Art Director; LUCIEN M. HAFLEY, Set Decorator; Western; Mission: Impossible (CBS)
JAN SCOTT Another Part Of The Forest; Hollywood Television Theatre; Special Of The Week (PBS)
JAN M. VAN TAMELEN, Art Director; FRED R. PRICE, Set Decorator; Mannix; Series (CBS)

B. For a Musical or Variety single program of a series or a special program.

BRIAN BARTHOLOMEW and KEATON S. WALKER The Julie Andrews Hour (with "Eliza Doolittle" and "Mary Poppins") (ABC)
PAUL BARNES and BOB SANSOM, Art Directors; BILL HARP, Set Decorator; The Doily Sisters; The Carol Burnett Show (CBS)
ROMAIN JOHNSTON The Flip Wilson Show (with Burt Reynolds, Tim Conway and Roberta Flack) (NBC)

LIGHTING DIRECTION (E-872)

A single program of a series or a special program, produced for electronic television only.

JOHN FRESCHI and JOHN CASAGRANDE 44th Annual Oscar Awards (NBC)
TRUCK KRONE Christmas Show; The Julie Andrews Hour (ABC)
JOHN R. BEAM The Sonny And Cher Comedy Hour (with William Conrad) (CBS)

COSTUME DESIGN (E-873)

A single program of a series or a special program.

JACK BEAR The Julie Andrews Hour (with Ken Berry and Jack Cassidy) (ABC)
THEONI V. ALDREDGE Much Ado About Nothing (CBS)
GRADY HUNT Dagger Of The Mind; Columbo; NBC Sunday Mystery Movie (NBC)
EMMA PORTEOUS Dr. Jekyll And Mr. Hyde (NBC)
CHRISTINA VON HUMBOLDT Cortez and Montezuma; Appointment With Destiny (CBS)

MAKE-UP (E-874)

A single program of a series or a special program.

DEL ARMSTRONG, ELLIS BURMAN and STAN WINSTON Gargoyles; The New CBS Tuesday Night Movies (CBS)
ROBERT A. SIDELL The Actress; The Waltons (CBS)
NEVILLE SMALLWOOD Dr. Jekyll & Mr. Hyde (NBC)
ALLAN SNYDER and RICHARD COBOS The Red Pony; Bell System Family Theatre (NBC)
FRANK C. WESTMORE Chains; Kung Fu (ABC)
MICHAEL WESTMORE and MARVIN WESTMORE Frankenstein - Parts I and II; ABC Wide World Of Entertainment (ABC)

CINEMATOGRAPHY - ENTERTAINMENT PROGRAMMING (E-875)

A. For a series or a single program of a series.

JACK WOOLF An Eye For An Eye; Kung Fu (ABC)
SAM LEAVITT Banacek; NBC Wednesday Mystery Movie; Series (NBC)
RUSSELL L. METTY The Waltons; Series (CBS)
B. For a special or feature length program made for television.

HOWARD SCHWARTZ, A.S.C. Night Of Terror; Tuesday Movie Of The Week (ABC)
ANDREW JACKSON The Red Pony; Bell System Family Theatre (NBC)
OWEN ROIZMAN Singer Presents Liza With A ''Z'' (NBC)

FILM EDITING - ENTERTAINMENT PROGRAMMING (E-876)

A. For a series or a single program of a series.

GENE FOWLER, JR., MARJORIE FOWLER, and ANTHONY WOLLNER The Literary Man; The Waltons (CBS)
DOUGLAS HINES The Mary Tyler Moore Show; Series (CBS)
STANFORD TISCHLER and FRED W. BERGER M*A*S*H; Series (CBS)
B. For a special or feature length program made for television

PETER C. JOHNSON and ED SPIEGEL Surrender At Appomattox; Appointment With Destiny (CBS)
HENRY BERMAN, A.C.E. Go Ask Alice; Wednesday Movie Of The Week (ABC)
ALAN HEIM Singer Presents Liza With A ''Z'' (NBC)

FILM SOUND EDITING (E-877)

A single program of a series or a special program.

ROSS TAYLOR, FRED BROWN and DAVID MARSHALL The Red Pony; Bell System Family Theatre (NBC)
PETER BERKOS, JOHN SINGLETON, BRIAN COURCIER, GORDON ECKER, JOHN STACY, JAMES NOWNES, GEORGE LUCKENBACHER, WALTER JENEVEIN and SIDNEY LUBOW Short Walk to Daylight; Tuesday Movie Of The Week (ABC)
CHARLES L. CAMPBELL, ROGER A. SWORD, ROBERT H. CORNETT and JERRY R. STANFORD The Smile Of The Walrus; The Undersea World Of Jacques Cousteau (ABC)

FILM SOUND MIXING (E-878)

A single program of a series or a special program.

RICHARD J. WAGNER, GEORGE E. PORTER, EDDIE J. NELSON and FRED LEROY GRANVILLE Surrender At Appomattox; Appointment With Destiny (CBS)
MELVIN M. METCALFE, SR. and THOM PIPER That Certain Summer; Wednesday Movie Of The Week (ABC)
GEORGE PORTER, EDDIE NELSON and HOPPY MEHTERIAN The Singing Whale; The Undersea World Of Jacques Cousteau (ABC)

LIVE OR TAPE SOUND MIXING (E-879)

A single program of a series or a special program.

AL GRAMAGLIA and MAHLON FOX Much Ado About Nothing (CBS)
WILLIAM J. LEVITSKY 44th Annual Oscar Awards (NBC)
PHILIP RAMONE Duke Ellington. . .We Love You Madly (CBS)

VIDEO TAPE EDITING (E-880)

A single program of a series or a special program.

NICK GIORDANO and ARTHUR SCHNEIDER The Julie Andrews Hour (with "Eliza Doolittle" and "Mary Poppins") (ABC)
WILLIAM H. BRESHEARS and ANDREW McINTYRE Ed Sullivan Presents The TV Comedy Years (CBS)
JAMES H. ROSE Burt Bacharach In Shangri-La (ABC)
CHARLES SHADEL and WALTER BALDERSON Democratic Convention Highlights; NBC Nightly News (NBC)
MIKE WENIG Love Is. . .Barbara Eden (ABC)

TECHNICAL DIRECTION AND ELECTRONIC CAMERAWORK (E-881)

A single program of a series or a special program.

ERNIE BUTTELMAN Technical Director; **ROBERT A. KEMP, JAMES ANGEL, JAMES BALDEN and DAVE HILMER,** Cameramen; The Julie Andrews Hour (with "Mary Poppins" And "Eliza Doolittle") (ABC)
CHARLES FRANKLIN, Technical Director; GORME ERICKSON, JACK JENNINGS, TOM McCONNELL, RICHARD NELSON and BARNEY NEELEY, Cameramen; The Sonny & Cher Comedy Hour (with Mike Connors) (CBS)
E.G. JOHNSON, Technical Director; SAM DRUMMY, Cameraman; Apollo 17 - Splashdown (Pool Coverage)

THE AREAS

(Possibility of One Award, More Than One Award, or No Award)

ACHIEVEMENT BY INDIVIDUALS IN DAYTIME DRAMA (E-882)

MARY FICKETT, Performer; All My Children; Series (ABC)
MACDONALD CAREY, Performer; Days Of Our Lives; Series (NBC)
NORMAN HALL, Director; The Doctors; January 9, 1973 (NBC)
H. WESLEY KENNEY, Director; Days Of Our Lives; March 6, 1973 (NBC)
PETER LEVIN, Director; Love Is A Many Splendored Thing; July 17, 1972 (CBS)
DAVID PRESSMAN, Director; One Life To Live; January 23, 1973 (ABC)
VICTOR PAGANUZZI, Scenic Designer; JOHN A. WENDELL, Set Decorator; Love Is A Many Splendored Thing; Series (CBS)

ACHIEVEMENT BY INDIVIDUALS IN DAYTIME PROGRAMMING (E-883)

An Award for individual achievements which do not qualify in Daytime Drama.

BILL CULLEN, Host; Three On A Match; Series (NBC)
PAUL LYNDE, Performer; The Hollywood Squares; Series (NBC)
PETER MARSHALL, Host; The Hollywood Squares; Series (NBC)

ACHIEVEMENT IN CHILDREN'S PROGRAMMING (E-884)

An Award for programs and individual achievements. A. Entertainment/Fictional

SESAME STREET Jon Stone, Executive Producer; Bob Cunniff, Producer; Series (PBS)
ZOOM Christopher Sarson, Producer; Series (PBS)
TOM WHEDON, JOHN BONI, SARA COMPTON, TOM DUNSMUIR, THAD MUMFORD, JEREMY STEVENS and JIM THURMAN, Writers; The Electric Company (PBS)
THE ELECTRIC COMPANY Samuel Y. Gibbon, Jr. and David D. Connell, Executive Producers; Andy Ferguson, Producer; Series (PBS)
HENRY BEHAR, Director; The Electric Company (PBS)
ROBERT G. MYHRUM, Director; Sesame Street (PBS)
CHARLES M. SCHULZ, Writer; You're Elected, Charlie Brown (CBS)
JOE RAPOSO, Music Director; Sesame Street (PBS)

B. International/Factual
LAST OF THE CURLEWS The ABC Afterschool Special; William Hanna and Joseph Barbera, Producers (ABC)
SHARI LEWIS, Performer; A Picture Of Us; NBC Children's Theatre (NBC)
IN THE NEWS Joel Heller, Executive Producer; Pat Lynch and Judy Towers Reemtsma, Producers; Series (CBS)
MAKE A WISH Lester Cooper, Executive Producer; Tom Bywaters, Producer; Series (ABC)
JAMESON BREWER, Writer; Last Of The Curlews; The ABC Afterschool Special (ABC)

ACHIEVEMENT IN SPORTS PROGRAMMING (E-885)

An Award for programs and for individuals contributing to the coverage of sporting events.

ABC'S WIDE WORLD OF SPORTS Roone Arledge, Executive Producer; Series (ABC)
1972 SUMMER OLYMPIC GAMES Roone Arledge, Executive Producer (ABC)
JOHN CROAK, CHARLES GARDNER, JAKOB HIERL, CONRAD KRAUS, EDWARD McCARTHY, NICK MAZUR, ALEX MOSKOVIC, JAMES PARKER, LOUIS RENDE, ROSS SKIPPER, ROBERT STEINBACK, JOHN DeLISA, GEORGE BOETTCHER, MERRIT ROESSER, LEO SCHARF, RANDY COHEN, VITO GERARDI, HAROLD BYERS, WINFIELD GROSS, PAUL SCOSKIE, PETER FRITZ, LEO STEPHAN, GERBER McBEATH, LOUIS TORINO, MICHAEL WENIG, TOM WIGHT and JAMES KELLEY, Video Tape Editors; 1972 Summer Olympic Games (ABC)
NCAA COLLEGE FOOTBALL Roone Arledge, Executive Producer; Chuck Howard, Producer; Series (ABC)
NFL MONDAY NIGHT FOOTBALL Roone Arledge, Executive Producer; Chet Forte and Dennis Lewin, Producers; Series (ABC)
SUPER BOWL VII Scotty Connal, Executive Producer; Roy Hammerman, Producer (NBC)
KEITH JACKSON, Commentator; 1972 Summer Olympic Games (ABC)
JIM McKAY, Commentator; l972 Summer Olympic Games (ABC)

ENGINEERING DEVELOPMENT (E-886)

SONY for the development of the Trinitron, a picture tube providing good picture quality in color television receivers.

CMX SYSTEMS, a CBS/Memorex company, for the development of a video tape editing system, utilizing a computer to aid the decision-making process, store the editing decisions and implement them in the final assembly of takes.

THE NATIONAL AWARD FOR COMMUNITY SERVICE (E-887)

TAKE DES MOINES. . .PLEASE; KDIN-TV (Educational Station); Des Moines, Iowa
BARS TO PROGRESS; WMAR-TV; Baltimore, Maryland
CARRASCOLENDAS, KLRN-TV (Educational Station); Austin, Texas

EGYPT VALLEY - AN EPITAPH/A CALL TO CONSCIENCE (Montage); WKYC-TV; Cleveland, Ohio
THE GREEN GRASS OF HOME; KFDA-TV; Amarillo, Texas
IN A CLASS. . .ALL BY HIMSELF; KNBC-TV; Los Angeles, California
NEWSIGN 4; KRON-TV; San Francisco, California
ONE AND ONE IS. . .DOS; WZZM-TV; Grand Rapids, Michigan
A SEED OF HOPE; WTVJ-TV; Miami, Florida
WILLOWBROOK: THE LAST GREAT DISGRACE; WABC-TV; New York, New York

NEWS AND DOCUMENTARY PROGRAM AND INDIVIDUAL ACHIEVEMENTS

(Possibility of One Award, More than One Award, or No Award)

ACHIEVEMENT WITHIN REGULARLY SCHEDULED NEWS PROGRAMS (E-888)

A. An Award for program segments, i.e. the presentation of individual stories (in single or multi-part) or elements within the program.

THE US/SOVIET WHEAT DEAL: IS THERE A SCANDAL? CBS Evening News with Walter Cronkite; Paul Greenberg and Russ Bensley, Executive Producers; Stanhope Gould and Linda Mason, Producers (CBS)
COVERAGE OF THE RETURN OF THE POW'S; NBC Nightly News; Robert Mulholland, Executive Producer; Richard Fischer, Producer (NBC)
COVERAGE OF THE SHOOTING OF GOVERNOR WALLACE; CBS Evening News With Walter Cronkite; Russ Bensley, Executive Producer; Ed Fouhy and John Lane, Producers (CBS)
THE TASADAY TRIBE OF THE PHILIPPINES; NBC Nightly News; Wallace Westfeldt, Executive Producer; Robert Mulholland and David Teitelbaum, Producers (NBC)
THE WATERGATE AFFAIR; CBS Evening News With Walter Cronkite; Paul Greenberg, Executive Producer; Stanhope Gould, Brian Healy, Ed Fouhy, Producers (CBS)

B. An Award for individuals contributing to the program segments.

WALTER CRONKITE, DAN RATHER, DANIEL SCHORR and JOEL BLOCKER, Correspondents; The Watergate Affair; CBS Evening News With Walter Cronkite (CBS)
DAVID DICK, DAN RATHER, ROGER MUDD and WALTER CRONKITE, Correspondents; Coverage of the Shooting of Governor Wallace; CBS Evening News With Walter Cronkite (CBS)
ERIC SEVAREID, Correspondent; LBJ - The Man And The President;- CBS Evening News with Walter Cronkite (CBS)
JOHN CHANCELLOR, Correspondent; Coverage of President Nixon's Visit to Russia; NBC Nightly News (NBC)
JACK REYNOLDS, Reporter; The Tasaday Tribe Of The Philippines; NBC Nightly News (NBC)
ERIC SEVAREID, Correspondent; The Paradox Of Special Privilege: Executive Immunity And Shield Laws; CBS Evening News With Walter Cronkite (CBS)

REGULARLY SCHEDULED MAGAZINE-TYPE PROGRAMS (E-889)

A. An Award for programs, program segments or series.

THE POPPY FIELDS OF TURKEY - THE HEROIN LABS OF MARSEILLES - THE N.Y. CONNECTION; 60 Minutes; Don Hewitt, Executive Producer; William McClure, John Tiffin, Philip Scheffler,Producers (CBS)
THE SELLING OF COLONEL HERBERT; 60 Minutes; Don Hewitt, Executive Producer; Barry Lando, Producer (CBS)
60 MINUTES Don Hewitt, Executive Producer; Series (CBS)
FIRST TUESDAY Eliot Frankel, Executive Producer; Series (NBC)
TODAY Stuart Schulberg, Executive Producer; Douglas P. Sinsel, Gene Farinet, Producers; Series (NBC)

B. An Award for individuals contributing to the program, program segments or series achievements.

MIKE WALLACE, Correspondent; The Selling Of Colonel Herbert; 60 Minutes (CBS)
MIKE WALLACE, Correspondent; 60 Minutes; Series (CBS)
MORLEY SAFER, Correspondent; 60 Minutes; Series (CBS)
MIKE WALLACE, Correspondent; Dita Beard Interview; 60 Minutes (CBS)
EDWIN NEWMAN, Writer; No Contest; Today (NBC)

COVERAGE OF SPECIAL EVENTS (E-890)

A. An Award for program achievements.

COVERAGE OF THE MUNICH OLYMPIC TRAGEDY; ABC Special; Roone Arledge, Executive Producer (ABC)
THE 1972 DEMOCRATIC NATIONAL CONVENTION; NBC News Special; George F. Murray, Executive Producer; Ray Lockhart, Producer (NBC)
ELECTION NIGHT '72; NBC News Special; Robert Northshield, Executive Producer (NBC)
JACKIE ROBINSON; CBS News Special; Robert Wussler, Executive Producer; Clarence Cross, Russ Bensley and Barry Jagoda, Producers (CBS)
THE RETURN OF THE POW'S; NBC News Special; Helen Marmor, Producer (NBC)

B. An Award for individuals contributing to the program achievement.

JIM McKAY, Commentator; Coverage Of The Munich Olympic Tragedy; ABC Special (ABC)
JOHN CHANCELLOR, DAVID BRINKLEY, EDWIN NEWMAN, CATHERINE MACKIN, DOUGLAS KIKER and GARRICK UTLEY, Correspondents; Election Night '72; NBC News Special (NBC)
HARRY REASONER and HOWARD K. SMITH Anchormen; Elections '72; ABC News Special (ABC)
DAVID FOX, Director; Apollo 17; Astronauts Splashdown in Pacific (Pool Coverage)
EDWIN NEWMAN, Writer; Decision '72: It Starts Tomorrow; NBC News Special (NBC)

DOCUMENTARY PROGRAM ACHIEVEMENT (E-891)

A. An Award for documentary programs dealing with events or matters of current significance.

THE BLUE COLLAR TRAP; NBC News White Paper; Fred Freed, Producer (NBC)
THE MEXICAN CONNECTION; CBS Reports; Burton Benjamin, Executive Producer; Jay McMullen, Producer (CBS)
ONE BILLION DOLLAR WEAPON And Now the War Is Over - The American Military In the 70's; NBC Reports; Fred Freed, Executive Producer; Craig Leake, Producer (NBC)
IF YOU WANT US TO STAND DOWN, TELL US And Now the War Is Over - The American Military in The 70's; NBC Reports; Fred Freed, Executive Producer; Al Davis, Producer (NBC)
PENSIONS: THE BROKEN PROMISE; NBC Reports; Eliot Frankel, Executive Producer; David Schmerler, Producer (NBC)

B. An Award for documentary programs dealing with artistic, historical or cultural subjects.

AMERICA Michael Gill, Executive Producer; Series (NBC)
JANE GOODALL AND THE WORLD OF ANIMAL BEHAVIOR The Wild Dogs Of Africa; Marshall Flaum, Executive Producer; Hugo Van Lawick, Bill Travers, and James Hill, Producers (ABC)
THE CAVE PEOPLE OF THE PHILIPPINES; NBC Reports; Gerald Green, Producer (NBC)
THE INCREDIBLE FLIGHT OF THE SNOW GEESE Aubrey Buxton, Executive Producer (NBC)
IN SEARCH OF ANCIENT ASTRONAUTS Laurence Savadove, Executive Producer; Alan Landsburg, Producer (NBC)

C. An Award for individuals contributing to Documentary Programs.

ALISTAIR COOKE, Narrator; America; Series (NBC)
ALISTAIR COOKE, Writer; A Firebell In The Night; America (NBC)
HUGO VAN LAWICK, Director; Jane Goodall And The World Of Animal Behavior: The Wild Dogs Of Africa (ABC)
MARSHALL FLAUM And BILL TRAVERS, Writers; Jane Goodall And the World Of Animal Behavior; The Wild Dogs of Africa (ABC)

TOM PRIESTLEY, Director; The Forbidden City; NBC Reports (NBC)

SPECIAL CLASSIFICATION OF OUTSTANDING PROGRAM AND INDIVIDUAL ACHIEVEMENT (E-892)

An Award for unique program and individual achievements, which does not fall into a specific category, or is not otherwise recognized.

THE ADVOCATES Greg Harney, Executive Producer; Tom Burrows, Russ Morash and Peter McGhee, Producers; Series (PBS)
VD BLUES Special Of The Week; Don Fouser, Producer (PBS)
LBJ: THE LAST INTERVIEW Burton Benjamin, Producer (CBS)
DICK CAVETT, Host; VD Blues; Special Of The Week (PBS)
WALTER CRONKITE, Correspondent; LBJ: The Last Interview; CBS News Special (CBS)

RELIGIOUS PROGRAMMING (E-893)

An Award for programs and individual achievements.

DUTY BOUND Doris Ann, Executive Producer; Martin Hoade, Producer (NBC)
INSIGHT Father Ellwood Kieser, Executive Producer; John Meredyth Lucas and John Furia, Jr., Producers; Series (Synd)
MARTIN HOADE, Director; Duty Bound (NBC)
JOHN B. BOXER, Costume Designer; Duty Bound (NBC)

ACHIEVEMENT IN ANY AREA OF CREATIVE TECHNICAL CRAFTS (E-894)

An Award for individual technical craft achievement which does not fall into a specific category, and is not otherwise recognized.

DONALD FELDSTEIN, ROBERT FONTANA and JOE ZUCKERMAN, Animation Layout of Da Vinci's Art; Leonardo: To Know How To See (NBC)
PHILIPPE COUSTEAU, Underwater Cameraman; The Singing Whale; The Undersea World of Jacques Cousteau (ABC)
BIDDY CHRYSTAL, Hairdresser; Dr. Jekyll And Mr. Hyde (NBC)

(One Award Only In Each of the Following Categories)

CINEMATOGRAPHY FOR NEWS AND DOCUMENTARY PROGRAMMING (E-895)

A. Regularly scheduled News programs and coverage of Special Events.

LAURENS PIERCE Coverage of the Shooting of Governor Wallace; CBS Evening News With Walter Cronkite (CBS)
ISADORE BLECKMAN Roadside Garden; On The Road; CBS Evening News With Walter Cronkite (CBS)
DANG VAN MINH Vietnamese Orphans; ABC Evening News With Howard K. Smith And Harry Reasoner (ABC)

B. Documentary, Magazine-type or Mini-documentary programs.

DES and JEN BARTLETT The Incredible Flight Of The Snow Geese (NBC)
PHILIPPE COUSTEAU and JACQUES RENOIR The Smile Of The Walrus; The Undersea World Of Jacques Cousteau (ABC)
PHILIPPE COUSTEAU, FRANCOIS CHARLET and WALTER BAL The Singing Whale; The Undersea World Of Jacques Cousteau (ABC)

FILM EDITING FOR NEWS AND DOCUMENTARY PROGRAMMING (E-896)

A. Regularly scheduled News programs and coverage of Special Events.

PATRICK MINERVA, MARTIN SHEPPARD, GEORGE JOHNSON, WILLIAM J. FREEDA, MIGUEL E. PORTILLO, ALBERT J. HELIAS, IRWIN GRAF, JEAN VENABLE, RICK HESSEL, LOREN BERRY, NICK WILKINS, GERRY BREESE, MICHAEL SHUGRUE, K. SU, EDWIN EI-

NARSEN, THOMAS DUNPHY, RUSSEL MOORE and ROBERT MOLE; NBC Nightly News; Series (NBC)
MICHAEL C. SHUGRUE; I Am Woman; NBC Nightly News (NBC)
PATRICK MINERVA, THOMAS DUNPHY, JEAN VENABLE, EDWIN EINARSEN and GERALD BREESE Coverage Of President Nixon's Trip To Russia; NBC Nightly News (NBC)
Documentary, Magazine-type or Mini-documentary programs.
LES PARRY The Incredible Flight Of The Snow Geese (NBC)
CARL KRESS The Singing Whale; The Undersea World Of Jacques Cousteau (ABC)
JOHN SOH The Smile Of The Walrus; The Undersea World Of Jacques Cousteau (ABC)

1973/74

ENTERTAINMENT PROGRAM AND INDIVIDUAL ACHIEVEMENTS
(One Award Only In Each of the Following Categories)

COMEDY SERIES (E-897)
Award to Executive Producer(s) and/or Producer(s)
M*A*S*H, Gene Reynolds, and Larry Gelbart, Producers (CBS)
THE MARY TYLER MOORE SHOW, James Brooks, and Allan Burns, Executive Producers; Ed Weinberger, Producer (CBS)
ALL IN THE FAMILY, Norman Lear, Executive Producer; John Rich, Producer (CBS)
THE ODD COUPLE, Garry Marshall, and Harvey Miller, Executive Producers; Tony Marshall, Producer (ABC)

DRAMA SERIES (E-898)
Award to Executive Producer(s) and/or Producer(s)
UPSTAIRS, DOWNSTAIRS, Masterpiece Theatre; Rex Firkin, Executive Producer; John Hawkesworth, Producer (PBS)
KOJAK, Abby Mann, and Matthew Rapf, Executive Producers; James McAdams, Producer (CBS)
THE STREETS OF SAN FRANCISCO, Quinn Martin, Executive Producer; John Wilder, Producer (ABC)
POLICE STORY, David Gerber, Executive Producer; Stanley Kallis, Producer (NBC)
THE WALTONS, Lee Rich, Executive Producer; Robert L. Jacks, Producer (CBS)

MUSIC-VARIETY SERIES (E-899)
Award to Executive Producer(s) and/or Producer(s) and Star (if applicable)
THE CAROL BURNETT SHOW, Joe Hamilton, Executive Producer; Ed Simmons, Producer; Carol Burnett, Star (CBS)
THE SONNY AND CHER COMEDY HOUR, Allan Blye, and Chris Bearde, Producers; Sonny and Cher, Stars (CBS)
THE TONIGHT SHOW STARRING JOHNNY CARSON, Fred de Cordova, Producer; Johnny Carson, Star (NBC)

LIMITED SERIES (E-900)
Award to Executive Producer(s) and/or Producer(s)
COLUMBO, NBC Sunday Mystery Movie; Dean Hargrove, and Roland Kibbee, Executive Producers; Douglas Benton, Robert F. O'Neill, and Edward K. Dodds, Producers (NBC)
McCLOUD, NBC Sunday Mystery Movie; Glen Larson, Executive Producer; Michael Gleason, Producer (NBC)
THE BLUE KNIGHT, Lee Rich, Executive Producer; Walter Coblenz, Producer (NBC)

SPECIAL - COMEDY OR DRAMA (E-901)
A Single Special Program Award to Executive Producer(s) and/or Producer(s)
THE AUTOBIOGRAPHY OF MISS JANE PITTMAN, Robert Christiansen, and Rick Rosenberg, Producers (CBS)
THE MIGRANTS, CBS Playhouse 90; Tom Gries, Producer (CBS)
THE EXECUTION OF PRIVATE SLOVIK, NBC Wednesday Night At The Movies; Richard Levinson, and William Link, Executive Producers; Richard Dubelman, Producer (NBC)
STEAMBATH, Hollywood Television Theatre; Norman Lloyd, Executive Producer (PBS)
6 RMS RIV VU, Joe Hamilton, Producer (CBS)

SPECIAL - COMEDY-VARIETY, VARIETY OR MUSIC (E-902)
A Single Special Program Award to Executive Producer(s) and/or Producer(s) and Star (if applicable)
LILY, Irene Pinn, Executive Producer; Herb Sargent, and Jerry McPhie, Producers; Lily Tomlin, Star (CBS)
BARBRA STREISAND. . .AND OTHER MUSICAL INSTRUMENTS, Martin Erlichman, Executive Producer; Gary Smith, Dwight Hemion, and Joe Layton, Producers; Barbra Streisand, Star (CBS)
MAGNAVOX PRESENTS FRANK SINATRA, Howard W. Koch, Producer; Frank Sinatra, Star (NBC)
THE JOHN DENVER SHOW, Jerry Weintraub, Executive Producer; Rich Eustis, and Al Rogers, Producers; John Denver, Star (ABC)

SPECIAL - CHILDREN'S (E-903)
For programs which were broadcast during the evening
Award to Executive Producer(s) and Producer(s)
MARLO THOMAS AND FRIENDS IN FREE TO BE. . .YOU AND ME, Marlo Thomas, and Carole Hart, Producers; Marlo Thomas, Star (ABC)
THE BORROWERS, Hallmark Hall of Fame; Duane C. Bogie, Executive Producer; Walt DeFaria, and Warren Lockhart, Producers (NBC)
A CHARLIE BROWN THANKSGIVING, Lee Mendelson, and Bill Melendez, Producers (CBS)

ACTOR - COMEDY SERIES (E-904)
ALAN ALDA, M*A*S*H (CBS)
REDD FOXX, Sanford and Son (NBC)
JACK KLUGMAN, The Odd Couple (ABC)
CARROLL O'CONNOR, All In The Family (CBS)
TONY RANDALL, The Odd Couple (ABC)

ACTOR - DRAMA SERIES (E-905)
TELLY SAVALAS, Kojak (CBS)
WILLIAM CONRAD, Cannon (CBS)
KARL MALDEN, The Streets of San Francisco (ABC)
RICHARD THOMAS, The Waltons (CBS)

ACTOR - LIMITED SERIES (E-906)
WILLIAM HOLDEN, The Blue Knight (NBC)
PETER FALK, Columbo; NBC Sunday Mystery Movie (NBC)
DENNIS WEAVER, McCoud; NBC Sunday Mystery Movie (NBC)

ACTOR - DRAMA SPECIAL (E-907)
For a special program--Comedy or Drama; or a single appearance in a Drama or Comedy Series
HAL HOLBROOK, Pueblo; ABC Theatre (ABC)
DICK VAN DYKE, The Morning After; Wednesday Movie Of The Week (ABC)
LAURENCE OLIVIER, The Merchant Of Venice; ABC Theatre (ABC)
MARTIN SHEEN, The Execution of Private Slovik; NBC Wednesday Night At The Movies (NBC)
ALAN ALDA, 6 Rms Riv Vu (CBS)

ACTOR OF THE YEAR - SERIES (E-908)
ALAN ALDA, M*A*S*H (CBS)

ACTOR OF THE YEAR - SPECIAL (E-909)
HAL HOLBROOK, Pueblo; ABC Theatre (ABC)

ACTRESS - COMEDY SERIES (E-910)
MARY TYLER MOORE, The Mary Tyler Moore Show (CBS)
BEA ARTHUR, Maude (CBS)
JEAN STAPLETON, All In The Family (CBS)

ACTRESS - DRAMA SERIES (E-911)
MICHAEL LEARNED, The Waltons (CBS)
JEANETTE NOLAN, Dirty Sally (CBS)
JEAN MARSH, Upstairs, Downstairs; Masterpiece (PBS)

ACTRESS - LIMITED SERIES (E-912)
MILDRED NATWICK, The Snoop Sisters; NBC Tuesday Mystery Movie (NBC)
LEE REMICK, The Blue Knight (NBC)
HELEN HAYES, The Snoop Sisters; NBC Tuesday Mystery Movie (NBC)

ACTRESS - DRAMA SPECIAL (E-913)
For a special program--Comedy or Drama; or a single appearance in a Drama or Comedy Series
CICELY TYSON, The Autobiography of Miss Jane Pittman (CBS)
ELIZABETH MONTGOMERY, A Case of Rape; NBC Wednesday Night At The Movies (NBC)
KATHARINE HEPBURN, The Glass Menagerie (ABC)
CLORIS LEACHMAN, The Migrants; CBS Playhouse 90 (CBS)
CAROL BURNETT, 6 Rms Riv Vu (CBS)

ACTRESS OF THE YEAR - SERIES (E-914)
MARY TYLER MOORE, The Mary Tyler Moore Show (CBS)

ACTRESS OF THE YEAR - SPECIAL (E-915)
CICELY TYSON, The Autobiography of Miss Jane Pittman (CBS)

SUPPORTING ACTOR - COMEDY (E-916)
For a special program, a one-time appearance in a series; or a continuing role
ROB REINER, All In The Family (CBS)
TED KNIGHT, The Mary Tyler Moore Show (CBS)
EDWARD ASNER, The Mary Tyler Moore Show (CBS)
GARY BURGHOFF, M*A*S*H (CBS)
McLEAN STEVENSON, M*A*S*H (CBS)

SUPPORTING ACTOR - DRAMA (E-917)
For a special program; a one-time appearance in a series; or a continuing role
MICHAEL MORIARTY, The Glass Menagerie (ABC)
MICHAEL DOUGLAS, The Streets of San Francisco (ABC)
WILL GEER, The Waltons (CBS)
SAM WATERSTON, The Glass Menagerie (ABC)

SUPPORTING ACTOR - COMEDY-VARIETY, VARIETY OR MUSIC (E-918)
For a special program; a one-time appearance in a series; or a continuing role
HARVEY KORMAN, The Carol Burnett Show (CBS)
TIM CONWAY, The Carol Burnett Show (with Tim Conway and Petula Clark) (CBS)
FOSTER BROOKS, The Dean Martin Comedy Hour (NBC)

SUPPORTING ACTOR OF THE YEAR (E-919)
MICHAEL MORIARTY, The Glass Menagerie (ABC)

SUPPORTING ACTRESS - COMEDY (E-920)
For a special program; a one-time appearance in a series; or a continuing role
CLORIS LEACHMAN, The Lars Affair; The Mary Tyler Moore Show (CBS)
VALERIE HARPER, The Mary Tyler Moore Show (CBS)
LORETTA SWIT, M*A*S*H (CBS)
SALLY STRUTHERS, All In The Family (CBS)

SUPPORTING ACTRESS - DRAMA (E-921)
For a special program; a one-time appearance in a series; or a continuing role
JOANNA MILES, The Glass Menagerie (ABC)
ELLEN CORBY, The Waltons (CBS)
NANCY WALKER, McMillan And Wife; NBC Sunday Mystery Movie (NBC)

SUPPORTING ACTRESS - COMEDY-VARIETY, VARIETY OR MUSIC (E-922)
For a special program; a one-time appearance in a series; or a continuing role
BRENDA VACCARO, The Shape Of Things (CBS)
VICKI LAWRENCE, The Carol Burnett Show (CBS)
LEE GRANT, The Shape of Things (CBS)
RUTH BUZZI, The Dean Martin Comedy Hour (NBC)

SUPPORTING ACTRESS OF THE YEAR (E-923)
JOANNA MILES, The Glass Menagerie (ABC)

DIRECTOR - DRAMA (E-924)
A single program of a series with continuing characters and/or theme
ROBERT BUTLER, The Blue Knight, Part III (NBC)
HARRY HARRIS, The Journey; The Waltons (CBS)
PHILIP LEACOCK, The Thanksgiving Story; The Waltons (CBS)

DIRECTOR - DRAMA (E-925)
A single program--Comedy or Drama
JOHN KORTY, The Autobiography of Miss Jane Pittman (CBS)
TOM GRIES, The Migrants; CBS Playhouse 90 (CBS)
BORIS SAGAL, A Case of Rape; NBC Wednesday Night At The Movies (NBC)
ANTHONY PAGE, Pueblo; ABC Theatre (ABC)
LAMONT JOHNSON, The Execution of Private Slovik; NBC Wednesday Night At The Movies (NBC)

DIRECTOR - COMEDY (E-926)
A single program of a series with continuing characters and/or theme
JACKIE COOPER, Carry On, Hawkeye; M*A*S*H (CBS)
JAY SANDRICH, Lou's First Date; The Mary Tyler Moore Show (CBS)
GENE REYNOLDS, Deal Me Out; M*A*S*H (CBS)

DIRECTOR - VARIETY OR MUSIC (E-927)
A single program of a series
DAVE POWERS, The Australia Show; The Carol Burnett Show (CBS)
ART FISHER, The Sonny And Cher Comedy Hour (with Ken Berry and George Foreman) (CBS)
JOSHUA WHITE, In Concert (with Cat Stevens); ABC Wide World Of Entertainment (ABC)

DIRECTOR - COMEDY-VARIETY, VARIETY OR MUSIC - SPECIAL (E-928)

DWIGHT HEMION, Barbra Streisand. . .And Other Musical Instruments (CBS)
MARTY PASETTA, Magnavox Presents Frank Sinatra (NBC)
TONY CHARMOLI, Mitzi. . .A Tribute To The American Housewife (CBS)
STERLING JOHNSON, Peggy Fleming Visits The Soviet Union; Bell System Family Theatre (NBC)

DIRECTOR OF THE YEAR - SERIES (E-929)

ROBERT BUTLER, The Blue Knight, Part III (NBC)

DIRECTOR OF THE YEAR - SPECIAL (E-930)

DWIGHT HEMION, Barbra Streisand. . .And Other Musical Instruments (CBS)

WRITING - DRAMA (E-931)

A single program of a series with continuing characters and/or theme

JOANNA LEE, The Thanksgiving Story; The Waltons (CBS)
GENE R. KEARNEY, Death Is Not A Passing Grade; Kojak (CBS)
JOHN McGREEVEY, The Easter Story; The Waltons (CBS)

WRITING - DRAMA, ORIGINAL TELEPLAY (E-932)

A single program--Comedy or Drama

FAY KANIN, Tell Me Where It Hurts; GE Theatre (CBS)
WILL LORIN, Cry Rape!; The New CBS Tuesday Night Movies (CBS)
LANFORD WILSON, The Migrants; CBS Playhouse 90 (CBS)

WRITING - DRAMA, ADAPTATION (E-933)

A single program--Comedy or Drama

TRACY KEENAN WYNN, The Autobiography Of Miss Jane Pittman (CBS)
BRUCE JAY FRIEDMAN, Steambath; Hollywood Television Theare (PBS)
RICHARD LEVINSON and WILLIAM LINK, The Execution Of Private Slovik; NBC Wednesday Night At The Movies (NBC)

WRITING - COMEDY (E-934)

A single program of a series with continuing characters and/or theme

TREVA SILVERMAN, The Lou And Edie Story; The Mary Tyler Moore Show (CBS)
LINDA BLOODWORTH, and MARY KAY PLACE, Hot Lips And Empty Arms; M*A*S*H (CBS)
McLEAN STEVENSON, The Trial Of Henry Blake; M*A*S*H (CBS)

WRITING - VARIETY OR MUSIC (E-935)

A Single program of a series

ED SIMMONS, GARY BELKIN, ROGER BEATTY, ARNIE KOGEN, BILL RICHMOND, GENE PERRET, RUDY DE LUCA, BARRY LEVINSON, DICK CLAIR, JENNA McMAHON, and BARRY HARMAN, The Carol Burnett Show (with Tim Conway and Bernadette Peters) (CBS)
CHRIS BEARDE, ALLAN BLYE, BOB ARNOTT, GEORGE BURDITT, BOB EINSTEIN, PHIL HAHN, COSLOUGH JOHNSON, JIM MULLIGAN, and PAUL WAYNE, The Sonny and Cher Comedy Hour (with Chuck Connors and Howard Cosell) (CBS)
STAN HART, LARRY SIEGEL, GAIL PARENT, WOODY KLING, ROGER BEATTY, TOM PATCHETT, JAY TARSES, ROBERT HILLIARD, ARNIE KOGEN, BUZ KOHAN, and BILL ANGELOS, The Family Show; The Carol Burnett Show (CBS)

WRITING - COMEDY-VARIETY, VARIETY OR MUSIC (E-936)

A special program

HERB SARGENT, ROSALYN DREXLER, LORNE MICHAELS, RICHARD PRYOR, JIM RUSK, JAMES R. STEIN, ROBERT ILLES, LILY TOMLIN, GEORGE YANOK, JANE WAGNER, ROD WARREN, ANN ELDER, and KARYL GELD, Lily (CBS)
LARRY GELBART, MITZIE WELCH, and KEN WELCH, Barbra Streisand. . .And Other Musical Instruments (CBS)
RENEE TAYLOR, and JOSEPH BOLOGNA, Paradise (CBS)

WRITER OF THE YEAR - SERIES (E-937)

TREVA SILVERMAN, The Lou And Edie Story; The Mary Tyler Moore Show (CBS)

WRITER OF THE YEAR - SPECIAL (E-938)

FAY KANIN, Tell Me Where It Hurts; GE Theater (CBS)

CHOREOGRAPHY (E-939)

A single program of a series or a special program

TONY CHARMOLI, Mitzi. . .A Tribute To The American Housewife (CBS)
ERNEST O. FLATT, The Australia Show; The Carol Burnett Show (CBS)
CARL JABLONSKI, Sammy Davis Starring In NBC Follies (with Milton Berle, Johnny Brown, Michael Landon and Carol Lawrence) (NBC)

MUSIC COMPOSITION (E-940)

A. For a series or a single program of a series (in the first year of music's use only)

MORTON STEVENS, Hookman; Hawaii Five-O (CBS)
DON B. RAY, Nightmare In Blue; Hawaii Five-O (CBS)
BRUCE BROUGHTON, The $100,000 Nickel; Hawaii Five-O (CBS)
B. For a special program
FRED KARLIN, The Autobiography Of Miss Jane Pittman (CBS)
BILLY GOLDENBERG, The Migrants; CBS Playhouse 90 (CBS)
LAURENCE ROSENTHAL, Portrait: A Man Whose Name Was John (ABC)

BEST SONG OR THEME (E-941)

A series or a single program of a series or a special program written for television

MARTY PAICH and DAVID PAICH, "Light The Way"; Once More For Joey; Ironside (NBC)
FRED KARLIN "The Love That Lights Our Way"; The Autobiography Of Miss Jane Pittman (CBS)
BILLY GOLDENBERG, Kojak; Series (CBS)

MUSIC DIRECTION - VARIETY, MUSICAL OR DRAMATIC PROGRAM (E-942)

A single program of a series or a special program

JACK PARNELL, KEN WELCH and MITZIE WELCH, Barbra Streisand. . .And Other Musical Instruments (CBS)
PETER MATZ, The Australia Show; The Carol Burnett Show (CBS)
MARTY PAICH, The Sonny And Cher Years; The Sonny And Cher Comedy Hour (CBS)

MUSICIAN OF THE YEAR (E-943)

JACK PARNELL, KEN WELCH and MITZIE WELCH, Barbra Streisand. . .And Other Musical Instruments (CBS)

ART DIRECTION OR SCENIC DESIGN (E-944)

A. For a dramatic program or feature length film made for television; for a series, a single program of a series, or a special program

JAN SCOTT, Art Director; CHARLES KREINER, Set Decorator; The Lie; CBS Playhouse 90 (CBS)
MICHAEL HALLER, The Autobiography Of Miss Jane Pittman (CBS)
WALTER H. TYLER, Art Director; RICHARD FRIEDMAN, Set Decorator; The Execution Of Private Slovik; NBC Wednesday Night At The Movies (NBC)

B. For a Musical or Variety single program of a series or a special program

BRIAN C. BARTHOLOMEW, Barbra Streisand. . .And Other Musical Instruments (CBS)
PAUL BARNES, and BOB SANSOM, Art Directors; BILL HARP, Set Decorator; The Carol Burnett Show (with Bernadette Peters and Tim Conway) (CBS)
RENE LAGLER, and LYNN GRIFFIN, Art Directors; The Andy Williams Christmas Show (NBC)

ART DIRECTOR AND SET DECORATOR OF THE YEAR (E-945)

JAN SCOTT, Art Director; CHARLES KREINER, Set Decorator; The Lie; CBS Playhouse 90 (CBS)

COSTUME DESIGN (E-946)

A single program of a series or a special program

BRUCE WALKUP and SANDY STEWART, The Autobiography Of Miss Jane Pittman (CBS)
GRADY HUNT, The Devil Made Me Do It; The Snoop Sisters; NBC Tuesday Mystery Movie (NBC)
BARBARA MURPHY, The New Treasure Hunt (Synd)
RET TURNER, and BOB MACKIE, The Sonny And Cher Years; The Sonny And Cher Comedy Hour (CBS)
CHARLES KNODE, Concluding Episode; War And Peace (PBS)

MAKE-UP (E-947)

A single program of a series or a special program

STAN WINSTON, and RICK BAKER, The Autobiography Of Miss Jane Pittman (CBS)
NICK MARCELLINO, and JAMES LEE McCOY, Portrait: A Man Whose Name Was John (ABC)
BEN NYE II, Judgment--The Trial Of Julius And Ethel Rosenberg; ABC Theatre (ABC)
WILLIAM TUTTLE, The Phantom Of Hollywood; The New CBS Tuesday Night Movies (CBS)

CINEMATOGRAPHY - ENTERTAINMENT PROGRAMMING (E-948)

A. For a series or a single program of a series

HARRY WOLF, A.S.C., Any Old Port In A Storm; Columbo; NBC Sunday Mystery Movie (NBC)
GERALD PERRY FINNERMAN, A.S.C., Kojak (CBS)
ROBERT MORRISON, JACK WHITMAN, and BILL HUFFMAN, Hawaii Five-O (CBS)

B. For a special or feature length program made for television

TED VOIGTLANDER, A.S.C., It's Good To Be Alive; GE Theater (CBS)
RICHARD C. KRATINA, The Migrants; CBS Playhouse 90 (CBS)
WALTER STRENGE, A.S.C., Portrait: A Man Whose Name Was John (ABC)
ANDREW LASZLO, The Man Without A Country (ABC)
FRED MANDL, Trapped; Wednesday Movie Of The Week (ABC)

CINEMATOGRAPHER OF THE YEAR (E-949)

TED VOIGTLANDER, A.S.C., It's Good To Be Alive; GE Theater (CBS)

FILM EDITING - ENTERTAINMENT PROGRAMMING (E-950)

A. For a series or a single program of a series

GENE FOWLER, JR., MARJORIE FOWLER, and SAMUEL E. BEETLEY, The Blue Knight (NBC)
DOUGLAS HINES, and BUD ISAACS, The Mary Tyler Moore Show (CBS)
STANFORD TISCHLER, and FRED W. BERGER, M*A*S*H (CBS)

B. For a special or feature length program made for television

FRANK MORRISS, The Execution Of Private Slovik; NBC Wednesday Night At The Movies (NBC)
RICHARD BRACKEN, A Case Of Rape; NBC Wednesday Night At The Movies (NBC)
SIDNEY LEVIN, The Autobiography Of Miss Jane Pittman (CBS)

FILM EDITOR OF THE YEAR (E-951)

FRANK MORRISS, The Execution Of Private Slovik; NBC Wednesday Night At The Movies (NBC)

FILM SOUND EDITING (E-952)

A single program of a series or a special program

BUD NOLAN, Pueblo; ABC Theatre (ABC)
SID LUBOW, SAM CAYLOR, JACK KIRSCHNER, RICHARD RADERMAN, STANLEY FRAZEN, and JOHN SINGLETON, Marker For A Dead Bookie; Kojak (CBS)
JERRY ROSENTHAL, RON ASHCROFT, AL KAJITA, RICHARD BURROW, JACK MILNER, TONY GARBER, WILLIAM M. ANDREWS, EDWARD L. SANDLIN, and MILTON C. BURROW, Collision Course; Police Story (NBC)

FILM OR TAPE SOUND MIXING (E-953)

A single program of a series or a special program

ALBERT A. GRAMAGLIA, and MICHAEL SHINDLER, Pueblo; ABC Theatre (ABC)
JOHN K. KEAN, and THOM K. PIPER, The Execution Of Private Slovik; NBC Wednesday Night At The Movies (NBC)
CHARLES T. KNIGHT, and DON MINKLER, The Autobiography Of Miss Jane Pittman (CBS)

VIDEO TAPE EDITING (E-954)

A single program of a series or a special program

ALFRED MULLER, Pueblo; ABC Theatre (ABC)
LEWIS W. SMITH, The Lie; CBS Playhouse 90 (CBS)
NICK V. GIORDANO, and GEORGE GURUNIAN, The John Denver Show (ABC)

TECHNICAL DIRECTION AND ELECTRONIC CAMERAWORK (E-955)

A single program of a series or a special program

GERRY BUCCI, Technical Director; KENNETH TAMBURRI, DAVE HILMER, DAVE SMITH, JIM BALDEN, and RON BROOKS, Cameramen; In Concert (with Cat Stevens); ABC Wide World Of Entertainment (ABC)
PARKER ROE, Technical Director; LEW ADAMS, KEN LAMKIN, JOHN POLIAK, and GARY STANTON, Cameramen; Judgment--The Trial Of Julius And Ethel Rosenberg; ABC Theatre (ABC)
LOU MARCHAND, Technical Director; RICHARD KERR, MORRIS MANN, JOHN MORREALE, MICHAEL W. REBICH, and ROBERT WOLFF, Cameramen; Pueblo; ABC Theatre (ABC)

LIGHTING DIRECTION (E-956)

A single program of a series or a special program, produced for electronic television only

WILLIAM M. KLAGES, The Lie; CBS Playhouse 90 (CBS)
JOHN FRESCHI, Mitzi. . .A Tribute To The American Housewife (CBS)

LON STUCKY, and JOHN NANCE, Dean Martin Presents Music Country (with Johnny Cash and Loretta Lynn) (NBC)

THE AREAS

(Possibility of One Award, More Than One Award, or No Award)

INDIVIDUAL ACHIEVEMENT IN CHILDRENS PROGRAMMING (E-957)

CHARLES M. SCHULZ, Writer; A Charlie Brown Thanksgiving (CBS)
WILLIAM ZAHARUK, Art Director; PETER RAZMOFSKI, Set Decorator; The Borrowers; Hallmark Hall Of Fame (NBC)
DAME JUDITH ANDERSON, Performer; The Borrowers; Hallmark Hall Of Fame (NBC)
WALTER C. MILLER, Director; The Borrowers; Hallmark Hall Of Fame (NBC)
BILL DAVIS, Director; Marlo Thomas And Friends In Free To Be. . .You And Me (ABC)
JUUL HAALMEYER, Costume Designer; The Borrowers; Hallmark Hall Of Fame (NBC)

SPECIAL CLASSIFICATION OF OUTSTANDING PROGRAM AND INDIVIDUAL ACHIEVEMENT (E-958)

An Award for unique program and individual achievements, which does not fall into a specific category, or is not otherwise recognized

THE DICK CAVETT SHOW, John Gilroy, Producer; Dick Cavett, Star; Series (ABC)
TOM SNYDER, Host; Tomorrow (NBC)
WARNER BROS. MOVIES--A 50 YEAR SALUTE, ABC Wide World Of Entertainment; Rick Rosner, Executive Producer; Lawrence Einhorn, Producer (ABC)
CBS ALL-AMERICAN THANKSGIVING DAY PARADE, Mike Gargiulo, Executive Producer (CBS)
PAUL LYNDE, Performer; The Hollywood Squares (NBC)
BETTE DAVIS, Hostess; Warner Bros. Movies--A 50 Year Salute; ABC Wide World Of Entertainment (ABC)

SPORTS PROGRAMMING (E-959)

An Award for programs and for individuals contributing to the coverage of sporting events

ABC'S WIDE WORLD OF SPORTS, Roone Arledge, Executive Producer; Dennis Lewin, Producer (ABC)
JIM McKAY, Host; ABC'S Wide World Of Sports (ABC)
BOBBY RIGGS VS. BILLIE JEAN KING, TENNIS BATTLE OF THE SEXES, Roone Arledge, and Jackie Barnett, Executive Producers; Chuck Howard, Producer (ABC)
1973 WORLD SERIES, Allan B. Connal, Executive Producer; Roy Hammerman, Producer (NBC)
MONDAY NIGHT FOOTBALL, Roone Arledge, Executive Producer Don Ohlmeyer, Producer; (ABC)
HOWARD COSELL, Announcer; Monday Night Football (ABC)
FRANK GIFFORD, Announcer; Monday Night Football (ABC)
TONY VERNA, Director; The Triple Crown Of Racing: The Kentucky Derby, The Preakness And The Belmont Stakes (CBS)
HARRY COYLE, Director; 1973 World Series (NBC)

ACHIEVEMENT IN ANY AREA OF CREATIVE TECHNICAL CRAFTS (E-960)

An Award for individual technical craft achievement which does not fall into a specific category, and is not otherwise recognized

LYNDA GURASICH, Hair Stylist; The Autobiography Of Miss Jane Pittman (CBS)

JORDON WHITELAW, Orchestral Treatment Director; Evening At Pops (with Ella Fitzgerald) (PBS)
RENA LEUSCHNER, Hairdresser; The Sonny And Cher Comedy Hour (with Paul Anka and Neil Sedaka) (CBS)

SPECIAL AWARDS

ACHIEVEMENT IN ENGINEERING DEVELOPMENT (E-961)

CONSOLIDATED VIDEO SYSTEMS, INC. for the application of digital video technique to the Time Base Corrector, permitting use of smaller, lighter weight, more portable video tape equipment on news and other outside events in television broadcasting.
RCA for its leading role in the development of the quadraplex video tape cartridge equipment, providing improved production reliability and efficiency in broadcasting video taped program segments, promos, and commercials.
THE TELECOPTER To JOHN D. SILVA for the conception and expertise and To GOLDEN WEST BROADCASTERS for its realization.

INTERNATIONAL NON-FICTION AWARD (E-962)

HORIZON: THE MAKING OF A NATURAL HISTORY FILM, British Broadcasting Corporation, London, England
OMNIBUS: FIDELIO FINCKE, WHERE ARE YOU NOW?, British Broadcasting Corporation, London, England
GREY OWL, Canadian Broadcasting Corporation, Toronto, Ontario, Canada
BUNNY, Thames Television Limited, London, England
TOO LONG A WINTER, Yorkshire Television Ltd., London, England

INTERNATIONAL FICTION AWARD (E-963)

LA CABINA, Television Espanola, Madrid, Spain
HIGH SUMMER, Armchair Theatre; Thames Television Limited, London, England
COUNTRY MATTERS: THE LITTLE FARM, Granada Television, Ltd., Manchester, England
THE DUCHESS OF MALFI, British Broadcasting Corporation, London, England
SARAH, Yorkshire Television, Yorkshire, England

THE INTERNATIONAL DIRECTORATE AWARD (E-964)

CHARLES CURRAN, President, European Broadcasting Union; Director-General, British Broadcasting Corporation

THE NATIONAL AWARD FOR COMMUNITY SERVICE (E-965)

THROUGH THE LOOKING GLASS DARKLY, WKY-TV, Oklahoma City, Oklahoma
FROM PROTEST TO POLITICS, WXYZ-TV, Southfield, Michigan
THE RAPE OF PAULETTE, WBBM-TV, Chicago, Illinois
PROBE: UNCLE SAM IS A SLUMLORD, WRC-TV, Washington, D.C.
LIVING WITH DEATH, WCCO-TV, Minneapolis, Minnesota
FOCUS 30, KYTV, Springfield, Missouri
MEDICINE: WHERE DOES IT HURT? WNBC-TV, New York, New York
THE FRIGHTENING FEELING YOU'RE GOING TO DIE, WCVB-TV, Needham, Massachusetts
A MATTER OF LIFE AND DEBT, KOOL-TV, Phoenix, Arizona
WHAT HAPPENS TO ME?, KPEC-TV, Tacoma, Washington (Educational Station)
THE NINE-YEAR-OLD IN NORFOLK PRISON, WTIC-TV, Hartford, Connecticut
THE ELDERS, KDIN, Des Moines, Iowa (Educational Station)

DAYTIME PROGRAM AND INDIVIDUAL ACHIEVEMENTS
(One Award Only in Each of the Followig Categories)

DAYTIME DRAMA SERIES (E-966)
Award to Executive Producer(s) and/or Creator, and Producer(s)

THE DOCTORS, Joseph Stuart, Producer (NBC)
GENERAL HOSPITAL, Jim Young, Producer; Frank and Doris Hursley, Creators (ABC)
DAYS OF OUR LIVES, Betty Corday, Executive Producer; Ted Corday, Irna Phillips, and Allan Chase, Creators; H. Wesley Kenney, Producer (NBC)

DAYTIME DRAMA SPECIAL (E-967)
Award to Executive Producer(s) and Producer(s)

THE OTHER WOMAN, ABC Matinee Today; John Conboy, Producer (ABC)
A SPECIAL ACT OF LOVE, ABC Afternoon Playbreak; John Choy, Producer (ABC)
TIGER ON A CHAIN, CBS Daytime 90; Tony Converse, and Darryl Hickman, Executive Producers; Linda Fidler Wendell, Producer (CBS)

DAYTIME GAME SHOW (E-968)
Award to Executive Producer(s) and Producer(s)

PASSWORD, Frank Wayne, Executive Producer; Howard Felsher, Producer (ABC)
THE HOLLYWOOD SQUARES, Merrill Heatter and Robert Quigley, Executive Producers; Jay Redack, Producer (NBC)
JEOPARDY!, Robert H. Rubin, Producer (NBC)

DAYTIME TALK, SERVICE OR VARIETY SERIES (E-969)
Award to Executive Producer(s) and Producer(s)

THE MERV GRIFFIN SHOW, Bob Murphy, Producer (Synd)
DINAH'S PLACE, Henry Jaffe, Executive Producer; Fred Tatashore, Producer (NBC)
THE MIKE DOUGLAS SHOW, Woody Fraser, Producer (Synd)

DAYTIME ENTERTAINMENT CHILDREN'S SERIES (E-970)
Award to Executive Producer(s) and Producer(s)

ZOOM, Jim Crum, and Christopher Sarson, Producers (PBS)
CAPTAIN KANGAROO, Jim Krayer, Executive Producer; Jim Hirschfeld, Producer (CBS)
FAT ALBERT AND THE COSBY KIDS, Norman Prescott, and Lou Scheimer, Producers (CBS)
STAR TREK, Lou Scheimer, and Norman Prescott, Producers (NBC)

DAYTIME ENTERTAINMENT CHILDREN'S SPECIAL (E-971)
Award to Executive Producer(s) and Producer(s)

ROOKIE OF THE YEAR, The ABC Afterschool Special; Dan Wilson, Producer (ABC)
MY DAD LIVES IN A DOWNTOWN HOTEL, The ABC Afterschool Special; Gerald Isenberg, Executive Producer; Richard Marx, Producer (ABC)
THE SWISS FAMILY ROBINSON, Famous Classic Tales; Walter E. Hucker, Executive Producer (CBS)

ACTOR - DAYTIME DRAMA (E-972)
A. For a Series

MACDONALD CAREY, Days Of Our Lives (NBC)
JOHN BERADINO, General Hospital (ABC)
PETER HANSEN, General Hospital (ABC)

B. For a Special Program
PAT O'BRIEN, The Other Woman; ABC Matinee Today (ABC)
PETER COFFIELD, Legacy Of Fear; CBS Daytime 90 (CBS)
DON PORTER, Mother Of The Bride; ABC Afternoon Playbreak (ABC)

DAYTIME ACTOR OF THE YEAR (E-973)
PAT O'BRIEN, The Other Woman; ABC Matinee Today (ABC)

ACTRESS - DAYTIME DRAMA (E-974)
A. For a Series

ELIZABETH HUBBARD, The Doctors (NBC)
MARY STUART, Search For Tomorrow (CBS)
RACHEL AMES, General Hospital (ABC)
MARY FICKETT, All My Children (ABC)
B. For a Special Program
CATHLEEN NESBITT, The Mask Of Love; ABC Matinee Today (ABC)
EVE ARDEN, Mother Of The Bride; ABC Afternoon Playbreak (ABC)
CONSTANCE TOWERS, Once In Her Life; CBS Daytime 90 (CBS)

DAYTIME ACTRESS OF THE YEAR (E-975)
CATHLEEN NESBITT, The Mask Of Love; ABC Matinee Today (ABC)

GAME SHOW HOST OR HOSTESS (E-976)
PETER MARSHALL, The Hollywood Squares (NBC)
ALLEN LUDDEN, Password (ABC)
ART FLEMING, Jeopardy! (NBC)

TALK, SERVICE OR VARIETY SERIES HOST OR HOSTESS (E-977)
DINAH SHORE, Dinah's Place (NBC)
MIKE DOUGLAS, The Mike Douglas Show (Synd)
MERV GRIFFIN, The Merv Griffin Show (Synd)
BARBARA WALTERS, Not For Women Only (Synd)

DAYTIME HOST OF THE YEAR (E-978)
PETER MARSHALL, The Hollywood Squares (NBC)

DIRECTOR - DAYTIME DRAMA SERIES (E-979)
H. WESLEY KENNEY, Days Of Our Lives (NBC)
HUGH McPHILLIPS, The Doctors (NBC)
NORMAN HALL, The Doctors (NBC)

DIRECTOR - DAYTIME SPECIAL PROGRAM (E-980)
H. WESLEY KENNEY, Miss Kline, We Love You; ABC Afternoon Playbreak (ABC)
PETER LEVIN, The Other Woman; ABC Matinee Today (ABC)
LELA SWIFT, The Gift Of Terror, ABC Afternoon Playbreak (ABC)
BURT BRINCKERHOFF, The Mask Of Love; ABC Matinee Today (ABC)

DIRECTOR - DAYTIME GAME SHOW (E-981)
MIKE GARGIULO, Jackpot! (NBC)
JEROME SHAW, The Hollywood Squares (NBC)
STUART PHELPS, Password (with Carol Burnett and Elizabeth Montgomery) (ABC)

DIRECTOR - DAYTIME TALK, SERVICE OR VARIETY PROGRAM (E-982)
DICK CARSON, The Merv Griffin Show (with Rosemary Clooney, Helen O'Connell, Fran Warren and Kay Starr) (Synd)
RON A. APPLING, The Merv Griffin Show (with Clint Eastwood, Forrest Tucker and Stanley Myron Handleman) (Synd)
GLEN SWANSON, Dinah's Place (with Jose Feliciano) (NBC)

DAYTIME DIRECTOR OF THE YEAR (E-983)

H. WESLEY KENNEY, Miss Kline, We Love You; ABC Afternoon Playbreak (ABC)

WRITING - DAYTIME DRAMA SERIES (E-984)

HENRY SLESAR, The Edge Of Night (CBS)
EILEEN and ROBERT MASON POLLOCK, and JAMES LIPTON, The Doctors (NBC)
FRANK and DORIS HURSLEY, BRIDGET DOBSON, and DEBORAH HARDY, General Hospital (ABC)

WRITING - DAYTIME SPECIAL PROGRAM (E-985)

LILA GARRETT, and SANDY KRINSKI, Mother Of The Bride; ABC Afternoon Playbreak (ABC)
ROBERT SHAW, Once In Her Life; CBS Daytime 90 (CBS)
ART WALLACE, Alone With Terror; ABC Matinee Today (ABC)

WRITING - DAYTIME GAME SHOW (E-986)

JAY REDACK, HARRY FRIEDMAN, HAROLD SCHNEIDER, GARY JOHNSON, STEVE LEVITCH, RICK KELLARD, and ROWBY GOREN; The Hollywood Squares (NBC)
ROBERT SHERMAN, PATRICK NEARY, JOE NEUSTEIN, and DICK DeBARTOLO; Match Game '74 (CBS)
LYNETTE WILLIAMS, ELIZABETH M. CAMP, LESLIE COOPER, MARK EISMAN, G. ROSS PARKER, and JAMES J. THESING; Jeopardy! (NBC)

WRITING - DAYTIME TALK, SERVICE OR VARIETY PROGRAM (E-987)

TONY GARAFALO, BOB MURPHY, and MERV GRIFFIN; The Merv Griffin Show (with Billie Jean King, Mark Spitz, Hank Aaron and Johnny Unitas) (Synd)
BILL WALKER, BOB HOWARD and FRED TATASHORE; The Child Abuse Show; Dinah's Place (NBC)
DON CORNELIUS, Soul Train (with Johnny Mathis) (Synd)

DAYTIME WRITER OF THE YEAR (E-988)

LILA GARRETT, and SANDY KRINSKI, Mother Of The Bride; ABC Afternoon Playbreak (ABC)

DAYTIME MUSICAL DIRECTION (E-989)

RICHARD CLEMENTS, A Special Act Of Love; ABC Afternoon Playbreak (ABC)
JOHN GELLER, The Doctors (NBC)
PAUL TAUBMAN, Edge Of Night (CBS)

DAYTIME ART DIRECTION OR SCENIC DESIGN (E-990)

TOM TRIMBLE, Art Director; BROCK BROUGHTON, Set Decorator; The Young And The Restless (CBS)
OTIS RIGGS, JR., Another World (NBC)
VICTOR L. PAGANUZZI, Scenic Desiner; JOHN WENDELL, Set Decorator; Once In Her Life; CBS Daytime 90 (CBS)
LLOYD R. EVANS, Scenic Designer; TOM CUNNINGHAM, and JOHN WENDELL, Set Decorators; Love of Life; Series (CBS)

DAYTIME COSTUME DESIGN (E-991)

BILL JOBE, The Mask Of Love; ABC Matinee Today (ABC)
LEWIS BROWN, Another World (NBC)
JULIA SZE, Somerset (NBC)
HAZEL ROY, All My Children; Series (ABC)

DAYTIME MAKE-UP (E-992)

DOUGLAS D. KELLY, The Mask Of Love; ABC Matinee Today (ABC)
ANDREW EGER, The Edge of Night (CBS)
LEE BAYGAN, The Doctors (NBC)
SYLVIA LAWRENCE, All My Children (ABC)

TECHNICAL DIRECTION AND ELECTRONIC CAMERAWORK - DAYTIME (E-993)

LOU MARCHAND, Technical Director; GERALD M. DOWD, FRANK MELCHIORRE, and JOHN MORRIS, Cameramen; One Life To Live (ABC)
HAROLD SCHUTZMAN, Technical Director; HAL WELDON, WILLIAM UNKEL, and ROBERT TOERPER, Cameramen; The Edge Of Night (CBS)
A.J. CUNNINGHAM, Technical Director; RICK TANZI, JOE ARVIZU, JACK JENNINGS, and WAYNE ORR, Cameramen; The Price Is Right (CBS)
GORDON C. JAMES, Technical Director; GEORGE SIMPSON, GEORGE MEYER, and JOHN KULLMAN, Cameramen; Days Of Our Lives (NBC)
CLIVE BASSETT, Technical Director; PAUL JOHNSON, RICK TANZI, DICK OUDERKIRK, MARVIN DRESSER, and GORDON SWEENEY, Cameramen; The Young And The Restless (CBS)
J.J. LUPATKIN and BILL DEGENHARDT, Technical Directors; JOHN WOOD, FRANK ZUCCARO, JAMES WOODLE, JOE SOLOMITO, AL GIANETTA, and LEN GELARDI, Cameramen; All My Children (ABC)

LIGHTING DIRECTION - DAYTIME (E-994)

RICHARD HOLBROOK, The Young And The Restless (CBS)
ALAN E. SCARLETT, Days Of Our Lives (NBC)
RON HOLDEN, General Hospital (ABC)
MEL HANDLESMAN, All My Children (ABC)

SOUND MIXING - DAYTIME (E-995)

ERNEST DELLUTRI, Days Of Our Lives (NBC)
DICK ELLIS, General Hospital (ABC)
ALBIN S. LEMANSKI, All My Children (ABC)

EDITING - DAYTIME (E-996)

GARY ANDERSON, Miss Kline, We Love You; ABC Afternoon Playbreak (ABC)
JERRY GREENE, The Mask Of Love; ABC Matinee Today (ABC)
JEFF LAING, Once In Her Life; CBS Daytime 90 (CBS)

NEWS AND DOCUMENTARY PROGRAM AND INDIVIDUAL ACHIEVEMENTS

(Possibility of One Award, More than One Award, or No Award)

ACHIEVEMENT WITHIN REGULARLY SCHEDULED NEWS PROGRAMS (E-997)

For program segments, i.e. presentation of individual stories (in single or multi-part) or elements within the programs Emmy Awards may possibly be given to: Executive Producer(s), Producer(s), Broadcaster(s)

COVERAGE OF THE OCTOBER WAR FROM ISRAEL'S NORTHERN FRONT, CBS Evening News With Walter Cronkite; John Laurence, Correspondent (CBS)
THE AGNEW RESIGNATION, CBS Evening News With Walter Cronkite; Paul Greenberg, Executive Producer; Ron Bonn, Ed Fouhy, John Lane, Don Bowers, John Armstrong, and Robert Mean, Producers; Walter Cronkite, Robert Schakne, Fred Graham, Robert Pierpoint, Roger Mudd, Dan Rather, John Hart, and Eric Sevareid, Correspondents (CBS)
THE KEY BISCAYNE BANK CHARTER STRUGGLE, CBS Evening News With Walter Cronkite; Ed Fouhy, Producer; Robert Pierpoint, Correspondent (CBS)
REPORTS ON WORLD HUNGER, NBC Nightly News; Lester M. Crystal, Executive Producer; Richard Fisher and Joseph Angotti, Producers; Tom Streithorst, Phil Brady, John Palmer, and Liz Trotta, Correspondents (NBC)
INSIDE CHINA, ABC Evening News; Ted Koppel, and Steve Bell, Correspondents (ABC)
THE ARAB WORLD, ABC Evening News; Peter Jennings, and Barry Dunsmore, Correspondents (ABC)
DEPROGRAMMING: THE CLASH BETWEEN RELIGION AND CIVIL

RIGHTS, CBS Evening News With Walter Cronkite; Roger Sims, Producer; Steve Young, Correspondent (CBS)

ACHIEVEMENT FOR REGULARLY SCHEDULED MAGAZINE-TYPE PROGRAMS (E-998)

For program segments, i.e. the presentation of individual stories, individual segments, or a single program of a series Emmy Awards may possibly be given to: Executive Producer(s), Producer(s), Broadcaster(s)

AMERICA'S NERVE GAS ARSENAL, First Tuesday; Eliot Frankel, Executive Producer; William B. Hill, and Anthony Potter, Producers; Tom Pettit, Correspondent (NBC)
THE ADVERSARIES, Behind The Lines; Carey Winfrey, Executive Producer; Peter Forbath, Producer/Reporter; Brendan Gill, Host/Moderator (PBS)
A QUESTION OF IMPEACHMENT, Bill Moyers' Journal; Jerome Toobin, Executive Producer; Martin Clancy, Producer; Bill Moyers, Broadcaster (PBS)
IT'S ENOUGH TO MAKE YOU SICK, The Reasoner Report; Ernest Leiser, Executive Producer; Frank Reynolds, Correspondent (ABC)
THE END OF A SALESMAN, 60 Minutes; Don Hewitt, Executive Producer; Joseph Wershba, Producer; Morley Safer, Correspondent (CBS)
LOCAL NEWS AND THE RATING WAR, 60 Minutes; Don Hewitt, Executive Producer; Harry Moses, Producer; Mike Wallace, Correspondent (CBS)

ACHIEVEMENT IN COVERAGE OF SPECIAL EVENTS (E-999)

For program achievements Emmy Awards may possibly be given to: Executive Producer(s), Producer(s), Broadcaster(s)

WATERGATE: THE WHITE HOUSE TRANSCRIPTS, Russ Bensley, Executive Producer; Sylvia Westerman, Barry Jagoda, Mark Harrington, and Jack Kelly, Producers; Walter Cronkite, Dan Rather, Barry Serafin, Bob Schieffer, Daniel Schorr, Nelson Benton, Bruce Morton, Roger Mudd, and Fred Graham, Correspondents (CBS)
WATERGATE COVERAGE, Martin Clancy, Executive Producer; The NPACT Staff, Producers; Jim Lehrer, Peter Kaye, and Robert Mac-Neil, Reporters (PBS)
ABC NEWS AT EASE, Walter J. Pfister, Producer; Howard K. Smith, and Harry Reasoner, Anchormen (ABC)
WATERGATE: THIS WEEK, Helen Marmor, Producer; John Chancellor, and Carl Stern, Correspondents (NBC)

DOCUMENTARY PROGRAM ACHIEVEMENTS (E-1000)

A. For documentary programs dealing with events or matters of current significance Emmy Awards may possibly be given to: Executive Producer(s), Producer(s), Broadcaster(s)

FIRE!, ABC News Close Up; Pamela Hill, Producer; Jules Bergman, Correspondent/Narrator (ABC)
CBS NEWS SPECIAL REPORT: THE SENATE AND THE WATERGATE AFFAIR, Leslie Midgley, Executive Producer; Hal Haley, Bernard Birnbaum, and David Browning, Producers; Dan Rather, Roger Mudd, Daniel Schorr, and Fred Graham, Correspondents (CBS)
ACTION BIOGRAPHY: HENRY KISSINGER, Ted Koppel, Producer; Howard K. Smith, Correspondent (ABC)
JUVENILE COURT, Special of the Week; Fred Wiseman, Producer (PBS)
THE UNQUIET DEATH OF JULIUS AND ETHEL ROSENBERG, Special of the Week; Alvin Goldstein, Producer (PBS)
OIL: THE POLICY CRISIS, ABC News Close-up; Steven Fleischman, Producer (ABC)
B. For documentary programs dealing with artistic, historial or cultural subjects Emmy Awards may possibly

be given to: Executive Producer(s), Producer(s), (Broadcaster(s)

JOURNEY TO THE OUTER LIMITS, National Geographic Society; Nicholas Clapp, and Dennis Kane, Executive Producers; Alex Grasshoff, Producer (ABC)
THE WORLD AT WAR, Series; Jeremy Isaacs, Producer (Synd)
CBS REPORTS: THE ROCKEFELLERS, Burton Benjamin, Executive Producer; Howard Stringer, Producer; Walter Cronkite, Correspondent (CBS)
THE BABOONS OF GOMBE, Jane Goodall and The World of Animal Behavior; Marshall Flaum, Executive Producer; Hugo van Lawick, and Bill Travers, Producers (ABC)
CULTURE THIEVES, ABC News Close-up; Martin Carr, Producer; Howard K. Smith, Correspondent (ABC)
RAOUL WALSH, The Men Who Made The Movies; Richard Schickel, Producer (PBS)
POWER AND THE PRESIDENCY, The American Parade; Joel Heller, Executive Producer; Jack Willis, Producer (CBS)

INTERVIEW PROGRAM (E-1001)

For a single program or one entire program of a series produced by a network news division or dealing with public affairs exclusively Emmy Awards may possibly be given to: Executive Producer(s), Producer(s), Broadcaster(s)

SOLZHENITSYN, CBS News Special; Burton Benjamin, Producer; Walter Cronkite, Correspondent (CBS)
HENRY STEELE COMMAGER, Bill Moyers' Journal; Jerome Toobin, Executive Producer; Martin Clancy, Producer; Bill Moyers, Broadcaster (PBS)
WATERGATE: AN INTERVIEW WITH JOHN DEAN, CBS News Special Report; Ed Fouhy, Executive Producer; Don Bowers, Producer; Walter Cronkite, Correspondent (CBS)
CRISIS OF THE PRESIDENCY, ABC News Special; Ernest Leiser, Executive Producer; Arthur Holch and Joan Richman, Producers (ABC)

TELEVISION NEWS BROADCASTER (E-1002)

For achievements within program segments, one program of a series, or a single program; for reporting, interviewing, interpretation, commentary, analysis within Regularly Scheduled News programs, Magazine-type programs, Coverage of Special Events, interview programs, and Documentary programs dealing with events or matters of current significance. Emmy Award will be given to the News Broadcaster

HARRY REASONER, ABC News (ABC)
BILL MOYERS, Essay On Watergate; Bill Moyers' Journal (PBS)
MIKE WALLACE, 60 Minutes (CBS)
WALTER CRONKITE, CBS Evening News With Walter Cronkite and Various Specials (CBS)
CARL STERN, Coverage of Watergate and Justice Department; NBC Nightly News (NBC)
JOHN CHANCELLOR, NBC Nightly News (NBC)

INDIVIDUAL ACHIEVEMENT IN CHILDREN'S PROGRAMMING (E-1003)

RONALD BALDWIN, Art Director; NAT MONGIOI, Set Decorator; The Electric Company (PBS)
THE MUPPETS (JIM HENSON, FRANK OZ, CARROLL SPINNEY, JERRY NELSON, RICHARD HUNT, and FRAN BRILL), Performers; Sesame Street; Series (PBS)
JON STONE, JOSEPH A. BAILEY, JERRY JUHL, EMILY PERL KINGSLEY, JEFFREY MOSS, RAY SIPHERD, and NORMAN STILES, Writers; Sesame Street (PBS)
HENRY BEHAR, Director; The Electric Company (PBS)
THOMAS A. WHEDON, JOHN BONI, SARA COMPTON, TOM DUNS-

MUIR, THAD MUMFORD, JEREMY STEVENS, and JIM THURMAN, Writers; The Electric Company (PBS)

RELIGIOUS PROGRAMMING (E-1004)

KEN LAMKIN, Technical Director; SAM DRUMMY, GARY STANTON, and ROBERT HATFIELD, Cameramen; Gift Of Tears; This Is The Life (Synd)
JOHN WARD, Scenic Designer; MYRON BLEAM, Set Decorator; St Francis of Assisi, The Tower of Babel, David and Goliath; Marshall Efron's Illustrated, Simplified and Painless Sunday School (CBS)
HOLY LAND, Doris Ann, Producer (NBC)
DIRECTIONS, Sid Darion, Executive Producer (ABC)
CHRISTMAS IN WALES, Directions; Paul E. Wilson, Producer (ABC)

NEWS AND DOCUMENTARY DIRECTING (E-1005)

For program segments, one program of a series, or a single program; for Regularly Scheduled News programs, Magazine-type programs, Coverage of Special Events, Interview programs, Documentary programs dealing with events or matters of current significance, and Cultural Documentaries

PAMELA HILL, Fire!; ABC News Close-up (ABC)
VICTORIA HOCHBERG, The Right To Die; ABC News Close-up (ABC)
WILLIAM LINDEN, Watergate: The White House Transcripts; CBS News Special Report (CBS)

NEWS AND DOCUMENTARY WRITING (E-1006)

For program segments, one program of a series, or a single program; for Regularly Scheduled News programs, Magazine-type programs, Coverage of Special Events, Interview programs, Documentary programs dealing with events or matters of current significance, and Cultural Documentaries
ROBERT NORTHSHIELD, The Sins Of The Fathers; NBC Reports (NBC)
MARLENE SANDERS, The Right To Die; ABC News Close-up (ABC)
HOWARD STRINGER, and BURTON BENJAMIN, The Rockefellers; CBS Reports (CBS)
ALVIN H. GOLDSTEIN, The Unquiet Death of Julius and Ethel Rosenberg; Special Of The Week (PBS)

ACHIEVEMENT IN ANY AREA OF CREATIVE TECHNICAL CRAFTS (E-1007)

An Award for individual craft achievement which does not fall into a specific category, and is not otherwise recognized

PHILIPPE COUSTEAU, Under Ice Photography; Beneath the Frozen World; The Undersea World of Jacques Cousteau (ABC)
JOHN CHAMBERS, and TOM BURMAN, Make-up; Struggle for Survival; Primal Man (ABC)
AGGIE WHELAN, Courtroom Drawings; The Mitchell-Stans Trial; CBS Evening News with Walter Cronkite (CBS)
FRANCOIS CHARLET, Aerial Photography; Beneath the Frozen World; The Undersea World of Jacques Cousteau (ABC)
ROBERT R. DUNN, Cameraman; C. FRED GAYTON, Videotape Recorder Operator; Electronic Newsgathering using minicam; The Hearst Kidnapping; CBS Evening News (CBS)

INFORMATIONAL CHILDREN'S SERIES (E-1008)

MAKE A WISH, Lester Cooper, Executive Producer; Tom Bywaters, Producer (ABC)
THE ELECTRIC COMPANY, Samuel Y. Gibbon, Jr., Executive Producer; Andrew B. Ferguson, Jr., Producer (PBS)
IN THE NEWS, Joel Heller, Executive Producer; Judy Towers Reemtsma, Producer (CBS)

INFORMATIONAL CHILDREN'S SPECIAL (E-1009)

THE RUNAWAYS, Joseph Barbera and William Hanna, Executive Producers; Bill Schwartz, Producer (ABC)
WHAT'S IMPEACHMENT ALL ABOUT?, Joel Heller, Executive Producer; Walter Lister, Producer (CBS)
WHAT'S THE ENERGY CRISIS ALL ABOUT?, Joel Heller, Executive Producer; Walter Lister, Producer (CBS)

INSTRUCTIONAL CHILDREN'S PROGRAMMING (E-1010)

INSIDE/OUT, Larry Walcoff, Executive Producer (Synd)
MISTER ROGERS' NEIGHBORHOOD, Leland Hazard, Executive Producer; Fred Rogers, Producer; Series (PBS)
MULTIPLICATION ROCK, Tom Yohe, Executive Producer; Radford Stone, Producer; Series (ABC)
SESAME STREET, Jon Stone, Executive Producer; Bob Cunniff, Producer (PBS)

CINEMATOGRAPHY - NEWS AND DOCUMENTARY PROGRAMMING (E-1011)

For a series, a single program of a series, a special program, program segments or elements within: A. Regularly scheduled News Programs and coverage of Special Events

DELOS HALL, Clanking Savannah Blacksmith; On The Road With Charles Kuralt; CBS Evening News with Walter Cronkite (CBS)
ROBERT O. BROWN, and ELIA RAVASZ, SLA Shootout, Los Angeles; CBS Evening News with Dan Rather (CBS)
ISADORE BLECKMAN, Bird Lady; On The Road With Charles Kuralt; CBS Evening News with Walter Cronkite (CBS)
B. Documentary, Magazine-type or Mini-documentary programs
WALTER DOMBROW, Ballerina; 60 Minutes (CBS)
PHILIPPE COUSTEAU, Beneath the Frozen World; The Undersea World of Jacques Cousteau (ABC)
JOHN J. LANDI, and RALPH MAYHER, Fire!; ABC News Close-up (ABC)
DICK MINGALONE, Inside Attica; The Reasoner Report (ABC)

MUSIC COMPOSITION (E-1012)

For a series, a single program of a series or a special program
WALTER SCHARF, Beneath the Frozen World; The Undersea World of Jacques Cousteau (ABC)
LYN MURRAY, Struggle For Survival; Primal Man (ABC)
BILLY GOLDENBERG, Journey to the Outer Limits; National Geographic Society (ABC)

ART DIRECTION OR SCENIC DESIGN (E-1013)

For a series, a single program of a series or a special program
WILLIAM SUNSHINE, 60 Minutes; Series (CBS)
FRANK SKINNER, Soviet Prison Camps; NBC News Presents: Special Edition (NBC)
MERRILL SINDLER, The Cost of Living: Up, Up and Away; Today (NBC)

FILM EDITING - NEWS AND DOCUMENTARY PROGRAMMING (E-1014)

For a series, a single program of a series, a special program, program segments or elements within: A. Regularly scheduled News programs and coverage of Special Events

WILLIAM J. FREEDA, Profile of Poverty in Appalachia; NBC Nightly News (NBC)
PATRICK MINERVA, THOMAS E. DUNPHY, WILLIAM J. FREEDA, IR-

WIN GRAF, ALBERT J. HELIAS, GEORGE JOHNSON, MIGUEL POR-TILLO, MARTIN SHEPPARD, JEAN VENABLE, EDWIN EINARSEN, CONSTANTINE S. GOCHIS, LOFTUS McDONOUGH, DESMOND McEL-ROY, ROBERT MOLE, RUSSELL MOORE, LOREN BERRY, TINA GRUETTNER, NICK WILKINS, GERRY BREESE, K TU-HUEI SU, MI-CHAEL SHUGRUE, and NINA JACKSON; NBC Nightly News (NBC)
GILBERT LeVEQUE, SLA Shootout; CBS Evening News with Dan Rather (CBS)

B. Documentary, Magazine-type or Mini-documentary programs

ANN CHEGWIDDEN, The Baboons of Gombe; Jane Goodall and The World of Animal Behavior (ABC)
DAVID H. NEWHOUSE, Journey to the Outer Limits National Geographic Society (ABC)
JOHN SOH, Beneath the Frozen World; The Undersea World of Jacques Cousteau (ABC)

FILM OR TAPE SOUND MIXING (E-1015)

For a series, a single program of a series or a special program

PETER PILAFIAN, GEORGE E. PORTER, EDDIE J. NELSON, and ROB-ERT L. HARMAN; Journey to the Outer Limits; National Geographic Society (ABC)
ROBERT L. HARMAN, GEORGE E. PORTER, EDDIE J. NELSON, and GUY JOUAS; The Flight of the Penguins; The Undersea World of Jacques Cousteau (ABC)
GEORGE E. PORTER, EDDIE J. NELSON, and ROY GRANVILLE; South to Fire and Ice; The Undersea World of Jaques Cousteau (ABC)
ROBERT L. HARMAN, GEORGE E. PORTER, and EDDIE J. NELSON; The Baboons of Gombe; Jane Goodall and The World of Animal Behavior (ABC)

FILM SOUND EDITING (E-1016)

For a series, a single program of a series or a special program

CHARLES L. CAMPBELL , ROBERT CORNETT, LARRY CAROW, LARRY KAUFMAN, COLIN MOUAT, DON WARNER, and FRANK R. WHITE, The Baboons of Gombe; Jane Goodall and The World of Animal Behavior (ABC)
STEPHEN E. PRICE, Bigger is Better; 60 Minutes (CBS)
CHARLES L. CAMPBELL, COLIN MOUAT, JERRY R. STANFORD, and LARRY CAROW; The Flight of the Penguins; The Undersea World of Jacques Cousteau (ABC)

VIDEO TAPE EDITING (E-1017)

For a series, a single program of a series or a special program

GARY ANDERSON, Paramount Presents. . .ABC Wide World of Entertainment (ABC)
GEORGE KIYAK, ROBERT BAILEY, LLOYD CAMPBELL, JOSEPH D. COLVIN, DON DUNN, BUDDY FLECK, VINCENT GABRIELE, RICHARD LEIBLE, RALPH MARTUCCI, ARTHUR SCHWEIGER, MORTON SMITH, JERRY VALDIVIA, and RICHARD WEDEKING; Watergate: This Week; NBC News Special (NBC)
JACK STANLEY, and ERNEST ALLEN TOBIN, Watergate Hearings; CBS Evening News with Walter Cronkite (CBS)

TECHNICAL DIRECTION AND ELECTRONIC CAMERAWORK (E-1018)

For a series, a single program of a series or a special program

CARL SCHUTZMAN, Technical Director; JOSEPH SCHWARTZ, and WILLIAM BELL, Cameramen; 60 Minutes (CBS)
DAVID FEE, Technical Director; STUART GOODMAN, RICHARD KERR, EUGENE WOOD, and PHIL FONTANA, Cameramen; Geraldo Rivera: Goodnight America; ABC Wide World of Entertainment (ABC)
MARTIN SOLOMON, Technical Director; HARRY HAIGOOD, DAVID DORSETT, and CASS GAYLORD, Cameramen; CBS Evening News with Walter Cronkie (CBS)

1974/75

ENTERTAINMENT PROGRAM AND INDIVIDUAL ACHIEVEMENTS

COMEDY SERIES (E-1019)

Emmy(s) to Executive Producer(s) and/or Producer(s)

THE MARY TYLER MOORE SHOW, James L. Brooks and Allan Burns, Executive Producers; Ed Weinberger and Stan Daniels, Producers (CBS)
M*A*S*H, Gene Reynolds and Larry Gelbart, Producers (CBS)
ALL IN THE FAMILY, Don Nicholl, Executive Producer; Michael Ross and Bernie West, Producers (CBS)
RHODA, James L. Brooks and Allan Burns, Executive Producers; David Davis and Lorenzo Music, Producers (CBS)

DRAMA SERIES (E-1020)

Emmy(s) to Executive Producer(s) and/or Producer(s)

UPSTAIRS, DOWNSTAIRS, Masterpiece Theatre; Rex Firkin, Executive Producer; John Hawkesworth, Producer (PBS)
THE STREETS OF SAN FRANCISCO, Quinn Martin, Executive Producer; John Wilder and William Robert Yates, Producers (ABC)
POLICE STORY, Stanley Kallis and David Gerber, Executive Producers; Chris Morgan, Producer (NBC)
THE WALTONS, Lee Rich, Executive Producer; Robert L. Jacks, Producer (CBS)
KOJAK, Matthew Rapf, Executive Producer; Jack Laird and James McAdams, Producers (CBS)

COMEDY-VARIETY OR MUSIC SERIES (E-1021)

Emmy(s) to Executive Producer(s) and/or Producer(s) and Star(s), if applicable

THE CAROL BURNETT SHOW, Joe Hamilton, Executive Producer; Ed Simmons, Producer; Carol Burnett, Star (CBS)
CHER, George Schlatter, Producer; Cher, Star (CBS)

LIMITED SERIES (E-1022)

Emmy(s) to Executive Producer(s) and/or Producer(s)

BENJAMIN FRANKLIN, Lewis Freedman, Executive Producer; George Lefferts and Glenn Jordan, Producers (CBS)
McCLOUD, NBC Sunday Mystery Movie; Glen A Larson, Executive Producer; Michael Gleason and Ronald Satlof, Producers (NBC)
COLUMBO, NBC Sunday Mystery Movie; Roland Kibbee and Dean Hargrove, Executive Producers; Everett Chambers and Edward K. Dodds, Producers (NBC)

SPECIAL - DRAMA OR COMEDY (E-1023)

Emmy(s) to Executive Producer(s) and/or Producer(s)

THE LAW, NBC World Premiere Movie; William Sackheim, Producer (NBC)
THE MISSILES OF OCTOBER, ABC Theatre; Irv Wilson, Executive Producer; Herbert Brodkin and Buzz Berger, Producers (ABC)
QUEEN OF THE STARDUST BALLROOM, Robert W. Christiansen and Rick Rosenberg, Producers (CBS)
LOVE AMONG THE RUINS, ABC Theatre; Allan Davis, Producer (ABC)
QB VII, Parts 1 & 2; ABC Movie Special; Douglas S. Cramer, Producer (ABC)

SPECIAL - COMEDY-VARIETY OR MUSIC (E-1024)

Emmy(s) to Executive Producer(s) and/or Producer(s) and Star(s) if applicable

AN EVENING WITH JOHN DENVER, Jerry Weintraub, Executive Producer; Al Rogers and Rich Eustis, Producers; John Denver, Star (ABC)
LILY, Irene Pinn, Executive Producer; Jane Wagner and Lorne Michaels, Producers; Lily Tomlin, Star (ABC)

SHIRLEY MacLAINE: IF THEY COULD SEE ME NOW, Bob Wells, Producer; Shirley MacLaine, Star (CBS)

CLASSICAL MUSIC PROGRAM (E-1025)
For a special program or for a series Emmy(s) to Executive Producer(s) and/or Producer(s) and Star(s), if applicable

PROFILE IN MUSIC: BEVERLY SILLS, Festival '75; Patricia Foy, Producer; Beverly Sills, Star (PBS)
RUBINSTEIN, Great Performances; Fritz Buttenstedt, Executive Producer; Helmut Bauer and David Griffiths, Producers; Artur Rubinstein, Star (PBS)
BERNSTEIN AT TANGLEWOOD, Great Performances; Klaus Hallig and Harry Kraut, Executive Producers; David Griffiths, Producer; Leonard Bernstein, Star (PBS)
EVENING AT POPS, William Cosel, Producer; Arthur Fiedler, Star; Series (PBS)

ACTOR - COMEDY SERIES (E-1026)
TONY RANDALL, The Odd Couple (ABC)
ALAN ALDA, M*A*S*H (CBS)
JACK ALBERTSON, Chico And The Man (NBC)
JACK KLUGMAN, The Odd Couple (ABC)
CARROLL O'CONNOR, All In The Family (CBS)

ACTOR - DRAMA SERIES (E-1027)
ROBERT BLAKE, Baretta (ABC)
KARL MALDEN, The Streets of San Francisco (ABC)
BARRY NEWMAN, Petrocelli (NBC)
TELLY SAVALAS, Kojak (CBS)

ACTOR - LIMITED SERIES (E-1028)
PETER FALK, Columbo; NBC Sunday Mystery Movie (NBC)
DENNIS WEAVER, McCloud; NBC Sunday Mystery Movie (NBC)

ACTOR - DRAMA OR COMEDY SPECIAL (E-1029)
For a special program; or a single appearance in a Drama or Comedy Series
LAURENCE OLIVIER, Love Among The Ruins; ABC Theatre (ABC)
RICHARD CHAMBERLAIN, The Count Of Monte Cristo; Bell System Family Theatre (NBC)
WILLIAM DEVANE, The Missiles Of October; ABC Theatre (ABC)
CHARLES DURNING, Queen Of The Stardust Ballroom (CBS)
HENRY FONDA, IBM Presents Clarence Darrow (NBC)

ACTRESS - COMEDY SERIES (E-1030)
VALERIE HARPER, Rhoda (CBS)
MARY TYLER MOORE, The Mary Tyler Moore Show (CBS)
JEAN STAPLETON, All In The Family (CBS)

ACTRESS - DRAMA SERIES (E-1031)
JEAN MARSH, Upstairs, Downstairs; Masterpiece Theatre (PBS)
ANGIE DICKINSON, Police Woman (NBC)
MICHAEL LEARNED, The Waltons (CBS)

ACTRESS - LIMITED SERIES (E-1032)
JESSICA WALTER, Amy Prentiss; NBC Sunday Mystery Movie (NBC)
SUSAN SAINT JAMES, McMillan & Wife; NBC Sunday Mystery Movie (NBC)

ACTRESS - DRAMA OR COMEDY SPECIAL (E-1033)
For a special program; or a single appearance in a Drama or Comedy Series

KATHARINE HEPBURN, Love Among The Ruins; ABC Theatre (ABC)

JILL CLAYBURGH, Hustling; Special World Premiere ABC Saturday Night Movie (ABC)
ELIZABETH MONTGOMERY, The Legend of Lizzie Borden; Special World Premiere ABC Monday Night Movie (ABC)
DIANA RIGG, In This House Of Brede; GE Theater (CBS)
MAUREEN STAPLETON, Queen of the Stardust Ballroom (CBS)

SUPPORTING ACTOR - COMEDY SERIES (E-1034)
For a regular or limited series
ED ASNER, The Mary Tyler Moore Show (CBS)
ROB REINER, All In The Family (CBS)
TED KNIGHT, The Mary Tyler Moore Show (CBS)
GARY BURGHOFF, M*A*S*H (CBS)
McLEAN STEVENSON, M*A*SH (CBS)

SUPPORTING ACTOR - DRAMA SERIES (E-1035)
For a regular or limited series
WILL GEER, The Waltons (CBS)
MICHAEL DOUGLAS, The Streets Of San Francisco (ABC)
J.D. CANNON, McCloud; NBC Sunday Mystery Movie (NBC)

SUPPORTING ACTOR - CONTINUING OR SINGLE PERFORMANCE - VARIETY OR MUSIC (E-1036)
For a continuing role in a regular or limited series; or a one-time appearance in a series; or a special
JACK ALBERTSON, Cher (CBS)
TIM CONWAY, The Carol Burnett Show (CBS)
JOHN DENVER, Doris Day Today (CBS)

SUPPORTING ACTOR - SINGLE PERFORMANCE - COMEDY OR DRAMA SPECIAL (E-1037)
ANTHONY QUAYLE, QB VII, Parts 1 & 2; ABC Movie Special (ABC)
RALPH BELLAMY, The Missiles Of October; ABC Theatre (ABC)
TREVOR HOWARD, The Count of Monte Cristo; Bell System Family Theatre (NBC)
JACK HAWKINS, QB VII, Parts 1 & 2; ABC Movie Special (ABC)

SUPPORTING ACTOR - SINGLE PERFORMANCE - COMEDY OR DRAMA SERIES (E-1038)
For a one-time appearance in a regular or limited series
PATRICK McGOOHAN, By Dawn's Early Light; Columbo; NBC Sunday Mystery Movies (NBC)
LEW AYRES, The Vanishing Image; Kung Fu (ABC)
HAROLD GOULD, Fathers And Sons; Police Story (NBC)
HARRY MORGAN, The General Flipped At Dawn; M*A*S*H (CBS)

SUPPORTING ACTRESS - COMEDY SERIES (E-1039)
For a regular or limited series
BETTY WHITE, The Mary Tyler Moore Show (CBS)
JULIE KAVNER, Rhoda (CBS)
NANCY WALKER, Rhoda (CBS)
LORETTA SWIT, M*A*S*H (CBS)

SUPPORTING ACTRESS - DRAMA SERIES (E-1040)
For a regular or limited series
ELLEN CORBY, The Waltons (CBS)
NANCY WALKER, McMillan & Wife; NBC Sunday Mystery Movie (NBC)
ANGELA BADDELEY, Upstairs, Downstairs; Masterpiece Theatre (PBS)

SUPPORTING ACTRESS - CONTINUING OR SINGLE PERFORMANCE - VARIETY OR MUSIC (E-1041)

For a continuing role in a regular or limited series; or a one-time appearance in a series; or a special

CLORIS LEACHMAN, Cher (CBS)
RITA MORENO, Out To Lunch (ABC)
VICKI LAWRENCE, The Carol Burnett Show (CBS)

SUPPORTING ACTRESS - SINGLE PERFORMANCE - COMEDY OR DRAMA SPECIAL (E-1042)

JULIET MILLS, QB VII, Parts 1 & 2; ABC Movie Special (ABC)
CHARLOTTE RAE, Queen of The Stardust Ballroom (CBS)
LEE REMICK, QB VII, Parts 1 & 2; ABC Movie Special (ABC)
EILEEN HECKART, Wedding Band; ABC Theatre (ABC)

SUPPORTING ACTRESS - SINGLE PERFORMANCE - COMEDY OR DRAMA SERIES (E-1043)

For a one-time appearance in a regular or limited series

CLORIS LEACHMAN, Phyllis Whips Inflation; The Mary Tyler Moore Show (CBS)
ZOHRA LAMPERT, Queen Of The Gypsies; Kojak (CBS)
SHELLEY WINTERS, The Barefoot Girls Of Bleecker Street; McCloud; NBC Sunday Mystery Movie (NBC)

DIRECTOR - DRAMA SERIES (E-1044)

A single episode of a regular or limited series with continuing characters and/or theme

BILL BAIN, A Sudden Storm; Uptairs, Downstairs; Masterpiece Theatre (PBS)
HARRY FALK, The Mask Of Death; The Streets of San Francisco (ABC)
DAVID FRIEDKIN, Cross Your Heart And Hope to Die; Kojak (CBS)
TELLY SAVALAS, I Want To Report A Dream. . .; Kojak (CBS)
GLENN JORDAN, The Ambassador; Benjamin Franklin (CBS)

DIRECTOR - COMEDY SERIES (E-1045)

A single episode of a regular or limited series with continuing characters and/or theme

GENE REYNOLDS, O.R.; M*A*S*H (CBS)
HY AVERBACK, Alcoholics Unanimous; M*A*S*H (CBS)
ALAN ALDA, Bulletin Board; M*A*S*H (CBS)

DIRECTOR - COMEDY-VARIETY OR MUSIC SERIES (E-1046)

A single episode of a regular or limited series

DAVE POWERS, The Carol Burnett Show (with Alan Alda) (CBS)
ART FISHER, Cher (with Bette Midler, Flip Wilson and Elton John) (CBS)

DIRECTOR - COMEDY-VARIETY OR MUSIC SPECIAL (E-1047)

BILL DAVIS, An Evening With John Denver (ABC)
ROBERT SCHEERER, Shirley MacLaine: If They Could See Me Now (CBS)
DWIGHT HEMION, Ann-Margret Olsson (NBC)

DIRECTOR - SPECIAL PROGRAM - DRAMA OR COMEDY (E-1048)

GEORGE CUKOR, Love Among The Ruins; ABC Theatre (ABC)
JOHN BADHAM, The Law; NBC World Premiere Movie (NBC)
SAM O'STEEN, Queen of The Stardust Ballroom (CBS)
TOM GRIES, QB VII, Parts 1 & 2; ABC Movie Special (ABC)
ANTHONY PAGE, The Missiles Of October; ABC Theatre (ABC)

WRITING - DRAMA SERIES (E-1049)

A single episode of a regular or limited series with continuing characters and/or theme

HOWARD FAST, The Ambassador; Benjamin Franklin (CBS)
ROBERT COLLINS, Robbery: 48 Hours; Police Story (NBC)
ALFRED SHAUGHNESSY, Miss Forrest; Upstairs, Downstairs; Masterpiece Theatre (PBS)
LORING MANDEL, The Whirlwind; Benjamin Franklin (CBS)
JOHN HAWKESWORTH, The Bolter; Upstairs, Downstairs; Masterpiece Theatre (PBS)

WRITING - COMEDY SERIES (E-1050)

A single episode of a regular or limited series with continuing characters and/or theme

ED WEINBERGER and STAN DANIELS, Mary Richards Goes To Jail; The Mary Tyler Moore Show (CBS)
DAVID LLOYD, Lou And That Woman; The Mary Tyler Moore Show (CBS)
NORMAN BARASCH, CARROLL MOORE, DAVID LLOYD, LORENZO MUSIC, ALLAN BURNS, JAMES L. BROOKS and DAVID DAVIS, Rhoda's Wedding; Rhoda (CBS)

WRITING - COMEDY-VARIETY OR MUSIC SERIES (E-1051)

A single episode of a regular or limited series

ED SIMMONS, GARY BELKIN, ROGER BEATTY, ARNIE KOGEN, BILL RICHMOND, GENE PERRET, RUDY DeLUCA, BARRY LEVINSON, DICK CLAIR and JENNA McMAHON, The Carol Burnett Show (with Alan Alda) (CBS)
DIGBY WOLFE, DON REO, ALAN KATZ, IRIS RAINER, DAVID PANICH, RON PEARLMAN, NICK ARNOLD, JOHN BONI, RAY TAYLOR and GEORGE SCHLATTER, Cher (with Raquel Welch, Tatum O'Neal and Wayne Rogers) (CBS)

WRITING - COMEDY-VARIETY OR MUSIC SPECIAL (E-1052)

BOB WELLS, JOHN BRADFORD and CY COLEMAN, Shirley MacLaine: If They Could See Me Now (CBS)
SYBIL ADELMAN, BARBARA GALLAGHER, GLORIA BANTA, PAT NARDO, STUART BIRNBAUM, MATT NEUMAN, LORNE MICHAELS, MARILYN MILLER, EARL POMERANTZ, ROSIE RUTHCHILD, LILY TOMLIN and JANE WAGNER, Lily (ABC)

WRITING, SPECIAL PROGRAM - DRAMA OR COMEDY - ORIGINAL TELEPLAY (E-1053)

JAMES COSTIGAN, Love Among The Ruins; ABC Theatre (ABC)
JEROME KASS, Queen Of The Stardust Ballroom (CBS)
STANLEY R. GREENBERG, The Missiles Of October; ABC Theatre (ABC)
FAY KANIN, Hustling; Special World Premiere ABC Saturday Night Movie (ABC)
JOEL OLIANSKY, Story by William Sackheim and Joel Oliansky; The Law; NBC World Premiere Movie (NBC)

WRITING, SPECIAL PROGRAM - DRAMA OR COMEDY - ADAPTATION (E-1054)

DAVID W. RINTELS, IBM Presents Clarence Darrow (NBC)
EDWARD ANHALT, QB VII, Parts 1 & 2; ABC Movie Special (ABC)

CHOREOGRAPHY (E-1055)

For a single episode of a series or a special program

MARGE CHAMPION, Queen Of The Stardust Ballroom (CBS)
ALAN JOHNSON, Shirley MacLaine: If They Could See Me Now (CBS)
DEE DEE WOOD, Cher (with Freddie Prinze and The Pointer Sisters) (CBS)

MUSIC COMPOSITION - SERIES (E-1056)

Dramatic Underscore For a single episode of a regular or limited series

BILLY GOLDENBERG, The Rebel; Benjamin Franklin (CBS)
PAT WILIAMS, One Last Shot; The Streets Of San Francisco (ABC)

MUSIC COMPOSITION - SPECIAL (E-1057)

Dramatic Underscore

JERRY GOLDSMITH, QB VII, Parts 1 & 2; ABC Movie Special (ABC)
BILLY GOLDENBERG, ALAN and MARILYN BERGMAN; Queen Cf The Stardust Ballroom (CBS)

ART DIRECTION OR SCENIC DESIGN - COMEDY, DRAMA OR LIMITED SERIES (E-1058)

CHARLES LISANBY, Art Director; ROBERT CHECCHI, Set Decorator; The Ambassador; Benjamin Franklin (CBS)
MICHAEL BAUGH, Art Director; JERRY ADAMS, Set Decorator; Playback; Columbo; NBC Sunday Mystery Movie (NBC)

ART DIRECTION OR SCENIC DESIGN - COMEDY-VARIETY OR MUSIC (E-1059)

For a single episode of a comedy-variety or music series; or a comedy-variety or music special

ROBERT KELLY, Art Director; ROBERT CHECCHI, Set Decorator; Cher (with Bette Midler, Flip Wilson and Elton John) (CBS)
KEN JOHNSON and DWIGHT JACKSON, Art Directors; An Evening With John Denver (ABC)

ART DIRECTION OR SCENIC DESIGN - DRAMA SPECIAL OR FILM (E-1060)

For a dramatic special or a feature length film made for television

CARMEN DILLON, Art Director; TESSA DAVIES, Set Decorator; Love Among The Ruins; ABC Theatre (ABC)
JACK DeSHEILDS, Art Director; HARRY GORDON, Set Decorator; The Legend Of Lizzie Borden; Special World Premiere; ABC Monday Night Movie (ABC)
ROSS BELLAH and MAURICE FOWLER, Art Directors; AUDREY BLESDEL-GODDARD and TERRY PARR, Set Decorators; QB VII, Parts 1 & 2; ABC Movie Special (ABC)

GRAPHIC DESIGN AND TITLE SEQUENCES (E-1061)

For a single episode of a series; or for a special program. This includes animation only when created for use in titling

PHILL NORMAN, QB VII, Parts 1 & 2; ABC Movie Special (ABC)
RICK ANDREOLI, The Tonight Show Starring Johnny Carson (NBC)
SUSAN CUSCUNA, The Tonight Show Starring Johnny Carson (NBC)

CINEMATOGRAPHY - ENTERTAINMENT SERIES (E-1062)

For a single episode of a regular or limited series

RICHARD C. GLOUNER, A.S.C., Playback; Columbo; NBC Sunday Mystery Movie (NBC)
WILLIAM JURGENSEN, Bombed; M*A*S*H (CBS)
VILIS LAPENIEKS, A.S.C. and SOL NEGRIN, A.S.C., Wall Street Gunslinger; Kojak (CBS)

CINEMATOGRAPHY, ENTERTAINMENT SPECIAL (E-1063)

For a special or feature length program made for television

DAVID M. WALSH, Queen Of the Stardust Ballroom (CBS)
HOWARD SCHWARTZ, A.S.C., Sad Figure, Laughing; Sandburg's Lincoln (NBC)
PAUL BEESON and ROBERT L. MORRISON, QB VII, Parts 1 & 2; ABC Movie Special (ABC)
MICHAEL CHAPMAN, Death Be Not Proud; Tuesday Movie of the Week (ABC)

FILM EDITING - ENTERTAINMENT SERIES (COMEDY) (E-1064)

For a single episode of a comedy series

DOUGLAS HINES, An Affair To Forget; The Mary Tyler Moore Show (CBS)
STANFORD TISCHLER and FRED W. BERGER, The General Flipped At Dawn; M*A*S*H (CBS)

FILM EDITING - ENTERTAINMENT SERIES (DRAMA) (E-1065)

For a single episode of a drama series

DONALD R. RODE, Mirror, Mirror On The Wall; Petrocelli (NBC)
RAY DANIELS, Cry Help!; The Streets Of San Francisco (ABC)
JERRY YOUNG, The Mask Of Death; The Streets Of San Francisco (ABC)

FILM EDITING - ENTERTAINMENT SPECIAL (E-1066)

For a special or film made for television

JOHN A. MARTINELLI, A.C.E., The Legend Of Lizzie Borden; Special World Premiere; ABC MMonday Night Movie (ABC)
BYRON "BUZZ" BRANDT and IRVING C. ROSENBLUM, QB VII, Parts 1 & 2; ABC Movie Special (ABC)
JERRY YOUNG, Attack on Terror: The FBI Versus The Ku Klux Klan, Parts 1 & 2 (CBS)

FILM SOUND EDITING (E-1067)

For a single episode of a regular or limited series; or for a special program

MARVIN I. KOSBERG, RICHARD BURROW, MILTON C. BURROW, JACK MILNER, RONALD ASHCROFT, JAMES BALLAS, JOSEF VON STROHEIM, JERRY ROSENTHAL, WILLIAM ANDREWS, EDWARD SANDLIN, DAVID HORTON, ALVIN KAJITA, TONY GARBER and JEREMY HOENACK, QB VII, Parts 1 & 2; ABC Movie Special (ABC)
DONALD ISAACS, DON HIGGINS, LARRY KAUFMAN, JACK KIRSCHNER, DICK LeGRAND, GARY VAUGHAN, GENE WAHRMAN, FRANK WHITE, and HAROLD WOOLEY, The Legend Of Lizzie Borden; Special World Premiere; ABC Monday Night Movie (ABC)

FILM OR TAPE SOUND MIXING (E-1068)

For a single episode of a regular or limited series; or for a special program

MARSHALL KING, The American Film Institute Salute To James Cagney (CBS)
DOUG NELSON, The Missiles Of October; ABC Theatre (ABC)
DOUG NELSON and NORM SCHWARTZ, California Jam; Wide World In Concert (ABC)

VIDEO TAPE EDITING (E-1069)

For a single episode of a regular or limited series; or for a special program

GARY ANDERSON and JIM McELROY, Judgement: The Court-Martial Of Lt. William Calley; ABC Theatre (ABC)
NICK V. GIORDANO and GEORGE GURUNIAN, California Jam; Wide World in Concert (ABC)
JERRY GREENE, The Missiles Of October; ABC Theatre (ABC)

TECHNICAL DIRECTION AND ELECTRONIC CAMERAWORK (E-1070)

For a single episode of a regular or limited series; or for a special program

ERNIE BUTTELMAN, Technical Director; JIM ANGEL, JIM BALDEN, RON BROOKS and ART LaCOMBE, Cameramen; The Missiles Of October; ABC Theatre (ABC)
HEINO RIPP, Technical Director; JON OLSON, BOB KEYS, JOHN JAMES and KURT TONNESSEN, Cameramen; IBM Presents Clarence Darrow (NBC)
HEINO RIPP and LOU FUSARI, Technical Directors; ROY HOLM, TONY YARLETT, RICK LOMBARDO, BOB KEYS and RAY FIGELSKI, Cameramen; The Perry Como Christmas Show (CBS)

LIGHTING DIRECTION (E-1071)

For a single episode of a regular or limited series, or for a special program

JOHN FRESCHI, The Perry Como Christmas Show (CBS)
LON STUCKY, IBM Presents Clarence Darrow (NBC)

CHILDREN'S SPECIAL (E-1072)

For specials which were broadcast during the evening Emmy(s) to Executive Producer(s) and Producer(s)

YES, VIRGINIA, THERE IS A SANTA CLAUS, Burt Rosen, Executive Producer; Bill Melendez and Mort Green, Producers (ABC)
BE MY VALENTINE, CHARLIE BROWN, Lee Mendelson, Executive Producer; Bill Melendez, Producer (CBS)
DR. SEUSS' THE HOOBER-BLOOB HIGHWAY, David H. DePatie, Executive Producer; Friz Freleng and Ted Geisel, Producers (CBS)
IT'S THE EASTER BEAGLE, CHARLIE BROWN, Lee Mendelson, Executive Producer; Bill Melendez, Producer (CBS)

SPORTS EVENT (E-1073)

For a non-edited program (for a program which, when broadcast, was not edited)

JIMMY CONNORS VS. ROD LAVER TENNIS CHALLENGE, Frank Chirkinian, Executive Producer (CBS)
NFL MONDAY NIGHT FOOTBALL, Roone Arledge, Executive Producer; Don Ohlmeyer, Producer (ABC)
NCAA FOOTBALL, Roone Arledge, Executive Producer; Chuck Howard, Producer (ABC)
ABC CHAMPIONSHIP GOLF, Roone Arledge, Executive Producer; Chuck Howard, Producer (ABC)
NBA CHAMPIONSHIP GAME, Chuck Milton, Producer (CBS)
NATIONAL FOOTBALL LEAGUE GAME - WASHINGTON VS. DALLAS, Chuck Milton and Tom O'Neill, Producers (CBS)
JACKIE GLEASON INVERRARY CLASSIC, John Koushouris, Executive Producer; Joe O'Rourke and Herb Kaplan, Producers (HTN)
ANDY WILLIAMS SAN DIEGO OPEN, John Koushouris, Producer (HTN)

MADISON SQUARE GARDEN EVENTS, Jack Simon, Producer (HTN)
1974 WORLD SERIES, Scotty Connal, Executive Producer; Roy Hammerman, Producer (NBC)
NBC MONDAY NIGHT BASEBALL, Scotty Connal, Executive Producer; Roy Hammerman, Producer (NBC)
AFC FOOTBALL PLAYOFFS, Scotty Connal, Executive Producer; Don Ellis and Ted Nathanson, Producers (NBC)
SPALDING INTERNATIONAL MIXED DOUBLES TENNIS CHAMPIONSHIP, Ron Devillier, Executive Producer; Renate Cole, Producer (PBS)
NATIONAL BICYCLE TRACK CHAMPIONSHIPS, Alf Steele, Executive Producer (PBS)
ATP SUMMER TENNIS TOUR, Greg Harney, Executive Producer (PBS)
WORLD FOOTBALL LEAGUE CHAMPIONSHIP, Edward Einhorn, Executive Producer; Joe Gallagher, Producer (TVS)
UCLA-NOTRE DAME BASKETBALL, Edward Einhorn, Executive Producer; Howard Zuckerman, Producer (TVS)
NCAA BASKETBALL, Edward Einhorn, Executive Producer; Howard Zuckerman, Producer (TVS)

SPORTS PROGRAM (E-1074)

For an edited program (for a program which, when broadcast, contained edited segments)

WIDE WORLD OF SPORTS, Roone Arledge, Executive Producer; Doug Wilson, Ned Steckel, Dennis Lewin, John Martin and Chet Forte, Producers (ABC)
THE SUPERSTARS, Roone Arledge, Executive Producer; Don Ohlmeyer, Producer (ABC)
THE AMERICAN SPORTSMAN, Roone Arledge, Executive Producer; Neil Cunningham, Pat Smith, Curt Gowdy, Bob Duncan, Neil Goodwin, Producers (ABC)
CBS SPORTS SPECTACULAR, Frank Chirkinian, Executive Producer; Perry Smith, Producer (CBS)
NFL ON CBS, William Fitts, Executive Producer; Tom O'Neill, Producer (CBS)
NBA ON CBS, Perry Smith and Chuck Milton, Producers (CBS)
THE BASEBALL WORLD OF JOE GARAGIOLA, Gates Brown-Parts 1 & 2; Joe Garagiola, Executive Producer; Don Ellis, Producer (NBC)
THE BASEBALL WORLD OF JOE GARAGIOLA, Old Ball Parks; Joe Garagiola, Executive Producer; Don Ellis, Producer (NBC)
SUPER BOWL IX PRE-GAME SHOW, Scotty Connal, Executive Producer; Dick Auerbach, Producer (NBC)
THE WAY IT WAS, Gerry Gross, Executive Producer (PBS)
VICTOR AWARDS, David Marmel, Executive Producer; Lou Rudolph, Producer (TVS)
USA-CHINA BASKETBALL HIGHLIGHTS, Edward Einhorn, Executive Producer; Howard Zuckerman, Producer (TVS)

SPORTS BROADCASTER (E-1075)

JIM McKAY, Wide World Of Sports (ABC)
HOWARD COSELL, Monday Night Football (ABC)
KEITH JACKSON, NCAA Football (ABC)
FRANK GIFFORD, Monday Night Football (ABC)
CHRIS SCHENKEL, ABC Championship Golf (ABC)
VIN SCULLY, Jimmy Connors Vs. Rod Laver Tennis Challenge (CBS)
PAT SUMMERALL, NFL Football (CBS)
BRENT MUSBURGER, NBA Basketball (CBS)
JACK WHITAKER, NBA All Star Game (CBS)
KEN SQUIER, CBS Sports Spectacular (CBS)
CURT GOWDY, AFC Football Playoffs (NBC)
DON MEREDITH, Super Bowl IX (NBC)
JOE GARAGIOLA, The Baseball World of Joe Garagiola; Gates Brown-Parts 1 & 2 (NBC)
JIM SIMPSON, Wimbledon Tennis (NBC)
TIM RYAN, 1974 Stanley Cup Playoffs (NBC)
BUDD COLLINS, Spalding International Mixed Doubles Tennis Championship (PBS)
JUDY DIXON, Spalding International Mixed Doubles Tennis Championship (PBS)
CURT GOWDY, The Way It Was (PBS)

THE AREAS
(Possibility of One Award, More Than One Award, or No Award)

SPECIAL CLASSIFICATION OF OUTSTANDING PROGRAM AND INDIVIDUAL ACHIEVEMENT (E-1076)
An Award for unique program and individual achievements, which does not fall into a specific category, or is not otherwise recognized

THE AMERICAN FILM INSTITUTE SALUTE TO JAMES CAGNEY, George Stevens, Jr., Executive Producer; Paul W Keyes, Producer (CBS)
THE AMERICAN FILM INSTITUTE SALUTE TO ORSON WELLS, George Stevens, Jr., Executive Producer; Paul W Keyes, Producer (CBS)
ALISTAIR COOKE, Host, Masterpiece Theatre (PBS)
THE DICK CAVETT SHOW, John Gilroy, Producer; Dick Cavett, Star (ABC)
THAT'S ENTERTAINMENT: 50 YEARS OF MGM, ABC Wide World of Entertainment, Jack Haley, Jr., Executive Producer; Jimmie Baker, Producer (ABC)
86TH ANNUAL PASADENA TOURNAMENT OF ROSES PARADE, Dick Schneider, Producer (NBC)
TOM SNYDER, Host, Tomorrow (NBC)
JACK STEWART, Art Director; JOHN HUENERS, Set Decorator; Bicentennial Minutes (CBS)

SPECIAL MUSICAL MATERIAL (E-1077)
For a song (which must have both music and lyrics), a theme for a series, or special material for a variety program providing the first usage of this material was written expressly for television

ALAN and MARILYN BERGMAN, and BILLY GOLDENBERG, Queen Of The Stardust Ballroom (CBS)
CY COLEMAN and BOB WELLS, Shirley MacLaine: If They Could See Me Now (CBS)
MORTON STEVENS, Police Woman; Theme (NBC)
EARL BROWN and BILLY BARNES, Cher (with Bette Midler, Flip Wilson and Elton John) (CBS)
JOSE FELICIANO and JANNA MERLYN FELICIANO; Chico and The Man; Theme (NBC)

COSTUME DESIGN (E-1078)
For a single episode of a series; or for a special program
GUY VERHILLE, The Legend of Lizzie Borden; Special World Premiere; ABC Monday Night Movie (ABC)
MARGARET FURSE, Love Among The Ruins; ABC Theatre (ABC)
BRUCE WALKUP, Queen Of The Stardust Ballroom (CBS)
BOB MACKIE, Cher (with Bette Midler, Flip Wilson and Elton John) (CBS)
RET TURNER, The Sonny Comedy Revue (with McLean Stevenson and Joey Heatherton) (ABC)

MAKE-UP (E-1079)
For a single episode of a series; or for a special program
HARRY BLAKE, STAN WINSTON, JIM KAIL, RALPH GULKO, BOB OSTERMANN, TOM COLE and LARRY ABBOTT; Masquerade Party (Synd)
MARK R. BUSSAN, The Ambassador; Benjamin Franklin (CBS)
DAN STRIEPEKE and JOHN CHAMBERS, Twigs (CBS)

ACHIEVEMENT IN ANY AREA OF CREATIVE TECHNICAL CRAFTS (E-1080)
An Award for individual technical craft achievement which does not fall into a specific category, and is not otherwise recognized

EDIE PANDA, Hairstylist; The Ambassador; Benjamin Franklin (CBS)
DOUG NELSON and NORM SCHWARTZ, Wide World In Concert; Double System Sound Editing and Synchronization For Stereophonic Broadcasting Of Television Programs; Series (ABC)
LARRY GERMAIN, Hairstylist; If I Should Wake Before I Die; Little House On The Prairie (NBC)

INDIVIDUAL ACHIEVEMENT IN SPORTS PROGRAMMING (E-1081)
For individuals who may be directors, writers, cinematographers, technical directors and electronic cameramen, sound mixers, film editors, video tape editors, lighting directors and graphic designers (for graphic design and title sequences)

GENE SCHWARZ, Technical Director; 1974 World Series (NBC)
HERB ALTMAN, Film Editor; The Baseball World Of Joe Garagiola (NBC)
COREY LEIBLE, LEN BASILE, JACK BENNETT, LOU GERARD and RAY FIGELSKI, Electronic Cameramen; 1974 Stanley Cup Playoffs (NBC)
JOHN PUMO, CHARLES D'ONOFRIO, FRANK FLORIO, Technical Directors; GEORGE KLIMCSAK, ROBERT KANIA, HAROLD HOFFMANN, HERMAN LANG, GEORGE DRAGO, WALT DENIEAR, STAN GOULD, AL DIAMOND, CHARLES ARMSTRONG, AL BRANTLEY, SIG MEYERS, FRANK McSPEDON, GEORGE F. NAEDER, JAMES MURPHY, JAMES McCARTHY, VERN SURPHLIS, AL LORETO, GORDON SWEENEY, JO SIDLO, WILLIAM HATHAWAY, GENE PESCALEK and CURLY FONOROW, Cameramen; Masters Tournament (CBS)
LARRY KAMM, LOU VOLPICELLI, BRICE WEISMAN, NED STECKEL, ANDY SIDARIS and CHET FORTE, Directors; WIDE WORLD OF SPORTS (ABC)
WERNER GUNTHER, JOHN BRODERICK and JOHN IRVINE, Technical Directors; ANDY ARMENTANI, DREW DeROSA, JIM HENEGHAN, JOHN MORREALE, JOE NESI, MIKE REBICH, JACK HIMELFARB, STEVE CILIBERTO, JESSE KOHN, JOE STEFANONI, STU GOODMAN, JOE SCHIAVO, BOB HAMMOND, ART PEFFER, DICK SPANOS, ART FERRARE, GENE WOOD, ROY HUTCHINGS, BILL KARVELAS, RONNIE STERCKX, JOE SAPIENZA, BOB WOLFE, JOHN CRONIN, CARL BROWN, ROBERT COPPER, DICK KERR, MORT LEVIN, BOB BERNSTEIN, JERRY DOUD and JACK DORFMAN, Cameramen; U.S. Open (ABC)
WILLIAM MORRIS and WERNER GUNTHER, Technical Directors; ANDY ARMENTANI, DREW DeROSA, JIM HENEGHAN, JOHN MORREALE, JOE NESI, MIKE REBICH, JACK HIMELFARB, STEVE CILIBERTO, JESSE KOHN, JOE STEFANONI, STU GOODMAN, JOE SCHIAVO, BILL SULLIVAN, STEVE NIKIFOR, JACK DORFMAN and BOB LOPES, Cameramen; Indianapolis 500 (ABC)
JOHN PETERSON and TONY ZACCARO, Film Editors; Wide World Of Sports (ABC)
JOHN CROAK, JOHN DeLISA, CHESTER PAWLAK, MARV GENCH, ALEX MOSKOVIC, JACK HIERL, TONY GRECO, ERSKINE ROBERTS, ART VOLK and HARVEY BEAL, Video Tape Editors; Wide World Of Sports (ABC)
JOHN CROAK, JOHN DeLISA, ART VOLK, RON ACKERMAN, MARV GENCH, ALEX MOSKOVIC and NICK MAZUR, Video Tape Editors; The Superstars (ABC)
PAT SMITH, Writer; The American Sportsman (ABC)
JACK SIMON, Director; New York Mets Baseball (HTN)
JOE O'ROURKE, Director; Professional Championship Golf (HTN)
HARRY COYLE, Director; 1974 World Series (NBC)
TED NATHANSON, Director; AFC Football Playoffs (NBC)
HOWARD NEEF and BARRY WINNIK, Cinematographers; The Baseball World Of Joe Garagiola; Gates Brown-Parts 1 & 2 (NBC)
MURRAY VECCHIO, BILL TOBEY, BILL ROSE, JOHN O'CONNOR, Videotape (Slow Motion) Editors; Orange Bowl (NBC)
SANDY BELL, FRANK VILOT, CHUCK FRANKLIN, JIM ANGERAMI and JOHN BURKHART, Technical Directors; DICK DOUGLAS, GEORGE KLIMCSAK, AL DIAMOND, FRANK McSPEDON, JOHN LINCOLN, PHIL

WALSH, STAN GOULD, MIKE ENGLISH, ROBERT HELLER, DAVID GRAHAM, WALT DENIEAR, ROBERT CHANDLER, HAROLD HOFFMAN, GENE SAVITT, DAVE LEVENSON, GEORGE ERICKSON, CURLY FONAROW, TOM McCONNELL, FRED DANSEREAU, BOB FAETH, GEORGE DRAGO, JIM MURPHY, GEORGE F. NAEDER, JO SOKOTA, PAT McBRIDE, AL LORETO, DAVE LEAVEL, JERRY WEAVER, BOB CHANEY, FRED SCHULTZ, TONY BUTTS, DANNY IRELAND, Cameramen; NBA Basketball (CBS)

ANGEL J. GULINO, BOB BROWN, ED DAHLBERG, DICK OHLDACKER, SAM LANE, TOM DUFFY and FRANK HICKS, Sound Mixers; NBA Basketball (CBS)

PETE REED, Sound Mixer; Jimmy Connors Vs. Rod Laver Tennis Challenge (CBS)

SANDY GROSSMAN, Director; NBA Basketball (CBS)

BOB DAILEY, Director; Jimmy Connors Vs. Rod Laver Tennis Challenge (CBS)

SPECIAL AWARDS

ENGINEERING DEVELOPMENT (E-1082)

COLUMBIA BROADCASTING SYSTEM for spearheading the development and realization of the Electronic News Gathering System
NIPPON ELECTRIC COMPANY for development of digital television Frame Synchronizers
Citation to THE SOCIETY OF MOTION PICTURE AND TELEVISION ENGINEERS for the technical development of the Unversal Video Tape Time Code

TRUSTEES AWARDS (E-1083)

ELMER LOWER, Vice President, Corporate Affairs, American Broadcastiing Companies, Inc.
DR. PETER GOLDMARK, President, Goldmark Laboratories, Stamford, Connecticut

THE NATIONAL AWARD FOR COMMUNITY SERVICE (E-1084)

THE WILLOWBROOK CASE: THE PEOPLE VS. THE STATE OF NEW YORK, WABC-TV, New York, New York
BREAST SURGERY: REBIRTH OR BETRAYAL, WXYZ-TV Detroit, Michigan
FOCUS 30, KYTV, Springfield, Missouri
GRANDPEOPLE, WPBT(Educational Station), No. Miami, Florida
THE OCCUPANT IN THE SINGLE ROOM, WNET (Educational Station), New York, New York
SENILITY, A STATE OF MIND, KSL, Salt Lake City, Utah
SMOKE AND STEEL, WKY-TV,Oklahoma City, Oklahoma
TROUBLE IN THE GHETTO, WAGA-TV, Atlanta, Georgia
WHY ME? KNXT, Los Angeles, California
WITHOUT FEAR, WKYC-TV, Cleveland, Ohio

1973/74 INTERNATIONAL FICTION AWARDS (E-1085)

MR AXELFORD'S ANGEL, Yorkshire Television Limited, Lonndon, England
DON JUAN, Television Espanola, Madrid, Spain
THE BENNY HILL SHOW, Thames Television Limited, London, England
SIX DAYS OF JUSTICE: THE COMPLAINT,Thames Televisin Limited, London, England
THE GOODIES AND THE BEANSTALK, British Broadcastig Corporation, London, England

1973/74 INTERNATIONAL NON-FICTION AWARDS (E-1086)

AQUARIUS: HELLO DALI!, London Weekend Television, London, England
CTV INQUIRY: KEEP OUT OF THE REACH OF ADULTS, CTV Television Network, Limited, Ontario, Canada

KATARAGAMA: A GOD FOR ALL SEASONS, Granada Television Limited, Manchester, Great Britain
ELLESMERE LAND, Canadian Broadcasting Corporation, Ontario, Canada
UNTAMED WORLD: THE GREY GOOSE, CTV Television Network, Limited, Ontario, Canada

THE 1973/74 INTERNATIONAL DIRECTORATE AWARD (E-1087)

DR. JOSEPH V. CHARYK, President Communications Satellite Corporation

1974/75 INTERNATIONAL FICTION AWARDS (E-1088)

COMETS AMONG THE STARS, ATV Network Limited, Hertfordshire, England
MAD IN AUSTRIA, ORF, Vienna, Austria
JENNIE: HIS BORROWED PLUMES, Thames Television Limited, London, England
MR. SING MY HEART'S DELIGHT, Radio Telefis Eireann, Dublin, Ireland
THE EVACUEES, British Broadcasting Corporation, London, England
DE VERRASSING, Nederlandse Omroep Stichting, The Netherlands

1974/75 INTERNATIONAL NON-FICTION AWARDS (E-1089)

TRAVELS THROUGH LIFE WITH LEACOCK, Canadian Broacasting Corporation, Ontario, Canada
AFTER 30 YEARS IN JUNGLE: HOMECOMING OF A JAPANESE SOLDIER, Fuji Telecasting Company, Limited, Tokyo, Japan
PILGER: MR. NIXON'S SECRET LEGACY, ATV Network Limited, Hertfordshire, England
INSIDE STORY: MAREK, British Broadcasting Corporation, London, England
THE SEARCH FOR THE SHINOHARA, Survival Anglia Limited, London, England

THE 1974/75 INTERNATIONAL DIRECTORATE AWARD (E-1090)

MR. JUNZO IMAMICHI, Chairman Of The Board Tokyo Broadcasting System, Inc

DAYTIME PROGRAM AND INDIVIDUAL ACHIEVEMENTS

(One Award Only in Each of the Following Categories)

DAYTIME DRAMA SERIES (E-1091)

Emmy(s) to Executive Producer(s) and/or Creator(s) and Producer(s)

THE YOUNG AND THE RESTLESS, John J. Conboy, Producer; William J. Bell and Lee Phillip Bell, Creators (CBS)
DAYS OF OUR LIVES, Mrs. Ted Corday, Executive Producer; Ted Corday, Irna Phillips and Allan Chase, Creators; Jack Herzberg, Producer (NBC)
ANOTHER WORLD, Paul Rauch, Executive Producer; Joe Rothenberger and Mary E. Bonner, Producers; Irna Phillips and William J. Bell, Creators (NBC)

DAYTIME DRAMA SPECIAL (E-1092)

Emmy(s) to Executive Producer(s) and Producer(s)

THE GIRL WHO COULDN'T LOSE, ABC Afternoon Playbreak; Ira Barmak, Executive Producer; Lila Garrett, Producer (ABC)
THE LAST RIDE OF SALEM, ABC Afternoon Playbreak; Robert Michael Lewis, Executive Producer; George Paris, Producer (ABC)

GAME OR AUDIENCE PARTICIPATION SHOW (E-1093)
Emmy(s) to Executive Producer(s) and Producer(s)

HOLLYWOOD SQUARES, Merrill Heatter and Bob Quigley, Executive Producers; Jay Redack, Producer (NBC)
THE $10,000 PYRAMID, Bob Stewart, Executive Producer; Anne Marie Schmitt, Producer (ABC)
JEOPARDY!, Robert H. Rubin, Executive Producer; Lynette Williams, Producer (NBC)
LET'S MAKE A DEAL, Stefan Hatos, Executive Producer; Alan Gilbert, Producer (ABC)

TALK, SERVICE OR VARIETY SERIES (E-1094)
Emmy(s) to Executive Producer(s) and Producer(s)

DINAH!, Henry Jaffe and Carolyn Raskin, Executive Producers; Fred Tatashore, Producer (Synd)
THE MIKE DOUGLAS SHOW, Jack Reilly, Executive Producer; Woody Fraser, Producer (Synd)
TODAY, Stuart Schulberg, Executive Producer; Douglas P. Sinsel and Gene Farinet, Producers (NBC)

CHILDREN'S ENTERTAINMENT SPECIAL (E-1095)
Emmy(s) to Executive Producer(s) and Producer(s)

HARLEQUIN, The CBS Festival Of Lively Arts For Young People; Edward Villella, Executive Poducer; Gardner Compton, Producer (CBS)
AILEY CELEBRATES ELLINGTON, The CBS Festival Of Lively Arts For Young People; Herman Krawitz, Executive Producer; Bob Weiner, Producer (CBS)
WHAT MAKES A GERSHWIN TUNE A GERSHWIN TUNE?, New York Philharmonic Young People's Concert; Roger Englander, Producer (CBS)

CHILDREN'S ENTERTAINMENT SERIES (E-1096)
Emmy(s) to Executive Producer(s) and Producer(s)

STAR TREK, Lou Scheimer and Norm Prescott, Producers (NBC)
CAPTAIN KANGAROO, Jimmy Hirshfeld, Producer (CBS)
THE PINK PANTHER, David H. DePatie and Friz Freleng, Producers (NBC)

ACTOR - DAYTIME DRAMA SERIES (E-1097)
MACDONALD CAREY, Days Of Our Lives (NBC)
JOHN BERADINO, General Hospital (ABC)
BILL HAYES, Days Of Our Lives (NBC)

ACTOR - DAYTIME DRAMA SPECIAL (E-1098)
BRADFORD DILLMAN, The Last Bride Of Salem; ABC Afternoon Playbreak (ABC)
JACK CARTER, The Girl Who Couldn't Lose; ABC Afternoon Playbreak (ABC)
BERT CONVY, Oh! Baby, Baby, Baby. . .; ABC Afternoon Playbreak (ABC)

ACTRESS - DAYTIME DRAMA SERIES (E-1099)
SUSAN FLANNERY, Days Of Our Lives (NBC)
RACHEL AMES, General Hospital (ABC)
SUSAN SEAFORTH, Days Of Our Lives (NBC)
RUTH WARRICK, All My Children (ABC)

ACTRESS - DAYTIME DRAMA SPECIAL (E-1100)
KAY LENZ, Heart In Hiding; ABC Afternoon Playbreak (ABC)
DIANE BAKER, Can I Save My Children?; ABC Afternoon Playbreak (ABC)
JULIE KAVNER, The Girl Who Couldn't Lose; ABC Afternoon Playbreak (ABC)

LOIS NETTLETON, The Last Bride Of Salem; ABC Afternoon Playbreak (ABC)

HOST - GAME OR AUDIENCE PARTICIPATION SHOW (E-1101)
PETER MARSHALL, The Hollywood Squares (NBC)
MONTY HALL, Let's Make A Deal (ABC)
GENE RAYBURN, Match Game '75 (CBS)

HOST OR HOSTESS - TALK, SERVICE OR VARIETY SERIES (E-1102)
BARBARA WALTERS, Today (NBC)
MIKE DOUGLAS, The Mike Douglas Show (Synd)
DINAH SHORE, Dinah! (Synd)
JIM HARTZ, Today (NBC)

DIRECTOR - DAYTIME DRAMA SERIES (E-1103)
For a single episode

RICHARD DUNLAP, The Young and The Restless (CBS)
IRA CIRKER, Another World (NBC)
JOSEPH BEHAR, Days Of Our Lives (NBC)

DIRECTOR - DAYTIME SPECIAL PROGRAM (E-1104)
MORT LACHMAN, The Girl Who Couldn't Lose; ABC Afternoon Playbreak (ABC)
WALTER C. MILLER, Can I Save My Children?; ABC Afternoon Playbreak (ABC)

DIRECTOR - GAME OR AUDIENCE PARTICIPATION SHOW (E-1105)
For a single episode

JEROME SHAW, The Hollywood Squares; October 28, 1974 (NBC)
JOSEPH BEHAR, Let's Make A Deal; March 6, 1975 (ABC)

DIRECTOR - DAYTIME VARIETY PROGRAM (E-1106)
For a single episode

GLEN SWANSON, Dinah!; Dinah Salutes Broadway (with Ethel Merman, Bobby Morse, Michelle Lee, Phil Silvers and Jack Cassidy) (Synd)
DICK CARSON, The Merv Griffin Show (with Robert Goulet, Louis Prima and Shecky Greene) (Synd)

WRITING - DAYTIME DRAMA SERIES (E-1107)
For a single episode of a series; or for the entire series

HARDING LEMAY, TOM KING, CHARLES KOZLOFF, JAN MERLIN and DOUGLAS MARLAND, Another World; Series (NBC)
WILLIAM J. BELL, The Young and The Restless; October 22, 1974 (CBS)
WILLIAM J. BELL, PAT FALKEN SMITH and BILL REGA; Days Of Our Lives; November 21, 1974 (NBC)

WRITING - DAYTIME SPECIAL PROGRAM (E-1108)
AUDREY DAVIS LEVIN, Heart In Hiding; ABC Afternoon Playbreak (ABC)
RUTH BROOKS FLIPPEN, Oh! Baby, Baby, Baby. . .; ABC Afternoon Playbreak (ABC)
LILA GARRETT and SANFORD KRINSKI, The Girl Who Couldn't Lose; ABC Afternoon Playbreak (ABC)

THE DAYTIME AREAS

(Possibility of One Award, More Than One Award, or No Award)

INDIVIDUAL ACHIEVEMENT - DAYTIME PROGRAMMING (E-1109)

For a single episode of a series or for a special program

PAUL LYNDE, Performer; The Hollywood Squares (NBC)
JAY REDACK, HARRY FRIEDMAN, GARY JOHNSON, HAROLD SCHNEIDER, RICK KELLARD and STEVE LEVITCH, Writers; The Hollywood Squares; November 22, 1974 (NBC)
STAS PYKA, Graphic Design and Title Sequence, How To Survive A Marriage (NBC)

INDIVIDUAL ACHIEVEMENT - CHILDREN'S PROGRAMMING (E-1110)

For a single episode of a series; or for a special program

ELINOR BUNIN, Graphic Design and Title Sequences; Funshine Saturday & Sunday; Umbrella Title Animations For Saturday & Sunday Morning Children's Programming (ABC)
BOB KEESHAN, Performer; Captain Kangaroo (CBS)
BILL COSBY, Performer; Highlights Of Ringling Bros. Barnum & Bailey Circus; Bell System Family Theatre; (NBC)
CHARLES M. SCHULZ, Writer; Be My Valentine, Charlie Brown (CBS)

1975/76

ENTERTAINMENT PROGRAM AND INDIVIDUAL ACHIEVEMENTS

(One Award Only In Each of the Following Categories)

COMEDY SERIES (E-1111)

Emmy(s) to Executive Producer(s) and/or Producer(s)

THE MARY TYLER MOORE SHOW; James L. Brooks and Allan Burns, Executive Producers; Ed Weinberger and Stan Daniels, Producers (CBS)
ALL IN THE FAMILY; Hal Kanter, Norman Lear and Woody Kling, Executive Producers; Lou Derman and Bill Davenport, Producers (CBS)
M*A*S*H; Gene Reynolds and Larry Gelbart, Producers (CBS)
WELCOME BACK KOTTER; James Komack, Executive Producer; Alan Sacks, George Yanok and Eric Cohen, Producers (ABC)
BARNEY MILLER; Danny Arnold, Executive Producer; Chris Hayward and Arne Sultan, Producers (ABC)

DRAMA SERIES (E-1112)

Emmy(s) to Executive Producer(s) and/or Producer(s)

POLICE STORY; David Gerber and Stanley Kallis, Executive Producers; Liam O'Brien and Carl Pingitore, Producers (NBC)
BARETTA; Bernard L. Kowalski, Executive Producer; Jo Swerling, Jr., Robert Harris, Howie Horwitz and Robert Lewin, Producers (ABC)
COLUMBO; NBC Sunday Mystery Movie; Everett Chambers, Producer (NBC)
THE STREETS OF SAN FRANCISCO; Quinn Martin, Executive Producer; William Robert Yates, Producer (ABC)

COMEDY-VARIETY OR MUSIC SERIES (E-1113)

Emmy(s) to Executive Producer(s) and/or Producer(s) and Star(s), if applicable

NBC'S SATURDAY NIGHT; Lorne Michaels, Producer (NBC)
THE CAROL BURNETT SHOW; Joe Hamilton, Executive Producer; Ed Simmons, Producer; Carol Burnett, Star (CBS)

LIMITED SERIES (E-1114)

Emmy(s) to Executive Producer(s) and/or Producer(s)

UPSTAIRS, DOWNSTAIRS; Masterpiece Theatre; Rex Firkin, Executive Producer; John Hawkesworth, Producer (PBS)
JENNIE: LADY RANDOLPH CHURCHILL; Great Performances; Stella Richman, Executive Producer; Andrew Brown, Producer (PBS)
RICH MAN, POOR MAN; Harve Bennett, Executive Producer; Jon Epstein, Producer (ABC)
THE ADAMS CHRONICLES; Jac Venza, Executive Producer; Virginia Kassel, Series Producer; Paul Bogart, Robert Costello, James Cellan Jones and Fred Coe, Producers (PBS)
THE LAW; William Sackheim, Producer (NBC)

SPECIAL - DRAMA OR COMEDY (E-1115)

Emmy(s) to Executive Producer(s) and/or Producer(s)

ELEANOR AND FRANKLIN; ABC Theatre; David Susskind, Executive Producer; Harry Sherman and Audrey Maas, Producers (ABC)
BABE; Norman Felton and Stanley Rubin, Producers (CBS)
A MOON FOR THE MISBEGOTTEN; ABC Theatre; David Susskind and Audrey Maas, Producers (ABC)
FEAR ON TRIAL; Alan Landsburg and Larry Savadove, Executive Producers; Stanley Chase, Producer (CBS)
THE LINDBERGH KIDNAPPING CASE; NBC World Premiere Movie; David Gerber, Executive Producer; Buzz Kulik, Producer (NBC)

SPECIAL - COMEDY-VARIETY OR MUSIC (E-1116)

Emmy(s) to Executive Producer(s) and/or Producer(s), and Star(s), if applicable

GYPSY IN MY SOUL; William O. Harbach, Executive Producers; Cy Coleman and Fred Ebb, Producers; Shirley MacLaine, Star (CBS)
THE MONTY PYTHON SHOW; Wide World: Special; Ian McNaughton, Producer (ABC)
JOHN DENVER ROCKY MOUNTAIN CHRISTMAS; Jerry Weintraub, Executive Producer; Al Rogers and Rich Eustis, Producers; John Denver, Star (ABC)
STEVE AND EYDIE: 'OUR LOVE IS HERE TO STAY'; Gary Smith, Executive Producer; Dwight Hemion, Producer; Steve Lawrence and Eydie Gorme, Stars (CBS)
LILY TOMLIN; Irene Pinn, Executive Producer; Jane Wagner and Lorne Michaels, Producers; Lily Tomlin, Star (ABC)

CLASSICAL MUSIC PROGRAM (E-1117)

For a special program or a series Emmy(s) to Executive Producers(s) and/or Producer(s) and Stars, if applicable

BERNSTEIN AND THE NEW YORK PHILHARMONIC; Great Performances; Klaus Hallig and Harry Kraut, Executive Producers; David Griffiths, Producer; Leonard Bernstein, Star (PBS)
THREE BY BALANCHINE WITH THE NEW YORK CITY BALLET; Great Performances; Dr. Reiner E. Moritz and Emile Ardolino, Producers (PBS)
ARTUR RUBINSTEIN - CHOPIN; Great Performances; Fritz Buttenstedt, Executive Producer; Fritz Buttenstedt, and David Griffiths, Producers; Artur Rubinstein, Star (PBS)
DANCE IN AMERICA: CITY CENTER JOFFREY BALLET; Jac Venza, Executive Producer; Merrill Brockway, Series Producer; Emile Ardolino, Producer (PBS)
LIVE FROM LINCOLN CENTER; John Goberman, Executive Producer; David Griffiths and Ken Campbell, Producers; Andre Previn and Van Cliburn, Stars (PBS)

ACTOR - COMEDY SERIES (E-1118)

JACK ALBERTSON; Chico And The Man (NBC)
HAL LINDEN; Barney Miller (ABC)
ALAN ALDA; M*A*S*H (CBS)
HENRY WINKLER; Happy Days (ABC)

ACTOR - DRAMA SERIES (E-1119)

PETER FALK; Columbo, NBC Sunday Mystery Movie (NBC)
KARL MALDEN; The Streets Of San Francisco (ABC)
JAMES GARNER; The Rockford Files (NBC)

ACTOR - LIMITED SERIES (E-1120)

HAL HOLBROOK; Sandburg's Lincoln (NBC)
NICK NOLTE; Rich Man, Poor Man (ABC)
PETER STRAUSS; Rich Man, Poor Man (ABC)
GEORGE GRIZZARD; The Adams Chronicles (PBS)

ACTOR - DRAMA OR COMEDY SPECIAL (E-1121)

ANTHONY HOPKINS; The Lindbergh Kidnapping Case; NBC World Premiere Movie (NBC)
WILLIAM DEVANE; Fear On Trial (CBS)
JACK LEMMON; The Entertainer (NBC)
EDWARD HERRMANN; Eleanor And Franklin; ABC Theatre (ABC)
JASON ROBARDS; A Moon For The Misbegotten; ABC Theater (ABC)

ACTOR - SINGLE PERFORMANCE - DRAMA OR COMEDY SERIES (E-1122)

EDWARD ASNER; Rich Man, Poor Man (ABC)
ROBERT REED; The Fourth Sex; Medical Center, Parts 1 & 2 (CBS)
TONY MUSANTE; The Quality Of Mercy; Medical Story (NBC)
BILL BIXBY; Police Buff; The Streets Of San Francisco (ABC)

ACTRESS - COMEDY SERIES (E-1123)

MARY TYLER MOORE; The Mary Tyler Moore Show (CBS)
BEATRICE ARTHUR; Maude (CBS)
VALERIE HARPER; Rhoda (CBS)
LEE GRANT; Fay (NBC)
CLORIS LEACHMAN; Phyllis (CBS)

ACTRESS - DRAMA SERIES (E-1124)

MICHAEL LEARNED; The Waltons (CBS)
ANNE MEARA: Kate McShane (CBS)
ANGIE DICKINSON; Police Woman (NBC)
BRENDA VACCARO; Sara (CBS)

ACTRESS - LIMITED SERIES (E-1125)

ROSEMARY HARRIS; Notorious Woman; Masterpiece Theatre (PBS)
LEE REMICK; Jennie: Lady Randolph Churchill; Great Performances (PBS)
SUSAN BLAKELY; Rich Man, Poor Man (ABC)
JEAN MARSH; Upstairs, Downstairs; Masterpiece Theatre (PBS)

ACTRESS - DRAMA OR COMEDY SPECIAL (E-1126)

SUSAN CLARK; Babe (CBS)
COLLEEN DEWHURST; A Moon For The Misbegotten; ABC Theatre (ABC)
JANE ALEXANDER; Eleanor And Franklin; ABC Theatre (NBC)
SADA THOMPSON; The Entertainer (NBC)

ACTRESS - SINGLE PERFORMANCE - DRAMA OR COMEDY SERIES (E-1127)

KATHRYN WALKER; John Adams, Lawyer; The Adams Chronicles (PBS)
HELEN HAYES; Retire In Sunny Hawaii . . . Forever; Hawaii Five-O (CBS)
SHEREE NORTH; How Do You Know What Hurts Me?; Marcus Welby, M.D. (ABC)
PAMELA PAYTON-WRIGHT; John Quincy Adams, Diplomat; The Adams Chronicles (PBS)
MARTHA RAYE; Greed; McMillan & Wife; NBC Sunday Mystery Movie (NBC)

SUPPORTING ACTOR - COMEDY SERIES (E-1128)

For a regular or limited series
TED KNIGHT; The Mary Tyler Moore Show (CBS)
GARY R. BURGHOFF; M*A*S*H (CBS)
ABE VIGODA; Barney Miller (ABC)
EDWARD ASNER; The Mary Tyler Moore Show (CBS)
HARRY MORGAN; M*A*S*H (CBS)

SUPPORTING ACTOR - DRAMA SERIES (E-1129)

For a regular or limited series
ANTHONY ZERBE; Harry O (ABC)
WILL GEER; The Waltons (CBS)
RAY MILLAND; Rich Man, Poor Man (ABC)
ROBERT REED; Rich Man, Poor Man (ABC)
MICHAEL DOUGLAS; The Streets Of San Francisco (ABC)

SUPPORTING ACTOR - VARIETY OR MUSIC (E-1130)

For a continuing role in a regular or limited series; or a one-time appearance in a series; or a special
CHEVY CHASE; NBC's Saturday Night, January 17, 1976 (NBC)
HARVEY KORMAN; The Carol Burnett Show, Series (CBS)
TIM CONWAY; The Carol Burnett Show, November 15, 1975 (CBS)

SUPPORTING ACTOR - COMEDY OR DRAMA SPECIAL (E-1131)

ED FLANDERS; A Moon For The Misbegotten; ABC Theatre (ABC)
ART CARNEY; Katherine; The ABC Sunday Night Movie (ABC)
RAY BOLGER; The Entertainer (NBC)

SUPPORTING ACTOR - COMEDY OR DRAMA SERIES (E-1132)

For a one-time appearance in a regular or limited series
GORDON JACKSON; The Beastly Hun; Upstairs, Downstairs; Masterpiece Theatre (PBS)
ROSCOE LEE BROWNE; The Escape Artist; Barney Miller (ABC)
BILL BIXBY; Rich Man, Poor Man (ABC)
NORMAN FELL; Rich Man, Poor Man (ABC)
VAN JOHNSON; Rich Man, Poor Man (ABC)

SUPPORTING ACTRESS - COMEDY SERIES (E-1133)

For a regular or limited series
BETTY WHITE; The Mary Tyler Moore Show (CBS)
GEORGIA ENGEL; The Mary Tyler Moore Show (CBS)
NANCY WALKER; Rhoda (CBS)
JULIE KAVNER; Rhoda (CBS)
LORETTA SWIT; M*A*S*H (CBS)

SUPPORTING ACTRESS - DRAMA SERIES (E-1134)

For a regular or limited series
ELLEN CORBY; The Waltons (CBS)
SUSAN HOWARD; Petrocelli (NBC)
ANGELA BADDELEY; Upstairs, Downstairs; Masterpiece Theatre (PBS)
DOROTHY McGUIRE; Rich Man, Poor Man (ABC)
SADA THOMPSON; Sandburg's Lincoln (NBC)

SUPPORTING ACTRESS - VARIETY OR MUSIC SHOW (E-1135)

For a continuing role in a regular or limited series; or a special
VICKI LAWRENCE; The Carol Burnett Show (CBS)
CLORIS LEACHMAN; Telly. . .Who Loves Ya Baby? (CBS)

SUPPORTING ACTRESS - COMEDY OR DRAMA SPECIAL (E-1136)

ROSEMARY MURPHY; Eleanor And Franklin; ABC Theatre (ABC)
IRENE TEDROW; Eleanor and Franklin; ABC Theatre (ABC)
LILIA SKALA; Eleanor And Franklin; ABC Theatre (ABC)
LOIS NETTLETON; Fear On Trial (CBS)

SUPPORTING ACTRESS - COMEDY OR DRAMA SERIES (E-1137)

For a one-time appearance in a regular or limited series

FIONNUALA FLANAGAN; Rich Man, Poor Man (ABC)
EILEEN HECKART; Mary's Aunt; The Mary Tyler Moore Show (CBS)
RUTH GORDON; Kiss Your Epaulets Goodbye; Rhoda (CBS)
KIM DARBY; Rich Man, Poor Man (ABC)
KAY LENZ; Rich Man, Poor Man (ABC)

DIRECTOR - DRAMA SERIES (E-1138)

A single episode of a regular or limited series with continuing characters and/or theme

DAVID GREENE; Rich Man, Poor Man (ABC)
JAMES CELLAN JONES; Jennie: Lady Randolph Churchill, Part IV; Great Performances (PBS)
BORIS SAGAL; Rich Man, Poor Man, Episode 5 (ABC)
GEORGE SCHAEFER; Crossing Fox River; Sandburg's Lincoln (NBC)
FIELDER COOK; Beacon Hill; Pilot (CBS)
CHRISTOPHER HODSON; Women Shall Not Weep; Upstairs, Downstairs (PBS)

DIRECTOR - COMEDY SERIES (E-1139)

A single episode of a regular or limited series with continuing characters and/or theme

GENE REYNOLDS; Welcome To Korea; M*A*S*H (CBS)
HAL COOPER; The Analyst; Maude (CBS)
JOAN DARLING; Chuckles Bites The Dust; The Mary Tyler Moore Show (CBS)
ALAN ALDA; The Kids; M*A*S*H (CBS)

DIRECTOR - COMEDY-VARIETY OR MUSIC SERIES (E-1140)

A single episode of a regular or limited series

DAVE WILSON; NBC's Saturday Night (with host Paul Simon) (NBC)
DAVE POWERS; The Carol Burnett Show (with Maggie Smith) (CBS)
TIM KILEY; The Sonny And Cher Show; Premiere (CBS)

DIRECTOR - COMEDY-VARIETY OR MUSIC SPECIAL (E-1141)

DWIGHT HEMION; Steve And Eydie: 'Our Love Is Here To Stay' (CBS)
BILL DAVIS; John Denver Rocky Mountain Christmas (ABC)
TONY CHARMOLI; Mitzi. . .Roarin' In The 20's (CBS)

DIRECTOR - SPECIAL PROGRAM - DRAMA OR COMEDY (E-1142)

DANIEL PETRIE; Eleanor And Franklin; ABC Theatre (ABC)
LAMONT JOHNSON; Fear On Trial (CBS)
BUZZ KULIK; Babe (CBS)
JOSE QUINTERO and GORDON RIGSBY; A Moon For The Misbegotten; ABC Theatre (ABC)

WRITING - DRAMA SERIES (E-1143)

A single episode of a regular or limited series with continuing characters and/or theme

SHERMAN YELLEN; John Adams, Lawyer; The Adams Chronicles (PBS)
DEAN RIESNER; Rich Man, Poor Man (ABC)
JULIAN MITCHELL; Jennie: Lady Randolph Churchill; Great Performances (PBS)
JOEL OLIANSKY; Complaint Amended; The Law (NBC)
ALFRED SHAUGHNESSY; Another Year; Upstairs, Downstairs; Masterpiece Theatre (PBS)

WRITING - COMEDY SERIES (E-1144)

A single episode of a regular or limited series with continuing characters and/or theme

DAVID LLOYD; Chuckles Bites The Dust; The Mary Tyler Show (CBS)
DANNY ARNOLD and CHRIS HAYWARD; The Hero; Barney Miller (ABC)
JAY FOLB; The Analyst; Maude (CBS)
LARRY GELBART and GENE REYNOLDS; The More I See You; M*A*S*H (CBS)
LARRY GELBART and SIMON MUNTER; Hawkeye; M*A*S*H (CBS)

WRITING - COMEDY-VARIETY OR MUSIC SERIES (E-1145)

A single episode of a regular or limited series

ANNE BEATTS, CHEVY CHASE, AL FRANKEN, TOM DAVIS, LORNE MICHAELS, MARILYN SUZANNE MILLER, MICHAEL O'DONOGHUE, HERB SARGENT, TOM SCHILLER, ROSIE SCHUSTER and ALAN ZWEIBEL; NBC's Saturday Night (with Host Elliott Gould) (NBC)
ED SIMMONS, GARY BELKIN, ROGER BEATTY, BILL RICHMOND, GENE PERRET, ARNIE KOGEN, RAY JESSEL, RUDY DeLUCA, BARRY LEVINSON, DICK CLAIR and JENNA McMAHON; The Carol Burnett Show (with Jim Nabors) (CBS)
PHIL HAHN, BOB ARNOTT, JEANINE BURNIER, COSLOUGH JOHNSON, IRIS RAINER, STUART GILLARD, FRANK PEPPIATT, JOHN AYLESWORTH and TED ZEIGLER; The Sonny And Cher Show, Premiere (CBS)

WRITING - COMEDY-VARIETY OR MUSIC SPECIAL (E-1146)

JANE WAGNER, LORNE MICHAELS, ANN ELDER, CHRISTOPHER GUEST, EARL POMERANTZ, JIM RUSK, LILY TOMLIN, ROD WARREN and GEORGE YANOK; Lily Tomlin (ABC)
FRED EBB; Gypsy In My Soul (with Shirley Maclaine) (CBS)
DICK VAN DYKE, ALLAN BLYE, BOB EINSTEIN, JAMES STEIN, GEORGE BURDITT, ROBERT ILLES, STEVE MARTIN, JACK MENDELSOHN and RICK MITTLEMAN; Van Dyke And Company (NBC)
JERRY MAYER; Mitzi. . .Roarin' In The 20's (CBS)

WRITING, SPECIAL PROGRAM - DRAMA OR COMEDY - ORIGINAL TELEPLAY (E-1147)

JAMES COSTIGAN; Eleanor And Franklin; ABC Theatre (ABC)
JOANNA LEE; Babe (CBS)
J.P. MILLER; The Lindbergh Kidnapping Case; NBC World Premiere Movie (NBC)
NICHOLAS MEYER and ANTHONY WILSON; The Night That Panicked America; The ABC Friday Night Movie (ABC)
JEB ROSEBROOK and THEODORE STRAUSS; I Will Fight No More Forever; ABC Theatre (ABC)

WRITING, SPECIAL PROGRAM - DRAMA OR COMEDY - ADAPTATION (E-1148)

DAVID W. RINTELS; Fear On Trial (CBS)
JEANNE WAKATSUKI HOUSTON, JAMES D. HOUSTON and JOHN KORTY; Farewell To Manzanar; NBC World Premiere Movie (NBC)
ELLIOTT BAKER; The Entertainer (NBC)

CHILDREN'S SPECIAL (E-1149)
For specials which were broadcast during the evening
Emmy(s) to Executive Producer(s) and Producer(s)

YOU'RE A GOOD SPORT, CHARLIE BROWN; Lee Mendelson, Executive Producer; Bill Melendez, Producer (CBS)
HUCKLEBERRY FINN; Steven North, Producer (ABC)

LIVE SPORTS SPECIAL (E-1150)
Emmy(s) To Executive Producer(s) and Producer(s)

1975 WORLD SERIES; Scotty Connal, Executive Producer; Roy Hammerman, Producer (NBC)
NCAA BASKETBALL CHAMPIONSHIP; Scotty Connal, Executive Producer; Roy Hammerman, Producer (NBC)
ROSE BOWL; Scotty Connal, Executive Producer; Dick Auerbach, Producer (NBC)
THE SUPER BOWL TODAY AND SUPER BOWL X; Robert Wussler, Executive Producer; Robert Stenner, Producer (CBS)
1975 MASTERS GOLF TOURNAMENT; Frank Chirkinian, Producer (CBS)

LIVE SPORTS SERIES (E-1151)
Emmy(s) to Executive Producer(s) and Producer(s)

NFL MONDAY NIGHT FOOTBALL; Roone Arledge, Executive Producer; Don Ohlmeyer, Producer (ABC)
NCAA FOOTBALL; Roone Arledge, Executive Producer; Chuck Howard and Terry Jastrow, Producers (ABC)
ABC'S GOLF; Roone Arledge, Executive Producer; Chuck Howard, Producer (ABC)
NFL ON CBS; Robert Wussler, Executive Producer (CBS)

EDITED SPORTS SPECIAL (E-1152)
Emmy(s) to Executive Producer(s) and Producer(s)

XII WINTER OLYMPICS GAMES; Roone Arledge, Executive Producer; Chuck Howard, Don Ohlmeyer, Geoff Mason, Chet Forte, Bob Goodrich, Ellie Riger, Brice Weisman, Doug Wilson, and John Wilcox, Producers (ABC)
TRIUMPH AND TRAGEDY. . .THE OLYMPIC EXPERIENCE; Roone Arledge, Executive Producer; Don Ohlmeyer, Producer (ABC)

EDITED SPORTS SERIES (E-1153)
Emmy(s) to Executive Producer(s) and Producer(s)

ABC's WIDE WORLD OF SPORTS; Roone Arledge, Executive Producer; Doug Wilson, Chet Forte, Ned Steckel, Brice Weisman, Terry Jastrow, Bob Goodrich, John Martin, Dennis Lewin, Chuck Howard and Don Ohlmeyer, Producers (ABC)
THE SUPERSTARS; Roone Arledge, Executive Producer; Don Ohlmeyer, Terry Jastrow and Chet Forte, Producers (ABC)
THE BASEBALL WORLD OF JOE GARAGIOLA; Joe Garagiola, Executive Producer; Don Ellis, Producer (NBC)
THE WAY IT WAS; Gerry Gross, Executive Producer; Dick Enberg and Dan Merrin, Producers (PBS)

SPORTS PERSONALITY (E-1154)
JIM MCKAY; ABC's Wide World Of Sports; ABC's XII Winter Olympics (ABC)
JOE GARAGIOLA; 1975 World Series--Game 6 (NBC)
FRANK GIFFORD; NFL Monday Night Football; ABC's XII Winter Olympics (ABC)
VIN SCULLY; Masters Golf (NBC)
HEYWOOD HALE BROUN; CBS Sports Programs (CBS)

THE NATIONAL AWARD FOR COMMUNITY SERVICE (E-1155)
FORGOTTEN CHILDREN; WBBM-TV Chicago, Illinois
A DAY WITHOUT SUNSHINE; WPBT, North Miami, Florida
THE GIFT OF LIFE; KWTV, Oklahoma City, Oklahoma
BLOOD BANK; WCIX-TV Miami, Florida
CENTRE FOUR; WJXT-TV, Jacksonville, Florida

CLOSING THE GAP; WITF-TV, Hershey, Pennsylvania
BUDDY, CAN YOU SPARE A DIME?; WBAL-TV, Baltimore, Maryland
THE EDELIN CONVICTION; WGBH, Boston, Massachusetts

THE AREAS
(Possibility of One Award, More Than One Award, or No Award)

SPECIAL CLASSIFICATION OF OUTSTANDING PROGRAM AND INDIVIDUAL ACHIEVEMENT (E-1156)
An award for unique program and individual achievements, which does not fall into a specific category, or is not otherwise recognized

BICENTENNIAL MINUTES; Bob Markell, Executive Producer; Gareth Davies and Paul Waigner, Producers, Series (CBS)
THE TONIGHT SHOW STARRING JOHNNY CARSON; Fred De Cordova, Producer; Johnny Carson, Star, Series (NBC)
ANN MARCUS, JERRY ADELMAN and DANIEL GREGORY BROWNE, Writers; Mary Hartman, Mary Hartman, Pilot (Synd)
THE AMERICAN FILM INSTITUTE SALUTE TO WILLIAM WYLER; George Stevens, Jr., Executive Producer; Paul Keyes, Producer (CBS)
TOMORROW; Joel Tator, Pamela Burke and Bruce McKay, Producers (NBC)
MARY HARTMAN, MARY HARTMAN; Norman Lear, Executive Producer; Viva Knight, Producer (Synd)
TOM SNYDER, Host; Tomorrow (NBC)
LOUISE LASSER, Performer; Mary Hartman, Mary Hartman (Synd)
ARTIE MALVIN, KEN WELCH and MITZIE WELCH, Mini Musical - Irving Berlin Finale; The Carol Burnett Show (CBS)

INDIVIDUAL ACHIEVEMENT IN SPORTS PROGRAMMING (E-1157)
For a single episode of a series; or for a special program

ANDY SIDARIS, DON OHLMEYER, ROGER GOODMAN, LARRY KAMM, RONNIE HAWKINS and RALPH MELLANBY, Directors; XII Winter Olympic Games (ABC)

THE CREATIVE ARTS AWARDS
(One Award Only in Each of the Following Categories)

CHOREOGRAPHY (E-1158)
For a single episode of a series or a special program

TONY CHARMOLI; Gypsy In My Soul (with Shirley MacLaine) (CBS)
JAIME ROGERS; Mary's Incredible Dream (with Mary Tyler Moore) (CBS)
ERNEST O. FLATT; The Carol Burnett Show (with Roddy McDowell and Bernadette Peters) (CBS)
ROB ISCOVE; Ann-Margaret Smith; Bell System Family Theatre (NBC)
LESTER WILSON; Lola! (ABC)

MUSIC COMPOSITION FOR A SERIES (E-1159)
Dramatic Underscore For a single episode of a regular or limited series

ALEX NORTH; Rich Man, Poor Man (ABC)
JOHN CACAVAS; A Question Of Answers; Kojak (CBS)
JACK URBONT; Next Of Kin; Bronk (CBS)
DAVID ROSE; Remember Me (Parts 1 & 2); Little House On The Prairie (NBC)

MUSIC COMPOSITION FOR A SPECIAL (E-1160)
Dramatic Underscore

JERRY GOLDSMITH; Babe (CBS)
CY COLEMAN; Gypsy In My Soul (with Shirley MacLaine) (CBS)
BILLY GOLDENBERG; Dark Victory (NBC)
JACK URBONT; Supercops; A CBS Friday Night Double Feature (CBS)

MUSIC DIRECTION (E-1161)

For a single episode of a series or a special program whether it be variety or music

SEIJI OZAWA; Central Park In The Dark/A Hero's Life; Evening At Symphony (PBS)
DON TRENNER, Conductor; CY COLEMAN, Arranger; Gypsy In My Soul (with Shirley MacLaine) (CBS)

ART DIRECTION OR SCENIC DESIGN (E-1162)

For a single episode of a comedy, drama or limited series

TOM JOHN, Art Director; JOHN WENDELL and WES LAWS, Set Decorators; Beacon Hill; Pilot (CBS)
ED WITTSTEIN, Art Director; The Adams Chronicles (PBS)
WILLIAM HINEY, Art Director; JOSEPH J. STONE, Set Decorator; Rich Man, Poor Man (ABC)
MICHAEL HALL and FRED PUSEY, Scenic Designers; Jennie: Lady Randolph Churchill; Great Performances (PBS)

ART DIRECTION OR SCENIC DESIGN (E-1163)

For a single episode of a comedy-variety or music series; or for a comedy-variety or music special

RAYMOND KLAUSEN, Art Director; ROBERT CHECCHI, Set Decorator; Cher (with Anthony Newley and Ike and Tina Turner) (CBS)
EUGENE T. McAVOY, Art Director; Mary's Incredible Dream (with Mary Tyler Moore) (CBS)
KEN JOHNSON, Art Director; John Denver (Rocky Mountain Christmas) (ABC)
PAUL BARNES and BOB SANSOM, Art Directors; BILL HARP, Set Decorator; The Carol Burnett Show (with The Pointer Sisters) (CBS)

ART DIRECTION OR SCENIC DESIGN (E-1164)

For a dramatic special or a feature length film made for television

JAN SCOTT, Art Director; ANTONY MONDELLO, Set Decorator; Eleanor And Franklin; ABC Theatre (ABC)
JACK F. DE SHIELDS, Art Director; REG ALLEN, Set Decorator; Barbary Coast; The ABC Sunday Night Movie (ABC)
ROY CHRISTOPHER, Art Director; FRANCISCO LOMBARDO, Set Decorator; The Legendary Curse Of The Hope Diamond (CBS)

GRAPHIC DESIGN AND TITLE SEQUENCES (E-1165)

For a single episode of a series; or for a special program. This includes animation only when created for use in titling

NORMAN SUNSHINE; Addie And The King Of Hearts (CBS)
PHIL NORMAN; The New, Original Wonder Woman; The ABC Friday Night Movie Special Double Feature (ABC)
ANTHONY GOLDSCHMIDT; Eleanor And Franklin; ABC Theatre (ABC)
GIRSH BHARGAVA and BILL MANDEL; The Adams Chronicles (PBS)
EDIE BASKIN and BOB POOK; NBC's Saturday Night (with Host Buck Henry) (NBC)

COSTUME DESIGN - DRAMA SPECIAL (E-1166)

JOE I. TOMPKINS; Eleanor And Franklin; ABC Theatre (ABC)
BOB CHRISTENSON and DENITA CAVETT; The Lindbergh Kidnapping Case; NBC World Premiere Movie (NBC)

COSTUME DESIGN - MUSIC-VARIETY (E-1167)

For a single episode of a series; or for a special program

BOB MACKIE; Mitzi. . .Roarin' In The 20's (CBS)
BOB MACKIE and RET TURNER; Cher (with Wayne Rogers and Nancy Walker) (CBS)

COSTUME DESIGN - DRAMA OR COMEDY SERIES (E-1168)

For a single episode of a Drama, Comedy or Limited series

JANE ROBINSON and JILL SILVERSIDE; Recovery; Jennie: Lady Randolph Churchill; Great Performances (PBS)
CHARLES WALDO; Rich Man, Poor Man (ABC)
ALVIN COLT; John Adams, Diplomat; The Adams Chronicles (PBS)

MAKE-UP (E-1169)

For a single episode of a series or for a special program

DEL ARMSTRONG and MIKE WESTMORE; Eleanor And Franklin; ABC Theatre (ABC)
ALLAN WHITEY SNYDER; The 1975 Fashion Awards (ABC)
WILLIAM TUTTLE; Babe (CBS)

CINEMATOGRAPHY - ENTERTAINMENT SERIES (E-1170)

HARRY L. WOLF, A.S.C.; Keep Your Eye On The Sparrow; Baretta (ABC)
TED VOIGTLANDER, A.S.C.; Remember Me (Parts 1 & 2); Little House On The Prairie (NBC)
HOWARD SCHWARTZ; Rich Man, Poor Man (ABC)
SOL NEGRIN. A.S.C.; A Question Of Answers; Kojak (CBS)
WILLIAM JURGENSEN; Hawkeye; M*A*S*H (CBS)

CINEMATOGRAPHY - ENTERTAINMENT SPECIAL (E-1171)

PAUL LOHMANN and EDWARD R. BROWN, SR; Eleanor and Franklin; ABC Theatre (ABC)
CHARLES F. WHEELER. A.S.C.; Babe (CBS)
HIRO NARITA; Farewell To Manzanar; NBC World Premiere Movie (NBC)
RICHARD C. GLOUNER, A.S.C.; Griffin And Phoenix: A Love Story; The ABC Friday Night Movie (ABC)
JAMES CRABE; The Entertainer (NBC)

FILM EDITING - COMEDY SERIES (E-1172)

STANFORD TISCHLER and FRED W. BERGER; Welcome To Korea; M*A*S*H (CBS)
DOUGLAS HINES; Chuckles Bites The Dust; The Mary Tyler Moore Show (CBS)

FILM EDITING - DRAMA OR LIMITED SERIES (E-1173)

SAMUEL E. BEETLEY, A.C.E. and KEN ZEMKE; The Quality Of Mercy; Medical Story (NBC)
DOUGLAS STEWART; Rich Man, Poor Man (ABC)
DOUGLAS VAN ENGER, JR.; The Right To Die; Medical Story (NBC)
RICHARD BRACKEN; Rich Man, Poor Man (ABC)

FILM EDITING - ENTERTAINMENT SPECIAL (E-1174)

MICHAEL KAHN; Eleanor And Franklin; ABC Theatre (ABC)
HENRY BERMAN; Babe (CBS)
BUD S. ISAACS, TONY RADECKI and GEORGE NICHOLSON, A.C.E; The Night That Panicked America; The ABC Friday Night Movie (ABC)
ROBERT K. LAMBERT; I Will Fight No More Forever; ABC Theatre (ABC)
RITA ROLAND, A.C.E.; The Lindbergh Kidnapping Case; NBC World Premiere Movie (NBC)

FILM SOUND EDITING (E-1175)

For a single episode of a regular or limited series

DOUGLAS H. GRINDSTAFF, AL KAJITA, MARVIN I. KOSBERG, HANS NEWMAN, LEON SELDITZ, DICK FRIEDMAN, STAN GILBERT, HANK SALERNO, LARRY SINGER and WILLIAM ANDREWS; The Quality Of

Mercy; Medical Story (NBC)
JERRY CHRISTIAN, KEN SWEET, THOMAS M. PATCHETT, JACK JACKSON, DAVID A. SCHONLEBER, JOHN W. SINGLETON, DALE JOHNSTON, GEORGE E. LUCKENBACHER, WALTER JENEVEIN and DENNIS DILTZ; The Secret Of Bigfoot (Parts 1 & 2); The Six Million Dollar Man (ABC)
MARVIN I. KOSBERG, BOB HUMAN, HANS NEWMAN, LEON SELDITZ, JEREMY HOENACK, JACK MILNER, AL KAJITA, LUKE WOLFRAM, DICK FRIEDMAN, HANK SALERNO, LARRY SINGER, STAN GILBERT and WILLIAM ANDREWS; Task Force (Parts 1 & 2); Police Woman (NBC)

FILM SOUND EDITING - SPECIAL (E-1176)

CHARLES L. CAMPBELL. LARRY NEIMAN, COLIN MOUAT, LARRY CAROW, DON WARNER, JOHN SINGLETON, TOM McMULLEN, JOSEPH DiVITALE, CARL KRESS, JOHN KLINE and JOHN HANLEY; The Night That Panicked America; The ABC Friday Night Movie (ABC)
DON HALL, WILLIAM HARTMAN, MIKE CORRIGAN, ED ROSSI, DICK SPERBER, RON SMITH, JOHN JOLLIFFE, BOB PEARSON, JOHN KLINE, AL LA MASTRA and JAY ENGEL; Eleanor And Franklin; ABC Theatre (ABC)
MARVIN I. KOSBERG, LARRY KAUFMAN, JACK MILNER and WILLIAM ANDREWS; The Lindbergh Kidnapping Case; NBC World Premiere Movie (NBC)

FILM SOUND MIXING (E-1177)

For a single episode of a regular or limited series; or for a special program

DON BASSMAN and DON JOHNSON; Eleanor And Franklin (Parts 1 & 2); ABC Theatre (ABC)
CHARLES LEWIS, ROBERT L. HARMAN, GEORGE PORTER and EDDIE NELSON; Prairie Lawyer; Sandburg's Lincoln (NBC)

TAPE SOUND MIXING (E-1178)

For a single episode of a regular or limited series; or for a special program

DAVE WILLIAMS; Anniversary Show; The Tonight Show Starring Johnny Carson (NBC)
VERNON COLEMAN; New Year's Eve At Pops (Arthur Fiedler) (PBS)
JOHN F. PFEIFFER; Live From Lincoln Center (PBS)

VIDEO TAPE EDITING - SERIES (E-1179)

For a single episode of a regular or limited series

GIRISH BHARGAVA and MANFORD SCHORN; The Adams Chronicles (PBS)
KEN DENISOFF and ROBERT VEATCH; Earthquake II; Sanford and Son (NBC)
SUSAN JENKINS and MANUEL MARTINEZ; The Telethon; Welcome Back, Kotter (ABC)
HOMER POWELL, FRED GOLAN and PAUL SCHATZKIN; Happy New Year; Barney Miller (ABC)

VIDEO TAPE EDITING - SPECIAL (E-1180)

NICK V. GIORDANO; Alice Cooper–The Nightmare; Wide World: In Concert (ABC)
ROY STEWART; The Hemingway Play; Hollywood Television Theatre (PBS)
HAL COLLINS and DANNY WHITE; Texaco Presents A Quarter Century of Bob Hope On Television (NBC)
REX BAGWELL and FRANK PHILLIPS; Mitzi... Roarin' In The 20's (CBS)

TECHNICAL DIRECTION AND ELECTRONIC CAMERAWORK (E-1181)

For a single episode of a regular or limited series; or for a special program

LEONARD CHUMBLEY, Technical Director; WALTER EDEL, JOHN FEHER, STEVE ZINK, Cameramen; The Adams Chronicles (PBS)
KEN LAMKIN, Technical Director; LEW ADAMS, JOHN POLIAK, SAMUEL E. DOWLEN and RONALD SHELDON, Cameramen; Mary's Incredible Dream (with Mary Tyler Moore) (CBS)
LOUIS FUSARI, Technical Director; JOHN OLSON, ROY HOLM, RICK LOMBARDO and IAN TAYLOR, Cameramen; Mitzi And A Hundred Guys (CBS)
JERRY WEISS, Technical Director; FRED DONELSON, BRUCE GRAY, GEORGE MEYER and ROY HOLM, Cameramen; Mitzi. . .Roarin' In The 20's (CBS)

LIGHTING DIRECTION (E-1182)

For a single episode of a regular or limited series; or for a special program

WILLIAM KLAGES and LON STUCKY; Mitzi And A Hundred Guys (CBS)
JOHN FRESCHI; Mitzi. . .Roarin'In The 20's (CBS)
BILLY KNIGHT and DICK WEISS; John Quincy Adams--Diplomat; The Adams Chronicles (PBS)

THE CREATIVE ARTS AREAS

(Possibility of One Award, More Than One Award or No Award)

SPECIAL MUSICAL MATERIAL (E-1183)

For a song (which must have both music and lyrics), a theme for a series, or special material for a variety program providing the first usage of this material was written expressly for television

KEN WELCH, MITZIE WELCH and ARTIE MALVIN; Cinderella Gets It On; The Carol Burnett Show (with The Pointer Sisters) (CBS)
CY COLEMAN and FRED EBB; Gypsy In My Soul (with Shirley MacLaine) (CBS)

OUTSTANDING ACHIEVEMENT IN ANY AREA OF CREATIVE TECHNICAL CRAFTS (E-1184)

An award for individual technical craft achievement which does not fall into a specific category and is not otherwise recognized

JEAN BURT REILLY and BILLIE LAUGHRIDGE, Hairstylists; Eleanor And Franklin; ABC Theatre (ABC)
DONALD SAHLIN, KERMIT LOVE, CAROLY WILCOX, JOHN LOVELADY and ROLLIE KREWSON, Costumes and Props for the Muppets; Sesame Street (PBS)
JOHN LEAY and MARK SCHUBIN, Live Stereo Simulcast Nationwide, First Stereo Simulcast Via Satellite; Live From Lincoln Center (Andre Previn/Van Cliburn) (PBS)
WERNER G. SHERER, Hairdresser; First Ladies' Diaries: Martha Washington (NBC)
LOUIS SCHMITT, SOPHIE QUINN and TRUDY PHILION, Animated Characters Designers; The Tiny Tree; Bell System Family Theatre (NBC)

INDIVIDUAL ACHIEVEMENT IN DAYTIME PROGRAMMING (E-1185)

For a single episode of a series; or for a special program

RENE LAGLER, Art Director; RICHARD HARVEY, Set Decorator; Dinah! (Synd)
STAS PYKA, Graphic Design and Title Sequence; First Ladies' Diaries: Edith Wilson (NBC)
LEE BAYGAN, Make-Up; First Ladies' Diaries: Martha Washington

(NBC)
RICHARD W. WILSON, Tape Sound Mixer; The Merv Griffin Show (with Tony Bennett, Peggy Lee and Fred Astaire) (Synd)

INDIVIDUAL ACHIEVEMENT IN SPORTS PROGRAMMING (E-1186)

For a single episode of a series; or for a special program

JEFF COHAN, JOE ACETI, JOHN DELISA, LOU FREDERICK, JACK GALLIVAN, JIM JENNETT, CAROL LEHTI, HOWARD SHAPIRO, KATSUMI ASEADA, JOHN FERNANDEZ, PETER FRITZ, EDDIE C. JOSEPH, KEN KLINGBEIL, LEO STEPHAN, TED SUMMERS, MICHAEL WENIG, RON ACKERMAN, MICHAEL BONIFAZIO, BARBARA BOWMAN, CHARLIE BURNHAM, JOHN CROAK, CHARLES GARDNER, MARVIN GENCH, VICTOR GONZALES, JAKOB HIERL, NICK MAZUR, ED McCARTHY, ALEX MOSKOVIC, ARTHUR NACE, LOU RENDE, ERSKINE ROBERTS, MERRITT ROESSER, ARTHUR VOLK, ROGER HAENELT, CURT BRAND, PHIL MOLLICA, GEORGE BOETTCHER and HERB OHLANDT, Video Tape Editors; XII Winter Olympic Games (ABC)
DICK ROES, JACK KELLY, BILL SANDREUTER, FRANK BAILEY and JACK KESTENBAUM, Tape Sound Mixers; XII Winter Olympic Games (ABC)
LARRY CANSLER, Music Composition; Theme/CBS Sports Spectacular (CBS)
MIKE DELANEY, HARVEY HARRISON, HARRY HART, D'ARCY MARSH, BRUCE BUCKLEY, DON SHAPIRO and ERIC VAN HAREN NOMAN, Cameramen; XII Winter Olympic Games (ABC)
JOHN PETERSEN, TONY ZACCARO, DON SHOEMAKER, PETER SILVER, ALAN SPENCER, IRWIN KRECHAF and MARGARET MURPHY, Film Editors; XII Winter Olmpic Games (ABC)

RELIGIOUS PROGRAMMING (E-1187)

For a single episode of a series; or a special program

JOSEPH J. H. VADALA, Cinematographer; A Determining Force (NBC)
SHARON KAUFMAN, Film Sound Editor; The Will To Be Free (ABC)
HARVEY HOLOCKER, Make-Up; Good News; The Rex Humbard World Outreach Ministry (Synd)

INDIVIDUAL ACHIEVEMENT IN CHILDREN'S PROGRAMMING (E-1188)

For a single episode of a series; or for a special program

BUD NOLAN and JIM COOKMAN, Film Sound Editors; Bound For Freedom (NBC)
ROBERT L. HARMAN, TED GOMILLION and BILL EDMUNDSON, Film Sound Mixers; Papa And Me; Special Treat (NBC)
GERRI BRIOSO, Graphic Design; Sesame Street (PBS)
MICHAEL WESTMORE and LOUIS PHILLIPPI, Make-Up; Blackout; Land Of The Lost (NBC)

ENGINEERING DEVELOPMENT (E-1189)

SONY CORPORATION for the U-matic video cassette concept
EASTMAN KODAK for the development of Eastman Ektachrome Video News Film
Citation to TEKTRONIX for leadership in development of equipment for verifying television transmission performance in the vertical interval

DAYTIME PROGRAM AND INDIVIDUAL ACHIEVEMENTS

(One Award Only in Each of the Following Categories)

DAYTIME DRAMA SERIES (E-1190)

Emmy(s) to Executive Producer(s) and Producer(s)

ANOTHER WORLD; Paul Rauch, Executive Producer; Joe Rothenberger and Mary S. Bonner, Producers (NBC)
DAYS OF OUR LIVES; Mrs Ted Corday, Executive Producer; Jack Herzberg and Al Rabin, Producers (NBC)
THE YOUNG AND THE RESTLESS; John J. Conboy, Executive Pro-

ducer; Patricia Wenig, Producer (CBS)
ALL MY CHILDREN; Bud Kloss, Producer (ABC)

DAYTIME DRAMA SPECIAL (E-1191)

Emmy(s) to Executive Producer(s) and Producer(s)

FIRST LADIES' DIARIES: EDITH WILSON; Jeff Young, Producer (NBC)
FIRST LADIES' DIARIES: RACHEL JACKSON; Paul Rauch, Producer (NBC)
FIRST LADIES' DIARIES: MARTHA WASHINGTON; Linda Wendell, Producer (NBC)

DAYTIME GAME OR AUDIENCE PARTICIPATION SHOW (E-1192)

Emmy(s) to Executive Producer(s) and Producer(s)

THE $20,000 PYRAMID; Bob Stewart, Executive Producer; Anne Marie Schmitt, Producer (ABC)
THE PRICE IS RIGHT; Frank Wayne, Executive Producer; Jay Wolpert, Producer (CBS)
MATCH GAME '75; Ira Skutch, Producer (CBS)
THE HOLLYWOOD SQUARES; Merrill Heatter and Bob Quigley, Executive Producers; Jay Redack, Producer (NBC)
LET'S MAKE A DEAL; Stefan Hatos, Executive Producer; Alan Gilbert, Producer (ABC)

DAYTIME TALK, SERVICE OR VARIETY SERIES (E-1193)

Emmy(s) to Executive Producer(s) and Producer(s)

DINAH! Henry Jaffe and Carolyn Raskin, Executive Producers; Fred Tatashore, Producer (Synd)
GOOD MORNING, AMERICA; Mel Ferber, Executive Producer; George Merlis and Bob Lissit, Producers (ABC)
THE MIKE DOUGLAS SHOW; Jack Reilly, Executive Producer; Woody Fraser, Producer (Synd)

CHILDREN'S ENTERTAINMENT SERIES (E-1194)

Emmy(s) to Executive Producer(s) and Producer(s)

BIG BLUE MARBLE; Henry Fownes, Producer (Synd)
CAPTAIN KANGAROO; Jimmy Hirshfield, Producer (CBS)
ZOOM; Austin Hoyt, Executive Producer (PBS)
FAT ALBERT AND THE COSBY KIDS; Norman Prescott and Lou Scheimer, Producers (CBS)

CHILDREN'S ENTERTAINMENT SPECIAL (E-1195)

Emmy(s) to Executive Producer(s) and Producer(s)

DANNY KAYE'S LOOK-IN AT THE METROPOLITAN OPERA; The CBS Festival Of Lively Arts For Young People; Sylvia Fine, Executive Producer; Bernard Rothman, Jack Wohl and Herbert Bonis, Producers (CBS)
ME AND DAD'S NEW WIFE; ABC Afterschool Special; Daniel Wilson, Producer (ABC)
IT MUST BE LOVE ('CAUSE I FEEL SO DUMB!); ABC Afterschool Special; Arthur Barron and Evelyn Barron, Producers (ABC)
WHAT IS NOISE? WHAT IS MUSIC?; New York Philharmonic Young People's Concert; Roger Englander, Producer (CBS)
PAPA AND ME; Special Treat; William P. D'Angelo, Ray Allen and Harvey Bullock, Executive Producers; Michael McLean, Producer (NBC)

CHILDREN'S INFORMATIONAL SERIES (E-1196)

Emmy(s) to Executive Producer(s) and Producer(s)

GO; George A. Heinemann, Executive Producer; Rift Fournier, J. Philip Miller, William W. Lewis and Joan Bender, Producers (NBC)
THE ELECTRIC COMPANY; Andrew B. Ferguson, Producer (PBS)
MAKE A WISH; Lester Cooper, Executive Producer; Peter Weinberg, Producer (ABC)

CHILDREN'S INFORMATIONAL SPECIAL (E-1197)

Emmy(s) to Executive Producer(s) and Producer(s)

HAPPY ANNIVERSARY, CHARLIE BROWN; Lee Mendelson and Warren Lockhart, Producers (CBS)
WHAT ARE THE LOCH NESS AND OTHER MONSTERS ALL ABOUT?; Joel Heller, Executive Producer; Walter Lister, Producer (CBS)
WINNING AND LOSING: DIARY OF A CAMPAIGN; ABC Afterschool Special; Daniel Wilson, Producer (ABC)

CHILDREN'S INSTRUCTIONAL PROGRAMMING - SERIES AND SPECIALS (E-1198)

Emmy(s) to Executive Producer(s) and Producer(s)

GRAMMAR ROCK; Thomas G. Yohe, Executive Producer; Radford Stone, Producer (ABC)
MISTER ROGERS' NEIGHBORHOOD; Fred Rogers, Executive Producer; Bill Moates, Producer (PBS)
SESAME STREET; Jon Stone, Executive Producer; Dulcy Singer, Producer (PBS)

ACTOR - DAYTIME DRAMA SERIES (E-1199)

LARRY HAINES; Search For Tomorrow (CBS)
JOHN BERADINO; General Hospital (ABC)
BILL HAYES; Days Of Our Lives (NBC)
MacDONALD CAREY; Days Of Our Lives (NBC)
SHEPPERD STRUDWICK; One Life To Live (ABC)
MICHAEL NOURI; Search For Tomorrow (CBS)

ACTOR - DAYTIME DRAMA SPECIAL (E-1200)

GERALD GORDON; First Ladies' Diaries: Rachel Jackson (NBC)
JAMES LUISI; First Ladies' Diaries: Martha Washington (NBC)

ACTRESS - DAYTIME DRAMA SERIES (E-1201)

HELEN GALLAGHER; Ryan's Hope (ABC)
SUSAN SEAFORTH HAYES; Day Of Our Lives (NBC)
MARY STUART; Search For Tomorrow (CBS)
DENISE ALEXANDER; General Hospital (ABC)
FRANCES HEFLIN; All My Children (ABC)

ACTRESS - DAYTIME DRAMA SPECIAL (E-1202)

ELIZABETH HUBBARD; First Ladies' Diaries; Edith Wilson (NBC)
SUSAN BROWNING; First Ladies' Diaries: Martha Washington (NBC)

HOST OR HOSTESS - GAME OR AUDIENCE PARTICIPATION SHOW (E-1203)

ALLEN LUDDEN; Password (ABC)
PETER MARSHALL; The Hollywood Squares (NBC)
GEOFF EDWARDS; Jackpot (NBC)

HOST OR HOSTESS - TALK, SERVICE OR VARIETY SERIES (E-1204)

DINAH SHORE; Dinah! (Synd)
DAVID HARTMAN; Good Morning, America (ABC)
MIKE DOUGLAS; The Mike Douglas Show (Synd)
MERV GRIFFIN; The Merv Griffin Show (Synd)

DIRECTOR - DAYTIME DRAMA SERIES (E-1205)

For a single episode

DAVID PRESSMAN; One Life To Live (ABC)
HUGH McPHILLIPS; The Doctors (NBC)
RICHARD DUNLAP; The Young And The Restless (CBS)

DIRECTOR - DAYTIME SPECIAL PROGRAM (E-1206)

NICHOLAS HAVINGA; First Ladies' Diaries: Edith Wilson (NBC)
JOHN J. DESMOND; First Ladies' Diaries: Martha Washington (NBC)
IRA CIRKER; First Ladies' Diaries: Rachel Jackson (NBC)

DIRECTOR - GAME OR AUDIENCE PARTICIPATION SHOW (E-1207)

For a single episode

MIKE GARGIULO; The $20,000 Pyramid (ABC)
JEROME SHAW; The Hollywood Squares (NBC)

DIRECTOR - DAYTIME VARIETY PROGRAM (E-1208)

For a single episode

GLEN SWANSON; Dinah Salutes Tony Orlando and Dawn On Their 5th Anniversary; Dinah! (Synd)
DONALD R. KING; The Mike Douglas Show (with Fred Astaire and Gene Kelly) (Synd)

WRITING - DAYTIME DRAMA SERIES (E-1209)

For a single episode of a series; or for the entire series

WILLIAM J. BELL, KAY LENARD, PAT FALKEN SMITH, BILL REGA, MARGARET STEWART, SHERI ANDERSON and WANDA COLEMAN; Days Of Our Lives; Series (NBC)
HENRY SLESAR; The Edge of Night; Series (ABC)
JEROME DOBSON, BRIDGET DOBSON and JEAN ROUVEROL; The Guiding Light (CBS)
WILLIAM J. BELL and KAY ALDEN; The Young And The Restless (CBS)
AGNES NIXON, WISNER WASHAM, KATHRYN McCABE, MARY K. WELLS and JACK WOOD; All My Children; Series (ABC)

WRITING - DAYTIME SPECIAL PROGRAM (E-1210)

AUDREY DAVIS LEVIN; First Ladies' Diaries: Edith Wilson (NBC)
ETHEL FRANK; First Ladies' Diaries: Martha Washington (NBC)

THE DAYTIME AREAS

(Possibility of One Award, More Than One Award or No Award)

INDIVIDUAL ACHIEVEMENT - DAYTIME PROGRAMMING (E-1211)

For a single episode of a series; or a special program
PAUL LYNDE, Performer; The Hollywood Squares (NBC)

INDIVIDUAL ACHIEVEMENT - CHILDREN'S PROGRAMMING (E-1212)

For a single episode of a series; or for a special program
THE MUPPETS; Performers (JIM HENSON, FRANK OZ, JERRY NELSON, CARROLL SPINNEY and RICHARD HUNT); Sesame Street; April 25, 1975 (PBS)

1976/77

COMEDY SERIES (E-1213)

Award(s) to Executive Producer(s) and/or Producer(s)

THE MARY TYLER MOORE SHOW, Allan Burns and James L. Brooks, Executive Producers; Ed. Weinberger and Stan Daniels, Producers (CBS)
ALL IN THE FAMILY, Mort Lachman, Executive Producer; Milt Josefsberg, Producer (CBS)
BARNEY MILLER, Danny Arnold, Executive Producer; Roland Kibbee, Danny Arnold, Producers (ABC)
THE BOB NEWHART SHOW, Tom Patchett, Jay Tarses, Executive Producers; Michael Zinberg, Gordon Farr and Lynne Farr, Producers (CBS)
M*A*S*H, Gene Reynolds, Executive Producer; Allan Katz, Don Reo and Burt Metcalfe, Producers (CBS)

DRAMA SERIES (E-1214)

Award(s) to Executive Producer(s) and/or Producer(s)

UPSTAIRS, DOWNSTAIRS, Masterpiece Theatre; John Hawkesworth and Joan Sullivan, Producers (PBS)
BARETTA, Anthony Spinner, Bernard Kowalski and Leigh Vance, Executive Producers; Charles E. Dismukes, Producer (ABC)
COLUMBO, NBC Sunday Mystery Movie; Everett Chambers, Producer (NBC)
FAMILY, Aaron Spelling, Leonard Goldberg and Mike Nichols, Executive Producers; Nigel McKeand, Producer; (ABC)
POLICE STORY, David Gerber, Executive Producer; Liam O'Brien, Producer; Mel Swope, Co-Producer (NBC)

COMEDY-VARIETY OR MUSIC SERIES (E-1215)

Award(s) to Executive Producer(s) and/or Producer(s) and Star(s), if applicable

VAN DYKE AND COMPANY, Byron Paul, Executive Producer; Allan Blye and Bob Einstein, Producers; Dick Van Dyke, Star (NBC)
THE CAROL BURNETT SHOW, Joe Hamilton, Executive Producer; Ed Simmons, Producer; Carol Burnett, Star (CBS)
EVENING AT POPS, William Cosel, Producer; Arthur Fiedler, Star (PBS)
THE MUPPET SHOW, Jim Henson and David Lazer, Executive Producers; Jack Burns, Producer; The Muppets (Frank Oz, Richard Hunt, Dave Goelz, Eren Ozker, John Lovelady, and Jerry Nelson) Stars (SYND)
NBC's SATURDAY NIGHT, Lorne Michaels, Producer (NBC)

LIMITED SERIES (E-1216)

Award(s) to Executive Producer(s) and/or Producer(s)

ROOTS, ABC Novel For Television; David L. Wolper, Executive Producer; Stan Margulies, Producer (ABC)
THE ADAMS CHRONICLES, Jac Venza, Executive Producer; Virginia Kassel, Series Producer; Robert Costello, Coordinating Producer; Fred Coe and James Cellan-Jones, Producers (PBS)
CAPTAINS AND THE KINGS, NBC's Best Seller; Roy Huggins, Executive Producer; Jo Swerling, Jr., Producer (NBC)
MADAME BOVARY, Masterpiece Theatre; Richard Beynon, Producer (PBS)
THE MONEYCHANGERS, NBC World Premiere Movie; The Big Event; Ross Hunter and Jacque Mapes, Producers (NBC)

SPECIAL - DRAMA OR COMEDY (E-1217)

Award(s) to Executive Producer(s) and/or Producer(s)

ELEANOR AND FRANKLIN: THE WHITE HOUSE YEARS, ABC Theatre; David Susskind, Executive Producer; Harry R. Sherman, Producer (ABC)
SYBIL, NBC World Premiere Movie; The Big Event; Peter Dunne and Philip Capice, Executive Producers; Jacqueline Babbin, Producer (NBC)
HARRY S. TRUMAN: PLAIN SPEAKING, David Susskind, Producer (PBS)
RAID ON ENTEBBE, The Big Event; Edgar J. Scherick and Daniel H. Blatt, Executive Producers (NBC)
21 HOURS AT MUNICH, The ABC Sunday Night Movie; Edward S. Feldman, Executive Producer; Frank von Zerneck and Robert Greenwald, Producers (ABC)

SPECIAL - COMEDY-VARIETY OR MUSIC (E-1218)

Award(s) to Executive Producer(s) and/or Producer(s) and Star(s), if applicable

THE BARRY MANILOW SPECIAL, Miles Lourie, Executive Producer; Steve Binder, Producer; Barry Manilow, Star (ABC)
DOUG HENNING'S WORLD OF MAGIC, Jerry Goldstein, Executive Producer; Walter C. Miller, Producer; Doug Henning, Star (NBC)
THE NEIL DIAMOND SPECIAL, Jerry Weintraub, Executive Producer; Gary Smith and Dwight Hemion Producers; Neil Diamond, Star (NBC)
THE SHIRLEY MacLAINE SPECIAL: WHERE DO WE GO FROM HERE?, George Schlatter, Producer; Shirley MacLaine, Star (CBS)

SILLS AND BURNETT AT THE MET, Joe Hamilton, Producer; Beverly Sills and Carol Burnett, Stars (CBS)

CLASSICAL PROGRAM IN THE PERFORMING ARTS (E-1219)

For a special program, or for a series (excluding drama)
Award(s) to Executive Producer(s) and/or Producer(s) and Star(s), if applicable

AMERICAN BALLET THEATRE: SWAN LAKE, Live From Lincoln Center; (Great Performances); John Goberman, Producer (PBS)
AMERICAN BALLET THEATRE; DANCE IN AMERICA; (Great Performances); Jac Venza, Executive Producer; Emile Ardolino, Series Coordinating Producer; Merrill Brockway, Series Producer (PBS)
ARTUR RUBINSTEIN AT 90; (Great Performances); Jac Venza, Klaus Hallig and Herbert Kloiber, Executive Producers; David Griffiths and Fritz Buttenstadt, Producers; Artur Rubinstein, Star (PBS)
THE BOLSHOI BALLET: ROMEO AND JULIET, Lothar Bock, Executive Producer; Alvin Cooperman, Producer (CBS)
MARTHA GRAHAM DANCE COMPANY, Dance In America; (Great Performances); Jac Venza, Executive Producer; Emile Ardolino, Series Coordinating Producer; Merrill Brockway, Series Producer; Martha Graham, Star (PBS)

CHILDREN'S SPECIAL (E-1220)

For specials which were broadcast during the evening.
Award(s) to Executive Producer(s) and Producer(s)

BALLET SHOES, PARTS 1 & 2, Piccadilly Circus; John McRae and Joan Sullivan, Producers (PBS)
IT'S ARBOR DAY, CHARLIE BROWN, Lee Mendelson, Executive Producer; Bill Melendez, Producer (CBS)
PETER PAN, Hallmark Hall Of Fame; The Big Event; Gary Smith and Dwight Hemion, Executive Producers; Gary Smith, Producer (NBC)
PINOCCHIO, Bernard Rothman and Jack Wohl, Producers (CBS)
THE LITTLE DRUMMER BOY, BOOK II, Arthur Rankin, Jr. and Jules Bass, Producers (NBC)

COVERAGE OF SPECIAL EVENTS - PROGRAMS (E-1221)

An Award for unique program achievement. A special event is a single program presented as live coverage; i.e., parades, pageants, awards presentations, salutes and coverage of other live events which were not covered by the news division. (Possibility of one Award, more than one Award, or no Award)

THE GOOD OLD DAYS OF RADIO, Loring d'Usseau, Producer (PBS)
GRAMMY AWARDS SHOW, Marty Pasetta, Producer (CBS)
THE 28th ANNUAL EMMY AWARDS, Norman Rosemont, Producer (ABC)
30th ANNUAL TONY AWARDS, Alexander H. Cohen, Producer (ABC)
48th ANNUAL OSCAR AWARDS, Howard W. Koch, Producer (ABC)

SPECIAL CLASSIFICATION OF OUTSTANDING PROGRAM ACHIEVEMENT (E-1222)

An Award for unique program achievement, which does not fall into a specific category, and is not otherwise recognized. (Possibility of one Award, more than one Award, or no Award)

THE TONIGHT SHOW STARRING JOHNNY CARSON, Fred De Cordova, Producer; Johnny Carson, Star; Series (NBC)
BICENTENNIAL MINUTES, Bob Markell, Executive Producer; Series (CBS)
THE FIRST FIFTY YEARS, The Big Event; Greg Garrison, Executive Producer; Lee Hale, Chet Hagan, Producers (NBC)
LIFE GOES TO THE MOVIES, The Big Event; Jack Haley, Jr., Executive Producer; Mel Stuart, Richard Schickel, Malcolm Leo, Producers (NBC)

THE WONDERFUL WORLD OF DISNEY, Ron Miller, Executive Producer; Series (NBC)

ACTOR - COMEDY SERIES (E-1223)

CARROLL O'CONNOR, All In The Family (CBS)
JACK ALBERTSON, Chico and the Man (NBC)
ALAN ALDA, M*A*S*H (CBS)
HAL LINDEN, Barney Miller (ABC)
HENRY WINKLER, Happy Days (ABC)

ACTOR - DRAMA SERIES (E-1224)

JAMES GARNER, The Rockford Files (NBC)
ROBERT BLAKE, Baretta (ABC)
PETER FALK, Columbo (NBC)
JACK KLUGMAN, Quincy, M. E. (NBC)
KARL MALDEN, The Streets Of San Francisco (ABC)

ACTOR - LIMITED SERIES (E-1225)

CHRISTOPHER PLUMMER, The Moneychangers; NBC World Premiere Movie; The Big Event (NBC)
STANLEY BAKER, How Green Was My Valley; Masterpiece Theatre (PBS)
RICHARD JORDAN, Captains And The Kings; NBC's Best Seller (NBC)
STEVEN KEATS, Seventh Avenue; NBC's Best Seller (NBC)

ACTOR - DRAMA OR COMEDY SPECIAL (E-1226)

ED FLANDERS, Harry S. Truman: Plain Speaking (PBS)
PETER BOYLE, Tail Gunner Joe; NBC World Premiere Movie; The Big Event (NBC)
PETER FINCH, Raid On Entebbe; The Big Event (NBC)
EDWARD HERRMANN, Eleanor and Franklin: The White House Years; ABC Theatre (ABC)
GEORGE C. SCOTT, Beauty And The Beast; Hallmark Hall Of Fame (NBC)

ACTOR - SINGLE PERFORMANCE - DRAMA OR COMEDY SERIES (E-1227)

LOUIS GOSSETT, JR., Roots, Part 2 (ABC)
JOHN AMOS, Roots, Part 5 (ABC)
LEVAR BURTON, Roots, Part 1 (ABC)
BEN VEREEN, Roots, Part 6 (ABC)

ACTRESS - COMEDY SERIES (E-1228)

BEATRICE ARTHUR, Maude (CBS)
VALERIE HARPER, Rhoda (CBS)
MARY TYLER MOORE, The Mary Tyler Moore Show (CBS)
SUZANNE PLESHETTE, The Bob Newhart Show (CBS)
JEAN STAPLETON, All In The Family (CBS)

ACTRESS - DRAMA SERIES (E-1229)

LINDSAY WAGNER, The Bionic Woman (ABC)
ANGIE DICKINSON, Police Woman (NBC)
KATE JACKSON, Charlie's Angels (ABC)
MICHAEL LEARNED, The Waltons (CBS)
SADA THOMPSON, Family (ABC)

ACTRESS - LIMITED SERIES (E-1230)

PATTY DUKE ASTIN, Captains And The Kings; NBC's Best Seller (NBC)
SUSAN FLANNERY, The Moneychangers; NBC World Premiere Movie; The Big Event (NBC)
DORI BRENNER, Seventh Avenue; NBC's Best Seller (NBC)
EVA MARIE SAINT, How The West Was Won (ABC)
JANE SEYMOUR, Captains And The Kings; NBC's Best Seller (NBC)

ACTRESS - DRAMA OR COMEDY SPECIAL (E-1231)

SALLY FIELD, Sybil; NBC World Premiere Movie; The Big Event (NBC)

JANE ALEXANDER, Eleanor and Franklin: The White House Years; ABC Theatre (ABC)
SUSAN CLARK, Amelia Earhart; NBC Monday Night At The Movies, (NBC)
JULIE HARRIS, The Last Of Mrs. Lincoln; Hollywood Television Theatre (PBS)
JOANNE WOODWARD, Sybil; NBC World Premiere Movie; The Big Event (NBC)

ACTRESS - SINGLE PERFORMANCE - DRAMA OR COMEDY SERIES (E-1232)

BEULAH BONDI, The Waltons; The Pony Cart (CBS)
SUSAN BLAKELY, Rich Man, Poor Man, Book II, Ch. 1 (ABC)
MADGE SINCLAIR, Roots, Part 4 (ABC)
LESLIE UGGAMS, Roots, Part 6 (ABC)
JESSICA WALTER, The Streets of San Francisco; 'Til Death Us Do Part (ABC)

SUPPORTING ACTOR - COMEDY SERIES (E-1233)

For a regular or limited series

GARY BURGHOFF, M*A*S*H (CBS)
EDWARD ASNER, The Mary Tyler Moore Show (CBS)
TED KNIGHT, The Mary Tyler Moore Show (CBS)
HARRY MORGAN, M*A*S*H (CBS)
ABE VIGODA, Barney Miller (ABC)

SUPPORTING ACTOR - DRAMA SERIES (E-1234)

For a regular or limited series

GARY FRANK, Family (ABC)
NOAH BEERY, The Rockford Files (NBC)
DAVID DOYLE, Charlie's Angels (ABC)
TOM EWELL, Baretta (ABC)
WILL GEER, The Waltons (CBS)

SUPPORTING ACTOR - CONTINUING OR SINGLE PERFORMANCE - VARIETY OR MUSIC (E-1235)

For a continuing role in a regular or limited series; or a one-time appearance in a series; or a special

TIM CONWAY, The Carol Burnett Show; Series (CBS)
JOHN BELUSHI, NBC's Saturday Night (with Candice Bergen) (NBC)
CHEVY CHASE, NBC's Saturday Night (with Elliott Gould) (NBC)
HARVEY KORMAN, The Carol Burnett Show; Entire Series (CBS)
BEN VEREEN, The Bell Telephone Jubilee (NBC)

SUPPORTING ACTOR - COMEDY OR DRAMA SPECIAL (E-1236)

BURGESS MEREDITH, Tail Gunner Joe; NBC World Premiere Movie; The Big Event (NBC)
MARTIN BALSAM, Raid On Entebbe; The Big Event (NBC)
MARK HARMON, Eleanor And Franklin: The White House Years; ABC Theatre (ABC)
YAPHET KOTTO, Raid On Entebbe; The Big Event (NBC)
WALTER McGINN, Eleanor And Franklin: The White House Years; ABC Theatre (ABC)

SUPPORTING ACTOR - SINGLE PERFORMANCE - COMEDY OR DRAMA SERIES (E-1237)

For a one-time appearance in a regular or limited series

EDWARD ASNER, Roots, Part 1 (ABC)
CHARLES DURNING, Captains And The Kings, Chapter 2; NBC's Best Seller (NBC)
MOSES GUNN, Roots, Part 1 (ABC)
ROBERT REED, Roots, Part 5 (ABC)
RALPH WAITE, Roots, Part 1 (ABC)

SUPPORTING ACTRESS - COMEDY SERIES (E-1238)

For a regular or limited series

MARY KAY PLACE, Mary Hartman, Mary Hartman (SYND)
GEORGIA ENGEL, The Mary Tyler Moore Show (CBS)
JULIE KAVNER, Rhoda (CBS)
LORETTA SWIT, M*A*S*H (CBS)
BETTY WHITE, The Mary Tyler Moore Show (CBS)

SUPPORTING ACTRESS - DRAMA SERIES (E-1239)

For a regular or limited series

KRISTY McNICHOL, Family (ABC)
MEREDITH BAXTER-BIRNEY, Family (ABC)
ELLEN CORBY, The Waltons (CBS)
LEE MERIWETHER, Barnaby Jones (CBS)
JACQUELINE TONG, Upstairs, Downstairs; Masterpiece Theatre (PBS)

SUPPORTING ACTRESS - CONTINUING OR SINGLE PERFORMANCE - VARIETY OR MUSIC (E-1240)

For a continuing role in a regular or limited series; or a one-time appearance in a series; or a special

RITA MORENO, The Muppet Show (SYND)
VICKI LAWRENCE, The Carol Burnett Show; Entire Series (CBS)
GILDA RADNER, NBC's Saturday Night (with Steve Martin) (NBC)

SUPPORTING ACTRESS - COMEDY OR DRAMA SPECIAL (E-1241)

DIANA HYLAND, The Boy In The Plastic Bubble; The ABC Friday Night Movie (ABC)
RUTH GORDON, The Great Houdinis; The ABC Friday Night Movie (ABC)
ROSEMARY MURPHY, Eleanor And Franklin: The White House Years; ABC Theatre (ABC)
PATRICIA NEAL, Tail Gunner Joe; NBC World Premiere Movie; The Big Event (NBC)
SUSAN OLIVER, Amelia Earhart; NBC Monday Night At The Movies (NBC)

SUPPORTING ACTRESS - SINGLE PERFORMANCE - COMEDY OR DRAMA SERIES (E-1242)

For a one-time appearance in a regular or limited series

OLIVIA COLE, Roots, Part 8 (ABC)
SANDY DUNCAN, Roots, Part 5 (ABC)
EILEEN HECKART, The Mary Tyler Moore Show; Lou Proposes (CBS)
CICELY TYSON, Roots, Part 1 (ABC)
NANCY WALKER, Rhoda; The Separation (CBS)

WRITING - COMEDY SERIES (E-1243)

A single episode of a regular or limited series with continuing characters and/or theme

ALLAN BURNS, JAMES L. BROOKS, ED. WEINBERGER, STAN DANIELS, DAVID LLOYD and BOB ELLISON, The Mary Tyler Moore Show; The Last Show (CBS)
ALAN ALDA, M*A*S*H; Dear Sigmund (CBS)
DANNY ARNOLD, TONY SHEEHAN, Barney Miller; Quarantine, Part 2 (ABC)
DAVID LLOYD, The Mary Tyler Moore Show; Mary Midwife (CBS)
EARL POMERANTZ, The Mary Tyler Moore Show; Ted's Change Of Heart (CBS)

WRITING - DRAMA SERIES (E-1244)

A single episode of a regular or limited series with continuing characters and/or theme

ERNEST KINOY, WILLIAM BLINN, Roots, Part 2 (ABC)
JAMES LEE, Roots, Part 5 (ABC)
ROGER O. HIRSON, The Adams Chronicles; Charles Francis Adams: Minister To Great Britian (PBS)
M. CHARLES COHEN, Roots, Part 8 (ABC)
TAD MOSEL, The Adams Chronicles; John Quincy Adams: President (PBS)

WRITING - COMEDY-VARIETY OR MUSIC SERIES (E-1245)

A single episode of a regular or limited series

ANNE BEATTS, DAN AYKROYD, AL FRANKEN, TOM DAVIS, JAMES DOWNEY, LORNE MICHAELS, MARILYN SUZANNE MILLER, MICHAEL O'DONOGHUE, HERB SARGENT, TOM SCHILLER, ROSIE SHUSTER, ALAN ZWEIBEL, JOHN BELUSHI and BILL MURRAY, NBC's Saturday Night (with Sissy Spacek) (NBC)
JIM HENSON, JACK BURNS, MARC LONDON and JERRY JUHL, The Muppet Show (with Paul Williams) (SYND)
ANNE BEATTS, CHEVY CHASE, AL FRANKEN, TOM DAVIS, LORNE MICHAELS, MARILYN SUZANNE MILLER, MICHAEL O'DONOGHUE, HERB SARGENT, TOM SCHILLER, ROSIE SHUSTER and ALAN ZWEIBEL NBC's Saturday Night (with Elliott Gould) (NBC)
ED SIMMONS, ROGER BEATTY, ELIAS DAVIS, DAVID POLLOCK, RICK HAWKINS, LIZ SAGE, ADELE STYLER, BURT STYLER, TIM CONWAY, BILL RICHMOND, GENE PERRET, DICK CLAIR and JENNA McMAHON, The Carol Burnett Show (with Eydie Gorme) (CBS)
BOB EINSTEIN, ALLAN BLYE, GEORGE BURDITT, GARRY FERRIER, KEN FINKELMAN, MITCH MARKOWITZ, TOMMY McLOUGHLIN, DON NOVELLO, PAT PROFT, LEONARD RIPPS, MICKEY ROSE, AUBREY TADMAN, DICK VAN DYKE and PAUL WAYNE, Van Dyke & Company (with John Denver) (NBC)

WRITING - COMEDY-VARIETY OR MUSIC SPECIAL (E-1246)

ALAN BUZ KOHAN, TED STRAUSS, American Salutes Richard Rodgers: The Sound Of His Music (CBS)
ALAN THICKE, DON CLARK, SUSAN CLARK, RONNY PEARLMAN, STEVE BINDER, BARRY MANILOW and BRUCE VILANCH, The Barry Manilow Special (ABC)
BILL DYER, NTOZAKE SHANGE, An Evening With Diana Ross; The Big Event (NBC)
KEN WELCH, MITZIE WELCH, KENNY SOLMS and GAIL PARENT, Sills And Burnett At The Met (CBS)
DIGBY WOLFE and GEORGE SCHLATTER, John Denver And Friend (ABC)

WRITING, SPECIAL PROGRAM - DRAMA OR COMEDY - ORIGINAL TELEPLAY (E-1247)

LANE SLATE, Tail Gunner Joe; NBC World Premiere Movie; The Big Event (NBC)
BARRY BECKERMAN, Raid On Entebbe; The Big Event (NBC)
JAMES COSTIGAN, Eleanor And Franklin: The White House Years; ABC Theatre (ABC)
ERNEST KINOY, Victory At Entebbe (ABC)
DOUGLAS DAY STEWART, Teleplay; JOE MORGENSTERN and DOUGLAS DAY STEWART, Story; The Boy In The Plastic Bubble; The ABC Friday Night Movie (ABC)

WRITING, SPECIAL PROGRAM - DRAMA OR COMEDY - ADAPTATION (E-1248)

STEWART STERN, Sybil; NBC World Premiere Movie; The Big Event (NBC)
WILLIAM BAST, The Man In The Iron Mask; The Bell System Presents (NBC)
JOHN McGREEVEY, Judge Horton And The Scottsboro Boys; NBC World Premiere (NBC)
CAROL SOBIESKI, Harry S. Truman: Plain Speaking (PBS)
STEVEN GETHERS, A Circle Of Children (CBS)

DIRECTOR - COMEDY SERIES (E-1249)

A single episode of a regular or limited series with continuing characters and/or theme

ALAN ALDA, M*A*S*H; Dear Sigmund (CBS)
PAUL BOGART, All In The Family; The Draft Dodger (CBS)
JOAN DARLING, M*A*S*H; The Nurses (CBS)
ALAN RAFKIN, M*A*S*H; Lt. Radar O'Reilly (CBS)
JAY SANDRICH, The Mary Tyler Moore Show; The Last Show (CBS)

DIRECTOR - DRAMA SERIES (E-1250)

A single episode of a regular or limited series with continuing characters and/or theme

DAVID GREENE, Roots, Part 1 (ABC)
MARVIN CHOMSKY, Roots, Part 3 (ABC)
FRED COE, The Adams Chronicles; John Quincy Adams: President (PBS)
JOHN ERMAN, Roots, Part 2 (ABC)
GILBERT MOSES, Roots, Part 6 (ABC)

DIRECTOR, SPECIAL PROGRAM - DRAMA OR COMEDY (E-1251)

DANIEL PETRIE, Eleanor And Franklin: The White House Years; ABC Theatre (ABC)
FIELDER COOK, Judge Horton And The Scottsboro Boys; NBC World Premiere Movie (NBC)
TOM GRIES, Helter Skelter (CBS)
IRVIN KERSHNER, Raid On Entebbe; The Big Event (NBC)
JUD TAYLOR, Tail Gunner Joe; NBC World Premiere Movie; The Big Event (NBC)

DIRECTOR - COMEDY-VARIETY OR MUSIC SERIES (E-1252)

A single episode of a regular or limited series

DAVE POWERS, The Carol Burnett Show (with Eydie Gorme) (CBS)
JOHN C. MOFFITT, Van Dyke And Company (with John Denver) (NBC)
DAVE WILSON, NBC's Saturday Night (with Host Paul Simon) (NBC)

DIRECTOR - COMEDY-VARIETY OR MUSIC SPECIAL (E-1253)

DWIGHT HEMION, America Salutes Richard Rodgers: The Sound Of His Music (CBS)
STEVE BINDER, The Barry Manilow Special (ABC)
TONY CHARMOLI, The Shirley MacLaine Special: Where Do We Go From Here? (CBS)
WALTER C. MILLER, Doug Henning's World Of Magic (NBC)
DAVID POWERS, Sills And Burnett At The Met (CBS)

INDIVIDUALS - SPECIAL EVENTS COVERAGE (E-1254)

An Award for unique program achievement. A special event is a a single program presented as live coverage; i.e., pageants, parades, awards presentations, salutes and coverage of other live events which were not covered by the news division. (Possibility of one Award, more than one Award, or no Award)

JOHN C. MOFFITT, Director; The 28th Annual Emmy Awards (ABC)
HELEN O'CONNELL, Hostess; Miss Universe Beauty Pageant (CBS)
MARTY PASETTA, Director; 48th Annual Oscar Awards (ABC)

DAYTIME TALK, SERVICE, OR VARIETY SERIES (E-1255)

Emmy(s) to Executive Producer(s) and Producer(s)

DINAH! Henry Jaffe and Carolyn Raskin, Executive Producers; Fred Tatashore, Producer (SYND)
THE GONG SHOW, Chuck Barris, Executive Producer; Gene Banks, Producer (NBC)
THE MERV GRIFFIN SHOW, Bob Murphy, Producer (SYND)
THE MIKE DOUGLAS SHOW, David Salzman, Executive Producer; Jack Reilly, Producer (SYND)

HOST OR HOSTESS - TALK, SERVICE OR VARIETY SERIES (E-1256)

PHIL DONAHUE, Donahue (SYND)
MIKE DOUGLAS, The Mike Douglas Show (SYND)
MERV GRIFFIN, The Merv Griffin Show (SYND)
DINAH SHORE, Dinah! (SYND)

DIRECTOR - DAYTIME VARIETY PROGRAM (E-1257)

For a single episode
DICK CARSON, The Merv Griffin Show; Merv Griffin in Israel (SYND)
JOHN DORSEY, The Gong Show (NBC)
DONALD R. KING, The Mike Douglas Show; Mike in Hollywood (with Ray Charles & Michel Le Grand) (SYND)
GLEN SWANSON, Dinah!; Dinah from Australia (SYND)

GAME OR AUDIENCE PARTICIPATION SHOW (E-1258)

For Daytime and Nightime Programs. Emmy(s) to Executive Producer(s) and Producer(s)

THE $20,000 PYRAMID, Bob Stewart, Executive Producer; Anne Marie Schmitt, Producer (ABC)
FAMILY FEUD, Howard Felsher, Producer (ABC)
HOLLYWOOD SQUARES, Robert Quigley and Merrill Heatter, Executive Producers; Jay Redack, Producer (NBC)
MATCH GAME '76, Ira Skutch, Producer (CBS)
TATTLETALES, Ira Skutch, Executive Producer; Paul Alter, Producer (CBS)

HOST OR HOSTESS - GAME OR AUDIENCE PARTICIPATION SHOW (E-1259)

For Daytime or Nighttime Programs
DICK CLARK, The $20,000 Pyramid (ABC)
BERT CONVY, Tattletales (CBS)
GENE RAYBURN, Match Game '76 (CBS)

DIRECTOR - GAME OR AUDIENCE PARTICIPATION SHOW (E-1260)

For a single episode of a Daytime or Nighttime Series
JOSEPH BEHAR, Let's Make a Deal (ABC)
MIKE GARGIULO, The $20,000 Pyramid (with Tony Randall & Jo Anne Worley) (ABC)

CHILDREN'S ENTERTAINMENT SERIES (E-1261)

Emmy(s) to Executive Producer(s) and Producer(s)
CAPTAIN KANGAROO, Jim Hirschfeld, Producer (CBS)
DAVID COPPERFIELD, Once Upon A Classic; Jay Rayvid, Executive Producer; John McRae and Don Coney, Producers (PBS)
HEIDI, Once Upon A Classic; Jay Rayvid, Executive Producer; John McRae and Don Coney, Producers (PBS)
THE PRINCE AND THE PAUPER; Once Upon A Classic; Jay Rayvid, Executive Producer; Barry Letts and Don Coney, Producers (PBS)
ZOOM! Cheryl Susheel Bibbs, Executive Producer; Monia Joblin and Mary Benjamin, Producers (PBS)

CHILDREN'S ENTERTAINMENT SPECIAL (E-1262)
Emmy(s) to Executive Producer(s) and Producer(s)

BIG HENRY AND THE POLKA DOT KID, Special Treat; Linda Gottlieb, Producer (NBC)

BLIND SUNDAY, ABC Afterschool Specials; Daniel Wilson, Producer (ABC)

FRANCESCA BABY, ABC Afterschool Specials; Martin Tahse, Producer (ABC)

LUKE WAS THERE, Special Treat; Linda Gottlieb, Executive Producer; Richard Marquand, Producer (NBC)

THE ORIGINAL ROMPIN' STOMPIN' HOT AND HEAVY, COOL AND GROOVY ALL STAR JAZZ SHOW, The CBS Festival Of Lively Arts For Young People; Ron Kass and Edgar Bronfman, Jr., Executive Producers; Gary Keys, Producer (CBS)

P. J. AND THE PRESIDENT'S SON, ABC Afterschool Specials; Danny Wilson, Executive Producer; Fran Sears, Producer (ABC)

CHILDREN'S INFORMATIONAL SERIES (E-1263)
Emmy(s) to Executive Producer(s) and Producer(s)

ABC MINUTE MAGAZINE, Thomas H. Wolf, Producer (ABC)

AMERICA ROCK, Tom Yohe, Executive Producer; Radford Stone, Producer (ABC)

ANIMALS, ANIMALS, ANIMALS, Lester Cooper, Executive Producer; Peter Weinberg, Producer (ABC)

THE ELECTRIC COMPANY, Samuel Y. Gibbon, Jr., Executive Producer (PBS)

CHILDREN'S INFORMATIONAL SPECIAL (E-1264)
Emmy(s) to Executive Producer(s) and Producer(s)

HOW TO FOLLOW THE ELECTION, Sid Darion, Producer (ABC)

MY MOM'S HAVING A BABY, ABC Afterschool Specials; David H. DePatie and Friz Freleng, Executive Producers; Bob Chenault, Producer (ABC)

CHILDREN'S INSTRUCTIONAL PROGRAMMING - SERIES AND SPECIALS (E-1265)
Emmy(s) to Executive Producer(s) and Producer(s)

SESAME STREET, Jon Stone, Executive Producer; Dulcy Singer, Producer (PBS)

VILLA ALEGRE, Claudio Guzman, Executive Producer; Larry Gottlieb, Producer (PBS)

DIRECTOR - DAYTIME DRAMA SERIES (E-1266)
For a single episode

JOSEPH BEHAR, Days Of Our Lives (NBC)

IRA CIRKER, Another World (NBC)

PAUL E. DAVIS, LEONARD VALENTA, As The World Turns (CBS)

AL RABIN, Days Of Our Lives; Julie And Doug's Wedding (NBC)

JOHN SEDWICK, The Edge Of Night (ABC)

LELA SWIFT, Ryan's Hope (ABC)

DAYTIME DRAMA SERIES (E-1267)
Emmy(s) to Executive Producer(s) and Producer(s)

ALL MY CHILDREN, Bud Kloss and Agnes Nixon, Producers (ABC)

ANOTHER WORLD, Paul Rauch, Executive Producer; Mary S. Bonner and Joseph H. Rothenberger, Producers (NBC)

DAYS OF OUR LIVES, Mrs. Ted Corday, Executive Producer; H. Wesley Kenny and Jack Herzberg, Producers (NBC)

THE EDGE OF NIGHT, Erwin Nicholson, Producer (ABC)

RYAN'S HOPE, Paul Avila Mayer and Claire Labine, Executive Producers; Robert Costello, Producer (ABC)

THE INTERNATIONAL DIRECTORATE AWARD (E-1268)

TALBOT DUCKMANTON, Chairman, and **SIR CHARLES MOSES**, Secretary-General, Asian Broadcasting Union

SPECIAL INTERNATIONAL DIRECTORATE AWARD CITATIONS (E-1269)

HOWARD THOMAS, Chairman of Thames Television, Ltd. and Dr. **ROBERTO MARINHO**, President, TV-Globo Network of Brazil

INTERNATIONAL FICTION AWARD (E-1270)

THE NAKED CIVIL SERVANT, Thames Television Limited, London, England

THE STANLEY BAXTER PICTURE SHOW PART III, London Weekend Television, London, England

FAWLTY TOWERS, British Broadcasting Corporation, London, England

LES LAVANDES ET LE RESEDA, Societe Nationale de Programme France Regions, Paris, France

IT'S A LOVELY DAY TOMORROW, ATV Network Limited, Hertfordshire, England

INTERNATIONAL NON-FICTION AWARD (E-1271)

REACH FOR TOMORROW, Nippon Television Network, Tokyo, Japan

PROFESSOR MENGLEBERG, Nederlandse Omroep Stichting, The Netherlands

PINCHAS ZUKERMAN, British Broadcasting Corporation, London, England

THE BATTLE OF THE SOMME, British Broadcasting Corporation, London, England

W5-CHILDREN'S HOSPITAL, CTV Canada, Toronto, Ontario, Canada

THE NATIONAL AWARD FOR COMMUNITY SERVICE (E-1272)

RAPE (WGBH-TV) Boston, Massachusetts

EQUALITY, New Jersey Public Television, Trenton, New Jersey

BREAST CANCER: A FACT OF LIFE (KTBS-TV) Shreveport, Louisiana

EYEWITNESS NEWS: YEAR 2000 (KPIX) San Francisco, California

SIGHT AND SOUND: I AM OLD, I AM OLD (WNBC-TV) New York, New York

BEHIND THESE BARS (KAIT-TV) Jonesboro, Arkansas

THE NUCLEAR REACTION (KMGH-TV) Denver, Colorado

GENESIS, JUBA AND OTHER JEWELS (WTOP-TV) Washington, D.C.

ACTRESS - DAYTIME DRAMA SERIES (E-1273)

NANCY ADDISON, Ryan's Hope (ABC)

HELEN GALLAGHER, Ryan's Hope (ABC)

BEVERLEE McKINSEY, Another World (NBC)

MARY STUART, Search For Tomorrow (CBS)

RUTH WARRICK, All My Children (ABC)

DAYTIME DRAMA SPECIAL (E-1274)

The Academy's rules specify the possibility of no winners in this 'Area'. For this reason, the nominees' names have been omitted to spare any possible embarassment in the event there are no winners.

THE AMERICAN WOMAN: PORTRAITS OF COURAGE, Gaby Monet, Producer; Lois Nettleton, Performer; Writers, Gaby Monet, Anne Grant (ABC)

WRITING - DAYTIME DRAMA SERIES (E-1275)
For a single episode of a series; or for the entire series

WILLIAM J. BELL, PAT FALKEN SMITH, WILLIAM REGA, KAY LENARD, MARGARET STEWART, Days of Our Lives; Series (NBC)

CLAIRE LABINE, PAUL AVILA MAYER, MARY MUNISTERI, Ryan's Hope; Series (ABC)

HARDING LEMAY, TOM KING, PETER SWET, BARRY BERG, JAN MERLIN, ARTHUR GIRON, KATHY CALLAWAY, Another World; Series (NBC)

AGNES NIXON, WISNER WASHAM, KATHRYN McCABE, MARY K. WELLS, JACK WOOD, All My Children; Series (ABC)

ROBERT SODERBERG, EDITH SOMMER, RALPH ELLIS, EUGENIE HUNT, THEODORE APSTEIN, GILLIAN SPENCER, As The World Turns; October 27, 1976 (CBS)

ACTOR - DAYTIME DRAMA SERIES (E-1276)

VAL DUFOUR, Search For Tomorrow (CBS)
FARLEY GRANGER, One Life to Live (ABC)
LARRY HAINES, Search For Tomorrow (CBS)
LAWRENCE KEITH, All My Children (ABC)
JAMES PRITCHETT, The Doctors (NBC)

CREATIVE ARTS IN TELEVISION

ART DIRECTION OR SCENIC DESIGN - COMEDY SERIES (E-1277)

For a single episode of a regular or limited series

THOMAS E. AZZARI, Art Director; Fish; The Really Longest Day (ABC)
SEYMOUR KLATE, Art Director; MARY ANN BIDDLE, Set Decorator; Sirota's Court; The Happy Hooker (NBC) C. MURAWSKI, Art Director; Maude; Walter's Crisis (CBS) DON ROBERTS, Art Director; All In The Family; The Unemployment Story, Part 2 (CBS)
ROY CHRISTOPHER, Art Director; MARY ANN BIDDLE, Set Decorator; Mr. T & Tina; The Americanization of Michi (ABC)

ART DIRECTION OR SCENIC DESIGN - DRAMA SERIES (E-1278)

For a single episode of a regular or limited series

TIM HARVEY, Scenic Designer; The Pallisers, Episode No. 1 (PBS)
JOHN CORSO, Art Director; JERRY ADAMS, Set Decorator; Captains And The Kings, Chapter 2; NBC's Best Seller (NBC)
JOSEPH R. JENNINGS, Art Director; SOLOMON BREWER, Set Decorator; Roots, Part 6 (ABC)
JAN SCOTT, Art Director; CHARLES BENNETT, Set Decorator; Roots, Part 2 (ABC)
ED WITTSTEIN, Production Designer; The Adams Chronicles; John Quincy Adams: Congressman (PBS)

ART DIRECTION OR SCENIC DESIGN - COMEDY-VARIETY OR MUSIC SERIES (E-1279)

For a single episode of a regular or limited series

ROMAIN JOHNSTON, Art Director; The Mac Davis Show (with Susan St. James, The Pointer Sisters, and Shields & Yarnell) (NBC)
PAUL BARNES and BOB SANSOM, Art Directors; BILL HARP, Set Decorator; The Carol Burnett Show (with Glen Campbell) (CBS)
BILL BOHNERT, Art Director; JOHN TOLD, Set Decorator; Donny And Marie (with Chad Everett and Florence Henderson) (ABC)
EUGENE LEE, LEO YOSHIMURA and FRANNE LEE, NBC's Saturday Night (with Sissy Spacek) (NBC)

ART DIRECTION OR SCENIC DESIGN - DRAMATIC SPECIAL (E-1280)

JAN SCOTT, Art Director; ANNE D. McCULLEY, Set Decorator; Eleanor And Franklin: The White House Years; ABC Theatre (ABC)
WILLIAM H. TUNTKE, Art Director; RICHARD FRIEDMAN, Set Decorator; Amelia Earhart; NBC Monday Night At The Movies (NBC)
ROY CHRISTOPHER, Art Director; BEULAH FRANKEL, Set Decorator; The Last Of Mrs. Lincoln; Hollywood Television Theatre (PBS)
TREVOR WILLIAMS, Art Director; ROBERT CHECCHI, Set Decorator; Eccentricities Of A Nightingale; Theater In America; Great Performances (PBS)

ART DIRECTION OR SCENIC DESIGN - COMEDY-VARIETY OR MUSIC SPECIAL (E-1281)

ROBERT KELLY, Art Director; America Salutes Richard Rodgers: The Sound Of His Music (CBS)
JAC VENZA, Scenic Designer; American Ballet Theatre: Billy The Kid; Dance In America; (Great Performances) (PBS)
ROY CHRISTOPHER, Art Director; JOHN HUENERS, Set Decorator; The George Burns Comedy Special (CBS)

WILLIAM MICKLEY, Art Director; American Ballet Theatre: Les Painteurs; Dance In America; (Great Performances) (PBS)

CHOREOGRAPHY (E-1282)

For a single episode of a regular or limited series, or for a special program.

RON FIELD, America Salutes Richard Rodgers: The Sound Of His Music (CBS)
DAVID BLAIR, Swan Lake; Live From Lincoln Center; Great Performances (PBS)
ERNEST O. FLATT, The Carol Burnett Show (with The Pointer Sisters) (CBS)
ALAN JOHNSON, The Shirley MacLaine Special: Where Do We Go From Here? (CBS)
DONALD McKAYLE, Minstrel Man (CBS)

CINEMATOGRAPHY - ENTERTAINMENT SERIES (E-1283)

For a single episode of a regular or limited series

RIC WAITE, Captains And The Kings, Chapter 1; NBC's Best Seller (NBC)
JOSEPH BIROC, The Moneychangers, Part 1; NBC World Premiere Movie; The Big Event (NBC)
JOHN J. JONES, Once An Eagle, Part 1; NBC's Best Seller (NBC)
WILLIAM JURGENSEN, M*A*S*H; Dear Sigmund (CBS)
SHERMAN KUNKEL, Baretta; Soldier In The Jungle (ABC)
STEVAN LARNER, Roots, Part 2 (ABC)
SOL NEGRIN, A.S.C., Kojak; Shield For Murder, Part 2 (CBS)
JOSEPH M. WILCOTS, Roots, Part 7 (ABC)

CINEMATOGRAPHY - ENTERTAINMENT SPECIAL (E-1284)

WILMER C. BUTLER, Raid On Entebbe; The Big Event (NBC)
JAMES CRABE, Eleanor And Franklin: The White House Years; ABC Theatre (ABC)
MARIO TOSI, Sybil; NBC World Premiere Movie; The Big Event (NBC)
TED VOIGTLANDER, A.S.C., The Loneliest Runner (NBC)
RIC WAITE, Tail Gunner Joe; NBC World Premiere Movie; The Big Event (NBC)

COSTUME DESIGN - DRAMA OR COMEDY SERIES (E-1285)

For a single episode of a regular or limited series

RAYMOND HUGHES, The Pallisers, Episode No. 1 (PBS)
ALVIN COLT, The Adams Chronicles; Henry Adams: Historian (PBS)
JACK F. MARTELL, Roots, Part 1 (ABC)
JOAN ELLACOTT, Madame Bovary, Episode No. 3; Masterpiece Theatre (PBS)
GRADY HUNT, The Quest; Prairie Woman (NBC)

COSTUME DESIGN - MUSIC-VARIETY (E-1286)

For a single episode of a regular or limited series, or for a special program

JAN SKALICKY, The Barber Of Seville; Live From Lincoln Center; Great Performances (PBS)
BILL HARGATE, Neil Sedaka Steppin' Out (NBC)
FRANK THOMPSON, America Salutes Richard Rodgers: The Sound Of His Music (CBS)
RET TURNER, BOB MACKIE, The Sonny & Cher Show (with Barbara Eden and The Smothers Brothers) (CBS)
BOB MACKIE, An Evening With Diana Ross; The Big Event (NBC)

COSTUME DESIGN - DRAMA SPECIAL (E-1287)

JOE I. TOMPKINS, Eleanor And Franklin: The White House Years; ABC Theatre (ABC)
OLGA LEHMANN, The Man In The Iron Mask; A Bell System Special (NBC)
ALBERT WOLSKY, Beauty And The Beast; Hallmark Hall Of Fame (NBC)

FILM EDITING - COMEDY SERIES (E-1288)

For a single episode of a regular or limited series

DOUGLAS HINES, A.C.E., The Mary Tyler Moore Show; Murray Can't Lose (CBS)
SAMUEL E. BEETLEY, A.C.E., STANFORD TISCHLER, A.C.E., M*A*S*-H; Dear Sigmund (CBS)

FILM EDITING - DRAMA SERIES (E-1289)

For a single episode of a regular or limited series

NEIL TRAVIS, Roots, Part 1 (ABC)
JAMES T. HECKERT, Roots, Part 8 (ABC)
PETER KIRBY, Roots, Part 3 (ABC)
JERROLD LUDWIG, Rich Man, Poor Man, Book II, Ch. 3 (ABC)
NEIL TRAVIS, JAMES HECKERT, Roots, Part 2 (ABC)

FILM EDITING - SPECIAL (E-1290)

RITA ROLAND, A.C.E. and MICHAEL S. McLEAN, A.C.E., Eleanor And Franklin: The White House Years; ABC Theatre (ABC)
BYRON "BUZZ" BRANDT, A.C.E. and BUD ISAACS, A.C.E., Helter Skelter (CBS)
RONALD J. FAGAN, A.C.E., 21 Hours At Munich; The ABC Sunday Night Movie (ABC)
BUD S. ISAACS, A.C.E., ART SEID, A.C.E. and NICK ARCHER, A.C.E., Raid On Entebbe; The Big Event (NBC)
JOHN L. LOEFFLER, The Loneliest Runner (NBC)

FILM SOUND EDITING - SERIES (E-1291)

For a single episode of a regular or limited series

LARRY CAROW, LARRY NEIMAN, DON WARNER, COLIN MOUAT, GEORGE FREDRICK, DAVE PETTIJOHN, and PAUL BRUCE RICHARDSON; Roots, Part 2 (ABC)
DALE JOHNSTON, JAMES A. BEAN, CARL J. BRANDON, JOE DiVITALE, DON TOMLINSON, DON WEINMAN and GENE CRAIG, The Six Million Dollar Man; The Return Of Bigfoot, Part 1 (ABC)
DOUGLAS H. GRINDSTAFF, RICHARD RADERMAN, SID LUBOW, HANS NEWMAN, AL KAJITA, LUKE WOLFRAM, DON V. ISAACS, HANK SALERNO, LARRY SINGER and STANLEY M. GILBERT, Fantastic Journey; Atlantium (NBC)
JERRY ROSENTHAL, WILLIAM L. STEVENSON and MICHAEL CORRIGAN, Charlie's Angels; The Mexican Connection (ABC)

FILM SOUND EDITING - SPECIAL (E-1292)

BERNARD F. PINCUS, MILTON C. BURROW, GENE ELIOT, DON ERNST, TONY GARBER, DON V. ISAACS, LARRY KAUFMAN, WILLIAM L. MANGER, A. DAVID MARSHALL, RICHARD OSWALD, EDWARD L. SANDLIN and RUSS TINSLEY, Raid On Entebbe; The Big Event (NBC)
DOUGLAS H. GRINDSTAFF, DON V. ISAACS, LARRY KAUFMAN, BOB HUMAN, BUZZ COOPER, JACK A. FINLEY, MARVIN I. KOSBERG, HAROLD LEE CHANEY, DICK FRIEDMAN, BILL ANDREWS, RICHARD RADERMAN, LARRY SINGER, STANLEY M. GILBERT, HANK SALERNO, AL KAJITA and JACK MILNER, The Quest; NBC Thursday Night At The Movies (NBC)
RICHARD HARRISON, Eleanor And Franklin: The White House Years; ABC Theatre (ABC)
JERRY ROSENTHAL, WILLIAM PHILLIPS, JOHN STRAUSS, WILLIAM JACKSON, JAMES YANT, JERRY PIROZZI, and BRUCE BELL, The Boy In The Plastic Bubble; The ABC Friday Night Movie (ABC)

FILM SOUND MIXING (E-1293)

For a single episode of a regular or limited series, or for a special program

ALAN BERNARD, GEORGE E. PORTER, EDDIE J. NELSON and ROBERT L. HARMAN, The Savage Bees; NBC Monday Night At The Movies (NBC)
WILLIE D. BURTON, GEORGE E. PORTER, EDDIE J. NELSON and ROBERT L. HARMAN, Roots, Part 4 (ABC)

HOPPY MEHTERIAN, GEORGE E. PORTER, EDDIE J. NELSON and ARNOLD BRAUN, Roots, Part 7 (ABC)
GEORGE E. PORTER, EDDIE J. NELSON, ROBERT L. HARMAN and ARNOLD BRAUN, Roots, Part 8 (ABC)
RICHARD PORTMAN, DAVID RONNE, DONALD W. MAC DOUGALL and EDWARD "CURLY" THIRLWELL, Eleanor And Franklin: The White House Years; ABC Theatre (ABC)
BILL VARNEY, LEONARD PETERSON, ROBERT LITT and WILLIE D. BURTON, Roots, Part 1 (ABC)

GRAPHIC DESIGN AND TITLE SEQUENCES (E-1294)

For a single episode of a series, or for a special program. This includes animation only when created for use in titling

EYTAN KELLER, STU BERNSTEIN, Bell Telephone Jubilee (NBC)
PHILL NORMAN, The Moneychangers, Part 1; NBC World Premiere Movie; NBC Saturday Night At The Movies (NBC)
GENE PIOTROWSKY, Visions; The Gardener's Son (PBS)
MARTINE SHEON, DAVID SUMMERS, Previn And The Pittsburgh; Mozart As Keyboard Prodigy (PBS)

LIGHTING DIRECTION (E-1295)

For a single episode of a regular or limited series, or for a special program

WILLIAM M. KLAGES and PETER EDWARDS, The Dorothy Hamill Special (ABC)
IMERO FIORENTINO and SCOTT JOHNSON, The Neil Diamond Special (NBC)
GEORGE RIESENBERGER and WILLIAM KNIGHT, The Adams Chronicles; John Quincy Adams: President (PBS)
DICK WEISS and WILLIAM KNIGHT, The Adams Chronicles; Henry Adams: Historian (PBS)
KEN DETTLING and LEARD DAVIS, Visions; The Gold Watch (PBS)

MAKE-UP (E-1296)

For a single episode of a series, or for a special program

KEN CHASE, Make-Up Design; JOE DiBELLA, Make-up Artist; Eleanor And Franklin: The White House Years; ABC Theatre (ABC)
DEL ACEVEDO, JOHN CHAMBERS and DAN STRIEPEKE, Beauty And The Beast; Hallmark Hall Of Fame (NBC)
DICK SMITH, Harry S. Truman: Plain Speaking (PBS)
MICHAEL G. WESTMORE, ED BUTTERWORTH and CHARLIE SCHRAM, The Million Dollar Rip-Off; NBC World Premiere Movie; NBC Wednesday Night At The Movies (NBC)
STAN WINSTON, An Evening With Diana Ross; The Big Event (NBC)

MUSIC COMPOSITION - SERIES (DRAMATIC UNDERSCORE) (E-1297)

For a single episode of a regular or limited series

QUINCY JONES, GERALD FRIED, Roots, Part 1 (ABC)
ELMER BERNSTEIN, Captains And The Kings, Chapter 8; NBC's Best Seller (NBC)
GERALD FRIED, Roots, Part 8 (ABC)
DICK DE BENEDICTIS, Police Story; Monster Manor (NBC)
JACK URBONT, Bronk; The Vigilante (CBS)

MUSIC COMPOSITION - SPECIAL (DRAMATIC UNDERSCORE) (E-1298)

LEONARD ROSENMAN, ALAN BERGMAN and MARILYN BERGMAN, Sybil; NBC World Premiere Movie; The Big Event (NBC)
JOHN BARRY, Eleanor And Franklin: The White House Years; ABC Theatre (ABC)
FRED KARLIN, Minstrel Man (CBS)
DAVID SHIRE, Raid On Entebbe; The Big Event (NBC)
BILLY GOLDENBERG, Helter Skelter (CBS)

MUSIC DIRECTION (E-1299)

For a single episode of a series, or a special program, whether it be variety or music

IAN FRASER, America Salutes Richard Rodgers: The Sound Of His Music (CBS)
ANDRE PREVIN, Previn And The Pittsburgh; Mozart As Keyboard Prodigy (PBS)
JACK URBONT, Bronk; The Vigilante (CBS)
PETER MATZ, Sills And Burnett At The Met (CBS)
RAFAEL KUBELIK, New York Philharmonic: Rafael Kubelik; Live From Lincoln Center; Great Performances (PBS)

SPECIAL MUSICAL MATERIAL (E-1300)

For a song (which must have both music and lyrics), a theme for a series, or special material for a variety program providing that the first usage of this material was written expressly for television. (Possibility of one Award, more than one Award, or no Award)

BILL DYER and BILLY GOLDENBERG, An Evening with Diana Ross; The Big Event (NBC)
JERROLD IMMEL, How The West Was Won; Series Theme (ABC)
FRED KARLIN (Music) and MEG KARLIN (Lyrics), Minstrel Man; Song: "Early In The Morning" (CBS)
MORTON STEVENS (Music) and HERMINE HILTON (Lyrics), Police Woman; Killer Cowboys; Song: "Leave Me Tomorrow" (NBC)
LARRY GROSSMAN, America Salutes Richard Rodgers: The Sound Of His Music (CBS)

TAPE SOUND MIXING (E-1301)

For a single episode of a regular or limited series, or for a special program

DOUG NELSON, John Denver And Friend (ABC)
MICHAEL T. GANNON, JERRY CLEMANS, TOM HUTH and PHIL SERETTI, Police Story; Ice Time (NBC)
DOUG NELSON, NORMAN H. SCHWARTZ and JOHN BLACK, The American Music Awards (ABC)
EMIL NERODA, The Adams Chronicles; John Quincy Adams: President (PBS)

TECHNICAL DIRECTION AND ELECTRONIC CAMERAWORK (E-1302)

For a single episode of a regular or limited series, or for a special program

KARL MESSERSCHMIDT, Technical Director; JON OLSON, BRUCE GRAY, JOHN GUTIERREZ, JIM DODGE and WAYNE McDONALD, Cameramen, Doug Henning's World Of Magic (NBC)
ERNIE BUTTELMAN, Technical Director; DAVID HILMER, JAMES BALDEN, JACK DENTON, and MAYO PARTEE, Cameramen, A Special Olivia Newton-John (ABC)
GENE CROWE, Technical Director; SAMUEL E. DOWLEN, TOM DOAKES, LARRY HEIDER, BOB KEYS, WAYNE ORR, BILL PHILBIN and RON SHELDON, Cameramen, The Neil Diamond Special (NBC)
KEN LAMKIN, Technical Director; LEW ADAMS, MIKE KEELER, GARY STANTON and SAMUEL E. DOWLEN, ameramen, Victory At Entebbe (ABC)
KEN ANDERSON, Technical Director; ARTHUR G. VOGEL, JR., Cameraman, Harry S. Truman: Plain Speaking (PBS)

VIDEO TAPE EDITING FOR A SERIES (E-1303)

For a single episode of a regular or limited series
ROY STEWART, Visions; The War Widow (PBS)
TERRY PICKFORD, Meeting Of Minds, Episode No. 3 (PBS)
KEN DENISOFF and STOWELL WERDEN, C.P.O. Sharkey; Sharkey

Boogies On Down (NBC)
JIMMY B. FRAZIER, Police Story; Ice Time (NBC)

VIDEO TAPE EDITING FOR A SPECIAL (E-1304)

GARY H. ANDERSON, American Bandstand's 25th Aniversary (ABC)
THOMAS KLEIN and BILL BRESHEARS, The Barry Manilow Special (ABC)
SUSAN JENKINS and MANUEL MARTINEZ, The Captain And Tennille Special (ABC)
JIMMY B. FRAZIER and DANNY WHITE, The Dorothy Hamill Special (ABC)
JAMES McELROY, MIKE GAVALDON and DAVID SAXON, Victory At Entebbe (ABC)
WILLIAM BRESHEARS and BARBARA BABCOCK, The Neil Diamond Special (NBC)

OUTSTANDING INDIVIDUAL ACHIEVEMENT IN ANY AREA OF CREATIVE TECHNICAL CRAFTS (E-1305)

An Award for individual technical craft achievement which does not fall into a specific category, and is not otherwise recognized. (Possibility of one Award, more than one Award, or no Award)

EMMA di VITTORIO (Hairstylist), VIVIENNE WALKER (Hairstylist), Eleanor and Franklin: The White House Years, ABC Theatre (ABC)
LARRY GERMAIN (Hairstylist), Little House on the Prairie, To Live with Fear (NBC)
NAOMI CAVIN (Hairstylist), The Great Houndinis; The ABC Friday Night Movie (ABC)
DICK WILSON (Live Sound Mixing), DOUG NELSON (Live Sound Mixing), The 28th Annual Emmy Awards (ABC)
ROBERT BIGGART (Tape Sound Editing), PATRICK SOMERSET (Tape Sound Editing), Victory At Entebbe (ABC)

SPECIAL CLASSIFICATION OF OUTSTANDING INDIVIDUAL ACHIEVEMENT (E-1306)

An Award for unique individual achievement which does not fall into a specific category, and is not otherwise recognized. (Possibility of one Award, more than one Award, or no Award)

ALLEN BREWSTER, BOB ROETHLE, WILLIAM LORENZ, MANUEL MARTINEZ, RON FLEURY, MIKE WELCH, JERRY BURLING, WALTER BALDERSON, CHUCK DROEGE (Video Tape Editing), The First Fifty Years; The Big Event (NBC)
GEORGE PITTS, CLAY CASSELL (Film Editing), The First Fifty Years; The Big Event (NBC)
ENZO MARTINELLI (Cinematography), Nancy Drew/Hardy Boys Mysteries; Mystery of the Haunted House (ABC)
ROBERT K. LAMBERT, PETER C. JOHNSON (Film Editing), Life Goes to the Movies; The Big Event (NBC)

INDIVIDUAL ACHIEVEMENT IN CHILDREN'S PROGRAMMING (E-1307)

For a single episode of a regular or limited series, or for a special program (Possibility of one Award, more than one Award, or no Award)

JEAN DE JOUX (Videoanimation), ELIZABETH SAVEL (Videoanimation), Peter Pan; Hallmark Hall of Fame; The Big Event (NBC)
BILL HARGATE (Costume Designer), Pinocchio (CBS)
JERRY GREENE (Video Tape Editor), Pinocchio (CBS)
MICHAEL TILSON THOMAS (Music Director), CBS Festival of Lively Arts For Young People; New York Philharmonic Young People's Concert; Making Pictures With Music (CBS)
STAN WINSTON (Make-up Artist), ED BUTTERWORTH (Make-up Artist) Pinocchio (CBS)

INDIVIDUALS - SPECIAL EVENTS COVERAGE (E-1308)

An Award for individual achievement. A special event is a ingle program presented as live coverage; i.e., parades, pageants, awards presentations, salutes and coverage of other live events which were not covered by the news division. (Possibility of one Award, more than one Award, or no Award)

BRIAN C. BARTHOLOMEW, KEATON S. WALKER, ART Directors, The 28th Annual Emmy Awards (ABC)

ACHIEVEMENT IN BROADCAST JOURNALISM (E-1309)

ATAS Broadcast Journalism Awards to:

MacNEIL-LEHRER REPORT; ERIC SEVAREID; LEAGUE OF WOMEN VOTERS; 60 MINUTES

ENGINEERING DEVELOPMENT (E-1310)

An Award to an individual, a company or an organization for developments in engineering which are either so extensive an improvement on existing methods or so innovative in nature that they materially affect the transmission, recording or reception of television.

An Emmy was awarded to the AMERICAN BROADCASTING COMPANY for leadership in establishing Circularly Polarized Transmission to improve television reception, and a citation was awarded to VARIAN ASSOCIATES for improving the efficiency of UHF Klystrons.

LIVE SPORTS SPECIAL (E-1311)

Emmy(s) to Executive Producer(s) and Producer(s)

SUPER BOWL XI, Scotty Connal, Executive Producer; George Finkel and Ted Nathanson Producers (NBC)

1976 MASTERS GOLF TOURNAMENT, Frank Chirkinian, Producer (CBS)

1976 WORLD SERIES, Scotty Connal, Executive Producer; Roy Hammerman, Producer (NBC)

1977 ROSE BOWL, Scotty Connal, Executive Producer; Dick Auerbach, Producer (NBC)

1976 OLYMPIC GAMES/Montreal, Canada, Roone Arledge, Executive Producer; Chuck Howard, Don Ohlmeyer, Chet Forte, Dennis Lewin, Bob Goodrich, Geoffrey Mason, Terry Jastrow, Eleanor Riger, Ned Steckel, Brice Weisman, John Wilcox, Doug Wilson, Producers (ABC)

LIVE SPORT SERIES (E-1312)

Emmy(s) to Executive Producer(s) and Producer(s)

ABC'S NCAA FOOTBALL, Roone Arledge, Executive Producer; Chuck Howard and Terry Jastrow, Producers (ABC)

ABC'S NFL MONDAY NIGHT FOOTBALL, Roone Arledge, Executive Producer; Don Ohlmeyer and Dennis Lewin, Producers (ABC)

COLLEGE BASKETBALL 1977, Scotty Connal, Executive Producer; George Finkel and Roy Hammerman, Producers (NBC)

NFL FOOTBALL, Scotty Connal, Executive Producer; Dick Auerbach, George Finkel, Roy Hammerman, Ted Nathanson, Larry Circillo, Jim Marooney, Producers (NBC)

THE NFL TODAY/NFL FOOTBALL ON CBS, Michael Pearl, Hal Classon, Sid Kaufman, Producers (CBS)

EDITED SPORTS SPECIAL (E-1313)

Emmy(s) to Executive Producer(s) and Producer(s)

BASEBALL WORLD OF JOE GARAGIOLA (World Series Pre-Game), Joe Garagiola, Executive Producer; Ginny Seipt, Producer; October 16-21, 1976 (NBC)

THE GLORY OF THEIR TIMES, Cappy Petrash Greenspan, Executive Producer; Bud Greenspan, Producer (PBS)

TO THE TOP OF THE WORLD, AN ASSAULT ON EVEREST, Ed Goren and Mike Hoover, Producers (CBS)

WIDE WORLD OF SPORTS, 15TH ANNIVERSARY SPECIAL, Roone Arledge, Executive Producer; Dennis Lewin, Producer (ABC)

A SPECIAL PREVIEW OF THE 1976 OLYMPIC GAMES FROM MONT-REAL, CANADA, Roone Arledge, Executive Producer; Chuck Howard, Don Ohlmeyer, Chet Forte, Dennis Lewin, Bob Goodrich, Geoffrey Mason, Terry Jastrow, Eleanor Riger, Ned Steckel, Brice Weisman, John Wilcox, Doug Wilson, Producers (ABC)

EDITED SPORTS SERIES (E-1314)

Emmy(s) to Executive Producer(s) and Producer(s)

ABC'S WIDE WORLD OF SPORTS, Roone Arledge, Executive Producer; Dennis Lewin, Ned Steckel, Doug Wilson, Chet Forte, Chuck Howard, Producers (ABC)

GRANDSTAND, Don Ellis, Executive Producer; Bill Fitts, Producer (NBC)

THE OLYMPIAD, Cappy Petrash Greenspan, Executive Producer; Bud Greenspan, Producer (PBS)

THE WAY IT WAS, Gerry Gross, Executive Producer; Gary Brown and Dick Enberg, Producers (PBS)

SPORTS PERSONALITY (E-1315)

Jim McKay (ABC)

Frank Gifford (ABC)
Keith Jackson (ABC)
Don Meredith (NBC)
Joe Garagiola (NBC)

DIRECTING IN SPORTS PROGRAMMING (E-1316)

HARRY COYLE, World Series of Baseball (Yankees VS Cincinnati); October 16, 1976 (NBC)

CHET FORTE, ABC NFL Monday Night Football (ABC)
RONALD HAWKINS, JOE ACETI, CHET FORTE, ROGER GOODMAN, LARRY KAMM, DON OHLMEYER, ANDY SIDARIS, LOU VOLPICELLI, ROBERT RIGER, RALPH MELLANEY; 1976 Olympic Games, Montreal Canada (ABC)

ROBERT RIGER, ABC'S Wide World of Sports-Men's World Cup Downhill Skiing Championships, Laax, Switzerland; February 27, 1977 (ABC)

DOUG WILSON, ABC'S Wide World of Sports-Grand Prix of Monaco, June 5 1976 (ABC)

INDIVIDUAL ACHIEVEMENT IN SPORTS PROGRAMMING

(For a single episode of a series or for a special program. The following are "Areas" where there is a possibility of one Award, more than one Award or no Award.)

CINEMATOGRAPHY (E-1317)

PETER HENNING, HARVEY HARRISON, HARRY HART, D'ARCY MARCH, DON SHAPIRO, DON SHOEMAKER, JOE VALENTINE; 1976 Olympic Games (ABC)

TAPE SOUND MIXING (E-1318)

DICK ROSS, RICH SLOAN, JACK BLACK, GARY LARKINS, BILL SANDRUETER, JOHN McCULLOUGH, WILLIE EARL, ART MORGANSTERN, JACK BRANDES, CHARLES BUCKAGE, WAYNE CALUGER, MAX GOLDSTEIN, JACK HUGHES, LES SCHEYER, RAY TOMASZESKI; 1976 Olympic Games (ABC)

GRAPHIC DESIGN (E-1319)

MICHAEL WEBSTER and JIM DUFFY, Challenge of the Sexes-Show #1; January 16, 1977 (CBS)

FILM EDITING (E-1320)

JOHN PETERSEN, ANGELO BERNADUCCI, IRWIN KRECHAF, MARGARET MURPHY, VINCENT REDA, ANTHONY ZACCARO; 1976 Olympic Games (ABC)

ENGINEERING SUPERVISION/TECHNICAL DIRECTION/ELECTRONIC CAMERAWORK (E-1321)

JULIUS BARNATHAN, PHIL LEVENS, JOE DEBONIS, JOE MALTZ, BEN GREENBERG, WILLIAM H JOHNSON, ABDELNOUR TADROS, JACK NEITLICH, HERB KRAFT, JACQUES LESGARDS, BOB CZINKE, FRANK GENEREUX, DICK HORAN, MEL MOREHOUSE, MORT ROMANOFF, JACK WILKEY, Engineering Supervisors; ERNIE BUTTLEMAN, BILL MORRIS, DAVE SMITH, GENE AFFRUNTI, BOB MYERS, VIC BARY, JOHN ALLEN, JOHN BRODERICK, CHARLIE GILES, TOM SUMNER, WERNER GUNTHER, BOB BERNTHAL, JOE NESI, Technical Directors; KEITH BROCK, EVAN BAKER, JOHN LEE, BILL SULLIVAN, SIMON MELROSE, JIM ANGEL, ANDY ARMENTANI, JOHN CRONIN, DREW DEROSA, JACK DORFMAN, SAL FOLINO, JAMES HENNEGHAN, WILLIAM KARVELAS, MORT LEVIN, JOHN MORREALE, STEVE NIKIFOR, ROGER PIERCE, MIKE REBICH, JOE SAPIENZA, JOE SCARPA, JOE STEFANONI, LARRY STENMAN, JOE TALOSI, DALE WALSH, Electronic Cameramen, 1976 Olympic Games (ABC)

VIDEOTAPE EDITING (INCLUDES ASSOCIATE DIRECTION) (E-1322)

CAROL LEHTI, DICK BUFFINTON, JEFF COHAN, VINCE DeDARIO, JOHN DeLISA, LOU FREDERICK, JACK GALLIVAN, JIM JENNETT, BOB LANNING, JEAN MacLEAN, DAVE MALENOFSKI, NORM SAMET, HOWARD SHAPIRO, STAN SPIRO, Associate Directors: EMIL RICH, JOHN STEVENS, MIKE RAFFAELE, RON ACKERMAN, HARRY ALLEN, HARVEY BEAL, RONALD BLACHUT, BARBARA BOWMAN, BUD CROWE, PETER FRITZ, CHARLES GARDNER, VITO GERARDI, NICK GIORDANO, JAMES HEPPER, JACOB HIERL, HECTOR KICELIAN, CONRAD KRAUS, FRED LABIB, HAL LEA, PAT MALIK, ED McCARTHY, PETER MECCA, ALEX MOSKOVIC, HARVEY OTTO, NICHOLAS PANTELAKIS, CHESTER PAWLAK, CARL POLLACK, DOUGLAS RIDSEL, ERSKIN ROBERTS, DANNY ROSENSON, WINSTON SADDO, GENE SMEJKAL, LEO STEPHEN, TED SUMMERS, MARTIN THIBEAU, ARTHUR VOLK, MIKE WENIG, MIKE BIONDI, ROCCO COTUGNO, JIM FLORENCE, MARVIN GENCH, VICTOR GONZALEZ, FRANK GUIGLIANO, GALON HALLOWAY, EMERSON LAWSON, NICK MAZUR, MERRIT ROESSER, NATHAN ROGERS, MARIO SCHENCMAN, TRUETT SMITH, CHARLES STEPHENSON, GEORGE STEVENS, TOM WIGHT, HECTOR KIERL, KEN KLINGBEIL, Videotape Editors; 1976 Olympic Games (ABC)

1977/78

NIGHTTIME PROGRAMMING

COMEDY SERIES (E-1323)

Award(s) to Executive Producer(s) and/or Producer(s)

ALL IN THE FAMILY, Mort Lachman, Executive Producer; Milt Josefsberg, Producer (CBS)
BARNEY MILLER, Danny Arnold, Executive Producer; Tony Sheehan, Producer (ABC)
M*A*S*H, Burt Metcalfe, Producer (CBS)
SOAP, Paul Junger Witt, Tony Thomas, Executive Producers; Susan Harris, Producer (ABC)
THREE'S COMPANY, Don Nicholl, Michael Ross, Bernie West, Producers (ABC)

DRAMA SERIES (E-1324)

Award(s) to Executive Producer(s) and/or Producer(s)

THE ROCKFORD FILES, Meta Rosenberg, Executive Producer; Stephen J. Cannell, Supervising Producer; David Chase, Chas. Floyd Johnson, Producers (NBC)
COLUMBO, Richard Alan Simmons, Executive Producer (NBC)
FAMILY, Aaron Spelling, Leonard Goldberg, Executive Producers; Nigel McKeand, Producer (ABC)
LOU GRANT, James L Brooks, Allan Burns, Gene Reynolds, Executive Producers; Gene Reynolds, Producer (CBS)
QUINCY, Glen A. Larson, Jud Kinberg, Richard Irving, Executive Pro-

ducers; B. W. Sandefur, Supervising Producer; Chris Morgan, Peter J. Thompson, Edward J. Montagne, Robert F. O'Neill, Producers; Michael Sloan, Associate Executive Producer (NBC)

SPECIAL ATAS GOVERNORS AWARD (E-1325)

LARRY STEWART, President of ATAS, 1975-1977.

COMEDY-VARIETY OR MUSIC SERIES (E-1326)

Award(s) to Executive Producer(s) and/or Producer(s) and Star(s), if applicable

THE MUPPET SHOW, David Lazer, Executive Producer; Jim Henson, Producer; The Muppets (Frank Oz, Jerry Nelson, Richard Hunt, Dave Goelz, Jim Henson), Stars (Synd)
AMERICA 2NIGHT, Alan Thicke, Producer (Synd)
THE CAROL BURNETT SHOW, Joe Hamilton, Executive Producer; Ed Simmons, Producer; Carol Burnett, Star (CBS)
EVENING AT POPS, Bill Cosel, Producer; Arthur Fiedler, Star (PBS)
NBC'S SATURDAY NIGHT LIVE, Lorne Michaels, Producer (NBC)

LIMITED SERIES (E-1327)

Award(s) to Executive Producer(s) and/or Producer(s)

HOLOCAUST, Herbert Brodkin, Executive Producer; Robert Berger, Producer (NBC)
KING, Edward S. Feldman, Executive Producer; Paul Maslansky, Producer; William Finnegan, Supervising Producer (NBC)
WASHINGTON: BEHIND CLOSED DOORS, Stanley Kallis, Executive Producer; Eric Bercovici, David W. Rintels, Supervising Producers; Norman Powell, Producer (ABC)
ANNA KARENINA, (Masterpiece Theatre), Ken Riddington, Executive Producer; Donald Wilson, Producer; Joan Sullivan, Series Producer (PBS)
I, CLAUDIUS, (Masterpiece Theatre), Joan Sullivan, Series Producer; Martin Lisemore, Producer (PBS)

FIRST ANNUAL ATAS GOVERNORS AWARD (E-1328)

To WILLIAM S. PALEY, Chairman of the Board, CBS

SPECIAL - DRAMA OR COMEDY (E-1329)

Award(s) to Executive Producer(s) and/or Producer(s)

THE GATHERING, Joseph Barbera, Executive Producer; Harry R. Sherman, Producer, (ABC)
A DEATH IN CANAAN, Robert W. Christiansen, Rick Rosenberg, Producers (CBS)
JESUS OF NAZARETH, Bernard J. Kingham, Executive Producer; Vincenzo Labella, Producer (NBC)
OUR TOWN, (Bell System Special), Saul Jaffe, Executive Producer; George Schaefer, Producer (NBC)
YOUNG JOE, THE FORGOTTEN KENNEDY, William McCutchen, Producer (ABC)

SPECIAL - COMEDY-VARIETY OR MUSIC (E-1330)

Award(s) to Executive Producer(s) and/or Producer(s) and Star(s), if applicable

BETTE MIDLER - OL' RED HAIR IS BACK, Aaron Russo, Executive Producer; Gary Smith, Dwight Hemion, Producers; Bette Midler, Star, (NBC)
DOUG HENNING'S WORLD OF MAGIC, Jerry Goldstein, Executive Producer; Walter C. Miller, Producer; Doug Henning, Star, (NBC)
THE GEORGE BURNS ONE-MAN SHOW, Irving Fein, Executive Producer; Stan Harris, Producer; George Burns, Star, (CBS)
NEIL DIAMOND: I'M GLAD YOU'RE HERE WITH ME TONIGHT, Jerry Weintraub, Executive Producer; Art Fisher, Producer; Neil Diamond, Star, (NBC)

THE SECOND BARRY MANILOW SPECIAL, Miles J. Lourie, Executive Producer; Ernest Chambers, Barry Manilow, Producers; Barry Manilow, Star, (ABC)

CLASSICAL PROGRAM IN THE PERFORMING ARTS (E-1331)
For a special program, or for a series (excluding drama). Award(s) to Executive Producer(s) and/or Producer(s) and Star(s), if applicable **AMERICAN BALLET THEATRE'S "GISELLE", Live From Lincoln Center; John Goberman, Producer (PBS)**
AMERICAN BALLET THEATRE, Live From Lincoln Center; John Goberman, Executive Producer; Emile Ardolino, Producer, (PBS)
DANCE IN AMERICA: CHOREOGRAPHY BY BALANCHINE; Jac Venza, Executive Producer; Emile Ardolino, Merrill Brockway, Producers, (PBS)
LA BOHEME, LIVE FROM THE MET; Michael Bronson, Executive Producer; John Goberman, Producer, (PBS)
THE NUTCRACKER (BARYSHNIKOV), Herman Krawitz, Executive Producer; Yanna Kroyt Brandt, Producer (CBS)

CHILDREN'S SPECIAL (E-1332)
For specials which were broadcast in the evening. Award(s) to Executive Producer(s) and/or Producer(s)
HALLOWEEN IS GRINCH NIGHT, David H. DePatie, Friz Freleng, Executive Producers; Ted Geisel, Producer (ABC)
A CONNECTICUT YANKEE IN KING ARTHUR'S COURT, Jay Rayvid, Executive Producer; Jay Rayvid, Chiz Schultz and Shep Greene, Producers (PBS)
THE FAT ALBERT CHRISTMAS SPECIAL, Lou Scheimer, Norm Prescott, Producers, (CBS)
ONCE UPON A BROTHERS GRIMM, Bernard Rothman, Jack Wohl, Producers, (CBS)
PETER LUNDY AND THE MEDICINE HAT STALLION Ed Friendly, Producer, (NBC)

INFORMATIONAL SERIES (E-1333)
Award(s) to Executive Producer(s) and/or Producer(s)
THE BODY HUMAN, Thomas W. Moore, Executive Producer; Alfred R. Kelman, Producer (CBS)
BETWEEN THE WARS, Alan Landsburg, Executive Producer; Anthony Potter, Series Producer (Synd)
COUSTEAU OASIS IN SPACE, Philippe Cousteau, Executive Producer; Andrew Solt, Producer (PBS)
MUTUAL OF OMAHA'S WILD KINGDOM, Don Meir, Producer (Synd)
NOVA, John Angier, Executive Producer (PBS)

INFORMATIONAL SPECIAL (E-1334)
Award(s) to Executive Producer(s) and/or Producer(s)
THE GREAT WHALES, NATIONAL GEOGRAPHIC, Thomas Skinner, Dennis B. Kane, Executive Producers; Nicolas Noxon, Producer, (PBS)
BING CROSBY: HIS LIFE AND LEGEND, Franklin Konigsberg, Executive Producer; Marshall Flaum, Producer, (ABC)
CALYPSO'S SEARCH FOR ATLANTIS, COUSTEAU ODYSSEY, Jacques Cousteau, Philippe Cousteau, Executive Producers; Andrew Solt, Producer, (PBS)
THE TREASURES OF TUTANKHAMUN, Donald Knox, Executive Producer; Valerie Gentile, Producer, (PBS)
TUT: THE BOY KING, George A. Heinemann, Executive Producer (NBC)

SPECIAL EVENTS PROGRAMS (E-1335)
(Possibility of one Award, more than one Award, or no Award)
50th ANNUAL AWARDS OF THE ACADEMY OF MOTION PICTURE ARTS AND SCIENCES, Howard Koch, Producer (ABC)

SPECIAL CLASSIFICATION OF OUTSTANDING PROGRAM ACHIEVEMENT (E-1336)
(Possibility of one Award, more than one Award, or no Award)
THE TONIGHT SHOW STARRING JOHNNY CARSON, Fred de Cordova, Producer; Johnny Carson, Star (NBC)
THE AMERICAN FILM INSTITUTE SALUTE TO BETTE DAVIS, George Stevens, Jr., Executive Producer; Perry Lafferty, Supervising Producer; Robert Scheerer, Producer, (CBS)
THE AMERICAN FILM INSTITUTE SALUTE TO HENRY FONDA, George Stevens, Jr., Executive Producer; George Stevens, Jr., Eric Lieber, Producers, (CBS)
THE DICK CAVETT SHOW, Joan Konner, Executive Producer; Christopher Porterfield, Julie Rubenstein, Lynda Sheldon, Tom O'Malley, Producers, Dick Cavett; Star (PBS)
NBC: THE FIRST FIFTY YEARS - A CLOSER LOOK, Greg Garrison, Executive Producer; Lee Hale, Producer, (NBC)

ACTOR - COMEDY SERIES (E-1337)
CARROLL O'CONNOR, All In The Family (CBS)
ALAN ALDA, M*A*S*H (CBS)
HAL LINDEN, Barney Miller (ABC)
JOHN RITTER, Three's Company (ABC)
HENRY WINKLER, Happy Days (ABC)

ACTOR - DRAMA SERIES (E-1338)
EDWARD ASNER, Lou Grant (CBS)
JAMES BRODERICK, Family (ABC)
PETER FALK, Columbo (NBC)
JAMES GARNER, Rockford Files (NBC)
JACK KLUGMAN, Quincy (NBC)
RALPH WAITE, The Waltons (CBS)

ACTOR - LIMITED SERIES (E-1339)
MICHAEL MORIARTY, Holocaust (NBC)
HAL HOLBROOK, The Awakening Land (NBC)
JASON ROBARDS, JR., Washington: Behind Closed Doors (ABC)
FRITZ WEAVER, Holocaust (NBC)
PAUL WINFIELD, King (NBC)

ACTOR - DRAMA OR COMEDY SPECIAL (E-1340)
FRED ASTAIRE, A Family Upside Down, (NBC)
ALAN ALDA, Kill Me If You Can, (NBC)
HAL HOLBROOK, Our Town, Bell System, (NBC)
MARTIN SHEEN, Taxi!!!, Hallmark Hall of Fame, (NBC)
JAMES STACY, Just a Little Inconvenience, (NBC)

ACTOR - SINGLE PERFORMANCE - DRAMA OR COMEDY SERIES (E-1341)
BARNARD HUGHES, Lou Grant, Judge, (CBS)
DAVID CASSIDY, Police Story, A Chance to Live, (NBC)
WILL GEER, The Love Boat, The Old Man and the Runaway, (ABC)
JUDD HIRSCH, Rhoda, Rhoda Likes Mike, (CBS)
JOHN RUBINSTEIN, Family, And Baby Makes Three, (ABC)
KEENAN WYNN, Police Woman, Good Old Uncle Ben, (NBC)

ACTRESS - COMEDY SERIES (E-1342)
JEAN STAPLETON, All In The Family (CBS)
BEATRICE ARTHUR, Maude (CBS)
CATHRYN DAMON, Soap (ABC)
VALERIE HARPER, Rhoda (CBS)
KATHERINE HELMOND, Soap (ABC)
SUZANNE PLESHETTE, The Bob Newhart Show (CBS)

ACTRESS - DRAMA SERIES (E-1343)
SADA THOMPSON, Family (ABC)

MELISSA SUE ANDERSON, Little House On The Prairie (NBC)
FIONNULA FLANAGAN, How The West Was Won (ABC)
KATE JACKSON, Charlie's Angels (ABC)
MICHAEL LEARNED, The Waltons (CBS)
SUSAN SULLIVAN, Julie Farr, M.D. (ABC)

ACTRESS - LIMITED SERIES (E-1344)

MERYL STREEP, Holocaust (NBC)
ROSEMARY HARRIS, Holocaust (NBC)
ELIZABETH MONTGOMERY, The Awakening Land (NBC)
LEE REMICK, Wheels (NBC)
CICELY TYSON, King (NBC)

ACTRESS - DRAMA OR COMEDY SPECIAL (E-1345)

JOANNE WOODWARD, See How She Runs, GE Theatre (CBS)
HELEN HAYES, A Family Upside Down, (NBC)
EVA MARIE SAINT, Taxi!!!, Hallmark Hall of Fame, (NBC)
MAUREEN STAPLETON, The Gathering, (ABC)
SADA THOMPSON, Our Town, Bell System, (NBC)

ACTRESS - SINGLE APPEARANCE - DRAMA OR COMEDY SERIES (E-1346)

RITA MORENO, The Rockford Files, The Paper Palace, (NBC)
PATTY DUKE ASTIN, Having Babies, Having Babies III, (ABC)
KATE JACKSON, James at 15/16, James at 15, (NBC)
JAYNE MEADOWS, Meeting of The Minds, Luther, Voltaire, Plato, Nightingale, (PBS)
IRENE TEDROW, James at 15/16, Ducks, (NBC)

SUPPORTING ACTOR - COMEDY SERIES (E-1347)

For a regular or limited series
ROB REINER, All In The Family (CBS)
TOM BOSLEY, Happy Days (ABC)
GARY BURGHOFF, M*A*S*H (CBS)
HARRY MORGAN, M*A*S*H (CBS)
VIC TAYBACK, Alice (CBS)

SUPPORTING ACTOR - DRAMA SERIES (E-1348)

For a regular or limited series
ROBERT VAUGHN, Washington: Behind Closed Doors (ABC)
OSSIE DAVIS, King (NBC)
WILL GEER, The Waltons (CBS)
SAM WANAMAKER, Holocaust (NBC)
DAVID WARNER, Holocaust (NBC)

SUPPORTING ACTOR - CONTINUING OR SINGLE PERFORMANCE - VARIETY OR MUSIC (E-1349)

For a continuing role in a regular or limited series, or for a one-time appearance in a series or a special
TIM CONWAY, The Carol Burnett Show (Series) (CBS)
DAN AYKROYD, NBC'S Saturday Night Live (Series) (NBC)
JOHN BELUSHI, NBC'S Saturday Night Live (Series) (NBC)
LOUIS GOSSETT, JR. The Sentry Collection Presents Ben Vereen - His Roots, (ABC)
PETER SELLERS, The Muppet Show (Synd)

SUPPORTING ACTOR - COMEDY OR DRAMA SPECIAL (E-1350)

HOWARD DA SILVA, Verna: USO Girl, Great Performances, (PBS)
JAMES FARENTINO, Jesus Of Nazareth, (NBC)
BURGESS MEREDITH, The Last Hurrah, Hallmark Hall of Fame, (NBC)
DONALD PLEASENCE, The Defection of Simas Kudirka (CBS)
EFREM ZIMBALIST, JR., A Family Upside Down, (NBC)

SUPPORTING ACTOR - SINGLE PERFORMANCE - COMEDY OR DRAMA SERIES (E-1351)

For a one-time appearance in a regular or limited series
RICARDO MONTALBAN, How The West Was Won, Part II, (ABC)
WILL GEER, Eight Is Enough, Yes Nicholas. . .There Is A Santa Claus, (ABC)
LARRY GELMAN, Barney Miller, Goodbye Mr. Fish - Part II, (ABC)
HAROLD GOULD, Rhoda, Happy Anniversary, (CBS)
ABE VIGODA, Barney Miller, Goodbye Mr. Fish - Part II, (ABC)

SUPPORTING ACTRESS - COMEDY SERIES (E-1352)

For a regular or limited series
JULIE KAVNER, Rhoda (CBS)
POLLY HOLLIDAY, Alice (CBS)
SALLY STRUTHERS, All In The Family (CBS)
LORETTA SWIT, M*A*S*H (CBS)
NANCY WALKER, Rhoda (CBS)

SUPPORTING ACTRESS - DRAMA SERIES (E-1353)

For a regular or limited series
NANCY MARCHAND, Lou Grant (CBS)
MEREDITH BAXTER-BIRNEY, Family (CBS)
TOVAH FELDSHUH, Holocaust (NBC)
LINDA KELSEY, Lou Grant (CBS)
KRISTY McNICHOL, Family (ABC)

SUPPORTING ACTRESS - CONTINUING OR SINGLE PERFORMANCE - VARIETY OR MUSIC (E-1354)

For a continuing role in a regular or limited series, or for a one-time appearance in a series or a special
GILDA RADNER, NBC'S Saturday Night Live, (Series) (NBC)
BEATRICE ARTHUR, Laugh-In, (NBC)
JANE CURTIN, NBC'S Saturday Night Live (Series) (NBC)
DOLLY PARTON, Cher. . .Special, (ABC)
BERNADETTE PETERS, The Muppet Show (Synd)

SUPPORTING ACTRESS - DRAMA OR COMEDY SPECIAL (E-1355)

EVA LE GALLIENNE, The Royal Family, (PBS)
PATTY DUKE ASTIN, A Family Upside Down, (NBC)
TYNE DALY, Intimate Strangers, (ABC)
MARIETTE HARTLEY, The Last Hurrah, Hallmark Hall Of Fame, (NBC)
CLORIS LEACHMAN, It Happed One Christmas, (ABC)
VIVECA LINDFORS, A Question Of Guilt, (CBS)

SUPPORTING ACTRESS - SINGLE PERFORMANCE - COMEDY OR DRAMA SERIES (E-1356)

For a one-time appearance in a regular or limited series
BLANCHE BAKER, Holocaust, Part I (NBC)
ELLEN CORBY, The Waltons, Grandma Comes Home, (CBS)
JEANETTE NOLAN, The Awakening Land, Part I, (NBC)
BEULAH QUO, Meeting Of The Minds, Douglass, Tz'u-Hsi, Beccaria, De Sade, (PBS)
BEATRICE STRAIGHT, The Dain Curse, Part I, (CBS)

WRITING - COMEDY SERIES (E-1357)

For a single episode of a regular or limited series with continuing characters and/or theme
BOB WEISKOPF and BOB SCHILLER, Teleplay, BARRY HARMAN and HARVE BROSTEN, Story; All In The Family, Cousin Liz, (CBS)
ALAN ALDA, M*A*S*H, Fallen Idol, (CBS)
MEL TOLKIN, LARRY RHINE, Teleplay, ERIK TARLOFF, Story; All In The Family, Edith's Crisis Of Faith - Part II, (CBS)
BOB WEISKOPF and BOB SCHILLER, All In The Family, Edith's 50th Birthday, (CBS)

WRITING - DRAMA SERIES (E-1358)

For an episode of a regular or limited series with continuing characters and/or theme

GERALD GREEN, Holocaust, (NBC)
STEVE ALLEN, Meeting of The Minds, (PBS)
ALAN AYCKBOURN, The Norman Conquests, (CBS)
ROBERT W. LENSKI, The Dain Curse, (CBS)
ABBY MANN, King, (NBC)

WRITING - COMEDY-VARIETY OR MUSIC SERIES (E-1359)

For an episode of a regular or limited series

ED SIMMONS, ROGER BEATTY, RICK HAWKINS, LIZ SAGE, ROBERT ILLES, JAMES STEIN, FRANELLE SILVER, LARRY SIEGEL, TIM CONWAY, BILL RICHMOND, GENE PERRET, DICK CLAIR and JENNA McMAHON, The Carol Burnett Show with Steve Martin, Betty White, (CBS)
ED SIMMONS, ROGER BEATTY, ELIAS DAVIS, DAVID POLLOCK, RICK HAWKINS, LIZ SAGE, ADELE STYLER, BURT STYLER, TIM CONWAY, BILL RICHMOND, GENE PERRET, DICK CLAIR and JENNA McMAHON, The Carol Burnett Show with Ken Berry, (CBS)
JERRY JUHL, DON HINKLEY, JOSEPH BAILEY and JIM HENSON, The Muppet Show with Dom De Luise (Synd)
ALAN THICKE, JOHN BONI, NORMAN STILES, JEREMY STEVENS, TOM MOORE, ROBERT ILLES, JAMES STEIN, HARRY SHEARER, TOM DUNSMUIR and DAN WILCOX, America 2Night with Carol Burnett (Synd)
DAN AYKROYD, ANNE BEATTS, TOM DAVIS, JAMES DOWNEY, BRIAN DOYLE-MURRAY, AL FRANKEN, LORNE MICHAELS, MARILYN SUZANNE MILLER, DON NOVELLO, MICHAEL O'DONOGHUE, HERB SARGENT, TOM SCHILLER, ROSIE SHUSTER and ALAN ZWEIBEL, NBC's Saturday Night Live, Host Steve Martin (NBC)

WRITING - COMEDY-VARIETY OR MUSIC SPECIAL (E-1360)

LORNE MICHAELS, PAUL SIMON, CHEVY CHASE, TOM DAVIS, AL FRANKEN, CHARLES GRODIN, LILY TOMLIN and ALAN ZWEIBEL, The Paul Simon Special, (NBC)
ALAN BUZ KOHAN, ROD WARREN, PAT McCORMICK, TOM EYEN, JERRY BLATT, BETTE MIDLER and BRUCE VILANCH, Bette Midler - Ol' Red Hair Is Back, (NBC)
ELON PACKARD, FRED FOX and SEAMAN JACOBS The George Burns One-Man Show, (CBS)
ERNEST CHAMBERS and BARRY MANILOW, The Second Barry Manilow Special, (ABC)
MICHAEL H. KAGAN, The Sentry Collection Presents Ben Vereen - His Roots, (ABC)

WRITING - SPECIAL PROGRAM - DRAMA OR COMEDY - ORIGINAL TELEPLAY (E-1361)

GEORGE RUBINO, The Last Tenant, (ABC)
BRUCE FELDMAN, The Defection of Simas Kudirka, (CBS)
RICHARD LEVINSON and WILLIAM LINK, The Storyteller, (NBC)
LORING MANDEL, Breaking Up, (ABC)
JERRY McNEELY, Something For Joey, (CBS)
JAMES POE, The Gathering, (ABC)

WRITING - SPECIAL PROGRAM - DRAMA OR COMEDY - ADAPTATION (E-1362)

CARYL LEDNER, Mary White, (ABC)
BLANCHE HANALIS, A Love Affair: The Eleanor and Lou Gehrig Story (NBC)
ALBERT INNAURATO, Verna: USO Girl, Great Performances, (PBS)
JEROME LAWRENCE and ROBERT E. LEE, Actor, Hollywood Television Theatre (PBS)
BARBARA TURNER, The War Between The Tates, (NBC)

DIRECTOR - COMEDY SERIES (E-1363)

For an episode of a regular or limited series with continuing characters and/or theme

PAUL BOGART, All In The Family, Edith's 50th Birthday (CBS)
HAL COOPER, Maude, Vivian's Decision, (CBS)
BURT METCALFE, ALAN ALDA, M*A*S*H, Comrades In Arms - Part I, (CBS)
JERRY PARIS, Happy Days, Richie Almost Dies, (ABC)
JAY SANDRICH, Soap, #24, (ABC)

DIRECTOR - DRAMA SERIES (E-1364)

For an episode of a regular or limited series with continuing characters and/or theme

MARVIN J. CHOMSKY, Holocaust (NBC)
ABBY MANN, King (NBC)
GARY NELSON, Washington: Behind Closed Doors (ABC)
E. W. SWACKHAMER, The Dain Curse (CBS)
HERBERT WISE, I Claudius, Masterpiece Theatre (PBS)

DIRECTOR - SPECIAL PROGRAM - DRAMA OR COMEDY (E-1365)

DAVID LOWELL RICH, The Defection of Simas Kudirka (CBS)
LOU ANTONIO, Something For Joey (CBS)
RANDAL KLEISER, The Gathering (ABC)
DELBERT MANN, Breaking Up (ABC)
RONALD MAXWELL, Verna: USO Girl, Great Performances (PBS)
GEORGE SCHAEFER, Our Town, Bell System (NBC)

DIRECTOR - COMEDY-VARIETY OR MUSIC SERIES (E-1366)

For an episode of a regular or limited series

DAVE POWERS, The Carol Burnett Show with Steve Martin, Betty White, (CBS)
STEVE BINDER, Shields and Yarnell with John Aylesworth, (CBS)
PETER HARRIS, The Muppet Show with Elton John (Synd)
JOHN C. MOFFITT, The Richard Pryor Show with Paula Kelly (NBC)
DAVE WILSON, NBC's Saturday Night Live with Steve Martin (NBC)

DIRECTOR - COMEDY-VARIETY OR MUSIC SPECIAL (E-1367)

DWIGHT HEMION, The Sentry Collection Presents Ben Vereen - His Roots (ABC)
TONY CHARMOLI, Mitzi. . .Zings Into Spring (CBS)
WALTER C. MILLER, Doug Henning's World of Magic (NBC)
GEORGE SCHAEFER, The Second Barry Manilow Special (ABC)
DAVE WILSON, The Paul Simon Special (NBC)

DAYTIME PROGRAMMING

HOST OR HOSTESS - TALK, SERVICE, OR VARIETY SERIES (E-1368)

JAMES CROCKETT Crockett's Victory Garden (PBS)
PHIL DONAHUE Donahue (Synd)
JIM NABORS The Jim Nabors Show (Synd)
DINAH SHORE Dinah! (Synd)

INDIVIDUAL DIRECTOR - VARIETY PROGRAM (E-1369)

For a single episode

DONALD R. KING The Mike Douglas Show, Mike in Hollywood (Synd)
MARTIN HAIG MACKEY Over Easy (PBS)
GLEN SWANSON Dinah! Dinah and the Philadelphians (Synd)

TALK, SERVICE, OR VARIETY SERIES (E-1370)

Emmy(s) to Executive Producer(s) and Producer(s)

DINAH! Henry Jaffe, Executive Producer; Fred Tatashore, Producer (Synd)

MERV GRIFFIN SHOW Bob Murphy, Producer (Synd)

THE MIKE DOUGLAS SHOW Frank Miller, Executive Producer; Brad Lachman, Producer (Synd)

DONAHUE Richard Mincer, Executive Producer; Patricia McMillen, Producer (Synd)

INDIVIDUAL DIRECTOR - DAYTIME GAME OR AUDIENCE PARTICIPATION SHOW (E-1371)

For a single episode

PAUL ALTER, Family Feud, Valentine's Day Celebration Special (ABC)

MIKE GARGIULO, The $20,000 Pyramid (ABC)

HOST OR HOSTESS - GAME OR AUDIENCE PARTICIPATION SHOW (E-1372)

DICK CLARK, The $20,000 Pyramid (ABC)

RICHARD DAWSON, Family Feud (ABC)

GENE RAYBURN, Match Game (CBS)

CHUCK WOOLERY, SUSAN STAFFORD, Wheel of Fortune (NBC)

GAME OR AUDIENCE PARTICIPATION SHOW (E-1373)

Emmy(s) to Executive Producer(s) and Producer(s)

FAMILY FEUD, Howard Felsher, Producer (ABC)

HOLLYWOOD SQUARES, Merrill Heatter and Bob Quigley, Executive Producers; Jay Redack, Producer (NBC)

THE $20,000 PYRAMID, Bob Stewart, Executive Producer; Anne Marie Schmitt, Producer (ABC)

SPECIAL CLASSIFICATION OF OUTSTANDING PROGRAM ACHIEVEMENT (E-1374)

(Possibility of one Award, more than one Award or no Award)

CAMERA THREE John Musilli, Executive Producer; John Musilli, Roger Englander, Producers (CBS)

GOOD MORNING AMERICA, Woody Fraser, Executive Producer; George Merlis, Merrill Mazuer, Bob Blum, Producers (ABC)

LIVE FROM LINCOLN CENTER: RECITAL OF TENOR LUCIANO PAVAROTTI FROM THE MET John Goberman, Executive Producer (PBS)

MUTUAL OF OMAHA'S WILD KINGDOM, Don Meir, Executive Producer (Synd)

CHILDREN'S INFORMATIONAL SERIES (E-1375)

Emmy(s) to Executive Producer(s) and Producer(s)

ABC MINUTE MAGAZINE, Tom Wolf, Executive Producer (ABC)

ANIMALS, ANIMALS, ANIMALS, Lester Cooper, Executive Producer; Paul Weinberg, Producer (ABC)

VILLA ALEGRE, Claudio Guzman, Executive Producer; Larry Gotlieb, Producer (PBS)

CHILDREN'S INSTRUCTIONAL SERIES (E-1376)

Emmy(s) to Executive Producer(s) and Producer(s)

SCHOOLHOUSE ROCK, Tom Yohe, Executive Producer; Radford Stone, George Newall, Producers (ABC)

SESAME STREET, Al Hyslop, Producer (PBS)

CHILDREN'S ENTERTAINMENT SPECIAL (E-1377)

Emmy(s) to Executive Producer(s) and Producer(s)

A PIECE OF CAKE, (Special Treat); Marilyn Olin, Lee Polk, Producers (NBC)

HEWITT'S JUST DIFFERENT, (ABC Afterschool Special); Daniel Wilson, Executive Producer; Fran Sears, Producer (ABC) HOW THE BEATLES CHANGED THE WORLD, (Special Treat); Charles E. Andrews, Ken Greengrass, Executive Producers (NBC)

I CAN, (The Winners); Robert Guenette, Executive Producer; Paul Asselin, Diane Asselin, Producers (CBS)

JOURNEY TOGETHER, (The Winners); Robert Guenette, Executive Producer, Paul Asselin and Diane Asselin, Producers (CBS)

MAN FROM NOWHERE, Once Upon A Classic; Jay Rayvid, Executive Producer; Shep Greene, Producer (PBS)

THE PINBALLS, ABC Afterschool Special; Martin Tahse, Producer (ABC)

CHILDREN'S ENTERTAINMENT SERIES (E-1378)

Emmy(s) to Executive Producer(s) and Producer(s)

CAPTAIN KANGAROO, Jim Hirschfeld, Producer (CBS)

ROBIN HOOD, Once Upon A Classic; Jay Rayvid, Executive Producer; Shep Greene, Producer (PBS)

ZOOM, Terri Payne Francis, Executive Producer; Bob Glover, Janet Weaver, Producers (PBS)

COVERAGE OF SPECIAL EVENTS (E-1379)

(Possibility of one Award, more than one Award or no Award)

ALL-AMERICAN THANKSGIVING DAY PARADE, Mike Gargiulo, Executive Producer; Vern Diamond, Clarence Schimmel, Jim Hirschfeld, Wilfred Fielding, Malachy Wienges, Producers (CBS)

TOURNAMENT OF ROSES PARADE AND PAGEANT, Mike Gargiulo, Executive Producer; Vern Diamond, Producer (CBS)

FOURTH ANNUAL DAYTIME EMMY AWARDS, Walter Miller, Producer (NBC)

MACY'S 51st ANNUAL THANKSGIVING DAY PARADE, Dick Schneider, Producer (NBC)

THE GREAT ENGLISH GARDEN PARTY - PETER USTINOV LOOKS AT 100 YEARS OF WIMBLEDON, Ken Ashton, Allison Hawkes, Pamela Moncur, Producers (NBC)

RELIGIOUS PROGRAMMING (E-1380)

(Possibility of one Award, more than one Award or no Award)

DIRECTIONS, Sid Darion, Executive Producer (ABC)

FRANCIS OF ASSISI: A SEARCH FOR THE MAN AND HIS MEANING, Doris Ann, Executive Producer; Martin Hoade, Producer (NBC)

WOMAN OF VALOR, Doris Ann, Executive Producer; Martin Hoade, Producer (NBC)

CHILDREN'S INFORMATIONAL SPECIAL (E-1381)

Emmy(s) to Executive Producer(s) and Producer(s)

HENRY WINKLER MEETS WILLIAM SHAKESPEARE, CBS Festival of Lively Arts for Young People; Daniel Wilson, Producer (CBS)

VERY GOOD FRIENDS, ABC Afterschool Special; Matin Tahse, Producer (ABC)

WRITING - DAYTIME DRAMA SERIES (E-1382)

For a single episode of a series; or for the entire series

WILLIAM J. BELL, KAY LENARD, BILL REGA, PAT FALKEN SMITH, MARGARET STEWART, Days of Our Lives (NBC)

JEROME and BRIDGET DOBSON, NANCY FORD, JEAN RUVEROL, ROBERT and PHYLLIS WHITE, The Guiding Light, Series (CBS)

CLAIRE LABINE, PAUL AVILA MAYER, MARY MUNISTERI, ALLAN LEICHT, JUDITH PINSKER, Ryan's Hope, Series (ABC)

AGNES NIXON, CATHY CHICOS, DORIS FRANKEL, KEN HARVEY, KATHRYN McCABE, WISNER WASHAM, MARY K. WELLS, JACK WOOD, All My Children, Series (ABC)

ANN MARCUS, RAY GOLDSTONE, JOYCE PERRY, MICHAEL ROBERT DAVID, LAURA OLSHER, ROCCI CHATFIELD, ELIZABETH HARROWER, Days of Our Lives, Series (NBC)

ACTOR - DAYTIME DRAMA SERIES (E-1383)
MATTHEW COWLES, All My Children (ABC)
LARRY KEITH, All My Children (ABC)
MICHAEL LEVIN, Ryan's Hope (ABC)
JAMES PRITCHETT, The Doctors (NBC)
ANDREW ROBINSON, Ryan's Hope (ABC)
MICHAEL STORM, One Life to Live (ABC)

INDIVIDUAL DIRECTOR - DAYTIME DRAMA SERIES (E-1384)
For a single episode
IRA CIRKER, Another World, December 20, 1977 (NBC)
RICHARD DUNLAP, The Young and The Restless, March 3, 1978 (CBS)
RICHARD T. McCUE, As The World Turns, March 15, 1977 (CBS)
ROBERT MYHRUM, Love Of Life, August 31, 1977 (CBS)
AL RABIN, Days Of Our Lives, February 21, 1978 (NBC)
LELA SWIFT, Ryan's Hope, November 3, 1977 (ABC)

ACTRESS - DAYTIME DRAMA SERIES (E-1385)
MARY FICKETT, All My Children (ABC)
SUSAN SEAFORTH HAYES, Days Of Our Lives (NBC)
JENNIFER HARMON, One Life To Live (ABC)
LAURIE HEINEMAN, Another World (NBC)
SUSAN LUCCI, All My Children (ABC)
BEVERLEE Mc KINSEY, Another World (NBC)
VICTORIA WYNDHAM, Another World (NBC)

DAYTIME DRAMA SERIES (E-1386)
Emmy(s) to Executive Producer(s) and Producer(s)
ALL MY CHILDREN, Bud Kloss and Agnes Nixon, Producers (ABC)
DAYS OF OUR LIVES, Betty Corday and Wesley Kenny, Executive Producers; Jack Herzberg, Producer (NBC)
RYAN'S HOPE, Claire Labine and Paul Avila Mayer, Executive Producers; Robert Costello, Producer (ABC)
THE YOUNG AND THE RESTLESS, John Conboy, Executive Producer; Patricia Wenig, Producer (CBS)

THE NATIONAL AWARD FOR COMMUNITY SERVICE (E-1387)
BUBBLE GUM DIGEST (WMAQ-TV) Chicago, Illinois
CO-OP CONSPIRACY: PYRAMID OF SHAME (KTVI-TV) St. Louis, Missouri
DYING TO GROW UP (WCVB-TV) Needham, Massachusetts
HOT SPOT: A REPORT ON ROCKY FLATS (KMGH-TV) Denver, Colorado
IS THERE ANY HOPE FOR HOPE STREET? (KAIT-TV) Jonesboro, Arkansas
MISERY, MONEY & WHITEWASH (KBTV) Denver, Colorado
ONE MAN'S STRUGGLE (WBAL-TV) Baltimore, Maryland
VOLUNTEER-A-THON (WRAL-TV) Raleigh, North Carolina
WATER (KOOL-TV) Phoenix, Arizona

THE INTERNATIONAL DIRECTORATE AWARD (E-1388)
ALPHONSE OUIMET, Chairman of the Board of TELESAT CANADA

INTERNATIONAL FICTION AWARD (E-1389)
THE COLLECTION, Granada Television Ltd. Manchester, England
THE LAST FLICKERS OF SUNSET, TV Asahi, Tokyo, Japan
SARAH, Canadian Broadcasting Corporation, Toronto, Canada
RED FLOWER, (NHK) Japan Broadcasting Corporation, Tokyo, Japan
ROGUE MALE, British Broadcasting Corporation, London, England

INTERNATIONAL NON-FICTION AWARD (E-1390)
HENRY FORD'S AMERICA, Canadian Broadcasting Corporation, Toronto, Canada

TIDES OF WAR, Global Communications Ltd., Don Mills, Canada
THE GOOD, BAD AND THE INDIFFERENT, Yorkshire Television Ltd., Leeds, England
HOMAGE TO CHAGALL, Canadian Broadcasting Corporation, Toronto, Canada
TWENTY-ONE, Granada Television Ltd., Manchester, England

CREATIVE ARTS IN TELEVISION

ART DIRECTION - COMEDY SERIES (E-1391)
For a single episode of a regular or limited series
EDWARD STEPHENSON, Production Designer, ROBERT CHECCHI, Set Decorator, Soap, Episode #1 (ABC)
THOMAS E. AZZARI, A.E.S. Hudson Street, In The Black (ABC)
ROY CHRISTOPHER, Art Director, JAMES SHANAHAN, Art Director, Welcome Back, Kotter, Barbarino In Love, Part I (ABC)
PAUL SYLOS and EUGENE H. HARRIS, Art Directors, ROBERT SIGNORELLI and JOHN McCARTHY, Set Decorators, The Love Boat, (ABC)
C. MURAWSKI, Maude, The Wake (CBS)

ART DIRECTION - DRAMA SERIES (E-1392)
For a single episode of a regular or limited series
TIM HARVEY, Art Director, I, Claudius, Masterpiece Theatre, Episode #1 (PBS)
JACK DE SHIELDS, Production Designer, JAMES F. CLAYTOR, Art Director, BARBARA KREIGER, Set Decorator, Washington: Behind Closed Doors-Episode #3 (ABC)
DEREK DODD, Anna Karenina, Masterpiece Theatre Episode #1 (PBS)
WILFRED J. SHINGLETON, Production Designer, THEO HARISCH, JURGEN KIEBACH, Art Directors, MAXI HAREITER, Set Decorator, Holocaust (NBC)

ART DIRECTION - COMEDY-VARIETY OR MUSIC SERIES (E-1393)
For a single episode of a regular or limited series
ROY CHRISTOPHER, The Richard Pryor Show (NBC)
PAUL BARNES and BOB SANSOM Art Directors, BILL HARP, Set Decorator, The Carol Burnett Show, The Final Show (CBS)
BILL BOHNERT, Art Director, ARLENE ALEN, Set Decorator, Donny and Marie, Opening Show (ABC)
ROMAIN JOHNSTON, Captain and Tennille (ABC)
EUGENE LEE and LEO YOSHIMURA, Art Directors, FRANNE LEE and LEE MAYMAN, Set Decorators NBC's Saturday Night Live, host Steve Martin ((NBC)

ART DIRECTION - DRAMATIC SPECIAL (E-1394)
JOHN DE CUIR, Production Designer, RICHARD C. GODDARD, Set Decorator, Ziegfeld: The Man And His Women (NBC)
ROY CHRISTOPHER, Production Designer, JAMES SHANAHAN, Set Decorator, Our Town, Bell System (NBC)
JOHN J. LLOYD, Art Director, HAL GAUSMAN, Set Decorator, It Happened One Christmas (ABC)
LOYD S. PAPEZ, Art Director, RICHARD FRIEDMAN, Set Decorator, The Bastard (Synd)
JAN SCOTT, Art Director, ANNE D. McCULLEY, Set Decorator, The Gathering (ABC)

ART DIRECTION - COMEDY-VARIETY OR MUSIC SPECIAL (E-1395)
ROMAIN JOHNSTON, Art Director, KERRY JOYCE, Set Decorator, The Sentry Collection Presents Ben Vereen - His Roots (ABC)
BRIAN C. BARTHOLOMEW, Art Director, Cher. . .Special (ABC)
ROY CHRISTOPHER, Art Director, DON REMACLE, Set Decorator, How To Survive the 70s and Maybe Even Bump Into Happiness (CBS)
ROMAIN JOHNSTON and JOHN DAPPER, Art Directors, ROBERT

CHECCI, Set Decorator, They Said It With Music: Yankee Doodle To Ragtime (CBS)
ROBERT KELLY, Mitzi. . .Zings Into Spring (CBS)

CHOREOGRAPHY (E-1396)
For an episode of a regular or limited series
RON FIELD, The Sentry Collection Presents Ben Vereen - His Roots (ABC)
GEORGE BALANCHINE, ALEXANDRA DANILOVA, New York City Ballet: Coppelia, Live From Lincoln Center (PBS)
TONY CHARMOLI, Mitzi. . .Zings Into Spring (CBS)
ERNEST O. FLATT, The Carol Burnett Show, The Final Show (CBS)
MIRIAM NELSON, Ziegfeld: The Man And His Women (NBC)

CINEMATOGRAPHY - ENTERTAINMENT SERIES (E-1397)
For a single episode of a regular or limited series
TED VOIGTLANDER, ASC, Little House On The Prairie, The Fighter (NBC)
LLOYD AHERN, The Love Boat, (The Inspector; A Very Special Girl; Until The Last Goodbye) (ABC)
JOSEPH BIROC, ASC, Washington: Behind Closed Doors, Part I (ABC)
ROBERT HAUSER, Roll Of Thunder, Hear My Cry (ABC)
MICHAEL HUGO, ASC, The Awakening Land (NBC)

CINEMATOGRAPHY - ENTERTAINMENT SPECIAL (E-1398)
For a special or feature length program made for television
GERALD PERRY FINNERMAN, ASC, Ziegfeld: The Man And His Women (NBC)
JOSEPH BIROC, ASC, A Family Upside Down (NBC)
SOL NEGRIN, ASC, The Last Tenant (ABC)
HOWARD SCHWARTZ, ASC, The Ghost of Flight 401 (NBC)
RICHARD WAITE, The Life And Assassination Of The Kingfish (NBC)

COSTUME DESIGN - DRAMA OR COMEDY SERIES (E-1399)
For a single episode of a regular or limited series
PEGGY FARRELL, EDITH ALMOSLINO, Holocaust (NBC)
DONFELD, The New Adventures of Wonder Woman, Anschluss '77 (CBS)
GRADY HUNT, Quark, The Emperor's Quasi Norms, Part II (NBC)
BILL JOBE, Testimony Of Two Men, Part III (Synd)
YVONNE WOOD, 79 Park Avenue (NBC)

COSTUME DESIGN - MUSIC-VARIETY (E-1400)
For a single episode of a regular or limited series, or for a special program
BOB MACKIE, RET TURNER, Mitzi. . .Zings Into Spring (CBS)
DAVID DOUCETTE, Dorothy Hamill Presents Winners (ABC)
BILL HARGATE, Doug Henning's World Of Magic (NBC)
WARDEN NEIL, The John Davidson Christmas Special (ABC)
SANDRA STEWART, Cindy (ABC)

COSTUME DESIGN - DRAMA SPECIAL (E-1401)
NOEL TAYLOR, Actor, Hollywood Television Theatre (PBS)
JEAN-PIERRE DORLEAC, The Bastard (Synd)
GRADY HUNT, Ziegfeld: The Man And His Women (NBC)
BILL JOBE, The Dark Secret of Harvest Home (NBC)
OLGA LEHMANN, The Four Feathers, Bell System (NBC)

FILM EDITING - COMEDY SERIES (E-1402)
For a single episode of a regular or limited series

ED COTTER, Happy Days, Richie Almost Dies (ABC)
M. PAM BLUMENTHAL, The Bob Newhart Show, A Jackie Story (CBS)
STANFORD TISCHLER and LARRY L. MILLS, M*A*S*H, Fade Out, Fade In, (CBS)
NORMAN WALLERSTEIN, A.C.E. and ROBERT MOORE, A.C.E., Love Boat, (Masquerade; The Caper; Eyes Of Love; Hollywood Royalty) (ABC)

FILM EDITING - DRAMA SERIES (E-1403)
For a single episode of a regular or limited series
STEPHEN A. ROTTER, ROBERT M. REITANO, CRAIG McKAY, ALAN HEIM and BRIAN SMEDLEY-ASTON, Holocaust (NBC)
DAVID G. BLANGSTED, A.C.E., HOWARD TERRILL, A.C.E., Eight Is Enough, Yes Nicholas, There Is A Santa Claus (ABC)
BYRON "BUZZ" BRANDT, A.C.E., RICHARD MEYER and DAVID BERLATSKY, King (NBC)
JIM FARIS, Family, Acts Of Love, Part I (ABC)
BILL MOSHER, The Waltons, Grandma Comes Home (CBS)
ROBERT WATTS, Columbo, How To Dial A Murder (NBC)

FILM EDITING - SPECIAL (E-1404)
For a drama, comedy or music-variety special or film made for television
JOHN A. MARTINELLI, A.C.E., The Defection of Simas Kudirka (CBS)
RONALD J. FAGAN, A.C.E., Young Joe, The Forgotten Kennedy (ABC)
LESLIE L. GREEN, Ziegfeld: The Man And His Women (NBC)
HARRY KAYE, A.C.E., DONALD RODE, To Kill A Cop (NBC)
KENNETH R. KOCH, Mary Jane Harper Cried Last Night (CBS)
BERNARD J. SMALL, Just A Little Inconvenience (NBC)
KEN ZEMKE, A Killing Affair (CBS)

FILM SOUND EDITING - SERIES (E-1405)
For a single episode of a regular or limited series
DOUGLAS H. GRINDSTAFF, HANK SALERNO, LARRY SINGER, CHRISTOPHER CHULACK, RICHARD RADERMAN, DON CROSBY, H. LEE CHANEY, MARK DENNIS, DON V. ISAACS, STEVE OLSON and AL KAJITA, Police Story, River Of Promises (NBC)
LARRY CAROW, DAVID PETTIJOHN, DON WARNER, COLIN MOUAT, CHUCK MORAN and PETER HUBBARD, Baa Baa Black Sheep/Black Sheep Squadron, The Hawk Flies On Sunday (NBC)
TONY GARBER, DALE JOHNSTON and RON CLARK, Lou Grant, Nazi (CBS)
DOUGLAS H. GRINDSTAFF, LARRY SINGER, HANK SALERNO, CHRISTOPHER CHULACK, LUKE WOLFRAM, AL KAJITA, DWAYNE AVERY, RICHARD FRIEDMAN and DON V. ISAACS, Fantasy Island, Racer and Lady Of The Evening (ABC)
WILLIAM STEVENSON and RICHARD RADERMAN, Roll Of Thunder, Hear My Cry (ABC)

FILM SOUND EDITING - SPECIAL (E-1406)
JERRY ROSENTHAL, MICHAEL CORRIGAN, JERRY PIROZZI, WILLIAM JACKSON, JAMES YANT, RICHARD LE GRAND, DONALD HIGGINS, JOHN STRAUSS and JOHN KLINE, The Amazing Howard Hughes (CBS)
DOUGLAS H. GRINDSTAFF, H. LEE CHANEY, DON V. ISAACS, LARRY KAUFMAN, STEVE OLSON, DON CROSBY, AL KAJITA, BOB HUMAN, HANK SALERNO and LARRY SINGER, The Last Hurrah, Hallmark Hall Of Fame (NBC)
DOUGLAS H. GRINDSTAFF, HANK SALERNO, LARRY SINGER, CHRISTOPHER CHULACK, MARK DENNIS, DON CROSBY, H. LEE CHANEY and DON V. ISAACS, To Kill A Cop, Part I (NBC)
DON HALL, DWAYNE AVERY, TOM BURKE and CHICK CAMERA, Standing Tall (NBC)
BERNARD F. PINCUS, PATRICK R. SOMERSET, JEFFREY BUSHELMAN, A. JEREMY HOENACK, JOHN BUSHELMAN, EDWARD L. SANDLIN, ROBERT A. BIGGART and JERRY ROSENTHAL, The Dark Secret Of Harvest Home (NBC)

DON WARNER, LARRY CAROW, COLIN MOUAT, DAVID PETTIJOHN, GARY VAUGHAN, CHUCK MORAN, PETER HUBBARD and FRED STAFFORD, Tarantulas: The Deadly Cargo (CBS)

FILM SOUND MIXING (E-1407)

For a single episode of a regular or limited series, or for a special program

WILLIAM TEAGUE, GEORGE E. PORTER, EDDIE J. NELSON and ROBERT L. HARMAN, Young Joe, The Forgotten Kennedy (ABC)
ALAN BERNARD, GEORGE E. PORTER, EDDIE J. NELSON and HOPPY MEHTERIAN, Having Babies II (ABC)
EDDIE KNOWLES, GEORGE E. PORTER, EDDIE J. NELSON, and J. ROBERT PETTIS, Tarantulas: The Deadly Cargo, (CBS)
HOPPY MEHTERIAN, GEORGE E. PORTER, EDDIE J. NELSON and DEAN HODGES, A Sensitive, Passionate Man (NBC)
J. ROBERT PETTIS, GEORGE E. PORTER, EDDIE J. NELSON and CA-BELL SMITH, See How She Runs, G.E. Theatre (CBS)
TOMMY THOMPSON, GEORGE E. PORTER, EDDIE J. NELSON and HOPPY MEHTERIAN, In The Matter Of Karen Ann Quinlan (NBC)

GRAPHIC DESIGN AND TITLE SEQUENCES (E-1408)

For a single episode of a regular or limited series, or for a special program This includes animation only when created for use in titling.

BILL DAVIS, NBC: The First Fifty Years - A Closer Look - Variety (NBC)
EYTAN KELLER and STEWART BERNSTEIN, 50th Annual Awards of the Academy of Motion Picture Arts and Sciences (ABC)
MAURY NEMOY, ROBERT BRANHAM and JOHN DE CUIR, Ziegfeld: The Man And His Women (NBC)
PHILL NORMAN, Washington: Behind Closed Doors (ABC)

LIGHTING DIRECTION (E-1409)

For a single episode of a regular or limited series or for a special program

GREG BRUNTON, Cher. . .Special (ABC)
LEARD DAVIS, Lighting Designer, KEN DETTLING, Lighting Director, You Can Run But You Can't Hide, Visions (PBS)
IMERO FIORENTINO, The Neil Diamond Special: I'm Glad You're Here With Me Tonight (NBC) FRED Mc KINNON and CARL J. VITELLI, JR., Happy Birthday, Las Vegas (ABC)
ALAN K. WALKER and BILL KLAGES, Olivia (ABC)
GEORGE RIESENBERGER, Best Of Families, The Great Trolley Strike of 1895 (PBS)

MAKE-UP (E-1410)

For a single episode of a series, or for a special program

RICHARD COBOS and WALTER SCHENCK, How The West Was Won, Part II (ABC)
HANK EDDS, ALLAN "WHITEY" SNYDER, Little House On The Prairie, The Fighter (NBC)
CHRISTINA SMITH, King (NBC)
FRANK C. WESTMORE and MICHAEL G. WESTMORE, A Love Affair: The Eleanor And Lou Gehrig Story (NBC)
MICHAEL G. WESTMORE, HANK EDDS and LYNN REYNOLDS, The Amazing Howard Hughes (CBS)

MUSIC COMPOSITION - SERIES (DRAMATIC UNDERSCORE) (E-1411)

For a single episode of a regular or limited series

BILLY GOLDENBERG, King (NBC)
MORTON GOULD, Holocaust (NBC)
FRED KARLIN, The Awakening Land (NBC)
MORTON STEVENS, Wheels (NBC)
PATRICK WILLIAMS, Columbo, Try And Catch Me (NBC)

MUSIC COMPOSITION - SPECIAL (DRAMATIC UNDERSCORE) (E-1412)

JIMMIE HASKELL, See How She Runs, G.E. Theatre (CBS)
DICK DE BENEDICTIS, Ziegfeld: The Man And His Women (NBC)
BILLY GOLDENBERG, Actor, Hollywood Television Theatre (PBS)
DAVID SHIRE, The Defection Of Simas Kudirka (CBS)

MUSIC DIRECTION (E-1413)

For a single episode of a regular or limited series, or a special program, whether it be variety or music

IAN FRASER, The Sentry Collection Presents Ben Vereen - His Roots (ABC)
JIMMIE HASKELL, The Second Barry Manilow Special (ABC)
ZUBIN MEHTA, The New York Philharmonic/Mehta, Live From Lincoln Center (PBS)
ANDRE PREVIN, Previn And The Pittsburgh, The Music That Made The Movies (PBS)

SPECIAL MUSICAL MATERIAL (E-1414)

For a song (which must have both music and lyrics), a theme for a series, or special material for a variety program providing that the first usage of this material was written expressly for television. (Possibility of one Award, more than one Award, or no Award)

STAN FREEMAN and ARTHUR MALVIN, Music and Lyrics The Carol Burnett Show, Mini Musical: "Hi-Hat", (CBS)
MITZIE WELCH and KEN WELCH, Music and Lyrics, The Sentry Collection Presents Ben Vereen - His Roots, Song: "See You Tomorrow In Class" (ABC)
EARL BROWN, The Donny And Marie Show, Song: "Leading Lady" (ABC)
BILL DYER, Lyrics, DICK DE BENEDICTIS, Music, Ziegfeld: The Man And His Women, Song: "Until The Music Ends" (NBC)
KENYON EMRYS-ROBERTS, Poldark, Masterpiece Theatre, Poldark Theme (PBS)

TAPE SOUND MIXING (E-1415)

For a single episode of a regular or limited series or for a special program

THOMAS J. HUTH, EDWARD J. GREENE and RON BRYAN, Bette Midler - Ol' Red Hair Is Back (NBC)
RON ESTES, Our Town, Bell System (NBC)
PHILLIP J. SERETTI, BOB GAUDIO, VAL GARAY, RICK RUGGIERI and JOHN WALKER, The Neil Diamond Special: I'm Glad You're Here With Me Tonight (NBC)
LARRY STEPHENS, THOMAS J. HUTH, RON BRYAN, ERIC LEVINSON and GROVER HELSLEY, Perry Como's Easter By The Sea (ABC)
DICK WILSON, The Lawrence Welk Show with Roger Williams at the Piano (Synd)

TECHNICAL DIRECTION AND ELECTRONIC CAMERAWORK (E-1416)

For a single episode of a regular or limited series, or for a special program

GENE CROWE, Technical Director; WAYNE ORR, LARRY HEIDER, DAVE HILMER, BOB KEYS, Cameramen, The Sentry Collection Presents Ben Vereen - His Roots (ABC)
CHARLES FRANKLIN, STEVE CUNNINGHAM, HARRY TATARIAN, MARK MILLER, Technical Directors; GORMAN ERICKSON, JOHN AGUIRRE, STANLEY ZITNICK, DAVID FINCH, RICHARD NELSON, HECTOR RAMIREZ, LOUIS SHORE, BEN WOLF, THOMAS BROWN, GORDON SWEENEY, ROBERT WELSH and BRIAN CUNNEEN, Cameramen, CBS: On The Air (CBS)
LOUIS FUSARI, Technical Director; RODGER HARBAUGH, ROY HOLM, RICK LOMBARDO and PEGGY MAHONEY, Camerapersons,

Mitzi. . .What's Hot, What's Not (CBS)
KARL MESSERSCHMIDT, Technical Director; JON OLSON, MIKE STRAMISKY, GEORGE LOOMIS, GEORGE FALARDEAU, MIKE HIGUERA and JIM DODGE, Cameramen, Doug Henning's World Of Magic (NBC)
O. TAMBURRI, Technical Director; JON OLSON, ROY HOLM and REED HOWARD, Cameramen, Our Town, Bell System (NBC)

VIDEO TAPE EDITING - SERIES (E-1417)

For a single episode of a regular or limited series

TUCKER WIARD, The Carol Burnett Show, The Final Show (CBS)
GARY H. ANDERSON, Soap, Episode #2 (ABC)
ED. J. BRENNAN, Laugh-In, Show #6 (NBC)
CHIP BROOKS, The Betty White Show, Pilot, (CBS)
JERRY DAVIS, Three's Company, Chrissy, Come Home (ABC)
MARCO ZAPPIA, Husbands, Wives & Lovers, The One Where Everybody Is Looking For A Little Action (CBS)

VIDEO TAPE EDITING - SPECIAL (E-1418)

PAM MARSHALL and ANDY ZALL, The Sentry Collection Presents Ben Vereen - His Roots (ABC)
ED. J. BRENNAN, The Goldie Hawn Special (CBS)
CHIP BROOKS and HAL COLLINS, Texaco Presents Bob Hope In A Very Special Special - On The Road With Bing (NBC)
JIMMY B. FRAZIER, The Carpenters - Space Encounters (ABC)
MARCO ZAPPIA, TERRY GREENE, HARVEY BERGER and JIMMY B. FRAZIER, Superstunt (NBC)

INDIVIDUAL ACHIEVEMENT IN ANY AREA OF CREATIVE TECHNICAL CRAFTS (E-1419)

(Possibility of one Award, more than one Award, or no Award)

WILLIAM F. BROWNELL and JOHN H. KANTROWE, JR. (Sound Effects), Our Town, Bell System (NBC)
SUGAR BLYMER (Hairstylist), The Awakening Land, Part III (NBC)
LARRY GERMAIN and GLADYS WITTEN (Hairstylists), Little House On The Prairie, Here Come The Brides (NBC)
MARK SCHUBIN (Technical Designer), Live From Lincoln Center (Series) (PBS)
FRANK VAN DER VEER (Optical Effects), L. B. ABBOTT (Special Photographic Effects), The Return Of Captain Nemo (CBS)

SPECIAL CLASSIFICATION OF INDIVIDUAL ACHIEVEMENT (E-1420)

(Possibility of one Award, more than one Award or no Award)

WILLIAM PITKIN (Costume Designer), Romeo and Juliet (PBS)
MIKHAIL BARYSHNIKOV (Dancer), The Nutcracker (CBS)
WILLIAM T. CARTWRIGHT (Film Editor), JEFFREY WESTON (Film Editor), Oscar Presents The War Movies And John Wayne (ABC)
JAN SCOTT (Production Designer), EARL CARLSON (Set Decorator), CBS: On The Air (CBS)

CHILDREN'S PROGRAMMING - INDIVIDUAL ACHIEVEMENT (E-1421)

(Possibility of one Award, more than one Award, or no Award)

KEN JOHNSON, Art Director, ROBERT CHECCHI, Set Decorator, Once Upon A Brothers Grimm (CBS)
BILL HARGATE (Costume Designer), Once Upon A Brothers Grimm (CBS)
JERRY GREENE (Video Tape Editor), Once Upon A Brothers Grimm (CBS)
NICHOLAS SPIES and ROBERT MILLSLAGLE (Video Tape Editors), A Connecticut Yankee In King Arthur's Court (PBS)
TOMMY COLE, LARRY ABBOTT, MICHAEL G. WESTMORE (Make-Up), Once Upon A Brothers Grimm (CBS)

INDIVIDUALS - SPECIAL EVENTS COVERAGE (E-1422)

(Possibility of one Award, more than one Award, or no Award)

RODGER HARBAUGH (Aerial Photography), The 29th Annual Emmy Awards Show (NBC)
WILLIAM W. LANDERS (Technical Direction and Electronic Camerawork), The 29th Annual Emmy Awards Show (NBC)
ALAN BUZ KOHAN (Music), 50th Annual Awards Of The Academy Of Motion Picture Arts And Sciences, Opening Production Number: "Look How Far We've Come" (ABC)
CLARK JONES (Director), Footlights: The 1978 Tony Awards (CBS)

ACHIEVEMENT IN BROADCAST JOURNALISM (E-1423)

ATAS Broadcast Journalism Awards

CHARLES KURALT, "On The Road" (CBS News).
BILL MOYERS (CBS Reports):
"THE FIRE NEXT DOOR" (CBS Reports), Howard Stringer, Executive Producer.
"EXPLODING GAS TANKS" (ABC News, 20/20 segment), Sylvia Chase, Correspondent, Stanhope Gould, Producer.

ENGINEERING DEVELOPMENT (E-1424)

An Award to an individual, a company or an organization for developments in engineering which are either so extensive an improvement on existing methods or so innovative in nature that they materially affect the transmission, recording or reception of television.

PETRO VLAHOS of Vlahos-Gottschalk Research Corporation for the invention and development of the ULTIMATTE video-matting device. Society of Motion Picture and Television Engineers, a citation, for expeditiously achieving the difficult task of obtaining industry agreement on the One-Inch Type C Continuous Field Helical Recording Standards.

SPECIAL ATAS GOVERNORS MEDALLION (E-1424A)

Frederick Wolcott, for his thirty years of service on the ATAS Engineering Awards Panel.

LIVE SPORTS SPECIALS (E-1425)

Emmys(s) to Executive Producer(s) and Producer(s)
1977 LEAGUE CHAMPIONSHIP SERIES - AMERICAN AND NATIONAL LEAGUES, Scotty Connal, Executive Producer; Roy Hammerman, George Finkel and Mike Weisman, Producers; (NBC)
MASTERS GOLF TOURNAMENT, Frank Chirkinian, Producer; (CBS)
NCAA BASKETBALL CHAMPIONSHIP GAME, Don Ohlmeyer, Executive Producer; George Finkel, Producer; (NBC)
SUPERBOWL XII, Robert Stenner, Producer; (CBS)
U.S. OPEN TENNIS CHAMPIONSHIPS, Frank Chirkinian, Producer; (CBS)
WORLD CHAMPIONSHIP BOXING(ALI/SPINKS), Frank Chirkinian, Producer; (CBS)

LIVE SPORTS SERIES (E-1426)

Emmy(s) to Executive Producer(s) and Producer(s)
MAJOR LEAGUE BASEBALL: GAME OF THE WEEK, Scotty Connal, Executive Producer; Jim Marooney, David Stern, Larry Cirillo, Mike Weisman, Roy Hammerman and George Finkel, Producers (NBC)
NCAA BASKETBALL, Don Ohlmeyer, Executive Producer; David Stern, Dick Auerbach, Jim Marooney, George Finkel, Roy Hammerman and Mike Weisman, Producers (NBC)
NFL FOOTBALL, Scotty Connal, Executive Producer; Jim Marooney, David Stern, Ken Edmundson, Larry Cirillo, Mike Weisman, Roy Hammerman, George Finkel and Dick Auerbach, Producers (NBC)

THE NFL TODAY/NFL FOOTBALL ON CBS, Michael Pearl, Producer (CBS)

EDITED SPORTS SPECIAL (E-1427)

Emmy(s) to Executive Producer(s) and Producer(s)

THE BASEBALL WORLD OF JOE GARAGIOLA, Joe Garagiola, Executive Producer; Ginny Seipt, Producer; July 19, 1977 (NBC)

THE IMPOSSIBLE DREAM: BALLOONING ACROSS THE ATLANTIC, Ed Goren, Producer; (CBS)

TARGET: NEW ORLEANS (NFL PREVIEW '77), Michael Pearl, Producer; (CBS)

EDITED SPORTS SERIES (E-1428)

Emmy(s) to Executive Producer(s) and Producer(s)

CBS SPORTS SPECTACULAR, Ed Goren, Producer (CBS)

SOCCER MADE IN GERMANY, James Scalen, Executive Producer; Christian Viertel, Producer (PBS)

SPORTS WORLD, Don Ohlmeyer, Executive Producer; Don Ellis, Coordinating Producer; Larry Cirillo, Peter Diamond, Les Dennis, Ken Edmundson, Chris Glidden, Linda Jonsson, Rex Lardner, Jr., Jim Marooney, Don McGuire, Ginny Seipt, David Stern, Mike Weisman, Dick Auerbach, Geoff Mason, Ted Nathanson, John Kerwin, George Finkel, Ed Connel, Bill Sheehan, Peter Bonventre, Bud Greenspan, Producers (NBC)

THE WAY IT WAS, Gerry Gross, Executive Producer; Gary Brown and Dick Enberg, Producers (SYND)

SPORTS PERSONALITY (E-1429)

Dick Enberg (NBC)
Al McGuire (NBC)
Brent Musburger (CBS)
Vince Scully (CBS)
Pat Summerall (CBS)
Jack Whitaker (CBS)

DIRECTING - SPORTS PROGRAMMING (E-1430)

FRANK CHIRKINIAN, World Championship Boxing (Ali/Spinks); (CBS)

HARRY COYLE, NCAA College Basketball Championships; (NBC)

TED NATHANSON, AFC Championship Football; (NBC)

TONY VERNA, Superbowl XII; (CBS)

INDIVIDUAL ACHIEVEMENT IN SPORTS PROGRAMMING

The following are "AREAS", Not "CATEGORIES". The Academy's rules specify the possibility of one Award, more than one Award or no Award for any of the following "AREAS"

WRITING (E-1431)

STEVE SABOL, "Joe And The Magic Bean: The Story Of Superbowl III" (Segment of NFL Today); December 1977 (CBS)

CINEMATOGRAPHY (E-1432)

JOE JAY JALBERT and KIM TAKAL, Aerial Acrobatic Skiing Championship (SportsWorld); Mar. 26, 1978 (NBC)

STEVE SABOL, Skateboard Fever (SportsWorld); February 1978 (NBC)

BARRY WINIK, Downhill Skiing; (NBC)

FILM EDITING (E-1433)

JOE JAY JALBERT and KIM TAKAL, Aerial Acrobatic Skiing Championship (SportsWorld); Mar. 26, 1978 (NBC)

YALE NELSON, Downhill Skiing; (NBC)

STEVE SABOL, Skateboard (SportsWorld); February 1978 (NBC)

NORM SMITH, The Impossible Dream: Ballooning Across The Atlantic; (CBS)

ENGINEERING SUPERVISION/TECHNICAL DIRECTION/ELECTRONIC CAMERAMEN (E-1434)

JAMES MARTENS, Engineering Supervisor; ROBERT BROWN, Technical Director-The NFL Today; (SERIES) (CBS)

ARTHUR TINN, Engineering Supervisor-The Superbowl Today/ SuperBowl XII; (CBS)

WILLIAM TOBEY, Technical Director, PHIL CANTRELL, ROBER HABAUG, BUDDY JOSEPH, BILL LANDERS, GEORGE LOOMIS, DONALD J. MULVANEY, ROY V. RATLIFF, MIKE STRAMISKY, Electronic Cameramen: American League Championship, 5th Game-Yankees at Kansas City; Oct. 8, 1977 (NBC)

VIDEOTAPE EDITING (INCLUDES ASSOCIATE DIRECTORS) (E-1435)

BOB LEVY, Associate Director; JEROME HAGGART, RICHARD LEIBLE, CHARLES LIOTTA, JOHN OSZEWSKI, Videotape Editors - "Sportsworld"; (SERIES) (NBC)

JOE BILL WORTHINGTON, Videotape Editor; Colgate Triple Crown LPGA Match Play Championships; (PBS)

ART DIRECTION/SCENIC DESIGN AND GRAPHIC DESIGN/TITLE SEQUENCES (E-1436)

NEIL DeLUCA, Scenic Designer; The NFL Today; (SERIES) (CBS)

MATTHEW F. McCARTHY AND PETER CAESAR, Graphic Designers; Sportsworld (SERIES) (NBC)

1978/79

NIGHTTIME PROGRAMMING

COMEDY SERIES (E-1437)

Emmy(s) to Executive Producer and/or Producer

TAXI, James L. Brooks, Stan Daniels, David Davis and Ed. Weinberger, Executive Producers; Glen Charles, Les Charles, Producers (ABC)

MORK & MINDY, Garry Marshall and Tony Marshall, Executive Producers; Dale McRaven, Bruce Johnson, Producers (ABC)

M*A*S*H, Burt Metcalfe, Producer (CBS)

BARNEY MILLER, Danny Arnold, Executive Producer; Tony Sheehan, Reinhold Weege, Co-Producers (ABC)

ALL IN THE FAMILY, Mort Lachman, Executive Producer; Milt Josefsberg, Producer (CBS)

COMEDY-VARIETY OR MUSIC PROGRAM (E-1438)

For a special or a series, Emmy(s) to Executive Producer and/or Producer and Star, if applicable

STEVE & EYDIE CELEBRATE IRVING BERLIN, Steve Lawrence, Gary Smith, Executive Producers; Gary Smith, Dwight Hemion, Producers; Steve Lawrence, Eydie Gorme, Stars (NBC)

SHIRLEY MacLAINE AT THE LIDO, Gary Smith, Dwight Hemion, Producers; Shirley MacLaine, Star (CBS)

NBC'S SATURDAY NIGHT LIVE, Lorne Michaels, Producer; Dan Aykroyd, John Belushi, Jane Curtin, Garrett Morris, Bill Murray, Laraine Newman, Gilda Radner, Stars; (NBC)

THE MUPPET SHOW, David Lazer, Executive Producer; Jim Henson, Producer; The Muppets (Frank Oz, Jerry Nelson, Richard Hunt, Dave Goelz, Jim Henson Stars) (Synd)

ARTHUR FIEDLER: JUST CALL ME MAESTRO, William Cosel, Producer; Arthur Fiedler, Star (PBS)

DRAMA SERIES (E-1439)

Emmy(s) to Executive Producer and/or Producer

LOU GRANT, Gene Reynolds, Executive Producer; Seth Freeman,

Gary David Goldberg, Producers (CBS)
THE ROCKFORD FILES, Meta Rosenberg, Executive Producer; Stephen J. Cannell, Supervising Producer; Chas. Floyd Johnson, David Chase, Juanita Bartlett, Producers (NBC)
THE PAPER CHASE, Robert C. Thompson, Executive Producer; Robert Lewin, Albert Aley, Producers (CBS)

LIMITED SERIES (E-1440)

Emmy(s) to Executive Producer and/or Producer

ROOTS: THE NEXT GENERATIONS, David L. Wolper, Executive Producer; Stan Margulies, Producer (ABC)
BLIND AMBITION, David Susskind, Executive Producer; George Schaefer, Renee Valente, Producers (CBS)
BACKSTAIRS AT THE WHITE HOUSE, Ed Friendly, Executive Producer; Ed Friendly, Michael O'Herlihy, Producers (NBC)

DRAMA OR COMEDY SPECIAL (E-1441)

Emmy(s) to Executive Producer and/or Producer

FRIENDLY FIRE, Martin Starger, Executive Producer; Philip Barry, Producer; Fay Kanin, Co-Producer (ABC)
SUMMER OF MY GERMAN SOLDIER, Linda Gottlieb, Producer (NBC)
THE JERICHO MILE, Tim Zinnemann, Producer (ABC)
FIRST YOU CRY, Philip Barry, Producer (CBS)
DUMMY, Frank Konigsberg, Executive Producer; Sam Manners, Ernest Tidyman, Producers (CBS)

INFORMATIONAL PROGRAM (E-1442)

For a special or a series. Emmy(s) to Executive Producer and/or Producer

SCARED STRAIGHT!, Arnold Shapiro, Producer (Synd)
WHO ARE THE DEBOLTS--AND WHERE DID THEY GET 19 KIDS?, Henry Winkler, Executive Producer; John Korty, Warren Lockhart, Dan McCann, Producers (ABC)
THE BODY HUMAN: THE SEXES, Thomas W. Moore, Executive Producer; Alfred R. Kelman, Robert E. Fuisz, M.D., Producers; Vivian R. Moss, Charles A. Bangert, Co-Producers (CBS)

CLASSICAL PROGRAM IN THE PERFORMING ARTS (E-1443)

For a special or a series. Emmy(s) to Executive Producer and/or Producer and Star, if applicable

BALANCHINE IV, DANCE IN AMERICA; (Great Performances); Jac Venza, Executive Producer; Merrill Brockway, Series Producer; Emile Ardolino, Series Coordinating Producer; Judy Kinberg, Producer (PBS)
LIVE FROM LINCOLN CENTER (with Luciano Pavarotti and Joan Sutherland), John Goberman, Producer (PBS)
THE SLEEPING BEAUTY; The American Ballet Theatre; Live From Lincoln Center; John Goberman, Producer (PBS)
GIULINI'S BEETHOVEN'S 9TH LIVE - A GIFT FROM LOS ANGELES, Jeanne Mulcahy, Executive Producer; John Goberman, Producer (PBS)
BALANCHINE III, DANCE IN AMERICA; (Great Performances); Jac Venza, Executive Producer; Merrill Brockway, Series Producer; Emile Ardolino, Series Coordinating Producer; Judy Kinberg, Producer (PBS)

ANIMATED PROGRAM (E-1444)

For a special or a series. Emmy(s) to Executive Producer and/or Producer (Possibility of one Award, more than one Award, or no Award)

THE LION, THE WITCH AND THE WARDROBE, David Connell, Executive Producer; Steve Melendez, Producer (CBS)
YOU'RE THE GREATEST, CHARLIE BROWN, Lee Mendelson, Executive Producer; Bill Melendez, Producer (CBS)

HAPPY BIRTHDAY, CHARLIE BROWN, Lee Mendelson, Producer (CBS)

CHILDREN'S PROGRAM (E-1445)

For a special or a series. Emmy(s) to Executive Producer and/or Producer (Possibility of one Award, more than one Award, or no Award)

CHRISTMAS EVE ON SESAME STREET, Jon Stone, Executive Producer; Dulcy Singer, Producer (PBS)
ONCE UPON A CLASSIC, Jay Rayvid, Executive Producer; Graham McDonald, James A. DeVinney, Producers; Series (PBS)
BENJI'S VERY OWN CHRISTMAS STORY, Joe Camp, Producer (ABC)
A SPECIAL SESAME STREET CHRISTMAS, Bob Banner, Executive Producer; Stephen Pouliot, Producer (CBS)

PROGRAM ACHIEVEMENT - SPECIAL EVENTS (E-1446)

Emmy(s) to Executive Producer and/or Producer. (Possibility of one Award, more than one Award, or no Award)

51ST ANNUAL AWARDS PRESENTATION OF THE ACADEMY OF MOTION PICTURE ARTS AND SCIENCES, Jack Haley, Jr., Producer (ABC)
GOOD LUCK TONIGHT - THE 1979 TONY AWARDS, Alexander H. Cohen, Executive Producer; Hildy Parks, Producer; Roy A. Somlyo, Co-Producer (CBS)
BARYSHNIKOV AT THE WHITE HOUSE, Gerald Slater, Executive Producer; Emile Ardolino, Producer (PBS)

PROGRAM ACHIEVEMENT - SPECIAL CLASS (E-1447)

Emmy(s) to Executive Producer and/or Producer and Star, if applicable. (Possibility of one Award, more than one Award, or no Award)

THE TONIGHT SHOW STARRING JOHNNY CARSON, Fred de Cordova, Producer; Johnny Carson, Star (NBC)
LIFELINE, Thomas W. Moore and Robert E. Fuisz, M.D., Executive Producers; Alfred Kelman, Producer; Geof Bartz, Co-Producer (NBC)
STEVE ALLEN'S MEETING OF MINDS, Loring d'Usseau, Producer; Steve Allen, Star (PBS)
THE DICK CAVETT SHOW, Chris Porterfield, Producer; Dick Cavett, Star (PBS)

SUPPORTING ACTRESS - COMEDY OR COMEDY-VARIETY OR MUSIC SERIES (E-1448)

For a continuing or single performance in a regular series

SALLY STRUTHERS, All In The Family, (California Here We Are) (CBS)
POLLY HOLLIDAY, Alice (CBS)
MARION ROSS, Happy Days (CBS)
LORETTA SWIT, M*A*S*H (CBS)

SUPPORTING ACTOR - COMEDY OR COMEDY-VARIETY OR MUSIC SERIES (E-1449)

For a continuing or single performance in a regular series

ROBERT GUILLAUME, Soap (ABC)
GARY BURGHOFF, M*A*S*H (CBS)
DANNY DE VITO, Taxi (ABC)
MAX GAIL, Barney Miller (ABC)
HARRY MORGAN, M*A*S*H (CBS)

SUPPORTING ACTRESS - DRAMA SERIES (E-1450)
For a continuing or single performance in a regular series

KRISTY McNICHOL; Family (ABC)
LINDA KELSEY; Lou Grant (CBS)
NANCY MARCHAND; Lou Grant (CBS)

SUPPORTING ACTOR - DRAMA SERIES (E-1451)
For a continuing or single performance in a regular series

STUART MARGOLIN, The Rockford Files (NBC)
MASON ADAMS, Lou Grant (CBS)
NOAH BEERY, The Rockford Files (NBC)
JOE SANTOS, The Rockford Files (NBC)
ROBERT WALDEN, Lou Grant (CBS)

SUPPORTING ACTRESS - LIMITED SERIES OR A SPECIAL (E-1452)
For a continuing role in a limited series, or for a single appearance in a limited series or a special

ESTHER ROLLE, Summer Of My German Soldier (NBC)
RUBY DEE, Roots: The Next Generations (ABC)
COLLEEN DEWHURST, Silent Victory: The Kitty O'Neil Story (CBS)
EILEEN HECKART, Backstairs At The White House (NBC)
CELESTE HOLM, Backstairs At The White House (NBC)

SUPPORTING ACTOR - LIMITED SERIES OR A SPECIAL (E-1453)
For a continuing role in a limited series, or for a single appearance in a limited series or a special

MARLON BRANDO, Roots: The Next Generations, Episode Seven (ABC)
ED FLANDERS, Backstairs At The White House, Book Two (NBC)
AL FREEMAN, JR., Roots: The Next Generations, Episode Seven (ABC)
ROBERT VAUGHN, Backstairs At the White House, Book One (NBC)
PAUL WINFIELD, Roots: The Next Generations, Episode Five (ABC)

ACTRESS - COMEDY SERIES (E-1454)

RUTH GORDON, Taxi, Sugar Mama (ABC)
KATHERINE HELMOND, Soap (ABC)
LINDA LAVIN, Alice (CBS)
ISABEL SANFORD, The Jeffersons (CBS)
JEAN STAPLETON, All In The Family (CBS)

ACTOR - COMEDY SERIES (E-1455)
For a continuing or single performance in a regular series

CARROLL O'CONNOR, All In The Family (CBS)
ALAN ALDA, M*A*S*H (CBS)
JUDD HIRSCH, Taxi (ABC)
HAL LINDEN, Barney Miller (ABC)
ROBIN WILLIAMS, Mork & Mindy (ABC)

ACTRESS - DRAMA SERIES (E-1456)
For a continuing or single performance in a regular series

MARIETTE HARTLEY, The Incredible Hulk, Married (CBS)
BARBARA BEL GEDDES, Dallas (CBS)
RITA MORENO, The Rockford Files, Rosendahl And Gilda Stern Are Dead (NBC)
SADA THOMPSON, Family (ABC)

ACTOR - DRAMA SERIES (E-1457)
For a continuing or single performance in a regular series

RON LEIBMAN, Kaz (CBS)
ED ASNER, Lou Grant (CBS)
JAMES GARNER, The Rockford Files (NBC)
JACK KLUGMAN, Quincy, M.E. (NBC)

ACTRESS - LIMITED SERIES OR A SPECIAL (E-1458)
For a continuing role in a limited series, or for a single appearance in a limited series or a special

BETTE DAVIS, Strangers: The Story of a Mother and Daughter (CBS)
CAROL BURNETT, Friendly Fire (ABC)
OLIVIA COLE, Backstairs At The White House (NBC)
KATHARINE HEPBURN, The Corn Is Green (CBS)
MARY TYLER MOORE, First You Cry (CBS)

ACTOR - LIMITED SERIES OR A SPECIAL (E-1459)
For a continuing role in a limited series, or for a single appearance in a limited series or a special

PETER STRAUSS, The Jericho Mile (ABC)
NED BEATTY, Friendly Fire (ABC)
LOUIS GOSSETT, JR., Backstairs At The White House (NBC)
KURT RUSSELL, Elvis (ABC)

DIRECTOR - COMEDY OR COMEDY-VARIETY OR MUSIC SERIES (E-1460)
For a single episode of a regular series

NOAM PITLIK, Barney Miller, The Harris Incident (ABC)
ALAN ALDA, M*A*S*H; Dear Sis (CBS)
PAUL BOGART, All In The Family, California, Here We Are, Part II (CBS)
CHARLES DUBIN, M*A*S*H, Point Of View (CBS)
JAY SANDRICH, Soap, Episode 27 (ABC)

DIRECTOR - DRAMA SERIES (E-1461)
For a single episode of a regular series

JACKIE COOPER, the White Shadow, Pilot (CBS)
BURT BRINCKERHOFF, Lou Grant, Schools (CBS)
MEL DAMSKI, Lou Grant, Murder (CBS)
GENE REYNOLDS, Lou Grant, Prisoner (CBS)

DIRECTOR - LIMITED SERIES OR A SPECIAL (E-1462)

DAVID GREENE, Friendly Fire (ABC)
LOU ANTONIO, Silent Victory: The Kitty O'Neil Story (CBS)
GLENN JORDAN, Les Miserables (CBS)

WRITING - COMEDY OR COMEDY-VARIETY OR MUSIC SERIES (E-1463)
For a single episode of a regular series

ALAN ALDA, M*A*S*H, Inga (CBS)
DAN AYKROYD, ANNE BEATTS, TOM DAVIS, JAMES DOWNEY, BRIAN DOYLE-MURRAY, AL FRANKEN, BRIAN McCONNACHIE, LORNE MICHAELS, DON NOVELLO, HERB SARGENT, TOM SCHILLER, ROSIE SHUSTER, WALTER WILLIAMS, ALAN ZWEIBEL, NBC's Saturday Night Live, Host: Richard Benjamin (NBC)
MILT JOSEFSBERG, PHIL SHARP, BOB SCHILLER, BOB WEISKOPF, All In The Family, California Here We Are, Part Two (CBS)
MICHAEL LEESON, Taxi, Blind Date (ABC)
KEN LEVINE and DAVID ISAACS, M*A*S*H, Point of View (CBS)

WRITING - DRAMA SERIES (E-1464)

For a single episode of a regular series

MICHELE GALLERY, Lou Grant, Dying (CBS)
JIM BRIDGES, The Paper Chase, The Late Mr. Hart (CBS)
GENE REYNOLDS, Lou Grant, Marathon (CBS)
LEON TOKATYAN, Lou Grant, Vet (CBS)

WRITING - LIMITED SERIES OR A SPECIAL (E-1465)

For a single episode of a limited series, or for a special, whether the writing is an original teleplay or an adaptation

PATRICK NOLAN and MICHAEL MANN, The Jericho Mile (ABC)
GWEN BAGNI and PAUL DUBOV, Backstairs At The White House, Book One (NBC)
JANE HOWARD HAMMERSTEIN, Summer Of My German Soldier (NBC)
FAY KANIN, Friendly Fire (ABC)
ERNEST KINOY, Roots: The Next Generations, Episode One (ABC)

INDIVIDUAL ACHIEVEMENT - ANIMATION PROGRAM (E-1466)

(Possibility of one Award, more than one Award, or no Award)

BILL MELENDEZ and DAVID CONNELL, Writers; The Lion, The Witch and The Wardrobe (CBS)

INDIVIDUAL ACHIEVEMENT - INFORMATION PROGRAM (E-1467)

(Possibility of one Award, more than one Award, or no Award)

JOHN KORTY, Director; Who Are The Debolts--And Where Did They Get 19 Kids? (ABC)
ARNOLD SHAPIRO, Writer; Scared Straight! (Synd)

INDIVIDUAL ACHIEVEMENT - SPECIAL EVENTS (E-1468)

(Possibility of one Award, more than one Award, or no Award)

MIKHAIL BARYSHNIKOV, Baryshnikov At The White House (PBS)

A SPECIAL PRESENTATION (E-1469)

To MILTON BERLE, "Mr. Television"

SECOND ANNUAL ATAS GOVERNORS AWARD (E-1470)

To WALTER CRONKITE

ACADEMY TRIBUTE (E-1471)

DON HARRIS, ROBERT BROWN and BILL STEWART, news broadcasters who lost their lives in Guyana and Nicaragua

DAYTIME PROGRAMMING

HOST OR HOSTESS - GAME OR AUDIENCE PARTICIPATION SHOW (E-1472)

BOB BARKER, The Price Is Right (CBS)
DICK CLARK, The $20,000 Pyramid (ABC)
PETER MARSHALL, The Hollywood Squares (NBC)

GAME OR AUDIENCE PARTICIPATION SHOW (E-1473)

Emmy(s) to Executive Produucer(s) and Producer(s)
FAMILY FEUD, Mark Goodson and Bill Todman, Executive Producers; Howard Felsher, Producer (ABC)
HOLLYWOOD SQUARES, Merrill Heatter, Bob Quigley, Executive Producers; Jay Redack, Producer (NBC)
THE $20,000 PYRAMID, Bob Stewart, Executive Producer; Anne Marie Schmitt, Producer (ABC)

HOST OR HOSTESS IN A TALK, SERVICE OR VARIETY SERIES (E-1474)

JOHN BENNETT-PERRY, Everyday (Synd)
PHIL DONAHUE, Donahue (Synd)
STEPHANIE EDWARDS, Everyday (Synd)

TALK, SERVICE OR VARIETY SERIES (E-1475)

Emmy(s) to Executive Producer(s) and Producer(s)
DINAH! Henry Jaffe, Executive Producer; Fred Tatashore, Producer (Synd)
DONAHUE, Richard Mincer, Executive Producer; Patricia McMillen, Producer (Synd)
GOOD MORNING AMERICA, George Merlis, Senior Producer; John Kippycash, Jack Reilly, Sonya Selby-Wright, Producers (ABC)
MIKE DOUGLAS SHOW, Frank R. Miller, Executive Producer; Vince Calandra, E.V. DiMassa, Jr., Producers (Synd)

SPECIAL CLASSIFICATION OF OUTSTANDING PROGRAM ACHIEVEMENT (E-1476)

(Possibility of one Award, more than one Award, or no Award)

A BEETHOVEN FESTIVAL, Jack Costello, Executive Producer (PBS)
CAMERA THREE, John Musilli, Executive Producer (CBS)
CINEMATIC EYE, Peter Anderson, Executive Producer; Benjamin Dunlap, Co-Producer; Ruth Sproat, Coordinating Producer; Sidney Palmer, Diana Weynand, Producers (PBS)

ACHIEVEMENT IN COVERAGE OF SPECIAL EVENTS (E-1477)

(Possibility of one Award, or more than one Award, or no Award)

THE FIFTH ANNUAL EMMY AWARDS FOR DAYTIME TELEVISION, William Carruthers, Joel Stein, Producers (ABC)
HOROWITZ: LIVE! Herbert Kloiber, Executive Producer; John Goberman, Producer (NBC)
LEONTYNE PRICE AT THE WHITE HOUSE, Hal Hutkoff, Producer (PBS)
ROSTROPOVICH AT THE WHITE HOUSE, Hal Hutkoff, Producer (PBS)

SUPPORTING ACTOR - DAYTIME DRAMA SERIES (E-1478)

LEWIS ARLT, Search for Tomorrow (CBS)
BERNARD BARROW, Ryan's Hope (ABC)
JOE GALLISON, Days of Our Lives (NBC)
RON HALE, Ryan's Hope (ABC)
PETER HANSEN, General Hospital (ABC)
MANDEL KRAMER, Edge of Night (ABC)

SUPPORTING ACTRESS - DAYTIME DRAMA SERIES (E-1479)

RACHEL AMES, General Hospital (ABC)
SUSAN BROWN, General Hospital (ABC)
LOIS KIBBEE, Edge of Night (ABC)
FRANCES REID, Days of Our Lives (NBC)
SUZANNE ROGERS, Days of Our Lives (NBC)

CHILDREN'S INFORMATIONAL SPECIAL (E-1480)

Emmy(s) to Executive Producer(s) and Producer(s)

RAZZMATAZZ, Joel Heller, Executive Producer; Vern Diamond, Producer (CBS)

THE SECRET OF CHARLES DICKENS, CBS Festival of Lively Arts for Young People; Daniel Wilson, Executive Producer; Linda Marmelstein, Producer (CBS)

CHILDREN'S INSTRUCTIONAL SERIES (E-1481)

Emmy(s) to Executive Producer(s) and Producer(s)

DEAR ALEX & ANNIE, (Kids Are People Too); Ken Greengrass and Phil Lawrence, Executive Producers; Lynn Ahrens, Producer (ABC)

METRIC MARVELS, George Newall, Tom Yohe, Producers (NBC)

SESAME STREET, David D. Connell, Vice President for Production; Al Hyslop, Producer (PBS)

SCIENCE ROCK, (Schoolhouse Rock); Tom Yohe, Executive Producer; George Newall, Radford Stone, Producers (ABC)

CHILDREN'S ENTERTAINMENT SERIES (E-1482)

Emmy(s) to Executive Producer(s) and Producer(s)

CAPTAIN KANGAROO, Frank Alesia, Joel Kosofsky, Producers (CBS)

JOHN HALIFAX: GENTLEMAN, (Once Upon a Classic); Jay Rayvid, Executive Producer; James A. DeVinney, John McRae, Producers (PBS)

KIDS ARE PEOPLE TOO, Lawrence Einhorn, Executive Producer; Laura Schrock, Producer; Noreen Conlin, Co-Producer (ABC)

LORNA DOONE, (Once Upon a Classic); Jay Rayvid, Executive Producer; Shep Greene, Barry Letts, Producers (PBS)

THE SECRET GARDEN, (Once Upon a Classic); Jay Rayvid, Executive Producer; Dorothea Brooking, James A. DeVinney, Producers (PBS)

CHILDREN'S ENTERTAINMENT SPECIAL (E-1483)

Emmy(s) to Executive Producer(s) and Producer(s)

JOEY & REDHAWK, Daniel Wilson, Executive Producer; Fran Sears, Producer (CBS)

MAKE BELIEVE MARRIAGE, (ABC Afterschool Special); Linda Gottlieb, Executive Producer; Evelyn Barron, Producer (ABC)

MOM AND DAD CAN'T HEAR ME, (ABC Afterschool Special); Daniel Wilson, Executive Producer; Fran Sears, Producer (ABC)

NYC TOO FAR FROM TAMPA BLUES, (Special Treat); Daniel Wilson, Executive Producer; Linda Marmelstein, Phyllis Minoff, Producers (NBC)

RODEO RED AND THE RUNAWAY, (Special Treat); Linda Gottlieb, Executive Producer; Doro Bachrach, Producer (NBC)

THE TAP DANCE KID, (Special Treat); Linda Gottlieb, Executive Producer; Evelyn Barron, Producer (NBC)

INDIVIDUAL DIRECTION - GAME OR AUDIENCE PARTICIPATION SHOW (E-1484)

For a single episode

MIKE GARGIULO, The $20,000 Pyramid (ABC)

RICHARD SCHNEIDER, Jeopardy (NBC)

JEROME SHAW, The Hollywood Squares (NBC)

INDIVIDUAL DIRECTION - VARIETY PROGRAM (E-1485)

For a single episode

RON WEINER, Donahue; Nazis and the Klan (Synd)

DONALD R. KING, America Alive (NBC)

GLEN SWANSON, Dinah!; The 5th Anniversary Show (Synd)

DIRECTOR - DAYTIME DRAMA SERIES (E-1486)

For the entire series

IRA CIRKER, MELVIN BERNHARDT, PAUL LAMMERS, ROBERT CALHOUN, Another World (NBC)

JACK COFFEY, DEL HUGHES, HENRY KAPLAN, All My Children (ABC)

RICHARD DUNLAP, BILL GLENN, The Young and The Restless (CBS)

JERRY EVANS, LELA SWIFT, Ryan's Hope (ABC)

AL RABIN, JOE BEHAR, FRANK PACELLI, Days of our Lives (NBC)

JOHN SEDWICK, RICHARD PEPPERMAN, The Edge of Night (NBC)

WRITING - DAYTIME DRAMA SERIES (E-1487)

For the entire series

WILLIAM J. BELL, KAY ALDEN, ELIZABETH HARROWER, The Young and The Restless (CBS)

CLAIRE LABINE, PAUL AVILA MAYER, MARY MUNISTERI, JUDITH PINSKER, JEFFREY LANE, Ryan's Hope (ABC)

ANN MARCUS, MICHAEL ROBERT DAVID, RAYMOND E. GOLDSTONE, JOYCE PERRY, ELIZABETH HARROWER, ROCCI CHATFIELD, LAURA OLSHER, Days of Our Lives (NBC)

AGNES NIXON, WISNER WASHAM, JACK WOOD, MARY K. WELLS, KENNETH HARVEY, CATHY CHICOS, CAROLINE FRANZ, DORIS FRANKEL, WILLIAM DELLIGAN, All My Children (ABC)

ACTOR - DAYTIME DRAMA SERIES (E-1488)

JED ALLAN, Days of Our Lives (NBC)

NICHOLAS BENEDICT, All My Children (ABC)

JOHN CLARKE, Days of Our Lives (NBC)

JOEL CROTHERS, Edge of Night (ABC)

AL FREEMAN, JR., One Life to Live (ABC)

MICHAEL LEVIN, Ryan's Hope (ABC)

ACTRESS - DAYTIME DRAMA SERIES (E-1489)

NANCY ADDISON, Ryan's Hope (ABC)

IRENE DAILEY, Another World (NBC)

HELEN GALLAGHER, Ryan's Hope (ABC)

BEVERLEE McKINSEY, Another World (NBC)

SUSAN SEAFORTH HAYES, Days of Our Lives (NBC)

VICTORIA WYNDHAM, Another World (NBC)

DAYTIME DRAMA SERIES (E-1490)

Emmy(s) to Executive Producer(s) and Producer(s)

ALL MY CHILDREN, Agnes Nixon, Executive Producer; Bud Kloss, Producer (ABC)

DAYS OF OUR LIVES, Betty Corday, H. Wesley Kenney, Executive Producers; Jack Herzberg, Producer (NBC)

RYAN'S HOPE, Claire Labine, Paul Avila Mayer, Executive Producers; Ellen Barrett, Robert Costello, Producers (ABC)

THE YOUNG AND THE RESTLESS, John Conboy, Executive Producer; Ed Scott, Patricia Wenig, Producers (CBS)

CHILDREN'S INFORMATIONAL SERIES (E-1491)

Emmy(s) to Executive Producer(s) and Producer(s)

30 MINUTES, Joel Heller, Executive Producer; Madeline Amgott, Elliot Bernstein, JoAnn Caplin, Christine Huneke, Robert Rubin, Patti Obrow White, Producers (CBS)

ABC MINUTE MAGAZINE, Thomas H. Wolf, Producer (ABC)

ANIMALS, ANIMALS, ANIMALS, Lester Cooper, Executive Producer; Jake Haselkorn, Producer (ABC)

BIG BLUE MARBLE, Robert Wiemer, Executive Producer; Richard Berman, Producer (Synd)

IN THE NEWS, Joel Heller, Executive Producer; Susan Mills, Producer (CBS)

WHEN YOU TURN OFF THE SET, TURN ON A BOOK, Mary Alice Dwyer, Executive Producer; George Newall, Tom Yohe, Producers (NBC)

ACHIEVEMENT IN TECHNICAL EXCELLENCE - DAYTIME DRAMA SERIES (E-1492)

Emmy(s) to Program Representative(s), Emmy Certificates to Respective Individuals

ALL MY CHILDREN, Technical Team (ABC)

ANOTHER WORLD, Technical Team (ABC)

THE EDGE OF NIGHT, Technical Team (ABC)

ONE LIFE TO LIVE, Technical Team (ABC)

RYAN'S HOPE, Technical Team (ABC)

THE YOUNG AND THE RESTLESS, Technical Team (CBS)

ACHIEVEMENT IN DESIGN EXCELLENCE - DAYTIME DRAMA SERIES (E-1493)

Emmy(s) to Program Representatives, Emmy Certificates to Respective Individuals

DAYS OF OUR LIVES, Design Team (NBC)

LOVE OF LIFE, Design Team (CBS)

ONE LIFE TO LIVE, Design Team (ABC)

RYAN'S HOPE, Design Team (ABC)

THE NATIONAL AWARD FOR COMMUNITY SERVICE (E-1494)

1978 KENTUCKY GENERAL ASSEMBLY IN OPEN SESSION (KET NETWORK) Lexington, Kentucky

THE BIGGEST STING (KBTV) Denver, Colorado

A RACE WITH DEATH (WJLA-TV) Washington, D.C.

OLD AGE: DO NOT GO GENTLE (KGO-TV) San Francisco, California

NO ROOM IN SUBURBIA (WBZ-TV) Allston, Massachusetts

ZOOT SUIT: THE PLAY AND THE PROMISE (KNXT) Hollywood, California

THE DESERT PEOPLE (KOOL-TV) Phoenix, Arizona

SCANDAL AT C.E.T.A. (WPLG) Miami, Florida

WE THE VICTIMS (WCBS-TV) New York, New York

30 MINUTES (WIIC-TV) Pittsburgh, Pennsylvania

POISONS IN THE WIND (KMGH-TV) Denver, Colorado

THE UNIVERSITY OF THE THIRD AGE (KCST-TV) San Diego, California

NEWS AND DOCUMENTARIES

PROGRAMS AND PROGRAM SEGMENTS (E-1495)

Emmy(s) to Producer(s)

PAPAL SELECTION--JOHN PAUL II/CHURCH IN CHANGE, Jeff Gralnick, Executive Producer (ABC)

THE CRASH OF FLIGHT 191, Paul Beavers, Producer (NBC)

SHOWDOWN IN IRAN--CBS REPORTS, Leslie Midgley, Executive Producer

THE BOAT PEOPLE--CBS REPORTS, Andrew Lack, Producer

NORMALIZATION OF U.S. RELATIONS WITH CHINA--CBS EVENING NEWS WITH BOB SCHIEFFER, Joan Richman, Executive Producer

MISSISSIPPI FLOODS--CBS MORNING NEWS, Roberta Hollander, Producer (segment)

UNREST IN EL SALVADOR--CBS MORNING, EVENING & WEEKEND NEWS, Robert Bahr, Producer

MID-EAST PEACE SIGNING--CBS EVENING NEWS WITH WALTER CRONKITE, John Armstrong, Producer (segment)

3-MILE ISLAND--CBS EVENING NEWS WITH WALTER CRONKITE, Ronald S. Bonn and Jonathan Ward, Producers (segment)

TERROR IN THE PROMISED LAND, Malcolm Clarke, Producer (ABC)

HOW MUCH FOR THE HANDICAPPED?--CBS REPORTS, Marlene Sanders, Producer

READING, WRITING AND REEFER-NBC REPORTS, Robert Rogers, Producer

ANYPLACE BUT HERE--CBS REPORTS, Tom Spain, Producer

A HOUSE DIVIDED, Dick Hubert, Executive Producer; Mike Joseloff, Producer (for Capital Cities Communications, Inc. in association with Gateway Productions, Inc.) (SYN)

IS ANYONE OUT THERE LEARNING--CBS REPORT CARD ON AMERICAN EDUCATION, Jane Bartels, Bernard Birnbaum and Hal Haley, Producers

THE POLICE TAPES--ABC NEWS CLOSE-UP, Alan Raymond and Susan Raymond, Producers

THE EARTH REVISITED--CBS EVENING NEWS WITH WALTER CRONKITE, Jonathan Ward, Producer (segment series)

THE RATING GAME--CBS "CBS 60 MINUTES", Marion Goldin, Producer (segment)

SOMOZA--CBS "60 MINUTES", Stephen Glauber, Producer (segment)

HAITIAN REFUGEES--NBC "WEEKEND", Peter Jeffries, Producer (segment)

MIGRANTS--NBC NIGHTLY NEWS, Brian Ross and Janet Pearce, Co-Producers (segment series)

CHILDREN OF HOPE--NBC "WEEKEND", Christine Huneke, Producer (segment)

IN THE MAINSTREAM--CBS "60 MINUTES", Philip Scheffler, Producer (segment)

THE ELDERLY-OUT OF THE SHADOWS--ABC WORLD NEWS TONIGHT, Ellen Rossen, Producer (segment)

ERASING VIETNAM--NBC NIGHTLY NEWS-SEGMENT III, John Hart, Producer/Correspondent

WHO OWNS WHAT IN AMERICA?--A FEW MINUTES WITH ANDY ROONEY--CBS "60 MINUTES", Andrew A Rooney, Producer (segment)

MISSION: MIND CONTROL, Paul Altmeyer, Producer (ABC)

F-16: SALE OF THE CENTURY, David Boulton,Producer (for the current affairs series, "Inside Europe") (PBS)

THE KILLING GROUND, Steve Singer, Producer (ABC)

PAUL JACOBS AND THE NUCLEAR GANG, Jack Willis, Producer (PBS)

GOING, GOING.ᵧ.ᵧ.GONE--CBS REPORTS, Philip Burton, Jr., Producer

MENTAL--ABC NEWS "20/20", Peter Lance, Producer (segment)

FROM BURGERS TO BANKRUPTCY--CBS "60 MINUTES", Marion Goldin, Producer; Ken Dalglish and Janet Harshman, Associate Producers (segment)

THE THORNWELL FILE--CBS "60 MINUTES", Harry Moses, Producer (segment)

RUNAWAYS, THROWAWAYS--CBS "60 MINUTES", Frank Little, Producer (segment)

FLEECING THE PENTAGON--ABC NEWS "20/20", Anthony Van Witsen, Producer (segment)

MISHA--CBS "60 MINUTES", David Lowe, Jr., Producer; Mike Wallace, Interviewer (segment)

TEDDY KOLLECK'S JERUSALEM--CBS "60 MINUTES", Joseph Wershba, Producer; Morley Safer, Interviewer (segment)

INCEST: THE BEST KEPT SECRET--CBS MARCH MAGAZINE, Jo Ann Caplin, Producer; Sharon Lovejoy, Interviewer (segment)

ZIMBABWE: THE OTHER SIDE--CBS "60 MINUTES", Leslie Edwards, Producer; Dan Rather, Interviewer (segment)

POPS--CBS "60 MINUTES", Mary Drayne, Producer; Morley Safer, Interviewer (segment)

GUNSITE--NBC "WEEKEND", Beth Polson, Producer and Interviewer (segment)

INTERVIEW WITH FATHER OF BOY WITH DOWN'S SYNDROME--NBC "TODAY", Eric Burns, Producer and Interviewer (segment)

PALESTINE, Mike Wooller, Executive Producer (for Thames Television, London, England) (PBS)

1968--CBS NEWS SPECIAL, Shareen Blair Brysac, Producer

GOLD!--NATIONAL GEOGRAPHIC SPECIAL, Irwin Rosten, Producer (PBS)

EINSTEIN--NOVA, Patrick Griffin, Producer (PBS)

THE BOSTON GOES TO CHINA--CBS REPORTS, Howard Stringer, Executive Producer

BUT WHAT ABOUT THE CHILDREN--CBS REPORTS, Grace Diekhaus, Producer

HONG KONG: A FAMILY PORTRAIT--NATIONAL GEOGRAPHIC SPECIAL, Thomas Skinner and Dennis B. Kane, Executive Producers (PBS)

HARVEST--BILL MOYER'S JOURNAL, David Grubin, Producer (PBS)

ANDREW YOUNG REMEMBERS MARTIN LUTHER KING--BILL MOYER'S JOURNAL, Betsy McCarthy, Producer (PBS)

HOW MUCH IS A HOUSEWIFE WORTH--CBS DECEMBER MAGAZINE, Grace Diekhause and Judith Hole, Producers

A VERY, VERY SPECIAL PLACE--NBC "WEEKEND", Craig Leake, Producer; Janet Janjigian, Associate Producer (segment)

NOAH--CBS "60 MINUTES", Imre Horvath, Producer (segment)

25th ANNIVERSARY OF THE BROWN VS BOARD OF EDUCATION--CBS NEWS THURSDAY MORNING, John C. O'Regan and Karen Curry, Producers (segment)

EUBIE--CBS EVENING NEWS WITH BOB SCHIEFFER, James Ganser, Producer

INDIVIDUALS (E-1496)

Emmy(s) to Individuals(s)

WRITERS

RICHARD GERDAU, Arson: Fire For Hire--ABC News Close-up
ED BRADLEY, ANDREW LACK & HOWARD STRINGER, The Boat People--CBS Reports
GEORGIE CRILE, III & BILL MOYERS, Battle For South Africa--CBS Reports
ANDREW A ROONEY, Who Owns What In America--A Few Minutes with Andy Rooney--CBS "60 Minutes" (segment)
MARLENE SANDERS, How Much For The Handicapped?--CBS Reports
TOM SPAIN, Anyplace But Here--CBS Reports
PERRY WOLFF, 1968--CBS News Special

DIRECTORS

TOM PRIESTLY, The Killing Ground--ABC News Close-up
JUDY CRICHTON, Battle For South Africa--CBS Reports
GRACE DIEKHAUS, But What About The Children--CBS Reports
ANDREW LACK, The Boat People--CBS Reports
MAURICE MURAD, Anyplace But Here--CBS Reports
MARLENE SANDERS, How Much For The Handicapped?--CBS Reports
HOWARD STRINGER, The Boston Goes To China--CBS Reports

CINEMATOGRAPHERS

ALAN RAYMOND, The Police Tapes--ABC News Close-up
GREG COOKE & IAN WILSON, The Boat People--CBS Reports
TOM SPAIN, Anyplace But Here--CBS Reports
WOLFGANG BAYER, Last Stand In Eden--National Geographic Special (PBS)
DAVID GRUBIN, Harvest--Bill Moyer's Journal (PBS)

FILM EDITORS

MILI BONSIGNORI, But What About The Children--CBS Reports
JOHN DULLAGHAN, SARA STEIN & NABUKO OGANESOFF, 1968--CBS News Special
MAURICE MURAD, The Boston Goes To China--CBS Reports
JOSEPH MURANIA, Baryshnikov--CBS "60 Minutes" (segment)
PATRICK M. COOK, Callas (PBS)

VIDEOTAPE EDITORS

SUSAN RAYMOND, The Police Tapes--ABC News Close-up
JIM ALKINS, 1968--CBS News Special

AUDIO

JAMES R. CAMERY & PHILLIP GLEASON, SOUND RECORDISTS, The Boston Goes To China--CBS Reports
JOEL H. DULBERG, SOUND RE-RECORDING MIXER, Baryshnikov--CBS "60 Minutes" (segment)

GRAPHICS

NED STEINBERG, GRAPHIC ART DIRECTOR (Opening & Internal Graphics) Election Night '78 (CBS)

LIGHTING

DONALD ("PETE") HOWARD, LIGHTING DIRECTOR, Live Coverage--House of Representatives (PBS)

MUSIC

RITA ABRAMS, MUSIC COMPOSER/DIRECTOR/LYRICIST, I Want It All Now: Utopia Beyond The Golden Gate (NBC)

INTERNATIONAL NON-FICTION AWARD (E-1497)

FACES OF COMMUNISM-CZECHOSLOVAKIA LIVING ON THEIR KNEES (Yorkshire Television, United Kingdom)
THE CASE OF YOLANDE MCSHANE (Yorkshire Television, United Kingdom)
LIVES: MUHAMMAD ALI, THE BLACK BALLOON (Global Television Network, Canada)
FOUR WOMEN (Canadian Broadcasting Corporation, Canada)

DUDH KOSI - RELENTLESS RIVER OF EVEREST (HTV Wales, Wales, United Kingdom)
LIFE ON A SILKEN THREAD (Maran Film for Suddeutscher Rundfunk, Federal Rep. of Germany)

INTERNATIONAL FICTION AWARD (E-1498)

THE PRIME OF MISS JEAN BRODIE EPISODE # 1 - NEWCASTLE (Scottish Television Ltd., Scotland)
DAVE ALLEN AT LARGE (British Broadcasting Corp., United Kingdom)
LIGABUE (RAI-Radio Televisione Italiana-Rete TV 1, Italy)
1847 - THE NEWCOMERS (Nielsen-Ferns Inc., Canada)
THE FLY (Televisie Radio Omroep Stichting, The Netherlands)
TOMMY STEELE AND A SHOW (Thames Television Ltd., United Kingdom)

NATAS TRUSTEES AWARD (E-1498A)

WILLIAM S. PALEY

CREATIVE ARTS IN TELEVISION

ACHIEVEMENT IN ENGINEERING DEVELOPMENT (E-1499)

EMMY AWARD to AMPEX CORPORATION, for the development of their Automatic Scan Tracking system for helical video tape equipment.
CITATION to MAGICAM, INC., for development of real time tracking of independent scenes.

ART DIRECTION - SERIES (E-1500)

For a single episode of a regular series

HOWARD E. JOHNSON, Art Director, RICHARD B. GODDARD, Set Decorator, Little Women, Part I (NBC)
JOHN E. CHILBERG II, Art Director, MICKEY S. MICHAELS, Set Decorator, LOWELL CHAMBERS, Set Decorator, Battlestar Galactica, Saga Of A Star World (ABC)
RENE LAGLER, Art Director, EARL CARLSON, Set Decorator, The Mary Tyler Moore Hour (with Gene Kelly) (CBS)

ART DIRECTION - LIMITED SERIES OR A SPECIAL (E-1501)

For a single episode of a regular or a limited series, or for a special program

JAN SCOTT, Art Director and Production Designer, BILL HARP, Set Decorator, Studs Lonigan, Part III (NBC)
MICHAEL BAUGH, Art Director, ROBERT CHECCHI, Set Decorator, ARTHUR JEPH PARKER, Set Decorator, Blind Ambition, Part 3 (CBS)
RICHARD Y. HAMAN, Art Director, ANNE D. McCULLEY, Set Decorator, Backstairs At The White House, Book One (NBC)
JAN SCOTT, Art Director and Production Designer, EDWARD J. McDONALD, Set Decorator, BILL HARP, Set Decorator, Studs Lonigan, Part I (NBC)
JACK SENTER, Production Designer, JOHN W. CORSO, Art Director, SHERMAN LOUDERMILK, Art Director, JOSPEH J. STONE, Set Decorator, JOHN M. DWYER, Set Decorator, ROBERT G. FREER, Set Decorator, Centennial, The Shepherds, Chapter Seven (NBC)

CHOREOGRAPHY (E-1502)

For a single episode of a regular or limited series, or for a special program

KEVIN CARLISLE, The 3rd Barry Manilow Special (ABC)
MARTHA GRAHAM, The Martha Graham Dance Company; Clytemnestra; Dance In America; Great Performances (PBS)
ANITA MANN, The Muppets Go Hollywood (CBS)

CINEMATOGRAPHY - SERIES (E-1503)

For a single episode of a regular series

TED VOIGTLANDER, ASC, Little House On The Prairie, The Craftsman (NBC)
JOSEPH BIROC, Little Women, Part II (NBC)
WILLIAM W. SPENCER, ASC, Barnaby Jones, Memory Of A Nightmare (CBS)

CINEMATOGRAPHY - LIMITED SERIES OR A SPECIAL (E-1504)

For a single episode of a limited series, or for a special program

HOWARD SCHWARTZ, ASC, Rainbow (NBC)
ARCH R. DALZELL (U.S.A.), FREDDIE YOUNG, B.S.C. (U.K.), Ike, Part II (ABC)
DENNIS DALZELL, the Winds Of Kitty Hawk (NBC)
DONALD M. MORGAN, Elvis (ABC)

COSTUME DESIGN - SERIES (E-1505)

For a single episode of a regular series

JEAN-PIERRE DORLEAC, Battlestar Galactica, Furlon (ABC)
ALFRED E. LEHMAN, Laverne & Shirley, The Third Annual Shotz Talent Show (ABC)

COSTUME DESIGN - LIMITED SERIES OR A SPECIAL (E-1506)

For a single episode of a limited series, or for a special program

ANN HOLLOWOOD, SUE LE CASH, CHRISTINE WILSON, Edward The King; King At Last (Synd)
BOB MACKIE, RET TURNER, Cher. . .And Other Fantasies (NBC)
WARDEN NEIL, The John Davidson Christmas Show (ABC)
DAVID WALKER, The Corn Is Green (CBS)

FILM EDITING - SERIES (E-1507)

For a single episode of a regular series

M. PAM BLUMENTHAL, Taxi, Paper Marriage (ABC)
FRED W. BERGER, A.C.E., Dallas, Reunion, Part II (CCBS)
JAMES GALLOWAY, A.C.E., Lou Grant, Hooker (CBS)
LARRY L. MILLS, STANFORD TISCHLER, M*A*S*H, The Billfold Syndrome (CBS)

FILM EDITING - LIMITED SERIES OR A SPECIAL (E-1508)

For a single episode of a limited series, or for a special program

ARTHUR SCHMIDT, The Jericho Mile (ABC)
JAMES GALLOWAY, First You Cry (CBS)
JOHN A. MARTINELLI, A.C.E., The Winds of Kitty Hawk (NBC)
ROBERT WATTS, A.C.E., Centennial, Only The Rocks Live Forever, Chapter One (NBC)
JOHN M. WOODCOCK, A.C.E., BILL LENNY, PAUL DIXON, Ike, Part III (ABC)

ACHIEVEMENT IN FILM SOUND EDITING (E-1509)

For a single episode of a regular or limited series or for a special program

WILLIAM H. WISTROM, Friendly Fire (ABC)
DOUGLAS H. GRINDSTAFF, DON ISAACS, MARK DENNIS, BOB HUMAN, LARRY KAUFMAN, LARRY SINGER and HANK SALERNO, A Fire In The Sky (NBC)
LAWRENCE E. NEIMAN, CHARLES L. CAMPBELL, COLIN MOUAT, DON WARNER, DAVID PETTIJOHN, PIETER S. HUBBARD, GARY VAUGHAN, CHARLES E. MORAN, BOB CANTON and MARTIN VARNO, The Triangle Factory Fire Scandal (NBC)

MICHAEL REDBOURN, PETER HARRISON, RUSS TINSLEY, LINDA DOVE and LEONARD CORSO, Ike, Part II (ABC)

FILM SOUND MIXING (E-1510)

For a single episode of a regular or limited series, or for a special program

BILL TEAGUE, GEORGE E. PORTER, EDDIE J. NELSON, RAY WEST, The Winds Of Kitty Hawk(NBC)
STANLEY P. GORDON, GEORGE E. PORTER, EDDIE J. NELSON, HOPPY MEHTERIAN, A Christmas To Remember (CBS)
GEORGE E. PORTER, EDDIE J. NELSON, RAY WEST, MAURY HARRIS, The Triangle Factory Fire Scandal (NBC)
BILL TEAGUE, GEORGE E. PORTER, EDDIE J. NELSON, HOPPY MEHTERIAN, Ike, Part II (ABC)

GRAPHIC DESIGN AND TITLE SEQUENCES (E-1511)

For a single episode of a regular or limited series, or for a special program. This includes animation only when created for use in titling

STU BERNSTEIN, EYTAN KELLER, Cinderella At The Palace (CBS)
PHILL NORMAN, Vega$; Centerfold (ABC)

LIGHTING DIRECTION (ELECTRONIC) (E-1512)

For a single episode of a regular or limited series, or for a special program

GEORGE REISENBERGER, Lighting Consultant & Designer; ROY A. BARNETT, Director of Photography "E"; You Can't Take It With You (CBS)
WILLIAM M. KLAGES, GEORGE REISENBERGER, A Salute To American Imagination (CBS)
WILLIAM KNIGHT, The Homecoming; Mourning Becomes Electra; Great Performances (PBS)
FRED McKINNON, Cinderella At The Palace (CBS)

MAKE-UP (E-1513)

For a single episode of a regular or limited series, or for a special program

TOMMY COLE, MARK BUSSAN, RON WALTERS, Backstairs At The White House, Book Four (NBC)
KEN CHASE, Makeup Design; JOE DiBELLA, ZOLTAN ELEK, TOM MILLER, DAVID DITTMAR, Makeup Artists; Roots: The Next Generations, Episode Three (ABC)
LEO L. LOTITO, JR., NICK PAGLIARO, Lady Of The House (NBC)
MARVIN G. WESTMORE, Elvis (ABC)

HAIRSTYLING (E-1514)

For a single episode of a regular or limited series, or for a special program

JANICE D. BRANDOW, The Triangle Factory Fire Scandal (NBC)
SUSAN GERMAINE, LOLA KEMP, VIVIAN McATEER, Backstairs At The White House, Book Four (NBC)
JEAN BURT REILLY, Ike, Part III (ABC)

MUSIC COMPOSITION - SERIES (E-1515)

(Dramatic underscore, theme, song, or special material - with or without lyrics) For a single episode of a regular series

DAVID ROSE, Little House On The Prairie, The Craftsman, (NBC)
DICK DeBENEDICTIS, DEAN DeBENEDICTIS, Dear Detective (CBS)
CHARLES FOX, NORMAN GIMBEL (Lyrics), The Paper Chase, A Day In The Life (CBS)
PATRICK WILLIAMS, Lou Grant, Prisoner (CBS)

MUSIC COMPOSITION - LIMITED SERIES OR A SPECIAL (E-1516)

(Dramatic underscore, theme, song, or special material - with or without lyrics) For a single episode of a limited series, or for a special program

LEONARD ROSENMAN, Friendly Fire (ABC)
PETER MATZ, First You Cry (CBS)
ALEX NORTH, The Word (CBS)
KEN WELCH, MITZIE WELCH, The Hal Linden Special (ABC)

TAPE SOUND MIXING (E-1517)

For a single episode of a regular or limited series, or for a special program

ED GREENE, PHILLIP J. SERETTI, DENNIS S. SANDS, GARRY ULMER, Steve & Eydie Celebrate Irving Berlin (NBC)
ED GREENE, The Muppets Go Hollywood (CBS)
GORDON KLIMUCK, TOM HUTH, Perry Como's Early American Christmas (ABC)
DOUG NELSON, The 3rd Barry Manilow Special (ABC)
GEORJA SKINNER, PHILLIP J. SERETTI, Return Engagement, Hallmark Hall Of Fame (NBC)

TECHNICAL DIRECTION AND ELECTRONIC CAMERAWORK (E-1518)

For a single episode of a regular or limited series, or for a special program

JERRY WEISS, Technical Director; DON BARKER, PEGGY MAHONEY, REED HOWARD, KURT TONNESSEN, WILLIAM LANDERS, LOUIS CYWINSKI, GEORGE LOOMIS, BRIAN SHERRIFFE, Camerapersons, Dick Clark's Live Wednesday, Show #1 (NBC)
ROBERT G. HOLMES, Technical Director; BRUCE BOTTONE, JIM HERRING, ROYDEN HOLM, BILL LANDERS, PEGGY MAHONEY, Camerapersons, The Midnight Special, Host Dolly Parton (NBC)
ROBERT C. JONES, Technical Director; BARRY A. BROWN, LARRY HEIDER, WAYNE ORR, HANK GEVING, DIANNE BIEDERBECK, RICHARD PRICE, TOM KARNOWSKI, DAVE LEVISOHN, Camerapersons, You Can't Take It With You (CBS)
HEINO RIPP, Technical Director; AL CAMOIN, PETER BASIL, TOM DE ZENDORF, JOHN PINTO, VINCE DI PIETRO, Camperpersons, NBC's Saturday Night Live, Host Richard Benjamin (NBC)

VIDEO TAPE EDITING FOR A SERIES (E-1519)

For a single episode of a regular series

ANDY ZALL, Stockard Channing In Just Friends, Pilot (CBS)
HAL COLLINS, HARVEY BERGER, The 200th Episode Celebration Of All In The Family (CBS)

VIDEO TAPE EDITING - LIMITED SERIES OR A SPECIAL (E-1520)

For a single episode of a limited series, or for a special program

KEN DENISOFF, TUCKER WIARD, JANET McFADDEN, The Scarlet Letter, Part Two (PBS)
DARRYL SUTTON, The Muppets Go Hollywood (CBS)
ANDY ZALL, The Cheryl Ladd Special (ABC)
MARCO ZAPPIA, Liberace - A Valentine Special (CBS)

INDIVIDUAL ACHIEVEMENT - ANIMATION PROGRAM (E-1521)

(Possibility of one Award, more than one Award, or no Award)
JOHNNY BRADFORD (Lyrics), DOUG GOODWIN (Music), A Pink Christmas (main title song) (ABC)
DOUG GOODWIN (Music & Lyrics), A Pink Christmas (songs) (ABC)
PETER YARROW and DAVID CAMPBELL (Music & Lyrics), Puff The Magic Dragon (CBS)

INDIVIDUAL ACHIEVEMENT - CHILDREN'S PROGRAM (E-1522)

(Possibility of one Award, more than one Award, or no Award)
GERRI BRIOSO, Graphic Artist, Christmas Eve on Sesame Street (PBS)
TONY DI GIROLAMO, Lighting Director, DAVE CLARK, Lighting Director, Christmas Eve on Sesame Street (PBS)

INDIVIDUAL ACHIEVEMENT - CREATIVE TECHNICAL CRAFTS (E-1523)

(Possibility of one Award, more than one Award, or no Award)
JOHN DYKSTRA, Special Effects Coordinator, RICHARD EDLUND, Director of Miniature Photography, JOSEPH GOSS, Mechanical Special Effects, Battlestar Galactica, Saga Of A Star World (ABC)
TOM ANCELL (Live Stereo Sound Mixing), Giulini's Beethoven's 9th Live - A Gift From Los Angeles (PBS)
JOE UNSINN, Special Effects, Explosion and Destruction, Pyrotechnical Work, A Fire In The Sky (NBC)
DICK WILSON, (Sound Effects), Welcome Back Kotter, Barbarino's Baby (ABC)

INDIVIDUAL ACHIEVEMENT - INFORMATIONAL PROGRAM (E-1524)

(Possibility of one Award, more than one Award, or no Award)
ROBERT NEIMACK, Film Editor, Scared Straight! (Synd)

INDIVIDUAL ACHIEVEMENT - SPECIAL CLASS (E-1525)

(Possibility of one Award, more than one Award, or no Award)
HARRY BLAKE, BOB OSTERMANN and DAVID A. DITTMAR, Makeup Artists, General Electric's All-Star Aniversary (ABC)
WILLIAM M. KLAGES, Lighting Director, Rockette: A Holiday Tribute To Radio City Music Hall (NBC)
CARL VITELLI, Lighting Director, A Gift Of Song - The Music for UNICEF Special (NBC)
DAVE CLARK, Lighting Designer, MICHAEL ROSATTI and HARRY BOTTORF, Lighting Directors, Baryshnikov At The White House (PBS)
DAVID W. FOSTER and EDDIE C. JOSEPH, Videotape Editors, The Television Annual: 1978/1979 (ABC)

INDIVIDUAL ACHIEVEMENT - SPECIAL EVENTS (E-1526)

(Possibility of one Award, more than one Award, or no Award)
MICHAEL L. WENIG and TERRY PICKFORD, Videotape Editors, 51st Annual Awards Presentation of the Academy of Motion Picture Arts and Sciences (ABC)
ROY CHRISTOPHER, Art Director, 51st Annual Awards Presentation of the Academy of Motion Picture Arts and Sciences (ABC)

LIVE SPORTS SPECIAL (E-1527)

Emmy(s) to Executive Producer(s) and Producer(s)
THE MASTERS GOLF TOURNAMENT, Frank Chirkinian, Executive Producer (CBS)
NCAA BASKETBALL CHAMPIONSHIP, Don Ohlmeyer, Executive Producer; George Finkel, Producer (NBC)
SUPER BOWL XIII, Don Ohlmeyer, Executive Producer; George Finkel & Michael Weisman, Producers (NBC)
U.S. OPEN TENNIS CHAMPIONSHIPS, Frank Chirkinian, Executive Producer (CBS)
WIMBLEDON '79, Don Ohlmeyer, Executive Producer; Geoff Mason and Ted Nathanson, Producers (NBC)

1978 WORLD SERIES, Don Ohlmeyer, Executive Producer; George Finkel & Michael Weisman, Producers (NBC)

LIVE SPORTS SERIES (E-1528)
Emmy(s) to Executive Producer(s) and Producer(s)

ABC'S NFL MONDAY NIGHT FOOTBALL, Roone Arledge, Executive Producer; Dennis Lewin, Producer (ABC)

AFC/NFL FOOTBALL, Don Ohlmeyer, Executive Producer; Michael Weisman, David Stern, Jim Marooney, George Finkel, Larry Cirillo, Roy Hammerman and Kenneth Edmundson, Producers (NBC)

MAJOR LEAGUE BASEBALL, Don Ohlmeyer, Executive Producer; Michael Weisman, George Finkel, David Stern and Jim Marooney, Producers (NBC)

NCAA BASKETBALL, Doh Ohlmeyer, Executive Producer; Roy Hammerman, George Finkel, Michael Weisman, David Stern, Kenneth Edmundson, Producers (NBC)

THE NFL TODAY/NFL FOOTBALL ON CBS, Michael Pearl, Producer (CBS)

EDITED SPORTS SPECIAL (E-1529)
Emmy(s) to Executive Producer(s) and Producer(s)

INDIANAPOLIS 500, Roone Arledge, Executive Producer; Chuck Howard, Bob Goodrich, Producers (ABC)

OLYMPIC DIARY, Don Ohlmeyer, Executive Producer; Bernie Hoffman, Peter Diamond, Producers (NBC)

PAN AMERICAN GAMES, Eddie Einhorn, Executive Producer; Ed Goren, Producer (CBS)

SPIRIT OF '78 - THE FLIGHT OF DOUBLE EAGLE II, Roone Arledge, Executive Producer; John Wilcox, Producer (ABC)

SUPER BOWL XIII - PRE-GAME, Don Ohlmeyer, Executive Producer, Don McGuire, Producer (NBC)

EDITED SPORTS SERIES (E-1530)
Emmy(s) to Executive Producer(s) and Producer(s)

ABC'S WIDE WORLD OF SPORTS, Roone Arledge, Executive Producer; Chet Forte, Chuck Howard, Doug Wilson, Ned Steckel, Bob Goodrich, Dennis Lewin, Eleanor Riger, Carol Lehti, Joe Aceti, Terry O'Neil, Producers (ABC)

THE AMERICAN SPORTSMAN, Roone Arledge, Executive Producer; John Wilcox, Producer (ABC)

SPORTSWORLD, Doh Ohlmeyer, Executive Producer; Linda Jonsson, Virginia Seipt, Hilary Cosell, Ted Nathanson, Michael Weisman, Jim Marooney, Bernie Hoffman, Matthew McCarthy, David Stern, George Finkel, Larry Cirillo, Don McGuire, Producers (NBC)

SPORTS PERSONALITY (E-1531)
Dick Enberg (NBC)
Frank Gifford (ABC)
Keith Jackson (ABC)
Jim McKay (ABC)
Merlin Olsen (NBC)
Pat Summerall (CBS)
Jack Whitaker (CBS)

DIRECTING IN SPORTS PROGRAMMING (E-1532)
FRANK CHIRKINIAN, ROBERT DAILEY, The Masters Golf Tournament (CBS)
HARRY COYLE, 1978 World Series (NBC)
CHET FORTE, ABC's NFL Monday Night Football (ABC)
TED NATHANSON, Super Bowl XIII (NBC)
ANDY SIDARIS, NCAA Football (ABC)

INDIVIDUAL ACHIEVEMENT IN SPORTS PROGRAMMING
Emmy(s) to Individual(s). In case of group winners, the producing organization will be awarded the Emmy, with Certificates to winning team members.

WRITING (E-1533)
STEVE SABOL, DAVE MORCOM; Pigskin Poetry (Part of NFL '78 for Pre-Game show) (NBC)

TECHNICAL DIRECTION/ENGINEERING SUPERVISION/ELECTRONIC CAMERAWORK (E-1534)
SANDY BELL & BOB BROWN, Technical Directors;RALPH SAVIGNANO & ART TINN, Engineering Supervisors; BARRY DRAGO, JIM McCARTHY, JOE SOKOTA, GEORGE ROTHWEILER, GEORGE NAEDER, JOHN LINCOLN, TOM McCARTHY, HANS SINGER, KEITH LAWRENCE, JIM MURPHY, NEIL McCAFFREY, HERMAN LANG, FRANK McSPEDON, Electronic Camerapersons; ANTHONY HLAVATY, WAYNE WRIGHT, JOHNNY MORRIS, ED AMBROSINI, FRANK FLORIO, TOM SPALDING, Electronic Camerapersons for Minicam & Microwave Systems; Daytona 500 (CBS)

SANDY BELL & CHARLES D'ONOFRIO, Technical Directors; ART TINN & LOU SCANNAPIECO, Engineering Supervisors; GEORGE KLIMCSAK, FRED HOLST, GAVIN BLANE, DAVID GRAHAM, HARRY HAIGOOD, GEORGE ROTHWEILER, HERMAN LANG, HANS SINGER, FRANK McSPEDON, BARRY DRAGO, JAMES MURPHY, ALAN DIAMOND, NEIL McCAFFREY, GEORGE NAEDER, JAMES McCARTHY, ALFRED LORETO, JOHN LINCOLN, DENNIS McBRIDE, STANLEY GOULD, ROBERT WELSH, DAVID FINCH, GORDON SWEENEY, JOSEPH VICENS, ROBERT SKORUP, R. WOELCK, Electronic Camerapersons; The Masters Golf Tournament (CBS)

HORACE RUIZ, Technical Director; JOE COMMARE, BOB McKEARNIN, JACK BENNETT, Engineering Supervisors; GEORGE LOOMIS, RODGER HARBAUGH, WILLIAM W. LANDERS, MICHAEL C. STRAMISKY, ROY V. RATLIFF, LEONARD BASILE, MARIO J. CIARLO, TOM C. DEZONDORF, STEVE CIMINO, WILLIAM M. GOETZ, LOUIS GERARD, LEN STUCKER, STEVEN H. GONZALES, JIM JOHNSON, CORY LIEBLE, DON MULVANEY, AL RICE, JR., RUSS K. ROSS, Electronic Camerapersons; Superbowl XIII (NBC)

HORACE RUIZ, DICK ROECKER & RAY FIGELSKI, Technical Directors; ROBERT McKEARNIN, JACK BENNETT, ERNEST THIEL, JERRY IRELAND & BOB BROWN, Engineering Supervisors; LEONARD G. BASILE, MARIO J. CIARLO, ROY RATLIFF, GEORGE LOOMIS, BERNARD JOSEPH, LOUIS GERARD, STEVE CIMINO, MIKE STRAMISKY, RODGER HARBAUGH, AL RICE, JR., WILLIAM M. GOETZ, JIM JOHNSON, BRIAN CHERRIFFE, PHIL CANTRELL, STEVEN H. GONZALES, RUSS C. ROSS, ART PARKER, BILL LANDERS, JIM BRAGG, JAMES CULLEY, CORY LIEBLE, LEN STUCKER, Electronic Camerapersons; 1978 World Series (NBC)

BOB VERNUM & CHARLES D'DONOFRIO, Technical Directors; JOSEPH TIER, Engineering Supervisor; JAMES McCARTHY, RICK BLANE, GEORGE KLIMCSAK, AL DIAMOND, HANS SINGER, FRANK McSPEDON, DAVID GRAHAM, DICK DOUGLAS, AL LORETO, STEVE GORSUCH, HERMAN LANG, FRED HOLTZ & ARTHUR JACKSON, Electronic Camerapersons; U.S. Open Tennis Championships (CBS)

CINEMATOGRAPHY (E-1535)
BOB ANGELO, ERNIE ERNST, JAY GERBER, STAN LESHNER, HANK McELWEE, HOWARD NEEF, JACK NEWMAN, STEVE SABOL, BOB SMITH, ART SPIELER & PHIL TUCKETT, Cinematographers for NFL Films; NFL Game Of The Week (SERIES) (SYND)

ASSOCIATE DIRECTION/VIDEOTAPE EDITING (E-1536)
TED SHAKER, RICHARD DRAKE & RICK SHARP, Associate Directors; Daytona 500 (CBS)

JEFF RINGEL, JEFF LAING, BOB HICKSON, CHRIS BALOMATIS, Videotape Editors; Daytona 500 (CBS)

BOB LEVY & MATTHEW McCARTHY, Associate Directors; RICHARD LEIBLE, MARK BELTRAN, MARK JANKELOFF, Videotape Editors; Sportsworld (SERIES) (NBC)

RALPH J. MOLE, Associate Director; ODEN KITZMILLER, CYRUS McROE, ED EBLIK, LEN JORDAN, HAL SOMMER, FRANK O'CONNELL, Videotape Editors; Pan American Games (CBS)

MUSIC COMPOSITION/MUSIC DIRECTION (E-1537)
ROGER NICHOLS; Olympathon '79 ("Olympic Theme") (NBC)

GRAPHIC DESIGN/TITLE SEQUENCES (E-1538)
ROBERT ANGELO & JAY GERBER, Graphic Designers; The NFL Today (CBS)

JAMES W. GRAU, Graphic Designer/Titles; All CBS Sports Programs (CBS)

SPECIAL CLASSIFICATION OF OUTSTANDING PROGRAM AND INDIVIDUAL ACHIEVEMENT
Emmy(s) to Producing Organization(s) or Individual(s), whichever applicable.

PROGRAM (E-1539)
SPORTSJOURNAL: "THE COCAINE CONNECTION: KEN STABLER AND THE SET-UP?" Don Ohlmeyer, Executive Producer; Hilary Cosell, Producer, (NBC)

INDIVIDUAL (E-1540)
TOM SPALDING, Inventor/Developer of the in-car racing system; Daytona 500 (CBS)

1979/80

PRIME TIME EMMY AWARDS

COMEDY SERIES (E-1541)
Emmy(s) to Executive Producer(s) and/or Producer(s)
BARNEY MILLER, Danny Arnold, Executive Producer; Tony Sheehan, Noam Pitlik, Producers; Gary Shaw, Co-Producer (ABC)
M*A*S*H, Burt Metcalfe, Executive Producer; Jim Mulligan, John Rappaport, Producers (CBS)
SOAP, Paul Junger Witt, Tony Thomas, Executive Producers; Susan Harris, Producer (ABC)
TAXI, James L. Brooks, Stan Daniels, Ed. Weinberger, Executive Producers; Glen Charles, Les Charles, Producers (ABC)
WKRP IN CINCINNATI, Hugh Wilson, Executive Producer; Rod Daniel, Bill Dial, Producers (CBS)

DRAMA SERIES (E-1542)
Emmy(s) to Executive Producer(s) and/or Producer(s)
DALLAS, Philip Capice, Lee Rich, Executive Producers; Leonard Katzman, Producer (CBS)
FAMILY, Aaron Spelling, Leonard Goldberg, Executive Producers; Edward Zwick, Producer (ABC)
LOU GRANT, Gene Reynolds, Executive Producer; Seth Freeman, Producer (CBS)
THE ROCKFORD FILES, Meta Rosenberg, Executive Producer; Stephen J. Cannell, Supervising Producer; David Chase, Chas. Floyd Johnson, Juanita Bartlett, Producers (NBC)
THE WHITE SHADOW, Bruce Paltrow, Executive Producer; Mark Tinker, Producer (CBS)

LIMITED SERIES (E-1543)
Emmy(s) to Executive Producer(s) and/or Producer(s)
DISRAELI: PORTRAIT OF A ROMATIC, (Masterpiece Theatre); Joan Wilson, Series Producer; Cecil Clarke, Producer (PBS)
EDWARD & MRS. SIMPSON, Andrew Brown, Producer (Synd)
THE DUCHESS OF DUKE STREET II, (Masterpiece Theatre); Joan Wilson, Series Producer; John Hawkesworth, Producer (PBS)
MOVIOLA, David L. Wolper, Executive Producer; Stan Margulies, Producer (NBC)

VARIETY OR MUSIC PROGRAM (E-1544)
For a special or a series Emmy(s) to Executive Producer(s) and/or Producer(s) and Star, if applicable
THE BENNY HILL SHOW, Dennis Kirkland, Keith Beckett, Mark Stuart, Producers (Synd)
GOLDIE AND LIZA TOGETHER, George Schlatter, Executive Producer; Don Mischer, Fred Ebb, Producers (CBS)
IBM PRESENTS BARYSHNIKOV ON BROADWAY, Herman Krawitz, Executive Producer; Gary Smith, Dwight Hemion, Producers (ABC)
THE MUPPET SHOW, David Lazer, Executive Producer; Jim Henson, Producer (Synd)
SHIRLEY MACLAINE. . .'EVERY LITTLE MOVEMENT' Gary Smith, Dwight Hemion, Producers (CBS)

DRAMA OR COMEDY SPECIAL (E-1545)
Emmy(s) to Executive Producer(s) and/or Producer(s)
ALL QUIET ON THE WESTERN FRONT (Hallmark Hall of Fame) Martin Starger, Executive Producer; Norman Rosemont, Producer (CBS)
AMBER WAVES, Philip Mandelker, Executive Producer; Stanley Kallis, Producer (ABC)
GIDEON'S TRUMPET (Hallmark Hall of Fame) John Houseman, Executive Producer; David W. Rintels, Producer (CBS)
GUYANA TRAGEDY: THE STORY OF JIM JONES, Frank Konigsberg, Executive Producer; Ernest Tidyman, Sam Manners, Producers (CBS)
THE MIRACLE WORKER, Raymond Katz, Sandy Gallin, Executive Producers; Fred Coe, Producer (NBC)

CLASSICAL PROGRAM IN THE PERFORMING ARTS (E-1546)
For a special or a series: Emmy(s) to Executive Producer(s) and/or Producer(s) and Star, if applicable
AGNES deMILLE AND THE JOFFREY BALLET IN CONVERSATIONS ABOUT THE DANCE Loring d'Usseau, Producer (PBS)
BEVERLY SILLS IN CONCERT, Thomas L. Merklinger, Executive Producer (PBS)
LIVE FROM STUDIO 8H: A TRIBUTE TO TOSCANINI, Judith De Paul, Alvin Cooperman, Producers (NBC)
LUCIANO PAVAROTTI AND THE NEW YORK PHILHARMONIC LIVE FROM LINCOLN CENTER, John Goberman, Producer (PBS)

INFORMATION PROGRAM (E-1547)
For a special or a series Emmy(s) to Executive Producer(s) and/or Producer(s)
BILL MOYERS' JOURNAL, Joan Konner, Executive Producer (PBS)
THE BODY HUMAN: THE BODY BEAUTIFUL, Thomas W. Moore, Executive Producer; Robert E. Fuisz, M.D., Alfred R. Kelman, Producers; Charles A. Bangert, Geof Bartz, Co-Producers (CBS)
THE BODY HUMAN: THE MAGIC SENSE, Thomas W. Moore, Executive Producer; Alfred R. Kelman, Robert E. Fuisz, M.D., Producers; Charles A. Bangert, Vivian R. Moss, Co-Producers (CBS)
THE NILE: THE COUSTEAU ODYSSEY, Jacques-Yves Cousteau, Philippe Cousteau, Executive Producers (PBS)
PICASSO--A PAINTER'S DIARY, George Page, Executive Producer; Perry Miller Adato, Producer (PBS)

SPECIAL EVENTS PROGRAM (E-1548)
Emmy(s) to Executive Producer(s) and/or Producer(s) (Possibility of one Award, more than one Award, or no Award)
THE AMERICAN FILM INSTITUTE SALUTE TO JIMMY STEWART, George Stevens, Jr., Producer (CBS)
52nd ANNUAL AWARDS PRESENTATION OF THE ACADEMY OF MOTION PICTURE ARTS AND SCIENCES, Howard W. Koch, Producer (ABC)
THE KENNEDY CENTER HONORS: A CELEBRATION OF THE PERFORMING ARTS, George Stevens, Jr., Nick Vanoff, Producers (CBS)
THE 34th ANNUAL TONY AWARDS, Alexander H. Cohen, Executive

1978/79—Milton Berle (Special Presentation to "Mr. Television")

1980/81—Barbara Babcock (Best Actress—Drama Series) and Daniel J. Travanti (Best Actor—Drama Series)

1979/80—Powers Booth (Best Actor—Limited Series or a Special)

1978/79—Alan Alda (Best Writing—Comedy or Comedy-Variety or Music Series)

1980/81 (on outside of photo) Rocco Urbisci and Lily Tomlin, producers of *Lily: Sold Out* (Best Variety, Music or Comedy Program). (middle of photo) Isabel Sanford (Best Actress—Comedy Series) with Sherman Hemsley

1982/83—Jean Simmons (Best Supporting Actress—Limited Series or a Special)

1982/83—Barbara Stanwyck (Best Actress—Limited Series or a Special)

1982/83—Doris Roberts (Best Supporting Actress—Drama Series) and James Coco (Best Supporting Actor—Drama Series)

1981/82—Michael Conrad (Best Supporting Actor—Drama Series)

1982/83—Carol Kane (Best Supporting Actress—Comedy, Variety or Music Series)

Producer; Hildy Parks, Producer; Roy A. Somlyo, Co-Producer (CBS)

SPECIAL CLASS PROGRAM (E-1549)

Emmy(s) to Executive Producer(s) and/or Producer(s) (Possibility of one Award, more than one Award or no Award)

FRED ASTAIRE: CHANGE PARTNERS AND DANCE, George Page, Jac Venza, Executive Producers; David Heeley, Producer (PBS)

FRED ASTAIRE: PUTTIN' ON HIS TOP HAT, George Page, Jac Venza, Executive Producers; David Heeley, Producer (PBS)

REAL PEOPLE, George Schlatter, Executive Producer; John Barbour, Bob Wynn, Producers (NBC)

THE TONIGHT SHOW STARRING JOHNNY CARSON, Fred de Cordova, Producer (NBC)

WINTER OLYMPICS '80 - THE WORLD COMES TO AMERICA Roone Arledge, Executive Producer; Don Wilson, Producer (ABC)

CHILDREN'S PROGRAM (E-1550)

For a special or a series. Emmy(s) to Executive Producer(s) and/or Producer(s) (Possibility of one Award, more than one Award, or no Award)

BENJI AT WORK, Joe Camp, Executive Producer; Fielder Baker, Producer (ABC)

THE HALLOWEEN THAT ALMOST WASN'T, Richard Barclay, Executive Producer; Gaby Monet, Producer (ABC)

SESAME STREET IN PUERTO RICO, Al Hyslop, Executive Producer (PBS)

ANIMATED PROGRAM (E-1551)

For a special or a series. Emmy(s) to Executive Producer(s) and/or Producer(s) (Possibility of one Award, more than one Award, or no Award)

CARLTON YOUR DOORMAN, Lorenzo Music, Barton Dean, Producers (CBS)

DR SEUSS' PONTOFFEL POCK, WHERE ARE YOU? David H. De Patie, Friz Freleng, Executive Producers; Ted Geisel, Producer (ABC)

PINK PANTHER IN OLYM-PINKS, David H. De Patie, Friz Freleng, Producers (ABC)

SHE'S A GOOD SKATE, CHARLIE BROWN, Lee Mendelson, Executive Producer; Bill Melendez, Producer (CBS)

ACTOR - COMEDY SERIES (E-1552)

For a continuing or single performance in a regular series

ALAN ALDA; M*A*S*H (CBS)
ROBERT GUILLAUME; Benson (ABC)
JUDD HIRSCH; Taxi (ABC)
HAL LINDEN; Barney Miller (ABC)
RICHARD MULLIGAN; Soap (ABC)

ACTOR - DRAMA SERIES (E-1553)

For a continuing or single performance in a regular series

ED ASNER; Lou Grant (CBS)
JAMES GARNER; The Rockford Files (NBC)
LARRY HAGMAN; Dallas (CBS)
JACK KLUGMAN; Quincy, M.E. (NBC)

ACTOR - LIMITED SERIES OR A SPECIAL (E-1554)

For a continuing role in a limited series, or for a single appearance in a limited series or a special

POWERS BOOTHE; Guyana Tragedy: The Story of Jim Jones (CBS)
TONY CURTIS; Moviola, The Scarlett O'Hara War (NBC)
HENRY FONDA; Gideon's Trumpet (CBS)
JASON ROBARDS; F.D.R. The Last Year (NBC)

ACTRESS - COMEDY SERIES (E-1555)

For a continuing or single performance in a regular series

CATHRYN DAMON; Soap (ABC)
KATHERINE HELMOND; Soap (ABC)
POLLY HOLLIDAY; Flo (CBS)
SHEREE NORTH; Archie Bunker's Place (CBS)
ISABEL SANFORD; The Jeffersons (CBS)

ACTRESS - DRAMA SERIES (E-1556)

For a continuing or single performance in a regular series

LAUREN BACALL; The Rockford Files, Lions, Tigers, Monkeys and Dogs (NBC)
BARBARA BEL GEDDES; Dallas (CBS)
MARIETTE HARTLEY; The Rockford Files, Paradise Cove (CBS)
KRISTY McNICHOL; Family (ABC)
SADA THOMPSON; Family (ABC)

ACTRESS - LIMITED SERIES OR A SPECIAL (E-1557)

For a continuing role in a limited series, or for a single appearance in a limited series or a special

PATTY DUKE ASTIN; The Miracle Worker (NBC)
BETTE DAVIS; White Mama (CBS)
MELISSA GILBERT; The Miracle Worker (NBC)
LEE REMICK; Haywire (CBS)

SUPPORTING ACTOR - COMEDY OR VARIETY OR MUSIC SERIES (E-1558)

For a continuing or single performance in a regular series

MIKE FARRELL; M*A*S*H (CBS)
MAX GAIL; Barney Miller (ABC)
HOWARD HESSEMAN; WKRP in Cincinnati (CBS)
STEVE LANDESBERG; Barney Miller (ABC)
HARRY MORGAN; M*A*S*H (CBS)

SUPPORTING ACTOR - DRAMA SERIES (E-1559)

For a continuing or single performance in a regular series

MASON ADAMS; Lou Grant (CBS)
NOAH BEERY; The Rockford Files (NBC)
STUART MARGOLIN; The Rockford Files (NBC)
ROBERT WALDEN; Lou Grant (CBS)

SUPPORTING ACTOR - LIMITED SERIES OR A SPECIAL (E-1560)

For a continuing role in a limited series, or for a single appearance in a limited series or a special

ERNEST BORGNINE; All Quiet On The Western Front (Hallmark Hall of Fame) (CBS)
JOHN CASSAVETES; Flesh and Blood (CBS)
CHARLES DURNING; Attica (ABC)
HAROLD GOULD; Moviola, The Scarlett O'Hara War (NBC)
GEORGE GRIZZARD; The Oldest Living Graduate (NBC)

SUPPORTING ACTRESS - COMEDY OR VARIETY OR MUSIC SERIES (E-1561)

For a continuing or single performance in a regular series

LONI ANDERSON; WKRP In Cincinnati (CBS)
POLLY HOLLIDAY; Alice (CBS)
INGA SWENSON; Benson (ABC)
LORETTA SWIT; M*A*S*H (CBS)

SUPPORTING ACTRESS - DRAMA SERIES (E-1562)

For a continuing or single performance in a regular series

NINA FOCH; Lou Grant, Hollywood (CBS)
LINDA KELSEY; Lou Grant CBS
NANCY MARCHAND; Lou Grant (CBS)
JESSICA WALTER; Trapper John, M.D. (CBS)

SUPPORTING ACTRESS - LIMITED SERIES OR A SPECIAL (E-1563)

For a continuing role in a limited series, or for a single appearance in a limited series or a special

EILEEN HECKART; F.D.R. The Last Year (NBC)
PATRICIA NEAL; All Quiet On The Western Front (Hallmark Hall of Fame) (CBS)
CARRIE NYE; Moviola, The Scarlett O'Hara War (NBC)
MARE WINNINGHAM; Amber Waves (ABC)

DIRECTOR - COMEDY SERIES (E-1564)

For a single episode of a regular series

ALAN ALDA; M*A*S*H, Dreams (CBS)
JAMES BURROWS; Taxi, Louie And The Nice Girl (ABC)
CHARLES S. DUBIN; M*A*S*H, Period of Adjustment (CBS)
BURT METCALFE; M*A*S*H, Bottle Fatigue (CBS)
HARRY MORGAN; M*A*S*H, Stars And Stripe (CBS)

DIRECTOR - DRAMA SERIES (E-1565)

For a single episode of a regular series

BURT BRINCKERHOFF; Lou Grant, Hollywood (CBS)
PETER LEVIN; Lou Grant, Andrew Part II: Trial (CBS)
FRANK PERRY; Skag, Premiere (NBC)
GENE REYNOLDS; Lou Grant, Influence (CBS)
ROGER YOUNG; Lou Grant, Cop (CBS)

DIRECTOR - VARIETY OR MUSIC PROGRAM (E-1566)

For a single episode of a regular or limited series or for a special

STEVE BINDER; The Big Show, with Mariette Hartley, Dean Martin (NBC)
TONY CHARMOLI; John Denver And The Muppets, A Christmas Get Together (ABC)
PETER HARRIS; The Muppet Show, with Liza Minnelli (Synd)
DWIGHT HEMION; IBM Presents Baryshnikov On Broadway (ABC)

DIRECTOR - LIMITED SERIES OR A SPECIAL (E-1567)

For a single episode of a limited series, or for a special

MARVIN J. CHOMSKY; Attica (ABC)
JOHN ERMAN; Moviola, The Scarlett O'Hara War (NBC)
WILLIAM A. GRAHAM; Guyana Tragedy: The Story Of Jim Jones (CBS)
DELBERT MANN; All Quiet On The Western Front (CBS)
JOSEPH SARGENT; Amber Waves (ABC)

CHOREOGRAPHY (E-1568)

For a single episode of a regular or limited series, or for a special

RON FIELD; IBM Presents Baryshnikov On Broadway (ABC)
ALAN JOHNSON; Shirley MacLaine. . .'Every Little Movement' (CBS)
LESTER WILSON; Uptown - A Musical Comedy History Of Harlem's Apollo Theatre (NBC)

WRITING - COMEDY SERIES (E-1569)

For a single episode of a regular series

GLEN CHARLES, LES CHARLES; Taxi, Honor Thy Father (ABC)
BOB COLLEARY; Barney Miller, Photographer (ABC)
STAN DANIELS, ED. WEINBERGER; The Associates, The Censors (ABC)
DAVID ISAACS, KEN LEVINE; M*A*S*H, Goodbye, Radar, Part II (CBS)
MICHAEL LEESON, Teleplay; CHARLIE HAUCK, Story; The Associates, The First Day (ABC)

WRITING - DRAMA SERIES (E-1570)

For a single episode of a regular series

ALLAN BURNS, GENE REYNOLDS; Lou Grant, Brushfire (CBS)
STEPHEN J. CANNELL; Tenspeed And Brown Shoe, Pilot (ABC)
SETH FREEMAN; Lou Grant, Cop (CBS)
MICHELE GALLERY; Lou Grant, Lou (CBS)
ABBY MANN; Skag, Premiere (NBC)

WRITING - VARIETY OR MUSIC PROGRAM (E-1571)

For a single episode of a regular or limited series, or for a special

PETER AYKROYD, ANNE BEATTS, TOM DAVIS, JAMES DOWNEY, BRIAN DOYLE-MURRAY, AL FRANKEN, TOM GAMMELL, LORNE MICHAELS, MATT NEUMAN, DON NOVELLO, SARAH PALEY, MAX PROSS, HERB SARGENT, HARRY SHEARER, TOM SCHILLER, ROSIE SHUSTER, ALAN ZWEIBEL; Saturday Night Live, Host: Teri Garr (NBC)
FRED EBB; Goldie And Liza Together (CBS)
JIM HENSON, DON HINKLEY, JERRY JUHL, DAVID ODELL; The Muppet Show, Guest: Alan Arkin (Synd)
BUZ KOHAN; Shirley MacLaine. . .'Every Little Movement' (CBS)
BOB ARNOTT, ROGER BEATTY, DICK CLAIR, TIM CONWAY, ANN ELDER, ARNIE KOGEN, BUZ KOHAN, JENNA MC MAHON, KENNY SOLMS; Carol Burnett & Company, Guest: Sally Field (ABC)

WRITING - LIMITED SERIES OR A SPECIAL (E-1572)

For a single episode of a limited series, or for a special, whether the writing is an original teleplay or an adaptation

DAVID CHASE; Off The Minnesota Strip (ABC)
JAMES S. HENERSON; Attica (ABC)
JAMES LEE; Moviola, This Year's Blonde (NBC)
DAVID W. RINTELS; Gideon's Trumpet (Hallmark Hall of Fame) (CBS)
KEN TREVEY; Amber Waves (ABC)

CREATIVE CRAFT EMMY AWARDS

CINEMATOGRAPHY - SERIES (E-1573)

For a single episode of a regular series

EMMETT BERGHOLZ; Fantasy Island, The Wedding (ABC)
ALRIC EDENS, A.S.C.; Quincy, M.E., Riot (NBC)
GERALD PERRY FINNERMAN, A.S.C.; From Here To Eternity, Pearl Harbor (NBC)
ENZO A. MARTINELLI, A.S.C.; The Contender, Breakthrough (CBS)
JOHN McPHERSON, A.S.C.; The Incredible Hulk, Broken Image (CBS)
TED VOIGTLANDER, A.S.C.; Little House On The Prairie, May We Make Them Proud (NBC)

CINEMATOGRAPHY - LIMITED SERIES OR A SPECIAL (E-1574)

For a single episode of a limited series, or for a special

JOE BIROC, A.S.C.; Kenny Rogers As The Gambler CBS
GAYNE RESCHER, A.S.C.; Moviola, The Silent Lovers (NBC)
TED VOIGTLANDER, A.S.C.; The Miracle Worker (NBC)
HARRY L. WOLF, A.S.C.; Brave New World (NBC)

ART DIRECTION - SERIES (E-1575)
For a single episode of a regular series
JAMES J. AGAZZI, Art Director; PAUL SYLOS, Art Director BOB SIGNORELLI, Set Decorator; Hart To Hart, Man With Jade Eyes (ABC)
MICHAEL BAUGH, Production Designer; EDWARD McDONALD, Set Decorator; Beyond Westworld, Pilot (CBS)
JAMES D. BISSELL, Art Director; WILLIAM WEBB, Set Decorator; Palmerstown, U.S.A. The Old Sister (CBS)
HUB BRADEN, Art Director; FRED LUFF, Art Director; FRANK LOMBARDO, Set Decorator; Buck Rogers In The 25th Century; Ardala Returns (NBC)
DAVID MARSHALL, Art Director; WILLIAM CRAIG SMITH, Art Director; LEONARD MAZZOLA, Set Decorator; Skag, Premiere (NBC)

ART DIRECTION - LIMITED SERIES OR A SPECIAL (E-1576)
For a single episode of a limited series, or for a special
MICHAEL BAUGH, Production Designer; JERRY ADAMS, Set Decorator; Moviola, The Silent Lovers (NBC)
JACK F. DE SHIELDS, Art Director; IRA BATES, Set Decorator; The Ordeal Of Dr. Mudd (CBS)
TOM H. JOHN, Art Director; MARY ANN BIDDLE, Set Decorator; Brave New World (NBC)
JAN SCOTT, Art Director & Production Designer; BILL HARP, Set Decorator; Orphan Train (CBS)
WILFRID SHINGLETON, Production Designer; JULIAN SACKS, Art Director; JEAN TAILLANDIER, Art Director; CHERYAL KEARNEY, Set Decorator; Gauguin The Savage (CBS)
JOHN STOLL, Production Designer; KAREL VACEK, Art Director; All Quiet On The Western Front (Hallmark Hall of Fame) (CBS)

ART DIRECTION - VARIETY OR MUSIC PROGRAM (E-1577)
For a single episode of a single or regular series, or for a special
BRIAN C. BARTHOLOMEW, BOB KEENE, Production Designers; TONY BUGENHAGEN, Set Decorator; The Big Show, with Hosts Sarah Purcell, Flip Wilson (NBC)
ROMAIN JOHNSTON, Art Director; DEBE HENDRICKS, Set Decorator; Shirley MacLaine. . .'Every Little Movement' (CBS)
CHARLES LISANBY, Art Director; DWIGHT JACKSON, Set Decorator; IBM Presents Baryshnikov On Broadway (ABC)
MALCOLM STONE, Art Director; The Muppet Show, with Beverly Sills (Synd)

MUSIC COMPOSITION - SERIES (DRAMATIC UNDERSCORE) (E-1578)
for a single episode of a regular series
BRUCE BROUGHTON; Dallas, The Lost Child (CBS)
JOHN CACAVAS; Eischied, Only The Pretty Girls Die - Part II (NBC)
BILLY GOLDENBERG; Skag, Premiere (NBC)
FRED KARLIN; Paris, Decisions (CBS)
PATRICK WILLIAMS; Lou Grant, Hollywood (CBS)

MUSIC COMPOSITION - LIMITED SERIES OR A SPECIAL (DRAMATIC UNDERSCORE) (E-1579)
For a single episode of a limited series, or for a special
JERRY FIELDING; High Midnight (CBS)
GERALD FRIED; Moviola, The Silent Lovers (NBC)
PETE RUGOLO; The Last Convertible, Episode One (NBC)
HARRY SUKMAN; Salem's Lot (CBS)

MUSIC DIRECTION (E-1580)
For a single episode of a regular or limited series, or for a special, whether it be variety or music
ARTIE BUTLER;Barry Manilow - One Voice (ABC)
IAN FRASER, Music Director; RALPH BURNS AND BILLY BYERS, Principle Arrangers; IBM Presents Baryshnikov on Broadway (ABC)
NICK PERITO; The Big Show, hosts Steve Lawrence, Don Rickles (NBC)

COSTUME DESIGN - SERIES (E-1581)
For a single episode of a regular series
JEAN-PIERRE DORLEAC; Galactica 1980, Starbuck's Great Journey (ABC)
CALISTA HENDRICKSON; The Muppet Show, with Guest Beverly Sills (Synd)
GRADY HUNT; Fantasy Island, Tatoo: The Love God/Magnolia Blossom (ABC)
ALFRED E. LEHMAN; Buck Rogers In The 25th Century Flight Of The War Witch, Part Two (NBC)
PETE MENEFEE; The Big Show, hosts Tony Randall, Herve Villechaize (NBC)

COSTUME DESIGN - LIMITED SERIES OR A SPECIAL (E-1582)
For a single episode of a limited series, or for a special
BILL BELEW; The Carpenters, Music, Music, Music (ABC)
GRADY HUNT; The Dream Merchants (Synd)
BOB MACKIE; Ann-Margaret - Hollywood Movie Girls (ABC)
TRAVILLA; Moviola, The Scarlett O'Hara War (NBC)
RET TURNER; The Beatrice Arthur Special (ABC)

MAKE-UP (E-1583)
For a single episode of a regular or limited series, or for a special
RICHARD BLAIR; Moviola, The Scarlett O'Hara War (NBC)
JOHN CHAMBERS, ROBERT A. SIDELL; Beyond Westworld, Pilot (CBS)
LORRAINE DAWKINS, ANITA HARRIS, SHEILA MANN, MARY SOUTHGATE, BRENDA YEWDELL; Disraeli: Portrait Of A Romantic, Masterpiece Theatre; Dizzy (PBS)
JACK FREEMAN; Haywire (CBS)
BEN LANE; JACK YOUNG, S.M.A.; Salem's Lot (CBS)

HAIRSTYLING (E-1584)
For a single episode of a regular or limited series, or for a special
NAOMA CAVIN, MARY HADLEY; Murder Can Hurt You! (ABC)
LEONARD DRAKE; Moviola, The Silent Lovers (NBC)
CAROLINE ELLIAS, BETTE IVERSON; Haywire (CBS)
LARRY GERMAIN, DONNA GILBERT; The Miracle Worker (NBC)
JOAN PHILLIPS; Fantasy Island, Dr. Jekyll and Ms. Hyde/Aphrodite (ABC)

GRAPHIC DESIGN AND TITLE SEQUENCES (E-1585)
For a single episode of a regular or limited series, or for a special, This includes animation only when created for use in titling
GENE KRAFT; Salem's Lot (CBS)
PHILL NORMAN; The French Atlantic Affair, Part I (ABC)

FILM EDITING - SERIES (E-1586)
For a single episode of a regular series
M. PAM BLUMENTHAL; Taxi, Louie And The Nice Girl (ABC)
SIDNEY M. KATZ, A.C.E.; Skag, Premiere (NBC)
LARRY MILLS, STANFORD TISCHLER; M*A*S*H, The Yalu Brick Road

(CBS)
LARRY STRONG, A.C.E.; Skag, The Working Girl, Part I (NBC)

FILM EDITING - LIMITED SERIES OR A SPECIAL (E-1587)

For a single episode of a limited series, or for a special
BILL BLUNDEN, ALAN PATTILLO; All Quiet On The Western Front (Hallmark Hall Of Fame) (CBS)
PAUL LA MASTRA; Attica (ABC)
JERROLD L. LUDWIG, A.C.E.; Kenny Rogers As The Gambler (CBS)
JOHN A. MARTINELLI, A.C.E., RUSTY COPPLEMAN; S.O.S. Titanic (ABC)
DAVID NEWHOUSE, A.C.E.; Moviola, The Silent Lovers (NBC)
JOHN WOODCOCK, A.C.E.; When Hell Was In Session (NBC)

FILM SOUND EDITING (E-1588)

For a single episode of a regular or limited series, or for a special
MICHAEL L. HILKENE, TOM CORNWELL, DAVE ELLIOTT, DON ERNST, DIMITRY GORTINSKY, PETER HARRISON, ANDREW HERBERT, FRED JUDKINS, RUSS TINSLEY, CHRISTOPHER T. WELCH; The Plutonium Incident (CBS)
MICHAEL L. HILKENE, TOM CORNWELL, PETER HARRISON, ANDREW HERBERT, FRED JUDKINS, RUSS TINSLEY, JILL TAGGERT; Amber Waves (ABC)
MICHAEL REDBOURN, TOM CORNWELL, LINDA DOVE, DON ERNST, PETER HARRISON, ANDREW HERBERT, FRED JUDKINS, RUSS TINSLEY; Attica (ABC)
DON CROSBY, MARK DENNIS, TONY GARBER, DOUG GRINDSTAFF, DON V. ISAACS, HANK SALERNO, LARRY SINGER; Power, Part I (NBC)

FILM SOUND MIXING (E-1589)

For a single episode of a regular or limited series, or for a special
RAY BARONS, DAVID CAMPBELL, BOB PETTIS, JOHN REITZ; The Ordeal Of Dr. Mudd (CBS)
DAVID CAMPBELL, JOHN REITZ, BOB PETTIS, JACQUE NOSCO; Guyana Tragedy: The Story Of Jim Jones, Part II (CBS)
CHRISTOPHER LARGE, EDDIE NELSON, GEORGE E. PORTER, TERRY PORTER; Amber Waves (ABC)
WILLIAM L. MC CAUGHEY, DAVID E. DOCKENDORF, ROBERT L. HARMAN, JACK SOLOMON; Skag Premiere (NBC)
JOHN WILKENSON, ROBERT GLASS, JR., ROBERT THIRWELL, PATRICK MITCHELL; The Golden Moment: An Olympic Love Story (NBC)

TAPE SOUND MIXING (E-1590)

For a single episode of a regular or limited series, or for a special
BRUCE BURNS, JERRY CLEMANS; Sinatra: The First 40 Years (NBC)
JERRY CLEMANS, GORDON F. KLIMUCK, DOUG NELSON; Olivia Newton-John--Hollywood Nights (ABC)
JERRY CLEMANS, JUERGEN KOPPERS, DOUG NELSON; The Donna Summer Special (ABC)
JERRY CLEMANS, BILL SHERRILL; Kenny Rogers and the American Cowboy (CBS)
TERRY FARRIS, TOM HUTH, BLAKE NORTON; The Crystal Gayle Special (CBS)
DONALD WORSHAM; The Oldest Living Graduate (NBC)

VIDEO TAPE EDITING - SERIES (E-1591)

For a single episode of a regular series
KEN DENISOFF, KEVIN MULDOON, ANDY ZALL; The Big Show, hosts Tony Randall, Herve Villechaize (NBC)
JOHN HAWKINS; The Muppet Show, with Guest Liza Minnelli (Synd)
TERRY PICKFORD; Fridays, Show #5, with Boz Scaggs (ABC)
MARCO ZAPPIA; A New Kind Of Family, I Do (ABC)

VIDEO TAPE EDITING - LIMITED SERIES OR A SPECIAL (E-1592)

For a single episode of a limited series or for a special
TERRY CLIMER; The Donna Summer Special (ABC)
DANNY WHITE; Olivia Newton-John–Hollywood Nights (ABC)
ANDY ZALL; IBM Presents Baryshnikov On Broadway (ABC)
MARCO ZAPPIA; Perry Como's Christmas In New Mexico (ABC)

TECHNICAL DIRECTION AND ELECTRONIC CAMERWORK (E-1593)

For a single episode of a regular or limited series or for a special program
ROBERT G. HOLMES, Technical Director; BRUCE BUTTONE, GEORGE FALARDEAU, BILL LANDERS, PEGGY MAHONEY, MIKE STRAMISKY, Camerapersons; The Midnight Special, Host: The Cars (NBC)
ROBERT A. KEMP, Technical Director; RALPH ALCOCER, JIM ANGEL, DAVE BANKS, RON BROOKS, BUD HOLLAND, ART LA CONBE, DAN LANGFORD, Camerpersons; Goldie and Liza Together (CBS)
WAYNE PARSONS, Technical Director; TOM GEREN, DEAN HALL, BOB HIGHTON, BILL LANDERS, RON SHELDON, Camerapersons; The Oldest Living Graduate (NBC)
JERRY WEISS, Technical Director; LESLIE B. ATKINSON, ROY HOLM, PEGGY MAHONEY, MIKE STRAMISKY, Camerapersons; The Magic Of David Copperfield (CBS)
JERRY WEISS, Technical Director; LARRY HEIDER, ROY HOLM, BILL LANDERS, PEGGY MAHONEY, WAYNE ORR, MIKE STRAMISKY, Camerapersons; A Christmas Special. . .With Love, Mac Davis (NBC)

LIGHTING DIRECTION (ELECTRONIC) (E-1594)

For a single episode of a regular or limited series, or for a special
TONY DI GIROLAMO; The Tender Land (PBS)
PETER G. EDWARDS, WILLIAM KNIGHT, PETER S. PASSAS; F.D.R. The Last Year (NBC)
DANIEL FLANNERY, Lighting Director; WILLIAM M. KLAGES, Lighting Consultant; Goldie And Liza Together (CBS)
WILLIAM M. KLAGES; The Big Show, hosts: Sarah Purcell, Flip Wilson (NBC)
FRED McKINNON, MARK PALIUS; The Cheryl Ladd Special: Souvenirs (ABC)
GEORGE W. RIESENBERGER, JOHN FRESCHI; The Unbroken Circle: A Tribute To Mother Maybelle Carter (CBS)

INDIVIDUAL ACHIEVEMENT - SPECIAL EVENTS (E-1595)

(Possibility of one Award, more than one Award, or no Award)
CARL VITELLI, Lighting Director; The 34th Annual Tony Awards (CBS)
DONALD O'CONNOR, Performer; 52nd Annual Awards Presentation Of The Academy Of Motion Picture Arts And Sciences (ABC)
LARRY GROSSMAN, Music, BUZ KOHAN, Lyrics; 52nd Annual Awards Presentation Of The Academy Of Motion Picture Arts And Sciences, "Dancin' On The Silver Screen" (ABC)
WALTER PAINTER, Choreographer; 52nd Annual Awards Presentation Of The Academy Of Motion Picture Arts And Sciences, "Dancin' On The Silver Screen" (ABC)
RAY KLAUSEN, Art Director; 52nd Annual Awards Presentation Of The Academy Of Motion Picture Arts And Sciences (ABC)

INDIVIDUAL ACHIEVEMENT - INFORMATIONAL PROGRAM (E-1596)

(Possibility of one Award, more than one Award, or no Award)
DAVID CLARK, JOEL FEIN, ROBERT L. HARMAN, GEORGE E. PORTER, Film Sound Mixers; Dive To The Edge Of Creation, National Geographic Special (PBS)
BRYAN ANDERSON, BOB ELFSTROM, AL GIDDINGS, Cinematogra-

phers; Mysteries Of The Sea (ABC)
ROBERT E. FUISZ, M.D., LOUIS H. GORFAIN, Writers; The Body Human: The Body Beautiful (CBS)
HENRI COLPI, JOHN SOH, Film Editors; The Nile, The Cousteau Odyssey (PBS)
ROBERT EISENHARDT, HANK O'KARMA, JANE KURSON, Film Editors; The Body Human: The Body Beautiful (CBS)

INDIVIDUAL ACHIEVEMENT - SPECIAL CLASS (E-1597)

(Possibility of one Award, more than one Award or no Award)

HARRY BOTTORF, JOHN GISONDI, WILLIAM C. KNIGHT, DICK WEISS, Lighting; A Christmas Carol (PBS)
ORLAND TAMBURRI, Technical Director; READ HOWARD, WILLIAM LANDERS, VICTORIA WALKER, Camerapersons; Skinflint: A Country Christmas Carol (NBC)
GEOF BARTZ, Film Editor; Operation: Lifeline, Dr. James "Red" Duke, Trauma Surgeon (NBC)
DARRYL SUTTON, Video Tape Editor; Bob Hope's Overseas Christmas Tours: Around The World With The Troops (NBC)
CLIFFORD L. CHALLY, PAT ZINN, Costumes; The Dream Merchants (Synd)

INDIVIDUAL ACHIEVEMENT - CREATIVE TECHNICAL CRAFTS (E-1598)

(Possibility of one Award, more than one Award, or no Award)

SCOTT SCHACHTER, Live Audio Mixing; Live From Studio 8h: A Tribute To Toscanini (NBC)
ROY WHYBROW, Special Effects - Cinematography; All Quiet On The Western Front (Hallmark Hall of Fame) (CBS)
LESLIE ASCH, ED CHRISTIE, BARBARA DAVIS, FAZ FAZAKAS, NOMI FREDRICK, MICHAEL FRITH, AMY VAN GILDER, DAVE GOELZ, MARIANNE HARMS, LARRY JAMESON, MARI KAESTLE, ROLLIN KREWSON, TIM MILLER, ROBERT PAYNE, JAN ROSENTHAL, DON SAHLIN, CAROLY WILCOX, Muppet Design - Art Direction; The Muppet Show, with Guest Alan Arkin (Synd)
ED CHRISTIE, BARBARA DAVIS, FAZ FAZAKAS, NOMI FREDRICK, MICHAEL FRITH, AMY VAN GILDER, DAVE GOELZ, LARRY JAMESON, MARI KAESTLE, ROLLIN KREWSON, TIM MILLER, ROBERT PAYNE, JAN ROSENTHAL, DON SAHLIN, CAROLY WILCOX, Muppet Design - Art Direction; The Muppet Show, with Guest Kenny Rogers (Synd)
MARK SCHUBIN, Liveo Stereo Simulcast; Luciano Pavarotti And The New York Philharmonic; Live From Lincoln Center (PBS)

INDIVIDUAL ACHIEVEMENT - CHILDREN'S PROGRAM (E-1599)

(Possibility of one Award, more than one Award, or no Award)

ARTHUR GINSBURG, Film Editor; The Halloween That Almost Wasn't (ABC)
NAT MONGIOI, Art Director; Sesame Street in Puerto Rico (PBS)
BOB O'BRADOVICH, MakeUp; The Halloween That Almost Wasn't (ABC)
MARIETTE HARTLEY, Performer; The Halloween That Almost Wasn't (ABC)
OZZIE ALFONSO, Director; Sesame Street In Puerto Rico (PBS)

INDIVIDUAL ACHIEVEMENT - ANIMATION PROGRAM (E-1600)

(Possibility of one Award, more than one Award, or no Award)

FRIZ FRELENG, Director; Pink Panther In Olym-Pinks (ABC)
CHUCK JONES, Director; Bugs Bunny's Bustin' Out All Over (CBS)

NATIONAL DAYTIME EMMY AWARDS

DAYTIME DRAMA SERIES (E-1601)
Emmy(s) to Executive Producer(s) and Producer(s)

ALL MY CHILDREN, Agnes Nixon, Executive Producer; Jorn Winther, Producer (ABC)
ANOTHER WORLD, Paul Rauch, Executive Producer; Mary S. Bonner, Robert Costello, Producers (NBC)
GUIDING LIGHT, Allen M. Potter, Executive Producer; Leslie Kwartin, Joe Willmore, Producers (CBS)

GAME OR AUDIENCE PARTICIPATION SHOW (E-1602)
Emmy(s) to Executive Producer(s) and Producer(s)

FAMILY FEUD, Mark Goodson, Executive Producer; Howard Felsher, Producer (ABC)
HOLLYWOOD SQUARES, Merrill Heatter, Robert Quigley, Executive Producers; Jay Redack, Producer (NBC)
THE $20,000 PYRAMID, Bob Stewart, Executive Producer; Ann Marie Schmitt, Jane Rothchild, Producers (ABC)

TALK, SERVICE OR VARIETY SERIES (E-1603)
Emmy(s) to Executive Producer(s) and Producer(s)

DONAHUE, Richard Mincer, Executive Producer; Patricia McMillen, Senior Producer; Darlene Hayes, Sheri Singer, Producers (Synd)
GOOD MORNING AMERICA, George Merlis, Executive Producer; John Kippycash, Jack Reilly, Jan Rifkinson, Sonya Selby-Wright, Producers (ABC)
MIKE DOUGLAS SHOW, Frank Miller, Executive Producer; Vince Calandra, E.V. DiMassa, Jr., Producers (Synd)

ACTOR - DAYTIME DRAMA SERIES (E-1604)

JOHN GABRIEL; Ryan's Hope (ABC)
MICHAEL LEVIN; Ryan's Hope (ABC)
FRANC LUZ; The Doctors (NBC)
JAMES MITCHELL; All My Children (ABC)
WILLIAM MOONEY; All My Children (ABC)
DOUGLASS WATSON; Another World (NBC)

ACTRESS - DAYTIME DRAMA SERIES (E-1605)

JULIA BARR; All My Children (ABC)
LESLIE CHARLESON; General Hospital (ABC)
KIM HUNTER; The Edge Of Night (ABC)
JUDITH LIGHT; One Life To Live (ABC)
BEVERLEE McKINSEY; Another World (NBC)
KATHLEEN NOONE; All My Children (ABC)

SUPPORTING ACTOR - DAYTIME DRAMA SERIES (E-1606)

VASILI BOGAZIANOS; The Edge Of Night (ABC)
WARREN BURTON; All My Children (ABC)
LARRY HAINES; Search For Tomorrow (CBS)
RON HALE; Ryan's Hope (ABC)
JULIUS LA ROSA; Another World (NBC)
SHEPPERD STRUDWICK; Love Of Life (CBS)

SUPPORTING ACTRESS - DAYTIME DRAMA SERIES (E-1607)

DEIDRE HALL; Days Of Our Lives (NBC)
FRANCESCA JAMES; All My Children (ABC)
LOIS KIBBEE; The Edge Of Night (ABC)
ELAINE LEE; The Doctors (NBC)
VALERIE MAHAFFEY; The Doctors (NBC)
LOUISE SHAFFER; Ryan's Hope (ABC)

GUEST/CAMEO APPEARANCE - DAYTIME DRAMA SERIES (E-1608)

For five or less appearances
SAMMY DAVIS, JR. One Life To Live (ABC)
JOAN FONTAINE Ryan's Hope (ABC)
KATHRYN HARROW; The Doctors (NBC)
HUGH McPHILLIPS; Days Of Our Lives (NBC)
ELI MINTZ; All My Children (ABC)

HOST OR HOSTESS - GAME OR AUDIENCE PARTICIPATION SHOW (E-1609)

RICHARD DAWSON; Family Feud (ABC)
PETER MARSHALL; The Hollywood Squares (NBC)

HOST OR HOSTESS - TALK, SERVICE OR VARIETY SERIES (E-1610)

PHIL DONAHUE; Donahue (Synd)
DINAH SHORE; Dinah! And Friends (Synd)

DIRECTOR - DAYTIME DRAMA SERIES (E-1611)

For the Entire Series
HENRY KAPLAN, JACK COFFEY, SHERRELL HOFFMAN, JORN WINTHER; All My Children (ABC)
IRA CIRKER, MELVIN BERNHARDT, ROBERT CALHOUN, BARNET KELLMAN, JACK HOFSISS, ANDREW WEYMAN; Another World (NBC)
JOHN SEDWICK, RICHARD PEPPERMAN; The Edge Of Night (ABC)
MARLENA LAIRD, ALAN PULTZ, PHIL SOGARD; General Hospital (ABC)
LARRY AUERBACH, ROBERT SCINTO; Love Of Life (CBS)
LELA SWIFT, JERRY EVANS; Ryan's Hope (ABC)

INDIVIDUAL DIRECTOR - GAME OR AUDIENCE PARTICIPATION SHOW (E-1612)

For a single episode
PAUL ALER; Family Feud 4/10/79 (ABC)
JEROME SHAW; The Hollywood Squares, 6/14/79 (NBC)

INDIVIDUAL DIRECTOR - TALK, SERVICE OR VARIETY SERIES (E-1613)

For a single episode
DUKE STRUCK; Henry Fonda Tribute, Good Morning America (ABC)
GLEN SWANSON Dinah! And Friends In Singapore (Synd)
RON WEINER; Pimps, Donahue (Synd)

WRITING - DAYTIME DRAMA SERIES (E-1614)

AGNES NIXON, WISNER WASHAM, JACK WOOD, CAROLINE FRANZ, MARY K. WELLS, CATHY CHICOS, CLARICE BLACKBURN, ANITA JAFFE, KEN HARVEY; All My Children (ABC)
HENRY SLESAR, STEVE LEHRMAN; The Edge Of Night (ABC)
GORDON RUSSELL, SAM HALL, PEGGY O'SHEA, DON WALLACE, LANIE BERTRAM, CYNTHIA BENJAMIN, MARISA GIOFFRE; One Life To Live (ABC)
CLAIRE LABINE, PAUL AVILA MAYER, MARY MUNISTERI, JUDITH PINSKER, JEFFREY LANE; Ryan's Hope (ABC)

ACHIEVEMENT IN TECHNICAL EXCELLENCE - DAYTIME DRAMA SERIES (E-1615)

Emmys to individuals
JOSEPH SOLOMITO, HOWARD ZWEIG, Technical Directors; LAWRENCE HAMMOND, ROBERT AMBRICO, DIANE CATES-CANTRELL, CHRISTOPHER N MAURO, LARRY STRACK, VINCENT SENATORE, Electronic Camera; ALBIN S. LEMANSKI, Audio Engineer; LEN WALAS, Video Engineer; DIANA WENMAN, JEAN DADARIO, Associate Producers; ROGER HAENELT, JOHN L. GRELLA, Videotape Editors; IRVING ROBBIN, JIM REICHERT, Music Composers; TERI SMITH, Music Director; All My Children (ABC)

FRANK GAETA, STEVE CIMINO, FRANK DeRIENZO, Technical Directors; CARL ECKETT, DAVID WEINBERG, OLONZO ROBERTS, WAYNE NORMAN, Electronic Camera; PHILIP BERGE, MEL HENCH, Audio Engineers; ARNOLD DICK, HAROLD MOFSEN, Video Engineers; KEVIN KELLY, JOHN LIBRETTO, Associate Directors; LLOYD CAMPBELL, JOHN O'CONNOR, Videotape Editors; SCORE PRODUCTIONS; Music Composer/Director; Another World (NBC)
RAYMOND BARRETT, Technical Director; JACK DOLAN, STEVE JAMBECK, JAN KASSOFF, Electronic Camera; GEORGE CORRADO, Audio Engineer; FRANK VIERLING, Video Engineer; DAVID HANDLER, Associate Director; LEE GOLDMAN, Videotape Editor; BOB ISRAEL, Music Coordinator; JOHN GELLER, Music Director; The Doctors (NBC)
WILLIAM EDWARDS, Technical Director; WILLIAM HUGHES, THOMAS STALLONE, ARIE HEFTER, Electronic Camera; EDWARD ATCHISON, Audio Engineer; ROBERT SAXON, Sound Effects; JOHN VALENTINO, Video Engineer; JOANNE GOODHART, Associate Director; STEPHEN SCOTT, LENNY DAVIDOWITZ, Videotape Editors; ELIOT LAWRENCE, Music Composer; BARBARA MILLER, Music Coordinator; The Edge Of Night (ABC)
DAVID SMITH, JOHN COCHRAN, Technical Directors; DAVE BANKS, LUIS ROJAS, CAROL WETOVICH, JAMES ANGEL, JACK DENTON, Electronic Camera; KEN QUAYLE, ZOLI OSAZE, Audio Engineers; NICK KLEISSAS, Sound Effects; SAM POTTER, Video Engineer; HAL ALEXANDER, GEORGE THOMPSON, Associate Directors; DAN BLEVENS, JACK MOODY, Videotape Editors; CHARLES PAUL, Music Composer/Director; General Hospital (ABC)
GEORGE WHITAKER, Technical Director; DICK KERR, MARY FLOOD, FRANK J MERKLEIN, Electronic Camera; WILLIAM deBLOCK, LEE M. GOLDMAN, Audio Engineers; RUDY PICARILLO, DICK WILLIAMS, LINDA WALLACH, Video Engineers; SUELLEN GOLDSTEIN, Associate Director; PAT MALIK, WALTER URBANSKI, Video Editors; CAREY GOLD, Music Composer; SYBIL WEINBERGER, Music Supervisor; Ryan's Hope (ABC)

DESIGN - DAYTIME DRAMA SERIES (E-1616)

Emmys to individuals
WILLIAM MICKLEY, Scenic Designer; WILLIAM ITKIN, DONNA LARSON, MEL HANDELSMAN, Lighting Directors; CAROL LUIKEN, Costume Designer; SYLVIA LAWRENCE, Make-up Designer; MICHAEL HUDDLE, Hair Designer; HY BLEY, Graphic Designer; All My Children (ABC)
ROBERT FRANKLIN, Art Director; RUSSELL CHRISTIAN, RICHARD HANKINS, Scenic Designers; LEO FARRENKOPF, MAURY VERSCHOORE, Lighting Designer; LEWIS BROWN, Costume Designer; FRANK RUBERTONE, Hair Designer; EDWARD JACKSON, Make-up Designer; Another World (NBC)
JIM ELLINGWOOD, MERCER BARROWS, Art Directors; GRANT VELIE, JOHN ZAK, TOM MARKLE, Lighting Directors; GEORGE WHITTAKER, Costume Designer; JAMES COLA, Make-up Designer; KATHY KOTARAKOS, Hair Designer; General Hospital (ABC)
SY TOMASHOFF, Scenic Designer; HERB GRUBER, Scenic Artist; JOHN CONNOLY, Lighting Director; BILL KELLARD, Costume Designer; JAMES COLA, Make-up Designer; JOHN K. QUINN, Hairdesigner; Ryan's Hope (ABC)

CHILDREN'S ENTERTAINMENT SERIES (E-1617)

Emmy(s) to Executive Producer(s) and Producer(s)
CAPTAIN KANGAROO, Robert Keeshan, Executive Producer; Joel Kosofsky, Producer (CBS)
HOT HERO SANDWICH, Bruce Hart, Carole Hart, Executive Producers; Howard G. Malley, Producer (NBC)
KIDS ARE PEOPLE TOO, Lawrence Einhorn, Executive Producer; Laura Schrock, Producer; Noreen Conlin, Co-Producer (ABC)

CHILDREN'S ENTERTAINMENT SPECIAL (E-1618)

Emmy(s) to Executive Producer(s) and Producer(s)
THE BOY WITH TWO HEADS, (Once Upon A Classic); Jay Rayvid, Executive Producer; Frank Good, Producer (PBS)
THE HOUSE AT 12 ROSE STREET (NBC Special Treat) Daniel Wilson, Executive Producer; Fran Sears, Producer (NBC)
I DON'T KNOW WHO I AM (NBC Special Treat) Daniel Wilson, Executive Producer; Joanne A. Curley, Producer (NBC)
THE LATE GREAT ME: STORY OF A TEENAGE ALCOHOLIC, (ABC

Afterschool Special) Daniel Wilson, Executive Producer; Linda Marmelstein, Producer (ABC)

THE ROCKING CHAIR REBELLION (NBC Special Treat) Daniel Wilson, Executive Producer; Phyllis Minoff, Producer (NBC)

CHILDREN'S ANTHOLOGY/DRAMATIC PROGRAMMING (E-1619)

Emmy(s) to Executive Producer(s) and Producer(s)

ANIMAL TALK (CBS Library) Diane Asselin, Executive Producer; Paul Asselin, Producer (CBS)

THE GOLD BUG (ABC Weekend Special) Linda Gottlieb, Executive Producer; Doro Bachrach, Producer (ABC)

LEATHERSTOCKING TALES (Once Upon A Classic); Jay Rayvid, Executive Producer; Bob Walsh, Producer (PBS)

ONCE UPON A MIDNIGHT DREARY (CBS Library) Diane Asselin, Paul Asselin, Producers (CBS)

THE REVENGE OF RED CHIEF (ABC Weekend Special) Robert Chenault, Executive Producer (ABC)

CHILDREN'S INFORMATIONAL/INSTRUCTIONAL SERIES/SPECIAL (E-1620)

Emmy(s) to Executive Producer(s) and Producer(s)

MISTER ROGERS' NEIGHBORHOOD, Fred Rogers, Executive Producer; Hugh Martin, Producer (PBS)

SESAME STREET, Al Hyslop, Executive Producer; Dave Freyss, Producer (PBS)

THIRTY MINUTES, Joel Heller, Executive Producer; Madeline Amgott, Diego Echeverria, Horace Jenkens, Elizabeth Lawrence, Patti Obrow White, Robert Rubin, Producers (CBS)

MAKE 'EM LAUGH: A YOUNG PEOPLE'S COMEDY CONCERT (CBS Festival of Lively Arts For Young People) Jack Wohl, Bernard Rothman, Executive Producers; Robert Arnott, Sid Smith, Producers (CBS)

WHY A CONDUCTOR? (CBS Festival of Lively Arts For Young People) Kirk Browning, Executive Producer (CBS)

CHILDREN'S INFORMATION/INSTRUCTIONAL PROGRAMMING - SHORT FORMAT (E-1621)

Emmy(s) to Executive Producer(s) and Producer(s)

ABC SCHOOLHOUSE ROCK, Thomas Yohe, Executive Producer; George Newall, Radford Stone, Producers (ABC)

ASK NBC NEWS, Lester Crystal, Senior Executive Producer; Beryl Pfizer, Producer (NBC)

H.E.L.P.!!! (Dr. Henry's Emergency Lessons For People) Lynn Ahrens, Producer (ABC)

IN THE NEWS, Joel Heller, Executive Producer; Walter Lister, Producer (CBS)

WHEN YOU TURN OFF THE SET, TURN ON A BOOK, Mary Alice Dwyer, Executive Producer; George Newall, Tom Yohe, Producers (NBC)

INDIVIDUAL ACHIEVEMENT - CHILDREN'S PROGRAMMING

For a single episode of a series or for a special program. (Possibility of one Award, more than one Award or no Award).

PERFORMERS (E-1622)

MELISSA SUE ANDERSON; Which Mother Is Mine?, ABC Afterschool Special (ABC)

RENE AUBERJONOIS; Once Upon A Midnight Dreary, CBS Library (CBS)

MAIA DANZIGER; The Late Great Me: Story Of A Teenage Alcoholic, ABC Afterschool Special (ABC)

BOB KEESHAN; Captain Kangaroo (CBS)

BUTTERFLY McQUEEN; The Seven Wishes Of A Rich Kid, ABC Afterschool Special (ABC)

FRED ROGERS; Mister Rogers Goes To School, Mister Rogers' Neighborhood (PBS)

WRITERS (E-1623)

MARY BATTEN; Forces/Friday, 3-2-1 Contact (PBS)

DAVID AXELROD, JOSEPH BAILEY, ANDY BRACKMAN, RICHARD CAMP, SHERRY COBEN, BRUCE HART, CAROLE HART, MARIANNE MEYER; Hot Hero Sandwich, #5 (NBC)

JAN HARTMAN; The Late Great Me: Story Of A Teenage Alcoholic, ABC Afterschool Special (ABC)

JOHN O'TOOLE; The Leatherstocking Tales, Once Upon A Classic (PBS)

FRED ROGERS; Mister Rogers Goes To School, Mister Rogers' Neighborhood (PBS)

DIRECTORS (E-1624)

JOSEPH CONSENTINO; Divorce, Big Blue Marble (Synd)

ANTHONY LOVER; The Late Great Me: Story Of A Teenage Alcoholic, ABC Afterschool Special (ABC)

J. PHILIP MILLER; The Bloodhound Gang, 3-2-1 Contact (PBS)

ARTHUR ALLAN SEIDELMAN; Which Mother Is Mine? ABC Afterschool Special (ABC)

THOMAS TRBOVICH; Hot Hero Sandwich, #4 (NBC)

TECHNICAL DIRECTOR/ELECTRONIC CAMERA (E-1625)

WILLIAM P. KELLEY, Technical Director;

GENE MARTIN, JOHN PINTO, VINCENT DiPIETRO, THOMAS C. DEZENDORF, EDWARD CORSI, DONALD MULVANEY, Electronic Camerapersons; Hot Hero Sandwich, #4 (NBC)

STEVEN ZINK, Director of Photography; Sesame Street, #1320 - Puerto Rico (PBS)

AUDIO (E-1626)

GEORGE ALCH, Audio Engineer; A Special Gift, ABC Afterschool Special (ABC)

LEE DICHTER, Film Sound Mixer; Big Blue Marble, #105 (Synd)

PETER PAGE, Film Sound Mixer; Shark, Animals, Animals, Animals (ABC)

SCOTT A. SCHACHTER, JOEL G. SPECTOR, Tape Sound Mixers; Hot Hero Sandwich, #4 (NBC)

ASSOCIATE DIRECTION/VIDEO TAPE EDITING (E-1627)

JEROME HAGGART, HARVEY BERGER, BILL BRESHEARS, Videotape Editors; Hot Hero Sandwich, #1 (NBC)

CHARLES J. LIOTTA, JOHN A. SERVIDIO, GEORGE A. MAGDA, Videotape Editors; Time Out (NBC)

DON SULLIVAN, Associate Director; JAN MORGAN, Videotape Editor; Fast/Slow, 3-2-1 Contact (PBS)

CINEMATOGRAPHY (E-1628)

JOHN BEYMER, MIKE FASH; A Movie Star's Daughter, ABC Afterschool Special (ABC)

ROBERT COLLINS; Heartbreak Winner, (ABC Afterschool Special) (ABC)

TOM McDONOUGH; Mountain Climbing, Hot/Cold, 3-2-1 Contact (PBS)

DAVID SANDERSON; Once Upon A Midnight Dreary (CBS Library) (CBS)

ALEX THOMPSON; The Gold Bug, (ABC Weekend Special) (ABC)

FILM EDITING (E-1629)

NORMAN GAY; Communication - Mets, 3-2-1 Contact (PBS)

JACK SHOLDER; Noisy/Quiet - Hearing, 3-2-1 Contact (PBS)

VINCENT SKLENA; The Late Great Me: Story Of A Teenage Alcoholic, (ABC Afterschool Special) (ABC)

MERLE WORTH; Fast/Slow - Speed Up/Slow Down, 3-2-1- Contact (PBS)

MUSIC COMPOSITION/DIRECTION (E-1630)

TOM ANTHONY, Music Composer/Director; Theme, Noisy/Quiet, 3-2-1 Contact (PBS)
DANNY EPSTEIN, Music Director; Forces, 3-2-1 Contact (PBS)
WALT LEVINSKY, Music Composer; Forces, 3-2-1 Contact (PBS)
GLENN PAXTON, Music Composer; Which Mother Is Mine?, (ABC Afterschool Special) (ABC)
HOD DAVID SCHUDSON, Music Composer; Heartbreak Winner, ABC Afterschool Special (ABC)

ART DIRECTION/SCENIC DESIGN/SET DECORATION (E-1631)

RONALD BALDWIN, Art Director; Growth/Decay, 3-2-1 Contact (PBS)
SHAWN CALLAHAN, HENRY HUBBERT, Set Decorators; Captain Kangaroo (CBS)
BIL MIKULEWICZ, Art Director/Scenic Designer; Space Chicken And The Disappearing Stars, Captain Kangaroo (CBS)
NAT MONGIOI, Set Decorator; Hot/Cold, 3-2-1 Contact (PBS)

LIGHTING DIRECTION (E-1632)

TONY DiGIROLAMO, Lighting Director; Sesame Street, #1285 (PBS)

COSTUME/MAKE-UP/HAIR DESIGN (E-1633)

STEVEN ATHA, Make-up/Hair Designer; The Gold Bug, ABC Weekend Special (ABC)
BILL GRIFFIN, Costume Designer; Captain Kangaroo, #791030 (CBS)
CONSTANCE WEXLER, Costume Designer; Growth/Decay, 3-2-1 Contact (PBS)

GRAPHIC DESIGN (E-1634)

MICHAEL BAUGH; I Can Sing A Rainbow, Villa Alegre (PBS)
R. GREENBERG (Greenberg Associates); Noisy/Quiet, 3-2-1 Contact (PBS)
ROBERT POOK, Internal Graphics; Hot Hero Sandwich, #9 (NBC)

RELIGIOUS SERIES (E-1635)

Emmy(s) to Executive Producer(s) and Producer(s) (Possibility of one Award, more than one Award or no Award).

DIRECTIONS, Sid Darion, Executive Producer (ABC)
FOR OUR TIMES, Pamela Ilott, Executive Producer; Joseph Clement, Chalmers Dale, Marlene DiDonato, Ted Holmes, Producers (CBS)

RELIGIOUS SPECIALS (E-1636)

Emmy(s) to Executive Producer(s) and Producer(s). (Possibility of one Award, more than one Award, or no Award).

AS WE WITH CANDLES DO, Doris Ann, Executive Producer (NBC)
A CONVERSATION ON PASSOVER: Renewing Ancient Traditions; Doris Ann, Executive Producer; Martin Hoade, Producer (NBC)
A TALENT FOR LIFE: Jews of the Italian Renaissance; Helen Marmor, Executive Producer; Martin Hoade, Producer (NBC)

INDIVIDUAL ACHIEVEMENT IN RELIGIOUS PROGRAMMING

For a single episode of a series or for a special program (Possibility of one Award, more than one Award or no Award).

PERFORMERS (E-1637)

NORMAN ROSE, Narrator; A Talent For Life: Jews of the Italian Renaissance (NBC)
WILLIAM SCHALLERT; The Stableboy's Christmas, This Is The Life (Synd)
DEAN JAGGER; Independence And 76, This Is The Life (Synd)

WRITERS (E-1638)

RICHARD F. MOREAN; If No Birds Sang, This Is The Life (Synd)
ALLAN E. SLOANE; As We With Candles Do (NBC)
ARTHUR ZEGARD; Aging In Venice, Directions (ABC)

DIRECTOR (E-1639)

LYNWOOD KING; As We With Candles Do (NBC)

TECHNICAL DIRECTION/ELECTRONIC CAMERA (E-1640)

HEINO RIPP, Technical Director; AL CAMOIN, GENE MARTIN, DON MULVANEY, Electronic Camerapersons; As We With Candles Do (NBC)

AUDIO (E-1641)

JUSTUS TAYLOR, Sound Recordist; Seeds Of Revolution, Directions (ABC)

FILM EDITING (E-1642)

EDWARD R. WILLIAMS; A Talent For Life: Jews of the Italian Renaissance (NBC)

MUSIC COMPOSITION/DIRECTION (E-1643)

JOHN DUFFY, Music Composer/Director; A Talent For Life: Jews of The Italian Renaissance (NBC)

ART DIRECTION (E-1644)

THOMAS E. AZZARI; Stable Boy's Christmas, This Is The Life (Synd)

SPECIAL CLASSIFICATION - PROGRAM ACHIEVEMENT (E-1645)

Emmy(s) to Executive Producer(s) and Producer(s)

AMERICAN BANDSTAND, Dick Clark, Executive Producer; Larry Klein, Producer; Barry Glazer, Co-Producer (ABC)
FYI (with Hal Linden) Yanna Kroyt Brandt, Producer (ABC)
GISELLE, E. Grigorian, Producer (for Gosteleradio - USSR) (NBC)
A MEMORIAL TRIBUTE TO JIM CROCKETT, Russell Marash, Producer (for WGBH - Boston) (PBS)

SPECIAL CLASSIFICATION - INDIVIDUAL ACHIEVEMENT

(Possibility of one Award, more than one Award or no Award).

WRITERS (E-1646)

JAY REDACK, HARRY FRIEDMAN, BRIAN POLLACK, GARY JOHNSON, STEVE KREINBERG, JUSTIN ANTONOW, PHIL KELLARD; The Hollywood Squares (NBC)

DIRECTOR (E-1647)

MICHAEL R. GARGUILO; FYI (ABC)

CHOREOGRAPHER (E-1648)

JOSEPH CAROW; Nightmare Ballet Sequence, Witch's Sister, Chapter 2, Big Blue Marble (Synd)

PUPPET DESIGN AND CONSTRUCTION (E-1649)

DANNY SEAGREN; Miss Peach Of The Kelly School, The Annual Thanksgiving Turkey Day Raffle (Synd)

SPECIAL EVENTS COVERAGE (E-1650)

Possibility of one Award, more than one Award or no Award). Emmy(s) to Executive Producer(s) and Producer(s)

LA GIOCONDA, Jeanne Mulcahy, Executive Producer; John Goberman, Producer (For KCET - Los Angeles) (PBS)
MACY'S 53rd ANNUAL THANKSGIVING DAY PARADE, Dick Schneider, Producer (NBC)
91st TOURNAMENT OF ROSES PARADE, Dick Schneider, Producer (NBC)

INDIVIDUAL ACHIEVEMENT - SPECIAL EVENTS COVERAGE

(Possibility of one Award, more than one Award or no Award).

PERFORMERS (E-1651)

LUCIANO PAVAROTTI, La Gioconda (PBS)
RENATA SCOTTO, La Gioconda (PBS)

DIRECTOR (E-1652)

KIRK BROWNING; La Gioconda (PBS)

TECHNICAL DIRECTION/ELECTRONIC CAMERA (E-1653)

RON GRAFT, Technical Director; KENNETH PATTERSON, GARY EMRICK, LUIS A. FUERTE, DANIEL J. WEBB, Electronic Camerapersons; GREG HARMS, Video Engineer; La Gioconda (PBS)

AUDIO (E-1654)

TOM ANCELL, Audio Mixer; La Gioconda (PBS)

ASSOCIATE DIRECTION/VIDEOTAPE EDITING (E-1655)

VAL RIOLO, Associate Director; ROY STEWART, Videotape Editor; La Gioconda (PBS)

SCENIC DESIGN/SET DECORATION (E-1656)

ZACK BROWN; La Gioconda (PBS)

LIGHTING DIRECTION (E-1657)

KEN DETTLING; Lighting Director; La Gioconda (PBS)

COSTUME DESIGN (E-1658)

ZACK BROWN; La Gioconda (PBS)

INDIVIDUAL ACHIEVEMENT IN ANY AREA OF CREATIVE TECHNICAL CRAFTS

(Possibility of one Award, more than one Award or no Award).

TECHNICAL DIRECTION/ELECTRONIC CAMERA (E-1659)

MIKE MALOOF, Technical Director; DICK WATSON, GALEN WESTFALL, JOHN GILLIS, Electronic Camerapersons; Dinah! And Friends (Synd)

ASSOCIATE DIRECTION/VIDEOTAPE EDITING (E-1660)

BECKY GREENLAW, Associate Director; GARY NESTRA, Videotape Editor; The Mike Douglas Show (Synd)

MUSIC COMPOSITION/DIRECTION (E-1661)

JOE MASSIMINO, Music Composer/Director; The Mike Douglas Show (Synd)

LIVE SPORTS SPECIAL (E-1662)

Emmy(s) to Executive Producer(s) and Producer(s)

NCAA CHAMPIONSHIP BASKETBALL (Louisville vs. UCLA) - Don Ohlmeyer, Exec Producer; George Finkel, Producer (NBC)
SUPERBOWL XIV - Robert Stenner, Producer (CBS)
WIMBLEDON '80 - Don Ohlmeyer, Exec Producer; Geoffrey Mason, Producer; Ted Nathanson, Coproducer (NBC)
1980 WINTER OLYMPIC GAMES (Lake Placid, NY) - Roone Arledge, Exec Producer; Chuck Howard, Chet Forte, Dennis Lewin, Senior Producers; Bob Goodrich, Curt Gowdy Jr., Terry Jastrow, Terry O'Neil, Eleanor Riger, Ned Steckel, Doug Wilson, Producers; Jeff Ruhe, Coordinating Producer; Brice Weisman, Producer for "Up Close And Personals"; Robert Riger, Bud Greenspan, Special Projects Producers (ABC)
1979 WORLD SERIES (Baltimore Orioles vs. Pittsburgh Pirates) - Roone Arledge, Exec Producer; Chuck Howard, Producer (ABC)

LIVE SPORTS SERIES (E-1663)

Emmy(s) to Executive Producer(s) and Producer(s)

ABC'S NFL MONDAY NIGHT FOOTBALL - Roone Arledge, Exec Producer; Dennis Lewin, Producer (ABC)
NCAA BASKETBALL - Don Ohlmeyer, Exec Producer; George Finkel, Coordinating Producer; Ken Edmundson, Producer (NBC)
NCAA COLLEGE FOOTBALL - Roone Arledge, Exec Producer; Chuck Howard, Senior Producer; Bob Goodrich, Eleanor Riger, Curt Gowdy Jr., Dick Buffinton, Chris Carmody, Ned Steckel, Doug Wilson, Producers (ABC)
NFL FOOTBALL ON CBS - Bill Barnes, David Fox, Robert Stenner, Robert Rowe, Perry Smith, Chuck Will, Tom O'Neill, Howard Reifsnyder, Producers (CBS)
PGA ON CBS - Frank Chirkinian, Exec Producer-Producer (CBS)

SPORTS SPECIAL EDITING (E-1664)

Emmy(s) to Executive Producer(s) and Producer(s)

GOSSAMER ALBATROSS-FLIGHT OF IMAGINATION - Eddie Einhorn, Exec Producer; Joseph A. Thompson, Producer (CBS)
1980 INDIANAPOLIS 500 - Roone Arledge, Exec Producer; Chuck Howard, Bob Goodrich, Producers (ABC)
OLYMPIC TRIALS - Don Ohlmeyer, Exec Producer; Don McGuire, Coordinating Producer; Peter Diamond, Bernie Hoffman, Linda Jonsson, Producers (NBC)
UPSETS AND UNDERDOGS, HOT DOGS AND HEROES: THE STORY OF THE 1979 NFL SEASON - Steve Sabol, Ed Sabol, Producers (NBC)
1980 WINTER OLYMPIC PREVIEW SPECIAL: ADIRONDACK GOLD RUSH - Roone Arledge, Exec Producer; Terry O'Neill, Producer (ABC)

SPORTS SERIES EDITING (E-1665)

Emmy(s) to Executive Producer(s) and Producer(s)

ABC'S WIDE WORLD OF SPORTS - Roone Arledge, Exec Producer; Dennis Lewin, Coordinating Producer; Chuck Howard, Chet Forte, Joe Aceti, Carol Lehti, Terry O'Neil, Ned Steckel, Doug Wilson, Bob Goodrich, Producers (ABC)
AMERICAN SPORTSMAN - Roone Arledge, Exec Producer; John Wilcox, Series Producer; Robert Duncan, Curt Gowdy, Robert Nixon, Producers (ABC)
CBS SPORTS SPECTACULAR - Eddie Einhorn, Exec Producer; Ed Goren, Coordinating Producer; David Fox, Ted Shaker, Perry Smith, Brad Schrieber, Charles Milton, Jim Silman, Michael Pearl, Dave Berman, Ken Squire, Sherman Eagan, Tom O'Neill, Tony Verna, Robert Stenner, Howard Reifsynder, Producers (CBS)
NFL GAME OF THE WEEK - Ed Sabol, Exec Producer; Steve Sabol, Producer (Synd)
THIS WEEK IN BASEBALL - Larry Parker, Exec Producer; Jody Shapiro, Geoff Belinfante, Supervising Producers; Tim Parker, Bill Brown, Producers (Synd)

SPORTS PERSONALITY (E-1666)

Emmy to sports personality for overall broadcasting achievement

HOWARD COSELL (ABC)
FRANK GIFFORD (ABC)
KEITH JACKSON (ABC)
AL McGUIRE (NBC)
JIM McKAY (ABC)
DON MEREDITH (ABC)
VIN SCULLY (CBS)
JACK WHITAKER (CBS)

DIRECTING IN SPORTS PROGRAMMING (E-1667)

Emmy(s) to Director(s) for a series, episode of a series of for a special

1980 WINTER OLYMPIC GAMES (Lake Placid, NY) - Joe Aceti, Roger Goodman, Coordinating Directors; Chet Forte, John DeLisa, Jack Gallivan, Mac Hemion, Craig Janoff, Jim Jennett, Larry Kamm, Bob Lanning, Raimo Piltz, Andy Sidaris, Ken Wolfe, Lou Volpicelli, Larry Cavolina, Ron Harrison, Directors (ABC)
THE MASTERS - Frank Chirkinian, Robert Dailey (CBS)
1979 WORLD SERIES - Chet Forte (ABC)
SUPER BOWL XIV - Sandy Grossman (CBS)
WIMBLEDON '80 (Men's Final-McEnroe vs. Borg) - Ted Nathanson (NBC)
NFL FOOTBALL ON CBS - Duke Struck, Robert Dailey, Sandy Grossman, Marvin Mews, Jim Silman, Robert Dunphy, Chris Erskine, Tony Verna, John McDonough (CBS)
ABC'S WIDE WORLD OF SPORTS (World Figure Skating Championships) - Doug Wilson (ABC)

FOLLOWING ARE AREAS WHERE THERE IS A POSSIBILITY OF ONE WINNER, MORE THAN ONE WINNER OR NO WINNER IN EACH AREA.

INDIVIDUAL ACHIEVEMENT IN SPORTS PROGRAMMING (E-1668)

Emmy(s) to individual(s) for a single episode of a series or for a special

ABC'S NFL MONDAY NIGHT FOOTBALL - Ron Ackerman, Tom Capace, Phil Mollica, Cyril Tywang, Videotape Editors (ABC)
NFL GAME OF THE WEEK - Bob Angelo, Ernie Ernst, Jay Gerber, Stan Leshner, Don Marx, Hank McElwee, Howard Neff, Jack Newman, Steve Sabol, Bob Smith, Art Spiller, Phil Tuckett, Cinematographers (Synd)
UP CLOSE AND PERSONALS (1980 Winter Olympic Games, Lake Placid, NY) - Angelo Bernarducci, Jon Day, Sam Fine, John Petersen, Vincent Reda, Anthony Scandiffio, Wayne Weiss, Ted Winterburn, Film Editors (ABC)
1980 WINTER OLYMPIC GAMES (Lake Placid, NY) - Barbara Bowman, Paul Fanelli, Charles Gardner, Marvin Gench, Roger Haenelt, Connie Kraus, Alex Moskovic, Lou Rende, Nathan Rogers, Erskine Roberts, Mario Schenchman, Ann Stone, Arthur Volk, Frank Guigliano, Videotape Editors (ABC)
UP CLOSE AND PERSONALS (1980 Winter Olympic Games, Lake Placid, NY) - Trevor Carless, George Hause, Jim Lynch, Jan Schulte, **Location Sound Mixers (ABC)**
ABC'S NFL MONDAY NIGHT FOOTBALL - Loren Coltran, Technical Manager; Bill Morris, Technical Director; Andrew J. Armentani, Jack Dorfman, Steve Nikifor, Joe Cotugno, Gary Donatelli, Jim Heneghan, Roy Hutchings, Tom O'Connell, Jack Savoy, Dick Spanos, Electronic Cameramen (ABC)
1980 WINTER OLYMPIC GAMES (Lake Placid, NY) - Roger Goodman, Creative Director in charge; Hy Bley, Director of Graphic Arts; Maxwell Berry, Director of Electronic Graphics (ABC)
1980 WINTER OLYMPIC GAMES (Lake Placid, NY) - Mel Handelsman, Lighting Director (ABC)

UP CLOSE AND PERSONALS (1980 Winter Olympic Games, Lake Placid, NY) - Harvey Harrison, Harry Hart, Don Shapiro, Cinematographers (ABC)
1980 WINTER OLYMPIC GAMES (Lake Placid, NY) - Dick Horan, Robert Armbruster, Bill Blumel, Coach Coltran, Geoffrey Felger, Mike Jochim, Jacques Lesgards, Bill Maier, Joseph Polito, Elliott R. Reed, Martin Sandberg, Tony Versley, Mike Fisher, Joseph Kresnicka, B. Untiedt, Technical Managers; Les Weiss, Werner Gunther, Chester Mazurek, William Morris, Joseph Schiavo, Joe Nesi, E. Buttleman, J. Allen, G. Bucci, H. Falk, D. Smith, Technical Directors; Diane Cates, Gary Donatelli, Danny LaMothe, Charles Mitchell, Steve Nikifor, William Sullivan, Don Farnum, Rick Knipe, Morton Kipow, Joseph Montesano (minicam), Electronic Cameramen (ABC)
1980 WINTER OLYMPIC GAMES (Lake Placid, NY) - Carol Lehti, Rob Beiner, Jeff Cohan, Vince DeDario, Bob Dekas, Lou Frederick, Bob Hersh, Ronald Hawkins, Jean MacLean, Norm Samet, Howard Shapiro, Toni Slotkin, Stan Spiro, Doug Towey, Pat Tuite, Associate Directors (live-tape) (ABC)
1980 WINTER OLYMPIC GAMES (Lake Placid, NY, including original theme "Give It All You Got") - Chuck Mangione, Music Composer-Director (ABC)
1980 WINTER OLYMPIC GAMES (Lake Placid, NY) - Dick Roes, Jim Davis, Tom Glazner, Jack Hughes, George Meyer, Joe Vernum, Jonathan M. Lory, Gary Larson, D. Nelson, J. Eaton, R. Emerson, A. Morgenstern, Live-Tape Sound Mixers (ABC)
THE MASTERS - Lou Scannapieco, Arthur Tinn, Engineering Supervisors; Charles D'Onofrio, Sandy Bell, Technical Directors; George Klimcsak, George Rothweller, David Graham, Herman Lang, Hans Singer, Harry Haigood, Rick Blane, Frank McSpedon, Barry Drago, Jim Murphy, Mike Zwick, George Naeder, Jim McCarthy, Al Loreto, Al Diamond, Mike English, John Lincoln, Pat McBride, Stan Gould, Joe Sokota, Neil McCaffrey, Bob Welsh, David Finch, Gordon Sweeney, Gorm Erickson, Electronic Cameramen (CBS)

SPECIAL CLASSIFICATION OF PROGRAM AND INDIVIDUAL ACHIEVEMENT

Emmy(s) to Executive Producer(s) and Producer(s) for program; Emmy(s) to individual(s) for individual achievement; for programs and individual achievements which are so unique and different that they do not fall in any previous categories or areas

PROGRAM (E-1669)

A TRIBUTE TO THURMAN MUNSON - (Preempted regular Major League Baseball pregame programming - Terry Ewert, Producer (NBC)

INDIVIDUAL (E-1670)

JERRY P. CARUSO, HARRY SMITH, creators-developers of radio frequency golf cup mic - "Bob Hope Golf Classic" (NBC)

NEWS AND DOCUMENTARIES

PROGRAMS AND PROGRAM SEGMENTS (E-1671)

Emmy(s) to Producer(s) and Correspondent(s)

ABORTED RAID BROADCAST (CBS Evening News with Walter Cronkite) (CBS) Sanford Socolow, Executive Producer; Mark Harrington, Sam Roberts, Linda Mason & Lane Venardos, Producers; Walter Cronkite, Doug Tunnell, Ike Pappas, Lesley Stahl, Phil Jones & Marvin Kalb, Correspondents
THE POPE IN AMERICA: JOURNEY FOR UNDERSTANDING (ABC) Jeff Gralnick, Producer, Frank Reynolds, Correspondent
POPE JOHN PAUL II IN POLAND (NBC) Helen Marmor, Producer; Philip Scharper & Sally Scharper, Correspondents
POST ELECTION SPECIAL EDITION (ABC News, "Nightline") (ABC) Jeff Gralnick & William Lord, Producers; Ted Koppel, Frank Reynolds, Barbara Walters, Max Robinson & Lynn Sherr, Correspondents
AFTER THE DELUGE (Segment: CBS News "Sunday Morning") (CBS) James Houtrides, Producer; Ed Rabel, Correspondent

FISHING BOAT SINKS (Segment: NBC Nightly News) (NBC) Nancy Fernandez & Jeff Weinstock, Producers; Lee McCarthy, Correspondent

THE FIXER (Segment: ABC News "20/20') (ABC) Lowell Bergman, Producer; Geraldo Rivera, Correspondent

HOSTAGES--300 DAYS (Segment: CBS Evening News with Walter Cronkite) (CBS) Rita Braver, Producer; Diane Sawyer, Correspondent

IRAN-IRAQ WAR (5-part Segment: CBS News with Walter Cronkite) (CBS) William Willson, Producer; Larry Pintak, Correspondent

MURDER OF A CORRESPONDENT (Segment: ABC World News Tonight) (6/21/79) (ABC) Ken Luckoff, Producer; Al Dale, Correspondent

CAMPAIGN REPORT # 3: THE NEW RIGHT, THE EVANGELICALS (Bill Moyers' Journal) (PBS) Martin Koughan, Producer; Bill Moyers, Correspondent

CAMPAIGN REPORT # 8: ESSENTIAL CARTER/ESSENTIAL REAGAN (Bill Moyers' Journal) (PBS) Randy Bean & Howard Weinberg, Producers; Bill Moyers, Correspondent

CBS REPORTS: MIAMI: THE TRIAL THAT SPARKED THE RIOTS (CBS) Eric F. Saltzman, Producer; Ed Bradley, Correspondent

LIGHTS, CAMERA

LIGHTS, CAMERAS. . .POLITICS (ABC News, "Closeup") (ABC) Ann G Black & Tom Priestley, Producers; Richard Reeves, Correspondent

NBC WHITE PAPER: WE'RE MOVING UP: THE HISPANIC MIGRATION (NBC) Anthony Potter, Producer; Bill McLaughlin, Correspondent

B-52'S: TOO OLD TO FLY? (Segment: ABC News, "20/20") (ABC) Richard Clark, Producer; Jules Bergman, Correspondent

CHILD SNATCHING (Segment: ABC News, "20/20") (ABC) David Meyer, Producer; Bob Brown, Correspondent

ENERGY ALTERNATIVES: BEATING OPEC NOW (3-part Special Assignment Segment: ABC World News Tonight) (ABC) Sharon Young, Producer; Roger Peterson, Correspondent

THE IRAN FILE (Segment: CBS News, "60 Minutes") (CBS) Barry Lando, Producer; Mike Wallace, Correspondent

MONEY TALKS (Segment: ABC News "20/20) (ABC) Martin Clancy, Producer; Barry Serafin, Correspondent

NICARAGUA (Segment: ABC News, "20/20") (ABC) Lowell Bergman & Neil Cunningham, Producers; Dave Marash, Correspondent

ONWARD CHRISTIAN VOTERS (Segment: CBS News, "60 Minutes") (CBS) Joel Bernstein, Producer; Dan Rather, Correspondent

TOO LITTLE, TOO LATE? (Segment: CBS News, "Magazine") (CBS) Janet Roach, Producer; Ed Bradley, Correspondent

HOT SHELLS: U.S. ARMS FOR SOUTH AFRICA ("World") (PBS) William Cran, Producer

NBC REPORTS: THE MIGRANTS, 1980 (NBC) Morton Silverstein, Producer; Chris Wallace, Correspondent

A PLAGUE ON OUR CHILDREN ("Nova") (PBS) Robert Richter, Producer/Correspondent

SONG OF THE CANARY (PBS) Josh Hanig & David Davis, Producers

WHO KILLED GEORGI MARKOV? ("World") (PBS) Phil Harding, Producer; Michael Cockerell, Correspondent

ARSON FOR PROFIT--PARTS I & II (Segment: ABC News, "20/20") (ABC) Peter Lance, Producer; Geraldo Rivera, Correspondent

CARNIVAL CAPERS (Segment: ABC News, "20/20") (ABC) Barbara Newman, Producer; Geraldo Rivera, Correspondent

EQUAL JUSTICE? (Segment: CBS News, "60 Minutes") (CBS) Leslie Edwards, Producer; Dan Rather, Correspondent

INJUSTICE FOR ALL (Segment: ABC News, "20/20") (4/17/80) (ABC) Charles C. Thompson, Producer; Geraldo Rivera, Correspondent

PRISON BENEFITS (Segment: NBC News, "Prime Time Saturday") (NBC) Beth Polson, Producer; Jack Perkins, Correspondent

SCIENTOLOGY: THE CLEARWATER CONSPIRACY (Segment: CBS News, "60 Minutes") (CBS) Allan Maraynes, Producer; Mike Wallace, Correspondent

URETHANE (Segment: NBC News, "Prime Time Saturday") (NBC) Peter Jeffries, Producer; John Dancy, Correspondent

VW BEETLE: THE HIDDEN DANGER (Segment: ABC News, "20/20") (ABC) Jeff Diamond, Producer; Sylvia Chase, Correspondent

CBS REPORTS: TEDDY (CBS) Andrew Lack, Producer; Roger Mudd, Interviewer

A CONVERSATION WITH ZBIGNIEW BRZEZINSKI (Bill Moyers' Journal) (PBS) Betsy McCarthy, Producer; Bill Moyers, Interviewer

JUDGE: PARTS I & II (Bill Moyers' Journal) (PBS) Randy Bean, Producer; Bill Moyers, Interviewer

LORIN HOLLANDER (Old Friends. . .New Friends) (PBS) Jayne Adair, Producer; Fred Rogers, Interviewer

BETTE DAVIS (Segment: CBS News, "60 Minutes") (CBS) Nancy Lea, Producer; Mike Wallace, Interviewer

HERE'S. . .JOHNNY! (Segment: CBS News "60 Minutes") (CBS) David Lowe, Jr., Producer; Mike Wallace, Interviewer

THE UMP (RON LUCIANO) (Segment: ABC News, "20/20") (ABC) Bernard I. Cohen, Producer/Interviewer

AMERICAN DREAM, AMERICAN NIGHTMARE (CBS News Special Report) (CBS) Perry Wolff, Executive Producer; Shareen Blair Brysac, Producer; Harry Reasoner, Correspondent

CBS REPORTS: ON THE ROAD (CBS) Bernard Birnbaum & Charles Kuralt, Producers; Charles Kuralt, Correspondent

CBS REPORTS: WHAT SHALL WE DO ABOUT MOTHER? (CBS) Judy Reemtsma, Producer; Marlene Sanders, Correspondent

CHOOSING SUICIDE (PBS) Richard Ellison, Producer/Correspondent

DIVE TO THE EDGE OF CREATION (National Geographic Special) (PBS) James Lipscomb, Producer

THE INVISIBLE WORLD (National Geographic Special) (PBS) Alex Pomasanoff, Producer

MYSTERIES OF THE MIND (National Geographic Special) (PBS) Irwin Rosten, Producer

NBC REPORTS: TO BE A DOCTOR (NBC) Tom Spain, Producer; Tom Brokaw, Correspondent

TO DIE FOR IRELAND (ABC News, "Closeup") (ABC) Alan Raymond & Susan Raymond, Producers

ANNE LINDBERGH (Segment: CBS News "60 Minutes) (CBS) Joseph Wershba, Producer; Morley Safer, Correspondent

ANNIE (Segment: NBC News, "Prime Time Saturday") (NBC) Fred Flamenhaft, Producer; Jessica Savitch, Correspondent

BACK IN THE WORLD; VIETNAM VETS (Segment: CBS News, "Sunday Morning") (CBS) William Moran, Producer; Jerry Landay, Correspondent

BILLY JOEL (Segment: ABC News "20/20") (ABC) Donovan Moore, Producer; Tom Hoving, Correspondent

BILLY MARTIN #1 (Segment: ABC News, "20/20") (ABC) Peggy Brim, Producer; Sylvia Chase, Correspondent

THE ENDLESS WAR (Segment: ABC News "20/20") (ABC) Phyllis McGrady, Producer; Sylvia Chase, Correspondent

GEORGE BURNS: AN UPDATE (Segment: ABC News, "20/20") (ABC) Betsy Osha, Producer; Bob Brown, Producer

HEART TRANSPLANT (Segment: NBC News, "Prime Time Sunday") (NBC) Robert Eaton, George Lewis & Arthur Lord, Producers; Jack Perkins, Correspondent

PLENTY FOR EVERYONE (Segment: CBS News, "Magazine") (CBS) Jean Abounader, Producer; Sharron Lovejoy, Correspondent

A TALE OF TWO CITIES (Segment: CBS News, "Sunday Morning") (9/9/79) (CBS) Robert Northshield, Executive Producer; Elliot Bernstein, Producer; Tom Fenton & Don Kladstrup, Correspondents

TO SAVE A LIFE (Segment: ABC News, "20/20") (ABC) Peter W. Kunhardt, Producer; Tom Jarriel, Correspondent

WALKING SMALL IN PITKIN COUNTY (Segment: CBS News, "60 Minutes") (CBS) Greg Cooke, Producer; Morley Safer, Correspondent

INDIVIDUAL(S)
Emmy(s) to Individual(s)

WRITERS (E-1672)

MALCOLM CLARKE & RAY BRADBURY Infinite Horizons: Space Beyond Apollo (ABC)

LLOYD DOBYNS & REUVEN FRANK NBC White Paper: If Japan Can, Why Can't We? (NBC)

BILL MOYERS Our Times (Bill Moyers' Journal) (PBS)

ROGER MUDD CBS Reports: Teddy (CBS)

IRWIN ROSTEN Mysteries of the Mind (National Geographic Special) (PBS)

MARLENE SANDERS & JUDY TOWERS REEMTSMA CBS Reports: What Shall We Do About Mother? (CBS)

MORTON SILVERSTEIN & CHRIS WALLACE NBC Reports: The Migrants, 1980 (NBC)

PERRY WOLFF American Dream, American Nightmare (CBS News Special Report) (CBS)

DIRECTORS (E-1673)

PATRICK M. COOK Death in a Southwest Prison (ABC News, "Closeup") (ABC)
ANDREW LACK Inside Afghanistan (Segment: CBS News, "60 Minutes") (CBS)
RAY LOCKHART NBC White Paper: If Japan Can, Why Can't We? (NBC)
ROGER PHENIX NBC Reports: To Be a Doctor (NBC)
DICK SCHNEIDER Who's Choosing Our President? (Bill Moyers' Journal) (PBS)
MORTON SILVERSTEIN NBC Reports: The Migrants, 1980 (NBC)

TECHNICAL DIRECTION/ELECTRONIC CAMERA (E-1674)

JON ALPERT, Camera; Third Avenue: Only the Strong Survive (PBS)
DON BASIL, Camera; The Ump (Ron Luciano) (Segment: ABC News, "20/20") (ABC)
JACK CLARK, Camera; Shooting of Bill Stuart–Nicaragua (Segment: ABC World News Tonight) (ABC)
J. RANDALL FAIRBAIRN, Camera; Haitians Expelled From Cayo Lobos (3-part Segment: NBC Nightly News) (NBC)
MARTIN MURPHY, BOB McKENNY & JOHN WASZAK, Engineering Supervisors; GILBERT A. MILLER, BOB VERNUM & JOSEPH DUENAS, Technical Directors; Democratic National Convention: CBS News, "Campaign '80" (CBS)

CINEMATOGRAPHY (E-1675)

GREGORY ANDRACKE Infinite Horizons: Space Beyond Apollo (ABC)
MIKE EDWARDS Inside Afghanistan (Segment: CBS News, "60 Minutes") (CBS)
DAVID GRUBIN The World of David Rockefeller (Bill Moyers' Journal) (PBS)
ALAN RAYMOND To Die For Ireland (ABC News, "Closeup") (ABC)
TOM SPAIN & DAVID GRUBIN NBC Reports: To Be a Doctor (NBC)
IVAN STRASBURG & RICHARD ROY Escape From Justice: Nazi War Criminals in America (ABC News, "Closeup") (ABC)

ASSOCIATE DIRECTION AND/OR VIDEOTAPE EDITING (E-1676)

JERRY CHERNAK, Associate Director; THOMAS R. GUBAR, Videotape Editor; The Ump (Ron Luciano) (Segment: ABC News, "20/20") (ABC)
JOHN GODFREY, JON ALPERT & KEIKO TSUNO, Videotape Editors; Third Avenue: Only the Strong Survive (PBS)
RUTH NEUWALD, Videotape Editor; CBS Reports: Miami: The Trial That Sparked The Riots (CBS)
DENNIS S. OSIK, Associate Director; EDWARD BUDA, CONSUELO GONZALEZ & PETER MURPHY, Videotape Editors; The Elvis Coverup (Segment: ABC News, "20/20") (ABC)
MITCHEL RUDICK, Videotape Editor; The Iran File (Segment: CBS News, "60 Minutes) (CBS)
TRESSA ANNE VERNA, Videotape Editor; Terry Bradshaw--Cashing In (Segment: NBC News, "Prime Time Saturday") (NBC)

FILM EDITING (E-1677)

KENNETH J. DALGLISH Leonard Bernstein (Segment: CBS News, "60 Minutes") (CBS)
RICHARD MANICHELLO Pavarotti (Segment: CBS News, "60 Minutes") (CBS)
MAURICE MURAD CBS Reports: The Saudis (CBS)
STEVE SHEPPARD Inside Afghanistan (Segment: CBS News, "60 Minutes") (CBS)
KENNETH E. WERNER & NILS RASMUSSEN Death in a Southwest Prison (ABC News, "Closeup") (ABC)
MERLE WORTH NBC Reports: To Be a Doctor (NBC)

AUDIO (E-1678)

JIM CEFALO, Sound Recordist; Shooting of Bill Stuart – Nicaragua (Segment: ABC World News Tonight) (ABC)
ANTHONY GAMBINO, Sound Recordist; The Ump (Ron Luciano) (Seg-
ment: ABC News, "20/20") (ABC)
JOHN HAMPTON, Sound Recordist -- Court; RON YOSHIDA, Sound Recordist -- Location; The Shooting of Big Man: Anatomy of a Criminal Case (ABC News, "Closeup") (ABC)
ROBERT ROGOW, Location Sound Recordist; JOEL DULBERG, Re-Recording Mixer; Pavarotti (Segment: CBS News, "60 Minutes") (CBS)

SCENIC/SET DESIGN (E-1679)

DAVID M. CLARK, IMERO FIORENTINO & GEORGE HONCHAR, Scenic Designers; Democratic National Convention (POOL)
VICTOR PAGANUZZI & NEIL J. DELUCA, Set Designers; Sports (Segment: CBS News, "Morning with Charles Kuralt") (CBS)

LIGHTING DIRECTION (E-1680)

CARL VITELLI, JR. & EVERETT MELOSH (ABC), Lighting Directors; Democratic National Convention (POOL)

GRAPHIC DESIGN (E-1681)

WILLIAM SUNSHINE & ELLEN DENTON, Graphic Designers; Pavarotti (Segment: CBS News, "60 Minutes") (CBS)

MUSIC (E-1682)

LIONEL HAMPTON, No Maps On My Taps (PBS)

INTERNATIONAL AWARDS

DOCUMENTARY (E-1683)

60 MINUTES, TCN Channel Nine, Australia
THE SECRET HOSPITAL, PART I, RAMPTON, Yorkshire Television Ltd. United Kingdom
PROCESSOR PER STUPRO (TRIAL FOR RAPE), RAI, Rete 2, Italy

PERFORMING ARTS (E-1684)

ELEGIES FOR THE DEATHS OF THREE SPANISH POTES, Allegro Films United Kingdom
THE MEDIUM BY GIAN CARLO MENOTTI, Comus/CBC, Canada
OSCAR PETERSON-CANADIANA SUITE, CBC, Canada

POPULAR ARTS (E-1685)

TOLLER CRANSTON - DREAM WEAVER, CBC Canada
RICH LITTLE'S CHRISTMAS CAROL, Tel Pro/CBC, Canada
SOME MOTHERS DO 'AVE 'EM, BBC, United Kingdom

DRAMA (E-1686)

COLLISION COURSE, Granada Television International, Ltd., United Kingdom
ON GIANTS SHOULDERS, BBC, United Kingdom
THOMAS GUERIN. . .RETRAITE Societe Nationale De Programme, FR 3, France

INTERNATIONAL DIRECTORATE AWARD (E-1687)

PRIX ITALIA

THE NATIONAL AWARD FOR COMMUNITY SERVICE (E-1688)

THE WELFARE BLUES: NEW YORK CITY (WABC-TV) New York, NY
A CASE OF NEGLECT (KPNX-TV) Phoenix, AZ.
ANGEL DEATH (KTTV-TV) Los Angeles, CA.
WEDNESDAY'S CHILD (KOCO-TV) Oklahoma City, OK.
POLITICS OF POISON (KRON-TV) San Francisco, CA.
AGENT ORANGE: THE HUMAN HARVEST (WBBM-TV) Chicago, IL.
SLOW MOTION TRAGEDY (WSM-TV) Nashville, TN.
SEVEN ON YOUR SIDE (WJLA-TV) Washington, DC.
THE LAST HURRAH: CHICAGO STYLE (WLS-TV) Chicago, IL.
PINEY: THE RURAL FACE OF NEW JERSEY(WNEW-TV) New York, NY.
EMERGENCY MEDICAL SERVICES: PROBE (WDVM-TV) Washington, DC.

TRUSTEES AWARD (E-1689)

LEONARD H. GOLDENSON for his role in forming the American Broadcasting Corp. and guiding its growth to become one of the leading forces in American communications.

ENGINEERING AWARDS (E-1690)

PANASONIC CO. for the introduction of digital techniques for the production of video special effects.
NIPPON ELECTRIC CO., QUANTEL LTD., and VITAL INDUSTRIES for the development and implementation of digital techniques for the production of video special effects.

1980/81

PRIMETIME

COMEDY SERIES (E-1691)

Emmy(s) to Executive Producer(s) and/or Producer(s)
BARNEY MILLER, Danny Arnold, Executive Producer; Tony Sheehan, Noam Pitlik, Producers; Gary Shaw, Co-Producer (ABC)
M*A*S*H, Burt Metcalfe, Executive Producer; John Rappaport, Producer (CBS)
SOAP, Paul Junger Witt, Tony Thomas, Susan Harris, Executive Producers; Stu Silver, Dick Clair, Jenna McMahon, Producers (ABC)
TAXI, James L. Brooks, Stan Daniels, Ed Weinberger, Executive Producers; Glen Charles, Les Charles, Producers (ABC)
WKRP IN CINCINNATI, Hugh Wilson, Executive Producer; Rod Daniel, Supervising Producer; Blake Hunter, Steven Kampmann, Peter Torokvei, Producers (CBS)

DRAMA SERIES (E-1692)

Emmy(s) to Executive Producer(s) and/or Producer(s)
DALLAS, Philip Capice, Executive Producer; Leonard Katzman, Producer (CBS)
HILL STREET BLUES, Steven Bochco, Michael Kozoll, Executive Producers; Gregory Hoblit, Producer (NBC)
LOU GRANT, Gene Reynolds, Executive Producer; Seth Freeman, Producer (CBS)
QUINCY, David Moessinger, Executive Producer; William O. Cairncross, Lester William Berke, Supervising Producers; Sam Egan, Producer (NBC)
THE WHITE SHADOW, Bruce Paltrow, Executive Producer; Mark Tinker, Producer; John Masius Coordinating Producer (CBS)

LIMITED SERIES (E-1693)

Emmy(s) to Executive Producer(s) and/or Producer(s)
JOHN STEINBECK'S EAST OF EDEN, Mace Neufeld, Executive Producer; Barney Rosenzweig, Producer; Ken Wales, Co-Producer (ABC)
MASADA, George Eckstein, Producer (ABC)
RUMPOLE OF THE BAILEY, (Mystery!), Joan Wilson, Series Producer; Jacqueline Davis, Producer (PBS)
SHOGUN, James Clavell, Executive Producer, Eric Bercovici, Producer (NBC)
TINKER, TAILOR, SOLDIER, SPY, (Great Performances), Jac Venza, Executive Producer; Jonathan Powell, Producer; Sam Paul, Series Producer (PBS)

VARIETY, MUSIC OR COMEDY PROGRAM (E-1694)

For A Variety Or Music Special Or Series Or For A Comedy Special. Emmy(s) to Executive Producer(s) and/or Producer(s) and Star(s), if Applicable
THE AMERICAN FILM INSTITUTE SALUTE TO FRED ASTAIRE, George Stevens, Jr., Producer. (CBS)
THE BENNY HILL SHOW, Philip Jones, John Robins, Dennis Kirkland, Mark Stuart, Keith Beckett, Producers; Benny Hill, Star. (SERIES) (SYN)
LILY: SOLD OUT, Lily Tomlin, Jane Wagner, Executive Producers; Rocco Urbisci, Producer; Lily Tomlin, Star. (CBS)

THE MUPPET SHOW, David Lazer, Executive Producer; Jim Henson, Producer; Frank Oz, Jerry Nelson, Richard Hunt, Dave Goelz, Louise Gold, Steve Whitmire, Kathryn Mullen, Brian Muehl, Karen Prell, Jim Henson, Stars. (SERIES) (SYN)
THE TONIGHT SHOW STARRING JOHNNY CARSON, Fred de Cordova, Producer; Peter Lasally, Co-Producer; Johnny Carson, Star. (SERIES) (NBC)

DRAMA SPECIAL (E-1695)

Emmy(s) to Executive Producer(s) and/or Producer(s)
EVITA PERON, Harry Evans Sloan, Lawrence L. Kuppin, Selma Jaffe, Executive Producers; Fred Baum, Supervising Producer; Marvin Chomsky, Producer; David R. Ames, Co-Producer. (NBC)
FALLEN ANGEL, Jim Green, Allen Epstein, Executive Producers; Lew Hunter, Audrey Blasdel-Goddard, Producers. (CBS)
PLAYING FOR TIME, Linda Yellen, Executive Producer; Linda Yellen, Producer, John E. Quill, Co-Producer. (CBS)
THE SHADOW BOX, Jill Marti, Susan Kendall Newman, Producers. (ABC)
THE WOMEN'S ROOM, Philip Mandelker, Executive Producer; Glenn Jordan, Supervising Producer; Kip Gowans, Anna Cottle, Producers. (ABC)

CLASSICAL PROGRAM IN THE PERFORMING ARTS (E-1696)

For a Special or a Series. Emmy(s) to Executive Producers(s) and/or Producer(s) and Star(s) if Applicable
JOAN SUTHERLAND, MARILYN HORNE AND LUCIANO PAVAROTTI LIVE FROM LINCOLN CENTER, John Goberman, Series Producer; Joan Sutherland, Marilyn Horne, Luciano Pavarotti, Stars. (PBS)
A LINCOLN CENTER SPECIAL: BEVERLY! HER FAREWELL PERFORMANCE, (Great Performances), John Goberman, Producer; Beverly Sills, Star. (PBS)
LIVE FROM STUDIO 8H: AN EVENING OF JEROME ROBBIN'S BALLETS WITH MEMBERS OF THE NEW YORK CITY BALLET, Alvin Cooperman, Judith De Paul, Producers (NBC)
NUREYEV AND THE JOFFREY BALLET/IN TRIBUTE TO NIJINSKY, (Dance In America), Jac Venza, Executive Producer; Emile Ardolino, Judy Kinberg, Producers; Rudolf Nureyev, Star. (PBS)
ZUBIN MEHTA, ITZHAK PERLMAN AND PINCHAS ZUKERMAN CELEBRATE ISAAC STERN'S 60TH BIRTHDAY, (Live From Lincoln Center), John Goberman, Series Producer; Zubin Mehta, Itzhak Perlman, Pinchas Zukerman, Isaac Stern, Stars. (PBS)

INFORMATIONAL SPECIAL (E-1697)

Emmy(s) to Executive Producer(s) and/or Producer(s)
THE BODY HUMAN: THE BIONIC BREAKTHROUGH, Thomas W. Moore, Executive Producer; Robert E. Fuisz, M.D., Alfred R. Kelman, Producers; Charles A. Bangert, Nancy Smith, Co-Producers. (CBS)
THE BODY HUMAN: THE SEXES II, Thomas W. Moore, Executive Producer; Alfred R. Kelman, Robert E. Fuisz, M.D., Producers; Charles A. Bangert, Vivian R. Moss, Co-Producers. (CBS)
GORILLA, (National Geographic Special), Dennis B. Kane, Thomas Skinner, Executive Producers; Barbara Jampel, Producer. (PBS)
MAKING M*A*S*H, Michael Hirsch, Producer. (PBS)
STARRING KATHARINE HEPBURN, George Page, Executive Producer; David Heeley, Producer. (PBS)

INFORMATIONAL SERIES (E-1698)

Emmy(s) to Executive Producer(s) and/or Producer(s)
THE BARBARA WALTERS SPECIALS, Don Mischer, Executive Producer; Jo Ann Goldberg, Producer (ABC)
COSMOS, Adrian Malone, Executive Producer; Geoffrey Haines-Stiles, David Kennard, Senior Producers; Gregory Andorfer, Producer (PBS)
PROFILE: LILLIAN HELLMAN, David Dowe, Producer (PBS)
REAL PEOPLE, George Schlatter, Executive Producer; John Barbour, Bob Wynn, Producers (NBC)
STEVE ALLEN'S MEETING OF MINDS, Loring d'Usseau, Producer (PBS)

ANIMATED PROGRAM (E-1699)

For a Series or a Special. Emmy(s) to Executive Producer(s) and/or Producer(s)

BUGS BUNNY: ALL AMERICAN HERO, Hal Geer, Executive Producer; Friz Freleng, Producer. (CBS)

FAERIES, Thomas W. Moore, Jean Moore Edwards, Anne E. Upson, Executive Producers; Lee Mishkin, Fred Hellmich, Norton Virgien, Producers. (CBS)

GNOMES, Thomas W. Moore, Anne E. Upson, Executive Producers; Jack Zander, Producer. (CBS)

IT'S MAGIC, CHARLIE BROWN, Lee Mendelson, Executive Producer; Bill Melendez, Producer. (CBS)

LIFE IS A CIRCUS, CHARLIE BROWN, Lee Mendelson, Executive Producer; Bill Melendez, Producer. (CBS)

CHILDRENS PROGRAM (E-1700)

For a Series or a Special. Emmy(s) to Executive Producer(s) and/or Producer(s)

THE ART OF DISNEY ANIMATION---DISNEY'S WONDERFUL WORLD, William Robert Yates, Executive Producer; Bob King, Phil May, William Reid, Producers. (NBC)

DONAHUE AND KIDS, (Project Peacock), Walter Bartlett, Executive Producer; Don Mischer, Producer; Jan Cornell, Co-Producer. (NBC)

EMMET OTTER'S JUG-BAND CHRISTMAS, David Lazer, Executive Producer, Jim Henson, Producer. (ABC)

THE LEGEND OF SLEEPY HOLLOW, Charles E. Sellier, Jr, Executive Producer; James L. Conway, Producer. (NBC)

PADDINGTON BEAR, Pepper Weiss, Executive Producer; Renate Cole, Graham Clutterbuck, Producers. (SERIES) (PBS)

ACTOR - COMEDY SERIES (E-1701)

For a continuing or single performance in a regular series

ALAN ALDA; M*A*S*H (CBS)

JUDD HIRSCH; Taxi (ABC)

HAL LINDEN; Barney Miller (ABC)

RICHARD MULLIGAN; Soap (ABC)

JOHN RITTER; Three's Company (ABC)

ACTOR - DRAMA SERIES (E-1702)

For a continuing or single performance in a regular series

EDWARD ASNER; Lou Grant (CBS)

JIM DAVIS; Dallas (CBS)

LOUIS GOSSETT, JR.; Palmerstown, (Future City) 4/7/81 (CBS)

LARRY HAGMAN; Dallas (CBS)

PERNELL ROBERTS; Trapper John, M.D. (CBS)

DANIEL J. TRAVANTI; Hill Street Blues (NBC)

ACTOR - LIMITED SERIES OR SPECIAL (E-1703)

For a continuing role in a limited series, or for a single appearance in a limited series or a special

RICHARD CHAMBERLAIN; Shogun (NBC)

ANTHONY HOPKINS, The Bunker (CBS)

TOSHIRO MIFUNE; Shogun (NBC)

PETER O'TOOLE; Masada (ABC)

PETER STRAUSS; Masada (ABC)

ACTRESS - COMEDY SERIES (E-1704)

For a continuing or single performance in a regular series

EILEEN BRENNAN; Taxi (Thy Boss' Wife) 2/12/81 (ABC)

CATHRYN DAMON; Soap (ABC)

KATHERINE HELMOND; Soap (ABC)

LYNN REDGRAVE; House Calls (CBS)

ISABEL SANFORD; The Jeffersons (CBS)

ACTRESS - DRAMA SERIES (E-1705)

For a continuing or single performance in a regular series

BARBARA BABCOCK; Hill Street Blues (Fecund Hand Rose) 3/25/81 (NBC)

BARBARA BEL GEDDES; Dallas (CBS)

LINDA GRAY; Dallas (CBS)

VERONICA HAMEL; Hill Street Blues (NBC)

MICHAEL LEARNED; Nurse (CBS)

STEFANIE POWERS; Hart to Hart (ABC)

ACTRESS - LIMITED SERIES OR SPECIAL (E-1706)

For a continuing role in a limited series, or for a single appearance in a limited series or a special

ELLEN BURSTYN; People vs Jean Harris (NBC)

CATHERINE HICKS; Marilyn, The Untold Story (ABC)

VANESSA REDGRAVE; Playing For Time (CBS)

YOKO SHIMADA; Shogun (NBC)

JOANNE WOODWARD; Crisis At Central High (CBS)

SUPPORTING ACTOR - COMEDY OR VARIETY OR MUSIC SERIES (E-1707)

For a continuing or single performance in a regular series

DANNY De VITO; Taxi (ABC)

HOWARD HESSEMAN; WKRP In Cincinnati (CBS)

STEVE LANDESBERG; Barney Miller (ABC)

HARRY MORGAN; M*A*S*H (CBS)

DAVID OGDEN STIERS; M*A*S*H (CBS)

SUPPORTING ACTOR - DRAMA SERIES (E-1708)

For a continuing or single performance in a regular series

MASON ADAMS; Lou Grant (CBS)

MICHAEL CONRAD; Hill Street Blues (NBC)

CHARLES HAID; Hill Street Blues (NBC)

ROBERT WALDEN; Lou Grant (CBS)

BRUCE WEITZ; Hill Street Blues (NBC)

SUPPORTING ACTOR - LIMITED SERIES OR SPECIAL (E-1709)

For a continuing role in a limited series, or for a single appearance in a limited series or a special

ANDY GRIFFITH; Murder in Texas (NBC)

YUKI MEGURO; Shogun (NBC)

ANTHONY QUAYLE; Masada (ABC)

JOHN RHYS-DAVIES; Shogun (NBC)

DAVID WARNER; Masada (ABC)

SUPPORTING ACTRESS - COMEDY OR VARIETY OR MUSIC SERIES (E-1710)

LONI ANDERSON; WKRP In Cincinnati (CBS)

EILEEN BRENNAN; Private Benjamin (CBS)

MARLA GIBBS; The Jeffersons (CBS)

ANN MEARA; Archie Bunker's Place (CBS)

LORETTA SWIT; M*A*S*H (CBS)

SUPPORTING ACTRESS - DRAMA SERIES (E-1711)

For a continuing or single performance in a regular series

BARBARA BARRIE; Breaking Away (ABC)

BARBARA BOSSON; Hill Street Blues (NBC)

LINDA KELSEY; Lou Grant (CBS)

NANCY MARCHAND; Lou Grant (CBS)

BETTY THOMAS; Hill Street Blues (NBC)

SUPPORTING ACTRESS - LIMITED SERIES OR SPECIAL (E-1712)

For a continuing role in a limited series, or for a single appearance in a limited series or a special

JANE ALEXANDER; Playing For Time (CBS)
PATTY DUKE ASTIN; The Women's Room (ABC)
COLLEEN DEWHURST; The Women's Room (ABC)
SHIRLEY KNIGHT; Playing For Time (CBS)
PIPER LAURIE; The Bunker (CBS)

DIRECTOR - COMEDY SERIES (E-1713)

For a single episode of a regular series
ALAN ALDA; M*A*S*H (The Life You Save) 5/4/81 (CBS)
JAMES BURROWS; Taxi (Elaine's Strange Triangle) 12/10/80 (ABC)
ROD DANIEL; WKRP In Cincinnati (Venus Flytrap Explains The Atom) 1/31/81 (CBS)
LINDA DAY; Archie Bunker's Place (Tough Love) 3/15/81 (CBS)
BURT METCALFE; M*A*S*H (No Laughing Matter) 2/16/81 (CBS)
JERRY PARIS; Happy Days (Hello Mrs. Arcola) 2/24/81 (ABC)
NOAM PITLIK; Barney Miller (Liquidation) 5/21/81 (ABC)

DIRECTOR - DRAMA SERIES (E-1714)

For a single eposode of a regular series
COREY ALLEN; Hill Street Blues (Jungle Madness) 5/26/81 (NBC)
BURT BRINCKERHOFF; Lou Grant (Pack) 10/27/80 (CBS)
GEORG STANFORD BROWN; Hill Street Blues (Up In Arms) 2/21/81 (NBC)
ROBERT BUTLER; Hill Street Blues (Hill Street Station) 1/15/81 (NBC)
MEL DAMSKI; American Dream (Pilot) 4/26/81 (ABC)
GENE REYNOLDS; Lou Grant (Strike) 2/16/81 (CBS)

DIRECTOR - VARIETY, MUSIC OR COMEDY PROGRAM (E-1715)

For a single episode of a regular or limited series, or for a special

EMILE ARDOLINO; Nureyev And The Joffrey Ballet/ In Tribute To Nijinsky (Dance In America). (PBS)
TONY CHARMOLI; Sylvia Fine Kaye's Musical Comedy Tonight II. (PBS)
DWIGHT HEMION; Linda In Wonderland. (CBS)
BOB HENRY; Barbara Mandrell And The Mandrell Sisters With: Dolly Parton & John Schneider. 11/18/80 (NBC)
DON MISCHER; The Kennedy Center Honors: A National Celebration Of The Performing Arts. (CBS)
MARTY PASETTA; The 53rd Annual Academy Awards. (ABC)

DIRECTOR - LIMITED SERIES OR A SPECIAL (E-1716)

For a single episode of a limited series, or for a special
JAMES GOLDSTONE; Kent State. (NBC)
JERRY LONDON; Shogun (Episode 5). 9/19/80 (NBC)
PAUL NEWMAN; The Shadow Box. (ABC)
BORIS SAGAL; Masada (Episode 4). 4/8/81 (ABC)
ROGER YOUNG; Bitter Harvest. (NBC)

CHOREOGRAPHY (E-1717)

For a single episode of a regular or limited series, or for a special
TONY CHARMOLI; Lily: Sold Out (CBS)
DON CRICHTON; The Tim Conway Show (Episode 219) 1/31/81 (CBS)
WALTER PAINTER; Lynda Carter's Celebration (CBS)
MICHAEL SMUIN; The Tempest, Live With The San Francisco Ballet

(Dance In America) (PBS)
LESTER WILSON; Sixty Years Of Seduction (ABC)

WRITING - COMEDY SERIES (E-1718)

For a single episode of a regular series
STEPHEN J. CANNELL; The Greatest American Hero (Pilot) 3/18/81 (ABC)
GLEN CHARLES, LES CHARLES; Taxi (Going Home) 12/17/80 (ABC)
MIKE FARRELL, JOHN RAPPAPORT, DENNIS KOENIG, Teleplay; THAD MUMFORD, DAN WILCOX, BURT METCALFE, Story; M*A*S*H (Death Takes The Holiday) 12/15/80 (CBS)
MICHAEL LEESON; Taxi (Tony's Sister And Jim) 11/26/80 (ABC)
DAVID LLOYD; Taxi (Elaine's Strange Triangle) 12/10/80 (ABC)

WRITING - DRAMA SERIES (E-1719)

For a single episode of a regular series
MICHAEL KOZOLL, STEVEN BOCHCO; Hill Street Blues (Hill Street Station) 1/15/81 (NBC)
MICHAEL KOZOLL, STEVEN BOCHCO, ANTHONY YERKOVICH; Hill Street Blues (Jungle Madness) 5/26/81 (NBC)
RONALD M. COHEN, BARBARA CORDAY, KEN HECHT; American Dream (Pilot) 4/26/81 (ABC)
SETH FREEMAN; Lou Grant (Rape) 1/12/81 (CBS)
APRIL SMITH; Lou Grant (Strike) 2/16/81 (CBS)

WRITING - VARIETY, MUSIC OR COMEDY PROGRAM (E-1720)

For a variety or music special or series, or for a comedy special
NANCY AUDLEY, ANN ELDER, IRENE MECCHI, ELAINE POPE, ZIGGY STEINBERG, ROCCO URBISCI, JANE WAGNER, ROD WARREN; Lily: Sold Out (CBS)
JERRY JUHL, DAVID ODELL, CHRIS LANGHAM, JIM HENSON, DON HINKLEY; The Muppet Show With: Carol Burnett (SYN)
SYLVIA FINE KAYE; Sylvia Fine Kaye's Musical Comedy Tonight II (PBS)
RAY SILLER, JR., HAL GOODMAN, LARRY KLEIN, MICHAEL BARRIE, JIM MULHOLLAND, KEVIN MULHOLLAND, BOB SMITH, GARY MURPHY, GREG FIELDS, PAT Mc CORMICK; The Tonight Show Starring Johnny Carson (18th Anniversary Show) 9/29/80 (NBC)
GEORGE STEVENS, JR., JOSEPH Mc BRIDE; The American Film Institute Salute To Fred Astaire (CBS)

WRITING - LIMITED SERIES OR A SPECIAL (E-1721)

For a single episode of a limited series, or for a special
ERIC BERCOVICI; Shogun (Episode 5). 9/19/80 (NBC)
MICHAEL CRISTOFER; The Shadow Box (ABC)
RICHARD FRIEDENBERG; Bitter Harvest (NBC)
ARTHUR MILLER; Playing For Time (CBS)
JOEL OLIANSKY; Masada (Episode 4) 4/8/81 (ABC)

GOVERNOR'S AWARD (E-1722)

ELTON H. RULE

CINEMATOGRAPHY - SERIES (E-1723)

For a single episode of a regular series
BEN COLMAN; Buck Rogers (Hawk) 1/9/81 (NBC)
WILLIAM H. CRONJAGER; Hill Street Blues (Hill Street Station) 1/15/81 (NBC)
GERALD PERRY FINNERMAN, A.S.C.; The Gangster Chronicles (Pilot) 2/12/81 (NBC)
BRIANNE MURPHY, A.S.C.; Breaking Away (La Strada) 1/10/81 (ABC)
CHARLES W. SHORT; Nero Wolf (Death And The Dolls) 4/10/81 (NBC)
TED VOIGTLANDER, A.S.C; Little House On The Prairie (Sylvia) 2/9/81 & 2/16/81 (NBC)

CINEMATOGRAPHY - LIMITED SERIES OR A SPECIAL (E-1724)

For a single episode of a limited series, or for a special

ARTHUR F IBBETSON, B.S.C.; Little Ford Fauntleroy (CBS)
ANDREW LASZLO; Shogun (Episode 4) 9/18/80 (NBC)
TERRY K. MEADE; Marilyn: The Untold Story (ABC)
GAYNE RESCHER; Bitter Harvest (NBC)
FRANK W. STANLEY, A.S.C.; John Steinbeck's East Of Eden (Episode 2) 2/9/81 (ABC)
TED VOIGTLANDER, A.S.C; The Diary Of Anne Frank (NBC)

ART DIRECTION - SERIES (E-1725)

For a single episode of a regular series

JAMES J. AGAZZI, PAUL SYLOS, Art Directors; ROBERT SIGNORELLI, Set Decorator; Hart To Hart (Blue Chip Murders) 5/26/81 (ABC)
THOMAS E. AZZARI, Production Design; JAMES I. COLBURN, Set Decorator; Goodtime Harry (Wally Smith) 7/26/80 (NBC)
JOHN E. CHILBERG, II, PAUL SYLOS, FRANK SWIG, Art Directors; BROCK BROUGHTON, Set Decorator; Dynasty (Episode 1) 1/12/81 (ABC)
JEFFERY GOLDSTEIN, Art Director; JOSEPH A. ARMETTA, Set Decorator; Hill Street Blues (Hill Street Station) 1/15/81 (NBC)
HOWARD E. JOHNSON, Art Director; JOHN M. DWYER, ROBERT GEORGE FREER, Set Decorators; The Gangster Chronicles (The Eleventh Hour) 5/1/81 (NBC)

ART DIRECTION - LIMITED SERIES OR A SPECIAL (E-1726)

For a single episode of a limited series, or for a special
ROBERT GUNDLACH, Art Director; GARY JONES, Set Decorator; Playing For Time (CBS)
JOSEPH R. JENNINGS, Production Designer; SHINOBU NISHIOKA, Art Director; THOMAS R. PEDIGO, SHOICHI YASUDA, Set Decorators; Shogun (Episode 5) 9/19/80 (NBC)
JAN SCOTT, SIDNEY Z. LITWACK, Art Directors; BILL HARP, Set Decorator; Marilyn; The Untold Story (ABC)
JOHN H. SENTER, Production Designer; GEORGE RENNE, KULI SANDER, Art Directors; JOSEPH J. STONE, EDWARD M. PARKER, Set Decorators; Masada (Episode 4) 4/8/81 (ABC)
RAY STOREY, Art Director, DENNIS PEEPLES, DAVID LOVE, Set Decorators; John Steinbeck's East Of Eden (Episode 3) 2/11/81 (ABC)

ART DIRECTION - VARIETY OR MUSIC PROGRAM (E-1727)

For a single episode of a regular or limited series, or for a special

ROY CHRISTOPHER, Art Director; 53rd Annual Academy Awards (ABC)
ROMAIN JOHNSTON, Art Director; JIM WAGNER, Set Decorator; Barbara Mandrell And The Mandrell Sisters With: Charlie Pride 12/6/80 (NBC)
RAY KLAUSEN, Art Director; WALTER L. GOODWIN, Set Decorator; Lynda Carter's Celebration (CBS)
CHARLES LISANBY, Art Director; DWIGHT JACKSON, Set Decorator; Diana (CBS)
JOHN SHRUM, Art Director; The Tonight Show Starring Johnny Carson With: Charles Nelson Reilly 12/31/80 (NBC)
MALCOLM STONE, Art Director; The Muppet Show With: Brooke Shields (SYN)

MUSIC COMPOSITION - SERIES (DRAMATIC UNDERSCORE) (E-1728)

For a single episode of a regular series. Emmy(s) to composer(s)

BRUCE BROUGHTON; Buck Rogers (The Satyr) 3/12/81 (NBC)
BILLY GOLDENBERG; The Gangster Chronicles (Episode 1) 2/12/81 (NBC)
MIKE POST; Hill Street Blues (Hill Street Station) 1/15/81 (NBC)
DAVID ROSE; Little House On The Prairie (The Lost Ones) (Part 2) 5/11/81 (NBC)
PATRICK WILLIAMS; Lou Grant (Stroke) 5/4/81 (CBS)

MUSIC COMPOSITION - LIMITED SERIES OR A SPECIAL (DRAMTIC UNDERSCORE) (E-1729)

For a single episode of a limited series or for a special Emmy(s) to composer(s)

PAUL CHIHARA; The Tempest, Live With The San Francisco Ballet (Dance In America) (PBS)
JERRY GOLDSMITH; Masada (Episode 2) 4/6/81 (ABC)
FRED KARLIN; Homeward Bound (CBS)
PETER MATZ; Father Damien: The Leper Priest (NBC)
MORTON STEVENS; Masada (Episode 4) 4/8/81 (ABC)

MUSIC DIRECTION (E-1730)

For a single episode of a regular or limited series, or for a special, whether it be variety or music. Emmy(s) to music director and principal arranger(s)

JACK ELLIOT, Music Director; ALF CLAUSEN, BILL GOLDSTEIN, Arrangers; Omnibus 12/28/80 (ABC)
IAN FRASER, Music Director; BILLY BYERS, CHRIS BOARDMAN, BOB FLORENCE, Arrangers; Linda In Wonderland (CBS)
EARLE HAGEN, Music Director; CARL BRANDT, DEANE HAGEN, Arrangers; Stand By Your Man (CBS)
NICK PERITO, Music Director & Arranger; Perry Como's Christmas In The Holy Land (ABC)
GEORGE WYLE, Music Director; SID FELLER, NORMAN MAMEY, Arrangers; The Magic Of David Copperfield (CBS)

MUSIC AND LYRICS (E-1731)

For a song (which must have both music and lyrics), whether it be for a single episode of a regular or limited series, or for a special. Emmy(s) to composer(s) and lyricist(s)

EARL BROWN, Composer & Lyricist; All Commercials (Song: "Truman Capote Jeans") (NBC)
RAY CHARLES, Composer & Lyricist; Perry Como's Christmas In The Holy Land (Song: "The City of Tradition") (ABC)
LARRY GROSSMAN, Composer; SHELDON HARNICK, Lyricist; The Way They Were (Song: "In The Beginning") (SYN)
FRED KARLIN, Composer; DAVID POMERANZ, Lyricist; Homeward Bound (Song: "Home") (CBS)
KEN WELCH, Composer; MITZIE WELCH, Lyricist; Linda In Wonderland (Song: "This Is My Night") (CBS)

COSTUME DESIGN - SERIES (E-1732)

For a single episode of a regular or limited series
GRADY HUNT; Beulah Land (Episode 3) 10/9/80 (NBC)
ALFRED E. LEHMAN; Buck Rogers (The Dorian Secret) 4/16/81 (NBC)
SHIN NISHIDA; Shogun (Episode 5) 9/19/80 (NBC)
NINO NOVARESE; Masada (Episode 4) 4/8/81 (ABC)

COSTUME DESIGN - SPECIAL (E-1733)

For a comedy, drama, variety or music special
WILLA KIM, The Tempest, Live With The San Francisco Ballet

(Dance In America) (PBS)
OLGA LEHMANN; A Tale Of Two Cities (Hallmark Hall Of Fame) (CBS)
WARDEN NEIL; The Jayne Mansfield Story (CBS)
NINO NOVARESE; Peter and Paul (CBS)
TRAVILLA; Evita Peron (NBC)

MAKEUP (E-1734)

For a single episode of a regular or limited series, of for a special

DEL ACEVEDO, ALBERT PAUL JEYTE; Masada (Episode 4) 4/8/81 (ABC)
SCOTT H. EDDO, STAN SMITH; The Diary Of Anne Frank (NBC)
ALAN FRIEDMAN, LONA MARDOCK JEFFERS; The Jayne Mansfield Story (CBS)
JOHN INZERELLA; Father Damien: The Leper Priest (NBC)
ALBERT PAUL JEYTE, JAMES KAIL; Peter And Paul (CBS)
ALLAN "WHITEY" SNYDER; Marilyn: The Untold Story (ABC)

HAIRSTYLING (E-1735)

For a single episode of a regular or limited series, or for a special

SYLVIA ABASCAL, JANIS CLARK; The Jayne Mansfield Story (CBS)
JEAN AUSTIN; Lou Grant (Stroke) 5/4/81 (CBS)
JANICE D. BRANDOW; Father Damien: The Leper Priest (NBC)
LARRY GERMAIN; Little House On The Prairie (To See The Light) 12/1/80 (NBC)
SHIRLEY PADGETT; Madame X (NBC)

GRAPHIC DESIGN AND TITLE SEQUENCES (E-1736)

For a single episode of a regular or limited series, or for a special

GENE KRAFT; Freebie And The Bean (Health Nuts) 12/13/80 (CBS)
PHILL NORMAN; Shogun (Episode 1) 9/15/80 (NBC)

FILM EDITING - SERIES (E-1737)

For a single episode of a regular series

BERNARD BALMUTH, A.C.E.; Palmerstown (Crossroads) 6/9/81 (CBS)
CLAY BARTELS; Hill Street Blues (Jungle Madness) 5/26/81 (NBC)
FRED W. BERGER; Dallas (Ewing-Gate) 5/1/81 (CBS)
M. PAM BLUMENTHAL, JACK MICHON; Taxi (Elaine's Strange Triangle) 12/10/80 (ABC)
RAY DANIELS, A. DAVID MARSHALL; Hill Street Blues (Hill Street Station) 1/15/81 (NBC)
RICHARD W. DARLING, JR.; Dynasty (Episode 3) 1/26/81 (ABC)
TONY De ZARRAGA; The White Shadow (A Day In The Life) 3/16/81 (CBS)
JAMES GALLOWAY, A.C.E.; Lou Grant (Strike) 2/16/81 (CBS)
CHRISTOPHER NELSON; The Greatest American Hero (Pilot) 3/18/81 (ABC)
THOMAS H. STEVENS, JR., CLAY BARTELS; Hill Street Blues (Rites Of Spring) 5/19/81 (NBC)
STANFORD TISCHLER, A.C.E.; LARRY L. MILLS, A.C.E.; M*A*S*H ((Death Takes The Holiday) 12/15/80 (CBS)

FILM EDITING - LIMITED SERIES OR SPECIAL (E-1738)

For a single episode of a limited series, or for a special
JOHN BLOOM, Supervising Editor; EDWIN F. ENGLAND, PETER KIRBY; Masada (Episode 4) 4/8/81 (ABC)
BARBARA DIES, MICHAEL S. Mc LEAN, A.C.E.; The Best Little Girl In The World (ABC)
MICHAEL ELIOT, ROBERT FLORIO; A Whale For The Killing (ABC)
THOMAS FRIES; Bitter Harvest (NBC)
JOHN A. MARTINELLI, A.C.E.; Murder In Texas (NBC)

DONALD R. RODE, BENJAMIN A. WEISSMAN, JERRY YOUNG, BILL LUCIANO; Shogun (Episode 5) 9/19/80 (NBC)

FILM SOUND EDITING (E-1739)

For a single episode of a regular or limited series, or for a special

MICHAEL HILKENE, RUSS TINSLEY, Supervising Editors; ALBERT CAVIGGA, TOM CORNWELL, LINDA DOVE, DAVE ELLIOTT, DON ERNST, DIMITRY GORTINSKY, PETER HARRISON, JERRY M. JACOBSON, FRED JUDKINS, JOHN KLINE, CORINNE SESSAREGO, RUSTY TINSLEY, CHRIS WELCH, Editors; The Women's Room (ABC)
SAMUEL HORTA, Supervising Editor; ROBERT CORNETT, DENISE HORTA, EILEEN HORTA, Editors; Hill Street Blues (Hill Street Station) 1/15/81 (NBC)
JOHN KLINE, RUSS TINSLEY, Supervising Editors; TOM CORNWELL, DIMITRY GORTINSKY, MICHAEL HILKENE, BILL MANGER, BOB PEARSON, CHRIS WELCH, Editors; A Whale For The Killing (ABC)
STANLEY M. PAUL, Supervising Editor; BILL ANDREWS, LEONARD CORSO, DENNIS DUTTON, JACK FINLEY, SEAN HANLEY, PIERRE JALBERT, JACK KEATH, ALAN NINEBERG, LEE OSBORNE, TALLEY PAULOS, Editors; Shogun (Episode 3) 9/17/80 (NBC)
RUSS TINSLEY, BILL WISTROM, Supervising Editors; TOM CORNWELL, PETER HARRISON, BILL MANGER, R. WILLIAM THIEDERMAN, CHRISTOPHER T. WELCH, Editors; Evita Peron (NBC)

FILM SOUND MIXING (E-1740)

For a single episode of a regular or limited series, or for a special

ALAN BERNARD, Production Mixer; ROBERT L. HARMAN, WILLIAM L. Mc CAUGHEY, HOWARD WOLLMAN; Re-Recording Mixers; Baby Comes Home (CBS)
NICK GAFFEY, Production Mixer; GARY BOURJEOIS, LEE MINKLER, TERRY PORTER, Re-Recording Mixers; Nero Wolfe (Gambit) 4/03/81 (NBC)
STANLEY P. GORDON, Production Mixer; ROBERT L. HARMAN, WILLIAM L. Mc CAUGHEY, LEE MINKLER; Re-Recording Mixers; Dial "M" For Murder (NBC)
RENE MAGNOL, Production Mixer; ROBERT L. HARMAN, WILLIAM L. Mc CAUGHEY, HOWARD WOLLMAN; Re-Recording Mixers; The Bunker (CBS)
JOHN Mc CLOUD, Production Mixer; ROBERT L. HARMAN, WILLIAM L. Mc CAUGHEY, TERRY PORTER; Re-Recording Mixers; Word Of Honor (CBS)
RICHARD RAGUSE, Production Mixer; ROBERT L. HARMAN, WILLIAM L. Mc CAUGHEY, HOWARD WOLLMAN, Re-Recording Mixers; The Killing Of Randy Webster (CBS)
WILLIAM R. TEAGUE; Production Mixer; JOEL FINE, GEORGE E. PORTER, HOWARD WOLLMAN, Re-Recording Mixers; A Time For Miracles (ABC)
WILLIAM R. TEAGUE, Production Mixer; ROBERT L. HARMAN, WILLIAM L. Mc CAUGHEY, HOWARD WOLLMAN, Re-Recording Mixers; Evita Peron (Part I) 2/23/81 (NBC)
MANUEL TOPETE, Production Mixer; HARRY ALPHIN, ROBERT L. HARMAN, WILLIAM L. Mc CAUGHEY, Re-Recording Mixers; A Rumor Of War (CBS)
BLAKE WILCOX, Production Mixer; ROBERT L. HARMAN, WILLIAM L. Mc CAUGHEY, HOWARD WOLLMAN, Re-Recording Mixers; Hart To Hart (Tis The Season To Be Murdered) 12/16/80 (ABC)

TAPE SOUND MIXING (E-1741)

For a single episode of a regular or limited series, or for a special

TOM L. ANCELL; San Francisco Inaugural Gala (PBS)
JERRY CLEMANS, ED GREENE, PHILLIP J. SERETTI; Perry Como's Spring In San Francisco (ABC)
JERRY CLEMANS, MATTHEW HYDE, DONALD WORSHAM; Barbara Mandrell And The Mandrell Sisters With: The Gatlin Brothers 2/14/81 (NBC)
JERRY CLEMANS, DOUG NELSON, DONALD WORSHAM; John Denver With His Special Guest George Burns–Two Of A Kind 3/30/81

(ABC)
DON JOHNSON, PHILLIP J. SERETTI; Kent State (NBC)

VIDEO TAPE EDITING - SERIES (E-1742)

For a single episode of a regular series

ANDY ACKERMAN; WKRP In Cincinnati (Bah, Humbug) 12/20/80 (CBS)
KEN DENNISOFF; Barbara Mandrell And The Mandrell Sisters With: Ray Stevens 12/13/80 (NBC)
JOHN HAWKINS; The Muppet Show With: Brooke Shields (SYN)
ANDY ZALL; Barbara Mandrell And The Mandrell Sisters With: Dolly Parton & John Schneider 11/18/80 (NBC)

VIDEO TAPE EDITING - LIMITED SERIES OR SPECIAL (E-1743)

For a single episode of a limited series, or for a special

HARVEY W. BERGER, ANDY SCHUBERT; The American Film Institute Salute To Fred Astaire (CBS)
RAYMOND M. BUSH; Tom And Dick Smothers Brothers Special I (NBC)
TERRY W. GREENE, RON MENZIES; Diana (CBS)
PAM MARSHALL; John Schneider - Back Home (CBS)
MARCO ZAPPIA; Perry Como's Christmas In The Holy Land (ABC)

TECHNICAL DIRECTION AND ELECTRONIC CAMERAWORK (E-1744)

For a single episode of a regular or limited series, or for a special

JOHN B. FIELD, Technical Director; RICK CASWELL, ROCKY DANIELSON, BOB EBERLINE, HANK GEVING, DEAN HALL, LARRY HEIDER, BOB HEIGHTON, DAVE HILMER, DAVE LEVISHOHN, DAN PRESTON, LARRY TRAVIS, WAYNE WOMACK, Camerapersons; Kenny Rogers' America (CBS)
HEINO RIPP, Technical Director; PETER BASIL, AL CAMOIN, TOM DEZENDORF, VINCE Di PIETRO, GENE MARTIN, Camerapersons; Live From Studio 8H: An Evening Of Jerome Robbins' Ballets With Members Of The New York City Ballet (NBC)
CREW A-- TOM SABOL, Technical Director; GEORGE CILIBERTO, BARRY FRISHER, JODI GREENBERG, PAMELA SCHNEIDER, Camerapersons; CREW B-- O. TAMBURRI, Technical Director; GEORGE LOOMIS, MIKE STRAMISKY, Camerapersons; Tomorrow Coast To Coast (Charles Manson Interview) 6/12/81 (NBC)
O. TAMBURRI, Technical Director; GEORGE FALARDEAU, ROYDEN HOLM, REED HOWARD, Camerapersons; People Vs Jean Harris (NBC)
JERRY WEISS, Technical Director; DON BARKER, BRUCE BOTTONE, JIM HERRING, ROYDEN HOLM, Camerapersons; The Magic Of David Copperfield (CBS)

LIGHTING DIRECTION (E-1745)

For a single episode of a regular or limited series, or for a special

GREGORY BRUNTON; Sixty Years Of Seduction (ABC)
GREGORY BRUNTON, Lighting Director; ALAN BRANTON, Lighting Designer; Diana (CBS)
LEARD DAVIS; The Osmond Family Christmas Show (NBC)
RALPH HOLMES; Nureyev And The Joffrey Ballet/ In Tribute To Nijinsky (Dance In America) (PBS)
FRED Mc KINNON; Command Performance: The Stars Salute To The President (NBC)
GEORGE W. RIESENBERGER; A Bayou Legend (PBS)
CARL J. VITELLI, JR.; The 35th Annual Tony Awards (CBS)

INDIVIDUAL ACHIEVEMENT - INFORMATIONAL PROGRAMMING (E-1746)

(Possibility of one award, more than one or no award)

KENT GIBSON, GERALD ZELINGER, Tape Sound Mixers; Cosmos (Blues For A Red Planet) 10/26/80 (PBS)
ROY STEWART, Video Tape Editor; Cosmos (The Shores Of The Cosmic Ocean) 9/29/80 (PBS)
KENNETH LOVE, Production Mixer; GARY BOURGEOIS, HOPPY MEHTERIAN, HOWARD WOLLMAN, Re-Recording Mixers; Living Treasures Of Japan (National Geographic Special) 2/11/81 (PBS)
DAVID HUGHES, Production Mixer; DAVE DOCKENDORF, HOPPY MEHTERIAN, GEORGE PORTER, Re-Recording Mixers; Etosha: Place Of Dry Water (National Geographic Special) 1/7/81 (PBS)
KENNETH LOVE, Production Mixer; GARY BOURGEOIS, GEORGE PORTER, TERRY PORTER, Re-Recording Mixers; National Parks: Playground Paradise (National Geographic Special) 3/11/81 (PBS)
DICK RECTOR, Production Mixer; GARY BOURGEOIS, DAVE DOCKENDORF; JOHN MACK, Re-Recording Mixers; Gorilla (National Geographic Special) 4/8/81 (PBS)

INDIVIDUAL ACHIEVEMENT - SPECIAL CLASS (E-1747)

(Possibility of one award, more than one or no award)

NICK PERITO, Music Director, ZUBIN MEHTA, MICHAEL TILSON THOMAS, ALAN BARKER, Guest Conductors; The Kennedy Center Honors: A Celebration Of The Performing Arts (CBS)
RITA BENNETT, Women's Costumer; BILL BLACKBURN, Men's Costumer; The Diary Of Anne Frank (NBC)
ROBERT MAGAHAY, Men's Costumer; JUDY TRUCHAN, Women's Costumer; John Steinbeck's East Of Eden (Episode 1) 2/8/81 (ABC)
ADRIANNE LEVESQUE, Women's Costumer; HARRY CURTIS, Men's Costumer; Crazy Times (ABC)
SARAH VAUGHAN, Performer; Rhapsody & Song - A Tribute To George Gershwin (PBS)

INDIVIDUAL ACHIEVEMENT - CREATIVE TECHNICAL CRAFTS (E-1748)

(Possibility of one award, more than one or no award)

MARK SCHUBIN, Technical Designer, Stereo Simulcast; Joan Sutherland, Marilyn Horne and Luciano Pavarotti Live From Lincoln Center 3/23/81 (PBS)
DICK WILSON, Sound Effects; Fridays (Episode 8) 11/14/80 (ABC)
JON ALLISON, ADOLF SCHAUER, DON DAVIS, RICK STERNBACH, JOHN LOMBERG, Astronomical Artists; Cosmos (The Shores Of The Cosmic Ocean) 9/29/80 (PBS)
CAREY MELCHER, Technical Designer; BOB BUCKNER, STEVE BURUM, JIM DOW, JOHN GALE, LARRY HEIDER, MIKE JOHNSON, CLEVE LANDESBERG, JOSEPH MATZA, CHUCK RILEY, JOE WOLCOTT, Magicam Crew; Cosmos (The Shores Of The Cosmic Ocean) 9/28/80 (PBS)
JOHN L. MARLOW, M.D., Live Fetal Photography; The Body Human: The Bionic Breakthrough (CBS)

INDIVIDUAL ACHIEVEMENT - CHILDREN'S PROGRAMMING (E-1749)

(Possibility of one award, more than one or no award)

TOM WRIGHT, Lighting; Emmet Otter's Jug-Band Christmas (ABC)
PAUL WILLIAMS, Composer & Lyricist; Emmet Otter's Jug-Band Christmas (Song: When The River Meets The Sea) (ABC)
PATTY DUKE ASTIN, Performer; Girl On The Edge Of Town, (Family Specials) (SYN)
DON MISCHER, Director; Donahue And Kids (Project Peacock) (NBC)
CALISTA HENDRICKSON, SHERRY AMMOTT, Costume Designers; Emmet Otter's Jug-Band Christmas (ABC)

INDIVIDUAL ACHIEVEMENT - ANIMATED PROGRAMMING (E-1750)

(Possibility of one award, more than one or no award)

HOYT S. CURTIN, Composer; The Flintstones (Flintstones New Neighbors) 9/26/80 (NBC)

PETER ARIES, Film Editor; Faeries (CBS)
PETER ARIES, Film Sound Editor; Faeries (CBS)
ALAN ALDRIDGE, LEE MISHKIN, Teleplay; CHRISTOPHER GORE, Story; Faeries (CBS)

NATIONAL DAYTIME EMMY AWARDS

DAYTIME DRAMA SERIES (E-1751)
Emmy(s) to Executive Producer(s) and Producer(s)
ALL MY CHILDREN, Agnes Nixon, Executive Producer; Jorn Winther, Producer (ABC)
GENERAL HOSPITAL, Gloria Monty, Producer (ABC)
RYAN'S HOPE, Paul Avila Mayer, Claire Labine, Executive Producers; Ellen Barrett, Producer (ABC)

GAME OR AUDIENCE PARTICIPATION SHOW (E-1752)
Emmy(s) to Executive Producer(s) and Producer(s)
FAMILY FEUD, Mark Goodson, Executive Producer; Howard Felsher, Producer (ABC)
HOLLYWOOD SQUARES, Merrill Heatter, Bob Quigley, Executive Producers; Jay Redack, Producer (ABC)
THE $20,000 PYRAMID, Bob Stewart, Executive Producer; Anne Marie Schmitt, Jane Rothchild, Producers (ABC)

TALK OR SERVICE SERIES (E-1753)
Emmy(s) to Executive Producer(s) and Producer(s)
OVER EASY, Richard R. Rector, Executive Producer; Jules Power, Senior Producer; Ben Bayol, Janice Tunder, Studio Producers (Synd)
DONAHUE, Richard Mincer, Executive Producer; Patricia McMillen, Senior Producer; Darlene Hayes, Sheri Singer, Producers (Synd)
THE RICHARD SIMMONS SHOW, Woody Fraser, Executive Producer; Nora Fraser, Producer (Synd)

VARIETY SERIES (E-1754)
Emmy(s) to Executive Producer(s) and Producer(s)
THE DAVID LETTERMAN SHOW, Jack Rollins, Executive Producer; Barry Sand, Producer (NBC)
THE MERV GRIFFIN SHOW, Peter Barsocchini, Producer (Synd)

ACTOR - DAYTIME DRAMA SERIES (E-1755)
JAMES MITCHELL; All My Children (ABC)
DOUGLASS WATSON; Another World (NBC)
LARRY BRYGGMAN; As The World Turns (CBS)
HENDERSON FORSYTHE; As The World Turns (CBS)
ANTHONY GEARY; General Hospital (ABC)

ACTRESS - DAYTIME DRAMA SERIES (E-1756)
JULIA BARR; All My Children (ABC)
SUSAN LUCCI; All My Children (ABC)
JUDITH LIGHT; One Life To Live (ABC)
ROBIN STRASSER; One Life To Live (ABC)
HELEN GALLAGHER; Ryan's Hope (ABC)

SUPPORTING ACTOR - DAYTIME DRAMA SERIES (E-1757)
MATTHEW COWLES; All My Children (ABC)
WILLIAM MOONEY; All My Children (ABC)
JUSTIN DEAS; As The World Turns (CBS)
RICHARD BACKUS; Ryan's Hope (ABC)
LARRY HAINES; Search For Tomorrow (CBS)

SUPPORTING ACTRESS - DAYTIME DRAMA SERIES (E-1758)
ELIZABETH LAWRENCE; All My Children (ABC)

LOIS KIBBEE; The Edge Of Night (ABC)
JANE ELLIOT; General Hospital (ABC)
JACKLYN ZEMAN; General Hospital (ABC)
RANDALL EDWARDS; Ryan's Hope (ABC)

HOST OR HOSTESS - GAME OR AUDIENCE PARTICIPATION SHOW (E-1759)
DICK CLARK; The $20,000 Pyramid (ABC)
RICHARD DAWSON; Family Feud (ABC)
PETER MARSHALL; The Hollywood Squares (NBC)

HOST OR HOSTESS - TALK OR SERVICE SERIES (E-1760)
PHIL DONAHUE; Donahue (Synd)
HUGH DOWNS; Over Easy (PBS)

HOST OR HOSTESS - VARIETY SERIES (E-1761)
MERV GRIFFIN; The Merv Griffin Show (Synd)
DAVID LETTERMAN; The David Letterman Show (NBC)
DINAH SHORE; Dinah & Friends (Synd)

DIRECTOR - DAYTIME DRAMA SERIES (E-1762)
For the Entire Series
LARRY AUERBACH, JACK COFFEY, SHERRELL HOFFMAN, JORN WINTHER; All My Children (ABC)
MARLENA LAIRD, ALAN PULTZ, PHILLIP SOGARD; General Hospital (ABC)
DAVID PRESSMAN, PETER MINER, NORMAN HALL; One Life To Live (ABC)

INDIVIDUAL DIRECTION - GAME OR AUDIENCE PARTICIPATION SHOW (E-1763)
For a single episode
PAUL ALTER; Family Feud 12/16/80 (ABC)
MIKE GARGIULO; The $20,000 Pyramid 5/15/80 (ABC)

INDIVIDUAL DIRECTION - TALK OR SERVICE SERIES (E-1764)
For a single episode
VINCENT CASALAINA; Over Easy 10/14/80 (PBS)
JERRY KUPCINET; The Richard Simmons Show 3/13/80 (Synd)
RON WEINER; Wives Who Kill Husbands, Donahue 9/23/80 (Synd)

INDIVIDUAL DIRECTION - VARIETY SERIES (E-1765)
For a single episode
DICK CARSON; Salute To New York Dance, The Merv Griffin Show 10/30/80 (Synd)
STERLING JOHNSON; Dinah & Friends in Israel 9/10/80 (Synd)

WRITING - DAYTIME DRAMA SERIES (E-1766)
For the Entire Series
AGNES NIXON, WISNER WASHAM, JACK WOOD, MARY K. WELLS, CLARICE BLACKBURN, CAROLINE FRANZ, CATHY CHICOS, CYNTHIA BENJAMIN; All My Children (ABC)
PAT FALKEN SMITH, MARGARET DePRIEST, SHERI ANDERSON, FRANK SALISBURY, MARGARET STEWART; General Hospital (ABC)
DOUGLAS MARLAND, ROBERT DWYER, NANCY FRANKLIN, HARDING LEMAY; The Guiding Light (CBS)
SAM HALL, PEGGY O'SHEA, DON WALLACE, LANIE BERTRAM, GORDON RUSSELL, FRED CORKE; One Life To Live (ABC)

ACHIEVEMENT IN TECHNICAL EXCELLENCE - DAYTIME DRAMA SERIES (E-1767)

For The Entire Series--Emmys to individuals

JOSEPH SOLOMITO, HOWARD ZWEIG, Technical Directors; LAWRENCE HAMMOND, DIANNE CATES-CANTRELL, ROBERT AMBRICO, CHRISTOPHER MAURO, LARRY STRACK, SALVATORE AUGUGLIARO, VINCENT SENATORE, THOMAS McGRATH, Electronic Camera; LEN WALAS, Sr. Video Engineer; ALBIN S. LEMANSKI,PETER BOHM, CHARLES EISEN, Sr. Audio Engineers; BARBARA WOOD, Sound Effects Eng.; DIANA WENMAN, JEAN DADARIO, Associate Directors; ROGER HAENELT, Videotape Editor; All My Children (ABC)

JOHN COCHRAN, DAVID SMITH, Technical Directors; JACK DENTON, JAMES ANGEL, DAVID BANKS, D.J. DIOMEDES, WILLIAM POPE, JOHN RAGO, LUIS ROJAS, WILLIAM SCOTT, JOSEPH TALOSI, DALE WALSH, CAROL WETOVICH, SAL FOLINO, Electronic Camera; VICTOR BAGDADI, SAM POTTER, ERIC CLAY, RICHARD ENGSTROM, Sr. Video Engineers; ROBERT MILLER, ZOLI OSAZE, Sr. Audio Engineers; HAL ALEXANDER, GEORGE THOMPSON, Associate Directors; BOB LANHAM, JOSE GALVEZ, JACK MOODY, Videotape Editors; General Hospital (ABC)

MARTIN GAVRIN, LOUIS MARCHAND, Technical Directors; JOHN MORRIS, THOMAS FRENCH, EUGENE KELLY, RICHARD WESTLEIN, JOHN WOOD, EARL MOORE, GENEVIEVE TWOHIG, BILL PHYPERS, KEITH MORRIS, NANCY KRIEGEL, Electronic Camera; HERBERT SEGALL, Sr. Video Engineer; FRANK BAILEY, JEFFERY SCHLOSS, Sr. Audio Engineers; JACK SULLIVAN, STUART SILVER, Associate Directors; TONY GRECO, ROBERT STEINBACK, AL FORMAN; One Life To Live (ABC)

DESIGN - DAYTIME DRAMA SERIES (E-1768)

For The Entire Series--Emmys to individuals

WILLIAM MICKLEY, Scenic Designer; WILLIAM ITKIN, DONNA LARSON, DONALD GAVITT, Lighting Directors; CAROL LUIKEN, Costume Designer;SYLVIA LAWRENCE, Make-up Designer; MICHAEL HUDDLE, MARIE ANGE RIPKA, Hair Designers; TERI SMITH, Music Director; SID RAMIN, IRVING ROBBINS, Music Composers; HY BLEY, Graphic Designer; All My Children (ABC)

JAMES ELLINGWOOD, Art Director; MERCER BARROWS, Set Decorator; GRANT VELIE, JOHN ZAK, TOM MARKLE, Lighting Directors; JIM O'DANIEL, GEORGE WHITTAKER, Costume Designers; PAM K. COLE, Make-up Designer; KATHY KOTARAKOS, Hair Designer; DOMINIC MESSINGER, JIM PHELPS, Music Directors; CHARLES PAUL, Music Composer; General Hospital (ABC)

CHARLES BRANDON, Scenic Designer; HOWARD SHARROT, JO MAYER, Lighting Directors; JOSEPH MILLER, Costume Designer; JOSEPHINE FOERDERER, TRACEY KELLY, Make-up Designers; KAREN CREHAN, WILLIS HANCHETT, Hair Designers; IRVING ROBBINS, JOHN ANTHONY, Music Directors; JACK URBONT, Music Composer; One Life To Live (ABC)

SY TOMASHOFF, Scenic Designer; JOHN CONNOLLY, Lighting Director; DAVID MURIN, MICHELE REISCH, Costume Designers; JAMES COLA, Make-up Designer; JOHN K. QUINN, Hair Designer; SYBIL WEINBERGER, Music Supervisor; Ryan's Hope (ABC)

CHILDREN'S ENTERTAINMENT SERIES (E-1769)

Emmy(s) to Executive Producer(s) and Producer(s)

ABC WEEKEND SPECIALS, Robert Chenault, Executive Producer (ABC)

CAPTAIN KANGAROO, Joel Kosofsky, Producer (CBS)

THE LEGEND OF KING ARTHUR (Once Upon A Classic) Jay Rayvid, Executive Producer; James A. DeVinney, Producer (PBS)

A TALE OF TWO CITIES (Once Upon A Classic) Jay Rayvid, Executive Producer; James A. DeVinney, Producer; Christine Ochtun, Co-Producer (PBS)

CHILDREN'S ENTERTAINMENT SPECIALS (E-1770)

Emmy(s) to Executive Producer(s) and Producer(s)

FAMILY OF STRANGERS (ABC Afterschool Special) 9/24/80 Linda Gottlieb, Executive Producer; Doro Bachrach & Franklin Getchell, Producers

I THINK I'M HAVING A BABY (The CBS Afternoon Playhouse) 3/3/81 Joe Stern, Executive Producer; Eda Godel Hallinan & Keetje Van Benschoten, Producers (CBS)

A MATTER OF TIME (ABC Afterschool Special) 2/11/81 Martin Tahse, Executive Producer/Producer (ABC)

SUNSHINE'S ON THE WAY (NBC Special Treat) 11/11/80 Linda Gottlieb, Executive Producer; Doro Bachrach, Producer (NBC)

CHILDREN'S INFORMATIONAL/INSTRUCTIONAL SERIES (E-1771)

Emmy(s) to Executive Producer(s) and Producer(s)

ANIMALS ANIMALS ANIMALS, Lester Cooper, Executive Producer; Jake Haselkorn, Producer (ABC)

KIDS ARE PEOPLE TOO, Laura Schrock, Producer; Lyn Butler, Coordinating Producer; Burt Dubrow, Studio Producer (ABC)

SESAME STREET, Dulcy Singer, Executive Producer; Lisa Simon, Producer (PBS)

30 MINUTES, Joel Heller, Executive Producer; Madeline Amgott, Vern Diamond, Allen Ducovny, Diego Echeverria, Virginia Gray, Susan Mills, Patti Obrow White, Catherine Olian, Robert Rubin, Martin Smith, Producers (CBS)

CHILDREN'S INFORMATIONAL/INSTRUCTIONAL SPECIAL (E-1772)

Emmy(s) to Executive Producer(s) and Producer(s)

JULIE ANDREWS' INVITATION TO THE DANCE WITH RUDOLF NUREYEV (The CBS Festival of Lively Arts for Young People) 11/30/80 Jack Wohl & Bernard Rothman, Producers (CBS)

SIDE BY SIDE - PREJUDICE (On The Level) 11/14/80 Lawrence Walcoff, Executive Producer (PBS)

CHILDREN'S INFORMATIONAL/INSTRUCTIONAL PROGRAMMING-SHORT FORM (E-1773)

Emmy(s) to Executive Producer(s) and Producer(s)

ABC NUTRITION SPOTS, George Newall & Tom Yohe, Executive Producers (ABC)

ASK NBC NEWS, Beryl Pfizer, Producer (NBC)

THE DOUGHNUTS, Ken Greengrass & Phil Lawrence, Executive Producers; Lynn Ahrens, Producer (ABC)

IN THE NEWS, Walter Lister, Producer (CBS)

INDIVIDUAL ACHIEVEMENT IN CHILDREN'S PROGRAMMING

For a single episode of a series or for a special program (Possibility of one Award, more than one Award or no Award).

PERFORMERS (E-1774)

JULIE ANDREWS; Julie Andrew's Invitation To The Dance With Rudolf Nureyev (The CBS Festival of Lively Arts for Young People) 2/30/80 (CBS)

BILL BIXBY; A Tale Of Two Cities (Part I) (Once Upon A Classic) 10/4/80 (PBS)

BILL COSBY; The Secret (The New Fat Albert Show) 9/13/80 (CBS)

KEN HOWARD; The Body Human: Facts For Boys 11/6/80 (CBS)

MARLO THOMAS; The Body Human: Facts For Girls 10/7/80 (CBS)

DANNY AIELLO; Family of Strangers (ABC Afterschool Special) 9/24/80 (ABC)

SCOTT BAIO; Stoned (ABC Afterschool Special) 11/12/80 (ABC)

HAL LINDEN; Llama (Animals Animals Animals) 9/28/80 (ABC)

WRITERS (E-1775)

BOB BRUSH; Captain Kangaroo 12/26/80 (CBS)

PAUL W. COOPER; A Matter Of Time (ABC Afterschool Special) 2/11/81 (ABC)

BLOSSOM ELFMAN; I Think I'm Having a Baby (The CBS Afternoon

Playhouse) 3/3/81 (CBS)
ROBERT E. FUISZ, M.D.; The Body Human: Facts For Girls 10/7/80 (CBS)
JOHN HERZFELD; Stoned (ABC Afterschool Special) 11/12/80 (ABC)
MARY MUNISTERI; Mandy's Grandmother (Young People's Special) 4/1/80 (Synd)
NORMAN STILES, SARA COMPTON, JUDY FREUDBERG, TONY GEISS, JOHN GLINES, EMILY KINGSLEY, LOUIS SANTEIRO, RAY SIPHERD, PETER SWET; Sesame Street 1/29/81 (Show #1494) (PBS)

DIRECTORS (E-1776)

JOHN HERZFELD; Stoned (ABC Afterschool Special) 11/12/80 (ABC)
DON ROY KING; Kids Are People Too 9/21/80 (ABC)

ELECTRONIC CAMERA (E-1777)

CHUCK CLIFTON; Reflections: From the Ghetto 1/14/71 (PBS)

AUDIO (E-1778)

DICK MAITLAND, Sound Effects Engineer; Tuning The Engine (Sesame Street) 4/14/80 (PBS)

CINEMATOGRAPHERS: (E-1779)

CHUCK CLIFTON; Mandy's Grandmother (Young People's Special) 4/1/80 (Synd)
JOE CONSENTINO; Globetrotters (Big Blue Marble) 9/6/80 (Synd)
ROBERT ELFSTROM; The Body Human; Facts For Boys 11/6/80 (CBS)
LARRY PIZER; Stoned (ABC Afterschool Special) 11/12/80 (ABC)
ERIC VAN HAREN NOMEN; Egyptian Weavers (Big Blue Marble) 9/13/80 (Synd)

FILM EDITORS (E-1780)

GEOF BARTZ; The Body Human: Facts For Girls 10/7/80 (CBS)
PETER HAMMER; Do Me A Favor. . .Don't Vote For My Mom Pt 3 (Big Blue Marble) 11/22/80 (Synd)
ALLEN KIRKPATRICK; Bike Racing (Big Blue Marble) 10/11/80 (Synd)

MUSIC COMPOSERS AND/OR DIRECTORS (E-1781)

BOB COBERT, Composer/Conductor; I Think I'm Having A Baby (The CBS Afternoon Playhouse) 3/3/81 (CBS)
DICK HYMAN, Composer; Sunshine's On The Way (NBC Special Treat) 11/11/80 (NBC)

LIGHTING DIRECTORS (E-1782)

DAVE CLARK, WILLIAM KNIGHT; Sesame Street 5/9/80 (PBS)

COSTUME DESIGNERS (E-1783)

DIANNE FINN-CHAPMAN; Stoned (ABC Afterschool Special) 11/12/80 (ABC)
BILL KELLARD; The Great Space Coaster 1/6/81 (Synd)
BARBARA WARWICH; A Matter Of Time (ABC Afterschool Special) 2/11/81 (ABC)
DOROTHY WEAVER; Family Of Strangers (ABC Afterschool Special) 9/24/80 (ABC)

MAKE-UP & HAIR DESIGNERS (E-1784)

CHRISTY ANN NEWQUIST, Make-up Designer; A Matter Of Time (ABC Afterschool Special) 2/11/81 (ABC)
STEVE ATHA Make-up & Hair Designer; Sunshine's On The Way (NBC Special Treat) 11/11/80 (NBC)

GRAPHIC & ANIMATION DESIGNERS (E-1785)

GERRI BRIOSO, Graphic Designer; Sesame Street series (PBS)
FRED CRIPPEN, ROY MORITA, ROSEMARY O'CONNOR, ROBERT ZAMBONI, Animation Layout Designers; The Incredible Book Escape (The CBS Library) 6/3/80 (CBS)
LEWIS GIFFORD, PAUL KIM, TOM YOHE, Animation Layout Designers; Drawing Power 10/11/80 (NBC)

ACHIEVEMENT IN RELIGIOUS PROGRAMMING (E-1786)

Emmys(s) to Executive Producer(s) and Producer(s) (Possibility of one Award, more than one Award or no Award).

DIRECTIONS, Sid Darion, Producer (ABC)
INSIGHT, Ellwood E. Kieser, C.S.P., Executive Producer; Mike Rhodes, Producer (Synd)

INDIVIDUAL ACHIEVEMENT IN RELIGIOUS PROGRAMMING

For a single episode of a series or for a special program. (Possibility of one Award, more than one Award or no Award).

PERFORMER (E-1787)

MARTIN SHEEN; Long Road Home (Insight) 11/30/80 (Synd)

CINEMATOGRAPHER (E-1788)

JOSEPH J.H. VADALA; Work And Worship: The Legacy Of St. Benedict 4/27/80 (NBC)

ART DIRECTORS/SET DECORATOR (E-1789)

C. MURAWSKI & DAHL DELU, Art Directors; SCOTT HEINEMAN, Set Decorator; Long Road Home (Insight) 11/30/80 (Synd)

SPECIAL CLASSIFICATION OF OUTSTANDING PROGRAM ACHIEVEMENT (E-1790)

Emmy(s) to Executive Producer(s) and Producer(s) (Possibility of one Award, more than one Award or no Award).

F.Y.I., Yanna Kroyt Brandt, Producer; Mary Ann Donahue, Coordinating Producer (ABC)
GOOD MORNING AMERICA, George Merlis, Executive Producer; Jack Reilly, Susan Winston & Sonya Selby-Wright, Producers; David Horwitz, Senior Producers of News (ABC)

SPECIAL CLASSIFICATION OF OUTSTANDING INDIVIDUAL ACHIEVEMENT

(Possibility of one Award, more than one Award or no Award).

PERFORMERS (E-1791)

DICK CLARK; American Bandstand 2/28/81 (ABC)
HAL LINDEN; F.Y.I. series (ABC)

WRITERS (E-1792)

JUSTIN ANTONOW, HARRY FRIEDMAN, GARY JOHNSON, PHIL KELLARD, STEVE KREINBERG, BRIAN POLLACK, JAY REDACK; The Hollywood Squares series (NBC)
BETTY S. CORNFELD, MARY ANN DONAHUE, ED TIVNAN; F.Y.I series (ABC)
MERRIL MARKOE, RICH HALL, DAVID LETTERMAN, GERARD MULLIGAN, PAUL RALEY, RON RICHARDS; The David Letterman Show 10/23/80 (NBC)

DIRECTORS (E-1793)

MICHAEL R. GARGIULO; F.Y.I series (ABC)
BARRY GLAZER; American Bandstand 2/28/81 (ABC)

PUPPET DESIGN, CONSTRUCTION & COSTUMING (E-1794)

CAROLY WILCOX, CHERYL BLALOCK, EDWARD G. CHRISTIE; Sesame Street series (PBS)

COVERAGE OF SPECIAL EVENTS (E-1795)

Emmy(s) to Executive Producer(s) and Producer(s) (Possibility of one Award, more than one Award or no Award).

CBS TOURNAMENT OF ROSES PARADE, Mike Gargiulo, Executive Producer; Vern Diamond, Producer 1/1/81 (CBS)
MACY'S THANKSGIVING DAY PARADE, Dick Schneider, Producer 11/27/80 (NBC)
THE SEVENTH ANNUAL EMMY AWARDS FOR DAYTIME PROGRAMMING, William Carruthers, Executive Producer; Joel Stein, Producer 6/4/80 (NBC)
92nd TOURNAMENT OF ROSES PARADE, Dick Schneider, Producer 1/1/81 (NBC)

INDIVIDUAL ACHIEVEMENT IN THE COVERAGE OF SPECIAL EVENTS

(Possibility of one Award, more than one Award or no Award).

DIRECTOR (E-1796)

DICK SCHNEIDER, Macy's Thanksgiving Day Parade 11/27/80 (NBC)

WRITER (E-1797)

BARRY E. DOWNES, Macy's Thanksgiving Day Parade 11/27/80 (NBC)

TECHNICAL DIRECTION AND/OR ELECTRONIC CAMERA (E-1798)

TERRY ROHNKE, Technical Director; Macy's Thanksgiving Day Parade 11/27/80 (NBC)
TERRY ROHNKE, Technical Director; PETER BASIL, AL CAMOIN, TOM DEZENDORF, BARRY FRISCHER, JOHN PINTO, BRYAN RUSSO, Electronic Camera; The Seventh Annual Emmy Awards For Daytime Programming 6/4/80 (NBC)

LIGHTING DIRECTOR (E-1799)

ROBERT WARREN DAVIS; The Seventh Annual Emmy Awards For Daytime Programming 6/4/80 (NBC)

MUSIC DIRECTOR (E-1800)

MILTON DELUGG; Macy's Thanksgiving Day Parade 11/27/80 (NBC)

INDIVIDUAL ACHIEVEMENT IN ANY AREA OF CREATIVE TECHNICAL CRAFTS

(Possibility of one Award, more than one Award or no Award).

TECHNICAL DIRECTOR/ELECTRONIC CAMERA (E-1801)

ROBERT HOFFMAN, Tech. Director; ANTHONY GAMBINO, LAWRENCE HAMMOND, Electronic Camera; Remote: Savannah (All My Children) 2/23-24/81 (ABC)

ART DIRECTOR (E-1802)

KATHLEEN ANKERS; The David Letterman Show 10/23/80 (NBC)

LIGHTING DIRECTOR (E-1803)

TONY DiGIROLAMO (Location); Remote: Anita Bryant Interview (Donahue) 3/24/80 (Synd)

COSTUME DESIGNER (E-1804)

DAYTON ANDERSON; The Mike Douglas Show 2/9/81 (Synd)

GRAPHIC & ANIMATION DESIGNERS (E-1805)

ELINOR BUNIN, Graphic Designer, Title Sequence; F.Y.I (Premier: 3/2/81) (ABC)
MICHAEL GASS, Graphic Designer; Good Morning America series (ABC)
BOB POOK, BILL SHORTRIDGE, JR., Graphic Designers; The David Letterman Show 10/23/80 (NBC)
DONALD SPAGNOLIA, Graphic Designer, Opening Logo; THOMAS BURTON, CLAUDIA ZEITLIN BURTON, Animation Designers, Opening; The John Davidson Show 6/30/80 (Synd)

INTERNATIONAL AWARDS

DOCUMENTARY (E-1806)

CHARTERS POUR L'ENFER (CHARTERS TO HELL), Societe Nationale de Television Francaise-1, France
THE CLIVE JAMES PARIS FASHION SHOW, London Weekend Television Ltd., United Kingdom
VICTIMS OF VIOLENCE IN NORTHERN IRELAND, Radio Telefis Eireann, Ireland

DRAMA (E-1807)

THE GOOD SOLDIER, Granada Television Ltd., United Kingdom
THE REASON OF THINGS, Yorkshire Television Ltd., United Kingdom
A TOWN LIKE ALICE, Mariner Films & Channel 7, Australia

PERFORMING ARTS (E-1808)

HOMENAJE A LA PINTURA, Radiotelevision Espanola, Spain
RIGHT ROYAL COMPANY, British Broadcasting Corporation, United Kingdom
SWEENEY TODD: SCENES FROM THE MAKING OF A MUSICAL, London Weekend Television Ltd., United Kingdom

POPULAR ARTS (E-1809)

END OF PART I, London Weekend Television Ltd., United Kingdom
PETER COOK & CO., London Weekend Television Ltd., United Kingdom
VINICIUS PARA CRIANCAS OR ARCA DE NOE (NOAH'S ARK), Teve Globo, Ltda., Brazil

INTERNATIONAL DIRECTORATE AWARD (E-1810)

SIR HUW WELDON

FOUNDERS AWARD (E-1811)

ROONE ARLEDGE

LIVE SPORTS SPECIAL (E-1812)

Emmy(s) to Executive Producer(s) and Producer(s) and Director(s)

1980 AMERICAN & NATIONAL LEAGUE CHAMPIONSHIP SERIES, Roone Arledge, Executive Producer. National League--Dennis Lewin, Producer; Joe Aceti, Director. American League--Chuck Howard, Producer; Chet Forte, Director (ABC)
1981 KENTUCKY DERBY, Roone Arledge, Executive Producer; Chuck Howard, Producer; Chet Forte, Director (ABC)
1981 SUGAR BOWL, Roone Arledge, Executive Producer; Chuck Howard, Producer; Andy Sidaris, Director (ABC)

SUPER BOWL XV, Don Ohlmeyer, Executive Producer; Ted Nathanson, Coordinating Producer; Larry Cirillo & George Finkel, Producers; Ted Nathanson, Director; Ken Fouts, Replay Director (NBC)
1980 WORLD SERIES, Don Ohlmeyer, Executive Producer; Michael Weisman, Coordinating Producer; George Finkel & Michael Weisman, Producers; Harry Coyle & Ken Fouts, Directors (NBC)

LIVE SPORTS SERIES (E-1813)
Emmy(s) to Executive Producer(s) and Producer(s) and Director(s)
1980-1981 COLLEGE BASKETBALL, Don Ohlmeyer, Executive Producer; George Finke, Coordinating Producer; Kenneth Edmundson, George Finkel, David Stern & Michael Weisman, Producers; Harry Coyle, Ken Fouts, John Gonzalez & Andy Rosenberg, Directors (NBC)
1980-1981 NFL FOOTBALL, Don Ohlmeyer, Executive Producer; Ted Nathanson, Coordinating Producer; Larry Cirillo, Kenneth Edmundson, Terry Ewert, George Finkel, J Michael Hadley, Roy Hammerman, Don McGuire, Peter M Rolfe, David Stern & Michael Weisman, Producers; Richard Cline, Harry Coyle, Jim Cross, Ken Fouts, John Gonzalez, James Marcione, Ted Nathanson, Lou Rainone, Andy Rosenberg & Barry Stoddard, Directors (NBC)
1980-81 NFL MONDAY NIGHT FOOTBALL, Roone Arledge, Executive Producer, Bob Goodrich, Producer; Chet Forte, Director (ABC)
PGA TOUR ON CBS, Frank Chirkinian, Executive Producer; Bob Bailey & Frank Chirkinian, Directors (CBS)
PRO BOWLERS TOUR, Roone Arledge, Executive Producer; Curt Gowdy, Jr & Peter Englehart, Producers; Larry Cavolina, John DeLisa & Ralph Abraham, Directors (ABC)

EDITED SPORTS SPECIAL (E-1814)
Emmy(s) to Executive Producer(s) and Producer(s) and Director(s)
ABC'S WIDE WORLD OF SPORTS 20TH ANNIVERSARY SHOW, Roone Arledge, Executive Producer; Dennis Lewin & Doug Wilson, Producers; Larry Kamm, Director (ABC)
1981 INDIANAPOLIS 500, Roone Arledge, Executive Producer; Dennis Lewin, Coordinating Producer; Chuck Howard & Bob Goodrich, Producers; Chet Forte & Roger Goodman, Directors (ABC)
NFL '80: SUPER SUNDAY COUNTDOWN, Don Ohlmeyer, Executive Producer; David Stern, Producer; Les Dennis & David Neal, Feature Producers; Bob Levy, Director (NBC)
SUGAR RAY LEONARD VS ROBERTO DURAN II, Roone Arledge, Executive Producer; Bob Goodrich, Producer; Chet Forte, Director (ABC)
WIMBLEDON '81, Don Ohlmeyer, Executive Producer; Geoff Mason & Ted Nathanson, Producers; Terry Ewert, Tape Producer; Ted Nathanson, Director; Bob Levy, Tape Director (NBC)

EDITED SPORTS SERIES (E-1815)
Emmy(s) to Executive Producer(s) and Producer(s) and Director(s)
ABC'S WIDE WORLD OF SPORTS, Roone Arledge, Executive Producer; Dennis Lewin, Coordinating Producer; Bob Goodrich, Eleanor Riger, Doug Wilson, Mike Pearl, Brice Weisman, Ralph Abraham, Ken Wolfe, Jeff Ruhe, Chuck Howard & Carol Lehti Producers; Larry Kamm, Chet Forte, Roger Goodman, Craig Janoff, Andy Sidaris, Jim Jennett, Joe Aceti & Lou Volpicelli, Directors (ABC)
AMERICAN SPORTSMAN, Roone Arledge, Executive Producer; John Wilcox, Series Producer; Chris Carmody, Coordinating Producer; Robert Nixon & Curt Gowdy, Producers; John Wilcox & Bob Nixon, Directors (ABC)
CBS SPORTS SATURDAY/SUNDAY, Terry O'Neil, Executive Producer; Jean Harper, Coordinating Producer; John Faratzis, David Dinkins, Jr, Ed Goren, David Winner, Dan Forer, Dan Lauck, George Veras, Sherman Eagan, Perry Smith, Chuck Milton, Ted Shaker & Mike Burks, Producers; Richard Drake, Larry Cavolina, John McDonough, Andy Kindle, Bob Dunphy, Peter Bleckner & Bob Fishman, Directors (CBS)
NBC SPORTSWORLD, Don Ohlmeyer, Executive Producer; Linda Jonsson, Coordinating Producer; Hilary Cosell, Terry Ewert, Matthew McCarthy, Peter M Rolfe, Ginny Seipt, Michael Weisman, Producers; Bob Levy, Coordinating Director; Richard Cline, Harry Coyle, Ken Fouts, John Gonzalez & Ted Nathanson, Directors (NBC)

NFL '80, Don Ohlmeyer, Executive Producer; David Stern, Producer; Les Dennis, David Israel & David Neal, Feature Producers; Bob Levy, Director (NBC)

SPORTS PERSONALTY - HOST (Play by Play) (E-1816)
Dick Enberg (NBC)
Keith Jackson (ABC)
Jim McKay (ABC)
Al Michaels (ABC)
Vin Scully (CBS)

SPORTS PERSONALITY - ANALYST (Commentary) (E-1817)
Dick Button (ABC)
Al McGuire (NBC)
Don Meredith (ABC)
Merlin Olsen (NBC)
Jack Whitaker (CBS)

OUTSTANDING INDIVIDUAL ACHIEVEMENT IN SPORTS PROGRAMMING:
This is an "AREA" where there is a possiblilty of one Award, more than one Award or no Award

CINEMATOGRAPHY (E-1818)
EDGAR BOYLES, DAVID CONLEY, JON HAMMOND, PETER HENNING, MIKE HOOVER, D'ARCY MARSH, DAN MERKLE, STANTON WATERMAN, STEVE PETROPOULOS & ROGER BROWN, American Sportsman; Apr. 5, 1981 (ABC)
STEVE SABOL, ERNIE ERNST, HOWARD NEEF, PHIL TUCKETT, BOB SMITH, BOB ANGELO, DONNIE MARX, JAY GERBER, ART SPIELLER, JACK NEWMAN, HANK McELWEE, The Super Seventies; Aug. 26, 1980 (NBC)

ASSOCIATE DIRECTION/VIDEOTAPE EDITING (E-1819)
ROB BEINER, DICK BUFFINTON, JEFF COHAN, KATHY COOK, VINCE DEDARIO, JOHN DELISA, JOEL FELD, BEN HARVEY, BOB HERSH, JACK GRAHAM, BOB LANNING, PETER LASSER, CAROL LEHTI, BRIAN McCULLOUGH, DENNIS MAZZOCCO, BOB ROSBURG, NORM SAMET, NED SIMON, TONI SLOTKIN, LARRY CAVOLINA, BOB DEKAS, Associate Directors; ABC'S Wide World of Sports; Jul. 19, 1980 (ABC)
TONY TOCCI, KEN BROWNE & GARY BRADLEY, Videotape Editors; The Baseball Bunch; May 1, 1981 (SYN)
MATTHEW McCARTHY, Associate Director; MARK KANKELOFF, RICHARD LEIBLE, JIM McQUEEN & JEFF U'REN, Videotape Editors; NBC Sportsworld; Jul. 20, 1981 (NBC)
LOU RENDE, RON ACKERMAN, CHARLES GARDNER, RON FESZCHUR, MARTIN BELL, WINSTON SADOO, Videotape Editors; NFL Football - Sunday Night; Oct. 26, 1980 (ABC)
CATHY BARRETO, Associate Director; JOEL ARONOWITZ, JACK BLACK, BOB COFFEY, JOE D'ORNELLAS, STANLEY FAER, BOB HALPER, BETH HERMELIN, HOWARD MILLER, GADY REINHOLD, RONI SCHERMAN, STEVE DELLAPIETRA & BARRY HICKS, Associate Directors - Highlights and Coords; GEORGE PALMISANO & JOHN WELLS, Videotape Supervisors; JIM ALKINS, CURTIS CAMPBELL, BOB CLARK, TED DEMERS, JOE DRAKE, TOM DURKIN, BOB FOSTER, HARVE GILMAN, AL GOLLY, SIG GORDON, ELLIOTT GREENBLATT, BOB HICKSON, FRANK HODNETT, GEORGE JOANITIS, ANDY KLEIN, GARY KOZAK, ED KNUDHOLDT, PETE LACORTE, MARVIN LEE, GEORGE MAGEE, MARIO MARINO, WALTER MATWICHUK, JOHN MAYER, HENRY MENUSAN, JESSE MICHNICK, JEFF RINGEL, CHARLOTTE ROBINSON, ALLAN SEGAL, BILL VANDENORT, IRV VILLAFANA, HANK WOLF & BILL ZIZZA, Videotape Editors; NFL Today; Sep. 7, 1980 (CBS)
TOM WIGHT, DICK VELASCO, HECTOR KICELIAN, BRUCE A GIARRAFFA & MERRIT ROESSER, Videotape Editors; Sugar Bowl; Jan. 1,

1981 (ABC)
MIKE KOSTEL, MARIO BUCICH, KEN McILWAINE & TONY TOCCI, Videotape Editors; This Week in Baseball; Sep. 11, 1980 (SYN)

FILM EDITING (E-1820)

ANGELO BERNARDUCCI, VINCENT REDA, RICHARD ROSSI, ANTHONY SCANDIFFIO, NORMAN SMITH, CHRIS RIGER, TED WINTERBURN & ANTHONY ZACCARO, Film Editors; The American Sportsman; Apr. 5, 1981 (ABC)
MIKE ADAMS, BOB RYAN, PHIL TUCKETT, Film Editors; NFL Symfunny; Jan. 17, 1981 (SYN)

AUDIO (E-1821)

JACK NEWMAN, DAVE PAUL, DON PARAVATI & BILL GRAY, Location Sound Recordists; Saviors, Saints and Sinners; Jan. 25, 1981 (NBC)

TECHNICAL DIRECTION/ELECTRONIC CAMERAWORK (E-1822)

SANDY BELL, ROBERT BROWN, Technical Directors; EDWARD AMBROSINI, ROBERT SQUITTIERI, RONALD RESCH, Senior Video Operators; JAMES MURPHY, NEIL MC CAFFREY, HERMAN LANG, FRANK MC SPEDON, THOMAS MC CARTHY, BARRY DRAGO, JOSEPH SOKOTA, STEPHEN GORSUCH, GEORGE ROTHWEILER, GEORGE NAEDER, DAVID GRAHAM, JEFFREY POLLACK, JAMES MC CARTHY, HANS SINGER, SIGMUND MEYERS, Electronic Camerapersons; 1981 Daytona 500 (CBS)
RAY SIGELSKI, KEITH KNIEP, Technical Directors; CARROLL BOLSTAD, Senior Video Operator; JIM BRAGG, PHIL CANTRELL, JIM HERRING, GEORGE LOOMIS, HUGH MORELLI, JAY O'NEIL, MIKE STRAMISKY, DAN SUTTON, Electronic Camerapersons; John Denver Pro Celebrity Ski Tournament (NBC Sportsworld)
CHARLES D'ONOFRIO, SANDY BELL, Technical Directors; ROBERT HANFORD, EDWARD AMBROSINI, ROBERT PIERENGER, FRANK FLORIO, Video Supervisors; ROBERT SQUITTIERI, LOUIS LEDGER, DANIEL CHAN, WILLIAM BERRIDGE, THOMAS DELILLA, Video Operators; RICK BLANE, GEORGE KLIMCSAK, GEORGE NAEDER, JAMES MC CARTHY, GEORGE ROTHWEILER, AL LORETO, HERMAN LANG, HANS SINGER, NICHOLAS LAURIA, JAMES MURPHY, HARRY HAIGOOD, MICHAEL ENGLISH, JOHN LINCOLN, FRANK MC SPEDON, STAN GOULD, DENNIS MC BRIDE, JOSEPH SOKOTA, BARRY DRAGO, NEIL MC CAFFREY, DAVID GRAHAM, WALTER SOUCY, ROBERT WELSH, DAVID FINCH, R. KEARNY, J. SIDIO, W. HAIGOOD, Electronic Camerapersons; The 1981 Masters Golf Tournament (CBS)
H CAL SHADWELL & BRUCE SHAPIRO, Technical Supervisors; WILLIAM TOBEY, Technical Director; LENNY STUCKER, Facilities Technical Director; ARNOLD REIF, Director, Sports Technical Operations; ROBERT McKEARNIN, Manager, Sports Technical Operation; LENNY BASILE, MARIO CIARLO, JAMES J CULLEY, BARRY JON FRISCHER, LOU GERARD, STEVE GONZALEZ, DAVID A HAGEN, JIM JOHNSON, BUDDY JOSEPH, DON MULVANEY & BRYAN RUSSO, Electronic Camerapersons; 1981 NCAA College Basketball Championship; Mar. 30, 1981 (NBC)
JOHN ALLEN, Technical Director; KEN AMOW, Senior Video Operator; FRANK MELCHIORRE, JOE PULEO, EVAN BAKER, ED PAYNE, SAL FOLINO, MIKE FREEDMAN, WARREN CRESS & JOHN DUKEWICH, Electronic Camerapersons; NCAA Football; Nov. 14, 1980 (ABC)
ROBERT BROWN & E KUSCHNER, Technical Directors; ROBERT HANFORD & FRANK FLORIO, Senior Video Operators; RICK BLANE, STAN GOULD, STEPHEN GORSUCH, JOHN LINCOLN, GEORGE KLIMSCAK, ROBERT JAMIESON, DAVID GRAHAM, JAMES MURPHY, FRANK McSPEDON, JEFFREY POLLACK, JOSEPH VINCENS & DAVID FINCH, Electronic Camerapersons; NFC Championship Game; Jan. 11, 1981 (CBS)
JOE SCHIAVO, Technical Director; JOSEPH LEE, Senior Video Operator; DREW DEROSA, JIM HENEGHAN, ANDREW ARMENTANI, GARY DONATELLI, JACK DORFMAN, JESSE KOHN, JACK SAVOY, TOM O'CONNELL, STEVE NIKIFOR, JOE COTUGNO & ROY HUTCHINGS, Electronic Camerapersons; NFL Football - Sunday Night; Oct. 26, 1980 (ABC)
GILBERT A MILLER, Technical Director; RONALD RESCH & EMANUEL KAUFMAN, Senior Video Operators; JOHN CURTIN, THOMAS McCARTHY, JAMES McCARTHY, NEIL McCAFFREY, STEPHEN GOR-

SUCH & MICHAEL ENGLISH, Electronic Camerapersons; NFL Today; Sep. 7, 1980 (CBS)
JOHN ALLEN, Technical Director; KEN AMOW, Senior Video Operator; JOHN MORREALE, JOHN DUKEWICH, EVAN BAKER, MIKE FREEDMAN, SAL FOLINO, FRANK MELCHIORE & WARREN CRESS, Electronic Camerapersons; Sugar Bowl; Jan. 1, 1981 (ABC)
RICK CORTRIGHT, Technical Supervisor; HORACE RUIZ, Technical Director; WILLIAM TOBEY, Facilities Technical Director; ARNOLD REIF, Director, Sports Technical Operations; ROBERT McKEARNIN, Manager, Sports Technical Operations; JIM MARSHALL, Senior Video Operator; LENNY BASILE, JIM BRAGG, PHILLIP E CANTRELL, MARIO CIARLO, GEORGE CILIBERTO, LOU GERARD, STEVE GONZALEZ, DAVID A HAGEN, RODGER G HARBAUGH, KEN HARVEY, JIM JOHNSON, BUDDY JOSEPH, CORY LIEBLE, GEORGE LOOMIS, R V RATLIFF, ALBERT RICE, BRYAN RUSSO, BRIAN D. SHERIFFE, MICHAEL C STRAMISKY, VICTORIA WALKER, Electronic Camerapersons; Super Bowl XV; Jan 25, 1981 (NBC)
RICK CORTRIGHT, KEITH SCAMMAHORN, H CAL SHADWELL, & ERNEST A THIEL, JR, Technical Supervisors; HORACE RUIZ, Technical Director; BUTCH BERQUIST & WILLIAM TOBEY, Facilities Technical Director; LENNY BASILE, JIM BRAGG, AL CAMOIN, PHILLIP E CANTRELL, MARIO CIARLO, GEORGE CILIBERTO, LOUIS CYWINSKI, LOU GERARD, BILL GOETZ, DAVID A HAGEN, RODGER G HARBAUGH, KEN HARVEY, JIM JOHNSON, BUDDY JOSEPH, CORY LIEBLE, GEORGE LOOMIS, DON MULVANEY, ART PARKER, R V RATLIFF, ALBERT RICE, BRYAN RUSSO, BRIAN D SHERIFFE, MICHAEL C STRAMISKY & DAN SUTTON, Electronic Camerapersons; 1980-1981 World Series; Oct 14-21, 1980 (NBC)

PRIMARY GRAPHIC DESIGNERS (E-1823)

JAMES W GRAU, Graphic Designer, NBA on CBS (Show Opening); Nov 27, 1980 (CBS)
MATTHEW McCARTHY, Graphic Designer, NBC Sports Presents: The Summer Season; Jul 25, 1980 (NBC)
ROGER GOODMAN, Graphic Designer, Prudential College Scoreboard Show; Sep 6, 1980 (ABC)
JAMES W GRAU, Graphic Designer, U S Open (Show Opening); Aug 8, 1980 (CBS)

WRITING (E-1824)

MARK DURAND, MIKE TOLLIN & GARY COHEN, writers
The Baseball Bunch; May 1, 1981 (SYN)
MARK DURAND, WARNER FUSSELLE, HAL FISCHER, writers
This Week In Baseball; Aug 1, 1980 (SYN)

SPECIAL CLASSIFICATION OF OUTSTANDING PROGRAM AND INDIVIDUAL ACHIEVEMENT
Emmy(s) to Producer(s) for PROGRAM: Emmys to Individuals for INDIVIDUAL ACHIEVEMENT

PROGRAM (E-1825)

THE BASEBALL BUNCH, Larry Parker, Executive Producer; Jody Shapiro, Producer; May 1, 1981 (SYN)
THE ARLBERG KANDAHAR DOWNHILL FROM ST ANTON, (NBC Sportsworld) Don Ohlmeyer, Executive Producer, Linda Jonsson, Coordinating Producer, Terry Ewert & Geoff Mason, Producers; Bob Levy, Coordinating Director; Feb 1, 1981 (NBC)

INDIVIDUAL (E-1826)

AMY SACKS, Producer ABC Sports On-Air Promotions; ABC
DON OHLMEYER, TED NATHANSON, Producers , LOUMA CAMERA CRANE, Friday Night Fights; (NBC)
DENNIS LEWIN, Producer, GONDOLA CAMERA (OVER SECOND BASE) 1980 National League Championship Series; (ABC)
BOB LEVY, Coordinating Director, NBC Sportsworld; (NBC)
STEVE GONZALES, Electronic Camera, Super Bowl XV; (NBC)
CHUCK HOWARD, Producer, ELECTRONIC CAMERA LOGISTICS; U.S. Open Golf Championship (ABC)

NEWS AND DOCUMENTARIES

PROGRAMS AND PROGRAM SEGMENTS (E-1827)
Emmy(s) to Producer(s) and Correspondent(s)

INSIDE AWACS, (Segment: NBC News, 'Magazine with David Brinkley), Sid Feders, Producer; Garrick Utley, Correspondent (NBC)

ITALIAN EARTHQUAKE, (5-part Segment: ABC World News Tonight), Dean Johnsos, Producer; Gregg Dobbs & Bill Blakemore, Correspondents (ABC)

MOMENT OF CRISIS-HYATT DISASTER, (Segment: ABC News, '20/20'), Stanhope Gould & Peter W Kunhardt, Producers; Tom Jarriel, Correspondent (ABC)

CBS REPORTS: MURDER TEENAGE STYLE, Irina Posner, Producer; Ed Bradley, Correspondent (CBS)

SOLDIERS OF THE TWILIGHT, (ABC News, 'Closeup'), Malcolm Clarke, Producer; Marshall Frady, Correspondent (ABC)

DEATH IN THE FAST LANE, (Segment: ABC News, '20/20'), Danny Schechter, Producer; Catherine Mackin, Correspondent (ABC)

GHOST TOWN, (Segment: ABC News, '20/20'), Pete Simmons & Ellen Rossen, Producers; John Laurence, Correspondent (ABC)

'GRAIN' A FEW MINUTES WITH ANDY ROONEY, (Segment: CBS News, '60 Minutes'); Andrew A Rooney, Producer/Reporter (CBS)

LIBYA, (2-part Special Assignment Segment: ABC World News Tonight); Liz Colton & Denise Schreiner, Producers; Lou Cioffi, Correspondent (ABC)

THE WAR ON OPIUM, (Segment: ABC News, 'Nightline'); Tom Yellin, Producer; Mark Litke, Correspondent (ABC)

CBS REPORTS: THE DEFENSE OF THE UNITED STATES: NUCLEAR BATTLEFIELD; Judy Crichton, Producer; Harry Reasoner, Correspondent (CBS)

CBS REPORTS: THE DEFENSE OF THE UNITED STATES: THE WAR MACHINE; Craig Leake, Producer; Richard Threlkeld, Correspondent (CBS)

THE HUNTER AND THE HUNTED, Thomas F Madigan, Executive Producer; John Oakley & Lisa Cantini-Sequin, Bill Bemister, Producers; Bill Bemister, Correspondent (PBS)

NEAR ARMAGEDDON: THE SPREAD OF NUCLEAR WEAPONS IN THE MIDDLE EAST, (ABC News, 'Closeup'); Christopher Isham, Producer; Marshall Frady & William Sherman, Correspondents (ABC)

WHY AMERICA BURNS, (Nova); Brian Kaufman, Producer (PBS)

FORMULA FOR DISASTER, (Segment: ABC News, '20/20'); John Fager, Producer; Geraldo Rivera, Correspondent (ABC)

KILLER WHEELS, (Segment: CBS News, '60 Minutes'), Allan Maraynes, Producer; Mike Wallace, Correspondent (CBS)

ROCKETS FOR SALE, (Segment: NBC News, 'Magazine with David Brinkley'); Tony Van Witsen, Producer; Garrick Utley, Correspondent (NBC)

TEEN MODELS, (Segment: NBC News, 'Magazine with David Brinkley'); Beth Polson, Producer; Jack Perkins, Correspondent (NBC)

UNNECESSARY SURGERY, (Segment: ABC News, '20/20'); Peter Lance & Janice Tomlin, Producers; Peter Lance, Correspondent (ABC)

CLARK CLIFFORD ON PRESIDENTS AND POWER (Part 1), (Bill Moyers' Journal); Douglas Lutz, Producer; Bill Moyers, Interviewer (PBS)

GEORGE STEINER ON LITERATURE, LANGUAGE & CULTURE (Bill Moyers' Journal); Douglas Lutz, Producer; Bill Moyers, Interviewer (PBS)

THE LAST MAFIOSO (JIMMY FRATIANNO), (Segment: CBS News, '60 Minutes'); Marion F Goldin, Producer; Mike Wallace, Interviewer (CBS)

WANTED (TERPIL/KORKALA INTERVIEW), (Segment: CBS News, '60 Minutes'); Barry Lando, Producer; Mike Wallace, Interviewer (CBS)

CLOSE HARMONY; Nigel Noble, Producer (PBS)

THE COLONEL COMES TO JAPAN, (Enterprise); John Nathan, Producer (PBS)

LOUIS IS 13 (Segment: ABC News, 'Sunday Morning'); Lee Reichenthal, Producer; Morton Dean, Correspondent (CBS)

MOMENT OF CRISIS:BERLIN WALL, (Segment: ABC News, '20/20'); Richard O'Regan & Rolfe Tessem, Producers; Tom Jarriel, Correspondent (ABC)

MOMENT OF CRISIS: VIETNAM WITHDRAWAL, (Segment: ABC News, '20/20'); Peter W Kunhardt, Producer; Tom Jarriel, Correspondent (ABC)

RAY CHARLES, (Segment: ABC News, '20/20'); Betsy Osha, Producer; Bob Brown, Correspondent (ABC)

ST. PAUL'S BELLS, (Segment: ABC World News Tonight); Phil Bergman, Producer; Hughes Rudd, Correspondent (ABC)

NBC Nightly News, Paul Greenberg, Executive Producer; Bill Wheatley, Senior Producer; Lloyd Siegel (Domestic), Harry Griggs (Foreign), Bob McFarland (Washington), Joan Carrigan (Germany), Producers; Jim Bitterman, John Hart, Judy Woodruff, Tom Pettit, John Palmer, Bob Jamieson, Linda Ellerbee, Correspondents (NBC) (1/20/81)

NBC Nightly News; Paul Greenberg, Executive Producer; Bill Wheatley, Senior Producer; Lloyd Siegel (Domestic), Harry Griggs (Foreign), Bob McFarland (Washington), Producers; John Chancellor & Roger Mudd, Anchors; Tom Pettit, John Palmer, John Dancy, Bob Jamieson, Robert Hager, John Cochran, Correspondents (NBC) (1/27/81)

EL SALVADOR FIREFIGHT, (Segment: Today Show); Dave Riggs, Producer; Jim Cimmins, Correspondent (NBC)

THE OTHER EGYPT, (Segment: NBC News, 'Magazine'); Sid Feders, Bill Theodore, Ron Bonn, Producers; Garrick Utley, Correspondent (NBC)

RELUCTANT HERO, (Segment: NBC News, 'Magazine with David Brinkley'), Sid Feders, Producer; Doug Kiker, Correspondent (NBC)

SADAT, (Segment: CBS Evening News with Dan Rather), Sanford Socolow, Mark Harrington, David Buksbaum, Linda Mason, Lane Venardos, Producers; Dan Rather, Correspondent (CBS)

THE SHATTERED BADGE, (ABC News, 'Closeup'), Paul Altmeyer, Producer/Correspondent (ABC)

ANATOMY OF A MANHUNT, (Segment: CBS News, 'Sunday Morning'), James Houtrides, Producer; Ed Rabel, Correspondent (CBS)

ART/SCIENCE, (Segment: Walter Cronkite's Universe), Michele Dumont, Producer; Charles Osgood, Correspondent (CBS)

BOSTON IRISH-IRA, (Segment: ABC News, 'Nightline'), Robert Jordan, Producer; Mike Barnicle, Correspondent (ABC)

THE CHEAPEST WAY TO GO, (Segment: ABC News, '20/20'), Richard R. Clark, Producer; John Stossel, Correspondent (ABC)

CRIME/ELDERLY, (Segment: ABC News, 'Nightline'), Herb Holmes, Producer; Bob Greene, Correspondent (ABC)

HUNGER IN AFRICA, (Segment: CBS Evening News with Dan Rather), Harry Radliffe, Producer; Tom Fenton, Correspondent (CBS)

INSANITY AND MURDER, (3-part Segment: NBC Nightly News) Chuck Collins, Producer; James Polk, Correspondent (NBC)

MAGIC BULLETS, (Segment: Walter Cronkite's Universe), Elena Mannes, Producer; Jacqueline Adams, Correspondent (CBS)

NORTHERN IRELAND'S HISTORY, (Segment: CBS Evening News with Morton Dean), Joan Richman, Executive Producer; Bill Higley, Producer; John Blackstone, Correspondent (CBS)

RESCUING THE HOSTAGES: THE UNTRIED MISSION, (2-part: NBC Nightly News Special Segment), Ellen McKeefe, Producer; George Lewis, Mike Snyder (KXAS), Correspondents (NBC)

THE RITES OF PASSAGE, (Segment: ABC News, '20/20'), Jeff Diamond, Producer; Bob Brown, Correspondent (ABC)

TOUGH GUYS/TOUGH TIMES, (Segment: CBS Evening News with Dan Rather), Bob McNamara, Producer/Correspondent (CBS)

UNEMPLOYMENT IN BRITAIN, (Segment: NBC Nightly News), Dina Modianot, Producer; John Hart, Correspondent (NBC)

THE GENE MERCHANTS, (ABC News, 'Closeup'), Stephen Fleischman, Producer; Marshall Frady & William Sherman, Correspondents (ABC)

SIRHAN-SIRHAN (2-part Segment: ABC News, 'Nightline'), David Bohrman, Bob Jordan, Susan Mercandetti, Producers; Ted Koppel, Interviewer (ABC)

EISENSTAEDT: GERMANY, Gordon Bowman, Producer (PBS)

CHINESE ISLAND, (Segment: CBS Evening News with Dan Rather), Barry Peterson, Producer/Correspondent (CBS)

THE HOLOCAUST, (Segment: ABC News, 'Nightline'), Pamela L. Kahn, Producer (ABC)

A PLACE TO GO, (Segment: CBS News, '60 Minutes'), Joel Bernstein, Producer; Dan Rather, Correspondent (CBS)

ROMARE BEARDEN, (Segment: CBS News, 'Sunday Morning') Kathy Sulkes, Producer; David Culhane, Correspondent (CBS)

SUNSHINE FOUNDATIONS, (Segment: Today Show), Bert Medley, Producer; Bob Dotson, Correspondent (NBC)

A TIME OF MAGIC, (Segment: CBS News, 'Sunday Morning'), Philip Garvin, Producer; David Culhane, Correspondent (CBS)

INDIVIDUALS

WRITERS (E-1828)

Emmy(s) to Individual(s)

PHILIP BUTON, JR. & LARRY L. KING, CBS Reports: The Best Little Statehouse in Texas (CBS)

WALTER PINCUS, ANDREW LACK, HOWARD STRINGER & BOB SCHIEFFER, CBS Reports: The Defense of the United States: Ground Zero (CBS)

JUDY CRICHTON, HOWARD STRINGER & LESLIE COCKBURN, CBS Reports: The Defense of the United States: Nuclear Battlefield (CBS)

JUDY TOWERS REEMTSMA & MARLENE SANDERS, CBS Reports: Nurse, Where Are You? (CBS)

PERRY WOLFF, Inside Hollywood: The Movie Business (A CBS News Special) (CBS)

PIERRE SALINGER, (Narrative), GEORGE ORICK, (Studio & Background Material), America Held Hostage: The Secret Negotiations (ABC)

LLOYD DOBYNS, DAROLD MURRAY & PAT TRESE, An American Adventure: The Rocket Pilots (NBC)

MAURICE MURAD, CBS Reports: The Defense of the United States: A Call to Arms (CBS)

ANDREW LACK, CBS Reports: The Defense of the United States: The Russians (CBS)

CRAIG LEAKE & RICHARD THRELKELD, CBS Reports: The Defense of the United States: The War Machine (CBS)

IRINA POSNER & ED BRADLEY, CBS Reports: Murder Teenage Style (CBS)

HELEN WHITNEY, The Monastery (ABC News) (ABC)

LINDSAY MILLER, News in Review (CBS)

DIRECTORS (E-1829)

CRAIG LEAKE, CBS Reports: The Defense of the United States: The War Machine (CBS)

CHARLES HEINZ, Four Presidents, (Segment: ABC World News Tonight) (ABC)

HELEN WHITNEY, The Monastery, (ABC News, 'Closeup') (ABC)

TECHNICAL DIRECTION/ELECTRONIC CAMERA (E-1830)

RICHARD JEFFREYS, Electronic Camera, The Assassination of Anwar Sadat, (Segment: CBS Evening News with Dan Rather) (CBS)

TOM WOODS, Electronic Camera, Inside Afghanistan, (Segment: NBC News, 'Magazine with David Brinkley') (NBC)

RUPEN VOSGIMORUKIAN & BARRY FOX, Electronic Camera, Italian Earthquake, (5 part segment), (ABC World News Tonight) (ABC)

STEPHEN N. STANFORD, Electronic Camera, Monarch Butterflies, (Segment: ABC News, '20/20') (ABC)

SHELDON FIELMAN, Electronic Camera, President Reagan Shooting, (NBC News Special Report) (NBC)

DON BASIL, RICHARD KUHNE, JOHN CORDONE, JOHN LANDI, ELLIOT BUTLER, JACK CLARK, SIDNEY DOBISH, KEN SANBORN, BOB FREEMAN, RUPEN VOSGIMORUKIAN, TONY HIRASHIKI, RON HEADFORD & FABRICE MOUSSUS, Electronic Camera, America Held Hostage: The Secret Negotiations, (ABC News Special) (ABC)

ROLFE TESSEM, Electronic Camera, Carter's Final Hours, (Segment: ABC News, 'Nightline') (ABC)

JOHN J. LANDI, (Location & Game), LES SOLIN, GORDON HOOVER & SCOTT LEVINE, (Game), Electronic Camera, If You Were the President, (ABC News, '20/20') (ABC)

HENRY BROWN, Electronic Camera, President Reagan Assassination Attempt, (Segment: ABC World News Tonight) (ABC)

FABRICE MOUSSUS, Electronic Camera, Sadat Assassination, (ABC News Special Events) (ABC)

CINEMATOGRAPHY (E-1831)

BILLY WAGNER, JAN MORGAN, JOHN BOULTER & JOHN PETERS, Cinematographers, CBS Reports: The Defense of the United States: Nuclear Battlefield (CBS)

ASSOCIATE DIRECTION AND/OR VIDEOTAPE EDITING (E-1832)

NEIL PHILPSON, Senior Associate Director, (Post Production); JERRY CHERNAK, Associate Director (Post Production); ED BUDA & THOMAS R. GUBAR, Senior Videotape Editors; SAM HADLEY, ROBERT BRANDT, ALAN CAMPBELL, HENRIETTE HUEHNE, DAVID HARTEN, ROBERT KERR, VICKI PAPAZIAN, DAVE RUMMEL, DONNA ROWLINSON, Videotape Editors; HARVEY BEAL, EILEEN CLANCY, JOHN CROAK, DEAN IRWIN, CATHERINE ISABELLA, CONRAD KRAUS, MIKE MAZELLA, TOM MILLER, PETER MURPHY, ERSKIN ROBERTS, MARIO SCHENCMAN, MIKE SIEGEL, BARRY SPITZER & CHRIS VON BENGE, Videotape Editors (Post Production); America Held Hostage: The Secret Negotiations (ABC News Special) (ABC)

DAVID G. RUMMEL, JR., Videotape Editor, Monarch Butterflies, (Segment: ABC News, '20/20') (ABC)

JOHN J. GILLEN, Videotape Editor, Robots: The Coming Revolution; (Segment: ABC World News Tonight) (ABC)

FILM EDITING (E-1833)

JOHN J. MARTIN, Film Editor; An American Adventure: The Rocket Pilots, (An NBC News Special Program) (NBC)

MILI BONSIGNORI, Film Editor; CBS Reports: The Defense of the United States: Call to Arms (CBS)

ARA CHEKMAYAN & CHRISTOPHER DALRYMPLE, Film Editors; CBS Reports: The Defense of the United States: The War Machine (CBS)

DAVID R. WARD, Film Editor; Jackie Gleason: How Sweet It Is; (Segment: ABC News, '20/20') (ABC)

PETER ELISCU, Film Editor; CBS Reports: The Defense of the United States: Nuclear Battlefield (CBS)

ALAN RAYMOND & NILS RASMUSSEN, Film Editors; Hooray for Hollywood; (ABC News, 'Closeup') (ABC)

AUDIO (E-1834)

ED JENNINGS, Tape Sound Editor; Carter's Final Hours; (Segment: ABC News, 'Nightline') (ABC)

RUDY BOYER, ANTHONY PAGANO, ALFONSO BURNEY, MARK FRENCH, JAY LAMONACO, JACK GRAY, NEAL HARVEY, JIM FITZGERALD, LEONARD JENSEN, ALAN LEWIS, ALI ASHMAWY, Live/Location Tape Sound Recordists; GEORGE MYER, Re-recording Mixer/Editor; America Held Hostage: The Secret Negotiations; (ABC News Special) (ABC)

JAMES A. CEFALO, Location Sound Recordist, Monarch Butterflies; (Segment: ABC News, '20/20') (ABC)

HARRY WELDON, Location Sound Recordist, President Reagan Assassination Attempt; (Segment: ABC World News Tonight) (ABC)

ALY EL ASHNAWY, Location Sound Recordist, Sadat Assassination; ABC News Special Events (ABC)

LIGHTING DIRECTION (E-1835)

JEROME SLATTERY, Location Lighting Director, America Held Hostage: The Secret Negotiations; (ABC News Special) (ABC)

GRAPHIC DESIGN (E-1836)

FREIDA REITER, Graphic Artist/Illustrator, America Held Hostage: The Secret Negotiations; (ABC News Special) (ABC)

GERRY ANDREA, Graphic Designer/Illustrator, Shooting of Pope John Paul II; (Segments: ABC World News Tonight) (ABC)

BARBARA M. INCOGNITO, Electronic Graphic Designer; ABC News, '20/20'; (Title Sequence) (ABC)

THE NATIONAL AWARD FOR COMMUNITY SERVICE (E-1837)

KLAN (WTHR-TV) Indianapolis, IN.

STILL FIGHTING (WXXI-TV) Rochester, NY.

CRIME'S CHILDREN (WSMV-TV) Nashville, TN.

CENTRAL STATES WATERPROOFING (WCCO-TV) Minneapolis, MN.

CRUSADE FOR CHILDREN (WHAS-TV) Louisville, KY.

THE WAR WITHIN (WFAA-TV) Dallas, TX.

UNTIL WE SAY GOODBYE (WJLA-TV) Washington, DC.

SEX & CHILDREN (WXYZ-TV) Detroit, MI.
THE DAY (KOOL-TV) Phoenix, AZ.
DISABLED ARE ABLE (WITI-TV) Milwaukee, WI.
THE PEOPLE NEXT DOOR (WDIV-TV) Detroit, MI.
QUALIFIED AND ABLE (WNAC-TV) Boston, MA.

TRUSTEES AWARD (E-1838)

AGNES NIXON, for continued distinguished service to Television and the public this medium serves.

ENGINEERING AWARDS (E-1839)

AMPEX CORP.
COLUMBIA BROADCASTING SYSTEM
IKEGAMI ELECTRONICS.
MARCONI ELECTRONICS.
RCA-CCSD.

1981/82

PRIMETIME

COMEDY SERIES (E-1840)

Emmy(s) to Executive Producer(s) and/or Producer(s)

BARNEY MILLER, Danny Arnold, Roland Kibbee, Executive Producers; Frank Dungan, Jeff Stein, Producers; Gary Shaw, Coproducer (ABC)
LOVE, SIDNEY, George Eckstein, Executive Producer; Ernest Chambers, Bob Brunner, Ken Hecht, Supervising Producers; April Kelly, Mel Tolkin, Jim Parker, Producers (NBC)
M*A*S*H, Burt Metcalfe, Executive Producer; John Rappaport, Supervising Producer; Thad Mumford, Dan Wilcox, Dennis Koenig, Producers (CBS)
TAXI, James L. Brooks, Stan Daniels, Ed Weinberger, Executive Producers; Glen Charles, Les Charles, Supervising Producers; Ken Estin, Howard Gewirtz, Ian Praiser, Producers; Richard Sakai, Coproducer (ABC)
WKRP IN CINCINNATI, Hugh Wilson, Executive Producer; Blake Hunter, Peter Torokvei, Dan Guntzelman, Steve Marshall, Producers (CBS)

DRAMA SERIES (E-1841)

Emmy(s) to Executive Producer(s) and/or Producer(s)

HILL STREET BLUES, Steven Bochco, Executive Producer; Gregory Hoblit, Supervising Producer; David Anspaugh, Anthony Yerkovich, Producers (NBC)
DYNASTY, Aaron Spelling, Douglas S. Cramer, Executive Producers; E. Duke Vincent, Supervising Producer; Ed Ledding, Elaine Rich, Producers (ABC)
FAME, William Blinn, Gerald I. Isenberg, Executive Producers; Stan Rogow, Mel Swope, Producers (NBC)
LOU GRANT, Gene Reynolds, Executive Producer; Seth Freeman, Producer (CBS)
MAGNUM, P.I., Donald P. Bellisario, Executive Producer; Douglas Green, Andrew Schneider, Rick Weaver, Producers (CBS)

LIMITED SERIES (E-1842)

Emmy(s) to Executive Producer(s) and/or Producer(s)

MARCO POLO, Vincenzo Labella, Producer (NBC)
BRIDESHEAD REVISITED, Jac Venza, Robert Kotlowitz, Executive Producers; Sam Paul, Series Producer; Derek Granger, Producer (PBS)
MASTERPIECE THEATRE: FLICKERS, Joan Wilson, Executive Producer; Joan Brown, Producer (PBS)
AMERICAN PLAYHOUSE: OPPENHEIMER, Peter Goodchild, Producer; Lindsay Law, Coordinating Producer (PBS)
MASTERPIECE THEATRE: A TOWN LIKE ALICE, Joan Wilson, Executive Producer; Henry Crawford, Producer (PBS)

VARIETY, MUSIC OR COMEDY PROGRAM (E-1843)

For a variety or music special or series or for a comedy special. Emmy(s) to Executive Producer(s) and/or Producer(s) and Star(s), if Applicable

NIGHT OF 100 STARS, Alexander H. Cohen, Executive Producer; Hildy Parks, Producer; Roy A. Somlyo, Coproducer (ABC)
AIN'T MISBEHAVIN', Alvin Cooperman, Executive Producer; Cooperman, Buddy Bregman, Producers (NBC)
AMERICAN FILM INSTITUTE SALUTE TO FRANK CAPRA, George Stevens Jr., Producer (CBS)
BARYSHNIKOV IN HOLLYWOOD, Herman E. Krawitz, Executive Producer; Don Mischer, Producer; Mikhail Baryshnikov, Star (CBS)
SCTV NETWORK, Andrew Alexander, Doug Holtby, Len Stuart, Jack Rhodes, Executive Producers; Patrick Whitley, Supervising Producer; Barry Sand, Don Novello, Producers; Nicholas Wry, Coproducer (NBC)

DRAMA SPECIAL (E-1844)

Emmy(s) to Executive Producer(s) and/or Producer(s)

A WOMAN CALLED GOLDA, Harve Bennett, Executive Producer; Gene Corman, Producer (SYN)
BILL, Alan Landsburg, Executive Producer; Mel Stuart, Producer (CBS)
ELEPHANT MAN, Martin Starger, Executive Producer; Richmond Crinkley, Producer (ABC)
INSIDE THE THIRD REICH, E. Jack Neuman, Producer (ABC)
SKOKIE, Herbert Brodkin, Executive Producer; Robert Berger, Producer (CBS)

CLASSICAL PROGRAM IN THE PERFORMING ARTS (E-1845)

For a special or a series. Emmy(s) to Executive Producer(s) and/or Producer(s) and Star(s) if Applicable

LIVE FROM THE MET: LA BOHEME, Michael Bronson, Executive Producer; Clement D'Alessio, Producer (PBS)
BERNSTEIN/BEETHOVEN, Horant H. Hohlfeld, Harry Kraut, Executive Producers; David Griffiths, Producer; Leonard Bernstein, Star (PBS)
HOROWITZ IN LONDON: A ROYAL CONCERT, Peter Gelb, John Vernon, Producers; Vladimir Horowitz, Star (PBS)
LIVE FROM LINCOLN CENTER: AN EVENING WITH DANNY KAYE AND THE NEW YORK PHILHARMONIC, Herbert Bonis, Executive Producer; John Goberman, Producer; Danny Kaye, Star (PBS)
LIVE FROM LINCOLN CENTER: AN EVENING WITH ITZHAK PERLMAN AND THE NEW YORK PHILHARMONIC, John Goberman, Producer; Itzhak Perlman, Star (PBS)

INFORMATIONAL SPECIAL (E-1846)

Emmy(s) to Executive Producer(s) and/or Producer(s)

MAKING OF 'RAIDERS OF THE LOST ARK', Sidney Ganis, Executive Producer; Howard Kazanjian, Producer (PBS)
GREAT MOVIE STUNTS: RAIDERS OF THE LOST ARK, Sidney Ganis, Executive Producer; Robert Guenette, Producer (CBS)
HIGH HOPES: THE CAPRA YEARS, Carl Pingitore, Frank Capra Jr., Producers (NBC)
HOLLYWOOD: THE GIFT OF LAUGHTER, David L Wolper, Executive Producer; Jack Haley Jr., Producer (ABC)
MARVA COLLINS: EXCELLENCE IN EDUCATION, Kathleen Maloney, Producer (PBS)

INFORMATIONAL SERIES (E-1847)

Emmy(s) to Executive Producer(s) and/or Producer(s)

CREATIVITY WITH BILL MOYERS, Merton Koplin, Charles Grinker, Executive Producers; Betsy McCarthy, Coordinating Producer (PBS)
BARBARA WALTERS SPECIALS, Don Mischer, Executive Producer; Jo Ann Goldberg, Producer (ABC)
DICK CAVETT SHOW, Robin Breed, Producer (PBS)
ENTERTAINMENT TONIGHT, Jim Bellows, Executive Producer; Andy Friendly, John Goldhammer, Vin DiBona, Producers (SYN)
MIDDLETOWN, Peter Davis, Producer (PBS)

ANIMATED PROGRAM (E-1848)

For a series or a special. Emmy(s) to Executive Producer(s) and/or Producer(s)

GRINCH GRINCHES THE CAT IN THE HAT, David H. DePatie, Executive Producer; Ted Geisel, Friz Freleng, Producers (ABC)
CHARLIE BROWN CELEBRATION, Lee Mendelson, Bill Melendez, Producers (CBS)
SMURF SPRINGTIME SPECIAL, Joseph Barbera, William Hanna, Executive Producers; Gerard Baldwin, Producer (NBC)
SMURFS, William Hanna, Joseph Barbera, Executive Producers; Gerard Baldwin, Kay Wright, Producers (NBC)
SOMEDAY YOU'LL FIND HER, CHARLIE BROWN, Lee Mendelson, Executive Producer; Bill Melendez, Producer (CBS)

CHILDRENS PROGRAM (E-1849)

For a series or a special. Emmy(s) to Executive Producer(s) and/or Producer(s)

THE WAVE, Virginia L Carter, Executive Producer; Fern Field, Producer (ABC)
PROJECT PEACOCK: ALICE AT THE PALACE, Joseph Papp, Producer (NBC)
PROJECT PEACOCK: ELECTRIC GRANDMOTHER, Linda Gottlieb, Executive Producer; Doro Bachrach, Producer (NBC)
PLEASE DON'T HIT ME, MOM, Virginia L. Carter, Executive Producer; Fern Field, Producer (ABC)
THROUGH THE MAGIC PYRAMID, Ron Howard, Executive Producer; Rance Howard, Herbert J. Wright, Producers (NBC)

ACTOR - COMEDY SERIES (E-1850)

For a continuing or single performance in a regular series

ALAN ALDA, M*A*SH (CBS)
ROBERT GUILLAUME, Benson (ABC)
JUDD HIRSCH, Taxi (ABC)
HAL LINDEN, Barney Miller (ABC)
LESLIE NIELSEN, Police Squad! (ABC)

ACTOR - DRAMA SERIES (E-1851)

For a continuing or single performance in a regular series

DANIEL J. TRAVANTI, Hill Street Blues (NBC)
EDWARD ASNER, Lou Grant (CBS)
JOHN FORSYTHE, Dynasty (ABC)
JAMES GARNER, Bret Maverick (NBC)
TOM SELLECK, Magnum P.I. (CBS)

ACTOR - LIMITED SERIES OR SPECIAL (E-1852)

For a continuing role in a limited series, or for a single appearance in a limited series or a special

MICKEY ROONEY, Bill (CBS)
ANTHONY ANDREWS, Brideshead Revisited (PBS)
PHILIP ANGLIM, Elephant Man (ABC)
ANTHONY HOPKINS, Hallmark Hall of Fame: Hunchback Of Notre Dame (CBS)
JEREMY IRONS, Brideshead Revisited (PBS)

ACTRESS - COMEDY SERIES (E-1853)

For a continuing or single performance in a regular series

CAROL KANE, Taxi: Simka Returns (ABC)
NELL CARTER, Gimme A Break (NBC)
BONNIE FRANKLIN, One Day At A Time (CBS)
SWOOSIE KURTZ, Love Sidney (NBC)
CHARLOTTE RAE, Facts Of Life (NBC)
ISABEL SANFORD, Jeffersons (CBS)

ACTRESS - DRAMA SERIES (E-1854)

For a continuing or single performance in a regular series

MICHAEL LEARNED, Nurse (CBS)
DEBBIE ALLEN, Fame (NBC)
VERONICA HAMEL, Hill Street Blues (NBC)
MICHELE LEE, Knots Landing (CBS)
STEFANIE POWERS, Hart To Hart (ABC)

ACTRESS - LIMITED SERIES OR SPECIAL (E-1855)

For a continuing role in a limited series, or for a single appearance in a limited series or a special

INGRID BERGMAN, A Woman Called Golda (SYN)
GLENDA JACKSON, Patricia Neal Story (CBS)
ANN JILLIAN, Mae West (ABC)
JEAN STAPLETON, Eleanor, First Lady Of The World (CBS)
CICELY TYSON, Hallmark Hall Of Fame: Marva Collins Story (CBS)

SUPPORTING ACTOR - COMEDY OR VARIETY OR MUSIC SERIES (E-1856)

For a continuing or single performance in a regular series

CHRISTOPHER LLOYD, Taxi (ABC)
DANNY De VITO, Taxi (ABC)
RON GLASS, Barney Miller (ABC)
STEVE LANDESBERG, Barney Miller (ABC)
HARRY MORGAN, M*A*S*H (CBS)
DAVID OGDEN STIERS, M*A*S*H (CBS)

SUPPORTING ACTOR - DRAMA SERIES (E-1857)

For a continuing or single performance in a regular series

MICHAEL CONRAD, Hill Street Blues (NBC)
TAUREAN BLACQUE, Hill Street Blues (NBC)
CHARLES HAID, Hill Street Blues (NBC)
MICHAEL WARREN, Hill Street Blues (NBC)
BRUCE WEITZ , Hill Street Blues (NBC)

SUPPORTING ACTOR - LIMITED SERIES OR SPECIAL (E-1858)

For a continuing role in a limited series, or for a single appearance in a limited series or a special

LAURENCE OLIVIER, Brideshead Revisited (PBS)
JACK ALBERTSON, My Body, My Child (ABC)
JOHN GIELGUD, Brideshead Revisited: Et In Arcadia Ego (PBS)
DEREK JACOBI, Inside The Third Reich (ABC)
LEONARD NIMOY, A Woman Called Golda (SYN)

SUPPORTING ACTRESS - COMEDY OR VARIETY OR MUSIC SERIES (E-1859)

For a continuing or single performance in a regular series

LORETTA SWIT, M*A*S*H (CBS)
EILEEN BRENNAN, Private Benjamin (CBS)
MARLA GIBBS, Jeffersons (CBS)
ANDREA MARTIN, SCTV Network (NBC)
ANNE MEARA, Archie Bunker's Place: Relapse (CBS)
INGA SWENSON, Benson (ABC)

SUPPORTING ACTRESS - DRAMA SERIES (E-1860)

For a continuing or single performance in a regular series

NANCY MARCHAND, Lou Grant (CBS)
BARBARA BOSSON, Hill Street Blues (NBC)
JULIE HARRIS, Knots Landing (CBS)

LINDA KELSEY, Lou Grant (CBS)
BETTY THOMAS, Hill Street Blues (NBC)

SUPPORTING ACTRESS - LIMITED SERIES OR SPECIAL (E-1861)

For a continuing role in a limited series, or for a single appearance in a limited series or a special

PENNY FULLER, Elephant Man (ABC)
CLAIRE BLOOM, Brideshead Revisited: Sebastian Against The World (PBS)
JUDY DAVIS, A Woman Called Golda (SYN)
VICKI LAWRENCE, Eunice (CBS)
RITA MORENO, Portrait Of A Showgirl (CBS)

DIRECTOR - COMEDY SERIES (E-1862)

For a single episode of a regular series

ALAN RAFKIN, One Day At A Time: Barbara's Crisis (CBS)
ALAN ALDA, M*A*S*H: Where There's A Will, There's A War (CBS)
HY AVERBACK, M*A*S*H: Sons And Bowlers (CBS)
JAMES BURROWS, Taxi: Jim The Psychic (ABC)
CHARLES S DUBIN, M*A*S*H: Pressure Points (CBS)
BURT METCALFE, M*A*S*H: Picture This (CBS)

DIRECTOR - DRAMA SERIES (E-1863)

For a single episode of a regular series

HARRY HARRIS, Fame: To Soar And Never Falter (NBC)
JEFF BLECKNER, Hill Street Blues: The World According To Freedom (NBC)
ROBERT BULTER, Hill Street Blues: The Second Oldest Profession (NBC)
GENE REYNOLDS, Lou Grant: Hometown (CBS)
ROBERT SCHEERER, Fame: Musical Bridge (NBC)

DIRECTOR - VARIETY, MUSIC OR COMEDY PROGRAM (E-1864)

For a single episode of a regular or limited series, or for a special

DWIGHT HEMION, Goldie And Kids. . .Listen To Us (ABC)
CLARK JONES, Night Of 100 Stars (ABC)
DON MISCHER, Baryshnikov In Hollywood (CBS)
MARTY PASETTA, Fifty-Fourth Annual Academy Awards (ABC)
ROBERT SCHEERER, Live From Lincoln Center: An Evening With Danny Kaye And The New York Philharmonic (PBS)

DIRECTOR - LIMITED SERIES OR A SPECIAL (E-1865)

For a single episode of a limited series, or for a special

MARVIN J. CHOMSKY, Inside The Third Reich (ABC)
LEE PHILIPS, Mae West (ABC)
CHARLES STURRIDGE, MICHAEL LINDSAY-HOGG, Brideshead Revisited: Et In Arcadia Ego (PBS)
HERBERT WISE, Skokie (CBS)

CHOREOGRAPHY (E-1866)

For a single episode of a regular or limited series, or for a special

DEBBIE ALLEN, Fame: Come One, Come All (NBC)
PETER ANASTOS, MICHAEL KIDD, Baryshnikov In Hollywood (CBS)
ARTHUR FARIA, Ain't Misbehavin' (NBC)
ALAN JOHNSON, Shirley MacLaine. . .Illusions (CBS)
WALTER PAINTER, Fifty-Fourth Annual Academy Awards (ABC)

WRITING - COMEDY SERIES (E-1867)

For a single episode of a regular series

KEN ESTIN, Taxi: Elegant Iggy (ABC)
ALAN ALDA, M*A*S*H: Follies Of The Living, Concerns Of The Dead (CBS)
FRANK DUNGAN, JEFF STEIN, TONY SHEEHAN, Barney Miller: Landmark, Part III (ABC)
BARRY KEMP (Teleplay), HOLLY HOLMBERG BROOKS (Story), Taxi: Jim The Psychic (ABC)
DAVID ZUCKER, JIM ABRAHAMS, JERRY ZUCKER, Police Squad!: A Substantial Gift (ABC)

WRITING - DRAMA SERIES (E-1868)

For a single episode of a regular series

STEVEN BOCHCO, ANTHONY YERKOVICH, JEFFREY LEWIS, MICHAEL WAGNER, (Teleplay), MICHAEL KOZOLL, BOCHCO, (Story); Hill Street Blues: Freedom's Last Stand (NBC)
STEVEN BOCHCO, ANTHONY YERKOVICH, ROBERT CRAIS, (Teleplay), MICHAEL KOZOLL, BOCHCO, YERKOVICH, (Story); Hill Street Blues: The Second Oldest Profession (NBC)
STEVEN BOCHCO, ANTHONY YERKOVICH, JEFFREY LEWIS, MICHAEL WAGNER, Hill Street Blues: Personal Foul (NBC)
SETH FREEMAN, Lou Grant: Black List (CBS)
MICHAEL WAGNER, Hill Street Blues: The World According To Freedom (NBC)

WRITING - VARIETY, MUSIC OR COMEDY PROGRAM (E-1869)

For a variety or music special or series, or for a comedy special

JOHN CANDY, JOE FLAHERTY, EUGENE LEVY, ANDREA MARTIN, RICK MORANIS, CATHERINE O'HARA, DAVE THOMAS, DICK BLASUCCI, PAUL FLAHERTY, BOB DOLMAN, JOHN McANDREW, DOUG STECKLER, BERT RICH, JEFFREY BARRON, MICHAEL SHORT, CHRIS CLUESS, STUART KREISMAN, BRIAN McCONNACHIE, SCTV Network: Moral Majority Show (NBC)
RICHARD ALFIERI, RITA MAE BROWN, RICK MITZ, ARTHUR ALLAN SEIDELMAN, NORMAN LEAR, I Love Liberty (ABC)
JOHN CANDY, JOE FLAHERTY, EUGENE LEVY, ANDREA MARTIN, RICK MORANIS, CATHERINE O'HARA, DAVE THOMAS, DICK BLASUCCI, PAUL FLAHERTY, BOB DOLMAN, JOHN McANDREW, DOUG STECKLER, JEFFREY BARRON, SCTV Network: Cycle Two, Show Two (NBC)
JOHN CANDY, JOE FLAHERTY, EUGENE LEVY, ANDREA MARTIN, RICK MORANIS, CATHERINE O'HARA, DAVE THOMAS, DICK BLASUCCI, PAUL FLAHERTY, BOB DOLMAN, JOHN McANDREW, DOUG STECKLER, MICHAEL SHORT, TOM COUCH, EDDIE GORODETSKY, DON NOVELLO, SCTV Network: Cycle Three, Show One (NBC)
JOHN CANDY, JOE FLAHERTY, EUGENE LEVY, ANDREA MARTIN, RICK MORANIS, CATHERINE O'HARA, DAVE THOMAS, DICK BLASUCCI, PAUL FLAHERTY, BOB DOLMAN, JOHN McANDREW, DOUG STECKLER, MERT RICH, JEFFREY BARRON, SCTV Network: Christmas Show (NBC)

WRITING - LIMITED SERIES OR A SPECIAL (E-1870)

For a single episode of a limited series, or for a special

COREY BLECHMAN, (Teleplay), BARRY MORROW, (Story); Bill (CBS)
OLIVER HAILEY, Sidney Shorr (NBC)
ERNEST KINOY, Skokie (CBS)
JOHN MORTIMER, Brideshead Revisited: Et In Arcadia Ego (PBS)
PETER PRINCE, American Playhouse Part 5: Oppenheimer (PBS)

GOVERNOR'S AWARD (E-1871)

HALLMARK HALL OF FAME

CINEMATOGRAPHY - SERIES (E-1872)

For a single episode of a regular series

WILLIAM W. SPENCER, Fame: Alone In A Crowd (NBC)
ROBERT F. LIU, Lou Grant: Ghosts (CBS)
SOL NEGRIN, Baker's Dozen: A Class By Himself (CBS)
WOODY OMENS, Magnum, P.I.: Memories Are Forever (CBS)
TED VOIGTLANDER, Little House On The Prairie: He Was Only Twelve-Part 2 (NBC)

CINEMATOGRAPHY - LIMITED SERIES OR A SPECIAL (E-1873)

For a single episode of a limited series, or for a special

JAMES CRABE, The Letter (ABC)
PASQUALINO DE SANTIS, Marco Polo: Part 4 (NBC)
GAYNE RESCHER, Princess And The Cabbie (CBS)

ART DIRECTION - SERIES (E-1874)

For a single episode of a regular series

IRA DIAMOND, Art Director; JOSEPH STONE, Set Decorator; Fame: Tomorrow's Farewell (NBC)
JAMES J. AGAZZI, PAUL SYLOS, Art Directors; ROBERT SIGNORELLI, Set Decorator; Hart To Hart: Hart Of The Matter (ABC)
JEFFREY L. GOLDSTEIN, Art Director; JAMES G. CANE, Set Decorator; Hill Street Blues: Personal Foul (NBC)
SCOTT T. RITTENOUR, Art Director; ROBERT L. ZILLIOX, Set Decorator; Bret Maverick: The Yellow Rose (NBC)

ART DIRECTION - LIMITED SERIES OR A SPECIAL (E-1875)

For a single episode of a limited series, or for a special

JAMES HULSEY, Art Director; JERRY ADAMS, Set Decorator; The Letter (ABC)
PETER PHILLIPS, Production Designer, Brideshead Revisited: Et In Arcadia Ego (PBS)
LUCIANO RICCERI, Production Designer; BRUNO CESARI, Set Decorator; Marco Polo: Part 2 (NBC)
ROLF ZEHETBAUER, Production Designer; KULI SANDER, HERBERT STRABEL, Art Directors; Inside The Third Reich (ABC)

ART DIRECTION - VARIETY OR MUSIC PROGRAM (E-1876)

For a single episode of a regular or limited series, or for a special

RAY KLAUSEN, Art Director, Fifty-Fourth Annual Academy Awards (ABC)
ROY CHRISTOPHER, Art Director, Baryshnikov In Hollywood (CBS)
KIM COLFAX, Production Designer, Olivia Newton-John: Let's Get Physical (ABC)
ROMAIN JOHNSTON, Art Director; JIM WAGNER, Set Decorator; Barbara Mandrell And The Mandrell Sisters: With Tom Jones, R.C. Bannon (NBC)
CHARLES LISANBY, Art Director; DWIGHT JACKSON, Set Decorator; American Playhouse: Working (PBS)

MUSIC COMPOSITION - SERIES (DRAMATIC UNDERSCORE) (E-1877)

For a single episode of a regular series. Emmy(s) to Composer(s)

DAVID ROSE, Little House On The Prairie: He Was Only Twelve-Part 2 (NBC)
BRUCE BROUGHTON, Dallas: The Search (CBS)
JOE HARNELL, Incredible Hulk: Triangle (CBS)
PATRICK WILLIAMS, Lou Grant: Hometown (CBS)

MUSIC COMPOSITION - LIMITED SERIES OR A SPECIAL (DRAMATIC UNDERSCORE) (E-1878)

For a single episode of a limited series or for a special. Emmy(s) to composer(s)

PATRICK WILLIAMS, Princess And The Cabbie (CBS)
BRUCE BROUGHTON, Killjoy (CBS)
ALLYN FERGUSON, Ivanhoe (CBS)
BILLY GOLDENBERG, Jacqueline Bouvier Kennedy (ABC)
MICHEL LEGRAND, A Woman Called Golda (SYN)
LAURENCE ROSENTHAL, The Letter (ABC)

MUSIC DIRECTION (E-1879)

For a single episode of a regular or limited series, or for a special, whether it be variety or music. Emmy(s) to music director and principal arranger(s)

ELLIOT LAWRENCE, Music Director; BILL ELTON, TOMMY NEWSOM, TORRIE ZITO, LANNY MEYERS, JONATHAN TUNICK, Principal Arrangers; Night Of 100 Stars (ABC)
ALLYN FERGUSON, Music Director and Principal Arranger; American Movie Awards (NBC)
IAN FRASER, Music Director; BILLY BYERS, CHRIS BOARDMAN, Principal Arrangers; Walt Disney. . .One Man's Dream (CBS)
LUTHER HENDERSON, Music Director and Principal Arranger; Ain't Misbehavin' (NBC)
PETER MATZ, Music Director and Principal Arranger; Shirley MacLaine. . .Illusions (CBS)

MUSIC AND LYRICS (E-1880)

For a song (which must have both music and lyrics), whether it be for a single episode of a regular or limited series, or for a special. Emmy(s) to Composer(s) and Lyricist(s)

LARRY GROSSMAN, Composer; ALAN BUZ KOHAN, Lyricist; Shirley MacLaine. . .Illusions Song: On The Outside Looking In (CBS)
BILLY GOLDENBERG, Composer; CAROL CONNORS, Lyricist; Love, Sidney: Welcome Home. Song: Friends Forever (NBC)
MITZIE WELCH, KEN WELCH, Composers and Lyricists; Walt Disney-. . .One Man's Dream. Song: Marceline (CBS)

COSTUME DESIGN - SERIES (E-1881)

For a single episode of a regular or limited series

ENRICO SABBATINI, Marco Polo: Part 3 (NBC)
RICKIE A. HANSEN, Solid Gold With Andy Gibb, Marilyn McCoo (SYN)
BILL HARGATE, Barbara Mandrell And The Mandrell Sisters With Brenda Lee, Paul Williams (NBC)
GRADY HUNT, Fantasy Island: La Liberatora/Mr Nobody (ABC)
JANE ROBINSON, Brideshead Revisited: Home And Abroad (PBS)

COSTUME DESIGN - SPECIAL (E-1882)

For a comedy, drama, variety or music special

DONALD BROOKS, The Letter (ABC)
JEAN-PIERRE DORLEAC, Mae West (ABC)
NOEL TAYLOR, Eleanor, First Lady Of The World (CBS)
TRAVILLA, Jacqueline Bouvier Kennedy (ABC)
JULIE WEISS, Elephant Man (ABC)

MAKEUP (E-1883)

For a single episode of a regular or limited series, of for a special

PAUL STANHOPE, World War III (NBC)
DEL ACEVEDO, PAULINE HEYS, Oliver Twist (CBS)
RICHARD BLAIR, Mae West (ABC)
JACK FREEMAN, JACK BARRON, The Letter (ABC)
LEO L. LOTITO JR., NORA DE LA TORRE, Fantasy Island: Case Against Mr. Roarke/Save Sherlock Holmes (ABC)

HAIRSTYLING (E-1884)

For a single episode of a regular or limited series, or for a special

HAZEL CATMULL, Eleanor, First Lady Of The World (CBS)
EMMA DI VITTORIO, DIONE TAYLOR, Jacqueline Bouvier Kennedy (ABC)
RENATA MAGNANTI, ELDA MAGNANTI, Marco Polo: Part 4 (NBC)
GLORIA MONTEMAYOR, Fame: The Strike (NBC)
STEVE ROBINETTE, Cagney & Lacey: Street Scene (CBS)

GRAPHIC DESIGN AND TITLE SEQUENCES (E-1885)

For a single episode of a regular or limited series, or for a special

MICHAEL LEVINE, MICHAEL HOEY, Fame: Metamorphosis (NBC)
BOB POOK, WILLIAM SHORTRIDGE JR., ARLEN SCHUMER, Late Night With David Letterman With Bob Denver, Tony Bill (NBC)
VALERIE PYE, Brideshead Revisited: Brideshead Revisited (PBS)

FILM EDITING - SERIES (E-1886)

For a single episode of a regular series

ANDREW CHULACK, Hill Street Blues: Of Mouse And Man (NBC)
JEANENE AMBLER, Quincy: For Love Of Joshua (NBC)
FRED W. BERGER, Dallas: The Split (CBS)
RAY DANIELS, Hill Street Blues: The Second Oldest Profession (NBC)
MICHAEL A. HOEY, Fame: Passing Grade (NBC)
MARK MELNICK, Fame: Musical Bridge (NBC)

FILM EDITING - LIMITED SERIES OR SPECIAL (E-1887)

For a single episode of a limited series, or for a special

ROBERT F. SHUGRUE, Woman Called Golda (SYN)
JAMES T. HECKERT, RICHARD BELDING, LES GREEN, Inside The Third Reich (ABC)
JOHN A. MARTINELLI, Marco Polo: Part 4 (NBC)
RITA ROLAND, A Piano For Mrs. Cimino (CBS)

FILM SOUND EDITING (E-1888)

For a single episode of a regular or limited series, or for a special

WILLIAM H. WISTROM, RUSS TINSLEY, Supervising Editors; PETER BOND, TOM CORNWELL, DAVID ELLIOTT, TONY GARBER, PETER HARRISON, CHARLES W. McMANN, JOSEPH MAYER, JOSEPH MELODY, R. WILLIAM A. THIEDERMAN, RUSTY TINSLEY, Editors; Inside The Third Reich (ABC)
JEFF BUSHELMAN, STEVE BUSHELMAN, IAN MacGREGOR-SCOTT, Supervising Editors; BARNEY CABRAL, WILLIAM DE NICHOLAS, JERELYN GOLDING, FRANK HOWARD, BOBBE KURTZ, LETTIE OD-NEY, BERNARD PINCUS, SAM SHAW, PATRICK SOMERSET, FRANK SPENCER, DAVE STONE, ASCHER YATES, Editors; Marco Polo: Part 4 (NBC)
JOSEPH MELODY, RUSS TINSLEY, Supervising Editors; TOM CORN-WELL, DAVID ELLIOTT, DON ERNST, MICHAEL L. HILKENE, FRED JUDKINS, JOHN KLINE, R. WILLIAM A. THIEDERMAN, RUSTY TINS-LEY, Editors; Marian Rose White (CBS)
RUSS TINSLEY, MICHAEL HILKENE, Supervising Editors; TOM CORN-WELL, DAVID ELLIOTT, PETER HARRISON, FRED JUDKINS, JOHN KLINE, JOSEPH MELODY, R. WILLIAM A. THIEDERMAN, WILLIAM H. WISTROM, Editors; Capture Of Grizzly Adams (NBC)

FILM SOUND MIXING (E-1889)

For a single episode of a regular or limited series, or for a special

WILLIAM MARKY, Production Mixer; ROBERT W. GLASS JR., BILL M. NICHOLSON, HOWARD WILMARTH, Rerecording Mixers; Hill Street Blues: Personal Foul (NBC)
THOMAS CAUSEY, Production Mixer; DAVID J. HUDSON, MEL MET-

CALFE, GEORGE R. WEST, Rerecording Mixers; Fire On The Mountain (NBC)
WILLIAM MARKY, Production Mixer; DONALD CAHN, JAMES R. COOK, ROBERT L. HARMAN, Rerecording Mixers; Hill Street Blues: The Second Oldest Profession (NBC)
JACQUES NOSCO, Production Mixer; DON CAHN, JAMES R. COOK, ROBERT L. HARMAN, Rerecording Mixers; World War III (NBC)
ELI YORKIN, Production Mixer; DONALD CAHN, JAMES R. COOK, ROBERT L. HARMAN, Rerecording Mixers; A Woman Called Golda (SYN)

TAPE SOUND MIXING (E-1890)

For a single episode of a regular or limited series, or for a special

CHRIS HAIRE, RICHARD J. MASCI, DOUG NELSON, Perry Como's Easter In Guadalajara (ABC)
JERRY CLEMANS, MATT HYDE, DON WORSHAM, Barbara Mandrell And The Mandrell Sisters with Ray Charles, Sylvia (NBC)
JERRY CLEMANS, JOE RALSTON, Sinatra, The Man And His Music (NBC)
BILL COLE, JOE RALSTON, Ain't Misbehavin' (NBC)
CHRISTOPHER L. HAIRE, DON WORSHAM, Debby Boone. . .One Step Closer (NBC)

VIDEO TAPE EDITING - SERIES (E-1891)

For a single episode of a regular series

KEN DENISOFF, Barbara Mandrell And The Mandrell Sisters With Brenda Lee, Paul Williams (NBC)
ANDY ACKERMAN, WKRP In Cincinnati: Fire (CBS)
RAYMOND BUSH, Report To Murphy: High Noon (CBS)
JOHN CARROL, MARIO DiMAMBRO, DAVE GOLDSON, ART SCHNEIDER, Greatest American Hero: Lost Diablo Mine (ABC)
ROY STEWART, American Playhouse: Working (PBS)

VIDEO TAPE EDITING - LIMITED SERIES OR SPECIAL (E-1892)

For a single episode of a limited series, or for a special

WILLIAM H. BREASHERS SR., PAM MARSHALL, TUCKER WIARD, American Bandstand's 30th Anniversary Special (ABC)
ED J. BRENNAN, Ain't Misbehavin' (NBC)
JIMMY B. FRAZIER, KEN LASKI, Lily For President? (CBS)
PAM MARSHALL, Perry Como's French-Canadian Christmas (ABC)

TECHNICAL DIRECTION AND ELECTRONIC CAMERAWORK (E-1893)

For a single episode of a regular or limited series, or for a special

JERRY WEISS, Technical Director; BRUCE BOTTONE, KEN DAHL-QUIST, DEAN HALL, JIM HERRING, ROYDEN HOLM, TOM MUN-SHOWER, WANE NOSTAJA, DAVID NOWELL, Camerapersons; Magic Of David Copperfield (CBS)
GERRY BUCCI, Technical Director; RON BROOKS, WARREN CRESS, D. J. DIOMEDES, DON LANGFORD, JAN LOWRY, BILL SCOTT, Camerapersons; Lynda Carter: Street Life (CBS)
TERRY DONOHUE, Technical Director; ROCKY DANIELSON, JOE EP-PERSON, JOHN GILLIS, DEAN HALL, DON JONES, MIKE KEELER, BRUCE OLDHAM, KENNETH A. PATTERSON, JOHN REPCZYNSKI, KEN TAMBURRI, Camerapersons; Rod Stewart: Tonight He's Yours (SYN)
KARL MESSERSCHMIDT, Technical Director; LES ATKINSON, GEORGE FALARDEAU, JAMES HERRING, MIKE HIGUERA, ROYDEN HOLM, MIKE STRAMISKY, Camerapersons; All The Way Home (NBC)
O. TAMBURRI, Technical Director; DONALD BARKER, GEORGE FALARDEAU, MIKE HIGUERA, ROYDEN HOLM, REED HOWARD, Camerapersons; Ain't Misbehavin' (NBC)

LIGHTING DIRECTION (E-1894)

For a single episode of a regular or limited series, or for a special

GEORGE W. REISENBERGER, Lighting Designer; KEN DETTLING, Lighting Director; American Playhouse: Working (PBS)
GREGORY BRUNTON, Lighting Director, Debby Boone. . .One Step Closer (NBC)
LEARD DAVIS, Lighting Designer, Nashville Palace With Tammy Wynette, George Jones and Minnie Pearl (NBC)
BOB DICKINSON, Lighting Consultant; HAROLD GUY, Lighting Director; Solid Gold With Marilyn McCoo And Charlie Daniels Band (SYN)
WILLIAM KLAGES, Lighting Designer, Night Of 100 Stars (ABC)
FRED McKINNON, Lighting Consultant; MARCH PALIUS, Lighting Director; I Love Liberty (ABC)

INDIVIDUAL ACHIEVEMENT - INFORMATIONAL PROGRAMMING

PERFORMERS (E-1895)

Continuing or single performance in a regular or limited series, or special
PETER USTINOV, Omni: The New Frontier (SYN)

CINEMATOGRAPHY (E-1896)

Single episode of an informational series, or informational special
PHILLIP SCHUMAN, GIL HUBBS, Great Movie Stunts: Raiders Of The Lost Ark (CBS)

GRAPHIC DESIGN AND TITLE SEQUENCES (E-1897)

Single episode of an informational series, or informational special
JAMES CASTLE, BRUCE BRYANT, Hollywood: The Gift Of Laughter (ABC)
RON HAYS, RICHARD FROMAN, Omni: The New Fronter: Terminal Man/Ciani (SYN)

FILM SOUND MIXING (E-1898)

Single episode of an informational series, or informational special
MICHAEL DENEKE, Production Mixer; GARY BOURGEOIS, HOPPY MEHTERIAN, HOWARD WOLLMAN, Re-recording Mixers; Great Movie Stunts: Raiders Of The Lost Ark (CBS)

INDIVIDUAL ACHIEVEMENT - CHILDREN'S PROGRAMMING

ART DIRECTION (E-1899)

Single episode of a children's seriees, or children's special
ALBERT HESCHONG, Art Director; WARREN E. WELCH, Set Decorator; Rascals And Robbers: The Secret Adventures Of Tom Sawyer And Huck Finn (CBS)

COSTUME DESIGN (E-1900)

Single episode of a children's series, or children's special
THEONI V. ALDREDGE, Project Peacock: Alice At The Palace (NBC)

FILM EDITING (E-1901)

Single episode of a children's series, or children's special
BYRON (BUZZ) BRANDT, Rascals And Robbers: The Secret Adventures of Tom Sawyer And Huckleberry Finn (CBS)

FILM SOUND MIXING (E-1902)

Single episode of a children's series, or children's special
KEITH A. WESTER, Production Mixer; ROBERT W. GLASS JR., WILLIAM NICHOLSON, HOWARD WILMARTH, Re-recording Mixers; Rascals And Robbers: The Secret Adventures Of Tom Sawyer And Huck Finn (CBS)

LIGHTING DIRECTION (E-1903)

Single episode of a children's series, or children's special
RALPH HOLMES, Lighting Designer, Project Peacock: Alice At The Palace (NBC)

INDIVIDUAL ACHIEVEMENT - ANIMATED PROGRAM DIRECTION (E-1904)

Single episode of an animated series, or for an animated special
BILL PEREZ, Grinch Grinches The Cat In The Hat (ABC)
PHIL ROMAN, Someday You'll Find Her, Charlie Brown (CBS)

INDIVIDUAL ACHIEVEMENT - SPECIAL CLASS

PERFORMERS (E-1905)

Continuing or single performance in a regular or limited series, or special
NELL CARTER, Ain't Misbehavin' (NBC)
ANDREW De SHIELDS, Ain't Misbehavin' (NBC)
GREGORY HINES, I Love Liberty (ABC)

COSTUMERS (E-1906)

Single episode of a regular or limited series, or for a special
MARILYN MATTHEWS, Costume Supervisor; Fame: The Strike (NBC)
ELSA FENNELL, Costume Supervisor; GLORIA BARNES, Costume Mistress; COLIN WILSON, Costume Master; Agatha Christie's Murder Is Easy (CBS)

INDIVIDUAL ACHIEVEMENT - CREATIVE SPECIAL ACHIEVEMENT

GRAPHIC DESIGN AND TITLE SEQUENCES (E-1907)

WILLIAM MESA, TIM DONAHUE, Inside The Third Reich (ABC)
ALEX TKACH, MICHAEL GROSS, WAYNE SCHNEIDER, SCTV Network: Cycle Two-Show One (NBC)

VIDEOTAPE EDITING (E-1908)

Single episode of a regular or limited series, or special
ANDY ZALL, Shirley MacLaine. . .Illusions (CBS)

FILM SOUND EDITING (E-1909)

Single episode of a regular or limited series, or special
JEFF BUSHELMAN, STEVE BUSHELMAN, IAN MacGREGOR-SCOTT, Supervising Editors; BARNEY CABRAL, WILLIAM De NICHOLAS, JERELYN GOLDING, FRANK HOWARD, BOBBE KURTZ, LETTIE OD-

NEY, BERNARD PINCUS, PATRIC SOMERSET, Editors; Marco Polo: Part 4 (NBC)

DAYTIME EMMY AWARDS

DAYTIME DRAMA SERIES (E-1910)
Emmy(s) to Executive Producer(s) and Producer(s)

THE GUIDING LIGHT, Allen Potter, Producer (CBS)
ALL MY CHILDREN, Jorn Winther, Producer (ABC)
GENERAL HOSPITAL, Gloria Monty, Producer (ABC)
RYAN'S HOPE, Ellen Barrett, Producer (ABC)

GAME OR AUDIENCE PARTICIPATION SHOW (E-1911)
Emmy(s) to Executive Producer(s) and Producer(s)

PASSWORD PLUS, Robert Sherman, Producer (NBC)
FAMILY FEUD, Mark Goodson, Executive Producer; Howard Felsher, Producer (ABC)
THE PRICE IS RIGHT, Frank Wayne, Executive Producer; Barbara Hunter, Phillip Wayne, Co-Producers (CBS)
WHEEL OF FORTUNE, Nancy Jones, Producer (NBC)

TALK OR SERVICE SERIES (E-1912)
Emmy(s) to Executive Producer(s) and Producer(s)

THE RICHARD SIMMONS SHOW, Woody Fraser, Executive Producer; Nora Fraser, Producer (SYN)
LOUIS RUKEYSER'S BUSINESS JOURNAL, Paul Galan, Dick Hubert, Executive Producers; Craig Fisher, Senior Producer (SYN)
THE PHIL DONAHUE SHOW, Richard Mincer, Executive Producer; Patricia McMillen, Senior Producer; Darlene Hayes & Sheri Singer, Producers (SYN)
HOUR MAGAZINE, Martin M. Berman, Executive Producer; Steve Clements, Producer (SYN)

VARIETY SERIES (E-1913)
Emmy(s) to Executive Producer(s) and Producer(s)

THE REGIS PHILBIN SHOW, E. V. Di Massa, Jr., Fred Tatashore, Producers (NBC)
THE JOHN DAVIDSON SHOW, Frank Brill, Executive Producer; Vince Calandra, Producer (SYN)
THE MERV GRIFFIN SHOW, Peter Barsocchini, Producer (SYN)

ACTOR - DAYTIME DRAMA SERIES (E-1914)

ANTHONY GEARY, General Hospital, (ABC)
JAMES MITCHELL, All My Children (ABC)
RICHARD SHOBERG, All My Children (ABC)
LARRY BRYGGMAN, As The World Turns (CBS)
STUART DAMON, General Hospital (ABC)

ACTRESS - DAYTIME DRAMA SERIES (E-1915)

ROBIN STRASSER, One Life To Live (ABC)
SUSAN LUCCI, All My Children (ABC)
ANN FLOOD, The Edge Of Night (ABC)
SHARON GABET, The Edge Of Night (ABC)
LESLIE CHARLESON, General Hospital (ABC)

SUPPORTING ACTOR - DAYTIME DRAMA SERIES (E-1916)

DAVID LEWIS, General Hospital (ABC)
DARNELL WILLIAMS, All My Children (ABC)
DOUG SHEEHAN, General Hospital (ABC)
GERALD ANTHONY, One Life To Live (ABC)

SUPPORTING ACTRESS - DAYTIME DRAMA SERIES (E-1917)

DOROTHY LYMAN, All My Children (ABC)
ELIZABETH LAWRENCE, All My Children (ABC)
MEG MUNDY, The Doctors (NBC)
LOUISE SHAFFER, Ryan's Hope (ABC)

HOST OR HOSTESS - GAME OR AUDIENCE PARTICIPATION SHOW (E-1918)

BOB BARKER, The Price Is Right (CBS)
BILL CULLEN, Blockbusters (NBC)
RICHARD DAWSON, Family Feud (ABC)

HOST OR HOSTESS - TALK OR SERVICE SERIES (E-1919)

PHIL DONAHUE, Donahue (SYN)
GARY COLLINS, Hour Magazine (SYN)

HOST OR HOSTESS - VARIETY SERIES (E-1920)

MERV GRIFFIN, The Merv Griffin Show (SYN)
MIKE DOUGLAS, The Mike Douglas Show (SYN)

DIRECTOR - DAYTIME DRAMA SERIES (E-1921)
For the entire series

MARLENA LAIRD, ALAN PULTZ, PHILLIP SOGARD, General Hospital (ABC)
LARRY AUERBACH, JACK COFFEY, SHERREL HOFFMAN, JORN WINTHERALI My Children (ABC)
RICHARD PEPPERMAN, JOHN SEDWICK, The Edge Of Night (ABC)
NORMAN HALL, PETER MINER, DAVID PRESSMAN, One Life To Live (ABC)

INDIVIDUAL DIRECTION - GAME OR AUDIENCE PARTICIPATION SHOW (E-1922)
For a single episode

PAUL ALTER, Family Feud, May 29, 1981 (ABC)
DICK CARSON, Wheel Of Fortune, March 3, 1982, (NBC)

INDIVIDUAL DIRECTION - TALK OR SERVICE SERIES (E-1923)
For a single episode

RON WEINER, The Phil Donahue Show, January 21, 1982, (SYN)
GLEN SWANSON, Hour Magazine, January 11, 1982, (SYN)

INDIVIDUAL DIRECTION - VARIETY SERIES (E-1924)
For a single episode

BARRY GLAZER, American Bandstand, April 18, 1981, (ABC)
DICK CARSON, The Merv Griffin Show In Paris (The Merv Show), November 10, 1981, (SYN)

WRITING - DAYTIME DRAMA SERIES (E-1925)
For the entire series

DOUGLAS MARLAND, NANCY FRANKLIN, PATRICK MULCAHEY, GENE PALUMBO, FRANK SALISBURY, The Guiding Light (CBS)
AGNES NIXON, WISNER WASHAM, JACK WOOD, MARY K. WELLS, CLARICE BLACKBURN, CAROLYN FRANZ, LORRAINE BRODERICK, CYNTHIA BENJAMIN, JOHN SAFFRON, ELIZABETH WALLACE, All My Children (ABC)
HENRY SLESAR, LOIS KIBBEE, The Edge Of Night (ABC)
SAM HALL, PEGGY O'SHEA, DON WALLACE, LANIE BERTRAM, FRED CORKE, S. MICHAEL SCHNESSEL, One Life To Live (ABC)

ACHIEVEMENT IN TECHNICAL EXCELLENCE - DAYTIME DRAMA SERIES (E-1926)

For the entire series--Emmys to Individuals

ALL MY CHILDREN, Joseph Solomito, Howard Zweig, Technical Directors; Diana Wenman, Jean Dadario, Barbara Martin Simmons, Associate Directors; Lawrence Hammond, Robert Ambrico, Larry Strack, Vincent Senatore, Jay Kenn, Trevor Thompson, Electronic Camera; Len Walas, Sr. Video Engineer; Al Lemanski, Charles Eisen, Audio Engineers; Roger Haenelt, Video Tape Editor; Barbara Wood, Sound Effects Eng; (ABC)

GENERAL HOSPITAL, John Cochran, David Smith, Technical Directors; Ritch Kenney, John Rago, James Angel, Barry Kirstein, Jack Denton, David Banks, Jan Lowry, Blair White, Dale Walsh, Carol Wetovich, William Scott, D.J. Diomedes, Sal Folino, Bud Holland, Electronic Camera; Sam Potter, Victor Bagdadi, Robert Miller, Zoli Osaze, Sr. Video Engineers; Hal Alexander, George Thompson, Associate Directors; Bob Lanham, Jose Galvez, Jack Moody, Videotape Editors (ABC)

DESIGN - DAYTIME DRAMA SERIES (E-1927)

For the entire series--Emmys to Individuals

GENERAL HOSPITAL, James Ellingwood, Art Director; Mercer Barrows, Set Decorator; Grant Velie, Thomas Markle, John Zak, Lighting Directors; Jim O'Daniel, Costume Designer; P.K. Cole, Vikki McCarter, Diane Lewis, Make-up Designers; Katherine Kotarakos, Debbie Holmes, Hair Designers; Dominic Messinger, Jill Farren Phelps, Music Directors; Charles Paul, Music Composer (ABC)

ALL MY CHILDREN, John Pitts, Scenic Designer; William Itkin, Donna Larson, Donald Gavitt, Lighting Directors; Carol Luiken, Costume Designer; Sylvia Lawrence, Scott Hersh, Make-up Designers; Marie Ange Ripka, Richard Green, Hair Designers; Teri Smith, Music Director; Sid Ramin, Irving Robbin, Music Composers; Hy Bley, Graphic Designer (ABC)

RYAN'S HOPE, Sy Tomashoff, Scenic Designer; John Connolly, Dennis Size, Lighting Directors; Alex Tolken, Costume Designer; James Cola, Tracy Kelly McNevin, Make-up Designers; John Keith Quinn, John DeLaat, Hair Designers; Sybil Weinberger, Music Director (ABC)

CHILDREN'S ENTERTAINMENT SERIES (E-1928)

Emmy(s) to Executive Producer(s) and Producer(s)

CAPTAIN KANGAROO, Robert Keeshan, Executive Producer; Joel Kosofsky, Producer (CBS)

ABC WEEKEND SPECIALS, Robert Chenault, Executive Producer (ABC)

CHILDREN'S ENTERTAINMENT SPECIALS (E-1929)

Emmy(s) to Executive Producer(s) and Producer(s)

STARSTRUCK, (ABC Afterschool Special) Paul Freeman, Producer, October 14, 1981 (ABC)

ME AND MR. STENNER, (CBS Afternoon Playhouse) Diana Karew, Producer, January 5, 1982 (CBS)

CHILDREN'S INFORMATIONAL/INSTRUCTIONAL SERIES (E-1930)

Emmy(s) to Executive Producer(s) and Producer(s)

30 MINUTES, Joel Heller, Producer (CBS)

KIDS ARE PEOPLE TOO, Marilyn Olin, Executive Producer (ABC)

SESAME STREET, Dulcy Singer, Executive Producer (PBS)

CHILDREN'S INFORMATIONAL/INSTRUCTIONAL SPECIAL (E-1931)

Emmy(s) to Executive Producer(s) and Producer(s)

KATHY, Kier Cline, Barry Teicher, Producers (PBS)

THE BODY HUMAN: "BECOMING A MAN", Thomas W. Moore, Executive Producer; Alfred R. Kelman, Robert E. Fuisz, M.D., Producers (CBS)

THE BODY HUMAN: "BECOMING A WOMAN", Thomas W. Moore, Executive Producer; Alfred R. Kelman, Robert E. Fuisz, M.D., Producers (CBS)

INFORMATIONAL/INSTRUCTIONAL PROGRAMMING–SHORT FORM (E-1932)

Emmy(s) to Executive Producer(s) and Producer(s)

IN THE NEWS, Joel Heller, Executive Producer; Walter Lister, Producer (CBS)

ASK NBC NEWS, Lester Crystal, Executive Producer; Beryl Pfizer, Producer (NBC)

BETCHA DON'T KNOW, Chiz Schultz, Executive Producer; Bob Glover, Producer (NBC)

INDIVIDUAL ACHIEVEMENT IN CHILDREN'S PROGRAMMING

PERFORMERS (E-1933)

BOB KEESHAN, Captain Kangaroo Show, Feburary 8, 1982 (CBS)

MIKE FARRELL, The Body Human: Becoming A Man (CBS)

RITA MORENO, Orphans, Waifs and Wards (CBS)

CICELY TYSON, The Body Human: Becoming A Woman (CBS)

WRITERS (E-1934)

PAUL W. COOPER, She Drinks A Little (ABC Afterschool Special) (ABC)

ROBERT E. FUISZ, M.D., The Body Human: Becoming A Woman (CBS)

NORMAN STILES, SARA COMPTON, TOM DUNSMUIR, JUDY FREUDBERG, TONY GEISS, JOHN GLINES, EMILY KINGLSEY, DAVID KORR, LUIS SANTEIRO, RAY SIPHERD, JOE BAILEY, Sesame Street, November 23, 1981 (PBS)

DIRECTORS (E-1935)

For a single episode of a series or for a special program

ARTHUR ALLAN SEIDELMAN, She Drinks A Little (ABC Afterschool Special) (ABC)

JEFF BLECKNER, Daddy, I'm Their Mama Now (ABC Afterschool Special) (ABC)

JIM HIRSCHFELD, Captain Kangaroo Show, Feburary 8, 1982 (CBS)

TECHNICAL DIRECTOR/ELECTRONIC CAMERA (E-1936)

JAMES ANGERAME, Technical Director; An Orchestra Is A Team, Too! (CBS)

FRANK FLORIO, Technical Director; Orphans, Waifs and Wards (CBS)

AUDIO (E-1937)

STEVE J. PALACEK, Tape Sound Recordist; An Orchestra Is A Team, Too! (CBS)

CINEMATOGRAPHERS (E-1938)

For a single episode of a series or for a special program

TOM HURWITZ, Horsemen Of Inner Mongolia, (Big Blue Marble) (SYN)

HANANIA BAER, Daddy, I'm Their Mama Now, (ABC Afterschool Special) (ABC)

DON LENZER, The Body Human: Becoming A Woman (CBS)

FILM EDITORS (E-1939)

For a single episode of a series or for a special program

PETER HAMMER, ALLEN KIRKPATRICK, Horsemen Of Inner Mongolia, (Big Blue Marble) (SYN)

ROBERT EISENHARDT, The Body Human: Becoming A Woman (CBS)

GLORIA WHITTENMORE, My Mother Was Never A Kid, (ABC Afterschool Special) (ABC)

MUSIC COMPOSERS AND/OR DIRECTORS (E-1940)

For a single episode of a series or for a special program

ELLIOT LAWRENCE, Composer/Director, The Unforgiveable Secret, (ABC Afterschool Special) (ABC)
CHRISTOPHER CERF, DAVID CONNER, NORMAN STILES, Composers, Sesame Street, December 18, 1981 (PBS)

LIGHTING DIRECTORS (E-1941)

RANDY NORDSTROM, Sesame Street, January 27, 1982 (PBS)

COSTUME DESIGNERS (E-1942)

JEAN BLACKBURN, She Drinks A Little, (ABC Afterschool Special) (ABC)
ALFRED E. LEHMAN, Bill Bixby and the Adventures of a Young Magician, (CBS Festival of the Lively Arts For Young People) (CBS)
DELPHINE WHITE, My Mother Was Never A Kid, (ABC Afterschool Special) (ABC)

ART DIRECTORS (E-1943)

CLAUDE BONNIERE, My Mother Was Never A Kid, (ABC Afterschool Special) (ABC)
CARY WHITE, Daddy, I'm Their Mama Now, (ABC Afterschool Special) (ABC)

MAKE-UP & HAIR DESIGNERS (E-1944)

JUDI COOPER SEALY, Hair Designer, My Mother Was Never A Kid, (ABC Afterschool Special) (ABC)
NANCY FERGUSON, Make-up Designer, She Drinks A Little, (ABC Afterschool Special) (ABC)
SHONAGH JABOUR, Make-up Designer, My Mother Was Never A Kid, (ABC Afterschool Special) (ABC)

GRAPHIC DESIGN (E-1945)

RAY FAVATA, MICHAEL J. SMOLLIN, Graphic Designers–Opening Animation, The Great Space Coaster #93, October 9, 1981 (SYN)
LOU PALISANO, Graphic Designer, An Orchestra Is A Team, Too!, (CBS Festival of Lively Arts for Young People) (CBS)
STAS PYKA, Graphic Designer, Louis Rukeyser's Business Journal (SYN)

ACHIEVEMENT IN RELIGIOUS PROGRAMMING - SERIES (E-1946)

Emmy(s) to Executive Producer(s) and Producer(s)

INSIGHT, Ellwood Kieser, Executive Producer; Mike Rhodes, Producer (SYN)
DIRECTIONS, Sid Darion, Executive Producer; Adela E. Lowe, Producer (ABC)

ACHIEVEMENT IN RELIGIOUS PROGRAMMING - SPECIALS (E-1947)

HARRY CHAPIN'S COTTON PATCH, Feburary 28, 1982 (NBC)
WHAT SHALL WE DO ABOUT THE CHILDREN, September 27, 1981 (NBC)

INDIVIDUAL ACHIEVEMENT IN RELIGIOUS PROGRAMMING

PERFORMERS (E-1948)

STEVE ALLEN, Host; Wait Till We're 65 (NBC)
EDWIN NEWMAN, Moderator; Ambassadors Of Hope (NBC)

SPECIAL CLASSIFICATION OF OUTSTANDING PROGRAM ACHIEVEMENT (E-1949)

Emmy(s) to Executive Producer(s) and Producer(s)

FYI, Yanna Kroyt Brandt, Producer (ABC)
THE BODY HUMAN: THE LOVING PROCESS--MEN, Thomas W. Moore, Executive Producer; Alfred R. Kelman and Robert E. Fuisz, Producers (CBS)
THE BODY HUMAN: THE LOVING PROCESS--WOMEN, Thomas W. Moore, Executive Producer; Alfred R. Kelman and Robert E. Fuisz, Producers (CBS)

SPECIAL CLASSIFICATION OF OUTSTANDING INDIVIDUAL ACHIEVEMENT

(Possibility of One Award, more than one Award or no Award).

PERFORMERS (E-1950)

HAL LINDEN, Host; FYI (ABC)

WRITERS (E-1951)

ELAINE MERYL BROWN, BETTY CORNFELD, MARY ANN DONAHUE, JOE FUSTAITIS, ROBIN WESTEN, FYI (ABC)

DIRECTORS (E-1952)

ALFRED R. KELMAN, The Body Human: The Loving Process–Women (CBS)
CHARLES A. BANGERT, ALFRED R. KELMAN, The Body Human: The Loving Process--Men (CBS)
MICHAEL GARGIULO, FYI (ABC)

COVERAGE OF SPECIAL EVENTS (E-1953)

Emmy(s) to Executive Producer(s) and Producer(s)

MACY'S THANKSGIVING DAY PARADE, Dick Schneider, Producer (NBC)
THE EIGHTH ANNUAL EMMY AWARDS FOR DAYTIME PROGRAMMING, William Carruthers, Executive Producer; Joel Stein, Producer (ABC)

INDIVIDUAL ACHIEVEMENT IN THE COVERAGE OF SPECIAL EVENTS

(Possibility of one Award, more than one Award or no Award).

DIRECTOR (E-1954)

DICK SCHNEIDER, Macy's Thanksgiving Day Parade (NBC)

WRITER (E-1955)

BERNARD N. EISMAN, The Body Human: The Loving Process--Women (CBS)

TECHNICAL DIRECTION AND/OR ELECTRONIC CAMERA (E-1956)

TERRY ROHNKE, Technical Director; TOM DEZENDORF, VINCENT DiPIETRO, CARL ECKETT, ERIC EISENSTEIN, BARRY FRISCHER, BILL GOETZ, STEVE GONZALEZ, DAVE HAGEN, JOHN HILLYER, JIM JOHNSON, GENE MARTIN, DON MULVANEY, AL ROBERTS, Electronic Camera; Macy's Thanksgiving Day Parade (NBC)

MUSIC COMPOSER/DIRECTOR (E-1957)

MILTON DeLUGG, Composer/Director, Macy's Thanksgiving Day Parade (NBC)
WALTER LEVINSKY, Composer/Director, 1981 Daytime Emmy Show (ABC)

INDIVIDUAL ACHIEVEMENT IN ANY AREA OF CREATIVE TECHNICAL CRAFTS

(Possibility of one Award, more than one Award or no Award).

TECHNICAL DIRECTOR/ELECTRONIC CAMERA (E-1958)

SANFORD BELL, HAL CLASSON, Technical Directors; Remote: Kent Falls State Park–Danbury, Connecticut; The Guiding Light (CBS)
LAWRENCE HAMMOND, NICHOLAS HUTAK, THOMAS WOODS, Electronic Camera; Remote: Switzerland; All My Children (ABC)
FRANK FLORIO, MALACHY G. WIENGES, Technical Directors; Remote: Canary Island, Spain; The Guiding Light (CBS)
WILLIAM H. POPE, Electronic Camera; Remote: Luke and Laura's Wedding; General Hospital (ABC)

ASSOCIATE DIRECTION/VIDEOTAPE EDITING (E-1959)

NICK GIORDANO, LOU TORINO, Vidotape Editors; Remote: Luke And Laura's Wedding; General Hospital (ABC)

CINEMATOGRAPHY (E-1960)

CHUCK LEVEY, The Body Human: The Loving Process--Men (CBS)

FILM EDITING (E-1961)

GEOF BARTZ, The Body Human: The Loving Process--Women (CBS)
CHARLOTTE GROSSMAN, The Body Human: The Loving Process--Men (CBS)

ART DIRECTION/SCENIC DESIGN/SET DECORATION (E-1962)

BOB KEENE, GRIFF LAMBERT, Art Directors, The Richard Simmons Show (SYN)
JACK McADAM, KATE MURPHY, Art Directors, The John Davidson Show (SYN)

LIGHTING DIRECTION (E-1963)

EVERETT MELOSH, Remote: Gallery Basement; One Life to Live (ABC)
JAMES TETLAW, Remote: Switzerland; All My Children (ABC)

COSTUME DESIGN (E-1964)

NANCY SIMMONS, The Richard Simmons Show (SYN)

SPECIAL AWARDS

TRUSTEES AWARD (E-1965)

Walter Cronkite for continued distinguished service to television and the public this medium serves.

ENGINEERING AWARDS (E-1966)

Eastman Kodak Co., and Fuji Photo Film Co., Ltd. for the research and development of a new film technology which led to the introduction of the new high speed negative color film.
Rank Cintel Co. (Citation) for its research and introduction of the Digiscan Frame Store for the flying spot telecine system.
Bosch Fernseh (Citation) for the development and implementation of the CCD telecine technology.
British Broadcasting Corp. (Citation) for the early development and research work on the CCD scanner telecine technology.
Arthur C. Clarke (Citation) for his early theory studies and writings concerning the possibility of stationary satellite transmission to large areas of the earth.

INTERNATIONAL AWARDS

DOCUMENTARY (E-1967)

IS THERE ONE WHO UNDERSTANDS ME? THE WORLD OF JAMES JOYCE, Radio Telefis Eireann, Ireland
ALL FIVE TOGETHER, NHK, Japan
THE SPIES WHO NEVER WERE, PARTS I & II, Canadian Broadcasting Corporation, Canada

DRAMA (E-1968)

A VOYAGE ROUND MY FATHER, Thames Television Ltd., United Kingdom
MISS MORRISON'S GHOSTS, Anglia Television Ltd., United Kingdom
NORTHERN LIGHTS, Scottish Television, United Kingdom
THE WORLD CUP: A CAPTAIN'S TALE, Tyne Tees Television, United Kingdom

PERFORMING ARTS (E-1969)

A LOT OF HAPPINESS, Granada Television Ltd., United Kingdom
THE MOON PRINCESS, NHK, Japan
OTTORINO RESPIGHI: A DREAM OF ITALY, Allegro Films, United Kingdom

POPULAR ARTS (E-1970)

DEATH AND LIFE SEVERINIAN, TV Globo Ltda., Brazil
"AUSTRALIAN WOMAN'S WEEKLY" AUSTRALIAN FASHION AWARDS, National Nine Network, Australia
THE MORECAMBE & WISE SHOW, Thames Television Ltd., United Kingdom

INTERNATIONAL DIRECTORATE AWARD (E-1971)

AKIO MORITA

FOUNDERS AWARD (E-1972)

Michael Landon

SPORTS PROGRAMMING

LIVE SPORTS SPECIAL: (E-1973)

Emmy(s) to Executive Producer(s) and Producer(s) and Director(s)

NCAA BASKETBALL CHAMPIONSHIP FINAL, Kevin O'Malley, Executive Producer; Rick Sharp, Robert Fishman, Director (CBS)
1982 KENTUCKY DERBY, Roone Arledge, Executive Producer; Chuck Howard, Producer; Jim Jennett, Director (ABC)
1982 U.S. OPEN, Roone Arledge, Executive Producer; Chuck Howard, Producer; Terry Jastrow, Jim Jennett & Bob Goodrich, Directors (ABC)
SUPER BOWL XVI, Charles H Milton, III, Senior Producer; Terry O'Neil, Producer; Sandy Grossman, Director (CBS)
THE MASTERS, Frank Chirkinian, Producer; Bob Dailey, Director (CBS)

LIVE SPORTS SERIES (E-1974)

Emmy(s) to Executive Producer(s) and Producer(s) and Directors

NFL FOOTBALL, Terry O'Neil, Executive Producer; Charles H Milton III, Senior Producer; Michael Burks, David Dinkins, Jr, Sherman Eagan, John Faratis, Ed Goren, Bob Rowe, Perry Smith, Jim Silman, Robert D Stenner & David Winner, Producers;, Peter Bleckner, Larry Cavolina, Joe Carolie, Bob Dailey, Bob Dunphy, Robert Fishman, Sandy Grossman, Andy Kindle, John McDonough, Jim Silman & Tony Verna, Directors (CBS)
ABC'S NFL MONDAY NIGHT FOOTBALL, Roone Arledge, Executive Producer; Bob Goodrich, Producer; Chet Forte, Director (ABC)
NCAA FOOTBALL, Roone Arledge, Executive Producer; Chuck Howard, Senior Producer; Curt Gowdy, Jr, Ken Wolfe & Eleanor Sanger Riger, Producers; Andy Sidaris, Jim Jennett, Larry Kamm & Ken Fouts,

Directors (ABC)
THE NBA ON CBS, James F Harrington, Executive Producer; Michael Burks & Robert Stenner, Producers; Sandy Grossman & Tony Verna, Directors (CBS)
NCAA BASKETBALL, Kevin O'Malley, Executive Producer; Rick Sharp, David Dinkins, Jr, George Veras, David Michaels, Dave Blatt, Bob Mansbach, Jean Harper & Ted Shaker (CBS)

EDITED SPORTS SPECIAL (E-1975)
Emmy(s) to Executive Producer(s) and Producer(s) and Director(s)

1982 INDIANAPOLIS "500", Roone Arledge, Executive Producer; Mike Pearl & Bob Goodrich, Producers; Chuck Howard, Cooordinating Producer; Larry Kamm & Roger Goodman, Directors (ABC)
1981 NATIONAL SPORTS FESTIVAL, Roone Arledge, Executive Producer; Chuck Howard, Senior Producer; Mike Pearl, Doug Wilson, Jeff Ruhe, Peter Lasser & Ned Simon, Producers; Joe Aceti, Andy Sidaris, Larry Kamm, John DeLisa, & Ken Fouts, Directors (ABC)
WBC WORLD HEAVYWEIGHT CHAMPIONSHIP (LARRY HOLMES VS. GERRY COONEY), Roone Arledge, Executive Producer; Chet Forte, Producer; Joe Aceti, Director (ABC)
THE SUPER BOWL TODAY, Ted Shaker, Producer; Daniel H Forer, Co-Ord Feature Producer; Andy Kindle, Dan Lauck, & David Winner, Segment Producers; David Michaels & George Veras, Remote Producers; Richard Drake, Director; Jim Silman & Patti Tuite, Remote Directors (CBS)
THE HEISMAN TROPHY AWARD '81, Michael Lepiner, Executive Producer; Cappy Petrash Greenspan, Senior Producer; Nancy Beffa, Producer; Bud Greenspan, Director (SYNDICATED)

EDITED SPORTS SERIES/ANTHOLOGIES (E-1976)
Emmy(s) to Executive Producer(s) and Producer(s) and Directors(s)

ABC'S WIDE WORLD OF SPORTS, Roone Arledge, Executive Producer; Dennis Lewin, Coordinating Producer; Chuck Howard, Mike Pearl, Jeff Ruhe, Brice Weisman, Doug Wilson, Eleanor Sanger Riger, Ken Wolfe, Bob Goodrich, Curt Gowdy, Jr, & Carol Lehti, Producers; Craig Janoff, Larry Kamm, Ralph Abraham, Jim Jennett, Joe Aceti, Roger Goodman, Ken Fouts, Chet Forte & Andy Sidaris, Directors (ABC)
ABC SPORTSBEAT (ABC)
CBS SPORTS SATURDAY, Terry O'Neil, Executive Producer; David Winner & Jean Harper, Coordinating Producers; Michael Arnold, Michael Burks, David Blatt, Bill Brown, David Dinkins, Jr, Bob Dekas, Sherman Eagan, John Faratzis, Robert Fishman, Daniel H Forer, Ed Goren, Dan Lauck, Robert Matina, David Michaels, Charles H Milton III, Bob Mansbach, Pat O'Brien, David Segal, Craig Silver, Perry Smith, Robert D Stenner, George Veras, John Tesh & Mark Wolff, Producers; Peter Bleckner, Cathy Barreto, Larry Cavolina, Bob Dailey, Richard Drake, Bob Dekas, Bob Dunphy, Robert Fishman, Sandy Grossman, Andy Kindle, John McDonough, Arthur Struck, Patti Tuite, Directors (CBS)
THE NFL TODAY, Ted Shaker, Producer; Daniel H Forer, Coordinating Producer; Sherman Eagan, Jean Harper, Andy Kindle, Bob Mansbach & David Winner, Feature Producers; Richard Drake, Director (CBS)
THE AMERICAN SPORTSMAN, Roone Arledge, Executive Producer; John Wilcox, Series Producer; Chris Carmody, Coordinating Producer; Bob Nixon & Curt Gowdy, Producers (ABC)

SPORTS PERSONALITY-HOST: (E-1977)
(Play-By-Play)

Jim McKay (ABC)
Keith Jackson (ABC)
Brent Musburger (CBS)
Al Michaels (ABC)
Pat Summerall (CBS)

SPORTS PERSONALITY-ANALYST: (E-1978)
(Commentary)

John Madden, (CBS)
Nelson Burton, Jr, (ABC)
Dick Button, (ABC)
Dave Marr, (ABC)
Billy Packer, (CBS)

INDIVIDUAL ACHIEVEMENT IN SPORTS PROGRAMMING:
(Possibility of one award, more than one award or no award)

CINEMATOGRAPHERS: (E-1979)
ERNIE ERNST, HANK McELWEE, HOWARD NEEF, STEVE SABOL & PHIL TUCKETT, Sports Illustrated: A Series for Television (SYNDICATED)
JOSEPH H KLIMOVITZ, A Celebration of Sports (NBC)
JAMES W GRAU & JAMES W BARRY GRAU, Super Bowl XVI Time Capsule, Program Titles (CBS)
PAUL BELLINGER, EDGAR BOYLES, JON HAMMOND, PETER HENNING, MIKE HOOVER, D'ARCY MARSH, STANTON WATERMAN & JONATHAN WRIGHT, The American Sportsman (ABC)

ASSOCIATE DIRECTORS: (E-1980)
JEFF COHAN, BOB LANNING & NED SIMON, 1982 Indianapolis "500" (ABC)
JOHN C McDONOUGH, JR, The Super Bowl XVI Close-"The Winner Takes It All" (CBS)
CATHY BARRETO, STEVE DELIAPIATRA & DANNY LEW, Superbowl Today (CBS)
DICK BUFFINTON, KATHY COOK, VINCE DEDARIO, JOHN DELISA, JACK GRAHAM, BEN HARVEY, BOB HERSH, PAUL HUTCHINSON, PETER LASSER, DENNIS MAZZOCCO, BRIAN McCULLOUGH, NORMAN SAMET, TONI SLOTKIN & MEG STREETER, ABC's Wide World of Sports (ABC)
BOB DEKAS & PATTI TUITE, NCAA Basketball Championship Final - Feature Endpiece (CBS)
JOEL ARONOWITZ, CATHY BARRETO, BOB COFFEY, STEVE DELIAPIATRA, STAN FAER, BOB HALPER, BETH HERMELIN, BARRY HICKS, DAVE KAPLAN, DANNY LEW, MUFFY McDONOUGH, HOWARD MILLER, GADY REINHOLD, RONI SCHERMAN STEIN, & TOMMY SIMPSON, NFL TODAY (CBS)

VIDEOTAPE/FILM EDITORS: (E-1981)
STEVE PURCELL, Reggie Jackson (CBS)
MARTIN BELL, JOE CLARK, FINBAR COLLINS, RON FESZCHUR, CHUCK GARDNER, BRUCE GIARAFFE, CLARE GILMOUR, HECTOR KICILIAN, M SCHENCMAN, MIKE SEIGEL, MIKE WENIG & TOM WHITE, Indianapolis "500" (ABC)
RASHA DRACHKOVITCH, Legend of Larry Mahan-Greatest Sports Legends (SYNDICATED)
JOE DRAKE, BOB HICKSON & GEORGE JOANITIS, NCAA Basketball Championship Final - Feature Endpiece (CBS)
PHIL TUCKETT, NFL Weekly Magazine/Week 14 (SYNDICATED)
SCOTT L RADER, The Spirit of Competition - A Celebration of Sports Segment: "Secretariat" (NBC)
MARIO BUCICH, KEN McILWAINE, BOB KLUG, ANDY PRASKAI, BRUCE SCHECHTER, TONY TOCCI & MIKE KOSTEL, This Week in Baseball, Episode #615 (SYNDICATED)
JIMMY ALKINS, STEVE BABB, ART BUCKNER, CURTIS CAMPBELL, SUMNER DEMAR, DAVID DIAZ, JOE DRAKE, TOM DURKIN, BOB ENRIONE, AL GOLLY, SIG GORDON, FRANK HODNETT, BERNIE JACOBS, MIKE KAYATTA, ANDY KLEIN, GARY KOZAK, JEFF LAING, MARK LEOCZKO, GEORGE MAGEE, WALTER MATWICHUK, JOHN MAYER, GARY MAZZACCA, HENRY MENUSAN, JESSE MICHNICK, GEORGE PALMISANO, FRED PINCIARO, JEFF RINGEL, CHARLOTTE ROBINSON, BRIAN ROSNER, JOE SCHOLNICK, ALLAN SEGAL, TOM FERRANTE, LARRY SHELLENBERGER, BILL VANDENNOORT, JIM WARDEN, JOHN WELLS & BILL ZIZZA, NFL Today (CBS)
ANDREW SQUICCIARINI, The Heisman Trophy Award '81 (SYN-

DICATED)
RICH DOMICH, KEN McILWAINE, BRUCE SCHECHTER & TONY TOCCI, The Baseball Bunch #4 (SYNDICATED)
ANGELO BERNARDUCCI, RICHARD ROSSI, ANTHONY SCANDIFFIO, TED WINTERBURN & ANTHONY ZACCARO, The American Sportsman (ABC)
FINBAR COLLINS, CLARE GILMOUR, PHIL JACKSON, DALE SILLS, ART VOLK, PAUL WEBER, MIKE WENIG & TOM WHITE, U.S. Open (ABC)
MARTIN BELL, RON FESCHUR, CHUCK GARDNER, LOU RENDE, WINSTON SADOO & ED ZLOTNIK, NFL Football (ABC)
NAT CHOMSKY, BRUCE GIARRAFFA, HECTOR KICELIAN, MERRITT ROESSER, MIKE WENIG & TOM WHITE, Sugar Bowl (ABC)

LIGHTING DIRECTORS: (E-1982)

NAT ALBIN, Indianapolis "500" (ABC)
TONY AZZOLINO, Sugar Bowl (ABC)

SENIOR AUDIO ENGINEERS: (E-1983)

JACK BRANDES, JIM DAVIS, JACK HUGHES, NORM KIERNAN & MORLEY LANG, U.S. Open (ABC)
JAMES J DAVIS JR, NCAA Football (ABC)
BRIAN WICKHAM, Spirit of Competition: A Celebration of Sports (NBC)
JACK NEWMAN & PHIL SPIELLER, NFL Weekly Magazine/Week 14 (SYNDICATED)
JOHN LORY, New York Marathon (ABC)
JIM DAVIS, Sugar Bowl (ABC)
JACK KESTENBAUM, NFL Football (ABC)
JIM DAVIS, JACK HUGHES & JACK KELLY, Indianapolis "500" (ABC)
JONATHON LORY, HESH YARMARK & ALAN JAMES, The Ironman Endurance Triathalon (ABC's Wide World of Sports) (ABC)

TECHNICAL DIRECTORS, ELECTRONIC CAMERAPERSONS, SENIOR VIDEO OPERATORS: (E-1984)

ANTHONY FILIPPI, ROBERT PIERINGER & ROBET SQUITTIERI, Senior Video Operators; JAMES MURPHY, NEIL McCAFFREY, STEVE GORSUCH, HERMAN LANG, BARRY DRAGO, JOSEPH SOKOTA, FRANK McSPEDON, GEORGE ROTHWEILER, JEFFREY POLLACK, GEORGE NAEDER, GEORGE GRAFFEO, THOMAS McCARTHY, SIGMUND MEYERS, SOL BRESS, JAMES McCARTHY, HANS SINGER & WALTER SOUCY, Electronic Camerapersons: 1982 Daytona 500 (CBS)
JOHN ALLEN, Technical Director; MIKE MICHAELS, Senior Video Operator; JOHN MORREALE, FRANK MELCHIORE, DIANE CATES, JOHN DUKEWICH, EVAN BAKER, MIKE FREEDMAN, SAL FOLINO, WARREN CRESS, DAN LANGFORD & DALE WELSH, Electronic Camerapersons: Sugar Bowl (ABC)
GENE AFFRUNTI, JOHN FIGER, RICH GELBER & WINK GUNTHER, Technical Directors; JOHN MONTELEONE, Senior Video Operator; MORT LEVIN, F MERKLEIN, J SAPIENZA, A BEST, JOHN CORDONE, D SPANOS, GEORGE MONTANEZ, D LAMOTHE, JACK CRONIN, J WOODLE, A DEMAMOS, R WESTLINE, J SCHAFER, TONY GAMBINO, KENNETH SANBORN, R WOLFF, PHIL FONTANA, A PEFFER, R HAMMOND, T MORTELLARO, SERF MENDUINA, W SULLIVAN, R BERNSTEIN, S MADJANSKI, & J STEFANONI, Electronic Camerapersons: New York Marathon (ABC)
WINK GUNTHER & CHET MAZUREK, Technical Directors; CYRIL TYWANG & KEN AMOW, Senior Video Operators; A PEFFER, W SULLIVAN, STEVE NIKIFOR, J MORREALE, R HAMMOND, A DeROSA, JOE COTUGNO, JESSE KOHN, ANDY ARMENTANI, JACK SAVOY, GENE WOOD, JACK DORFMAN, TOM O'CONNELL, JOE STEFANONI, FRANK MELCHIORRE, MORT LEVIN, JOE SAPIENZA, SERF MENDUINA, GARY DONATELLI & STEVE WOLFF, Electronic Camerapersons: Indianapolis "500" (ABC)
CHARLES D'ONOFRIO & ROBERT VERNUM, Technical Directors; EDWARD AMBROSINI, WILLIAM BERRIDGE, LOUIS LEGER & ROBERT PIERINGER, Senior Video Operators; JAMES McCARTHY, GEORGE ROTHWEILER, PATTI McBRIDE, FRANK McSPEDON, HANS SINGER, ROY JACKSON, RICK BLANE, GEORGE KLIMCSAK, BARRY DRAGO, ALFRED LORETO, NEIL McCAFFREY, ROBERT JAMIESON, WILLIAM MURPHY & HERMAN LANG, Electronic Camerapersons: U.S. Open

Tennis (CBS)
SANFORD BELL & CHARLES D'ONOFRIO, Technical Directors; WILLIAM BERRIDGE, THOMAS DeLILLA, D OHRLICH, FRANK FOSSO & LOUIS LEGER, Senior Video Operators; J VICENZ, R SKORUP, JAMES MURPHY, RICH BLANE, JOSEPH SOKOTA, JOHN LINCOLN, WALTER SOUCY, FRANK McSPEDON, STANLEY GOULD, DENNIS McBRIDE, BARRY DRAGO, G ERICKSON, D FINCA, DAVID C GRAHAM, ROBERT JAMIESON, NEIL McCAFFREY, G NAEDER, GEORGE ROTHWEILER, JAMES McCARTHY, ALFRED LORETO, HERMAN LANG, GEORGE KLIMCSAK, HANS SINGER, NICHOLAS LAURIA, GORDON SWEENEY & WILLIAM MURPHY, Electronic Camerapersons: 1982 MASTERS (CBS)
JAMES ANGERAME, STANFORD BELL, CHARLES D'ONOFRIO, GEORGE NAEDER, ROBERT BROWN & GILBERT MILLER, Technical Directors; ANTHONY FILIPPI, ROBERT HANFORD, ROBERT SQUITTIERI, THOMAS DeLILLA, WILLIAM BERRIDGE, DAVID FRUITMAN, FRANK FLORIO, NANCY STEVENSON, RONALD RESCH & ROBERT PIERINGER, Senior Video Operators; RICK BLANE, STEVE GORSUCH, MICHAEL DENNY, GEORGE KLIMCSAK, GORDON SWEENEY, JOSEPH VICENZ, DAVID FINCH, JAMES MURPHY, GEORGE ROTHWEILER, ROBERT JAMIESON, ROBERT WELCH, WALTER SOUCY, GORM ERICKSON, FRANK McSPEDON, HERMAN LANG, STANLEY GOULD, HAL HOFFMAN, JOHN LINCOLN, JOHN BRENNAN, DAVID DORSETT, MICHAEL ENGLISH, JEFFREY POLLACK, AL LORETO, DENNIS McBRIDE, GENE SAVITT, NEIL McCAFFREY, JOSEPH SOKOTA, SIG MEYER & ANTHONY CUCURULLO, Electronic Camerapersons: Super Bowl XVI (CBS)
BOB BROWN & STEVE CUNNINGHAM, Technical Directors; LOU LEGER & FRANK FLORIO, Senior Video Operators; JOHN AGUIRRE, SOL BRESS, BARRY DRAGO, STEVE GORSUCH, BOB JAMIESON, HERMAN LANG, TOM McCARTHY, JEFF POLLACK, JOE SAKOTA, PAUL SHERWOOD, JOE VICENS & BOB WELSH, Electronic Camerapersons: NCAA Basketball Championship Final (CBS)
SAL NIGITA, Technical Director; SCOTTY McCARTHY, Senior Video Operator; LENNY BASILE, MARIO CIARLO, STEVE GONZALES, BARRY FRISCHER, DAVE HAGEN, ROGER HARBAUGH, TOM HOGAN, JAMES JOHNSON, GEORGE LOOMIS, JOHN PINTO, OLONZO ROBERTS & BRIAN RUSSO, Electronic Camerapersons: C.A.R.T. Michigan 500 Indy Race Live (NBC)
JOE SCHIAVO, Technical Director; ROBERT GREENSETH, Senior Video Operator; FRANK CELECIA, JOE COTUGNO, A DeROSA, TOM O'CONNELL, GARY DONATELLI, STEVE NIKIFOR, JIM HENEGHAN, JACK SAVOY, ROY HUTCHINGS, STEVE WOLFF, JESSE KOHN, JACK DORFMAN & ANDY ARMENTANI, Electronic Camerapersons: NFL Football (ABC)
WINK GUNTHER, ERNIE BUTTLEMAN & GARY LARKINS, Technical Directors; MIKE MICHAELS, ROBERT GREENSETH & HUGO DILONARDO, Senior Video Operators; JOE SAPIENZA, RICHIE WESTLINE, GEORGE MONTANEZ, A DeROSA, ANDREW ARMENTANI, MORT LEVIN, JOE PULEO, SERF MENDUINA, TOM MORTELLARO, GREG CICCONE, STEVE WOLFF, JACK CRONIN, GENE KELLY, JACK DORFMAN, BOB BERNSTEIN, JIM HENEGHAN & J MORREALE, Electronic Camerapersons: U.S. Open (ABC)
JOHN ALLEN, Technical Director; KEN AMON, Senior Video Operator; WARREN CRESS, SAL FOLINO, DON LANGFORD, EVAN BAKER, JOSEPH PULEO, MIKE FREEDMAN, JOHN V MORREALE, FRANK MELCHIORRE & JOHN DUKEWICH, Electronic Camerapersons: NCAA Football (ABC)

TECHNICAL/ENGINEERING SUPERVISORS: (E-1985)

JAMES PATTERSON, JESSE RINEER, LOUIS SCANNA, ARTHUR TINN & PHILIP WILSON,
Super Bowl XVI (CBS)
BILL FREIBERGER, GEOFF FELGER, VERNE KERRICK, RICK OKULSKI, FRANK QUITONI &
HAROLD ROBBINS, New York Marathon (ABC)
JESSE RINEER & JOSEPH TIER, U.S. Open Tennis (CBS)
LOUIS SCANNAPIECO & ARTHUR TINN, 1982 Masters (CBS)
ROBERT ARMBRUSTER, U.S. Open (ABC)
VERNE KERRICK, Indianapolis "500" (ABC)
LOREN COLTRAN, NFL Football (ABC)
ROBERT ARMBRUSTER, Sugar Bowl (ABC)
WALTER PILE & ARTHUR TINN, 1982 Daytona 500 (CBS)
DOUG FLEETHAM, NCAA Basketball Championship Final (CBS)

GRAPHICS: (E-1986)

PEGGY HUGHES, NCAA College Football (ABC)
JAMES W GRAU, Super Bowl XVI Show Opening Title Sequences (CBS)
ERIC BUONAMASSA & JOE FLYNN, The NFL Today (CBS)
MARK HOWARD, ABC's NFL Monday Night Football (ABC)
HY BLEY & ROGER GOODMAN, 1982 Indianapolis "500" (ABC)

WRITING: (E-1987)

STEVE ROTFELD, The Legend of Jackie Robinson - Greatest Sports Legends (SYNDICATED)
MARK DURAND & WARNER FUSSELLE, This Week in Baseball, Episode #607 (SYNDICATED)
GEORGE BELL, The American Sportsman (ABC)
GARY COHEN, MARK DURAND & MIKE TOLLIN, The Baseball Bunch, Episode #204 (SYNDICATED)
JOHN MOSEDALE, The NFL Today (CBS)
THEODORE STRAUSS, Hillary's Challenge: Race to the Sky (PBS)
STEVE STERN, Super-Duper All-Star Bloopers (SYNDICATED)
PETER BENCHLEY & HANK WHITTEMORE, The American Sportsman (ABC)
BUD GREENSPAN, The Heisman Trophy Award '81 (SYNDICATED)
HAL FISHER, Once In A Lifetime (SYNDICATED)

MUSIC: (E-1988)

JON SILBERMANN, Super Bowl XVI Theme (CBS)
BOB ISRAEL, USA Vs. The World (ABC)

SPECIAL CLASSIFICATION OF OUTSTANDING PROGRAM

(Possibility of one award, more than one award or no award)

PROGRAM: (E-1989)

REGGIE JACKSON, (CBS)
THE BASEBALL BUNCH, Larry Parker, Executive Producer; Jody Shapiro & Gary Cohen, Producers (SYNDICATED)
ABC SPORTSBEAT, (ABC)
IRONMAN WORLD ENDURANCE TRIATHLON, Roone Arledge, Executive Producer;
Dennis Lewin, Coordinating Producer; Brice Weisman, Producer; Craig Janoff, Director (ABC)
JOCKEY SAFETY, Roone Arledge, Executive Producer; Maryann Grabavoy, Producer (ABC)
THEY SHOOT HORSES, DON'T THEY, Robert Fishman, Producer (CBS)
MATTERS OF LIFE AND DEATH: FOOTBALL IN AMERICA, Carol Brandenberg, Executive Producer;
Robert Carmichael, Producer (PBS)
SUPERMAN III, David Segal, Producer (CBS)

SPECIAL CLASSIFICATION FOR INDIVIDUAL ACHIEVEMENT

INDIVIDUALS: (E-1990)

(Possibility of one award, more than one award or no award)

RACECAM at the DAYTONA 500, Jim Harrington, Executive Producer;
Robert D Stenner, Producer; Robert Fishman, Director; Walter Pile, Field Technical Manager; John Porter, Peter Larsson, David Curtis, Engineers; George Graffeo, Cameraman (CBS)
ABC SPORTS' ON-AIR PROMOTIONS, Amy Sacks, Producer; Joe Novello, Director (ABC)
CLEMSON, Chuck Howard, Senior Producer; Jeff Ruhe, Producer; Jim Lampley, Reporter (ABC)
NEW YORK CITY MARATHON, Ken Wolfe, Producer; Craig Janoff, Director (ABC)
SPORTS PROMO - ON THE ROAD AGAIN, Douglas E Towey (CBS)

CBS CHALKBOARD, Terry O'Neil (CBS)
THE BASEBALL BUNCH, Johnny Bench (SYNDICATED)
LEGEND OF JACKIE ROBINSON, Ken Howard (SYNDICATED)
NBC SPORTS IMAGE DISPLAY, Paul Hammons (NBC)
THIS WEEK IN BASEBALL, Mel Allen (SYNDICATED)

NEWS AND DOCUMENTARY

COVERAGE OF A SINGLE BREAKING NEWS STORY (E-1991)
PROGRAMS:

DISASTER ON THE POTOMAC, (Nightline), William Lord, Vice President & Executive Producer; Stuart Schwartz, Senior Producer; Ted Koppel, Anchorman (ABC)
WASHINGTON MONUMENT SIEGE, (Nightline), William Lord, Vice President & Executive Producer; Stuart Schwartz, Tom Yellin, Senior Producers; Ted Koppel, Anchorman (ABC)
BREZHNEV DEATH, (Nightline), William Lord, Executive Producer; Stuart Schwartz, Tom Yellin, Bill Moore, Senior Producers; John Martin, Barry Serafin, Carl Bernstein, Reporters/Correspondents (ABC)
SEGMENTS:
NEW MEXICO'S YATES OIL COMPANY, (CBS Evening News with Dan Rather), Steve Kroft, Producer; Steve Kroft, Reporter/Correspondent (CBS)
PERSONAL NOTE/BEIRUT, (ABC World News Tonight), John Boylan, Producer; Peter Jennings, Reporter/Correspondent (ABC)
LINDA DOWN'S MARATHON, (ABC's World News This Morning), Peter Heller, Producer; Fred Wymore, Reporter/Correspondent (ABC)
AMERASIANS COME HOME, (CBS Evening News with Dan Rather), Rita Braver, Producer; Bruce Morton, Reporter/Correspondent (CBS)
HEART TREATMENT, (ABC World New Tonight), Sally Holm, Producer; George Strait, Reporter/Correspondent (ABC)

BACKGROUND/ANALYSIS OF A SINGLE CURRENT STORY (E-1992)
PROGRAMS:

CHRYSLER: ONCE UPON A TIME. . .AND NOW, Shelby Newhouse, Producer; Andrew Kokas, Reporter/Correspondent (PBS)
FROM THE ASHES. . .NICARAGUA TODAY, Helena Solberg Ladd & Glenn Silber, Producers (PBS)
GUATEMALA, (CBS Reports), Martin Smith, Producer; Ed Rabel, Reporter/Correspondent (CBS)
ROSES IN DECEMBER, Ann Carrigan, Bernard Stone, Producers; Ann Carrigan, Reporter/Correspondent (PBS)
WHAT PRICE CLEAN AIR?, Robert Richter, Producer; Robert Richter, Reporter/Correspondent (PBS)
BOOKS UNDER FIRE, Arnold Bennett, Grady Watts, Jr., Producer (PBS)
THE FALKLANDS/OH WHAT A SORRY WAR, Bill Brown, Producer; Lloyd Dobyns, Reporter/Correspondent (NBC)
OUR FRIENDS THE GERMANS, Catherine Olian, Producer; Bill Moyers, Reporter/Correspondent (CBS)
PEOPLE LIKE US, (CBS Reports), Judy Towers Reemtsma, Producer; Bill Moyers, Reporter/Correspondent (CBS)
THE AMERICAN-ISRAELI CONNECTION, Philip Burton, Jr., Producer; Andrew Lack, Reporter/Correspondent (CBS)
FORTRESS ISRAEL, Judy Crichton, Producer; Marshall Frady, Reporter/Correspondent (ABC)
THE MONEY MASTERS, Pamela Hill, Vice President & Executive Producer; Richard Richter, Senior Producer; Richard Gerdau, Producer & Director; Dan Cordtz, Michael Connor, Correspondents (ABC)
DRUG SMUGGLING, (Nightline), Herbert Holmes, Producer; David Garcia, Reporter/Correspondent (ABC)
SEGMENTS:
COLLEGE SPORTS, THE MONEY GAME, (NBC Nightly News), ML Flynn, Paul Hazzard, Barry Hohlfelder, Producers; Bob Jamieson, Co-Producer; Bob Jamieson, Reporter/Correspondent (NBC)
"TANKS" - A FEW MINUTES WITH ANDY ROONEY, Jane Bradford, Producer; Andrew A. Rooney, Reporter/Correspondent (CBS)
WELCOME TO PALERMO, (60 Minutes), William McClure, Producer; Harry Reasoner, Reporter/Correspondent (CBS)

SAVING THE SMALLEST HUMANS, (NBC Nightly News), Mary Laurence Flynn, Producer; Robert Bazell, Reporter/Correspondent (NBC)

TITLE V, (CBS Evening News), Elena Mannes, Producer; Bill Moyers, Reporter/Correspondent (CBS)

HOMELESS, (60 Minutes), Joel Bernstein, Producer; Ed Bradley, Reporter/Correspondent (CBS)

THE ALASKA GAS PIPELINE RIP-OFF, (CBS Evening News), Martin Koughan, Producer; Bill Moyers, Reporter/Correspondent (CBS)

. . .TO TAX, VALUE, JUDGE, (Sunday Morning), James Houtrides, Robert Northshield, Producers; David Culhane, Reporter/Correspondent (CBS)

INSIDE IRAN, (CBS Evening News with Dan Rather), Harry Radcliffe, Producer; Tom Fenton, Reporter/Correspondent (CBS)

CRIME AND PUNISHMENT, (20/20), Peter W. Kunhardt, Producer; Tom Jarriel, Reporter/Correspondent (ABC)

UNDER THE ISRAELI THUMB, (20/20), Stanhope Gould, Producer; Tom Jarriel, Reporter/Correspondent (ABC)

LEST WE FORGET, (60 Minutes), Tom Bettag, Producer; Morley Safer, Reporter/Correspondent (CBS)

CANDLE IN THE DARK, (60 Minutes), Al Wasserman, Producer; Harry Reasoner, Reporter/Correspondent (CBS)

MARTINA, (60 Minutes), Grace Diekhaus, Producer; Mike Wallace, Reporter/Correspondent (CBS)

LIFE AFTER DOOMSDAY?, (20/20), Danny Schecter, Bill Lichtenstein, Producers; Tom Jarriel, Reporter/Correspondent (ABC)

OUR ATOMIC LEGACY: A SPECIAL REPORT ON NUCLEAR TESTING AND ITS EFFECTS, (Good Morning America), Thomas A. Ryder, Steve Fox, Producers; Steve Fox, Reporter/Correspondent (ABC)

INVESTIGATIVE JOURNALISM (E-1993)

PROGRAMS:

FRANK TERPIL: CONFESSIONS OF A DANGEROUS MAN, David Fanning, Producer; Anthony Thomas, Reporter/Correspondent (PBS)

THE MAN WHO SHOT THE POPE: A STUDY IN TERRORISM, Anthony Potter, Executive Producer; Marvin Kalb, Bill McLaughlin, Reporter/Correspondents (NBC)

J. EDGAR HOOVER, Tom Bywaters, Producer; Marshall Frady, Correspondent; Pat Lynch, Reporter (ABC)

RAIN OF TERROR, Steve Singer, Producer; Bill Redeker, Reporter/Correspondent (ABC)

SEGMENTS:

THE NAZI CONNECTION, (60 Minutes), Ira Rosen, Producer; Mike Wallace, Reporter/Correspondent (CBS)

AIR FORCE SURGEON, (60 Minutes), Tom Bettag, Producer; Morley Safer, Reporter/Correspondent (CBS)

LAND HUSTLES, (NBC Nightly News), Robert Windrem, Charles Collins, Co-Producers; Mark Nykanen, Reporter/Correspondent (NBC)

SMALL TOWN, (60 Minutes), William H. Willson, Producer; Mike Wallace, Reporter/Correspondent (CBS)

THE TROUBLE WITH TEMIK, (CBS Evening News with Dan Rather), Elizabeth Karnes, Martin Koughan, Producers; Bill Moyers, Reporter/Correspondent (CBS)

MARIEL CUBANS SPREAD CRIME, (CBS Evening News with Dan Rather), Andrew Heyward, Producer; Bernard Goldberg, Reporter/Correspondent (CBS)

FORMALDEHYDE: THE DANGER WITHIN, (20/20), Peter Lance, Bill Lichtenstein, Co-Producers; Peter Lance, Reporter/Correspondent (ABC)

APACHE: THE TANK CHOPPER, (20/20), Jeff Diamond, Jay LaMonica, Producers; Tom Jarriel, Reporter/Correspondent (ABC)

THROWAWAY KIDS, Bill Lichtenstein, Karen Burnes, Co-Producers; Sylvia Chase, Reporter/Correspondent (ABC)

DEADLY CHEMICALS: DEADLY OIL, (20/20), Janice Tomlin, Producer; Peter Lance, Reporter/Correspondent (ABC)

WILLOWBROOK-TEN YEARS AFTER, (20/20), Kerry Smith, Producer; Geraldo Rivera, Reporter/Correspondent (ABC)

INTERVIEW/INTERVIEWER(S) (E-1994)

PROGRAMS:

THE PALESTINIANS VIEWPOINT, (Nightline), Bob Jordan, Producer; Ted Koppel, Interviewer (ABC)

THE BARBARA WALTERS SPECIAL, Beth Polson, Producer; Barbara Walters, Interviewer (ABC)

THE LAWMAKERS, Gregg Ramshaw, Producer; Paul Duke, Linda Wertheimer, Interviewers (PBS)

NEWS IN THE NETWORK, Joe Russin, Producer; Hodding Carter, Interviewer (PBS)

ABSENCE OF MALICE: FACT OR FICTION, Lois Cunniff, Producer; Hodding Carter, Interviewer (PBS)

SEGMENTS:

IN THE BELLY OF THE BEAST, (60 Minutes), Monika Jensen, Producer; Ed Bradley, Interviewer (CBS)

JACOB TIMERMAN, (60 Minutes), Barry Lando, Producer; Mike Wallace, Interviewer (CBS)

RICHARD NIXON, (CBS Morning News), Shirley Wershba, Producer; Diane Sawyer, Interviewer (CBS)

BEST IN THE WEST, (60 Minutes), Steve Glauber, Producer; Ed Bradley, Interviewer (CBS)

COVERAGE OF A CONTINUING NEW STORY (E-1995)

PROGRAMS:

THE PATERSON PROJECT, Howard Husock, Producer; Scott Simon, Reporter/Correspondent (PBS)

SMALL BUSINESS FAILURES, Kenneth Witty, Producer; Robert MacNeil, Jim Lehrer, Reporter/Correspondents (PBS)

THE WAR IN LEBANON, (Nightline), Stuart Schwartz, Senior Producer; Ted Koppel, Anchorman (ABC)

SEGMENTS:

COVERAGE OF AMERICAN UNEMPLOYMENT, (CBS Evening News with Dan Rather), Rita Braver, David Browning, Quentin Nuefeld, Terry Martin, David Gelber, Producers; Bruce Morton, Jerry Bowen, Terry Drinkwater, Ed Rabel, Ray Brady, Correspondents (CBS)

EL SALVADOR REPORTS, Jon Alpert, Producer; Jon Alpert, Reporter/Correspondent (NBC)

YOU'RE UNDER ARREST, (60 Minutes), James W. Jackson, Producer; Harry Reasoner, Reporter/Correspondent (CBS)

TO SERVE AND TO SHARE, (Sunday Morning), Larry Doyle, Producer; David Culhane, Reporter/Correspondent (CBS)

HONOR THY CHILDREN, (60 Minutes), Barry Lando, Producer; Mike Wallace, Reporter/Correspondent (CBS)

SAD NEW FACES, (Sunday Morning), Skip Brown, Producer; Barry Peterson, Reporter/Correspondent (CBS)

WATERGATE: AN UNTOLD STORY, (20/20), Gordon Freedman, Producer; Tom Jarriel, Reporter/Correspondent (ABC)

INFORMATIONAL, CULTURAL OR HISTORICAL PROGRAMMING (E-1996)

PROGRAMS:

HERE'S LOOKING AT YOU, KID, Andrew Maguire, Producer (PBS)

THE TAJ MAHAL, James M. Messenger, Stuart Sillery, Producers (PBS)

JAPAN: MYTHS BEHIND THE MIRACLE, Malcolm Clarke, Producer; Jim Laurie, Reporter/Correspondent (ABC)

EGYPT: QUEST FOR ETERNITY, (National Geographic Special), Miriam Birch, Producer; Richard Basehart, Reporter/Correspondent (PBS)

DON'T TOUCH THAT DIAL, Julian Krainin, Producer; Morley Safer, Reporter/Correspondent (CBS)

MIDDLETOWN: THE CAMPAIGN, Peter Davis, Producer (PBS)

JEAN SEBERG, (The Mike Wallace Profiles), Harry Moses, Producer; Mike Wallace, Reporter/Correspondent (CBS)

A PORTRAIT OF MAYA ANGELOU, David Grubin, Producer; Bill Moyers, Reporter/Correspondent (PBS)

SEGMENTS:

ECLECTIC: A PROFILE OF QUINCY JONES, (Sunday Morning), Brett Alexander, Producer; Billy Taylor, Reporter/Correspondent (CBS)

SID CAESAR, (20/20), Betsy Osha, Producers; Dick Schaap, Reporter/Correspondent (ABC)

LENA, (60 Minutes), Jeanne Solomon, Producer; Ed Bradley, Reporter/Correspondent (CBS)

NATHAN MILSTEIN, (Sunday Morning), Alan Harper, Producer; Eugenia Zukerman, Reporter/Correspondent (CBS)

SALTA PROVINCE, (NBC Nightly News), Charles McLean, Producer; Dan Molina, Reporter/Correspondent (NBC)

CUBAN MISSILE CRISIS 1962, (Nightline), William Lord, Executive Producer; Robert J. LeDonne, Jay LaMonica, Producers; Jay LaMonica, Reporter (ABC)

A REGAL WAY WITH WORDS, (Sunday Morning), Kathy Sulkes, Producer; Charles Kuralt, Reporter/Correspondent (CBS)

SOME OF OUR AIRMEN ARE HOME, (Sunday Morning), James Houtrides, Producer; John Blackstone, Reporter/Correspondent (CBS)

MUSICIAN PLAYS THE GLASSES, (CBS Evening News with Dan Rather), Charles Kuralt, Producer; Charles Kuralt, Reporter/Correspondent (CBS)

KEITH HARING, SUBWAY ARTIST, (CBS Evening News with Dan Rather), Peter Schweitzer, Producer; Charles Osgood, Reporter/Correspondent (CBS)

MONKEY SEE, (Walter Cronkite's Universe), Ruth Streeter, Producer; Walter Cronkite, Reporter/Correspondent (CBS)

ORBIS (DISTANT VISIONS), Richard R. Clark, Producer; Geraldo Rivera, Reporter/Correspondent (ABC)

DREAMS DO COME TRUE, (20/20), Rolfe Tessem, Producer; Steve Fox, Reporter/Correspondent (ABC)

THE BEST MOVIE EVER MADE (CASABLANCA), (60 Minutes), Drew Phillips, Producer; Harry Reasoner, Reporter/Correspondent (CBS)

NAME BRANDS, NO BRANDS, (20/20), Bob Lange, Producer; John Stossel, Reporter/Correspondent (ABC)

TINA TURNER, (20/20), Chip Kurzenhauser, Danny Schechter, Producers; Steve Fox, Reporter/Correspondent (ABC)

SEX & SCENTS, (20/20), Bob Lange, Producer; John Stossel, Reporter/Correspondent (ABC)

GREAT ARCTIC ADVENTURE, (20/20), Richard R. Clark, Producer; Geraldo Rivera, Reporter/Correspondent (ABC)

MOMENT OF CRISIS: THE MUNICH MASSACRE, (20/20), Judith Moses, Producer; Tom Jarriel, Reporter/Correspondent (ABC)

SPECIAL CLASSIFICATION FOR OUTSTANDING PROGRAM ACHIEVEMENT (E-1997)
PROGRAMS:

VIETNAM REQUIEM, Jonas McCord, William Couturie, Producers (ABC)

FIRE ON THE WATER, Robert Hillman, Producer (PBS)

CENTRAL AMERICA IN REVOLT, (CBS Reports), Martin Smith, Craig Leake, Barry Lando, Producers (CBS)

EYE ON THE MEDIA: BUSINESS AND THE PRESS, Mary Drayne, Producer (CBS)

SEGMENTS:

IT DIDN'T HAVE TO HAPPEN, (60 Minutes), Norman Gorin, Producer; Morley Safer, Correspondent (CBS)

DPT VACCINE, Lea Thompson, Stewart Dan, Producers (NBC)

HOT PROPERTY, (NBC Magazine), Robert Lissit, Producer (NBC)

GETTING STRAIGHT, (NBC Magazine), Beth Polson, Producer; Jack Perkins, Reporter (NBC)

SURVIVAL IN AMERICA, Steve Friedman, Producer (NBC)

INDIVIDUAL ACHIEVEMENT

WRITERS (E-1998)

SHARON BLAIR BRYSAC, PERRY WOLFF, Juilliard and Beyond: A Life in Music (CBS)

CHARLES KURALT, Cicada Invasion (CBS Evening News) (CBS)

JOSEPH ANGIER, JIM LAURIE, MALCOLM CLARKE, Japan: Myths Behind the Miracle (ABC News Closeup) (ABC)

DAVID BRINKLEY, RICHARD THRELKELD, ANN BLACK, RICHARD GERDAU, TOM PRIESTLY, KATHY SLOBOGIN, STEVE ZOUSMER, FDR (ABC)

PERRY WOLFF, Pablo Picasso: A Retrospective, Once In a Lifetime (CBS)

CATHERINE OLIAN, PERRY WOLFF, Our Friends the Germans (CBS)

MORLEY SAFER, Don't Touch that Dial (CBS Reports) (CBS)

MARVIN KALB, BILL McLAUGHLIN, ANTHONY POTTER, The Man Who Shot The Pope: A Study in Terrorism (NBC)

MIRIAM BIRCH, Egypt: Quest For Eternity (National Geographic) (PBS)

THEODORE STRAUSS, Hillary's Challenge: Race to the Sky (PBS)

SHELBY NEWHOUSE, DAN McCOSH, ANDREW KOKAS, ED BAUMEISTER, Chrysler: Once Upon A Time. . . and Now (PBS)

JAMES LIPSCOMB, Polar Bear Alert: (National Geographic Special) (PBS)

NICOLAS NOXON, The Sharks (National Geographic Special) (PBS)

DIRECTORS (E-1999)
JONAS McCORD, WILLIAM COUTURIE, Vietnam Requiem (ABC)
BILL JERSEY, Children of Violence (PBS)
PAUL R. FINE, The Saving of the President (ABC)
ANTHONY POTTER, The Man Who Shot the Pope: A Study in Terrorism (NBC)
MALCOLM CLARKE, Japan: Myths Behind the Miracle, (ABC News Closeup) (ABC)
CATHERINE OLIAN, Our Friends The Germans (CBS)
ANTHONY THOMAS, Frank Terpil: Confessions of a Dangerous Man (PBS)
TOM COHEN, Family Business (PBS)

CINEMATOGRAPHERS (E-2000)
NORRIS BROCK, Egypt: Quest for Eternity (National Geographic) (PBS)
ARNIE SERLIN, The Taj Mahal (PBS)
JAMES DECKARD, JAMES LIPSCOMB, Polar Bear Alert (National Geographic) (PBS)
TED HAIMES, Vietnam Requiem (ABC)
JERI SOPANEN, ROBERT LEACOCK, MICHAEL LIVESEY, VICTOR LOSICK, RICK MALKAMES, Juillard and Beyond: A Life in Music (CBS)
BILL BACON, Alaska: Story of a Dream (SYN)
JON ELSE, Palace of Delights (PBS)

ELECTRONIC CAMERAPERSONS: VIDEOGRAPHERS (E-2001)
(Studio & Location)
DAVID GREEN, Guerillas in Usulatan, (CBS Evening News with Dan Rather) (CBS)
GEORGE FRIDRICK, (Electronic Camera), Along Route 30 (NBC)
CHESTER PANZER, Plane Disaster (World News Tonight) (ABC)
ALAIN DEBOS, Ceasefire, (CBS Evening News with Dan Rather) (CBS)
JON ALPERT, El Salvador Reports (NBC)
ERIK P. PRENTNIEKS, Palace of Gold, (CBS Morning News) (CBS)
JOHN LANDI, FABRICE MOUSSUST, (Electronic Camera), Assassination of Anwar Sadat (ABC)
IZZY BLECKMAN, (Cameraperson), Woman Flyer (CBS News with Dan Rather) (CBS)
STEVE BYERLY, (Electronic Camera), Epidemic: Why Your Kid is On Drugs (SYN)

SOUND (E-2002)
AUDIO SWEETING (including Editors, mixers and effects, STUDIO AUDIO MIXERS, FILM SOUND MIXERS, including, RE-RECORDING MIXERS and Editors, LIVE LOCATION VIDEOTAPE AND SOUND RECORDIST, VIDEO AND FILM)

ROBERT SAMDBO, (Sound Editor); ALAN BERLINER, S. HYMOWITZ, F. MARTINEZ, JONATHAN M. LORY, (Audio Sweeting, Editors); TOM FLEISCHMAN (Mixer), FDR (ABC)
TOM COHEN, (Sound Recordist), The Campaign (PBS)
GARY BOURGEOIS, (Re-Recording Artist); LEE CHALOUKIAN, (Sound Director); KENNETH LOVE, (Production Mixer); ELLIOT TYSON, (Re-Recording Mixer); TROY S. PORTER, (Sound Recordist), Egypt: Quest for Eternity (National Geographic) (PBS)
VINCENT R. PERRY, (Audio Engineer); PAUL H. GLASER, (Audio Engineer), Nuclear Arms: What To Do About Them (ABC)
ALAN BERLINER, (Sound Editor), Battleships (ABC)
LARRY LOEWINGER, (Sound Recordist); Juilliard and Beyond: A Life in Music (CBS)
PETER MILLER, (Sound Recordist); LEE DICHTER, (Film Sound Mixer & Re-Recording Mixer); The Family Business (PBS)
EMILY PAINE, (Audio Sweeting, Sound Editor); Community of Praise (PBS)

INDIVIDUAL ACHIEVEMENT IN NEWS/DOCUMENTARY PROGRAMMING

ASSOCIATE DIRECTORS (E-2003)

CONSUELO GONZALEZ, NEILL PHILLIPSON, FDR (ABC)
LARRY M. WEISMAN, Throwaway Kids (20/20) (ABC)
STANLEY SPIRO, Barbara Mandrell (20/20) (ABC)

VIDEOTAPE EDITORS, VIDEOTAPE POST PRODUCTION EDITORS (E-2004)

THOMAS MICKLAS, (Videotape Editor), Ice Sculptor (CBS Evening News) (CBS)
ANTHONY CICCIMARRO, KATHY HARDIGAN, DON ORRICO, MATTY POWERS (Video tape Editors), The Man Who Shot the Pope: A Study in Terrorism (NBC)
CATHY BLACK, CATHERINE ISABELLA, DEAN IRWIN, CARLA MORGENSTERN, EDWARD BUDA, RUTH IWANO, CHRIS VON BENGE, MIKE SEIGAL, (Video tape Editors), Post Production, FDR (ABC)
DEAN IRWIN, (Post Production Videotape Editor), Throwaway Kids (ABC)
TIM GIBNEY, (Videotape Editor), Saving the Smallest Humans (NBC)
JOHN MATEJKO, (Videotape Editor), Viewpoint (ABC)
MITCH UDOFF, Vacation Dream, Vacation Nightmare (ABC)
ROBERT SHATTUCK, SUSAN OTTALINI, (Videotape Editors), Central America in Revolt, (El Salvador Segments) (CBS)
BERNARD ALTMAN, (Tape Editor), Monkey See (Walter Cronkite's Universe) (CBS)
JOHN J. GODFREY, JON ALPERT, (Video tape Editors), El Salvador Reports (NBC)
ARDEN RYNEW, CAREN MYERS, BRUCE OCHMANEK, (Video tape Editors); Artists in the Lab (PBS)
THOMAS C. GOODWIN, Bill COYLE, GERARDINE WURZBURG, (Video tape Editors) We Dig Coal, A Portrait of Three Women (PBS)

FILM EDITORS AND FILM POST PRODUCTION EDITORS (E-2005)

JAMES FLANAGAN, NILS RASMUSSEN, WILLIAM LONGO, WALTER ESSENFELD, (Film Editors); FDR (ABC)
NOBUKO OGANESOFF, (Film Editor); Juilliard and Beyond: A Life in Music (CBS)
BOB BRADY, (Film Editor); The Campaign (PBS)
ROB WALLACE, (Film Editor); Merle Haggard, A Profile (ABC)
LISA SHREVE, (Film Editor); Recipes for Life (ABC)
NANCY KANTER, (Film Editor); Japan: Myths Behind the Miracle (ABC)
TOM HANEKE, (Film Editor); Second Time Around (PBS)
BARRY NYE, (Film Editor); The Sharks (National Geographic) (PBS)
MICHAEL CHANDLER, (Film Editor); Fire on the Water (PBS)
STEVEN STEPT, (Film Editor); Vietnam Requiem (ABC)
JOHN J. MARTIN, ELIZABETH ACKERMAN, OTTO PFEFFER, (Film Editors); Bataan: The Forgotten Hell (NBC)

GRAPHIC DESIGNERS, ELECTRONIC GRAPHICS, GRAPHIC ILLUSTRATORS, ELECTRONIC & FILM ANIMATION (E-2006)

REBECCA ALLEN, (Graphic Designer); Walter Cronkite's Universe (CBS)
DAVID MILLMAN, (Graphic Artist Illustrator); The Cuban Missile Crisis (Nightline) (ABC)
BRUCE SOLOWAY, (Graphic Designer); World News Tonight (ABC)
GERRY ANDREA, (Grapic Illustrator); The Falklands (World News Tonight) (ABC)
T. CACIOPPO, (Art director); G. PETANI, J.DOMINICK, (Graphic Artists); CBS Evening News with Dan Rather (CBS)
BARBARA M. INCOGNITA, MADELINE DeVITO, (Electronic Animators); Special 20/20 Openings (ABC)

MUSIC COMPOSERS: (E-2007)

(Including Arrangers, Music Directors, Including Conductors, Music Lyricists)

JAMES G. PIRIE, (Music Composer, Conductor); Alaska: Story of A Dream (SYN)
KEN MELVILLE, DAWN ATKINSON, (Music Composers); Vietnam Requiem (ABC)
CHRIS ADELMAN, (Composer); Battleship (ABC)

THE NATIONAL AWARD FOR COMMUNITY SERVICE (E-2008)

SEXUAL ABUSE OF CHILDREN – I-TEAM (WCCO-TV) Minneapolis, MN.
DOWNWIND (KUTV) Salt Lake City, UT.
EPIDEMIC: WHY YOUR KID IS ON DRUGS (WXIA-TV) Atlanta, GA.
THE ULTIMATE GIFT (WTCN-TV) Minneapolis, MN.
PRESCRIPTION DRUG ABUSE: A TOTAL STATION CAMPAIGN (WBZ-TV) Boston, MA.
DWI: SORRY ISN'T ENOUGH (KIRO-TV) Seattle, WA.
THE ELECTRICAL STORM: A KIND OF NETWORK ENERGY PAPER (KING-TV) Seattle, WA.
VOTER FRAUD (KTVI-TV) St. Louis, MO.
WHERE WAS OUR PARADE (WLWT-TV) Cincinnati, OH.
OUR DAILY BREAD: A STUDY IN BLACK YOUTH UNEMPLOYMENT (WTBS-TV) Atlanta, GA.
DPT: VACCINE ROULETTE (WRC-TV) Washington, DC.

1982/83

PRIMETIME

COMEDY SERIES (E-2009)

Emmy(s) to Executive Producer(s) and/or Producer(s)

CHEERS, James Burrows, Glen Charles, Les Charles, Producers; Ken Levine, David Isaacs, Co-Producers (NBC)
BUFFALO BILL, Bernie Brillstein, Tom Patchett, Jay Tarses, Executive Producers; Dennis Klein, Carol Gary, Producers (NBC)
M*A*S*H, Burt Metcalfe, Executive Producer; John Rappaport, Supervising Producer; Dan Wilcox, Thad Mumford, Dennis Koenig, Producers (CBS)
NEWHART, Barry Kemp, Executive Producer; Sheldon Bull, Producer (CBS)
TAXI, James L. Brooks, Stan Daniels, Ed. Weinberger, Executive Producers; Ken Estin, Sam Simon, Richard Sakai, Producers (NBC)

DRAMA SERIES (E-2010)

Emmy(s) to Executive Producer(s) and/or Producer(s)

HILL STREET BLUES, Steven Bochco, Executive Producer, Gregory Hoblit, Co-Executive Producer; Anthony Yerkovich, Supervising Producer; David Anspaugh, Scott Brazil, Producers (NBC)
CAGNEY & LACEY, Barney Rosenzweig, Executive Producer; Richard M. Rosenbloom, Harry R. Sherman, Supervising Producers; April Smith, Joseph Stern, Terry Louise Fisher, Steve Brown, Producers (CBS)
FAME, William Blinn, Executive Producer, Mel Swope, Producer (NBC)
MAGNUM, P.I., Donald P. Bellisario, Executive Producer; Joel Rogosin, Supervising Producer; Douglas Green, Supervising Producer in Hawaii; Douglas Green, Chas. Floyd Johnson, Producers; Rick Weaver, Reuben Leder, Co-Producers (CBS)
ST. ELSEWHERE, Bruce Paltrow, Executive Producer; Mark Tinker, John Masius, John Falsey, Joshua Brand, Producers (NBC)

LIMITED SERIES (E-2011)

Emmy(s) to Executive Producer(s) and/or Producer(s)

NICHOLAS NICKLEBY, Colin Callender, Producer (SYN)
SMILEY'S PEOPLE, Jonathan Powell, Producer (SYN)
THORN BIRDS, David L. Wolper, Edward Lewis, Executive Producers; Stan Margulies, Producer (ABC)
TO SERVE THEM ALL MY DAYS (MASTERPIECE THEATRE), Ken Rid-

dington, Producer (PBS)
WINDS OF WAR, Dan Curtis, Producer (ABC)

VARIETY, MUSIC OR COMEDY PROGRAM (E-2012)

Emmy(s) to Executive Producer(s) and/or Producer(s), and Host, if name appears in the title of the program

MOTOWN 25: YESTERDAY, TODAY, FOREVER, Suzanne de Passe, Executive Producer; Don Mischer, Buz Kohan, Producers; Suzanne Coston, Producer for Motown. (05/16/83) (NBC)
KENNEDY CENTER HONORS: A CELEBRATION OF THE PERFORMING ARTS, George Stevens, Jr., Nick Vanoff, Producers. (12/25/82) (CBS)
SCTV NETWORK, Andrew Alexander, Senior Executive Producer; Andrew Alexander, Len Stuart, Jack E. Rhodes, Doug Holtby, Executive Producers; Patrick Whitley, Supervising Producer; Doug Holtby, Patrick Whitley, Nancy Geller, Don Novello, Producers (Series) (NBC)
TONIGHT SHOW STARRING JOHNNY CARSON, Fred de Cordova, Producer; Peter Lassally, Co-Producer; Johnny Carson, Host (Series) (NBC)
TONY AWARDS, 37TH ANNUAL, Alexander H. Cohen, Executive Producer; Hildy Parks, Producer; Roy A. Somlyo, Co-Producer. (06/05/83) (CBS)

DRAMA SPECIAL (E-2013)

Emmy(s) to Executive Producer(s) and/or Producers(s) (Includes all scripted specials that have a story with a beginning, middle and end, and performers portraying characters other than themselves.)

SPECIAL BULLETIN, Don Ohlmyer, Executive Producer; Marshall Herskovitz, Edward Zwick, Producers (NBC)
LITTLE GLORIA. . .HAPPY AT LAST, Edgar J. Scherick, Scott Rudin, Executive Producers; David Nicksay, Justine Heroux, Producers (NBC)
M.A.D.D.: THE CANDY LIGHTNER STORY, MOTHERS AGAINST DRUNK DRIVERS, David Moessinger, Executive Producer; Douglas Benton, Supervising Producer; Michael Braverman, Producer O(NBC)
SCARLET PIMPERNEL, Mark Shelmerdine, Executive Producer; David Conroy, Producer (CBS)
WHO WILL LOVE MY CHILDREN? Paula Levenback, Wendy Riche, Producers (ABC)

CLASSICAL PROGRAM IN THE PERFORMING ARTS (E-2014)

Emmy(s) to Executive Producer(s) and/or Producer(s), and Star(s) if name appears in the title of the program

PAVAROTTI IN PHILADELPHIA: LA BOHEME, Margaret Anne Everitt, Executive Producer; Clemente D'Alessio, Producer; Luciano Pavarotti, Star. (08/28/82) (PBS)
DANCE IN AMERICA, Jac Venza, Executive Producer; Judy Kinberg, Barbara Horgan, Producers. (Series) (PBS)
IN CONCERT AT THE MET: PRICE, HORNE, LEVINE, Michael Bronson, Executive Producer; Clemente d'Alessio, Producer; Leontyne Price, Marilyn Horne, James Levine, Stars. (12/04/82) (PBS)
LINCOLN CENTER SPECIAL: STRAVINSKY AND BALANCHINE - GENIUS HAS A BIRTHDAY!, John Goberman, Barbara Horgan, Producers. (10/04/82) (PBS)
WAGNER'S RING: THE BAYREUTH CENTENNIAL PRODUCTION, Horant H. Hohlfeld, Executive Producer; David Griffiths, Supervising Producer; Dietrich von Watzdorf, Peter Windgassen, Producers. (Series) (PBS)

INFORMATIONAL SPECIAL (E-2015)

Emmy(s) to Executive Producer(s) and/or Producer(s), and Host, if name appears in the title of the program

BODY HUMAN: THE LIVING CODE, Thomas W. Moore, Executive Producer; Robert E. Fuisz, M.D., Alfred R. Kelman, M.D., Producers; Charles A. Bangert, Franklin Getchell, Nancy Smith, Co-Producers. (CBS)
I, LEONARDO: A JOURNEY OF THE MIND, Chandler Cowles, Helen

Kristt Radin, Executive Producers, Lee R. Bobker, Producer. (CBS)
KING PENGUIN: STRANDED BEYOND THE FALKLANDS, Lord Aubrey Buxton, Executive Producer; Colin Willock, Producer. (CBS)
MAKING OF GANDHI: MR. ATTENBOROUGH AND MR. GANDHI, Jenny Barraclough, Producer (SYN)
MARIO LANZA: THE AMERICAN CARUSO, John Musilli, Stephan Chodorov, Executive Producers; Jo Ann G. Young, Producer. (PBS)

INFORMATIONAL SERIES (E-2016)

Emmy(s) to Executive Producer(s) and/or Producer(s), and Host, if name appears in the title of the program

BARBARA WALTERS SPECIALS, Beth Polson, Producer; Barbara Walters, Host (ABC)
ENTERTAINMENT TONIGHT/ENTERTAINMENT THIS WEEK, George Merlis, Jim Bellows, Executive Producers; Vin Di Bona, Producer; Bruce Cook, Coordinating Producer (SYN)
OVER EASY WITH MARY MARTIN & JIM HARTZ, Richard Rector, Jules Power, Executive Producers; Ben Bayol, Janice Tunder, Producers; Mary Martin, Jim Hartz, Hosts (PBS)
REAL PEOPLE, George Schlatter, Executive Producer; Bob Wynn, Producer (NBC)
SCREENWRITERS/WORD INTO IMAGE, Terry Sanders, Frida Lee Mock, Producers (PBS)

ANIMATED PROGRAM (E-2017)

Emmy(s) to Executive Producer(s) and/or Producer(s)

ZIGGY'S GIFT, Lena Tabori, Executive Producer; Richard Williams, Tom Wilson, Lena Tabori, Producers. (ABC)
HERE COMES GARFIELD, Jay Poyner, Executive Producer; Lee Mendelson, Bill Melendez, Producers. (CBS)
IS THIS GOODBYE, CHARLIE BROWN?, Lee Mendelson, Bill Melendez, Producers. (CBS)
SMURFS CHRISTMAS SPECIAL, Joseph Barbera, William Hanna, Executive Producers; Gerard Baldwin, Producer. (NBC)
WHAT HAVE WE LEARNED, CHARLIE BROWN?, Lee Mendelson, Executive Producer; Bill Melendez, Producer. (CBS)

CHILDRENS PROGRAM (E-2018)

Emmy(s) to Executive Producer(s) and/or Producer(s)

BIG BIRD IN CHINA, Jon Stone, Executive Producer; David Liu, Kuo Bao-Xiang, Xu Ja-Cha, Producers (NBC)
GRANDPA, WILL YOU RUN WITH ME?, Ken Ehrlich, Producer (NBC)
SKEEZER, Bill McCutchen, Executive Producer; Lee Levinson, Producer (NBC)
SNOW QUEEN - A SKATING BALLET, Gregory G. Harney; Executive Producer; Bernice Olenick, Producer (PBS)

ACTOR - COMEDY SERIES (E-2019)

For a continuing or single performance in a regular series.

JUDD HIRSCH, Taxi (NBC)
ALAN ALDA, M*A*S*H (CBS)
DABNEY COLEMAN, Buffalo Bill (NBC)
TED DANSON, Cheers (NBC)
ROBERT GUILLAUME, Benson (ABC)

ACTOR - DRAMA SERIES (E-2020)

For a continuing or single performance in a regular series

ED FLANDERS, St. Elsewhere (NBC)
WILLIAM DANIELS, St. Elsewhere (NBC)
JOHN FORSYTHE, Dynasty (ABC)
TOM SELLECK, Magnum, P.I. (CBS)
DANIEL J. TRAVANTI, Hill Street Blues (NBC)

ACTOR - LIMITED SERIES OR A SPECIAL (E-2021)
For a continuing or single performance in a limited series or for a special

TOMMY LEE JONES, Executioner's Song (NBC)
ROBERT BLAKE, Blood Feud (OPT)
RICHARD CHAMBERLAIN, Thorn Birds (ABC)
ALEC GUINNESS, Smiley's People (SYN)
ROGER REES, Nicholas Nickleby (SYN)

ACTRESS - COMEDY SERIES (E-2022)
For a continuing or single performance in a regular series

SHELLEY LONG, Cheers (NBC)
NELL CARTER, Gimme A Break (NBC)
MARIETTE HARTLEY, Goodnight, Beantown (CBS)
SWOOSIE KURTZ, Love Sidney, (NBC)
RITA MORENO, 9 To 5 (ABC)
ISABEL SANFORD, Jeffersons (CBS)

ACTRESS - DRAMA SERIES (E-2023)
For a continuing or single performance in a regular series

TYNE DALY, Cagney & Lacey (CBS)
DEBBIE ALLEN, Fame (NBC)
LINDA EVANS, Dynasty (ABC)
SHARON GLESS, Cagney & Lacey (CBS)
VERONICA HAMEL, Hill Street Blues (NBC)

ACTRESS - LIMITED SERIES OR A SPECIAL (E-2024)
For a continuing or single performance in a regular series NOTE: SINGLE PERFORMANCES INDICATED BY EPISODE TITLE AND AIR DATE

BARBARA STANWYCK, Thorn Birds Part 1, 03/27/83 (ABC)
ANN-MARGRET, Who Will Love My Children? (ABC)
ROSANNA ARQUETTE, Executioner's Song (NBC)
MARIETTE HARTLEY, M.A.D.D.: The Candy Lightner Story; Mothers Against Drunk Drivers (NBC)
ANGELA LANSBURY, Little Gloria. . .Happy At Last (NBC)

SUPPORTING ACTOR - COMEDY, VARIETY OR MUSIC SERIES (E-2025)
For a continuing or single performance in a regular series

CHRIS LLOYD, Taxi (NBC)
NICHOLAS COLASANTO, Cheers (NBC)
DANNY DE VITO, Taxi (NBC)
HARRY MORGAN, M*A*S*H (CBS)
EDDIE MURPHY, Saturday Night Live (NBC)

SUPPORTING ACTOR - DRAMA SERIES (E-2026)
For a continuing or single performance in a regular series (NOTE: SINGLE PERFORMANCES INDICATED BY EPISODE TITLE AND AIR DATE)

JAMES COCO, St. Elsewhere; Cora And Arnie, 11/23/82 (NBC)
ED BEGLEY JR., St. Elsewhere (NBC)
MICHAEL CONRAD, Hill Street Blues (Series) (NBC)
JOE SPANO, Hill Street Blues (NBC)
BRUCE WEITZ, Hill Street Blues (NBC)

SUPPORTING ACTOR - LIMITED SERIES OR A SPECIAL (E-2027)
For a continuing or single performance in a limited series or for a special (NOTE: SINGLE PERFORMANCES INDICATED BY EPISODE TITLE AND AIR DATE)

RICHARD KILEY, Thorn Birds Part I, 03/27/83 (ABC)
RALPH BELLAMY, Winds Of War (ABC)
BRYAN BROWN, Thorn Birds (ABC)
CHRISTOPHER PLUMMER, Thorn Birds (ABC)
DAVID THRELFALL, Nicholas Nickleby (SYN)

SUPPORTING ACTRESS - COMEDY, VARIETY OR MUSIC SERIES (E-2028)
For a continuing or single performance in a regular series

CAROL KANE, Taxi (NBC)
EILEEN BRENNAN, Private Benjamin (CBS)
MARLA GIBBS, Jeffersons (CBS)
RHEA PERLMAN, Cheers (NBC)
LORETTA SWIT, M*A*S*H (CBS)

SUPPORTING ACTRESS - DRAMA SERIES (E-2029)
For a continuing or single performance in a regular series (NOTE: SINGLE PERFORMANCES INDICATED BY EPISODE TITLE AND AIR DATE)

DORIS ROBERTS, St. Elsewhere; Cora And Arnie, 11/23/82 (NBC)
BARBARA BOSSON, Hill Street Blues (NBC)
CHRISTINA PICKLES, St. Elsewhere (NBC)
MADGE SINCLAIR, Trapper John, M.D. (CBS)
BETTY THOMAS, Hill Street Blues (NBC)

SUPPORTING ACTRESS - LIMITED SERIES OR A SPECIAL (E-2030)
For a continuing or single performance in a limited series or for a special (NOTE: SINGLE PERFORMANCES INDICATED BY EPISODE TITLE AND AIR DATE)

JEAN SIMMONS, Thorn Birds (ABC)
DAME JUDITH ANDERSON, Medea; Kennedy Center Tonight 04/20/83 (PBS)
POLLY BERGEN, Winds Of War (ABC)
BETTE DAVIS, Little Gloria. . .Happy At Last 10/24/82 & 10/25/82 (NBC)
PIPER LAURIE, Thorn Birds Part 3, 03/29/83 (ABC)

INDIVIDUAL PERFORMANCE - VARIETY OR MUSIC PROGRAM (E-2031)
For a continuing or single performance, lead or support, in a variety music series or special

LEONTYNE PRICE, Live From Lincoln Center Leontyne Price, Zubin Mehta And The New York Philharmonic (PBS)
CAROL BURNETT, Texaco Star Theater. . .Opening Night (NBC)
MICHAEL JACKSON, Motown 25: Yesterday, Today, Forever (NBC)
LUCIANO PAVAROTTI, Live From Lincoln Center Luciano Pavarotti And The New York Philharmonic (PBS)
RICHARD PRYOR, Motown 25: Yesterday, Today, Forever (NBC)

DIRECTOR - COMEDY SERIES (E-2032)
For a single episode of a regular series

JAMES BURROWS, Cheers, Showdown - Part 2, 03/31/83 (NBC)
ALAN ALDA, M*A*S*H, Goodbye, Farewell And Amen, 02/28/83 (CBS)
JIM DRAKE, Buffalo Bill, Woody Quits, 06/15/83 (NBC)
BURT METCALFE, M*A*S*H, The Joker Is Wild, 11/15/82 (CBS)
TOM PATCHETT, Buffalo Bill, Pilot, 06/01/83 (NBC)
BOB SWEENEY, Love Boat, The Dog Show, 03/26/83 (ABC)

DIRECTOR - DRAMA SERIES (E-2033)
For a single episode of a regular series

JEFF BLECKNER, Hill Street Blues, Life In The Minors, 02/24/83 (NBC)
MARC DANIELS, Fame, And The Winner Is, 09/30/82 (NBC)
LEO PENN, Mississippi, Old Hatreds Die Hard, 05/06/83 (CBS)
ROBERT SCHEERER, Fame, Feelings, 10/14/82 (NBC)

DIRECTOR - VARIETY OR MUSIC PROGRAM (E-2034)
For a single episode of a regular series or for a special

DWIGHT HEMION, Sheena Easton. . .Act I (NBC)
EMILE ARDOLINO, Lincoln Center Special: Stravinsky And Balanchine - Genius Has A Birthday! (PBS)
JOHN BLANCHARD and JOHN BELL, SCTV NETWORK The Energy Ball/Sweeps Week Show (NBC)
KIRK BROWNING, Live From Lincoln Center, Zubin Mehta Conducts Beethoven's Ninth With The New York Philharmonic (PBS)
DON MISCHER, Motown 25; Yesterday, Today, Forever (NBC)
MARTY PASETTA, 55th Annual Academy Awards Presentation (ABC)

DIRECTOR - LIMITED SERIES OR A SPECIAL (E-2035)
For a single episode of a limited series or for a special

JOHN ERMAN, Who Will Love My Children? (ABC)
DAN CURTIS, Winds Of War, Into The Maelstrom, 02/13/83 (ABC)
DARYL DUKE, Thorn Birds, Part 2, 03/28/83 (ABC)
SIMON LANGTON, Smiley's People, Part 2 (SYN)
EDWARD ZWICK, Special Bulletin (NBC)

CHOREOGRAPHY (E-2036)
For a single episode of a regular or limited series or for a special

DEBBIE ALLEN, Fame, Class Act, 10/21/82 (NBC)
WALTER PAINTER, 55th Annual Academy Awards Presentation (ABC)
TWYLA THARP, Catherine Wheel (PBS)
LESTER WILSON, Motown 25: Yesterday, Today, Forever (NBC)

WRITING - COMEDY SERIES (E-2037)
For a single episode of a regular series

GLEN CHARLES, LES CHARLES, Cheers, Give Me A Ring Sometime, 09/30/82 (NBC)
KEN ESTIN, Taxi, Jim's Inheritance, 10/07/82 (NBC)
KEN LEVINE, DAVID ISAACS, Cheers, The Boys In The Bar, 01/27/83 (NBC)
DAVID LLOYD, Cheers, Diane's Perfect Date, 02/10/83 (NBC)
TOM PATCHETT, JAY TARSES, Buffalo Bill Pilot, 06/01/83 (NBC)

WRITING - DRAMA SERIES (E-2038)
For a single episode of a regular series

DAVID MILCH, Hill Street Blues, Trial By Fury, 09/30/82 (NBC)
STEVEN BOCHCO, ANTHONY YERKOVICH, JEFFREY LEWIS, Hill Street Blues, A Hair Of The Dog, 11/25/82 (NBC)
KAREN HALL, Hill Street Blues, Officer Of The Year, 10/28/82 (NBC)
MICHAEL WAGNER, DAVID MILCH (Teleplay), STEVEN BOCHCO, ANTHONY YERKOVICH, JEFFREY LEWIS (story), Hill Street Blues, No Body's Perfect, 12/09/82 (NBC)
ANTHONY YERKOVICH, DAVID MILCH, KAREN HALL (Teleplay), STEVEN BOCHCO, ANTHONY YERKOVICH, JEFFREY LEWIS (Story), Hill Street Blues, Eugene's Comedy Empire Strikes Back, 03/03/83 (NBC)

WRITING - VARIETY OR MUSIC PROGRAM (E-2039)
For a single episode of a regular series or for a special

JOHN CANDY, JOE FLAHERTY, EUGENE LEVY, ANDREA MARTIN, MARTIN SHORT, DICK BLASUCCI, PAUL FLAHERTY, JOHN McAN-DREW, DOUG STECKLER, BOB DOLMAN, MICHAEL SHORT, MARY CATHERINE WILCOX, SCTV NETWORK, The Energy Ball/Sweeps Week, 02/25/83 (NBC)
JOHN CANDY, JOE FLAHERTY, EUGENE LEVY, ANDREA MARTIN, CATHERINE O'HARA, MARTIN SHORT, DICK BLASUCCI, PAUL FLAHERTY, JOHN McANDREW, DOUG STECKER, BOB DOLMAN, MICHAEL SHORT, MARY CHARLOTTE WILCOX, SCTV Network, The Christmas Show, 12/17/82 (NBC)
JOHN CANDY, JOE FLAHERTY, EUGENE LEVY, ANDREA MARTIN, MARTIN SHORT, DICK BLASUCCI, PAUL FLAHERTY, JOHN McANDREW, DOUG STECKLER, BOB DOLMAN, MICHAEL SHORT, MARY CHARLOTTE WILCOX, JOHN HEMPHILL, SCTV Network, Towering Inferno, 12/10/82 (NBC)
JOHN CANDY, JOE FLAHERTY, EUGENE LEVY, ANDREA MARTIN, MARTIN SHORT, DICK BLASUCCI, PAUL FLAHERTY, JOHN McANDREW, DOUG STECKLER, BOB DOLMAN, MICHAEL SHORT, MARY CHARLOTTE WILCOX, DAVE THOMAS, SCTV Network, With: Robin Williams, America, 11/26/82 (NBC)
JOHN CANDY, JOE FLAHERTY, EUGENE LEVY, ANDREA MARTIN, MARTIN SHORT, DICK BLASUCCI, PAUL FLAHERTY, JOHN McANDREW, DOUG STECKLER, BOB DOLMAN, MICHAEL SHORT, JEFFREY BARRON, MARY CHARLOTTE WILCOX, SCTV Network, With: Joe Walsh, 03/15/83 (NBC)

WRITING - LIMITED SERIES OR A SPECIAL (E-2040)
For a single episode of a limited series or for a special

MARSHALL HERSKOVITZ (Teleplay), EDWARD ZWICK, MARSHALL HERSKOVITZ (Story), Special Bulletin, (NBC)
MICHAEL BORTMAN, Who Will Love My Children? (ABC)
DAVID EDGAR, Nicholas Nickleby (Part 4) (SYN)
WILLIAM HANLEY, Little Gloria. . .Happy At Last (NBC)
NORMAN MAILER, Executioner's Song (NBC)

GOVERNOR'S AWARD (E-2041)
SYLVESTER (PAT) WEAVER

CINEMATOGRAPHY - SERIES (E-2042)
For a single episode of a regular series

JOSEPH BIROC, A.S.C., Casablanca, The Masterbuilder's Woman, 04/17/83 (NBC)
EMMETT BERGHOLZ, Fantasy Island, Curse Of The Moreaus/My Man Friday, 10/16/82 (ABC)
HARRY WOLF, A.S.C., Little House: A New Beginning, The Wild Boy - Part 1, 11/01/82 (NBC)

CINEMATOGRAPHY - LIMITED SERIES OR A SPECIAL (E-2043)
For a single episode of a limited series or for a special

CHARLES CORRELL, A.S.C., STEVEN LARNER, A.S.C., Winds Of War Part 7, 02/13/83 (ABC)
BILL BUTLER, Thorn Birds, Part 1, 03/28/83 (ABC)
AL FRANCIS, A.S.C., Blue And The Gray, Part 3, 11/17/82 (CBS)
ARTHUR F. IBBETSON, B.S.C., Witness For The Prosecution, Hallmark Hall Of Fame (CBS)
GAYNE RESCHER, Mickey Spillane's Mike Hammer, "Murder Me, Murder You" (CBS)

ART DIRECTION - SERIES (E-2044)
For a single episode of a regular series. Emmy(s) to Art Director(s) and Set Decorator(s)

JOHN W. CORSO (Production Designer), FRANK GRIECO, JR. (Art Director), ROBERT GEORGE FREER, (Set Decorator), Tales Of The Gold Monkey, Pilot, 09/22/82 (ABC)
E. PRESTON AMES (Production Designer), BILL HARP (Set Decorator), Casablanca, Jenny, 04/24/83 (NBC)
HUB BRADEN (Art Director), DON REMACLE (Set Decorator), Seven Brides For Seven Brothers, The Rescue, 02/09/83 (CBS)
IRA DIAMOND (Art Director), JOSEPH STONE (Set Decorator), Fame,

Not In Kansas Anymore, 02/24/83 (NBC)
JAMES HULSEY, JACQUELINE WEBBER, (Art Directors), ERNIE BISHOP, MICHELE GUIOL, (Set Decorators), St. Elsewhere, Pilot 10/26/82 (NBC)
RICHARD SYLBERT (Production Designer), GEORGE GAINES (Set Decorator), Cheers, Give Me A Ring Sometime, 09/30/82 (NBC)
TOM TRIMBLE, PAUL SYLOS, (Art Directors), BROCK BROUGHTON (Set Decorator), Dynasty, Fathers And Sons, 03/09/83 (ABC)

ART DIRECTION - LIMITED SERIES OR A SPECIAL (E-2045)

For a single episode of a limited series or for a special. Emmy(s) to Art Director(s) and Set Decorator(s)

ROBERT MacKICHAN (Art Director), JERRY ADAMS (Set Decorator), Thorn Birds, Part 1, 03/27/83 (ABC)
TONY CURTIS (Production Designer), CAROLYN SCOTT (Set Decorator), Scarlet Pimpernel (CBS)
JACKSON De GOVIA (Production Designer), JOHN CARTWRIGHT, MIKE MINOR, MALCOLM MIDDLETON, (Art Directors), TOM ROYSDEN, FRANCESCO CHIANESE, HERTA PISCHINGER (Set Decorators), Winds Of War, The Winds Rise, 02/06/83 (ABC)
JOHN NAPIER (Designer), Nicholas Nickleby, Part 4, 01/13/83 (SYN)
STUART WURTZEL (Production Designer), GUY COMTOIS (Art Director), ENRICO CAMPANA, DOUG KRANER, MAURICE Le BLANC, (Set Decorators), Little Gloria. . .Happy At Last (NBC)

ART DIRECTION - VARIETY OR MUSIC PROGRAM (E-2046)

For a single episode of a regular series or for a special. Emmy(s) to Art Director(s) and Set Decorator(s)

RAY KLAUSEN (Art Director), MICHAEL CORENBLITH (Set Decorator), 55th Annual Academy Awards Presentation (ABC)
ROMAIN JOHNSTON (Art Director), Sheena Easton. . .Act I (NBC)
RENE LAGLER, LARRY WIEMER (Art Directors), Solid Gold Christmas Special (SYN)
RENE LAGLER (Art Director), George Burns And Other Sex Symbols (NBC)

MUSIC COMPOSITION - SERIES (DRAMATIC UNDERSCORE) (E-2047)

For a single episode of a regular series. Emmy(s) to Composer(s)

BRUCE BROUGHTON, Dallas, The Ewing Blues, 01/07/83 (CBS)
WILLIAM GOLDSTEIN, Fame, Not In Kansas Anymore, 02/24/83 (NBC)
JERROLD IMMEL, Knots Landing, Loss Of Innocence (CBS)
DAVID ROSE, Father Murphy, Sweet Sixteen, 12/28/82 (NBC)
NAN SCHWARTZ, Devlin Connection, Ring Of Kings, Ring Of Thieves, 11/27/82 (NBC)

MUSIC COMPOSITION - LIMITED SERIES OR A SPECIAL (DRAMATIC UNDERSCORE) (E-2048)

For a single episode of a limited series or for a special. Emmy(s) to Composer(s)

BILLY GOLDENBERG, Rage Of Angels (NBC)
BRUCE BROUGHTON, Blue And The Gray, Part 2, 11/16/82 (CBS)
JOE HARNELL, V (NBC)
HENRY MANCINI, Thorn Birds, Part 1, 03/27/83 (ABC)
PETER MATZ, Drop-Out Father (CBS)
LAURENCE ROSENTHAL, Who Will Love My Children? (ABC)

MUSIC DIRECTION (E-2049)

For a single episode of a regular or limited series or for a special. Emmy(s) to Music Director and Principal Arranger(s)

DICK HYMAN (Music Director & Principal Arranger), Eubie Blake: A Century Of Music - Kennedy Center Tonight (05/07/83) (PBS)
MERCER ELLINGTON (Music Director & Principal Arranger), Ellington: The Music Lives On - Great Performances (03/07/83) (PBS)
IAN FRASER (Music Director), BILLY BYERS, CHRIS BOARDMAN (Principal Arrangers), EPCOT Center: The Opening Celebration (10/23/82) (CBS)
PETER MATZ (Music Director & Principal Arranger), Sheena Easton. . .Act I (NBC)
NICK PERITO (Music Director), NICK PERITO, JON CHARLES, (Principal Arrangers), Perry Como's Christmas In Paris (ABC)

MUSIC AND LYRICS (E-2050)

For a single episode of a regular or limited series or for a special. Emmy(s) to Composer(s) and Lyricist(s)

JAMES DiPASQUALE (Composer), DORY PREVIN (Lyricist), Two Of A Kind- G. E. Theater; Song: We'll Win This World (CBS)
BRUCE BROUGHTON (Composer), MARK MUELLER (Lyricist), Quincy, M.E. - Quincy's Wedding - Part 2; Song: Quincy's Wedding Song (NBC)
EARL BROWN, ARTIE BUTLER, (Composers & Lyricists), Suzanne Somers And 10,000 G.I.'s; Song: We're Not So Dumb (CBS)
BILLY GOLDENBERG (Composer), CAROL CONNORS (Lyricist), Bare Essence; Song: In Finding You, I Found Love (CBS)
WILLIAM GOLDSTEIN (Composer), MOLLY-ANN LEIKIN (Lyricist), Happy Endings; Song: Happy Endings Theme Song (CBS)
LARRY GROSSMAN (Composer), BUZ KOHAN (Lyricist), 55th Annual Academy Awards Presentation; Song: And It All Comes Down To This (ABC)
GARY PORTNOY, JUDY HART ANGELO, (Composers & Lyricists), Cheers - Pilot; Song: Where Everybody Knows Your Name (NBC)

COSTUME DESIGN - SERIES (E-2051)

For a single episode of a regular series

THEADORA VAN RUNKLE, Wizards And Warriors, Dungeon Of Death, 05/07/83 (CBS)
JEAN-PIERRE DORLEAC, Tales Of The Gold Monkey, Naka Jima Kill, 03/18/83 (ABC)
BOB MACKIE, RET TURNER, Mama's Family, Wedding Part 2, 02/12/83 (NBC)
NOLAN MILLER, Dynasty, La Mirage, 12/15/82 (ABC)
WARDEN NEIL, Filthy Rich, Town And Gown 08/23/82 (CBS)

COSTUME DESIGN - LIMITED SERIES OR A SPECIAL (E-2052)

For a single episode of a limited series or for a special

PHYLLIS DALTON, Scarlet Pimpernel (CBS)
RAY AGHAYAN, 55th Annual Academy Awards Presentation, (ABC)
WARDEN NEIL, Happy Birthday, Bob! (NBC)
TRAVILLA, Thorn Birds, Part 1, 03/27/83 (ABC)
JULIE WEISS, Little Gloria. . .Happy At Last (NBC)

INDIVIDUAL ACHIEVEMENT

COSTUMES (E-2053)

For a single episode of a regular or limited series or for a special. (Possibility of one, more than one or no award)

TOMMY WELSH, Costume Supervisor; JOHN NAPOLITANO, PAUL VAHON, JOHANNES NIKERK, Wardrobe, Winds Of War, The Storm Breaks, 02/07/83 (ABC)
ALBERT H. FRANKEL, Men's Costumer; RITA BENNETT, Women's Costumer, M*A*S*H, Goodbye, Farewell And Amen, 02/28/83 (CBS)
MARILYN MATTHEWS, Costume Supervisor; Fame, Not in Kansas Anymore, 02/24/83 (NBC)

MINA MITTLEMAN, Women's Costume Supervisor; ELLIS COHEN, Men's Costume Supervisor, Missing Children: A Mother's Story (CBS)

MAKEUP (E-2054)

For a single episode of a regular or limited series or for a special. Emmy(s) to Makeup Artist(s)

DEL ACEVEDO, Thorn Birds, Part 4, 03/30/83 (ABC)
ZOLTAN ELEK, MONTY WESTMORE, Who Will Love My Children? (ABC)
LEO L. LOTITO, JR., Makeup Supervisor; WERNER KEPPLER, V (NBC)
JACK WILSON, Fame, Not In Kansas Anymore, 02/24/83 (NBC)

HAIRSTYLING (E-2055)

For a single episode of a regular or limited series or for a special. Emmy(s) to Hairstylist(s)

EDIE PANDA, Rosie: The Rosemary Clooney Story (CBS)
JANICE D BRANDOW, Missing Children: A Mother's Story (CBS)
MARK NELSON, Nicholas Nickleby, Part 4, 01/13/83 (SYN)
SHARLEEN RASSI, Wizards And Warriors, The Rescue, 03/12/83 (CBS)

GRAPHIC DESIGN AND TITLE SEQUENCES (E-2056)

For a single episode of a regular or limited series or for a special (Possibility of one, more than one or no award)

JAMES CASTLE, BRUCE BRYANT, Cheers, Showdown, 03/24/83 (NBC)
EDIE BASKIN, JEFF CARPENTER, Square Pegs, Muffy's Bas Mitzvah, 11/29/82 (CBS)
ANDY EWAN, Nicholas Nickleby, Part 1 (SYN)
PHILL NORMAN, Scarlet And The Black (CBS)
JOHN RIDGWAY, PAM BLOCH, HARRY MARKS, Entertainment Tonight, Part 373 (SYN)

FILM EDITING - SERIES (E-2057)

For a single episode of a regular series

RAY DANIELS, Hill Street Blues, Phantom Of The Hill, 12/02/82 (NBC)
JEANENE AMBLER, Quincy, M.E., Quincy's Wedding, Part 2, 02/23/83 (NBC)
FRED W. BERGER, A.C.E., Dallas, Ewing's Inferno, 05/06/83 (CBS)
BOB BRING, A.C.E., Matt Houston, The Showgirl Murders, 03/20/83 (ABC)
ANDREW CHULACK, Cheers, Endless Slumper, 12/02/83 (NBC)
STANFORD TISCHLER, A.C.E., LARRY L. MILLS, A.C.E., M*A*S*H, Goodbye, Farewell And Amen, 02/28/83 (CBS)
JOHN M. WOODCOCK, A.C.E., (Supervising Film Editor); BOB BLAKE (Film Editor), Dynasty, La Mirage, 12/15/82 (ABC)

FILM EDITING - LIMITED SERIES OR A SPECIAL (E-2058)

For a single episode of a regular or limited series or for a special

C. TIMOTHY O'MEARA, Thorn Birds, Part 3, 03/29/83 (ABC)
FRED A. CHULACK, A.C.E., BUD FRIEDGEN, A.C.E., Blue And Gray, Part 1, 11/24/82 (CBS)
BERNARD GRIBBLE, A.C.E., PETER ZINNER, A.C.E,, JOHN F. BURNETT, A.C.E., JACK TUCKER, EARLE HERDAN, GARY SMITH, Winds Of War, Into The Maelstrom, 02/13/83 (ABC)
JERROLD L. LUDWIG, A.C.E., Who Will Love My Children? (ABC)
ROBERT F. SHUGRUE, Thorn Birds, Part 1, 03/27/83 (ABC)
BENJAMIN A. WEISSMAN, Scarlet And The Black (CBS)

FILM SOUND EDITING - SERIES (E-2059)

For a single episode of a regular series

SAM HORTA, (Supervising Editor); DON ERNST, AVRAM GOLD, EILEEN HORTA, CONNIE KAZMER, GARY KRIVACEK, (Editors), Hill Street Blues, Stan The Man, 11/04/82 (NBC)
SAM HORTA, (Supervising Editor); DON ERNST,JERE GOLDING, CONNIE KAZMER, GARY KRIVACEK, (Editors), St. Elsewhere, Working, 03/2/83 (NBC)
WALTER JENEVEIN, (Supervising Editor); JOHN DETRA, DENNIS DILTZ, SAMGEMETTE, PHIL HABERMAN, MARVIN J. KOSBERG, TONY POLK, KYLE WRIGHT, SAM SHAW, BRUCE STAMBLER, (Editors), Knight Rider, Pilot, 09/25/82 (NBC)
ED ROSSI, (Supervising Editor); WILLIAM HARTMAN, DAVID ICE, DON ISAACS, GODFREY MARKS, RICHARD SPERBER, (Editors), M*A*S*H, Goodbye, Farewell And Amen, 02/28/83 (CBS)
SAM SHAW, (Supervising Editor); JOHN DETRA, SAM GEMETTE, DONLEE JORGENSEN, MARK ROBERTS, ERIC SCHRADER, JOHN STACY, BOB WEATHERFORD, Tales Of The Gold Monkey, Honor Thy Brother, 11/24/82 (ABC)

FILM SOUND EDITING - LIMITED SERIES OR A SPECIAL (E-2060)

For a single episode of a regular or limited series or for a special

JIM TROUTMAN, (Supervising Editor); DAVE CALDWELL, PAUL CLAY, PAUL LAUNE, TONY MAGRO, DICK RADERMAN, KAREN RASCH, ASCHER YATES, BILL SHENBERG, DAN THOMAS, (Editors), Executioner's Song (NBC)
MICHAEL HILKENE, RUSS TINSLEY, (Supervising Editors); BILL JACKSON, JOE MAYER, RUSTY TINSLEY, BEN WONG, (Editors), Who Will Love My Children? (ABC)
JOSEPH MELODY, RUSS TINSLEY, (Supervising Editors); TOM CORNWELL, DAVID R. ELLIOTT, MICHAEL HILKENE, FRED JUDKINS, JOHN KLINE, RUSTY TINSLEY, (Editors), Blue And The Gray, Part 1, 11/14/82 (CBS)
KEITH STAFFORD, (Supervising Editor); RICHARD W. ADAMS, DENIS DUTTON, JAMES FRITCH, ROBERT GUTKNECHT, CARL K. MAHAKIAN, LEE OSBORNE, (Editors); EDWARD SANDLIN, IAN McGREGOR SCOTT, (Editors), Winds Of War, Part 7, 02/13/83 (ABC)
CHRISTOPHER T. WELCH, RUSS TINSLEY, (Supervising Editors);, CATHEYBURROW, GREG DILLON, JOHN KLINE, BILL MANGER, (Editors), Uncommon Valor (CBS)

FILM SOUND MIXING - SERIES (E-2061)

For a single episode of a regular series

WILLIAM B. MARKEY, C.A.S., (Production Mixer), JOHN B. ASMAN, BILL NICHOLSON, KEN S. POLK, (Re-Recording Mixers), Hill Street Blues, Trial By Fury, 09/30/82 (NBC)
MAURY HARRIS, (Production Mixer); JOHN B. ASMAN, WILLIAM NICHOLSON, KEN S. POLK, (Re-Recording Mixers), Cagney & Lacey, Recreational Use, 12/27/83 (CBS)
JOHN KEAN, (Production Mixer); MICHAEL CASPER, STANLEY H. POLINKSY, B. TENNYSON SEBASTION II, (Re-Recording Mixers), Tales Of The Gold Monkey, Pilot, 09/22/82 (ABC)
EDDIE MAHLER, (Production Mixer); JAMES R. COOK, JOHN NORMAN, ROBERTH HARMAN, (Re-Recording Mixers), A-Team, Pilot, 01/23/83 (NBC)
JIMMY ROGERS, (Production Mixer), MICHAEL CASPER, EARL M. MADERY, B.TENNYSON SEBASTION II, (Re-Recording Mixers), Magnum, P.I., Did You See The Sunrise?, 09/30/82 (NBC)
DEAN S. VERNON, (Production Mixer), JOHN B. ASMAN, BILL NICHOLSON, KEN S. POLK, (Re-Recording Mixers), St. Elsewhere, The Count, 03/08/83 (NBC)

FILM SOUND MIXING - LIMITED SERIES OR A SPECIAL (E-2062)

For a single episode of a limited series or for a special

JOHN MITCHELL, (Production Mixer), GORDON L. DAY, STAN WETZEL, HOWARD WILMARTH, (Re-Recording Mixers), Scarlet And The Black (CBS)
ALAN BERNARD, (Production Mixer); ROBERT W. GLASS, JR., WILLIAM L. McCAUGHEY, C.A.S., MEL METCALFE, (Re-Recording Mixers), Winds Of War, Part 4, 02/09/83 (ABC)
ALAN BERNARD, (Production Mixer); ROBERT W. GLASS, JR., WIL-

LIAM L. McCAUGHEY, C.A.S., ALAN STONE, (Re-Recording Mixers), Winds Of War, Part 3, 02/08/83 (ABC)
ROBIN GREGORY, (Production Mixer); ROBERT W. GLASS, JR., MEL METCALFE, WILLIAM L. McCAUGHEY, C.A.S., (Re-Recording Mixers), Winds Of War, Part 7, 02/13/83 (ABC)
STEVE MARLOWE, (Production Mixer); ROBERT W. GLASS, JR., DAVID J. HUDSON, RAY WEST, (Re-Recording Mixers), Executioner's Song (NBC)

TAPE SOUND MIXING - SERIES (E-2063)

For a single episode of a regular series

KEN HAHN, FRANK KALUGA, (Production), Dance In America, The Magic Flute, 04/25/83 (PBS)
PAUL DOBE, (Pre-Production); DICK SARTER, (Production); JERRY CLEMANS,C.A.S., (Post-Production); CRAIG PORTER, (Sound Effects); Solid Gold With: Barry Manilow, 01/22/83 (SYN)
DON HELVEY, (Production); JERRY CLEMANS, C.A.S., (Post-Production), Alice, The Secret Of Mel's Diner, 10/20/82 (CBS)
MATT HYDE, (Pre-Production); RICH JACOB, (Production), CHRIS HAIRE, (Post-Production), DICK WILSON, (Sound Effects), Star Of The Family, Show #1, 09/30/82 (ABC)
RICHARD JACOB, (Production), AL PATAPOFF, (Post-Production), ROSS DAVIS, (Sound Effects), Benson, Death In A Funny Position, 10/22/82 (ABC)

TAPE SOUND MIXING - LIMITED SERIES OR A SPECIAL (E-2064)

For a single episode of a limited series or for a special

EDWARD J. GREENE, (Pre-Production); RON ESTES, (Production); CARROLL PRATT, (Post-Production), Sheena Easton. . .Act I (NBC)
BARTON CHAITE, (Pre-Production); PHILLIP J. SERETTI, (Production); JERRY CLEMANS, C.A.S., (Post-Production), Andy Williams Early New England Christmas (CBS)
RUSS TERRANA, (Pre-Production); DON WORSHAM, (Production); JERRY CLEMANS, C.A.S., (Post-Production), Eddie Rabbitt Special (CBS)

VIDEO TAPE EDITING - SERIES (E-2065)

For a single episode of a regular series

LARRY M. HARRIS, Jeffersons, Change Of A Dollar, 03/13/83 (CBS)
ANDY ACKERMAN, Newhart, Grandma, What A Big Mouth You Have, 04/03/83 (CBS)
DIANE BLOCK, TEE BOSUSTOW, CARY GRIES, MICHAEL KELLY, DOUG LOVISKA, BRUCE MOTYER,
BILL PAULSEN, NICHOLAS STEIN, CYNTHIA VAUGHN, JOE WALSH, Real People, Show #502, 11/03/82 (NBC)
TUCKER WIARD, Alice, Vera, The Torch, 04/24/83 (CBS)
MARCO ZAPPIA, Archie Bunker's Place, Three Women, 01/16/83 (CBS)

VIDEO TAPE EDITING - LIMITED SERIES OR A SPECIAL (E-2066)

For a single episode of a limited series or for a special

ARDEN RYNEW, Special Bulletin (NBC)
KEN DENISOFF, David Frost Presents: The Fourth International Guinness Book Of World Records (ABC)
KEN GUTSTEIN, Big Bird In China (NBC)
DANNY WHITE, Motown 25: Yesterday, Today, Forever (NBC)

TECHNICAL DIRECTION AND ELECTRONIC CAMERAWORK - SERIES (E-2067)

For a single episode of a regular series

HEINO RIPP, (Technical Director); MIKE BENNETT, AL CAMOIN, JAN KASOFF, JOHN PINTO,
MAUREY VERSHORE, (Camerapersons), Saturday Night Live, With: Sid Caeser, And Joe Cocker, 02/05/83 (NBC)
GERRY BUCCI, (Technical Director); D. J. DIOMEDES, ARTOL La COMBE, CAROL WETOVICH,
BLAIR WHITE, (Camerapersons), It Takes Two, An Affair To Remember, 12/16/82 (ABC)
HERM FALK, (Technical Director), WILLIAM POPE, DONNA QUANTE, JOHN RAGO, IRIS ROSENTHAL,
(Camerapersons), Benson, The Honeymooners, 01/07/83 (ABC)
CAL SLATER, (Technical Director), LUIS FUERTE, LARRY HEIDER, ROBERT KEYES, WAYNE ORR,
KEN PATTERSON, (Camerapersons), Sound Festival, With: Flora Purim & Airto, 11/09/83 (PBS)

TECHNICAL DIRECTION AND ELECTRONIC CAMERAWORK - LIMITED SERIES OR A SPECIAL (E-2068)

For a single episode of a limited series or for a special

HANK GEVING, (Cameraperson), Special Bulletin (NBC)
GENE CROWE, (Technical Director); GREG COOK, TOM GEREN, LARRY HEIDER, BOB KEYS, DAVE LEVISOHN,
WAYNE ORR, KEN PATTERSN, RON SHELDON, (Camerapersons), Motown 25: Yesterday, Today, Forever (NBC)
GENE CROWE, GENE SCHWARTZ, (Technical Directors); JOE EPPERSON, LARRY HEIDER, ROY HOLM,
RON SHELDON, (Camerapersons), Sheena Easton. . .Act I (NBC)
JOHN B. FIELD, (Technical Director); JOHN KING, DAVE LEVISOHN, (Camerapersons), Rocky Mountain Holiday
With John Denver And The Muppets (ABC)
KARL MESSERSCHMIDT, (Technical Director); LES ATKINSON, GEORGE FALARDEAU, TOM GEREN, ROY HOLM,
MIKE STRAMISKY, (Camerapersons), Member Of The Wedding - An NBC Live Theater Presentation (NBC)

LIGHTING DIRECTION (ELECTRONIC) - SERIES (E-2069)

For a single episode of a regular series

ROBERT A. DICKINSON, (Lighting Consultant); FRANK C. OLIVAS, (Lighting Director), Solid Gold,
With: Dolly Parton, Laura Branagan (SYN)
MIKEL NEIERS, (Lighting Designer), Rock "N" Roll Tonight, With: Molly Hatchett, Quiet Riot (SYN)
ALAN K. WALKER, Benson, Boys Night Out, 02/04/83 (ABC)
JOHN C. ZAK, (Lighting Director); ALAN WALKER, (Lighting Designer), Benson, Death In A Funny
Position, 10/22/82 (ABC)

LIGHTING DIRECTION (ELECTRONIC) - LIMITED SERIES OR A SPECIAL (E-2070)

For a single episode of a limited series or for a special

JOHN ROOK, (Lighting Designer); KEN WILCOX, BOB PHOLE, (Lighting Directors),
Sheena Easton. . .Act I (NBC)
ROBERT A. DICKINSON, (Lighting Consultant), FRANK C. OLIVAS, (Lighting Director),
Solid Gold Christmas Special, '82 (SYN)
JOHN FRESCHI, Motown 25: Yesterday, Today, Forever (NBC)
CARL GIBSON, Special Bulletin (NBC)
GEORGE RIESENBERGER, (Director Of Photography "E",)
Rocky Mountain Holiday With John Denver And The Muppets (ABC)

INDIVIDUAL ACHIEVEMENT - ANIMATED PROGRAMMING

DIRECTORS (E-2071)

For a single episode of an Animated series or for an Animated special (Possibility of one, more than one or no award)

GERARD BALDWIN, My Smurfy Valentine (NBC)
PHIL ROMAN, Here Comes Garfield (CBS)

WRITERS (E-2072)

LEN JANSON, CHUCK MENVILLE, (Teleplay); PEYO CULLIFORD, YVAN DELPORTE, LEN JANSON, CHUCK MENVILLE, GERARD BALDWIN,(Story), My Smurfy Valentine (NBC)

OUTSTANDING INDIVIDUAL ACHIEVEMENT - INFORMATIONAL PROGRAMMING

DIRECTORS (E-2073)

For a single episode of an Informatioal series or for an Informational special (Area Award - Possibility of one, more than one or no award)

ALFRED R. KELMAN, CHARLES BANGERT, Body Human: The Living Code (CBS)

PERFORMERS (E-2074)

STEVE EDWARDS, Entertainment Tonight/Entertainment This Week (SYN)
FRANK LANGELLA, I, Leonardo: A Journey Of The Mind (CBS)

WRITERS (E-2075)

LOUIS H. GORFAIN, DR. ROBERT E. FUISZ, Body Human: The Living Code (CBS)
CHANDLER COWLES, I, Leonardo: A Journey Of The Mind (CBS)

INDIVIDUAL ACHIEVEMENT - SPECIAL VISUAL EFFECTS

ART DIRECTION (E-2076)

GENE WARREN JR., PETER KLEINOW, LESLIE HUNTLEY, (Special Visual Effects); JACKSON DE GOVIA, (Production Designer); MICHAEL MINOR, Art Director; Winds Of War, Defiance, 02/09/83 (ABC)

VIDEO TAPE EDITING (E-2077)

An Award for a special visual effects achievement which does not fall into a regular category and is not otherwise recognized

BILL GOODARD, GARY L. SMITH, (Video Tape Editors), SCTV Network, Energy Ball/Sweeps Week Show, 02/25/83 (NBC)

ACHIEVEMENT IN ENGINEERING DEVELOPMENT (E-2078)

(An award to an individual, a company or an organization for developments in engineering which are either so extensive an improvement on existing methods or so innovative in nature that they materially affect the transmission, recording or reception of television.)

Award to Eastman Kodak Company for the development of Eastman high-speed color film 5294/7294, a color negative film with improved picture quality under low-light level.
Citation To Ikegami Electronics and CBS Inc. for the engineering and development of the EC-35, a camera used for electronic cinematography.
Citation To The Ampex Corp. for the development of the ADO, a digital effects unit displaying unique capabilities with improved picture quality.

NATIONAL DAYTIME EMMY AWARDS

DAYTIME DRAMA SERIES (E-2079)

Emmy(s) to Executive Producer(s) and Producer(s)

THE YOUNG & THE RESTLESS, William J. Bell, Executive Producer; H. Wesley Kenney, Executive Producer; Edward Scott, Producer (CBS)
ALL MY CHILDREN, Jacqueline Babbin, Producer (ABC)
DAYS OF OUR LIVES, Mrs. Ted Corday, Executive Producer; Al Rabin, Supervising Executive Producer; Patricia Wenig, Supervising Producer; Ken Corday, Producer (NBC)
GENERAL HOSPITAL, Gloria Monty, Producer (ABC)
ONE LIFE TO LIVE, Joseph Stuart, Producer (ABC)

GAME OR AUDIENCE PARTICIPATION SHOW (E-2080)

Emmy(s) to Executive Producer(s) and Producer(s)

THE $25,000 PYRAMID, Bob Stewart, Executive Producer; Anne Marie Schmitt & Sande Stewart, Producers (CBS)
THE PRICE IS RIGHT, Frank Wayne, Executive Producer; Barbara Hunter, Co-Producer; Phillip Wayne, Co-Producer (CBS)
FAMILY FEUD, Howard Felsher, Producer (ABC)

TALK OR SERVICE SERIES (E-2081)

Emmy(s) to Executive Producer(s) and Producers(s)

THIS OLD HOUSE, Russell Morash, Producer (PBS)
PHIL DONAHUE, Richard Mincer, Executive Producer; Patricia McMillen, Senior Producer; Darlene Hayes & Sheri Singer, Producers (SYN)
HOUR MAGAZINE, Martin M. Berman, Executive Producer; Steve Clements, Producer (SYN)
THE RICHARD SIMMONS SHOW, Woody Fraser and Nora Fraser, Executive Producers; Noreen Friend, Producer (SYN)

VARIETY SERIES (E-2082)

Emmy(s) to Executive Producer(s) and Producers(s)

THE MERV GRIFFIN SHOW, Peter Barsocchini, Producer (SYN)
FANTASY, Merrill Heatter, Executive Producer; E.V. DiMassa, Jr., Producer (NBC)

CHILDREN'S ENTERTAINMENT SERIES (E-2083)

Emmy(s) to Executive Producers(s) and Producers(s)

SMURFS, William Hanna and Joseph Barbera, Executive Producers; Gerard Baldwin, Producer (NBC)
CAPTAIN KANGAROO, Robert Keeshan and Jim Hirschfeld, Executive Producers (CBS)

CHILDREN'S INFORMATIONAL/INSTRUCTIONAL SERIES (E-2084)

Emmy(s) to Executive Producer(s) and Producer(s)

SESAME STREET, Dulcy Singer, Executive Producer, Lisa Simon, Producer (PBS)
MISTER ROGERS NEIGHBORHOOD, Fred Rogers, Executive Producer; Sam Newbury, Producer (PBS)
ABC WEEKEND SPECIALS (ABC)

CHILDREN'S ENTERTAINMENT SPECIALS (E-2085)

Emmy(s) to Executive Producer(s) and Producer(s)

THE WOMAN WHO WILLED A MIRACLE, Dick Clark and Preston Fischer, Executive Producers; Joanne A. Curley and Sharon Miller, Producers (ABC)
THE SHOOTING (CBS)
JUST PALS, Peter Walz, Executive Producer; Bob Johnson and Nick Anderson, Producers (CBS)
OH, BOY! BABIES!, Bruce Hart and Carole Hart, Executive Producers; Carole Hart, Producer (NBC)
HELP WANTED, (CBS Afternoon Playhouse) Stephen Gyllenhaal, Producer (CBS)

CHILDREN'S INFORMATIONAL/INSTRUCTIONAL SPECIAL (2086)

Emmy(s) to Executive Producers(s) and Producer(s)

WINNERS, Tom Robertson, Producer 5/82 (SYN)

INFORMATIONAL/INSTRUCTIONAL PROGRAMMING–SHORT FORM (E-2087)

Emmy(s) to Executive Producer(s) and Producer(s)

IN THE NEWS, Joel Heller, Executive Producer; Walter Lister, Producer (CBS)
WILLIE SURVIVES, Lynn Ahrens, Producer (ABC)

ACTOR - DAYTIME DRAMA SERIES (E-2088)

ROBERT WOODS, One Life To Live (ABC)
PETER BERGMAN, All My Children (ABC)
JAMES MITCHELL, All My Children (ABC)
STUART DAMON, General Hospital (ABC)
ANTHONY GEARY, General Hospital (ABC)

ACTRESS - DAYTIME DRAMA SERIES (E-2089)

DOROTHY LYMAN, All My Children (ABC)
SUSAN LUCCI, All My Children (ABC)
LESLIE CHARLESON, General Hospital (ABC)
ERICA SLEZAK, One Life To Live (ABC)
ROBIN STRASSER, One Life To Live (ABC)

SUPPORTING ACTOR - DAYTIME DRAMA SERIES (E-2090)

DARNELL WILLIAMS, All My Children (ABC)
HOWARD E. ROLLINS, JR., Another World (NBC)
DAVID LEWIS, General Hospital (ABC)
JOHN STAMOS, General Hospital (ABC)
ANTHONY CALL, One Life To Live (ABC)
AL FREEMAN, JR., One Life To Live (ABC)

SUPPORTING ACTRESS - DAYTIME DRAMA SERIES (E-2091)

LOUISE SHAFFER, Ryan's Hope (ABC)
EILEEN HERLIE, All My Children (ABC)
KIM DELANEY, All My Children (ABC)
MARCY WALKER, All My Children (ABC)
ROBIN MATTSON, General Hospital (ABC)
BRYNN THAYER, One Life To Live (ABC)

HOST OR HOSTESS - GAME OR AUDIENCE PARTICIPATION SHOW (E-2092)

BETTY WHITE, Just Men! (NBC)
DICK CLARK, The New $25,000 Pyramid (CBS)
RICHARD DAWSON, Family Feud (ABC)

HOST OR HOSTESS - TALK OR SERVICE SERIES (E-2093)

PHIL DONAHUE, Donahue (SYN)
GARY COLLINS, Hour Magazine (SYN)
MARY MARTIN, Over Easy (PBS)

HOST OR HOSTESS - VARIETY SERIES (E-2094)

LESLIE UGGAMS, Fantasy (NBC)
MERV GRIFFIN, The Merv Show (SYN)
PETER MARSHALL, Fantasy (NBC)

PERFORMER - CHILDREN'S PROGRAMMING (E-2095)

CLORIS LEACHMAN, The Woman Who Willed A Miracle (ABC Afterschool Special) (ABC)
KEVIN DOBSON, Help Wanted (CBS Afternoon Playhouse) (CBS)
MOLLY PICON, Grandma Didn't Wave Back (Young People's Special) (SYN)
LYNN REDGRAVE, The Shooting (CBS Afternoon Playhouse) (CBS)
FRED ROGERS, Mister Roger's Neighborhood (PBS)

DIRECTOR - DAYTIME DRAMA SERIES (E-2096)

For the entire series

ALLEN FRISTOE, NORMAN HALL, PETER MINER, DAVID PRESSMAN, One Life To Live (ABC)
LAWRENCE AUERBACH, JACK COFFEY, SHERREL HOFFMAN, FRANCESCA JAMES, All My Children (ABC)
MARLENA LAIRD, ALAN PULTZ, PHILLIP SOGARD, General Hospital (ABC)

INDIVIDUAL DIRECTION - GAME OR AUDIENCE PARTICIPATION SHOW (E-2097)

For a single episode

MARC BRESLOW, The Price Is Right (CBS)
PAUL ALTER, Family Feud (ABC)
BRUCE BURMESTER, The New $25,000 Pyramid (CBS)

INDIVIDUAL DIRECTION - TALK OR SERVICE SERIES (E-2098)

For a single episode of a series

GLEN SWANSON, Hour Magazine (SYN)
RON WEINER, Donahue (SYN)

INDIVIDUAL DIRECTION - VARIETY SHOW (E-2099)

For a single episode

DICK CARSON, The Merv Griffin Show (SYN)
BARRY GLAZER, American Bandstand (ABC)

DIRECTOR - CHILDREN'S PROGRAMMING (E-2100)

For a single episode of a series or for a special program

SHARON MILLER, The Woman Who Willed a Miracle (ABC Afterschool Special) (ABC)
JIM HIRSCHFELD, Captain Kangaroo Show (CBS)
JON STONE, Sesame Street (PBS)

WRITING - DAYTIME DRAMA SERIES (E-2101)

For the entire series

CLAIRE LABINE, PAUL AVILA MAYER, MARY RYAN MUNISTERI, EUGENE PRICE, JUDITH PINSKER, NANCY FORD, B. K. PERLMAN, RORY METCALF, TRENT JONES, HAROLD APTER, Ryan's Hope (ABC)
AGNES NIXON, WISNER WASHAM, LORRAINE BRODERICK, JACK WOOD, MARY K. WELLS, CLARICE BLACKBURN, CAROLYN FRANZ, ELIZABETH WALLACE, JOHN SAFFRON, All My Children (ABC)
ANNE HOWARD BAILEY, A.J. RUSSELL, LEAH LAIMAN, THOM RACINA, JACK TURLEY, JEANNE GLYNN, ROBERT GUZA, JR., CHARLES PRATT, JR., ROBERT SHAW, General Hospital (ABC)
SAM HALL, PEGGY O'SHEA, S. MICHAEL SCHNESSEL, VICTOR MILLER, DON WALLACE, LANIE BERTRAM, FRED CORKE, CRAIG CARLSON, One Life To Live (ABC)

TECHNICAL EXCELLENCE - DAYTIME DRAMA SERIES (E-2102)

For the entire series -- Emmys to Individuals

HOWARD ZWEIG, HENRY ENRICO FERRO, Technical Directors; DIANA WENMAN, JEAN DADARIO, Associate Directors; LAWRENCE HAMMOND, ROBERT AMBRICO, TREVOR THOMPSON, VIN-

CENT SENATORE, ROBERT BALLAIRS, THOMAS FRENCH, RICHARD WESTLEIN, Electronic Camera; LEN WALAS, Senior Video Engineer; FRAN GERTLER, KATHRYN TUCKER-BACHELDER, Audio Engineers; ROGER HAENELT, Video Tape Editor; BARBARA WOODS, Sound Effects Engineer: All My Children (ABC)
DAVE SMITH, JOHN COCHRAN, Technical Directors; JIM ANGEL, JACK DENTON, STEVE JONES, BARRY KIRSTEN, BILL SCOTT, JAN LOWRY, RICH KENNEY, WARREN CRESS, JOHN RAGO, DALE WALSH, SAL FOLINO, CAROL WETOVICH, Electronic Camera; LEN GRICE, SAM POTTER, GUY TYLER, Senior Video Engineers; ROBERT MILLER, ZOLI OSAZE, Senior Audio Engineers; BOB LANHAM, JOSE GALVEZ, JACK MOODY, Video Tape Editors: General Hospital (ABC)
MARTIN GAVRIN, LOU MARCHAND, Technical Directors; JOHN MORRIS, GENE KELLY, JOHN WOOD, HOWIE ZEIDMAN, CHARLIE HENRY, FRANK SCHIRALDI, NANCY KRIEGEL, RICK SCHIAFFO, CARLA NATION REID, GENEVIEVE TWOHIG, Electronic Camera; HERB SEGALL, Senior Video Engineer; FRANK BAILEY, KEN HOFFMAN, Senior Audio Engineers; STUART SILVER, JOHN W. SULLIVAN, Associate Directors: AL FORMAN, TONY GRECO, Videotape Editors: One Life To Live (ABC)

DESIGN EXCELLENCE - DAYTIME DRAMA SERIES (E-2103)

For the entire series -- Emmys to Individuals

WILLIAM MICKLEY, Scenic Designer; WILLIAM ITKIN, DONNA LARSON, DONALD GAVITT, ROBERT GRIFFIN, Lighting Directors; CAROL LUIKEN, Costume Designer; SYLVIA LAWRENCE, Make-up; SCOTT HERSH, Make-up Designer; RICHARD GREENE, Hair; ROBERT CHUI, Hair Designer; TERI SMITH, Music Director: SID RAMIN, Music Composer: All My Children (ABC)
JIM ELLINGWOOD, Art Director; MERCER BARROWS, GREG STRAIN, Set Decorators; GRANT VELIE, TOM MARKLE, JOHN ZAK, RAE CREEVEY, Lighting Directors; JIM O'DANIEL, ROBERT BERDELL, JACKIE EIFERT, ALICE JACKSON, JIM CHRISTOPHERSON, EMMA TRENCHARD, DOLORES LAMPANO, Costume Designers; P.K., BECKY BOWEN, SUNDI MARTINO, CATHERINE MCCANN, WENDY PENNINGTON, DIANE LEWIS, Make-Up Designers; KATHERINE KOTARAKOS, DEBBIE HOLMES, MARY GUERREO, CATHERINE MARCOTTE, Hair Designers; DOMINIC MESSINGER, JILL FARREN PHELPS, Music Directors: CHARLES PAUL, Music Composer: General Hospital (ABC)
CHARLES BRANDON, Scenic Designer; JO MAYER, HOWARD SHARROTT, Lighting Directors; DON SHEFFIELD, Costume Designer; PAUL GEBBIA, ROBERT O'BRADOVICH, Make-Up Designers; TONY ANTHONY, WILLIS HANCHETT, Hair Designers; JOHN ANTHONY, Music Director; JACK URBONT, Music Director: One Life To Live (ABC)

WRITING - CHILDREN'S PROGRAMMING (E-2104)

ARTHUR HEINEMANN, The Woman Who Willed A Miracle (ABC Afterschool Special) (ABC)
BOB BRUSH, HARRY CROSSFIELD, MARTIN DONOFF, HOWARD FRIEDLANDER, MATT ROBINSON, Captain Kangaroo (CBS)
JOE BAILEY, SARA COMPTON, TOM DUNSMUIR, JUDY FREUDBERG, TONY GEISS, EMILY KINGSLEY, DAVID KORR, JEFF MOSS, LUIS SANTEIRO, RAY SIPHERD, NORMAN STILES, Sesame Street (PBS)
DARYL WARNER, CAROLYN MILLER, Sometimes I Don't Love My Mother (ABC Afternoon Special) (ABC)

MUSIC COMPOSITION/DIRECTION - CHILDREN'S PROGRAMMING (E-2105)

For a single episode of a series or for a special program

ELLIOT LAWRENCE, Music Director, Sometimes I Don't Love My Mother (ABC Afternoon Special) (ABC)
JEFF MOSS, TONY GEISS, RICHARD J. FREITAS, CHRIS CERF, GERRI BRIOSO, Composers, Sesame Street (PBS)

CINEMATOGRAPHY - CHILDREN'S PROGRAMMING (E-2106)

For a single episode of a series or for a special program

TERRY MEADE, The Shooting (CBS Afternoon Playhouse) (CBS)
PETER STEIN, Robbers, Rooftops and Witches, (CBS Library) (CBS)

FILM EDITING - CHILDREN'S PROGRAMMING (E-2107)

For a single episode of a series or for a special program

SCOTT McKINSEY, The Shooting (CBS Afternoon Playhouse) (CBS)
JENNIFER BOYD, JIM BURGESS, PAUL FISHER, KARL KELEMAN, DICK LANGENBACH, ANDRE MARCEL, CHUCK PENN, The Great Space Coaster: A Special Kind of Courage: The Special Olympics (SYN)
BOB BEHERENS, GARRY SEIDEL, LESLIE SMITH, CHRISTOPHER STOCK, DAN SWIELIK, JUDY VERDA, Kidsworld (SYN)

AREAS

Possibility Of More Than One Award, One Award Or No Award.

ACHIEVEMENT IN RELIGIOUS PROGRAMMING – SERIES (E-2108)

Emmy(s) to Executive Producer(s) and Producer(s)

INSIGHT, Ellwood E. Kieser, Paulist, Executive Producer; Lan Oikun, Executive Producer; Mike Rhodes and Terry Sweeney, S.J., Producers (SYN)
DIRECTIONS, Sid Darion, Executive Producer; Della Lowe, Producer (ABC)

ACHIEVEMENT IN RELIGIOUS PROGRAMMING – SPECIALS (E-2109)

Emmy(s) to Executive Producers(s) and Producers(s)

THE JUGGLER OF NOTRE DAME, Ellwood E. Kieser, Paulist, Executive Producer; Mike Rhodes and Terry Sweeney, S.J., Producers (SYN)
LAND OF FEAR, LAND OF COURAGE, Helen Marmor, Executive Producer (NBC)

SPECIAL CLASSIFICATION OF OUTSTANDING PROGRAM ACHIEVEMENT (E-2110)

Emmy(s) to Executive Producer(s) and Producer(s)

AMERICAN BANDSTAND, Dick Clark, Executive Producer; Larry Klein, Producer; Barry Glazer, Co-Producer (ABC)
FYI, Yanna Kroyt Brandt, Producer; Mary Ann Donahue, Coordinating Producer (ABC)

COVERAGE OF SPECIAL EVENTS (E-2111)

Emmy(s) to Executive Producers(s) and Producer(s)

MACY'S THANKSGIVING DAY PARADE, Dick Schneider, Producer (NBC)
THE NINTH ANNUAL DAYTIME EMMY AWARDS, Bill Carruthers, Executive Producer; Joel Stein, Producer (CBS)

ACHIEVEMENT IN THE PERFORMING ARTS (E-2112)

Emmy(s) to Executive Producer(s) and Producer(s)

HANSEL AND GRETEL: LIVE FROM THE MET, Michael Bronson, Executive Producer; Clemente D'Alessio, Producer (PBS)
ZUBIN AND THE I.P.O., Samuel Elfert, Producer (NBC)

PERFORMERS - RELIGIOUS PROGRAMMING (E-2113)

LOIS NETTLETON, Insight: "A Gun For Mandy" (SYN)
EDWIN NEWMAN, Kids, Drugs and Alcohol (NBC)

SPECIAL CLASSIFICATION OF OUTSTANDING INDIVIDUAL ACHIEVEMENT

PERFORMERS (E-2114)
HAL LINDEN, FYI (ABC)

WRITING: (E-2115)
MARY ANN DONAHUE, JOSEPH GUSTAITIS, LINDA KLINE, ROBIN WESTEN, ELAINE WHITLEY, FYI (ABC)

DIRECTING: (E-2116)
MIKE GARGIULO, FYI (ABC)
AL RABIN, Days Of Our Lives, Remote: Helicopter Sequence At Lake Arrowhead (NBC)

DIRECTION - SPECIAL EVENTS COVERAGE (E-2117)
DICK SCHNEIDER, Macy's Thanksgiving Day Parade (NBC)

INDIVIDUAL ACHIEVEMENT IN SPECIAL EVENTS – TECHNICAL DIRECTION/ELECTRONIC CAMERAWORK (E-2118)
TERRY ROHNKE, Technical Director; MIKE BENNETT, CARL ECK-ETT, ERIC EISENSTEIN, BARRY FRISCHER, BILL GOETZ, STEVE GONZALEZ, DAVE HAGEN, JOHN HILLYER, GENE MARTIN, DON MULVANEY, JOHN PINTO, Electronic Camera: Macy's Thanksgiving Day Parade (NBC)

INDIVIDUAL ACHIEVEMENT IN ANY AREA OF CREATIVE TECHNICAL CRAFTS – TECHNICAL DIRECTION/ ELECTRONIC CAMERAWORK (E-2119)
ROBERT HOFFMAN, Technical Director, Remote: Silver Springs, Florida "One Life To Live" (ABC)
ANTHONY L. GAMBINO, Electronic Camera, Remote: Silver Springs, Florida "One Life To Live" (ABC)
HOWARD ZWEIG, Technical Director; LAWRENCE HAMMOND, TREVOR THOMPSON, DIANA CATES-CANTRELL, Electronic Camera, Remote: Backstage Ramp "All My Children" (ABC)
HARVEY L. CLAVON, Electronic Camera, The Richard Simmons Show (SYN)

ACHIEVEMENT IN ANY AREA OF CREATIVE TECHNICAL CRAFTS – ASSOCIATE DIRECTION/VIDEOTAPE EDITING (E-2120)
NICK MARTINO, Associate Director & Videotape Editor; MIKE BELTRAN, MORT SMITH, DAVID DUNLAP, JEFFREY C. SMITH, Videotape Editors, Fantasy (NBC)
JEAN L. DADARIO, ROGER HAENELT, Associate Directors, Remote: Backstage Ramp "All My Children" (ABC)

INDIVIDUAL ACHIEVEMENT IN CHILDREN'S PROGRAMMING – ASSOCIATE DIRECTION/VIDEOTAPE EDITING (E-2121)
ILIE AGOPIAN, Videotape Editor, Young People's Specials (SYN)

INDIVIDUAL ACHIEVEMENT IN RELIGIOUS PROGRAMMING – ASSOCIATE DIRECTION/VIDEOTAPE EDITING (E-2122)
MATTY POWERS, Videotape Editor, Priceless Treasure (NBC)

ACHIEVEMENT IN ANY AREA OF CREATIVE TECHNICAL CRAFTS – CINEMATOGRAPHY (E-2123)
ROBERT RYAN, Lorne Green's New Wilderness (SYN)

INDIVIDUAL ACHIEVEMENT IN RELIGIOUS PROGRAMMING – FILM EDITING (E-2124)
SCOTT McKINSEY, Insight – Every 90 Seconds (SYN)
ED WILLIAMS, Land Of Fear, Land Of Courage (NBC)

INDIVIDUAL ACHIEVEMENT IN ANY AREA OF CREATIVE TECHNICAL CRAFTS – FILM EDITING (E-2125)
LES BROWN, Lorne Greene's New Wilderness (SYN)

INDIVIDUAL ACHIEVEMENT IN ANY AREA OF CREATIVE TECHNICAL CRAFTS – AUDIO (E-2126)
JOHN N. CASTALDO, Audio Engineer, Donahue (SYN)

INDIVIDUAL ACHIEVEMENT IN ANY AREA OF THE PERFORMING ARTS – AUDIO (E-2127)
JAY DAVID SAKS, Audio Director, Hansel And Gretel: Live From The Met (PBS)

INDIVIDUAL ACHIEVEMENT IN ANY AREA OF CREATIVE TECHNICAL CRAFTS – MUSIC COMPOSITION/DIRECTION (E-2128)
JACK URBONT, Composer/Director, Lorne Green's New Wilderness (SYN)

INDIVIDUAL ACHIEVEMENT IN THE COVERAGE OF SPECIAL EVENTS – MUSIC COMPOSITION/DIRECTION (E-2129)
MILTON DELUGG, Composer/Director; ANNE DELUGG, Lyricist, Macy's Thanksgiving Day Parade (NBC)

INDIVIDUAL ACHIEVEMENT IN CHILDREN'S PROGRAMMING – ART DIRECTION/SCENIC DESIGN/SET DECORATION (E-2130)
VICTOR DiNAPOLI, Art Director, Sesame Street (PBS)

INDIVIDUAL ACHIEVEMENT IN ANY AREA OF CREATIVE TECHNICAL CRAFTS – ART DIRECTION/SCENIC DESIGN/SET DECORATION (E-2131)
MATTHEW STODDART, JOHN ORBERG, CHRISTOPHER LYALL, ROBERT LOVETT, JIM KROUPA, Puppet Design & Construction, The Great Space Coaster: A Special Kind Of Courage: The Special Olympics (SYN)
BRUCE RYAN, Art Director, American Bandstand (ABC)
DON SHIRLEY, Scenic Designer, Daytime Emmy Awards (CBS)

INDIVIDUAL ACHIEVEMENT IN CHILDREN'S PROGRAMMING – LIGHTING DIRECTION (E-2132)
WILLIAM KNIGHT, Sesame Street (PBS)
RANDY NORDSTROM, Sesame Street (PBS)

INDIVIDUAL ACHIEVEMENT IN RELIGIOUS PROGRAMMING – LIGHTING DIRECTION (E-2133)
GEORGE RIESENBERGER, It Is Written: "Prophet In The House" (SYN)

INDIVIDUAL ACHIEVEMENT IN THE COVERAGE OF SPECIAL EVENTS – LIGHTING DIRECTION (E-2134)
CARL VITELLI, Jr., Daytime Emmy Awards (CBS)

INDIVIDUAL ACHIEVEMENT IN THE PERFORMING ARTS – LIGHTING DIRECTION (E-2135)

GIL WESCHLER, Hansel And Gretel: Live From The Met (PBS)

ACHIEVEMENT IN ANY AREA OF CREATIVE TECHNICAL CRAFTS – LIGHTING DIRECTION (E-2136)

NICHOLAS HUTAK, Remote: Franconia Notch "The Guiding Light" (CBS)

EVERETT R. MELOSH, Remote: Silver Springs, Florida "One Life To Live" (ABC)

INDIVIDUAL ACHIEVEMENT IN CHILDREN'S PROGRAMMING – COSTUME DESIGN (E-2137)

ROBERT TURTURICE, The Shooting (CBS Afternoon Playhouse) (CBS)

BILL GRIFFIN, Captain Kangaroo (CBS)

INDIVIDUAL ACHIEVEMENT IN ANY AREA OF CREATIVE TECHNICAL CRAFTS – COSTUME DESIGN (E-2138)

ROBERT O'HEARN, Hansel And Gretel: Live From The Met (PBS)

INDIVIDUAL ACHIEVEMENT IN CHILDREN'S PROGRAMMING – MAKE-UP DESIGN & HAIR DESIGN (E-2139)

STEVE ATHA, Hair/Make-up Designer, Robbers, Rooftops And Witches (CBS Library) (CBS)

SCOTT HAMILTON, Make-Up Designer, The Woman Who Willed A Miracle (ABC Afterschool Special) (ABC)

CARLA WHITE, Hair-Make-Up Designer, Amy And The Angel (ABC Afterschool Special) 9/22/82 (ABC)

INDIVIDUAL ACHIEVEMENT IN ANY AREA OF CREATIVE TECHNICAL CRAFTS – MAKE-UP AND AND HAIR DESIGN (E-2140)

VICTOR CALLEGARI, Make-Up Designer, Hansel And Gretel: Live From The Met (PBS)

NINA LAWSON, Hair and Wig Designer, Hansel And Gretel: Live From The Met (PBS)

INDIVIDUAL ACHIEVEMENT IN CHILDREN'S PROGRAMMING – GRAPHIC DESIGN (E-2141)

GERRIO BRIOSO, Sesame Street (PBS)

ACHIEVEMENT IN ANY AREA OF CREATIVE TECHNICAL CRAFTS – GRAPHIC DESIGN (E-2142)

JACQUELINE A. FRAZIER, JIM STERLING, Fantasy (NBC)

LARRY FERGUSON, Over Easy (PBS)

INDIVIDUAL ACHIEVEMENT SPECIAL EVENTS – PERFORMERS (E-2143)

BRYANT GUMBEL, Macy's Thanksgiving Day Parade (NBC)

INDIVIDUAL ACHIEVEMENT IN THE PERFORMING ARTS – PERFORMERS (E-2144)

ZUBIN MEHTA, Zubin And The I.P.O. (NBC)

TRUSTEES AWARD (E-2145)

Robert E. Short

ENGINEERING AWARDS (E-2146)

The Ampex Corrporation.
The International Radio Consultive Committee of the I.T.U. (CCIR).
The European Broadcasting Union.
RCA CCSD Video Systems.
SMPTE.
3 M Corporation.
Xerox Corporation.
Mel Slater.
Richard Shoup.

SPORTS AWARDS

LIVE SPORTS SPECIAL (E-2146)

Emmy(s) to Executive Producer(s) and Producer(s) and Director(s)

THE 79TH WORLD SERIES, Michael Weisman, George Finkel, Producers; Harry Coyle, Andy Rosenberg, Directors (NBC)
DAYTONA 500, Robert D. Stenner, Ted Shaker, Dan Forer, Producers; Robert Fishman, Director (CBS)
THE BELMONT STAKES, Robert D. Stenner, Robert Fishman, Producers; Robert Fishman, Director (CBS)
1983 NCAA BASKETBALL CHAMPIONSHIP GAME, Kevin O'Malley, Executive Producer; Rick Sharp, Ted Shaker, Dan Forer, Patti Tuite, Producers; Bob Fishman, Duke Struck, Directors (CBS)
50th ANNIVERSARY ALL-STAR GAME, Michael Weisman, Executive Producer; Harry Coyle, George Finkel, David Neal, Producers; Andy Rosenberg, Harry Coyle, Directors (NBC)

LIVE SPORTS SERIES (E-2147)

Emmy(s) to Executive Producer(s) and Director(s)

CBS SPORTS PRESENTS THE NATIONAL FOOTBALL LEAGUE, Terry O'Neil, Executive Producer; Charles Milton, Michael Burks, Bob Stenner, David Dinkins, John Faratzis, Ed Goren, David Michaels, Jim Silman, David Winner, Producers; Sandy Grossman, Andrew Kindle, Joe Aceti, Bob Dunphy, John McDonough, Peter Bleckner, Bob Dailey, Larry Cavolina, Directors (CBS)
NCAA FOOTBALL '82, Roone Arledge, Executive Producer; Chuck Howard, Ken Wolfe, Mike Pearl, Producers; Andy Sidaris, Larry Kamm, Dick Buffington, Directors (ABC)
MAJOR LEAGUE BASEBALL GAME OF THE WEEK, Michael Weisman, Executive Producer; Harry Coyle, Larry Cirillo, Kenneth Edmundson, Terry Ewert, George Finkel, Producers; Richard Cline, Harry Coyle, John Gonzalez, Andy Rosenberg, Directors (NBC)
PROFESSIONAL BOWLERS TOUR '83, Roone Arledge, Executive Producer; Peter Lasser, Peter Englehart, Producers; Bob Lanning, Norm Sammet, Directors (ABC)
NCAA FOOTBALL ON CBS, Kevin O'Malley, Executive Producer; Ric La Civita, Rick Sharp, Jim Silman, Jean Harper, Mike Burks, Don McGuire, David Dinkins, Producers; Robert Fishman, Larry Cavolina, John McDonough, Bob Dailey, Sandy Grossman, Patti Tuite, Joe Cavolei, Peter Blechner, Directors (CBS)

EDITED SPORTS SPECIAL (E-2148)

Emmy(s) to Executive Producer(s) and Producer(s) and Director(s)

WIMBLEDON '83, Michael Weisman, Executive Producer; Ted Nathanson, Coordinating Producer; Geoffrey Mason, Producer; Ted Nathanson, Bob Levy, Directors; Richard Cline, Producer/Director; Terry Ewert, Videotape Producer (NBC)
1982 U.S. OPEN HIGHLIGHTS, Frank Chirkinian, Executive Producer; David Winner, Producer; Larry Cavolina, Director (CBS)
WAKE UP THE ECHOES. . .THE HISTORY OF NOTRE DAME FOOTBALL, Ed Sabol, Executive Producer; Steve Sabol, Producer; Phil Tuckett, Director (IND)
INDIANAPOLIS "500" '83, Roone Arledge, Executive Producer; Chuck Howard, Bob Goodrich, Producers; Dennis Lewin, Coordinating Producer; Larry Kamm, Roger Goodman, Jim Jennett, Directors (ABC)
THE GAME AND THE GLORY, Larry Parker, Executive Producer; Jody Shapiro, Gary Cohen, Tim Parker, Producers (SYN)

EDITED SPORTS SERIES/ANTHOLOGIES (E-2149)

THE AMERICAN SPORTSMAN, Roone Arledge, Executive Producer; John Wilcox, Senior Producer; Chris Carmody, Co-ordinating Producer; Bob Nixon, Curt Gowdy, Producers (ABC)
NFL TODAY, Ted Shaker, George Veras, Producers; Duke Struck, Director (CBS)
THIS IS THE U.S.F.L., Michael Tollin, Alan Lubell, Gary Cohen, Producers (SYN)
ABC'S WIDE WORLD OF SPORTS, Roone Arledge, Executive Producer; Dennis Lewin, Carol Lehti, Curt Gowdy, Jr., Ken Wolfe, Eleanor Riger, Bob Goodrich, Alex Wallau, Jeff Ruhe, Joel Feld, Producers; Doug Wilson, Producer-Director; Jim K Jennett, Andy Sidaris, Ken Fouts, Larry Kamm, Directors (ABC)
SPORTSWORLD, Michael Weisman, Linda Johnson, Hilary Cosell, Kenneth Edmundson, Terry Ewert, John Gonzalez, Jay Hansen, Matthew McCarthy, Peter M. Rolfe, Ginny Seipt, Producers; Bob Levy, Richard Cline, Ted Nathanson, Directors (NBC)

SPORTS PERSONALITY - HOST (E-2150)

DICK ENBERG (NBC)
AL MICHAELS (ABC)
BRENT MUSBURGER (CBS)
JIM McKAY (ABC)
VIN SCULLY (NBC)

SPORTS PERSONALITY - ANALYST (Commentary) (E-2151)

JOHN MADDEN (CBS)
FRANK BROYLES (ABC)
JOE GARAGIOLA (NBC)
AL McGUIRE (NBC)
MERLIN OLSEN (NBC)

SPECIAL CLASSIFICATION OF OUTSTANDING ACHIEVEMENT INNOVATIVE TECHNICAL ACHIEVEMENT (E-2152)

MICROWAVE TRANSMISSION FROM THE SUMMIT OF MT. EVEREST - THE AMERICAN SPORTSMAN - TRIUMPH ON MT. EVEREST - David Breashears, Randy Hermes, Allen Wechsler, John Wilcox, Nick Pantelakis, Peter Pilafian, Steve Marts (ABC)
2 WAY AUDIO WITH DRIVER - '83 DAYTONA 500 - John Porter, David Curtis, Peter Larsson, Robert Seiderman (CBS)
AIR TO AIR COMPETITION COVERAGE - ABC'S WIDE WORLD OF SPORTS - U.S. NATIONAL SKYDIVING CHAMPIONSHIPS - Roone Arledge, Executive Producer; Dennis Lewin, Carol Lehti, Producers; Andy Sidaris, Director; Norm Kent, Mike Sisemore, Jim Baker, Ken Crabtree, Mike Kurtgis, Cameramen; Dick Horan, Engineering Supervisor (ABC)

SPORTS JOURNALISM (E-2153)

ABC SPORTSBEAT, Michael Marley, Ed Silverman, Howard Cosell, Producers; Maury Rubin, Noubar Stone, Rob Beiner, Directors; (1) Cal State (2) Herschel Walker (ABC)
NFL HIGHS, NFL LOWS, Dan Lauck, Producer (IND)
ABC SPORTSBEAT, Michael Marley, Ed Silverman, Howard Cosell, Producers; Maurv Rubin, Noubar Stone, Rob Beiner, Directors; (1) Boxing Reform (2) Steroid Segment (ABC)
WIMBLEDON '83, Segment: BURNOUT, Michael Weisman, Ted Nathanson, Geoffrey Mason, Terry Ewert, Producers (NBC)
CBS SPORTS SATURDAY & SUNDAY, Segments: LANDON TURNER, BILL KUNKEL, JIMMY PIERSALL, Michael Arnold (CBS)
ALEXIS ARGUELLO, David Michaels, Pat O'Brien (CBS)

PROGRAM ACHIEVEMENT (E-2154)

ABC'S WIDE WORLD OF SPORTS, "Great American Bike Race", Roone Arledge, Executive Producer; Dennis Lewin, Larry Kamm, Producers; Larry Kamm, Peter Lasser, Directors (ABC)
FOOTBALL IN AMERICA, Robert Carmichael, Producer (PBS)
THE AMERICAN SPORTSMAN, "Triumph on Mt. Everest", John Wilcox, Producer/Director (ABC)

CBS SPORTS SATURDAY, "The Iditarod", Terry O'Neil, Ed Goren, Peter Henning, Producers (CBS)
CBS SPORTS SATURDAY/SUNDAY - "Top to Bottom Coverage of America's Downhill," Terry O'Neil, David Dinkins, Jr., Andy Kindle, Peter Bleckner, Producers (CBS)
NFL PRO MAGAZINE, "A Man to Match the Mountains", Steve Sabol, Phil Tuckett, Producers (SYN)

WRITING (E-2155)

GEORGE BELL, JR., The American Sportsman, A Retrospective of William Holden's Africa (ABC)
STEVE SABOL, PHIL TUCKETT, Wake Up The Echoes: The History of Notre Dame Football (IND)
BUD GREENSPAN, Time Capsule: The Los Angeles Olympic Games of 1932 (SYN)
BUD GREENSPAN, The 1982 Heisman Trophy Award Special (SYN)

ENGINEERING/TECHNICAL SUPERVISORS (E-2156)

DAYTONA "500", Walter Pile, John Pumo (CBS)
THE NEW YORK CITY MARATHON, Frank Quitoni, Harold Robbins, Rick Okulski, Geoff Felger and John Partyka (ABC)
NFL '82 SUPER BOWL XVII, Ernest A. Thiel, Jr. (NBC)
50th ANNIVERSARY ALL STAR GAME, H. Calvin Shadwell, John W. Haynes, Jack Signorelli (NBC)
79th WORLD SERIES, Robert McKearnin, Garfield Ricketts, Keith Scammahorn, H. Calvin Shadwell, Robert Brydon (NBC)

TECHNICAL DIRECTORS, ELECTRONIC CAMERAPERSONS, SENIOR VIDEO OPERATORS, SENIOR AUDIO ENGINEERS (TECHNICAL TEAM) (E-2157)

DAYTONA 500, Sandy Bell, Bob Brown, Anthony Filippi, Technical Directors; Bob Seiderman, Tom Jimenez, Audio; Robert Pieringer, Tom Delilla, Bill Berridge, Ron Rasch, Video; Jim Murphy, Neil McCaffrey, Tom McCarthy, Herman Lang, Barry Drago, Joe Sokota, Jim McCarthy, Jeff Pollack, Frank McSpedon, George Rothweiler, George Neader, George Graffeo, Ray Chiste, Hans Sincer, Sig Meyer, Walt Soucy, Camera; Walter Pile, John Pumo, Electronic Camera (CBS)
THE NCAA BASKETBALL FINAL FOUR, Bob Brown, Steve Cunningham, Technical Directors; Bob Seiderman, Mark Radulovich, Audio; Frank Florio, Ed Ambrosini, Lou Lecer, Dave Orlich, Video; Jeff Pollack, Gordon Sweeney, Joe Vicens, Bob Jamieson, Sol Baess, Tom McCarthy, Joel Solofsky, David Finch, Terry Clark, Bob Welsh, Camera (CBS)
THE NEW YORK CITY MARATHON, John Fider, W. Gunther, Rich Gelber, Gene Affrunti, Technical Directors; Mike Michaels, Bob Shultis, Paul Hurney, Ed Garofalo, M. Janklow, Danny Cahn, R. Ahrens, D. Brown, Harold Gordon, Gary Paparello, Marv Bronstein, Lloyd Lynch, T. McMurray, Senior Video Operators; John Lory, Jerry Cudmore, Fran Gertler, Audio; W. Maisch, A. Demammos, Steve Wolff, Richie Westline, J. Sapienza, Mort Levin, Nick Karas, Jerry Dowd, Jack Cronin, M. Hoffman, J. Cordone, D. Dragonetti, A. Peffer, George Montanez, Serf Menduina, J. Shaffer, Tony Gambino, R. Hammond, W. Sullivan, K. Sanborn, J. Stefanoni, Phil Fontana, R. Bernstein, V. Senatore, R. Theodore, E. Wood, Camera (ABC)
KENTUCKY DERBY, Joe Schiavo, John Fider, Technical Directors; Mike Michaels, Ken Amow, Senior Video Operators; Jim Davis, Jack Kestenbaum, Norm Kiernan, Bill Sandreuter, Audio; L. Stenman, A. Armentani, J. Morreale, Jim Heneghan, Tom O'Connell, Jesse Kohn, Gary Donatelli, A. DeRosa, Steve Nikifor, Frank Melchiorre, Jack Dorfman, Bill Sullivan, Jack Cronin, Roy Hutchings, E. Wood, Mort Levin, J. Stefanoni, T. Thompson, Bob Bernstein, Camera (ABC)
SUPER BOWL XVII, Lenny Stucker, Steven Cimino, William Tobey, Rick Lombardo, Technical Directors; Billy Kidd, Bill Parinello, Jim Blaney, Sr., Senior Audio Engineers; Jim Marshall, Scott McCartney, Senior Video Operators; Dayne Adams, Leonard Basile, Rodney Batten, Jim Bragg, Phil Cantrell, Mario Ciarlo, Jim Culley, Eric Eisenstein, Barry Frischer, Lou Gerard, Steve Gonzalez, David A. Hagen, Roger Harbaugh, Ken Harvey, James Herring, Jim Johnson, Buddy Joseph, Joe Klimovitz, Cory Leible, George Loomis, Gene Martin, Roy Ratliff, Al

Rice, George Simpson, Bailey Stortz, Mike Stramisky, Vickie Walker, Camera (NBC)

THE 79th WORLD SERIES, Lenny Stucker, Steven Cimino, William Tobey, Technical Directors; Jerry Caruso, Bill Parinello, Senior Audio Engineers; Jim Sunder, Sal Benza, Senior Video Operators; Leonard Basile, Al Camoin, Phil Cantrell, Mario Ciarlo, Jim Culley, Russ Diven, Eric Eisenstein, Barry Frischer, Lou Gerard, Bill Boetz, Steve Gonzalez, David A. Hagen, Tom Hogan, Jim Johnson, Buddy Joseph, Cory Leible, George Loomis, Albert Rice, Bryan Russo, George Simpson, Mike Straminsky, Vickie Walker, Camera (NBC)

ASSOCIATE DIRECTORS (E-2158)

THE AMERICAN SPORTSMAN - TRIUMPH ON MT. EVEREST, Angelo Bernaducci, Jean MacLean (ABC)
CLOSING SEGMENT - NCAA BASKETBALL CHAMPIONSHIP GAME, Patti Tuite, Bob Dekas (CBS)
INDIANAPOLIS "500", Norm Samet, Ned Simon, John Bessone, Garland Peete (ABC)
ABC'S WIDE WORLD OF SPORTS, Norm Samet, Ned Simon, Toni Slotkin, Jeff Cohan (ABC)
U.S. TENNIS OPEN HIGHLIGHTS, Cathy Barreto, Bob Howe, Bob Matina (CBS)
CAESARS PALACE GRAND PRIX, J.D. Hansen, John Libretto, Brian Orentreich (NBC)

LIGHTING DIRECTORS (E-2159)

NCAA FOOTBALL ON CBS, Joe Crookham (CBS)
ABC'S WIDE WORLD OF SPORTS, International Pro Figure Skating Championships, Melvin B. Handelsman (ABC)
PROFESSIONAL BOWLERS TOUR--Akron, Ohio, Tony Azzolino (ABC)

CINEMATOGRAPHERS (E-2160)

THE AMERICAN SPORTSMAN–Mt. Everest East Face, Kurt Diemburger, David Breashears (ABC)
THE IDITAROD SLED DOG RACE, Peter Henning, Bill Philbin (CBS)
ABC'S WIDE WORLD OF SPORTS--Great American Bike Race, Don Shoemaker, Joe Longo (ABC)
SPORTWORLD EPISODE: SURVIVAL OF THE FITTEST, Don Burgess, Steve Confer, Bill Philbin, Mark Zavad, Bob Carmichael, Steve Bridge, Wallack Axle, Mosh Levin, Jim Birdwell, Robert Bagley, Linton Diegle, Chris Woods (NBC)

VIDEOTAPE EDITORS (E-2161)

BOB HICKSON, GEORGE JOANITIS, LITO MAGPAYO, Closing Segment - NCAA Basketball Championship Game (CBS)
MIKE KOSTEL, RICK REED, RICH DOMICH, JOHN SERVIDEO, 1982 World Series Pre-Game Show (NBC)
RICHARD LEIBLE, JIM McQUEEN, SCOTT RADER, JEFF U'REN, Caesars Palace Grand Prix (NBC)
STEVE BABB, MARIO R. MARINO, Daytona 500 Opening (CBS)
RICHARD LEIBLE, JIM McQUEEN, SAM PATTERSON, SCOTT RADER, BRIAN WICKHAM, JEFF WURTZ, Sportsworld (NBC)
MIKE KOSTEL, RICK REED, RICH DOMICH, JOHN SERVIDEO, NBC Baseball Pre-Game/Major League Baseball: An Inside Look (NBC)
BOB KLUG, MARK KING, JAMES WALTON, This is the USFL - "What A Feeling" (SYN)
HARVEY BEAL, MARVIN GENCH, JOE LONGO, GARY MOSCATO, ALEX MOSKOVIC, PAM PETERSON, MARIO SCHENCMAN, MIKE SIEGEL, ABC's Wide World of Sports - Ironman Triathlon World Championship (ABC)

FILM EDITORS (E-2162)

YALE NELSON, The 79th World Series (NBC)
TED WINTERBURN, ABC's Wide World of Sports - Great American Bike Race (ABC)
STEVE SABOL, Wake Up the Echoes: The History of Notre Dame Football - (IND)

GRAPHIC DESIGNERS (E-2163)

DOUGLAS E. TOWEY, BILL FEIGENBAUM, NBA World Championship Series (CBS)
SONNY KING, PAUL HAMMONS, 1982 NBC Sports World Series (NBC)
KRISTIN STROMQUIST, JAMES R. STERLING II, John Denver Ski Classic (NBC)
MATTHEW McCARTHY, JAMES R. STERLING II, STACEY McDONOUGH, Sportsworld (NBC)

MUSIC COMPOSERS, MUSIC DIRECTORS (E-2164)

JOHN TESH, World University Games (CBS)
PAUL HAMMONS, ROGER TALLMAN, 1983 NBC Sports Super Bowl XVII (NBC)

INTERNATIONAL AWARDS

DOCUMENTARY (E-2165)

THE MIRACLE OF LIFE, Swedish Television (SVT); Sweden
THE GREAT PYRAMID, Nippon Television Network Corporation; Japan
THE UNKNOWN CHAPLIN, Thames Television Ltd.; United Kingdom

DRAMA (E-2166)

KING LEAR, Granada Television Ltd.; United Kingdom
CONNAISSEZ-VOUS BIGOT?, Nippon Hoso Kyokai; Japan
HARRY'S GAME, Yorkshire Television; United Kingdom

PERFORMING ARTS (E-2167)

DANGEROUS MUSIC, HTV, Ltd.; United Kingdom
OMNIBUS: SERGIO CELIBIDACHE, British Broadcasting Corp.; United Kingdom
THE TURN OF THE SCREW, Westdeutscher Rundfunk; Federal Republic of Germany

POPULAR ARTS (E-2168)

THE BLACK ADDER, British Broadcasting Corp.; United Kingdom
THE MAGIC PLANET, CTV Television Network Ltd.; Canada
NI EN VIVO, NI EN DIRECTO, Television Espanola, S.A.; Spain

CHILDREN'S PROGRAMMING (E-2169)

FRAGGLE ROCK, Canadian Broadcasting Corp.; Canada
GOLD IN THE CHIMNEY, Swiss National Television (RTS 1), Sudwestfunk (SWF), Polivideo; Switzerland-Federal Republic of Germany
THINK AGAIN: DOORS, British Broadcasting Corp.; United Kingdom

INTERNATIONAL DIRECTORATE AWARD (E-2170)

Dr. Robert Marinho

FOUNDERS AWARD (E-2171)

Herbert Brodkin

TONY®S

NOTE: Tony®s were awarded without prior nominations through 1956.

The American Theatre Wing's Antoinette Perry "TONY®" Award

1947

ACTORS (DRAMATIC) (T-01)

Jose Ferrer, Cyrano de Bergerac
Fredric March, Years Ago

ACTRESSES (DRAMATIC) (T-02)

Ingrid Bergman, Joan of Lorraine
Helen Hayes, Happy Birthday

ACTRESS, SUPPORTING OR FEATURED (DRAMATIC) (T-03)

Patricia Neal, Another Part of the Forest

ACTOR, SUPPORTING OR FEATURED (MUSICAL) (T-04)

David Wayne, Finian's Rainbow

DIRECTOR (T-05)

Elia Kazan, All My Sons

COSTUMES (T-06)

Lucinda Ballard, Happy Birthday/Another Part of the Forest/Street Scene/John Loves Mary/The Chocolate Soldier
David Ffolkes, Henry VIII

CHOREOGRAPHERS (T-07)

Agnes de Mille, Brigadoon
Michael Kidd, Finian's Rainbow

SPECIAL AWARDS (T-08)

Dora Chamberlain
Mr. and Mrs. Ira Katzenberg
Jules Leventhal
Burns Mantle
P. A. MacDonald
Arthur Miller
Vincent Sardi, Sr.
Kurt Weill

1948

ACTORS (DRAMATIC) (T-09)

Henry Fonda, Mister Roberts
Paul Kelly, Command Decision
Basil Rathbone, The Heiress

ACTRESSES (DRAMATIC) (T-10)

Judith Anderson, Medea
Katharine Cornell, Antony and Cleopatra
Jessica Tandy, A Streetcar Named Desire

ACTOR (MUSICAL) (T-11)

Paul Hartman, Angel in the Wings

ACTRESS (MUSICAL) (T-12)

Grace Hartman, Angel in the Wings

PLAY (T-13)

Mister Roberts by Thomas Heggen and Joshua Logan, based on the Thomas Heggen novel

PRODUCER (T-14)

Leland Hayward, Mister Roberts

AUTHORS (T-15)

Thomas Heggen and Joshua Logan, Mister Roberts

COSTUMES (T-16)

Mary Percy Schenck, The Heiress

SCENIC DESIGNER (T-17)

Horace Armistead, The Medium

CHOREOGRAPHER (T-18)

Jerome Robbins, High Button Shoes

STAGE TECHNICIANS (T-19)

George Gebhardt
George Pierce

SPECIAL AWARDS (T-20)

Vera Allen
Paul Beisman
Joe E. Brown
Robert Dowling
Experimental Theatre, Inc.
Rosamond Gilder
June Lockhart
Mary Martin
Robert Porterfield
James Whitmore

1949

ACTOR (DRAMATIC) (T-21)

Rex Harrison, Anne of the Thousand Days

ACTRESS (DRAMATIC) (T-22)

Martita Hunt, The Madwoman of Chaillot

ACTOR, SUPPORTING OR FEATURED (DRAMATIC) (T-23)

Arthur Kennedy, Death of a Salesman

ACTRESS, SUPPORTING OR FEATURED (DRAMATIC) (T-24)

Shirley Booth, Goodbye, My Fancy

ACTOR (MUSICAL) (T-25)

Ray Bolger, Where's Charley?

ACTRESS (MUSICAL) (T-26)

Nanette Fabray, Love Life

PLAY (T-27)

Death of a Salesman by Arthur Miller

PRODUCERS (DRAMATIC) (T-28)

Kermit Bloomgarden and Walter Fried, Death of a Salesman

AUTHOR (T-29)

Arthur Miller, Death of a Salesman

DIRECTOR (T-30)

Elia Kazan, Death of a Salesman

MUSICAL (T-31)

Kiss Me Kate, music and lyrics by Cole Porter, book by Bella and Samuel Spewack

PRODUCERS (MUSICAL) (T-32)

Saint-Subber and Lemuel Ayers, Kiss Me Kate

AUTHORS (MUSICAL) (T-33)

Bella and Samuel Spewack, Kiss Me Kate

COMPOSER AND LYRICIST (T-34)

Cole Porter, Kiss Me Kate

COSTUMES (T-35)

Lemuel Ayers, Kiss Me Kate

SCENIC DESIGNER (T-36)

Jo Mielziner, Sleepy Hollow/Summer and Smoke/Anne of the Thousand Days/Death of a Salesman/South Pacific

CHOREOGRAPHER (T-37)

Gower Champion, Lend An Ear

CONDUCTOR AND MUSICAL DIRECTOR (T-38)

Max Meth, As The Girls Go

1950

ACTOR (DRAMATIC) (T-39)

Sidney Blackmer, Come Back, Little Sheba

ACTRESS (DRAMATIC) (T-40)

Shirley Booth, Come Back, Little Sheba

ACTOR (MUSICAL) (T-41)

Ezio Pinza, South Pacific

ACTRESS (MUSICAL) (T-42)

Mary Martin, South Pacific

ACTOR, SUPPORTING OR FEATURED (MUSICAL) (T-43)

Myron McCormick, South Pacific

ACTRESS, SUPPORTING OR FEATURED (MUSICAL) (T-44)

Juanita Hall, South Pacific

PLAY (T-45)

The Cocktail Party by T. S. Eliot

PRODUCER (DRAMATIC) (T-46)

Gilbert Miller, The Cocktail Party

AUTHOR (DRAMATIC) (T-47)

T. S. Eliot, The Cocktail Party

DIRECTOR (T-48)

Joshua Logan, South Pacific

MUSICAL (T-49)

South Pacific, music by Richard Rodgers, lyrics by Oscar Hammerstein II, book by Oscar Hammerstein II and Joshua Logan

PRODUCERS (MUSICAL) (T-50)

Richard Rodgers, Oscar Hammerstein II, Leland Hayward and Joshua Logan, South Pacific

AUTHORS (MUSICAL) (T-51)

Oscar Hammerstein II and Joshua Logan, South Pacific

COMPOSER (T-52)

Richard Rodgers, South Pacific

COSTUMES (T-53)

Aline Bernstein, Regina

SCENIC DESIGNER (T-54)

Jo Mielziner, The Innocents

CHOREOGRAPHER (T-55)

Helen Tamiris, Touch and Go

CONDUCTOR AND MUSICAL DIRECTOR (T-56)

Maurice Abravanel, Regina

STAGE TECHNICIAN (T-57)

Joe Lynn, master propertyman, Miss Liberty

SPECIAL AWARDS (T-58)

Maurice Evans
Mrs. Eleanor Roosevelt presented a special award to a volunteer worker of the American Theatre Wing's hospital program.

1951

ACTOR (DRAMATIC) (T-59)

Claude Rains, Darkness At Noon

ACTRESS (DRAMATIC) (T-60)

Uta Hagen, The Country Girl

ACTOR, SUPPORTING OR FEATURED (DRAMATIC) (T-61)

Eli Wallach, The Rose Tattoo

ACTRESS, SUPPORTING OR FEATURED (DRAMATIC) (T-62)

Maureen Stapleton, The Rose Tattoo

ACTOR (MUSICAL) (T-63)

Robert Alda, Guys and Dolls

ACTRESS (MUSICAL) (T-64)

Ethel Merman, Call Me Madam

ACTOR, SUPPORTING OR FEATURED (MUSICAL) (T-65)

Russell Nype, Call Me Madam

ACTRESS, SUPPORTING OR FEATURED (MUSICAL) (T-66)

Isabel Bigley, Guys and Dolls

PLAY (T-67)

The Rose Tattoo by Tennessee Williams

PRODUCER (DRAMATIC) (T-68)

Cheryl Crawford, The Rose Tattoo

AUTHOR (DRAMATIC) (T-69)

Tennessee Williams, The Rose Tattoo

DIRECTOR (T-70)

George S. Kaufman, Guys and Dolls

MUSICAL (T-71)

Guys and Dolls, music and lyrics by Frank Loesser, book by Jo Swerling and Abe Burrows

PRODUCERS (MUSICAL) (T-72)

Cy Feuer and Ernest H. Martin, Guys and Dolls

AUTHORS (MUSICAL) (T-73)

Jo Swerling and Abe Burrows, Guys and Dolls

COMPOSER AND LYRICIST (T-74)

Frank Loesser, Guys and Dolls

COSTUMES (T-75)

Miles White, Bless You All

SCENIC DESIGNER (T-76)

Boris Aronson, The Rose Tattoo/The Country Girl/Season In The Sun

CHOREOGRAPHER (T-77)

Michael Kidd, Guys and Dolls

CONDUCTOR AND MUSICAL DIRECTOR (T-78)

Lehman Engel, The Consul

STAGE TECHNICIAN (T-79)

Richard Raven, The Autumn Garden

SPECIAL AWARD (T-80)

Ruth Green

1952

ACTOR (DRAMATIC) (T-81)

Jose Ferrer, The Shrike

ACTRESS (DRAMATIC) (T-82)

Julie Harris, I Am a Camera

ACTRESS (MUSICAL) (T-83)

Gertrude Lawrence, The King & I

ACTOR (MUSICAL) (T-84)

Phil Silvers, Top Banana

ACTOR, SUPPORTING OR FEATURED (DRAMATIC) (T-85)

John Cromwell, Point of No Return

ACTRESS, SUPPORTING OR FEATURED (DRAMATIC) (T-86)

Marian Winters, I Am a Camera

ACTOR, SUPPORTING OR FEATURED (MUSICAL) (T-87)

Yul Brynner, The King & I

ACTRESS, SUPPORTING OR FEATURED (MUSICAL) (T-88)

Helen Gallagher, Pal Joey

PLAY (T-89)

The Fourposter by Jan de Hartog

MUSICAL (T-90)

The King & I, book and lyrics by Oscar Hammerstein II, music by Richard Rodgers

DIRECTOR (T-91)

Jose Ferrer, The Shrike/The Fourposter/Stalag 17

COSTUMES (T-92)

Irene Sharaff, The King & I

SCENIC DESIGNER (T-93)

Jo Mielziner, The King & I

CHOREOGRAPHER (T-94)

Robert Alton, Pal Joey

CONDUCTOR AND MUSICAL DIRECTOR (T-95)

Max Meth, Pal Joey

STAGE TECHNICIAN (T-96)

Peter Feller, master carpenter for Call Me Madam

SPECIAL AWARDS (T-97)

Edward Kook
Judy Garland
Charles Boyer

1953

ACTOR (DRAMATIC) (T-98)

Tom Ewell, The Seven Year Itch

ACTRESS (DRAMATIC) (T-99)

Shirley Booth, Time of the Cuckoo

ACTOR, SUPPORTING OR FEATURED (DRAMATIC) (T-100)

John Williams, Dial M for Murder

ACTRESS, SUPPORTING OR FEATURED (DRAMATIC) (T-101)

Beatrice Straight, The Crucible

ACTOR (MUSICAL) (T-102)

Thomas Mitchell, Hazel Flagg

ACTRESS (MUSICAL) (T-103)

Rosalind Russell, Wonderful Town

ACTOR, SUPPORTING OR FEATURED (MUSICAL) (T-104)

Hiram Sherman, Two's Company

ACTRESS, SUPPORTING OR FEATURED (MUSICAL) (T-105)

Sheila Bond, Wish You Were Here

PLAY (T-106)

The Crucible by Arthur Miller

PRODUCER (DRAMATIC) (T-107)

Kermit Bloomgarden, The Crucible

AUTHOR (DRAMATIC) (T-108)

Arthur Miller, The Crucible

DIRECTOR (T-109)

Joshua Logan, Picnic

MUSICAL (T-110)

Wonderful Town, book by Joseph Fields and Jerome Chodorov, music by Leonard Bernstein, lyrics by Betty Comden and Adolph Green

PRODUCER (MUSICAL) (T-111)

Robert Fryer, Wonderful Town

AUTHORS (MUSICAL) (T-112)
Joseph Fields and Jerome Chodorov, Wonderful Town

COMPOSER (T-113)
Leonard Bernstein, Wonderful Town

COSTUME DESIGNER (T-114)
Miles White, Hazel Flagg

SCENIC DESIGNER (T-115)
Raoul Pene du Bois, Wonderful Town

CHOREOGRAPHER (T-116)
Donald Saddler, Wonderful Town

CONDUCTOR AND MUSICAL DIRECTOR (T-117)
Lehman Engel, Wonderful Town and Gilbert and Sullivan Season

STAGE TECHNICIAN (T-118)
Abe Kurnit, Wish You Were Here

SPECIAL AWARDS (T-119)
Beatrice Lillie
Danny Kaye
Equity Community Theatre

1954

ACTOR (DRAMATIC) (T-120)
David Wayne, The Teahouse of the August Moon

ACTRESS (DRAMATIC) (T-121)
Audrey Hepburn, Ondine

ACTOR, SUPPORTING OR FEATURED (DRAMATIC) (T-122)
John Kerr, Tea and Sympathy

ACTRESS, SUPPORTING OR FEATURED (DRAMATIC) (T-123)
Jo Van Fleet, The Trip to Bountiful

ACTOR (MUSICAL) (T-124)
Alfred Drake, Kismet

ACTRESS (MUSICAL) (T-125)
Dolores Gray, Carnival in Flanders

ACTOR, SUPPORTING OR FEATURED (MUSICAL) (T-126)
Harry Belafonte, John Murray Anderson's Almanac

ACTRESS, SUPPORTING OR FEATURED (MUSICAL) (T-127)
Gwen Verdon, Can-Can

PLAY (T-128)
The Teahouse of the August Moon by John Patrick

PRODUCER (DRAMATIC) (T-129)
Maurice Evans and George Schaefer, The Teahouse of the August Moon

AUTHOR (DRAMATIC) (T-130)
John Patrick, The Teahouse of the August Moon

DIRECTOR (T-131)
Alfred Lunt, Ondine

MUSICAL (T-132)
Kismet, book by Charles Lederer and Luther Davis, music by Alexander Borodin, adapted and with lyrics by Robert Wright and George Forrest

PRODUCER (MUSICAL) (T-133)
Charles Lederer, Kismet

AUTHOR (MUSICAL) (T-134)
Charles Lederer and Luther Davis, Kismet

COMPOSER (T-135)
Alexander Borodin, Kismet

COSTUME DESIGNER (T-136)
Richard Whorf, Ondine

SCENIC DESIGNER (T-137)
Peter Larkin, Ondine and The Teahouse of the August Moon

CHOREOGRAPHER (T-138)
Michael Kidd, Can-Can

MUSICAL CONDUCTOR (T-139)
Louis Adrian, Kismet

STAGE TECHNICIAN (T-140)
John Davis, Picnic

1955

ACTOR (DRAMATIC) (T-141)
Alfred Lunt, Quadrille

ACTRESS (DRAMATIC) (T-142)
Nancy Kelly, The Bad Seed

ACTOR, SUPPORTING OR FEATURED (DRAMATIC) (T-143)
Francis L. Sullivan, Witness for the Prosecution

ACTRESS, SUPPORTING OR FEATURED (DRAMATIC) (T-144)
Patricia Jessel, Witness for The Prosecution

ACTOR (MUSICAL) (T-145)
Walter Slezak, Fanny

ACTRESS (MUSICAL) (T-146)
Mary Martin, Peter Pan

ACTOR, SUPPORTING OR FEATURED (MUSICAL) (T-147)
Cyril Ritchard, Peter Pan

ACTRESS, SUPPORTING OR FEATURED (MUSICAL) (T-148)
Carol Haney, The Pajama Game

PLAY (T-149)
The Desperate Hours by Joseph Hayes

PRODUCERS (DRAMATIC) (T-150)
Howard Erskine and Joseph Hayes, The Desperate Hours

AUTHOR (DRAMATIC) (T-151)
Joseph Hayes, The Desperate Hours

DIRECTOR (T-152)
Robert Montgomery, The Desperate Hours

MUSICAL (T-153)
The Pajama Game, book by George Abbott and Richard Bissell, music and lyrics by Richard Adler and Jerry Ross

PRODUCERS (MUSICAL) (T-154)
Frederick Brisson, Robert Griffith and Harold S. Prince, The Pajama Game

AUTHORS (MUSICAL) (T-155)
George Abbott and Richard Bissell, The Pajama Game

COMPOSER AND LYRICIST (T-156)
Richard Adler and Jerry Ross, The Pajama Game

COSTUME DESIGNER (T-157)
Cecil Beaton, Quadrille

SCENIC DESIGNER (T-158)
Oliver Messel, House of Flowers

CHOREOGRAPHER (T-159)
Bob Fosse, The Pajama Game

CONDUCTOR AND MUSICAL DIRECTOR (T-160)
Thomas Schippers, The Saint of Bleecker Street

STAGE TECHNICIAN (T-161)
Richard Rodda, Peter Pan

SPECIAL AWARD (T-162)
Proscenium Productions

1956

ACTOR (DRAMATIC) (T-163)
Ben Gazzara, A Hatful of Rain
Boris Karloff, The Lark
Paul Muni, Inherit the Wind
Michael Redgrave, Tiger at the Gates
Edward G. Robinson, The Middle of the Night

ACTRESS (DRAMATIC) (T-164)
Barbara Bel Geddes, Cat on a Hot Tin Roof
Gladys Cooper, The Chalk Garden
Ruth Gordon, The Matchmaker
Julie Harris, The Lark
Siobhan McKenna, The Chalk Garden
Susan Strasberg, The Diary of Anne Frank

ACTOR, SUPPORTING OR FEATURED (DRAMATIC) (T-165)
Ed Begley, Inherit the Wind
Anthony Franciosa, A Hatful of Rain
Andy Griffith, No Time for Sergeants
Anthony Quayle, Tamburlaine the Great
Fritz Weaver, The Chalk Garden

ACTRESS, SUPPORTING OR FEATURED (DRAMATIC) (T-166)
Diane Cilento, Tiger at the Gates
Anne Jackson, The Middle of the Night

Una Merkel, The Ponder Heart
Elaine Stritch, Bus Stop

ACTOR (MUSICAL) (T-167)
Stephen Douglass, Damn Yankees
William Johnson, Pipe Dream
Ray Walston, Damn Yankees

ACTRESS (MUSICAL) (T-168)
Carol Channing, The Vamp
Gwen Verdon, Damn Yankees
Nancy Walker, Phoenix '55

ACTOR, SUPPORTING OR FEATURED (MUSICAL) (T-169)
Russ Brown, Damn Yankees
Mike Kellin, Pipe Dream
Will Mahoney, City Center Finian's Rainbow
Scott Merrill, The Threepenny Opera

ACTRESS, SUPPORTING OR FEATURED (MUSICAL) (T-170)
Rae Allen, Damn Yankees
Pat Carroll, Catch a Star
Lotte Lenya, The Threepenny Opera
Judy Tyler, Pipe Dream

PLAY (T-171)
Bus Stop by William Inge; Producers Robert Whitehead and Roger L. Stevens
Cat on a Hot Tin Roof by Tennessee Williams; Producer The Playwrights' Company
The Diary of Anne Frank by Frances Goodrich and Albert Hackett; Producer Kermit Bloomgarden
Tiger at the Gates by Jean Giraudoux, adapted by Christopher Fry; Producers Robert L. Joseph, The Playwrights' Company and Henry M. Margolis
The Chalk Garden by Enid Bagnold; Producer Irene Mayer Selznick

AUTHORS (DRAMATIC) (T-172)
Frances Goodrich and Albert Hackett, The Diary of Anne Frank

PRODUCER (DRAMATIC) (T-173)
Kermit Bloomgarden, The Diary of Anne Frank

DIRECTOR (T-174)
Joseph Anthony, The Lark
Harold Clurman, Bus Stop/Pipe Dream/Tiger at the Gates
Tyrone Guthrie, The Matchmaker/Six Characters in Search of an Author/Tamburlaine the Great
Garson Kanin, The Diary of Anne Frank
Elia Kazan, Cat on a Hot Tin Roof
Albert Marre, The Chalk Garden
Herman Shumlin, Inherit the Wind

MUSICAL (T-175)
Damn Yankees by George Abbott and Douglass Wallop. Music by Richard Adler and Jerry Ross; Producers Frederick Brisson, Robert Griffith, Harold S. Prince in association with Albert B. Taylor
Pipe Dream. Book and lyrics by Oscar Hammerstein II, music by Richard Rodgers; Producers Rodgers and Hammerstein

AUTHORS (MUSICAL) (T-176)
George Abbott and Douglass Wallop, Damn Yankees

PRODUCERS (MUSICAL) (T-177)
Frederick Brisson, Robert Griffith, Harold S. Prince in association with Albert B. Taylor, Damn Yankees

COMPOSER AND LYRICIST (T-178)
Richard Adler and Jerry Ross, Damn Yankees

CONDUCTOR AND MUSICAL DIRECTOR (T-179)

Salvatore Dell'Isola, Pipe Dream
Hal Hastings, Damn Yankees
Milton Rosenstock, The Vamp

SCENIC DESIGNER (T-180)

Boris Aronson, The Diary of Anne Frank/Bus Stop/Once Upon a Tailor/A View from the Bridge
Ben Edwards, The Ponder Heart/Someone Waiting/The Honeys
Peter Larkin, Inherit the Wind/No Time for Sergeants
Jo Mielziner, Cat on a Hot Tin Roof/The Lark/The Middle of the Night/Pipe Dream
Raymond Sovey, The Great Sebastians

COSTUME DESIGNER (T-181)

Mainbocher, The Great Sebastians
Alvin Colt, The Lark/Phoenix '55/*Pipe Dream
Helene Pons, The Diary of Anne Frank/Heavenly Twins/A View from the Bridge

CHOREOGRAPHER (T-182)

Robert Alton, The Vamp
Bob Fosse, Damn Yankees
Boris Runanin, Phoenix '55/Pipe Dream
Anna Sokolow, Red Roses for Me

STAGE TECHNICIAN (T-183)

Larry Bland, carpenter, The Middle of the Night/The Ponder Heart/Porgy and Bess
Harry Green, electrician and sound man, The Middle of the Night/Damn Yankees

SPECIAL AWARDS (T-184)

The Threepenny Opera
The Theatre Collection of the N. Y. Public Library

1957

ACTOR (DRAMATIC) (T-185)

Maurice Evans, The Apple Cart
Wilfred Hyde-White, The Reluctant Debutante
Fredric March, Long Day's Journey Into Night
Eric Portman, Separate Tables
Ralph Richardson, The Waltz Of The Toreadors
Cyril Ritchard, A Visit To A Small Planet

ACTRESS (DRAMATIC) (T-186)

Florence Eldridge, Long Day's Journey Into Night
Margaret Leighton, Separate Tables
Rosalind Russell, Auntie Mame
Sybil Thorndike, The Potting Shed

ACTOR, SUPPORTING OR FEATURED (DRAMATIC) (T-187)

Frank Conroy, The Potting Shed
Eddie Mayehoff, A Visit To A Small Planet
William Podmore, Separate Tables
Jason Robards, Jr., Long Day's Journey Into Night

ACTRESS, SUPPORTING OR FEATURED (DRAMATIC) (T-188)

Peggy Cass, Auntie Mame
Anna Massey, The Reluctant Debutante
Beryl Measor, Separate Tables
Mildred Natwick, The Waltz Of The Toreadors
Phyllis Neilson-Terry, Separate Tables
Diana Van Der Vlis, The Happiest Millionaire

ACTOR (MUSICAL) (T-189)

Rex Harrison, My Fair Lady
Fernando Lamas, Happy Hunting
Robert Weede, The Most Happy Fella

ACTRESS (MUSICAL) (T-190)

Julie Andrews, My Fair Lady
Judy Holliday, Bells Are Ringing
Ethel Merman, Happy Hunting

ACTOR, SUPPORTING OR FEATURED (MUSICAL) (T-191)

Sydney Chaplin, Bells Are Ringing
Robert Coote, My Fair Lady
Stanley Holloway, My Fair Lady

ACTRESS, SUPPORTING OR FEATURED (MUSICAL) (T-192)

Edith Adams, Li'l Abner
Virginia Gibson, Happy Hunting
Irra Petina, Candide
Jo Sullivan, The Most Happy Fella

PLAY (T-193)

Long Day's Journey Into Night by Eugene O'Neill; Producers Leigh Connell, Theodore Mann and Jose Quintero
Separate Tables by Terence Rattigan; Producers The Producers Theatre and Hecht-Lancaster
The Potting Shed by Graham Greene; Producers Carmen Capalbo and Stanley Chase
The Waltz Of The Toreadors by Jean Anouilh, translated by Lucienne Hill; Producer The Producers Theatre (Robert Whitehead)

AUTHOR (DRAMATIC) (T-194)

Eugene O'Neill, Long Day's Journey Into Night

PRODUCER (DRAMATIC) (T-195)

Leigh Connell, Theodore Mann and Jose Qintero, Long Day's Journey Into Night

DIRECTOR (T-196)

Joseph Anthony, A Clearing in the Woods/The Most Happy Fella
Harold Clurman, The Waltz of the Toreadors
Peter Glenville, Separate Tables
Moss Hart, My Fair Lady
Jose Quintero, Long Day's Journey Into Night

MUSICAL (T-197)

Bells Are Ringing. Book and lyrics by Betty Comden and Adolph Green, music by Jule Styne; Producer The Theatre Guild
Candide. Book by Lillian Hellman, music by Leonard Bernstein, lyrics by Richard Wilbur; Producer Ethel Linder Reiner in association with Lester Osterman, Jr.
My Fair Lady. Book and lyrics by Alan Jay Lerner, music by Frederick Loewe; Producer Herman Levin
The Most Happy Fella. Book, music and lyrics by Frank Loesser; Producers Kermit Bloomgarden and Lynn Loesser

AUTHOR (MUSICAL) (T-198)

Alan Jay Lerner, My Fair Lady

PRODUCER (MUSICAL) (T-199)

Heman Levin, My Fair Lady

COMPOSER (T-200)

Frederick Loewe, My Fair Lady

CONDUCTOR AND MUSICAL DIRECTOR (T-201)

Franz Allers, My Fair Lady
Herbert Greene, The Most Happy Fella
Samuel Krachmalnick, Candide

SCENIC DESIGNER (T-202)

Boris Aronson, A Hole In The Head/Small War on Murray Hill
Ben Edwards, The Waltz Of The Toreadors
George Jenkins, The Happiest Millionaire/Too Late The Phalarope
Donald Oenslager, Major Barbara

Oliver Smith, A Clearing in the Woods/Candide/Auntie Mame/*My Fair Lady/Eugenia/A Visit To A Small Planet

COSTUME DESIGNER (T-203)

Cecil Beaton, Little Glass Clock/*My Fair Lady
Alvin Colt, Li'l Abner/The Sleeping Prince
Dorothy Jeakins, Major Barbara/Too Late The Phalarope
Irene Sharaff, Candide/Happy Hunting/Shangri La/Small War on Murray Hill

CHOREOGRAPHER (T-204)

Hanya Holm, My Fair Lady

Michael Kidd, Li'l Abner
Dania Krupska, The Most Happy Fella
Jerome Robbins and Bob Fosse, Bells Are Ringing

STAGE TECHNICIAN (T-205)

Thomas Fitzgerald, sound man, Long Day's Journey Into Night
Joseph Harbach, carpenter, Auntie Mame

Howard McDonald (posthumous), carpenter, Major Barbara

SPECIAL AWARDS (T-206)

American Shakespeare Festival
Jean-Louis Barrault French Repertory
Robert Russell Bennett
William Hammerstein
Paul Shyre

1958

ACTOR (DRAMATIC) (T-207)

Ralph Bellamy, Sunrise At Campobello
Richard Burton, Time Remembered
Hugh Griffith, Look Homeward, Angel
Laurence Olivier, The Entertainer
Anthony Perkins, Look Homeward, Angel
Peter Ustinov, Romanoff and Juliet
Emlyn Williams, A Boy Growing Up

ACTRESS (DRAMATIC) (T-208)

Wendy Hiller, A Moon For The Misbegotten
Eugenie Leontovich, The Cave Dwellers

Helen Hayes, Time Remembered
Siobhan McKenna, The Rope Dancers
Mary Ure, Look Back In Anger
Jo Van Fleet, Look Homeward, Angel

ACTOR, SUPPORTING OR FEATURED (DRAMATIC) (T-209)

Henry Jones, Sunrise At Campobello

ACTRESS, SUPPORTING OR FEATURED (DRAMATIC) (T-210)

Anne Bancroft, Two For The Seesaw

ACTOR (MUSICAL) (T-211)

Ricardo Montalban, Jamaica

Robert Preston, The Music Man
Eddie Foy, Jr., Rumple
Tony Randall, Oh, Captain!

ACTRESS (MUSICAL) (T-212)

Thelma Ritter, New Girl In Town
Lena Horne, Jamaica
Beatrice Lillie, Ziegfeld Follies
Gwen Verdon, New Girl In Town

ACTOR, SUPPORTING OR FEATURED (MUSICAL) (T-213)

David Burns, The Music Man

ACTRESS, SUPPORTING OR FEATURED (MUSICAL) (T-214)

Barbara Cook, The Music Man

PLAY (T-215)

The Rope Dancers by Morton Wishengrad
Two For The Seesaw by William Gibson
Time Remembered by Jean Anouilh. English version by Patricia Moyes
The Dark at the Top of the Stairs by William Inge
Look Back In Anger by John Osborne
Romanoff and Juliet by Peter Ustinov
Sunrise At Campobello by Dore Schary

AUTHOR (DRAMATIC) (T-216)

Dore Schary, Sunrise At Campobello

PRODUCERS (DRAMATIC) (T-217)

Lawrence Langner, Theresa Helburn, Armina Marshall and Dore Schary, Sunrise At Campobello

DIRECTOR (DRAMATIC) (T-218)

Vincent J. Donehue, Sunrise At Campobello

MUSICAL (T-219)

West Side Story. Book by Arthur Laurents, music by Leonard Bernstein, lyrics by Stephen Sondheim
New Girl In Town. Book by George Abbott, music and lyrics by Bob Merrill
The Music Man. Book by Meredith Willson and Franklin Lacey, music and lyrics by Meredith Willson
Oh, Captain!. Book by Al Morgan and Jose Ferrer, music and lyrics by Jay Livingston and Ray Evans
Jamaica. Book by E. Y. Harburg and Fred Saidy, music by Harold Arlen, lyrics by E. Y. Harburg

AUTHOR (MUSICAL) (T-220)

Meredith Willson and Franklin Lacey, The Music Man

PRODUCER (MUSICAL) (T-221)

Kermit Bloomgarden, Herbert Greene, Frank Productions, The Music Man

COMPOSER AND LYRICIST (T-222)

Meredith Willson, The Music Man

CONDUCTOR AND MUSICAL DIRECTOR (T-223)

Herbert Greene, The Music Man

SCENIC DESIGNER (T-224)

Oliver Smith, West Side Story

COSTUME DESIGNER (T-225)

Motley, The First Gentleman

CHOREOGRAPHER (T-226)

Jerome Robbins, West Side Story

STAGE TECHNICIAN (T-227)

Harry Romar, Time Remembered

SPECIAL AWARDS (T-228)

The New York Shakespeare Festival
Mrs. Martin Beck

1959

ACTOR (DRAMATIC) (T-229)
Cedric Hardwicke, A Majority of One
Alfred Lunt, The Visit
Christopher Plummer, J. B.
Cyril Ritchard, The Pleasure of His Company
Jason Robards, Jr., The Disenchanted
Robert Stephens, Epitaph for George Dillon

ACTRESS (DRAMATIC) (T-230)
Gertrude Berg, A Majority of One
Claudette Colbert, The Marriage-Go-Round
Lynn Fontanne, The Visit
Kim Stanley, A Touch of the Poet
Maureen Stapleton, The Cold Wind and the Warm

ACTOR, SUPPORTING OR FEATURED (DRAMATIC) (T-231)
Marc Connelly, Tall Story
George Grizzard, The Disenchanted
Walter Matthau, Once More, With Feeling
Robert Morse, Say, Darling
Charlie Ruggles, The Pleasure of His Company
George Scott, Comes a Day

ACTRESS, SUPPORTING OR FEATURED (DRAMATIC) (T-232)
Maureen Delany, God and Kate Murphy
Dolores Hart, The Pleasure of His Company
Julie Newmar, The Marriage-Go-Round
Nan Martin, J. B.
Beatrice Reading, Requiem for a Nun

ACTOR (MUSICAL) (T-233)
Larry Blyden, Flower Drum Song
Richard Kiley, Redhead

ACTRESS (MUSICAL) (T-234)
Miyoshi Umeki, Flower Drum Song
Gwen Verdon, Redhead

ACTOR, SUPPORTING OR FEATURED (MUSICAL) (T-235)
Russell Nype, Goldilocks
Leonard Stone, Redhead
Cast of La Plume de Ma Tante

ACTRESS, SUPPORTING OR FEATURED (MUSICAL) (T-236)
Julienne Marie, Whoop-Up
Pat Stanley, Goldilocks
Cast of La Plume de Ma Tante

PLAY (T-237)
A Touch of the Poet by Eugene O'Neill; Producers The Producers Theatre, Robert Whitehead and Roger L. Stevens
Epitaph for George Dillon by John Osborne and Anthony Creighton; Producer David Merrick and Joshua Logan
J. B. by Archibald MacLeish; Producer Alfred de Liagre, Jr.
The Disenchanted by Budd Schulberg and Harvey Breit; Producers William Darrid and Eleanor Saidenberg
The Visit by Friedrich Duerrenmatt, adapted by Maurice Valency; Producer The Producers Theatre

AUTHOR (DRAMATIC) (T-238)
Archibald MacLeish, J. B.

PRODUCER (DRAMATIC) (T-239)
Alfred de Liagre, Jr., J. B.

DIRECTOR (T-240)
Peter Brook, The Visit
Robert Dhery, La Plume de Ma Tante
William Gaskill, Epitaph for George Dillon
Peter Glenville, Rashomon
Elia Kazan, J. B.
Cyril Ritchard, The Pleasure of His Company
Dore Schary, A Majority of One

MUSICAL (T-241)
Flower Drum Song, book by Oscar Hammerstein II and Joseph Fields, lyrics by Oscar Hammerstein II, music by Richard Rodgers
La Plume de Ma Tante, written, devised and directed by Robert Dhery, music by Gerard Calvi, English lyrics by Ross Parker. (David Merrick and Joseph Kipness present the Jack Hylton Production)
Redhead by Herbert and Dorothy Fields, Sidney Sheldon and David Shaw, music by Albert Hague, lyrics by Dorothy Fields

AUTHORS (MUSICAL) (T-242)
Herbert and Dorothy Fields, Sidney Sheldon and David Shaw, Redhead

PRODUCERS (MUSICAL) (T-243)
Robert Fryer and Lawrence Carr, Redhead

COMPOSER (T-244)
Albert Hague, Redhead

CONDUCTOR AND MUSICAL DIRECTOR (T-245)
Jay Blackston, Redhead
Salvatore Dell'Isola, Flower Drum Song
Lehman Engel, Goldilocks
Gershon Kingsley, La Plume de Ma Tante

SCENIC DESIGNER (T-246)
Boris Aronson, J. B.
Ballou, The Legend of Lizzie
Ben Edwards, Jane Eyre
Oliver Messel, Rashomon
Donald Oenslager, A Majority of One
Teo Otto, The Visit

COSTUME DESIGNER (T-247)
Castillo, Goldilocks
Dorothy Jeakins, The World of Suzie Wong
Oliver Messel, Rashomon
Irene Sharaff, Flower Drum Song
Rouben Ter-Arutunian, Redhead

CHOREOGRAPHER (T-248)
Agnes de Mille, Goldilocks
Bob Fosse, Redhead
Carol Haney, Flower Drum Song
Onna White, Whoop-Up

STAGE TECHNICIAN (T-249)
Thomas Fitzgerald, Who Was That Lady I Saw You With?
Edward Flynn, The Most Happy Fella (City Center Revival)
Sam Knapp, The Music Man

SPECIAL AWARDS (T-250)
John Gielgud
Howard Lindsay and Russel Crouse

1960

ACTOR (DRAMATIC) (T-251)

Melvyn Douglas, The Best Man
Lee Tracy, The Best Man
Jason Robards, Jr., Toys in the Attic
Sidney Poitier, A Raisin in the Sun
George C. Scott, The Andersonville Trial

ACTRESS (DRAMATIC) (T-252)

Anne Bancroft, The Miracle Worker
Margaret Leighton, Much Ado About Nothing
Claudia McNeil, A Raisin in the Sun
Geraldine Page, Sweet Bird of Youth
Maureen Stapleton, Toys in the Attic
Irene Worth, Toys in the Attic

ACTOR, SUPPORTING OR FEATURED (DRAMATIC) (T-253)

Warren Beatty, A Loss of Roses
Harry Guardino, One More River
Roddy McDowall, The Fighting Cock
Rip Torn, Sweet Bird of Youth
Lawrence Winters, The Long Dream

ACTRESS, SUPPORTING OR FEATURED (DRAMATIC) (T-254)

Leora Dana, The Best Man
Jane Fonda, There Was a Little Girl
Sarah Marshall, Goodbye, Charlie
Juliet Mills, Five Finger Exercise
Anne Revere, Toys in the Attic

ACTOR (MUSICAL) (T-255)

Jackie Gleason, Take Me Along
Robert Morse, Take Me Along
Walter Pidgeon, Take Me Along
Andy Griffith, Destry Rides Again
Anthony Perkins, Greenwillow

ACTRESS (MUSICAL) (T-256)

Carol Burnett, One Upon a Mattress
Dolores Gray, Destry Rides Again
Eileen Herlie, Take Me Along
Mary Martin, The Sound of Music
Ethel Merman, Gypsy

ACTOR, SUPPORTING OR FEATURED (MUSICAL) (T-257)

Theodore Bikel, The Sound of Music
Kurt Kasznar, The Sound of Music
Tom Bosley, Fiorello!
Howard Da Silva, Fiorello!
Jack Klugman, Gypsy

ACTRESS, SUPPORTING OR FEATURED (MUSICAL) (T-258)

Sandra Church, Gypsy
Pert Kelton, Greenwillow
Patricia Neway, The Sound of Music
Lauri Peters, The Sound of Music
The Children, The Sound of Music

PLAY (T-259)

A Raisin in the Sun by Lorraine Hansberry; Producers Philip Rose and David J. Cogan

The Best Man by Gore Vidal; Producer The Playwrights' Company
The Miracle Worker by William Gibson. Produced by Fred Coe
The Tenth Man by Paddy Chayefsky; Producers Saint-Subber and Arthur Cantor
Toys in the Attic by Lillian Hellman; Producer Kermit Bloomgarden

AUTHOR (DRAMATIC) (T-260)

William Gibson, The Miracle Worker

PRODUCER (DRAMATIC) (T-261)

Fred Coe, The Miracle Worker

DIRECTOR (DRAMATIC) (T-262)

Joseph Anthony, The Best Man
Tyrone Guthrie, The Tenth Man
Elia Kazan, Sweet Bird of Youth
Arthur Penn, The Miracle Worker
Lloyd Richards, A Raisin in the Sun

MUSICAL (T-263)

Fiorello! by Jerome Weidman and George Abbott. Lyrics by Sheldon Harnick, music by Jerry Bock; Producers Robert E. Griffith and Harold S. Prince
Gypsy by Arthur Laurents. Lyrics by Stephen Sondheim, music by Jule Styne; Producers David Merrick and Leland Hayward
Once Upon a Mattress, book by Jay Thompson, Marshall Barer, Dean Fuller, lyrics by Marshall Barer, music by Mary Rodgers; Producers T. Edward Hambleton, Norris Houghton, William and Jean Eckart
Take Me Along. Book by Joseph Stein and Robert Russell, lyrics and music by Bob Merrill; Producer David Merrick.
The Sound of Music. Book by Howard Lindsay and Russel Crouse, lyrics by Oscar Hammerstein II, music by Richard Rodgers; Producers Leland Hayward, Richard Halliday, Rodgers and Hammerstein

AUTHORS (MUSICAL) (T-264)

Jerome Weidman and George Abbott, Fiorello!
Howard Lindsay and Russel Crouse, The Sound of Music

PRODUCER (MUSICAL) (T-265)

Robert Griffith and Harold Prince, Fiorello!
Leland Hayward and Richard Halliday, The Sound of Music

DIRECTOR (MUSICAL) (T-266)

George Abbott, Fiorello!
Vincent J. Donehue, The Sound of Music
Peter Glenville, Take Me Along
Michael Kidd, Destry Rides Again
Jerome Robbins, Gypsy

COMPOSERS (T-267)

Jerry Bock, Fiorello!
Richard Rodgers, The Sound of Music

CONDUCTOR AND MUSICAL DIRECTOR (T-268)

Abba Bogin, Greenwillow
Frederick Dvonch, The Sound of Music
Lehman Engel, Take Me Along
Hal Hastings, Fiorello!
Milton Rosenstock, Gypsy

SCENIC DESIGNER (DRAMATIC) (T-269)

Will Steven Armstrong, Caligula
Howard Bay, Toys in the Attic
David Hays, The Tenth Man
George Jenkins, The Miracle Worker
Jo Mielziner, The Best Man

SCENIC DESIGNER (MUSICAL) (T-270)
Cecil Beaton, Saratoga
William and Jean Eckart, Fiorello!
Peter Larkin, Greenwillow
Jo Mielziner, Gypsy
Oliver Smith, The Sound of Music

COSTUME DESIGNER (T-271)
Cecil Beaton, Saratoga
Alvin Colt, Greenwillow
Raoul Pene Du Bois, Gypsy
Miles White, Take Me Along

CHOREOGRAPHER (T-272)
Peter Gennaro, Fiorello!
Michael Kidd, Destry Rides Again
Joe Layton, Greenwillow
Lee Scott, Happy Town
Onna White, Take Me Along

STAGE TECHNICIAN (T-273)
Al Alloy, chief electrician, Take Me Along
James Orr, chief electrician, Greenwillow
John Walters, chief carpenter, The Miracle Worker

SPECIAL AWARDS (T-274)
John D. Rockefeller III
James Thurber and Burgess Meredith, A Thurber Carnival

1961

ACTOR (DRAMATIC) (T-275)
Hume Cronyn, Big Fish, Little Fish
Sam Levene, The Devil's Advocate
Zero Mostel, Rhinoceros
Anthony Quinn, Becket

ACTRESS (DRAMATIC) (T-276)
Tallulah Bankhead, Midgie Purvis
Barbara Baxley, Period of Adjustment
Barbara Bel Geddes, Mary, Mary
Joan Plowright, A Taste of Honey

ACTOR, SUPPORTING OR FEATURED (DRAMATIC) (T-277)
Philip Bosco, The Rape of the Belt
Eduardo Ciannelli, The Devil's Advocate
Martin Gabel, Big Fish, Little Fish
George Grizzard, Big Fish, Little Fish

ACTRESS, SUPPORTING OR FEATURED (DRAMATIC) (T-278)
Colleen Dewhurst, All the Way Home
Eileen Heckart, Invitation to a March
Tresa Hughes, The Devil's Advocate
Rosemary Murphy, Period of Adjustment

ACTOR (MUSICAL) (T-279)
Richard Burton, Camelot
Phil Silvers, Do Re Mi
Maurice Evans, Tenderloin

ACTRESS (MUSICAL) (T-280)
Julie Andrews, Camelot
Carol Channing, Show Girl
Elizabeth Seal, Irma la Douce
Nancy Walker, Do Re Mi

ACTOR, SUPPORTING OR FEATURED (MUSICAL) (T-281)
Clive Revill, Irma la Douce
Dick Gautier, Bye, Bye Birdie
Ron Husmann, Tenderloin
Dick Van Dyke, Bye, Bye Birdie

ACTRESS, SUPPORTING OR FEATURED (MUSICAL) (T-282)
Nancy Dussault, Do Re Mi
Tammy Grimes, The Unsinkable Molly Brown
Chita Rivera, Bye, Bye Birdie

PLAY (T-283)
All the Way Home by Tad Mosel; Producer Fred Coe in association with Arthur Cantor
Becket by Jean Anouilh, translated by Lucienne Hill; Producer David Merrick
The Devil's Advocate by Dore Schary; Producer Dore Schary
The Hostage by Brendan Behan; Producers S. Field and Caroline Burke Swann

AUTHOR (DRAMATIC) (T-284)
Jean Anouilh, Becket

PRODUCER (DRAMATIC) (T-285)
David Merrick, Becket

DIRECTOR (DRAMATIC) (T-286)
Joseph Anthony, Rhinoceros
Sir John Gielgud, Big Fish, Little Fish
Joan Littlewood, The Hostage
Arthur Penn, All the Way Home

MUSICAL (T-287)
Bye, Bye Birdie. Book by Michael Stewart, music by Charles Strouse, lyrics by Lee Adams; Producer Edward Padula in association with L. Slade Brown
Do Re Mi. Book by Garson Kanin, music by Jule Styne, lyrics by Betty Comden and Adolph Green; Producer David Merrick
Irma la Douce. Book and lyrics by Alexandre Breffort, music by Marguerite Monnot. English book and lyrics by Julian More, David Heneker and Monty Norman. Producer David Merrick in association with Donald Albery and H. M. Tennent, Ltd.

AUTHOR (MUSICAL) (T-288)
Michael Stewart, Bye, Bye Birdie

PRODUCER (MUSICAL) (T-289)
Edward Padula, Bye, Bye Birdie

DIRECTOR (MUSICAL) (T-290)
Peter Brook, Irma la Douce
Gower Champion, Bye, Bye Birdie
Garson Kanin, Do Re Mi

CONDUCTOR AND MUSICAL DIRECTOR (T-291)
Franz Allers, Camelot
Pembroke Davenport, 13 Daughters
Stanley Lebowsky, Irma la Douce
Elliott Lawrence, Bye, Bye Birdie

SCENIC DESIGNER (DRAMATIC) (T-292)
Roger Furse, Duel of Angels
David Hays, All the Way Home
Jo Mielziner, The Devil's Advocate
Oliver Smith, Becket
Rouben Ter-Arutunian, Advise and Consent

A Photo Gallery of Tony Winners

Lauren Bacall

Anne Bancroft

Shirley Booth

Richard Burton

Gower Champion

Sandy Dennis

Bob Fosse

Julie Harris

Helen Hayes

Dustin Hoffman

Margaret Leighton

Walter Matthau

Mike Nichols

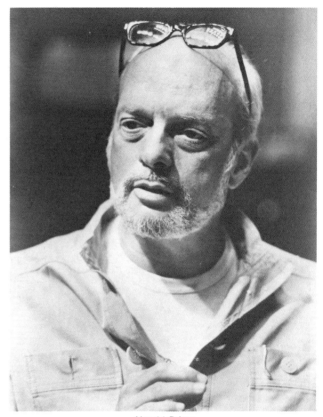

Harold Prince

Jason Robards

George C. Scott

SCENIC DESIGNER (MUSICAL) (T-293)

George Jenkins, 13 Daughters
Robert Randolph, Bye, Bye Birdie
Oliver Smith, Camelot

COSTUME DESIGNER (DRAMATIC) (T-294)

Theoni V. Aldredge, The Devil's Advocate
Motley, Becket
Raymond Sovey, All the Way Home

COSTUME DESIGNER (MUSICAL) (T-295)

Adrian, and Tony Duquette, Camelot
Rolf Gerard, Irma la Douce
Cecil Beaton, Tenderloin

CHOREOGRAPHER (T-296)

Gower Champion, Bye, Bye Birdie
Onna White, Irma la Douce

STAGE TECHNICIAN (T-297)

Teddy Van Bemmel, Becket

SPECIAL AWARDS (T-298)

David Merrick
The Theatre Guild

1962

ACTOR (DRAMATIC) (T-299)

Fredric March, Gideon
John Mills, Ross
Donald Pleasence, The Caretaker
Paul Scofield, A Man for All Seasons

ACTRESS (DRAMATIC) (T-300)

Gladys Cooper, A Passage to India
Colleen Dewhurst, Great Day in the Morning
Margaret Leighton, Night of the Iguana
Kim Stanley, A Far Country

ACTOR, SUPPORTING OR FEATURED (DRAMATIC) (T-301)

Godfrey M. Cambridge, Purlie Victorious
Joseph Campanella, A Gift of Time
Walter Matthau, A Shot in the Dark
Paul Sparer, Ross

ACTRESS, SUPPORTING OR FEATURED (DRAMATIC) (T-302)

Elizabeth Ashley, Take Her, She's Mine
Zohra Lampert, Look: We've Come Through
Janet Margolin, Daughter of Silence
Pat Stanley, Sunday in New York

ACTOR (MUSICAL) (T-303)

Ray Bolger, All American
Alfred Drake, Kean
Richard Kiley, No Strings
Robert Morse, How to Succeed in Business Without Really Trying

ACTRESS (MUSICAL) (T-304)

Anna Maria Alberghetti, Carnival
Diahann Carroll, No Strings
Molly Picon, Milk and Honey
Elaine Stritch, Sail Away

ACTOR, SUPPORTING OR FEATURED (MUSICAL) (T-305)

Orson Bean, Subways Are for Sleeping
Severn Darden, From the Second City
Pierre Olaf, Carnival
Charles Nelson Reilly, How to Succeed. . .

ACTRESS, SUPPORTING OR FEATURED (MUSICAL) (T-306)

Elizabeth Allen, The Gay Life
Barbara Harris, From the Second City
Phyllis Newman, Subways Are for Sleeping
Barbra Streisand, I Can Get It for You Wholesale

PLAY (T-307)

A Man for All Seasons by Robert Bolt; Producers Robert Whitehead and Roger L. Stevens
Gideon by Paddy Chayefsky; Producers Fred Coe and Arthur Cantor
The Caretaker by Harold Pinter; Producers Roger L. Stevens, Frederick Brisson and Gilbert Miller
The Night of the Iguana by Tennessee Williams; Producers Charles Bowden and Viola Rubber

AUTHOR (DRAMATIC) (T-308)

Robert Bolt, A Man for All Seasons

PRODUCER (DRAMATIC) (T-309)

Charles Bowden and Viola Rubber, Night of the Iguana
Fred Coe and Arthur Cantor, Gideon
David Merrick, Ross
Robert Whitehead and Roger L. Stevens, A Man for All Seasons

DIRECTOR (DRAMATIC) (T-310)

Tyrone Guthrie, Gideon
Donald McWhinnie, The Caretaker
Jose Quintero, Great Day In the Morning
Noel Willman, A Man for All Seasons

MUSICAL (T-311)

Carnival. Book by Michael Stewart and Helen Deutsch, music and lyrics by Bob Merrill; Producer David Merrick
How to Succeed in Business Without Really Trying. Book by Abe Burrows, Jack Weinstock and Willie Gilbert, music and lyrics by Frank Loesser; Producers Cy Feuer and Ernest Martin.
Milk and Honey. Book by Don Appell, lyrics and music by Jerry Herman; Producer Gerard Oestreicher.
No Strings. Book by Samuel Taylor, music and lyrics by Richard Rodgers; Producer Richard Rodgers in association with Samuel Taylor.

AUTHOR (MUSICAL) (T-312)

Abe Burrows, Jack Weinstock and Willie Gilbert, How to Succeed. . .
Michael Stewart and Helen Deutsch, Carnival

PRODUCER (MUSICAL) (T-313)

Helen Bonfils, Haila Stoddard and Charles Russell, Sail Away
Cy Feuer and Ernest Martin, How to Succeed. . .
David Merrick, Carnival
Gerard Oestreicher, Milk and Honey

DIRECTOR (MUSICAL) (T-314)

Abe Burrows, How to Succeed. . .
Gower Champion, Carnival
Joe Layton, No Strings
Joshua Logan, All American

COMPOSER (T-315)

Richard Adler, Kwamina
Jerry Herman, Milk and Honey
Frank Loesser, How to Succeed. . .
Richard Rodgers, No Strings

CONDUCTOR AND MUSICAL DIRECTOR (T-316)

Pembroke Davenport, Kean
Herbert Greene, The Gay Life
Elliot Lawrence, How to Succeed. . .
Peter Matz, No Strings

SCENIC DESIGNER (T-317)

Will Steven Armstrong, Carnival
Rouben Ter-Arutunian, A Passage to India
David Hays, No Strings
Oliver Smith, The Gay Life

COSTUME DESIGNER (T-318)

Lucinda Ballard, The Gay Life
Donald Brooks, No Strings
Motley, Kwamina
Miles White, Milk and Honey

CHOREOGRAPHER (T-319)

Agnes de Mille, Kwamina
Michael Kidd, Subways Are for Sleeping
Dania Krupska, The Happiest Girl in the World
Joe Layton, No Strings

STAGE TECHNICIAN (T-320)

Al Alloy, Ross
Michael Burns, A Man for All Seasons

SPECIAL AWARDS (T-321)

Brooks Atkinson
Franco Zeffirelli
Richard Rodgers

1963

ACTOR (DRAMATIC) (T-322)

Charles Boyer, Lord Pengo
Paul Ford, Never Too Late
Arthur Hill, Who's Afraid of Virginia Woolf?
Bert Lahr, The Beauty Part

ACTRESS (DRAMATIC) (T-323)

Hermione Baddeley, The Milk Train Doesn't Stop Here Anymore
Uta Hagen, Who's Afraid of Virginia Woolf?
Margaret Leighton, Tchin-Tchin
Claudia McNeill, Tiger, Tiger Burning Bright

ACTOR, SUPPORTING OR FEATURED (DRAMATIC) (T-324)

Alan Arkin, Enter Laughing
Barry Gordon, A Thousand Clowns
Paul Rogers, Photo Finish
Frank Silvera, The Lady of the Camellias

ACTRESS, SUPPORTING OR FEATURED (DRAMATIC) (T-325)

Sandy Dennis, A Thousand Clowns
Melinda Dillon, Who's Afraid of Virginia Woolf?
Alice Ghostley, The Beauty Part
Zohra Lampert, Mother Courage and Her Children

ACTOR (MUSICAL) (T-326)

Sid Caesar, Little Me
Zero Mostel, A Funny Thing Happened on the Way to the Forum
Anthony Newley, Stop the World - I Want to Get Off
Clive Revill, Oliver!

ACTRESS (MUSICAL) (T-327)

Georgia Brown, Oliver!
Nanette Fabray, Mr. President
Sally Ann Howes, Brigadoon
Vivien Leigh, Tovarich

ACTOR, SUPPORTING OR FEATURED (MUSICAL) (T-328)

David Burns, A Funny Thing Happened on the Way to the Forum
Jack Gilford, A Funny Thing Happened on the Way to the Forum
David Jones, Oliver!
Swen Swenson, Little Me

ACTRESS, SUPPORTING OR FEATURED (MUSICAL) (T-329)

Ruth Kobart, A Funny Thing Happened on the Way to the Forum
Virginia Martin, Little Me
Anna Quayle, Stop the World - I Want to Get Off
Louise Troy, Tovarich

PLAY (T-330)

A Thousand Clowns by Herb Gardner; Producers Fred Coe and Arthur Cantor
Mother Courage and Her Children by Bertolt Brecht, adapted by Eric Bentley; Producers Cheryl Crawford and Jerome Robbins
Tchin-Tchin by Sidney Michaels; Producer David Merrick.
Who's Afraid of Virginia Woolf? by Edward Albee; Producers Theatre 1963, Richard Barr and Clinton Wilder

PRODUCER (DRAMATIC) (T-331)

The Actors Studio Theatre, Strange Interlude
Richard Barr and Clinton Wilder, Theatre 1963, Who's Afraid of Virginia Woolf?
Cheryl Crawford and Jerome Robbins, Mother Courage and Her Children
Paul Vroom, Buff Cobb and Burry Fredrik, Too True To Be Good

DIRECTOR (DRAMATIC) (T-332)

George Abbott, Never Too Late
John Gielgud, The School for Scandal
Peter Glenville, Tchin-Tchin
Alan Schneider, Who's Afraid of Virginia Woolf?

MUSICAL (T-333)

A Funny Thing Happened on the Way to the Forum. Book by Burt Shevelove and Larry Gelbart, music and lyrics by Stephen Sondheim; Producer Harold Prince
Little Me. Book by Neil Simon, music by Cy Coleman, lyrics by Carolyn Leigh; Producers Cy Feuer and Ernest Martin
Oliver!. Book, music and lyrics by Lionel Bart; Producers David Merrick and Donald Albery
Stop the World - I Want to Get Off. Book, music and lyrics by Leslie Bricusse and Anthony Newley; Producer David Merrick in association with Bernard Delfont

AUTHOR (MUSICAL) (T-334)

Lionel Bart, Oliver!
Leslie Bricusse and Anthony Newley, Stop the World - I Want to Get Off
Burt Shevelove and Larry Gelbart, A Funny Thing Happened on the Way to the Forum
Neil Simon, Little Me

PRODUCER (MUSICAL) (T-335)

Cy Feuer and Ernest Martin, Little Me
David Merrick and Donald Albery, Oliver!
Harold Prince, A Funny Thing Happened on the Way to the Forum

DIRECTOR (MUSICAL) (T-336)

George Abbott, A Funny Thing Happened on the Way to the Forum
Peter Coe, Oliver!
John Fearnley, Brigadoon
Cy Feuer and Bob Fosse, Little Me

COMPOSER AND LYRICIST (T-337)

Lionel Bart, Oliver!
Leslie Bricusse and Anthony Newley, Stop the World - I Want to Get Off
Cy Coleman and Carolyn Leigh, Little Me
Milton Schafer and Ronny Graham, Bravo Giovanni

CONDUCTOR AND MUSICAL DIRECTOR (T-338)

Jay Blackton, Mr. President
Anton Coppola, Bravo Giovanni
Donald Pippin, Oliver!
Julius Rudel, Brigadoon

SCENIC DESIGNER (T-339)

Will Steven Armstrong, Tchin-Tchin
Sean Kenny, Oliver!
Anthony Powell, The School for Scandal
Franco Zeffirelli, The Lady of the Camellias

COSTUME DESIGNER (T-340)

Marcel Escoffier, The Lady of the Camellias
Robert Fletcher, Little Me
Motley, Mother Courage and Her Children
Anthony Powell, The School for Scandal

CHOREOGRAPHER (T-341)

Bob Fosse, Little Me
Carol Haney, Bravo Giovanni

STAGE TECHNICIAN (T-342)

Solly Pernick, Mr. President
Milton Smith, Beyond the Fringe

SPECIAL AWARDS (T-343)

W. McNeil Lowry
Irving Berlin
Alan Bennett
Peter Cook
Jonathan Miller
Dudley Moore

1964

ACTOR (DRAMATIC) (T-344)

Richard Burton, Hamlet
Albert Finney, Luther
Alec Guinness, Dylan
Jason Robards, Jr, After the Fall

ACTRESS (DRAMATIC) (T-345)

Elizabeth Ashley, Barefoot in the Park
Sandy Dennis, Any Wednesday
Colleen Dewhurst, The Ballad of the Sad Cafe
Julie Harris, Marathon '33

ACTOR, SUPPORTING OR FEATURED (DRAMATIC) (T-346)

Lee Allen, Marathon '33
Hume Cronyn, Hamlet
Michael Dunn, The Ballad of the Sad Cafe
Larry Gates, A Case of Libel

ACTRESS, SUPPORTING OR FEATURED (DRAMATIC) (T-347)

Barbara Loden, After the Fall
Rosemary Murphy, Any Wednesday
Kate Reid, Dylan
Diana Sands, Blues for Mister Charlie

ACTOR (MUSICAL) (T-348)

Sydney Chaplin, Funny Girl
Bob Fosse, Pal Joey (City Center revival)
Bert Lahr, Foxy
Steve Lawrence, What Makes Sammy Run?

ACTRESS (MUSICAL) (T-349)

Carol Channing, Hello, Dolly!
Beatrice Lillie, High Spirits
Barbra Streisand, Funny Girl
Inga Swenson, 110 in the Shade

ACTOR, SUPPORTING OR FEATURED (MUSICAL) (T-350)

Jack Cassidy, She Loves Me
Will Geer, 110 in the Shade
Danny Meehan, Funny Girl
Charles Nelson Reilly, Hello, Dolly!

ACTRESS, SUPPORTING OR FEATURED (MUSICAL) (T-351)

Julienne Marie, Foxy
Kay Medford, Funny Girl
Tessie O'Shea, The Girl Who Came to Supper
Louise Troy, High Spirits

PLAY (T-352)

The Ballad of the Sad Cafe by Edward Albee; Producers Lewis Allen and Ben Edwards
Barefoot in the Park by Neil Simon; Producer Saint Subber
Dylan by Sidney Michaels; Producers George W. George and Frank Granat
Luther by John Osborne; Producer David Merrick

AUTHOR (DRAMATIC) (T-353)

John Osborne, Luther

PRODUCER (DRAMATIC) (T-354)

Lewis Allen and Ben Edwards, The Ballad of the Sad Cafe
George W. George and Frank Granat, Dylan
Herman Shumlin, The Deputy
Saint Subber, Barefoot in the Park

DIRECTOR (DRAMATIC) (T-355)

June Havoc, Marathon '33
Mike Nichols, Barefoot in the Park
Alan Schneider, The Ballad of the Sad Cafe
Herman Shumlin, The Deputy

MUSICAL (T-356)

Funny Girl. Book by Isobel Lennart, music by Jule Styne, lyrics by Bob Merrill; Producer Ray Stark
Hello, Dolly! Book by Michael Stewart, music and lyrics by Jerry Herman; Producer David Merrick
High Spirits. Book, lyrics and music by Hugh Martin and Timothy Gray; Producers Lester Osterman, Robert Fletcher and Richard Horner
She Loves Me. Book by Joe Masteroff, music by Jerry Bock, lyrics by Sheldon Harnick; Producer Harold Prince in association with Lawrence N. Kasha and Philip C. McKenna

AUTHOR (MUSICAL) (T-357)

Noel Coward and Harry Kurnitz, The Girl Who Came To Supper
Joe Masteroff, She Loves Me
Hugh Martin and Timothy Gray, High Spirits
Michael Stewart, Hello, Dolly!

PRODUCER (MUSICAL) (T-358)

City Center Light Opera Company, West Side Story
David Merrick, Hello, Dolly!
Harold Prince, She Loves Me
Ray Stark, Funny Girl

DIRECTOR (MUSICAL) (T-359)

Joseph Anthony, 110 in the Shade
Gower Champion, Hello, Dolly!
Noel Coward, High Spirits
Harold Prince, She Loves Me

COMPOSER AND LYRICIST (T-360)

Jerry Herman, Hello, Dolly!
Hugh Martin and Timothy Gray, High Spirits
Harvey Schmidt and Tom Jones, 110 in the Shade
Jule Styne and Bob Merrill, Funny Girl

CONDUCTOR AND MUSICAL DIRECTOR (T-361)

Shepard Coleman, Hello, Dolly!
Lehman Engel, What Makes Sammy Run?
Charles Jaffe, West Side Story
Fred Werner, High Spirits

SCENIC DESIGNER (T-362)

Raoul Pene Du Bois, The Student Gypsy
Ben Edwards, The Ballad of the Sad Cafe
David Hays, Marco Millions
Oliver Smith, Hello, Dolly!

COSTUME DESIGNER (T-363)

Irene Sharaff, The Girl Who Came To Supper
Beni Montresor, Marco Millions
Rouben Ter-Arutunian, Arturo Ui
Freddy Wittop, Hello, Dolly!

CHOREOGRAPHER (T-364)

Gower Champion, Hello, Dolly!
Danny Daniels, High Spirits
Carol Haney, Funny Girl
Herbert Ross, Anyone Can Whistle

SPECIAL AWARD (T-365)

Eva Le Gallienne

1965

ACTOR (DRAMATIC) (T-366)

John Gielgud, Tiny Alice
Walter Matthau, The Odd Couple
Donald Pleasence, Poor Bitos
Jason Robards, Hughie

ACTRESS (DRAMATIC) (T-367)

Marjorie Rhodes, All In Good Time
Beah Richards, The Amen Corner
Diana Sands, The Owl and the Pussycat
Irene Worth, Tiny Alice

ACTOR, SUPPORTING OR FEATURED (DRAMATIC) (T-368)

Jack Albertson, The Subject Was Roses
Murray Hamilton, Absence of a Cello
Martin Sheen, The Subject Was Roses
Clarence Williams III, Slow Dance on the Killing Ground

ACTRESS, SUPPORTING OR FEATURED (DRAMATIC) (T-369)

Rae Allen, Traveller Without Luggage
Alexandra Berlin, All In Good Time
Carolan Daniels, Slow Dance on the Killing Ground
Alice Ghostley, The Sign in Sidney Brustein's Window

ACTOR (MUSICAL) (T-370)

Sammy Davis, Golden Boy
Zero Mostel, Fiddler On The Roof
Cyril Ritchard, The Roar of the Greasepaint - The Smell of the Crowd
Tommy Steele, Half A Sixpence

ACTRESS (MUSICAL) (T-371)

Elizabeth Allen, Do I Hear A Waltz?
Nancy Dussault, Bajour
Liza Minnelli, Flora, the Red Menace
Inga Swenson, Baker Street

ACTOR, SUPPORTING OR FEATURED (MUSICAL) (T-372)

Jack Cassidy, Fade Out - Fade In
James Grout, Half A Sixpence
Victor Spinetti, Oh, What A Lovely War!
Jerry Orbach, Guys and Dolls

ACTRESS, SUPPORTING OR FEATURED (MUSICAL) (T-373)

Maria Karnilova, Fiddler On The Roof
Luba Lisa, I Had A Ball
Carrie Nye, Half A Sixpence
Barbara Windsor, Oh, What A Lovely War!

PLAY (T-374)

Luv by Murray Schisgal; Producer Claire Nichtern
The Odd Couple by Neil Simon; Producer Saint-Subber
The Subject Was Roses by Frank Gilroy; Producer Edgar Lansbury
Tiny Alice by Edward Albee; Producers Theatre 1965, Richard Barr, Clinton Wilder

AUTHOR (DRAMATIC) (T-375)

Edward Albee, Tiny Alice
Frank Gilroy, The Subject Was Roses
Murray Schisgal, Luv
Neil Simon, The Odd Couple

PRODUCER (DRAMATIC) (T-376)

Hume Cronyn, Allen-Hogdon Inc., Stevens Productions Inc., Bonfils-Seawell Enterprises, Slow Dance on the Killing Ground
Claire Nichtern, Luv
Theatre 1965, Richard Barr, Clinton Wilder, Tiny Alice
Robert Whitehead, Tartuffe

DIRECTOR (DRAMATIC) (T-377)

William Ball, Tartuffe
Ulu Grosbard, The Subject Was Roses
Mike Nichols, Luv/The Odd Couple
Alan Schneider, Tiny Alice

MUSICAL (T-378)

Fiddler On The Roof. Book by Joseph Stein, music by Jerry Bock, lyrics by Sheldon Harnick; Producer Harold Prince
Golden Boy. Book by Clifford Odets and William Gibson, music by Charles Strouse, lyrics by Lee Adams; Producer Hillard Elkins
Half A Sixpence. Book by Beverly Cross, music and lyrics by David Heneker; Producers Allen Hodgdon, Stevens Productions and Harold Fielding
Oh, What A Lovely War! Devised by Joan Littlewood for Theatre Workshop, Charles Chilton and Members of the Cast; Producers David Merrick and Gerry Raffles

AUTHOR (MUSICAL) (T-379)
Jerome Coopersmith, Baker Street
Beverly Cross, Half A Sixpence
Sidney Michaels, Ben Franklin In Paris
Joseph Stein, Fiddler On The Roof

PRODUCER (MUSICAL) (T-380)
Allen Hodgdon, Stevens Productions and Harold Fielding, Half A Sixpence
Hillard Elkins, Golden Boy
David Merrick, The Roar of the Greasepaint - The Smell of the Crowd
Harold Prince, Fiddler On The Roof

DIRECTOR (MUSICAL) (T-381)
Joan Littlewood, Oh, What A Lovely War!
Anthony Newley, The Roar of the Greasepaint - The Smell of the Crowd
Jerome Robbins, Fiddler On The Roof
Gene Saks, Half A Sixpence

COMPOSER AND LYRICIST (T-382)
Jerry Bock and Sheldon Harnick, Fiddler On The Roof
Leslie Bricusse and Anthony Newley, The Roar of the Greasepaint - The Smell of The Crowd
David Heneker, Half A Sixpence
Richard Rodgers and Stephen Sondheim, Do I Hear A Waltz?

SCENIC DESIGNER (T-383)
Boris Aronson, Fiddler On The Roof and Incident At Vichy
Sean Kenny, The Roar of the Greasepaint - The Smell of the Crowd
Beni Montresor, Do I Hear A Waltz?
Oliver Smith, *Baker Street/Luv/The Odd Couple

COSTUME DESIGNER (T-384)
Jane Greenwood, Tartuffe
Motley, Baker Street
Freddy Wittop, The Roar of the Greasepaint - The Smell of the Crowd
Patricia Zipprodt, Fiddler On The Roof

CHOREOGRAPHER (T-385)
Peter Gennaro, Bajour
Donald McKayle, Golden Boy
Jerome Robbins, Fiddler On The Roof
Onna White, Half A Sixpence

SPECIAL AWARDS (T-386)
Gilbert Miller
Oliver Smith

1966

ACTOR (DRAMATIC) (T-387)
Roland Culver, Ivanov
Donal Donnelly and Patrick Bedford, Philadelphia, Here I Come!
Hal Holbrook, Mark Twain Tonight!
Nicol Williamson, Inadmissible Evidence

ACTRESS (DRAMATIC) (T-388)
Sheila Hancock, Entertaining Mr. Sloane
Rosemary Harris, The Lion in Winter
Kate Reid, Slapstick Tragedy
Lee Remick, Wait Until Dark

ACTOR, SUPPORTING OR FEATURED (DRAMATIC) (T-389)
Burt Brinckerhoff, Cactus Flower
A. Larry Haines, Generation
Eamon Kelly, Philadelphia
Patrick Magee, Marat/Sade

ACTRESS, SUPPORTING OR FEATURED (DRAMATIC) (T-390)
Zoe Caldwell, Slapstick Tragedy
Glenda Jackson, Marat/Sade
Mairin D. O'Sullivan, Philadelphia
Brenda Vaccaro, Cactus Flower

ACTOR (MUSICAL) (T-391)
Jack Cassidy, Superman
John Cullum, On A Clear Day You Can See Forever
Richard Kiley, Man of La Mancha
Harry Secombe, Pickwick

ACTRESS (MUSICAL) (T-392)
Barbara Harris, On A Clear Day
Julie Harris, Skyscraper
Angela Lansbury, Mame
Gwen Verdon, Sweet Charity

ACTOR, SUPPORTING OR FEATURED (MUSICAL) (T-393)
Roy Castle, Pickwick
John McMartin, Sweet Charity
Frankie Michaels, Mame
Michael O'Sullivan, Superman

ACTRESS, SUPPORTING OR FEATURED (MUSICAL) (T-394)
Beatrice Arthur, Mame
Helen Gallagher, Sweet Charity
Patricia Marand, Superman
Charlotte Rae, Pickwick

PLAY (T-395)
Inadmissible Evidence by John Osborne; Producer The David Merrick Arts Foundation
Marat/Sade by Peter Weiss. English version by Geoffrey Skelton; Producer The David Merrick Arts Foundation
Philadelphia, Here I Come! by Brian Friel; Producer The David Merrick Arts Foundation
The Right Honourable Gentleman by Michael Dyne; Producers Peter Cookson, Amy Lynn and Walter Schwimmer

DIRECTOR (DRAMATIC) (T-396)
Peter Brook, Marat/Sade
Hilton Edwards, Philadelphia
Ellis Rabb, You Can't Take It With You
Noel Willman, The Lion in Winter

MUSICAL (T-397)
Mame. Book by Jerome Lawrence and Robert E. Lee, music and lyrics by Jerry Herman. Producers Sylvia and Joseph Harris, Robert Fryer and Lawrence Carr
Man of La Mancha. Book by Dale Wasserman, music by Mitch Leigh, lyrics by Joe Darion. Producers Albert W. Selden and Hal James
Skyscraper. Book by Peter Stone, music by James Van Heusen, lyrics by Sammy Cahn. Producers Cy Feuer and Ernest M. Martin
Sweet Charity. Book by Neil Simon, music by Cy Coleman, lyrics by Dorothy Fields. Producers Sylvia and Joseph Harris, Robert Fryer and Lawrence Carr

DIRECTOR (MUSICAL) (T-398)
Cy Feuer, Skyscraper
Bob Fosse, Sweet Charity
Albert Marre, Man of La Mancha
Gene Saks, Mame

COMPOSER AND LYRICIST (T-399)

Cy Coleman and Dorothy Fields, Sweet Charity
Jerry Herman, Mame
Mitch Leigh and Joe Darion, Man of La Mancha
Burton Lane and Alan Jay Lerner, On A Clear Day

SCENIC DESIGNER (T-400)

Howard Bay, Man of La Mancha
William and Jean Eckart, Mame
David Hays, Drat! The Cat!
Robert Randolph, Anya/Skyscraper/Sweet Charity

COSTUME DESIGNER (T-401)

Loudon Sainthill, The Right Honourable Gentleman
Howard Bay and Patton Campbell, Man of La Mancha
Irene Sharaff, Sweet Charity
Gunilla Palmstierna-Weiss, Marat/Sade

CHOREOGRAPHER (T-402)

Jack Cole, Man of La Mancha
Bob Fosse, Sweet Charity
Michael Kidd, Skyscraper
Onna White, Mame

SPECIAL AWARD (T-403)

Helen Menken (posthumous)

1967

ACTOR (DRAMATIC) (T-404)

Hume Cronyn, A Delicate Balance
Donald Madden, Black Comedy
Donald Moffat, Right You Are and The Wild Duck
Paul Rogers, The Homecoming

ACTRESS (DRAMATIC) (T-405)

Eileen Atkins, The Killing of Sister George
Vivien Merchant, The Homecoming
Rosemary Murphy, A Delicate Balance
Beryl Reid, The Killing of Sister George

ACTOR, SUPPORTING OR FEATURED (DRAMATIC) (T-406)

Clayton Corzatte, The School for Scandal
Stephen Elliott, Marat/Sade
Ian Holm, The Homecoming
Sydney Walker, The Wild Duck

ACTRESS, SUPPORTING OR FEATURED (DRAMATIC) (T-407)

Camila Ashland, Black Comedy
Brenda Forbes, The Loves of Cass McGuire
Marian Seldes, A Delicate Balance
Maria Tucci, The Rose Tattoo

ACTOR (MUSICAL) (T-408)

Alan Alda, The Apple Tree
Jack Gilford, Cabaret
Robert Preston, I Do! I Do!
Norman Wisdom, Walking Happy

ACTRESS (MUSICAL) (T-409)

Barbara Harris, The Apple Tree
Lotte Lenya, Cabaret
Mary Martin, I Do! I Do!
Louise Troy, Walking Happy

ACTOR, SUPPORTING OR FEATURED (MUSICAL) (T-410)

Leon Bibb, A Hand is on the Gate
Gordon Dilworth, Walking Happy
Joel Grey, Cabaret
Edward Winter, Cabaret

ACTRESS, SUPPORTING OR FEATURED (MUSICAL) (T-411)

Peg Murray, Cabaret
Leland Palmer, A Joyful Noise
Josephine Premice, A Hand is on the Gate
Susan Watson, A Joyful Noise

PLAY (T-412)

A Delicate Balance, by Edward Albee; Producers Theatre 1967, Richard Barr and Clinton Wilder
Black Comedy, by Peter Shaffer; Producer Alexander H. Cohen
The Homecoming, by Harold Pinter; Producer Alexander Cohen
The Killing of Sister George by Frank Marcus; Producers Helen Bonfils and Morton Gottlieb

DIRECTOR (DRAMATIC) (T-413)

John Dexter, Black Comedy
Donald Driver, Marat/Sade
Peter Hall, The Homecoming
Alan Schneider, A Delicate Balance

MUSICAL (T-414)

Cabaret. Book by Joe Masteroff, music by John Kander, lyrics by Fred Ebb; Producer Harold Prince in association with Ruth Mitchell
I Do! I Do! Book and lyrics by Tom Jones, music by Harvey Schmidt. Producer David Merrick
The Apple Tree. Book by Sheldon Harnick and Jerry Bock, music by Jerry Bock, lyrics by Sheldon Harnick; Producer Stuart Ostrow
Walking Happy. Book by Roger O. Hirson and Ketti Frings, music by James Van Heusen, lyrics by Sammy Cahn; Producers Cy Feuer and Ernest H. Martin

DIRECTOR (MUSICAL) (T-415)

Gower Champion, I Do! I Do!
Mike Nichols, The Apple Tree
Jack Sydow, Annie Get Your Gun
Harold Prince, Cabaret

COMPOSER AND LYRICIST (T-416)

Jerry Bock and Sheldon Harnick, The Apple Tree
Sammy Cahn and James Van Heusen, Walking Happy
Tom Jones and Harvey Schmidt, I Do! I Do!
John Kander and Fred Ebb, Cabaret

SCENIC DESIGNER (T-417)

Boris Aronson, Cabaret
John Bury, The Homecoming
Oliver Smith, I Do! I Do!
Alan Tagg, Black Comedy

CHOREOGRAPHER (T-418)

Michael Bennett, A Joyful Noise
Danny Daniels, Walking Happy/Annie Get Your Gun
Ronald Field, Cabaret
Lee Theodore, The Apple Tree

COSTUME DESIGNER (T-419)

Nancy Potts, The Wild Duck/The School for Scandal
Tony Walton, The Apple Tree
Freddy Wittop, I Do! I Do!
Patricia Zipprodt, Cabaret

1968

ACTOR (DRAMATIC) (T-420)

Martin Balsam, You Know I Can't Hear You When the Water's Running
Albert Finney, Joe Egg
Milo O'Shea, Staircase
Alan Webb, I Never Sang for My Father

ACTRESS (DRAMATIC) (T-421)

Zoe Caldwell, The Prime of Miss Jean Brodie
Colleen Dewhurst, More Stately Mansions
Maureen Stapleton, Plaza Suite
Dorothy Tutin, Portrait of a Queen

ACTOR, SUPPORTING OR FEATURED (DRAMATIC) (T-422)

Paul Hecht, Rosencrantz and Guildenstern Are Dead
Brian Murray, Rosencrantz and Guildenstern Are Dead
James Patterson, The Birthday Party
John Wood, Rosencrantz and Guildenstern Are Dead

ACTRESS, SUPPORTING OR FEATURED (DRAMATIC) (T-423)

Pert Kelton, Spofford
Zena Walker, Joe Egg
Ruth White, The Birthday Party
Eleanor Wilson, Weekend

ACTOR (MUSICAL) (T-424)

Robert Goulet, The Happy Time
Robert Hooks, Hallelujah, Baby!
Anthony Roberts, How Now, Dow Jones
David Wayne, The Happy Time

ACTRESS (MUSICAL) (T-425)

Melina Mercouri, Illya, Darling
Patricia Routledge, Darling of the Day
Leslie Uggams, Hallelujah, Baby!
Brenda Vaccaro, How, Now, Dow Jones

ACTOR, SUPPORTING OR FEATURED (MUSICAL) (T-426)

Scott Jacoby, Golden Rainbow
Nikos Kourkoulos, Illya, Darling
Mike Rupert, The Happy Time
Hiram Sherman, How Now, Dow Jones

ACTRESS, SUPPORTING OR FEATURED (MUSICAL) (T-427)

Geula Gill, The Grand Music Hall of Israel
Julie Gregg, The Happy Time
Lillian Hayman, Hallelujah, Baby!
Alice Playten, Henry, Sweet Henry

PLAY (T-428)

Joe Egg, by Peter Nichols; Producers Joseph Cates and Henry Fownes
Plaza Suite, by Neil Simon; Producer Saint-Subber
Rosencrantz and Guildenstern Are Dead, by Tom Stoppard; Producer The David Merrick Arts Foundation
The Price, by Arthur Miller; Producer Robert Whitehead

PRODUCER (DRAMATIC) (T-429)

The David Merrick Arts Foundation, Rosencrantz and Guildenstern Are Dead

DIRECTOR (DRAMATIC) (T-430)

Michael Blakemore, Joe Egg
Derek Goldby, Rosencrantz and Guildenstern Are Dead
Mike Nichols, Plaza Suite
Alan Schneider, You Know I Can't Hear You When the Water's Running

MUSICAL (T-431)

Hallelujah, Baby! Book by Arthur Laurents, music by Jule Styne, lyrics by Betty Comden and Adolph Green; Producers Albert Selden, Hal James, Jane C. Nusbaum, and Harry Rigby
The Happy Time. Book by N. Richard Nash, music by John Kander, lyrics by Fred Ebb; Producer David Merrick
How Now, Dow Jones. Book by Max Shulman, music by Elmer Bernstein, lyrics by Carolyn Leigh; Producer David Merrick
Illya, Darling. Book by Jules Dassin, music by Manos Hadjidakis, lyrics by Joe Darion; Producer Kermit Bloomgarden

PRODUCER (MUSICAL) (T-432)

Albert Selden, Hal James, Jane C. Nusbaum and Harry Rigby, Hallelujah, Baby!

DIRECTOR (MUSICAL) (T-433)

George Abbott, How Now, Dow Jones
Gower Champion, The Happy Time
Jules Dassin, Illya, Darling
Burt Shevelove, Hallelujah, Baby!

COMPOSER AND LYRICIST (T-434)

Elmer Bernstein and Carolyn Leigh, How Now, Dow Jones
Manos Hadjidakis and Joe Darion, Illya, Darling
John Kander and Fred Ebb, The Happy Time
Jule Styne, Betty Comden and Adolph Green, Hallelujah, Baby!

SCENIC DESIGNER (T-435)

Boris Aronson, The Price
Desmond Heeley, Rosencrantz and Guildenstern Are Dead
Robert Randolph, Golden Rainbow
Peter Wexler, The Happy Time

COSTUME DESIGNER (T-436)

Jane Greenwood, More Stately Mansions
Desmond Heeley, Rosencrantz and Guildenstern Are Dead
Irene Sharaff, Hallelujah, Baby!
Freddy Wittop, The Happy Time

CHOREOGRAPHER (T-437)

Michael Bennett, Henry, Sweet Henry
Kevin Carlisle, Hallelujah, Baby!
Gower Champion, The Happy Time
Onna White, Illya, Darling

SPECIAL AWARDS (T-438)

Audrey Hepburn
Carol Channing
Pearl Bailey
David Merrick
Maurice Chevalier
APA-Phoenix Theatre
Marlene Dietrich

1969

ACTOR (DRAMATIC) (T-439)

Art Carney, Lovers
James Earl Jones, The Great White Hope
Alec McCowen, Hadrian VII
Donald Pleasence, The Man in the Glass Booth

ACTRESS (DRAMATIC) (T-440)

Julie Harris, Forty Carats
Estelle Parsons, Seven Descents of Myrtle
Charlotte Rae, Morning, Noon and Night
Brenda Vaccaro, The Goodbye People

ACTOR, SUPPORTING OR FEATURED (DRAMATIC) (T-441)

Al Pacino, Does a Tiger Wear a Necktie?
Richard Castellano, Lovers and Other Strangers
Anthony Roberts, Play It Again, Sam
Louis Zorich, Hadrian VII

ACTRESS, SUPPORTING OR FEATURED (DRAMATIC) (T-442)

Jane Alexander, The Great White Hope
Diane Keaton, Play It Again, Sam
Lauren Jones, Does a Tiger Wear a Necktie?
Anna Manahan, Lovers

ACTOR (MUSICAL) (T-443)

Herschel Bernardi, Zorba
Jack Cassidy, Maggie Flynn
Joel Grey, George M!
Jerry Orbach, Promises, Promises

ACTRESS (MUSICAL) (T-444)

Maria Karnilova, Zorba
Angela Lansbury, Dear World
Dorothy Loudon, The Fig Leaves Are Falling
Jill O'Hara, Promises, Promises

ACTOR, SUPPORTING OR FEATURED (MUSICAL) (T-445)

A. Larry Haines, Promises, Promises
Ronald Holgate, 1776
Edward Winter, Promises, Promises

ACTRESS, SUPPORTING OR FEATURED (MUSICAL) (T-446)

Sandy Duncan, Canterbury Tales
Marian Mercer, Promises, Promises
Lorraine Serabian, Zorba
Virginia Vestoff, 1776

PLAY (T-447)

The Great White Hope by Howard Sackler; Producer Herman Levin
Hadrian VII by Peter Luke; Producers Lester Osterman Productions, Bill Freedman, Charles Kasher
Lovers by Brian Friel; Producers Helen Bonfils and Morton Gottlieb
The Man in the Glass Booth by Robert Shaw; Producers Glasshouse Productions and Peter Bridge, Ivor David Balding & Associates Ltd. and Edward M. Meyers with Leslie Ogden

DIRECTOR (DRAMATIC) (T-448)

Peter Dews, Hadrian VII
Joseph Hardy, Play It Again Sam
Harold Pinter, The Man in the Glass Booth
Michael A. Schultz, Does a Tiger Wear a Necktie?

MUSICAL (T-449)

Hair. Book by Gerome Ragni and James Rado, music by Galt MacDermot, lyrics by James Rado; Producer Michael Butler
Promises, Promises. Book by Neil Simon, music and lyrics by Burt Bacharach; Producer David Merrick
1776. Book by Peter Stone, music and lyrics by Sherman Edwards; Producer Stuart Ostrow
Zorba. Book by Joseph Stein, music by John Kander, lyrics by Fred Ebb; Producer Harold Prince

DIRECTOR (MUSICAL) (T-450)

Peter Hunt, 1776
Robert Moore, Promises, Promises
Tom O'Horgan, Hair
Harold Prince, Zorba

SCENIC DESIGNER (T-451)

Boris Aronson, Zorba
Derek Cousins, Canterbury Tales
Jo Mielziner, 1776
Oliver Smith, Dear World

COSTUME DESIGNER (T-452)

Michael Annals, Morning, Noon and Night
Robert Fletcher, Hadrian VII
Louden Sainthill, Canterbury Tales
Patricia Zipprodt, Zorba

CHOREOGRAPHER (T-453)

Sammy Bayes, Canterbury Tales
Ronald Field, Zorba
Joe Layton, George M!
Michael Bennett, Promises, Promises

SPECIAL AWARDS (T-454)

The National Theatre Company of Great Britain
The Negro Ensemble Company
Rex Harrison
Leonard Bernstein
Carol Burnett

1970

ACTOR (DRAMATIC) (T-455)

James Coco, Last of the Red Hot Lovers
Frank Grimes, Borstal Boy
Stacy Keach, Indians
Fritz Weaver, Child's Play

ACTRESS (DRAMATIC) (T-456)

Geraldine Brooks, Brightower
Tammy Grimes, Private Lives (Revival)
Helen Hayes, Harvey (Revival)

ACTOR, SUPPORTING OR FEATURED (DRAMATIC) (T-457)

Joseph Bova, The Chinese and Dr. Fish
Ken Howard, Child's Play
Dennis King, A Patriot for Me

ACTRESS, SUPPORTING OR FEATURED (DRAMATIC) (T-458)

Blythe Danner, Butterflies Are Free
Alice Drummond, The Chinese and Dr. Fish
Eileen Heckart, Butterflies Are Free
Linda Lavin, Last of the Red Hot Lovers

ACTOR (MUSICAL) (T-459)

Len Cariou, Applause
Cleavon Little, Purlie
Robert Weede, Cry For Us All

ACTRESS (MUSICAL) (T-460)

Lauren Bacall, Applause
Katharine Hepburn, Coco
Dilys Watling, Georgy

ACTOR, SUPPORTING OR FEATURED (MUSICAL) (T-461)

Rene Auberjonois, Coco
Brandon Maggart, Applause
George Rose, Coco

ACTRESS, SUPPORTING OR FEATURED (MUSICAL) (T-462)

Bonnie Franklin, Applause
Penny Fuller, Applause
Melissa Hart, Georgy
Melba Moore, Purlie

PLAY (T-463)

Borstal Boy by Frank McMahon; Producers Michael McAloney, Burton C. Kaiser
Child's Play by Robert Marasco; Producer David Merrick
Indians by Arthur Kopit; Producers Lyn Austin, Oliver Smith, Joel Schenker, Roger L. Stevens
Last of the Red Hot Lovers by Neil Simon; Producer Saint-Subber

DIRECTOR (DRAMATIC) (T-464)

Joseph Hardy, Child's Play
Milton Katselas, Butterflies Are Free
Tomas MacAnna, Borstal Boy
Robert Moore, Last of the Red Hot Lovers

MUSICAL (T-465)

Applause. Book by Betty Comden and Adolph Green, music by Charles Strouse, lyrics by Lee Adams; Producers Joseph Kipness and Lawrence Kasha
Coco. Book and lyrics by Alan Jay Lerner, music by Andre Previn; Producer Frederick Brisson
Purlie. Book by Ossie Davis, Philip Rose, Peter Udell, music by Gary Geld, lyrics by Peter Udell; Producer Philip Rose

DIRECTOR (MUSICAL) (T-466)

Michael Benthall, Coco
Ron Field, Applause
Philip Rose, Purlie

SCENIC DESIGNER (T-467)

Howard Bay, Cry for Us All
Ming Cho Lee, Billy
Jo Mielziner, Child's Play
Robert Randolph, Applause

COSTUME DESIGNER (T-468)

Ray Aghayan, Applause
Cecil Beaton, Coco
W. Robert Lavine, Jimmy
Freddy Wittop, A Patriot for Me

CHOREOGRAPHER (T-469)

Michael Bennett, Coco
Grover Dale, Billy
Ron Field, Applause
Louis Johnson, Purlie

LIGHTING DESIGNER (T-470)

Jo Mielziner, Child's Play
Tharon Musser, Applause
Thomas Skelton, Indians

SPECIAL AWARDS (T-471)

Noel Coward
Alfred Lunt and Lynn Fontanne
The New York Shakespeare Festival
Barbra Streisand

1971

ACTOR (DRAMATIC) (T-472)

Brian Bedford, The School for Wives
John Gielgud, Home
Alec McCowen, The Philanthropist
Ralph Richardson, Home

ACTRESS (DRAMATIC) (T-473)

Estelle Parsons, And Miss Reardon Drinks a Little
Diana Rigg, Abelard and Heloise
Marian Seldes, Father's Day
Maureen Stapleton, Gingerbread Lady

ACTOR, SUPPORTING OR FEATURED (DRAMATIC) (T-474)

Ronald Radd, Abelard and Heloise
Donald Pickering, Conduct Unbecoming
Paul Sand, Story Theatre
Ed Zimmermann, The Philanthropist

ACTRESS, SUPPORTING OR FEATURED (DRAMATIC) (T-475)

Rae Allen, And Miss Reardon Drinks a Little
Lili Darvas, Les Blancs
Joan Van Ark, The School for Wives
Mona Washbourne, Home

ACTOR (MUSICAL) (T-476)

David Burns, Lovely Ladies, Kind Gentlemen
Larry Kert, Company
Hal Linden, The Rothschilds
Bobby Van, No, No, Nanette (Revival)

ACTRESS (MUSICAL) (T-477)

Susan Browning, Company
Sandy Duncan, The Boy Friend
Helen Gallagher, No, No, Nanette
Elaine Stritch, Company

ACTOR, SUPPORTING OR FEATURED (MUSICAL) (T-478)

Keene Curtis, The Rothschilds
Charles Kimbrough, Company
Walter Willison, Two By Two

ACTRESS, SUPPORTING OR FEATURED (MUSICAL) (T-479)

Barbara Barrie, Company
Patsy Kelly, No, No, Nanette
Pamela Myers, Company

PLAY (T-480)

Home by David Storey; Producer Alexander H. Cohen
Sleuth by Anthony Shaffer; Producers Helen Bonfils, Morton Gottlieb and Michael White
Story Theatre by Paul Sills; Producer Zev Bufman
The Philanthropist by Christopher Hampton; Producers David Merrick and Byron Goldman

PRODUCER (DRAMATIC) (T-481)

Alexander H. Cohen, Home
David Merrick, The Philanthropist
Helen Bonfils, Morton Gottlieb and Michael White, Sleuth
Zev Bufman, Story Theatre

DIRECTOR (DRAMATIC) (T-482)

Lindsay Anderson, Home
Peter Brook, Midsummer Night's Dream
Stephen Porter, The School for Wives
Clifford Williams, Sleuth

MUSICAL (T-483)

Company; Producer Harold Prince
The Me Nobody Knows; Producer Jeff Britton
The Rothschilds. Producers Lester Osterman and Hillard Elkins

PRODUCER (MUSICAL) (T-484)

Harold Prince, Company
Jeff Britton, The Me Nobody Knows
Hillard Elkins and Lester Osterman, The Rothschilds

DIRECTOR (MUSICAL) (T-485)

Michael Kidd, The Rothschilds
Robert H. Livingston, The Me Nobody Knows
Harold Prince, Company
Burt Shevelove, No, No, Nanette

BOOK (MUSICAL) (T-486)

George Furth, Company
Robert H. Livingston and Herb Schapiro, The Me Nobody Knows
Sherman Yellen, The Rothschilds

LYRICS (MUSICAL) (T-487)

Sheldon Harnick, The Rothschilds
Will Holt, The Me Nobody Knows
Stephen Sondheim, Company

SCORE (MUSICAL) (T-488)

Jerry Bock, The Rothschilds
Gary William Friedman, The Me Nobody Knows
Stephen Sondheim, Company

SCENIC DESIGNER (T-489)

Boris Aronson, Company
John Bury, The Rothschilds
Sally Jacobs, Midsummer Night's Dream
Jo Mielziner, Father's Day

COSTUME DESIGNER (T-490)

Raoul Pene Du Bois, No, No, Nanette
Jane Greenwood, Hay Fever/Les Blancs
Freddy Wittop, Lovely Ladies, Kind Gentlemen

CHOREOGRAPHER (T-491)

Michael Bennett, Company
Michael Kidd, The Rothschilds
Donald Saddler, No, No, Nanette

LIGHTING DESIGNER (T-492)

Robert Ornbo, Company
H. R. Poindexter, Story Theatre
William Ritman, Sleuth

SPECIAL AWARDS (T-493)

Elliot Norton
Ingram Ash
Playbill
Roger L. Stevens

1972

ACTOR (DRAMATIC) (T-494)

Tom Aldredge, Sticks and Bones
Donald Pleasence, Wise Child
Cliff Gorman, Lenny
Jason Robards, The Country Girl

ACTRESS (DRAMATIC) (T-495)

Eileen Atkins, Vivat! Vivat Regina!
Colleen Dewhurst, All Over
Rosemary Harris, Old Times
Sada Thompson, Twigs

ACTOR, SUPPORTING OR FEATURED (DRAMATIC) (T-496)

Vincent Gardenia, The Prisoner of Second Avenue
Douglas Rain, Vivat! Vivat Regina!
Lee Richardson, Vivat! Vivat Regina!
Joe Silver, Lenny

ACTRESS, SUPPORTING OR FEATURED (DRAMATIC) (T-497)

Cara Duff-MacCormick, Moonchildren
Mercedes McCambridge, The Love Suicide at Schofield Barracks
Frances Sternhagen, The Sign in Sidney Brustein's Window (Revival)
Elizabeth Wilson, Sticks and Bones

ACTOR (MUSICAL) (T-498)

Clifton Davis, Two Gentlemen of Verona
Barry Bostwick, Grease
Raul Julia, Two Gentlemen of Verona
Phil Silvers, A Funny Thing Happened on the Way to the Forum (Revival)

ACTRESS (MUSICAL) (T-499)

Jonelle Allen, Two Gentlemen of Verona
Dorothy Collins, Follies
Mildred Natwick, 70 Girls 70
Alexis Smith, Follies

ACTOR, SUPPORTING OR FEATURED (MUSICAL) (T-500)

Larry Blyden, A Funny Thing Happened on the Way to the Forum (Revival)
Timothy Meyers, Grease
Gene Nelson, Follies
Ben Vereen, Jesus Christ Superstar

ACTRESS, SUPPORTING OR FEATURED (MUSICAL) (T-501)

Adrienne Barbeau, Grease
Linda Hopkins, Inner City
Bernadette Peters, On The Town (Revival)
Beatrice Wind, Ain't Supposed to Die a Natural Death

PLAY (T-502)

Old Times by Harold Pinter; Producer Roger L. Stevens
The Prisoner of Second Avenue by Neil Simon; Producer Saint-Subber
Sticks and Bones by David Rabe; Producer The New York Shakespeare Festival - Joseph Papp
Vivat! Vivat Regina! by Robert Bolt; Producers David Merrick and Arthur Cantor

DIRECTOR (DRAMATIC) (T-503)

Jeff Bleckner, Sticks and Bones
Gordon Davidson, The Trial Of The Catonsville Nine
Peter Hall, Old Times
Mike Nichols, The Prisoner of Second Avenue

MUSICAL (T-504)

Ain't Supposed to Die a Natural Death; Producers Eugene V. Wolsk, Charles Blackwell, Emanuel Azenberg, Robert Malina
Follies. Producer Harold Prince
Two Gentlemen of Verona. Producer The New York Shakespeare Festival - Joseph Papp
Grease. Producers Kenneth Waissman and Maxine Fox

DIRECTOR (MUSICAL) (T-505)

Gilbert Moses, Ain't Supposed to Die a Natural Death
Harold Prince and Michael Bennett, Follies
Mel Shapiro, Two Gentlemen of Verona
Burt Shevelove, A Funny Thing Happened on the Way to the Forum

BOOK (MUSICAL) (T-506)

Ain't Supposed to Die a Natural Death by Melvin Van Peebles
Follies by James Goldman
Grease by Jim Jacobs and Warren Casey
Two Gentlemen of Verona by John Guare and Mel Shapiro

SCORE (T-507)

Ain't Supposed to Die a Natural Death. Composer: Melvin Van Peebles.
Lyricist: Melvin Van Peebles
Follies. Composer: Stephen Sondheim. Lyricist: Stephen Sondheim
Jesus Christ Superstar. Composer: Andrew Lloyd Webber. Lyricist:
Tim Rice
Two Gentlemen of Verona. Composer: Galt MacDermot. Lyricist: John
Guare

SCENIC DESIGNER (T-508)

Boris Aronson, Follies
John Bury, Old Times
Kert Lundell, Ain't Supposed to Die a Natural Death
Robin Wagner, Jesus Christ Superstar

COSTUME DESIGNER (T-509)

Theoni V. Aldredge, Two Gentlemen of Verona
Randy Barcelo, Jesus Christ Superstar
Florence Klotz, Follies
Carrie F. Robbins, Grease

CHOREOGRAPHER (T-510)

Michael Bennett, Follies
Patricia Birch, Grease
Jean Erdman, Two Gentlemen of Verona

LIGHTING DESIGNER (T-511)

Martin Aronstein, Ain't Supposed to Die a Natural Death
John Bury, Old Times
Jules Fisher, Jesus Christ Superstar
Tharon Musser, Follies

SPECIAL AWARDS (T-512)

The Theatre Guild-American Theatre Society
Richard Rodgers
Fiddler on the Roof
Ethel Merman

1973

ACTOR (DRAMATIC) (T-513)

Jack Albertson, The Sunshine Boys
Alan Bates, Butley
Wilfrid Hyde White, The Jockey Club Stakes
Paul Sorvino, That Championship Season

ACTRESS (DRAMATIC) (T-514)

Jane Alexander, 6 Rms Riv Vu
Colleen Dewhurst, Mourning Becomes Electra
Julie Harris, The Last of Mrs. Lincoln
Kathleen Widdoes, Much Ado About Nothing

ACTOR, SUPPORTING OR FEATURED (DRAMATIC) (T-515)

Barnard Hughes, Much Ado About Nothing
John Lithgow, The Changing Room
John McMartin, Don Juan
Hayward Morse, Butley

ACTRESS, SUPPORTING OR FEATURED (DRAMATIC) (T-516)

Maya Angelou, Look Away
Leora Dana, The Last of Mrs. Lincoln
Katherine Helmond, The Great God Brown
Penelope Windust, Elizabeth I

ACTOR (MUSICAL) (T-517)

Len Cariou, A Little Night Music
Robert Morse, Sugar
Brock Peters, Lost in the Stars
Ben Vereen, Pippin

ACTRESS (MUSICAL) (T-518)

Glynis Johns, A Little Night Music
Leland Palmer, Pippin
Debbie Reynolds, Irene (Revival)
Marcia Rodd, Shelter

ACTOR, SUPPORTING OR FEATURED (MUSICAL) (T-519)

Laurence Guittard, A Little Night Music
George S. Irving, Irene
Avon Long, Don't Play Us Cheap
Gilbert Price, Lost in the Stars

ACTRESS, SUPPORTING OR FEATURED (MUSICAL) (T-520)

Patricia Elliott, A Little Night Music
Hermione Gingold, A Little Night Music
Patsy Kelly, Irene
Irene Ryan, Pippin

PLAY (T-521)

Butley by Simon Gray; Producers Lester Osterman and Richard
Horner
That Championship Season by Jason Miller; Producer The New York
Shakespeare Festival - Joseph Papp
The Changing Room by David Storey; Producers Charles Bowden, Lee
Reynolds, Isobel Robins
The Sunshine Boys by Neil Simon; Producers Emanuel Azenberg and
Eugene V. Wolsk

DIRECTOR (DRAMATIC) (T-522)

A. J. Antoon, That Championship Season
A. J. Antoon, Much Ado About Nothing
Alan Arkin, The Sunshine Boys
Michael Rudman, The Changing Room

MUSICAL (T-523)

A Little Night Music. Producer Harold Prince
Don't Bother Me, I Can't Cope; Producers Edward Padula and Arch
Lustberg
Pippin. Producer Stuart Ostrow
Sugar. Producer David Merrick

DIRECTOR (MUSICAL) (T-524)

Vinnette Carroll, Don't Bother Me, I Can't Cope
Gower Champion, Sugar
Bob Fosse, Pippin
Harold Prince, A Little Night Music

BOOK (MUSICAL) (T-525)

A Little Night Music by Hugh Wheeler
Don't Bother Me, I Can't Cope by Micki Grant
Don't Play Us Cheap by Melvin Van Peebles
Pippin by Roger O. Hirson

SCORE (MUSICAL) (T-526)

A Little Night Music. Music and lyrics: Stephen Sondheim
Don't Bother Me, I Can't Cope. Music and Lyrics: Micki Grant
Much Ado About Nothing. Music: Peter Link
Pippin. Music and Lyrics: Stephen Schwartz

SCENIC DESIGNER (T-527)

Boris Aronson, A Little Night Music
David Jenkins, The Changing Room
Santo Loquasto, That Championship Season
Tony Walton, Pippin

COSTUME DESIGNER (T-528)

Theoni V. Aldredge, Much Ado About Nothing
Florence Klotz, A Little Night Music
Miles White, Tricks
Patricia Zipprodt, Pippin

CHOREOGRAPHER (T-529)

Gower Champion, Sugar
Bob Fosse, Pippin
Peter Gennaro, Irene
Donald Saddler, Much Ado About Nothing

LIGHTING DESIGNER (T-530)

Martin Aronstein, Much Ado About Nothing
Ian Calderon, That Championship Season
Jules Fisher, Pippin
Tharon Musser, A Little Night Music

SPECIAL AWARDS (T-531)

John Lindsay
Actor's Fund of America
Shubert Organization

1974

ACTOR (DRAMATIC) (T-532)

Michael Moriarty, Find Your Way Home
Zero Mostel, Ulysses in Nighttown
Jason Robards, A Moon for the Misbegotten (Revival)
George C. Scott, Vanya (Revival)
Nicol Williamson, Uncle Vanya

ACTRESS (DRAMATIC) (T-533)

Jane Alexander, Find Your Way Home
Colleen Dewhurst, A Moon for the Misbegotten (Revival)
Julie Harris, The Au Pair Man
Madeline Kahn, In The Boom Boom Room
Rachel Roberts, performances with The New Phoenix Repertory Company

ACTOR, SUPPORTING OR FEATURED (DRAMATIC) (T-534)

Rene Auberjonois, The Good Doctor
Ed Flanders, A Moon for the Misbegotten (Revival)
Douglas Turner Ward, The River Niger
Dick A. Williams, What the Wine-Sellers Buy

ACTRESS, SUPPORTING OR FEATURED (DRAMATIC) (T-535)

Regina Baff, Veronica's Room
Fionnuala Flanagan, Ulysses in Nighttown
Charlotte Moore, Chemin de Fer
Roxie Roker, The River Niger
Frances Sternhagen, The Good Doctor

ACTOR (MUSICAL) (T-536)

Alfred Drake, Gigi
Joe Morton, Raisin
Christopher Plummer, Cyrano
Lewis J. Stadlen, Candide

ACTRESS (MUSICAL) (T-537)

Virginia Capers, Raisin
Carol Channing, Lorelei
Michele Lee, Seesaw

ACTOR, SUPPORTING OR FEATURED (MUSICAL) (T-538)

Mark Baker, Candide
Ralph Carter, Raisin
Tommy Tune, Seesaw

ACTRESS, SUPPORTING OR FEATURED (MUSICAL) (T-539)

Leigh Berry, Cyrano
Maureen Brennan, Candide
June Gable, Candide
Ernestine Jackson, Raisin
Janie Sell, Over Here!

PLAY (T-540)

In The Boom Boom Room by David Rabe; Producer Joseph Papp
The Au Pair Man by Hugh Leonard; Producer Joseph Papp
The River Niger by Joseph A. Walker; Producer The Negro Ensemble Co., Inc.
Ulysses in Nighttown by Marjorie Barkentin; Producers Alexander H. Cohen and Bernard Delfont

DIRECTOR (DRAMATIC) (T-541)

Burgess Meredith, Ulysses in Nighttown
Mike Nichols, Uncle Vanya
Stephen Porter, Chemin de Fer
Jose Quintero, A Moon for the Misbegotten (Revival)
Edwin Sherin, Find Your Way Home

MUSICAL (T-542)

Over Here! Producers Kenneth Waissman and Maxine Fox
Raisin. Producer Robert Nemiroff
Seesaw. Producers Joseph Kipness, Lawrence Kasha, James Nederlander, George M. Steinbrenner III, Lorin E. Price

DIRECTOR (MUSICAL) (T-543)

Michael Bennett, Seesaw
Donald McKayle, Raisin
Harold Prince, Candide
Tom Moore, Over Here!

BOOK (MUSICAL) (T-544)

Candide by Hugh Wheeler
Raisin by Robert Nemiroff and Charlotte Zaltzberg
Seesaw by Michael Bennett

SCORE (T-545)

Gigi. Music: Frederick Loewe. Lyrics: Alan Jay Lerner
The Good Doctor. Music: Peter Link. Lyrics: Neil Simon
Raisin. Music: Judd Woldin. Lyrics: Robert Brittan
Seesaw. Music: Cy Coleman. Lyrics: Dorothy Fields

SCENIC DESIGNER (T-546)

John Conklin, The Au Pair Man
Franne and Eugene Lee, Candide
Santo Loquasto, What the Wine-Sellers Buy
Oliver Smith, Gigi
Ed Wittstein, Ulysses in Nighttown

COSTUME DESIGNER (T-547)

Theoni V. Aldredge, The Au Pair Man
Finlay James, Crown Matrimonial
Franne Lee, Candide
Oliver Messel, Gigi
Carrie F. Robbins, Over Here!

CHOREOGRAPHER (T-548)

Michael Bennett, Seesaw
Patricia Birch, Over Here!
Donald McKayle, Raisin

LIGHTING DESIGNER (T-549)

Martin Aronstein, In The Boom Boom Room
Ken Billington, The Visit (Revival)
Ben Edwards, A Moon for the Misbegotten (Revival)
Jules Fisher, Ulysses in Nighttown
Tharon Musser, The Good Doctor

SPECIAL AWARDS (T-550)

Liza Minnelli
Bette Midler
Peter Cook and Dudley Moore, Good Evening
A Moon for the Misbegotten (Revival)
Candide
Actor's Equity Association
Theatre Development Fund
John F. Wharton
Harold Friedlander

1975

ACTOR (DRAMATIC) (T-551)

James Dale, Scapino
Peter Firth, Equus
Henry Fonda, Clarence Darrow
Ben Gazzara, Hughie & Duet
John Kani & Winston Ntshona, Sizwe Banzi Is Dead & The Island
John Wood, Sherlock Holmes

ACTRESS (DRAMATIC) (T-552)

Elizabeth Ashley, Cat On A Hot Tin Roof
Ellen Burstyn, Same Time, Next Year
Diana Rigg, The Misanthrope
Maggie Smith, Private Lives
Liv Ullman, A Doll's House

ACTOR, SUPPORTING OR FEATURED (DRAMATIC) (T-553)

Larry Blyden, Absurd Person Singular
Leonard Frey, The National Health
Frank Langella, Seascape
Philip Locke, Sherlock Holmes
George Rose, My Fat Friend
Dick Anthony Williams, The Black Picture Show

ACTRESS, SUPPORTING OR FEATURED (DRAMATIC) (T-554)

Linda Miller, The Black Picture Show
Rita Moreno, The Ritz
Geraldine Page, Absurd Person Singular
Carole Shelley, Absurd Person Singular
Elizabeth Spriggs, London Assurance
Frances Sternhagen, Equus

ACTOR (MUSICAL) (T-555)

John Cullum, Shenandoah
Joel Grey, Goodtime Charley
Raul Julia, Where's Charley?
Eddie Mekka, The Lieutenant
Robert Preston, Mack and Mabel

ACTRESS (MUSICAL) (T-556)

Lola Falana, Doctor Jazz
Angela Lansbury, Gypsy
Bernadette Peters, Mack and Mabel
Ann Reinking, Goodtime Charley

ACTOR, SUPPORTING OR FEATURED (MUSICAL) (T-557)

Tom Aldredge, Where's Charley?
John Bottoms, Dance With Me
Douglas Henning, The Magic Show
Gilbert Price, The Night That Made America Famous
Ted Ross, The Wiz
Richard B. Shull, Goodtime Charley

ACTRESS, SUPPORTING OR FEATURED (MUSICAL) (T-558)

Dee Dee Bridgewater, The Wiz
Susan Browning, Goodtime Charley
Zan Charisse, Gypsy
Taina Elg, Where's Charley?
Kelly Garrett, The Night That Made America Famous
Donna Theodore, Shenandoah

PLAY (T-559)

Equus, by Peter Shaffer; producers Kermit Bloomgarden and Doris Cole Abrahams
Same Time, Next Year, by Bernard Slade; producer Morton Gottlieb
Seascape, by Edward Albee; producers Richard Barr, Charles Woodward and Clinton Wilder
Short Eyes, by Miguel Pinero; producer Joseph Papp
Sizwe Banzi Is Dead & The Island, by Athol Fugard, John Kani and Winston Ntshona; producers Hillard Elkins, Lester Osterman Prodns, Bernard Delfont, Michael White
The National Health, by Peter Nichols; producer Circle In the Square Inc.

DIRECTOR (DRAMATIC) (T-560)

Arvin Brown, The National Health
John Dexter, Equus
Frank Dunlop, Scapino
Ronald Eyre, London Assurance
Athol Fugard, Sizwe Banzi Is Dead & The Island
Gene Saks, Same Time, Next Year

MUSICAL (T-561)

Mack and Mabel, producer David Merrick
Shenandoah, producers Philip Rose, Gloria and Louis K. Sher
The Lieutenant, producers Spofford Beadle and Joseph Kutrzeba
The Wiz, producer Ken Harper

DIRECTOR (MUSICAL) (T-562)

Gower Champion, Mack and Mabel
Grover Dale, The Magic Show
Geoffrey Holder, The Wiz
Arthur Laurents, Gypsy

BOOK (MUSICAL) (T-563)

Mack and Mabel, Michael Stewart
Shenandoah, James Lee Barrett
The Lieutenant, Gene Curty, Nitra Scharfman, Chuck Strand
The Wiz, William F. Brown

SCORE (T-564)

A Letter for Queen Victoria, Music and Lyrics, Alan Lloyd
Shenandoah, Music and Lyrics, Gary Geld
The Lieutenant, Music and Lyrics, Gene Curty, Nitra Scharfman, Chuck Strand
The Wiz, Music and Lyrics, Charlie Smalls

SCENIC DESIGNER (T-565)
Scott Johnson, Dance With Me
Tanya Moiseiwitsch, The Misanthrope
William Ritman, God's Favorite
Rouben Ter-Arutunian, Goodtime Charley
Carl Toms, Sherlock Holmes
Robert Wagner, Mack and Mabel

COSTUME DESIGNER (T-566)
Arthur Boccia, Where's Charley?
Raoul Pene du Bois, Doctor Jazz
Geoffrey Holder, The Wiz
Willa Kim, Goodtime Charley
Tanya Moiseiwitsch, The Misanthrope
Patricia Zipprodt, Mack and Mabel

CHOREOGRAPHER (T-567)
Gower Champion, Mack and Mabel
George Faison, The Wiz
Donald McKayle, Doctor Jazz
Margo Sappington, Where's Charley?
Robert Tucker, Shenandoah
Joel Zwick, Dance With Me

LIGHTING DESIGNER (T-568)
Chip Monck, The Rocky Horror Show
Abe Feder, Goodtime Charley
Neil Patrick Jampolis, Sherlock Holmes
Andy Phillips, Equus
Thomas Skelton, All God's Chillun
James Tilton, Seascape

SPECIAL AWARDS (T-569)
Neil Simon
Al Hirschfeld

1976

ACTOR (DRAMATIC) (T-570)
Moses Gunn, The Poison Tree
George C. Scott, Death of a Salesman
Donald Sinden, Habeas Corpus
John Wood, Travesties

ACTRESS (DRAMATIC) (T-571)
Tovah Feldshuh, Yentl
Rosemary Harris, The Royal Family
Lynn Redgrave, Mrs. Warren's Profession
Irene Worth, Sweet Bird of Youth

ACTOR, FEATURED ROLE (DRAMATIC) (T-572)
Barry Bostwick, They Knew What They Wanted
Gabriel Dell, Lamppost Reunion
Edward Herrmann, Mrs. Warren's Profession
Daniel Seltzer, Knock Knock

ACTRESS, FEATURED ROLE (DRAMATIC) (T-573)
Marybeth Hurt, Trelawny of the 'Wells'
Shirley Knight, Kennedy's Children
Lois Nettleton, They Knew What They Wanted
Meryl Streep, 27 Wagons Full of Cotton

ACTOR (MUSICAL) (T-574)
Mako, Pacific Overtures
Jerry Orbach, Chicago
Ian Richardson, My Fair Lady
George Rose, My Fair Lady

ACTRESS (MUSICAL) (T-575)
Donna McKechnie, A Chorus Line
Vivian Reed, Bubbling Brown Sugar
Chita Rivera, Chicago
Gwen Verdon, Chicago

ACTOR, FEATURED ROLE (MUSICAL) (T-576)
Robert LuPone, A Chorus Line
Charles Repole, Very Good Eddie
Isao Sato, Pacific Overtures
Sammy Williams, A Chorus Line

ACTRESS, FEATURED ROLE (MUSICAL) (T-577)
Carole Bishop, A Chorus Line
Priscilla Lopez, A Chorus Line
Patti LuPone, The Robber Bridegroom
Virginia Seidel, Very Good Eddie

PLAY (T-578)
First Breeze of Summer, by Leslie Lee; producer Negro Ensemble Company
Knock Knock, by Jules Feiffer; producers Harry Rigby & Terry Allen Kramer
Lamppost Reunion, by Louis La Russo II; producer Joe Garofalo
Travesties, by Tom Stoppard; producers David Merrick, Doris Cole Abrahams, Burry Fredrik

DIRECTOR (DRAMATIC) (T-579)
Arvin Brown, Ah, Wilderness!
Marshall W. Mason, Knock Knock
Ellis Rabb, The Royal Family
Peter Wood, Travesties

MUSICAL (T-580)
A Chorus Line, producer Joseph Papp
Bubbling Brown Sugar, producers J. Lloyd Grant, Richard Bell, Robert M. Cooper & Ashton Springer
Chicago, producers Robert Fryer, James Cresson
Pacific Overtures, producer Harold Prince

DIRECTOR (MUSICAL) (T-581)
Michael Bennett, A Chorus Line
Bob Fosse, Chicago
Bill Gile, Very Good Eddie
Harold Prince, Pacific Overtures

BOOK (MUSICAL) (T-582)
A Chorus Line, James Kirkwood & Nicholas Dante
Chicago, Fred Ebb & Bob Fosse
Pacific Overtures, John Weidman
The Robber Bridegroom, Alfred Uhry

SCORE (T-583)
A Chorus Line, Music Marvin Hamlish; Lyrics Edward Kleban
Chicago, Music John Kander; Lyrics Fred Ebb
Pacific Overtures, Music & Lyrics, Stephen Sondheim
Treemonisha, Music & Lyrics, Scott Joplin

SCENIC DESIGNER (T-584)
Boris Aronson, Pacific Overtures
Ben Edwards, A Matter of Gravity
David Mitchell, Trelawny of the 'Wells'
Tony Walton, Chicago

COSTUME DESIGNER (T-585)
Theoni V. Aldredge, A Chorus Line
Florence Klotz, Pacific Overtures
Ann Roth, The Royal Family
Patricia Zipprodt, Chicago

LIGHTING DESIGNER (T-586)
Ian Calderon, Trelawny of the 'Wells'
Jules Fisher, Chicago
Tharon Musser, A Chorus Line
Tharon Musser, Pacific Overtures

CHOREOGRAPHER (T-587)
Michael Bennett & Bob Avian, A Chorus Line
Patricia Birch, Pacific Overtures
Bob Fosse, Chicago
Billy Wilson, Bubbling Brown Sugar

SPECIAL AWARDS (T-588)
Mathilde Pincus
Circle in the Square
Thomas H. Fitzgerald
The Arena Stage

1977

ACTOR (DRAMATIC) (T-589)
Tom Courtenay, Otherwise Engaged
Ben Gazzara, Who's Afraid of Virginia Woolf?
Al Pacino, The Basic Training of Pavlo Hummel
Ralph Richardson, No Man's Land

ACTRESS (DRAMATIC) (T-590)
Colleen Dewhurst, Who's Afraid of Virginia Woolf?
Julie Harris, The Belle of Amherst
Liv Ullmann, Anna Christie
Irene Worth, The Cherry Orchard

ACTOR, FEATURED ROLE (DRAMATIC) (T-591)
Bob Dishy, Sly Fox
Joe Fields, The Basic Training of Pavlo Hummel
Laurence Luckinbill, The Shadow Box

Jonathan Pryce, Comedians

ACTRESS, FEATURED ROLE (DRAMATIC) (T-592)
Trazana Beverley, For Colored Girls Who Have Considered Suicide/When The Rainbow Is Enuf
Patricia Elliott, The Shadow Box
Rose Gregorio, The Shadow Box
Mary McCarty, Anna Christie

ACTOR (MUSICAL) (T-593)
Barry Bostwick, The Robber Bridegroom
Robert Guillaume, Guys and Dolls
Raul Julia, The Threepenny Opera
Reid Shelton, Annie

ACTRESS (MUSICAL) (T-594)
Clamma Dale, Porgy and Bess
Ernestine Jackson, Guys and Dolls
Dorothy Loudon, Annie
Andrea McArdle, Annie

ACTOR, FEATURED ROLE (MUSICAL) (T-595)
Lenny Baker, I Love My Wife
David Kernan, Side By Side By Sondheim
Larry Marshall, Porgy and Bess
Ned Sherrin, Side By Side By Sondheim

ACTRESS, FEATURED ROLE (MUSICAL) (T-596)
Ellen Greene, The Threepenny Opera
Delores Hall, Your Arms Too Short To Box With God
Millicent Martin, Side By Side By Sondheim
Julie N. McKenzie, Side By Side By Sondheim

PLAY (T-597)
For Colored Girls Who Have Considered Suicide/When The Rainbow Is Enuf, by Ntozake Shange; producer Joseph Papp
Otherwise Engaged, by Simon Gray; producers Michael Codron, Frank Milton and James M. Nederlander
The Shadow Box, by Michael Cristofer; producers Allan Francis, Ken Marsolais, Lester Osterman, Leonard Soloway
Streamers, by David Rabe; producer Joseph Papp

DIRECTOR (DRAMATIC) (T-598)
Gordon Davidson, The Shadow Box
Ulu Grosbard, American Buffalo
Mike Nichols, Comedians
Mike Nichols, Streamers

MUSICAL (T-599)
Annie, producers Mike Nichols, Irwin Meyer, Stephen R. Friedman, Lewis Allen
Happy End, producers Michael Harvey and Chelsea Theatre Centre
I Love My Wife, producers Terry Allen Kramer and Harry Rigby
Side By Side By Sondheim, producer Harold Prince

DIRECTOR (MUSICAL) (T-600)
Vinnette Carroll, Your Arms Too Short To Box With God
Martin Charnin, Annie
Jack O'Brien, Porgy and Bess
Gene Saks, I Love My Wife

BOOK (MUSICAL) (T-601)
Annie, Thomas Meehan
Happy End, Elisabeth Hauptmann
I Love My Wife, Michael Stewart
Your Arms Too Short To Box With God, Vinnette Carroll

SCORE (T-602)
Annie, Music Charles Strouse; Lyrics Martin Charnin
Happy End, Music Kurt Weill; Lyrics Bertolt Brecht
Godspell, Music and Lyrics, Stephen Schwartz
I Love My Wife, Music Cy Coleman; Lyrics Michael Stewart

SCENIC DESIGNER (T-603)
Santo Loquasto, American Buffalo
Santo Loquasto, The Threepenny Opera
David Mitchell, Annie
Robert Randolph, Porgy and Bess

COSTUME DESIGNER (T-604)
Theoni V. Aldredge, Annie
Theoni V. Aldredge, The Threepenny Opera
Santo Loquasto, The Cherry Orchard
Nancy Potts, Porgy and Bess

LIGHTING DESIGNER (T-605)
John Bury, No Man's Land
Pat Collins, The Threepenny Opera
Neil Peter Jampolis, The Innocents
Jennifer Tipton, The Cherry Orchard

CHOREOGRAPHER (T-606)
Talley Beatty, Your Arms Too Short To Box With God
Patricia Birch, Music Is
Peter Gennaro, Annie
Onna White, I Love My Wife

MOST INNOVATIVE PRODUCTION OF A REVIVAL (T-607)
The Cherry Orchard
Guys and Dolls
Porgy and Bess
The Threepenny Opera

SPECIAL AWARDS (T-608)

Lily Tomlin
Barry Manilow
Diana Ross
National Theatre For The Deaf
Mark Taper Forum
Equity Library Theatre

1978

ACTOR (DRAMATIC) (T-609)

Hume Cronyn, The Gin Game

Barnard Hughes, Da
Frank Langella, Dracula
Jason Robards, A Touch of the Poet

ACTRESS (DRAMATIC) (T-610)

Anne Bancroft, Golda
Anita Gillette, Chapter Two
Estelle Parsons, Miss Margarida's Way

Jessica Tandy, The Gin Game

ACTOR, FEATURED ROLE (DRAMATIC) (T-611)

Morgan Freeman, The Mighty Gents
Victor Garber, Deathtrap
Cliff Gorman, Chapter Two

Lester Rawlins, Da

ACTRESS, FEATURED ROLE (DRAMATIC) (T-612)

Starletta DuPois, The Mighty Gents
Swoosie Kurtz, Tartuffe
Marian Seldes, Deathtrap

Ann Wedgeworth, Chapter Two

ACTOR (MUSICAL) (T-613)

Eddie Bracken, Hello, Dolly!

John Cullum, On The Twentieth Century
Barry Nelson, The Act
Gilbert Price, Timbuktu!

ACTRESS (MUSICAL) (T-614)

Madeline Kahn, On The Twentieth Century
Eartha Kitt, Timbuktu!

Liza Minnelli, The Act
Frances Sternhagen, Angel

ACTOR, FEATURED ROLE (MUSICAL) (T-615)

Steven Boockvor, Working
Wayne Cilento, Dancin'
Rex Everhart, Working

Kevin Kline, On The Twentieth Century

ACTRESS, FEATURED ROLE (MUSICAL) (T-616)

Nell Carter, Ain't Misbehavin'
Imogene Coca, On The Twentieth Century
Ann Reinking, Dancin'
Charlaine Woodard, Ain't Misbehavin'

PLAY (T-617)

Chapter Two, by Neil Simon; producer Emanuel Azenberg

Da, by Hugh Leonard; Hudson Guild Theatre prodn presented by Lester Osterman, Marilyn Strauss and Marc Howard
Deathtrap, by Ira Levin, presented by Alfred de Liagre Jr., and Roger L. Stevens
The Gin Game, by D.L. Coburn; Shubert Organization Presentation of Mike Nichols and Hume Cronyn prodn

DIRECTOR (DRAMATIC) (T-618)

Melvin Bernhardt, Da
Robert Moore, Deathtrap
Mike Nichols, The Gin Game
Dennis Rosa, Dracula

MUSICAL (T-619)

Ain't Misbehavin', Manhattan Theatre Club Prodn
Dancin', Jules Fisher, Shubert Organization and Columbia Pictures presentation of Jules Fisher prodn
On The Twentieth Century, Producers Circle 2 Inc. prodn in association with Joseph Harris and Ira Bernstein
Runaways, New York Shakespeare Festival Production

DIRECTOR (MUSICAL) (T-620)

Bob Fosse, Dancin'

Richard Maltby, Jr., Ain't Misbehavin'
Harold Prince, On The Twentieth Century
Elizabeth Swados, Runaways

BOOK (MUSICAL) (T-621)

A History Of The American Film, Christopher Durang

On The Twentieth Century, Betty Comden & Adolph Green
Runaways, Elizabeth Swados
Working, Stephen Schwartz

SCORE (T-622)

The Act, Music and Lyrics John Kander & Fred Ebb

On The Twentieth Century, Music Cy Coleman; Lyrics Comden & Green
Runaways, Music and Lyrics, Elizabeth Swados
Working, Music and Lyrics Craig Cornelia, Micki Grant, Mary Rodgers Susan Birkenhead, Stephen Schwartz, James Taylor

SCENIC DESIGNER (T-623)

Zack Brown, The Importance of Being Earnest
Edward Gorey, Dracula
David Mitchell, Working

Robin Wagner, On The Twentieth Century

COSTUME DESIGNER (T-624)

Edward Gorey, Dracula
Halston, The Act
Geoffrey Holder, Timbuktu!
Willa Kim, Dancin'

LIGHTING DESIGNER (T-625)

Jules Fisher, Beatlemania

Jules Fisher, Dancin'
Tharon Musser, The Act
Ken Billington, Working

CHOREOGRAPHER (T-626)

Arthur Faria, Ain't Misbehavin'

Bob Fosse, Dancin'
Ron Lewis, The Act
Elizabeth Swados, Runaways

MOST INNOVATIVE PRODUCTION OF A REVIVAL (T-627)

Dracula
Tartuffe
Timbuktu!
A Touch of the Poet

SPECIAL AWARD (T-628)

The Long Wharf Theatre

1979

ACTOR (DRAMATIC) (T-629)

Phillip Anglim, The Elephant Man

Tom Conti, Whose Life Is It Anyway?
Jack Lemmon, Tribute
Alec McCowen, St. Mark's Gospel

ACTRESS (DRAMATIC) (T-630)

Jane Alexander, First Monday In October
Constance Cummings, Wings
Carole Shelley, The Elephant Man
Frances Sternhagen, On Golden Pond

ACTOR, FEATURED ROLE (DRAMATIC) (T-631)

Bob Balaban, The Inspector General
Michael Gough, Bedroom Farce
Joseph Maher, Spokesong
Edward James Olmos, Zoot Suit

ACTRESS, FEATURED ROLE (DRAMATIC) (T-632)

Joan Hickson, Bedroom Farce
Laurie Kennedy, Man and Superman
Susan Littler, Bedroom Farce
Mary-Joan Negro, Wings

ACTOR (MUSICAL) (T-633)

Len Cariou, Sweeney Todd
Vincent Gardenia, Ballroom
Joel Grey, The Grand Tour
Robert Klein, They're Playing Our Song

ACTRESS (MUSICAL) (T-634)

Tovah Feldshuh, Sarava
Angela Lansbury, Sweeney Todd
Dorothy Loudon, Ballroom
Alexis Smith, Platinum

ACTOR, FEATURED ROLE (MUSICAL) (T-635)

Richard Cox, Platinum
Henderson Forsythe, The Best Little Whorehouse In Texas
Gregory Hines, Eubie!
Ron Holgate, The Grand Tour

ACTRESS, FEATURED ROLE (MUSICAL) (T-636)

Joan Ellis, The Best Little Whorehouse In Texas
Carlin Glynn, The Best Little Whorehouse In Texas
Millicent Martin, King Of Hearts
Maxine Sullivan, My Old Friends

PLAY (T-637)

Bedroom Farce by Alan Ayckbourn; producers Robert Whitehead, Roger L. Stevens, George W. George, Frank Milton
The Elephant Man by Bernard Pomerance; producers Richmond Crinkley, Elizabeth I. McCann, Nelle Nugent
Whose Life Is It Anyway? by Brian Clark; producers Emanuel Azenberg, James Nederlander, Ray Cooney
Wings by Arthur Kopit; producer Kennedy Center for the Performing Arts

DIRECTOR (DRAMATIC) (T-638)

Alan Ayckbourn & Peter Hall, Bedroom Farce
Paul Giovanni, The Crucifer Of Blood
Jack Hofsiss, The Elephant Man
Michael Lindsay-Hogg, Whose Life Is It Anyway?

MUSICAL (T-639)

Ballroom, producers Michael Bennett, Bob Avian, Bernard Gersten, Susan MacNair
Sweeney Todd, producers Richard Barr, Charles Woodward, Robert Fryer, Mary Lea Johnson, Martin Richards
The Best Little Whorehouse In Texas, producer Universal Pictures
They're Playing Our Song, producer Emanuel Azenberg

DIRECTOR (MUSICAL) (T-640)

Michael Bennett, Ballroom
Peter Masterson & Tommy Tune, The Best Little Whorehouse In Texas
Robert Moore, They're Playing Our Song
Harold Prince, Sweeney Todd

BOOK (MUSICAL) (T-641)

Ballroom, Jerome Kass
Sweeney Todd, Hugh Wheeler
The Best Little Whorehouse In Texas, Larry L. King, Peter Masterson
They're Playing Our Song, Neil Simon

SCORE (T-642)

Carmelina, Music Alan Jay Lerner; Lyrics Burton Lane
Eubie!, Music and Lyrics, Eubie Blake
Sweeney Todd, Music and Lyrics, Stephen Sondheim
The Grand Tour, Music and Lyrics, Jerry Herman

SCENIC DESIGNER (T-643)

Karl Eigsti, Knockout
David Jenkins, The Elephant Man
Eugene Lee, Sweeney Todd
John Wulp, The Crucifer Of Blood

COSTUME DESIGNER (T-644)

Theoni V. Aldredge, Ballroom
Franne Lee, Sweeney Todd
Ann Roth, The Crucifer Of Blood
Julie Weiss, The Elephant Man

LIGHTING DESIGNER (T-645)

Ken Billington, Sweeney Todd
Beverly Emmons, The Elephant Man
Roger Morgan, The Crucifer Of Blood
Tharon Musser, Ballroom

CHOREOGRAPHER (T-646)

Michael Bennett & Bob Avian, Ballroom
Henry LeTang & Billy Wilson, Eubie!
Dan Siretta, Whoopee!
Tommy Tune, The Best Little Whorehouse In Texas

SPECIAL AWARDS (T-647)

Henry Fonda
Walter F. Diehl
Eugene O'Neill Memorial Theatre Center
American Conservatory Theatre

1980

ACTOR (DRAMATIC) (T-648)

Charles Brown, Home
Gerald Hiken, Strider
Judd Hirsch, Talley's Folly
John Rubinstein, Children Of a Lesser God

ACTRESS (DRAMATIC) (T-649)

Blythe Danner, Betrayal
Phyllis Frelich, Children Of a Lesser God
Maggie Smith, Night And Day
Anne Twomey, Nuts

ACTOR, FEATURED ROLE (DRAMATIC) (T-650)

David Dukes, Bent
George Hearn, Watch On The Rhine
Earle Hyman, The Lady From Dubuque
Joseph Maher, Night And Day
David Rounds, Morning's At Seven

ACTRESS, FEATURED ROLE (DRAMATIC) (T-651)

Maureen Anderman, The Lady From Dubuque
Pamela Burrell, Strider
Lois de Banzie, Morning's At Seven
Dinah Manoff, I Ought To Be In Pictures

ACTOR (MUSICAL) (T-652)
Jim Dale, Barnum
Gregory Hines, Comin' Uptown
Mickey Rooney, Sugar Babies
Giorgio Tozzi, The Most Happy Fella

ACTRESS (MUSICAL) (T-653)
Christine Andreas, Oklahoma!
Sandy Duncan, Peter Pan
Patti LuPone, Evita
Ann Miller, Sugar Babies

ACTOR, FEATURED ROLE (MUSICAL) (T-654)
David Garrison, A Day In Hollywood, A Night In The Ukraine
Harry Groener, Oklahoma!
Bob Gunton, Evita
Mandy Patinkin, Evita

ACTRESS, FEATURED ROLE (MUSICAL) (T-655)
Debbie Allen, West Side Story
Glenn Close, Barnum
Jossie de Guzman, West Side Story
Priscilla Lopez, A Day In Hollywood, A Night In The Ukraine

PLAY (T-656)
Bent, by Martin Sherman; producers, Jack Schissel, Steven Steinlauf
Children Of a Lesser God, by Mark Medoff; producers, Emanuel Azenberg, The Shubert Organization, Dasha Epstein, Ron Dante
Home, by Samm-Art Williams; producers, Elizabeth I. McCann, Nelle Nugent, Gerald S. Krone, Ray Larsen
Talley's Folly, by Lanford Wilson; producers, Nancy Cooperstein, Porter Van Zandt, Marc Howard

DIRECTOR (DRAMATIC) (T-657)
Gordon Davidson, Children Of A Lesser God
Peter Hall, Betrayal
Marshall W. Mason, Talley's Folly
Vivian Matalon, Morning's At Seven

MUSICAL (T-658)
A Day In Hollywood, A Night In The Ukraine, producers, Alexander H. Cohen, Hildy Parks
Barnum, producers, Judy Gordon, Cy Coleman, Lois Rosenfield, Maurice Rosenfield
Evita, producer, Robert Stigwood
Sugar Babies, producers, Terry Allen Kramer, Harry Rigby

DIRECTOR (MUSICAL) (T-659)
Ernest Flatt, Rudy Tronto, Sugar Babies
Joe Layton, Barnum
Harold Prince, Evita
Tommy Tune, A Day In Hollywood, A Night In The Ukraine

BOOK (MUSICAL) (T-660)
A Day In Hollywood, A Night In The Ukraine, Dick Vosburgh
Barnum, Mark Bramble
Evita, Tim Rice
Sugar Babies, Ralph G. Allen and Harry Rigby

SCORE (T-661)
A Day In Hollywood, A Night In The Ukraine, Music, Frank Lazarus; Lyrics, Dick Vosburgh
Barnum, Music, Cy Coleman; Lyrics, Michael Stewart
Evita, Music, Andrew Lloyd Webber; Lyrics, Tim Rice
Sugar Babies, Music, Arthur Malvin; Lyrics, Arthur Malvin

SCENIC DESIGNER (T-662)
John Lee Beatty, Talley's Folly
David Mitchell, Barnum
Timothy O'Brien, Tazeena Firth, Evita
Tony Walton, A Day In Hollywood, A Night In The Ukraine

COSTUME DESIGNER (T-663)
Theoni V. Aldredge, Barnum
Pierre Balmain, Happy New Year
Timothy O'Brien, Tazeena Firth, Evita
Raoul Pene du Bois, Sugar Babies

LIGHTING DESIGNER (T-664)
Beverly Emmons, A Day In Hollywood, A Night In The Ukraine
David Hersey, Evita
Craig Miller, Barnum
Dennis Parichy, Talley's Folly

CHOREOGRAPHER (T-665)
Ernest Flatt, Sugar Babies
Larry Fuller, Evita
Joe Layton, Barnum
Tommy Tune, Thommie Walsh, A Day In Hollywood, A Night In The Ukraine

REPRODUCTION OF A PLAY OR MUSICAL (T-666)
Major Barbara, producer, Circle in the Square
Morning's At Seven, producers, Elizabeth I. McCann, Nelle Nugent, Ray Larsen
Peter Pan, producers, Zev Bufman, James M. Nederlander
West Side Story, producers, Gladys Rackmil, Kennedy Center, James M. Nederlander, Ruth Mitchell

SPECIAL AWARDS (T-667)
Actors Theatre of Louisville
Goodspeed Opera House
Mary Tyler Moore

LAWRENCE LANGNER AWARD
Helen Hayes

THEATRE AWARD '80
Richard Fitzgerald
Hobe Morrison

1981

ACTOR (DRAMATIC) (T-668)
Tim Curry, Amadeus
Roy Dotrice, A Life
Ian McKellen, Amadeus
Jack Weston, The Floating Light Bulb

ACTRESS (DRAMATIC) (T-669)
Glenda Jackson, Rose
Jane Lapotaire, Piaf
Eva Le Gallienne, To Grandmother's House We Go
Elizabeth Taylor, The Little Foxes

ACTOR, FEATURED ROLE (DRAMATIC) (T-670)
Tom Aldredge, The Little Foxes
Brian Backer, The Floating Light Bulb
Adam Redfield, A Life
Shepperd Strudwick, To Grandmother's House We Go

ACTRESS, FEATURED ROLE (DRAMATIC) (T-671)
Swoosie Kurtz, Fifth of July
Maureen Stapleton, The Little Foxes
Jessica Tandy, Rose
Zoe Wanamaker, Piaf

ACTOR (MUSICAL) (T-672)
Gregory Hines, Sophisticated Ladies
Kevin Kline, The Pirates of Penzance
George Rose, The Pirates of Penzance
Martin Vidnovic, Brigadoon

ACTRESS (MUSICAL) (T-673)
Lauren Bacall, Woman of the Year
Meg Bussert, Brigadoon
Chita Rivera, Bring Back Birdie
Linda Ronstadt, The Pirates of Penzance

ACTOR, FEATURED ROLE (MUSICAL) (T-674)
Tony Azito, The Pirates of Penzance
Hinton Battle, Sophisticated Ladies
Lee Roy Reams, 42d Street
Paxton Whitehead, Camelot

ACTRESS, FEATURED ROLE (MUSICAL) (T-675)
Marilyn Cooper, Woman of the Year
Phyllis Hyman, Sophisticated Ladies
Wanda Richert, 42d Street
Lynne Thigpen, Tintypes

PLAY (T-676)
A Lesson From Aloes, by Athol Fugard; producers, Jay J. Cohen, Richard Press, Louis Bush Hager Assocs., Yale Repertory Theatre
A Life, by Hugh Leonard; producers, Lester Osterman, Richard Horner, Hinks Shimberg, Freyberg-Cutler-Diamond Prods.
Amadeus, by Peter Shaffer; producers, Shubert Organization, Elizabeth McCann, Nelle Nugent, Roger S. Berlind
Fifth of July, by Lanford Wilson; producers, Jerry Arrow, Robert Lussier, Warner Theatre Prods.

DIRECTOR (DRAMATIC) (T-677)
Peter Coe, A Life
Peter Hall, Amadeus
Marshall W. Mason, Fifth of July
Austin Pendleton, The Little Foxes

MUSICAL (T-678)
42d St, producer, David Merrick
Sophisticated Ladies, producers, Roger S. Berlind, Manheim Fox, Sondra Gilman, Burton L. Litwin, Louise Westergaard, Belwin Mills Publishing Corp., Norzar Prods. Inc.
Tintypes, producers, Richmond Crinkley, Royal Pardon Prods., Ivan Bloch, Larry J. Silva, Eve Skina, Joan F. Tobin
Woman of the Year, producers, Lawrence Kasha, David S. Landay, James M. Nederlander, Warner Theatre Prods., Claire Nichtern, Carole J. Shorenstein, Stewart F. Lane

DIRECTOR (MUSICAL) (T-679)
Gower Champion, 42d Street
Wilford Leach, The Pirates of Penzance
Robert Moore, Woman of the Year
Michael Smuin, Sophisticated Ladies

BOOK (MUSICAL) (T-680)
42d St, Michael Stewart, Mark Bramble
The Moony Shapiro Songbook, Monty Norman, Julian More
Tintypes, Mary Kyte
Woman of the Year, Peter Stone

SCORE (T-681)
Charlie And Algernon, Music, Charles Strouse; Lyrics, David Rogers
Copperfield, Music and Lyrics, Al Kasha, Joel Hirschhorn
Shakespeare's Cabaret, Music, Lance Mulcahy
Woman of the Year, Music, John Kander; Lyrics, Fred Ebb

SCENIC DESIGNER (T-682)
John Lee Beatty, Fifth of July
John Bury, Amadeus
Santo Loquasto, The Suicide
David Mitchell, Can-Can

COSTUME DESIGNER (T-683)
Theoni V. Aldredge, 42d Street
John Bury, Amadeus
Willa Kim, Sophisticated Ladies
Franca Squarciapino, Can-Can

LIGHTING DESIGNER (T-684)
John Bury, Amadeus
Tharon Musser, 42d Street
Dennis Parichy, Fifth of July
Jennifer Tipton, Sophisticated Ladies

CHOREOGRAPHER (T-685)
Gower Champion, 42d Street
Graciela Daniele, The Pirates of Penzance
Henry Le Tang, Donald McKayle, Michael Smuin, Sophisticated Ladies
Roland Petit, Can-Can

REPRODUCTION OF A PLAY OR MUSICAL (T-686)
Brigadoon, producers, Zev Bufman, Shubert Organization
Camelot, producers, Mike Merrick, Don Gregory
The Little Foxes, producers, Zev Bufman, Donald C. Carter, John Cutler
The Pirates of Penzance, producer, Joseph Papp

SPECIAL AWARDS (T-687)
Lena Horne
Trinity Square Repertory Co.

1982

ACTOR (DRAMATIC) (T-688)
Roger Rees, The Life and Adventures of Nicholas Nickleby
Tom Courtenay, The Dresser
Milo O'Shea, Mass Appeal
Christopher Plummer, Othello

ACTRESS (DRAMATIC) (T-689)
Zoe Caldwell, Medea
Katharine Hepburn, The West Side Waltz
Geraldine Page, Agnes of God
Amanda Plummer, A Taste of Honey

ACTOR, FEATURED ROLE (DRAMATIC) (T-690)
Zakes Mokae, Master Harold. . .and the Boys
Richard Kavanaugh, The Hothouse
Edward Petherbridge, The Life and Adventures of Nicholas Nickleby
David Threlfall, The Life and Adventures of Nicholas Nickleby

ACTRESS, FEATURED ROLE (DRAMATIC) (T-691)
Amanda Plummer, Agnes of God
Judith Anderson, Medea
Mia Dillon, Crimes of the Heart
Mary Beth Hurt, Crimes of the Heart

ACTOR (MUSICAL) (T-692)
Ben Harney, Dreamgirls
Herschel Bernardi, Fiddler On The Roof
Victor Garber, Little Me
Raul Julia, "Nine"

ACTRESS (MUSICAL) (T-693)
Jennifer Holliday, Dreamgirls
Lisa Mordente, Marlowe
Mary Gordon Murray, Little Me
Sheryl Lee Ralph, Dreamgirls

ACTOR, FEATURED ROLE (MUSICAL) (T-694)
Cleavant Derricks, Dreamgirls
Obba Babatunde, Dreamgirls
David Alan Grier, The First
Bill Hutton, Joseph and The Amazing Technicolor Dreamcoat

ACTRESS, FEATURED ROLE (MUSICAL) (T-695)
Liliane Montevecchi, "Nine"
Karen Akers, "Nine"
Laurie Beechman, Joseph and The Amazing Technicolor Dreamcoat
Anita Morris, "Nine"

PLAY (T-696)

The Life and Adventures of Nicholas Nickleby, by David Edgar; producers James M. Nederlander, The Shubert Organization, Elizabeth I. McCann, Nelle Nugent
Crimes of the Heart, by Beth Henley; producers, Warner Theatre Productions, Inc., Claire Nichtern, Mary Lea Johnson, Martin Richards, Francine LeFrak
The Dresser, by Ronald Harwood; producers, James M. Nederlander, Elizabeth I. McCann, Nelle Nugent, Warner Theatre Productions, Inc., Michael Codron
Master Harold. . .and the boys, by Athol Fugard; producers, The Shubert Organization, Freydberg/Bloch Productions, Dasha Epstein, Emanuel Azenberg, David Geffen

DIRECTOR (DRAMATIC) (T-697)

Trevor Nunn and John Caird, The Life and Adventures of Nicholas Nickleby
Melvin Bernhardt, Crimes of the Heart
Geraldine Fitzgerald, Mass Appeal
Athol Fugard, Master Harold. . .and the boys

MUSICAL (T-698)

"Nine", producers, Michel Stuart, Harvey J. Klaris, Roger S. Berlind, James M. Nederlander, Francine LeFrak, Kenneth D. Greenblatt
Dreamgirls, producers, Michael Bennett, Bob Avian, Geffen Records, The Shubert Organization
Joseph and the Amazing Technicolor Dreamcoat, producers, Zev Bufman, Susan R. Rose, Melvyn J. Estrin, Sidney Shlenker, Gail Berman
Pump Boys and Dinettes, producers, Dodger Productions, Louis Busch Hager, Marilyn Strauss, Kate Studley, Warner Theatre Productions, Inc., Max Weitzenhoffer

DIRECTOR (MUSICAL) (T-699)

Tommy Tune, "Nine"
Michael Bennett, Dreamgirls
Martin Charnin, The First
Tony Tanner, Joseph and the Amazing Technicolor Dreamcoat

BOOK (MUSICAL) (T-700)

Dreamgirls, Tom Eyen
Joseph and the Amazing Technicolor Dreamcoat, Tim Rice
"Nine," Arthur Kopit
The First, Joel Siegel, Martin Charnin

SCORE (T-701)

"Nine", Music and Lyrics, Maury Yeton
Dreamgirls, Music, Henry Krieger; Lyrics, Tom Eyen
Joseph and the Amazing Technicolor Dreamcoat, Music, Andrew Lloyd Webber; Lyrics, Tim Rice
Merrily We Roll Along, Music and Lyrics, Stephen Sondheim

SCENIC DESIGNER (T-702)

John Napier and Dermot Hayes, The Life and Adventures of Nicholas Nickleby
Ben Edwards, Medea
Lawrence Miller, "Nine"
Robin Wagner, Dreamgirls

COSTUME DESIGNER (T-703)

William Ivey Long, "Nine"
Theoni V. Aldredge, Dreamgirls
Jane Greenwood, Medea
John Napier, The Life and Adventures of Nicholas Nickleby

LIGHTING DESIGNER (T-704)

Tharon Musser, Dreamgirls
Martin Aronstein, Medea
David Hersey, The Life and Adventures of Nicholas Nickleby
Marcia Madeira, "Nine"

CHOREOGRAPHER (T-705)

Michael Bennett and Michael Peters, Dreamgirls
Peter Gennaro, Little Me
Tony Tanner, Joseph and the Amazing Technicolor Dreamcoat
Tommy Tune, "Nine"

REPRODUCTION OF A PLAY OR MUSICAL (T-706)

Othello, producers, Barry & Fran Weissler, CBS Video Enterprises, Don Gregory
A Taste Of Honey, producers, Roundabout Theatre Co., Inc. Gene Feist, Michael Fried
Medea, producers, Barry & Fran Weissler, Kennedy Center, Bunny & Warren Austin
My Fair Lady, producers, Mike Merrick, Don Gregory

SPECIAL AWARDS (T-707)

The Guthrie Theatre, Minneapolis
The Actors' Fund of America

THEATRE AWARD '82

Warner Communications, Inc.
Radio City Music Hall, N.Y.

1983

ACTOR (DRAMATIC) (T-708)

Harvey Fierstein, Torch Song Trilogy
Jeffrey De Munn, K2
Edward Herrmann, Plenty
Tony Lo Bianco, A View From The Bridge

ACTRESS (DRAMATIC) (T-709)

Jessica Tandy, Foxfire
Kathy Bates, 'Night, Mother
Kate Nelligan, Plenty
Anne Pitoniak, 'Night, Mother

ACTOR, FEATURED ROLE (DRAMATIC) (T-710)

Matthew Broderick, Brighton Beach Memoirs
Zeljko Ivanek, Brighton Beach Memoirs
George N. Martin, Plenty
Stephen Moore, All's Well That Ends Well

ACTRESS, FEATURED ROLE (DRAMATIC) (T-711)

Judith Ivey, Steaming
Elizabeth Franz, Brighton Beach Memoirs
Roxanne Hart, Passion
Margaret Tyzack, All's Well That Ends Well

ACTOR (MUSICAL) (T-712)

Tommy Tune, My One and Only
Al Green, Your Arms Too Short to Box With God
George Hearn, A Doll's Life
Michael V. Smartt, Porgy and Bess

ACTRESS (MUSICAL) (T-713)

Natalia Makarova, On Your Toes
Lonette McKee, Show Boat
Chita Rivera, Merlin
Twiggy, My One and Only

ACTOR, FEATURED ROLE (MUSICAL) (T-714)

Charles "Honi" Coles, My One and Only
Harry Groener, Cats
Stephen Hanan, Cats
Lara Teeter, On Your Toes

ACTRESS, FEATURED ROLE (MUSICAL) (T-715)

Betty Buckley, Cats
Christine Andreas, On Your Toes
Karla Burns, Show Boat
Denny Dillon, My One and Only

PLAY (T-716)
Torch Song Trilogy, by Harvey Fierstein. Producers, Kenneth Waissman, Martin Markinson, Lawrence Lane, John Glines, BetMar, Donald Tick
Angels Fall, by Lanford Wilson. Producers, Elliot Martin, Circle Repertory Co., Lucille Lortel, Shubert Organization, Kennedy Center
'Night, Mother, by Marsha Norman. Producers, Dann Byck, Wendell Cherry, Shubert Organization, Frederick M. Zollo
Plenty, by David Hare. Producer, Joseph Papp

DIRECTOR (DRAMATIC) (T-717)
Gene Saks, Brighton Beach Memoirs
Marshall W. Mason, Angels Fall
Tom Moore, 'Night, Mother
Trevor Nunn, All's Well That Ends Well

MUSICAL (T-718)
Cats, producers, Cameron Mackintosh, The Really Useful Co., Ltd., David Geffen, Shubert Organization
Blues in the Night, producers, Mitchell Maxwell, Alan J. Schuster, Fred H. Krones, M2 Entertainment, Inc
Merlin, producers, Ivan Reitman, Columbia Pictures Stage Productions, Inc., Marvin A. Krauss, James M. Nederlander
My One and Only, producers, Paramount Theatre Productions, Francine LeFrak, Kenneth-Mark Productions

DIRECTOR (MUSICAL) (T-719)
Trevor Nunn, Cats
Michael Kahn, Show Boat
Ivan Reitman, Merlin
Tommy Tune and Thommie Walsh, My One and Only

BOOK (MUSICAL) (T-720)
Cats, by T.S. Eliot
A Doll's Life, by Betty Comden and Adolph Green
Merlin, by Richard Levinson and William Link
My One and Only, by Peter Stone and Timothy S. Mayer

SCORE (T-721)
Cats, music by Andrew Lloyd Webber, lyrics by T.S. Eliot
A Doll's Life, music by Larry Grossman, lyrics by Betty Comden and Adolph Green
Merlin, music by Elmer Bernstein, lyrics by Don Black
Seven Brides for Seven Brothers, music by Gene de Paul, Al Kasha and Joel Hirschhorn, lyrics by Johnny Mercer, Al Kasha and Joel Hirschhorn

SCENIC DESIGNER (T-722)
Ming Cho Lee, K2
John Gunter, All's Well That Ends Well
David Mitchell, Foxfire
John Napier, Cats

COSTUME DESIGNER (T-723)
John Napier, Cats
Lindy Hemming, All's Well That Ends Well
Rita Ryack, My One And Only
Patricia Zipprodt, Alice in Wonderland

LIGHTING DESIGNER (T-724)
David Hersey, Cats
Ken Billington, Foxfire
Robert Bryan, All's Well That Ends Well
Allen Lee Hughes, K2

CHOREOGRAPHER (T-725)
Thommie Walsh and Tommy Tune, My One and Only
George Faison, Porgy and Bess
Gillian Lynne, Cats
Donald Saddler, On Your Toes

REPRODUCTION OF A PLAY OR MUSICAL (T-726)
On Your Toes, producers, Alfred De Liagre, Jr., Roger L. Stevens, John Mauceri, Donald R. Seawell, Andre Pastoria
All's Well That Ends Well, producer, Royal Shakespeare Co
A View From The Bridge, producers, Zev Bufman, Sidney Shlenker
The Caine Mutiny Court-Martial, producers, Circle in the Square Theatre, Kennedy Center

SPECIAL AWARD (T-727)
Oregon Shakespearean Festival Association, Ashland, OR

THEATRE AWARD '83
The Theatre Collection, Museum of The City of New York

GRAMMY®S

All the photographs in this section are reproduced courtesy of the Margaret Herrick Library, Academy Foundation.

© NARAS

1958

RECORD OF THE YEAR (G-01)
CATCH A FALLING STAR - Perry Como (RCA)
THE CHIPMUNK SONG - David Seville (Lib)
FEVER - Peggy Lee (Cap)
NEL BLU DIPINTO DI BLU (VOLARE) - Domenico Modugno (Decca)
WITCHCRAFT - Frank Sinatra (Cap)

ALBUM OF THE YEAR (G-02)
ELLA FITZGERALD SINGS THE IRVING BERLIN SONG BOOK - Ella Fitzgerald (Verve)
COME FLY WITH ME - Frank Sinatra (Cap)
THE MUSIC FROM PETER GUNN - Henry Mancini (Victor)
ONLY THE LONELY - Frank Sinatra (Cap)
TCHAIKOVSKY: CONCERTO NO. 1, IN B FLAT MINOR OP. 23 - Van Cliburn (Victor)

SONG OF THE YEAR (G-03)
(Songwriter's Award)
CATCH A FALLING STAR - Paul Vance and Lee Pockriss (Victor)
FEVER - Johnny Davenport and Eddie Cooley (Cap)
GIGI - Alan J. Lerner and Frederick Loewe (MGM)
NEL BLU DIPINTO DI BLU (VOLARE) - Domenico Modugno (Decca)
WITCHCRAFT - Cy Coleman and Carolyn Leigh (Cap)

VOCAL - FEMALE (G-04)
ELLA FITZGERALD SINGS THE IRVING BERLIN SONG BOOK - Ella Fitzgerald (Verve)
EVERYBODY LOVES A LOVER - Doris Day (Col)
EYDIE IN LOVE - Eydie Gorme (Am-Par)
FEVER - Peggy Lee (Cap)
I WISH YOU LOVE - Keely Smith (Cap)

VOCAL - MALE (G-05)
CATCH A FALLING STAR - Perry Como (RCA)
COME FLY WITH ME - Frank Sinatra (Cap)
HAWAIIAN WEDDING SONG - Andy Williams (Cadence)
NEL BLU DIPINTO DI BLU (VOLARE) - Domenico Modugno (Decca)
WITCHCRAFT - Frank Sinatra (Cap)

ORCHESTRA (G-06)
BURNISHED BRASS - George Shearing (Cap)
CROSS COUNTRY SUITE - Buddy DeFranco (Dot)
PETER GUNN - Henry Mancini (RCA)
I WANT TO LIVE - Johnny Mandel (UA)
KANE IS ABLE - Jack Kane (Coral)
BILLY MAY'S BIG FAT BRASS - Billy May (Cap)
OTHER WORLDS, OTHER SOUNDS - Esquivel (RCA)
YOUNG MAN'S LAMENT - David Rose & His Orchestra with Andre Previn (MGM)

DANCE BAND (G-07)
BASIE - Count Basie (Roulette)
BAUBLES, BANGLES & BEADS - Jonah Jones (Cap)
PETER GUNN - Ray Anthony (Cap)
PATRICIA - Perez Prado (RCA)
TEA FOR TWO CHA CHA - Warren Covington & The Tommy Dorsey Orchestra (Decca)

VOCAL GROUP OR CHORUS (G-08)
BAUBLES, BANGLES AND BEADS - Kirby Stone Four (Col)
TOM DOOLEY - Kingston Trio (Cap)
IMAGINATION - The King Sisters (Cap)
SING A SONG OF BASIE - Lambert, Henricks, & Ross (Am-Par)
THAT OLD BLACK MAGIC - Louis Prima, Keely Smith (Cap)

JAZZ - INDIVIDUAL (G-09)
BAUBLES, BANGLES & BEADS - Jonah Jones (Cap)
BURNISHED BRASS - George Shearing (Cap)
DIXIELAND STORY - Matty Matlock (WB)
ELLA FITZGERALD SINGS THE DUKE ELLINGTON SONG BOOK - Ella Fitzgerald (Verve)
JUMPIN' WITH JONAH - Jonah Jones (Cap)

JAZZ - GROUP (G-10)
BASIE - Count Basie (Roulette)
BAUBLES, BANGLES & BEADS - Jonah Jones (Cap)
BURNISHED BRASS - George Shearing (Cap)
FOUR FRESHMAN IN PERSON (Cap)
SING A SONG OF BASIE - Basie Rhythm Section, Dave Lambert Singers (Am-Par)

COMEDY PERFORMANCE (G-11)
BEST OF THE STAN FREBERG SHOWS - Stan Freberg (Cap)
CHIPMUNK SONG - David Seville (Lib)
THE FUTURE LIES AHEAD - Mort Sahl (Verve)
GREEN CHRISTMAS - Stan Freberg (Cap)
IMPROVISATIONS TO MUSIC - Mike Nichols & Elaine May (Merc)

COUNTRY & WESTERN PERFORMANCE (G-12)
ALL I HAVE TO DO IS DREAM - Everly Brothers (Cadence)
BIRD DOG - Everly Brothers (Cadence)
TOM DOOLEY - Kingston Trio (Cap)
OH LONESOME ME - Don Gibson (Victor)
OH, OH, I'M FALLING IN LOVE AGAIN - Jimmie Rodgers (Roulette)

RHYTHM & BLUES PERFORMANCE (G-13)
BELAFONTE SINGS THE BLUES - Harry Belafonte (Victor)
THE END - Earl Grant (Decca)
LOOKING BACK - Nat King Cole (Cap)
PATRICIA - Perez Prado (Victor)
TEQUILA - Champs (Challenge)

ARRANGEMENT (G-14)
(Arranger's Award)
COME FLY WITH ME (Frank Sinatra) - Billy May (Cap)
FEVER (Peggy Lee) - Jack Marshall (Cap)
THE MUSIC FROM PETER GUNN - Henry Mancini (RCA)
BILLY MAY'S BIG FAT BRASS - Billy May (Cap)
WITCHCRAFT (Frank Sinatra) - Nelson Riddle (Cap)

BEST ENGINEERED RECORD - CLASSICAL (G-15)
(Engineer's Award)
DUETS WITH A SPANISH GUITAR (Almeida & Terri) Eng: Sherwood Hall III (Cap)
GAIETE PARISIENNE (Felix Slatkin) Eng: Sherwood Hall III (Cap)
PROKOFIEFF: LIEUTENANT KIJI/STRAVINSKY; SONG OF THE NIGHTINGALE (Fritz Reiner) (Victor)
STRAVINSKY: RITE OF SPRING (Bernstein) (Col)

BEST ENGINEERED RECORDING - OTHER THAN CLASSICAL (G-16)
(Engineer's Award)
THE CHIPMUNK SONG (David Seville) Eng: Ted Keep (Lib)
COME FLY WITH ME (Frank Sinatra) Eng: Luis P. Valentin (Cap)
BILLY MAY'S BIG FAT BRASS (Billy May) Eng: Hugh Davies (Cap)
OTHER WORLDS, OTHER SOUNDS (Esquivel) Eng: Rafael O. Valentin (Victor)
WITCHCRAFT (Frank Sinatra) Eng: Luis P. Valentin (Cap)

ALBUM COVER (G-17)
(Art Director's Award)
COME FLY WITH ME (Frank Sinatra) Art Dir: Marvin Schwartz (Cap)
FOR WHOM THE BELLS TOLL (Ray Heindorf) Photog: Paramount Pictures Corp., Ray Rennahan, A.S.C. (WB)
IRA IRONSTRINGS PLAY MUSIC FOR PEOPLE WITH $3.98 - Art Dir: David Rose (WB)
JULIE (Julie London) Art Dir: Charles Ward (Lib)
ONLY THE LONELY (Frank Sinatra) Art Dir: Frank Sinatra (Cap)

COMPOSITION - OVER 5 MINS. DURATION (G-18)
VANESSA: Samuel Barber (Victor)
CROSS COUNTRY SUITE - Nelson Riddle
I WANT TO LIVE - Johnny Mandel (UA)
VICTORY AT SEA, VOL. III: Richard Rodgers (Victor)
MAHOGONNY: Kurt Weill (Col)

ORIGINAL CAST ALBUM - BROADWAY OR TV (G-19)
FLOWER DRUM SONG - Orig. Cast Album, Salvatore dell'Isola, Musical Dir. Richard Rodgers, Music (Col)
THE MUSIC MAN - Orig. Broadway Cast, Meredith Willson (Cap)
SOUND OF JAZZ - from CBS TV "Seven Lively Arts" with Basie, Giuffre, Holiday, etc. (Col)
VICTORY AT SEA VOL. 11 - from NBC TV prod. RCA Victor Sym. Orch., Richard Rodgers (RCA)
PETER GUNN - Henry Mancini (RCA)

SOUND TRACK ALBUM - DRAMATIC PICTURE SCORE OR ORIGINAL CAST (G-20)
AUNTIE MAME SOUND TRACK - Ray Heindorf Orchestra (WB)
THE BRIDGE ON THE RIVER KWAI - Malcolm Arnold (Col)
GIGI - Orig. Motion Picture Sound Track, Andre Previn (MGM)
I WANT TO LIVE - Johnny Mandel (UA)
SOUTH PACIFIC - Orig. Sound Track Orch. cond. Alfred Newman (Victor)

DOCUMENTARY OR SPOKEN WORD RECORDING (G-21)
THE BEST OF THE STAN FREBERG SHOWS (Cap)
GREAT AMERICAN SPEECHES - Melvyn Douglas, Vincent Price, Carl Sandburg, Ed Begley (Caedmon)
GREEN CHRISTMAS - Stan Freberg (Cap)
IMPROVISATIONS TO MUSIC - Mike Nichols, Elaine May (Merc)
TWO INTERVIEWS OF OUR TIME - Henry Jacobs, Woody Leafer (Fantasy)
THE LADY FROM PHILADELPHIA - Marion Anderson (Rupp, Morrow) (Victor)

RECORDING FOR CHILDREN (G-22)
CHILDREN'S MARCHING SONG - Cyril Stapleton (London)
THE CHIPMUNK SONG - David Seville (Lib)
FUN IN SHARILAND - Shari Lewis (Victor)
MOMMY, GIVE ME A DRINKA WATER - Danny Kaye (Cap)
TUBBY THE TUBA - Jose Ferrer (MGM)
THE WITCH DOCTOR - David Seville (Lib)

CLASSICAL PERFORMANCE - ORCHESTRA (G-23)
BARBER: MEDITATION AND DANCE OF VENGEANCE - Charles Munch, Boston Symphony (Victor)
BEETHOVEN: SYMPHONY No. 6 IN F MAJOR - Bruno Walter, Columbia Symphony Orch. (Col)
GAIETE PARISIENNE - Felix Slatkin, Hollywood Bowl Symphony (Cap)
MAHLER: SYMPHONY No. 2 IN C MINOR (Emilia Cundari, Maureen Forrester, Westminster Choir) - Bruno Walter, N.Y. Philharmonic (Col)
PROKOFIEV: SYMPHONY No. 5 IN B FLAT MAJOR - Eugene Ormandy, Philadelphia Orchestra (Col)
RIMSKY-KORSAKOFF: SCHEHEREZADE - Pierre Monteux, London Symphony (Victor)
STRAVINSKY: LE SACRE DU PRINTEMPS - Leonard Bernstein, N.Y. Philharmonic (Col)

CLASSICAL PERFORMANCE - INSTRUMENTAL (WITH CONCERTO SCALE ACCOMPANIMENT) (G-24)
BARTOK: CONCERTO FOR VIOLIN - Isaac Stern (Bernstein, cond. N.Y. Philharmonic) (Col)
BRAHMS: PIANO CONCERTO No. 2 - Emil Gilels (Fritz Reiner, cond. Chicago Symphony) (Victor)
RACHMANINOFF: RHAPSODY ON A THEME OF PAGANINI - Leonard Pennario (Cap)
SAINT-SAENS: PIANO CONCERTO No. 2 - Artur Rubinstein (Wallenstein, cond. Symphony of the Air) (Victor)
(Andres) SEGOVIA GOLDEN JUBILEE (last record in set) (Decca)
TCHAIKOVSKY: CONCERTO No. 1 IN B FLAT MINOR, OP. 23 - Van Cliburn (Kondrashin Symphony) (Victor)

CLASSICAL PERFORMANCE - INSTRUMENTAL (OTHER THAN CONCERTO SCALE ACCOMPANIMENT) (G-25)
ART OF THE HARPSICHORD - Wanda Landowska (RCA)
BEETHOVEN SONATA No. 9 AND SONATA No. 8 - Nathan Milstein (Cap)
HOROWITZ PLAYS CHOPIN - Vladimir Horowitz (Victor)
MUSIC FOR THE HARP - Marcel Grandjany (Cap)
SEGOVIA GOLDEN JUBILEE - Andres Segovia (Decca)

CLASSICAL PERFORMANCE - CHAMBER MUSIC (INCLUDING CHAMBER ORCHESTRA) (G-26)
BEETHOVEN QUARTET 130 - Hollywood String Quartet (Cap)
BEETHOVEN: TRIO IN E FLAT, OP. 3 - Jascha Heifetz, William Primrose, Gregor Piatigorsky (Victor)
BEETHOVEN: TRIO IN E FLAT MAJOR; TRIO IN D MAJOR - Pablo Casals, Eugene Istomin, Fuchs (Col)
BEETHOVEN: TRIO IN G, OP. 9, NO. 1; TRIO IN C MINOR, OP. 9, NO. 3 - Jascha Heifetz, William Primrose, Gregor Piatigorsky (Victor)
RAVEL: QUARTET IN F MAJOR; DEBUSSY: QUARTET IN G MINOR - The Budapest String Quartet (Col)

CLASSICAL PERFORMANCE - VOCAL SOLOIST (WITH OR WITHOUT ORCHESTRA) (G-27)
CHERUBINI: MEDEA - Maria Callas (Merc)
DUETS FOR SPANISH GUITAR - Salli Terri (Cap)
EILEEN FARRELL AS MEDEA - Eileen Farrell (Col)
OPERATIC RECITAL - Renata Tebaldi (London)
WAGNER: PRELUDE & LIEBESTOD/"TRISTAN & ISOLDE", BRUNNHILDE'S IMMOLATION, DIE GOTTERDAMERUNG - Eileen Farrell (Munch, Boston Symphony) (Victor)

CLASSICAL PERFORMANCE - OPERATIC OR CHORAL (G-28)
BARBER: VANESSA - Dimitri Mitropoulos, Metropolitan Opera Chorus & Orch. (Steber, Elias, Resnick, Gedda, Nagy, Cehanovsky, Tozzi) (Victor)
DONIZETTI: LUCIA DE LAMMERMOOR - Erich Leinsdorf, Rome Opera House Chorus & Orch. (Peters, Pace, Carlin, Palma, Peerce, Maero, Tozzi) (Victor)
PUCCINI: MADAME BUTTERFLY - Erich Leinsdorf, Rome Opera House Chorus & Orch. (Cifferi, Mattioli, Moffo, Zeri, Elias, Pace, Carlin, Valletti, Catalani Cesari, Mineo, Corena, Monreale) (Victor)
ROSSINI: BARBER OF SEVILLE - Maria Callas, Tito Gobbi (Angel)
VICTORIA: REQUIEM MASS - Dom David Nicholson, Dir., Choir of the Abbey of Mt. Angel/C. Robert Zimmerman, Dir., Portland Symphony Choir (Victor)
VIRTUOSO - Roger Wagner Chorale (Cap)

1959

RECORD OF THE YEAR (G-29)
A FOOL SUCH AS I - Elvis Presley (RCA)
HIGH HOPES - Frank Sinatra (Cap)
LIKE YOUNG - Andre Previn (MGM)
MACK THE KNIFE - Bobby Darin (Atco)
THE THREE BELLS - The Browns (RCA)

ALBUM OF THE YEAR (G-30)
BELAFONTE AT CARNEGIE HALL - Harry Belafonte (RCA)
COME DANCE WITH ME - Frank Sinatra (Cap)
MORE MUSIC FROM PETER GUNN - Henry Mancini (RCA)
RACHMANINOFF PIANO CONCERTO No. 3 - Van Cliburn, Kiril Kondrashin (RCA)
VICTORY AT SEA, VOL. I - Robert Russell Bennett (Remake) (RCA)

SONG OF THE YEAR (G-31)
(Songwriter's Award)

BATTLE OF NEW ORLEANS - Jimmy Driftwood
HIGH HOPES - Sammy Cahn, Jimmy van Heusen
I KNOW - Karl Stutz, Edith Lindeman
LIKE YOUNG - Paul Francis Webster, Andre Previn
SMALL WORLD - Jule Styne, Stephen Sondheim

VOCAL - FEMALE (G-32)
ALRIGHT, OKAY - Peggy Lee (Cap)
BROADWAY '59 - Pat Suzuki (RCA)
BUT NOT FOR ME - Ella Fitzgerald (Verve)
LA STRADA DEL AMORE - Caterina Valente (RCA)
PORGY AND BESS - Lena Horne (RCA)

VOCAL - MALE (G-33)
AN EVENING WITH LERNER AND LOWE - Robert Merrill (RCA)
BELAFONTE AT CARNEGIE HALL - Harry Belafonte (RCA)
COME DANCE WITH ME - Frank Sinatra (Cap)
GUESS WHO - Jesse Belvin (RCA)
MACK THE KNIFE - Bobby Darin (Atco)

DANCE BAND (G-34)
ANATOMY OF A MURDER - Duke Ellington (Col)
BREAKFAST DANCE AND BARBECUE - Count Basie (Roulette)
FOR THE VERY FIRST TIME - Glenn Miller (RCA)
NEW SOUNDS AT THE ROOSEVELT - Larry Elgart (RCA)
POPS AND PRADO - Perez Prado (RCA)
SOUND SPECTACULAR - Ray Anthony (Cap)

ORCHESTRA (G-35)
JUST FOR KICKS - Bob Thompson & Orch.
LIKE YOUNG - David Rose & Orch. with Andre Previn (MGM)
MORE MUSIC FROM PETER GUNN - Henry Mancini (RCA)
MUSIC FROM M SQUAD - Stanley Wilson (RCA)
STRINGS AFLAME - Esquivel (RCA)
TWO SIDES OF WINTERHALTER - Hugo Winterhalter

VOCAL GROUP OR CHORUS (G-36)
AMES BROTHERS SING FAMOUS HITS OF FAMOUS QUARTETS - Ames Brothers (RCA)
BATTLE HYMN OF THE REPUBLIC - Mormon Tabernacle Choir, Richard Condi, Cond. (Col)
KINGSTON TRIO AT LARGE - Kingston Trio (Cap)
THE THREE BELLS - The Browns (RCA)
THE STEPHEN FOSTER SONG BOOK - Robert Shaw Chorale (RCA)

JAZZ - SOLOIST (G-37)
BEST OF NEW BROADWAY SHOW HITS - Urbie Green (RCA)
BOBBY TROUP AND HIS STARS OF JAZZ - Bobby Troup (RCA)
EASY NOW - Ruby Braff (RCA)
ELLA SWINGS LIGHTLY - Ella Fitzgerald (Verve)
LIKE YOUNG - Andre Previn (MGM)
RED NORVO IN HI-FI - Red Norvo (RCA)

JAZZ - GROUP (G-38)
CHANCES ARE IT SWINGS - Shorty Rogers (RCA)
I DIG CHICKS - Jonah Jones (Cap)
MORE MUSIC FROM PETER GUNN - Henry Mancini (RCA)
RED NORVO IN HI-FI - Red Norvo (RCA)
ELLINGTON JAZZ PARTY - Duke Ellington (Col)

CLASSICAL PERFORMANCE - ORCHESTRA (G-39)
BEETHOVEN: SYMPHONY No. 6 - Pierre Monteux cond. Vienna Philharmonic (RCA)
DEBUSSY: IMAGES FOR ORCHESTRA - Charles Munch cond. Boston Symphony (RCA)
ROSSINI: OVERTURES - Fritz Reiner cond. Chicago Symphony (RCA)
TCHAIKOVSKY: CAPRICCIO ITALIEN; RIMSKY-KORSAKOV: CAPRICCIO ESPAGNOL - Kiril Kondrashin cond. RCA Victor Symphony (RCA)
TCHAIKOVSKY: 1812 OVERTURE/RAVEL: BOLERO - Morton Gould & His Orch. (RCA)

CLASSICAL PERFORMANCE - CONCERTO OR INSTRUMENTAL SOLOIST (WITH FULL ORCHESTRAL ACCOMPANIMENT) (G-40)
BRAHMS: VIOLIN CONCERTO IN D - Henryk Szeryng (Monteux cond. London Symphony) (RCA)
BRAHMS: PIANO CONCERTO No.2 - Artur Rubinstein (J. Kripps cond. RCA Victor Symphony) (RCA)
MENDELSSOHN: VIOLIN CONCERTO No. 2 IN E MINOR OP. 64; PROKOFIEFF: VIOLIN CONCERTO No. 2 IN G MINOR - Jascha Heifetz (Munch cond. Boston Symphony) (RCA)
RACHMANINOFF: PIANO CONCERTO No. 3 - Van Cliburn (Kondrashin cond. Symphony of the Air) (RCA)
TCHAIKOVSKY: PIANO CONCERTO No. 1 - Vladimir Horowitz (Toscanini cond. NBC Symphony) (RCA)

CLASSICAL PERFORMANCE - OPERA CAST OR CHORAL (G-41)
MOZART: THE MARRIAGE OF FIGARO - Erich Leinsdorf, Vienna Philharmonic (Peters, London, Della, Casa) (RCA)
ROSSINI: THE BARBER OF SEVILLE - Erich Leinsdorf, Metropolitan Orch. & Chorus (Peters, Valetti, Merrill, Tozzi) (RCA)
SAINT-SAENS: SAMPSON AND DELILAH - Fausto Cleva cond. Metropolitan Opera Orch. & Chorus (Stevens, Del Monago) (RCA)
THE BELOVED CHORUSES - Mormon Tabernacle Choir, Richard Condie cond. (Col)
VERDI: THE FORCE OF DESTINY - Fernado Previtali cond. Accademia de Santa Cecilia, Rome, Orch. & Chorus (Milanov, Tozzi) (RCA)

CLASSICAL PERFORMANCE - VOCAL SOLOIST (G-42)
A BRAHMS/SCHUMANN RECITAL - Maureen Forrester (Decca)
BJOERLING IN OPERA - Jussi Bjoerling (London)
MARIA CALLAS PORTRAYS VERDI HEROINES - Maria Callas (Angel)
MILANOV OPERATIC ARIAS - Zinka Milanov (RCA)
THE ART OF SONG - Cesare Valletti (RCA)

CLASSICAL PERFORMANCE - CHAMBER MUSIC (G-43)
BEETHOVEN: SONATA No. 21, IN C OP. 53/"WALDSTEIN" SONATA NO. 18 IN E FLAT OP. 53 NO. 3 - Artur Rubinstein (RCA)

BEETHOVEN: PIANO QUARTET IN E FLAT OP. 16; SCHUMAN PIANO QUARTET IN E FLAT OP. 47 - The Festival Quartet (RCA)
CELLO GALAXY - Felix Slatkin (Cap)
FOUR ITALIAN SONATAS - Nathan Milstein (Cap)
VILLA LOBOS: STRING QUARTET - Felix Slatkin (Cap)

CLASSICAL PERFORMANCE - INSTRUMENTAL SOLOIST (WITHOUT ORCHESTRAL ACCOMPANIMENT) (G-44)

BEETHOVEN: SONATA NO. 21 IN C OP. 53/"WALDSTEIN" SONATA NO. 18 IN E FLAT OP. 53 NO. 3 - Artur Rubinstein (RCA)
DANZAS - Laurindo Almeida (Cap)
FOUR ITALIAN SONATAS - Nathan Milstein (Cap)
BERG: SONATA FOR PIANO, OP. 1; KRENEK: SONATA NO. 3, OP. 92 NO 4; SCHOENBERG: THREE PIANO PIECES OP. 11 - Glenn Gould (Col)
PENNARIO PLAYS - Leonard Pennario (Cap)
PRESENTING JAIME LAREDO - Jaime Laredo (RCA)

COMPOSITION - MORE THAN 5 MIN. (G-45)

ANATOMY OF A MURDER - Duke Ellington
MORE MUSIC FROM PETER GUNN - Henry Mancini
PROKOFIEFF: THE OVERTURE RUSSE OP. 72 - Serge Prokofieff
ST. LAWRENCE SUITE - Morton Gould
SHOSTAKOVITCH: CONCERTO NO. 2 FOR PIANO AND ORCH., OP. 101 - Dimitri Shostakovitch

SOUND TRACK ALBUM - SCORE, MOTION PICTURE OR TELEVISION (G-46)

ANATOMY OF A MURDER - Duke Ellington (Col)
MORE MUSIC FROM PETER GUNN - Henry Mancini (RCA)
PETE KELLY'S BLUES - Dick Cathcart (WB)
THE MUSIC FROM M SQUAD - Stanley Wilson (RCA)
THE NUN'S STORY - Franz Waxman (WB)

SOUND TRACK ALBUM - ORIGINAL CAST, MOTION PICTURE OR TELEVISION (G-47)

FOR THE FIRST TIME - Mario Lanza (RCA)
PORGY AND BESS - Andre Previn, Ken Darby (Col)
SLEEPING BEAUTY (Disneyland)
SOME LIKE IT HOT (U.A.)
THE FIVE PENNIES (Dot)

BROADWAY SHOW ALBUM (G-48)

A PARTY WITH BETTY COMDEN AND ADOLPH GREEN - Betty Comden, Adolph Green (Cap)
AGES OF MAN - Sir John Gielgud (Col)
GYPSY - Ethel Merman (Col)
ONCE UPON A MATTRESS - Hal Hastings, cond. (Kapp)
REDHEAD - Gwen Verdon (RCA)

COMEDY - SPOKEN WORD (G-49)

HAMLET - Andy Griffith (Cap)
INSIDE SHELLEY BERMAN - Shelley Berman (Verve)
LOOK FORWARD IN ANGER - Mort Sahl (Verve)
SICK HUMOR - Lenny Bruce (Fantasy)
STAN FREBERG WITH ORIGINAL CAST - Stan Freberg (Cap)

COMEDY - MUSICAL (G-50)

A PARTY WITH BETTY COMDEN AND ADOLPH GREEN - Betty Comden, Adolph Green (Cap)
CHARLIE WEAVER SINGS FOR HIS PEOPLE - Cliff Arquette (Col)
MONSTER RALLY - Hans Conreid, Alice Pearce
MUSICALLY MAD - Bernie Green (RCA)
THE BATTLE OF KOOKAMONGA - Homer & Jethro (RCA)

DOCUMENTARY OR SPOKEN WORD RECORDING (G-51)

A LINCOLN PORTRAIT - Carl Sandburg (Col)
AGES OF MAN - Sir John Gielgud (Col)
BASIL RATHBONE READS SHERLOCK HOLMES - Basil Rathbone (Audio Book)
MARK TWAIN TONIGHT - Hal Holbrook (Col)
NEW YORK TAXI DRIVER - Tony Schwartz (Col)

PERFORMANCE BY "TOP 40" ARTIST (G-52)

A BIG HUNK O'LOVE - Elvis Presley (RCA)
BROKEN HEARTED MELODY - Sarah Vaughan (Merc)
CHARLIE BROWN - The Coasters (Atco)
MAKIN' LOVE - Floyd Robinson (RCA)
MIDNIGHT FLYER - Nat King Cole (Cap)
NEIL SEDAKA - Neil Sedaka (RCA)

COUNTRY AND WESTERN PERFORMANCE (G-53)

BATTLE OF NEW ORLEANS - Johnny Horton (Col)
DON'T TELL ME YOUR TROUBLES - Don Gibson (RCA)
HOME - Jim Reeves (RCA)
SET HIM FREE - Skeeter Davis (RCA)
TENNESSEE STUD - Eddy Arnold (RCA)

RHYTHM AND BLUES PERFORMANCE (G-54)

A BIG HUNK O'LOVE - Elvis Presley (RCA)
CHARLIE BROWN - The Coasters (Atco)
GUESS WHO - Jesse Belvin (RCA)
MIDNIGHT FLYER - Nat King Cole (Cap)
WHAT A DIFFERENCE A DAY MAKES - Dinah Washington (Merc)

FOLK PERFORMANCE (G-55)

BELAFONTE AT CARNEGIE HALL - Harry Belafonte (RCA)
KINGSTON TRIO AT LARGE - Kingston Trio (Cap)
TENNESSEE STUD - Eddy Arnold (RCA)
ATHE WILD WILD WEST - Ralph Hunter Choir (RCA)
THE WILDERNESS ROAD - Jimmy Driftwood (RCA)

RECORDING FOR CHILDREN (G-56)

HANSEL AND GRETEL - Franz Allers (RCA)
PETER AND THE WOLF - Peter Ustinov (von Karajan, Philharmonia Orch.) (Angel)
POPEYE'S FAVORITE SEA CHANTIES - Capt. Allen Swift (RCA)
THE ARABIAN NIGHTS - Marla Ray (RCA)
THREE TO MAKE MUSIC/CINDERELLA - Mary Martin (RCA)

ARRANGEMENT (G-57)

AN EVENING WITH LERNER & LOWE - Johnny Green (RCA)
COME DANCE WITH ME - Billy May (Frank Sinatra) (Cap)
MACK THE KNIFE - Richard Wess (Bobby Darin) (Atco)
MORE MUSIC FROM PETER GUNN - Henry Mancini (RCA)
STRINGS AFLAME - Esquivel (RCA)
VICTORY AT SEA, VOL. 1 (Re-make) - Robert Russell Bennett cond. RCA Symphony Orch. (RCA)

BEST ENGINEERED RECORDING, CLASSICAL (G-58)

(Engineer's Award)
DOUBLING IN BRASS - Lewis W. Layton (Morton Gould) (RCA)
ROSSINI OVERTURES - Lewis W. Layton (Fritz Reiner) (RCA)
TCHAIKOVSKY: CAPRICCIO ITALIEN; RIMSKY KORSAKOV: CAPRICCIO ESPAGNOL - Lewis W. Layton (Kiril Kondrashin) (RCA)
TCHAIKOVSKY: 1812 OVERTURE; RAVEL: BOLERO - Lewis W. Layton (Morton Gould) (RCA)
VICTORY AT SEA, VOL. 1 - Lewis W. Layton (Robert Russell Bennett) (RCA)

ENGINEERING - NOVELTY RECORDING (G-59)
(Engineer's Award)

ALVIN'S HARMONICA - Ted Keep (David Seville) (Cap)
ORIENTA - Thorne Nogar (Markko Polo Adventurers) (RCA)
SUPERSONICS IN FLIGHT - Robert Simpson (Billy Mure) (RCA)
THE BAT - Luis P. Valentin (Alvino Rey) (Cap)
THE WILD WILD WEST - Robert Simpson (Ralph Hunter Choir) (RCA)

ENGINEERING CONTRIBUTION - OTHER THAN CLASSICAL OR NOVELTY (G-60)
(Engineer's Award)

BELAFONTE AT CARNEGIE HALL - Robert Simpson (RCA)
BIG BAND GUITAR - Robert Simpson (Buddy Morrow) (RCA)
COMPULSION TO SWING - Robert Simpson (Henri Rene) (RCA)
NEW SOUNDS AT THE ROOSEVELT - Robert Simpson (Larry Elgart) (RCA)
STRINGS AFLAME - Ernest Oelrich (Esquivel) (RCA)

ALBUM COVER (G-61)
(Art Director's Award)
ANATOMY OF A MURDER - Saul Bass (Duke Ellington) (Col)
FOR LP FANS ONLY - Col. Tom Parker (Elvis Presley) (RCA)
PORGY AND BESS - Acy R. Lehman (Lena Horne, Harry Belafonte) (RCA)
SHOSTAKOVICH: SYMPHONY NO. 5 - Robert M. Jones (Howard Mitchell) (RCA)
THE SOUTH SHALL RISE AGAIN - Robert L. Yorke, Acy R. Lehmann (Phil Harris) (RCA)

NEW ARTIST OF 1959 (G-62)
EDD BYRNES
BOBBY DARIN
MARK MURPHY
JOHNNY RESTIVO
MAVIS RIVERS

SPECIAL TRUSTEES AWARDS FOR ARTISTS & REPERTOIRE CONTRIBUTION (G-63)
Record of the Year, MACK THE KNIFE, Bobby Darin; A & R Producer, Ahmet Ertegun (ATCO).
Album of the Year, COME DANCE WITH ME, Frank Sinatra; A & R Producer; Dave Cavanaugh (Cap).

1960

RECORD OF THE YEAR (G-64)
ARE YOU LONESOME TONIGHT? - Elvis Presley (RCA)
GEORGIA ON MY MIND - Ray Charles (ABC)
MACK THE KNIFE - Ella Fitzgerald (Verve)
NICE 'N' EASY - Frank Sinatra (CAP)
THEME FROM A SUMMER PLACE - Percy Faith (Col)

ALBUM OF THE YEAR (G-65)
BELAFONTE RETURNS TO CARNEGIE HALL - Harry Belafonte (RCA)
BRAHMS: CONCERTO NO. 2 IN B FLAT - Sviatoslav Richter (RCA)
BUTTON DOWN MIND - Bob Newhart (WB)
NICE 'N' EASY - Frank Sinatra (Cap)
PUCCINI: TURANDOT - Erich Leinsdorf (RCA)
WILD IS LOVE - Nat King Cole (Cap)

SONG OF THE YEAR (G-66)
(Songwriter's Award)
HE'LL HAVE TO GO - Charles Green, Joe Allison, Audrey Allison
NICE 'N' EASY - Lew Spence, Marilyn Keith, Alan Bergman
SECOND TIME AROUND - Sammy Cahn, Jimmy Van Heusen
THEME FROM A SUMMER PLACE - Max Steiner
THEME FROM EXODUS - Ernest Gold

VOCAL - FEMALE - SINGLE OR TRACK (G-67)
SOUND OF MUSIC - Doris Day (Col)
I'VE GOTTA RIGHT TO SING THE BLUES - Eileen Farrell (Col)
MACK THE KNIFE - Ella Fitzgerald (Verve)
I'M SORRY - Brenda Lee (Decca)
I'M GONNA GO FISHIN' - Peggy Lee (Cap)

VOCAL - FEMALE - ALBUM (G-68)
CLAP HANDS, HERE COMES ROSIE - Rosemary Clooney (Col)
MACK THE KNIFE/ELLA IN BERLIN - Ella Fitzgerald (Verve)
LATIN ALA LEE - Peggy Lee (Cap)
MIRIAM MAKEBA - Miriam Makeba (RCA)
DELLA - Della Reese (RCA)

VOCAL - MALE - SINGLE OR TRACK (G-69)
GEORGIA ON MY MIND - Ray Charles (ABC)
MISTY - Johnny Mathis (Col)
ARE YOU LONESOME TONIGHT? - Elvis Presley (RCA)
HE'LL HAVE TO GO - Jim Reeves (RCA)
NICE 'N' EASY - Frank Sinatra (Cap)

VOCAL - MALE - ALBUM (G-70)
BELAFONTE RETURNS TO CARNEGIE HALL - Harry Belafonte (RCA)
GENIUS OF RAY CHARLES - Ray Charles (Atl)
WILD IS LOVE - Nat King Cole (Cap)
G.I. BLUES - Elvis Presley (RCA)
NICE 'N' EASY - Frank Sinatra (Cap)

BAND FOR DANCING (G-71)
DANCE WITH BASIE - Count Basie (Roulette)
BANDLAND - Les Brown (Col)
THE BLUES AND THE BEAT - Henry Mancini (RCA)
GIRLS & BOYS ON BROADWAY - Billy May (Cap)
BIG HITS BY PRADO - Perez Prado (RCA)

ARRANGEMENT (G-72)
(Arranger's Award)
THEME FROM THE APARTMENT (Ferrante/Teicher) Arr: Don Costa (UA)
THEME FROM A SUMMER PLACE - Arr: Percy Faith (Col)
I'M GONNA GO FISHING' (Gerry Mulligan) Arr: Bill Holman (Verve)
LET THE GOOD TIMES ROLL (Ray Charles) Arr: Quincy Jones (Atl)
MR. LUCKY - Arr: Henry Mancini (RCA)
HONEYSUCKLE ROSE (Shearing) Arrs: George Shearing, Billy May (Cap)
NICE N' EASY (Frank Sinatra) Arr: Nelson Riddle (Cap)
WILD PERCUSSION AND HORNS A'PLENTY (Dick Schory) Arr: Dick Schory (RCA)

ORCHESTRA (G-73)
COUNT BASIE STORY - Count Basie (Roulette)
INFINITY IN SOUND - Esquivel (RCA)
THEME FROM A SUMMER PLACE - Percy Faith (Col)
MR. LUCKY - Henry Mancini (RCA)
THE CONCERT JAZZ BAND - Gerry Mulligan (Verve)

VOCAL GROUP (G-74)
GREENFIELDS - The Brothers Four (Col)
WE GOT US - Eydie Gorme, Steve Lawrence (ABC)
ALL OVER THE PLACE - The Hi Los (Col)
HERE WE GO AGAIN - Kingston Trio (Cap)
SCANDINAVIAN SHUFFLE - Swe-Danes (WB)

CHORUS (G-75)
BELAFONTE RETURNS TO CARNEGIE HALL - Belafonte Folk Singers (RCA)
DEEP NIGHT - Ray Charles Singers (Decca)
MY FAVORITE THINGS - Pete King Chorale (Kapp)

SONGS OF THE COWBOY - Norman Luboff Choir (Col)
WHAT WONDROUS LOVE - Robert Shaw Choral (RCA)

JAZZ - SOLO OR SMALL GROUP (G-76)

JAZZ TRACK - Miles Davis (Col)
BACK TO BACK - Duke Ellington, Johnny Hodges (Verve)
THE GREATEST TRUMPET OF THEM ALL - Dizzy Gillespie and his Octet (Verve)
THE HOTTEST NEW GROUP IN JAZZ - Lambert, Hendricks and Ross (Col)
WEST SIDE STORY - Andre Previn (Contempo)
WHITE SATIN - George Shearing (Cap)
GREATEST PIANO OF THEM ALL - Art Tatum (Verve)
PYRAMID - Modern Jazz Quartet (Atl)

JAZZ - LARGE GROUP (G-77)

THE COUNT BASIE STORY - Count Basie (Roulette)
SKETCHES OF SPAIN - Miles Davis, Gil Evans (Col)
THE GREAT WIDE WORLD OF QUINCY JONES - Quincy Jones (Merc)
BLUES AND THE BEAT - Henry Mancini (RCA)
I'M GONNA GO FISHIN' - Gerry Mulligan (Verve)
SPIRITUALS TO SWING CONCERT - The Recording Artists (Vanguard)

CLASSICAL PERFORMANCE - ORCHESTRA (G-78)

HAYDN: SALOMON SYMPHONIES VOL. 2 - Sir Thomas Beecham cond. Royal Philharmonic (Cap)
IVES: SYMPHONY NO. 2 - Leonard Bernstein cond. New York Philharmonic (Col)
COPLAND: APPALACHIAN SPRING - Aaron Copland cond. Boston Symphony (RCA)
GROFE: GRAND CANYON SUITE - Morton Gould cond. Morton Gould Orchestra (RCA)
SCHUBERT: SYMPHONY NO. 9 - Josef Krips cond. London Symphony (London)
STRAVINSKY: PETROUCHKA - Pierre Monteux cond. Boston Symphony (RCA)
TCHAIKOVSKY: SIXTH SYMPHONY - Eugene Ormandy cond. Philadelphia Symphony (Col)
BARTOK: MUSIC FOR STRINGS, PERCUSSION AND CELESTE - Fritz Reiner cond. Chicago Symphony (RCA)

CLASSICAL PERFORMANCE - VOCAL OR INSTRUMENTAL - CHAMBER MUSIC (G-79)

CONVERSATIONS WITH THE GUITAR - Laurindo Almeida (Cap)
SCHUBERT: "TROUT" QUINTET - Clifford Curzon and Vienna Octet (London)
BRAHMS: HORN TRIO; BEETHOVEN: SONATA FOR HORN AND PIANO - Joseph Eger, Henryk Szeryng, Victor Babin (RCA)
HAYDN: QUARTETS, OPUS 71 and 74 - Griller Quartet (Vanguard)
DEBUSSY AND RAVEL QUARTETS - Juilliard Quartet (RCA)
BACH: THE COMPLETE BRANDENBURG CONCERTI - Yehudi Menuhin and Bach Festival Chamber Orchestra (Cap)
BACH: CANTATA NO. 4; CHRIST LAG IN TODESBADEN - Robert Shaw Chorale (RCA)
JANACEK STRING QUARTETS Nos. 1 and 2 - Smetana Quartet (Artia)

CLASSICAL PERFORMANCE - CONCERTO OR INSTRUMENTAL SOLOIST (G-80)

SCHUMANN: PIANO CONCERTO IN A - Van Cliburn (Reiner cond. Chicago Symphony) (RCA)
MOZART: CLARINET CONCERTO - Gervase De Peyer (Maag cond. London Symphony) (London)
PROKOFIEFF: CONCERTO NO. 2 - Malcolm Frager (Leibowitz cond. Paris Conservatoire) (RCA)
BRAHMS: DOUBLE CONCERTO (CONCERTO FOR VIOLIN AND CELLO IN A MINOR) - Zino Francescatti, Pierre Fournier (Walter cond. Columbia Symphony) (Col)
BACH: CONCERTO NO. 5 - Glenn Gould (Golschmann cond. Columbia Symphony) (Col)
SIBELIUS: VIOLIN CONCERTO IN D - Jascha Heifetz (Hendl cond. Chicago Symphony) (RCA)
BRAHMS: PIANO CONCERTO No. 2 IN B-FLAT - Sviatoslav Richter
(Leinsdorf cond. Chicago Symphony) (RCA)
BRAHMS: PIANO CONCERTO No. 2 - Rudolf Serkin (Ormandy cond. Philadelphia Symphony) (Col)

CLASSICAL PERFORMANCE - INSTRUMENTAL SOLOIST OR DUO (OTHER THAN WITH ORCHESTRA) (G-81)

THE SPANISH GUITARS OF LAURINDO ALMEIDA - Laurindo Almeida (Cap)
THE ART OF JULIAN BREAM - Julian Bream (RCA)
PICTURES AT AN EXHIBITION - Vladimir Horowitz (RCA)
HAYDN. . .LANDOWSKA - Wanda Landowska (RCA)
BACH: PARTITA No. 3 In E; BRAHMS: SONATA No. 3 IN D MINOR - Jaime Laredo (RCA)
BRAHMS: KEYBOARD MUSIC OF THE FRENCH COURT - Paul Maynard (Am. Soc Concerts in Home)
PROKOFIEFF: SONATA No. 7 AND PICTURES AT AN EXHIBITION - Sviatoslav Richter (Artia)
CHOPIN: BALLADES - Artur Rubinstein (RCA)

CLASSICAL PERFORMANCE - VOCAL SOLOIST (G-82)

CONVERSATIONS WITH THE GUITAR - Salli Terri (Cap)
ARIAS IN GREAT TRADITION - Eileen Farrell (Col)
SCHUBERT: SONGS, ALBUM 3 - Dietrich Fischer-Dieskau (Angel)
MAHLER: KINDERTOTENLIEDER - Maureen Forrester (RCA)
BRITTEN: NOCTURNE - Peter Pears (London)
A PROGRAM OF SONG - Leontyne Price (RCA)
HANDEL: ARIAS - Joan Sutherland (Oiseau-Lyre)
SCHUMANN: DICHTERLIEBE - Cesare Valletti (RCA)

OPERA PRODUCTION (G-83)

VERDI: AIDA - Herbert von Karajan (Solos: Tebaldi, Bergonzi, Simionato, Corena) (London)
PUCCINI: LA BOHEME - Tullio Serafin (Solos: Tebaldi, Bergonzi, Bastianini, Corena) (London)
MOZART: DON GIOVANNI - Josef Krips (Solos: Siepi, Danco, Dermote, Corena) (London)
VERDI: SHAKESPEARE: MACBETH - Erich Leinsdorf (Solos: Warren, Hines, Rysanek, Bergonzi) (RCA)
BOITA: MEFISTOFELE - Tullio Serafin (Solos: Siepi, Tebaldi, Del Monaco) (London)
BRITTEN: PETER GRIMES - Benjamin Britten (Solos: Pears, Pease, Watson) (London)
VERDI: LA TRAVIATA - Tullio Serafin (Solos: de los Angeles, Del Monte, Sereni) (Cap)
PUCCINI: TURANDOT - Erich Leinsdorf (Solos: Tebaldi, Nilsson, Bjoerling, Tozzi) (RCA)
POULENC, COCTEAU: LA VOIX HUMAINE - Georges Pretre cond. Paris Opera Comique & National Theatre Orch. (Solos: Duval) (RCA)

CONTEMPORARY CLASSICAL COMPOSITION (G-84)

SYMPHONY NO. 1 - Easley Blackwood (RCA)
ORCHESTRAL SUITE FROM TENDER LAND SUITE - Aaron Copland (RCA)
SONATA FOR CELLO AND PIANO - Paul Hindemith (RCA)
SYMPHONY No. 2 - Charles Ives (Col)
LA VOIX HUMAINE - Francis Poulenc (RCA)
SYMPHONY No. 1 - Roger Sessions (Comp. Rcds)
THRENI - Igor Stravinsky (Col)
DENSITY 21.5 - Edgard Varese (Col)

CLASSICAL PERFORMANCE - CHORAL (G-85)

HANDEL: THE MESSIAH - Sir Thomas Beecham cond. Royal Philharmonic & Chorus (Solos: Vyvyan, Sinclair, Vicki, Tozzi) (RCA)
ARIAS, ANTHEMS AND CHORALES OF AMERICAN MORAVIANS, VOL. 1 - Moravian Festival Chorus (Col)
BERLIOZ: REQUIEM - Charles Munch & The New England Conservatory Chorus (RCA)

VERDI: REQUIEM - Fritz Reiner, Vienna Philharmonic Society of Friends of Music of Vienna (RCA)
BACH: MOTET No. 3 "JESU MEINE FREUDE" - Robert Shaw Chorale (RCA)
DVORAK: REQUIEM - Maria Stader, Sieglinde Wagner, Hans Ernst Haefliger, Kim Borg (DGG)
VAUGHAN WILLIAMS: MASS IN G MINOR; BACH: CHRIST LAY IN THE BONDS OF DEATH - Roger Wagner Chorale (Cap)

SOUND TRACK ALBUM - SCORE, MOTION PICTURE OR TV (G-86)

(Composer's Award)
THE APARTMENT - Comp: Adolph Deutsch (S-T) (UA)
BEN HUR - Comp: Dr. Miklos Rozsa (S-T) (MGM)
EXODUS - Comp: Ernest Gold (S-T) (RCA)
MR. LUCKY - Comp: Henry Mancini (RCA)
THE UNTOUCHABLES - Comp: Nelson Riddle (Cap)

SOUND TRACK ALBUM - ORIGINAL CAST, MOTION PICTURE OR TV (G-87)

(Composer's Award)
BELLS ARE RINGING (Judy Holiday, Dean Martin, Orig. Cast) Comps: Betty Comden, Adolph Green, Jule Styne (Cap)
CAN CAN (Frank Sinatra, Orig. Cast) Comp: Cole Porter (Cap)
G.I. BLUES - Elvis Presley (RCA)
LI'L ABNER (S-T) - Comp: Nelson Riddle (Col)

SHOW ALBUM - ORIGINAL CAST (G-88)

(Composer's Award)
BYE BYE BIRDIE - Charles Strouse, Lee Adams (Col)
CAMELOT - Alan Jay Lerner, Frederick Loewe (Col)
FIORELLO! - Jerry Bock, Sheldon Harnick (Cap)
THE SOUND OF MUSIC - Richard Rodgers, Oscar Hammerstein (Col)
THE UNSINKABLE MOLLY BROWN - Meredith Willson (Cap)

COMEDY - SPOKEN WORD (G-89)

THE EDGE OF SHELLEY BERMAN - Shelley Berman (Verve)
BUTTON DOWN MIND STRIKES BACK - Bob Newhart (WB)
2,000 YEAR OLD MAN - Carl Reiner and Mel Brooks (World Pac.)
THE WONDERFUL WORLD OF JONATHAN WINTERS - Jonathan Winters (Verve)

COMEDY - MUSICAL (G-90)

JONATHAN AND DARLENE EDWARDS IN PARIS - Paul Weston, Jo Stafford (Col)
THE OLD PAYOLA ROLL BLUES - Stan Freberg (Cap)
HOMER AND JETHRO AT THE COUNTRY CLUB - Homer and Jethro (RCA)
AN EVENING WASTED WITH TOM LEHRER - Tom Lehrer (Lehrer)
ALVIN FOR PRESIDENT - David Seville (Lib)

DOCUMENTARY OR SPOKEN WORD (G-91)

AGES OF MAN, VOL. 2 (ONE MAN IN HIS TIME) PART TWO - SHAKESPEARE - Sir John Gielgud (Col)
VOICES OF THE TWENTIETH CENTURY - Henry Fonda (Decca)
J.B. - Archibald MacLeish (RCA)
F.D.R. SPEAKS - Franklin D. Roosevelt, Robert Bialek, A&R Prod. (Wash.)

POP SINGLE ARTIST (G-92)

GEORGIA ON MY MIND - Ray Charles (ABC)
MACK THE KNIFE - Ella Fitzgerald (Verve)
HEART - Peggy Lee (Cap)
ARE YOU LONESOME TONIGHT? - Elvis Presley (RCA)
NICE N' EASY - Frank Sinatra (Cap)

COUNTRY AND WESTERN PERFORMANCE (G-93)

NORTH TO ALASKA - Johnny Horton (Col)
WINGS OF A DOVE - Ferlin Husky (Cap)
PLEASE HELP ME, I'M FALLING - Hank Locklin (RCA)
HE'LL HAVE TO GO - Jim Reeves (RCA)
EL PASO - Marty Robbins (Col)

RHYTHM AND BLUES PERFORMANCE (G-94)

SHAKE A HAND - LaVerne Baker (Atl)
FINGER POPPIN' TIME - Hank Ballard (King)
LET THE GOOD TIMES ROLL - Ray Charles (Atl)
WALKIN' AND TALKIN' - Bo Diddley (Checker)
TRAVELIN' - John Lee Hooker (VeeJay)
ALL I COULD DO WAS CRY - Etta James (Argo)
GOT MY MOJO WORKING - Muddy Waters (Chess)
LONELY TEARDROPS - Jackie Wilson (Brunswick)

FOLK PERFORMANCE (G-95)

SWING DAT HAMMER - Harry Belafonte (RCA)
CHEERS - Belafonte Singers (RCA)
GREENFIELDS - The Brothers Four (Col)
SONGS OF BILLY YANK AND JOHNNY REB - Jimmy Driftwood (RCA)
HERE WE GO AGAIN - Kingston Trio (Cap)
SOUTHERN FOLK HERITAGE SERIES - Alan Lomax (Atl)
SONGS OF ROBERT BURNS - Ewan MacColl (Flkwy)
MIRIAM MAKEBA - Miriam Makeba (RCA)

ALBUM FOR CHILDREN (G-96)

ADVENTURES IN MUSIC, GRADE 3, VOLUME 1 - Howard Mitchell (RCA)
LET'S ALL SING WITH THE CHIPMUNKS - David Seville (Lib)
DR. SEUSS PRESENTS: BARTHOLOMEW AND THE OOBLECK - Dr. Seuss (Camden)
FOLK SONGS FOR YOUNG PEOPLE - Pete Seeger (Flkways)
MOTHER GOOSE NURSERY RHYMES - Sterling Holloway (Disneyland)
STORIES AND SONGS OF THE CIVIL WAR - Ralph Bellamy (RCA)

ENGINEERING CONTRIBUTION - CLASSICAL (G-97)

(Engineer's Award)
PROKOFIEFF: ALEXANDER NEVSKY (Reiner cond. Chicago Symphony) Eng: Lewis Layton (RCA)
BARTOK: MUSIC FOR STRINGS, PERCUSSION AND CELESTE (Reiner cond. Chicago Symphony) Eng: Lewis Layton (RCA)
BERLIOZ: REQUIEM (Munch cond. New England Conservatory Chorus & Boston Symphony) Eng: Lewis Layton (RCA)
R. STRAUSS: DON QUIXOTE (Reiner cond. Chicago Symphony) Eng: Lewis Layton (RCA)
SPANISH GUITARS OF LAURINDO ALMEIDA (Laurindo Almeida) Eng: Hugh Davies (Cap)
THE TWO PIANOS OF LEONARD PENNARIO (Leonard Pennario) Eng: John Kraus (Cap)
PUCCINI: TURANDOT (Tebaldi, Nilsson, Bjoerling, Tozzi, Leinsdorf, cond.) Eng: Lewis Layton (RCA)

ENGINEERING CONTRIBUTION - POPULAR (G-98)

(Engineer's Award)
BELAFONTE RETURNS TO CARNEGIE HALL (Harry Belafonte) Eng: Robert Simpson (RCA)
LOUIS BELLSON SWINGS JULE STYNE - Eng: Luis P. Valentin (Verve)
ELLA FITZGERALD SINGS THE GEORGE AND IRA GERSHWIN SONG BOOK - Eng: Luis P. Valentin (Verve)
INFINITY IN SOUND (Esquivel) Eng: John Norman (RCA)
PERSUASIVE PERCUSSION NO. 2 (Terry Snyder & the All Stars) Eng: Robert Fine (Cmmd)
WILD IS LOVE (Nat King Cole) Eng: John Kraus (Cap)
WILD PERCUSSION AND HORNS A'PLENTY (Dick Schory) Eng: Robert Simpson (RCA)

ENGINEERING CONTRIBUTION - NOVELTY (G-99)

(Engineer's Award)

ALVIN FOR PRESIDENT (David Seville & the Chipmunks) Eng: Ted Keep (Lib)
JUNE NIGHT (Jack Cookerly) Eng: John Kraus (Cap)
LET'S ALL SING WITH THE CHIPMUNKS (David Seville) Eng: Ted Keep (Lib)
MR. CUSTER (Larry Verne) Eng: George Fernandez (Era)
NEW SOUNDS AMERICA LOVES BEST (John Klein) Engs: Robert Simpson, John Crawford, Tony Salvatore (RCA)
THE OLD PAYOLA ROLL BLUES (Stan Freberg) Eng: John Kraus (Cap)
SPIKE JONES IN HI-FI - Eng: Thorne Nogar (WB)

ALBUM COVER (G-100)

(Art Director's Award)

PROKOFIEFF: ALEXANDER NEVSKY (Reiner cond. Chicago Symphony) Art Dir: Bob Jones (RCA)
BEAN BAGS (Milt Jackson) Art Dir: Marvin Israel (Atl)
CARLOS MONTOYA - Art Dir: Bob Jones (RCA)
ELLA FITZGERALD SINGS THE GEORGE AND IRA GERSHWIN SONG BOOK - Art Dir: Sheldon Marks (Verve)
LATIN ALA LEE (Peggy Lee) Art Dir: Marvin Schwartz (Cap)
NOW! FRED ASTAIRE - Art Dir: Irving Werbin (Kapp)
TCHAIKOVSKY: NUTCRACKER SUITE EXCERPTS (Reiner, Chicago Symphony) Art Dir: Bob Jones (RCA)
STRAVINSKY: PETROUCHKA (Monteux, Boston Symphony) Art Dir: Bob Jones (RCA)
WILD PERCUSSION AND HORNS A'PLENTY (Dick Schory) Art Dir: Bob Jones (RCA)

NEW ARTIST OF 1960 (G-101)

THE BROTHERS FOUR (Col)
MIRIAM MAKEBA (RCA)
BOB NEWHART (WB)
LEONTYNE PRICE (RCA)
JOANIE SOMMERS (WB)

JAZZ COMPOSITION - MORE THAN 5 MIN. (G-102)

(Composer's Award)

BLUE RONDO A LA TURK - Dave Brubeck (Col)
BLUES SUITE - Bob Brookmeyer (Atl)
IDIOM '59 (FESTIVAL SESSION) - Duke Ellington (Col)
NEWPORT SUITE - Maynard Ferguson (Roulette)
SKETCH FROM THIRD STREAM MUSIC - John Lewis (Atl)
SKETCHES OF SPAIN - Miles Davis, Gil Evans (Col)
WESTERN SUITE - Jimmy Giuffre (Atl)

SPECIAL NATIONAL TRUSTEES AWARDS FOR ARTISTS AND REPERTOIRE CONTRIBUTION (G-103)

Record Of The Year, THEME FROM A SUMMER PLACE, A&R Prod: Ernest Altschuler (Col).
BUTTON DOWN MIND, A&R Prod: George Avakian (WB).

1961

RECORD OF THE YEAR (G-104)

BIG BAD JOHN - Jimmy Dean (Col)
UP A LAZY RIVER - Si Zentner (Lib)
MOON RIVER - Henry Mancini (RCA)
THE SECOND TIME AROUND - Frank Sinatra (Rep)
TAKE FIVE - Dave Brubeck (Col)

ALBUM OF THE YEAR - (NON-CLASSICAL) (G-105)

BREAKFAST AT TIFFANY'S - Henry Mancini (RCA)
GENIUS ∎ SOUL JAZZ - Ray Charles (Impulse)
GREAT BAND WITH GREAT VOICES - Si Zentner, Johnny Mann Singers (Lib)
JUDY AT CARNEGIE HALL - Judy Garland (Cap)
THE NAT COLE STORY - Nat King Cole (Cap)
WEST SIDE STORY (Soundtrack) - Johnny Green, Music Director (Col)

ALBUM OF THE YEAR - CLASSICAL (G-106)

THE ART OF THE PRIMA DONNA - Joan Sutherland, (Molinari - Pradelli, Royal Opera House Orch.) (London)
BLOCK: SACRED SERVICE - Leonard Bernstein, New York Philharmonic (Col)
BRAHMS: SYMPHONY NO. 2 - William Steinberg, Pittsburgh Symphony (Command)
REVERIE FOR SPANISH GUITARS - Laurindo Almeida (Cap)
STRAVINSKY CONDUCTS, 1960: LE SACRE DU PRINTEMPS; PETROUCHKA - Igor Stravinsky cond. Columbia Symphony (Col)

SONG OF THE YEAR (G-107)

(Songwriter's Award)

A LITTLE BITTY TEAR - Hank Cochran (Decca)
BIG BAD JOHN - Jimmy Dean (Col)
LOLLIPOPS AND ROSES - Tony Velona (Kapp)
MAKE SOMEONE HAPPY - Jule Styne, Betty Comden, Adolph Green
MOON RIVER - Henry Mancini, Johnny Mercer (RCA)

INSTRUMENTAL THEME OR INSTRUMENTAL VERSION OF SONG (G-108)

(Composer's Award)

AFRICAN WALTZ - Galt MacDermott (Roulette)
THE GUNS OF NAVARONE - Dimitri Tiomkin (Col)
LA DOLCE VITA - Nino Rota (RCA)
PARIS BLUES - Duke Ellington (Col)
THEME FROM "CARNIVAL" - Robert Merrill (MGM)

VOCAL - FEMALE (G-109)

(Following are all album nominations)

BASIN STREET EAST - Peggy Lee (Cap)
THE ESSENTIAL BILLIE HOLIDAY (CARNEGIE HALL CONCERT) - Billie Holiday (Verve)
JUDY AT CARNEGIE HALL - Judy Garland (Cap)
LENA AT THE SANDS - Lena Horne (RCA)
MR. PAGANINI - Ella Fitzgerald (Verve)

VOCAL - MALE (G-110)

(Following are all single nominations)

A LITTLE BITTY TEAR - Burl Ives (Decca)
BIG BAD JOHN - Jimmy Dean (Col)
DANNY BOY - Andy Williams (Col)
LOLLIPOPS AND ROSES - Jack Jones (Kapp)
PORTRAIT OF MY LOVE - Steve Lawrence (UA)

JAZZ - SOLOIST OR SMALL GROUP (INSTRUMENTAL) (G-111)

ANDRE PREVIN PLAYS HAROLD ARLEN - Andre Previn (Contemporary)
BILL EVANS AT THE VILLAGE VANGUARD - Bill Evans Trio (Riverside)
DREAMSTREET - Erroll Garner (Am-Par)
EUROPEAN CONCERT - The Modern Jazz Quartet (Atl)
THE GREATEST HORN IN THE WORLD - Al Hirt (RCA)

JAZZ - LARGE GROUP (INSTRUMENTAL) (G-112)

A TOUCH OF ELEGANCE - Andre Previn (Col)
BASIE AT BIRDLAND - Count Basie & Orch. (Roulette)
GILLESPIANA - Dizzy Gillespie (Verve)
OUT OF THE COOL - Gil Evans (ABC)
WEST SIDE STORY - Stan Kenton (Cap)

ORIGINAL JAZZ COMPOSITION (G-113)

(Composer's Award)
A TOUCH OF ELEGANCE - Andre Previn (Col)
AFRICAN WALTZ - Galt MacDermott (Rvrsde)
GILLESPIANA - Lalo Schifrin (Verve)
PERCEPTIONS - J.J. Johnson (Verve)
UNSQUARE DANCE - Dave Brubeck (Col)

ORCHESTRA - FOR DANCING (G-114)

CALCUTTA - Lawrence Welk (Dot)
I DIG DANCERS - Quincy Jones (Merc)
UP A LAZY RIVER - Si Zentner (Lib)
THE LERNER AND LOEWE BANDBOOK - Les Brown (Col)
MR. LUCKY GOES LATIN - Henry Mancini (RCA)
SHALL WE SWING? - Glen Gray, Billy May (Cap)

ORCHESTRA - OTHER THAN DANCING (G-115)

A CONCERT IN JAZZ - Gerry Mulligan (Verve)
A TOUCH OF ELEGANCE - Andre Previn (Col)
BREAKFAST AT TIFFANY'S - Henry Mancini (RCA)
THE GREATEST HORN IN THE WORLD - Al Hirt (RCA)
WEST SIDE STORY - Stan Kenton (Cap)

ARRANGEMENT (G-116)

(Arranger's Award)
ALL ABOUT ROSIE - George Russell (Mulligan) (Verve)
UP A LAZY RIVER - Bob Florence (Si Zentner) (Lib)
MOON RIVER - Henry Mancini (RCA)
NEW PIANO IN TOWN - Peter Nero (RCA)
PERCEPTIONS - J.J. Johnson (Dizzy Gillespie) (Verve)

VOCAL GROUP (G-117)

CLOSE UP - Kingston Trio (Cap)
HIGH FLYING - Lambert, Hendricks & Ross (Col)
THE SLIGHTLY FABULOUS LIMELITERS - The Limeliters (RCA)
VOICES IN FUN - Four Freshmen (Cap)
THE WAY YOU LOOK TONIGHT - The Lettermen (Cap)

CHORUS (G-118)

A SONG AT TWILIGHT - Roger Wagner Chorale (Cap)
BELAFONTE FOLK SINGERS AT HOME AND ABROAD - Belafonte Folk Singers (RCA)
GREAT BAND WITH GREAT VOICES (Si Zentner Orch) Johnny Mann Singers (Lib)
HEY, LOOK ME OVER - The Pete King Chorale (Kapp)
THIS IS NORMAN LUBOFF - Norman Luboff Choir (RCA)

SOUND TRACK ALBUM - SCORE, MOTION PICTURE OR TELEVISION (G-119)

BREAKFAST AT TIFFANY'S - Henry Mancini (RCA)
CHECKMATE - Johnny Williams (Col)
THE GUNS OF NAVARONE - Dimitri Tiomkin (Col)
LA DOLCE VITA - Nino Rota (RCA)
PARIS BLUES - Duke Ellington, Louis Armstrong (UA)

SOUND TRACK ALBUM - ORIGINAL CAST, MOTION PICTURE OR TELEVISION (G-120)

BABES IN TOYLAND - Tutti Camarata (Buena Vista)
BLUE HAWAII - Elvis Presley (RCA)
FLOWER DRUM SONG - Alfred Newman, Ken Darby (Decca)
PARENT TRAP - Tutti Camarata (Buena Vista)
WEST SIDE STORY - Johnny Green, Saul Chaplin, Sid Ramin, Irwin Kostal (Col)

ORIGINAL CAST SHOW ALBUM (G-121)

(Composer's Award)
CARNIVAL - Robert Merrill (MGM)
DO RE MI - Jule Styne, Betty Comden, Adolph Green (RCA)
HOW TO SUCCEED IN BUSINESS WITHOUT REALLY TRYING - Frank Loesser (RCA)
MILK AND HONEY - Jerry Herman (RCA)
WILDCAT - Cy Coleman, Carolyn Leigh (RCA)

COMEDY PERFORMANCE (G-122)

AN EVENING WITH MIKE NICHOLS AND ELAINE MAY - Mike Nichols, Elaine May (Merc)
HERE'S JONATHAN - Jonathan Winters (Verve)
JOSE JIMENEZ THE ASTRONAUT - Bill Dana (Kapp)
STAN FREBERG PRESENTS THE UNITED STATES OF AMERICA - Stan Freberg (Cap)
2001 YEARS WITH CARL REINER AND MEL BROOKS - Carl Reiner, Mel Brooks (Cap)

DOCUMENTARY OR SPOKEN WORD RECORDING (G-123)

THE COMING OF CHRIST - Alexander Scourby, Robert Russell Bennett, cond. (Decca)
HUMOR IN MUSIC - Leonard Bernstein, cond. New York Philharmonic (Col)
MORE OF HAL HOLBROOK IN MARK TWAIN TONIGHT! - Hal Holbrook (Col)
WISDOM, VOL. 1 (Sandburg, Shapley, Nehru, Lipschitz) Milt Gabler, Prod. (Decca)
WORLD OF DOROTHY PARKER - Dorothy Parker (Verve)

ENGINEERING CONTRIBUTION - POPULAR RECORDING (G-124)

(Engineer's Award)
BREAKFAST AT TIFFANY'S (Henry Mancini) Eng: Al Schmitt (RCA)
COZY (Steve Lawrence, Eydie Gorme) Eng: Bill MacMeekin (UA)
GREAT BAND WITH GREAT VOICES (Johnny Mann Singers) Eng: Al Schmitt (Lib)
JUDY AT CARNEGIE HALL (Judy Garland) Eng: Robert Arnold (Cap)
STEREO 35/MM. (Enoch Light) Eng: Robert Fine (Command)

ENGINEERING CONTRIBUTION - NOVELTY (G-125)

(Engineer's Award)
THE ALVIN SHOW (David Seville) Eng: Ted Keep (lib)
CARTOONS IN STEREO (Bob Prescott) Eng: Bruno Vineis (Audio Fld.)
THE SOUPY SALES SHOW - Eng: Eddie Brackett (Rep)
STAN FREBERG PRESENTS THE UNITED STATES OF AMERICA - Eng: John Kraus (Cap)
X-15 AND OTHER SOUNDS: ROCKETS MISSILES & JETS - Eng: Rafael O. Valentin (Rep)

ALBUM COVER (G-126)

(Other than Classical) (Art Director's Award)
A TOUCH OF ELEGANCE (Andre Previn) Art Dir: Bob Cato (Col)
BREAKFAST AT TIFFANY'S (Henry Mancini) Art Dir: Robert Jones (RCA)
JACKIE'S BAG (Jackie McLean) Art Dir: Reid Miles (Blue Note)
JUDY AT CARNEGIE HALL (Judy Garland) Art Dir: Jim Silke (Cap)
NEW ORLEANS - THE LIVING LEGEND (Peter Bocage) Art Dir: Ken Deardoff (Rvrsd)

RECORDING FOR CHILDREN (G-127)

GOLDEN TREASURY OF GREAT MUSIC AND LITERATURE - Arthur Shimkin, Producer (Golden)
101 DALMATIANS - Tutti Carmarata, Prod. (Disney)
PROKOFIEV: PETER AND THE WOLF - Leonard Bernstein, New York Philharmonic (Col)

THE SOUPY SALES SHOW - Soupy Sales (Rep)
YOUNG ABE LINCOLN - Arthur Shimkin, Producer (Original Broadway Cast) (Golden)

ROCK AND ROLL RECORDING (G-128)
GOODBYE CRUEL WORLD - James Darren (Colpix)
I LIKE IT LIKE THAT - Chris Kenner (Instnt)
IT'S GONNA WORK OUT FINE - Ike & Tina Turner (Sue)
LET'S TWIST AGAIN - Chubby Checker (Pkwy)
THE LION SLEEPS TONIGHT - The Tokens (RCA)

COUNTRY AND WESTERN RECORDING (G-129)
A LITTLE BITTY TEAR - Burl Ives (Decca)
BIG BAD JOHN - Jimmy Dean (Col)
HELLO WALLS - Faron Young (Cap)
HILLBILLY HEAVEN - Tex Ritter (Cap)
WALK ON BY - Leroy Van Dyke (Merc)

RHYTHM & BLUES RECORDING (G-130)
BRIGHT LIGHTS, BIG CITY - Jimmy Reed (Vee Jay)
FOOL THAT I AM - Etta James (Argo)
HIT THE ROAD JACK - Ray Charles (Am-Par)
MOTHER IN LAW - Ernie K-Doe (Minit)
SAVED - LaVerne Baker (Atl)

FOLK RECORDING (G-131)
BELAFONTE FOLK SINGERS AT HOME AND ABROAD - Belafonte Folk Singers (RCA)
THE BIG BILL BROONZY STORY - Bill Broonzy (Verve)
THE CLANCY BROTHERS AND TOMMY MAKEM - The Clancy Brothers and Tommy Makem (Col)
FOLK SONGS OF BRITAIN, VOL. 1 - Alan Lomax (Caedmon)
THE SLIGHTLY FABULOUS LIMELITERS - The Limeliters (RCA)

GOSPEL OR OTHER RELIGIOUS RECORDING (G-132)
EVERYTIME I FEEL THE SPIRIT - Mahalia Jackson (Col)
HYMNS AT HOME - Tennessee Ernie Ford (Cap)
JESUS KEEP ME NEAR THE CROSS - Prof. Alex Bradford (Choice)
LINCOLN HYMNS - Tex Ritter (Cap)
SWING LOW - Staple Singers (VeeJay)

NEW ARTIST OF 1961 (G-133)
ANN-MARGRET (RCA)
DICK GREGORY (Colpix)
THE LETTERMEN (Cap)
PETER NERO (RCA)
TIMI YURO (Lib)

CLASSICAL PERFORMANCE - ORCHESTRA (G-134)
BARTOK: MUSIC FOR STRING INSTRUMENTS, PERCUSSION & CELESTA; HINDEMITH: MATHIS DER MAHLER - Herbert von Karajan cond. Philharmonia (Angel)
BRUCKNER: SYMPHONY NO. 4 IN E FLAT MAJOR; WAGNER: TANNHAUSER OVERTURE & VENUSBERG MUSIC - Bruno Walter cond. Boston Symphony (Col)
RAVEL: DAPHNIS ET CHLOE - Charles Munch cond. Boston Symphony (RCA)
R. STRAUSS: DON JUAN; DEBUSSY: LA MER - Fritz Reiner cond. Chicago Symphony (RCA)
R. STRAUSS: DON QUIXOTE - George Szell cond. Cleveland Orchestra (Epic)

CLASSICAL PERFORMANCE - CHAMBER MUSIC (G-135)
BEETHOVEN: SERENADE, OP. 8; KODALY: DUO FOR VIOLIN &
CELLO, OP. 7 - Jascha Heifetz, Gregor Piatigorsky, William Primrose (RCA)
BERG: LYRIC SUITE; SEBERN: 5 PIECES FOR STRING QUARTET, OP. 5, 6 BAGATELLES, OP. 9 - Juilliard String Quartet (RCA)
FAURE: FIRST QUARTET, OP. 15; SCHUMANN: CLAVIER QUARTET, OP. 47 - Leonard Pennario, Eudice Shapiro, Sanford Schonbach, Victor Gottlieb (Cap)
FAURE: SONATA NO. 1; DEBUSSY: SONATA NO. 3 - Gary Graffman, Berl Senofsky (RCA)
FRANCK AND MOZART SONATAS - Erica Morini, Rudolf Firkusny (Decca)

CLASSICAL PERFORMANCE - INSTRUMENTAL SOLOIST (WITH ORCHESTRA) (G-136)
BARTOK: CONCERTO NO. 1 FOR VIOLIN & ORCH. - Isaac Stern (Ormandy, Philadelphia Orchestra) (Col)
BEETHOVEN: EMPEROR CONCERTO - Leon Fleisher (Szell cond. Cleveland Orchestra) (Epic)
BOCCHERINI, CASSADO: CONCERTO FOR GUITAR - Andres Segovia (Jorda cond. Symphony of Air) (Decca)
BRAHMS: DOUBLE CONCERTO (CONCERTO IN A FOR VIOLIN & CELLO) - Jascha Heifetz, Gregor Piatigorsky (Wallenstein cond.) (RCA)
R. STRAUSS: DON QUIXOTE - Pierre Founier (Szell cond. Cleveland Orchestra) (Epic)

CLASSICAL PERFORMANCE - INSTRUMENTAL SOLOIST (WITHOUT ORCHESTRA) (G-137)
BACH: SUITE NO. 3 - Andres Segovia (Decca)
BARTOK, HINDEMITH, PROKOFIEFF: SOLO VIOLIN SONATAS - Ruggerio Ricci (London)
BEETHOVEN: APPASSIONATA SONATAS, FUNERAL MARCH SONATA - Sviatoslav Richter (RCA)
HOMAGE TO LISZT - Vladimir Horowitz (RCA) REVERIE FOR SPANISH GUITARS - Laurindo Almeida (Cap)

OPERA RECORDING (G-138)
(Conductor's Award)
DONIZETTI: LUCIA DI LAMMERMOOR - John Pritchard cond. Chorus & Orch. of L'Accademia di Santa Cecilia (Sutherland, Cioni, Merrill, Siepi) (London)
MOZART: THE MARRIAGE OF FIGARO - Carlo Maria Giulini cond. Philharmonic Orchestra & Chorus (Schwarzkopf, Moffo, Taddei, Wachter, Cossotto) (Angel)
PUCCINI: MADAME BUTTERFLY - Gabriele Santini cond. Rome Opera Chorus & Orch. (de Los Angeles, Bjoerling, Piarzzini, Serini) (Cap)
R. STRAUSS: ELEKTRA - Karl Bohm cond. Orch & Chorus of Dresden State Opera (Borkh, Schech, Madeira, Fischer-Dieskau, Uhl) (DGG)
WAGNER: THE FLYING DUTCHMAN - Antal Dorati cond. Royal Opera House Orchestra (London, Rysanek, Tozzi, Elias, Liebl, Lewis) (RCA)

CLASSICAL PERFORMANCE - CHORAL (OTHER THAN OPERA) (G-139)
BACH: B MINOR MASS - Robert Shaw Chorale, Robert Shaw cond. (RCA)
BEETHOVEN: MISSA SOLEMNIS - Westminster Choir, Warren Martin, Dir; Leonard Bernstein cond. New York Philharmonic (Col)
BERLIOZ: L'ENFANCE DU CHRIST - St. Anthony Singers w/Pears, Morrison; Goldsbrough Orch., Colin Davis, cond. (Oiseau-Lyre)
POULENC: GLORIA IN G MAJOR FOR SOPRANO SOLO, CHORUS & ORCHESTRA - French Natl Radio-TV Chorus & Orch., Yvonne Gouverne, dir., Georges Pretre, cond. (Angel)
RESPIGHI: LAUD TO THE NATIVITY; MONTEVERDI: MAGNIFICAT - Rober Wagner Chorale, Roger Wagner, dir., Alfred Wallenstein cond. LA Philharmonic (Cap)
WALTON: BELSHAZZAR'S FEAST - Rutgers Univ. Choir, F. Austin Walter, dir., Eugene Ormandy cond. Philadelphia Orchestra (Col)

CLASSICAL PERFORMANCE - VOCAL SOLOIST (G-140)

THE ART OF THE PRIMA DONNA - Joan Sutherland (Molinari-Pradelli cond. Royal Opera House Orch.) (London)
BACH: CANTATAS NO. 58 & NO. 202 - Eileen Farrell, Bach Aria Group Orch. (Decca)
THE FABULOUS VICTORIA DE LOS ANGELES - Victoria de los Angeles, (Moore, pianist) (Angel)
OPERATIC ARIAS - Leontyne Price (deFabrutis and Rome Opera House Orch.) (RCA)
TRIMBLE: FOUR FRAGMENTS FROM THE CANTERBURY TALES - Adele Addison (Conant, Russo, Orenstein) (Col)

CONTEMPORARY CLASSICAL COMPOSITION (G-141)

(Composer's Award)

DISCANTUS - Laurindo Almeida (Cap)
GLORIA IN G MAJOR - Francis Poulenc (Angel)
MOVEMENTS FOR PIANO AND ORCHESTRA - Igor Stravinsky (Col)
MUSIC FOR BRASS QUINTET - Gunther Schuller (Comp. Recordings)
STRING QUARTET NO. 2 - Elliott Carter (RCA)

ENGINEERING CONTRIBUTION - CLASSICAL RECORDING (G-142)

(Engineer's Award)
BRAHMS: SYMPHONY NO. 2 (Steinberg cond. Pittsburgh Symphony) Eng: Robert Fine (Cmmnd)
POULENC: CONCERTO IN G FOR ORGAN, STRINGS AND TIMPANI (Durufle, soloist; Pretre cond. French Natl Radio-TV Orch.) Engs: Paul Vavasseur, Walter Ruhlmann (Angel)
PROKOFIEV: CONCERTO NO. 3 (Browning, solo; Leinsdorf Philharmonia Orch.) Eng: Chris Parker (Cap)
RAVEL: DAPHNIS ET CHLOE (Munch cond. Boston Symphony) Eng: Lewis W. Layton (RCA)
R. STRAUSS: ELEKTRA (Borkh, Schech, Madeira, Fischer-Dieskau, Uhl; Bohm cond. Orch. & Chorus of Dresden State Opera) Eng: Heinrich Keiholtz (DGG)

ALBUM COVER - CLASSICAL (G-143)

(Art Director's Award)
ALBENIZ: IBERIA; RAVEL: RAPSODIE ESPAGNOLE (Morel cond. Paris Conservatory Orch.) Art Dir: Robert Jones (RCA)
BEETHOVEN: NINE SYMPHONIES (Klemperer cond. Philharmonia Orch.) Art Dir: Marvin Schwartz (Angel)
GOLDEN AGE OF ENGLISH LUTE MUSIC (Julian Bream) Art Dir: Meyer Miller (RCA)
GOULD BALLET MUSIC: FALL RIVER LEGEND, INTERPLAY, LATIN AMERICAN SYMPHONETTE (Gould & his Orch.) Art Dir: Robert Jones (RCA)
PUCCINI: MADAME BUTTERFLY (de los Angeles, Bjoerling, Pirazzini, Serini; Santini cond. Rome Opera Chorus & Orch.) Art Dir: Marvin Schwartz (RCA)

1962

RECORD OF THE YEAR (G-144)

DESAFINADO - Stan Getz, Charlie Byrd (Verve)
FLY ME TO THE MOON BOSSA NOVA - Joe Harnell & His Orchestra (Kapp)
I CAN'T STOP LOVING YOU - Ray Charles (ABC)
I LEFT MY HEART IN SAN FRANCISCO - Tony Bennett (Col)
RAMBLIN' ROSE - Nat King Cole (Cap)
WHAT KIND OF FOOL AM I - Sammy Davis, Jr. (Reprise)

ALBUM OF THE YEAR (G-145)

(Other than Classical)

THE FIRST FAMILY - Vaughn Meader (Cadence)
I LEFT MY HEART IN SAN FRANCISCO - Tony Bennett (Col)
JAZZ SAMBA - Stan Getz, Charlie Byrd (Verve)
MODERN SOUNDS IN COUNTRY & WESTERN MUSIC - Ray Charles (ABC)
MY SON, THE FOLK SINGER - Allan Sherman (WB)

ALBUM OF THE YEAR - CLASSICAL (G-146)

BACH: ST. MATTHEW PASSION - Otto Klemperer cond. Philharmonia Orch. & Choir (Angel)
Columbia Records Presents VLADIMIR HOROWITZ - Vladimir Horowitz (Col)
THE HEIFETZ - PIATIGORSKY CONCERTS WITH PRIMROSE, PENNARIO AND GUESTS - Jascha Heifetz, Gregor Piatigorsky, William Primrose (RCA)
MAHLER: SYMPHONY NO. 9 IN D MINOR - Bruno Walter cond. Columbia Symphony (Col)
STRAVINSKY: THE FIREBIRD BALLET - Igor Stravinsky cond. Columbia Symphony (Col)

SONG OF THE YEAR (G-147)

(Songwriter's Award)
AS LONG AS HE NEEDS ME - Lionel Bart (RCA)
I LEFT MY HEART IN SAN FRANCISCO - Douglass Cross, George Cory (Col)
MY COLORING BOOK - John Kander, Fred Ebb (Colpix)
THE SWEETEST SOUNDS - Richard Rodgers (Cap)
WHAT KIND OF FOOL AM I - Leslie Bricusse, Anthony Newley (London)

INSTRUMENTAL THEME (G-148)

(Composer's Award)

A TASTE OF HONEY - Bobby Scott, Ric Marlow (Reprise)
BABY ELEPHANT WALK - Henry Mancini (RCA)
ROUTE 66 THEME - Nelson Riddle (Cap)
STRANGER ON THE SHORE - Acker Bilk, Robert Mellin (Atco)
THE STRIPPER - David Rose (MGM)
WALK ON THE WILD SIDE - Elmer Bernstein, Mack David (Ava)

VOCAL - FEMALE (G-149)

ELLA SWINGS BRIGHTLY WITH NELSON RIDDLE - Ella Fitzgerald (album) (Verve)
I'M A WOMAN - Peggy Lee (single) (Cap)
LENA. . .LOVELY AND ALIVE - Lena Horne (album) (RCA)
LOVE LETTERS - Ketty Lester (album) (Era)
MY COLORING BOOK - Sandy Stewart (single) (Colpix)
NO STRINGS - Diahann Carroll (album) (Cap)
SLIGHTLY OUT OF TUNE (DESAFINADO) - Pat Thomas (Verve)

VOCAL - MALE (G-150)

COMIN' HOME BABY - Mel Torme (album) (Atl)
I CAN'T STOP LOVING YOU - Ray Charles (album) (ABC)
I LEFT MY HEART IN SAN FRANCISCO - Tony Bennett (album) (Col)
WHAT KIND OF FOOL AM I - Sammy Davis, Jr. (album) (Reprise)
WHAT KIND OF FOOL AM I - Anthony Newley (single) (London)

JAZZ - SOLOIST OR SMALL GROUP (INSTRUMENTAL) (G-151)

A TASTE OF HONEY - Eddie Cano (Reprise)
DESAFINADO - Stan Getz (Verve)
NAT KING COLE SINGS, GEORGE SHEARING PLAYS - George Shearing Quintet (Cap)
TIJUANA MOODS - Charlie Mingus (RCA)
UNDERCURRENT - Bill Evans, Jim Hall (UA)
VIVA BOSSA NOVA! - Laurindo Almeida (Cap)
WEST SIDE STORY - Oscar Peterson Trio (Verve)

JAZZ - LARGE GROUP (INSTRUMENTAL) (G-152)

ADVENTURES IN JAZZ - Stan Kenton (Cap)
BIG BAND BOSSA NOVA - Stan Getz, Gary McFarland (Verve)
CARNEGIE HALL CONCERT - Dizzy Gillespie (Verve)
FIRST TIME! - Duke Ellington, Count Basie (Col)
THE LEGEND - Count Basie (Roulette)
MILES DAVIS AT CARNEGIE HALL - Miles Davis, Gil Evans (Orch.) (Col)
WALK ON THE WILD SIDE - Jimmy Smith (Verve)

ORIGINAL JAZZ COMPOSITION (G-153)

(Composer's Award)

CAST YOUR FATE TO THE WIND - Vince Guaraldi (Fantasy)
DESMOND BLUE - Paul Desmond (RCA)
FOCUS - Eddie Sauter (Verve)
QUINTESSENCE - Quincy Jones (Impulse)
SOUNDS OF HATARI - Henry Mancini (RCA)
TIJUANA MOODS - Charlie Mingus (RCA)
TUNISIAN FANTASY - Lalo Schifrin (Verve)

ORCHESTRA - FOR DANCING (G-154)

BIG BAND BOSSA NOVA - Stan Getz, Gary McFarland (Verve)
BIG BAND BOSSA NOVA - Quincy Jones (Merc)
FLY ME TO THE MOON BOSSA NOVA - Joe Harnell (Kapp)
JAZZ POPS - Neal Hefti (Reprise)
THE STRIPPER - David Rose (MGM)
VIVA BOSSA NOVA! - Laurindo Almeida (Cap)

ORCHESTRA OR INSTRUMENTALIST WITH ORCHESTRA - NOT JAZZ OR DANCING (G-155)

THE COLORFUL PETER NERO - Peter Nero (RCA)
HATARI! - Henry Mancini (RCA)
HOEDOWN! - Felix Slatkin (Lib)
STRANGER ON THE SHORE - Acker Bilk (Atco)
WALK ON THE WILD SIDE - Elmer Bernstein (Ava)

INSTRUMENTAL ARRANGEMENT (G-156)

(Arranger's Award)

BABY ELEPHANT WALK (Mancini & Orch.) Arr: Henry Mancini (RCA)
FLY ME TO THE MOON BOSSA NOVA (Harnell & Orch.) Arr: Joe Harnell (Kapp)
FOCUS (Stan Getz) Arr: Eddie Sauter (Verve)
QUINTESSENCE (Jones) Arr: Quincy Jones (ABC)
ROUTE 66 THEME (Riddle & His Orch.) Arr: Nelson Riddle (Cap)
SENSUOUS STRINGS OF ROBERT FARNON (Farnon & Orch.) Arr: Robert Farnon (Merc.)
THE STRIPPER (Rose & Orch.) Arr: David Rose (MGM)

BACKGROUND ARRANGEMENT (G-157)

(Arranger's Award)

BORN TO LOSE (Ray Charles) Arr: Marty Paich (ABC)
GO AWAY LITTLE GIRL (Steve Lawrence) Arr: Marion Evans (Col)
I CAN'T STOP LOVING YOU (Ray Charles) Arr: Marty Paich (Impulse)
I LEFT MY HEART IN SAN FRANCISCO (Tony Bennett) Arr: Marty Manning (Col)
JOAO GILBERTO (Joao Gilberto) Arr: Antonio Carlos Jobim (Cap)
MY SHIP (Carol Sloane) Arr: Bill Finegan (Col)
WHAT KIND OF FOOL AM I? (Sammy Davis, Jr.) Arr: Marty Paich (Reprise)

VOCAL GROUP (G-158)

A SONG FOR YOUNG LOVE - The Lettermen (Cap)
THE HI-LO'S HAPPEN TO FOLK SONGS - The Hi-Lo's (Reprise)
IF I HAD A HAMMER - Peter, Paul & Mary (WB)
THE SWINGERS - The Four Freshmen (Cap)
THROUGH CHILDREN'S EYES - The Limeliters (RCA)

CHORUS (G-159)

A CHORAL SPECTACULAR - Norman Luboff (RCA)
CONSIDER YOURSELF - Pete King Chorale (Kapp)
GREAT BAND WITH GREAT VOICES SWING THE GREAT VOICES OF THE GREAT BAND - Johnny Mann Singers, Si Zentner Orch. (Lib)
PRESENTING THE NEW CHRISTY MINSTRELS - The New Christy Minstrels (Col)
THE WARING BLEND - Fred Waring and the Pennsylvanians (Cap)

ORIGINAL CAST SHOW ALBUM (G-160)

(Composer's Award)

A FUNNY THING HAPPENED ON THE WAY TO THE FORUM (Orig. Broadway Cast) Comp: Stephen Sondheim (Cap)
BEYOND THE FRINGE (Alan Bennett, Peter Cook, Jonathan Miller, Dudley Moore) Comp: Dudley Moore (Cap)
NO STRINGS (Orig. Broadway Cast) Comp: Richard Rodgers (Cap)
OLIVER! (Orig. Broadway Cast Recording) Comp: Lionel Bart (RCA)
STOP THE WORLD - I WANT TO GET OFF (Anthony Newley, Anna Quayle & Cast) Comps: Leslie Bricusse, Anthony Newley (London)

CLASSICAL PERFORMANCE - ORCHESTRA (G-161)

BRUCKNER: SYMPHONY No. 7 IN E MAJOR - Otto Klemperer cond. Philharmonia Orch. (Angel)
MAHLER: SYMPHONY No. 3 IN D MINOR - Leonard Bernstein cond. New York Philharmonic (Col)
MAHLER: SYMPHONY No. 9 IN D MINOR - Bruno Walter cond. Columbia Symphony (Col)
R. STRAUSS: ALSO SPRACH ZARATHUSTRA, OP. 30 - Fritz Reiner cond. Chicago Symphony (RCA)
STRAVINSKY: THE FIREBIRD BALLET - Igor Stravinsky cond. Columbia Symphony (Col)

CLASSICAL PERFORMANCE - CHAMBER MUSIC (G-162)

BACH: SONATAS FOR VIOLIN & HARPSICHORD - Yehudi Menuhin, George Malcolm (Angel)
BARTOK: COMPLETE QUARTETS - Hungarian Quartet (DGG)
BEETHOVEN: THE LATE QUARTETS - The Budapest String Quartet (Col)
THE HEIFETZ-PIATIGORSKY CONCERTS WITH PRIMROSE, PENNARIO AND GUESTS - Jascha Heifetz, Gregor Piatigorsky, William Primrose (RCA)
THE INTIMATE BACH - Laurindo Almeida, Virginia Majewski, Vincent De Rosa (Cap)
RUBINSTEIN and SZERYNG VIOLIN SONATAS, BRAHMS: SONATA NO. 1; BEETHOVEN: SONATA No. 8 OP. 30, No. 3 - Artur Rubinstein, Henryk Szeryng (RCA)

CLASSICAL PERFORMANCE - INSTRUMENTAL SOLOIST(S) (WITH ORCHESTRA) (G-163)

BRAHMS: CONCERTO IN D FOR VIOLIN - David Oistrakh (Klemperer cond. French Natl Radio Orch.) (Angel)
BRUCH: SCOTTISH FANTASY, VIEUXTEMPS: CONCERTO No. 5 - Jascha Heifetz (Sargent cond. New Symphony Orch. of London) (RCA)
LISZT: CONCERTOS 1 AND 2 FOR PIANO & ORCH. - Sviatoslav Richter (Kondrashin cond. London Symphony) (Merc.)
RACHMANINOFF: CONCERTO NO. 2 - Van Cliburn (Reiner cond. Chicago Symphony) (RCA)
STRAVINSKY: CONCERTO IN D FOR VIOLIN - Isaac Stern (Stravinsky cond. Columbia Symphony) (Col)

CLASSICAL PERFORMANCE - INSTRUMENTAL SOLOIST OR DUO (WITHOUT ORCHESTRA) (G-164)

THE ART OF LEON GOOSSENS - Leon Goossens (Angel)
BACH: THE ART OF THE FUGUE, VOL. 1 - Glenn Gould (Col)
BACH: THE SIX SONATAS & PARTITAS FOR VIOLIN UNACCOM-

1958—1st ANNUAL GRAMMY AWARDS—Johnny Mercer and Nelson Riddle © N.A.R.A.S.

1964—7th ANNUAL GRAMMY AWARDS—Gregor Piatigorsky with Leonard Pennario and Morris Stoloff © N.A.R.A.S.

1960—3rd ANNUAL GRAMMY AWARDS—Bobby Darin, Mort Sahl, Henry Mancini (Winner), and Giselle Mackenzie © N.A.R.A.S.

1966—9th ANNUAL GRAMMY AWARDS—The Mamas & The Papas (John Phillips, Michelle Phillips, Dennis Donerty) and Herb Alpert © N.A.R.A.S.

1972—15th ANNUAL GRAMMY AWARDS—Michel LeGrand
© N.A.R.A.S.

1970—13th ANNUAL GRAMMY AWARDS—Paul and Linda
McCartney
© N.A.R.A.S.

1967—10th ANNUAL GRAMMY AWARDS—Glen Campbell
© N.A.R.A.S.

1970—13th ANNUAL GRAMMY AWARDS—Simon and Garfunkel
© N.A.R.A.S.

PANIED - Joseph Szigeti (Vanguard)
BEETHOVEN: SONATA No. 22 FOR PIANO - Sviatoslav Richter (RCA)
Columbia Records Presents VLADIMIR HOROWITZ - Vladimir Horowitz (Col)
Five Pieces from PLATERO AND I - Andres Segovia (Decca)
FRENCH PIANO MUSIC - FOUR HANDS - Robert and Gaby Casadesus (Col)
HIGHLIGHTS OF RUBINSTEIN AT CARNEGIE HALL RECORDED DURING THE HISTORIC TEN RECITALS OF 1961 - Artur Rubinstein (RCA)

OPERA RECORDING (G-165)

(Conductor's Award)

BEETHOVEN: FIDELIO - Otto Klemperer cond. Philharmonia Orch. & Chorus (Solos: Ludwig, Vickers, Frick, Hallstein, Berry) (Angel)
BIZET: THE PEARL FISHERS - Pierre Dervaux cond. Chorus & Orch. of Theatre Natl de l'Opera Comique (Solos: Micheau, Gedda) (Angel)
PUCCINI: LA BOHEME - Erich Leinsdorf cond. Rome Opera House Orch. & Chorus (Solos: Moffo, Tucker, Costa, Merrill, Tozzi, Maero) (RCA)
R. STRAUSS: SALOME - Georg Solti cond. Vienna Philharmonic (Solos: Nilsson, Wachter, Stolze) (London)
VERDI: AIDA - Georg Solti cond. Rome Opera House Orch. & Chorus (Solos: Price, Vickers, Gorr, Merrill, Tozzi) (RCA)
WAGNER: DIE WALKURE - Erich Leinsdorf cond. London Symphony (Solos: Nilsson, Brouwenstien, Gorr, Vickers, London, Ward) (RCA)

CLASSICAL PERFORMANCE - CHORAL (OTHER THAN OPERA) (G-166)

BACH: ST. MATTHEW PASSION - Philharmonia Choir, Wilhelm Pitz, Choral Director, Otto Klemperer cond. Philharmonia Orch. (Angel)
BERLIOZ: ROMEO AND JULIET - New England Conservatory Chorus, Lorna Cooke de Varon, Dir. Charles Munch cond. Boston Symphony (RCA)
FAURE: REQUIEM - Roger Wagner Chorale; Orch. de la Societe des Concerts du Conservatoire de Paris, Roger Wagner, cond. (Cap)
HONEGGER: KING DAVID (Le Roi David) - Univ. of Utah Chorus, Ardean Watts, Dir. Maurice Abravanel cond. Utah Symphony (Vanguard)
MAHLER: SYMPHONY No. 3 IN D MINOR - Women's Chorus of Schola Cantorum, Hugh Ross, Dir. Boy's Choir, Church of Transfiguration, Stuart Gardner, Dir. Leonard Bernstein cond. New York Philharmonic (Col)
PROKOFIEV: ALEXANDER NEVSKY, OP. 78 - Westminster Choir, Warren Martin, Dir. Thomas Schippers cond. New York Philharmonic (Col)

CLASSICAL PERFORMANCE - VOCAL SOLOIST (WITH OR WITHOUT ORCHESTRA) (G-167)

FOSS: TIME CYCLE - Adele Addison (Bernstein cond. New York Philharmonic) (Col)
GREAT ARIAS FROM FRENCH OPERA - Maria Callas (Pretre cond. Orch. Natl de la Radio Diffusion Francaise) (Angel)
SCHUBERT: DIE SCHONE MULLERIN - Dietrich Fischer-Dieskau (Moore, piano) (Angel)
SPANISH SONGS OF THE 20th CENTURY - Victoria de los Angeles (Soriano, piano) (Angel)
R. STRAUSS: SALOME - Birgit Nilsson (Solti cond. Vienna Philharmonic) (London)
WAGNER: GOTTERDAMERUNG, BRUNNHILDE'S IMMOLATION SCENE; WESENDONCK: SONGS - Eileen Farrell (Bernstein cond. New York Philharmonic) (Col)

CLASSICAL COMPOSITION BY CONTEMPORARY COMPOSER (G-168)

ARCANA - Comp: Edgard Varese (Col)
CONNOTATIONS FOR ORCHESTRA - Comp: Aaron Copland (Col)
THE FLOOD - Comp: Igor Stravinsky (Col)
NOYE'S FLUDDE - Comp: Benjamin Britten (London)
SONG OF SONGS - Comp: Lukas Foss (Col)
SYMPHONY No. 2 - Comp: Sir William Walton (Epic)
TIME CYCLE - Comp: Lukas Foss (Col)

ENGINEERING CONTRIBUTION - CLASSICAL RECORDING (G-169)

(Engineer's Award)

Columbia Records Presents VLADIMIR HOROWITZ - Eng: Fred Plaut (Col)
COPLAND: BILLY THE KID; APPALACHIAN SPRING (Dorati cond. London Symphony) Eng: Robert Fine (Merc)
HOLST: THE PLANETS (Karajan cond. Vienna Philharmonic) Eng: London Recording Team (col)
MAHLER: SYMPHONY No. 3 IN D MINOR - (Bernstein cond. New York Philharmonic) Eng: Fred Plaut (Col)
MAHLER: SYMPHONY No. 9 IN D MINOR (Walter cond. Columbia Symphony Orch.) Eng: William Britten (Col)
PROKOFIEV: CONCERTO No. 3 FOR PIANO; RACHMANINOFF: CONCERTO No. 1 FOR PIANO (Janis, piano; Kondrashin cond. Moscow Philharmonic) Eng: Robert Fine (Merc)
STRAUSS: ALSO SPRACH ZARATHUSTRA OP. 30 (Reiner cond. Chicago Symphony) Eng: Lewis W. Layton (RCA)

ALBUM COVER - CLASSICAL (G-170)

(Art Director's Award)

BARTOK: THE MIRACULOUS MANDARIN; SHOSTAKOVICH: THE AGE OF GOLD (Irving cond. Philharmonia Orchestra) Art Dir: Jim Silke (Cap)
BEETHOVEN: FIDELIO (Klemperer cond. Philharmonia Orch. & Chorus) Art Dir: Marvin Schwartz (Angel)
FAURE: REQUIEM (Wagner cond. Roger Wagner Chorale & Orch. de la Societe des Conservatoire de Paris) Art Dir: Marvin Schwartz (Cap)
THE INTIMATE BACH (Almeida, Majewski, de Rosa) Art Dir: Marvin Schwartz (Cap)
OTTO KLEMPERER CONDUCTS (WEILL: THREE PENNY OPERA SUITE and others) (Klemperer cond. Philharmonia Orch.) Art Dir: Marvin Schwartz (Angel)
WAGNER: PRELUDE AND LOVE DEATH; R. STRAUSS DEATH AND TRANSFIGURATION (Leinsdorf cond. Los Angeles Philharmonic) Art Dir: Marvin Schwartz (Cap)

COMEDY PERFORMANCE (G-171)

ANOTHER DAY, ANOTHER WORLD - Jonathan Winters (Verve)
BEYOND THE FRINGE - Alan Bennett, Peter Cook, Jonathan Miller, Dudley Moore (Cap)
THE FIRST FAMILY - Vaughn Meader (Cadence)
MY SON, THE FOLKSINGER - Allan Sherman (WB)
NICHOLS AND MAY EXAMINE DOCTORS - Elaine May and Mike Nichols (Merc)

DOCUMENTARY OR SPOKEN WORD RECORDING (G-172)

CARL SANDBURG READING HIS POETRY - Carl Sandburg (Caedmon)
ENOCH ARDEN (MUSIC BY R. STRAUSS; POEM BY ALFRED TENNYSON) - Claude Rains, reader; Glenn Gould, pianist (Col)
FIRST PERFORMANCE: LINCOLN CENTER FOR THE PERFORMING ARTS - New York Philharmonic, Leonard Bernstein, cond. (Col)
MAMA SANG A SONG - Stan Kenton (Cap)
SIR MICHAEL REDGRAVE READS "THE HARMFULNESS OF TOBACCO", "A TRANSGRESSION", "THE FIRST CLASS PASSENGER" BY ANTON CHEKHOV - Sir Michael Redgrave (Spoken Arts)
SIX MILLION ACCUSE - Yehuda Lev, narr. (UA)
THE STORY-TELLER: A SESSION WITH CHARLES LAUGHTON - Charles Laughton (Cap)
THIS IS MY BELOVED - Laurence Harvey (Atl)

ENGINEERING CONTRIBUTION - OTHER THAN NOVELTY OR CLASSICAL (G-173)

(Engineer's Award)

ADVENTURES IN JAZZ (Stan Kenton) Eng: Carson C. Taylor (Cap)
GREAT BAND WITH GREAT VOICES SWING THE GREAT VOICES OF THE GREAT BANDS (Si Zentner Orch., Johnny Mann Singers) Eng: Al Schmitt (Lib)
HATARI! (Henry Mancini) Eng: Al Schmitt (RCA)

I CAN'T STOP LOVING YOU (Ray Charles) Eng: Bill Putnam (ABC)
JONAH JONES AND GLEN GRAY - Eng: Hugh Davies (Cap)
ROUTE 66 THEME (Nelson Riddle) Eng: John Kraus (Cap)
STEREO SPECTACULAR (Various Artists) Eng: William Hamilton (Audio Fld.)

ENGINEERING CONTRIBUTION - NOVELTY (G-174)

(Engineer's Award)

THE CHIPMUNK SONGBOOK (David Seville) Eng: Al Schmitt (Lib)
THE CIVIL WAR, VOL. 1 (Fennell cond. Eastman Wind Ensemble; Martin Gabel, narr.) Eng: Robert Fine (Merc)
THE FIRST FAMILY (Vaughn Meader) Eng: John Quinn (Cadence)
MY SON, THE FOLK SINGER (Allan Sherman) Eng: Lowell Frank (WB)
PEPINO, THE ITALIAN MOUSE (Lou Monte) Eng: Eddie Smith (Reprise)

ALBUM COVER (OTHER THAN CLASSICAL) (G-175)

(Art Director's Award)

THE COMEDY (The Modern Jazz Quartet) Art Dir: Loring Eutemey (Atl)
THE FIRST FAMILY (Vaughn Meader) Art Dir: Bill Longcore (Cadence)
THE GREAT YEARS (Frank Sinatra) Art Dir: Jim Silke (Cap)
JAZZ SAMBA (Stan Getz) Art Dir: John Murello (Verve)
LENA. . .LOVELY AND ALIVE (Lena Horne) Art Dir: Robert Jones (RCA)
LONELY WOMAN (The Modern Jazz Quartet) Art Dir: Loring Eutemey (Atl)
MY SON, THE FOLK SINGER (Allan Sherman) Art Dir: Ken Kim (WB)
POTPOURRI PAR PIAF (Edith Piaf) Art Dir: Ed Thrasher (Cap)

RECORDING FOR CHILDREN (G-176)

THE CAT WHO WALKED BY HERSELF - Boris Karloff (Caedmon)
THE CHIPMUNK SONGBOOK - David Seville (Lib)
GRIMM'S FAIRY TALES - Danny Kaye (Golden)
SAINT-SAEN'S: CARNIVAL OF THE ANIMALS; BRITTEN: YOUNG PERSON'S GUIDE TO THE ORCHESTRA - Leonard Bernstein (Col)
SHARI IN STORYLAND - Shari Lewis (RCA)
THROUGH CHILDREN'S EYES - The Limeliters (RCA)
YOU READ TO ME, I'LL READ TO YOU - John Ciardi (Spoken)

ROCK AND ROLL RECORDING (G-177)

ALLEY CAT - Bent Fabric (Atco)
BIG GIRLS DON'T CRY - Four Seasons (VeeJay)
BREAKING UP IS HARD TO DO - Neil Sedaka (RCA)
TWISTIN' THE NIGHT AWAY - Sam Cooke (RCA)
UP ON THE ROOF - The Drifters (Atl)
YOU BEAT ME TO THE PUNCH - Mary Wells (Motown)

COUNTRY AND WESTERN RECORDING (G-178)

DEVIL WOMAN - Marty Robbins (Col)
FUNNY WAY OF LAUGHIN' - Burl Ives (Decca)
IT KEEPS RIGHT ON A-HURTIN' - Johnny Tillotson (Cadence)
P.T. 109 - Jimmy Dean (Col)
SHE STILL THINKS I CARE - George Jones (UA)
WOLVERTON MOUNTAIN - Claude King (Col)

RHYTHM AND BLUES RECORDING (G-179)

BRING IT ON HOME TO ME - Sam Cooke (RCA)
COMIN' HOME BABY - Mel Torme (Atl)
I CAN'T STOP LOVING YOU - Ray Charles (ABC)
LOCO-MOTION - Little Eva (Dimension)
NUT ROCKER - B. Bumble and the Stingers (Rendezvous)
WHAT'D I SAY - Bobby Darin (Atco)

FOLK RECORDING (G-180)

THE BALLAD OF JED CLAMPETT - Flatt and Scruggs (Col)
BOB DYLAN - Bob Dylan (Col)
IF I HAD A HAMMER - Peter, Paul & Mary (WB)

JOAN BAEZ IN CONCERT - Joan Baez (Vanguard)
THE MIDNIGHT SPECIAL - Harry Belafonte (RCA)
PRESENTING THE NEW CHRISTY MINSTRELS - The New Christy Minstrels (Col)
SOMETHING SPECIAL - Kingston Trio (Cap)

GOSPEL OR OTHER RELIGIOUS RECORDING (G-181)

BLACK NATIVITY - Prof. Alex Bradford (Marion Williams & Stars of Faith) (VeeJay)
GREAT SONGS OF LOVE AND FAITH - Mahalia Jackson (Col)
HYMNS AT SUNSET - Ralph Carmichael (Cap)
I LOVE TO TELL THE STORY - Tennessee Ernie Ford (Cap)
INSPIRATION - GREAT MUSIC FOR CHORUS & ORCHESTRA - Norman Luboff Choir, Leopold Stokowki cond. New Symphony Orch. of London (RCA)
MARIAN ANDERSON - HE'S GOT THE WHOLE WORLD IN HIS HANDS, AND 18 OTHER SPIRITUALS - Marian Anderson (Franz Rupp, piano) (RCA)
SAME ME - The Clefs of Calvary (True Sound)

NEW ARTIST OF 1962 (G-182)

FOUR SEASONS (VeeJay)
ROBERT GOULET (Col)
VAUGHN MEADER (Cadence)
THE NEW CHRISTY MINSTRELS (Col)
PETER, PAUL AND MARY (WB)
ALLAN SHERMAN (WB)

1963

RECORD OF THE YEAR (G-183)

THE DAYS OF WINE AND ROSES - Henry Mancini (RCA)
DOMINIQUE - Soeur Sourire (Philips)
HAPPY DAYS ARE HERE AGAIN - Barbra Streisand (Col)
I WANNA BE AROUND - Tony Bennett (Col)
WIVES AND LOVERS - Jack Jones (Kapp)

ALBUM OF THE YEAR - OTHER THAN CLASSICAL (G-184)

BACH'S GREATEST HITS - The Swingle Singers (Philips)
THE BARBRA STREISAND ALBUM - Barbra Streisand (Col)
THE DAYS OF WINE AND ROSES - Andy Williams (Col)
HONEY IN THE HORN - Al Hirt (RCA)
THE SINGING NUN - Soeur Sourire (Philips)

ALBUM OF THE YEAR - CLASSICAL (G-185)

BRITTEN: WAR REQUIEM - Benjamin Britten cond. London Sym. Orch. & Chorus (Soloists: Vishnevskaya, Pears, Fischer-Dieskau; David Willocks, Dir. Bach Choir; Edward Chapman, Dir. Highgate School Choir (London)
DEBUSSY: LA MER; RAVEL: DAPHNIS AND CHLOE - George Szell cond. Cleveland Orch. (Epic)
GREAT SCENES FROM GERSHWIN'S PORGY & BESS - Leontyne Price and William Warfield (Skitch Henderson cond. RCA Sym. Orch. & Chorus) (RCA)
PUCCINI: MADAME BUTTERFLY - Erich Leinsdorf cond. RCA Italiana Opera Orch. & Chorus (Soloists: Price, Tucker, Elias) (RCA)
THE SOUND OF VLADIMIR HOROWITZ (Works of Schumann, Scarlatti, Schubert, Scriabin) Vladimir Horowitz (Col)

SONG OF THE YEAR (G-186)

(Composer's Award)

CALL ME IRRESPONSIBLE - Comps: Sammy Cahn, Jimmy Van Heusen (Reprise)
THE DAYS OF WINE AND ROSES - Comps: Johnny Mercer, Henry Mancini (RCA)
THE GOOD LIFE - Comps: Sacha Distel, Jack Reardon (Jay Gee)

I WANNA BE AROUND - Comps: Sadie Vimmerstedt, Johnny Mercer (Col)

WIVES AND LOVERS - Comps: Burt Bacharach, Hal David (Kapp)

INSTRUMENTAL THEME (G-187)

(Composer's Award)

BLUESETTE - Comp: Jean "Toots" Theilmans (ABC-Para)

GRAVY WALTZ - Comps: Ray Brown, Steve Allen (Dot)

LAWRENCE OF ARABIA - Comp: Maurice Jarre (Colpix)

MORE (THEME FROM "MONDO CANE") - Comps: Riz Ortolani, Nino Oliviero, Norman Newell (UA)

WASHINGTON SQUARE - Comps: Bob Goldstein, David Shire (Epic)

VOCAL - FEMALE (G-188)

THE BARBRA STREISAND ALBUM - Barbra Streisand (Col)

BLAME IT ON THE BOSSA NOVA - Eydie Gorme (single) (Col)

DOMINIQUE - Soeur Sourire (The Singing Nun) (single) (Philips)

I'M A WOMAN - Peggy Lee (album) (Cap)

THE WORLD OF MIRIAM MAKEBA - Miriam Makeba (album) (RCA)

VOCAL - MALE (G-189)

BUSTED - Ray Charles (single) (ABC-Para)

CATCH A RISING STAR - John Gary (album) (RCA)

THE DAYS OF WINE AND ROSES - Andy Williams (album) (Col)

I WANNA BE AROUND - Tony Bennett (single) (Col)

WIVES AND LOVERS - Jack Jones (single) (Kapp)

JAZZ - SOLOIST OR SMALL GROUP (G-190)

CONVERSATIONS WITH MYSELF - Bill Evans (Verve)

CRISS-CROSS - Thelonious Monk (Col)

DAVE BRUBECK AT CARNEGIE HALL - Dave Brubeck Quartet (Col)

4 TO GO! - Andre Previn, with Ray Brown, Herb Ellis, Shelly Manne (Col)

OUR MAN IN NEW ORLEANS - Al Hirt (RCA)

PETER NERO IN PERSON - Peter Nero (RCA)

SEVEN STEPS TO HEAVEN - Miles Davis (Col)

JAZZ - LARGE GROUP (G-191)

ENCORE: WOODY HERMAN, 1963 - Woody Herman Band (Philips)

FULL NELSON - Oliver Nelson Orch. (Verve)

GERRY MULLIGAN '63 - Gerry Mulligan Concert Jazz Band (Verve)

OUR MAN IN NEW ORLEANS - Al Hirt (RCA)

QUINCY JONES PLAYS THE HIP HITS - Quincy Jones (Mercury)

SEVEN STEPS TO HEAVEN - Miles Davis (Col)

ORIGINAL JAZZ COMPOSITION (G-192)

(Composer's Award)

BLACK SAINT AND THE SINNER LADY - Comp: Charlie Mingus (Impulse)

EAST SIDE-WEST SIDE - Comp: Kenyon Hopkins (Backbone Hill)

GRAVY WALTZ - Comp: Ray Brown, Steve Allen (Dot)

LITTLE BIRD - Comps: Dick Grove, Pete Jolly, Tommy Wolf (Ava)

MEDITATION - Comps: Newton Mendonco, Antonio Carlos Jobim (Riverside)

TAKE TEN - Comp: Paul Desmond (RCA)

ORCHESTRA - FOR DANCING (G-193)

ENCORE: WOODY HERMAN, 1963 - Woody Herman (Philips)

FLY ME TO THE MOON AND THE BOSSA NOVA POPS - Joe Harnell (Kapp)

THE PAGE 7. . .AN EXPLOSION IN POP MUSIC - Page Cavanaugh (RCA)

QUINCY JONES PLAYS THE HIP HITS - Quincy Jones (Mercury)

RICHARD RODGERS BANDBOOK - Les Brown (Col)

THIS TIME BY BASIE! HITS OF THE 50'S AND 60'S - Count Basie (Reprise)

ORCHESTRA OR INSTRUMENTALIST WITH ORCHESTRA - NOT JAZZ OR DANCING (G-194)

ANDRE PREVIN IN HOLLYWOOD - Andre Previn (Col)

HAIL THE CONQUERING NERO - Peter Nero (RCA)

JAVA - Al Hirt (RCA)

MORE - Kai Winding (Verve)

OUR MAN IN HOLLYWOOD - Henry Mancini (RCA)

THEMES FOR YOUNG LOVERS - Percy Faith (Col)

INSTRUMENTAL ARRANGEMENT (G-195)

(Arranger's Award)

GRAVY WALTZ (Steve Allen) Arr: Robert N. Enevoldsen (Dot)

I CAN'T STOP LOVING YOU (Count Basie) Arr: Quincy Jones (Reprise)

MORE (Kai Winding) Arr: Claus Ogerman (Verve)

MOUNTAIN GREENERY (Peter Nero) Arrs: Peter Nero & Marty Gold (RCA)

WASHINGTON SQUARE (The Village Stompers) Arr: Joe Sherman (Epic)

BACKGROUND ARRANGEMENT (G-196)

(Arranger's Award)

BLAME IT ON THE BOSSA NOVA (Eydie Gorme) Arr: Marion Evans (Col)

BUSTED (Ray Charles) Arr: Benny Carter (ABC)

CALL ME IRRESPONSIBLE (Frank Sinatra) Arr: Nelson Riddle (Reprise)

THE DAYS OF WINE AND ROSES (Henry Mancini) Arr: Henry Mancini (RCA)

TELL ME THE TRUTH (Nancy Wilson) Arr: Gerald Wilson (Cap)

WIVES AND LOVERS (Jack Jones) Arr: Pete King (Kapp)

VOCAL GROUP (G-197)

BLOWIN' IN THE WIND - Peter, Paul and Mary (WB)

HEY LOOK US OVER! - The J's with Jamie (Col)

THE HI LO'S HAPPEN TO BOSSA NOVA - The Hi Lo's (Reprise)

LIKE SING - JACKIE AND ROY KRAL - Jackie and Roy Kral (Col)

WAITIN' FOR THE EVENING TRAIN - Anita Kerr Singers (RCA)

CHORUS (G-198)

BACH'S GREATEST HITS - Swingle Singers (Philips)

CHARADE - Henry Mancini and his Orchestra with Chorus (RCA)

GREEN, GREEN - The New Christy Minstrels (Col)

THE JOY OF CHRISTMAS - The Mormon Tabernacle Choir, Richard P. Condie, Director; Leonard Bernstein cond. New York Phil. (Col)

THE MANY MOODS OF CHRISTMAS - Robert Shaw Chorale, RCA Orchestra, Robert Shaw cond.

ORIGINAL SCORE - MOTION PICTURE OR TELEVISION (G-199)

(Composer's Award)

CLEOPATRA - Comp: Alex North (20th Cen. Fox)

LAWRENCE OF ARABIA - Comp: Maurice Jarre (Colpix)

MONDO CANE - Comps: Riz Ortolani, Nino Oliviero (UA)

TOM JONES - Comp: John Addison (UA)

SCORE FROM AN ORIGINAL CAST SHOW ALBUM (G-200)

(Composer's Award)

HERE'S LOVE (Original Cast with Janis Paige, Craig Stevens, Laurence Naismith; Elliot Lawrence) Musical Director - Comp: Meredith Willson (Col)

JENNIE (Mary Martin, Original Cast with Ethel Shutta, George Wallace, Jack DeLon, Robbin Bailey) Comps: Arthur Schwartz, Howard Deitz (RCA)

110 IN THE SHADE (Original Cast with Robert Horton, Inga Swenson, Stephen Douglass, Will Peer, Steve Roland, Scooter Teague, Lesley Warren; Orchestra conducted by Donald W. Pippin) Comps: Harvey

Schmidt, Tom Jones (RCA)
SHE LOVES ME (Original Cast with Barbara Cook, Daniel Massey, Jack Cassidy) Comps: Jerry Bock, Sheldon Harnick (MGM)
TOVARICH (Original Cast with Vivien Leigh, Jean-Pierre Aumont) Comps: Lee Pockriss, Anne Croswell (Cap)

CLASSICAL PERFORMANCE - ORCHESTRA (G-201)

BARTOK: CONCERTO FOR ORCHESTRA - Erich Leinsdorf cond. Boston Sym. Orch. (RCA)
BEETHOVEN: THE NINE SYMPHONIES (COMPLETE) - Herbert von Karajan cond. Berlin Philharmonic (DGG)
BEETHOVEN: SYMPHONY No. 6 IN F MAJOR, OP. 68 ("PASTORALE") - Fritz Reiner cond. Chicago Symphony (RCA)
MAHLER: SYMPHONY No. 1 IN D MAJOR ("THE TITAN") - Bruno Walter cond. Columbia Symphony (Col)
RAVEL: DAPHNIS AND CHLOE - George Szell cond. the Cleveland Orchestra (Epic)
SCHUBERT: SYMPHONY No. 9 IN C MAJOR ("THE GREAT") - Arturo Toscanini cond. Philadelphia Symphony (RCA)

CLASSICAL PERFORMANCE - CHAMBER MUSIC (G-202)

BEETHOVEN: QUARTET No. 11 IN F MINOR, OP. 95; QUARTET NO. 16 IN F MAJOR, OP. 135 - Juilliard String Quartet (RCA)
BEETHOVEN: SONATAS FOR VIOLIN & PIANO (NOS. 3, 4 & 5) - Zino Francescatti, Violinist; Robert Casadesus, Pianist (Col)
BRAHMS: LIEBESLIEDER WALTZES; SCHUMANN: SPANISCHE LIEBESLIEDER - Arthur Gold and Robert Fizdale (with vocalists) (Col)
AN EVENING OF ELIZABETHAN MUSIC - Julian Bream Consort (RCA)
MOZART: WIND MUSIC, VOLS. 1-5 - London Wind Soloists (London)
SCHUBERT: QUINTET IN A MAJOR FOR PIANO & STRINGS, OP. 114 ("TROUT") - Members of Budapest String Quartet with Mieczyslaw Horszowski and Julius Levine (Col)

CLASSICAL PERFORMANCE - INSTRUMENTAL SOLOIST(S) (WITH ORCHESTRA) (G-203)

BARTOK: CONCERTO No. 1 FOR PIANO & ORCHESTRA - Rudolf Serkin (Szell cond. Columbia Symphony) (Col)
BRUCH: CONCERTO No. 1 IN G MINOR FOR VIOLIN, OP. 26; MOZART: CONCERTO No. 4 IN D MAJOR, FOR VIOLIN, K 218 - Jascha Heifetz (Sargent cond. New Symphony Orchestra of London) (RCA)
HINDEMITH: CONCERTO FOR VIOLIN - David Oistrakh (Hindemith cond. London Symphony) (London)
LISZT: CONCERTO No. 1 FOR PIANO & ORCHESTRA - Andre Watts (Bernstein cond. New York Philharmonic) (Col)
RACHMANINOFF: CONCERTO No. 3 IN D MINOR FOR PIANO - Vladimir Ashkenazy (Fistoulari cond. London Symphony) (London)
RAVEL: CONCERTO IN G FOR PIANO & ORCHESTRA; DELLO JOIO: FANTASY & VARIATIONS FOR PIANO & ORCHESTRA - Lorin Hollander (Leinsdorf cond. Boston Symphony) (RCA)
TCHAIKOVSKY: CONCERTO No. 1 IN B-FLAT MINOR FOR PIANO & ORCHESTRA - Artur Rubinstein (Leinsdorf cond. Boston Symphony) (RCA)

CLASSICAL PERFORMANCE - INSTRUMENTAL SOLOIST OR DUO (WITHOUT ORCHESTRA) (G-204)

BACH: THE SIX PARTITAS - Glenn Gould (Col)
BEETHOVEN: THREE FAVORITE SONATAS (SONATA NO. 8 "PATHETIQUE"; SONATA NO. 14 "MOONLIGHT"; SONATA NO. 23 "APPASSIONATA") - Rudolf Serkin (Col)
GRANADA (ALBENIZ: "GRANADA"; GRANADOS: "SPANISH DANCE IN E MINOR"; PONCE, TANSMAN, AGUADO: "EIGHT LESSONS FOR THE GUITAR"; SOR: "FOUR STUDIES") - Andres Segovia (Decca)
SCHUMANN: CARNAVAL; FANTASIESTUCKE - Artur Rubinstein (RCA)
THE SOUND OF HOROWITZ (Works of Schumann, Scarlatti, Schubert, Scriabin) - Vladimir Horowitz (Col)

OPERA RECORDING (G-205)
(Conductor's Award, Plaques to Principal Soloists)
BARTOK: BLUEBEARD'S CASTLE - Eugene Ormandy cond. Philadelphia Orchestra (Soloists: Elias, Hines) (Col)
MOZART: COSI FAN TUTTE - Eugen Jochum cond. RIAS Chamber Chorus, Berlin Philharmonic (Soloists: Seefried, Merriman, Koth, Haefliger, Prey, Fischer-Dieskau) (DGG)
MUSSORGSKY: BORIS GODOUNOV - Andre Cluytens cond. Paris Conservatoire Orchestra & Chorus of National Opera of Sofia (Soloist: Boris Christoff) (Angel)
PUCCINI: MADAMA BUTTERFLY - Erich Leinsdorf cond. RCA Italiana Orchestra & Chorus (Soloists: Price, Tucker, Elias) (RCA)
PUCCINI: TOSCA - Herbert von Karajan cond. Vienna Philharmonic (Soloists: Price, DiStefano, Taddei) (RCA)
WAGNER: SIEGFRIED - Georg Solti cond. Vienna Philharmonic (Soloists: Nilsson, Windgassen, Hotter, Stolze, Hoffgen, Neidlinger, Sutherland) (London)

CLASSICAL PERFORMANCE - CHORAL (OTHER THAN OPERA) (G-206)

BACH: ST. MATTHEW PASSION - Abraham Kaplan, Dir. Collegiate Chorale; Stuart Gardner, Dir. Boy's Choir, Church of Transfiguration; Leonard Bernstein cond. New York Philharmonic (Col)
BRAHMS: A GERMAN REQUIEM - Richard Condie Dir. Mormon Tabernacle Choir; Eugene Ormandy cond. Philadelphia Orchestra (Col)
BRITTEN: WAR REQUIEM - David Willcocks, Dir. Bach Choir; Edward Chapman, Dir. Highgate School Choir; Benjamin Britten cond. London Symphony Orchestra & Chorus (London)
HAYDN: "NELSON MASS" (MASS No. 9 IN D MINOR, MISSA SOLEMNIS) - David Willcocks cond. Choir of King's College & London Symphony (London)
MILHAUD: LES CHOEPHORES - Hugh Ross, Dir. Schola Cantorum of New York; Leonard Bernstein cond. New York Philharmonic (Col)
ROBERT SHAW CHORALE "ON TOUR" (Ives, Schoenberg, Mozart, Ravel) - Robert Shaw cond. Robert Shaw Chorale & Orch. (RCA)
STRAVINSKY: OEDIPUS REX - Igor Stravinsky cond. Chorus & Orch. of Opera Society of Washington (Col)

CLASSICAL PERFORMANCE - VOCAL SOLOIST (G-207)

A VERDI COLLABORATION - Anna Moffo (Ferrara cond. RCA Italiana Sym. Orch.) (RCA)
CANTELOUBE: SONGS OF THE AUVERGNE, VOL. 2 Netania Davrath (Orch. cond. by Pierre de la Roche) (Vanguard)
COMMAND PERFORMANCE - Joan Sutherland (Bonynge cond. London Symphony) (London)
GREAT SCENES FROM GERSHWIN'S PORGY & BESS - Leontyne Price (RCA)
MAHLER: DES KNABEN WUNDERHORN - Maureen Forrester (Prohaska cond. Symphony Orchestra of Vienna Festival) (Vanguard)
MELODIES DE FRANCE (Ravel, Debussy, Duparc) - Victoria de los Angeles (Pretre cond. Paris Conservatoire Orch.) (Angel)
RAVEL: SCHEHERAZADE; BERLIOZ: CLEOPATRE (Scene Lyrique) - Jennie Tourel (Bernstein cond. New York Philharmonic) (Col)
SCHUBERT: SCHWANENGESANG - Dietrich Fischer-Dieskau (Moore, Pianist) (Col)
STRAVINSKY: OEDIPUS REX - Shirley Verrett (Stravinsky cond. Chorus & Orch. of the Washington Opera Society) (Col)

CLASSICAL COMPOSITION BY CONTEMPORARY COMPOSER (G-208)
(Composer's Award)
ANDROMACHE'S FAREWELL, OP. 39 - Comp: Samuel Barber (Col)
CONCERTO FOR PIANO - Comp: John LaMontaine (Composers Recordings)
CONCERTO No. 2 FOR CELLO & ORCHESTRA - Comp: Heitor Villa-Lobos (Westminster)
SYMPHONY No. 4, OP. 43 - Comp. Dimitri Shostakovich (Col)
SYMPHONY No. 8 - Comp. William Schuman (Col)
WAR REQUIEM - Comp. Benjamin Britten (London))

BEST ENGINEERED RECORDING - CLASSICAL (G-209)

(Engineer's Award))

BERNSTEIN CONDUCTS TCHAIKOVSKY (Bernstein cond. New York Philharmonic) - Eng: Fred Plaut (Col)

BRITTEN: WAR REQUIEM (Britten cond. London Symphony Orch. & Chorus) - Eng: Kenneth Wilkenson (London)

GREAT SCENES FROM GERSHWIN'S PORGY & BESS (Price & Warfield) - Eng: Lewis Layton (RCA)

MAHLER: SYMPHONY No. 1 IN D ("THE TITAN") (Leinsdorf cond. Boston Symphony) - Eng: Lewis Layton (RCA)

PUCCINI: MADAME BUTTERFLY (Leinsdorf cond. RCA Italiana Orch. & Chorus) - Eng: Lewis Layton (Price, Tucker, Elias) (RCA)

WAGNER: SIEGFRIED (Solti cond. Vienna Philharmonic. Soloists: Nilsson, Windgassen, Hotter,Stolze, Hoffgen, Neidlinger, Sutherland) - Eng: Gordon Parry (London)

ALBUM COVER - CLASSICAL (G-210)

(Art Director's Award)

BEETHOVEN: SYMPHONY NO. 5 IN C MINOR, OP. 67 (Bernstein cond. New York Philharmonic) Art Dir: John Berg (Col)

BEETHOVEN: SYMPHONY No. 6 IN F MAJOR, OP. 68 ("PASTORALE") (Reiner cond. Chicago Sym. Orch.) Art Dir: Robert Jones (RCA)

EVENING OF ELIZABETHAN MUSIC (Julian Bream Consort) Art Dir: Dorle Soria (RCA)

PUCCINI: MADAMA BUTTERFLY (Leinsdorf cond. RCA Italiana Orch. & Chorus) Art Dir: Robert Jones (RCA)

PUCCINI: TOSCA (von Karajan cond. Vienna Philharmonic Orch.) Art Dir: Dorle Soria (RCA)

GRANADA (Albeniz: "Granada; Granados: "Spanish Dance in E Minor"; Ponce, Tansman, Aguado: "8 Lessons for Guitar"; Sor: "Four Studies") (Andres Segovia) Art Dir: Vladimir Bobri (Decca)

R. STRAUSS: DON QUIXOTE (Ormandy cond. Philadelphia Orch.) Art Dir: Bob Cato (Col)

MOST PROMISING NEW CLASSICAL ARTIST (G-211)

THE ABBEY SINGERS (Vocalists) (Decca)
REGINE CRESPIN (Vocalist) (London)
COLIN DAVIS (Conductor) (Angel)
ALIRIO DIAZ (Guitarist) (Vanguard)
JOHN OGDON (Pianist) (Angel)
FOU TS'ONG (Pianist) (Westminster)
ANDRE WATTS (Pianist) (Col)

COMEDY PERFORMANCE (G-212)

BILL COSBY IS A VERY FUNNY FELLOW, RIGHT! - Bill Cosby (WB)
CARL REINER AND MEL BROOKS AT THE CANNES FILM FESTIVAL - Carl Reiner, Mel Brooks (Cap)
HELLO MUDDUH, HELLO FADDAH - Allan Sherman (WB)
I AM THE GREATEST! - Cassius Clay (Col)
THINK ETHNIC - The Smothers Bros. (Merc)

DOCUMENTARY, SPOKEN WORD OR DRAMA RECORDING (OTHER THAN COMEDY) (G-213)

THE BADMEN (Pete Seeger and others) Goddard Lieberson, Producer (Col)

BRECHT ON BRECHT (Original Cast with Dane Clark, Anne Jackson, Lotte Lenya, Viveca Lindfors, George Voskovec, Michael Wager) Berthold Brecht, Playwright (Col)

JOHN F. KENNEDY - THE PRESIDENTIAL YEARS (David Teig, Narr) Norman Weiser, Producer (four Corners)

STRANGE INTERLUDE - Eugene O'Neill (Original Broadway Cast: Betty Field, Jane Fonda, Ben Gazzara, Pat Hingle, Geoff Horne, William Prince, Geraldine Page, Richard Thomas, Franchot Tone)

WE SHALL OVERCOME (The March on Washington. . .August 28, 1963) - Dr. Martin Luther King, Jr. (with Joan Baez, Marian Anderson, Odetta, Rabbi Joachim Prinz, Bob Dylan, Whitney M. Young, Jr., John Lewis, Roy Wilkins, Walter Reuther, Peter, Paul and Mary, Bayard Rustin, A. Philip Randolph) (United Civil Rights)

WHO'S AFRAID OF VIRGINIA WOOLF? - Edward Albee, Playwright (Original Cast: Uta Hagen, Arthur Hill, George Grizzard, with Melinda Dillon) (WB)

BEST ENGINEERED RECORDING - OTHER THAN CLASSICAL (G-214)

(Engineer's Award)

THE BARBRA STREISAND ALBUM (Barbra Streisand) Eng: Frank Laico (Col)

CHARADE (Henry Mancini Orch. & Chorus) Eng: James A. Malloy (RCA)

ELLA AND BASIE (Ella Fitzgerald, Count Basie) Eng: Luis P. Valentin (Verve)

EXOTIC SOUNDS OF BALI (Mantle Hood, Dir.) Eng: Harold Chapman (Col)

THE MANY MOODS OF CHRISTMAS (Robert Shaw Chorale) Eng: Anthony J. Salvatore (RCA)

OUR MAN IN HOLLYWOOD (Henry Mancini) Eng: Albert H. Schmitt (RCA)

POLITELY PERCUSSIVE (Dick Schory) Eng: Ronald A. Steele (RCA)

THE SECOND BARBRA STREISAND ALBUM (Barbra Streisand) Eng: Frank Laico (Col)

SUPERCUSSION (Dick Schory) Eng: Ronald A. Steele (RCA)

BEST ENGINEERED RECORDING - SPECIAL OR NOVEL EFFECTS (G-215)

(Engineer's Award)

CHEYENNE FRONTIER DAYS (Hank Thompson) Eng: John Kraus (Cap)

CIVIL WAR VOL. 2 (Frederick Fennell) Eng: Robert Fine (Mercury)

FAST, FAST, FAST RELIEF FROM TV COMMERCIALS (Bill McFadden, Bryna Rayburn) Eng: William Hamilton (Audio Fid.)

FOUR IN THE FLOOR (The Shut Downs) Engs: Scotty Shackner, Bob MacMeekin (Dimension)

HEARTSTRINGS (Dean Elliott) Engs: John Kraus, Hugh B. Davies (Cap)

PEPINO'S FRIEND PASQUALE (Lou Monte) Eng: Phil Macy,Al Weintraub (Reprise)

ZOUNDS! WHAT SOUNDS (Dean Elliott) Eng: John Kraus (Cap)

ALBUM COVER - OTHER THAN CLASSICAL (G-216)

(Art Director's Award)

ALOHA FROM NORMAN LUBOFF (The Norman Luboff Choir) Art Dir: Robert Jones (RCA)

BACH'S GREATEST HITS (The Swingle Singers) Art Dir: Jim Ladwig (Philips)

THE BARBRA STREISAND ALBUM (Barbra Streisand) Art Dir: John Berg (Col)

CARL REINER AND MEL BROOKS AT THE CANNES FILM FESTIVAL (Carl Reiner and Mel Brooks) Art Dir: Edward L. Thrasher (WB)

HOLLYWOOD MY WAY (Nancy Wilson) Art Dir: Jim Silke (Cap)

HONEY IN THE HORN (Al Hirt) Art Dir: Robert Jones (RCA)

NIGHT TRAIN (Oscar Peterson) Art Dir: John Murello (Verve)

ALBUM NOTES (G-217)

(Annotator's Award)

THE AMAZING AMANDA AMBROSE (Amanda Ambrose) Ann: Bob Bollard (RCA)

THE BADMEN (Pete Seeger and others) Ann: B.A. Botkin, Sylvester L. Vigilante, Harold Preece, James L. Horan (Col)

THE BARBRA STREISAND ALBUM (Barbra Streisand) Ann: Harold Arlen (Col)

THE ELLINGTON ERA (Duke Ellington) Ann: Leonard Feather, Stanley Dance (Col)

EVENING OF ELIZABETHAN MUSIC (Julian Bream Consort) Ann: Sidney Bock (RCA)

WHO'S AFRAID OF VIRGINIA WOOLF? (Original Cast) Ann: Edward Albee, Harold Clurman (Col)

RECORDING FOR CHILDREN (G-218)
ADDITION AND SUBTRACTION - Rica Owen Moore (Disney)
BERNSTEIN CONDUCTS FOR YOUNG PEOPLE - Leonard Bernstein cond. New York Phil. (Col)
CHILDREN'S CONCERT - Pete Seeger (Col)
LET'S GO TO THE ZOO - Fred V. Grunfeld, Producer (Various Artists) (Decca)
ON TOP OF SPAGHETTI - Tom Glazer (and The Do Re Mi Children's Chorus) (Kapp)
PUFF (THE MAGIC DRAGON) - Peter, Paul and Mary (WB)
WINNIE THE POOH - Jack Gilford (Golden)

ROCK AND ROLL RECORDING (G-219)
ANOTHER SATURDAY NIGHT - Sam Cooke (RCA)
DEEP PURPLE - Nino Tempo, April Stevens (Atco)
I WILL FOLLOW HIM - Little Peggy March (RCA)
IT'S MY PARTY - Lesley Gore (Merc)
OUR DAY WILL COME - Ruby & The Romantics (Kapp)
TEEN SCENE - Chet Atkins (RCA)

COUNTRY AND WESTERN RECORDING (G-220)
DETROIT CITY - Bobby Bare (RCA)
FLATT & SCRUGGS AT CARNEGIE HALL - Flatt & Scruggs (Col)
LOVE'S GONNA LIVE HERE - Buck Owens (Cap)
NINETY MILES AN HOUR (DOWN A DEAD END STREET) - Hank Snow (RCA)
THE PORTER WAGONER SHOW - Porter Wagoner (RCA)
RING OF FIRE - Johnny Cash (Col)
SAGINAW, MICHIGAN - Lefty Frizzell (Col)

RHYTHM AND BLUES RECORDING (G-221)
BUSTED - Ray Charles (ABC-Para)
FRANKIE AND JOHNNY - Sam Cooke (RCA)
(LOVE IS LIKE A) HEAT WAVE - Martha & The Vandellas (Gordy)
HEY, LITTLE GIRL - Major Lance (Okeh)
HELLO STRANGER - Barbara Lewis (Atl)
PART TIME LOVE - Little Johnny Taylor (Galaxy)
SINCE I FELL FOR YOU - Lenny Welch (Cadence)

FOLK RECORDING (G-222)
BLOWIN' IN THE WIND - Peter, Paul & Mary (WB)
GREEN, GREEN - The New Christy Minstrels (Col)
JUDY COLLINS No. 3 - Judy Collins (Elektra)
ODETTA SINGS FOLK SONGS - Odetta (RCA)
WALK RIGHT IN (album) - The Rooftop Singers (Vanguard))
WE SHALL OVERCOME - Pete Seeger (Col)
THE WORLD OF MIRIAM MAKEBA - Miriam Makeba (RCA)

GOSPEL OR OTHER RELIGIOUS RECORDING (MUSICAL) (G-223)
DOMINIQUE - Soeur Sourire (The Singing Nun) (Philips)
THE EARTH IS THE LORD'S (AND THE FULLNESS THEREOF) - George Beverly Shea (RCA)
MAKE A JOYFUL NOISE - Mahalia Jackson (Col)
MAKIN' A JOYFUL NOISE - The Limeliters (RCA)
PIANO IN CONCERT - Charles Magnuson and Fred Bock (Sacred)
RECORDED LIVE! - Bessie Griffin and the Gospel Pearls (Epic)
STEPPIN' RIGHT IN - Kings of Harmony (Kings of Harmony)
THE STORY OF CHRISTMAS - Tennessee Ernie Ford; The Roger Wagner Chorale (Col)

NEW ARTIST OF 1963 (G-224)
VIKKI CARR (Lib)
JOHN GARY (RCA)
J'S WITH JAMIE (Col)
TRINI LOPEZ (Reprise)
SWINGLE SINGERS (Philips)

1964

RECORD OF THE YEAR (G-225)
DOWNTOWN - Petula Clark (WB)
THE GIRL FROM IPANEMA - Stan Getz, Astrud Gilberto (Verve)
HELLO, DOLLY! - Louis Armstrong (Kapp)
I WANT TO HOLD YOUR HAND - The Beatles (Cap)
PEOPLE - Barbra Streisand (Col)

ALBUM OF THE YEAR (G-226)
COTTON CANDY - Al Hirt (RCA)
FUNNY GIRL - Robert Merrill, Jule Styne (Cap)
GETZ/GILBERTO - Stan Getz, Joao Gilberto (Verve)
PEOPLE - Barbra Streisand (Col)
THE PINK PANTHER - Henry Mancini (RCA)

ALBUM OF THE YEAR - CLASSICAL (G-227)
BERNSTEIN: SYMPHONY No. 3 ("KADDISH") - Leonard Bernstein cond. New York Philharmonic (Col)
BIZET: CARMEN - Herbert von Karajan cond. Vienna Philharmonic (Soloists: Price, Corelli, Merrill, Freni) (RCA)
MAHLER: SYMPHONY No. 5; BERG: WOZZECK EXCERPTS (Phyllis Curtin) - Erich Leinsdorf cond. Boston Symphony (RCA)
VERDI: FALSTAFF - Georg Solti cond. RCA Italiana Opera Orch. & Chorus (Soloists: Evans, Merrill, Kraus, Simionato, Ligabue, Elias, others) (RCA)
VERDI: REQUIEM MASS - Carlo Maria Giulini cond. Philharmonia Orch. (Soloists: Schwarzkopf, Gedda, Ludwig, Ghiaurov) (Angel)

SONG OF THE YEAR (G-228)
(Songwriter's Award)
A HARD DAY'S NIGHT - Songwrs: John Lennon, Paul McCartney (Cap)
DEAR HEART - Songwrs: Henry Mancini, Ray Evans, Jay Livingston (RCA)
HELLO, DOLLY! - Songwr: Jerry Herman (Kapp)
PEOPLE - Songwrs: Jule Styne, Bob Merrill (Col)
WHO CAN I TURN TO - Songwrs: Leslie Bricusse, Anthony Newley (Col)

INSTRUMENTAL COMPOSITION (OTHER THAN JAZZ) (G-229)
(Composer's Award)
COTTON CANDY - Comp: Russ Daymon (RCA)
THE PINK PANTHER THEME - Comp: Henry Mancini (RCA)
SUGAR LIPS - Comp: Buddy Killen, Billy Sherrill (RCA)
THEME FROM GOLDEN BOY - Comps: Charles Strouse, Lee Adams (Decca)
THEME FROM "THE MUNSTERS" - Comp: Jack Marshall (Cap)

VOCAL - FEMALE (G-230)
DOWNTOWN - Petula Clark (single) (WB)
THE GIRL FROM IPANEMA - Astrud Gilberto (single) (Verve)
HOW GLAD I AM - Nancy Wilson (single) (Cap)
PEOPLE - Barbra Streisand (single) (Col)
WE'LL SING IN THE SUNSHINE - Gale Garnett (single) (RCA)

VOCAL - MALE (G-231)
CALL ME IRRESPONSIBLE - Andy Williams (album) (Col)
EVERYBODY LOVES SOMEBODY - Dean Martin (album) (Reprise)
GETZ/GILBERTO - Joao Gilberto (album) (Verve)
HELLO, DOLLY! - Louis Armstrong (single) (Kapp)
WHO CAN I TURN TO? - Tony Bennett (single) (Col)

JAZZ - SMALL GROUP OR SOLOIST WITH SMALL GROUP (G-232)

COLLABORATION - The Modern Jazz Quartet with Laurindo Almeida (Atl)

GETZ/GILBERTO - Stan Getz (Verve)
MILES DAVIS IN EUROPE - Miles Davis (Col)
MUMBLES - Oscar Peterson and Clark Terry (Merc)
MY FAIR LADY - Andre Previn (Col)
SWEET SEPTEMBER (album) - Pete Jolly (Ava)

JAZZ - LARGE GROUP OR SOLOIST WITH LARGE GROUP (G-233)

DYNAMIC SOUND PATTERNS OF THE ROD LEVITT ORCHESTRA - Rod Levitt (Riverside)

GUITAR FROM IPANEMA - Laurindo Almeida (Cap)
THE INDIVIDUALISM OF GIL EVANS - Gil Evans (Verve)
MY FAIR LADY WITH THE UNORIGINAL CAST - Shelly Manne (Cap)
OSCAR PETERSON - NELSON RIDDLE - Oscar Peterson and Nelson Riddle (Verve)
QUIET NIGHTS - Miles Davis and Gil Evans (Col)
QUINCY JONES EXPLORES THE MUSIC OF HENRY MANCINI - Quincy Jones (Merc)
WOODY HERMAN '64 - Woody Herman (Phillips)

ORIGINAL JAZZ COMPOSITION (G-234)

(Composer's Award)

THE CAT - Comp: Lalo Schifrin (Verve)
HERE AND NOW - Comp: Bob Florence (Lib)
NIGHT CREATURE - Comp: Duke Ellington (Rep)
PACO - Comp: Gerald Wilson (World Pac.)
THEME FROM MR. BROADWAY - Comp: Dave Brubeck (Col)
THE WITCHING HOUR - Comp: Quincy Jones (Merc)

INSTRUMENTAL - NON-JAZZ (G-235)

AS LONG AS HE NEEDS ME - Peter Nero (RCA)
THE BEATLES SONG BOOK (Hollyridge Strings) Stu Phillips (Cap)
COTTON CANDY - Al Hirt (RCA)
GOLDEN BOY (string version) Quincy Jones (Merc)
PINK PANTHER - Henry Mancini (RCA)

INSTRUMENTAL ARRANGEMENT (G-236)

(Arranger's Award)

A SPOONFUL OF SUGAR - Duke Ellington - Arr: Billy Strayhorn (Reprise)
GOLDEN BOY (string version) - Quincy Jones - Arr: Quincy Jones (Merc)
I WANT TO HOLD YOUR HAND - Arthur Fiedler & the Boston Pops - Arr: Richard Hayman (RCA)
THEME FROM "THE LONG SHIPS" - Arr: Hugo Montenegro (RCA)
PINK PANTHER - Arr: Henry Mancini (RCA)
THE SONG IS YOU - Arr: Bob Florence (Lib)
SUGAR LIPS - Al Hirt - Arr: Anita Kerr (RCA)

ACCOMPANIMENT ARRANGEMENT FOR VOCALIST(S) OR INSTRUMENTALIST(S) (G-237)

(Arranger's Award)

HOW GLAD I AM - Nancy Wilson - Arr: Oliver Nelson (Cap)
PEOPLE - Barbra Streisand - Arr: Peter Matz (Col)
RINGO - Lorne Green - Arr: Don Ralke (RCA)
WE'LL SING IN THE SUNSHINE - Gale Garnett - Arr: Sid Bass (RCA)
WHERE LOVE HAS GONE - Jack Jones - Arr: Pete King (Kapp)
WHO CAN I TURN TO - Tony Bennett - Arr: George Siravo (Col)

VOCAL GROUP (G-238)

A HARD DAY'S NIGHT - The Beatles (Cap)
THE DOUBLE SIX SING RAY CHARLES - The Double Six of Paris (Philips)

GRAND OLE OPRY FAVORITES - The Browns (RCA)
MORE FOUR FRESHMEN AND FIVE TROMBONES - Four Freshmen (Cap)
PETER PAUL AND MARY IN CONCERT - Peter, Paul and Mary (WB)

CHORUS (G-239)

ARTISTRY IN VOICES & BRASS - Stan Kenton Orchestra: Chorus by Pete Rugolo (Cap)
DEAR HEART - Henry Mancini Orchestra & Chorus (RCA)
DON'T LET THE RAIN COME DOWN (CROOKED LITTLE MAN) - The Serendipity Singers (Philips)
LOVE ME WITH ALL YOUR HEART - The Ray Charles Singers (Col)
THE SWINGLE SINGERS GOING BAROQUE - The Swingle Singers (Philips)

ORIGINAL SCORE - MOTION PICTURE OR TV SHOW (G-240)

(Composer's Award)

A HARD DAY'S NIGHT - The Beatles - Comps: John Lennon, Paul McCartney (UA)
GOLDFINGER - John Barry Cond. - Comp: John Barry (UA)
MARY POPPINS - Julie Andrews, Dick Van Dyke, David Tomlinson, Glynis Johns, Ed Wynn - Comp: Richard M. Sherman, Robert B. Sherman (Buena Vista)
THE PINK PANTHER - Henry Mancini cond. - Comp: Henry Mancini (RCA)
ROBIN AND THE SEVEN HOODS - Frank Sinatra, Dean Martin, Bing Crosby,
Sammy Davis, Jr. - Comps: Sammy Cahn, Jimmy Van Heusen (Reprise)

SCORE FROM ORIGINAL CAST SHOW ALBUM (G-241)

(Composer's Award)

FIDDLER ON THE ROOF - Orig. Cast w/Zero Mostel, Tanya Everett, Joanna Merlin - Comps: Jerry Bock, Sheldon Harnick (RCA)
FUNNY GIRL - Barbra Streisand and Orig. Cast - Comps: Jule Styne, Bob Merrill (Cap)
HELLO DOLLY! - Carol Channing and Orig. Cast - Comp: Jerry Herman (RCA)
HIGH SPIRITS - Beatrice Lillie, Tammy Grimes, Edward Woodward and Orig. Cast - Comps: Hugh Martin, Timothy Gray (ABC)
WHAT MAKES SAMMY RUN? - Steve Lawrence and Orig. Cast - Comp: Ervin Drake (Col)

COMEDY PERFORMANCE (G-242)

FOR SWINGIN' LIVERS ONLY! - Allan Sherman (WB)
I STARTED OUT AS A CHILD - Bill Cosby (WB)
READY OR NOT, HERE COMES GODFREY CAMBRIDGE - Godfrey Cambridge (Epic)
WHISTLE STOPPING - Jonathan Winters (Verve)
WOODY ALLEN - Woody Allen (Colpix)

DOCUMENTARY, SPOKEN WORD OR DRAMA RECORDING (OTHER THAN COMEDY) (G-243)

BBC TRIBUTE TO JOHN F. KENNEDY - "That was The Week That Was" Cast (Decca)
DIALOGUE HIGHLIGHTS FROM "BECKET" - Richard Burton, Peter O'Toole (RCA)
DYLAN - Original Cast with Sir Alec Guinness and Kate Reid
THE KENNEDY WIT - John F. Kennedy, narrated by David Brinkley, introduction by Adlai Stevenson (RCA)
SHAKESPEARE: HAMLET - Richard Burton (Orig. Cast: Hume Cronyn, John Gielgud, Alfred Drake, George Voskovec, Ellen Herlie, William Redfield, George Ross) (Col)
SHAKESPEARE: OTHELLO - National Theatre of Great Britain Prod. - Sir Laurence Olivier (w/Maggie Smith, Joyce Redman, Frank Finlay) (RCA)

BEST ENGINEERED RECORDING (G-244)

(Engineer's Award)

ARTISTRY IN VOICES & BRASS - Stan Kenton - Eng: John Kraus (Cap)

GETZ/GILBERTO - Stan Getz, Joao Gilberto - Eng: Phil Ramona (Verve)

THE PINK PANTHER - Henry Mancini - Eng: James Malloy (RCA)

POPS GOES THE TRUMPET - Al Hirt, Arthur Fiedler & the Boston Pops - Eng: Bernie Keville (RCA)

SUGAR LIPS - Al Hirt - Eng: Chuck Seitz (RCA)

WHO CAN I TURN TO - Tony Bennett - Eng: George Kneurr, Frank Laico (Col)

BEST ENGINEERED RECORDING - SPECIAL OR NOVEL EFFECTS (G-245)

(Engineer's Award)

THE BIG SOUNDS OF THE SPORT CARS - Eng: Bill Robinson

THE CHIPMUNKS SING THE BEATLES - The Chipmunks - Eng: Dave Hassinger (Lib)

LES POUPEES DE PARIS - Various Artists - Eng: John Norman (RCA)

MAIN THEME: THE ADDAMS FAMILY - Vic Mizzy - Eng: James Malloy (RCA)

WALKIN' IN THE RAIN - The Ronettes - Eng: Larry Levine (Phillies)

ALBUM COVER (G-246)

(Awards to Art Director, Photographer or Graphic Artist)

GETZ/GILBERTO - Stan Getz, Joao Gilberto - Art Dir: Acy Lehman; Graphic: Olga Albizu (Verve)

GUITAR FROM IPANEMA - Laurindo Almeida - Art Dir: George Osaki; Photographer: George Jerman (Cap)

OSCAR PETERSON PLAYS MY FAIR LADY - Art Dir: Acy Lehman; Graphic: Tom Daly (Verve)

PEOPLE - Barbra Streisand - Art Dir: Robert Cato; Photog: Don Bronstein (Col)

POITIER MEETS PLATO - Art Dir: Ed Thrasher (WB)

THE SOUND OF HARLEM - Various Artists - Art Dir: Robert Cato; Graphic: Milton Glaser (Col)

RECORDING FOR CHILDREN (G-247)

A SPOONFUL OF SUGAR - Mary Martin and the Do-Re-Mi Children's Chorus (Kapp)

BRITTEN: YOUNG PERSON'S GUIDE TO THE ORCHESTRA - Hugh Downs, narrator: Arthur Fiedler cond. the Boston Pops Orch. (RCA)

BURL IVES CHIM CHIM CHEREE AND OTHER CHILDREN'S CHOICES - Burl Ives and Children's Chorus (Buena Vista)

DANIEL BOONE - Fess Parker (RCA)

MARY POPPINS - Julie Andrews and Dick Van Dyke (w/David Tomlinson, Glynis Johns, Ed Wynn) (Buena Vista)

ROCK AND ROLL RECORDING (G-248)

A HARD DAY'S NIGHT - The Beatles (Cap)

DOWNTOWN - Petula Clark (WB)

MR. LONELY - Bobby Vinton (Epic)

OH, PRETTY WOMAN - Roy Orbison (Monument)

YOU'VE LOST THAT LOVIN' FEELING - The Righteous Brothers (Phillies)

RHYTHM AND BLUES RECORDING (G-249)

BABY LOVE - The Supremes (Motown)

GOOD TIMES - Sam Cooke (RCA)

HOLD WHAT YOU'VE GOT - Joe Tex (Dial Lat)

HOW GLAD I AM - Nancy Wilson (Cap)

KEEP ON PUSHING - The Impressions (ABC)

WALK ON BY - Dionne Warwicke (Scepter)

FOLK RECORDING (G-250)

BELAFONTE AT THE GREEK THEATRE - Harry Belafonte (RCA)

PETER, PAUL AND MARY IN CONCERT - Peter, Paul and Mary (RCA)

THE TIMES, THEY ARE A'CHANGIN' - Bob Dylan (Col)

TODAY - The New Christy Minstrels (Col)

THE VOICE OF AFRICA - Miriam Makeba (RCA)

WE'LL SING IN THE SUNSHINE - Gale Garnett (RCA)

WOODY GUTHRIE: LIBRARY OF CONGRESS RECORDINGS - Woody Guthrie (Nonesuch)

GOSPEL OR OTHER RELIGIOUS RECORDING (MUSICAL) (G-251)

FAMILY ALBUM OF HYMNS - Roger Williams (Kapp)

GREAT GOSPEL SONGS - Tennessee Ernie Ford (Cap)

GREGORIAN CHANT - Dominican Nuns of Fichermont (Philips)

GEORGE BEVERLY SHEA SINGS HYMNS OF SUNRISE AND SUNSET - George Beverly Shea (RCA)

SWEET HOUR OF PRAYER - Jo Stafford (Cap)

STANDIN' ON THE BANKS OF THE RIVER - James Cleveland & The Angelic Choir (Savoy)

THIS I BELIEVE - Fred Waring (Cap)

NEW ARTIST OF 1964 (G-252)

THE BEATLES (Cap)

PETULA CLARK (WB)

ASTRUD GILBERTO (Verve)

ANTONIO CARLOS JOBIM (WB)

MORGANA KING (Mainstream)

COUNTRY & WESTERN SINGLE (G-253)

DANG ME - Roger Miller (Smash)

FOUR STRONG WINDS - Bobby Bare (RCA)

HERE COMES MY BABY - Dottie West (RCA)

ONCE A DAY - Connie Smith (RCA)

YOU'RE THE ONLY WORLD I KNOW - Sonny James (Cap)

COUNTRY & WESTERN ALBUM (G-254)

THE BEST OF BUCK OWENS - Buck Owens (Cap)

THE BEST OF JIM REEVES - Jim Reeves (RCA)

BITTER TEARS - Johnny Cash (Col)

DANG ME/CHUG-A-LUG - Roger Miller (Smash)

GUITAR COUNTRY - Chet Atkins (RCA)

HANK WILLIAMS, JR. SINGS SONGS OF HANK WILLIAMS - Hank Williams, Jr. (MGM)

COUNTRY & WESTERN VOCAL - FEMALE (G-255)

HE SAYS THE SAME THING TO ME (track) - Skeeter Davis (RCA)

HERE COMES MY BABY (single) - Dottie West (RCA)

ONCE A DAY (single) - Connie Smith (RCA)

SECOND FIDDLE (single) - Jean Shepard (Cap)

TWO SIDES OF WANDA JACKSON (album) - Wanda Jackson (Cap)

COUNTRY & WESTERN VOCAL - MALE (G-256)

DANG ME (single) - Roger Miller (Smash)

FORT WORTH, DALLAS OR HOUSTON (album) - George Hamilton IV (RCA)

FOUR STRONG WINDS (single) - Bobby Bare (RCA)

HANK LOCKLIN SINGS HANK WILLIAMS (album) - Hank Locklin (RCA)

I WALK THE LINE (album) - Johnny Cash (Col)

MY HEART SKIPS A BEAT (single) - Buck Owens (Cap)

YOU'RE THE ONLY WORLD I KNOW (single) - Sonny James (Cap)

COUNTRY & WESTERN SONG (G-257)

(Songwriter's Award)

DANG ME - Roger Miller (Smash)

HERE COMES MY BABY - Dottie West, Bill West (RCA)

ONCE A DAY - Bill Anderson (RCA)

WINE, WOMEN AND SONG - Betty Sue Perry (Decca)

YOU'RE THE ONLY WORLD I KNOW - Sonny James, Bob Tubert (Cap)

NEW COUNTRY & WESTERN ARTIST OF 1964 (G-258)

CHARLIE LOUVIN (Cap)
ROGER MILLER (Smash)
CONNIE SMITH (RCA)
DOTTIE WEST (RCA)
HANK WILLIAMS, JR. (MGM)

ALBUM NOTES (G-259)

(Annotator's Award)
BEYOND THE FRINGE '64 - Orgiinal Cast - Ann: Alexander Cohen (Cap)
THE DEFINITIVE PIAF - Edith Piaf - Ann: Rory Guy (Cap)
GETZ/GILBERTO - Stan Getz, Joao Gilberto - Anns: Stan Getz, Joao Gilberto, Gene Lees (Verve)
MAHLER: SYMPHONY NO. 5; BERG: WOZZECK EXCERPTS (Phyllis Curtin) - Erich Leinsdorf cond. Boston Symphony - Ann: Neville Cardus (RCA)
MEXICO (LEGACY COLLECTION) - Carlos Chavez - Anns: Stanton Catlin, Carleton Beals (Col)
QUINCY JONES EXPLORES THE MUSIC OF HENRY MANCINI - Quincy Jones - Ann: Jack Tracy (Merc)
THE YOUNG CHEVALIER - Maurice Chevalier - Ann: George Sponholtz (Cap)

CLASSICAL PERFORMANCE - ORCHESTRA (G-260)

BARTOK: CONCERTO FOR ORCHESTRA - Eugene Ormandy cond. Philadelphia Orchestra (Col)
HANDEL: CONCERTI GROSSI (12), OP. 6 - Yehudi Menuhin cond. Bath Festival Chamber Orchestra (Angel)
HAYDN: SYMPHONY No. 95 IN C MINOR, SYMPHONY No. 101 IN D MAJOR ("CLOCK") - Fritz Reiner cond. Chicago Symphony (RCA)
MAHLER: SYMPHONY No. 2 IN C ("RESURRECTION") - Leonard Bernstein cond. New York Philharmonic (Col)
MAHLER: SYMPHONY No. 5 IN C SHARP MINOR; BERG: WOZZECK EXCERPTS (Phyllis Curtin) - Erich Leinsdorf cond. Boston Symphony (RCA)
MOZART: LAST SIX SYMPHONIES - Bruno Walter cond. Columbia Symphony (Col)
R. STRAUSS: SYMPHONIA DOMESTICA - George Szell cond. Cleveland Orchestra (Col)

CHAMBER MUSIC PERFORMANCE - INSTRUMENTAL (G-261)

BEETHOVEN: QUARTET No. 15 IN A MINOR OP. 132 - Juilliard String Quartet (RCA)
BEETHOVEN: SONATAS (5) FOR PIANO & CELLO (Complete) - Sviatoslav Richter, Mstislav Rostropovich (Philips)
BEETHOVEN: TRIO No. 1 IN E FLAT, OP. 1, No. 1, - Jascha Heifetz, Gregor Piatigorsky (Jacob Lateiner, piano) (RCA)
BRAHMS: QUINTET IN F MINOR FOR PIANO AND STRINGS - Rudolph Serkin w/the Budapest Quartet (Col)
MOZART: THE COMPLETE FLUTE SONATAS - Jean-Pierre Rampal, Robert Veyron-Lacroix (Epic)
STRAVINSKY: L'HISTOIRE DU SOLDAT - Igor Markevich cond. Chamber Group (w/narrators Jean Cocteau, Peter Ustinov, Jean-Marie Fertey, Anne Tonietti) (Philips)

CHAMBER MUSIC PERFORMANCE - VOCAL

(G-262) DUFAY MOTETS - Le Petit Ensemble Vocal de Montreal (Vox)
IT WAS A LOVER AND HIS LASS (MORLEY, BYRD AND OTHERS) - New York Pro Musica, Noah Greenberg cond. (Decca)
MUSIC FOR VOICES AND VIOLS IN THE TIME OF SHAKESPEARE - Golden Age Singers (Westminster)
MUSIC OF THE RENNAISSANCE (DES PREZ, MORLEY) - Vocal Arts Ensemble (Counterpoint)
MUSIC OF MEDIEVAL FRANCE, 1200-1400,SACRED AND SECULAR - Deller Consort (Vanguard)
WALTON: FACADE - Hermione Gingold, Russell Oberlin, Thomas Dunn cond. (Decca)

CLASSICAL PERFORMANCE - INSTRUMENTAL SOLOIST(S) (WITH ORCHESTRA) (G-263)

BARBER: CONCERTO FOR PIANO & ORCHESTRA, OP. 38 - John Browning (Szell cond. Cleveland Orchestra) (Col)
BEETHOVEN: CONCERTO NO. 5 IN E FLAT - Artur Rubinstein (Leinsdorf cond. Boston Symphony) (RCA)
BLOCH: CONCERTO FOR VIOLIN - Yehudi Menuhin (Kletzki cond. Philharmonia Orchestra) (Angel)
BRAHMS: CONCERTO No. 1 IN D MINOR FOR PIANO - Van Cliburn (Leinsdorf cond. Boston Symphony) (RCA)
MOZART: SINFONIA CONCERTANTE IN E FLAT MAJOR FOR VIOLIN, VIOLA & ORCHESTRA - Rafael Druian and Abraham Skernick (Szell Cond. Cleveland Orchestra) (Col)
PROKOFIEFF: CONCERTO No. 1 IN D MAJOR FOR VIOLIN - Isaac Stern (Ormandy cond. Philadelphia Orchestra) (Col)
RODRIGO: CONCIERTO DE ARANJUEZ FOR GUITAR & ORCHESTRA; VIVALDI: CONCERTO IN D FOR LUTE & STRINGS - Julian Bream (Davis cond. Melos Chamber Orchestra) (RCA)

CLASSICAL PERFORMANCE - INSTRUMENTAL SOLOIST(S) (WITHOUT ORCHESTRA) (G-264)

A FRENCH PROGRAM (RAVEL, POULENC, FAURE, CHABRIER) - Artur Rubinstein (RCA)
BACH: TWO AND THREE PART INVENTIONS - Glenn Gould (Col)
FRENCH BAROQUE MUSIC FOR HARPSICHORD (COUPERIN, RAMEAU & BOISMORTIER) - Igor Kipnis (Epic)
POPULAR CLASSICS FOR SPANISH GUITAR (VILLA-LOBOS, FALLA, etc.) - Julian Bream (RCA)
RICHTER PLAYS SCHUBERT (SONATA IN A MAJOR FOR PIANO, "WANDERER" FANTASIA FOR PIANO) - Sviatoslav Richter (Angel)
VLADIMIR HOROWITZ PLAYS BEETHOVEN, DEBUSSY, CHOPIN (BEETHOVEN: SONATA No. 8 "PATHETIQUE"; DEBUSSY; PRELUDES; CHOPIN: ETUDES & SCHERZOS 1 THROUGH 4) - Vladimir Horowitz (Col)

OPERA RECORDING (G-265)

(Conductor's Award)
BIZET: CARMEN - Herbert Von Karajan cond. Vienna Philharmonic & Chorus (Soloists: Price, Corelli, Merrill, Freni) (RCA)
MUSSORGSKY: BORIS GODOUNOV - Alexander Melik-Pachaev cond. Orchestra & Chorus of the Bolshoi Theatre (Soloists: London, Arkhipova) (Col)
PUCCINI: LA BOHEME - Thomas Schippers cond. Orchestra & Chorus of Opera House,
Rome (Soloists: Freni, Gedda, Adani, Sereni) (Angel)
SMETANA: THE BARTERED BRIDE - Rudolf Kempe cond. Bamberg Symphony (Soloists: Lorengar, Wunderlich, Frick) (Angel)
WAGNER: LOHENGRIN - Rudolf Kempe cond. Vienna Philharmonic, Chorus of Vienna State Opera. (Soloists:
Thomas, Grummer, Fischer-Dieskau, Ludwig) (Angel)
VERDI: FALSTAFF: - Georg Solti cond. RCA Italiana Opera Orchestra & Chorus (Soloists: Evan, Merrill, Kraus, Simionato, Ligabue, Elias, Freni) (RCA)

CHORAL PERFORMANCE - OTHER THAN OPERA (G-266)

(Awards to Choral and Orchestra Conductors)
BRITTEN: A CEREMONY OF CAROLS - The Robert Shaw Chorale, Robert Shaw cond. (RCA)
MOZART: REQUIEM MASS IN D MINOR - Harvard Glee Club, Radcliffe Choral Society, Elliott Forbes cond.; Chorus Pro Musica, Alfred Nash Patterson cond.; New England Conservatory Chorus, Lorna Cooke de Varon cond.; St. John's Seminary Choir, Rt. Rev. Russell H.Davis cond.; Erich Leinsdorf cond. Boston Symphony (RCA)
POULENC: STABAT MATTER - Rene Duclos Chorus, Rene Duclos cond.; Georges Pretre & Paris Conservatoire (Angel)
STRAVINSKY: SYMPHONY OF PSALMS - Toronto Festival Chorus, Elmer Iseler cond. Igor Stravinsky cond. Canadian Broadcasting Corp. Orchestra (Col)
VERDI: REQUIEM MASS - Philharmonia Chorus, Wilhelm Pitz, dir.; Carlo Maria Giulini cond. Philharmonia Orchestra (Angel)

VERDI: REQUIEM MASS - Westminster Choir, George Lynn, dir.; Eugene Ormandy cond. Philadelphia Orchestra (Col)

CLASSICAL PERFORMANCE VOCAL SOLOIST - (G-267)

THE AGE OF BEL CANTO: OPERATIC SCENES - Joan Sutherland (Bonygne cond. London Symphony & New Symphony of London)
BERLIOZ: NUITS D'ETE (SONG CYCLE) - Regine Crespin (Ansermet cond. Suisse Romande Orchestra) (London)
BERLIOZ: NUITS D'ETE (SONG CYCLE); FALLA: EL AMOR BRUJO - Leontyne Price (Reiner cond. Chicago Symphony) (RCA)
BRITTEN: SERENADE FOR TENOR, HORN & STRINGS - Peter Pears (Britten cond. London Symphony) (London)
CALLAS SINGS VERDI - Maria Callas (Rescigno cond. Paris Conservatoire) (Angel)
SHUBERT DIE WINTERREISE - Dietrich Fischer-Dieskau (Angel)
TSARS AND KINGS (OPERA ARIAS) - Boris Christoff (Cluytens cond. Paris Conservatoire Orchestra) (Angel)

COMPOSITION BY A CONTEMPORARY COMPOSER (G-268)

(Composer's Award)
A FRENCHMAN IN NEW YORK - Darius Milhaud (RCA)
NEW ENGLAND HOLIDAYS - Charles E. Ives
PIANO CONCERTO - Samuel Barber (Col)
SERMON, NARRATIVE AND PRAYER - Igor Stravinsky (Col)
SYMPHONY No. 3 ("KADDISH") - Leonard Bernstein (Col)

BEST ENGINEERED RECORDING (G-269)

(Engineer's Award)
BRITTEN: YOUNG PERSON'S GUIDE TO THE ORCHESTRA - Carlo Maria Giulini cond. Philharmonia Orchestra - Eng: Douglas Larter (Angel)
MAHLER: SYMPHONY No. 2 IN C MINOR ("RESURRECTION") - Leonard Bernstein cond. New York Philharmonic - Eng: Fred Plaut (Col)
MAHLER: SYMPHONY No. 5 IN C SHARP MINOR - Erich Leinsdorf cond. Boston Symphony - Eng: Lewis Layton (RCA)
PROKOFIEFF: SYMPHONY No. 5, OP. 100 - Erich Leinsdorf cond. Boston Symphony - Eng: Lewis Layton (RCA)
VLADIMIR HOROWITZ PLAYS BEETHOVEN, DEBUSSY, CHOPIN - Vladimir Horowitz - Eng: Fred Plaut (Col)

ALBUM COVER - CLASSICAL (G-270)

(Awards to Art Director, Photographer or Graphic Artist)
COURT AND CEREMONIAL MUSIC OF THE 16TH CENTURY - Roger Blanchard Ensemble with the Poulteau Consort - Art Dir: Bill Harvey; Graphic: Lionel Kalish (Nonesuch)
MAHLER: SYMPHONY No. 5 IN C SHARP MINOR - Erich Leinsdorf cond. Boston Symphony - Art Dir: Robert Jones; Photog: David Hecht (RCA)
MEXICO: (LEGACY COLLECTION) - Carlos Chavez - Art Dir: Robert Cato (Col)
SAINT-SAENS: CARNIVAL OF THE ANIMALS; BRITTEN: YOUNG PERSON'S GUIDE TO THE ORCHESTRA - Arthur Fiedler cond. Boston Pops - Art Dir: Robert Jones; Graphic: Jan Balet (RCA)
R. STRAUSS: ALSO SPRACH ZARATHUSTRA - Eugene Ormandy cond. Philadelphia Orchestra - Art Dir: John Berg; Designer: Henrietta Condak (Col)
VERDI: REQUIEM MASS - Giulini cond. Philharmonia Orchestra - Art Dir: Marvin Schwartz (Angel)

MOST PROMISING NEW CLASSICAL ARTIST (G-271)

MIRELLA FRENI, Soprano (Angel)
MARILYN HORNE, Mezzo-Soprano (London)
IGOR KIPNIS, Harpsichord (Epic)
JUDITH RASKIN, Soprano (Decca)
JESS THOMAS, Tenor (DGG)

1965

RECORD OF THE YEAR (G-272)

(Grammys to Artist and A&R Producer)
A TASTE OF HONEY - Herb Alpert & the Tijuana Brass - A&R: Herb Alpert, Jerry Moss (A&M)
THE "IN" CROWD - Ramsey Lewis Trio - A&R: Esmond Edwards (Cadet)
KING OF THE ROAD - Roger Miller - A&R: Jerry Kennedy (Smash)
THE SHADOW OF YOUR SMILE (LOVE THEME FROM THE SANDPIPER) - Tony Bennett - A&R: Ernie Altschuler, Al Stanton (Col)
YESTERDAY - Paul McCartney - A&R: George Martin (Cap)

ALBUM OF THE YEAR (G-273)

(Grammys to Artist and A&R Producer)
HELP! - The Beatles - A&R: George Martin (Cap)
MY NAME IS BARBRA - Barbra Streisand - A&R: Bob Mersey (Col)
MY WORLD - Eddy Arnold - A&R: Chet Atkins
SEPTEMBER OF MY YEARS - Frank Sinatra - A&R: Sonny Burke (Reprise)
SOUND OF MUSIC - Julie Andrews and Cast - A&R: Neely Plumb (RCA)
WHIPPED CREAM & OTHER DELIGHTS - Herb Alpert & the Tijuana Brass - A&R: Herb Alpert and Jerry Moss (A&M)

ALBUM OF THE YEAR - CLASSICAL (G-274)

(Awards to the Artist and A&R Producer)
BERG: WOZZECK - Karl Bohm cond. Orchestra of German Opera, Berlin - A&R: Otto Gerdes (DGG)
CHOPIN: 8 POLONAISES, 4 IMPROMPTUS - Artur Rubinstein - A&R: Max Wilcox (RCA)
HOROWITZ AT CARNEGIE HALL, An Historic Return - Vladimir Horowitz - A&R: Thomas Frost (Col)
IVES: SYMPHONY NO. 4 - Leopold Stokowski cond. American Symphony - A&R: John McClure (Col)
STRAUSS: SALOME (DANCE OF THE SEVEN VEILS, INTERLUDE & FINAL SCENE); THE EGYPTIAN HELEN (AWAKENING SCENE) - Leontyne Price; Erich Leinsdorf cond. Boston Symphony - A&R: Richard Mohr (RCA)

SONG OF THE YEAR (G-275)

(Songwriter's Award)
I WILL WAIT FOR YOU (THEME FROM "UMBRELLAS OF CHERBOURG") - Michel Legrand, Norman Gimbel, Jacques Demy (Philips)
KING OF THE ROAD - Roger Miller (Smash)
SEPTEMBER OF MY YEARS - Jimmy Van Heusen, Sammy Cahn (Reprise)
THE SHADOW OF YOUR SMILE (LOVE THEME FROM "THE SANDPIPER") - Paul Francis Webster, Johnny Mandel (Mercury)
YESTERDAY - John Lennon, Paul McCartney (Cap)

VOCAL - FEMALE (G-276)

THE ASTRUD GILBERTO ALBUM - Astrud Gilberto (Verve)
DOWNTOWN (album) - Petula Clark (WB)
GENTLE IS MY LOVE (album) - Nancy Wilson (Cap)
MY NAME IS BARBRA (album) - Barbra Streisand (Col)
WHAT THE WORLD NEEDS NOW IS LOVE (single) - Jackie DeShannon (Imperial)

VOCAL - MALE (G-277)

BABY THE RAIN MUST FALL (album) - Glenn Yarbrough (RCA)
IT WAS A VERY GOOD YEAR (single) - Frank Sinatra (Reprise)
KING OF THE ROAD (single) - Roger Miller (Smash)
THE SHADOW OF YOUR SMILE (LOVE THEME FROM "THE SANDPIPER") (single) - Tony Bennett (Col)
YESTERDAY (single) - Paul McCartney (Cap)

INSTRUMENTAL - NON-JAZZ (G-278)

A TASTE OF HONEY - Herb Alpert & the Tijuana Brass (A&M)
GIRL TALK - Neal Hefti (Col)
THE GREAT RACE - Henry Mancini (RCA)
WALK IN THE BLACK FOREST - Horst Jankowski (Merc)
YAKETY AXE - Chet Atkins (RCA)

VOCAL GROUP (G-279)

FLOWERS ON THE WALL - The Statler Bros (Col)
HELP! - The Beatles (Cap)
MRS. BROWN YOU'VE GOT A LOVELY DAUGHTER - Herman's Hermits (MGM)
WE DIG MANCINI - Anita Kerr Singers (RCA)
YOU WERE ON MY MIND - We Five (A&M)

CHORUS (G-280)

ANYONE FOR MOZART? - The Swingle Singers (Philips)
CHIM CHIM CHER-EE & OTHER HAPPY SONGS - New Christy Minstrels (Col)
DEAR HEART & OTHER SONGS ABOUT LOVE - Henry Mancini Chorus and Orchestra (RCA)
JAZZ SUITE ON THE MASS TEXTS - Paul Horn and Chorus (RCA)
ROBERT SHAW CHORALE & ORCHESTRA ON BROADWAY - Robert Shaw Chorale and Orchestra (RCA)

ORIGINAL SCORE - MOTION PICTURE OR TV SHOW (G-281)

(Composer's Award)
HELP! (The Beatles) John Lennon, Paul McCartney, George Harrison, Ken Thorne (Cap)
THE MAN FROM U.N.C.L.E. (Hugo Montenegro Orch.) Lalo Schifrin, Mort Stevens, Walter Scharf, Jerry Goldsmith (RCA)
THE SANDPIPER (Robert Armbruster Orch.) Johnny Mandel (Mercury)
THE UMBRELLAS OF CHERBOURG (Michel Legrand Orch.) Michel Legrand, Jacques Demy (Philips)
ZORBA THE GREEK (M. Theodorakis Orch.) Mikis Theodorakis (20th)

SCORE FROM AN ORIGINAL CAST SHOW (G-282)

(Composer's Award)
BAJOUR - Walter Marks (Col)
BAKER STREET - Marian Grudeff, Raymond Jessell (MGM)
DO I HEAR A WALTZ - Richard Rodgers, Stephen Sondheim (Col)
HALF A SIXPENCE - David Heneker (RCA)
ON A CLEAR DAY - Alan Lerner, Burton Lane (RCA)

COMEDY PERFORMANCE (G-283)

MOM ALWAYS LIKED YOU BEST - Smothers Bros. (Merc)
THEM COTTON PICKIN' DAYS IS OVER - Godfrey Cambridge (Epic)
WELCOME TO THE L.B.J. RANCH - Earl Doud & Allen Robin (Cap)
WHY IS THERE AIR? - Bill Cosby (WB)
YOU DON'T HAVE TO BE JEWISH - Various Artists written by Bob Booker & George Foster (Kapp)

SPOKEN WORD OR DRAMA RECORDING (G-284)

A PERSONAL CHOICE - Sir Alec Guinness (RCA)
A TIME TO KEEP: 1964 - Chet Huntley and David Brinkley (RCA)
THE BRONTES - Margaret Webster (Vanguard)
JOHN F. KENNEDY: AS WE REMEMBER HIM - Produced by Goddard Lieberson (Col)
MUCH ADO ABOUT NOTHING - National Theatre of Great Britain (RCA)
THE VOICE OF THE UNCOMMON MAN - Adlai Stevenson (Produced by Mort Nasatir) (MGM)

NEW ARTIST (G-285)

THE BYRDS (Col)
HERMAN'S HERMITS (MGM)
HORST JANKOWSKI (Merc)

TOM JONES (Parrot)
MARILYN MAYE (RCA)
SONNY & CHER (Atco)
GLENN YARBROUGH (RCA)

RECORDING FOR CHILDREN (G-286)

DR. SEUSS PRESENTS "FOX IN SOX"; "GREEN EGGS AND HAM" - Marvin Miller (RCA)
LOVE SONGS FOR CHILDREN: "A" YOU'RE ADORABLE - Diahann Carroll (Golden)
PATRICK MULDOON & HIS MAGIC BALLOON - Carmel Quinn (RCA)
SUPERCALIFRAGELISTIC EXPIALIDOCIOUS - The Chipmunks (David Seville) (Lib)
WINNIE THE POOH & THE HONEY TREE - Sterling Holloway, Sebastian Cabot (Disney)

ALBUM NOTES (G-287)

(Annotator's Award)
BERG: WOZZECK - Karl Bohm cond. Orchestra of German Opera - Anns: Gustav Rudolf Sellner, Otto Gerdes (DGG)
FATHER & SON: HANK WILLIAMS & HANK WILLIAMS, JR. - Ann: Charles Lamb (MGM)
GRAND TERRACE BAND - Earl Hines - Ann: Stanley Dance (RCA)
SEPTEMBER OF MY YEARS - Frank Sinatra - Ann: Stan Cornyn (Reprise)
THE VOICE OF THE UNCOMMON MAN - Adlai Stevenson - Ann: Dom Cerulli (MGM)

JAZZ - SMALL GROUP OR SOLOIST WITH SMALL GROUP (G-288)

A LOVE SUPREME - John Coltrane (Imp)
CYCLE - Paul Horn (RCA)
GLAD TO BE UNHAPPY - Paul Desmond, Jim Hall (RCA)
THE "IN" CROWD - Ramsey Lewis Trio (Cadet)
THE POWER OF POSITIVE SWINGING - Clark Terry & Bob Brookmeyer Quintet (Mainstream)
SOFT SAMBA - Gary McFarland Group (Verve)
SOUL SAUCE - Cal Tjader (Verve)
TRIO '65 - Bill Evans Trio (Verve)

JAZZ - LARGE GROUP OR SOLOIST WITH LARGE GROUP (G-289)

BUMPIN' - Wes Montgomery w/String Orch. (Verve)
ELLINGTON '66 - Duke Ellington Orch. (Rep)
INSIGHT - Rod Levitt (RCA)
JAZZ SUITE ON THE MASS TEXTS - Paul Horn (RCA)
KENNY BURRELL: GUITAR FORMS - Kenny Burrell and Gil Evans Orch. (Verve)
LOVE THEME FROM "THE SANDPIPER" - Dizzy Gillespie (Fuller, Monterey Jazz Fest.) (World Pac)
MICKEY ONE - Stan Getz (Verve)

ORIGINAL JAZZ COMPOSITION (G-290)

(Composer's Award)
A LOVE SUPREME - John Coltrane (Imp)
BUMPIN' - Wes Montgomery (Verve)
CANADIANA SUITE - Oscar Peterson (Limelite)
JAZZ SUITE ON THE MASS TEXTS - Lalo Schifrin (RCA)
MICKEY ONE - Eddie Sauter (MGM)
VIRGIN ISLANDS SUITE - Duke Ellington and Billy Strayhorn (Reprise)

INSTRUMENTAL ARRANGEMENT (G-291)

(Arranger's Award)
A HARD DAY'S NIGHT (Fiedler, Boston Pops) Arr: Jack Mason (RCA)
A TASTE OF HONEY (Alpert & Tijuana Brass) Arr: Herb Alpert (A&M)
GIRL TALK (Neal Hefti) Arr: Neal Hefti (Col)

MISSION TO MOSCOW (Si Zentner Orch.) Arr: Bob Florence (RCA)
THE SHADOW OF YOUR SMILE (Armbruster Orch.) Arr: Johnny Mandel (Merc)
WALK IN THE BLACK FOREST (Jankowski Orch.) Arr: Horst Jankowski (Merc)

ARRANGEMENT ACCOMPANYING VOCALIST OR INSTRUMENTALIST (G-292)

(Arranger's Award)
DAY BY DAY (Astrud Gilberto) Arr: Claus Ogerman (Verve)
EVERYTHING I'VE GOT (Vikki Carr) Arr: Bob Florence (Lib)
GREENSLEEVES (Kenny Burrell) Arr: Gil Evans (Verve)
HE TOUCHED ME (Barbra Streisand) Arr: Don Costa (Col)
IT WAS A VERY GOOD YEAR (Frank Sinatra) Arr: Gordon Jenkins (Reprise)
IT'S NOT UNUSUAL (Tom Jones) Arr: Les Reed (Parrot)
WHAT THE WORLD NEEDS NOW IS LOVE (Jackie DeShannon) Arr: Burt Bacharach (Imp)
YESTERDAY (The Beatles) Arr: George Martin (Cap)

CONTEMPORARY (R&R) SINGLE (G-293)
BABY THE RAIN MUST FALL - Glenn Yarbrough (RCA)
IT'S NOT UNUSUAL - Tom Jones (Parrot)
KING OF THE ROAD - Roger Miller (Smash)
WHAT THE WORLD NEEDS NOW IS LOVE - Jackie DeShannon (Imp)
YESTERDAY - Paul McCartney (Cap)

CONTEMPORARY (R&R) VOCAL - FEMALE (G-294)
BABY I'M YOURS - Barbara Lewis (Atl)
I KNOW A PLACE - Petula Clark (WB)
RESCUE ME - Fontella Bass (Chess)
SUNSHINE, LOLLIPOPS AND RAINBOWS - Lesley Gore (Merc)
WHAT THE WORLD NEEDS NOW IS LOVE - Jackie DeShannon (Imp)

CONTEMPORARY (R&R) VOCAL - MALE (G-295)
HEARTACHES BY THE NUMBER - Johnny Tillotson (MGM)
KING OF THE ROAD - Roger Miller (Smash)
1-2-3 - Len Barry (Decca)
WHAT'S NEW PUSSYCAT - Tom Jones (Parrot)
YESTERDAY - Paul McCartney (Cap)

CONTEMPORARY (R&R) PERFORMANCE - GROUP (VOCAL OR INSTRUMENTAL) (G-296)
FLOWERS ON THE WALL - The Statler Brothers (Col)
HELP! - The Beatles (Cap)
MRS. BROWN YOU'VE GOT A LOVELY DAUGHTER - Herman's Hermits (MGM)
STOP IN THE NAME OF LOVE - The Supremes (Motown)
WOOLY BULLY - Sam the Sham & The Pharaohs (MGM)

RHYTHM & BLUES RECORDING (G-297)
IN THE MIDNIGHT HOUR - Wilson Pickett (Atl)
MY GIRL - The Temptations (Motown)
PAPA'S GOT A BRAND NEW BAG - James Brown (King)
SHAKE - Sam Cooke (RCA)
SHOTGUN - Jr. Walker & the All Stars (Soul)

FOLK RECORDING (G-298)
A SONG WILL RISE - Peter, Paul & Mary (WB)
AN EVENING WITH BELAFONTE/MAKEBA - Harry Belafonte, Miriam Makeba (RCA)
MAKEBA SINGS - Miriam Makeba (RCA)
ROSCOE HOLCOMB: THE HIGH LONESOME SOUND - Roscoe Holcomb (Folkways)
STRANGERS AND COUSINS - Pete Seeger (Col)
THERE BUT FOR FORTUNE - Joan Baez (Vanguard)
THE WOMENFOLK AT THE HUNGRY I - Womenfolk (RCA)

GOSPEL OR OTHER RELIGIOUS RECORDING (G-299)
ALL DAY SING AND DINNER ON THE GROUND - The Statesmen Quartet w/Hovie Lister (RCA)
BOB ASHTON'S SONGS OF LIVING FAITH - Ralph Carmichael Singers and Orchestra (Stylist)
HOW GREAT THOU ART - Kate Smith (RCA)
JUST KEEP ON SINGING - Marian Anderson (RCA)
LET ME WALK WITH THEE - Tennessee Ernie Ford (Cap)
SOMETHING OLD, SOMETHING NEW - Blackwood Bros. (RCA)
SOUTHLAND FAVORITES - George Beverly Shea and Anita Kerr Singers (RCA)
WHAT A HAPPY TIME - Happy Goodman Family (Word)

COUNTRY & WESTERN SINGLE (G-300)
FLOWERS ON THE WALL - The Statler Bros. (Col)
IS IT REALLY OVER - Jim Reeves (RCA)
KING OF THE ROAD - Roger Miller (Smash)
MAKE THE WORLD GO AWAY - Eddy Arnold (RCA)
MAY THE BIRD OF PARADISE FLY UP YOUR NOSE - "Little" Jimmy Dickens (Col)
YAKETY AXE - Chet Atkins (RCA)

COUNTRY & WESTERN ALBUM (G-301)
FATHER & SON: HANK WILLIAMS & HANK WILLIAMS, JR (MGM)
THE JIM REEVES WAY - Jim Reeves (RCA)
MORE OF THAT GUITAR COUNTRY - Chet Atkins (RCA)
MY WORLD - Eddy Arnold (RCA)
THE RETURN OF ROGER MILLER - Roger Miller (Smash)

COUNTRY & WESTERN VOCAL - FEMALE (G-302)
BABY - Wilma Burgess (Decca)
BEFORE THE RING ON YOUR FINGER TURNS GREEN - Dottie West (RCA)
QUEEN OF THE HOUSE - Jody Miller (Cap)
SINGLE GIRL AGAIN - Molly Bee (MGM)
SUNGLASSES - Skeeter Davis (RCA)

COUNTRY & WESTERN VOCAL - MALE (G-303)
CRYSTAL CHANDELIER - Carl Belew (RCA)
IS IT REALLY OVER - Jim Reeves (RCA)
KING OF THE ROAD - Roger Miller (Smash)
MAKE THE WORLD GO AWAY - Eddy Arnold (RCA)
TALK ME SOME SENSE - Bobby Bare (RCA)

COUNTRY & WESTERN SONG (G-304)
(Songwriter's Award)
CRYSTAL CHANDELIER - Ted Harris (RCA)
FLOWERS ON THE WALL - Lewis DeWitt (Col)
KING OF THE ROAD - Roger Miller (Smash)
MAY THE BIRD OF PARADISE FLY UP YOUR NOSE - Neal Merritt (Col)
WHAT'S HE DOING IN MY WORLD - Carl Belew, B.J. Moore, Eddie Busch (RCA)

NEW COUNTRY & WESTERN ARTIST (G-305)
WILMA BURGESS (Decca)
JODY MILLER (Cap)
NORMA JEAN (RCA)
DEL REEVES (UA)
STATLER BROTHERS (Col)

BEST ENGINEERED RECORDING (G-306)
(Engineer's Award)
A TASTE OF HONEY (Alpert & Tijuana Brass) - Eng: Larry Levine (A&M)
MORE OF THAT GUITAR COUNTRY (Chet Atkins) - Engs: Al Pachucki, Chuck Seitz (RCA)

LATIN SOUND OF HENRY MANCINI (Mancini) - Eng: Richard Bogert, James Malloy (RCA)
MY NAME IS BARBRA (Barbra Streisand) - Eng: Frank Laico (Col)
SEPTEMBER OF MY YEARS (Frank Sinatra) - Eng: Lowell Frank (Reprise)
THAT HONEY HORN SOUND (Al Hirt) - Eng: Chuck Seitz, Wm. Vandevort (RCA)

BEST ENGINEERED RECORDING, CLASSICAL (G-307)
(Engineer's Award)
GOULD: SPIRITUALS FOR ORCH./COPLAND: DANCE SYMPHONY (Gould, Chicago Sym.) - Eng: Bernard Keville (RCA)
HOROWITZ AT CARNEGIE HALL - An Historic Return (Vladimir Horowitz) - Eng: Fred Plaut (Col)
IVES: SYMPHONY NO. 4 (Stokowski cond. American Symphony Orch.) - Eng: Edward T. Graham (Col) Anthony Salvatore (RCA)
STRAUSS: SALOME/THE EGYPTIAN HELEN (Leontyne Price, Leinsdorf cond. Boston Sym.) - Eng: Anthony Salvatore (RCA)
STRAVINSKY: SYMPHONY OF PSALMS (Robert Shaw Chorale, RCA Sym.) - Eng: Bernard Keville (RCA)

ALBUM COVER - PHOTOGRAPHY (G-308)
(Awards to Art Director and Photographer)
THE AZNAVOUR STORY (Charles Aznavour) - Art Dir: Ed Thrasher - Photog: Sherman Weisburd (Reprise)
BRINGING IT ALL BACK HOME - (Bob Dylan) - Art Dir: John Berg - Photog: Dan Kramer (Col)
JAZZ SUITE ON THE MASS TEXTS (Paul Horn) - Art Dir: Bob Jones - Photog: Ken Whitmore (RCA)
KENNY BURRELL/GUITAR FORMS (Kenny Burrell) - Art Dir: Acy Lehman - Photog: Rudolph Regname (Verve)
MONK (Thelonious Monk) - Art Dir: Jerry Smokler - Photog: W. Eugene Smith (Col)
MY NAME IS BARBRA (Barbra Streisand) - Art Dir: Robert Cato - Photog: Sheldon Streisand (Col)
WHIPPED CREAM & OTHER DELIGHTS (Herb Alpert & the Tijuana Brass) - Art Dir. & Photog: Peter Whorf (A&M)

ALBUM COVER - GRAPHIC ARTS (G-309)
(Awards to Art Director and Graphic Artist)
BARTOK: CONCERTO NO. 2 FOR VIOLIN/STRAVINSKY: CONCERTO FOR VIOLIN (Silverstein, Leinsdorf, Boston Sym.) - Art Dir: George Estes - Graphic: James Alexander (RCA)
CONCERT IN THE VIRGIN ISLANDS (Duke Ellington) Art Dir: Ed Thrasher - Graphic: Patrick Blackwell (Reprise)
GOULD: SPIRITUALS FOR ORCH./COPLAND: DANCE SYMPHONY (Gould, Chicago Symphony) - Art Dir: George Estes - Graphic: Charles White (RCA)
HOROWITZ AT CARNEGIE HALL (Horowitz) - Art Dir. & Graphic: John Berg (Col)
SOLO MONK (Thelonious Monk) - Art Dir: Jerry Smokler - Graphic: Paul Davis (Col)
WILLIAM TELL & OTHER FAVORITE OVERTURES (Bernstein, New York Philharmonic) - Art Dir. & Graphic: John Berg (Col)

CLASSICAL PERFORMANCE - ORCHESTRA (G-310)
(Conductor's Award)
BACH: BRANDENBURG CONCERTOS - Herbert von Karajan cond. Berlin Philharmonic (DGG)
BERLIOZ: ROMEO AND JULIET - Arturo Toscanini cond. NBC Symphony (RCA)
GOULD: SPIRITUALS FOR ORCHESTRA/COPLAND: DANCE SYMPHONY - Morton Gould cond. Chicago Symphony (RCA)
IVES: SYMPHONY NO. 4 - Leopold Stokowski cond. American Symphony (Col)
PROKOFIEFF: SYMPHONY NO. 6 IN E-FLAT MINOR - Erich Leinsdorf cond. Boston Symphony (RCA)
RAVEL: DAPHNIS & CHLOE SUITE NO. 2/ROUSSEL: BACCHUS AND ARIADNE, SUITE NO. 2 - Jean Martinon cond. Chicago Symphony (RCA)

CHAMBER MUSIC PERFORMANCE - INSTRUMENTAL OR VOCAL (G-311)
A PURCELL ANTHOLOGY - Yehudi Menuhin and Members of Bath Festival Orch. (Angel)
BACH: THE SIX SONATAS FOR VIOLIN & HARPSICHORD - Erick Friedman, Bruce Prince-Joseph (RCA)
BARTOK: THE SIX STRING QUARTETS - Juilliard String Quartet (Col)
MOZART/SCHUMANN RECITAL - Vladimir Ashkenazy, Malcolm Frager (London)
SCHUBERT: TRIO NO. 1 IN B-FLAT FOR PIANO - Isaac Stern, Eugene Istomin, Leonard Rose (Col)
SONATA RECITAL BY SZIGETI & BARTOK (BARTOK/BEETHOVEN/DEBUSSY) - Joseph Szigeti, Bela Bartok (Vanguard)

CLASSICAL PERFORMANCE - INSTRUMENTAL SOLOIST(S) (WITH ORCHESTRA) (G-312)
BARBER: CONCERTO FOR VIOLIN & ORCHESTRA/HINDEMITH: CONCERTO FOR VIOLIN & ORCH. Isaac Stern (Bernstein cond. New York Philharmonic) (Col)
BEETHOVEN: CONCERTO NO. 4 IN G MAJOR FOR PIANO AND ORCHESTRA- Artur Rubinstein (Leinsdorf cond. Boston Symphony) (RCA)
BEETHOVEN: CONCERTO NO. 4 IN G MAJOR FOR PIANO AND ORCHESTRA - Rudolf Serkin (Toscanini cond. NBC Symphony) (RCA)
BEETHOVEN: TRIPLE CONCERTO - Isaac Stern, Leonard Rose, Eugene Istomin (Ormandy cond. Philadelphia Orchestra) (Col)
RACHMANINOFF: CONCERTO NO. 1 IN F SHARP FOR PIANO/CONCERTO NO. 4 IN G MINOR FOR PIANO - Leonard Pennario (Previn cond. Royal Philharmonic) (RCA)
TCHAIKOVSKY: CONCERTO NO. 2 IN G MAJOR FOR PIANO & ORCH/CONCERTO NO. 3 IN E-FLAT MAJOR FOR PIANO & ORCH. - Gary Graffman (Ormandy, Philadelphia Orchestra) (Col)

CLASSICAL PERFORMANCE - INSTRUMENTAL SOLOIST(S) (WITHOUT ORCHESTRA) (G-313)
ALKAN: PIANO MUSIC - Raymond Lewenthal (RCA)
BACH: WELL TEMPERED CLAVIER, BOOK 1, VOL. 3 (17-24) - Glenn Gould (Col)
CHOPIN BALLADES (1,2,3,4) - Vladimir Ashkenazy (London)
CHOPIN: 8 POLONAISES AND 4 IMPROMPTUS - Artur Rubinstein (RCA)
HOROWITZ AT CARNEGIE HALL - An Historic Return - Vladimir Horowitz (Col)
JULIAN BREAM IN CONCERT - Julian Bream (RCA)

OPERA RECORDING (G-314)
(Conductor's Award)
BELLINI: NORMA - Richard Bonynge cond. London Symphony & Chorus (Soloists: Sutherland, Horne, Alexander, Cross) (RCA)
BERG: WOZZECK - Karl Bohm cond. Orchestra of German Opera, Berlin (Soloists: Fischer-Dieskau, Lear, Wunderlich) (DGG)
VERDI: LA FORZA DEL DESTINO - Thomas Schippers cond. RCA Italiana Opera Orchestra & Chorus (Soloists: Price, Tucker, Verrett, Merrill, Tozzi, Flagello) (RCA)
VERDI: LUISA MILLER - Fausto Cleva cond. RCA Italiana Opera Orchestra & Chorus (Soloists: Moffo, Bergonzi, Verrett, MacNeil, Tozzi,-Flagello) (RCA)
WAGNER: GOTTERDAMMERUNG - Georg Solti cond. Vienna Philharmonic (Soloists: Nilsson, Windgassen, Fischer-Dieskau) (London)

CHORAL PERFORMANCE - OTHER THAN OPERA (G-315)
BERLIOZ: REQUIEM - Robert Page cond. Temple University Choir/Eugene Ormandy cond. Philadelphia Orchestra (Col)
BRAHMS: GERMAN REQUIEM - Herbert von Karajan cond. Vienna Singverein & Berlin Philharmonic (DGG)
BRITTEN: CANTATA MISERICORDIUM - Benjamin Britten cond. London Symphony Chorus & Orchestra (London)
HANDEL: MESSIAH - Wilhelm Pitz, Chorus Master, The Philharmonia Chorus/Otto Klemperer cond. Philharmonia Orchestra (Angel)

SCHOENBERG: GURRE LIEDER - Wolfgang Schubert cond. Bavarian Radio Symphony Chorus/Rafael Kubelik cond. Bavarian Radio Symphony (DGG)

STRAVINSKY: SYMPHONY OF PSALMS/POULENC: GLORIA - Robert Shaw cond. Robert Shaw Chorale, RCA Victor Symphony (RCA)

CLASSICAL PERFORMANCE - VOCAL SOLOIST - (G-316)

CANTELOUBE: SONGS OF THE AUVERGNE/RACHMANINOFF: VOCALISE/VILLA LOBOS: BACHIANAS BRASILEIRAS NO. 5 - Anna Moffo (Stokowski cond. American Symphony) (RCA)
FALLA: SEVEN POPULAR SPANISH SONGS - Shirley Verrett
MIRELLA FRENI - OPERATIC ARIAS - Mirella Freni (Ferraris cond. Rome Opera House Orchestra) (Angel)
MOUSSORGSKY: SONGS - Galina Vishnevskaya (Markevitch cond. Russian State Symphony)
RUSSIAN & FRENCH ARIAS - Nicolai Ghiaurov (Downes cond. London Symphony) (London)
SCHUMANN: LIEDERKREIS - Dietrich Fischer-Dieskau (Moore, Pianist) (Angel)
STRAUSS: SALOME (DANCE OF THE SEVEN VEILS INTERLUDE, FINAL SCENE)/THE EGYPTIAN HELEN (AWAKENING SCENE) - Leontyne Price (Leinsdorf cond. Boston Symphony) (RCA)

COMPOSITION BY A CONTEMPORARY CLASSICAL COMPOSER (G-317)

(Composer's Award)
CANTATA MISERICORDIUM - Benjamin Britten, (London)
CHICHESTER PSALMS - Leonard Bernstein, (London)
STRING QUARTET NO. 4 - David Diamond, (Epic)
SYMPHONY NO. 4 - Charles Ives, (Col)
VARIATIONS ON A THEME BY HINDEMITH - William Walton, (Col)
WORLD WAR I SUITE - Morton Gould, (RCA)

MOST PROMISING NEW CLASSICAL ARTIST (G-318)

NICOLAI GHIAUROV, Bass (London)
EVELYN LEAR, Soprano (DGG)
RAYMOND LEWENTHAL, Pianist (RCA)
PETER SERKIN, Pianist (RCA)
SHIRLEY VERRETT, Soprano (RCA)

1966

RECORD OF THE YEAR (G-319)

(Awards to the Artist and A&R Producer)
ALMOST PERSUADED - David Houston- A&R: Billy Sherrill (Epic)
MONDAY, MONDAY - The Mamas & The Papas - A&R: Lou Adler (Dunhill)
STRANGERS IN THE NIGHT - Frank Sinatra - A&R: Jimmy Bowen (Reprise)
WHAT NOW MY LOVE - Herb Alpert & the Tijuana Brass - A&R: Herb Alpert and Jerry Moss (A&M)
WINCHESTER CATHEDRAL - New Vaudeville Band - A&R: Geoff Stephens (Fontana)

ALBUM OF THE YEAR (G-320)

(Awards to the Artist and A&R Producer)
COLOR ME BARBRA - Barbra Streisand - A&R: Bob Mersey (Col)
DR. ZHIVAGO (Soundtrack) - Maurice Jarre - A&R: Jesse Kaye (MGM)
REVOLVER - The Beatles - A&R: George Martin (Cap)
SINATRA: A MAN & HIS MUSIC - Frank Sinatra - A&R: Sonny Burke (Reprise)
WHAT NOW MY LOVE - Herb Alpert & the Tijuana Brass - A&R: Herb Alpert and Jerry Moss (A&M)

SONG OF THE YEAR (G-321)

(Songwriter's Award)
BORN FREE - John Barry, Don Black (MGM)
THE IMPOSSIBLE DREAM - Mitch Leigh, Joe Darion (Kapp)
MICHELLE - John Lennon, Paul McCartney (Cap)
SOMEWHERE MY LOVE (Lara's Theme from Dr. Zhivago) - Paul Francis Webster,
Maurice Jarre (MGM)
STRANGERS IN THE NIGHT - Bert Kaempfert, Charles Singleton, Eddie Snyder (Reprise)

INSTRUMENTAL THEME (G-322)

(Composer's Award)
ARABESQUE - Henry Mancini (RCA)
BATMAN THEME - Neal Hefti (RCA)
PRISSY - Priscilla Hubbard (RCA)
TRUMPET PICKIN' - D.J. Edwards (RCA)
WHO'S AFRAID - Alex North (WB)

VOCAL PERFORMANCE - FEMALE (G-323)

BORN A WOMAN (Single) - Sandy Posey (MGM)
COLOR ME BARBRA (album) - Barbra Streisand (Col)
ELLA AT DUKE'S PLACE (album) - Ella Fitzgerald (Verve)
IF HE WALKED INTO MY LIFE (single) - Eydie Gorme (Col)
THESE BOOTS ARE MADE FOR WALKIN' (single) - Nancy Sinatra (Reprise)

VOCAL PERFORMANCE - MALE (G-324)

ALMOST PERSUADED (single) - David Houston (Epic)
DISTANT DRUMS (single) - Jim Reeves (RCA)
ELEANOR RIGBY (single) - Paul McCartney (Cap)
THE IMPOSSIBLE DREAM (single) Jack Jones (Kapp)
THE SHADOW OF YOUR SMILE (album) - Andy Williams (Col)
STRANGERS IN THE NIGHT (single) - Frank Sinatra (Reprise)

INSTRUMENTAL - OTHER THAN JAZZ (G-325)

BATMAN THEME - Neal Hefti (RCA)
BORN FREE - Roger Williams (Kapp)
CHET ATKINS PICKS ON THE BEATLES - Chet Atkins (RCA)
DR. ZHIVAGO (Soundtrack) Maurice Jarre (MGM)
WHAT NOW MY LOVE - Herb Alpert & the Tijuana Brass (A&M)

VOCAL GROUP (G-326)

A MAN AND A WOMAN - Anita Kerr Singers (WB)
CHERISH - The Association (Valiant)
GOOD VIBRATIONS - The Beach Boys (Cap)
GUANTANAMERA - The Sandpipers (A&M)
MONDAY, MONDAY - The Mamas & The Papas (Dunhill)

CHORUS (G-327)

A MAN AND A WOMAN - The Johnny Mann Singers (Lib)
BASIE SWINGIN', VOICES SINGIN' - The Alan Copeland Singers (With Count Basie) (ABC)
HENRY MANCINI PRESENTS THE ACADEMY AWARD SONGS - Henry Mancini, Orch. & Chorus (RCA)
ROCOCO A' GO GO - Swingle Singers (Philips)
SOMEWHERE, MY LOVE (Lara's Theme from Dr. Zhivago) - Ray Conniff & Singers (Col)

ORIGINAL SCORE - MOTION PICTURE OR TELEVISION SHOW (G-328)

(Composer's Award)
ARABESQUE - Henry Mancini (RCA)
BORN FREE - John Barry (MGM)
DR. ZHIVAGO - Maurice Jarre (MGM)
ORIGINAL MUSIC FROM THE SCORE "ALFIE" - Sonny Rollins (Impulse)
WHO'S AFRAID OF VIRGINIA WOOLF? - Alex North (WB)

SCORE FROM AN ORIGINAL CAST SHOW ALBUM (G-329)

(Composer's Award)

THE APPLE TREE - Jerry Bock, Sheldon Harnick (Col)
MAME - Jerry Herman (Col)
MAN OF LA MANCHA - Mitch Leigh, Joe Darion (Kapp)
SKYSCRAPER - Jimmy Van Heusen, Sammy Cahn (Cap)
SWEET CHARITY - Cy Coleman, Dorothy Fields (Col)

COMEDY PERFORMANCE (G-330)

DOWNTOWN - Mrs. Miller (Cap)
FUNNY WAY TO MAKE AN ALBUM - Don Bowman (RCA)
HAVE A LAUGH ON ME - Archie Campbell (RCA)
WANTED FOR MURDER - Homer and Jethro (RCA)
WONDERFULNESS - Bill Cosby (WB)

SPOKEN WORD, DOCUMENTARY OR DRAMA (G-331)

DAY FOR DECISION - Johnny Sea (WB)
DEATH OF A SALESMAN - Lee J. Cobb, Mildred Dunnock (Caedmon)
EDWARD R. MURROW - A REPORTER REMEMBERS - VOL. I THE WAR YEARS - Edward R. Murrow (Col)
HISTORY REPEATS ITSELF - Buddy Starcher (Decca)
THE STEVENSON WIT - Adlai Stevenson, David Brinkley, narrator (RCA)

RECORDING FOR CHILDREN (G-332)

ALICE THROUGH THE LOOKING GLASS - Orig. Cast- Moose Charlap & Elsie Simmons, Score (RCA)
THE CHRISTMAS THAT ALMOST WASN'T - Paul Tripp & Cast (RCA)
DR. SEUSS PRESENTS: "IF I RAN THE ZOO" AND "SLEEP BOOK" - Marvin Miller (RCA)
FOR THE CHILDREN OF THE WORLD ART LINKLETTER NARRATES "THE BIBLE" - Art Linkletter (RCA)
HAPPINESS IS - Marty Gold cond. Do-Re-Mi Children's Chorus (Kapp)

ALBUM NOTES (G-333)

(Annotator's Award)

BEN COLDER STRIKES AGAIN - Harvey Cowen (MGM)
DR. ZHIVAGO - Nelson Lyon (Maurice Jarre)
EDWARD R. MURROW - A REPORTER REMEMBERS - VOL. I THE WAR YEARS - Fred Friendly (Col)
THE ELLINGTON ERA, VOL. II - Stanley Dance, Ralph Gleason (Col)
SINATRA AT THE SANDS - Stan Cornyn (Reprise)

JAZZ - GROUP OR SOLOIST WITH GROUP (G-334)

AT THE "GOLDEN CIRCLE" - Ornette Coleman Trio (Blue Note)
BILL EVANS TRIO WITH SYMPHONY ORCHESTRA - Bill Evans Trio (Verve)
CONCERT OF SACRED MUSIC - Duke Ellington Orch. (RCA)
GOIN' OUT OF MY HEAD - Wes Montgomery (Verve)
INTERMODULATION - Bill Evans, Jim Hall (Verve)
JOHN HANDY RECORDED LIVE AT THE MONTEREY JAZZ FESTIVAL - John Handy Quintet (Col)
STAN KENTON CONDUCTS THE LOS ANGELES NEOPHONIC ORCHESTRA - Stan Kenton (Cap)
WOODY'S WINNERS - Woody Herman Orchestra (Col)

ORIGINAL JAZZ COMPOSITION (G-335)

(Composer's Award)

ABC BLUES - Bob Brookmeyer (Solid State)
IF ONLY WE KNEW - John Handy (Col)
IN THE BEGINNING GOD - Duke Ellington (RCA)
JAZZ SAMBA - Claus Ogerman (Verve)
MARQUIS DE SADE - Lalo Schifrin (Verve)
TIME REMEMBERED - Bill Evans (Rvrsd)

CONTEMPORARY (R&R) RECORDING (G-336)

CHERISH - The Association (Valiant)
ELEANOR RIGBY - Paul McCartney (Cap)
GOOD VIBRATIONS - The Beach Boys (Cap)
LAST TRAIN TO CLARKSVILLE - The Monkees (Colgems)
MONDAY, MONDAY - The Mamas & The Papas (Dunhill)
WINCHESTER CATHEDRAL - New Vaudeville Band (Fontana)

CONTEMPORARY (R&R) SOLO VOCAL - MALE OR FEMALE (G-337)

BORN A WOMAN - Sandy Posey (MGM)
ELEANOR RIGBY - Paul McCartney (Cap)
IF I WERE A CARPENTER - Bobby Darin (Atl)
THESE BOOTS ARE MADE FOR WALKIN' - Nancy Sinatra (Reprise)
YOU DON'T HAVE TO SAY YOU LOVE ME - Dusty Springfield (Philips)

CONTEMPORARY (R&R) GROUP - VOCAL OR INSTRUMENTAL (G-338)

CHERISH - The Association (Valiant)
GOOD VIBRATIONS - The Beach Boys (Cap)
GUANTANAMERA - The Sandpipers (A&M)
LAST TRAIN TO CLARKSVILLE - The Monkees (Colgm)
MONDAY, MONDAY - The Mamas & The Papas (Dunhill)

RHYTHM & BLUES RECORDING (G-339)

CRYING TIME - Ray Charles (ABC-Par)
IT'S A MAN'S MAN'S MAN'S WORLD - James Brown (King)
LOVE IS A HURTIN' THING - Lou Rawls (Cap)
UPTIGHT - Stevie Wonder (Tamla)
WHEN A MAN LOVES A WOMAN - Percy Sledge (Atl)

RHYTHM & BLUES SOLO VOCAL - MALE OR FEMALE (G-340)

CRYING TIME - Ray Charles (ABC-Par)
IT'S A MAN'S MAN'S MAN'S WORLD - James Brown (King)
LOVE IS A HURTIN' THING - Lou Rawls (Cap)
UPTIGHT - Stevie Wonder (Tamla)
WHEN A MAN LOVES A WOMAN - Percy Sledge (Alt)

RHYTHM & BLUES GROUP - VOCAL OR INSTRUMENTAL (G-341)

COOL JERK - Capitols (Atco)
HOLD IT RIGHT THERE - Ramsey Lewis (Cadet)
HOLD ON, I'M COMIN' - Sam & Dave (Stax)
I'M YOUR PUPPET - James & Bobby Purify (Bell)
SPANISH HARLEM - King Curtis (Atco)

FOLK RECORDING (G-342)

BLUES IN THE STREET - Cortelia Clark (RCA)
GOD BLESS THE GRASS - Pete Seeger (Col)
HURRY SUNDOWN - Peter, Paul & Mary (WB)
LEADBELLY - Leadbelly (Elektra)
OLIVER SMITH - Oliver Smith (Elektra)
REFLECTIONS IN A CRYSTAL WIND - Mimi & Richard Farina (Vanguard)
SOUND OF THE SITAR - Ravi Shankar (Wrld Pac)
VIOLETS OF DAWN - Mitchell Trio (Merc)

SACRED RECORDING (MUSICAL) (G-343)

BIGGER "N" BETTER - Happy Goodman Family (Canaan)
CONNIE SMITH SINGS GREAT SACRED SONGS - Connie Smith (RCA)
GRAND OLD GOSPEL - Porter Wagoner & the Blackwood Bros. (RCA)
HOW BIG IS GOD - The Blackwood Bros. (RCA)
THE OAK RIDGE BOYS AT THEIR BEST - The Oak Ridge Boys (UA)
SOUTHLAND SONGS THAT LIFT THE HEART - George Beverly Shea (RCA)

COUNTRY & WESTERN RECORDING (G-344)

ALMOST PERSUADED - David Houston (Epic)
DISTANT DRUMS - Jim Reeves (RCA)
DON'T TOUCH ME - Jeannie Seely (Monument)
I'M A NUT - Leroy Pullins (Kapp)
THERE GOES MY EVERYTHING - Jack Greene (Decca)

COUNTRY & WESTERN VOCAL - FEMALE (G-345)

AIN'T HAD NO LOVING - Connie Smith (RCA)
DON'T COME HOME A DRINKIN' - Loretta Lynn (Decca)
DON'T TOUCH ME - Jeannie Seely (Monument)
EVIL ON YOUR MIND - Jan Howard (Decca)
WOULD YOU HOLD IT AGAINST ME - Dottie West (RCA)

COUNTRY & WESTERN VOCAL - MALE (G-346)

ALMOST PERSUADED - David Houston
ALMOST PERSUADED NO. 2 - Ben Colder (Verve)
DISTANT DRUMS - Jim Reeves (RCA)
JUST BETWEEN YOU AND ME - Charley Pride (RCA)
THERE GOES MY EVERYTHING - Jack Greene (Decca)

COUNTRY & WESTERN SONG (G-347)

(Songwriter's Award)
ALMOST PERSUADED - Bill Sherrill, Glenn Sutton (Epic)
DON'T TOUCH ME - Hank Cochran (Monument)
HUSBANDS AND WIVES - Roger Miller (Smash)
STREETS OF BALTIMORE - Tompall Glaser, Harlan Howard (RCA)
THERE GOES MY EVERYTHING - Dallas Frazier (Decca)

INSTRUMENTAL ARRANGEMENT (G-348)

(Arranger's Award)
ARABESQUE - (Henry Mancini) - Arr: Henry Mancini (RCA)
BATMAN THEME (Neal Hefti) - Arr: Neal Hefti (RCA)
BORN FREE (track from soundtrack album) (John Barry) Arr: John Barry (MGM)
MICHELLE (Bud Shank) - Arr: Bob Florence (World Pac.)
WHAT NOW MY LOVE (Herb Alpert & the Tijuana Brass) Arr: Herb Alpert (A&M)

ARRANGEMENT ACCOMPANYING VOCALIST OR INSTRUMENTALIST (G-349)

(Arranger's Award)
ELEANOR RIGBY (Paul McCartney, Beatles) Arr: George Martin (Cap)
GOIN' OUT OF MY HEAD (Wes Montgomery) Arr: Oliver Nelson (Verve)
GOOD VIBRATIONS (Beach Boys) Arr: Brian Wilson (Cap)
IF HE WALKED INTO MY LIFE (Eydie Gorme) Arr: Don Costa (Col)
STRANGERS IN THE NIGHT (Frank Sinatra) Arr: Ernie Freeman (Reprise)
THESE BOOTS ARE MADE FOR WALKIN' (Nancy Sinatra) Arr: Billy Strange (Reprise)

BEST ENGINEERED RECORDING - NON-CLASSICAL (G-350)

(Engineer's Award)
ARABESQUE - Henry Mancini - Eng: Dick Bogert (RCA)
JOE WILLIAMS & THAD JONES - MEL LEWIS & THE JAZZ ORCHESTRA - - Eng: Phil Ramone (Sid. St.)
THE LAST WORD IN LONESOME IS ME (Eddy Arnold) Eng: James Malloy (RCA)
PRESENTING THAD JONES - MEL LEWIS & THE JAZZ ORCHESTRA - Eng: Phil Ramone (Sid. St)
STRANGERS IN THE NIGHT (Frank Sinatra) (album) Engrs: Eddie Brackett, Lee Herschberg (Reprise)

BEST ENGINEERED RECORDING - CLASSICAL (G-351)

(Engineer's Award)
IVES: SYMPHONY NO. 1 IN D MINOR (Gould cond. Chicago Symphony) - Eng: Bernard Keville (RCA)
MAHLER: SYMPHONY NO. 6 IN A MINOR (Leinsdorf cond. Boston Symphony) - Eng: Anthony Salvatore (RCA)
VARESE: ARCANA (Martinon cond. Chicago Symphony) - Eng: Bernard Keville (RCA)
VIVALDI: GLORIA IN D (Robert Shaw Orch. & Chorus) - Eng: Ernest Oelrich (RCA)
WAGNER: LOHENGRIN (Leinsdorf cond. Boston Symphony Pro Musica Chorus & Soloists) - Eng: Anthony Salvatore (RCA)

ALBUM COVER, PHOTOGRAPHY (G-352)

(Awards to the Art Director and Photographer)
BLONDE ON BLONDE (Bob Dylan) Art Dirs: Bob Cato and John Berg - Photog: Gerald Schatsberg (Col)
CONFESSIONS OF A BROKEN MAN (Porter Wagoner) Art Dir: Robert Jones - Photog: Les Leverette (RCA) GUANTANAMERA (Sandpipers) Art Dir. & Photog: Peter Whorf (A&M) SAMMY DAVIS, JR SINGS - LAURINDO ALMEIDA PLAYS - Art Dir: Ed Thrasher - Photog: Tom Tucker (Reprise)
THE TIME MACHINE (Gary Burton) Art Dir: Robert Jones - Photog: Tom Zimmerman (RCA)
TURN! TURN! TURN! (The Byrds) Art Dirs: Bob Cato And John Berg - Photog: Guy Webster (Col)
WHAT NOW MY LOVE (Herb Alpert & The Tijuana Brass) Art Dir: Peter Whorf - Photog: George Jerman (A&M)

ALBUM COVER, GRAPHIC ARTS (G-353)

(Awards to the Art Director and Graphic Artist)
BAROQUE FANFARES & SONATAS FOR BRASS (London Brass Players, Joshua Rifkin dir.) Art Dir: William S. Harvey - Graphic: Gordon Kibbee (Nonesuch)
CHARLIE BYRD CHRISTMAS CAROLS FOR SOLO GUITAR - Art Dirs: Bob Cato and John Berg - Graphic: Allen Weinberg (Col)
COLOR ME BARBRA (Barbra Streisand) Art Dirs: Bob Cato and John Berg - Graphic: Elinor Bunin (Col)
IVES: SYMPHONY NO. 1 IN D MINOR (Gould cond. Chicago Symphony) Art Dir: George Estes - Graphic: Mozelle Thompson (RCA)
REVOLVER (The Beatles) Graphic: Klaus Voormann (Cap)
STAN KENTON CONDUCTS THE LOS ANGELES NEOPHONIC ORCHESTRA - Art Dir: George Osaki - Graphic: Rod Dyer (Cap)
TALK THAT TALK (The Jazz Crusaders) Art Dir: Woody Woodward - Graphic - Peter Whorf (Pac. Jazz)

ALBUM OF THE YEAR - CLASSICAL (G-354)

(Awards to the Artist and A&R Producer)
AARON COPLAND CONDUCTS (Copland: Music for a Great City, Statements) - Aaron Copland cond. London Symphony - A&R: John McClure (Col)
HANDEL: MESSIAH - Colin Davis cond. London Symphony Orch. & Choir - A&R: Harold Lawrence (Philips)
HENZE: SYMPHONIES (1 thru 5) - H.W. Henze cond. Berlin Philharmonic - A&R: Otto Gerdes (DGG)
IVES: SYMPHONY NO. 1 IN D MINOR - Morton Gould cond. Chicago Symphony - A&R: Howard Scott (RCA)
MAHLER: SYMPHONY NO. 6 IN A MINOR - Erich Leinsdorf cond. Boston Symphony - A&R: Richard Mohr (RCA)
MAHLER: SYMPHONY NO. 10 - Eugene Ormandy cond. Philadelphia Orchestra - A&R: Thomas Frost (Col)
OPENING NIGHTS AT THE MET - Various Artists - A&R: Peter Dellheim (RCA)
PRESENTING MONTSERRAT CABALLE (Bellini & Donizetti Arias) - Montserrat Caballe - A&R: C. Gerhardt (RCA)
WAGNER: DIE WALKURE - Georg Solti cond. Vienna Philharmonic (Soloists: Nilsson, Crespin, Ludwig, King, Hotter, Frick) A&R: John Culshaw (London)

CLASSICAL PERFORMANCE - ORCHESTRA (G-355)
BARTOK: CONCERTO FOR ORCHESTRA - George Szell cond. Cleveland Orchestra (Col)
BOULEZ: LE SOLEIL DES EAUX; MESSIAEN: CHRONOCHROMIE; KOECHLIN: LES BANDAR-LOG (Angel) Pierre Boulez cond. BBC Symphony; Antal Dorati cond. BBC Symphony
IVES: FOURTH OF JULY - Leonard Bernstein cond. New York Philharmonic (Col)
IVES: SYMPHONY NO. 1 IN D MINOR - Morton Gould cond. Chicago Symphony (RCA)
MAHLER: SYMPHONY NO. 6 IN A MINOR - Erich Leinsdorf cond. Boston Symphony (RCA)
MAHLER: SYMPHONY NO. 10 - Eugene Ormandy cond. Philadelphia Orchestra (Col)
RAVEL: DAPHNIS AND CHLOE - Ernest Ansermet cond. L'Orchestre de la Suisse Romande (London)
VARESE: ARCANA/MARTIN: CONCERTO FOR SEVEN WIND INSTRUMENTS, TIMPANI, PERCUSSION & STRING ORCHESTRA - Jean Martinon cond. Chicago Symphony (RCA)

CHAMBER MUSIC PERFORMANCE - INSTRUMENTAL OR VOCAL (G-356)
ARENSKY: TRIO IN D MINOR FOR VIOLIN, CELLO & PIANO/MARTINU: DUO FOR VIOLIN & CELLO - Jascha Heifetz, Gregor Piatigorsky with Leonard Pennario (RCA)
BEETHOVEN: TRIO NO. 6 IN B FLAT, OP. 97 ("ARCHDUKE") - Eugene Istomin, Isaac Stern, Leonard Rose (Col)
BOSTON SYMPHONY CHAMBER PLAYERS (Selections by Mozart, Brahms, Beethoven, Fine, Copland, Carter, Piston) Boston Symphony Chamber Players (RCA)
FRANCK: SONATA IN A MAJOR FOR VIOLIN & PIANO/DEBUSSY: SONATA IN G MINOR FOR VIOLIN & PIANO - Erick Friedman, Andre Previn (RCA)
HAYDN: QUARTETS (OP. 33) - Weller Quartet (London)
MOZART: THE SIX QUINTETS FOR STRING QUARTET & VIOLA - Walter Trampler & Budapest Quartet (Col)
PROKOFIEV: SONATA FOR CELLO & PIANO, OP. 119/CHOPIN: SONATA IN G MINOR FOR PIANO & CELLO, OP. 65 - Gregor Piatigorsky and Rudolf Firkusny (RCA)
SCHUBERT: QUINTET IN C MAJOR - Vienna Philharmonic Quartet (London)

CLASSICAL PERFORMANCE - INSTRUMENTAL SOLOIST(S) (WITH OR WITHOUT ORCHESTRA) (G-357)
BAROQUE GUITAR (Bach, Sanz, Weiss, Etc.) Julian Bream (RCA)
CHOPIN: NOCTURNES - Ivan Moravec (Conn.Soc)
DVORAK: CONCERTO IN A MINOR FOR VIOLIN - Isaac Stern, Soloist (Eugene Ormandy cond. Philadelphia Orchestra) (Col)
ELGAR: CONCERTO FOR VIOLIN - Yehudi Menuhin, Soloist (Sir Adrian Boult cond. New Philharmonia Orchestra) (Angel)
OPERATIC LISZT - Raymond Lewenthal (RCA)
PROKOFIEV: CONCERTO NO. 1 IN D FLAT MAJOR FOR PIANO/CONCERTO NO. 2 IN G MINOR FOR PIANO - John Browning, Soloist (Erich Leinsdorf cond. Boston Symphony) (RCA)
RODRIGO: CONCIERTO DE ARANJUEZ FOR GUITAR & ORCHESTRA/CASTELNUOVO - TEDESCO: CONCERTO IN D MAJOR FOR GUITAR - John Williams, Soloist (Eugene Ormandy cond. Philadelphia Orchestra) (Col)
RUBINSTEIN & CHOPIN (Bolero, Tarentelle, Fantasie in F Minor Barcarolle, Berceuse & 3 Nouvelles Etudes) - Artur Rubinstein (RCA)

OPERA RECORDING (G-358)
(Conductor's Award)
BARTOK: BLUEBEARD'S CASTLE - Istvan Kertesz cond. London Symphony (Soloists: Ludwig, Berry) (London)
COPLAND: THE TENDER LAND - Aaron Copland cond. Choral Arts Society & New York Philharmonic (Soloists: Clements, Turner, Cassilly, Treigle, Fredericks) (Col)
PUCCINI: TURANDOT - Francesco Molinari - Pradelli cond. Rome Opera Chorus & Orchestra (Soloists: Nilsson, Corelli) (Angel)

WAGNER: DIE WALKURE - Georg Solti cond. Vienna Philharmonic (Soloists: Nilsson, Crespin, Ludwig, King, Hotter) (London)
WAGNER: LOHENGRIN - Erich Leinsdorf cond. Boston Symphony (Soloists: Konya, Amarca, Gorr, Dooley) (RCA)

CLASSICAL CHORAL PERFORMANCE - OTHER THAN OPERA (G-359)
BEETHOVEN: MISSA SOI EMNIS IN D MAJOR - Wilhelm Pitz cond. New Philharmonia Chorus Otto Klemperer cond. New Philharmonia Orchestra (Angel)
BLESS THIS HOUSE - Richard Condie, Dir., Mormon Tabernacle Choir - Eugene Ormandy cond. Philadelphia Orchestra (Col)
HANDEL: MESSIAH - Colin Davis cond. Soloists, London Symphony Orchestra & Choir (Philips)
HANDEL: MESSIAH - Robert Shaw cond. Robert Shaw Chorale & Orchestra (RCA)
IVES: MUSIC FOR CHORUS (Gen. Wm. Booth Enters Into Heaven, Serenity, The Circus Band, etc.) Gregg Smith cond. Columbia Chamber Orchestra, Gregg Smith Singers, Ithaca College Concert Choir - George Bragg cond. Texas Boys Choir (Col)
ORFF: CARMINA BURANA - Wilhelm Pitz cond. New Philharmonia Chorus - Rafael Fruhbeck de Burgos cond. New Philharmonia Orch. (Angel)
VAUGHAN WILLIAMS: HODIE - David Willcocks cond. Bach Choir & Choristers of Westminster Abbey/London Symphony (Angel)
VERDI: REQUIEM - Alfred Nash Patterson, Dir., Boston Symphony Chorus/Erich Leinsdorf cond. Boston Symphony Orchestra (RCA)

CLASSICAL PERFORMANCE - VOCAL SOLOIST - (G-360)
MAHLER: SYMPHONY NO. 4 IN G MAJOR - Judith Raskin, Soloist (Szell cond. Cleveland Orchestra) (Col)
MAHLER: THE YOUTH'S MAGIC HORN (Das Knaben Wunderhorn) - Janet Baker, Solo. (Wyn Morris cond. London Philharmonic) (Angel)
PRESENTING MONTSERRAT CABALLE (Bellini & Donizetti Arias) - Montserrat Caballe (Carlo Felice Cilario, cond.) (RCA)
PRIMA DONNA (Barber, Purcell, etc.) Leontyne Price, Soloist (Molinari-Pradelli cond. RCA Italiana Opera Orchestra) (RCA)
SCHUMANN: DICHTERLIEBE - Dietrich Fischer-Dieskau, Soloist (DGG)
STRAUSS: FOUR LAST SONGS - Elisabeth Schwarzkopf, Soloist (Szell cond. Berlin Radio Symphony) (Angel)

1967

RECORD OF THE YEAR (G-361)
(Awards to the Artist and A&R Producer)
BY THE TIME I GET TO PHOENIX - Glen Campbell - A&R: Al de Lory (Cap)
MY CUP RUNNETH OVER - Ed Ames - A&R: Jim Fogelsong, Joe Reisman (RCA)
ODE TO BILLIE JOE - Bobbie Gentry - A&R: Bobby Paris, Kelly Gordon (Cap)
SOMETHIN' STUPID - Nancy and Frank Sinatra - A&R: Jimmy Bowen, Lee Hazelwood (Reprise)
UP, UP AND AWAY - 5th Dimension - A&R: Marc Gordon, Johnny Rivers (Soul City)

ALBUM OF THE YEAR (G-362)
(Awards to the Artist and A&R Producer)
FRANCIS ALBERT SINATRA/ANTONIO CARLOS JOBIM - Francis Albert Sinatra, Antonio Carlos Jobim - A&R: Sonny Burke (Reprise)
IT MUST BE HIM - Vikki Carr - A&R: Dave Pell, Tommy Oliver (Lib)
MY CUP RUNNETH OVER - Ed Ames - A&R: Jim Fogelsong (RCA)
ODE TO BILLIE JOE - Bobbie Gentry - A&R: Bobby Paris, Kelly Gordon (Cap)
SGT. PEPPER'S LONELY HEARTS CLUB BAND - The Beatles - A&R: George Martin (Cap)

SONG OF THE YEAR (G-363)

(Songwriter's Award)

BY THE TIME I GET TO PHOENIX - Jim Webb (Cap)
GENTLE ON MY MIND - John Hartford (RCA)
MY CUP RUNNETH OVER - Tom Jones, Harvey Schmidt (RCA)
ODE TO BILLIE JOE - Bobbie Gentry (Cap)
UP, UP AND AWAY - Jim Webb (Soul City)

INSTRUMENTAL THEME (G-364)

(Composer's Award)

A BANDA - Chico Buarque De Hollanda (A&M)
CASINO ROYALE - Burt Bacharach, Hal David (A&M)
HURRY SUNDOWN - Hugo Montenegro (MGM)
MERCY, MERCY, MERCY - Joe Zawinul (Cap)
MISSION: IMPOSSIBLE - Lalo Schifrin (Dot)

VOCAL - FEMALE (G-365)

ALFIE (single) - Dionne Warwick (Scepter)
DON'T SLEEP IN THE SUBWAY (single) Petula Clark (WB)
IT MUST BE HIM (album) - Vikki Carr (Lib)
ODE TO BILLIE JOE (single) Bobbie Gentry (Cap)
RESPECT (single) Aretha Franklin (Atl)

VOCAL - MALE (G-366)

BY THE TIME I GET TO PHOENIX (single) Glen Campbell (Cap)
CAN'T TAKE MY EYES OFF YOU (single) Frankie Valli (Philips)
FRANCIS ALBERT SINATRA/ANTONIO CARLOS JOBIM - Francis Albert Sinatra (Reprise)
MY CUP RUNNETH OVER (album) - Ed Ames (RCA)
YESTERDAY (single) Ray Charles (ABC)

INSTRUMENTAL PERFORMANCE (G-367)

CASINO ROYALE - Herb Alpert & the Tijuana Brass (A&M)
CHET ATKINS PICKS THE BEST - Chet Atkins (RCA)
MERCY, MERCY, MERCY - Cannonball Adderley Quintet (Cap)
MISSION: IMPOSSIBLE - Lalo Schifrin (Dot)
MUSIC TO WATCH GIRLS BY - Bob Crewe Generation (DynoVoice)

VOCAL GROUP (G-368)

I'M A BELIEVER - The Monkees (Colgems)
THE LETTER - The Box Tops (Bell)
NEVER MY LOVE - The Association (WB)
SGT. PEPPER'S LONELY HEARTS CLUB BAND - The Beatles (Cap)
UP, UP AND AWAY - 5th Dimension (Soul City)

CHORUS (G-369)

BLAME IT ON ME - Ray Charles Singers (Command)
ENCOUNTER - Swingle Singers - with the Modern Jazz Quartet (Philips)
UP, UP AND AWAY - Johnny Mann Singers (Lib)
WINDY - Percy Faith Chorus and Orch. (Col)
WISH ME A RAINBOW - Living Voices - Ethel Gabriel, conductor (RCA)

ORIGINAL SCORE - MOTION PICTURE OR TV SHOW (G-370)

CASINO ROYALE (Various Artists, Bacharach cond.) Comp: Burt Bacharach (RCA)
DOCTOR DOOLITTLE (Rex Harrison & motion picture cast, Lionel Newman cond.) Comp: Leslie Bricusse (20th)
IN THE HEAT OF THE NIGHT (Quincy Jones cond.) Comp: Quincy Jones (UA)
MISSION: IMPOSSIBLE (Lalo Schifrin Orch.) Comp: Lalo Schifrin (Dot)
TO SIR WITH LOVE (Soundtrack W/Lulu & the Mindbenders) Comps: Ron Grainer, Don Black, Mark London (Fontana)

SCORE FROM AN ORIGINAL CAST SHOW ALBUM (G-371)

(Awards to Composers & A&R Producer)

CABARET - Fred Ebb & John Kander - A&R: Goddard Lieberson (Col)
HALLELUJAH, BABY - Jule Styne, Betty Comden, Adolph Green - A&R: Edward Kleban (Col)
I DO! I DO! - Harvey Schmidt & Tom Jones - A&R: Andy Wiswell (RCA)
WALKING HAPPY - Sammy Cahn & Jimmy Van Heusen - A&R: Richard C. Jones (Cap)
YOU'RE A GOOD MAN, CHARLIE BROWN - Clark Gesner - A&R: Bob Morgan, Herb Galewitz (MGM)

COMEDY RECORDING (G-372)

THE COCKFIGHT AND OTHER TALL TALES - Archie Campbell (RCA)
COWBOYS AND COLORED PEOPLE - Flip Wilson (Atl)
LENNY BRUCE IN CONCERT - Lenny Bruce (UA)
REVENGE - Bill Cosby (WB)
TAKE-OFFS AND PUT-ONS - George Carlin (RCA)

NEW ARTIST (G-373)

LANA CANTRELL (RCA)
5TH DIMENSION (Soul City)
BOBBIE GENTRY (Cap)
HARPERS BIZARRE (WB)
JEFFERSON AIRPLANE (RCA)

JAZZ - SMALL GROUP OR SOLOIST WITH SMALL GROUP (G-374)

(7 or less Persons)

DUSTER - Gary Burton Quartet (RCA)
FURTHER CONVERSATIONS WITH MYSELF - Bill Evans (Verve)
HAPPENINGS - Bobby Hutcherson (Blue Note)
MERCY, MERCY, MERCY - Cannonball Adderley Quintet (Cap)
MILES SMILES - Miles Davis (Col)
SWEET RAIN - Stan Getz (Verve)

JAZZ - LARGE GROUP OR SOLOIST WITH LARGE GROUP (G-375)

(8 or more Persons)

BIG SWING FACE - Buddy Rich (Pac. Jazz)
FAR EAST SUITE - Duke Ellington (RCA)
LIVE AT MONTEREY - Don Ellis Big Band (Pac. Jaz)
LIVE AT THE VILLAGE VANGUARD - Thad Jones and Mel Lewis (UA)
WOODY LIVE - EAST AND WEST - Woody Herman (Col)

CONTEMPORARY SINGLE (G-376)

(Awards to the Artist and A&R Producer)

BY THE TIME I GET TO PHOENIX - Glen Campbell - A&R: Al de Lory (Cap)
DON'T SLEEP IN THE SUBWAY - Petula Clark - A&R: Tony Hatch (WB)
ODE TO BILLIE JOE - Bobbie Gentry - A&R: Bobby Paris, Kelly Gordon (Cap)
UP, UP AND AWAY - 5th Dimension - A&R: Marc Gordon, Johnny Rivers (Soul City)
YESTERDAY - Ray Charles - A&R: Sid Feller, Tangerine Records (ABC)

CONTEMPORARY ALBUM (G-377)

(Awards to the Artist and A&R Producer)

INSIGHT OUT - The Association - A&R: Bones Howe (WB)
IT MUST BE HIM - Vikki Carr - A&R: Dave Pell, Tommy Oliver (Lib)
ODE TO BILLIE JOE - Bobbie Gentry - A&R: Bobby Paris, Kelly Gordon (Cap)
SGT. PEPPER'S LONELY HEARTS CLUB BAND - The Beatles - A&R: George Martin (Cap)
UP, UP AND AWAY - 5th Dimension - A&R: Marc Gordon, Johnny Rivers (Soul City)

CONTEMPORARY FEMALE SOLO - VOCAL (G-378)
DON'T SLEEP IN THE SUBWAY - Petula Clark (WB)
I SAY A LITTLE PRAYER - Dionne Warwicke (Scptr)
IT MUST BE HIM - Vikki Carr (album) (Lib)
A NATURAL WOMAN - Aretha Franklin (Atl)
ODE TO BILLIE JOE - Bobbie Gentry (Cap)

CONTEMPORARY MALE SOLO - VOCAL (G-379)
BY THE TIME I GET TO PHOENIX - Glen Campbell (Cap)
CAN'T TAKE MY EYES OFF YOU - Frankie Valli (Philips)
CHILD OF CLAY - Jimmie Rodgers (A&M)
SAN FRANCISCO (Be Sure to Wear Some Flowers in Your Hair) - Scott McKenzie (Col)
YESTERDAY - Ray Charles (ABC)

CONTEMPORARY - GROUP - VOCAL OR INSTRUMENTAL (G-380)
I'M A BELIEVER - The Monkees (Colgems)
THE LETTER - Box Tops (Bell)
SGT. PEPPER'S LONELY HEARTS CLUB BAND - The Beatles (Cap)
UP, UP AND AWAY - 5th Dimension (Soul City)
A WHITER SHADE OF PALE - Procul Harum (Deram)
WINDY - The Association (WB)

RHYTHM & BLUES RECORDING (G-381)
(Awards to the Artist and A&R Producer)
DEAD END STREET - Lou Rawls - A&R: David Axelrod (Cap)
RESPECT - Aretha Franklin - A&R: Jerry Wexler (Atl)
SKINNY LEGS AND ALL - Joe Tex - A&R: Buddy Killen (Dial)
SOUL MAN - Sam & Dave - A&R: David Porter & Isaac Hayes (Stax)
TRY A LITTLE TENDERNESS - Otis Redding - A&R: Steve Cropper (Atco)

RHYTHM & BLUES SOLO VOCAL - FEMALE (G-382)
I HEARD IT THROUGH THE GRAPEVINE - Gladys Knight & The Pips (Soul)
THE QUEEN ALONE - Carla Thomas (Stax)
RESPECT - Aretha Franklin (Atl)
TELL MAMA - Etta James (Cadet)
(YOU'LL) GO TO HELL - Nina Simone (RCA)

RHYTHM & BLUES SOLO VOCAL - MALE (G-383)
DEAD END STREET - Lou Rawls (Cap)
FUNKY BROADWAY - Wilson Pickett (Atl)
HIGHER AND HIGHER - Jackie Wilson (Brnswck)
SKINNY LEGS AND ALL - Joe Tex (Dial)
TRY A LITTLE TENDERNESS - Otis Redding (Atco)

RHYTHM & BLUES GROUP - VOCAL OR INSTRUMENTAL (G-384)
AIN'T NO MOUNTAIN HIGH ENOUGH - Marvin Gaye & Tammi Terrell (Tamla)
HIP HUG-HER - Booker T. & the M.G.'s (Stax)
THE KING & QUEEN - Carla Thomas and Otis Redding (Stax)
SOUL MAN - Sam & Dave (Stax)
I SECOND THAT EMOTION - Smokey Robinson & the Miracles (Tamla)

SACRED PERFORMANCE (G-385)
DOTTIE WEST SINGS SACRED BALLADS - Dottie West (RCA)
HOW GREAT THOU ART - Elvis Presley (RCA)
THE OLD COUNTRY CHURCH - The Browns (RCA)
SONGS FOR THE SOUL - Red Foley (Decca)
SURELY GOODNESS AND MERCY - George Beverly Shea & the Blackwood Bros. Quartet (RCA)

GOSPEL PERFORMANCE (G-386)
THE BLACKWOOD BROS. QUARTET SINGS FOR JOY - The Blackwood Bros. Quartet (RCA)
GOOD 'N' HAPPY - Happy Goodman Family (Canaan)
MORE GRAND OLD GOSPEL - Porter Wagoner & The Blackwood Bros. Quartet (RCA)
THE OAK RIDGE BOYS - Oak Ridge Boys (Heartwarming)
THE SINGING RAMBOS - GOSPEL BALLADS - The Singing Rambos (Heartwarming)

FOLK PERFORMANCE (G-387)
ALBUM 1700 - Peter, Paul & Mary (WB)
ALICE'S RESTAURANT - Arlo Guthrie (Reprise)
GENTLE ON MY MIND - John Hartford (RCA)
IN MY LIFE - Judy Collins (Elektra)
JANIS IAN - Janis Ian (Verve)
WAIST DEEP IN THE BIG MUDDY - Pete Seeger (Col)

COUNTRY & WESTERN RECORDING (G-388)
(Awards to the Artist and A&R Producer)
COLD HARD FACTS OF LIFE - Porter Wagoner - A&R: Bob Ferguson (RCA)
DOES MY RING HURT YOUR FINGER - Charley Pride - A&R: Chet Atkins, Jack Clement, and Felton Jarvis (RCA)
GENTLE ON MY MIND - Glen Campbell - A&R: Al de Lory (Cap)
POP A TOP - Jim Ed Brown - A&R: Felton Jarvis (RCA)
THROUGH THE EYES OF LOVE - Tompall & the Glaser Bros - A&R: Jack Clement (MGM)

COUNTRY & WESTERN SOLO VOCAL - FEMALE (G-389)
CINCINNATI, OHIO - Connie Smith (RCA)
I DON'T WANNA PLAY HOUSE - Tammy Wynette (Epic)
MAMA SPANK - Liz Anderson (RCA)
PAPER MANSIONS - Dottie West (RCA)
WHAT DOES IT TAKE - Skeeter Davis (RCA)

COUNTRY & WESTERN SOLO VOCAL - MALE (G-390)
ALL THE TIME - Jack Greene (Decca)
COLD HARD FACTS OF LIFE - Porter Wagoner (RCA)
DOES MY RING HURT YOUR FINGER - Charley Pride (RCA)
GENTLE ON MY MIND - Glen Campbell (Cap)
POP A TOP - Jim Ed Brown (RCA)

COUNTRY & WESTERN DUET, TRIO OR GROUP (VOCAL OR INSTRUMENTAL) (G-391)
CHET'S TUNE - Some of Chet's Friends (RCA)
GAME OF TRIANGLES - Liz Anderson, Bobby Bare, Norma Jean (RCA)
JACKSON - Johnny Cash, June Carter (Col)
THE LONESOME RHODES - The Lonesome Rhodes (RCA)
MY CUP RUNNETH OVER - The Blue Boys (RCA)
MY ELUSIVE DREAMS - David Houston, Tammy Wynette (Epic)
OUR WAY OF LIFE - Bobby Goldsboro, Del Reeves (UA)
THROUGH THE EYES OF LOVE - Tompall & the Glaser Bros. (MGM)

COUNTRY & WESTERN SONG (G-392)
(Songwriter's Award)
BREAK MY MIND - John Loudermilk (RCA)
COLD HARD FACTS OF LIFE - Bill Anderson (RCA)
DOES MY RING HURT YOUR FINGER - Don Robertson, John Crutchfield, Doris Clement (RCA)
GENTLE ON MY MIND - John Hartford (RCA)
IT'S SUCH A PRETTY WORLD TODAY - Dale Noe (Cap)

SPOKEN WORD, DOCUMENTARY OR DRAMA RECORDING (G-393)

THE BALCONY - Patrick Magee, Cyril Cusack (Caedmon)
THE EARTH - Rod McKuen (WB)
GALLANT MEN - Sen. Everett M. Dirksen (Cap)
A MAN FOR ALL SEASONS - Paul Scofield, Wendy Hiller, Robert Shaw (RCA)
MARK TWAIN TONIGHT, VOL. 3 - Hal Holbrook (Col)
AN OPEN LETTER TO MY TEENAGE SON - Victor Lundberg (Lib)
POEMS OF JAMES DICKEY - James Dickey (Spoken Arts)

RECORDING FOR CHILDREN (G-394)

THE CARNIVAL OF THE ANIMALS - Verses by Ogden Nash, narrated by Tutti Camarata (Symphonie-Orchester Graunke) (Buena Vista)
DR. SEUSS: HOW THE GRINCH STOLE CHRISTMAS (TV Soundtrack) - Boris Karloff (MGM)
A HAPPY BIRTHDAY PARTY WITH WINNIE THE POOH - Sterling Holloway (Disneyland)
THE JUNGLE BOOK - Motion Picture Cast (Phil Harris, Louis Prima, Sterling Holloway, Sebastian Cabot, George Saunders) Tutti Camarata, A&R Prod. (Disney)
JUNGLE BOOKS - Richard Kiley (MGM)
MAGIC FISHBONE/HAPPY PRINCE/POTTED PRINCESS - Julie Harris, Richard Kiley (MGM)

INSTRUMENTAL ARRANGEMENT (G-395)

(Arranger's Award)

ALFIE (Burt Bacharach Orch.) - Arr: Burt Bacharach (A&M)
CASINO ROYALE (Herb Alpert & the Tijuana Brass) Arr: Burt Bacharach (A&M)
MUSIC TO WATCH GIRLS BY (Bob Crewe Generation) Arr: Hutch Davie (Philips)
NORWEGIAN WOOD (Buddy Rich Orch.) Arr: Bill Holman (Pac. Jazz)
WAVE (Antonio Carlos Jobim) Arr: Claus Ogerman (A&M)
WEST SIDE MEDLEY (Buddy Rich Orch.) Arr: Bill Reddie (Pac. Jazz)

ARRANGEMENT ACCOMPANYING VOCALIST(S) OR INSTRUMENTALIST(S) (G-396)

(Arranger's Award)

BY THE TIME I GET TO PHOENIX (Glen Campbell) Arr: Al de Lory (Cap)
A DAY IN THE LIFE (The Beatles) Arr: The Beatles & George Martin (Cap)
DON'T SLEEP IN THE SUBWAY (Petula Clark) Arr: Tony Hatch (WB-7 Arts)
ODE TO BILLIE JOE (Bobbie Gentry) Arr: Jimmie Haskell (Cap)
WINDY (The Association) Arr: Bill Holman, Bones Howe, Ray Pohlman (WB-7 Arts)

BEST ENGINEERED RECORDING, NON-CLASSICAL (G-397)

(Engineer's Award)

CHET'S TUNE (Some of Chet's Friends) Eng: William Vandevort (RCA)
HOW GREAT THOU ART (Elvis Presley) Eng: James Malloy (RCA)
MISSION: IMPOSSIBLE (Lalo Schifrin) Eng: Hank Cicalo (Dot)
ODE TO BILLIE JOE (Bobbie Gentry) Eng: Joe Polito (Cap)
SGT. PEPPER'S LONELY HEARTS CLUB BAND (The Beatles) Eng: G.E. Emerick (Cap)

BEST ENGINEERED RECORDING - CLASSICAL (G-398)

(Engineer's Award)

THE GLORIOUS SOUND OF BRASS (Philadelphia Brass Ensemble) Eng: Edward T. Graham (Col)
MAHLER: DAS LIED VON DER ERDE (Bernstein, Vienna Philharmonic & Soloists) Eng: Gordon Parry (London)
MAHLER: SYMPHONY NO. 2 IN C MINOR ("RESURRECTION") (Solti cond. London Symphony Chorus & Orch.; Harper, Watts) Eng: Gordon Parry (London)
MAHLER: SYMPHONY NO. 3 IN D MINOR (Leinsdorf cond. Boston Symphony) Eng: Edwin Begley (RCA Red Seal)
MAHLER: SYMPHONY NO. 8 IN E FLAT (Bernstein cond. London Symphony) Eng: Hellmuth Kolbe (Col)
RACHMANINOFF: SYMPHONY NO. 1 IN D (Ormandy cond. Philadelphia Orchestra) Eng: Edward T. Graham (Col)
WAGNER: TRISTAN & ISOLDE "LIVE" (Bohm cond. Bayreuth Festival Orchestra/Nilsson, Windgassen) Eng: Gunter Hermanns (DGG)

ALBUM COVER - PHOTOGRAPHY (G-399)

(Awards to Art Director and Photographer)

BOB DYLAN'S GREATEST HITS (Bob Dylan) Art Dirs: John Berg and Bob Cato - Photog: Roland Scherman (Col)
BRAVO, BRAVO, AZNAVOUR (Charles Aznavour) Art Dir. & Photog: Ken Kim (Monument)
THE DOORS (The doors) Art Dir: Bill Harvey - Photogs: Guy Webster, Joel Brodsky (Elektra)
EARTHWORDS & MUSIC (John Harford) Art Dir: Robert Jones - Photog: New World Photography (RCA)
FROM MEXICO WITH LAUGHS (Don Bowman) Art Dir: Robert Jones - Photog: Howard Cooper (RCA)
SUBURBAN ATTITUDES IN COUNTRY VERSE (John Loudermilk) Art Dir: Bob Jones - Photog: Jimmy Moore(RCA)
THAT MAN, ROBERT MITCHUM, SINGS - Art Dir. & Photog: Ken Kim (Monument)

ALBUM COVER - GRAPHIC ARTS (G-400)

(Awards to Art Director and Graphic Artist)

THE GOLD STANDARD COLLECTION (Hank Thompson) Art Dir: Ed Thrasher - Graphic: Charles White (WB-7)
HAYDN: SYM. NO. 84 IN E FLAT MAJOR: SYM. NO. 85 IN B FLAT MAJOR "LA REINE" (Bernstein cond. New York Philharmonic) Art Dirs: John Berg and Bob Cato - Graphic: Henrietta Condak (Col)
MONK/STRAIGHT, NO CHASER (Thelonious Monk) Art Dirs: John Berg and Bob Cato - Graphic: Laslo Kubinyi (Col)
NASHVILLE CATS (Homer & Jethro) Art Dir: Robert Jones - Graphic: Jack Davis (RCA)
SGT. PEPPER'S LONELY HEARTS CLUB BAND (The Beatles) Art Dirs: Peter Blake & Jann Haworth (Cap)
UP, UP AND AWAY (5th Dimension) Art Dir: Woody Woodward - Graphic: Wayne Kimball (Soul City)

ALBUM NOTES (G-401)

(Annotator's Award)

THE EARTH (Rod McKuen, Music by Anita Kerr) Ann: Rod McKuen (WB)
EXTRA SPECIAL (Peggy Lee) Ann: Rory Guy (Cap)
THE FAR EAST SUITE (Duke Ellington) Ann: Stanley Dance (RCA)
FRANCIS ALBERT SINATRA/ANTONIO CARLOS JOBIM - Ann: Stan Cornyn (Reprise)
LISTEN! (Gary Lewis & the Playboys) Ann: Richard Oliver (Lib)
SUBURBAN ATTITUDES IN COUNTRY VERSE (John Loudermilk) Ann: John D. Loudermilk (RCA)

ALBUM OF THE YEAR - CLASSICAL (G-402)

(Awards to the Artist and A&R Producer)

BERG: WOZZECK - Pierre Boulez Cond. Orch. & Chorus of Paris National Opera (Solos: Berry, Strauss, Uhl, Doench) - A&R: Thomas Shepard (Col)
HOROWITZ IN CONCERT - Vladimir Horowitz - A&R: Thomas Frost (Col)
MAHLER: DAS LIED VON DER ERDE - Leonard Bernstein cond. Vienna Philharmonic (James King and Dietrich Fischer-Dieskau) - A&R: John Culshaw (London)
MAHLER: SYMPHONY NO. 8 IN E FLAT MAJOR ("SYMPHONY OF A THOUSAND") - Leonard Bernstein cond. London Symphony with soloists and choruses - A&R: John McClure (Col)
PUCCINI: LA RONDINE Francesco Molinari-Pradelli cond. RCA Italiana

Opera Orch. & Chorus (Soloists: Moffo, Barioni, Sereni, Sciutti, De Palma) - A&R: Richard Mohr (RCA)
THE WORLD OF CHARLES IVES - Robert Browning Overture - Leopold Stokowski cond. American Symphony/Washington's Birthday - Leonard Bernstein cond. New York Philharmonic - A&R: John McClure, Thomas Frost (Col)

CLASSICAL PERFORMANCE - ORCHESTRA (G-403)

(Conductor's Award)
HOLST: THE PLANETS - Sir Adrian Boult cond. New Philharmonia Orch. (Angel)
IVES: ORCHESTRAL SET NO. 2/ROBERT BROWNING OVERTURE/ PUTNAM'S CAMP - Morton Gould cond. Chicago Symphony (RCA)
MAHLER: DAS LIED VON DER ERDE - Leonard Bernstein cond. Vienna Philharmonic (with James King & Dietrich Fischer-Dieskau) (London)
MAHLER: SYMPHONY NO. 2 IN C MINOR ("RESURRECTION") - Georg Solti cond. London Symphony (London)
SHOSTAKOVICH: SYMPHONY NO. 10 IN E MINOR - Herbert von Karajan cond. Berlin Philharmonic (DGG)
STRAVINSKY: FIREBIRD & PETROUCHKA SUITES - Igor Stravinsky cond. Columbia Symphony (Col)

CHAMBER MUSIC PERFORMANCE (G-404)

BEETHOVEN: QUARTET NO. 15 IN A MINOR, OP. 132 - Yale Quartet (Vanguard)
BRAHMS: QUINTET IN F MINOR FOR PIANO, OP. 34 - Artur Rubinstein & Guarneri Quartet (RCA)
BRAHMS: (THE) TRIOS FOR PIANO, VIOLIN & CELLO (Nos. 1, 2, & 3) - Eugene Istomin, Isaac Stern, Leonard Rose (Col)
THE GLORIOUS SOUND OF BRASS - Philadelphia Brass Ensemble (Col)
IVES: QUARTETS NOS.1 & 3 - Juilliard Quartet (Col)
WEST MEETS EAST - Ravi Shankar and Yehudi Menuhin (Angel)

CLASSICAL PERFORMANCE - INSTRUMENTAL SOLOIST(S) (WITH OR WITHOUT ORCHESTRA) (G-405)

CHOPIN: NOCTURNES - Artur Rubinstein (RCA)
GRANADOS: GOYESCAS Complete/ESCENAS ROMANTICAS - Alicia de Larrocha (Epic)
HOROWITZ IN CONCERT - Vladimir Horowitz (Col)
IVES: SONATA NO. 1 FOR PIANO - William Masselos (RCA)
SEGOVIA ON STAGE - Andres Segovia (Decca)
20TH CENTURY GUITAR (Works by Brindle, Britten, Villa-Lobos, Martin, Henze) Julian Bream (RCA)

OPERA RECORDING (G-406)

(Awards to the Artist and A&R Producer)
BERG: WOZZECK - Pierre Boulez cond. orch. & Chorus of Paris National Opera (Soloists: Berry, Strauss, Uhl, Doench) A&R: Thomas Shepard (Col)
HANDEL: JULIUS CAESAR - Julius Rudel cond. New York City Opera Chorus & Orch. (Soloists: Treigle, Sills, Forrester, Wolff) A&R: Peter Dellheim (RCA) PUCCINI: LA RONDINE - Francesco Molinari-Pradelli cond. RCA Italiana Opera Orch. & Chorus (Soloists: Moffo, Barioni, Sereni Sciutti, De Palma) A&R: Richard Mohr (RCA)
PUCCINI: MADAME BUTTERFLY - Sir John Barbirolli cond. Rome Opera Orch. & Chorus (Soloists: Scotto, Bergonzi) A&R: Kinloch Anderson (Angel)
VERDI: FALSTAFF - Leonard Bernstein cond. Vienna Philharmonic Orch. & Chorus (Soloists: Fischer-Dieskau, Ligabue, Sciutti, Resnik) A&R: Erik Smith (Col)
WAGNER: DIE WALKURE - Herbert von Karajan cond. Berlin Philharmonic (Soloists: Crespin, Janowitz, Veasey, Vickers, Stewart, Talvela) A&R: Otto Gerdes (DGG)
WAGNER: TRISTAN & ISOLDE "LIVE" - Karl Bohm cond. Bayreuth Festival Chorus & Orch. (Soloists: Nilsson, Windgassen, Ludwig, Talvela, Wachter) A&R: Otto Gerdes, Hans Hirsch (DGG)

CLASSICAL CHORAL PERFORMANCE - OTHER THAN OPERA (G-407)

(Awards to Choral and Orchestra Conductors)
THE CHORAL MUSIC OF ARNOLD SCHOENBERG - Gregg Smith Singers (Everest)
COPLAND: IN THE BEGINNING, LARK, LAS AGACHADAS - Aaron Copland cond. New England Conservatory Chorus (CBS)
HANDEL: MESSIAH - John McCarthy cond. Ambrosian Singers - Charles Mackerras cond. English Chamber Orch. (Angel)
HAYDN: THE SEASON - Karl Bohm cond. Vienna Singverein & Vienna Symphony (DGG)
MAHLER: SYMPHONY NO. 8 IN E FLAT MAJOR ("SYMPHONY OF A THOUSAND") - Leonard Bernstein cond. London Symphony Chorus & Orch. Soloists & Chorus (Col)
ORFF: CATULLI CARMINA - Robert Page cond. Temple Univ. Chorus - Eugene Ormandy cond. Philadelphia Orch. (Col)
PENDERECKI: PASSION ACCORDING TO ST. LUKE - Janusz Przybylski & Jozef Suwara, cond. Boys Chorus of Cracow; Henryk Czyz cond. Cracow Philharmonic (Philips)

CLASSICAL PERFORMANCE - VOCAL SOLOIST - (G-408)

AN ELISABETH SCHWARZKOPF SONGBOOK - Elisabeth Schwarzkopf (Gerald Moore, Pianist) (Angel)
BEETHOVEN: SONGS - Dietrich Fischer-Dieskau (Jorg Demus, Pianist) (DGG)
COPLAND: 12 POEMS OF EMILY DICKENSON - Adele Addison (Aaron Copland, Pianist) (CBS)
PRIMA DONNA, VOLUME 2 - Leontyne Price (Molinari-Pradelli cond. RCA Italiana Opera Orch.) (RCA)
SCHUBERT: DIE SCHOENE MUELLERIN - Fritz Wunderlich (Hubert Giesen, Pianist) (DGG)
SCHUBERT: DIE WINTERREISE - Peter Pears (Benjamin Britten, Pianist) (London)
SHEPHERD ON THE ROCK & OTHER SONGS - Christa Ludwig (with Instrumental Ensemble) (Angel)
VICTORIA DE LOS ANGELES SINGS DEBUSSY AND RAVEL AND OTHER FRENCH SONGS - Victoria de los Angeles (Gonzalo Soriano, Pianist) (Angel)

1968

RECORD OF THE YEAR (G-409)

(Awards to the Artist and A&R Producer)
HARPER VALLEY P.T.A. - Jeannie C. Riley - A&R: Shelby S. Singleton, Jr. (Plantation)
HEY JUDE - The Beatles - A&R: George Martin (Cap)
HONEY - Bobby Goldsboro - A&R: Bob Montgomery, Bobby Goldsboro (UA)
MRS. ROBINSON - Simon & Garfunkel - A&R: Paul Simon, Art Garfunkel, Roy Halee (Col)
WICHITA LINEMAN - Glen Campbell - A&R: Al de Lory (Cap)

ALBUM OF THE YEAR (G-410)

(Awards to the Artist and A&R Producer)
BOOKENDS - Simon & Garfunkel - A&R: Paul Simon, Art Garfunkel, Roy Halee (Col)
BY THE TIME I GET TO PHOENIX - Glen Campbell - A&R: Al de Lory (Cap)
FELICIANO! - Jose Feliciano - A&R: Rick Jarrard (RCA)
MAGICAL MYSTERY TOUR - The Beatles - A&R: George Martin (Cap)
A TRAMP SHINING - Richard Harris - A&R: Jim Webb (Dunhill)

SONG OF THE YEAR (G-411)

(Songwriter's Award)
HARPER VALLEY P.T.A. - Tom T. Hall (Plantation)
HONEY - Bobby Russell(UA)
HEY JUDE - John Lennon, Paul McCartney (Cap)

LITTLE GREEN APPLES - Bobby Russell (Col)
MRS. ROBINSON - Paul Simon (Col)

NEW ARTIST OF 1968 (G-412)
CREAM (Atco)
JOSE FELICIANO (RCA)
GARY PUCKETT & THE UNION GAP (Col)
JEANNIE C. RILEY (Plantation)
O.C. Smith (Col)

INSTRUMENTAL ARRANGEMENT (G-413)
(Arranger's Award)
BAROQUE-A-NOVA (Mason Williams) Arr: Al Capps (WB)
CLASSICAL GAS (Mason Williams) Arr: Mike Post (WB)
THE GOOD, THE BAD AND THE UGLY (Hugo Montenegro) Arr: Hugo Montenegro (RCA)
SCARBOROUGH FAIR (Wes Montgomery) Arr: Don Sebesky (A&M)
THE WINDMILLS OF YOUR MIND (Michel Legrand) Arr: Michel Legrand (UA)

ARRANGEMENT ACCOMPANYING VOCALIST(S) (G-414)
(Arranger's Award)
FOOL ON THE HILL (Sergio Mendes & Brasil '66) Arr: Dave Grusin (A&M)
LIGHT MY FIRE (Jose Feliciano) Arr: George Tipton (RCA)
MAC ARTHUR PARK (Richard Harris) Arr: Jim Webb (Dunhill)
WICHITA LINEMAN (Glen Campbell) Arr: Al de Lory (Cap)
YESTERDAY I HEARD THE RAIN (Tony Bennett) Arr: Torrie Zito (Col)

BEST ENGINEERED RECORDING (OTHER THAN CLASSICAL) (G-415)
(Engineer's Award)
DAKTARI (album) (Shelly Manne) Eng: Dave Wiechman (Atl)
THE GOOD, THE BAD AND THE UGLY (album) (Hugo Montenegro) Eng: Richard Bogert (RCA)
MAN OF LA MANCHA (London Orig. Cast) (album) Engs: Jerry Boys, Peter Vince (Decca)
ROTARY CONNECTION TRIP I (album) (Rotary Connection) Eng: Doug Brand (Concept)
WICHITA LINEMAN (single) (Glen Campbell) Engs: Joe Polito, Hugh Davies (Cap)

ALBUM COVER (G-416)
(Awards to the Art Director, Photographer and/or Graphic Artist)
IVES; HOLIDAYS SYMPHONY (Bernstein cond. New York Philharmonic) Art Dirs: John Berg and Bob Cato - Des: Ron Coro - Photog: Don Huntstein (CBS)
RHINOCEROS (Rhinoceros) Art Dir: William S. Harvey - Graphic: Gene Szafran (Elektra)
ROAD SONG (Wes Montgomery) Art Dir: Sam Antupit - Photog: Pete Turner (A&M)
UNDERGROUND (Thelonius Monk) Art Dirs: John Berg, Richard Mantel - Photog: Horn/Griner Studio (Col)
WOW (Moby Grape) Art Dir. & Graphic: Bob Cato (Col)

ALBUM NOTES (G-417)
(Annotator's Award)
ANTHOLOGY OF INDIAN MUSIC, VOLUME ONE (Ravi Shankar, Ali Akbar Khan, Balachander) Ann: Richard Oliver (World Pacific)
ETHEL WATERS ON STAGE & SCREEN 1925-40 - Ann: Miles Kreuger (Col)
FRANCIS A. & EDWARD K. (Francis Albert Sinatra, Edward Kennedy Ellington) Ann: Stan Cornyn (Reprise)
JOHNNY CASH AT FOLSOM PRISON (Johnny Cash) Ann: Johnny Cash (Col)

PETE SEEGER'S GREATEST HITS (Pete Seeger) Ann: Pete Seeger (Col)

CONTEMPORARY - POP VOCAL - FEMALE (G-418)
ANGEL OF THE MORNING (single) Merrilee Rush (Bell)
DO YOU KNOW THE WAY TO SAN JOSE (single) Dionne Warwicke (Scepter)
FUNNY GIRL (album) Barbra Streisand (Col)
I SAY A LITTLE PRAYER (single) Aretha Franklin (Atlantic)
THOSE WERE THE DAYS (single) Mary Hopkin (Cap)

CONTEMPORARY - POP VOCAL - MALE (G-419)
HONEY (single) Bobby Goldsboro (UA)
LIGHT MY FIRE (single) Jose Feliciano (RCA)
LITTLE GREEN APPLES (single) O.C. Smith (CBS)
MAC ARTHUR PARK (single) Richard Harris (Dunhill)
WICHITA LINEMAN (single) Glen Campbell (Cap)

CONTEMPORARY - POP VOCAL - DUO OR GROUP (G-420)
CHILD IS FATHER TO THE MAN - Blood, Sweat & Tears (Col)
FOOL ON THE HILL - Sergio Mendes & Brasil '66 (A&M)
GOIN' OUT OF MY HEAD/CAN'T TAKE MY EYES OFF YOU (medley) The Lettermen (Cap)
HEY JUDE - The Beatles (Cap)
MRS. ROBINSON - Simon & Garfunkel (Col)
WOMAN, WOMAN (album) Gary Puckett & the Union Gap (Col)

CONTEMPORARY - POP - CHORUS (G-421)
ANGEL OF THE MORNING - Percy Faith Chorus and Orchestra (Col)
HONEY - Ray Conniff & the Singers (Col)
MAC ARTHUR PARK - Ray Charles Singers (Command)
MISSION IMPOSSIBLE/NORWEGIAN WOOD (medley) Alan Copeland Singers (ABC)
THIS GUY'S IN LOVE WITH YOU - Johnny Mann Singers (Lib)

CONTEMPORARY - POP - INSTRUMENTAL (G-422)
CLASSICAL GAS - Mason Williams (WB)
ELEANOR RIGBY - Wes Montgomery (A&M)
THE GOOD, THE BAD AND THE UGLY - Hugo Montenegro (RCA)
GRAZING IN THE GRASS - Hugh Masekela (Uni)
HERE, THERE AND EVERYWHERE - Jose Feliciano (RCA)

RHYTHM & BLUES VOCAL - FEMALE (G-423)
CHAIN OF FOOLS (single) Aretha Franklin (Atlantic)
HE CALLED ME BABY (single) Ella Washington (S.Stg7)
LOVE MAKES A WOMAN (single) Barbara Acklin (Brnswc)
PIECE OF MY HEART (single) Erma Franklin (Shout)
SECURITY (single) Etta James (Cadet)

RHYTHM & BLUES VOCAL - MALE (G-424)
(SITTIN' ON) THE DOCK OF THE BAY (single) Otis Redding (Volt)
FOR ONCE IN MY LIFE (single) Stevie Wonder (Tamla)
(YOU KEEP ME) HANGIN' ON (single) Joe Simon (Sd. Stge 7)
I HEARD IT THROUGH THE GRAPEVINE (single) Marvin Gaye (Tamla)
WHO'S MAKING LOVE (single) Johnnie Taylor (Stax)

RHYTHM & BLUES - DUO OR GROUP - VOCAL OR INSTRUMENTAL (G-425)
CLOUD NINE - The Temptations (Gordy)
I THANK YOU - Sam & Dave (Stax)
PICKIN' WILD MOUNTAIN BERRIES - Peggy Scott and Jo Jo Benson (Plantation)
SWEET INSPIRATION - The Sweet Inspiration (Atlantic)
TIGHTEN UP - Archie Bell & The Drells (Atlantic)

RHYTHM & BLUES SONG (G-426)

(Songwriter's Award)

CHAIN OF FOOLS - Don Covay (Atlantic)

(SITTIN' ON) THE DOCK OF THE BAY - Otis Redding and Steve Cropper (Volt)

I WISH IT WOULD RAIN - Norman Whitfield, Barrett Strong, Roger Penzabene (Gordy)

PICKIN' WILD MOUNTAIN BERRIES - Edward Thomas, Bob McRee, Clifton Thomas (Plantation)

WHO'S MAKING LOVE - Homer Banks, Bettye Crutcher, Raymond Jackson, Donald Davis (Stax)

COUNTRY VOCAL - FEMALE (G-427)

BIG GIRLS DON'T CRY (single) Lynn Anderson (Chart)

COUNTRY GIRL (single) Dottie West (RCA)

D-I-V-O-R-C-E (single) Tammy Wynette (Epic)

HARPER VALLEY P.T.A. (single) Jeannie C. Riley (Plantation)

MY SON (single) Jan Howard (Decca)

COUNTRY VOCAL - MALE (G-428)

THE CARROLL COUNTY ACCIDENT (single) Porter Wagoner (RCA)

FOLSOM PRISON BLUES (single) Johnny Cash (Col)

I WANNA LIVE (single) Glen Campbell (Cap)

LITTLE GREEN APPLES (single) Roger Miller (Smash)

SKIP A ROPE (single) Henson Cargill (Monument)

COUNTRY - DUO OR GROUP - VOCAL OR INSTRUMENTAL (G-429)

FOGGY MOUNTAIN BREAKDOWN - Flatt & Scruggs (Col)

IT'S MY TIME - The Everly Brothers (WB)

THE LOVERS - Bill Wilbourne and Kathy Morrison (UA)

MOUNTAIN DEW - Nashville Brass (RCA)

THROUGH THE EYES OF LOVE - Tompall & the Glaser Bros. (MGM)

COUNTRY SONG (G-430)

(Songwriter's Award)

D-I-V-O-R-C-E - Curly Putman and Bobby Braddock (Col)

HARPER VALLEY P.T.A. - Tom T. Hall (Plantation)

HONEY - Bobby Russell (Verve)

LITTLE GREEN APPLES - Bobby Russell (Smash)

SKIP A ROPE - Glenn Tubb, Jack Moran (Monument)

SACRED PERFORMANCE (G-431)

BEAUTIFUL ISLE OF SOMEWHERE - Jake Hess (RCA)

HOW GREAT THOU ART - Anita Bryant (Col)

I'LL FLY AWAY - Jim Bohi (Word)

102 STRINGS, VOL. 2 - Ralph Carmichael (Word)

WHISPERING HOPE - George Beverly Shea (RCA)

YOU'LL NEVER WALK ALONE (album) Elvis Presley (RCA)

GOSPEL PERFORMANCE (G-432)

THE FLORIDA BOYS SING KINDA COUNTRY - Florida Boys Quartet (Word)

FOR GOODNESS SAKE - Thrasher Bros. (Anchor)

A GREAT DAY - Oak Ridge Boys (Hrtwrmg)

THE HAPPY GOSPEL OF THE HAPPY GOODMANS - Happy Goodman Family (Word)

YOURS FAITHFULLY - Blackwood Bros. Quartet (RCA)

SOUL GOSPEL PERFORMANCE (G-433)

BREAD OF HEAVEN, Parts 1 & 2 - James Cleveland & Angelic Choir (Savoy)

LONG WALK TO D.C. - Staple Singers (Stax)

ONLY BELIEVE - Swan Silvertones (Scepter)

THE SOUL OF ME - Dottie Rambo (Hrtwrmg)

WAIT A LITTLE LONGER - Davis Sisters (Savoy)

WILLA DORSEY: THE WORLD'S MOST EXCITING GOSPEL SINGER - Willa Dorsey (Word)

FOLK PERFORMANCE (G-434)

BOTH SIDES NOW - Judy Collins (Elektra)

DID SHE MENTION MY NAME - Gordon Lightfoot (UA)

THE HANGMAN'S BEAUTIFUL DAUGHTER - The Incredible String Band (Elektra)

JOHN WESLEY HARDING - Bob Dylan (Col)

LATE AGAIN - Peter, Paul & Mary (WB-7)

THE UNICORN - Irish Rovers (Decca)

INSTRUMENTAL THEME (G-435)

(Composer's Award)

CLASSICAL GAS - Mason Williams (WB)

THE GOOD, THE BAD AND THE UGLY - Hugo Montenegro, Ennio Morricone (RCA)

THE ODD COUPLE - Neal Hefti (Dot)

ROSEMARY'S BABY - Christopher Komeda (Dot)

THEME FROM "THE FOX" - Lalo Schifrin (WB-7)

ORIGINAL SCORE - MOTION PICTURE OR TV SPECIAL (G-436)

(Composer's Award)

BONNIE AND CLYDE - Charles Strouse (WB-7)

THE FOX - Lalo Schifrin (WB-7)

THE GRADUATE - Paul Simon, Dave Grusin (Col)

THE ODD COUPLE - Neal Hefti (Dot)

VALLEY OF THE DOLLS - Andre Previn (20th)

SCORE FROM AN ORIGINAL CAST SHOW ALBUM (G-437)

(Awards to the Composer and A&R Producer)

GEORGE M! - George M. Cohan - A&R: Thomas Shepard (Col)

HAIR - Gerome Ragni, James Rado, Galt MacDermott - A&R: Andy Wiswell (RCA)

THE HAPPY TIME - Fred Ebb. John Kander - A&R: George R. Marek, Andy Wiswell (RCA)

JACQUES BREL IS ALIVE AND WELL AND LIVING IN PARIS - Jacques Brel - A&R: Ed Kleban (Col)

YOUR OWN THING - Hal Hester, Danny Apolinar - A&R: George R. Marek, Andy Wiswell (RCA)

COMEDY RECORDING (G-438)

W.C. FIELDS ORIGINAL VOICE TRACKS FROM GREAT MOVIES - Produced by Gil Rodin (Decca)

FLIP WILSON, YOU DEVIL YOU - Flip Wilson (Atlantic)

HELLO DUMMY! Don Rickles (WB-7)

ROWAN & MARTIN LAUGH-IN - Dan Rowan and Dick Martin (Epic)

TO RUSSELL, MY BROTHER, WHOM I SLEPT WITH - Bill Cosby (WB-7)

SPOKEN WORD RECORDING (G-439)

THE CANTERBURY PILGRIMS - Martin Starkie (DGG)

I HAVE A DREAM - Rev. Martin Luther King, Jr. (20)

KENNEDY-NIXON: THE GREAT DEBATES, 1960 - Produced by Joel Heller (Col)

LONESOME CITIES (album) Rod McKuen (WB-7)

MURDER IN THE CATHEDRAL - Paul Scofield (Caedmon)

JAZZ - SMALL GROUP OR SOLOIST WITH SMALL GROUP (G-440)

BILL EVANS AT THE MONTREUX JAZZ FESTIVAL - Bill Evans Trio (Verve)

COMPADRES - Dave Brubeck, Gerry Mulligan (Col)

THE ELECTRIFYING. . .EDDIE HARRIS - Eddie Harris (Atl)

GARY BURTON QUARTET IN CONCERT - Gary Burton (RCA)

JAZZ FOR A SUNDAY AFTERNOON, VOL. 1 - Produced by Sonny Lester (Various) (Solid St.)

MILES IN THE SKY - Miles Davis, Herbie Hancock (Col)

JAZZ - LARGE GROUP OR SOLOIST WITH LARGE GROUP (G-441)

AND HIS MOTHER CALLED HIM BILL-Duke Ellington (RCA)
CONCERTO FOR HERD - Woody Herman (Verve)
DOWN HERE ON THE GROUND - Wes Montgomery (A&M)
ELECTRIC BATH - Don Ellis (Col)
MERCY,MERCY - Buddy Rich (World Pac.)
UP IN ERROLL'S ROOM - Erroll Garner (Verve)

CLASSICAL PERFORMANCE - ORCHESTRA (G-442)

(Conductor's Award)
BACH: FOUR SUITES FOR ORCHESTRA - Nikolaus Harnoncourt cond. Concentus Musicus of Vienna (Telef)
BOULEZ CONDUCTS DEBUSSY - Pierre Boulez cond. New Philharmonia Orch. (Col)
MAHLER: SYMPHONY NO.6 IN A MINOR & SYMPHONY NO.9 IN D MAJOR - Leonard Bernstein cond. New York Philharmonic (Col)
MESSIAEN: TURANGALILA/TAKEMITSU: NOVEMBER STEPS - Seiji Ozawa cond. Toronto Symphony (RCA)
PROKOFIEFF: ROMEO & JULIET - Erich Leinsdorf cond. Boston Symphony (RCA)
RIMSKY-KORSAKOV: SCHEHERAZADE - Andre Previn cond. London Symphony (RCA)
STRAVINSKY: RITE OF SPRING - Seiji Ozawa cond. Chicago Symphony (RCA)

CHAMBER MUSIC PERFORMANCE (G-443)

BEETHOVEN: THE FIVE MIDDLE QUARTETS - Guarneri Quartet (RCA)
BEETHOVEN: TRIO NO. 3 IN C MINOR & MENDELSSOHN: TRIO NO. 1 IN D MINOR - Eugene Istomin, Isaac Stern, Leonard Rose (Col)
GABRIELI: CANZONI FOR BRASS, WINDS, STRINGS & ORGAN - E. Power Biggs with Edward Tarr Brass Ensemble & Gabrieli Consort, Vittorio Negri, cond. (Col)
HINDEMITH: SONATA FOR VIOLA & PIANO - Walter Trampler & Ronald Turini (RCA)
JULIAN BREAM AND HIS FRIENDS - Julian Bream & Cremona String Quartet (RCA)
MOZART: QUINTET K. 515/MENDELSSOHN: TRIO NO. 2 IN C MINOR - Jascha Heifetz, Gregor Piatigorsky, William Primrose, Leonard Pennario (RCA)
WORKS BY MOZART, BRAHMS, SCHUBERT, POULENC, HAIEFF, VILLA-LOBOS, COLGRASS - Boston Symphony Chamber Players (RCA)

OPERA RECORDING (G-444)

(Awards to Conductor and A&R Producer)
BERG: LULU - Karl Bohm cond. Orchestra of German Opera, Berlin (Soloists: Lear, Fischer-Dieskau) A&R: Dr. Hans Hirsch (DGG)
GINASTERA: BOMARZO - Julius Rudel cond. Opera Society of Washington (Soloists: Novoa, Turner, Penagos, Simon) A&R: Thomas Shepard (Col)
MOZART: COSI FAN TUTTE - Erich Leinsdorf cond. New Philharmonia Orch. & Ambrosian Opera Chorus (Soloists: Price, Troyanos, Raskin, Milnes, Shirley, Flagello) A&R: Richard Mohr (RCA)
STRAUSS: ELEKTRA - Georg Solti cond. Vienna Philharmonic (Soloists: Nilsson, Resnik, Collier, Krause, Stolze) A&R: John Culshaw (London)
WAGNER: DAS RHEINGOLD - Herbert von Karajan cond. Berlin Philharmonic (Soloists: Fischer-Dieskau, Stolze, Mitalvela, Veasey, Grobe, Keleman, Dominguez) A&R: Otto Gerdes (DGG)

INSTRUMENTAL SOLOIST(S) - CLASSICAL (G-445)

BERG: CONCERTO FOR VIOLIN & ORCHESTRA - Arthur Grumiaux (Markevitch cond. Concertgebouw Orch.) (Philips)
BUSONI: CONCERTO FOR PIANO WITH MALE CHORUS - John Ogdon (Daniell Revenaugh cond. Royal Philharmonic) (Angel)
CARTER: CONCERTO FOR PIANO - Jacob Lateiner (Leinsdorf cond. Boston Symphony) (RCA)
DANCES OF DOWLAND - Julian Bream (RCA)
HOROWITZ ON TELEVISION - Vladimir Horowitz (Col)
RACHMANINOFF: CONCERTO NO. 3 IN D MINOR FOR PIANO & OR-

CHESTRA - Alexis Weissenberg (Pretre cond. Chicago Symphony) (RCA)
SCHUMANN: CONCERTO IN A MINOR FOR PIANO & ORCHESTRA - Artur Rubinstein (Giulini cond. Chicago Symphony) (RCA)

CHORAL PERFORMANCE - OTHER THAN OPERA (G-446)

(Awards to Choral and Orchestra Conductors)
BERLIOZ: REQUIEM - Charles Munch cond. Bavarian Radio Chorus & Symphony (DGG)
THE GLORY OF GABRIELI - Vittorio Negri cond./Gregg Smith Singers/Texas Boys Choir, George Bragg, Dir./Edward Tarr Ensemble (with E. Power Biggs) (Col)
HANDEL: SOLOMON - Stephen Simon cond. Vienna Jeunesse Chorus & Vienna Volksoper Orch (with Shirley-Quirk, Endich, Brooks, Young) (RCA)
HAYDN: THE CREATION - Abraham Kaplan cond. Camerata Singers/Leonard Bernstein cond. New York Philharmonic (Col)
MOZART: REQUIEM - Colin Davis cond. John Alldis Choir & B.B.C. Symphony (Philips)
ORFF: CARMINA BURANA - Eugen Jochum cond. Schoenberg Children's Chorus/Chorus & Orch. of German Opera, Berlin (DGG)
PFITZNER: VON DEUTSCHER SEELE - Joseph Keilberth cond. Bavarian Symphony Chorus and Orch. (DGG)
SHOSTAKOVICH: SYMPHONY NO. 2 IN C MAJOR & SYMPHONY NO. 3 IN E FLAT MAJOR - John McCarthy cond. Ambrosian Singers/Morton Gould cond. Royal Philharmonia (RCA)

CLASSICAL PERFORMANCE - VOCAL SOLOIST - (G-447)

MAHLER: KINDERTOTENLIEDER & SONGS OF A WAYFARER - Janet Baker (Barbirolli cond. Halle Orch.) (Angel)
ROSSINI RARITIES - Montserrat Caballe (Cillario cond. RCA Italiana Opera Orch. & Chorus) (RCA)
SCHUMANN: SONGS - Dietrich Fischer-Dieskau (Jorg Demus, Pianist) (DGG)
SONGS OF POULENC - Gerard Souzay (Dalton Baldwin, Pianist) (RCA)
SONGS OF ANDALUCIA - Victoria de los Angeles (ARS Musicae Ensemble of Barcelona) (Angel)
VERRETT IN OPERA - Shirley Verrett (Pretre cond. RCA Italiana Opera Orch.) (RCA)

BEST ENGINEERED RECORDING - CLASSICAL (G-448)

(Engineer's Award)
BRITTEN: BILLY BUDD (Britten cond. London Symphony/Soloists: Glossop, Pears, Shirley-Quirk, Brannigan) Engs: Gordon Parry, Kenneth Wilkenson (London)
MAHLER: SYMPHONY NO. 9 IN D MAJOR - (Georg Solti cond. London Symphony) Eng: Gordon Parry (London)
MESSIAEN: TURANGALILA/TAKEMITSU: NOVEMBER STEPS (Ozawa cond. Toronto Symphony) Eng: Bernard Keville (RCA)
PROKOFIEFF: ROMEO & JULIET (Leinsdorf cond. Boston Symphony) Eng: Anthony Salvatore (RCA)
RACHMANINOFF: CONCERTO NO. 3 IN D MINOR FOR PIANO & ORCHESTRA (Weissenberg/Pretre cond. Chicago Symphony) Eng: Michael Moran (RCA)
STRAVINSKY: RITE OF SPRING (Ozawa cond. Chicago Symphony) Eng: Bernard Keville (RCA)
VERDI: ERNANI (Schippers cond. RCA Italiana Opera Orch. & Chorus) Eng: Anthony Salvatore (RCA)

1969

RECORD OF THE YEAR (G-449)

(Awards to the Artist and A&R Producer)
AQUARIUS/LET THE SUNSHINE IN - 5th Dimension - A&R: Bones Howe (Soul City)
A BOY NAMED SUE - Johnny Cash - A&R: Bob Johnston (Col)

IS THAT ALL THERE IS - Peggy Lee - A&R: Jerry Leiber, Mike Stoller (Cap)
LOVE THEME FROM ROMEO & JULIET - Henry Mancini - A&R: Joe Reisman (RCA)
SPINNING WHEEL - Blood, Sweat & Tears - A&R: James William Guercio (Col)

ALBUM OF THE YEAR (G-450)
(Awards to the Artist and A&R Producer)
ABBEY ROAD - The Beatles - A&R: George Martin (Apple)
THE AGE OF AQUARIUS - 5th Dimension - A&R: Bones Howe (Soul City)
BLOOD, SWEAT & TEARS - Blood, Sweat & Tears - A&R: James William Guercio (Col)
CROSBY, STILLS & NASH - Crosby, Stills & Nash - A&R: David Crosby, Stephen Stills, Graham Nash (Atl)
JOHNNY CASH AT SAN QUENTIN - Johnny Cash - A&R: Bob Johnston (Col)

SONG OF THE YEAR (G-451)
(Songwriter's Award)
GAMES PEOPLE PLAY - Joe South
I'LL NEVER FALL IN LOVE AGAIN - Burt Bacharach, Hal David
RAINDROPS KEEP FALLIN' ON MY HEAD - Burt Bacharach, Hal David
SPINNING WHEEL - David Clayton Thomas
A TIME FOR US (LOVE THEME FROM ROMEO & JULIET) - Larry Kusik, Eddie Snyder, Nino Rota

NEW ARTIST OF 1969 (G-452)
CHICAGO (Col)
CROSBY, STILLS & NASH (Atl)
LED ZEPPELIN (Atl)
OLIVER (Crewe)
NEON PHILHARMONIC (WB)

INSTRUMENTAL ARRANGEMENT (G-453)
(Arranger's Award)
LOVE THEME FROM ROMEO & JULIET (Mancini) Arr: Henry Mancini (RCA)
MIDNIGHT COWBOY (Ferrante & Teicher) Arrs: Arthur Ferrante, Lou Teicher (Lib)
WALKING IN SPACE (Quincy Jones) Arr: Quincy Jones (A&M)
VARIATIONS ON A THEME BY ERIC SATIE (Blood, Sweat & Tears) Arr: Dick Halligan (Col)

ARRANGEMENT ACCOMPANYING VOCALIST(S) (G-454)
(Arranger's Award)
AQUARIUS/LET THE SUNSHINE IN (5th Dimension) Arrs: Bill Holman, Bob Alcivar, Bones Howe (Soul City)
IS THAT ALL THERE IS (Peggy Lee) Arr: Randy Newman (Cap)
I'VE GOTTA BE ME (Tony Bennett) Arr: Torrie Zito (Col)
SPINNING WHEEL (Blood, Sweat & Tears) Arr: Fred Lipsius (Col)
YOU'VE MADE ME SO VERY HAPPY (Blood, Sweat & Tears) Arrs: Al Kooper, Fred Lipsius (Col)

BEST ENGINEERED RECORDING (OTHER THAN CLASSICAL) (G-455)
(Engineer's Award)
ABBEY ROAD (The Beatles) Engs: Geoff Emerick, Phillip McDonald (Apple)
THE AGE OF AQUARIUS (5th Dimension) Eng: Bones Howe (Soul City)
BLOOD, SWEAT & TEARS (Blood, Sweat & Tears) Eng: Roy Halee, Fred Catero (Col)
MOOG GROOVE (Electronic Concept Orch.) Engs: Bruce Swedien, Doug Brand, Hans Wurman, Chuck Lishon (Limelight)
VELVET VOICES & BOLD BRASS (Anita Kerr Singers) Engs: Lee Herschberg, Larry Cox, Chuck Britz (Para)

ALBUM COVER (G-456)
(Awards to the Art Director, Photographer and/or Graphic Artist)
AMERICA THE BEAUTIFUL (Gary McFarland) Painting: Evelyn J. Kelbish - Graphics: David Stahlberg (Skye)
BLIND FAITH (Blind Faith) Art Dir. & Photog: Bob Seideman (Atco)
LED ZEPPELIN II (Led Zeppelin) Art Work by David Juniper (Atl)
PIDGEON (Pidgeon) Art Dir: Tom Lazarus - Photog: Gene Brownell - Des: Bill Gordon (Decca)
RICHARD PRYOR (Richard Pryor) Art Dir: Gary Burden - Photog: Henry Diltz (Dove)

ALBUM NOTES (G-457)
(Annotator's Award)
CHICAGO MESS AROUND (Johnny Dodds) Ann: John Dodds, II (Milestone)
DAVID'S ALBUM (Joan Baez) Ann: Joan Baez (Vanguard)
JOHN HARTFORD (J. Hartford) Ann: John Hartford (RCA)
MABEL MERCER & BOBBY SHORT AT TOWN HALL - Ann: Rex Reed (Atl)
NASHVILLE SKYLINE (Bob Dylan) Ann: Johnny Cash (Col)

CONTEMPORARY VOCAL - FEMALE (G-458)
IS THAT ALL THERE IS (single) Peggy Lee (Cap)
JOHNNY ONE TIME (single) Brenda Lee (Decca)
PUT A LITTLE LOVE IN YOUR HEART (single) Jackie DeShannon (Lib-UA)
SON OF A PREACHER MAN (single) Dusty Springfield (Atl)
THIS GIRL'S IN LOVE WITH YOU (single) Dionne Warwicke (Scepter)
WITH PEN IN HAND (single) Vikki Carr (Lib)

CONTEMPORARY VOCAL - MALE (G-459)
EVERYBODY'S TALKIN' (track) Harry Nilsson (UA)
GAMES PEOPLE PLAY (single) Joe South (Cap)
GITARZAN (single) Ray Stevens (Monument)
MY WAY (single) Frank Sinatra (WB)
RAINDROPS KEEP FALLIN' ON MY HEAD (single) B.J. Thomas (Scepter)

CONTEMPORARY VOCAL - GROUP (G-460)
ABBEY ROAD - The Beatles (Apple)
BLOOD, SWEAT & TEARS - Blood, Sweat & Tears (Col)
AQUARIUS/LET THE SUNSHINE IN - 5th Dimension (SI Cty)
CROSBY, STILLS & NASH - Crosby, Stills & Nash (Atl)
MORNING GIRL - Neon Philharmonic (WB)

CONTEMPORARY - CHORUS (G-461)
ANGEL OF THE MORNING - Living Voices (RCA)
JEAN - Ray Conniff & the Singers (Col)
LOVE THEME FROM ROMEO & JULIET - Percy Faith Orch. & Chorus (Col)
MAC ARTHUR PARK - Brooks Arthur Ensemble (Verve)
SLICES OF LIFE - Ray Charles Singers (Command)

CONTEMPORARY INSTRUMENTAL (G-462)
AREA CODE 615 - Area Code 615 (Polydor)
LOVE THEME FROM ROMEO & JULIET - Henry Mancini (RCA)
MIDNIGHT COWBOY - Ferrante & Teicher (Lib-UA)
WITH LOVE - Boots Randolph (Monument)
VARIATIONS ON A THEME BY ERIC SATIE - Blood, Sweat & Tears (Col)

CONTEMPORARY SONG (G-463)
(Songwriter's Award)
GAMES PEOPLE PLAY - Joe South
IN THE GHETTO - Mac Davis
JEAN - Rod McKuen

RAINDROPS KEEP FALLIN' ON MY HEAD - Burt Bacharach, Hal David
SPINNING WHEEL - David Clayton Thomas

R&B VOCAL - FEMALE (G-464)
FOOLISH FOOL (single) Dee Dee Warwick (Merc)
THE HUNTER (album) Tina Turner (Blue Thumb)
SHARE YOUR LOVE WITH ME (single) Aretha Franklin (Atl)
YESTERDAY (single) Ruth Brown (Skye)
YOU GOTTA PAY THE PRICE (single) Gloria Taylor (Silver Fox)

R&B VOCAL - MALE (G-465)
DOING HIS THING (single) Ray Charles (Tang)
THE CHOKIN' KIND (single) Joe Simon (Sd. Stg.)
ICE MAN COMETH (album) Jerry Butler (Merc)
LIVE & WELL (album) B.B. King (ABC)
YOUR GOOD THING (IS ABOUT TO END) (single) Lou Rawls (Cap)

R&B VOCAL - DUO OR GROUP (G-466)
BACKFIELD IN MOTION - Mel & Tim (Scepter)
FRIENDSHIP TRAIN - Gladys Knight & The Pips (Mtn)
IT'S YOUR THING - The Isley Brothers (T-Neck)
COLOR HIM FATHER - The Winstons (Metromedia)
SOULSHAKE - Peggy Scott, Jo Jo Benson (SSS)

R&B INSTRUMENTAL (G-467)
A BLACK MAN'S SOUL - Ike Turner (Pompeii)
GAMES PEOPLE PLAY - King Curtis (Atco)
TRASH TALKIN' - Albert Collins (Imperial)
WHAT DOES IT TAKE - Walker & The All Stars (Soul)
WORKIN' ON A GROOVY THING - Richard "Groove" Holmes (World Pac.)

R&B SONG (G-468)
(Songwriter's Award)
BACKFIELD IN MOTION - Herbert McPherson, Melvin Harden
COLOR HIM FATHER - Richard Spencer
I'D RATHER BE AN OLD MAN'S SWEETHEART - Clarence Carter, George Jackson, Raymond Moore
IT'S YOUR THING - Rudolph Isley, O. Kelly Isley, Jr., Ronnie Isley
ONLY THE STRONG SURVIVE - Kenny Gamble, Leon Huff, Jerry Butler

SOUL GOSPEL (G-469)
CASSIETTA - Cassietta George (Audio Gosp.)
COME ON AND SEE ABOUT ME - James Cleveland and the Southern California Choir (Savoy)
GUIDE ME, O THOU GREAT JEHOVAH - Mahalia Jackson (Col)
PRECIOUS MEMORIES - Sister Rosetta Tharpe (Savoy)
OH HAPPY DAY - Edwin Hawkins Singers (Buddah)

COUNTRY VOCAL - FEMALE (G-470)
BACK SIDE OF DALLAS (single) Jeannie C. Riley (Plantation)
I FALL TO PIECES (single) Diana Trask (Par)
RIBBON OF DARKNESS (single) Connie Smith (RCA)
STAND BY YOUR MAN (album) Tammy Wynette (Epic)
THAT'S A NO NO (single) Lynn Anderson (Chart)

COUNTRY VOCAL - MALE (G-471)
ALL I HAVE TO OFFER YOU IS ME (single) Charley Pride (RCA)
ARE YOU FROM DIXIE (single) Jerry Reed (RCA)
A BOY NAMED SUE (single) Johnny Cash (Col)
FROM HEAVEN TO HEARTACHE (single) Bobby Lewis (UA)
SPRING (single) Clay Hart (Metromedia)

COUNTRY - DUO OR GROUP (G-472)
CALIFORNIA GIRL - Tompall & Glaser Bros. (MGM)
JUST SOMEONE I USED TO KNOW - Porter Wagoner & Dolly Parton (RCA)

MAC ARTHUR PARK - Waylon Jennings & The Kimberlys (RCA)
RINGS OF GOLD - Dottie West & Don Gibson (RCA)
WISH I DIDN'T HAVE TO MISS YOU - Jack Greene & Jeannie Seely (Decca)

COUNTRY INSTRUMENTAL (G-473)
THE HITS OF CHARLEY PRIDE - Tommy Allsup & The Nashville Survey (Metromedia)
LOVIN' SEASON - Floyd Cramer (RCA)
THE NASHVILLE BRASS FEATURING DANNY DAVIS PLAY MORE NASHVILLE SOUNDS - Danny Davis & The Nashville Brass (RCA)
NASHVILLE SKYLINE RAG - Bob Dylan (Col)
SOLID GOLD '69 - Chet Atkins (RCA)

COUNTRY SONG (G-474)
(Songwriter's Award)
ALL I HAVE TO OFFER YOU IS ME - Dallas Frazier, A.L. Owens
A BOY NAMED SUE - Shel Silverstein
STAND BY YOUR MAN - Tammy Wynette, Billy Sherrill
THE THINGS THAT MATTER - Don Sumner
YOU GAVE ME A MOUNTAIN - Marty Robbins

SACRED PERFORMANCE (G-475)
(Non-Classical)
AIN'T THAT BEAUTIFUL SINGING - Jake Hess (RCA)
HE TOUCHED ME - Bill Gaither Trio (Hrtwrmg)
HOLY, HOLY, HOLY - Tennessee Ernie Ford (Cap)
I BELIEVE - George Beverly Shea (RCA)
WHISPERING HOPE - Connie Smith & Nat Stuckey (RCA)

GOSPEL PERFORMANCE (G-476)
THE BEST IS YET TO COME - The LeFevres (Canaan)
IN GOSPEL COUNTRY - Porter Wagoner & the Blackwood Bros. (RCA)
IT'S HAPPENING - The Oak Ridge Boys (Hrtwrmg)
THIS HAPPY HOUSE - Happy Goodman Family (Word)
THIS IS MY VALLEY - The Singing Rambos (Hrtwrmg)

FOLK PERFORMANCE (G-477)
ANY DAY NOW - Joan Baez (Vanguard)
ATLANTIS - Donovan (Epic)
BIRD ON A WIRE - Judy Collins (Elektra)
CLOUDS - Joni Mitchell (WB)
DAY IS DONE - Peter, Paul & Mary (WB)
YOUNG VS. OLD - Pete Seeger (Col)

INSTRUMENTAL THEME (G-478)
(Composer's Award)
GROOVY GRUBWORM - Harlow Wilcox, Bobby Warren
MACKENNA'S GOLD - Quincy Jones
MEMPHIS UNDERGROUND - Herbie Mann
MIDNIGHT COWBOY - John Barry
QUENTIN'S THEME - Robert Cobert

ORIGINAL SCORE - MOTION PICTURE OR TV SPECIAL (G-479)
(Composer's Award)
BUTCH CASSIDY & THE SUNDANCE KID - Burt Bacharach (A&M)
THE LOST MAN - Quincy Jones (Uni)
MACKENNA'S GOLD - Quincy Jones (RCA)
ME, NATALIE - Henry Mancini (Col)
YELLOW SUBMARINE - John Lennon, Paul McCartney, George Harrison, George Martin (Cap)

SCORE FROM AN ORIGINAL CAST SHOW ALBUM (G-480)

(Awards to Composers and A&R Producer)

DAMES AT SEA - George Haimsohn, Robin Miller, Jim J. Wise - A&R: Thomas Shepard (Col)
OH! CALCUTTA! - Robert Dennis, Stanley Walden, Peter Schickle - A&R: Henry Jerome (Aidart)
PROMISES, PROMISES - Burt Bacharach, Hal David - A&R: Henry Jerome, Phil Ramone (Lib)
1776 - Sherman Edwards - A&R: Thomas Shepard (Col)
ZORBA - John Kander, Fred Ebb - A&R: Richard C. Jones (Cap)

RECORDING FOR CHILDREN (G-481)

CHITTY CHITTY BANG BANG - Do-Re-Mi Chorus (Kapp)
FOLK TALES OF THE TRIBES OF AFRICA - Eartha Kitt (Caedmon)
FOR ALL MY LITTLE FRIENDS - Tiny Tim (WB)
PETER, PAUL & MOMMY - Peter, Paul & Mary (WB)
YELLOW SUBMARINE - Richard Wolfe Children's Chorus (RCA)

COMEDY RECORDING (G-482)

BERKELEY CONCERT - Lenny Bruce (WB)
BILL COSBY - Bill Cosby (Uni)
DON RICKLES SPEAKS! - Don Rickles (WB)
LAUGH-IN '69 - Carolyn Raskin, Producer (WB)
W.C. FIELDS ON RADIO - Bruce Lundvall, A&R Producer (Col)

SPOKEN WORD RECORDING (G-483)

THE GREAT WHITE HOPE - James Earl Jones (Tetra.)
HOME TO THE SEA - Jesse Pearson, Narrator (WB)
MAN ON THE MOON - Walter Cronkite (WB)
ROBERT F. KENNEDY: A MEMORIAL - A&R: Thomas Shepard and Joel Heller (Col)
WE LOVE YOU, CALL COLLECT - Art Linkletter & Diane (Word/Cap)

JAZZ - SMALL GROUP OR SOLOIST WITH SMALL GROUP (G-484)

(7 or less)

THE 86 YEARS OF EUBIE BLAKE - Eubie Blake (Col)
THE GREAT OSCAR PETERSON ON PRESTIGE - Oscar Peterson (Prestige)
IN A SILENT WAY - Miles Davis (Col)
MEMPHIS UNDERGROUND - Herbie Mann (Atl)
VIOLIN SUMMIT - Stephane Grappelly, Stuff Smith, Sven Asmussen, Jean Luc-Ponty (Prestige)
WHAT'S NEW - Bill Evans, Jeremy Steig (Verve)
WILLOW WEEP FOR ME - Wes Montgomery (Verve)

JAZZ - LARGE GROUP OR SOLOIST WITH LARGE GROUP (G-485)

(8 or more)

AMERICA THE BEAUTIFUL - Gary McFarland (Skye)
BUDDY & SOUL - Buddy Rich Orch. (World Pac)
CENTRAL PARK NORTH - Thad Jones, Mel Lewis (SISt)
LIGHT MY FIRE - Woody Herman (Cadet)
THE NEW DON ELLIS BAND GOES UNDERGROUND - Don Ellis (Col)
THE MUSIC OF HOAGY CARMICHAEL - Bob Wilber (Monmouth)
STANDING OVATION - Count Basie (Para)
WALKING IN SPACE - Quincy Jones (A&M)

ALBUM OF THE YEAR - CLASSICAL (G-486)

(Awards to the Artist and A&R Producer)

BERIO: SINFONIA - Luciano Berio cond. New York Philharmonic & Swingle Singers - A&R: Thomas Z. Shepard (Col)
BOULEZ CONDUCTS BERG (THREE PIECES FOR ORCHESTRA/CHAMBER CONCERTO/ALTENBERG LIEDER) Pierre Boulez cond. BBC Symphony (Baremboim, Gawriloff, Lukomska) A&R: Thomas Z. Shepard (Col)
BOULEZ CONDUCTS DEBUSSY, VOL.2 "IMAGES POUR ORCHES-TRE" - Pierre Boulez cond. Cleveland Orch. - A&R: Thomas Z. Shepard (Col)
GABRIELI: ANTIPHONAL MUSIC OF GABRIELI (CANZONI FOR BRASS CHOIRS) - The Philadelphia, Cleveland and Chicago Brass Ensembles - A&R: Andrew Kazdin (Col)
STRAUSS: ALSO SPRACH ZARATHUSTRA - Zubin Mehta cond. Los Angeles Philharmonic - A&R: Raymond Minshull (London)
SWITCHED-ON BACH (Virtuoso Electronic Performance of BRANDENBURG CONCERTO NO. 3/AIR ON A G STRING/JESU, JOY OF MAN'S DESTINY, etc.) - performed on Moog Synthesizer - Walter Carlos - A&R: Rachel Elkind (Col)

CLASSICAL PERFORMANCE - ORCHESTRA (G-487)

(Conductor's Award)

BARTOK: MUSIC FOR STRINGS, PERCUSSION & CELESTA - Pierre Boulez cond. BBC Symphony (Col)
BOULEZ CONDUCTS DEBUSSY, VOL.2 "IMAGES POUR ORCHES-TRE" - Pierre Boulez cond. Cleveland Orchestra (Col)
RAVEL: RAPSODIE ESPAGNOLE/MOTHER GOOSE SUITE/ALBORADA DEL GRACIOSO/INTRODUCTION & ALLEGRO - Jean Martinon cond. Chicago Symphony (RCA)
STRAUSS: ALSO SPRACH ZARATHUSTRA - Zubin Mehta cond. Los Angeles Philharmonic (London)
WAGNER: GREAT ORCHESTRAL HIGHLIGHTS FROM "THE RING OF THE NIBELUNGS" - George Szell cond. Cleveland Orchestra (Col)

CHAMBER MUSIC PERFORMANCE (G-488)

BACH & VIVALDI SONATAS FOR LUTE & HARPSICHORD - Julian Bream, George Malcolm (RCA)
BEETHOVEN: TRIOS FOR STRINGS - Grumiaux Trio (Philips)
BRAHMS: QUARTETS FOR PIANO & STRINGS (3)/SCHUMANN: QUINTET IN E FLAT MAJOR FOR PIANO & STRINGS - Artur Rubinstein & Guarneri Quartet (RCA)
BRAHMS: SONATAS IN E MINOR & F MAJOR FOR CELLO AND PIANO - Jacqueline De Pre and Daniel Barenboim (Angel)
GABRIELI: ANTIPHONAL MUSIC OF GABRIELI (CANZONI FOR BRASS CHOIRS) - The Philadelphia, Cleveland and Chicago Brass Ensembles (Col)
PROKOFIEV: SONATAS FOR VIOLIN & PIANO - Itzhak Perlman, Vladimir Ashkenazy (RCA)
SHOSTAKOVICH: STRING QUARTETS (COMPLETE) Borodin Quartet (Seraphim)

CLASSICAL PERFORMANCE - INSTRUMENTAL SOLOIST(S) (WITH OR WITHOUT ORCHESTRA) (G-489)

BACH: SONATAS & PARTITAS FOR SOLO VIOLIN - Henryk Szeryng (DGG)
DVORAK: CONCERTO IN B MINOR FOR CELLO - Mstislav Rostropovich, Cello (Karajan cond. Berlin Philharmonic) (DGG)
GILELS AT CARNEGIE HALL - Emil Gilels (Melyd)
IVES: SONATA NO.2 "CONCORD MASS." - John Kirkpatrick (Col)
RAVEL: INTRODUCTION & ALLEGRO FOR HARP & STRINGS - Edward Druzinsky, Harp (Martinon cond. Chicago Symphony) (RCA)
SWITCHED-ON BACH - Walter Carlos, Moog Synthesizer (Col)

OPERA RECORDING (G-490)

(Awards to Conductor and A&R Producer)

CAVALLI: L'ORMINDO - Raymond Leppard cond. London Philharmonic (Soloists: Wakefield, van Bork, Howells, Berbie, Cuenod; Glyndebourne Festival Opera) A&R: Michael Bremner (Argo)
MOZART: THE MARRIAGE OF FIGARO - Karl Bohm cond. Chorus & Orch. of German Opera (Soloists: Prey, Mathis, Janowitz, Fischer-Dieskau) A&R: Gustav Rudolf Sellner (DGG)
STRAUSS: ARIADNE AUF NAXOS - Rudolf Kempe cond. Dresden State Opera (Soloists: Janowitz, King, Zylis-Gara, Geszty, Adam) A&R: R. Kinloch Anderson and Eberhard Geiler (Angel)
STRAUSS: SALOME - Erich Leinsdorf cond. London Symphony (Soloists: Caballe, Milnes, Lewis, Resnik, King) A&R: Richard Mohr (RCA)
VERDI: LA TRAVIATA - Lorin Maazel cond. Orch. & Chorus of Deutsche

Opera Berlin (Soloists: Lorengar, Aragall, Fischer-Dieskau) A&R: John Mordler (London)

VERDI: OTELLO - Sir John Barbirolli cond. New Philharmonia Orch. & Chorus (Soloists: McCracken, Fischer-Dieskau, Jones, Di Stasio) A&R: R. Kinloch Anderson (Angel)

WAGNER: SIEGFRIED - Herbert von Karajan cond. Berlin Philharmonic (Soloists: Thomas, Stewart, Stolze, Dernesch, Keleman, Dominguez, Gayer, Ridderbusch) A&R: Otto Gerdes (DGG)

CHORAL PERFORMANCE - OTHER THAN OPERA (G-491)

(Grammys to Conductor and Choral Director)

BACH: MASS IN B MINOR - Vienna Boys Choir & Chorus Viennensis - Hans Gillesberger, cond./Concentus Musicus - Nikolaus Harnoncourt, cond. (Telefunken)

BERIO: SINFONIA - Swingle Singers, Ward Swingle, Choral Master/New York Philharmonic, Luciano Berio, cond. (Col)

BERLIOZ: ROMEO ET JULIETTE - John Alldis Choir, London Symphony Orchestra & Chorus - Colin Davis, cond. (Philips)

BILLINGS: THE CONTINENTAL HARMONY - Gregg Smith Singers, Gregg Smith, cond. (Col)

DELIUS: SONGS OF SUNSET - Royal Liverpool Philharmonic Choir; Edmund Walters, cond. Royal Liverpool Philharmonic Orch.; Charles Groves cond. (Angel)

HENZE: THE RAFT OF THE FRIGATE "MEDUSA" Choirs of North German Radio/Berlin Radio/Boy's Chorus of St. Nicolai & North German Radio Symphony - Hans Werner Henze, cond. (DGG)

VAUGHAN WILLIAMS: SYMPHONY NO.1 (A SEA SYMPHONY) London Philharmonic Choir - Frederick Jackson, Choral Master/London Philharmonic - Adrian Boult, cond. (Angel)

CLASSICAL PERFORMANCE - VOCAL SOLOIST - (G-492)

BACH & HANDEL ARIAS (EXCERPTS FROM MAGNIFICAT, CHRISTMAS ORATORIO, ST. MATTHEW PASSION, MESSIAH, RODELINDA) - Marilyn Horne (Lewis cond. Vienna Cantata Orch.) (London)

BARBER: TWO SCENES FROM "ANTONY & CLEOPATRA"/KNOXVILLE: SUMMER OF 1915 - Leontyne Price (Schippers cond. New Philharmonia) (RCA)

BERG: ALTENBERG LIEDER - Halina Lukomska (Boulez cond. London Symphony in album "Boulez Conducts Berg") (Col)

BRAHMS: FOUR SERIOUS SONGS - Sherrill Milnes (From BRAHMS: REQUIEM recording by Erich Leinsdorf and Boston Symphony) (RCA)

BRITTEN: HOLY SONNETS OF DONNE, SONGS & PROVERBS OF BLAKE - Peter Pears, Dietrich Fischer-Dieskau (London)

MAHLER: DES KNABEN WUNDERHORN - Elisabeth Schwarzkopf & Dietrich Fischer-Dieskau (Szell cond. London Symphony) (Angel)

A MOST UNUSUAL SONG RECITAL (Beethoven, Rossini, Brahms, Reger, R. Strauss) Christa Ludwig, Walter Berry (Moore, Accom.) (Seraphim)

SCENES & ARIAS FROM FRENCH OPERA Beverly Sills (Mackerras cond. Royal Philharmonic) (Westminster)

STRAUSS (RICHARD): NINETEEN EARLY SONGS Dietrich Fischer-Dieskau (Gerald Moore, accomp.) (Angel)

BEST ENGINEERED RECORDING - CLASSICAL (G-493)

(Engineer's Award)

BERIO: SINFONIA (Berio cond. New York Philharmonic, Swingle Singers) Engs: Fred Plaut, Ed Michalski (Col)

BOULEZ CONDUCTS DEBUSSY, VOL.2 "IMAGES POUR ORCHESTRE" (Boulez cond. Cleveland Orchestra) Engs: Edward T. Graham, Arthur Kendy (Col)

GABRIELI: ANTIPHONAL MUSIC OF GABRIELI (CANZONI FOR BRASS CHOIRS) (Philadelphia, Cleveland & Chicago Brass Ensembles) Engs: Edward T. Graham, Milton Cherin (Col/Odyssey)

KHACHATURIAN: SYMPHONY NO.3/RIMSKY-KORSAKOV: RUSSIAN EASTER OVERTURE (Stokowski cond. Chicago Symphony) Eng: Paul Goodman (RCA)

MAHLER: SYMPHONY NO.1 (Ormandy cond. Philadelphia Symphony) Eng: Edwin Begley (RCA)

SWITCHED-ON BACH (Walter Carlos) Eng: Walter Carlos (Col)

1970

RECORD OF THE YEAR (G-494)

(Grammys to the Artist and A&R Producer)

BRIDGE OVER TROUBLED WATER - Simon & Garfunkel - A&R; Paul Simon, Art Garfunkel, Roy Halee (Col)

CLOSE TO YOU - Carpenters - A&R: Jack Daugherty (A&M)

EVERYTHING IS BEAUTIFUL - Ray Stevens - A&R: Ray Stevens (Barnaby)

FIRE AND RAIN - James Taylor - A&R: Peter Asher (WB)

LET IT BE - The Beatles - A&R: George Martin (Apple)

ALBUM OF THE YEAR (G-495)

(Grammys to the Artist and A&R Producer)

BRIDGE OVER TROUBLED WATER - Simon & Garfunkel - A&R: Paul Simon, Art Garfunkel, Roy Halee (Col)

CHICAGO - Chicago - A&R: James William Guercio (Col)

CLOSE TO YOU - Carpenters - A&R: Jack Daugherty (A&M)

DEJA VU - Crosby, Stills, Nash & Young - A&R: Crosby, Stills, Nash & Young (A&M)

ELTON JOHN - Elton John - A&R: Gus Dudgeon (Uni)

SWEET BABY JAMES - James Taylor - A&R: Peter Asher (WB)

SONG OF THE YEAR (G-496)

(Songwriter's Award)

BRIDGE OVER TROUBLED WATER - Paul Simon

EVERYTHING IS BEAUTIFUL - Ray Stevens

FIRE AND RAIN - James Taylor

LET IT BE - John Lennon, Paul McCartney

WE'VE ONLY JUST BEGUN - Roger Nichols, Paul Williams

NEW ARTIST OF THE YEAR (G-497)

CARPENTERS (A&M)

ELTON JOHN (Uni)

MELBA MOORE (Merc)

ANNE MURRAY (Cap)

THE PARTRIDGE FAMILY (Bell)

INSTRUMENTAL ARRANGEMENT (G-498)

(Arranger's Award)

BITCHES BREW (M. Davis) Arr: Miles Davis (Col)

GULA MATARI (Q. Jones) Arr: Quincy Jones (A&M)

THE MAGIC BUS ATE MY DONUT (Don Ellis) Arr: Fred Selden (Col)

OVERTURE FROM TOMMY (Assembled Multitude) Arr: Tom Sellers (Atl)

THEME FROM MEDICAL CENTER (Lalo Schifrin) Arr: Lalo Schifrin (MGM)

THEME FROM Z (Mancini) Arr: Henry Mancini (RCA)

ARRANGEMENT ACCOMPANYING VOCALIST(S) (G-499)

(Arranger's Award)

BRIDGE OVER TROUBLED WATER (Simon & Garfunkel) Arr: Paul Simon, Art Garfunkel, Jimmie Haskell, Ernie Freeman, Larry Knechtel (Col)

CLOSE TO YOU (Carpenters) Arr: Richard Carpenter (A&M)

EVERYTHING IS BEAUTIFUL - Ray Stevens, arr: (Barnaby)

LUCRETIA MAC EVIL (Blood, Sweat & Tears) arr: Dick Halligan (Col)

BEST ENGINEERED RECORDING (G-500)

(Engineer's Award)

BRIDGE OVER TROUBLED WATER (Simon & Garfunkel) Eng: Roy Halee (Col)

CLOSE TO YOU (Carpenters) Engs: Ray Gerhardt, Dick Bogert (A&M)

THE KAEMPFERT TOUCH (B. Kaempfert & Orch.) Eng: Peter Klemt (Decca)

TAP ROOT MANUSCRIPT (Neil Diamond) Eng: Armin Steiner (Uni)

TO OUR CHILDREN'S CHILDREN'S CHILDREN (The Moody Blues) Engs: Derek Varnals, Adrian Martins, Robin Thompson (Threshold)

ALBUM COVER (G-501)

(Awards to Art Director, Photographer and/or Graphic Artist)

CHICAGO (Chicago) Cover: John Berg - Cover Art: Nick Fasciano (Col)

HAND MADE (Mason Williams) Art Dir: Ed Thrasher - Design: Dave Bhang (WB)

INDIANOLA MISSISSIPPI SEEDS (B.B. King) - Design: Robert Lockart-Photog:Ivan Nagy (ABC)

MASON PROFFIT (Mason Profit) Photog: Peter Whorf - Designer: Martin Donald - Art Dir: Christopher Whorf (Happy Tiger)

THE NAKED CARMEN (Various) Art Dir: Desmond Strobel-Design: John Craig (Merc)

SCHUBERT "UNFINISHED" SYMPHONY - BEETHOVEN : FIFTH SYMPHONY (Philharmonic Symphony Orchestra of London, Rodzinski, cond.) Art Dir: Peter Whorf - Design: Christopher Whorf - Photog: Fred Poore (Westminster Gold)

UNCLE CHARLIE & HIS DOG TEDDY (Nitty Gritty Dirt Band) Art Dir: Woody Woodward - Photog: William E. McEuen - Album Design: Dean O. Torrence (UA) THE WORLD'S GREATEST BLUES SINGER (Bessie Smith) Art Dir: John Berg - Cover Art: Philip Hays - Album Design: Lloyd Ziff (Col)

ALBUM NOTES (G-502)

(Annotator's Award)

AS I SEE IT (Jack Moran) Ann: Billy Edd Wheeler (Athena)

BITCHES BREW (Miles Davis) Ann: Ralph J. Gleason (Col)

THE WORLD'S GREATEST BLUES SINGER (Bessie Smith) Ann: Chris Albertson (Col)

HOLD BACK THE WORLD (Alexander's Greyhound Brass) Ann: Rod McKuen (Stanyan)

I DO NOT PLAY NO ROCK 'N ROLL (Mississippi Fred McDowell) Ann: Anthony d'Oberoff (Cap)

JUDY. LONDON. 1969 (Judy Garland) Ann: Rex Reed (Juno)

SIXTEEN ALL TIME GREATEST HITS (Bill Monroe & Blue Grass Boys) Ann: James Goodfriend (Col)

THEY SHOOT HORSES, DON'T THEY? (John Green Orch.) Ann: Arthur Knight (ABC)

CONTEMPORARY VOCAL - FEMALE (G-503)

AIN'T NO MOUNTAIN HIGH ENOUGH (single) Diana Ross (Motown)

FANCY (album) Bobbie Gentry (Cap)

I'LL NEVER FALL IN LOVE AGAIN (album) Dionne Warwick (Scepter)

LONG LONG TIME (album) Linda Ronstadt (Cap)

SNOWBIRD (single) Anne Murray (Cap)

CONTEMPORARY VOCAL - MALE (G-504)

ELTON JOHN (album) Elton John (Uni)

EVERYTHING IS BEAUTIFUL (single) Ray Stevens (Barnaby)

MAD DOGS & ENGLISHMEN (album) Joe Cocker (A&M)

RAINY NIGHT IN GEORGIA (single) Brook Benton (Cotillion)

SWEET BABY JAMES (album) James Taylor (WB)

CONTEMPORARY VOCAL - DUO, GROUP OR CHORUS (G-505)

ABC - Jackson 5 (Motown)

BRIDGE OVER TROUBLED WATER - Simon & Garfunkel (Col)

CHICAGO - Chicago (Col)

CLOSE TO YOU - Carpenters (A&M)

LET IT BE - The Beatles (Apple)

CONTEMPORARY INSTRUMENTAL (G-506)

AIRPORT LOVE THEME - Vincent Bell (Decca)

OVERTURE FROM TOMMY- Assembled Multitude (Atl)

STAR SPANGLED BANNER - Jimi Hendrix (Cot)

SOUL FLOWER - Quincy Jones (UA)

THEME FROM Z AND OTHER FILM MUSIC - Henry Mancini (RCA)

CONTEMPORARY SONG (G-507)

(Songwriter's Award)

BRIDGE OVER TROUBLED WATER - Paul Simon

EVERYTHING IS BEAUTIFUL - Ray Stevens

FIRE AND RAIN - James Taylor

LET IT BE - John Lennon, Paul McCartney

WE'VE ONLY JUST BEGUN - Roger Nichols, Paul Williams

R&B VOCAL - FEMALE (G-508)

BLACK GOLD - Nina Simone (album) (RCA)

DON'T PLAY THAT SONG (single) Aretha Franklin (Atl)

SET ME FREE (single) Esther Phillips (Atl)

SHE DIDN'T KNOW (single) Dee Dee Warwick (Atco)

STAND BY YOUR MAN (single) Candi Staton (Fame)

R&B VOCAL - MALE (G-509)

ENGINE NO. 9 (single) Wilson Pickett (Atl)

PATCHES (single) Clarence Carter (Atl)

SIGNED, SEALED, DELIVERED (single) Stevie Wonder (Tamla)

THE THRILL IS GONE (single) B.B. King (ABC)

WAR (single) Edwin Starr (Gordy)

R&B - DUO OR GROUP - VOCAL OR INSTRUMENTAL (G-510)

DIDN'T I (BLOW YOUR MIND THIS TIME) The Delfonics (Philly Groove)

EXPRESS YOURSELF - Charles Wright & The Watts 103rd Street Rhythm Band (WB)

5-10-15-20 (25-30 YEARS OF LOVE) The Presidents (Buddah)

IT'S ALL IN THE GAME - Four Tops (Motown)

SOMEBODY'S BEEN SLEEPING IN MY BED - 100 Proof (Buddah)

RHYTHM & BLUES SONG (G-511)

(Songwriter's Award)

DIDN'T I (BLOW YOUR MIND THIS TIME) Thom Bell and William Hart (Phly Groove)

GROOVY SITUATION - Russell Lewis and Herman Davis (Merc)

PATCHES - Ronald Dunbar, General Johnson (Atl)

SIGNED, SEALED, DELIVERED - Stevie Wonder, Lee Garrett, Syreeta Wright, Lulu Hardaway (Tamla)

SOMEBODY'S BEEN SLEEPING IN MY BED Greg Perry, General Johnson, Angelo Bond (Buddah)

SOUL GOSPEL PERFORMANCE (G-512)

AMAZING GRACE - James Cleveland (Savoy)

CHRISTIAN PEOPLE - Andrae Crouch (Lib)

EVERY MAN WANTS TO BE FREE - Edwin Hawkins Singers (Buddah)

GOD GAVE ME A SONG - Myrna Summers (Cot)

HELLO SUNSHINE - Jessy Dixon (Savoy)

COUNTRY VOCAL - FEMALE (G-513)

(All nominations are singles)

MULE SKINNER BLUES - Dolly Parton (RCA)

ROSE GARDEN - Lynn Anderson (Col)

RUN WOMAN, RUN - Tammy Wynette (Epic)

THEN HE TOUCHED ME - Jean Shepard (Cap)

A WOMAN LIVES FOR LOVE - Wanda Jackson (Cap)

COUNTRY VOCAL - MALE (G-514)

AMOS MOSES - Jerry Reed (single) (RCA)

CHARLEY PRIDE'S 10TH ALBUM - Charley Pride (Col)

FOR THE GOOD TIMES - Ray Price (single) (Col)

OKIE FROM MUSKOGEE - Merle Haggard (album) (Cap)

SUNDAY MORNING COMING DOWN - Johnny Cash (single) (Col)

COUNTRY VOCAL - -DUO OR GROUP (G-515)

BED ROSES - Statler Brothers (Merc)
DADDY WAS AN OLD-TIME PREACHER MAN - Porter Waggoner & Dolly Parton (RCA)
IF I WERE A CARPENTER - Johnny Cash & June Carter (Col)
SUSPICIOUS MINDS - Waylon Jennings & Jessi Colter (RCA)
TENNESSEE BIRDWALK - Jack Blanchard & Misty Morgan (Wayside)

COUNTRY INSTRUMENTAL (G-516)

DRIVIN' HOME - Jerry Smith (Decca)
ME & JERRY - Chet Atkins, Jerry Reed (RCA)
STREET SINGER - Merle Haggard and the Stranger (Cap)
YESTERGROOVIN' - Chet Atkins (RCA)
YOU AIN'T HEARD NOTHIN' YET - Danny Davis & the Nashville Brass (RCA)

COUNTRY SONG (G-517)

(Songwriter's Award)
THE FIGHTIN' SIDE OF ME - Merle Haggard (Cap)
HELLO DARLIN' - Conway Twitty (Decca)
IS ANYBODY GOIN' TO SAN ANTONE - Glenn Martin & Dave Kirby (RCA)
MY WOMAN, MY WOMAN, MY WIFE - Marty Robbins (Col)
WONDER COULD I LIVE THERE ANYMORE - Bill Rice (RCA)

SACRED PERFORMANCE - MUSICAL (G-518)

THE CENTURION - Ralph Carmichael Orch & Chorus (Light)
EVERYTHING IS BEAUTIFUL - Jake Hess (RCA)
GOD OF OUR FATHERS - Richard Condie, cond. - Mormon Tabernacle Choir (Col)
RAPTURE - Pat Boone (Supreme)
THERE IS MORE TO LIFE - George Beverly Shea (RCA)

GOSPEL PERFORMANCE - OTHER THAN SOUL GOSPEL (G-519)

FANTASTIC THRASHERS AT FANTASTIC CAVERNS - Thrasher Brothers (Canaan)
THE LEFEVRES/MOVING UP - The LeFevres (Canaan)
THE MANY MOODS OF THE FLORIDA BOYS - The Florida Boys (Canaan)
TALK ABOUT THE GOOD TIMES - Wendy Bagwell & The Sunliters (Canaan)
TALK ABOUT THE GOOD TIMES - Oak Ridge Boys (Heartwarming)

ETHNIC OR TRADITIONAL RECORDING (INCLUDING TRADITIONAL BLUES) (G-520)

BLACK MUSIC OF SOUTH AMERICA - David Lewisohn (Nonesuch)
FOLK FIDDLING FROM SWEDEN - Bjorn Stabi and Ole Hjorth (Nonesuch)
GOOD FEELIN' - T-Bone Walker (Polydor)
I DO NOT PLAY NO ROCK N' ROLL - Mississippi Fred McDowell (Cap)
SAIL ON - Muddy Waters (Chess)
SHREE RAG - Ali Akbar Khan, accomp. by Shankar Ghosh, Tabla (Conn Soc)

INSTRUMENTAL COMPOSITION (G-521)

(Composer's Award)
AIRPORT LOVE THEME - Alfred Newman (Decca)
BITCHES BREW - Miles Davis (Col)
GULA MATARI - Quincy Jones (A&M)
LOVE THEME FROM SUNFLOWER - Henry Mancini (RCA)
THEME FROM MEDICAL CENTER - Lalo Schifrin (MGM)

ORIGINAL SCORE - MOTION PICTURE OR TV SPECIAL (G-522)

(Composer's Award)
AIRPORT - Alfred Newman (Decca)
DARLING LILI - Johnny Mercer, Henry Mancini (RCA)
LET IT BE - John Lennon, Paul McCartney, George Harrison, Ringo Starr (Apple)
M*A*S*H* - Johnny Mandel (Col)
THE STERILE CUCKOO - Fred Karlin (Para)

SCORE FROM AN ORIGINAL CAST SHOW ALBUM (G-523)

(Grammys to Composers and A&R Producer)
APPLAUSE - Charles Strouse, Lee Adams - A&R: Bob Arnold (ABC)
COCO - Alan Lerner, Andre Previn - A&R: Andy Wiswell (Para)
COMPANY - Stephen Sondheim, - A&R: Thomas Z. Shepard (Col)
JOY - Oscar Brown, Jr., Jean Pace, Sivuca - A&R: Ernie Altschuler (RCA)
PURLIE - Gary Geld, Peter Udell - A&R: Andy Wiswell (Ampex)

RECORDING FOR CHILDREN (G-524)

ARISTOCATS - Tutti Camarata, Musical Prod. (Camarata, Holloway, Harris, Lester, Mike Sammes Singers) (Disneyland)
A BOY NAMED CHARLIE BROWN (Soundtrack) A&R Prod. & Musical Dir: John Scott Trotter (Col)
RUBBER DUCKIE - Jim Henson (Col)
SESAME STREET (Sesame Street TV Cast) Children's TV Workshop, Joan Cooney, Producer (Col)
SUSAN SINGS SONGS FROM SESAME STREET - Loretta Long (Scepter)

COMEDY RECORDING (G-525)

THE BEGATTING OF THE PRESIDENT - Orson Welles (Mediarts)
DADDY PLAYED FIRST BASE - Homer & Jethro (RCA)
THE DEVIL MADE ME BUY THIS DRESS - Flip Wilson (Little David)
I AM THE PRESIDENT - David Frye (Elektra)
LIVE AT MADISON SQUARE GARDEN - Bill Cosby (Uni)

SPOKEN WORD RECORDING (G-526)

EVERETT DIRKSEN'S AMERICA - Everett Dirksen (Bell)
GROVER HENSON FEELS FORGOTTEN - Bill Cosby (Uni)
IN THE BEGINNING - Robert Cotterell, A&R Prod. (Apollo 8, 11, 12 Astronauts, Pres. Kennedy & Nixon) (Creative Sound)
POEMS AND BALLADS FROM 100-PLUS AMERICAN POETS - Paul Molloy, A&R Prod. (Ambrose, Dryden, Hecht, Molloy, Seeger) (Scholastic)
THE SOFT SEA - Jesse Pearson (WB)
WHY I OPPOSE THE WAR IN VIETNAM - Rev. Martin Luther King, Jr. (Black Forum)

JAZZ - SMALL GROUP OR SOLOIST WITH SMALL GROUP (G-527)

(7 or less)
ALONE - Bill Evans (MGM)
COLTRANE LEGACY - John Coltrane (Atl)
FAT ALBERT ROTUNDA - Herbie Hancock (WB)
FEELING IS BELIEVING - Erroll Garner (Octv)
GOOD-VIBES - Gary Burton (Atl)
SWISS MOVEMENT - Les McCann, Eddie Harris (Atl)
THAT'S THE WAY IT IS - Milt Jackson Quintet with Ray Brown (Impulse)

JAZZ - LARGE GROUP OR SOLOIST WITH LARGE GROUP (G-528)

(8 or more)
BITCHES BREW - Miles Davis (Col)

BRIDGE OVER TROUBLED WATER - Paul Desmond (A&R)
CONSUMMATION - Thad Jones & Mel Lewis (Ble/Nt)
DON ELLIS AT FILLMORE - Don Ellis (Col)
DUKE ELLINGTON - 70TH BIRTHDAY CONCERT - Duke Ellington (Solid State)
GULA MATARI - Quincy Jones (A&M)
LIVE AT THE ROOSEVELT GRILL - World's Greatest Jazzband (Atl)
THREE SHADES OF BLUE - Johnny Hodges (Flying Dutchman)

ALBUM OF THE YEAR, CLASSICAL (G-529)
(Grammys to Artist and A&R Producer)

BEETHOVEN EDITION 1970 Herbert von Karajan cond. Berlin Philharmonic (Oistrakh, Anda, Kempf, Goossens, Leitner, etc.) A&R: Dr. Wilfried Daenicke (DGG)
BERLIOZ: LES TROYENS - Colin Davis cond. Royal Opera House Orchestra & Chorus (Solos: Vickers, Veasey Lindholm) A&R: Erik Smith (Philips)
BRAHMS: DOUBLE CONCERTO (CONCERTO IN A MINOR FOR VIOLIN & CELLO) David Oistrakh & Mstislav Rostropovich (Szell cond. Cleveland Orchestra) A&R: Peter Andry (Angel)
IVES: THREE PLACES IN NEW ENGLAND/RUGGLES: SUN TREADER - Michael Tilson Thomas cond. Boston Symphony - A&R: Tom Mowrey (DGG)
SHOSTAKOVICH: SYMPHONY NO. 13 - Eugene Ormandy cond. Philadelphia Symphony (Krause, baritone/Male Chorus of Mendelsohn Club of Philadelphia, R. Page, dir.) - A&R: Peter Dellheim (RCA)
STRAVINSKY: LE SACRE DU PRINTEMPS - Pierre Boulez cond. Cleveland Orchestra - A&R: Thomas Z. Shepard (Col)

CLASSICAL PERFORMANCE - ORCHESTRA (G-530)
(Conductor's Award)

BARTOK: CONCERTO FOR ORCHESTRA - Seiji Ozawa cond. Chicago Symphony (Angel)
BERLIOZ: ROMEO & JULIET - Carlo Maria Giulini cond. Chicago Symphony (Angel)
BRUCKNER: SYMPHONY NO. 8 IN C MINOR - George Szell cond. Cleveland Orchestra (Col)
DVORAK: SYMPHONY NO. 8 IN G MAJOR - George Szell cond. Cleveland Orchestra (Angel)
IVES: THREE PLACES IN NEW ENGLAND/RUGGLES: SUN TREADER - Michael Tilson Thomas cond. Boston Symphony (DGG)
MAHLER: SYMPHONY NO. 2 IN C MINOR "RESURRECTION" - Eugene Ormandy cond. Philadelphia Symphony (RCA)
MAHLER: SYMPHONY NO. 6 IN A MINOR - Georg Solti cond. Chicago Symphony (London)
STRAVINSKY: LE SACRE DU PRINTEMPS - Pierre Boulez cond. Cleveland Orchestra (Col)

CLASSICAL PERFORMANCE - INSTRUMENTAL SOLOIST(S) (WITH OR WITHOUT ORCHESTRA) (G-531)

BACH: WELL TEMPERED CLAVIER BOOK 2, NOS. 9-16 - Glenn Gould (CBS)
BARTOK: CONCERTO NO. 2 FOR PIANO - Alexis Weissenberg (Ormandy cond. Philadelphia Symphony) (RCA)
BEETHOVEN: SONATAS NO. 26 OP. 81a ("LES ADIEUX") & NO. 15, OP. 28 ("PASTORAL") Ivan Moravec (Conn Soc)
BRAHMS: CONCERTO IN D MAJOR FOR VIOLIN - David Oistrakh (Szell Cond. Cleveland Orchestra) (Angel)
BRAHMS: DOUBLE CONCERTO (CONCERTO IN A MINOR FOR VIOLIN & CELLO) - David Oistrakh & Mstislav Rostropovich (Szell cond. Cleveland Orchestra) (Angel)
BRITTEN: SUITES FOR CELLO (2) - Mstislav Rostropovich (Britten cond.) (London)
CHOPIN: CONCERTO NO. 1 IN E MINOR FOR PIANO - Van Cliburn (Ormandy cond. Philadelphia Symphony) (RCA)
SCHUMANN: KREISLERIANA-Vladimir Horowitz (Col)
WELL-TEMPERED SYNTHESIZER - Walter Carlos (Col)

CHAMBER MUSIC PERFORMANCE (G-532)
(Inst. or Vocal)

BEETHOVEN: THE COMPLETE PIANO TRIOS - Eugene Istomin, Isaac Stern, Leonard Rose (Col)
BEETHOVEN: THE FIVE LATE QUARTETS - Guarneri Quartet (RCA)
CARTER: QUARTETS NOS. 1 & 2 FOR STRINGS - Composers Quartet (Nonesuch)
FRANCK: SONATA IN A MAJOR FOR VIOLIN & PIANO/BRAHMS: SONATA NO. 3 IN D MINOR - Sviatoslav Richter, David Oistrakh (Angel)
(GRAINGER) SALUTE TO PERCY GRAINGER - Benjamin Britten cond. English Chamber Orchestra & Ambrosian Singers (London)
IVES: CALCIUM LIGHT NIGHT - Gunther Schuller (CBS)
SCHUBERT: TRIO NO. 1 IN B FLAT MAJOR, MILHAUD: PASTORALE FOR OBOE, CLARINET & BASSOON/HINDEMITH: KLEINE KAMMERMUSIK - The Boston Symphony Chamber Players (RCA)

OPERA RECORDING (G-533)
(Grammys to Conductor and A&R Producer)

BERLIOZ: LES TROYENS - Colin Davis cond. Royal Opera House Orchestra & Chorus (Solos: Vickers, Veasey, Lindholm) A&R: Erik Smith (Philips)
DEBUSSY: PELLEAS ET MELISANDE - Pierre Boulez cond. Orchestra of Royal Opera House (Solos: McIntyre, Shirley, Soederstroem, David, Ward, etc.) A&R: Paul Myers (Col)
R. STRAUSS: DER ROSENKAVALIER - Georg Solti cond. Vienna Philharmonic (Solos: Crespin, Minton, Donath, Jungwirth) A&R: Christopher Raeburn (London)
VERDI: IL TROVATORE - Zubin Mehta cond. New Philharmonia Orchestra, Ambrosian Opera Chorus (Solos: Price, Domingo, Milnes, Cossotto) A&R: Richard Mohr (RCA)
WAGNER: GOTTERDAMMERUNG - Herbert von Karajan cond. Berlin Philharmonic, Deutsche Oper Chorus (Solos: Brilioth, Stewart, Keleman, Dernesch, Janowitz, Ludwig, Chookasian) A&R: Otto Gerdes (DGG)

CLASSICAL PERFORMANCE - VOCAL SOLOIST - (G-534)

BERLIOZ: THE TROJANS - FINAL SCENES "DEATH OF CLEOPATRA" - Janet Baker (Gibson cond. London Symphony) (Angel)
MAHLER: DES KNABEN WUNDERHORN - Christa Ludwig & Walter Berry (Bernstein cond. New York Philharmonic) (Col)
MAHLER: KINDERTOTENLIEDER/WAGNER: WESENDONCK LIEDER - Marilyn Horn (Henry Lewis cond.) (London)
MOZART & STRAUSS ARIAS - Beverly Sills (Ceccato cond. London Philharmonic) (Audio Treasury)
PRIMA DONNA VOLUME III - Leontyne Price (Downes cond. London Symphony) (RCA)
SCHUBERT: LIEDER - Dietrich Fischer-Dieskau (Gerald Moore, accomp.) (DGG)

CHORAL PERFORMANCE - OTHER THAN OPERA (G-535)
(Grammys to Conductor and Choral Director)

HAYDN: THE CREATION - Herbert von Karajan cond. Berlin Philharmonic/Reinhold Schmid & Helmut Froschauer cond. Vienna Singverien (DGG)
(IVES) NEW MUSIC OF CHARLES IVES - Gregg Smith cond. Gregg Smith Singers and Columbia Chamber Ensemble (Col)
MAHLER: DAS KLAGENDE LIED - Arthur Oldham cond. London Symphony Orchestra Chorus - Pierre Boulez cond. London Symphony (Col)
ORFF: CARMINA BURANA - Lorna Cooke de Varon, dir, New England Conservatory Chorus; Katherine Edmonds Pusztai, cond. Children's Chorus of New England Conservatory; Seiji Ozawa cond. Boston Symphony (RCA)
SHOSTAKOVICH: SYMPHONY NO. 13 - Eugene Ormandy cond. Philadelphia Symphony; Robert E. Page, dir., Male Chorus of Mendelssohn Club (RCA)
(STRAVINSKY): THE NEW STRAVINSKY - Gregg Smith cond. Ithaca

College Concert Choir/Robert Craft cond. Columbia Symphony (Col)
VAUGHAN WILLIAMS: FIVE TUDOR PORTRAITS - Bach Choir & New Philharmonia - David Willcocks, cond. (Angel)

BEST ENGINEERED RECORDING - CLASSICAL (G-536)

(Engineer's Award)
BRAHMS: DOUBLE CONCERTO (CONCERTO IN A MINOR FOR VIOLIN & CELLO) (Oistrakh & Rostropovich/Szell cond. Cleveland Orchestra - Eng: Carson C. Taylor (Angel)
IVES: THREE PLACES IN NEW ENGLAND/RUGGLES: SUN TREADER (Thomas cond. Boston Symphony) Eng: Gunter Hermanns (DGG)
SHOSTAKOVICH: SYMPHONY NO. 6 AND AGE OF GOLD (Stokowski cond. Chicago Symphony) Eng: Paul Goodman (RCA)
SHOSTAKOVICH: SYMPHONY NO. 13 (Ormandy cond. Philadelphia Symphony) Eng: Bernard Keville (RCA)
R. STRAUSS: DER ROSENKAVALIER (Solti cond. Vienna Philharmonic/Crespin, Minton) Engs: Gordon Parry, James Locke (London)
STRAVINSKY: LE SACRE DU PRINTEMPS (Boulez cond. Cleveland Orchestra) Engs: Fred Plaut, Ray Moore, Arthur Kendy (Col)
WELL-TEMPERED SYNTHESIZER (Walter Carlos) Eng: Walter Carlos (Col)

1971

RECORD OF THE YEAR (G-537)

(Grammys to the Artist and A&R Producer)
IT'S TOO LATE - Carole King - A&R: Lou Adler (Ode)
JOY TO THE WORLD - Three Dog Night - A&R: Richard Podolor (Dunhill)
MY SWEET LORD - George Harrison - A&R: George Harrison, Phil Spector (Apple)
THEME FROM SHAFT - Isaac Hayes - A&R: Isaac Hayes (Enterprise)
YOU'VE GOT A FRIEND - James Taylor - A&R: Peter Asher (WB)

ALBUM OF THE YEAR (G-538)

(Grammys to the Artist and A&R Producer)
ALL THINGS MUST PASS - George Harrison - A&R: George Harrison and Phil Spector (Apple)
CARPENTERS - Carpenters - A&R: Jack Daugherty (A&M)
JESUS CHRIST SUPERSTAR - London Production - A&R: Andrew Lloyd Webber, Tim Rice (Decca)
SHAFT - Isaac Hayes - A&R: Isaac Hayes (Enterprise)
TAPESTRY - Carole King - A&R: Lou Adler (A&M)

SONG OF THE YEAR (G-539)

(Songwriter's Award)
HELP ME MAKE IT THROUGH THE NIGHT - Kris Kristofferson
IT'S IMPOSSIBLE - Sid Wayne, Armando Manzanero
ME & BOBBY MC GEE - Kris Kristofferson, Fred Foster
ROSE GARDEN - Joe South
YOU'VE GOT A FRIEND - Carole King

NEW ARTIST OF THE YEAR (G-540)

CHASE (Epic)
EMERSON, LAKE & PALMER (Cot)
HAMILTON, JOE FRANK & REYNOLDS (Dunhill)
CARLY SIMON (Elektra)
BILL WITHERS (Sussex)

INSTRUMENTAL ARRANGEMENT (G-541)

(Arranger's Award)
EARTH - Arr: Michel Colombier (A&M)
NIGHTINGALE II - Arr: Joshua Rifkin (Elektra)
THE RITE OF SPRING (Hubert Laws) Arr: Don Sebesky (CTI)
THEME FROM SHAFT - Arrs: Isaac Hayes, Johnny Allen (Enterprises)
THEME FROM SUMMER OF '42 - Arr: Michel Legrand (WB)

ARRANGEMENT ACCOMPANYING VOCALIST(S) (G-542)

(Arranger's Award)
FREEDOM AND FEAR (Bill Medley) Arr: Michel Colombier (A&M)
LONG AGO TOMORROW (B.J. Thomas) Arrs: Burt Bacharach, Pat Williams (Scepter)
SUPERSTAR (Carpenters) Arr: Richard Carpenter (A&M)
UNCLE ALBERT/ADMIRAL HALSEY (Paul & Linda McCartney) Arr: Paul McCartney (Apple)
WHAT'S GOING ON (Marvin Gaye) Arr: David Van DePitte (Tamla)

BEST ENGINEERED RECORDING - NON-CLASSICAL (G-543)

(Engineer's Award)
CARPENTERS (Carpenters) Engs: Ray Gerhardt, Dick Bogert (A&M)
THE 5TH DIMENSION/LIVE! (5th Dimension) Eng: Bones Howe (Bell)
STONES (Neil Diamond) (single) Eng: Armin Steiner (Uni)
THEME FROM SHAFT (Isaac Hayes) Engs: Dave Purple, Henry Bush, Ron Capone (Enterprise)
WINGS (Michel Colombier) Engs: Larry Levine, Roger Roche (A&M)

ALBUM COVER (G-544)

(Awards to Art Director, Photographer and/or Graphic Artist)
B, S & T; 4 (Blood, Sweat & Tears) Art Dir: John Berg - Design: Robert Lockart - Photos and Art: Norman Seeff (Col)
BARK (Jefferson Airplane) Concept & Design: Acy Lehman - Photog: Nick Sangiamo (Grunt)
BLACK PEARL (Jimmy McGriff) Art Dir: Norman Seeff - Cover: John Van Hamersveld (UA)
HOT PLATTERS (Various) Art Dir: Ed Thrasher - Design: John Van Hamersveld (WB)
THE MUSIC OF ERIK SATIE: THROUGH A LOOKING GLASS (Camarata Contemporary Chamber Orch.) Art Dir: Vincent J. Biondi - Ilustration: Susan Obrant (Dream)
POLLUTION (Pollution) Art Dir: Gene Brownell - Design: Dean O. Torrance (Prophesy)
SHAREPICKERS (Mason Williams) Art Dir: Ed Thrasher - Photo: Terry Paul (WB)
STICKY FINGERS (The Rolling Stones) Photog: Andy Warhol - Graphics: Craigbraun (Rolling Stones)

ALBUM NOTES (G-545)

(Annotator's Award)
THE GENIUS OF LOUIS ARMSTRONG (Armstrong) Ann: Don DeMicheal (Col)
HONKY TONKIN' WITH CHARLIE WALKER (Walker) Ann: Tom West (Epic)
LOUIS ARMSTRONG JULY 4, 1900 - JULY 6, 1971 (Armstrong) Ann: Nat Hentoff (RCA)
MILES DAVIS (Davis) Ann: Colman Andrews (UA)
MUSIC OF VARESE (Simonovitch cond. Paris Instrumental Ensemble) Ann: James Lyons (Angel)
PIANO RAGS BY SCOTT JOPLIN (Rifkin) Ann: Joshua Rifkin (Nonesuch)
SAM HARD AND HEAVY (Samudio) Ann: Sam Samudio (Atlantic)
THIS IS BENNY GOODMAN (Goodman) Ann: George T. Simon (RCA)

POP VOCAL - FEMALE (G-546)

GYPSYS, TRAMPS & THIEVES - Cher (Kapp)
ME & BOBBY MC GEE - Janis Joplin (Col)
THE NIGHT THEY DROVE OLD DIXIE DOWN - Joan Baez (Vanguard)
TAPESTRY - Carole King (Ode)
THAT'S THE WAY I'VE ALWAYS HEARD IT SHOULD BE - Carly Simon (Elektra)

POP VOCAL - MALE (G-547)

AIN'T NO SUNSHINE - Bill Withers (Sussex)

I AM, I SAID - Neil Diamond (Uni)
IF YOU COULD READ MY MIND - Gordon Lightfoot (Reprise)
IT'S IMPOSSIBLE - Perry Como (RCA)
YOU'VE GOT A FRIEND - James Taylor (WB)

POP VOCAL - DUO, GROUP OR CHORUS (G-548)
ALL I EVER NEED IS YOU - Sonny & Cher (Kapp)
CARPENTERS - Carpenters (A&M)
HOW CAN YOU MEND A BROKEN HEART - Bee Gees (Atco)
JESUS CHRIST SUPERSTAR - London Production - Andrew Lloyd Webber, Geoffrey Mitchell, Alan Doggett, Horace James (Decca)
JOY TO THE WORLD - Three Dog Night (Dunhill)

POP INSTRUMENTAL (G-549)
BURT BACHARACH - Burt Bacharach (A&M)
SMACKWATER JACK - Quincy Jones (A&M)
THEME FROM LOVE STORY - Henry Mancini (RCA)
THEME FROM SUMMER OF '42 - Michel Legrand (WB)
THEME FROM SUMMER OF '42 - Peter Nero (Col)

R&B VOCAL - FEMALE (G-550)
BRIDGE OVER TROUBLED WATER - Aretha Franklin (Atlantic)
CONTACT - Freda Payne (Invictus)
I LOVE YOU (CALL ME) Diana Ross (Motown)
MR. BIG STUFF - Jean Knight (Stax)
PEARL - Janis Joplin (Col)

R&B VOCAL - MALE (G-551)
AIN'T NOBODY HOME - B.B. King (ABC)
INNER CITY BLUES (MAKE ME WANNA HOLLER) - Marvin Gaye (Tamla)
A NATURAL MAN - Lou Rawls (MGM)
NEVER CAN SAY GOODBYE - Isaac Hayes (Enterprise)
WE CAN WORK IT OUT - Stevie Wonder (Tamla)

R&B - DUO OR GROUP, VOCAL OR INSTRUMENTAL (G-552)
IF I WERE YOUR WOMAN - Gladys Knight and The Pips (Soul)
PROUD MARY - Ike and Tina Turner (UA)
RESPECT YOURSELF - Staple Singers (Stax)
THEME FROM SHAFT - Isaac Hayes (Enterprise)
YOU'VE GOT A FRIEND - Roberta Flack, Donny Hathaway (Atlantic)

RHYTHM & BLUES SONG (G-553)
(Songwriter's Award)
AIN'T NO SUNSHINE - Bill Withers
IF I WERE YOUR WOMAN - Clay McMurray, Laverne Ware, Pamela Sawyer
MR. BIG STUFF - Joseph Broussard, Ralph Williams, Carrol Washington
NEVER CAN SAY GOODBYE - Clifton Davis
SMILING FACES SOMETIMES - Norman Whitfield, Barrett Strong

SOUL GOSPEL PERFORMANCE (G-554)
THE FIVE BLIND BOYS OF ALABAMA - Blind Boys of Alabama (Hob)
GREAT MOMENTS IN GOSPEL - Clara Ward (Hob)
PASS ME NOT - Dottie Rambo (Heartwarming)
PUT YOUR HAND IN THE HAND OF THE MAN FROM GALILEE - Shirley Caesar (Hob)
THERE IS A GOD - Valerie Simpson (Tamla)

COUNTRY VOCAL - FEMALE (G-555)
GOOD LOVIN' - Tammy Wynette (Epic)
HELP ME MAKE IT THROUGH THE NIGHT - Sammi Smith (Mega)
HE'S SO FINE - Jody Miller (Epic)
HOW CAN I UNLOVE YOU - Lynn Anderson (Col)
JOSHUA - Dolly Parton (RCA)

COUNTRY VOCAL - MALE (G-556)
EASY LOVING - Freddie Hart (Capitol)
I WON'T MENTION IT AGAIN - Ray Price (Col)
KISS AN ANGEL GOOD MORNING - Charley Pride (RCA)
SHE'S ALL I GOT - Johnny Paycheck (Col)
WHEN YOU'RE HOT, YOU'RE HOT - Jerry Reed (RCA)

COUNTRY VOCAL - DUO OR GROUP (G-557)
AFTER THE FIRE IS GONE Conway Twitty and Loretta Lynn (Decca)
BETTER MOVE IT ON HOME - Porter Wagoner and Dolly Parton (RCA)
I SAW THE LIGHT - Roy Acuff with the Nitty Gritty Dirt Band (UA)
NO NEED TO WORRY - Johnny Cash and June Carter (Col)
RINGS - Tompall & The Glaser Bros. (MGM)

COUNTRY INSTRUMENTAL (G-558)
FOR THE GOOD TIMES - Floyd Cramer (RCA)
JERRY KENNEDY PLAYS: WITH ALL DUE RESPECT TO KRIS KRISTOFFERSON - Jerry Kennedy (Mer)
ROSE GARDEN - Bakersfield Brass (Capitol)
RUBY, DON'T TAKE YOUR LOVE TO TOWN - Danny Davis & The Nashville Brass (RCA)
SNOWBIRD - Chet Atkins (RCA)

COUNTRY SONG (G-559)
(Songwriter's Award)
EASY LOVING - Freddie Hart
FOR THE GOOD TIMES - Kris Kristofferson
HELP ME MAKE IT THROUGH THE NIGHT - Kris Kristofferson
ME & BOBBY MC GEE - Kris Kristofferson, Fred Foster
ROSE GARDEN - Joe South

SACRED PERFORMANCE (MUSICAL) (G-560)
ABIDE WITH ME - Anita Bryant (Word)
AMAZING GRACE - George Beverly Shea (RCA)
DID YOU THINK TO PRAY - Charley Pride (RCA)
GOLDEN STREETS OF GLORY - Dolly Parton (RCA)
PAT BOONE FAMILY - Pat Boone Family (Word)

GOSPEL PERFORMANCE - OTHER THAN SOUL GOSPEL (G-561)
HE'S STILL KING OF KINGS - Blackwood Bros. (RCA)
JESUS CHRIST, WHAT A MAN - Oak Ridge Boys (Impact)
LET ME LIVE - Charley Pride (RCA)
PUT YOUR HAND IN THE HAND - Hovie Lister with the Statesmen (Skylite)
TIME TO GET IT TOGETHER - The Imperials (Impact)

ETHNIC OR TRADITIONAL RECORDING (INCLUDING TRADITIONAL BLUES) (G-562)
18TH CENTURY TRADITIONAL MUSIC OF JAPAN - Keiko Matsuo (Everest)
THE ESSO TRINIDAD STEEL BAND - Esso Trinidad Steel Band (WB)
JAVANESE COURT GAMELAN - Javanese Players, Robert E. Brown, Producer (Nonesuch)
MESSAGE TO THE YOUNG - Howlin' Wolf (Chess)
MISSISSIPPI FRED MC DOWELL - Mississippi Fred McDowell (Everest)
STORMY MONDAY BLUES - T-Bone Walker (Blues-Time)
THEY CALL ME MUDDY WATERS - Muddy Waters (Chess)

INSTRUMENTAL COMPOSITION (G-563)
(Composer's Award)
HILL WHERE THE LORD HIDES - Chuck Mangione (Mercury)
NEW ORLEANS SUITE - Duke Ellington (Atl)
THEME FROM LOVE STORY - Francis Lai (Par)
THEME FROM SHAFT - Isaac Hayes (Enterprise)
THEME FROM SUMMER OF '42 - Michel Legrand (WB)

ORIGINAL SCORE - MOTION PICTURE OR A TELEVISION SPECIAL (G-564)

(Composer's Award)

BLESS THE BEASTS & CHILDREN - Barry DeVorzon, Perry Botkin, Jr. (A&M)
FRIENDS - Elton John, Bernie Taupin (Par)
LOVE STORY - Francis Lai (Par)
RYAN'S DAUGHTER - Maurice Jarre (MGM)
SHAFT - Isaac Hayes (MGM)

SCORE FROM AN ORIGINAL CAST SHOW ALBUM (G-565)

(Awards to Composers and A&R Producer)

FOLLIES - Stephen Sondheim - A&R: Richard C. Jones (Capitol)
GODSPELL - Composed and Produced by Stephen Schwartz (Bell)
THE ROTHSCHILDS - Jerry Bock, Sheldon Harnick - A&R: Thomas Z. Shepard (Col)
TOUCH - Kenn Long, Jim Crozier - A&R: Glenn Osser (Ampex)
TWO BY TWO - Richard Rodgers, Martin Charnin - A&R: Thomas Z. Shepard (Col)

RECORDING FOR CHILDREN (G-566)

BILL COSBY TALKS TO KIDS ABOUT DRUGS - Bill Cosby (Uni)
SESAME ST., RUBBER DUCKIE & OTHER SONGS FROM SESAME ST. - Richard Wolfe Children's Chorus (Camden)
SEX EXPLAINED FOR CHILDREN - Dr. Stanley Daniels (Carapan)
THE STORY OF SCHEHERAZADE - Julie Harris (Caedmon)
WILLY WONKA & THE CHOCOLATE FACTORY - Golden Orch. & Chorus, Peter Moore, Conductor (Golden)

COMEDY RECORDING (G-567)

AJAX LIQUOR STORE - Hudson & Landry (Dore)
CHEECH & CHONG - Cheech & Chong (Ode)
FLIP - THE FLIP WILSON SHOW - Flip Wilson (Little David)
THIS IS A RECORDING - Lily Tomlin (Polydor)
WHEN I WAS A KID - Bill Cosby (Uni)

SPOKEN WORD RECORDING (G-568)

DESIDERATA - Les Crane (WB)
HAMLET - Richard Chamberlain (RCA)
I CAN HEAR IT NOW - THE SIXTIES - Walter Cronkite (Col)
LONG DAY'S JOURNEY INTO NIGHT - Stacy Keach, Robert Ryan, Geraldine Fitzgerald (Caedmon)
WILL ROGERS' U.S.A. - James Whitmore (Col)

JAZZ - SOLOIST (G-569)

THE BILL EVANS ALBUM - Bill Evans (Col)
CARMEN MCRAE - Carmen McRae (Mainstream)
GYPSY QUEEN - Larry Coryell (Flying Dutchman)
PHIL WOODS & HIS EUROPEAN RHYTHM MACHINE AT THE FRANKFURT JAZZ FESTIVAL - Phil Woods -(Embryo)
PORTRAIT OF JENNY - Dizzy Gillespie (Perceptn)
QUINTESSENTIAL RECORDING SESSION - Earl Hines (Chiaroscuro)
THE YOU AND ME THAT USED TO BE - Jimmy Rushing (RCA)

JAZZ - GROUP (G-570)

THE BILL EVANS ALBUM - Bill Evans Trio (Col)
GARY BURTON & KEITH JARRETT (Atl)
GIANTS - Dizzy Gillespie, Bobby Hackett, Mary Lou Williams (Perception)
MILES DAVIS AT THE FILLMORE - Miles Davis (Col)
MWANDISHI - Herbie Hancock (WB)
THE NIFTY CAT - Roy Eldridge (Master Jazz)
PHIL WOODS & HIS EUROPEAN RHYTHM MACHINE AT THE FRANKFURT JAZZ FESTIVAL - Phil Woods (Embryo)

JAZZ - BIG BAND (G-571)

AFRIQUE - Count Basie (Flying Dutchman)
A DIFFERENT DRUMMER - Buddy Rich (RCA)
MAYNARD FERGUSON - M.F. HORN - Maynard Ferguson (Col)
NEW ORLEANS SUITE - Duke Ellington (Atl)
WOODY - Woody Herman (Cadet)

ALBUM OF THE YEAR - CLASSICAL (G-572)

(Grammys to the Artist and A&R Producer)

BERLIOZ: REQUIEM - Colin Davis cond. London Symphony/Russell Burgess cond. Wandsworth School Boys Choir/Arthur Oldham cond. London Symphony Chorus - A&R: Vittorio Negri (Philips)
BOULEZ CONDUCTS BOULEZ: PLI SELON PLI - Pierre Boulez cond. BBC Symphony -A&R: Paul Myers (Col)
CRUMB: ANCIENT VOICES OF CHILDREN - Jan DeGaetani & Michael Dash/Arthur Weisberg cond. Contemporary Chamber Ensemble - A&R: Teresa Sterne (Nonesuch)
HAYDN: SYMPHONIES NOS. 65-72 (Vol. I) Antal Dorati cond. Philharmonia Hungarica - A&R: James Mallinson (London)
HOROWITZ PLAYS RACHMANINOFF (Etudes - Tableaux, Piano Music, Sonatas) - Vladimir Horowitz - A&R: Richard Killough, Thomas Frost (Col.)
JANACEK: SINFONIETTA/LUTOSLAVSKI: CONCERTO FOR ORCHESTRA - Seiji Ozawa cond. Chicago Symphony - A&R: Peter Andry (Angel)
MAHLER: SYMPHONY NO. 1 IN D MAJOR - Carlo Maria Giulini cond. Chicago Symphony - A&R: Christopher Bishop (Angel)
PENDERECKI: UTRENJA, THE ENTOMBMENT OF CHRIST - Eugene Ormandy cond. Philadelphia Orchestra/Robert Page, Dir., Temple University Choirs - A&R: Peter Dellheim (RCA)
SHOSTAKOVICH: SYMPHONY NO. 14 - Phyllis Curtin, Simon Estes; Eugene Ormandy cond. Philadelphia Orchestra - A&R: Max Wilcox (RCA)
TIPPETT: THE MIDSUMMER MARRIAGE - Colin Davis cond. Royal Opera House Orchestra Covent Garden - A&R: Erik Smith (Philips)

CLASSICAL PERFORMANCE - ORCHESTRA (G-573)

(Conductor's Award)

BOULEZ CONDUCTS BOULEZ: PLI SELON PLI - Pierre Boulez cond. The BBC Symphony(Col)
BOULEZ CONDUCTS RAVEL - Pierre Boulez cond. The Cleveland Orchestra (Col)
HAYDN: SYMPHONIES NOS. 65-72 (Vol. I) - Antal Dorati cond. Philharmonia Hungarica (London)
HOLST: THE PLANETS - Bernard Haitink cond. London Philharmonic (Philips)
MAHLER: SYMPHONY NO. 1 IN D MAJOR - Carlo Maria Giulini cond. Chicago Symphony (Angel)
MAHLER: SYMPHONY NO. 3 IN D MIN. - Jascha Horenstein cond. London Symphony (Nonesuch)
RESPIGHI: THE FOUNTAINS OF ROME/THE PINES OF ROME - Eugene Ormandy cond Philadelphia Orchestra (Col)
VAUGHAN WILLIAMS: SYMPHONY NO. 4 IN F MINOR - Andre Previn cond. London Symphony (RCA)

CLASSICAL PERFORMANCE - INSTRUMENTAL SOLOIST(S) (WITH ORCHESTRA) (G-574)

BACH: COMPLETE CONCERTOS FOR HARPSICHORD & ORCHESTRA - Igor Kipnis (Marriner cond. London Strings) (Col)
BEETHOVEN: TRIPLE CONCERTO (CONCERTO IN C MAJOR FOR VIOLIN, PIANO & CELLO, OP. 56) David Oistrakh, Mstislav Rostropovich, Sviatoslav Richter (von Karajan cond. Berlin Philharmonic) (Angel)
BERG: CONCERTO FOR VIOLIN & ORCHESTRA/MARTINON: CONCERTO FOR VIOLIN - Henryk Szeryng (Kubelik cond. Bavarian Symphony) (DGG)
DVORAK: CONCERTO IN B MINOR FOR CELLO - Jacqueline du Pre (Barenboim cond. Chicago Symphony) (Angel)
RACHMANINOFF: RHAPSODY ON A THEME OF PAGANINI/LISZT: CONCERTO NO. 2 IN A MAJOR - Van Cliburn (Ormandy cond. Philadelphia Orchestra) (RCA)
SCHUMAN, WILLIAM: CONCERTO FOR VIOLIN - Paul Zukofsky

(Thomas cond. Boston Symphony) (DGG)
SIBELIUS: CONCERTO IN D MINOR FOR VIOLIN/TCHAIKOVSKY: CONCERTO IN D MAJOR FOR VIOLIN - Kyung-Wha Chung (Previn cond. London Symphony) (London)
VILLA-LOBOS: CONCERTO FOR GUITAR - Julian Bream (Previn cond. London Symphony) (RCA)
WALTON: CONCERTO FOR VIOLIN & ORCHESTRA/CONCERTO FOR VIOLA & ORCHESTRA - Yehudi Menuhin (Walton cond. New Philharmonia) (Angel)

CLASSICAL PERFORMANCE - INSTRUMENTAL SOLOIST(S) (WITHOUT ORCHESTRA) (G-575)
ALICIA DE LARROCHA PLAYS SPANISH PIANO MUSIC OF THE 20TH CENTURY - Alicia de Larrocha (London)
BACH: WELL-TEMPERED CLAVIER, BOOK 2, VOL. 3 PRELUDES & FUGUES 17-24 - Glenn Gould (Col)
BARBER: SONATA FOR PIANO/PROKOFIEFF: SONATA NO. 6 IN A MAJOR - Van Cliburn (RCA)
BARTOK: MIKROKOSMOS, VOL. 6/OUT OF DOORS SUITE/SONATINA - Stephen Bishop (Philips)
BEETHOVEN: SONATA NO. 29 IN B FLAT OP. 106 "HAMMERKLAVIER" - Rudolf Serkin (Col.)
THE BRAHMS I LOVE - Artur Rubinstein (RCA)
HOROWITZ PLAYS RACHMANINOFF (Etudes - Tableaux, Piano Music, Sonatas) Vladimir Horowitz (Col.)
PIANO RAGS BY SCOTT JOPLIN - Joshua Rifkin (Nonesuch)
SATIE: PIANO MUSIC OF ERIK SATIE, Vol. 5 - Aldo Ciccolini (Angel)

CHAMBER MUSIC PERFORMANCE (G-576)
CRUMB: ANCIENT VOICES OF CHILDREN - Jan DeGaitani, Michael M Dash; Arthur Weisberg cond. Contemporary Chamber Ensemble (Nonesuch)
DEBUSSY: QUARTET IN G MINOR/RAVEL: QUARTET IN F MAJOR - Juilliard Quartet (Col.)
DVORAK: PIANO TRIOS (Complete) Beaux Arts Trio (Philips)
FUX-SCHMELZER: MUSIC IN THE HAPSBURG PALACE - Nikolaus Harnoncourt cond. Concentus Musicus (Telefunken)
IVES: CHAMBER MUSIC - Paul Zukofsky, Gilbert Kalish, Charles Russo, Robert Sylvester (N.Y. String Quartet) (Col.)
THE MOZART QUARTETS FOR FLUTE - Jean-Pierre Rampal, Isaac Stern, Alexander Schneider, Leonard Rose (Col.)
SCHUBERT: FANTAISIE IN C MAJOR FOR VIOLIN (& PIANO) Op. 159 - Jascha Heifetz, - Brooks Smith (RCA)

OPERA RECORDING (G-577)
(Grammys to Conductor and A&R Producer)
MASSENET: MANON - Julius Rudel cond. New Philharmonia & Ambrosian Opera Chorus/(Solos: Sills, Gedda, Souzay, Bacquier) A&R: Michael Williamson (Audio Treas.)
MOZART: THE MAGIC FLUTE - Georg Solti cond. Vienna Philharmonic (Solos: Prey, Lorengar, Burrows, Fischer-Dieskau, Deutekom, Talvela) - A&R: Christopher Raeburn (London)
PUCCINI: IL TABARRO - Erich Leinsdorf cond. New Philharmonia; John Alldis Choir (Solos: Price, Domingo, Milnes) A&R: Richard Mohr (RCA)
TIPPETT: THE MIDSUMMER MARRIAGE - Colin Davis cond. Royal Opera House, Covent Garden (Solos: Remedios, Carlyle, Burrows, Herincx, Harwood) A&R: Erik Smith (Philips)
VERDI: AIDA - Erich Leinsdorf cond, London Symphony, John Alldis Choir (Solos: Price, Domingo, Milnes, Bumbry, Raimondi) A&R: Richard Mohr (RCA)
VERDI: DON CARLO - Carlo Maria Giulini cond. Orchestra of Royal Opera House, Covent Garden & Ambrosian Opera Chorus (Solos: Domingo, Caballe, Raimondi, Milnes, Verrett) A&R: Christopher Bishop (Angel)
WAGNER: DIE MEISTERSINGER VON NURNBERG - Herbert von Karajan cond. Dresden State Opera Orchestra & Choruses of Dresden State Opera & Leipzig Radio (Solos: Adam, Donath, Kollo, Evans, Schreier) A&R: R. Kinloch Anderson, Diether Gerhardt Worm (Angel)
WAGNER: PARSIFAL - Pierre Boulez cond. Bayreuth Festival Orchestra & Chorus (Solos: Stewart, Ridderbusch, Crass, King, Jones, McIntyre) A&R: Dr. Hans Hirsch (DGG)

CLASSICAL PERFORMANCE - VOCAL SOLOIST - (G-578)
AN EVENING OF DUETS - Janet Baket & Dietrich Fischer-Dieskau (Angel)
BERIO: EPIFANIE - Cathy Berberian (Berio cond. The B.B.C. Symphony) (RCA)
HAYDN & MOZART ARIAS - Dietrich Fischer-Dieskau (Peters cond. Vienna Haydn Orchestra) (London)
IVES: AMERICAN SCENES/AMERICAN POETS - Evelyn Lear, Thomas Stewart (Col.)
LEONTYNE PRICE SINGS ROBERT SCHUMANN - Leontyne Price (Garvey, accomp.) (RCA)
SHOSTAKOVICH: SYMPHONY NO. 14 - Phyllis Curtin, Simon Estes (Ormandy cond. Philadelphia Orchestra) (RCA)
WOLF: SONGS (Salzburg Festival 1953) Elisabeth Schwarzkopf (Furtwangler accomp.) (Seraphim)

CHORAL PERFORMANCE - OTHER THAN OPERA (G-579)
(Grammys to Conductor and Choral Director)
BERLIOZ: REQUIEM - Colin Davis cond. London Symphony/Russell Burgess cond. Wandsworth School Boys Choir/Arthur Oldham cond. London Symphony Chorus (Philips)
PENDERECKI: UTRENJA, THE ENTOMBMENT OF CHRIST - Robert Page, Dir., Temple University Choirs/Eugene Ormandy cond. Philadelphia Orchestra (RCA)
PROKOFIEV: SEVEN, THEY ARE SEVEN - Gennady Rozhdestvensky cond. Moscow Radio Chorus & Moscow Radio Symphony (Melodia/Angel)
SIBELIUS: KULLERVO, OP. 7 - Ensti Pohjola cond. Helsinki University Men's Choir: Paavo Berglund cond. Bournemout Symphony (Angel)
STOCKHAUSEN: STIMMUNG - Wolfgang Fromme cond. Collegium Vocale of Cologne (DGG)
VERDI: FOUR SACRED PIECES - Roger Wagner cond. Los Angeles Master Chorale/Zubin Mehta cond. Los Angeles Philharmonic (London)

BEST ENGINEERED RECORDING - CLASSICAL (G-580)
(Engineer's Award)
BERLIOZ: REQUIEM - Colin Davis cond. London Symphony/Russell Burgess cond. Wandsworth School Boys Choir/Arthur Oldham cond. London Symphony - Eng: Vittorio Negri (Philips)
BEETHOVEN: EGMONT - COMPLETE INCIDENTAL MUSIC - Georg Szell cond. Vienna Philharmonic - Eng: Gordon Parry (London)
CRUMB: ANCIENT VOICES OF CHILDREN - Jan de Gaetani, Michael Dash, Weisberg cond. Contemporary Chamber Ensemble - Eng: Marc J. Aubort (Nonesuch)
HOLST: THE PLANETS - William Steinberg cond. Boston Symphony - Eng: Gunter Hermanns (DGG)
JANACEK: SINFONIETTA - Seiji Ozawa cond. Chicago Symphony - Eng: Carson C. Taylor (Angel)
MAHLER: SYMPHONY NO. 1 IN D MAJOR - Carlo Maria Giulini cond. Chicago Symphony - Eng: Carson C. Taylor (Angel)
TCHAIKOVSKY: 1812 OVERTURE/BEETHOVEN: WELLINGTON'S VICTORY - Eugene Ormandy cond. Philadelphia Orchestra - Eng: Paul Goodman (RCA)

1972

RECORD OF THE YEAR (G-581)
(Grammys to the Artist and A&R Producer)
ALONE AGAIN (NATURALLY) - Gilbert O'Sullivan - Prod: Gordon Mills (MAM/London)
AMERICAN PIE - Don McLean - Prod: Ed Freeman (UA)
THE FIRST TIME EVER I SAW YOUR FACE - Roberta Flack - Prod: Joel Dorn (Atlantic)

SONG SUNG BLUE - Neil Diamond - Prods: Tom Catalano & Neil Diamond (Uni)
WITHOUT YOU - Nilsson - Prod: Richard Perry (RCA)

ALBUM OF THE YEAR (G-582)

(Grammys to the Artist and A&R Producer)
AMERICAN PIE - Don McLean - Prod: Ed Freeman (UA)
THE CONCERT FOR BANGLA DESH - George Harrison & Friends (Ravi Shankar, Bob Dylan, Leon Russell, Ringo Starr, Billy Preston, Eric Clapton, Klaus Voormann, others) - Prods: George Harrison & Phil Spector (Apple)
JESUS CHRIST SUPERSTAR - Orginial Broadway Cast - Composers: Andrew Lloyd Webber & Tim Rice - Prod: Tom Morgan (Decca)
MOODS - Neil Diamond - Prods: Tom Catalano & Neil Diamond (Uni)
NILSSON SCHMILSSON - Nilsson - Prod: Richard Perry (RCA)

SONG OF THE YEAR (G-583)

(Songwriter's Award)
ALONE AGAIN (NATURALLY) - Gilbert O'Sullivan
AMERICAN PIE - Don McLean
THE FIRST TIME EVER I SAW YOUR FACE - Ewan MacColl
SONG SUNG BLUE - Neil Diamond
THE SUMMER KNOWS - Marilyn & Alan Bergman & Michel Legrand

NEW ARTIST OF THE YEAR (G-584)

AMERICA (WB)
HARRY CHAPIN (Elektra)
EAGLES (Asylum/Atl.)
LOGGINS & MESSINA (Columbia)
JOHN PRINE (Atlantic)

INSTRUMENTAL ARRANGEMENT (G-585)

(Arranger's Award)
FLAT BAROQUE - Carpenters - Arr: Richard Carpenter (A&M)
LONELY TOWN - Freddie Hubbard - Arr: Don Sebesky (CTI)
MONEY RUNNER - Quincy Jones - Arr: Quincy Jones (Reprise)
THEME FROM THE FRENCH CONNECTION - Don Ellis Arr: Don Ellis (Columbia)
THEME FROM THE MANCINI GENERATION - Henry Mancini - Arr: Henry Mancini (RCA)

ARRANGEMENT ACCOMPANYING VOCALIST(S) (G-586)

(Arranger's Award)
BETCHA BY GOLLY, WOW - Stylistics - Arr: Thom Bell (Avco)
DAY BY DAY - Jackie & Roy - Arr: Don Sebesky (CTI)
LAZY AFTERNOON - Jackie & Roy - Arr: Don Sebesky (CTI)
THE SUMMER KNOWS - Sarah Vaughan - Arr: Michel Legrand (Mainstream)
WHAT ARE YOU DOING THE REST OF YOUR LIFE - Sarah Vaughan - Arr: Michel Legrand (Mainstream)

BEST ENGINEERED RECORDING (G-587)

(Engineer's Award)
BABY I'M-A WANT YOU - Bread - Eng: Armin Steiner (album) (Elektra)
FRAGILE - Yes - Eng: Eddy Offord (album) (Atlantic)
HONKY CHATEAU - Elton John - Eng: Ken Scott (album) (Uni)
MOODS - Neil Diamond - Eng: Armin Steiner (album) (Uni)
SONG OF SCHMILSSON - Nilsson - Eng: Robin Cable, Ken Scott and Phillip Mac Donald (album) (RCA)

ALBUM COVER (G-588)

(Award to Art Director, Photographer and/or Graphic Artist)
CHIEF (Dewey Terry) Album Design & Cover Art: Aaron Schumaker for Tumbleweed Graphics (Tumbleweed)
FIVE DOLLAR SHOES (Five Dollar Shoes) Art Director: Ron Levine,

Concept & Design: Pacific - Eye & Ear - Illustrations: Robert Rodriguez (Neighborhood/Famous)
FLASH (Flash) - Art Direction & Design: Hipgnosis - Photographer: Poe (Capitol)
HISTORICAL FIGURES AND ANCIENT HEADS - Canned Heat - Art Director & Cover Photog: Norman Seeff (UA)
SCHOOL'S OUT (Alice Cooper) Album Design: Wilkes & Braun, Inc. - Photog: Robert Otter (Desk, outside) - Jacket Concept: Sound Packaging Corp. (WB)
THE SIEGEL-SCHWALL BAND (The Siegel-Schwall Band) Art Director: Acy Lehman -Artist: Harvey Dinnerstein (Wooden Nickel)
SUNSET RIDE (Zephyr) Art Directors: Ed Thrasher and Chris Wolf/ Illustrator: Dave Willardson - Graphic: John & Barbara Casado (WB)
VIRGIN (The Mission) Art Director: Bill Levy - Design: Fred Marcellino (Paramount)

ALBUM NOTES (G-589)

(Annotator's Award)
BUNNY BERIGAN, HIS TRUMPET & HIS ORCHESTRA, VOLUME I (Bunny Berigan) Ann: Dan Morgenstern (Vintage)
LENNY BRUCE/CARNEGIE HALL (Lenny Bruce) Ann: Albert Goldman (UA)
TOM T. HALL'S GREATEST HITS (Tom T. Hall) Ann. Tom T. Hall (Mercury)
LET MY CHILDREN HEAR MUSIC (Charles Mingus) Ann: Charles Mingus (Col.)
SUPER CHIEF (Count Basie) Ann: Michael Brooks (Col.)

JAZZ - SOLOIST (G-590)

ALONE AT LAST - Gary Burton (album) (Atlantic)
GREAT SCOTT - Tom Scott - (album) (A&M)
THE HUB OF HUBBARD - Freddie Hubbard (album) (MPS/BASF)
SAHARA - McCoy Tyner (album) (Milestone)
TUNE-UP! - Sonny Stitt (album) (Cobblestone)

JAZZ - GROUP (G-591)

(All nominations are albums)
THE CHUCK MANGIONE QUARTET - Chuck Mangione (Mercury)
FIRST LIGHT - Freddie Hubbard (CTI)
I SING THE BODY ELECTRIC - Weather Report (Col.)
OUTBACK - Joe Farrell (CTI)
SAHARA - McCoy Tyner (Milestone)
WHITE RABBIT - George Benson (CTI)

JAZZ - BIG BAND (G-592)

(All nominations are albums)
THE AGE OF STEAM - Gerry Mulligan (A&M)
ALL SMILES - Kenny Clark - Francy Boland Big Band (MPS/BASF)
CONNECTION - - Don Ellis (Col.)
M.F. HORN TWO - Maynard Ferguson (Col.)
TOGO BRAVA SUITE - Duke Ellington (U.A.)

POP VOCAL - FEMALE (G-593)

ANTICIPATION - Carly Simon (album) (Elektra)
DAY DREAMING - Aretha Franklin (single) (Atl.)
I AM WOMAN - Helen Reddy (single) (Cap.)
QUIET FIRE - Roberta Flack (album) (Atl.)
SWEET INSPIRATION/WHERE YOU LEAD - Barbra Streisand (single) (Col.)

POP VOCAL - MALE (G-594)

(All nominations are singles)
ALONE AGAIN (NATURALLY) Gilbert O'Sullivan (MAM/London)
AMERICAN PIE - Don McLean (UA)
BABY, DON'T GET HOOKED ON ME - Mac Davis (Col.)
CANDY MAN - Sammy Davis, Jr. (MGM)
WITHOUT YOU - Nilsson (RCA)

POP VOCAL - DUO, GROUP OR CHORUS (G-595)

BABY I'M-A WANT YOU - Bread (album) (Elektra)
A HORSE WITH NO NAME - America (single) (WB)
I'D LIKE TO TEACH THE WORLD TO SING (IN PERFECT HARMONY) - New Seekers (single) (Elektra)
SUMMER BREEZE - Seals & Crofts (single) (W.B.)
WHERE IS THE LOVE - Roberta Flack & Donny Hathaway (single) (Atlantic)

POP INSTRUMENTAL (G-596)

AMAZING GRACE - Pipes & Drums & Military Band of the Royal Scots Dragoon Guards (album) (RCA)
DOC - Doc Severinsen (album) (RCA)
THE INNER MOUNTING FLAME - Mahavishnu Orchestra with John McLaughlin (album) (Col.)
JOY - Apollo 100 (single) (Mega)
OUTA-SPACE - Billy Preston (single) (A&M)

POP INSTRUMENTAL PERFORMANCE BY AN ARRANGER, COMPOSER, ORCHESTRA AND/OR CHORAL LEADER (G-597)

BLACK MOSES - Isaac Hayes (album) (Enterprise)
BRASS ON IVORY - Henry Mancini and Doc Severinsen (Album) (RCA)
CARAVANSERAI - Santana (album) (Col.)
MONEY RUNNER - Quincy Jones (single) (Reprise)
PICTURES AT AN EXHIBITION - Emerson, Lake and Palmer (album) (Cotillion/Atl.)
THEME FROM THE GARDEN OF THE FINZI CONTINIS - Cy Coleman (single) (London)

R&B VOCAL - FEMALE (G-598)

CLEAN UP WOMAN - Betty Wright (single) (Alston/Atl)
FROM A WHISPER TO A SCREAM - Esther Phillips (album) (Kudu/CTI)
IN THE GHETTO - Candi Staton (single) (Fame)
OH, NO NOT MY BABY - Merry Clayton (single) (Ode)
YOUNG, GIFTED & BLACK - Aretha Franklin (album) (Atlantic)

R&B VOCAL - MALE (G-599)

(All nominations are for singles)
DROWNING IN THE SEA OF LOVE - Joe Simon (Spring)
FREDDIE'S DEAD - Curtis Mayfield (Curtom)
I GOTCHA - Joe Tex (Dial/Merc.)
ME & MRS. JONES - Billy Paul (PIR)
WHAT HAVE THEY DONE TO MY SONG MA - Ray Charles (Tangerine)

R&B VOCAL - DUO, GROUP OR CHORUS (G-600)

(All nominations are singles)
HELP ME MAKE IT THROUGH THE NIGHT - Gladys Knight & The Pips (Soul/Motown)
IF YOU DON'T KNOW ME BY NOW - Harold Melvin & The Blue Notes (PIR)
I'LL BE AROUND - The Spinners (Atlantic)
I'LL TAKE YOU THERE - The Staple Singers (Stax)
PAPA WAS A ROLLING STONE - The Temptations (Gordy/Motown)

R&B INSTRUMENTAL (G-601)

CRUSADERS I - Crusaders (album) (Blue Thumb)
EVERYBODY'S TALKIN' - King Curtis (album) (Atco)
JUNKIE CHASE - Curtis Mayfield (Track) (Curtom)
LET'S STAY TOGETHER - Isaac Hayes (single) (Enterprise)
PAPA WAS A ROLLING STONE - The Temptations & Paul Riser, cond. (single) (Gordy/Motown)

RHYTHM & BLUES SONG (G-602)

(Songwriter's Award)
BACK STABBERS - Leon Huff, Gene McFadden and John Whitehead
EVERYBODY PLAYS THE FOOL - Rudy Clark, J.R. Bailey and Kenny Williams
FREDDIE'S DEAD - Curtis Mayfield
ME & MRS. JONES - Ken Gamble, Leon Huff and Cary Gilbert
PAPA WAS A ROLLING STONE - Barrett Strong and Norman Whitfield

SOUL GOSPEL PERFORMANCE (G-603)

AMAZING GRACE - Aretha Franklin (album) (Atlantic)
JESU - The Edwin Hawkins Singers - (single) (Buddah)
LAST MILE OF THE WAY - Clara Ward (single) (Nashboro)
MY SWEET LORD - The B.C. & M. Choir (album) (Creed)
PRECIOUS MEMORIES - Aretha Franklin & James Cleveland (track) (Atlantic)

COUNTRY VOCAL - FEMALE (G-604)

(All nominations are singles)
DELTA DAWN - Tanya Tucker (Col.)
HAPPIEST GIRL IN THE WHOLE USA - Donna Fargo (Dot)
MY MAN - Tammy Wynette (Epic)
ONE TIN SOLDIER - Skeeter Davis (RCA)
ONE'S ON THE WAY - Loretta Lynn (Decca)
TOUCH YOUR WOMAN - Dolly Parton (RCA)

COUNTRY VOCAL - MALE (G-605)

CHANTILLY LACE - Jerry Lee Lewis (single) (Mercury)
CHARLEY PRIDE SINGS HEART SONGS - Charley Pride (album) (RCA)
GOOD HEARTED WOMAN - Waylon Jennings (single) (RCA)
I TAKE IT ON HOME - Charlie Rich (single) (Epic)
IT'S NOT LOVE (BUT IT'S NOT BAD) - Merle Haggard (single) (Capitol)

COUNTRY VOCAL - DUO OR GROUP (G-606)

CLASS OF '57 - The Statler Bros (single) (Mercury)
IF I HAD A HAMMER - Johnny Cash & June Carter (single) (Col)
LEAD ME ON - Conway Twitty & Loretta Lynn (album) (Decca)
TAKE ME - George Jones & Tammy Wynette (single) (Epic)
WILL THE CIRCLE BE UNBROKEN - Mother Maybelle Carter, Earl Scruggs, Doc Watson, Roy Acuff, Merle Travis, Jimmy Martin, The Nitty Gritty Dirt Band (album) (UA)

COUNTRY INSTRUMENTAL (G-607)

CHET ATKINS PICKS ON THE HITS - Chet Atkins (album) (RCA)
FLOWERS ON THE WALL - Danny Davis & The Nashville Brass (album) (RCA)
FOGGY MOUNTAIN BREAKDOWN - Lester Flatt (single) (RCA)
ME AND CHET - Chet Atkins & Jerry Reed (Album) (RCA)
CHARLIE MC COY/THE REAL MC COY - Charlie McCoy (album) (Monument)

COUNTRY SONG (G-608)

(A Songwriter's Award)
DELTA DAWN - Alex Harvey & Larry Collins
FUNNY FACE - Donna Fargo
HAPPIEST GIRL IN THE WHOLE USA - Donna Fargo
KISS AN ANGEL GOOD MORNIN' - Ben Peters
WOMAN (SENSUOUS WOMAN) Gary S. Paxton

INSPIRATIONAL PERFORMANCE (G-609)

(Non-classical)
AMAZING GRACE - The Pipes & Drums & Military Band of the Royal Scots - Dragoon Guards (track) (RCA)
AWARD WINNING GUITAR - Little Jimmy Dempsey (album) (Skylite)
THE GREATEST HITS OF CHRISTMAS - Eugene Ormandy cond. Philadelphia Orchestra and Chorus (album) (RCA)
HE TOUCHED ME - Elvis Presley (album) (RCA)
LAND OF MANY CHURCHES - Merle Haggard (album) (Capitol)
LOVE LIFTED ME - Ray Stevens (single) (Barnaby)
SPREAD A LITTLE LOVE AROUND - Danny Lee & The Children of Truth (album) (RCA)

GOSPEL PERFORMANCE (OTHER THAN SOUL GOSPEL) (G-610)

(All nominations are albums)
AMERICA SINGS - The Thrasher Bros. (Canaan)
BY YOUR REQUEST - Wendy Bagwell & the Sunliters (Canaan)
LIGHT - Oak Ridge Boys (Heartwarming)
L-O-V-E - Blackwood Bros. (RCA)
SOUL IN THE FAMILY - The Rambos (Heartwarming)

ETHNIC OR TRADITIONAL RECORDING (INCLUDING TRADITIONAL BLUES) (G-611)

(All nominations are albums)
BLUES PIANO ORGY - Little Brother Montgomery, Roosevelt Sykes, Sunnyland Slim, Speckled Red, Otis Spann, Curtis Jones - Prod: Robert G. Koester (Delmark)
LIGHTNIN' STRIKES - Lightnin' Hopkins (Tradition/Everest)
LIVE AT SOLEDAD PRISON - John Lee Hooker (ABC)
THE LONDON MUDDY WATERS SESSION - Muddy Waters (Chess)
WALKING THE BLUES - Otis Spann (Barnaby)

RECORDING FOR CHILDREN (G-612)

(All nominations are albums)
THE ELECTRIC COMPANY - Lee Chamberlin, Bill Cosby, Rita Moreno (WB)
KUKLA, FRAN & OLLIE - Kukla,Fran & Ollie (RCA/Camden)
THE MUPPET ALPHABET ALBUM - Muppets (Jim Henson) (Col. Children's Album)
SESAME STREET II - Original TV Cast - Prods: Joe Raposo & Jeffrey Moss (WB)
SNOOPY, COME HOME - Original Cast - Composers: Robert B. & Richard M. Sherman(Columbia)

COMEDY RECORDING (G-613)

(All nominations are albums)
ALL IN THE FAMILY - The Bunkers (Carroll O'Connor, Jean Stapleton, Sally Struthers, Robert Reiner) (Atlantic)
AND THAT'S THE TRUTH - Lily Tomlin (Polydor)
BIG BAMBU - Cheech & Chong (Ode)
FM & AM - George Carlin (Little David)
GERALDINE - Flip Wilson (Little David)

SPOKEN WORD RECORDING (G-614)

(All nominations are albums)
ANGELA DAVIS SPEAKS - Angela Davis (Folkways)
CANNONBALL ADDERLEY PRESENTS SOUL ZODIAC - Narrator: Rick Holmes (Capitol)
LENNY - Original Cast - Prod: Bruce Botnick (Blue Thumb)
THE WORD - Rod McKuen (Discus/Stanyan)
YEVTUSHENKO - Yevtushenko (Col.)

INSTRUMENTAL COMPOSITION (G-615)

(Composer's Award)
BRASS ON IVORY - Henry Mancini (RCA)
BRIAN'S SONG - Michel Legrand (Bell)
OUTA-SPACE - Billy Preston & Joe Greene (A&M)
THEME FROM FRENCH CONNECTION - Don Ellis (Col.)
THEME FROM THE GODFATHER - Nino Rota (Paramount)

ORIGINAL SCORE - MOTION PICTURE OR A TELEVISION SPECIAL (G-616)

(Composer's Award)
$ SOUNDTRACK - Quincy Jones (Reprise)
THE GARDEN OF THE FINZI CONTINIS - Manuel DeSica (RCA)
THE GODFATHER - Nino Rota (Paramount)
NICHOLAS AND ALEXANDRA - Richard Rodney Bennett (Bell)
SUPERFLY - Curtis Mayfield (Curtom)

SCORE FROM THE ORIGINAL CAST SHOW ALBUM (G-617)

(Grammys to the Composers and A&R Producer)
AIN'T SUPPOSED TO DIE A NATURAL DEATH - Comp: Melvin Van Peebles - Prod: Melvin Van Peebles (A&M)
DON'T BOTHER ME I CAN'T COPE - Comp: Micki Grant - Prod: Jerry Ragavoy (Polydor)
GREASE - Comps: Warren Casey & Jim Jacobs - Prod: Arnold Maxin (MGM)
SUGAR - Comps: Jule Styne & Bob Merrill - Prod: Mitch Miller (UA)
TWO GENTLEMEN OF VERONA - Comps: John Guare & Galt MacDermott - Prods: Harold Wheeler & Galt MacDermott & Lee Young (ABC)

ALBUM OF THE YEAR - CLASSICAL (G-618)

(Grammys to the Artist and Producer; Certificates to the Engineer)
BERLIOZ: BENVENUTO CELLINI - Colin Davis cond. BBC Symphony Chorus of Covent Garden (Gedda, Eda-Pierre, Soyer, Berbie) Prod: Erik Smith (Philips)
BERNSTEIN: MASS - Leonard Bernstein cond. Choirs & Orchestra - Prods: John McClure & Richard Killough (Col.)
BRAHMS: CONCERTO NO. 2 IN B FLAT MAJOR FOR PIANO - Artur Rubinstein; Eugene Ormandy cond. Philadelphia Orchestra - Prod: Max Wilcox (RCA)
HOROWITZ PLAYS CHOPIN (Pol. in A-Flat Major Intro & Rondo, OP. 16, Etc.) Vladimir Horowitz - Prods: Richard Killough & Thomas Frost (Col.)
MAHLER: SYMPHONY NO. 8 IN E FLAT MAJOR ("SYMPHONY OF A THOUSAND") - Georg Solti cond. Chicago Symphony, Vienna Boys Choir, Vienna State Opera Chorus, Vienna Singverein Chorus & Soloists - Prod: David Harvey (London)
WAGNER: TANNHAUSER - Georg Solti cond. Vienna Philharmonic (Kollo, Dernesch, Ludwig, Braun, Sotin) Prod: Ray Minshull (London)

CLASSICAL PERFORMANCE - ORCHESTRA (G-619)

(A Conductor's Award)
BOULEZ CONDUCTS BARTOK/THE MIRACULOUS MANDARIN & DANCE SUITE - Pierre Boulez cond. New York Philharmonic (Col.)
GLIERE: ILYA MUROMETZ (SYMPHONY NO. 3) Eugene Ormandy cond. Philadelphia Orchestra (RCA)
HAYDN: SYMPHONIES (COMPLETE) VOL. 4 & 5 Antal Dorati cond. Philharmonia Hungarica (London)
IVES: ORCHESTRAL SET NO. 2 - Leopold Stokowski cond. London Symphony (London)
MAHLER: SYMPHONY NO. 7 IN E MINOR - Georg Solti cond. Chicago Symphony (London)
SCHUMANN: SYMPHONIES (4) Herbert von Karajan cond. Berlin Philharmonic (DG)
SHOSTAKOVICH: SYMPHONY NO. 15 - Maksim Shostakovich cond. Moscow Radio Symphony (Mel/Angel)
STRAVINSKY: RITE OF SPRING (SACRE DU PRINTEMPS) - Michael Tilson Thomas cond. Boston Symphony (DG)

OPERA RECORDING (G-620)

(Grammys to Conductor & Producer)
BERLIOZ: BENVENUTO CELLINI - Colin Davis cond. BBC Symphony/Chorus of Covent Garden/Prin. Solos: Nicolai Gedda, Christiane Eda-Pierre, Roger Soyer, Jeanne Berbie - Prod: Erik Smith (Philips)
BRITTEN: OWEN WINGRAVE - Benjamin Britten cond. English Chamber Orchestra/Prin. Solos: J. Baker, P. Pears, B. Luson, H. Harper - Prod: David Harvey (London)
MUSSORGSKY: BORIS GODUNOV - Herbert von Karajan cond. Vienna Philharmonic Vienna Boys Choir, Vienna State Opera Chorus/Prin. Solos: Nicolai Ghaiurov, Galina Vishnevskaya, Ludovic Spiess, Martti Talvela, Aleksei Maslennikov - Prod: Ray Minshull (London)
STRAUSS: DER ROSENKAVALIER - Leonard Bernstein cond. Vienna State Opera Chorus/Vienna Philharmonic/Prin. Solos: Christa Ludwig, Walter Berry, Lucia Popp, Jones - Prod: John Culshaw (Columbia)
WAGNER: THE RING OF THE NIBELUNG - Wilhelm Furtwangler cond. Rome Symphony/RAI Chorus/Prin. Solos: Martha Modl, Ludwig Su-

thaus, Ferdinand Frantz - Prods: J.D. Bicknell & Radiotelevisione Italiana (Seraphim)
WAGNER: TANNHAUSER - Georg Solti cond. Vienna Philharmonic/Prin. Solos: Rene Kollo, Helga Dernesch, Christa Ludwig, Victor Braun,Hans Sotin - Prod: Ray Minshull (London)

CHORAL PERFORMANCE - OTHER THAN OPERA (G-621)

(Grammys to the Conductor and Choral Director)

BERNSTEIN: MASS - Leonard Bernstein cond, the Orchestra and Norman Scribner and Berkshire Boys Choirs (Col.)
DELIUS: A MASS OF LIFE - Charles Groves cond. the London Philharmonic Choir and Orchestra (Angel)
THE GLORY OF VENICE (GABRIELI IN SAN MARCO - Music for Multiple Choirs, Brass & Organ) E. Power Biggs, Gregg Smith Singers, Texas Boys Choir, Gregg Smith/Tarr Brass Ensemble, Vittorio Negri, cond. (Col.)
MAHLER: SYMPHONY NO. 8 IN E FLAT MAJOR ("SYMPHONY OF A THOUSAND") - Georg Solti cond. Vienna State Opera chorus, Vienna Singverein Chorus, Vienna Boys Choir, Chicago Symphony & Soloists (London)
MONTEVERDI: MADRIGALS, Books 8, 9 and 10 - Raymond Leppard cond. Glyndebourne Opera Chorus/Ambrosian Singers/English Chamber Orchestra (Philips)
PROKOFIEV: ALEXANDER NEVSKY - Andre Previn cond. London Symphony Chorus and Orchestra (Angel)

CHAMBER MUSIC PERFORMANCE (G-622)

BARTOK: SONATAS NO. 1 & 2 FOR VIOLIN AND PIANO - Isaac Stern & Alexander Zakin (Col.)
DVORAK: QUINTET IN A MAJOR FOR PIANO - Artur Rubinstein & Guarneri Quartet (RCA)
JULIAN & JOHN (Sel. by Lawes, Carulli, Albeniz, Granados) Julian Bream & John Williams (RCA)
MUSIC FOR GUITAR & HARPSICHORD (Works by Straube, Ponce & Dodgson) John Williams & Rafael Puyana (Col.)
MUSIC FOR TWO HARPSICHORDS (Mozart, Byrd, Farnably, etc.) Igor Kipnis & Thurston Dart (Col.)
SCHUBERT: QUARTET NO. 13 IN A MINOR - Guarneri Quartet (RCA)
SHOSTAKOVICH: SONATA FOR VIOLIN & PIANO - David Oistrakh & Sviatoslav Richter (Mel/Angel)
STRING QUARTETS OF THE NEW VIENNESE SCHOOL - La Salle Quartet (DG)

CLASSICAL PERFORMANCE - INSTRUMENTAL SOLOIST(S) (WITH ORCHESTRA) (G-623)

BRAHMS: CONCERTO NO. 2 IN B FLAT MAJOR FOR PIANO - Artur Rubinstein (Ormandy cond. Philadelphia Orchestra) (RCA)
MOZART: COMPLETE WORKS FOR VIOLIN & ORCHESTRA - David Oistrakh (Berlin Philharmonic) (Angel)
MOZART: THE FOUR HORN CONCERTOS - Barry Tuckwell (Marriner cond. Academy of St. Martin-In-Fields) (Angel)
MUSIC FOR ORGAN, BRASS & PERCUSSION - E. Power Biggs (Peress cond. Col. Brass Percussion Ensemble) (Col)
RAVEL: CONCERTO IN D MAJOR FOR LEFT HAND - Philippe Entremont (Boulez cond. Cleveland Orchestra) (Col)
STRAUSS: CONCERTO IN D MAJOR FOR OBOE - Heinz Holliger (DeWaart cond. New Philharmonia) (Philips)

CLASSICAL PERFORMANCE - INSTRUMENTAL SOLOIST(S) (WITHOUT ORCHESTRA) (G-624)

THE ART OF LAURINDO ALMEIDA - Laurindo Almeida (Orion)
BEETHOVEN: THE LATE SONATAS FOR PIANO - Charles Rosen (Col.)
COUPERIN: HARPSICHORD PIECES - Rafael Puyana (Philips)
DEBUSSY: IMAGES, BOOKS 1 & 2 CHILDREN'S CORNER SUITE - Arturo Beneditti Michelangeli (DG)
HOROWITZ PLAYS CHOPIN - Vladimir Horowitz (Col)
JANACEK: PIANO WORKS (COMPLETE) - Rudolf Firkusny (DG)
PAGANINI: THE 24 CAPRICES - Itzhak Perlman (Angel)
SCHUMANN: DAVIDSBUNDLERTANZE/BRAHMS: SONATA NO. 1 - William Masselos (RCA)

CLASSICAL PERFORMANCE - VOCAL SOLOIST - (G-625)

BRAHMS: DIE SCHONE MAGELONE - Dietrich Fischer-Dieskau (Accom: Richter) (Angel)
ELGAR: SEA PICTURES - Janet Baker (Barbirolli cond. London Symphony) (Angel)
FIVE GREAT OPERATIC SCENES (Verdi: Traviata, Don Carlo/Tchaikovsky: Onegin/Strauss: Ariadne, etc.) - Leontyne Price (Cleva cond. London Symphony) (RCA)
SONGS BY STEPHEN FOSTER - Jan de Gaetani (Accom: Kalish) (Nonesuch)
SONGS OF DEBUSSY - Anna Moffo (accomp: Robert Casadesus) (RCA)
WAGNER: WESENDONCK LIEDER - Birgit Nilsson (Davis cond. London Symphony) (Philips)

ALBUM NOTES - CLASSICAL (G-626)

(Annotator's Award)

BERLIOZ: BENVENUTO CELLINI - Davis cond. BBC Symphony - Ann: David Cairns (Philips)
HAYDN: SYMPHONIES (COMPLETE) VOLS. 4 & 5 - Dorati cond. Philharmonia Hungarica - Ann: H. C. Robbins Landon (London)
JOHN OGDON PLAYS ALKAN - John Ogdon - Ann: Sacheverell Sitwell (RCA)
JULIAN & JOHN - Julian Bream & John Williams - Ann: Tom Eastwood (RCA)
MICHAEL RABIN - IN MEMORIAM - Michael Rabin - Ann: Karolynne Gee (Seraphim)
STRING QUARTETS OF THE NEW VIENNESE SCHOOL - La Salle Quartet - Ann: Dr. Ursula Von Rauchhaupt (DG)
VAUGHAN WILLIAMS: SYMPHONY NO. 2 ("A LONDON SYMPHONY") - Previn cond. London Symphony - ann: James Lyons (RCA)

BEST ENGINEERED RECORDING - CLASSICAL (G-627)

(Engineer's Award)

BERNSTEIN: MASS - Bernstein cond. Orchestra & Choir - Eng: Don Puluse (Col.)
BERLIOZ: BENVENUTO CELLINI - Davis cond. BBC Symphony/Chorus of Covent Garden - Eng: Hans Lauterslager (Philips)
BOULEZ CONDUCTS STRAVINSKY (PETRUSHKA) - Boulez cond. New York Philharmonic - Engs: Raymond Moore & Edward Graham (Col.)
BOULEZ CONDUCTS BARTOK/THE MIRACULOUS MANDARIN (Complete) & DANCE SUITE - Boulez cond. New York Philharmonic - Hugh Ross, Dir., Schola Cantorum - Engs: Edward Graham & Raymond Moore (Col.)
GLIERE: ILYA MUROMETZ (SYMPHONY NO. 3) Ormandy cond. Philadelphia Orchestra - Eng: Paul Goodman (RCA)
MAHLER: SYMPHONY NO. 8 ("SYMPHONY OF A THOUSAND") - Solti cond. Chicago Symphony - Engs: Gordon Parry & Kenneth Wilkinson
WAGNER: TANNHAUSER - Solti cond. Vienna Philharmonic - Engs: Gordon Parry, James Lock & Colin Moorfoot (London)

1973

RECORD OF THE YEAR (G-628)

(Grammys to the Artist and A&R Producer)

BAD, BAD LEROY BROWN - Jim Croce - Terry Cashman & Tommy West, Producers (ABC)
BEHIND CLOSED DOORS - Charlie Rich - Bill Sherrill, Producer (EPIC/Col.)
KILLING ME SOFTLY WITH HIS SONG - Roberta Flack - Joel Dorn, Producer (Atlantic)
YOU ARE THE SUNSHINE OF MY LIFE Stevie Wonder - Stevie Wonder, Producer (Tamla/Motown)
YOU'RE SO VAIN - Carly Simon - Richard Perry, Producer (Elektra)

ALBUM OF THE YEAR (G-629)

(Grammys to the Artist and A&R Producer)
BEHIND CLOSED DOORS - Charlie Rich - Billy Sherrill, Producer (Epic/Col.)
THE DIVINE MISS M - Bette Midler - Joel Dorn, Barry Manilow, Geoffrey Haslam & Ahmet Ertegun, Producers (Atlantic)
INNERVISIONS - Stevie Wonder - Stevie Wonder, Producer (Tamla/Motown)
KILLING ME SOFTLY - Roberta Flack - Joel Dorn, Producer (Atlantic)
THERE GOES RHYMIN' SIMON - Paul Simon - Paul Simon, Phil Ramone, Paul Samwell-Smith, Roy Halee and M.S.S. Rhythm Studio, Producers (Col)

SONG OF THE YEAR (G-630)

(A Songwriter's Award)
BEHIND CLOSED DOORS - Kenny O'Dell
KILLING ME SOFTLY WITH HIS SONG - Norman Gimbel, Charles Fox
TIE A YELLOW RIBBON ROUND THE OLE OAK TREE - Irwin Levine, L. Russell Brown
YOU ARE THE SUNSHINE OF MY LIFE - Stevie Wonder
YOU'RE SO VAIN - Carly Simon

NEW ARTIST OF THE YEAR (G-631)

EUMIR DEODATO (CTI)
MAUREEN McGOVERN (20th Century)
BETTE MIDLER (Atlantic)
MARIE OSMOND (MGM)
BARRY WHITE (20th Century)

INSTRUMENTAL ARRANGEMENT (G-632)

(An Arranger's Award)
THE DAILY DANCE - Stan Kenton & His Orchestra - Bill Holman, Arranger (Creative World)
EASY LIVING/AIN'T NOBODY'S BUSINESS IF I DO (Medley) - Grover Washing, Jr. - Bob James, Arranger (Kudu/CTI)
PROLOGUE/CRUNCHY GRANOLA SUITE - Neil Diamond - Lee Holdridge, Arranger (MCA)
SPAIN - Chick Corea and Return to Forever - Chick Corea, Arranger (Polydor)
SUMMER IN THE CITY - Quincy Jones - Quincy Jones, Arranger (A&M)

ARRANGEMENT ACCOMPANYING VOCALIST (G-633)

(An Arranger's Award)
LADY LOVE - Jon Lucien - Dave Grusin, Arranger (RCA)
LIVE AND LET DIE - Paul McCartney & Wings - George Martin, Arranger (Apple/Capitol)
MICHELLE - The Singers Unlimited - Gene Puerling, Arranger (MPS/BASF)
RASHIDA - Jon Lucien - Dave Grusin, Arranger (RCA)
SING - Carpenters - Richard Carpenter, Arranger (A&M)
TOUCH ME IN THE MORNING - Diana Ross - Tom Baird & Gene Page, Arrangers (Motown)

BEST ENGINEERED RECORDING - NON-CLASSICAL (G-634)

(An Engineer's Award)
THE DARK SIDE OF THE MOON - Pink Floyd - Alan Parson, Engineer (album) (Harvest/Capitol)
GOODBYE YELLOW BRICK ROAD - Elton John - David Hentschel, Engineer (album) (MCA)
INNERVISIONS - Stevie Wonder - Robert Margouleff & Malcolm Cecil Engineers (album) (Tamla/Motown)
LONG TRAIN RUNNIN' - The Doobie Brothers - Donn Landee, Engineer (track) (WB)
NO SECRETS - Carly Simon - Robin Geoffrey Cable & Bill Schnee, Engineers (album) (Elektra)

ALBUM PACKAGE (G-635)

(Grammy to Art Director)
BILLION DOLLAR BABIES (Alice Cooper) Pacific Eye and Ear, Art Director (WB)
CHICAGO VI - (Chicago) John Berg, Art director (Col)
CHUBBY CHECKER'S GREATEST HITS - (Chubby Checker) Al Steckler, Art director (ABKCO)
HOUSES OF THE HOLY - (Led Zeppelin) Hipgnosis, Art Director (Atl)
LOS COCHINOS - (Cheech & Chong) - Ode Visuals, Inc., Art Director (Ode/A&M)
OOH LA LA - (Faces) Jim Ladwig - AGI, Art Director (WB)
TOMMY - (London Symphony/Chambre Choir) Wilkes & Braun, Inc., Art Director (Ode/A&M)
THE WORLD OF IKE & TINA - (Ike & Tina Turner) Mike Salisbury, Art Director (UA)

ALBUM NOTES (G-636)

(An Annotator's Award)
GOD IS IN THE HOUSE - (Art Taum); Ann - Dan Morgenstern (Onyx)
LONESOME, ON'RY AND MEAN - (Waylon Jennings); Ann - Chet Flippo (RCA)
OL' BLUE EYES IS BACK - (Frank Sinatra); Ann - Stan Cornyn (Reprise/W.B.)
REMEMBER MARILYN - (Marilyn Monroe); Ann - Lionel Newman (20th Century)
THIS IS JIMMIE RODGERS - (Jimmie Rodgers); Ann - William Ivey (RCA)

JAZZ - SOLOIST (G-637)

THE BEGINNING AND THE END - Clifford Brown (Album) (Col)
GOD IS IN THE HOUSE - Art Tatum (album) (Onyx)
IN A MIST - Freddie Hubbard (track) (CTI)
MORNING STAR - Hubert Laws (Album) (CTI)
THE VERY THOUGHT OF YOU - Ray Brown (Milt Jackson Quintet) (track) (Impulse/ABC)

JAZZ - GROUP (G-638)

(All nominations are albums)
ALONE TOGETHER - Jim Hall, Ron Carter (Milestone)
INSIDE STRAIGHT - Cannonball Adderley Quintet (Fantasy)
LIGHT AS A FEATHER - Chick Corea and Return to Forever (Polydor)
MUSIC OF ANOTHER PRESENT ERA - Oregon (Vanguard)
SUPERSAX PLAYS BIRD - Supersax (Cap)

JAZZ - BIG BAND (G-639)

(All nominations are albums)
GIANT STEPS - Woody Herman (Fantasy)
SOARING - Don Ellis (MPS/BASF)
SVENGALI - Gil Evans (Atl)
SWISS SUITE - Oliver Nelson (Flying Dutchman)
TANJAH - Randy Weston (Polydor)

POP VOCAL - FEMALE (G-640)

(All nominations are singles)
BOOGIE WOOGIE BUGLE BOY - Bette Midler (Atl)
DANNY'S SONG - Anne Murray (Cap)
KILLING ME SOFTLY WITH HIS SONG - Roberta Flack (Atl)
TOUCH ME IN THE MORNING - Diana Ross (Motown)
YOU'RE SO VAIN - Carly Simon (Elektra)

POP VOCAL - MALE (G-641)

AND I LOVE YOU SO- Perry Como (single) (RCA)
BAD, BAD LEROY BROWN - Jim Croce (single) (ABC)
DANIEL - Elton John (single) (MCA)
THERE GOES RHYMIN' SIMON - Paul Simon (album) (Col)
YOU ARE THE SUNSHINE OF MY LIFE - Stevie Wonder (single) (Tamla/Motown)

POP VOCAL - DUO, GROUP OR CHORUS (G-642)
DIAMOND GIRL Seals & Crofts (track) (WB)
LIVE AND LET DIE - Paul McCartney & Wings (single) (Apple/Capitol)
NEITHER ONE OF US (WANTS TO BE THE FIRST TO SAY GOODBYE) - Gladys Knight & the Pips (single) (Soul/Motown)
SING - Carpenters (single) (A&M)
TIE A YELLOW RIBBON ROUND THE OLE OAK TREE - Dawn Featuring Tony Orlando (single) (Bell)

POP INSTRUMENTAL (G-643)
ALSO SPRACH ZARATHUSTRA (2001) Eumir Deodato (single) (CTI)
BIRD OF FIRE - Mahavishnu Orchestra (track) (Col)
FRANKENSTEIN - Edgar Winter (single) (Epic/Col.)
SPACE RACE - Billy Preston (single) (A&M)
YOU'VE GOT IT BAD GIRL (instrumental portions of album) Quincy Jones (A&M)

R&B VOCAL - FEMALE (G-644)
ALONE AGAIN (NATURALLY) Esther Phillips (album) (Kudu/CTI)
ETTA JAMES - Etta James (album) (Chess)
I CAN'T STAND THE RAIN - Ann Peebles (single) (Hi/London)
MASTER OF EYES - Aretha Franklin (single) (Atl)
PILLOW TALK - Sylvia (single) (Vibration)

R&B VOCAL - MALE (G-645)
CALL ME (COME BACK HOME) Al Green (single) (Hi/London)
I'M GONNA LOVE YOU JUST A LITTLE MORE BABY - Barry White (single) (20th Cent.)
KEEP ON TRUCKIN' - Eddie Kendricks (single) (Tamla/Motown)
LET'S GET IT ON - Marvin Gaye (album) (Motown)
SUPERSTITION- Stevie Wonder (track) (Tamla/Motown)

R&B VOCAL - DUO, GROUP OR CHORUS (G-646)
(All nominations are singles)
BE WHAT YOU ARE - The Staple Singers (Stax)
THE CISCO KID - War (UA)
COULD IT BE I'M FALLING IN LOVE - The Spinners (Atl)
LOVE TRAIN - The O'Jays (Phila. Int'l/Col)
MIDNIGHT TRAIN TO GEORGIA - Gladys Knight & The Pips (Buddah)

R&B INSTRUMENTAL (G-647)
BLACK BYRD - Donald Byrd (album) (Blue Note/UA)
HANG ON SLOOPY - Ramsey Lewis (single) (Col)
2ND CRUSADE - The Crusaders (album) (Blue Thumb)
SOUL MAKOSSA - Manu Dibango (album) (Atl)
YES WE CAN CAN - Young-Holt Unlimited (track) (Atl)

RHYTHM & BLUES SONG (G-648)
(A Songwriter's Award)
THE CISCO KID - War
FAMILY AFFAIR - Sylvester Stewart
LOVE TRAIN - Ken Gamble, Leon Huff
MIDNIGHT TRAIN TO GEORGIA - Jim Weatherly
SUPERSTITION - Stevie Wonder

SOUL GOSPEL PERFORMANCE (G-649)
DOWN MEMORY LANE - James Cleveland (track) (Savoy)
HE AIN'T HEAVY - Jessy Dixon (track) (Gospel/Savoy)
LOVES ME LIKE A ROCK - Dixie Hummingbirds (single) (ABC)
NEW WORLD - Edwin Hawkins Singers (album) (Buddah)
YOU'VE GOT A FRIEND - Swan Silvertones (album) (Hob/Scepter)

COUNTRY VOCAL - FEMALE (G-650)
(All nominations are singles)
COUNTRY SUNSHINE - Dottie West (RCA)
KIDS SAY THE DARNDEST THINGS - Tammy Wynette (Epic/Col.)
LET ME BE THERE - Olivia Newton-John (MCA)
PAPER ROSES - Marie Osmond (MGM)
TEDDY BEAR SONG - Barbara Fairchild (Columbia)

COUNTRY VOCAL - MALE (G-651)
(All nominations are singles)
AMAZING LOVE - Charley Pride (RCA)
BEHIND CLOSED DOORS - Charlie Rich (Epic/Col.)
(OLD DOGS. . .CHILDREN AND) WATERMELON WINE Tom T. Hall (Mercury)
REDNECKS, WHITE SOCKS & BLUE RIBBON BEER - Johnny Russell (RCA)
WHY ME - Kris Kristofferson (Monument)

COUNTRY VOCAL - DUO OR GROUP (G-652)
CARRY ME BACK - Statler Brothers (album) (Mercury)
FROM THE BOTTLE TO THE BOTTOM - Kris Kristofferson, Rita Coolidge (track) (A&M)
IF TEARDROPS WERE PENNIES - Dolly Parton, Porter Wagoner (single) (RCA)
LOUISIANA WOMAN, MISSISSIPPI MAN - Conway Twitty, Loretta Lynn (single) (MCA)
WE'RE GONNA HOLD ON - Tammy Wynette, George Jones (single) (Epic/Col.)

COUNTRY INSTRUMENTAL (G-653)
DUELING BANJOS - Eric Weissberg, Steve Mandell (track) (WB)
FIDDLIN'AROUND - Chet Atkins (track) (RCA)
GOOD TIME CHARLIE - Charlie McCoy (album) (Monument)
I'LL FLY AWAY - Danny Davis & The Nashville Brass (album) (RCA)
SUPERPICKERS - Chet Atkins (album) (RCA)

COUNTRY SONG (G-654)
(A Songwriter's Award)
BEHIND CLOSED DOORS Kenny O'Dell
COUNTRY SUNSHINE - Billy Davis & Dottie West
THE MOST BEAUTIFUL GIRL - Rory Bourke, Billy Sherill & Norris Wilson
(OLD DOGS. . .,CHILDREN AND) WATERMELON WINE - Tom T. Hall
WHY ME - Kris Kristofferson

INSPIRATIONAL PERFORMANCE (G-655)
(All nominations are albums)
ALL THE PRAISES - Connie Smith (RCA)
ANITA BRYANT. . .NATURALLY - Anita Bryant (Myrrh/Word)
IN THE SWEET BY AND BY - Roy Rogers & Dale Evans (Word)
LET'S JUST PRAISE THE LORD - Bill Gaither Trio (Impact/Hrtwarming)
THERE'S SOMETHING ABOUT THAT NAME - George Beverly Shea (RCA)

GOSPEL PERFORMANCE (OTHER THAN SOUL GOSPEL) (G-656)
(All nominations are albums)
I BELIEVE IN JESUS - Statesmen (Artistic)
JUST ANDRAE - Andrae Crouch (light/Word)
LIVE - The Imperials (Impact/Hrtwarming)
RELEASE ME (FROM MY SIN) - Blackwood Brothers (Skylite)
STREET GOSPEL - Oak Ridge Boys (Heartwarming)

ETHNIC OR TRADITIONAL RECORDING (G-657)

(All nominations are albums)
BLUES AT MONTREAUX - King Curtis & Champion Jack Dupree (Atl)
CAN'T GET NO GRINDIN' - Muddy Waters (Chess)
JOHN LEE HOOKER'S DETROIT (1948-1952) John Lee Hooker (UA)
LEADBELLY (LIVE IN CONCERT) - Leadbelly (Playboy)
THEN AND NOW - Doc Watson (UA)

RECORDING FOR CHILDREN (G-658)

(All nominations are albums)
FREE TO BE. . .YOU AN ME - Marlo Thomas and Friends (Bell)
THE LITTLE PRINCE - Peter Ustinov (Argo)
MULTIPLICATION ROCK - Bob Dorough, Grady Tate, Blossom Dearie (Cap)
SESAME STREET LIVE - Sesame Street Cast - Joe Raposo, Producer (Col)
SONGS FROM the Electric Co. TV Show Conducted by Buddy Baker, with Vocalists (Disneyland)

COMEDY RECORDING (G-659)

(All nominations are albums)
LOS COCHINOS - Cheech & Chong (Ode/A&M)
FAT ALBERT - Bill Cosby (MCA)
OCCUPATION: FOOLE - George Carlin (Little David/Atl.)
RICHARD NIXON: A FANTASY - David Frye (Buddah)
LEMMINGS - National Lampoon (Banana/Blue Thumb)
CHILD OF THE 50's - Robert Klein (Brut/Buddah)

SPOKEN WORD RECORDING (G-660)

(All nominations are albums)
AMERICA, WHY I LOVE HER - John Wayne (RCA)
JONATHAN LIVINGSTON SEAGULL - Richard Harris (Dunhill/ABC)
SLAUGHTERHOUSE-FIVE - Kurt Vonnegut, Jr. (Caedmon)
SONGS & CONVERSATIONS - Billie Holiday (Paramount)
WITCHES GHOSTS & GOBLINS - Vincent Price (Caedmon)

INSTRUMENTAL COMPOSITION (G-661)

(A Composer's Award)
FRANKENSTEIN - Edgar Winter
HOCUS POCUS - Thijs van Leer and Jan Akkerman
LAST TANGO IN PARIS - Gato Barbieri
SOUL MAKOSSA - Manu Dibango
SPACE RACE - Billy Preston

ORIGINAL SCORE - MOTION PICTURE OR A TELEVISION SPECIAL (G-662)

(A Composer's Award)
JONATHAN LIVINGSTON SEAGULL - Neil Diamond (Col)
LAST TANGO IN PARIS - Gato Barbieri (UA)
LIVE AND LET DIE - Paul & Linda McCartney & George Martin (UA)
PAT GARRETT & BILLY THE KID - Bob Dylan (Col)
SOUNDER - Taj Mahal (Col)

SCORE FROM THE ORIGINAL CAST SHOW ALBUM (G-663)

(Grammys to the Composers and A&R Producer)
CYRANO - Anthony Burgess, Michael J. Lewis, Composers; Jerry Moss, Phil Ramone, Producers (A&M)
A LITTLE NIGHT MUSIC - Stephen Sondheim, Composer; Goddard Lieberson, Producer (Col)
MAN FROM THE EAST - Stomu Yamashta, Composer; Stomu Yamashta, Producer (Island/Cap)
PIPPIN - Stephen Schwartz Composer; Stephen Schwartz, Phil Ramone, Producers (Motown)

SEESAW - Cy Coleman, Dorothy Fields, Composer; Cy Coleman, Producer (Buddah)

ALBUM OF THE YEAR - CLASSICAL (G-664)

(Grammys to the Artist and Producer)
BARTOK: CONCERTO FOR ORCHESTRA - Pierre Boulez cond. New York Philharmonic - Thomas Z. Shepard, Producer (Col)
BEETHOVEN: CONCERTI (5) FOR PIANO & ORCHESTRA - Vladimir Ashkenazy/Georg Solti cond. Chicago Symphony - David Harvey, Producer (London)
BIZET: CARMEN - Leonard Bernstein cond. Metropolitan Opera Orchestra/Manhattan Opera Chorus/Soloists: M. Horne, J. McCracken, A. Maliponte, T. Krause - Thomas W. Mowrey, Producer (D.G./Polydor)
JOPLIN: THE RED BACK BOOK - Gunther Schuller cond. NE Conservatory Ragtime Ensemble - George Sponhaltz, Producer (Angel/Cap)
PROKOFIEV: ROMEO AND JULIET - Lorin Maazel cond. Cleveland Orchestra - Michael Woolcock, Producer (London)
PUCCINI: HEROINES (La Boheme, La Rondine, Tosca, Manon, Lescaut) - Leontyne Price/Downes cond. New Philharmonia) Richard Mohr, Producer (RCA)
(RACHMANINOFF) THE COMPLETE RACHMANINOFF - Vols. 1, 2, 3 - Sergei Rachmaninoff - John Pfeiffer, Greg Benko, Producers (RCA)
RACHMANINOFF: CONCERTO NO. 2 IN C MINOR FOR PIANO - Artur Rubinstein/Eugene Ormandy cond. Philadelphia Orchestra - Max Wilcox, Producer (RCA)

CLASSICAL PERFORMANCE - ORCHESTRA (G-665)

(A Conductor's Award)
BARTOK: CONCERTO FOR ORCHESTRA - Pierre Boulez cond. New York Philharmonic (Col)
BEETHOVEN: SYMPHONY NO. 9 IN D MINOR - Georg Solti cond. Chicago Symphony (London)
BERLIOZ: SYMPHONIE FANTASTIQUE - Seiji Ozawa cond. Boston Symphony (E.G./Polydor)
HOLST: THE PLANETS - Leonard Bernstein cond. New York Philharmonic (Col)
PROKOFIEV: ROMEO AND JULIET - Lorin Maazel cond. Cleveland Orchestra (London)
PROKOFIEV: ROMEO AND JULIET (COMPLETE BALLET) - Andre Previn cond. London Symphony (Angel/Cap)
RUSSO: THREE PIECES FOR BLUES BAND AND ORCHESTRA - Seiji Ozawa cond. San Francisco Symphony (Seigel-Schwall Band) (D.G./Polydor)
SIBELIUS: SYMPHONY NO. 2 IN D MAJOR - Eugene Ormandy cond. Philadelphia Orchestra (RCA)

OPERA RECORDING (G-666)

(Grammys to the Conductor and Producer)
BIZET: CARMEN - Leonard Bernstein cond. Metropolitan Opera Orchestra, Manhattan Opera Chorus/Prin. Solos: M. Horne, J. McCracken, A. Maliponte, T. Krause; Thomas W. Mowrey, Producer (D.G./Poly)
DELIUS: A VILLAGE ROMEO AND JULIET - Meredith Davies cond. Royal Philharmonic/John Alldis Choir/Prin. Solos: Robert Tear, Elizabeth Harwood: Christopher Bishop, Producer (Angel/Cap.)
PUCCINI: TURANDOT - Zubin Mehta cond. London Philharmonic, John Alldis Choir & Wandsworth School Choir/Prin. Solos: Sutherland, Pavarotti, Caballe, Ghaiurov, Krause, Pears; Ray Minshull, Producer (London)
WAGNER: DER RING DES NIBELUNGEN - Karl Bohm cond. Bayreuth Festival Orchestra/Prin Solos: Nilsson, Rysanek, Burmeister, Windgassen, King, Wohlfart, Adam, Stewart, Talvela, Greindl, Neidlinger; Wolfgang Lohse, Producer (Philips/Merc.)
WAGNER: PARSIFAL - George Solti cond. Vienna Philharmonic, Vienna State Opera Chorus/Vienna Boys Choir/Prin. Solos: Kollo, Ludwig, Fischer-Dieskau, Frick, Keleman, Hotter; Christopher Raeburn, Producer (London)
WAGNER: TRISTAN UND ISOLDE - Herbert von Karajan cond. Berlin Philharmonic/Prin. Solos: Vickers, Dernesch; Michael Glotz, Producer (Angel/Cap.)

CHORAL PERFORMANCE - OTHER THAN OPERA (G-667)

(Grammys to the Conductor and Choral Director)

BACH: ST. MATTHEW PASSION - Helmuth Froschauer cond. Vienna Singverein/Herbert von Karajan cond. Berlin Philharmonic (D.G./Polydor)
BEETHOVEN: MISSA SOLEMNIS - Eugen Jochum cond. Netherlands Radio Chorus & Concertgoebouw Orchestra/Giebel, Hoffgen, Haefliger, Ridderbusch (Phil.)
ELGAR: THE DREAM OF GERONTIUS - David Willcocks cond. Choir of King's College, Cambridge/Benjamin Britten cond. London Symphony (London)
HAYDN: MASS IN TIME OF WAR (Leonard Bernstein's Concert for Peace) - Norman Scribner Choir Norman Scribner, Dir./Orchestra cond. by Leonard Bernstein (Col)
HAYDN: THE SEASON - Herbert von Karajan cond. Chorus of the Deutsche Oper, Berlin & Berlin Philharmonic (Angel/Cap.)
MONTEVERDI: MADRIGALS, BOOKS 3 & 4 - Raymond Leppard cond. Glyndebourne Opera Chorus (Philip)
WALTON: BELSHAZZAR'S FEAST - Andre Previn cond. London Symphony & Arthur Oldham cond. London Symphony Orchestra Chorus (Angel/Cap)

CHAMBER MUSIC PERFORMANCE (G-668)

BENNETT: CONCERTO FOR GUITAR & CHAMBER ENSEMBLE - Julian Bream/Melos Ensemble of London, David Atherton (RCA)
BRAHMS: QUARTETS FOR STRINGS (COMPLETE) The Cleveland Quartet (RCA)
DVORAK: PIANO QUARTET IN E FLAT MAJOR, OP. 87 - Artur Rubinstein/Guarneri Quartet (RCA)
EARLY AMERICAN VOCAL MUSIC - Western Wind Vocal Ensemble (Nonesuch)
JOPLIN: THE RED BACK BOOK - Gunther Schuller & New England Ragtime Ensemble (Angel/Cap.)
ROCHBERG: QUARTET NO. 3 FOR STRINGS - Concord String Quartet (Nonesuch)
SCHUBERT: DUETS - Janet Baker, Dietrich Fischer-Dieskau (D.G./Polydor)

CLASSICAL PERFORMANCE - INSTRUMENTAL SOLOIST(S) (WITH ORCHESTRA) (G-669)

BEETHOVEN: CONCERTI (5) FOR PIANO & ORCHESTRA - Vladimir Ashkenazy (Solti cond. Chicago Symphony) (London)
BRAHMS: CONCERTO NO. 1 IN D MINOR FOR PIANO & ORCHESTRA & CONCERTO NO. 2 IN B FLAT MAJOR FOR PIANO & ORCHESTRA - Emil Gilels (Jochum cond. Berlin Philharmonic) (D.G./Pol)
MOZART: CONCERTO NO. 21 IN C MAJOR & CONCERTO NO. 25 IN C MAJOR - Stephen Bishop (C. Davis cond. London Symphony) (Philips/Merc.)
PREVIN: CONCERTO FOR GUITAR & ORCHESTRA/PONCE: CONCIERTO DEL SUR FOR GUITAR & ORCHESTRA - John Williams (Previn cond. London Symphony (Col)
RACHMANINOFF: CONCERTO NO. 2 IN C MINOR FOR PIANO - Artur Rubinstein (Ormandy cond. Philadelphia Orchestra) (RCA)
SAINT-SAENS: CONCERTI FOR PIANO (COMPLETE) Aldo Ciccolini (Baudo cond. Orchestre de Paris) (Seraphim/Cap.)
VIVALDI: FOUR SEASONS - Pinchas Zukerman - (Zukerman cond. English Chamber Orchestra) (Col)

CLASSICAL PERFORMANCE - INSTRUMENTAL SOLOIST(S) (WITHOUT ORCHESTRA) (G-670)

BACH: FRENCH SUITES 1-4-Glenn Gould (Col)
BACH: WELL-TEMPERED KLAVIER - Sviatoslav Richter (Melodiya/Angel)
CHOPIN: ETUDES - Maurizio Pollini (D.G.Poly)
HEAVY ORGAN AT CARNEGIE HALL - Virgil Fox (RCA)
SCHUBERT: SONATA IN B FLAT, OP. 960 - Alfred Brendel (Philips/Merc.)
(SCRIABIN) HOROWITZ PLAYS SCRIABIN - Vladimir Horowitz (Col)
THE WOODS SO WILD - Julian Bream (RCA)

CLASSICAL PERFORMANCE - VOCAL SOLOIST - (G-671)

BERG: SEVEN EARLY SONGS - Heather Harper (Boulez cond. BBC Symphony) (Col)
BERIO: RECITAL 1 (FOR CATHY) - Cathy Berberian (Berio cond. London Sinfonietta) (RCA)
LA VOCE D'ORO - Placido Domingo (Santi cond. New Philharmonia) (RCA)
MAHLER: DAS LIED VON DER ERDE - Yvonne Minton, Rene Kollo (Solti cond. Chicago Symphony) (London)
MARILYN HORNE SINGS ROSSINI (Excerpts from Siege of Corinth & La Donna del Lago) - Marilyn Horne (Lewis cond. Royal Philharmonic) (London)
MARTTI TALVELA - A LIEDER RECITAL (Schumann) Martti Talvela; (Irwin Gage, Accomp.) (London)
PUCCINI: HEROINES (La Boheme, La Rondine, Tosca, Manon Lescaut) - Leontyne Price (Downes cond. New Philharmonia) (RCA)
SCHUBERT: SONGS - Janet Baker; (Gerald Moore, accomp.) (Seraphim/Cap.)

ALBUM NOTES - CLASSICAL (G-672)

(An Annotator's Award)

BACH: BRANDENBURG CONCERTI - Marriner cond. Acad. of St. Martin-in-the-Fields - Ann: Erik Smith (Philips/Merc.)
BERIO: RECITAL 1 (FOR CATHY) Berberian, Berio cond. London Sinfonietta - Ann: Misha Donat (RCA)
BIZET: CARMEN - Bernstein cond. Metropolitan Opera Orchestra, Horne, McCracken, Maliponte, Krause - Ann: Harvey Phillips (D.G.)
DEBUSSY: LA MER/PRELUDE A L'APRES MIDI D'UN FAUNE & RAVEL: DAPHNIS & CHLOE SUITE NO. 2 - Ormandy cond. Philadelphia Orchestra - Ann: Clair Van Ausdall (RCA)
DVORAK: PIANO QUARTET IN E FLAT MAJOR, OP. 87 - Guarneri Quartet/Artur Rubinstein - Ann: Irving Kolodin (RCA)
HINDEMITH: SONATAS FOR PIANO (COMPLETE) Glenn Gould - Ann: Glenn Gould (Col.)
HAYDN: SYMPHONY NO. 36 - SYMPHONY NO. 48 - Dorati cond. Philharmonica Hungarica - Ann: H.C. Robbins Landon (London)
HAYDN: SYMPHONY NO. 20 IN C MAJOR TO SYMPHONY NO. 35 IN B FLAT MAJOR - Dorati cond. Philharmonica Hungarica - Ann: H.C. Robbins Landon (London)
RACHMANINOFF: CONCERTO NO. 2 IN C MINOR FOR PIANO - Rubinstein/Ormandy cond. Philadelphia Orchestra - Ann: Alan Rich (RCA)
THE WOODS SO WILD - Julian Bream - Ann: Tom Eastwood (RCA)

BEST ENGINEERED RECORDING - CLASSICAL (G-673)

(An Engineer's Award)

BACH'S GREATEST FUGUES - Ormandy cond. Philadelphia Orchestra - Paul Goodman, Eng. (RCA)
BARTOK: CONCERTO FOR ORCHESTRA - Boulez cond. New York Philharmonic - Edward T. Graham, Raymond Moore, Engs. (Columbia)
BERLIOZ: SYMPHONIE FANTASTIQUE - Ozawa cond. Boston Symphony - Hans Schweigmann, Eng. (E.G./Poly.)
BIZET: CARMEN - Bernstein cond. Metropolitan Opera Orchestra & Soloists - Gunther Hermanns, Eng. (D.G./Poly.)
HOLST: THE PLANETS - Bernstein cond. New York Philharmonic - Edward T. Graham, Larry Keyes, Engs. (Columbia)
PROKOFIEV: ROMEO AND JULIET - Maazel cond. Cleveland Orchestra - Jack Law, Colin Moorfoot, Gordon Parry, Engs. (London)
PUCCINI: HEROINES - Leontyne Price/Downes cond. New Philharmonia - Tony Salvatore, Eng. (RCA)
WAGNER: PARSIFAL - Solti cond. Vienna Philharmonic & Soloists - Kenneth Wilkinson, Gordon Parry, Engs. (London)

1974 HALL OF FAME WINNERS (G-674)

BODY AND SOUL - Coleman Hawkins - Bluebird #B-10523-A Released in 1939
THE CHRISTMAS SONG - Nat "King" Cole - Capitol #311 Released in 1946
GERSHWIN: RHAPSODY IN BLUE - Paul Whiteman with George

Gershwin - Victor #35822-A Released in 1927
WEST END BLUES - Louis Armstrong - Okeh #8597 Released in
1928
WHITE CHRISTMAS - Bing Crosby - Decca #18429-A Released in
1942

1974

RECORD OF THE YEAR (G-675)

(Grammys to the Artist and A&R Producer) (Certificates
to the Arranger, Engineer and Songwriter)
DON'T LET THE SUN GO DOWN ON ME - Elton John - Gus Dudgeon,
Producer (MCA)
FEEL LIKE MAKIN' LOVE - Roberta Flack - Roberta Flack, Producer
(Atl.)
HELP ME - Joni Mitchell - Joni Mitchell & Henry Lewy, Producers
(Asylum)
**I HONESTLY LOVE YOU - Olivia Newton-John - John Farrar, Producer
(MCA)**
MIDNIGHT AT THE OASIS - Maria Muldaur - Lenny Waronker & Joe
Boyd, Producers (Reprise/WB)

ALBUM OF THE YEAR (G-676)

(Grammys to the Artist and A&R Producer) (Certificates
to the Arrangers and Engineer)
BACK HOME AGAIN - John Denver - Milton Okun, Producer (RCA)
BAND ON THE RUN - Paul McCartney & Wings - Paul McCartney,
Producer (Apple/Cap)
CARIBOU - Elton John - Gus Dudgeon, Producer (MCA)
COURT AND SPARK - Joni Mitchell - Joni Mitchell & Henry Lewy,
Producers (Asylum)
**FULFILLINGNESS' FIRST FINALE - Stevie Wonder - Stevie Wonder,
Producer (Tamla/Motown)**

SONG OF THE YEAR (G-677)

(A Songwriter's Award)
FEEL LIKE MAKIN' LOVE - Eugene McDaniels
I HONESTLY LOVE YOU - Jeff Barry & Peter Allen
MIDNIGHT AT THE OASIS - David Nichtern
THE WAY WE WERE - Marilyn & Alan Bergman, Marvin Hamlisch
YOU AN ME AGAINST THE WORLD - Paul Williams & Ken Ascher

NEW ARTIST OF THE YEAR (G-678)

(This category is for an artist or organized group whose
first recording was released during the Eligibility
Period.)
BAD COMPANY (Swan Song)
JOHNNY BRISTOL (MGM)
DAVID ESSEX (Col.)
GRAHAM CENTRAL STATION (WB)
MARVIN HAMLISCH (MCA)
PHOEBE SNOW (Shelter)

INSTRUMENTAL ARRANGEMENT (G-679)

(An Arranger's Award for a specific arrangement
released on either a single or a track from an album)
CIRCUMVENT - Les Hooper Big Band - Les Hooper, Arranger (Creative
Wrld)
FIREBIRD/BIRDS OF FIRE - Don Sebesky - Don Sebesky, Arranger
(CTI)
LOOK WHAT THEY'VE DONE - Les Hooper Big Band - Les Hooper,
Arranger (Creative Wrld)
NIGHT ON BALD MOUNTAIN - Bob James - Bob James, Arranger
(CTI)
THRESHOLD - Pat Williams - Pat Williams, Arranger (Capitol)

ARRANGEMENT ACCOMPANYING VOCALISTS (G-680)

(An Arranger's Award for a specific arrangement
released on either a single or a track from an album)
**DOWN TO YOU - Joni Mitchell - Joni Mitchell & Tom Scott, Arrangers
(Asylum)**
LAND OF MAKE BELIEVE - Esther Satterfield (Chuck Mangione, Hamil-
ton Philharmonic) - Chuck Mangione, Arranger (Mercury)
SMILE OF THE BEYOND - Carol Shive (Mahavishnu Orch., with London
Symphony) Michael Gibbs, Arranger (Col.)
WE'VE ONLY JUST BEGUN - The Singers Unlimited - Gene Puerling
& Les Hooper, Arrangers (MPS/BASF)
WHERE IS LOVE - The Singers Unlimited - Gene Puerling, Arranger
(MPS/BASF)

BEST ENGINEERED RECORDING - NON-CLASSICAL (G-681)

(An Engineer's Award)
**BAND ON THE RUN - Paul McCartney & Wings - Geoff Emerick,
Engineer (album) (Apple/Cap.)**
CRIME OF THE CENTURY - Supertramp - Ken Scott & John Jansen,
Engineers (album) (A&M)
LINCOLN MAYORGA AND DISTINGUISHED COLLEAGUES VOLUME
III - Lincoln Mayorga - Bill Schnee, Engineer (album) (Sheffield)
POWERFUL PEOPLE - Gino Vannelli - Tommy Vicari & Larry Forkner,
Engineers (album) (A&M)
SOUTHERN COMFORT - The Crusaders - Rik Pekkonen & Peter Gra-
net, Engineers (album) (Blue Thumb)

ALBUM PACKAGE (G-682)

(Grammys to Art Director. Certificates to Designer(s),
Photographer(s), Illustrator(s), etc. where applicable)
CHEECH & CHONG'S WEDDING ALBUM - Cheech & Chong - Ode
Visuals, Art Director (Ode)
**COME & GONE - Mason Proffit - Ed Thrasher & Christopher Whorf,
Art Directors (WB)**
IS IT IN - Eddie Harris - Bob Defrin & Basil Pao, Art Directors (Atl.)
ON STAGE - Loggins and Messina - Ron Coro, Art Director (Col.)
QUADROPHENIA - The Who - Ethan A. Russell, Art Director (MCA)
RIDE 'EM COWBOY - Paul Davis - Eddie Biscoe, Art Director (Bang)
SANTANA'S GREATEST HITS - Santana - John Berg, Art Director
(Col.)
THAT'S A PLENTY - The Pointer Sisters - Herb Greene, Art Director
(Blue Thumb)

ALBUM NOTES (G-683)

(An Annotator's Award)
50 YEARS OF FILM MUSIC - Original Motion Picture Soundtrack Re-
cordings - Rudy Behlmer, Annotator (WB)
**FOR THE LAST TIME - Bob Wills and His Texas Playboys - Charles
R. Townsend, Annotator (UA)**
**THE HAWK FLIES - Coleman Hawkins - Dan Morgenstern, Annotator
(Milestone)**
THE PIANIST - Duke Ellington - Ralph J. Gleason, Annotator (Fantasy)
THE WORLD IS STILL WAITING FOR THE SUNRISE - Les Paul & Mary
Ford - J.R. Young, Annotator (Capitol)

PRODUCER OF THE YEAR (G-684)

(A Producer's Award for consistently outstanding
creativity in producing. Listed below are examples of the
producer's activities. (A)Album; (S)Single; (T)Track.)
**THOM BELL - "Mighty Love" (S) - Spinners - "You Make Me Feel
Brand New" (S) - Stylistics; "Then Came You" (S) - Dionne Warwick
& Spinners; "Love Don't Love Nobody" (S) - Spinners; "I'm Coming
Home" (S) - Johnny Mathis; "Mighty Love"(A) - Spinners; "Rockin'
Roll Baby" (A) - Stylistics**
RICK HALL - "You're Having My Baby" (S) - Paul Anka; "One Hell Of
A Woman" (S) - Mac Davis; "As Long As He Takes Care Of Home"

1975—18th ANNUAL GRAMMY AWARDS—Joan Baez, The Captain
and Tennille, and Stevie Wonder

© N.A.R.A.S.

1974—17th ANNUAL GRAMMY AWARDS—Marvin Hamlisch

© N.A.R.A.S.

1973—16th ANNUAL GRAMMY AWARDS—Gladys Knight and The Pips

© N.A.R.A.S.

1973—16th ANNUAL GRAMMY AWARDS—Bette Midler and The
Carpenters

© N.A.R.A.S.

1975—18th ANNUAL GRAMMY AWARDS—Earth, Wind and Fire

© N.A.R.A.S.

1976—19th ANNUAL GRAMMY AWARDS—Ella Fitzgerald with Richard Pryor and George Benson

© N.A.R.A.S.

1978—21st ANNUAL GRAMMY AWARDS—Donna Summer

© N.A.R.A.S.

1977—20th ANNUAL GRAMMY AWARDS—Barbra Streisand and Paul Williams

© N.A.R.A.S.

1978—21st ANNUAL GRAMMY AWARDS—Barry Manilow

© N.A.R.A.S.

(T) - Candi Staton
BILLY SHERRILL - "Woman To Woman" (S) - Tammy Wynette; "The Grand Tour" (S) - George Jones; "I Love My Friend" (S) - Charlie Rich; "Very Special Love Songs" (A) - Charlie Rich; "Would You Lay With Me" (A) - Tanya Tucker
LENNY WARONKER - "Carefree Highway" (S) - Gordon Lightfoot; "Waitress In A Donut Shop" (A) - Maria Muldaur (co-prod.: Joe Boyd); "Good Old Boys " (A) - Randy Newman (co-prod.: Russ Titleman); "Sundown" (A) - Gordon Lightfoot; "Midnight At The Oasis" (S) - Maria Muldaur (co-prod.: Joe Boyd)
STEVIE WONDER - "Fulfillingness' First Finale" (A) - Stevie Wonder; "You Haven't Done Nothin' " (S) - Stevie Wonder; "Boogie On Reggae Woman" (S) - Stevie Wonder; "Spinnin' & Spinnin' " (T) - Syretta Wright

JAZZ - SOLOIST (G-685)
(This category is for a solo performance with or without a group or band.)
FIRST RECORDINGS! - Charlie Parker (album) (Onyx)
HIGH ENERGY - Freddie Hubbard (album) (Col.)
IN THE BEGINNING - Hubert Laws (album) (CTI)
NAIMA - McCoy Tyner (track) (Milestone)
SOLO-CONCERTS - Keith Jarrett (album) (ECM/Poly)

JAZZ - GROUP (G-686)
(All nominations are albums)
HIGH ENERGY - Freddie Hubbard (Col.)
SALT PEANUTS - Supersax (Capitol)
SAMA LAYUCA - McCoy Tyner (Milestone)
THE TOKYO CONCERT - Bill Evans (Fantasy)
THE TRIO - Oscar Peterson, Joe Pass, Niels Pedersen (Pablo)

JAZZ - BIG BAND (G-687)
(All nominations are albums)
GIANT BOX - Don Sebesky (CTI)
LAND OF MAKE BELIEVE - Chuck Mangione (with Hamilton Philharmonic Orch.) (Mercury)
LOOK WHAT THEY'VE DONE - Les Hooper Big Band (Creative Wrld)
THUNDERING HERD - Woody Herman (Fantasy)
THRESHOLD - Pat Williams (Capitol)

POP VOCAL - FEMALE (G-688)
(This category is for pop, rock and folk.)
CLEO LAINE LIVE AT CARNEGIE HALL - Cleo Laine (album) (RCA)
COURT AND SPARK - Joni Mitchell (album) (Asylum)
FEEL LIKE MAKIN' LOVE - Roberta Flack (single) (Atl.)
I HONESTLY LOVE YOU - Olivia Newton-John (single) (MCA)
JAZZMAN - Carole King (track) (Ode)

POP VOCAL - MALE (G-689)
(This category is for pop, rock and folk.)
CAT'S IN THE CRADLE - Harry Chapin (track) (Elektra)
DON'T LET THE SUN GO DOWN ON ME - Elton John (single) (MCA)
FULFLLINGNESS' FIRST FINALE - Steve Wonder (album) (Tamla/Motown)
NOTHING FROM NOTHING - Billy Preston (track) (A&M)
PLEASE COME TO BOSTON - Dave Loggins (single) (Epic/Col.)

POP VOCAL - DUO, GROUP OR CHORUS (G-690)
(This category is for pop, rock and folk. All recordings on which the group receives artist billing on the label are eligible here even though the vocal may feature only one member of the group.)
BAND OF THE RUN - Paul McCartney & Wings (single) (Apple/Cap.)
BODY HEAT - Quincy Jones (album) (A&M)
RIKKI DON'T LOSE THAT NUMBER - Steely Dan (single) (ABC)
THEN CAME YOU - Dionne Warwick & Spinners (single) (Atl.)
YOU MAKE ME FEEL BRAND NEW - Stylistics (track) (Avco)

POP INSTRUMENTAL (G-691)
(This category is for pop, rock and folk. All recordings are for either pure instrumentals or instrumentals with vocal coloring.)
ALONG CAME BETTY - Quincy Jones (track) (A&M)
THE ENTERTAINER - Marvin Hamlisch (single) (MCA)
HEAD HUNTERS - Herbie Hancock (album) (Col.)
JOURNEY TO THE CENTRE OF THE EARTH - Rick Wakeman (album) (A&M)
RHAPSODY IN WHITE - Love Unlimited Orchestra (album) (20th Cent.)

R & B VOCAL - FEMALE (G-692)
AIN'T NOTHING LIKE THE REAL THING - Aretha Franklin (single) (Atl.)
IF LOVING YOU IS WRONG I DON'T WANT TO BE RIGHT - Millie Jackson (track) (Spring)
ST. LOUIS BLUES - Etta James (track) (Chess)
TINA TURNS THE COUNTRY ON! - Tina Turner (album) (UA)
WOMAN TO WOMAN - Shirley Brown (single) (Truth/Stax)
(YOU KEEP ME) HANGIN' ON - Ann Peebles (track) (Hi/London)
YOU'VE BEEN DOING WRONG FOR SO LONG - Thelma Houston (single) (Motown)

R & B VOCAL - MALE (G-693)
BOOGIE DOWN - Eddie Kendricks (single) (Tamla/Motown)
BOOGIE ON REGGAE WOMAN - Stevie Wonder (track) (Tamla/Motown)
HANG ON IN THERE BABY - Johnny Bristol (single) ((MGM)
MARVIN GAYE - LIVE - Marvin Gaye (album) (Tamla/Motown)
ROCK YOUR BABY - George McCrae (single) (T.K.)

R & B VOCAL - DUO, GROUP OR CHORUS (G-694)
(All recordings on which the group receives artist billing on label are eligible here even though the vocal may feature only one member of the group. All nominations are singles.)
DANCING MACHINE - Jackson Five (Motown)
FOR THE LOVE OF MONEY - The O'Jays (Phila. Int./Epic)
I FEEL A SONG (IN MY HEART) - Gladys Knight & The Pips (Buddah)
MIGHTY LOVE - Spinners (Atl.)
TELL ME SOMETHING GOOD - Rufus (ABC)

R & B INSTRUMENTAL (G-695)
LIGHT OF WORLDS - Kool & The Gang (album) (De-Lite)
PICK UP THE PIECES - Average White Band (track) (Atl.)
SCRATCH - The Crusaders (album) (Blue Thumb)
STRUTTIN' - Billy Preston (track) (A&M)
TSOP (THE SOUND OF PHILADELPHIA) - MFSB (single) (Phila. Int./Epic)

RHYTHM & BLUES SONG (G-696)
(A Songwriter's Award)
DANCING MACHINE - Harold Davis, Don Fletcher & Dean Parts
FOR THE LOVE OF MONEY - Ken Gamble, Leon Huff & Anthony Jackson
LIVING FOR THE CITY - Stevie Wonder
ROCK YOUR BABY - Henry Wayne Casey & Richard Finch

SOUL GOSPEL PERFORMANCE (G-697)
EDWIN HAWKINS SINGERS LIVE - Edwin Hawkins Singers (album) (Buddah)
FATHER ALONE - Ike Turner (single) (UA)
THE GOSPEL ACCORDING TO IKE AND TINA - Ike & Tina Turner (album) (UA)
IN THE GHETTO - James Cleveland and the Southern California Community Choir (album) (Savoy)
MY DESIRE - Five Blind Boys (album) (Peacock/ABC)

COUNTRY VOCAL - FEMALE (G-698)

JOLENE - Dolly Parton (track) (RCA)
LAST TIME I SAW HIM - Dottie West (single) (RCA)
LOVE SONG - Anne Murray (album) (Capitol)
WOMAN TO WOMAN - Tammy Wynette (single) (Epic)
WOULD YOU LAY WITH ME (IN A FIELD OF STONE) - Tanya Tucker (single) (Col.)

COUNTRY VOCAL - MALE (G-699)

BONAPARTE'S RETREAT - Glen Campbell (single) (Capitol)
COUNTRY FEELIN' - Charley Pride (album) (RCA)
THE ENTERTAINER - Roy Clark (album) (Dot)
I'M A RAMBLIN' MAN - Waylon Jennings (single) (RCA)
PLEASE DON'T TELL ME HOW THE STORY ENDS - Ronnie Milsap (single) (RCA)

COUNTRY VOCAL - DUO OR GROUP (G-700)

AFTER THE FIRE IS GONE - Willie Nelson & Tracy Nelson (single) (Atl.)
DADDY WHAT IF - Bobby Bare, Bobby Bare Jr. (single) (RCA)
FAIRYTALE - The Pointer Sisters (track) (Blue Thumb)
LOVING ARMS - Kris Kristofferson & Rita Coolidge (single) (A&M)
WHATEVER HAPPENED TO RANDOLPH SCOTT - The Statler Brothers (single) (Mercury)

COUNTRY INSTRUMENTAL (G-701)

THE ATKINS -TRAVIS TRAVELING SHOW - Chet Atkins & Merle Travis (album) (RCA)
BOOGIE WOOGIE (A/K/A T.D.'S BOOGIE WOOGIE) - Charlie McCoy & Barefoot Jerry (single) (Monument)
NASHVILLE BRASS IN BLUE GRASS COUNTRY - Danny Davis & The Nashville Brass (album) (RCA)
THE NASHVILLE HIT MAN - Charlie McCoy (album) (Monument)
THE YOUNG AND THE RESTLESS - Floyd Cramer (album) (RCA)

COUNTRY SONG (G-702)

(A Songwriter's Award)

A VERY SPECIAL LOVE SONG - Norris Wilson & Billy Sherrill
FAIRYTALE - Anita Pointer and Bonnie Pointer
IF WE MAKE IT THROUGH DECEMBER - Merle Haggard
I'M A RAMBLIN' MAN - Ray Pennington
PAPER ROSES - Janice Torre and Fred Spielman

INSPIRATIONAL PERFORMANCE (NON-CLASSICAL) (G-703)

HOW GREAT THOU ART - Elvis Presley (track) (RCA)
LISTEN - Bill Pursell (album) (Word)
THE LORD'S PRAYER - Sister Janet Mead (single) (A&M)
MAKE A JOYFUL NOISE - Tennessee Ernie Ford (album) (Capitol)
THANKS FOR SUNSHINE - The Bill Gaither Trio (album) (Impact)

GOSPEL PERFORMANCE (OTHER THAN SOUL GOSPEL) (G-704)

THE BAPTISM OF JESSE TAYLOR - Oak Ridge Boys (single) (Col.)
THE CARPENTER'S TOOL - Wendy Bagwell & The Sunliters (album) (Canaan)
FOLLOW THE MAN WITH THE MUSIC - Imperials (album) (Impact)
STEPPING ON THE CLOUDS - The LeFevres (album) (Canaan)
THERE HE GOES - The Blackwood Brothers (album) (Skylite)

ETHNIC OR TRADITIONAL RECORDING (INCLUDING TRADITIONAL BLUES AND PURE FOLK) (G-705)

(All nominations are albums)

THE BACK DOOR WOLF - Howlin' Wolf (Chess)
BIG DADDY - Bukka White (Biograph)
CATALYST - Willie Dixon (Ovation)
LONDON REVISITED - Muddy Waters & Howlin' Wolf (Chess)
TWO DAYS IN NOVEMBER - Doc & Merle Watson (U.A.)

RECORDING FOR CHILDREN (G-706)

(All nominations are albums)

AMERICA SINGS - Burl Ives, Others, Orch. & Chorus - Buddy Baker cond. (Disneyland)
ELI WALLACH READS ISAAC BASHEVIS SINGER - Eli Wallach (Newbery)
NEW ADVENTURES OF BUGS BUNNY VOLUME II - Mel Blanc (Peter Pan)
ROBIN HOOD - Various Artists, narrated by Roger Miller (Disneyland)
WINNIE THE POOH & TIGGER TOO - Sebastian Cabot, Sterling Holloway, Paul Winchell (Disneyland)

COMEDY RECORDING (G-707)

(All nominations are albums)

BOOGA! BOOGA! - David Steinberg (Col.)
CHEECH & CHONG'S WEDDING ALBUM - Cheech & Chong (Ode)
MIND OVER MATTER - Robert Klein (Brut/Buddah)
MISSING WHITE HOUSE TAPES - National Lampoon (Blue Thumb)
THAT NIGGER'S CRAZY - Richard Pryor (Partee/Stax)

SPOKEN WORD RECORDING (G-708)

AN EAR TO THE SOUNDS OF OUR HISTORY - Eric Sevareid (album) (Col.)
AUTUMN - Rod McKuen (track) (Stanyan/WB)
GOOD EVENING - Peter Cook & Dudley Moore (album) (Island)
SENATOR SAM AT HOME - Sam Ervin (album) (Col.)
WATERGATE VOLUME THREE: "I HOPE THE PRESIDENT IS FORGIVEN" (John W. Dean III Testifies) - Compiled by Don Molner (Folkways)

INSTRUMENTAL COMPOSITION (G-709)

(This is a Composer's Award for an original composition with or without lyrics which first gained recognition as an instrumental)

ALONG CAME BETTY - Benny Golson
BARRY'S THEME - Barry White
CHAMELEON - Herbie Hancock, Paul Jackson, Bernie Maupin and Harvey Mason
RHAPSODY IN WHITE - Barry White
TUBULAR BELLS (THEME FROM "THE EXORCIST") - Mike Oldfield

ORIGINAL SCORE - MOTION PICTURE OR A TELEVISION SPECIAL (G-710)

(A Composer's Award)

DEATH WISH - Herbie Hancock (Col.)
QB VII - Jerry Goldsmith (ABC)
SERPICO - Mikis Theodorakis (Paramount/ABC)
THE THREE MUSKETEERS - Michel Legrand (Bell)
THE WAY WE WERE - Marvin Hamlisch, Alan & Marilyn Bergman (Col.)

SCORE FROM THE ORIGINAL CAST SHOW ALBUM (G-711)

(Grammys to the Composers and A&R Producers)

LET MY PEOPLE COME - Earl Wilson, Jr., & Phil Oesterman Composers; Henry Jerome, Producer (Col.)
THE MAGIC SHOW - Stephen Schwartz, Composer; Phil Ramone & Stephen Schwartz, Producers (Bell)
OVER HERE - Richard M. Sherman & Robert B. Sherman, Composers; Charles Koppelman & Teo Macero, Producers (Col.)
RAISIN - Judd Woldin & Robert Brittan, Composers; Thomas Z. Shepard, Producer (Col.)
THE ROCKY HORROR SHOW - Richard O'Brien, Composer; Lou Adler, Producer (Ode)

ALBUM OF THE YEAR - CLASSICAL (G-712)

(Grammys to the Artist and Producer; Certificates to the Engineer)

BERLIOZ: THE DAMNATION OF FAUST - Colin Davis cond. London Symphony Orchestra & Chorus/Ambrosian Singers/Wandsworth School Boys' Choir/Soloists: Gedda, Bastin, Veasey, Van Allan - Erik Smith, Producer (Philips)

BERLIOZ: SYMPHONIE FANTASTIQUE - Georg Solti cond. Chicago Symphony - David Harvey, Producer (London)

IVES: THE 100TH ANNIVERSARY - Various Orchestras, Conductors, Soloists, etc. - Leroy Parkins & Vivian Perlis, Producers (Col.)

MAHLER: SYMPHONY NO. 2 IN C MINOR ("RESURRECTION") Leonard Bernstein cond. London Symphony/Edinburgh Festival Chorus/Soloists: Baker, Armstrong/ John McClure, Producer (Col.)

SCHUMANN: FAUST - Benjamin Britten cond. English Chamber Orchestra/Soloists: Fischer-Dieskau, Pears, Shirley-Quirk - Christopher Raeburn & Michael Woolcock, Producers (London)

"SNOWFLAKES ARE DANCING" - Isao Tomita - Isao Tomita, Producer (RCA)

WEBER: DER FREISCHUTZ - Carlos Kleiber cond. Dresden State Orchestra/Leipzig Radio Chorus/Soloists: Mathis, Janowitz,Schreier, Adam, etc. - Dr. Ellen Hickmann, Producer (DG)

CLASSICAL PERFORMANCE - ORCHESTRA (G-713)

(A Conductor's Award)

BARTOK: CONCERTO FOR ORCHESTRA - Herbert von Karajan cond. Berlin Philharmonic (Angel)

BERLIOZ: SYMPHONIE FANTASTIQUE - Georg Solti cond. Chicago Symphony (London)

BERNSTEIN CONDUCTS RAVEL - Leonard Bernstein cond. New York Philharmonic (Col.)

HOLST: THE PLANETS - Andre Previn cond. London Symphony (Angel)

IVES: SYMPHONY NO. 4 - Jose Serebrier cond. London Philharmonic (RCA)

MAHLER: SYMPHONY NO. 2 IN C MINOR - Leonard Bernstein cond. London Symphony (Col.)

OPERA RECORDING (G-714)

(Grammys to the Conductor and Producer; special Plaques to the Principal Soloists)

HUMPERDINCK: HANSEL & GRETEL - Kurt Eichhorn cond. Bavarian Radio Orchestra/Soloists: Moffo, Ludwig, Fischer-Dieskau/Fritz Ganss, Theodor Holzinger (RCA)

MOZART: COSI FAN TUTTE - Georg Solti cond. London Philharmonic/Soloists: Lorengar, Berganza, Berbie, Davies, Krause, Bacquier - Christopher Raeburn, Producer (London)

MOZART: DON GIOVANNI - Colin Davis cond. Chorus & Orchestra Royal Opera House, Covent Garden/Soloists: Wixell, Ganzarolli, Arroyo, Te Kenawa, Freni, Burrows/Erik Smith, Producer (Philips)

PFITZNER: PALESTRINA - Rafael Kubelik cond. Bavarian Radio Chorus & Orchestra/Soloists: Donath, Fassbaender, Gedda, Fischer-Dieskau, Prey - Dr. Rudolf Werner, Producer (DG)

PUCCINI: LA BOHEME - Georg Solti cond. London Philharmonic/Soloists: Caballe, Domingo, Milnes, Blegen, Raimondi/Richard Mohr, Producer (RCA)

VERDI: I VESPRI SICILIANI - James Levine cond. New Philharmonia/John Alldis Choir/Soloists: Arroyo, Domingo, Milnes, Raimondi - Richard Mohr, Producer, (RCA)

WEBER: DER FREISCHUTZ - Carlos Kleiber cond. Dresden State Orchestra/Leipzig Radio Chorus/Soloists: Mathis, Janowitz, Schreier, Adam, Crass, Weikl - Dr. Ellen Hickman, Producer (DG)

CHORAL PERFORMANCE - OTHER THAN OPERA (G-715)

(Grammys to the Conductor and Choral Director)

BERLIOZ: THE DAMNATION OF FAUST - Colin Davis cond. London Symphony Orchestra & Chorus/Ambrosian Singers/Wandsworth School Boys' Choir/Gedda, Bastin, Veasey, Van Allan (Philips)

HOLST: CHORAL SYMPHONY - Sir Adrian Boult cond. London Philharmonic Choir & Orchestra (Angel)

JANACEK: GLAGOLITIC MASS (SLAVONIC MASS) - Rudolf Kempe cond. Royal Philharmonic & Brighton Festival Chorus (London)

PENDERECKI: UTRENJA - Andrzej Markowski cond. Symphony Orchestra of National Philharmonic/Chorus of National Philharmonic Warsaw-Jozef Bok, Chorus Master/Pioneer Choir - Wladyslaw Skoraczewski, Chorus Master (Philips)

RACHMANINOFF: THE BELLS - Eugene Ormandy cond. Philadelphia Orchestra/Temple University Choirs, Robert Page, Director (RCA)

RACHMANINOFF: VESPERS (MASS) OP. 37 - Aleksander Sveshnikov cond. U.S.S.R. Russian Chorus (Mel. Angel)

SCHUMANN: FAUST - Russell Burgess cond. Aldeburgh Festival Singers/Wandsworth School Choir/Benj. Britten cond. English Chamber Orchestra (London)

VAUGHAN WILLIAMS: DONA NOBIS PACEM - Sir Adrian Boult, cond./John Alldis, Chorus Master/London Philharmonic Choir & Orchestra (Angel)

CHAMBER MUSIC PERFORMANCE - INSTRUMENTAL OR VOCAL (G-716)

BEETHOVEN: LATE QUARTETS - Juilliard Quartet (Col.)

BRAHMS: TRIOS (COMPLETE)/SCHUMANN: TRIO NO. 1 IN D MINOR - Artur Rubinstein, Henryk Szeryng, Pierre Fournier (RCA)

COPLAND: APPALACHIAN SPRING - Aaron Copland cond. Columbia Chamber Orchestra (Col.)

HAYDN: STRING QUARTETS, OP. 50 NO. 1 & 2-Tokyo String Quartet (DG)

IVES: VIOLIN SONATAS NOS. 1 - 4-Paul Zukofsky, Gilbert Kalish (Nonesuch)

JOPLIN: PALM LEAF RAG - Ralph Grierson with George Sponholtz & The Southland Stingers (Angel)

JULIAN & JOHN, VOL. 2 (Albeniz, Giuliani, Granados, etc.) - Julian Bream & John Williams (RCA)

CLASSICAL PERFORMANCE - INSTRUMENTAL SOLOIST(S) (WITH ORCHESTRA) (G-717)

BARTOK: VIOLIN CONCERTO NO. 2 - Itzhak Perlman (Previn cond. London Symphony) (Angel)

BRAHMS: PIANO CONCERTO NO. 2 IN B FLAT MAJOR-Alfred Brendel (Haitink cond. Concertgebouw Orchestra) (Philips)

CHOPIN: VARIATIONS ON "LA CI DAREM LA MANO"/FANTASY ON POLISH AIRS, OP. 13/ANDANTE SPIANATO & GRANDE POLONAISE BRILLANTE IN E FLAT, OP. 22-Claudio Arrau (Inbal cond. London Philharmonic) (Philips)

LISZT: TODTENTANZ FOR PIANO & ORCH./FRANCK: SYMPHONIC VARIATIONS FOR PIANO & ORCH. Andre Watts (Leinsdorf cond. London Symphony) (Col.)

SHOSTAKOVICH: VIOLIN CONCERTO NO. 1 - David Oistrakh (M. Shostakovich cond. New Philharmonic) (Angel)

STRAUSS: HORN CONCERTO NO. 2 IN E FLAT MAJOR-Norbert Hauptmann (von Karajan cond. Berlin Philharmonic) (DG)

WALTON: VIOLIN CONCERTO/STRAVINSKY: VIOLIN CONCERTO IN D MAJOR - Kyung-Wha Chung (Previn cond. London Symphony) (London)

WEBER: CONCERTINO IN E MINOR FOR HORN & ORCH. Barry Tuckwell (Marriner cond. Academy of St. Martin-in-the-Fields) (Angel)

CLASSICAL PERFORMANCE - INSTRUMENTAL SOLOIST(S) (WITHOUT ORCHESTRA) (G-718)

ALBENIZ: IBERIA - Alicia de Larrocha (London)

BACH: FRENCH SUITES, VOL. 2 NOS. 5 & 6 - Glenn Gould (Col.)

BEETHOVEN: PIANO SONATAS NOS. 21 IN C MAJOR ("WALDSTEIN") & 23 IN F MINOR ("APPASSIONATA") - Vladimir Horowitz (Col.)

CRUMB: MAKRO KOSMOS - David Burge (Nonesuch)

PERPETUAL MOTION- Itzhak Perlman (Angel)

RAVEL & DEBUSSY: MUSIC FOR TWO PIANOS/4 HANDS - Alfons & Aloys Kontarsky (DG)

SNOWFLAKES ARE DANCING - Isao Tomita (RCA)

CLASSICAL PERFORMANCE - VOCAL SOLOIST - (G-719)

AMAZING GRACE (Agnus Dei, Bless the Lord, O My Soul, etc.) - Sherrill Milnes (RCA)
BRAHMS: ALTO RHAPSODY - Janet Baker (Angel)
CATHY BERBERIAN AT THE EDINBURGH FESTIVAL - Cathy Berberian (RCA)
CRUMB: NIGHT OF THE FOUR MOONS - Jan DeGaetani (Col.)
DAVIES: EIGHT SONGS FOR A MAD KING - Julius Eastman (Nonesuch)
FRENCH AND SPANISH SONGS - Marilyn Horne (London)
SCHUBERT: GOETHE-LIEDER - Elly Ameling (Philips)
(R. STRAUSS) LEONTYNE PRICE SINGS RICHARD STRAUSS - Leontyne Price (RCA)
THERE'S A MEETING HERE TONIGHT - Martina Arroyo (Angel)
WAGNER: DUETS FROM PARSIFAL & DIE WALKURE - Birgit Nilsson, Helge Brilioth (Philips)

ALBUM NOTES - CLASSICAL (G-720)

(An Annotator's Award)

BERLIOZ: THE DAMNATION OF FAUST - Davis cond. London Symphony; Ann - David Cairns (Philips)
HERRMANN: CITIZEN KANE - Gerhardt cond. National Philharmonic; Ann - Christopher Palmer (RCA) HUMPERDINCK: HANSEL & GRETEL - Eichhorn cond. Bavarian Radio/Moffo, Donath; Ann - George Jellinek (RCA)
KORNGOLD: THE CLASSIC ERICH WOLFGANG KORNGOLD - Hoelscher/Mattes, cond; Ann - Rory Guy (Angel)
MAHLER: SYMPHONY NO. 10 - Morris cond. New Philharmonia Orch; Ann - Deryck Cooke (Philips)
MOZART: DON GIOVANNI - Davis cond. Royal Opera House Chorus & Orchestra; Ann - Erik Smith (Philips)
RACHMANINOFF: THE BELLS & THREE RUSSIAN SONGS - Ormandy cond./Curtin, Shirley, Devlin/Temple University Choirs, Page; Ann - Clair W. Van Ausdall (RCA)
SCRIABIN: PIANO MUSIC (COMP.) VOL. II - Ponti; Ann - Donald Garvelmann (Vox)
VERDI: I VESPRI SICILIANI - Levine, New Philharmonia; Ann - Irving Kolodin (RCA)
WEBER: DER FREISCHUTZ - Kleiber cond. Mathis, Janowitz, etc; Ann - Wolfram Schwinger (DG)

BEST ENGINEERED RECORDING - CLASSICAL (G-721)

(An Engineer's Award)

BERLIOZ: SYMPHONIE FANTASTIQUE - Solti cond. Chicago Symphony; Eng - Kenneth Wilkinson (London)
BERNSTEIN: CANDIDE - Original Cast; Engs - Bud Graham and Ray Moore (Col.)
COPLAND: APPALACHIAN SPRING - Copland cond. Columbia Chamber Players; Engs - Stanley Tonkel, Ray Moore and Milt Cherin (Col.)
IVES: SYMPHONY NO. 4 - Serebrier cond. London Philharmonic; Engs - Paul Goodman & Robert Auger (RCA)
PERCUSSION MUSIC - New Jersey Percussion Ensemble; Engs - Marc Aubort & Joanna Nickrenz (Nonesuch)
PUCCINI: LA BOHEME - Solti cond. London Philharmonic/Domingo, Caballe; Eng - Anthony Salvatore (RCA)
SNOWFLAKES ARE DANCING - Isao Tomita; Eng - Isao Tomita (RCA)

1975 HALL OF FAME WINNERS (G-722)

BEETHOVEN: PIANO SONATAS (32) (12 Albums) Artur Schnabel - Beethoven Sonata Society/HMV Vols. I-XII - Released 1932-1938
CARNEGIE HALL JAZZ CONCERT (Album) - Benny Goodman - Columbia #OSL 160 - Released in 1950
I CAN'T GET STARTED - Bunny Berigan - Victor #36208-A - Released in 1937
LEONCAVALLO: PAGLIACCI, ACT 1: VESTI LA GIUBBA - Enrico Caruso - Victrola #88061 - Released in 1907
MOOD INDIGO - Duke Ellington - Brunswick #80003-A - Released in 1931

1975

RECORD OF THE YEAR (G-723)

(Grammys to the Artist and A&R Producer. Certificates to Arranger, Engineer and Songwriter)

AT SEVENTEEN - Janis Ian - Brooks Arthur, Producer (Col.)
LOVE WILL KEEP US TOGETHER - Captain & Tennille - Daryl Dragon, Producer (A&M)
LYIN' EYES - Eagles - Bill Szymczyk, Producer (Asylum)
MANDY - Barry Manilow - Clive Davis, Barry Manilow & Ron Dante, Producers (Arista)
RHINESTONE COWBOY - Glen Campbell - Dennis Lambert & Brian Potter, Producers (Capitol)

ALBUM OF THE YEAR (G-724)

(Grammys to the Artist and A&R Producer. Certificates to the Arranger and Engineer)

BETWEEN THE LINES - Janis Ian - Brooks Arthur, Producer (Col.)
CAPTAIN FANTASTIC AND THE BROWN DIRT COWBOY - Elton John - Gus Dudgeon, Producer (MCA)
HEART LIKE A WHEEL - Linda Ronstadt - Peter Asher, Producer (Capitol)
ONE OF THESE NIGHTS - Eagles - Bill Szymczyk, Producer (Asylum)
STILL CRAZY AFTER ALL THESE YEARS - Paul Simon - Paul Simon & Phil Ramone, Producers (Col.)

SONG OF THE YEAR (G-725)

(A Songwriter's Award)

AT SEVENTEEN - Janis Ian
FEELINGS - Morris Albert
LOVE WILL KEEP US TOGETHER - Neil Sedaka & Howard Greenfield
RHINESTONE COWBOY - Larry Weiss
SEND IN THE CLOWNS - Stephen Sondheim

NEW ARTIST OF THE YEAR (G-726)

(This category is for an artist or organized group whose first recording was released during the Eligibility Period)

MORRIS ALBERT (RCA)
AMAZING RHYTHM ACES (RCA)
BRECKER BROS. (Arista)
NATALIE COLE (Capitol)
K.C. & THE SUNSHINE BAND (T.K.)

INSTRUMENTAL ARRANGEMENT (G-727)

(An Arranger's Award for a specific arrangement released on either a single or a track from an album)

CHILDREN OF LIMA - Woody Herman - Alan Broadbent, Arranger (Fantasy)
LIVING FOR THE CITY - Thad Jones & Mel Lewis - Thad Jones, Arranger (PIR)
NO SHOW - Blood, Sweat & Tears - Ron McClure, Arranger (Col.)
THE ROCKFORD FILES - Mike Post - Mike Post, Pete Carpenter, Arrangers (MGM)
SOME SKUNK FUNK - The Brecker Bros. - Randy Brecker, Arranger (Arista)
THEME FOR "JAWS" - John Williams - Herbert Spencer, Arranger (MCA)

ARRANGEMENT ACCOMPANYING VOCALISTS (G-728)

(An Arranger's Award for a specific arrangement released on either a single or a track from an album)

APRIL IN PARIS - The Singers Unlimited - Gene Puerling, Arranger (MPS)
AUTUMN IN NEW YORK - The Singers Unlimited - Gene Puerling, Arranger (MPS)

GERSHWIN MEDLEY - Mel Torme - Mel Torme, Arranger (Atlantic)
KILLING ME SOFTLY WITH HIS SONG - The Singers Unlimited - Gene Puerling, Arranger (MPS)
MISTY - Ray Stevens - Ray Stevens, Arranger (Barnaby)

BEST ENGINEERED RECORDING - NON-CLASSICAL (G-729)

(An Engineer's Award) (all nominations are albums)
AMBROSIA - Ambrosia; Engs - Chuck Johnson, Freddie Piro, Billy Taylor, Tom Trefethen, & Alan Parson (20th Century)
BETWEEN THE LINES - Janis Ian; Engs - Brooks Arthur, Larry Alexander & Russ Payne (Col.)
I'VE GOT THE MUSIC IN ME - Thelma Houston & Pressure Cooker; Eng - Bill Schnee (Sheffield)
THE ORIGINAL SOUNDTRACK - 10cc; Eng - Eric Stewart (Mercury)
STORM AT SUNUP - Gino Vannelli; Eng - Tommy Vicari (A&M)

ALBUM PACKAGE (G-730)

(Grammy to Art Director. Certificates to Designer(s), Photographer(s), Illustrator(s), etc. where applicable)
ATLANTIC CROSSING - Rod Stewart - John Kosh, Art Director (WB)
DREAM - Nitty Gritty Dirt Band - William E. McEuen, Art Director (UA)
HONEY - Ohio Players - Jim Ladwig, Art Director (Mercury)
ONE OF THESE NIGHTS - Eagles - Gary Burden, Art Director (Asylum)
PHYSICAL GRAFFITI - Led Zeppelin - AGI, Art Director (Swan Song/Atl)
PLAYING POSSUM - Carly Simon - Gene Christensen, Art Director (Elktra)
SOLO PIANO - Phineas Newborn, Jr. - Bob Defrin, Art Director (Atlantic)
STEPPIN' - The Pointer Sisters - Mick Haggerty, Art Director (Blue Thumb)
WISH YOU WERE HERE - Pink Floyd - Hipgnosis, Art Director (Col.)

ALBUM NOTES (G-731)

(An Annotator's Award)
BLOOD ON THE TRACKS - Bob Dylan; Ann - Pete Hamill (Col.)
GREATEST HITS, VOL. 2 - Tom T. Hall; Ann - Tom T. Hall (Mercury)
A LEGENDARY PERFORMER - Glenn Miller and His Orchestra; Ann - George T. Simon (RCA)
THE REAL LENNY BRUCE - Lenny Bruce; Ann - Ralph J. Gleason (Fantasy)
THE TATUM SOLO MASTERPIECES - Art Tatum; Ann - Benny Green, Annotator (Pablo)

PRODUCER OF THE YEAR (G-732)

(A Producer's Award for consistently outstanding creativity in producing.) Listed below are examples of the producer's activities. (A)Album, (S)Single, (T)Track
PETER ASHER - " Heart Like A Wheel" (A) - Linda Ronstadt; "Heat Wave" (S) - Linda Ronstadt "It Doesn't Matter Any More" (S) - Linda Ronstadt; "Prisoner In Disguise" (A) - Linda Ronstadt "When Will I Be Loved" (S) - Linda Ronstadt; "You're No Good" (S) - Linda Ronstadt
GUS DUDGEON - "Captain Fantastic and the Brown Dirt Cowboy" (A) - Elton John; "How Glad I Am" (S) - Kicci Dee; "Island Girl" (S) - Elton John; "Philadelphia Freedom" (S) - Elton John Band; "Someone Saved My Life Tonight" (S) - Elton John
DENNIS LAMBERT and BRIAN POTTER - "Estate of Mind" (A) - Evie Sands; "I Love Makin' Love To You" (S) - Evie Sands; "It Only Takes A Minute" (S) - Tavares; "Rhinestone Cowboy" (A) - Glen Campbell; "Rhinestone Cowboy" (S) - Glen Campbell; "Yesterday Can't Hurt Me" (T) - Evie Sands; "You Brought the Woman Out of Me" (S) - Evie Sands
ARIF MARDIN - "Cut the Cake" (A) - Average White Band; "If I Ever Lose This Heaven" (T) - Average White Band; "Jive Talkin' " (S) - Bee Gees; "Judith" (A) - Judy Collins; "Main Course" (A) - Bee Gees; "Mama's Pride" (A) - Mama's Pride; "The Prophet" (A) - Richard Harris
BILL SZYMCZYK - "Hotline" (A) - The J. Geils Band - (Album with

Co-Producer); "Lyin' Eyes" (S) - Eagles; "One Of These Nights" (A) - Eagles; "One Of These Nights" (S) - Eagles

JAZZ - SOLOIST (G-733)

(This category is for a solo performance with or without a group or band.)
CONCIERTO - Jim Hall - (album) (CTI)
GIANT STEPS - (first release of alternate take) - John Coltrane (track) (Atlantic)
IMAGES - Phil Woods - (album) (Gryphon/RCA)
OSCAR PETERSON AND DIZZY GILLESPIE - Dizzy Gillespie - (album) (Pablo)
SOLO PIANO - Phineas Newborn, Jr. (album) (Atlantic)

JAZZ - GROUP (G-734)

BASIE JAM - Count Basie (album) (Pablo)
DIZZY GILLESPIE'S BIG 4 - Dizzy Gillespie Quartet (album) (Pablo)
GIANT STEPS - (first release of alternate take) - John Coltrane Quartet (track) (Atlantic)
NO MYSTERY - Return to Forever featuring Chick Corea (album) (Polydor)
SUPERSAX PLAYS BIRD WITH STRINGS - Supersax - (album) (Capitol)

JAZZ - BIG BAND (G-735)

(All nominations are albums)
CLARK TERRY'S BIG B-A-D BAND LIVE AT THE WICHITA JAZZ FESTIVAL - Clark Terry (Vanguard)
IMAGES - Phil Woods with Michel Legrand and His Orchestra (Gryphon/RCA)
LAB '75 - North Texas State University Lab Band - Leon Breeden, Director (NTSU)
POTPOURRI - Thad Jones & Mel Lewis (PIR)
THE TIGER OF SAN PEDRO - Bill Watrous and the Manhattan Wildlife Refuge (Col.)

POP VOCAL - FEMALE (G-736)

(This category is for pop, rock and folk.)
AIN'T NO WAY TO TREAT A LADY - Helen Reddy (single) (Capitol)
AT SEVENTEEN - Janis Ian (single) (Columbia)
HAVE YOU NEVER BEEN MELLOW - Olivia Newton-John (single) (MCA)
HEART LIKE A WHEEL - Linda Ronstadt (album) (Capitol)
SEND IN THE CLOWNS - Judy Collins (single) (Elektra)

POP VOCAL - MALE (G-737)

(This category is for pop, rock and folk.)
BAD BLOOD - Neil Sedaka (single) (Rocket/MCA)
CAPTAIN FANTASTIC AND THE BROWN DIRT COWBOY - Elton John (album) (MCA)
FEELINGS - Morris Albert (single) (RCA)
RHINESTONE COWBOY - Glen Campbell (single) (Capitol)
STILL CRAZY AFTER ALL THESE YEARS - Paul Simon (album) (Columbia)

POP VOCAL - DUO, GROUP OR CHORUS (G-738)

(This category is for pop, rock and folk. All recordings on which the group receives artist billing on the label are eligible here even though the vocal may feature only one member of the group.)
A CAPELLA 2 - The Singers Unlimited (album) (MPS)
LOVE WILL KEEP US TOGETHER - Captain & Tennille (single) (A&M)
LYIN' EYES - Eagles (single) (Asylum)
MY LITTLE TOWN - Simon & Garfunkel (single) (Columbia)
THE WAY WE WERE/TRY TO REMEMBER - Gladys Knight & The Pips (single) (Buddah)

POP INSTRUMENTAL (G-739)

(This category is for pop, rock and folk. All recordings are for either pure instrumentals or instrumentals with vocal coloring.)

BRAZIL - The Ritchie Family (single) (20th Century)
CHASE THE CLOUDS AWAY - Chuck Mangione (album) (A&M)
THE HUSTLE - Van McCoy and the Soul City Symphony (single) (AVCO)
THE ROCKFORD FILES - Mike Post (single) (MGM)
TOM CAT - Tom Scott & The L.A. Express (album) (Ode)

R & B VOCAL - FEMALE (G-740)

NEVER CAN SAY GOODBYE - Gloria Gaynor (album) (MGM)
ROCKIN' CHAIR - Gwen McCrae (single) (Cat/T.K.)
SHAME, SHAME, SHAME - Shirley (and Company) (single) (Vibration)
THIS WILL BE - Natalie Cole (single) (Capitol)
WHAT A DIFF'RENCE A DAY MAKES - Esther Phillips (album) (Kudu/CTI)

R & B VOCAL - MALE (G-741)

CHOCOLATE CHIP - Isaac Hayes (album) (Hot Buttered Soul)
LIVING FOR THE CITY - Ray Charles (single) (Crossover)
L-O-V-E (LOVE) - Al Green (single) (Hi/London)
LOVE WON'T LET ME WAIT - Major Harris (single) (Atlantic)
SUPERNATURAL THING - PART I - Ben E. King (single) (Atlantic)

R & B VOCAL - DUO, GROUP OR CHORUS (G-742)

(All recordings on which the group receives artist billing on label are eligible here even though the vocal may feature only one member of the group.)

CUT THE CAKE - Average White Band (album) (Atlantic)
FIRE - Ohio Players (album) (Mercury)
GET DOWN TONIGHT - K.C. & The Sunshine Band (single) (T.K.)
HOW LONG (BETCHA' GOT A CHICK ON THE SIDE) - The Pointer Sisters (single) (Blue Thumb)
SHINING STAR - Earth, Wind & Fire (single) (Columbia)

R & B INSTRUMENTAL (G-743)

(All recordings are for either pure instrumentals or instrumentals with vocal coloring.)

DISCO BABY - Van McCoy and the Soul City Symphony (album) (AVCO)
FLY, ROBIN, FLY - Silver Convention (single) (Midland/RCA)
HANG UP YOUR HANGUPS - Herbie Hancock (single) (Columbia)
SNEAKIN' UP BEHIND YOU - Brecker Bros. (single) (Arista)
EXPRESS - B. T. Express (single) (Scepter)

RHYTHM & BLUES SONG (G-744)

(A Songwriter's Award)

EASE ON DOWN THE ROAD - Charlie Smalls
GET DOWN TONIGHT - H.W. Casey & Richard Finch
THAT'S THE WAY (I LIKE IT) - H.W. Casey & Richard Finch
WALKING IN RHYTHM - Barney Perry
WHERE IS THE LOVE - H.W. Casey, Richard Finch, Willie Clarke, Betty Wright

SOUL GOSPEL PERFORMANCE (G-745)

GOD HAS SMILED ON ME - James Cleveland with Voices of Tabernacle (album) (Savoy)
JESUS IS THE BEST THING - James Cleveland & Chas. Fold Singers (track) (Savoy)
THE STORM IS PASSING OVER - The 21st Century (album) (Creed)
TAKE ME BACK - Andrae Crouch and the Disciples (album) (Light)
TO THE GLORY OF GOD - James Cleveland & Southern California Community Choir (album) (Savoy)

COUNTRY VOCAL - FEMALE (G-746)

I CAN'T HELP IT (IF I'M STILL IN LOVE WITH YOU) - Linda Ronstadt (single) (Capitol)
IF I COULD ONLY WIN YOUR LOVE - Emmylou Harris (single) (Reprise)
I'M NOT LISA - Jessi Colter (single) (Capitol)
JOLENE (track from "In Concert") - Dolly Parton (track) (RCA)
THE PILL - Loretta Lynn (single) (MCA)

COUNTRY VOCAL - MALE (G-747)

(All nominations are singles)

ARE YOU SURE HANK DONE IT THIS WAY? - Waylon Jennings (RCA)
BEFORE THE NEXT TEARDROP FALLS - Freddy Fender (Dot/ABC)
BLUE EYES CRYING IN THE RAIN - Willie Nelson (Columbia)
COUNTRY BOY (YOU GOT YOUR FEET IN L.A.) - Glen Campbell (Capitol)
MISTY - Ray Stevens (Barnaby)
THANK GOD I'M A COUNTRY BOY - John Denver (RCA)

COUNTRY VOCAL - DUO OR GROUP (G-748)

FEELINS' - Conway Twitty & Loretta Lynn (single) (MCA)
I'LL GO TO MY GRAVE LOVING YOU - Statler Brothers (single) (Mercury)
LIVE YOUR LIFE BEFORE YOU DIE - The Pointer Sisters (single) (Blue Thumb)
LOVER PLEASE - Kris Kristofferson & Rita Coolidge (single) (Monument)
TEXAS GOLD - Asleep At The Wheel (album) (Capitol)

COUNTRY INSTRUMENTAL (G-749)

CHARLIE MY BOY - Charlie McCoy (album) (Monument)
COLONEL BOGEY - Chet Atkins & Jerry Reed (track) (RCA)
THE ENTERTAINER - Chet Atkins (track) (RCA)
FAT BOY RAG - Asleep At The Wheel (track) (Capitol)
VASSAR CLEMENTS - Vassar Clements (album) (Mercury)

COUNTRY SONG (G-750)

(A Songwriter's Award)

BEFORE THE NEXT TEARDROP FALLS - Vivian Keith & Ben Peters
BLUE EYES CRYING IN THE RAIN - Fred Rose
(HEY WON'T YOU PLAY) ANOTHER SOMEBODY DONE SOMEBODY WRONG SONG - Chips Moman & Larry Butler
I'M NOT LISA - Jessi Colter
THANK GOD I'M A COUNTRY BOY - John Martin Sommers

INSPIRATIONAL PERFORMANCE (G-751)

(Non-classical)

AMAZING GRACE - Larry Hart (track) (Cam)
GENTLE AS MORNING - Anita Kerr (album) (Word)
JESUS, WE JUST WANT TO THANK YOU - The Bill Gaither Trio (album) (Impact)
SOMETHING GOOD IS ABOUT TO HAPPEN - The Speers (album) (Heartwarming)
THIS TIME LORD - Ray Price (album) (Myrrh)

GOSPEL PERFORMANCE (OTHER THAN SOUL GOSPEL) (G-752)

(All nominations are albums)

CONNIE SMITH SINGS HANK WILLIAMS GOSPEL - Connie Smith (Columbia)
HAPPY GOODMAN FAMILY HOUR - Happy Goodman Family (Canaan)
HOLY BIBLE - NEW TESTAMENT - Statler Brothers (Mercury)
JOHNNY CASH SINGS PRECIOUS MEMORIES - Johnny Cash (Columbia)
NO SHORTAGE - Imperials (Impact)

ETHNIC OR TRADITIONAL RECORDING (INCLUDING TRADITIONAL BLUES AND PURE FOLK) (G-753)

(All nominations are albums)

I GOT WHAT IT TAKES - Koko Taylor (Alligator)
MEMPHIS BLUES (first U.S release) - Memphis Slim (Olympic)
THE MUDDY WATERS WOODSTOCK ALBUM - Muddy Waters (Chess)
MUSIC OF GUATEMALA - San Lucas Band, Kathryn King, Producer (ABC/Command)
WAKE UP DEAD MAN - Black Convict Work Songs Recorded & Edited by Bruce Jackson (Rounder)

LATIN RECORDING (G-754)

AFRO-INDIO - Mongo Santamaria (album) (Fania)
BARRETTO - Ray Barretto (album) (Fania)
FANIA ALL-STARS LIVE AT YANKEE STADIUM, VOL.I - Fania All-Stars (album) (Fania)
THE GOOD, THE BAD & THE UGLY - Willie Colon (album) (Fania)
QUIERES SER MI AMANTE - Camilo Sesto (single) (Pronto)
PAUNETTO'S POINT - Bobby Paunetto (album) (Pathfinder)
SUN OF LATIN MUSIC - Eddie Palmieri (album) (Coco)

RECORDING FOR CHILDREN (G-755)

BERT & ERNIE SING-ALONG - Bert & Ernie (CRA)
THE LITTLE PRINCE - Richard Burton, Narrator (featuring Jonathan Winters, Billy Simpson) (PIP)
MERRY CHRISTMAS FROM SESAME STREET - Sesame Street Cast (CRA)
MR. POPPER'S PENGUINS - Jim Backus (Newbery Award)
REALLY ROSIE - Carole King (Ode)
SESAME STREET MONSTERS - Jim Henson's Sesame Street Monsters (CRA)

COMEDY RECORDING (G-756)

(All nominations are albums)

AN EVENING WITH WALLY LONDO FEATURING BILL SLASZO - George Carlin (Little David)
IS IT SOMETHING I SAID? - Richard Pryor (Reprise)
MATCHING TIE & HANDKERCHIEF - Monty Python (Arista)
MODERN SCREAM - Lily Tomlin (Polydor)
A STAR IS BOUGHT - Albert Brooks (Asylum)

SPOKEN WORD, DOCUMENTARY OR DRAMA RECORDING (G-757)

(All nominations are albums)

THE AUTOBIOGRAPHY OF MISS JANE PITTMAN - Claudia McNeil (Caedmon)
GIVE 'EM HELL HARRY - James Whitmore (U.A.)
IMMORTAL SHERLOCK HOLMES MERCURY THEATER ON THE AIR - Orson Welles (Radiola)
THE PROPHET - Richard Harris (Atlantic)
TALK ABOUT AMERICA - Alistair Cooke (Pye)
TO KILL A MOCKINGBIRD - Maureen Stapleton (Miller-Brody)

INSTRUMENTAL COMPOSITION (G-758)

(This is a Composer's Award for an original composition with or without lyrics which first gained recognition as an instrumental)

CHASE THE CLOUDS AWAY - Chuck Mangione
FLY, ROBIN, FLY - Silvester Levay, Stephan Praeger
THE HUSTLE - Van McCoy
IMAGES - Michel Legrand
THE ROCKFORD FILES - Mike Post, Pete Carpenter

ORIGINAL SCORE - MOTION PICTURE OR A TELEVISION SPECIAL (G-759)

(A Composer's Award)

JAWS - John Williams (MCA)
MURDER ON THE ORIENT EXPRESS - Richard Rodney Bennett (Capitol)
NASHVILLE - Carradine, Blakley, Baskin, Reicheg, Gibson, Black (ABC)
THE RETURN OF THE PINK PANTHER - Henry Mancini (RCA)
THE WIND AND THE LION - Jerry Goldsmith (Artista)

CAST SHOW ALBUM (G-760)

(Grammys to the Composers and A&R Producer)

CHICAGO - John Kander, Fred Ebb, Composers - Phil Ramone, Producer (Artist)
A CHORUS LINE - Marvin Hamlisch, Edward Kleban, Composers - Goddard Lieberson, Producer (Columbia)
A LITTLE NIGHT MUSIC (Original London Cast) Stephen Sondheim, Composer - Thomas Z. Shepard, Producer (RCA)
SHENANDOAH - Gary Geld, Peter Udell, Composers - Gary Geld, Peter Udell, Philip Rose, Producers (RCA)
THE WIZ - Charlie Smalls, Composer - Jerry Wexler, Producer

ALBUM OF THE YEAR - CLASSICAL (G-761)

(Grammys to the Artist and Producer. Certificates to the Engineer(s).)

BEETHOVEN: SYMPHONIES (9) COMPLETE - Sir Georg Solti cond. Chicago Symphony - Ray Minshull, Producer (London)
BEETHOVEN: SYMPHONY NO. 5 IN C MINOR- Carlos Kleiber cond. Vienna Philharmonic - Werner Mayer, Producer (DG)
MOZART: COSI FAN TUTTE - Colin Davis cond. Royal Opera House, Covent Garden/Prin. Solos: Caballe, Baker, Gedda, Ganzarolli, Cotrubas, Van Allen - Erik Smith, Producer (Philips)
ORFF: CARMINA BURANA - Michael Tilson Thomas cond. Cleveland Orchestra/Robert Page Dir. Cleveland Orchestra Chorus & Boys Choir/Soloists: Blegen, Riegel, Bindery - Andrew Kazdin, Producer (Columbia)
PENDERECKI: MAGNIFICAT - Kryzysztof Penderecki cond. Polish Radio National Symphony & Chorus - David Mottley, Producer (Angel)
RAVEL: DAPHNIS ET CHLOE (Complete Ballet) - Pierre Boulez cond. New York Philharmonic/Camarata Singers - Andrew Kazdin, Producer (Columbia)
ROSSINI: THE SIEGE OF CORINTH - Thomas Schippers cond. London Symphony & Ambrosian Opera Chorus/Prin. Solos: Sills, Verrett, Diaz, Theyard - John Mordler, Producer (Angel)

CLASSICAL PERFORMANCE - ORCHESTRA (G-762)

(A Conductor's Award)

BARTOK: CONCERTO FOR ORCHESTRA - Rafael Kubelik cond. Boston Symphony (DG)
BEETHOVEN: SYMPHONIES (9) COMPLETE - Sir Georg Solti cond. Chicago Symphony (London)
BEETHOVEN: SYMPHONY NO. 5 IN C MINOR - Carlos Kleiber cond. Vienna Philharmonic (DG)
BEETHOVEN: SYMPHONY NO. 9 IN D MINOR - Seiji Ozawa cond. New Philharmonic Orchestra (Philips)
BERLIOZ: SYMPHNOIE FANTASTIQUE - Colin Davis cond. Concertgebouw Orchestra, Amsterdam (Philips)
MAHLER: SYMPHONY NO. 4 IN G MAJOR - James Levine cond. Chicago Symphony (RCA)
MAHLER: SYMPHONY NO. 5 IN C SHARP MINOR - Herbert von Karajan cond. Berlin Philharmonic (DG)
RAVEL: DAPHNIS ET CHLOE (Complete Ballet) - Pierre Boulez cond. New York Philharmonic (Columbia)

OPERA RECORDING (G-763)

(Grammys to the Conductor and Producer; special plaques to the Principal Soloists)

DALLAPICCOLA: IL PRIGIONIERO - Antal Dorati cond. National Symphony Orchestra of Washington, D.C./University of Maryland Chorus,

Paul Traver, Dir./Prin. Solos: Mazzieri, Barrera, Emili - James Mallinson, Producer (London)

KORNGOLD: DIE TOTE STADT - Erich Leinsdorf cond. Munich Radio Orchestra/Bavarian Radio Chorus/Prin. Solos: Kollo, Neblett, Prey, Luxon - Charles Gerhardt, Producer (RCA)

MOZART: COSI FAN TUTTE - Colin Davis cond. Royal Opera House, Covent Garden/Prin. Solos: Caballe, Baker, Gedda, Ganzarolli, Van Allen, Cotrubas - Erik Smith, Producer (Philips)

ROSSINI: THE BARBER OF SEVILLE - James Levine cond. London Symphony & John Alldis Choir/Prin. Solos: Sills, Milnes, Gedda - Christopher Bishop, Producer (Angel)

ROSSINI: THE SIEGE OF CORINTH - Thomas Schippers cond. London Symphony Orchestra & Ambrosian Opera Chorus/Prin. Solos: Sills, Verrett, Diaz, Theyard/John Mordler, Producer (Angel)

SCHOENBERG: MOSES AND AARON - Michael Gielen cond. Orchestra & Chorus of the Austrian Radio/Prin. Solos: Reich, Devos, Csapo, Obrowsky, Lucas - Abkauf Von Orf, Producer (Philips)

VAUGHAN WILLIAMS: SIR JOHN IN LOVE - Meredith Davis cond. New Philharmonia Orchestra/John Alldis Choir/Prin. Solos: Herincx, Palmer, Tear - Christopher Bishop, Producer (Angel)

CHORAL PERFORMANCE - OTHER THAN OPERA (G-764)

(Grammys to the Conductor and Choral Director)

BEETHOVEN: MISSA SOLEMNIS - Vienna Singverein & Berlin Philharmonic - Herbert von Karajan, cond. (Angel)

BERLIOZ: LA DAMNATION DE FAUST - Tanglewood Festival Chorus - John Oliver, Chorus Master/Boston Boy Choir - Theodore Marier, Chorus Master/Boston Symphony Orchestra - Seiji Ozawa, cond. (DG)

CHERUBINI: REQUIEM IN D MINOR FOR MALE CHORUS & ORCHESTRA - Ambrosian Singers - John McCarthy, Dir./New Philharmonia Orchestra - Riccardo Muti, cond. (Angel)

HAYDN: HARMONIEMESSE - Westminster Choir & New York Philharmonic - Leonard Bernstein, cond. (Columbia)

ORFF: CARMINA BURANA - Cleveland Orchestra Chorus & Boys Choir - Robert Page, Dir./Cleveland Orchestra - Michael Tilson Thomas, cond./Soloists: Blegen, Binder, Riegel (Columbia)

PENDERECKI: MAGNIFICAT - Polish Radio Chorus of Krakow - Tadeusz Dobrzanski, Chorus Master/Soloists & Boys Chorus from Krakow Philharmonic Chorus - Palka & Wietrzny, Chorus Masters/ Polish Radio National Symphony - Krzysztof Penderecki, cond.(Angel)

SCHOENBERG: GURRE-LIEDER - BBC Symphony Chorus/Goldsmith's Choral Union/Gentlemen of London Philharmonic Choir/BBC Symphony - Pierre Boulez, cond./Soloists: Napier, Minton Thomas (Columbia)

CHAMBER MUSIC PERFORMANCE (G-765)

(Instrumental or Vocal)

BAROQUE OBOE RECITAL: WORKS BY BACH, COUPERIN & MARAIS - Heinz Holliger, Christiane Jaccottet, Marcal Cervera (Philips)

BOLLING: SUITE FOR FLUTE & PIANO - Jean Pierre Rampal, Claude Bolling (Columbia)

GERSHWIN'S WONDERFUL' (Side 1: America In Paris, 3 Preludes) - Ralph Grierson & Artie Kane (Angel)

IVES: QUARTETS NOS. 1 & 2 - Concord Quartet (Nonesuch)

JOPLIN: THE EASY WINNERS & OTHER RAG-TIME MUSIC OF SCOTT JOPLIN - Itzhak Perlman & Andre Previn (Angel)

RAVEL: TRIO FOR VIOLIN, CELLO & PIANO - Jaime Laredo, Ruth Laredo & Jeffery Solow (Columbia)

SCHUBERT: TRIOS NOS. 1 IN B FLAT MAJOR OPP. 99 & 2 IN E FLAT MAJOR, OP. 100 (THE TRIOS) Artur Rubinstein, Henryk Szeryng, Pierre Fournier (RCA)

R. STRAUSS: SONATA IN F FOR CELLO & PIANO Mstislav Rostropovich & Vasso Devetzi (Angel)

CLASSICAL PERFORMANCE - INSTRUMENTAL SOLOIST(S) (WITH ORCHESTRA) (G-766)

BERKELEY: GUITAR CONCERTO/RODRIGO: CONCIERTO DE ARANJUEZ FOR GUITAR - Julian Bream (Gardiner cond. Monteverdi Orchestra) (RCA)

DVORAK: CONCERTO IN B MINOR FOR CELLO - Lynn Harrell (Levine cond. London Symphony) (RCA)

FOUR TRUMPET CONCERTOS BY VIVALDI, TELEMANN, MOZART, HUMMEL - Maurice Andre (von Karajan cond. Berlin Philharmonic) (Angel)

MENDELSSOHN: CONCERTO NO. 1 IN G MINOR FOR PIANO & NO. 2 IN D MINOR FOR PIANO - Murray Perahia (Marriner cond. Academy of St. Martin-in-the-Fields) (Columbia)

MOZART: CONCERTOS FOR PIANO & ORCHESTRA COMPOSED IN 1784 (6) (NOS. 14 - 19) - Peter Serkin (Schneider cond. English Chamber Orchestra) (RCA)

MOZART: CONCERTOS NOS. 18 IN B FLAT MAJOR & 27 IN B FLAT MAJOR FOR PIANO & ORCHESTRA - Alfred Brendel (Marriner cond. Academy of St. Martin-in-the-Fields) (Philips)

RAVEL: CONCERTO FOR LEFT HAND & CONCERTO FOR PIANO IN G MAJOR/FAURE: FANTAISIE FOR PIANO & ORCHESTRA Alicia de Larrocha (De Burgos cond. London Philharmonic - Faure/Foster cond. London Philharmonic - Ravel) (London)

SAINT-SAENS: INTRODUCTION & RONDO CAPRICCIOSO, HAVANAISE/CHAUSSON: POEME/RAVEL: TZIGANE - Itzhak Perlman (Martinon cond. Orchestre de Paris) (Angel)

CLASSICAL PERFORMANCE - INSTRUMENTAL SOLOIST(S) (WITHOUT ORCHESTRA) (G-767)

BACH: SONATAS & PARTITAS FOR VIOLIN UNACCOMPANIED Nathan Milstein (DG)

BACH: SUITES FOR LUTE - John Williams (Columbia)

CHOPIN: ETUDES, OP. 10 & 25 - Vladimir Ashkenazy (London)

FALLA: "MUSIC OF FALLA" (Three Cornered Hat, El Amor Brujo, etc.) - Alicia de Larrocha (London)

MESSIAEN: VINGT REGARDS SUR L'ENFANT JESUS - Peter Serkin (RCA)

SCHUMAN: CARNAVAL, OP. 9 - Arturo Benedetti Michelangeli (Angel)

CLASSICAL PERFORMANCE - VOCAL SOLOIST - (G-768)

AFTER THE BALL (A Treasury of Turn-of-the-Century Popular Songs) - Joan Morris (Bolcom, accomp.) (RCA)

CANTELOUBE: SONGS OF THE AUVERGNE, ALBUM 2 - Victoria de los Angeles (Jacquillat cond. Lamoureux Concerts Orchestra) (Angel)

CLEO LAINE SINGS PIERROT LUNAIRE & SONGS BY IVES - Cleo Laine (Nash Ensemble, Howarth/Hymas, piano) (RCA)

MAHLER: KINDERTOTENLIEDER - Janet Baker (Bernstein cond. Israel Philhamonic) (Columbia)

SCHUMANN: FRAUENLIEBE UND LEBEN - Elly Ameling (Baldwin, accomp.) (Philips)

SCHUMANN: FRAUENLIEBE UND LEBEN, OP. 42 - Elisabeth Schwarzkopf (Parsons, accomp.) (Angel)

VERDI & PUCCINI DUETS (Othello, Ballo en Maschera, Manon Lescaut, Madame Butterfly) Leontyne Price & Placido Domingo (Santi cond. New Philharmonic) (RCA)

ALBUM NOTES - CLASSICAL (G-769)

(An Annotator's Award)

THE ENGLISH HARPSICHORD (Byrd, Farnaby, etc.) -Igor Kipnis - Judith Robison, Annotator (Angel)

"FOOTLIFTERS" (A Century of American Marches - Sousa, Joplin, Ives) - Gunther Schuller cond. All-Star Band - Gunther Schuller, Annotator (Columbia)

GAGLIANO: LA DAFNE - Paul Vorwerk cond. Musica Pacifica - James H. Moore, Annotator (ABC/Command)

GERSHWIN: "GERSHWIN'S WONDERFUL" - Ralph Grierson & Artie Kane - Rory Guy, Annotator (Angel)

HAYDN: SYMPHONIES 93 - 104 - Dorati cond. Philharmonia Hungarica - H.C. Robbins-Landon, Annotator (London)

JOPLIN: THE COMPLETE WORKS OF SCOTT JOPLIN - Dick Hyman - Rudi Blesh, Annotator (RCA)

JOPLIN: THE EASY WINNERS - Itzhak Perlman/Andre Previn - Rory Guy and Itzhak Perlman, Annotators (Angel)

KODALY: ORCHESTRAL WORKS (Complete) - Antal Dorati cond. Hungarian Phil. - Laszlo Eosze, Annotator (London)

KORNGOLD: DIE TOTE STADT - Leinsdorf cond. Munich Radio Orchestra/Kollo, Neblett, Prey, Luxon - Christopher Palmer, Annotator (RCA)

BEST ENGINEERED RECORDING - CLASSICAL (G-770)

(An Engineer's Award)
BARTOK: CONCERTO FOR ORCHESTRA - Rafael Kubelik cond. Boston Symphony - Heinz Wildhagen, Engineer (DG)
BEETHOVEN: SYMPHONIES (9) COMPLETE - Sir Georg Solti cond. Chicago Symphony - Kenneth Wilkinson, Engineer (London)
BEETHOVEN: SYMPHONY NO. 5 IN C MINOR - Carlos Kleiber cond. Vienna Philharmonic - H.P. Schweigmann, Engineer (DG)
ORFF: CARMINA BURANA - Thomas cond. Cleveland Orchestra/Cleveland Chorus & Boys Choir, Page/Soloists: Blegen, Riegel, Binder - Edward Graham & Raymond Moore, Engineers (Columbia)
RAVEL: DAPHNIS & CHLOE - Maazel cond. Cleveland Orchestra - Gordon Parry & Colin Moorfoot, Engineers (London)
RAVEL: DAPHNIS ET CHLOE (Complete Ballet) - Boulez cond. New York Philharmonic - Bud Graham, Ray Moore & Milton Cherin, Engineers (Columbia)
STRAVINSKY: RITE OF SPRING - Sir George Solti cond. Chicago Symphony - James Lock & Kenneth Wilkinson, Engineers (London)

1976 HALL OF FAME WINNERS (G-771)

GERSHWIN: PORGY & BESS (Opera) (Album) - Lehman Engel, Conductor; Cast: Lawrence Winters, Camilla Williams and others. Columbia #SL-162. Released in 1951
GOD BLESS THE CHILD - Billie Holiday. Okeh #6270. Released in 1941
OKLAHOMA! (Album) - Original Broadway Cast with Alfred Drake, Orchestra & Chorus directed by Jay Blackton. Decca #A 359. Released in 1943
RACHMANINOFF: PIANO CONCERTO NO. 2 IN C MINOR (Album) Sergei Rachmaninoff (Piano); Philadelphia Orchestra. Victrola #M 58. Released in 1929
TAKE THE "A" TRAIN - Duke Ellington & his Orchestra Victor #27380-A. Released in 1941.

1976

RECORD OF THE YEAR (G-772)

(Grammys to the Artist & Producer.) (This category is for singles. An album track released as a single during the Eligibility Year is eligible provided that the track itself did not receive a previous nomination or award.)
AFTERNOON DELIGHT - Starland Vocal Band - Milt Okun, Producer (Windsong/RCA)
50 WAYS TO LEAVE YOUR LOVER - Paul Simon - Paul Simon, Phil Ramone, Producers (Columbia)
I WRITE THE SONGS - Barry Manilow - Ron Dante, Barry Manilow, Producers (Arista)
IF YOU LEAVE ME NOW - Chicago - James William Guercio, Producer (Columbia)
THIS MASQUERADE - George Benson - Tommy Lipuma, Producer (Warner Bros.)

ALBUM OF THE YEAR (G-773)

(Grammys to the Artist and Producer. This category is for non-classical albums.)
BREEZIN' - George Benson - Tommy Lipuma, Producer (Warner Bros.)
CHICAGO X - Chicago - James William Guercio, Producer (Columbia)
FRAMPTON COMES ALIVE - Peter Frampton - Peter Frampton, Producer (A&M)
SILK DEGREES - Boz Scaggs - Joe Wissert, Producer (Columbia)
SONGS IN THE KEY OF LIFE - Stevie Wonder - Stevie Wonder, Producer (Tamla)

SONG OF THE YEAR (G-774)

(A Songwriter's Award.) (Any song is eligible if a new recording of it has been released during the Eligibility Year, provided it was not a previous final nomination in a songwriting category.)
AFTERNOON DELIGHT - Bill Danoff
BREAKING UP IS HARD TO DO - Neil Sedaka, Howard Greenfield
I WRITE THE SONGS - Bruce Johnston
THIS MASQUERADE - Leon Russell
THE WRECK OF THE EDMUND FITZGERALD - Gordon Lightfoot

NEW ARTIST OF THE YEAR (G-775)

(This category is for an artist or organized group whose first recording was released during the Eligibility Year.)
BOSTON (Epic)
DR. BUZZARD'S ORIGINAL "SAVANNAH" BAND (RCA)
THE BROTHERS JOHNSON (A&M)
STARLAND VOCAL BAND (Windsong/RCA)
WILD CHERRY (Epic)

INSTRUMENTAL ARRANGEMENT (G-776)

(An Arranger's Award. This category is for a specific arrangement released for the first time during the Eligibility Year on either a single or an album track.)
THE DISASTER MOVIE SUITE - Henry Mancini cond. - London Symphony - Henry Mancini, John Williams, Herb Spencer & Al Woodbury, Arrangers (RCA)
LEPRECHAUN'S DREAM - Chick Corea - Chick Corea, Arranger (Polydor)
LIFE IS JUST A GAME - Stanley Clarke - Stanley Clarke, Arranger (Emperor/Atlantic)
SAUDADE DO BRAZIL - Antonio Carlos Jobim - Claus Ogerman, Arranger (Warner Bros.)
WESTCHESTER LADY - Bob James - Bob James, Arranger (CTI)

ARRANGEMENT ACCOMPANYING VOCALISTS (G-777)

(An Arranger's Award. This category is for a specific arrangement released for the first time during the Eligibility Year on either a single or an album track.)
BOTO (PORPOISE) - Antonio Carlos Jobim - Claus Ogerman, Arranger (Warner Bros.)
GREEN DOLPHIN STREET - The Singers Unlimited - Clare Fischer, Arranger (MPS)
IF YOU LEAVE ME NOW - Chicago - Jimmie Haskell & James Wm. Guercio, Arrangers (Columbia)
LET 'EM IN - Wings - Paul McCartney, Arranger (Capitol)
SENTIMENTAL JOURNEY - The Singers Unlimited - Robert Farnon, Arranger (MPS)

ARRANGEMENT FOR VOICES (DUO, GROUP OR CHORUS) (G-778)

(An Arranger's Award.) (This category is for a specific arrangement released for the first time during the Eligibility Year on either a single or an album track. This category covers all voices on a recording excluding a featured soloist and includes a cappella and voices with instrumental accompaniment.)
AFTERNOON DELIGHT - Starland Vocal Band - Starland Vocal Band, Arrangers (Windsong/RCA)
AIN'T MISBEHAVIN' - Quire - Christian Chevallier, Arranger (RCA)
BOHEMIAN RHAPSODY - Queen - Queen, Arrangers (Elektra)
CAN'T HIDE LOVE - Earth, Wind & Fire - Earth, Wind & Fire, Arrangers (Columbia)

I GET ALONG WITHOUT YOU VERY WELL - The Singers Unlimited - Gene Puerling, Arranger (MPS)

BEST ENGINEERED RECORDING - NON-CLASSICAL (G-779)

(An Engineer's Award.) (All nominations are albums)

BREEZIN' - George Benson - Al Schmitt, Engineer (Warner Bros.)
THE DREAM WEAVER - Gary Wright - Jay Lewis, Engineer (Warner Bros.)
THE KING JAMES VERSION - Harry James and his Big Band - Ron Hitchcock, Engineer (Sheffield Lab)
SOMEWHERE I'VE NEVER TRAVELLED - Ambrosia - Alan Parsons & Tom Trefethen, Engineers (20th Cent.)
TALES OF MYSTERY AND IMAGINATION - EDGAR ALLAN POE - The Alan Parsons Project - Alan Parsons, Engineer (20th Cent.)

ALBUM PACKAGE (G-780)

(An Art Director's Award. This category is for either classical or non-classical single-jacket albums or multiple pocket album packages.)

BELLAVIA - Chuck Mangione - Roland Young, Art Director (A&M)
CHICAGO X - Chicago - John Berg, Art Director (Columbia)
CONEY ISLAND BABY - Lou Reed - Acy Lehman, Art Director (RCA)
THE END OF THE BEGINNING - Richie Havens - Roland Young, Art Director (A&M)
MIRRORS - Peggy Lee - Roland Young, Art Director (A&M)
PRESENCE - Led Zeppelin - Hipgnosis and Hardie, Art Directors (Swan Song)
SCHUMANN: SYMPHONY #1 IN B-FLAT, OP. 38; MANFRED: OVERTURE, Op. 115 - Charles Munch cond. Boston Symphony - J. Stelmach, Art Director (RCA)
SILK DEGREES - Boz Scaggs - Ron Coro & Nancy Donald, Art Directors (Columbia)

ALBUM NOTES (G-781)

(An Annotator's Award.) (This category is for original writing for a specific album. Either classical or non-classical albums qualify.)

BEETHOVEN: THE FIVE PIANO CONCERTOS - Rubinstein, Baremboim cond. London Philharmonic - George R. Marek, Annotator (RCA)
THE BLUE SKY BOYS (BILL & EARL BOLICK) - Douglas B. Green, Annotator (RCA)
CARUSO - A LEGENDARY PERFORMER - Enrico Caruso - Francis Robinson, Annotator (RCA)
THE CHANGING FACE OF HARLEM, THE SAVOY SESSIONS - Various Artists - Dan Morgenstern, Annotator (Savoy)
THE COMPLETE TOMMY DORSEY, VOLUME I/1935 - Mort Goode, Annotator (RCA)

PRODUCER OF THE YEAR (G-782)

(A Producer's Award for consistently outstanding creativity in producing. Listed below are examples of the producer's activities.) (A)Album (S)Single (T)Track

KENNETH GAMBLE & LEON HUFF: "Enjoy Yourself" (S) - The Jacksons; "Family Reunion" (A) - The O'Jays; "Message In The Music" (A) - The O'Jays; "Wake Up Everybody" (A) & (S) - Melvin & The Bluenotes; "All Things In Time" (A) - Lou Rawls; "You'll Never Find Another Love Like Mine" (S) - Lou Rawls; "Groovy People" (S) - Lou Rawls; "Living For The Weekend" (S) - The O'Jays
RICHARD PERRY: "Burton Cummings" (A) - Burton Cummings; "Stand Tall" (S) - Burton Cummings; "The Coming Out" (A) - Manhattan Transfer
LENNIE WARONKER: "Gord's Gold" (Album One) - Gordon Lightfoot; "Summertime Dream" (A) - Gordon Lightfoot; "Shower The People" (S) - James Taylor; "In The Pocket" (A) - James Taylor; "Sweet Harmony" (A) - Maria Muldaur; "The Wreck Of The Edmund Fitzgerald" (S) - Gordon Lightfoot (above product with co-producers)
JOE WISSERT: "It's Over" (S) - Boz Scaggs; "Silk Degrees" (A) - Boz Scaggs; "Lowdown" (S) - Boz Scaggs; "Music, Music" (A) - Helen Reddy; "I Can't Hear You No More" (S) - Helen Reddy; "Gratitude" (A) - Earth, Wind & Fire (with co-producers)
STEVIE WONDER: "Songs In The Key Of Life" (A) - Stevie Wonder

JAZZ VOCAL (G-783)

(This category is for a soloist, duo or group.) (All nominations are albums)

FITZGERALD & PASS. . .AGAIN - Ella Fitzgerald (Pablo)
MORE SARAH VAUGHAN LIVE IN JAPAN - Sarah Vaughan (Mainstream)
PORGY AND BESS - Ray Charles and Cleo Laine (RCA)
QUIRE - Quire (RCA)
WHERE IS LOVE? - Irene Kral (Choice)

JAZZ - SOLOIST (G-784)

(This category is for a solo instrumental performance with or without a group or band.)

BASIE & ZOOT - Count Basie (album) (Pablo)
COMMITMENT - Jim Hall (album) (Horizon/A&M)
DONNA LEE - Jaco Pastorius (track) (Epic)
CLARK TERRY AND HIS JOLLY GIANTS - Clark Terry (album) (Vanguard)
THE NEW PHIL WOODS ALBUM - Phil Woods (album) (RCA)
WORKS OF ART - Art Tatum (album) (Jazz)

JAZZ - GROUP (G-785)

(This category is for an instrumental group.) (All nominations are albums)

BASIE & ZOOT - Count Basie & Zoot Sims (Pablo)
THE PAUL DESMOND QUARTET LIVE - Paul Desmond Quartet (Horizon/A&M)
THE LEPRECHAUN - Chick Corea (Polydor)
JACO PASTORIUS - Jaco Pastorius (Epic)
SINCE WE MET - The Bill Evans Trio (Fantasy)

JAZZ - BIG BAND (G-786)

(This category is primarily for a big band sound.) (All nominations are albums)

AFRO-CUBAN JAZZ MOODS - Dizzy Gillespie and Machito (Pablo)
THE ELLINGTON SUITES - Duke Ellington (Pablo)
LONG YELLOW ROAD - Toshiko Akiyoshi-Lew Tabackin Big Band (RCA)
NEW LIFE - Thad Jones, Mel Lewis (Horizon/A&M)
THE NEW PHIL WOODS ALBUM - Phil Woods (RCA)

POP VOCAL - FEMALE (G-787)

(This category is for a solo performance in either pop, rock or folk.)

HASTEN DOWN THE WIND - Linda Ronstadt (album) (Asylum)
HERE, THERE AND EVERYWHERE - Emmylou Harris (track) (Reprise)
THE HISSING OF SUMMER LAWNS - Joni Mitchell (album) (Asylum)
NATALIE - Natalie Cole (album) (Capitol)
TURN THE BEAT AROUND - Vicki Sue Robinson (single) (RCA)

POP VOCAL - MALE (G-788)

(This category is for a solo performance in either pop, rock or folk.)

SILK DEGREES - Boz Scaggs (album) (Columbia)
SONGS IN THE KEY OF LIFE - Stevie Wonder (album) (Tamla)
THIS MASQUERADE - George Benson (track) (Warner Bros.)
THE WRECK OF THE EDMUND FITZGERALD - Gordon Lightfoot (single) (Reprise)
YOU'LL NEVER FIND ANOTHER LOVE LIKE MINE - Lou Rawls (single) (PIR)

POP VOCAL - DUO, GROUP OR CHORUS (G-789)

(This category is for pop, rock and folk. All recordings on which the group receives artist billing on the label are eligible here even though the vocal may feature only one member of the group.) (All nominations are singles)
AFTERNOON DELIGHT - Starland Vocal Band (Windsong/RCA)
BOHEMIAN RHAPSODY - Queen (Elektra)
DON'T GO BREAKING MY HEART - Elton John & Kiki Dee (Rocket/MCA)
I'D REALLY LOVE TO SEE YOU TONIGHT - England Dan and John Ford Coley (Big Tree)
IF YOU LEAVE ME NOW - Chicago (Columbia)

POP INSTRUMENTAL (G-790)

(This category is for pop, rock and folk. All recordings are for either pure instrumentals or instrumentals with vocal coloring.)
BACK TO BACK - The Brecker Brothers Band (album) (Arista)
BREEZIN' - George Benson (album) (Warner Bros.)
CONTUSION - Stevie Wonder (track) (Tamla)
A FIFTH OF BEETHOVEN - Walter Murphy & The Big Apple Band (Pri. Stock)
WIRED - Jeff Beck (album) (Epic)

R & B VOCAL - FEMALE (G-791)

(This category is for a solo performance.) (All nominations are singles)
LEAN ON ME - Melba Moore (Buddah)
LOVE HANGOVER - Diana Ross (Motown)
MISTY BLUE - Dorothy Moore (Malaco)
SOMETHING HE CAN FEEL - Aretha Franklin (Atlantic)
SOPHISTICATED LADY (SHE'S A DIFFERENT LADY) - Natalie Cole (Capitol)

R & B VOCAL - MALE (G-792)

(This category is for a solo performance.)
DISCO LADY - Johnnie Taylor (single) (Columbia)
GROOVY PEOPLE - Lou Rawls (track) (PIR)
I NEED YOU, YOU NEED ME - Joe Simon (single) (Spring)
I WANT YOU - Marvin Gaye (album) (Tamla)
I WISH - Stevie Wonder (track) (Tamla)
LOWDOWN - Boz Scaggs (single) (Columbia)

R & B VOCAL - DUO, GROUP OR CHORUS (G-793)

(All recordings on which the group receives artist billing on the label are eligible here even though the vocal may feature only one member of the group.)
GRATITUDE - Earth, Wind & Fire (album) (Columbia)
PLAY THAT FUNKY MUSIC - Wild Cherry (track) (Epic)
RUBBERBAND MAN - Spinners (single) (Atlantic)
(SHAKE, SHAKE, SHAKE) SHAKE YOUR BOOTY - KC & The Sunshine Band (single) (T.K.)
YOU DON'T HAVE TO BE A STAR (TO BE IN MY SHOW) - Marilyn McCoo, Billy Davis Jr. (single) (ABC)

R & B INSTRUMENTAL (G-794)

(All recordings are for either pure instrumentals or instrumentals with vocal coloring.)
AFTER THE DANCE - Marvin Gaye (track) (Tamla)
BRASS CONSTRUCTION - Brass Construction (album) (U.A.)
DOIN' IT - Herbie Hancock (single) (Columbia)
HOPE THAT WE CAN BE TOGETHER SOON - Stanley Turrentine (single) (Fantasy)
KEEP THAT SAME OLD FEELING - The Crusaders (single) (Blue Thumb)

THEME FROM GOOD KING BAD - George Benson (track) (CTI)

RHYTHM & BLUES SONG (G-795)

(A Songwriter's Award.) (Any song is eligible if a new recording of it has been released during the Eligibility Year, provided it was not a previous final nomination in a songwriting category.)
DISCO LADY - Harvey Scales, Al Vance, Don Davis
LOVE HANGOVER - Pam Sawyer, Marilyn McLeod
LOWDOWN - Boz Scaggs, David Paich
MISTY BLUE - Bob Montgomery
(SHAKE, SHAKE, SHAKE) SHAKE YOUR BOOTY - Harry Wayne Casey, Richard Finch

SOUL GOSPEL PERFORMANCE (G-796)

(All nominations are albums)
GIVE IT TO ME - James Cleveland & The Southern California Community Choir (Savoy)
HOW I GOT OVER - Mahalia Jackson (Columbia)
THIS IS ANOTHER DAY - Andrae Crouch and the Disciples (Light)
TOUCH ME - VOLUME II - James Cleveland & The Charles Fold Singers (Savoy)
WAR ON SIN - Inez Andrews (Songbird)

COUNTRY VOCAL - FEMALE (G-797)

(This category is for a solo performance)
ALL I CAN DO - Dolly Parton (album) (RCA)
ELITE HOTEL - Emmylou Harris (album) (Reprise)
I'LL GET OVER YOU - Crystal Gayle (single) (U.A.)
'TIL I CAN MAKE IT ON MY OWN - Tammy Wynette (single) (Epic)
TONITE! AT THE CAPRI LOUNGE LORETTA HAGGERS - Mary Kay Place (album) (Columbia)

COUNTRY VOCAL - MALE (G-798)

(This category is for a solo performance)
ARE YOU READY FOR THE COUNTRY - Waylon Jennings (album) (RCA)
BROKEN LADY - Larry Gatlin (single) (Monument)
FOREVER LOVERS - Mac Davis (album) (Columbia)
I'D HAVE TO BE CRAZY - Willie Nelson (single) (Columbia)
(I'M A) STAND BY MY WOMAN MAN - Ronnie Milsap (single) (RCA)

COUNTRY VOCAL - DUO OR GROUP (G-799)

(All nominations are singles)
THE END IS NOT IN SIGHT (THE COWBOY TUNE) - Amazing Rhythm Aces (ABC)
GOLDEN RING - George Jones, Tammy Wynette (Epic)
THE LETTER - Loretta Lynn, Conway Twitty (MCA)
ROUTE 66 - Asleep At The Wheel (Capitol)
YOUR PICTURE IN THE PAPER - The Statler Bros. (Mercury)

COUNTRY INSTRUMENTAL (G-800)

(This category is for an Orchestra, Group or Soloist and is for either pure instrumentals or instrumentals with vocal coloring.)
BLUE EYES CRYING IN THE RAIN - Ace Cannon (single) (Hi)
CHESTER & LESTER - Chet Atkins, Les Paul (album) (RCA)
I'M THINKING TONIGHT OF MY BLUE EYES - Floyd Cramer (single) (RCA)
LONG HARD RIDE - Marshall Tucker Band (single) (Capricorn)
TEXAS - Danny Davis and the Nashville Brass (album) (RCA)

COUNTRY SONG (G-801)

(A Songwriter's Award.) (Any song is eligible if a new recording of it has been released during the Eligibility Year, provided it was not a previous final nomination in a songwriting category.)

BROKEN LADY - Larry Gatlin
THE DOOR IS ALWAYS OPEN - Bob McDill, Dickey Lees
DROPKICK ME, JESUS - Paul Craft
EVERY TIME YOU TOUCH ME (I GET HIGH) - Charlie Rich, Billy Sherrill
HANK WILLIAMS, YOU WROTE MY LIFE - Paul Craft

INSPIRATIONAL PERFORMANCE (G-802)

(This category is for non-classical recordings.)
AMAZING GRACE - Willie Nelson (track) (Columbia)
THE ASTONISHING, OUTRAGEOUS, AMAZING, INCREDIBLE, UN-BELIEVABLE, DIFFERENT WORLD OF GARY S. PAXTON - Gary S. Paxton (album) (Newpax)
HAVE A TALK WITH GOD - Stevie Wonder (track) (Tamla)
JUST A CLOSER WALK WITH THEE - Sonny James (track) (Columbia)
PRECIOUS MEMORIES - Ray Price (album) (Word)
SILVER LININGS - Charlie Rich (album) (Epic)
SOMETHING SUPER NATURAL - Pat Boone (album) (Lamb & Lion)
SUNDAY MORNING WITH CHARLEY PRIDE - Charley Pride (album) (RCA)

GOSPEL PERFORMANCE (OTHER THAN SOUL GOSPEL) (G-803)

BETWEEN THE CROSS AND HEAVEN (THERE'S A WHOLE LOT OF LIVING GOING ON) - The Speers (album) (Heartwarming)
HERE THEY COME - The Florida Boys (album) (Canaan)
JUST BECAUSE - Imperials (album) (Impact)
LEARNING TO LEAN - The Blackwood Brothers (album) (Skylight)
WHERE THE SOUL NEVER DIES - Oak Ridge Boys (single) (Columbia)

ETHNIC OR TRADITIONAL RECORDING (G-804)

(This category includes traditional blues and pure folk recordings.) (All nominations are albums)
BAGPIPE MARCHES AND MUSIC OF SCOTLAND - Shotts & Dykehead Caledonia Pipe Band (Olympic)
BEWARE OF THE DOG - Hound Dog Taylor (Alligator)
IF YOU LOVE THESE BLUES, PLAY 'EM AS YOU PLEASE - Michael Bloomfield (Guitar Player)
MARK TWANG - John Hartford (Flying Fish)
PROUD EARTH - Chief Dan George, Arliene Nofchissey Williams, Rick Brosseau (Salt City)

LATIN RECORDING (G-805)

(This category is for pure Latin music.) (All nominations are albums)
COCINANDO LA SALSA - Joe Cuba (Tico)
EL MAESTRO - Johnny Pacheco (Fania)
LA GORME - Eydie Gorme (Gala)
"SALSA" SOUNDTRACK - Fania All-Stars (Fania)
SOFRITO - Mongo Santamaria (Vaya)
UNFINISHED MASTERPIECE - Eddie Palmieri (Coco)

RECORDING FOR CHILDREN (G-806)

(This category is intended for recordings created specifically for children.)
THE ADVENTURES OF ALI AND HIS GANG VS. MR. TOOTH DECAY - Muhammed Ali & His Gang (album) (St. John's Fruits & Vegetables)
DICKENS' CHRISTMAS CAROL - Mickey Mouse & Scrooge McDuck (album) (Disneyland)
PROKOFIEV: PETER AND THE WOLF; SAINT SAENS: CARNIVAL OF THE ANIMALS - Hermione Gingold, Bohm cond. Vienna Philharmonic (album) (D.G.)
SNOW WHITE AND THE SEVEN DWARFS - Original Soundtrack (album) (Buena Vista)
WINNIE THE POOH FOR PRESIDENT (CAMPAIGN SONG) - Sterling Holloway, Larry Groce (single) (Disneyland)

COMEDY RECORDING (G-807)

(Either spoken word or musical performances are eligible here.) (All nominations are albums)
BICENTENNIAL NIGGER - Richard Pryor (Warner Bros.)
BILL COSBY IS NOT HIMSELF THESE DAYS - RAT OWN, RAT OWN, RAT OWN - Bill Cosby (Capitol)
GOODBYE POP - National Lampoon (Epic)
SLEEPING BEAUTY - Cheech & Chong (Ode)
YOU GOTTA WASH YOUR ASS - Redd Foxx (Atlantic)

SPOKEN WORD RECORDING (G-808)

(This category is for spoken word, documentary or drama recordings.) (All nominations are albums)
ASIMOV: FOUNDATION - THE PSYCHOHISTORIANS - William Shatner (Caedmon)
DICKENS: A TALE OF TWO CITIES - James Mason (Caedmon)
FAHRENHEIT 451 - Ray Bradbury (Listening Library)
GREAT AMERICAN DOCUMENTS - Orson Welles, Henry Fonda, Helen Hayes, James Earl Jones (CBS)
HEMINGWAY: THE OLD MAN AND THE SEA - Charlton Heston (Caedmon)

INSTRUMENTAL COMPOSITION (G-809)

(A Composer's Award for an original, non-classical composition with or without lyrics which first gained recognition as an instrumental.)

BELLAVIA - Chuck Mangione
CONTUSION - Stevie Wonder
EARTH, WIND & FIRE - Maurice White, Skip Scarbrough
LEPRECHAUN'S DREAM - Chick Corea
MIDNIGHT SOUL PATROL - Quincy Jones, Louis Johnson, Dave Grusin
THE WHITE DAWN - Henry Mancini

ORIGINAL SCORE - MOTION PICTURE OR A TELEVISION SPECIAL (G-810)

(A Composer's Award for an original background score or original songs written specifically for the or motion picture television special.)

CAR WASH - Norman Whitfield (MCA)
THE OMEN - Jerry Goldsmith (Tattoo/RCA)
ONE FLEW OVER THE CUCKOO'S NEST - Jack Nitzsche (Fantasy)
RICH MAN, POOR MAN - Alex North (MCA)
TAXI DRIVER - Bernard Herrmann (Arista)
3 DAYS OF THE CONDOR - Dave Grusin (Capitol)

CAST SHOW ALBUM (G-811)

(Awards to the Composers and Album Producers.) (Original cast albums, albums by road casts, or working casts, including show revival casts, are eligible.)

BUBBLING BROWN SUGAR - Razaf, Goodman, Sampson, Webb, Strayhorn, Holgate, Kemp, Lopez, Rogers, Williams, Mills, Parish, Ellington, Hines, Sissle, Blake, Pinkard, Waller, Overstreet, Higgins, Herzog, Webster, Holiday, Comps. - Hugo and Luigi, Producers (H&L)
MY FAIR LADY - 20th Anniversary Production - Alan Jay Lerner, Frederick Loewe, Composers - Goddard Lieberson, Producer (Columbia)
PACIFIC OVERTURES - Stephen Sondheim, Composer - Thomas Z. Shepard, Producer (RCA)
REX - Richard Rodgers, Sheldon Harnick, Composers - Thomas Z. Shepard, Producer (RCA)

SIDE BY SIDE BY SONDHEIM - Stephen Sondheim, Composer - Thomas Z. Shepard, Producer (RCA)

ALBUM OF THE YEAR - CLASSICAL (G-812)

(Grammys to the Artist and Producer. Certificates to the Engineer(s).)

THE ART OF COURTLY LOVE (Machaut & His Age - 14th Century Avant-Garde - The Court of Burgundy) - David Munrow cond. The Early Music Consort of London - Christopher Bishop, Producer (Seraphim)

BEETHOVEN: (THE) FIVE PIANO CONCERTOS - Artur Rubinstein & Daniel Barenboim cond. London Philharmonic - Max Wilcox, Producer (RCA)

BIZET: CARMEN - Sir Georg Solti (cond. London Philharmonic - Prin. Solos: Troyanos, Domingo, Kanawa, Van Dam) - Christopher Raeburn, Producer (London)

GERSHWIN: PORGY & BESS - Lorin Maazel (cond. Cleveland Orchestra - Prin. Solos: Mitchell, White) - Michael Woolcock, Producer (London)

GERSHWIN: RHAPSODY IN BLUE - George Gershwin - (1925 Piano Roll) & Michael Tilson Thomas cond. Columbia Jazz Band; GERSHWIN: AN AMERICAN IN PARIS - Michael Tilson Thomas cond. New York Philharmonic - Andrew Kazdin, Producer (Columbia)

HOROWITZ CONCERTS 1975/76 (Schumann, Scriabin) Vladimir Horowitz - John Pfeiffer, Producer (RCA)

JOPLIN: TREEMONISHA - Gunther Schuller (cond. Original Cast Orchestra & Chorus - Prin. Solos: Balthrop, Allen, White) - Tom Mowrey, Producer (DG)

ARTURO TOSCANINI - THE PHILADELPHIA ORCHESTRA - (First Release of the Legendary 1941-42 Recording - Schubert, Debussy, Berlioz, Respighi, etc.) - Arturo Toscanini cond. The Philadelphia Orchestra - John Pfeiffer, Producer (RCA)

CLASSICAL PERFORMANCE ORCHESTRA - (G-813)

(Grammys to the Conductor and Producer. Certificates to the classical orchestra committee.)

BERLIOZ: SYMPHONIE FANTASTIQUE - Jean Martinon cond. Orchestra National of the ORFT - Rene Challan, Producer (Angel)

BRAHMS: SYMPHONY NO. 1 IN C MINOR - James Levine cond. Chicago Symphony - Thomas Z. Shepard & Jay David Saks, Producer (RCA)

ELGAR: SYMPHONY NO. 2 IN E FLAT MAJOR - Sir Georg Solti cond. London Philharmonic - Ray Minshull, Producer (London)

FALLA: THREE CORNERED HAT (Boulez Conducts Falla) Pierre Boulez cond. New York Philharmonic - Andrew Kazdin, Producer (Columbia)

THE FOURTH OF JULY! (Ives: Sym. No. 2, Var. on America/Copland: Appalachian Spring/Bernstein: Over. to Candide/Gershwin: Amer. In Paris) Zubin Mehta cond. Los Angeles Philharmonic - Ray Minshull, Producer (London)

GERSHWIN: RHAPSODY IN BLUE - Michael Tilson Thomas cond. Columbia Jazz Band (with Gershwin 1925 Piano Roll) - Andrew Kazdin, Producer (Columbia)

RAVEL: DAPHNIS ET CHLOE (Complete Ballet) - Jean Martinon cond. Orchestre de Paris - Rene Challan, Producer (Angel)

STRAUSS: ALSO SPRACH ZARATHUSTRA - Sir Georg Solti cond. Chicago Symphony - Ray Minshull, Producer (London)

OPERA RECORDING (G-814)

(Grammys to the Conductor and Producer; special plaques to the Principal Soloists.)

BIZET: CARMEN - Sir Georg Solti (cond. London Philharmonic - Prin. Solos: Tatiana Troyanos, Placido Domingo, Kiri Te Kanawa, Jose Van Dam) - Christopher Raeburn, Producer (London)

GERSHWIN: PORGY & BESS - Lorin Maazel (cond. Cleveland Orchestra & Chorus - Prin. Solos: Leona Mitchell, Willard White) - Michael Woolcock, Producer (London)

JOPLIN: TREEMONISHA - Gunther Schuller (cond. Original Cast Orchestra & Chorus - Prin. Solos: Carmen Balthrop, Betty Allen, Willard White) - Tom Mowrey, Producer (DG)

MASSENET: THAIS - Lorin Maazel (cond. New Philharmonia Orchestra, John Alldis Choir - Prin. Solos: Beverly Sills, Sherrill Milnes, Nicolai

Gedda) - Christopher Bishop, Producer (Angel)

SCHOENBERG: MOSES AND AARON - Pierre Boulez (cond. BBC Symphony, BBC Symphony Singers, Orpheus Boys Choir - Prin. Solos: Gunther Reich, Richard Cassilly, Richard Angus, Felicity Palmer, Roland Hermann) - Paul Myers, Producer (Columbia)

VERDI: MACBETH - Claudio Abbado (cond. Chorus & Orchestra of La Scala - Prin. Solos: Shirley Verrett, Placido Domingo, Nicolai Ghiaurov) - Rainer Brock, Producer (DG)

CHORAL PERFORMANCE - OTHER THAN OPERA (G-815)

(Grammys to the Conductor and Choral Director)

BEETHOVEN: MISSA SOLEMNIS - Walter Hagen-Groll (Chorus Master of New Philharmonia Chorus) - Carlo Maria Giulini (cond. London Philharmonic) (Angel)

BERLIOZ: REQUIEM - Leonard Bernstein (cond. Choeurs de Radio France, Orchestre National de France & Orchestre Philharmonique de Radio France - w/Burrows, Tenor) (Columbia)

BERNSTEIN: CHICHESTER PSALMS; BRITTEN: REJOICE IN THE LAMB - Phillip Ledger (cond. Kings College Choir, Cambridge) (Angel)

ELGAR: THE KINGDOM, OP. 51 - Sir Adrian Boult (cond. London Philharmonic Chorus & London Philharmonic Orchestra) (Connoisseur Society)

FAURE: REQUIEM - Franz Muller (Chorus Master of Netherlands Radio Chorus) - Jean Fournet (cond. Rotterdam Philharmonic) (Philips)

GREGORIAN CHANT - Dom Jean Claire (Director of Choir of the Monks of Saint-Pierre de Solesmes Abbey) (London)

RACHMANINOFF: THE BELLS - Arthur Oldham (Chorus Master of London Symphony Chorus) - Andre Previn (cond. London Symphony) (Angel)

TIPPETT: A CHILD OF OUR TIME - Colin Davis (cond. BBC Singers & Choral Society and BBC Symphony) (Philips)

VERDI: OPERA CHORUSES (From Nabucco, Il Trovatore, Otello, Aida, etc.) - Romano Gandolfi (Chorus Master of Chorus of La Scala, Milan) - Claudio Abbado (cond. Orchestra of La Scala, Milan) (DG)

CHAMBER MUSIC PERFORMANCE (G-816)

(Instrumental or Vocal)

THE ART OF COURTLY LOVE (Machaut & His Age - 14th Century Avant Garde - The Court of Burgundy) - David Munrow cond. The Early Music Consort of London (Seraphim)

BARBER: QUARTET FOR STRINGS, OP. 11, IVES: QUARTET NO. 2 FOR STRINGS (TWO AMERICAN MASTERPIECES) - The Cleveland Quartet (RCA)

BEETHOVEN: SONATAS FOR CELLO (Complete) - Jacqueline du Pre & Daniel Barenboim (Angel)

DVORAK: QUARTETS, OPP. 96 & 105 - Prague String Quartet (DG)

THE HEIFETZ PIATIGORSKY CONCERTS (Dvorak: Trio in F Min. for Piano w/Leonard Pennario, Stravinsky: Suite Italienne for Violin & Cello, Gliere: Duo for Violin & Cello, etc.) - Jascha Heifetz & Gregor Piatigorsky (Columbia)

HINDEMITH: SONATAS FOR BRASS & PIANO (Complete) - Glenn Gould & Philadelphia Brass Ensemble (Columbia)

MESSIAEN: QUARTET FOR THE END OF TIME - Tashi (Peter Serkin, Fred Sherry, Ida Kavafian, Richard Stoltzman) (RCA)

SCHUBERT: QUINTET IN C, OP. 163 - Thomas Igloi & Alberni Quartet (CRD)

SHOSTAKOVICH: QUARTET NO. 14 IN F SHARP MAJOR - Fitzwilliam Quartet (Oiseau Lyre)

CLASSICAL PERFORMANCE - INSTRUMENTAL SOLOIST(S) (WITH ORCHESTRA) (G-817)

BARTOK: CONCERTI FOR PIANO NOS. 1 & 3 - Stephen Bishop, Piano (David cond. London Symphony) (Philips)

BEETHOVEN: THE FIVE PIANO CONCERTOS - Artur Rubinstein, Piano (Barenboim cond. London Philharmonic) (RCA)

BRAHMS: CONCERTO IN D MAJOR FOR VIOLIN - Nathan Milstein, Violin (Jochum cond. Vienna Philharmonic) (DG)

PROKOFIEV: THE FIVE PIANO CONCERTOS - Vladimir Ashkenazy, Piano (Previn cond. London Symphony) (London)

RAVEL: CONCERTO IN G MAJOR FOR PIANO & ORCH. & CONCERTO IN D MAJOR FOR LEFT HAND - Aldo Ciccolini, Piano (Martinon cond. Orchestre de Paris) (Angel)

STRAUSS: DON QUIXOTE - Mstislav Rostropovich, Cello (Karajan cond. Berlin Philharmonic) (Angel)

CLASSICAL PERFORMANCE - INSTRUMENTAL SOLOIST(S) (WITHOUT ORCHESTRA) (G-818)

CHOPIN: PRELUDES, OP. 28 - Maurizio Pollini, Piano (DG)
(GERSHWIN) "WATTS BY GEORGE": ANDRE WATTS PLAYS GEORGE GERSHWIN (Rhapsody in Blue, Preludes for Piano (3), 13 Songs from Gershwin Songbook) - Andre Watts, Piano (Columbia)
HOROWITZ CONCERTS 1975/76 (Schumann, Scriabin) - Vladimir Horowitz, Piano (RCA)
THE INTIMATE GUITAR/2 (Bach, Sor, Albeniz, Molleda, San Sebastian, Samazeuilh) - Andres Segovia, Guitar (RCA)
(KREISLER) ITZHAK PERLMAN PLAYS FRITZ KREISLER - (Caprice Viennois, Andantino in the Style of Martini, Allegretto in the Style of Boccherini, La Gitana) - Itzhak Perlman, Violin (Angel)
LISZT: LEGENDARY SOVIET PIANIST - LAZAR BERMAN PLAYS LIZST - Lazar Berman, piano (Everest)
RACHMANINOFF: 23 PRELUDES - Vladimir Ashkenazy, Piano (London)
SCHUBERT: SONATA IN A MINOR, OP. 42 & HUNGARIAN MELODY IN B MINOR (D 817) - Alfred Brendel, Piano (Philips)

CLASSICAL PERFORMANCE - VOCAL SOLOIST - (G-819)

CLASSICAL BARBRA (Debussy: Beau Soir, Canteloube: Berceuse, Wolf: Verschwiegene, etc.) - Barbra Streisand - (Ogerman cond. Columbia Symphony) (Columbia)
(HERBERT) MUSIC OF VICTOR HERBERT (Kiss in The Dark, Italian Street Song, Kiss Me Again etc.) - Beverly Sills (Kostelanetz cond. London Symphony) (Angel)
IVES: SONGS - Jan de Gaetani (Gilbert Kalish, Accomp.) (Nonesuch)
MAHLER: DAS LIED VON DER ERDE - Janet Baker & James King - (Haitink cond. Concertgebouw Orchestra) (Philips)
MOZART: ARIAS (La Clemenza di Tito, Die Entfuhrung aus dem Serail, Nozze di Figaro, etc.) - Margaret Price - (Lockhart cond. English Chamber Orchestra) (RCA)
SCHOENBERG: NINE EARLY SONGS; THE CABARET SONGS OF ARNOLD SCHOENBERG - Marni Nixon (Leonard Stein, Accomp.) (RCA)
(VERDI) CARLO BERGONZI SINGS VERDI - Carlo Bergonzi (Santi cond. New Philharmonia & Gardelli cond. Royal Philharmonic) (Philips)
WOLF: MORIKE LIEDER - Dietrich Fischer-Dieskau (Sviatoslav Richter, Accomp.) (DG)

BEST ENGINEERED RECORDING - CLASSICAL (G-820)

(An Engineer's Award)

BEYOND THE SUN: AN ELECTRONIC PORTRAIT OF HOLST'S "THE PLANETS" - Patrick Gleeson - Patrick Gleeson, Skip Shimmin, Neil Schwartz, Seth Dworken, Engineers (Mercury)
BRAHMS: SYMPHONY NO. 1 IN C MINOR - James Levine cond. Chicago Symphony - Paul Goodman, Engineer (RCA)
BRITTEN: FOUR SEA INTERLUDES & PASSACAGLIA FROM "PETER GRIMES" - Previn cond. London Symphony - Christopher Parker, Engineer (Angel)
FALLA: THREE CORNERED HAT (BOULEZ CONDUCTS FALLA) - Boulez cond. New York Philharmonic/de Gaetani - E. T. (Bud) Graham, Ray Moore, Milton Cherin, Engineers (Columbia)
GERSHWIN: PORGY & BESS - Maazel cond. Cleveland Orchestra/Mitchell, White - James Lock, Arthur Lilley, Colin Moorfoot, Michael Mailes, Engineers (London)
GERSHWIN: RHAPSODY IN BLUE - George Gershwin (1925 Piano Roll) & Thomas cond. Columbia Jazz Band - E. T. (Bud) Graham, Ray Moore, Milt Cherin, Engineers (Columbia)
MAHLER: SYMPHONY NO. 2 IN C MINOR ("RESURRECTION") - Mehta cond. Vienna Philharmonic - James Lock, Colin Moorfoot, Jack Law, Engineers (London)
SAINT-SAENS: SYMPHONY NO. 3 IN C MINOR ("ORGAN") - Barenboim cond. Chicago Symphony - Klaus Scheibe, Engineer (DG)
STRAUSS: AN ALPINE SYMPHONY - Mehta cond. Los Angeles Philharmonic - James Lock, Engineer (London)

BACH: THE WELL TEMPERED CLAVIER (Complete) (Albums) Wanda Landowska - RCA Victor #LM1017, #LM1107, #LM1136 - Released 1949-1954
BEETHOVEN: SYMPHONIES (9) (Albums) - Arturo Toscanini conducting the NBC Symphony - RCA Victor #LM6009, #LM1723, #LM1042, #LM1755, #LM1756, #LM1757, #LM6009 - Released 1950-1953
BEGIN THE BEGUINE - Artie Shaw - Bluebird #B7746 - Released in 1938
MY FAIR LADY (Album) - Original Broadway Cast with Rex Harrison and Julie Andrews - Columbia #OL5090 - Released in 1956
SINGIN' THE BLUES - Frankie Trumbauer & His Orchestra, featuring Bix Beiderbecke on Cornet - Okeh #40772 - Released in 1927

1977

RECORD OF THE YEAR (G-822)

(Grammys to the Artist and A&R Producer. Certificates to the Arranger, Engineer and Songwriter)

BLUE BAYOU - Linda Ronstadt - Peter Asher, Producer (Asylum)
DON'T IT MAKE MY BROWN EYES BLUE - Crystal Gayle - Allen Reynolds, Producer (UA)
HOTEL CALIFORNIA - Eagles - Bill Szymczyk, Producer (Asylum)
LOVE THEME FROM A STAR IS BORN (EVERGREEN) - Barbra Streisand - Barbra Streisand, Phil Ramone, Producers (Columbia)
YOU LIGHT UP MY LIFE - Debby Boone - Joe Brooks, Producer (WB/Curb)

ALBUM OF THE YEAR (G-823)

(Grammys to the Artist and A&R Producer. Certificates to the Arranger and Engineer)

AJA - Steely Dan - Gary Katz, Producer (ABC)
HOTEL CALIFORNIA - Eagles - Bill Szymczyk, Producer (Asylum)
J T - James Taylor - Peter Asher, Producer (Columbia)
RUMOURS - Fleetwood Mac - Fleetwood Mac, Richard Dashut, Ken Caillat, Producers (W.B.)
STAR WARS - London Symphony - John Williams, Conductor - George Lucas, Producer (20th Cent.)

SONG OF THE YEAR (G-824)

(A Songwriter's Award)

DON'T IT MAKE MY BROWN EYES BLUE - Richard Leigh
HOTEL CALIFORNIA - Don Felder, Don Henley, Glenn Frey
LOVE THEME FROM A STAR IS BORN (EVERGREEN) - Barbra Streisand, Paul Williams
NOBODY DOES IT BETTER - Marvin Hamlisch, Carole Bayer Sager
SOUTHERN NIGHTS - Allen Toussaint
YOU LIGHT UP MY LIFE - Joe Brooks

NEW ARTIST OF THE YEAR (G-825)

(This category is for an artist or organized group whose first recording was released during the Eligibility Period)

STEPHEN BISHOP (ABC)
DEBBY BOONE (WB/CURB)
SHAUN CASSIDY (WB/CURB)
FOREIGNER (Atlantic)
ANDY GIBB (RSO)

INSTRUMENTAL ARRANGEMENT (G-826)

(An Arranger's Award for a specific arrangement released on either a single or album track)

FREE AS THE WIND - The Crusaders - The Crusaders, Arrangers (ABC)
MUSICMAGIC - Return to Forever - Chick Corea, Arranger (Columbia)
NADIA'S THEME (THE YOUNG AND THE RESTLESS) - (Barry De Vorzon) - Harry Betts, Perry Botkin, Jr., Barry De Vorzon, Arrangers

(Arista)
ROOTS MURAL THEME - Quincy Jones - Herb Spencer, Arranger (A&M)
SCHEHEREZADE - Hubert Laws - Bob James, Arranger (CTI)

ARRANGEMENT ACCOMPANYING VOCALIST(S) (G-827)

(An Arranger's Award for a specific arrangement released on either a single or an album track)
BESAME MUCHO - Joao Gilberto - Claus Ogerman, Arranger (W. B.)
CALLING OCCUPANTS OF INTERPLANETARY CRAFT - Carpenters - Richard Carpenter, Arranger (A & M)
THE DEVIL IS A LIAR - Seawind - Seawind, Arranger (CTI)
LOVE THEME FROM A STAR IS BORN (EVERGREEN) - (Barbra Streisand) - Ian Freebairn-Smith, Arranger (Columbia)
NATURE BOY - George Benson - Claus Ogerman, Arranger (W. B.)

ARRANGEMENT FOR VOICES (G-828)

(An Arranger's Award for a specific arrangement released on either a single or an album track)
ALL YOU DO IS DIAL - Heatwave - Heatwave, Arrangers (Epic)
BABY, I'LL GIVE IT TO YOU - Seals & Crofts - Jim Seals, Arranger (W. B.)
GO YOUR OWN WAY - Fleetwood Mac - Fleetwood Mac, Arrangers (W. B.)
NEW KID IN TOWN - Eagles - Eagles, Arrangers (Asylum)
OH LORD, COME BY HERE - Quincy Jones - Quincy Jones, James Cleveland, John Mandel, Arrangers (A & M)

BEST ENGINEERED RECORDING - NON-CLASSICAL (G-829)

(An Engineer's Award.) (All nominations are albums)
AJA - Steely Dan - Roger Nichols, Elliot Scheiner, Bill Schnee, Al Schmitt, Engineers (ABC)
DISCOVERED AGAIN! - Dave Grusin - Bill Schnee, Engineer (Sheffield Lab)
J T - James Taylor - Val Garay, Engineer (Columbia)
RUMOURS - Fleetwood Mac - Ken Caillat, Richard Dashut, Engineers (W. B.)
SIMPLE DREAMS - Linda Ronstadt - Val Garay, Engineer (Asylum)

ALBUM PACKAGE (G-830)

(Grammy to Art Director. Certificates to Designer, Photographer, Illustrator, etc. where applicable.)
COLOR AS A WAY OF LIFE (Lou Donaldson) Abie Sussman, Bob Defrin, Art Directors (Cotillion/Atlantic)
GINSENG WOMAN (Eric Gale) Paula Scher, Art Director (Columbia)
HEJIRA (Joni Mitchell) Glen Christensen, Art Director (Asylum)
LOVE NOTES (Ramsey Lewis) John Berg, Art Director (Columbia)
SIMPLE DREAMS (Linda Ronstadt) Kosh, Art Director (Asylum)
SINGIN' (Melissa Manchester) Kosh, Art Director (Arista)
WINGS OVER AMERICA (Wings) MPL/Hipgnosis, Art Director (Capitol)
YARDBIRDS FAVORITES (Yardbirds) Paula Scher, Art Director (Epic)

ALBUM NOTES (G-831)

(An Annotator's Award for original writing for a specific album.)
BING CROSBY: A LEGENDARY PERFORMER - George T. Simon, Ann (RCA)
GUY LOMBARDO: A LEGENDARY PERFORMER - George T. Simon, Ann (RCA)
JEFFERSON AIRPLANE - FLIGHT LOG - Jefferson Airplane - Patrick Snyder, Ann (Grunt/RCA)
THE LESTER YOUNG STORY VOL. I - Michael Brooks, Ann (Columbia)
STORMY BLUES - Billie Holiday, Chris Albertson, Ann (Verve/Polydor)

PRODUCER OF THE YEAR (G-832)

(A Producer's Award for consistently outstanding creativity in producing. Listed below are examples of the producer's activities.) AAlbum SSingle TTrack
PETER ASHER: "Handy Man" (S) - James Taylor; "JT" (A) - James Taylor; "Lonely Boy" (S) - Andrew Gold; "What's Wrong With This Picture" (A) - Andrew Gold; "Simple Dreams" (A) - Linda Ronstadt; "Blue Bayou" (S) - Linda Ronstadt
THE BEE GEES, ALBHY GALUTEN, KARL RICHARDSON: "Here at Last. . .Bee Gees Live" (A) - Bee Gees
KENNETH GAMBLE & LEON HUFF: "The Jacksons" (A) - The Jacksons; "See You When I Git There" (S) - Lou Rawls; "Teddy Pendergrass" (A) - Teddy Pendergrass; "Travelin' At The Speed of Thought" (A) - The O'Jays; "Unmistakably Lou" (A) - Lou Rawls
RICHARD PERRY: "Baby It's Me" (A) - Diana Ross; "Endless Flight" (A) - Leo Sayer; "How Much Love" (S) - Leo Sayer; "Nobody Does It Better" (S) - Carly Simon; "Thunder In My Heart" (S) - Leo Sayer; "When I Need You" (S) - Leo Sayer; "You Make Me Feel Like Dancing" (S) - Leo Sayer
BILL SZYMCZYK; "Hotel California" (A) - Eagles; "Hotel California" (S) - Eagles; "Hurry Sundown" (A) - Outlaws; "Life In The Fast Lane" (S) - Eagles

JAZZ VOCAL (G-833)

(This category is for a soloist, duo or group.) (All nominations are albums)
AMOROSO - Joao Gilberto (W. B.)
CARMEN MCRAE AT THE GREAT AMERICAN MUSIC HALL - Carmen McRae (Blue Note/U.A.)
HELEN MERRILL - JOHN LEWIS - Helen Merrill (Mercury)
KRAL SPACE - Irene Kral (Catalyst)
LOOK TO THE RAINBOW - Al Jarreau (WB)

JAZZ - SOLOIST (G-834)

(This category is for a solo instrumental performance with or without a group or band.)(All nominations are albums)
AFRO BLUE IMPRESSIONS - John Coltrane (Pablo)
'BOP REDUX - Hank Jones (Muse)
THE GIANTS - Oscar Peterson (Pablo)
HEAVY WEATHER - Jaco Pastorius (Col.)
THE PHIL WOODS SIX - LIVE FROM THE SHOWBOAT - Phil Woods (RCA)

JAZZ - GROUP (G-835)

(This category is for an instrumental group.) (All nominations are albums)
AFRO BLUE IMPRESSIONS - John Coltrane (Pablo)
ECLYPSO - Tommy Flanagan Trio (Inner City)
HOMECOMING - LIVE AT THE VILLAGE VANGUARD - Dexter Gordon (Columbia)
MEL LEWIS & FRIENDS - Mel Lewis (Horizon/A & M)
THE PHIL WOODS SIX - LIVE FROM THE SHOWBOAT - Phil Woods (RCA)

JAZZ - BIG BAND (G-836)

(This category is primarily for a big band sound.) (All nominations are albums)
BUDDY RICH PLAYS AND PLAYS AND PLAYS - Buddy Rich (RCA/Gryphon)
THE 40TH ANNIVERSARY, CARNEGIE HALL CONCERT - Woody Herman (RCA)
LAB '76 - North Texas State University Lab Band, Leon Breeden, dir (NTSU Lab Jazz)
PRIME TIME - Count Basie and his Orchestra (Pablo)
ROAD TIME - Toshiko Akiyoshi-Lew Tabackin Big Band (RCA)

POP VOCAL - FEMALE (G-837)

(This category is for a solo performance in either pop, rock or folk.) (All nominations are singles)
BLUE BAYOU - Linda Ronstadt (Asylum)
HERE YOU COME AGAIN - Dolly Parton (RCA)
LOVE THEME FROM A STAR IS BORN (EVERGREEN) - Barbra Streisand (Columbia)
NOBODY DOES IT BETTER - Carly Simon (Elektra)
YOU LIGHT UP MY LIFE - Debby Boone (WB/Curb)

POP VOCAL - MALE (G-838)

(This category is for a solo performance in either pop, rock or folk.)
AFTER THE LOVIN' (album) - Engelbert Humperdinck (Epic)
HANDY MAN (single) - James Taylor (Columbia)
I JUST WANT TO BE YOUR EVERYTHING (single) - Andy Gibb (RSO)
ON AND ON (single) - Stephen Bishop (ABC)
WHEN I NEED YOU (single) - Leo Sayer (W. B.)

POP VOCAL - DUO, GROUP OR CHORUS (G-839)

(This category is for pop, rock or folk. All recordings on which the group received artist billing on the label are eligible here even though the vocal may feature only one member of the group.)
AJA - Steely Dan (album) (ABC)
CSN - Crosby, Stills & Nash (album) (Atlantic)
HOTEL CALIFORNIA - Eagles (album) (Asylum)
HOW DEEP IS YOUR LOVE - Bee Gees (single) (RSO)
RUMOURS - Fleetwood Mac (album) (W. B.)

POP INSTRUMENTAL (G-840)

(This category is for pop, rock or folk. All recordings are for either pure instrumentals or instrumentals with vocal coloring.)
GONNA FLY NOW (THEME FROM "ROCKY") - Bill Conti (single) (UA)
GONNA FLY NOW (THEME FROM "ROCKY") - Maynard Ferguson (single) (Columbia)
NADIA'S THEME (THE YOUNG AND THE RESTLESS) - Barry De Vorzon (album) (Arista)
STAR WARS - London Symphony, John Williams, conductor (album) (20th Century)
STAR WARS THEME/CANTINA BAND - Meco (single) (Millennium)

R & B VOCAL - FEMALE (G-841)

(This category is for a solo performance.)
BREAK IT TO ME GENTLY - Aretha Franklin (single) (Atlantic)
DON'T LEAVE ME THIS WAY - Thelma Houston (single) (Motown)
I BELIEVE YOU - Dorothy Moore (single) (Malaco)
I'VE GOT LOVE ON MY MIND - Natalie Cole (single) (Capitol)
YOUR LOVE IS SO GOOD FOR ME - Diana Ross (track) (Motown)

R & B VOCAL - MALE (G-842)

(This category is for a solo performance.)
AIN'T GONNA BUMP NO MORE (WITH NO BIG FAT WOMAN) - Joe Tex (single) (Epic)
GOT TO GIVE IT UP (PART I) - Marvin Gaye (single) (Motown)
IT'S JUST A MATTER OF TIME - B. B. King (track) (ABC)
A REAL MOTHER FOR YA - Johnny "Guitar" Watson (track) (DJM)
UNMISTAKABLY LOU - Lou Rawls (album) (PIR/Epic)

R & B VOCAL - DUO, GROUP OR CHORUS (G-843)

(All recordings on which the group receives artist billing on the label are eligible here even though the vocal may feature only one member of the group.)
ASK RUFUS - Rufus featuring Chaka Khan (album) (ABC)
BABY DON'T CHANGE YOUR MIND - Gladys Knight and the Pips (track) (Buddah)
BEST OF MY LOVE - Emotions (track) (Columbia)
BOOGIE NIGHTS - Heatwave (single) (Epic)
EASY - Commodores (single) (Motown)

R & B INSTRUMENTAL (G-844)

(All recordings are for either pure instrumentals or instrumentals with vocal coloring.)
FUNKY SEA, FUNKY DEW - Brecker Brothers (track) (Arista)
GETAWAY - Salsoul Orchestra (single) (Salsoul)
MORE STUFF - Stuff (album) (W. B.)
Q - Brothers Johnson (track) (A & M)
THE UNFINISHED BUSINESS - The Blackbyrds (track) (Fantasy)

RHYTHM & BLUES SONG (G-845)

(A Songwriter's Award.) (Any song is eligible if a new recording of it has been released during the Eligibility Year.)
BEST OF MY LOVE - Maurice White, Al McKay
BRICK HOUSE - Milan Williams, Walter Orange, Thomas McClary, William King, Lionel Richie, Ronald LaPread
DON'T LEAVE ME THIS WAY - Kenny Gamble, Leon Huff, Carry Gilbert
EASY - Lionel Richie
YOU MAKE ME FEEL LIKE DANCING - Leo Sayer, Vini Poncia

GOSPEL PERFORMANCE - CONTEMPORARY OR INSPIRATIONAL (G-846)

(All nominations are albums)
ADAM AGAIN - Michael Omartian (Myrrh/Word)
HART AND SOUL - Larry Hart & The Soul Singers (Genesis)
MIRROR - Evie Tornquist (Word)
MORE, FROM THE ASTONISHING, OUTRAGEOUS, AMAZING, INCREDIBLE, UNBELIEVABLE GARY S. PAXTON - Gary S. Paxton (New Pax) REBA/LADY - Reba Rambo Gardner (Greentree)
SAIL ON - Imperials (Dayspring/Word)

GOSPEL PERFORMANCE - TRADITIONAL (G-847)

BILL GAITHER SONGS - Blackwood Brothers (album) (Skylite)
CORNERSTONE - The Speers (album) (Heartwarming)
HAVE A LITTLE TALK WITH JESUS - Oak Ridge Boys (track) (Rockland Road)
NATURALLY - The Rambos (album) (Heartwarming)
THEN AND NOW - The Cathedral Quartet (album) (Canaan)
TILL HE COMES - The Lefevres (album) (Canaan)

SOUL GOSPEL PERFORMANCE - CONTEMPORARY (G-848)

BORN AGAIN - Jessy Dixon (single) (Light)
GOD IS NOT DEAD - Mighty Clouds of Joy (track) (ABC)
HE IS KING - Danniebelle (album) (Light)
MORE - Larnelle Harris (album) (Word)
WONDERFUL! - Edwin Hawkins & The Edwin Hawkins Singers (album) (Birthright)

SOUL GOSPEL PERFORMANCE - TRADITIONAL (G-849)

I'M JUST ANOTHER SOLDIER - Five Blind Boys of Mississippi (single) (Jewel)
JAMES CLEVELAND LIVE AT CARNEGIE HALL - James Cleveland (album) (Savoy)

THE LORD IS MY LIFE - James Cleveland & The Greater Metropolitan Church of Christ Choir (album) (Savoy)
SATISFACTION GUARANTEED - Rev. Cleavant Derricks & Family (album) (Canaan)
STAND UP FOR JESUS - The Savannah Choir & Rev. Isaac Douglas (album) (Creed)

INSPIRATIONAL PERFORMANCE (G-850)

HOME WHERE I BELONG - B. J. Thomas (album) (Myrrh/Word)
HOW GREAT THOU ART - Ray Price (album) (Word)
OH LORD, COME BY HERE - Quincy Jones & James Cleveland conducting the Wattsline Choir (track) (A & M)
TELL ALL THE WORLD ABOUT LOVE - Carol Lawrence (album) (Word)
YOUR ARMS TOO SHORT TO BOX WITH GOD - Salome Bey, Clinton Derricks-Carroll, Sheila Ellis, Delores Hall, William Hardy, Jr., Hector Jaime Mercado, Stanley Perryman, Mabel Robinson, William Thomas, Jr. (album) (ABC)

COUNTRY VOCAL - FEMALE (G-851)

(This category is for a solo performance.)
AFTER THE LOVIN' - Barbara Mandrell (track) (ABC/DOT)
DON'T IT MAKE MY BROWN EYES BLUE - Crystal Gayle (single) (U. A.)
MAKING BELIEVE - Emmylou Harris (single) (W. B.)
WHAT'RE YOU DOING TONIGHT - Janie Fricke (single) (Columbia)
(YOUR LOVE HAS LIFTED ME) HIGHER AND HIGHER - Dolly Parton (track) (RCA)

COUNTRY VOCAL - MALE (G-852)

(This category is for a solo performance.)
I DON'T WANNA CRY - Larry Gatlin (single) (Monument)
IT WAS ALMOST LIKE A SONG - Ronnie Milsap (single) (RCA)
LUCILLE - Kenny Rogers (single) (UA)
LUCKENBACH, TEXAS - Waylon Jennings (single) (RCA)
MR. BOJANGLES - Jerry Jeff Walker (single) (MCA)

COUNTRY VOCAL - DUO OR GROUP (G-853)

DYNAMIC DUO - Loretta Lynn, Conway Twitty (album) (MCA)
HEAVEN'S JUST A SIN AWAY - The Kendalls (single) (Ovation)
NEAR YOU - George Jones, Tammy Wynette (single) (Epic)
THE WHEEL - Asleep At The Wheel (album) (Capitol)
Y'ALL COME BACK SALOON - Oak Ridge Boys (single) (ABC/Dot)

COUNTRY INSTRUMENTAL (G-854)

(This category is for an Orchestra, Group or Soloist and is for either pure instrumentals or instrumentals with vocal coloring.)
CHET, FLOYD & DANNY - Chet Atkins, Floyd Cramer, Danny Davis (album) (RCA)
COUNTRY INSTRUMENTALIST OF THE YEAR - Hargus "Pig" Robbins (album) (Elektra)
ME & MY GUITAR - Chet Atkins (album) (RCA)
RAGTIME ANNIE - Asleep At The Wheel (track) (Capitol)
WEST BOUND AND DOWN - Jerry Reed (track) (MCA)

COUNTRY SONG (G-855)

(A Songwriter's Award.) (Any song is eligible if a new recording of it has been released during the Eligibility Year.)
DESPERADO - Glenn Frey, Don Henley
DON'T IT MAKE MY BROWN EYES BLUE - Richard Leigh
IT WAS ALMOST LIKE A SONG - Archie Jordan, Hal David
LUCILLE - Roger Bowling, Hal Bynum
LUCKENBACH, TEXAS - Bobby Emmons, Chips Moman

ETHNIC OR TRADITIONAL RECORDING (G-856)

(This category includes traditional blues and pure folk recordings.) (All nominations are albums)
BLUES HIT BIG TOWN - Junior Wells (Delmark)
HARD AGAIN - Muddy Waters (Blue Sky/CBS)
RIGHT PLACE, WRONG TIME - Otis Rush (Bullfrog)
THINGS THAT I USED TO DO - Joe Turner (Pablo)
WHAT HAPPENED TO MY BLUES - Willie Dixon (Ovation)

LATIN RECORDING (G-857)

(This category is for pure Latin music.) (All nominations are albums)
DAWN - Mongo Santamaria (Vaya)
FIREWORKS - Machito Orchestra with Lalo Rodriguez
LA LEYENDA - Tito Puente (Tico/Fania)
MUY AMIGOS/CLOSE FRIENDS - Eydie Gorme & Danny Rivera (Gala/Coco)
TOMORROW: BARRETTO LIVE - Ray Barretto Band (Atlantic)

RECORDING FOR CHILDREN (G-858)

(This category is intended for recordings created specifically for children.)
AREN'T YOU GLAD YOU'RE YOU - Sesame Street Cast & Muppets (album) (Sesame Street)
A CHARLIE BROWN CHRISTMAS - Various (Written by Charles M. Schulz) (Charlie Brown Records) (7' LP)
DOPE! THE DOPE KING'S LAST STAND - Various Artists (Lily Tomlin, Muhammad Ali, Pres. Jimmy Carter, etc.) Arthur Morrison, Producer (album) (Cornucopia)
RUSSELL HOBAN: THE MOUSE AND HIS CHILD - Read by Peter Ustinov (album) (Caedmon)
THE SESAME STREET FAIRY TALE ALBUM - Jim Henson's Muppets (album) (Sesame Street)

COMEDY RECORDING (G-859)

(Either spoken word or musical performances are eligible here.) (All nominations are albums)
ARE YOU SERIOUS??? - Richard Pryor (Laff)
THE ERNIE KOVACS ALBUM - Ernie Kovacs (Columbia)
LET'S GET SMALL - Steve Martin (W. B.)
ON THE ROAD - George Carlin (Little David)
SATURDAY NIGHT LIVE - NBC's Saturday Night Live Cast (Arista)

SPOKEN WORD RECORDING (G-860)

(This category is for spoken word, documentary or drama) (All nominations are albums)
ALEX HALEY TELLS THE STORY OF HIS SEARCH FOR ROOTS - Alex Haley (W. B.)
THE BELLE OF AMHERST - Julie Harris (Credo)
FOR COLORED GIRLS WHO HAVE CONSIDERED SUICIDE/WHEN THE RAINBOW IS ENUF - (Original Cast) Ntozake Shange, writer (Buddah)
J.R.R. TOLKIEN: THE SILMARILLION OF BEREN AND LUTHIEN - Read by Christopher Tolkien (Caedmon)
THE TRUMAN TAPES - Harry Truman speaking with Ben Gradus (Caedmon)

INSTRUMENTAL COMPOSITION (G-861)

(A Composer's Award for an original, non-classical composition with or without lyrics which first gained recognition as an instrumental.)
BIRDLAND - Joe Zawinul
BOND '77/JAMES BOND THEME - Marvin Hamlisch
GONNA FLY NOW (THEME FROM "ROCKY") - Bill Conti, Carol Connors, Ann Robbins
MAIN TITLE FROM STAR WARS - John Williams
"ROOTS" MEDLEY (MOTHERLAND, ROOTS MURAL THEME) - Quincy Jones, Gerald Fried

ORIGINAL SCORE - MOTION PICTURE OR A TELEVISION SPECIAL (G-862)

(A Composer's Award for an original background score or original songs written specifically for the motion picture or television special.)

ROCKY - Bill Conti (UA)

THE SPY WHO LOVED ME - Marvin Hamlisch (UA)

A STAR IS BORN - Kenny Ascher, Alan & Marilyn Bergman, Rupert Holmes, Leon Russell, Barbra Streisand, Donna Weiss, Paul Williams, Kenny Loggins (Columbia)

STAR WARS - John Williams (20th Century)

YOU LIGHT UP MY LIFE - Joe Brooks (Arista)

CAST SHOW ALBUM (G-863)

(Awards to the Composers and Album Producers.) (Original cast albums, albums by road casts or working casts, including show revival casts, are eligible.)

ANNIE - Charles Strouse, Martin Charnin, Composers - Larry Morton, Charles Strouse, Producers (Columbia)

GUYS AND DOLLS - Frank Loesser, Composer - William Goldstein, Producer (Motown)

I LOVE MY WIFE - Cy Coleman, Michael Stewart, Composers - Cy Coleman, Producer (Atlantic)

STARTING HERE, STARTING NOW - Richard Maltby, Jr., David Shire, Composers - Jay David Saks, Producer (RCA)

YOUR ARMS TOO SHORT TO BOX WITH GOD - Micki Grant, Alex Bradford, Composers Esmond Edwards, Producer (ABC)

ALBUM OF THE YEAR - CLASSICAL (G-864)

(Grammys to the Artist and Producer.) (Certificates to the Engineer(s).

CONCERT OF THE CENTURY - (Recorded Live at Carnegie Hall May 18, 1976) - Leonard Bernstein, Vladimir Horowitz, Isaac Stern, Mstislav Rostropovich, Dietrich Fischer-Dieskau, Yehudi Menuhin, Lyndon Woodside - Thomas Frost, Producer (Columbia)

GERSHWIN: PORGY & BESS - John De Main (cond. Houston Grand Opera Production - Prin. Solos: Dale, Smith, Shakesnider, Lane, Brice, Smalls) - Thomas Z. Shepard, Producer (RCA)

HAYDN: ORLANDO PALADINO - Antal Dorati (cond. Orchestre de Chambre de Lausanne/Auger, Ameling, Killebrew, Ahnsjo, Luxon, Trimarchi, Shirley - Erik Smith, Producer (Philips)

MAHLER: SYMPHONY NO. 9 IN D MAJOR - Carlo Maria Giulini (cond. Chicago Symphony) - Gunther Breest, Producer (DG)

PARKENING AND THE GUITAR - Christopher Parkening - Patti Laursen, Producer (Angel)

RAVEL: BOLERO/DEBUSSY: LA MER & APRES MIDI D'UN FAUNE - Sir Georg Solti (cond. Chicago Symphony) - Ray Minshull, Producer (London)

CLASSICAL PERFORMANCE ORCHESTRA - (G-865)

(Grammys to the Conductor and Producer. Certificates to the classical orchestra committee.)

BARTOK: THE WOODEN PRINCE - Pierre Boulez cond. New York Philharmonic - Andrew Kazdin, Producer (Columbia)

BRUCKNER: SYMPHONY NO. 8 IN C MINOR - Herbert von Karajan cond. Berlin Philharmonic - Hans Hirsch, Producer (DG)

MAHLER: SYMPHONY NO. 3 IN D MINOR - James Levine cond. Chicago Symphony - Thomas Z. Shepard, Jay David Saks, Producers (RCA)

MAHLER: SYMPHONY NO. 9 IN D MAJOR - Carlo Maria Giulini cond. Chicago Symphony - Gunther Breest, Producer (DG)

RAVEL: BOLERO - Sir Georg Solti cond. Chicago Symphony - Ray Minshull, Producer (London)

TCHAIKOVSKY: SWAN LAKE - Andre Previn cond. London Symphony - Christopher Bishop, Producer (Angel)

OPERA RECORDING (G-866)

(Grammys to the Conductor and Producer; special

plaques to the Principal Soloists.)

GERSHWIN: PORGY & BESS - John De Main (cond. Houston Grand Opera Production - Prin. Solos: Albert, Dale, Smith, Shakesnider, Lane, Brice, Smalls); Thomas S. Shepard, Producer (RCA)

HAYDN: ORLANDO PALADINO - Antal Dorati (cond. Orchstre de Chambre de Lausanne - Prin. Solos: Auger, Ameling, Killbrew, Ahnsjo, Luxon, Shirley, Trimarchi); Erik Smith, Producer (Philips)

JANACEK: KATYA KABANOVA - Charles Mackerras (cond. Vienna Philharmonic - Prin. Solos: Soderstrom, Kniplova, Dvorsky); James Mallinson, Producer (London)

MUSSORGSKY: BORIS GODUNOV - Jerzy Semkow (cond. Polish National Radio Symphony Orchestra & Chorus - Prin. Solos: Talvela, Gedda); David Mottley, Producer (Angel)

PUCCINI: TOSCA - Colin Davis (cond. Chorus & Orchestra of Royal Opera House, Covent Garden - Prin. Solos: Caballe, Carreras, Wixell, Ramey); Erik Smith, Producer (Philips)

WAGNER: DIE MEISTERSINGER VON NURNBERG - Eugen Jochum cond. (Deutsche Oper Berlin Orchestra & Chorus - Prin. Solos: Fischer-Dieskau, Domingo, Ludwig, Ligendza) - Gunther Breest, Producer (DG)

WAGNER: THE FLYING DUTCHMAN - Sir Georg Solti (cond. Chicago Symphony Orchestra & Chorus - Prin. Solos: Bailey, Martin, Talvela, Kollo, Krenn, Jones); Ray Minshull, Producer (London)

WEILL: THREE PENNY OPERA - Original Cast (New York Shakespeare Festival, Stanley Silverman, cond. - Prin. Solos: Raul Julia, C.K. Alexander, Ellen Greene) - Larry Morton, Producer (Columbia)

CHORAL PERFORMANCE - OTHER THAN OPERA (G-867)

(Grammys to the Conductor and Choral Director)

BERLIOZ: L'ENFANCE DU CHRIST - Colin Davis (cond. John Alldis Choir; London Symphony) (Philips)

BRITTEN: SAINT NICHOLAS - David Willcocks (cond. King's College Choir, Cambridge; Academy of St. Martin-in-the-Fields) (Seraphim)

BRUCKNER: TE DEUM - Herbert von Karajan (cond. Vienna Singverein; Berlin Philharmonic) (DG)

DVORAK: STABAT MATER - Rafael Kubelik (cond. Chorus of Bavarian Radio & Bavarian Radio Symphony) (DG)

PURCELL: FUNERAL MUSIC FOR QUEEN MARY - Philip Ledger (cond. King's College Choir, Cambridge; Academy of St. Martin-in-the-Fields) (Angel)

ROUSSEL: PSALM 80, FOR TENOR, CHORUS & ORCHESTRA - Serge Baudo, Cond. (Stephen Caillat Chorus & Orchestre de Paris) (Conn. Soc.)

VERDI: REQUIEM - Sir Georg Solti, Conductor - Margaret Hillis, Choral Director (Chicago Symphony Chorus & Orchestra) (RCA)

CHAMBER MUSIC PERFORMANCE (G-868)

(Instrumental or vocal)

BARTOK: QUARTETS FOR STRINGS (6) - Guarneri Quartet. (RCA)

A CONTEMPORARY ELIZABETHAN CONCERT (Works of Dowland, Williams, Purcell, etc.) David Munrow cond. Early Music Consort of London (Angel)

DVORAK: QUARTETS NO. 8 IN E MAJOR, OP 80 & NO. 10 IN E FLAT MAJOR, OP. 51 - Prague String Quartet. (DG)

DVORAK: QUINTET FOR PIANO IN A MAJOR, OP. 81 - Emanuel Ax & Cleveland Quartet (RCA)

IMPROVISATIONS - WEST MEETS EAST - ALBUM 3 - Ravi Shankar, Yehudi Menuhin, Jean-Pierre Rampal, Martine Geliot, Alla Rakha (Angel)

RACHMANINOFF: SONATA FOR CELLO & PIANO IN G MINOR, OP. 19 - ANDANTE/TCHAIKOVSKY:

TRIO FOR PIANO IN A MINOR, OP. 50 - PEZZO ELEGIACO - Vladimir Horowitz, Isaac Stern, Mstislav Rostropovich (Columbia)

SCHOENBERG: QUARTETS FOR STRINGS (COMPLETE) - Juilliard Quartet (Columbia)

CLASSICAL PERFORMANCE - INSTRUMENTAL SOLOIST(S) (WITH ORCHESTRA) (G-869)

BEETHOVEN: CONCERTI FOR PIANO (5) - Alfred Brendel, Piano (Hai-

tink cond. London Philharmonic) (Philips)
BEETHOVEN: CONCERTO FOR PIANO NO. 4 IN G MAJOR - Maurizio Pollini, Piano (Bohm cond. Vienna Philharmonic) (DG)
BRAHMS: CONCERTO FOR PIANO NO. 2 IN B FLAT MAJOR, OP. 83 - Solomon, Piano (Dobrowen cond. Philharmonic) (Vox)
CONCERTOS FROM SPAIN - (Surinach: Piano Concerto Montsalvatge; Concerto Breve) - Alicia de Larrocha, Piano (De Burgos cond. Royal Philharmonic) (London)
ELGAR: CONCERTO FOR CELLO, OP. 85 - Jacqueline Du Pre, Cello (Barenboim cond. Philadelphia Orchestra) (Columbia)
RACHMANINOFF: CONCERTO FOR PIANO NO. 3 IN D MINOR - Lazar Berman, Piano (Abbado, London Symphony) (Columbia)
SCHUMANN: CONCERTO FOR CELLO & ORCHESTRA IN A MINOR - BLOCH: SCHELOMO - Mstislav Rostropovich, Cello (Bernstein cond. Orchestra National de France) (Angel)
VIVALDI: THE FOUR SEASONS - Itzhak Perlman, Violin (Perlman cond. London Philharmonic) (Angel)

CLASSICAL PERFORMANCE - INSTRUMENTAL SOLOIST(S) (WITHOUT ORCHESTRA) (G-870)
BACH: THE ENGLISH SUITES (Complete) - Glenn Gould, Piano (Columbia)
BACH: PARTITAS FOR HARPSICHORD NOS. 1 IN B FLAT MAJOR & 2 IN C MINOR - Igor Kipnis, Harpsichord (Angel)
BEETHOVEN: SONATA FOR PIANO NO. 18 IN E FLAT MAJOR, OP. 31 NO. 3 - SCHUMANN: FANTASIESTUCKE, OP. 12 - Artur Rubinstein, Piano (RCA)
GRAINGER: PIANO MUSIC OF PERCY GRAINGER - Daniel Adni, Piano (Seraphim)
GRANADOS: GOYESCAS - Alicia de Larrocha, Piano (London)
KREISLER: ITZHAK PERLMAN PLAYS FRITZ KREISLER: ALBUM 2 - Itzhak Perlman, Violin (Angel)
MESSAIEN: 20 REGARDS DE L'ENFANT JESUS - Michel Beroff, Piano (Conn. Soc.)

CLASSICAL PERFORMANCE - VOCAL SOLOIST - (G-871)
BACH: ARIAS - Janet Baker (Marriner cond. Academy of St. Martin-in-the-Fields) (Angel)
BUT YESTERDAY IS NOT TODAY (Songs by Barber, Bowles, Copland, Chanler, etc.) - Donald Gramm (Hassard, accomp.) (New World)
FAURE: SONGS (Complete) - Gerard Souzay (Baldwin, Accomp.) (Conn. Soc.)
IVES: SONGS - Dietrich Fischer-Dieskau (Ponti, accomp.) (DG)
LUCIANO PAVAROTTI - O HOLY NIGHT (O Holy Night, Sanctus, Schubert: Ave Maria, etc.) - Luciano Pavarotti (Adler cond. National Philharmonic) (London)
RACHMANINOFF: SONGS - Volume Two - Elisabeth Soderstrom (Ashkenazy, accomp.) (London)
ROSSINI/MOZART: OPERA ARIAS - Frederica von Stade (de Waart cond. Rotterdam Philharmonic) (Philips)
SCHUBERT ON STAGE - Elly Ameling (de Waart cond. Rotterdam Philharmonic) (Philips)
SHOSTAKOVICH: SYMPHONY NO. 14 - Galina Vishnevskaya, Soprano - Mark Reshetin, Bass (Rostropovich cond. Moscow Philharmonic) (Columbia)

BEST ENGINEERED RECORDING - CLASSICAL (G-872)
(An Engineer's Award)
BARTOK: THE WOODEN PRINCE - Boulez cond. N.Y. Philharmonic - Bud Graham, Ray Moore & Milt Cherin, Engineers (Columbia)
BERLIOZ: L'ENFANCE DU CHRIST - Davis cond. London Symphony - S.J.W. Witteveen, Dick van Dijk, Engineers (Philips)
GERSHWIN: PORGY & BESS - De Main cond. Houston Grand Opera - Paul Goodman, Anthony Salvatore, Engineers (RCA)
MAHLER: SYMPHONY NO. 2 IN C MINOR ("RESURRECTION") - Abbado cond. Chicago Symphony - Heinz Wildhagen, Engineer (DG)

MAHLER: SYMPHONY NO. 9 IN D MAJOR - Giulini cond. Chicago Symphony - Klaus Scheibe, Engineer (DG)
RAVEL: BOLERO - Solti cond. Chicago Symphony - Kenneth Wilkinson, Engineer (London)

1978 HALL OF FAME WINNERS (G-873)
BACH-STOKOWSKI: TOCCATA & FUGUE IN D MINOR - Leopold Stokowski conducting Philadelphia Orchestra - Victrola #6751 - Released in 1927
THE GENIUS OF ART TATUM, VOLS. 1-13 (Albums) Art Tatum - Clef #MGC612, #MGC613, #MGC614, #MGC615, #MGC618, #MGC643, #MGC657, #MGC658, #MGC659, #MGC660, #MGC661, #MGC679, #MGC712 - Released 1954 through 1955
I CAN HEAR IT NOW, VOLS. 1-3 (Albums) - Edward R. Murrow - Columbia #ML4095, #ML4261, #ML4340 - Released 1948 through 1950
MY BLUE HEAVEN - Gene Austin - Victor #20964 - Released in 1928
STRANGE FRUIT - Billie Holiday - Commodore #CMS526 - Released in 1939

1978

RECORD OF THE YEAR (G-874)
(Grammys to the Artist and Producer.) (Certificates to the Arranger, Engineer, Songwriter, Musicians and Background Singers.)
BAKER STREET - Gerry Rafferty - Hugh Murphy, Gerry Rafferty, Producers (UA)
FEELS SO GOOD - Chuck Mangione - Chuck Mangione, Producer (A&M)
JUST THE WAY YOU ARE - Billy Joel - Phil Ramone, Producer (Columbia)
STAYIN' ALIVE - The Bee Gees - The Bee Gees, Karl Richardson, Albhy Galuten, Producers (RSO)
YOU NEEDED ME - Anne Murray - Jim Ed Norman, Producer (Capitol)

ALBUM OF THE YEAR (G-875)
(Grammys to the Artist and Producer.) (Certificates to the Arranger, Engineer and Songwriter.)
EVEN NOW - Barry Manilow - Barry Manilow, Ron Dante, Producers (Arista)
GREASE (ORIGINAL SOUNDTRACK) - John Travolta, Olivia Newton-John, Frankie Valli, Frankie Avalon, Stockard Channing, Jeff Conaway, Cindy Bullens, Sha-Na-Na, Louis St. Louis - Barry Gibb, John Farrar, Louis St. Louis, Albhy Galuten, Karl Richardson, Producers (Arista)
RUNNING ON EMPTY - Jackson Browne - Jackson Browne, Producer (Asylum)
SATURDAY NIGHT FEVER (MOTION PICTURE SOUNDTRACK) - The Bee Gees, David Shire, Yvonne Elliman, Tavares, Kool & The Gang, K.C. & The Sunshine Band, MFSB, Trammps, Walter Murphy, Ralph MacDonald - The Bee Gees, Karl Richardson, Albhy Galuten, Freddie Perren, Bill Oakes, David Shire, Arif Mardin, Thomas J. Valentino, Ralph MacDonald, W. Walter, K.G. Productions, H.W. Casey, Richard Finch, obby Martin, Broadway Eddie, Ron Kersey, Producers (RSO)
SOME GIRLS - The Rolling Stones - The Glimmer Twins, Producers

SONG OF THE YEAR (G-876)
(A Songwriter's Award.)
JUST THE WAY YOU ARE - Billy Joel
STAYIN' ALIVE - Barry Gibb, Robin Gibb, Maurice Gibb
THREE TIMES A LADY - Lionel Richie
YOU DON'T BRING ME FLOWERS - Neil Diamond, Alan Bergman, Marilyn Bergman
YOU NEEDED ME - Randy Goodrum

NEW ARTIST OF THE YEAR (G-877)

(This category is for an artist or organized group whose first recording was released during the Eligibility Period)
THE CARS (Elektra)
ELVIS COSTELLO (Columbia)
CHRIS REA (UA)
A TASTE OF HONEY (Capitol)
TOTO (CBS)

POP VOCAL - FEMALE (G-878)

(This category is for a solo performance in either pop, rock or folk.)
HOPELESSLY DEVOTED TO YOU - Olivia Newton-John (single) (RSO)
MAC ARTHUR PARK - Donna Summer (single) (Casablanca)
YOU BELONG TO ME - Carly Simon (single) (Elektra)
YOU DON'T BRING ME FLOWERS - (Solo version, not duet) - Barbra Streisand (track) (Columbia)
YOU NEEDED ME - Anne Murray (single) (Capitol)

POP VOCAL - MALE (G-879)

(This category is for a solo performance in either pop, rock or folk.)
BAKER STREET - Gerry Rafferty (single) (UA)
COPACABANA (AT THE COPA) - Barry Manilow (single) (Arista)
I JUST WANNA STOP - Gino Vannelli (single) (A&M)
RUNNING ON EMPTY - Jackson Browne (album) (Asylum)
SOMETIMES WHEN WE TOUCH - Dan Hill (single) (20th Century)

POP VOCAL - DUO, GROUP OR CHORUS (G-880)

(This category is for pop, rock, or folk. All recordings on which the group received artist billing on the label are eligible here even though the vocal may feature only one member of the group.)
THE CLOSER I GET TO YOU - Roberta Flack, Donny Hathaway (single) (Atlantic)
FM (NO STATIC AT ALL) - Steely Dan (single) (MCA)
GOT TO GET YOU INTO MY LIFE - Earth, Wind & Fire (single) (Columbia)
SATURDAY NIGHT FEVER - The Bee Gees (album) (RSO)
THREE TIMES A LADY - Commodores (single) (Motown)

POP INSTRUMENTAL (G-881)

(This category is for pop, rock or folk. All recordings are for either pure instrumentals or instrumentals with vocal coloring.)
CHILDREN OF SANCHEZ - Chuck Mangione Group (album) (A&M)
CLOSE ENCOUNTERS OF THE THIRD KIND (ORIGINAL MOTION PICTURE SOUNDTRACK) - John Williams (album) (Arista)
GUITAR MONSTERS - Chet Atkins, Les Paul (album) (RCA)
THE PINK PANTHER THEME ('78) - Henry Mancini (single) (UA)
STAR WARS AND CLOSE ENOUNTERS OF THE THIRD KIND - Zubin Mehta cond. The Los Angeles Philharmonic (London)

R&B VOCAL - FEMALE (G-882)

(This category is for a solo performance.)
ALMIGHTY FIRE - Aretha Franklin (album) (Atlantic)
I LOVE THE NIGHTLIFE (DISCO ROUND) - Alicia Bridges (single) (Polydor)
I'M EVERY WOMAN - Chaka Khan (single) (WB)
LAST DANCE - Donna Summer (single) (Casablanca)
OUR LOVE - Natalie Cole (single) (Capitol)

R&B VOCAL - MALE (G-883)

(This category is for a solo performance.)

CLOSE THE DOOR - Teddy Pendergrass (single) (PIR)
DANCE WITH ME - Peter Brown (single) (T.K.Prod.)
I CAN SEE CLEARLY NOW - Ray Charles (single) (Atlantic)
ON BROADWAY - George Benson (single) (WB)
WHEN YOU HEAR LOU, YOU'VE HEARD IT ALL - Lou Rawls (album) (PIR/Columbia)

R&B VOCAL - DUO, GROUP OR CHORUS (G-884)

(All recordings on which the group receives artist billing on the label are eligible here even though the vocal may feature only one member of the group.)
ALL 'N ALL - Earth, Wind & Fire (album) (Columbia)
BOOGIE OOGIE OOGIE - A Taste of Honey (single) (Capitol)
EASE ON DOWN THE ROAD - Diana Ross & Michael Jackson (single) (MCA)
NATURAL HIGH - Commodores (album) (Motown)
USE TA BE MY GIRL - O'Jays (track) (Columbia)

R&B INSTRUMENTAL (G-885)

(All recordings are for either pure instrumentals or instrumentals with vocal coloring.)
IMAGES - The Crusaders (album) (ABC)
MODERN MAN - Stanley Clarke (album) (Nemperor)
RUNNIN' - Earth, Wind & Fire (track) (Columbia)
STREETWAVE - Brothers Johnson (track) (A&M)
SWEET & SOUR - Average White Band (track) (Atlantic)

RHYTHM & BLUES SONG (G-886)

(A Songwriter's Award.) (Any song is eligible if a new recording of it has been released during the Eligibility Year.)
BOOGIE OOGIE OOGIE - Perry Kibble, Janice Johnson
DANCE, DANCE, DANCE - Bernard Edwards, Kenny Lehman, Nile Rogers
FANTASY - Maurice White, Eddie de Barrio, Verdine White
LAST DANCE - Paul Jabara
USE TA BE MY GIRL - Kenneth Gamble, Leon Huff

COUNTRY VOCAL - FEMALE (G-887)

(This category is for a solo performance.)
HERE YOU COME AGAIN - Dolly Parton (album) (RCA)
QUARTER MOON IN A TEN CENT TOWN - Emmylou Harris (album) (WB)
SLEEPING SINGLE IN A DOUBLE BED - Barbara Mandrell (single) (ABC)
TALKIN' IN YOUR SLEEP - Crystal Gayle (single) (UA)
WALK RIGHT BACK - Anne Murray (single) (Capitol)

COUNTRY VOCAL - MALE (G-888)

(This category is for a solo performance.)
GEORGIA ON MY MIND - Willie Nelson (single) (Columbia)
I'VE ALWAYS BEEN CRAZY - Waylon Jennings (album) (RCA)
LET'S TAKE THE LONG WAY AROUND THE WORLD - Ronnie Milsap (single) (RCA)
LOVE OR SOMETHING LIKE IT - Kenny Rogers (album) (UA)
SOFTLY, AS I LEAVE YOU - Elvis Presley (single) (RCA/Victory)
TAKE THIS JOB AND SHOVE IT - Johnny Paycheck (single) (Epic)

COUNTRY VOCAL - DUO OR GROUP (G-889)

(All nominations are singles)
ANYONE WHO ISN'T ME TONIGHT - Kenny Rogers and Dottie West (UA)
CRYIN' AGAIN - Oak Ridge Boys (ABC)
DO YOU KNOW YOU ARE MY SUNSHINE - Statler Brothers (Mercury)
IF THE WORLD RAN OUT OF LOVE TONIGHT - Jim Ed Brown, Helen

Cornelius (RCA)
**MAMAS DON'T LET YOUR BABIES GROW UP TO BE COWBOYS -
Waylon Jennings and Willie Nelson (RCA)**
ON MY KNEES - Charlie Rich with Janie Fricke (Epic)

COUNTRY INSTRUMENTAL (G-890)

(This category is for an Orchestra, Group or Soloist and
is for either pure instrumentals or instrumentals with
vocal coloring.)
BANJO BANDITS - Roy Clark and Buck Trent (album) (ABC)
COOKIN' COUNTRY - Danny Davis & The Nashville Brass (album)
(RCA)
ONE O'CLOCK JUMP - Asleep At The Wheel (track) (Capitol)
STEEL GUITAR RAG - Roy Clark (track) (Dot/ABC)
UNDER THE DOUBLE EAGLE - Doc Watson & Merle Watson (single)
(UA)

COUNTRY SONG (G-891)

(A Songwriter's Award.) (Any song is eligible if a new
recording of it has been released during the Eligibility
Year.)
EVERY TIME TWO FOOLS COLLIDE - Jan Dyer and Jeffrey Tweel
THE GAMBLER - Don Schlitz
LET'S TAKE THE LONG WAY AROUND THE WORLD - Archie Jordan
and Naomi Martin
MAMAS DON'T LET YOUR BABIES GROW UP TO BE COWBOYS - Ed
and Patsy Bruce
TAKE THIS JOB AND SHOVE IT - David A. Coe

GOSPEL PERFORMANCE - CONTEMPORARY OR INSPIRATIONAL (G-892)

COME ON, RING THOSE BELLS - Evie (album) (Word)
COSMIC COWBOY - Barry McGuire (album) (Sparrow)
DESTINED TO BE YOURS - McGuire (album) (Greentree)
IMPERIALS LIVE - Imperials (album) (DaySpring)
THE LADY IS A CHILD - Reba (album) (Greentree/Heartwarming)
WHAT A FRIEND - Larry Hart (track) (Genesis)

GOSPEL PERFORMANCE - TRADITIONAL (G-893)

(All nominations are albums)
ELVIS' FAVORITE GOSPEL SONGS - J.D. Sumner & The Stamps Quar-
tet (RCA)
HIS AMAZING LOVE - Blackwood Brothers (Skylite Sing)
THE OLD RUGGED CROSS - George Beverly Shea (Word)
REFRESHING - The Happy Goodman Family (Canaan)
SUNSHINE & ROSES - Cathedral Quartet (Canaan)

SOUL GOSPEL PERFORMANCE - CONTEMPORARY (G-894)

BECAUSE HE'S JESUS - Highland Park Community Choir, Inc. (track)
(Davida)
DANNIEBELLE LIVE IN SWEDEN WITH CHORALERNA - Danniebelle
and The Choralerna (album) (Sparrow)
LIVE IN LONDON - Andrae Crouch & The Disciples (album) (Light)
LOVE ALIVE II - Walter Hawkins (album) (Light)
REACH OUT AND TOUCH - Shirley Caeser (track) (Hob/Roadshow)
YOU LIGHT UP MY LIFE - Loleatta Holloway (track) (Gold Mine)

SOUL GOSPEL PERFORMANCE - TRADITIONAL (G-895)

AMAZING GRACE - Gladys McFadden & Loving Sisters (track) (ABC)
I DON'T FEEL NOWAYS TIRED - James Cleveland & The Salem Inspira-
tional Choir, dir. by Doretha Wade (album) (Savoy)
LIVE AND DIRECT - Mighty Clouds of Joy (album) (ABC)
SPECIAL APPEARANCE - Rev. Isaac Douglas, featuring the San Fran-
cisco Community Singers and the 21st Century Singers (album)
(Creed/Nashboro)

TOMORROW - James Cleveland and the Charles Fold Singers, dir. by
CCharles Fold (album) (Savoy)

INSPIRATIONAL PERFORMANCE (G-896)

(All nominations are albums)
BEHOLD - Billy Preston (Myrrh)
FIRST CLASS - The Boones (Lamb & Lion)
GOIN' UP IN SMOKE - Larry Hart (Genesis)
HAPPY MAN - B. J. Thomas (Myrrh)
HE TOUCHED ME - Tennessee Ernie Ford (Word)
PRECIOUS MEMORIES - Anita Kerr (Word)

ETHNIC OR TRADITIONAL RECORDING (G-897)

(This category includes traditional blues and pure folk
recordings.) (All nominations are albums)
CHICAGO BLUES AT HOME - Louis Myers, John Littlejohn, Eddie
Taylor, Jimmy Rogers, Johnny Shines, Homesick James Williamson,
Bob Myers (Advent)
CLIFTON CHENIER AND HIS RED HOT LOUISIANA BAND IN NEW
ORLEANS - Clifton Chenier (Dixieland/Jubilee)
I HEAR SOME BLUES DOWNSTAIRS - Fenton Robinson (Alligator)
I'M READY - Muddy Waters (Blue Sky)
U.S.A. - Memphis Slim & His House Rockers, featuring Matt "Guitar"
Murphy (Pearl)

LATIN RECORDING (G-898)

(This category is for pure Latin music. It is not for Latin
oriented or Latin influenced recordings.)
CORO MIYARE - Fania All Stars (track) (Columbia)
LAURINDO ALMEIDA TRIO - Laurindo Almeida (album) (Dobre)
HOMENAJE A BENY MORE - Tito Puente (album) (Tico)
LA RAZA LATINA - Orchestra Harlow (album) (Fania)
LUCUMI, MACUMBA, VOODOO - Eddie Palmieri (album) (Epic)
MONGO A LA CARTE - Mongo Santamaria (album) (Vaya)

RECORDING FOR CHILDREN (G-899)

(This category is intended for recordings created
specifically for children.) (All nominations are albums)
CHARLIE BROWN'S ALL-STARS (TV SPECIAL) - Warren Lockhart &
Jymn Magon, Producers (Charlie Brown Productions)
THE HOBBIT (SOUNDTRACK) - Orson Bean, John Huston, Hans Con-
ried (Buena Vista/Disneyland)
THE MUPPET SHOW - The Muppets (Arista)
PETER AND THE WOLF - David Bowie & Eugene Ormandy cond. the
Philadelphia Orchestra (RCA)
SESAME STREET FEVER - The Muppets & Robin Gibb (Sesame St.)

COMEDY RECORDING (G-900)

(Either spoken word or musical performances are eligi-
ble here.) (All nominations are albums)
THE RUTLES (ALL YOU NEED IS CASH) - The Rutles (WB)
ON STAGE - Lily Tomlin (Arista)
SEX AND VIOLINS - Martin Mull (ABC)
A WILD AND CRAZY GUY - Steve Martin (WB)
THE WIZARD OF COMEDY - Richard Pryor (Laff)

SPOKEN WORD RECORDING (G-901)

(This category is for spoken word, documentary or
drama.) (All nominations are albums)
**CITIZEN KANE (ORIGINAL MOTION PICTURE SOUNDTRACK) Or-
son Welles (Mark 56)**
JOHN STEINBECK: THE GRAPES OF WRATH (EXCERPTS) - Read by
Henry Fonda (Caedmon)
THE NIXON INTERVIEWS WITH DAVID FROST - Richard Nixon & David
Frost (Polydor)
ROOTS (ORIGINAL SOUNDTRACK FOR TV) - Stan Cornyn, Producer
(WB)

WUTHERING HEIGHTS - Dame Judith Anderson, Claire Bloom, James Mason, George Rose, Gordon Gould (Caedmon)

INSTRUMENTAL COMPOSITION (G-902)

(A Composer's Award for an original, non-classical composition with or without lyrics which first gained recognition as an instrumental.)

THE CAPTAIN'S JOURNEY - Lee Ritenour
CONSUELO'S LOVE THEME - Chuck Mangione
END OF THE YELLOW BRICK ROAD - Quincy Jones, Nick Ashford, Valerie Simpson
FRIENDS - Chick Corea
THEME FROM "CLOSE ENCOUNTERS OF THE THIRD KIND" - John Williams

ORIGINAL SCORE - MOTION PICTURE OR A TELEVISION SPECIAL (G-903)

(A Composer's and/or Songwriter's Award for an original score or original songs written specifically for the motion picture or television special.)

BATTLESTAR GALACTICA - Stu Phillip, John Tartaglia, Sue Collins, Glen Larson, Composers (MCA)
CLOSE ENCOUNTERS OF THE THIRD KIND - John Williams, Composer (Arista)
HOLOCAUST: THE STORY OF THE FAMILY WEISS - Morton Gould, Composer (RCA Red Seal)
MIDNIGHT EXPRESS - Giorgio Moroder, Chris Bennett, David Castle, William Hayes, Oliver Stone, Composers (Casablanca)
REVENGE OF THE PINK PANTHER - Henry Mancini, Composer - Leslie Bricusse, Lyricist (UA)

CAST SHOW ALBUM (G-904)

(Awards to the Composers and Album Producers.)
(Original cast albums, albums by road casts or working casts, including show revival casts, are eligible.)

AIN'T MISBEHAVIN' - Thomas Fats Waller & Others, Composers - Thomas Z. Shepard, Producer (RCA Red Seal)
THE BEST LITTLE WHOREHOUSE IN TEXAS - Carol Hall, Composer - John Simon, Producer (MCA)
BEATLEMANIA - John Lennon, Paul McCartney, George Harrison, Ringo Starr, Composers - Sandy Yaguda, Kenny Laguna, Producers (RCA Red Seal)
THE KING AND I - Richard Rodgers, Oscar Hammerstein II, Composers - Thomas Z. Shepard, Producer (RCA Red Seal)
ON THE TWENTIETH CENTURY - Adolph Green, Betty Comden, Cy Coleman, Composers - Cy Coleman, Producer (Columbia)

JAZZ VOCAL (G-905)

(All nominations are albums)
ALL FLY HOME - Al Jarreau (WB)
GENTLE RAIN - Irene Kral (Choice)
HOW LONG HAS THIS BEEN GOING ON - Sarah Vaughan (Pablo)
THE MAIN MAN - Eddie Jefferson (Inner City)
TOGETHER AGAIN - FOR THE FIRST TIME - Mel Torme (Gryphon/Century)
TRUE TO LIFE - Ray Charles (Atlantic)

JAZZ - SOLOIST (G-906)

(All nominations are albums)
HEAVY LOVE (Al Cohn & Jimmy Rowles) - Al Cohn (Xanadu)
MONTREUX '77 - OSCAR PETERSON JAM - Oscar Peterson (Pablo)
ROSEWOOD - Woody Shaw (Columbia)
SOPHISTICATED GIANT - Dexter Gordon (Columbia)
STAN GETZ GOLD - Stan Getz (Inner City)

JAZZ - GROUP (G-907)

(All nominations are albums)
FRIENDS - Chick Corea (Polydor)
HEAVY LOVE - Al Cohn and Jimmy Rowles (Xanadu)
THE PEACOCKS - Stan Getz and Jimmy Rowles (Columbia)
ROSEWOOD - Woody Shaw Concert Ensemble (Columbia)
SONG FOR SISYPHUS - The Phil Woods Quintet (Gryphon/Century)

JAZZ - BIG BAND (G-908)

(All nominations are albums)
BIG BAND JAZZ - Rob McConnell & The Boss Brass (Umbrella)
INSIGHTS - Toshiko Akiyoshi, Lew Tabackin Big Band (RCA)
LIVE IN MUNICH - Thad Jones and Mel Lewis (Horizon/A&M)
SOPHISTICATED GIANT - Dexter Gordon & Orchestra (Columbia)
THAD JONES GREETINGS & SALUTATIONS - Thad Jones (Biograph)

INSTRUMENTAL ARRANGEMENT (G-909)

(An Arranger's Award for a specific arrangement released on either a single or album track.)

AJA - Woody Herman Band - Alan Broadbent, Arranger (Century)
GREEN EARRINGS - Woody Herman Band - Joe Roccisano, Arranger (Century)
MAD HATTER RHAPSODY - Chick Corea - Chick Corea, Arranger (Polydor)
MAIN TITLE (OVERTURE PART ONE) - Wiz Original Soundtrack - Quincy Jones & Robert Freedman, Arrangers (MCA)
RUNNIN' - Earth, Wind & Fire - Tom Tom 84, Arranger (Columbia)

ARRANGEMENT ACOMPANYING VOCALIST(S) (G-910)

(An Arranger's Award for a specific arrangement released on either a single or album track.)

FALLING ALICE - Chick Corea - Chick Corea, Arranger (Polydor)
FANTASY - Earth, Wind & Fire - Tom Tom 84, Arranger (Columbia)
GOT TO GET YOU INTO MY LIFE - Earth, Wind & Fire - Maurice White, Arranger (RSO)
IT HAPPENS VERY SOFTLY - Andrea Marcovicci - Robert Freedman, Arranger (Take Home Tunes)
WE THREE KINGS - Christmas Festival Choracle & Orchestra - William Pursell, Arranger (National Geographic)

ARRANGEMENT FOR VOICES (G-911)

(An Arranger's Award for a specific arrangement released on either a single or album track.)

CRY ME A RIVER - The Singers Unlimited - Gene Puerling. Arranger (MPS/Capitol)
HIGH CLOUDS - Vocal Jazz Incorporated - Ira Shankman, Arranger (Grapevine)
ROTUNDA - McCoy Tyner - McCoy Tyner, Arranger (Milestone)
STAYIN' ALIVE - The Bee Gees - The Bee Gees, Arranger (RSO)
STUFF LIKE THAT - Quincy Jones - Quincy Jones, Valerie Simpson, Nick Ashford, Arrangers (A&M)

ALBUM PACKAGE (G-912)

(Grammy to Art Director. Certificates to Designer, Photographer, Illustrator, etc. where applicable.)

BOYS IN THE TREES - Carly Simon - Johnny Lee & Tony Lane, Art Directors (Elektra)
BRUCE ROBERTS - Bruce Roberts - Tony Lane, Art Director (Elektra)
THE CARS - The Cars - Ron Coro, Art Director (Elektra)
CHILDREN OF SANCHEZ - Chuck Mangione - Juni Osaki, Art Director (A&M)
HEADS - Bob James - John Berg & Paula Scher, Art Directors (Columbia)
LAST KISS - Fandango - Gribbitt/Tim Bryant, Art Director (RCA)

NON-FICTION - Steve Kuhn - Barbara Wojirsch, Art Director (ECM)
OUT OF THE WOODS - Oregon - Ron Coro & Johnny Lee, Art Directors (Elektra)

ALBUM NOTES (G-913)

(An Annotator's Award for original writing for a specific album.)
BEETHOVEN: 9 SYMPHONIES - von Karajan; Berlin Philharmonic - Irving Kolodin & Bill Bender, Annotators (Polydor)
A BING CROSBY COLLECTION, VOL. I & II - Michael Brooks, Annotator (Columbia)
ELLINGTON AT CARNEGIE HALL 1943 - Leonard Feather, Annotator (Prestige)
GEORGIA SEA ISLAND SONGS - Various artists - Alan Lomax, Annotator (New World)
THE INDIVIDUALISM OF PEE WEE RUSSELL - Dan Morgenstern, Annotator (Savoy)
WORKS OF CARPENTER/GILBERT/WEISS/POWELL - L.A. Philharmonic - Phil David Baker & R.D. Darrell, Annotators (New World)

HISTORICAL REPACKAGE ALBUM (G-914)

(Grammy to the Repackage Album Producer. Certificates to Designer, Annotator, Engineer, etc.)
A BING CROSBY COLLECTION, VOLS. I & II - Michael Brooks, Producer (Columbia)
THE FIRST RECORDED SOUNDS 1888 TO 1929 - Edison - George Garabedian, Producer (Mark 56)
THE GREATEST GROUP OF THEM ALL - The Ravens - Bob Porter, Producer (Savoy)
LA DIVINA - Maria Callas - Peter Andry & Walter Legge, Producers (Angel)
LESTER YOUNG STORY VOL. 3 - Michael Brooks, Producer (Columbia)

BEST ENGINEERED RECORDING (G-915)

(Non-Classical) (An Engineer's Award.)
ALL 'N ALL - Earth, Wind & Fire - George Massenberg, Engineer (album) (Columbia)
CLOSE ENCOUNTERS OF THE THIRD KIND - John Williams - John Neal, Engineer (album) (Arista)
FM (NO STATIC AT ALL) - Steely Dan - Roger Nichols, Al Schmitt, Engineers (track) (MCA)
PYRAMID - The Alan Parsons Project - Alan Parsons, Engineer (album) (Arista)
SOUNDS. . .AND STUFF LIKE THAT - Quincy Jones - Bruce Swedien, Engineer (album) (A&M)
A TRIBUTE TO ETHEL WATERS - Diahann Carroll - Allen Sides & John Neal, Engineers (album) (Orinda)

PRODUCER OF THE YEAR (G-916)

(A Producer's Award for consistently outstanding creativity in producing. Listed below are examples of producer's activities. AAlbum; SSingle; TTrack)
THE BEE GEES, ALBHY GALUTEN, KARL RICHARDSON: "More Than A Woman" (T); "Night Fever" (S); "Stayin' Alive" (S) - The Bee Gees
PETER ASHER: "Living in The U.S.A." (A); "Back In The U.S.A." (S) - Linda Rondstadt
QUINCY JONES: "Blam" (A) - Bros. Johnson; "Ease On Down The Road" (S) - Diana Ross, Michael Jackson; "Sounds. . .And Stuff Like That" (A) - Quincy Jones; "The Wiz" (A) - Original Soundtrack
ALAN PARSONS: "Time Passages" (A) - Al Stewart; "Pyramid" (A) - The Alan Parsons Project
PHIL RAMONE - "Hot Streets" (A); "Alive Again" (T); "No Tell Lover" (T) - Chicago

ALBUM OF THE YEAR - CLASSICAL (G-917)

(Grammys to the Artist and Producer. Certificates to the Engineer(s) and Classical Orchestra Commitee.)
BACH: MASS IN B MINOR - Neville Marriner (cond. Academy of St. Martin-in-the-Fields) - Vittorio Negri, Producer (Philips)
BEETHOVEN: SYMPHONIES (9) Complete - Herbert von Karajan (cond. Berlin Philharmonic) - Michel Glotz, Producer (DG)
BRAHMS: CONCERTO FOR VIOLIN IN D MAJOR - Itzhak Perlman with Carlo Maria Giulini (cond. Chicago Symphony) - Christopher Bishop, Producer (Angel)
DVORAK: SYMPHONY NO. 9 IN E MINOR ("NEW WORLD") - Carlo Maria Giulini (cond. Chicago Symphony) - Gunther Breest, Producer (DG)
MAHLER: SYMPHONY NO. 4 IN G MAJOR - Claudio Abbado (cond. Vienna Philharmonic) - Rainer Brock, Producer (DG)
NIELSEN: MASKARADE - John Frandsen (cond. Danish Radio Symphony Orchestra & Chorus/Prin. Solos: Hansen, Landy, Johansen, Plesner, Bastian, Sorens) - Peter Willemoes, Producer (Unicorn)
RACHMANINOFF: CONCERTO NO. 3 IN D MINOR FOR PIANO (HOROWITZ GOLDEN JUBILEE) - Vladimir Horowitz with Eugene Ormandy (cond. New York Philharmonic) -John F. Pfeiffer, Producer (RCA)
SIBELIUS: SYMPHONIES (Complete) - Colin Davis (cond. Boston Symphony) (Philips)

CLASSICAL PERFORMANCE ORCHESTRA - (G-918)

(Grammys to the Conductor and Producer. Certificate to Classical Orchestra Comittee.)
BEETHOVEN: SYMPHONIES (9) Complete - Herbert von Karajan cond. Berlin Philharmonic - Michel Glotz, Producer (DG)
BRUCKNER: SYMPHONY NO. 9 IN D MINOR - Carlo Maria Giulini cond. Chicago Symphony - Christopher Bishop, Producer (Angel)
HOLST: THE PLANETS - Neville Marriner cond. Concertgebouw Orchestra - Vittorio Negri, Producer (Philips)
MAHLER: SYMPHONY NO. 9 IN D MAJOR - Claudio Abbado cond. Vienna Philharmonic - Rainer Brock, Producer (DG)
MEDELSSOHN: SYMPHONIES (5) Complete - Kurt Masur cond. Leipzig Gewandhaus Orchestra - Rainer Brock, Producer (Vanguard)
MESSIAEN: TURANGALILA SYMPHONY - Andre Previn cond. London Symphony Orchestra - Christopher Bishop, Producer (Angel)
RACHMANINOFF: SYMPHONY NO. 1 IN D MINOR - Leonard Slatkin cond. St. Louis Symphony - Marc Aubort & Joanna Nickrenz, Producers (Candide)
SHOSTAKOVICH: SYMPHONY NO. 5 - Andre Previn cond. Chicago Symphony - Christopher Bishop, Producer (Angel)
STRAVINSKY: RITE OF SPRING - Zubin Mehta cond. New York Philharmonic - Andrew Kazdin, Producer (Columbia)
VARESE: AMERIQUES/ARCANA/IONISATION (BOULEZ CONDUCTS VARESE) - Pierre Boulez cond. New York Philharmonic - Andrew Kazdin, Producer (Columbia)

OPERA RECORDING (G-919)

(Grammys to the Conductor and Producer.) (Special plaques to the Principal Soloists.)
CHARPENTIER: LOUISE - Julius Rudel (cond. Chorus & Orchestra of Paris Opera - Prin. Solos: Sills, Gedda) - Christopher Bishop, Producer (Angel)
LEHAR: THE MERRY WIDOW - Julius Rudel (cond. New York City Opera Orchestra & Chorus - Prin. Solos: Sills, Titus) - George Sponhaltz & John Coveney, Producers (Angel)
MOZART: LA CLEMENZA DI TITO - Colin Davis (cond. Orchestra & Chorus of Royal Opera House, Covent Garden - Prin. Solos: Baker, Popp, Minton, von Stade, Burrows) (Philips)
NIELSEN: MASKARADE - John Frandsen (cond. Danish Radio Symphony Orchestra & Chorus - Prin. Solos: Hansen, Landy, Johansen, Plesner, Bastian, Sorensen) - Peter Willemoes, Producer (Unicorn)
PUCCINI: LA FANCIULLA DEL WEST - Zubin Mehta (cond. Chorus & Orchestra of Royal Opera House, Covent Garden - Prin. Solos: Neblett, Domingo, Milnes) - Gunther Breest, Producer (DG)
SHOSTAKOVICH: THE NOSE - Gennady Rozhdestvensky (cond. Chorus & Orchestra of Moscow Chamber Opera with soloists) - Severin Pazukhin, Producer (Columbia)
(R.) STRAUSS: SALOME - Herbert von Karajan (cond. Berlin Philhar-

monic - Prin. Solos: Behrens, van Dam) - Michel Glotz, Producer (Angel)
VERDI: LA TRAVIATA - Carlos Kleiber (cond. Bavarian State Opera Chorus & Orchestra - Prin. Solos: Cotrubas, Domingo, Milnes) - Dr. Hans Hirsch, Producer (DG)

CHORAL PERFORMANCE - OTHER THAN OPERA (G-920)

(Grammys to the Conductor and Choral Director.)
BACH: MASS IN B MINOR - Neville Marriner (cond. Chorus & Academy of St. Martin-in-the-Fields) (Philips)
BEETHOVEN: MISSA SOLEMNIS - Sir Georg Solti, cond.; Margaret Hillis, Choral Director (Chicago Symphony Orchestra & Chorus) (London)
BLOCH: SACRED SERVICE - Maurice Abravanel (cond. Utah Chorale & Symphony Orchestra) (Angel)
HAYDN: MASS NO. 9 IN D MINOR ("LORD NELSON MASS") - Leonard Bernstein, Cond.; Joseph Flummerfelt, Choral Dir. (Westminster Choir & New York Philharmonic) (Columbia)
PROKOFIEV: ALEXANDER NEVSKY- Leonard Slatkin, Cond.; Thomas Peck, Choral Dir. (St. Louis Symphony Chorus & Orchestra) (Candide)
STRAVINSKY: LES NOCES & MASS - Leonard Bernstein (cond. Trinity Boys' Choir, English Bach Festival Chorus & English Bach Festival Orchestra) (DG)
VIVALDI: GLORIA IN D MAJOR & MAGNIFICAT - Riccardo Muti, Cond.; Norbert Balatsch, Choral Dir. (New Philharmonia Chorus & Orchestra) (Angel)
WALTON: BELSHAZZAR'S FEAST - Sir Georg Solti, Cond.; John Alldis, Choral Dir. (London Philharmonic Choir & Orchestra) (London)

CHAMBER MUSIC PERFORMANCE (G-921)

(Instrumental or vocal)
THE ART OF THE RECORDER - David Munrow cond. David Munrow Recorder Consort & Members of the Early Music Consort of London (Angel)
BARTOK: QUARTET NO. 2 FOR STRINGS, OP 17 & QUARTET NO. 6 - Tokyo String Quartet (DG)
BARTOK: SONATA FOR 2 PIANOS & PERCUSSION/MOZART: ANDANTE WITH 5 VARIATIONS FOR PIANO, 4 HANDS/DEBUSSY: EN BLANC ET NOIR FOR 2 PIANOS - Stephen Bishop-Kovacevich & Martha Argerich (Philips)
BEETHOVEN: SONATAS FOR VIOLIN & PIANO (Complete) - Itzhak Perlman & Vladimir Ashkenazy (London)
DUETS FOR TWO VIOLINS - Itzhak Perlman & Pincas Zukerman (Angel)
JOHN WILLIAMS & FRIENDS - John Williams, Carlos Bonell, Brian Gascoigne, Morris Pert, Keith Marjoram (Columbia)
MOZART: QUARTETS FOR PIANO & STRINGS - Artur Rubinstein & Members of Guarneri Quartet (RCA)
SCHUBERT: QUINTET IN C MAJOR FOR STRINGS - Melos Quartet with Mstislav Rostropovich (DG)

CLASSICAL PERFORMANCE - INSTRUMENTAL SOLOIST(S) (WITH ORCHESTRA) (G-922)

BRAHMS: CONCERTO FOR VIOLIN IN D MAJOR - Itzhak Perlman, Violin (Giulini cond. Chicago Symphony) (Angel)
CHOPIN: CONCERTO NO. 2 IN F MINOR FOR PIANO - Emanuel Ax, Piano (Ormandy cond. Philadelphia Orchestra) (RCA)
DVORAK: CONCERTO FOR CELLO IN B MINOR/SAINT-SAENS: CONCERTO FOR CELLO NO. 1 IN A MINOR - Mstislav Rostropovich, Cello (Giulini cond. London Philharmonic) (Angel)
MOZART: CONCERTOS FOR PIANO NOS. 21 IN C MAJOR & 9 IN E FLAT MAJOR - Murray Perahia, Piano (Perahia cond. English Chamber Orchestra) (Columbia)
RACHMANINOFF: CONCERTO NO. 3 IN D MINOR FOR PIANO (HOROWITZ GOLDEN JUBILEE) - Vladimir Horowitz, Piano (Ormandy cond. Philadelphia Orchestra) (RCA)
VAUGHAN WILLIAMS: CONCERTO FOR TUBA - Arnold Jacobs, Tuba (Barenboim cond. Chicago Symphony) (DG)

CLASSICAL PERFORMANCE - INSTRUMENTAL SOLOIST(S) (WITHOUT ORCHESTRA) (G-923)

BACH: ITALIAN CONCERTO/CHORAL PRELUDE/PRELUDE,S922/CHROMATIC FANTASY & FUGUE/FANTASY & FUGUE - Alfred Brendel, Piano (Philips)
BEETHOVEN: THE LATE PIANO SONATAS - Maurizio Pollini, Piano (DG)
BEETHOVEN: VARIATIONS ON A WALTZ BY DIABELLI - Charles Rosen, Piano (Peters)
DEBUSSY: PRELUDES FOR PIANO, BOOKS I & II - Paul Jacobs, Piano (Nonesuch)
THE HOROWITZ CONCERTS 1977/78 - Vladimir Horowitz, Piano (RCA)
LISZT: 12 TRANSCENDENTAL ETUDES & 3 ETUDES DE CONCERT - Claudio Arrau, Piano (Philips)
RUDOLF SERKIN ON TELEVISION - Rudolf Serkin, Piano (Columbia)

CLASSICAL PERFORMANCE - VOCAL SOLOIST - (G-924)

BRAHMS: ALTO RHAPSODY - Christa Ludwig (Bohm cond. Vienna Philharmonic) (DG)
LUCIANO PAVAROTTI - HITS FROM LINCOLN CENTER - Luciano Pavarotti (various Accomp.) (London)
MARIA CALLAS/THE LEGEND The Unreleased Recordings - Maria Callas (various Conds. & Orchs.) (Angel)
MUSSORGSKY: SONGS & DANCES OF DEATH - Galina Vishnevskaya (Rostropovich cond. London Philharmonic) (Angel)
RAVEL: SHEHERAZADE - Marilyn Horne (Bernstein cond. Orchestre Nationale de France) (Columbia)
TERESA BERGANZA - FAVORITE ZARZUELA ARIAS - Teresa Berganza (Asensio cond. English Chamber Orchestra) (Zambra)
WAGNER: ARIAS - Dietrich Fischer-Dieskau (Kubelik cond. Bavarian Radio Orchestra) (Angel)

BEST ENGINEERED RECORDING - CLASSICAL (G-925)

(An Engineer's Award.)
BACH: MASS IN B MINOR - Marriner cond. Chorus & Academy of St. Martin-in-the-Fields (Philips)
BEETHOVEN: SYMPHONIES (9) Complete - von Karajan cond. Berlin Philharmonic - Gunter Hermann, Engineer (DG)
BERLIOZ: SYMPHONIE FANTASTIQUE - Ormandy cond. Philadelphia Orchestra - Paul Goodman, Engineer (RCA)
BRUCKNER: SYMPHONY NO. 5 IN B FLAT MAJOR - von Karajan cond. Berlin Philharmonic - Gunter Hermann, Engineer (DG)
FREDRICK FENNELL - CLEVELAND SYMPHONIC WINDS - Jack Renner, Engineer (Telarc)
HOLST: THE PLANETS - Marriner cond. Concertgebouw Orchestra (Philips)
MESSIAEN: TURANGALILA SYMPHONY - Previn cond. London Symphony - Chris Parker, Engineer (Angel)
PROKOFIEV: ALEXANDER NEVSKY - Slatkin cond. St. Louis Symphony & Chorus - Marc Aubort, Engineer (Candide)
VARESE: AMERIQUES/ARCANA/IONISATION (BOULEZ CONDUCTS VARESE) - Boulez cond. New York Philharmonic - Bud Graham, Arthur Kendy & Ray Moore, Engineers (Columbia)
WAGNER: DIE WALKURE: RIDE OF THE VALKYRIES/TRISTAN: PRELUDE ACT I/GOTTERDAMMERUNG: SIEGFRIED'S FUNERAL MUSIC/SIEGFRIED: FOREST MURMURS - Leinsdorf cond. Los Angeles Philharmonic - Doug Sax & Bud Wyatt, Engineers (Sheffield Lab)

1979 HALL OF FAME WINNERS (G-926)

HOW HIGH THE MOON - Les Paul & Mary Ford - Capitol #1451 - Released in 1951
ONE O'CLOCK JUMP - Count Basie - Decca #1363 - Released in 1937
RACHMANINOFF: RHAPSODY ON A THEME OF PAGANINI (Album) - Sergei Rachmaninoff (Piano); Philadelphia Orchestra, Leopold Stokowski, Conductor - RCA Victor #M250 - Released in 1935

1979

RECORD OF THE YEAR (G-927)
(Grammy to the Artist and Producer if other than the Artist.) (Certificates to the Arranger, Engineer, Songwriter, Musicians and Background Singers.)
AFTER THE LOVE HAS GONE - Earth, Wind & Fire - Maurice White, Producer (ARC-CBS)
THE GAMBLER - Kenny Rogers - Larry Butler, Producer (UA)
I WILL SURVIVE - Gloria Gaynor - Dino Fekaris, Freddie Perren, Producers (Polydor)
WHAT A FOOL BELIEVES - The Doobie Brothers - Ted Templeman, Producer (WB)
YOU DON'T BRING ME FLOWERS - Barbra Streisand and Neil Diamond - Bob Gaudio, Producer (Columbia)

ALBUM OF THE YEAR (G-928)
(Grammys to the Artist and Producer if other than the Artist.) (Certificates to the Arranger, Engineer and Songwriter.)
BAD GIRLS - Donna Summer - Giorgio Moroder, Pete Bellotte, Producers (Casablanca)
BREAKFAST IN AMERICA - Supertramp - Supertramp, Peter Henderson, Producers (A&M)
52ND STREET - Billy Joel - Phil Ramone, Producer (Columbia)
THE GAMBLER - Kenny Rogers - Larry Butler, Producer (UA)
MINUTE BY MINUTE - The Doobie Brothers - Ted Templeman, Producer (WB)

SONG OF THE YEAR (G-929)
(A Songwriter's Award)
AFTER THE LOVE HAS GONE - David Foster, Jay Graydon, Bill Champlin
CHUCK E.'S IN LOVE - Rickie Lee Jones
HONESTY - Billy Joel
I WILL SURVIVE - Dino Fekaris, Freddie Perren
MINUTE BY MINUTE - Lester Abrams, Michael McDonald
REUNITED - Dino Fekaris, Freddie Perren
SHE BELIEVES IN ME - Steve Gibb
WHAT A FOOL BELIEVES - Kenny Loggins, Michael McDonald

NEW ARTIST (G-930)
(This Category is for an artist or organized group whose first recording was released during the Eligibility Period)
BLUES BROTHERS (Atlantic)
DIRE STRAITS (WB)
RICKIE LEE JONES (WB)
THE KNACK (Capitol)
ROBIN WILLIAMS (Casablanca)

POP VOCAL - FEMALE (G-931)
(This Category is for a solo performance)
BAD GIRLS - Donna Summer (Album) (Casablanca)
CHUCK E.'S IN LOVE - Rickie Lee Jones (Track) (WB)
DON'T CRY OUT LOUD - Melissa Manchester (Single) (Arista)
I WILL SURVIVE - Gloria Gaynor (Track) (Polydor)
I'LL NEVER LOVE THIS WAY AGAIN - Dionne Warwick (Single) (Arista)

POP VOCAL - MALE (G-932)
(This category is for a solo performance)
DA YA THINK I'M SEXY? - Rod Stewart (Single) (WB)
52ND STREET - Billy Joel (Album) (Columbia)
SAD EYES - Robert John (Single) (EMI-America)
SHE BELIEVES IN ME - Kenny Rogers (Single) (UA)
UP ON THE ROOF - James Taylor (Single) (Columbia)

POP VOCAL - DUO, GROUP OR CHORUS (G-933)
(All recordings on which the group receives artist billing on the label are eligible here even though the vocal may feature only one member of the group.)
BREAKFAST IN AMERICA - Supertramp (Album) (A&M)
LONESOME LOSER - Little River Band (Single) (Capitol)
MINUTE BY MINUTE - The Doobie Brothers (Album) (WB)
SAIL ON - Commodores (Track) (Motown)
YOU DON'T BRING ME FLOWERS - Barbra Streisand & Neil Diamond (Single) (Columbia)

POP INSTRUMENTAL (G-934)
(All recordings are for either pure instrumentals or instrumentals with vocal coloring.)
AN EVENING OF MAGIC - Chuck Mangione (Album) (A&M)
MANHATTAN (Music From The Film) - Zubin Mehta & The New York Philharmonic (Album - Side 2) (CBS)
MUSIC BOX DANCER - Frank Mills (Track) (Polydor)
RISE - Herb Alpert (Single) (A&M)
THEME FROM SUPERMAN (MAIN TITLE) - John Williams (Track) (WB)

ROCK VOCAL - FEMALE (G-935)
(This category is for a solo performance)
HOT STUFF - Donna Summer (Single) (Casablanca)
THE LAST CHANCE TEXACO - Rickie Lee Jones (Track) (WB)
SURVIVOR - Cindy Bullens (Single) (UA)
TNT - Tanya Tucker (Album) (MCA)
VENGEANCE - Carly Simon (Single) (Elektra)
YOU'RE GONNA GET WHAT'S COMING - Bonnie Raitt (Track) (WB)

ROCK VOCAL - MALE (G-936)
(This category is for a solo performance)
BAD CASE OF LOVING YOU (DOCTOR, DOCTOR) - Robert Palmer (Track) (Island/W.B.)
BLONDES (HAVE MORE FUN) - Rod Stewart (Track) (WB)
DANCIN' FOOL - Frank Zappa (Track) (Zappa)
GOTTA SERVE SOMEBODY - Bob Dylan (Single) (Columbia)
IS SHE REALLY GOING OUT WITH HIM? - Joe Jackson (Single) (A&M)

ROCK VOCAL - DUO OR GROUP (G-937)
(All recordings on which the group receives artist billing on the label are eligible here even though the vocal may feature only one member of the group.)
BRIEFCASE FULL OF BLUES - Blues Brothers (Album) (Atlantic)
CANDY-O - Cars (Album) (Elektra)
CORNERSTONE - Styx (Album) (A&M)
HEARTACHE TONIGHT - Eagles (Single) (Asylum)
MY SHARONA - The Knack (Single) (Capitol)
SULTANS OF SWING - Dire Straits (Single) (WB)

ROCK INSTRUMENTAL (G-938)
(All recordings are for either pure instrumentals or instrumentals with vocal coloring.)
HIGH GEAR - Neil Larsen (Single) (A&M)
NIGHT OF THE LIVING DREGS - Dixie Dregs (Album) (Capricorn)
PEGASUS - The Allman Brothers Band (Track) (Capricorn)
RAT TOMAGO - Frank Zappa (Track) (Zappa)
ROCKESTRA THEME - Wings (Track) (Columbia)

R & B VOCAL - FEMALE (G-939)
(This category is for a solo performance)
DEJA VU - Dionne Warwick (Track) (Arista)
DIM ALL THE LIGHTS - Donna Summer (Single) (Casablanca)

I LOVE YOU SO - Natalie Cole (Album) (Capitol)
KNOCK ON WOOD - Amii Stewart (Single) (Ariola)
MINNIE - Minnie Ripperton (Album) (Capitol)
RING MY BELL - Anita Ward (Single) (Juana)

R & B VOCAL - MALE (G-940)

(This category is for a solo performance.)
CRUISIN' - Smokey Robinson (Single) (Motown)
DON'T LET GO - Isaac Hayes (Single) (Polydor)
DON'T STOP 'TILL YOU GET ENOUGH - Michael Jackson (Single) (Epic)
LOVE BALLAD - George Benson (Track) (WB)
MAMA CAN'T BUY YOU LOVE - Elton John (Single) (MCA)
SOME ENCHANTED EVENING - Ray Charles (Single) (Atlantic)

R&B VOCAL - DUO, GROUP OR CHORUS (G-941)

(All recordings on which the group receives artist billing on the label are eligible here even though the vocal may feature only one member of the group.)
AFTER THE LOVE HAS GONE - Earth, Wind & Fire (Track) (ARC-CBS)
AIN'T NO STOPPIN' US NOW - McFadden & Whitehead (Single) (Philips International)
MIDNIGHT MAGIC - Commodores (Album) (Motown)
REUNITED - Peaches & Herb (Single) (Polydor)
WE ARE FAMILY - Sister Sledge (Single) (Atlantic)

R&B INSTRUMENTAL (G-942)

(All recordings are for either pure instrumentals or instrumentals with vocal coloring.)
BOOGIE WONDERLAND (Instrumental) - Earth, Wind & Fire (Single) (ARC-CBS)
LAND OF PASSION - Hubert Laws (Track) (Columbia)
READY OR NOT - Herbie Hancock (Track) (Columbia)
WAVE - Harvey Mason (Track) (Arista)
WISHING ON A STAR - Jr. Walker (Single) (Whitfield/W.B.)

RHYTHM & BLUES SONG (G-943)

(A Songwriter's Award.) (Any song is eligible if a new recording of it has been released during the eligibility year, provided it was not a previous final nomination in a songwriting category.)
AFTER THE LOVE HAS GONE - David Foster, Jay Graydon, Bill Champlin
AIN'T NO STOPPIN' US NOW - Gene McFadden, John Whitehead, Jerry Cohen
DEJA VU - Isaac Hayes, Adrienne Anderson
REUNITED - Dino Fekaris, Freddie Perren
WE ARE FAMILY - Nile Rodgers, Bernard Edwards

DISCO RECORDING (G-944)

(One Grammy to the Artist; one Grammy to the Producer if other than the Artist. This category is for singles, albums or tracks.)
BOOGIE WONDERLAND - Earth, Wind & Fire and The Emotions - Maurice White & Al McKay, Producers (Single) (ARC-CBS)
BAD GIRLS - Donna Summer - Giorgio Moroder & Pete Bellotte, Producers (Album) (Casablanca)
DA YA THINK I'M SEXY? - Rod Stewart - Tom Dowd, Producer (Single) (WB)
DON'T STOP 'TIL YOU GET ENOUGH - Michael Jackson - Quincy Jones, Producer (Single) (Epic)
I WILL SURVIVE - Gloria Gaynor - Dino Fekaris, Freddie Perren, Producers (Single) (Polydor)

COUNTRY VOCAL - FEMALE (G-945)

(This category is for a solo performance.)
BLUE KENTUCKY GIRL - Emmylou Harris (Album) (WB)
I WILL SURVIVE - Billie Jo Spears (Single) (UA)
JUST FOR THE RECORD - Barbara Mandrell (Album) (MCA)
TELL ME WHAT IT'S LIKE - Brenda Lee (Single) (MCA)
WE SHOULD BE TOGETHER - Crystal Gayle (Album) (UA)

COUNTRY VOCAL - MALE (G-946)

(This category is for a solo performance.)
BURGERS AND FRIES/WHEN I STOP LEAVING (I'LL BE GONE) - Charley Pride (Album) (RCA)
EVERY WHICH WAY BUT LOOSE - Eddie Rabbitt (Single) (Elektra)
FAMILY TRADITION - Hank Williams, Jr. (Album) (Elektra)
THE GAMBLER - Kenny Rogers (Single) (UA)
WHISKEY RIVER - Willie Nelson (Single) (Columbia)

COUNTRY VOCAL - DUO OR GROUP (G-947)

(All recordings on which the group receives artist billing on the label are eligible here even though the vocal may feature only one member of the group.) (All nominations are singles)
ALL I EVER NEED IS YOU - Kenny Rogers & Dottie West (UA)
ALL THE GOLD IN CALIFORNIA - Larry Gatlin and The Gatlin Brothers Band (Columbia)
THE DEVIL WENT DOWN TO GEORGIA - Charlie Daniels Band (Epic)
HEARTBREAK HOTEL - Willie Nelson & Leon Russell (Columbia)
IF I SAID YOU HAVE A BEAUTIFUL BODY WOULD YOU HOLD IT AGAINST ME - Bellamy Brothers (WB)

COUNTRY INSTRUMENTAL (G-948)

(This category is for an orchestra, group or soloist, and is for either pure instrumentals or instrumentals with vocal coloring.)
BIG SANDY/LEATHER BRITCHES - Doc & Merle Watson (Track) (UA)
BLUEGRASS CONCERTO - The Osborne Brothers (Album) (CMH)
FANTASTIC PICKIN' - Lester Flatt's Nashville Grass (Album) (CMH)
IN CONCERT - Floyd Cramer (Album) (RCA)
LIVE FROM AUSTIN CITY LIMITS - Nashville Super Pickers (Album) (Flying Fish)
NASHVILLE JAM - Vassar Clements, Doug Jernigan, Jesse McReynolds, Buddy Spicher (Album) (Flying Fish)

COUNTRY SONG (G-949)

(A Songwriter's award.) (Any song is eligible if a new recording of it has been released during the eligibility year, provided it was not a previous final nomination in a songwriting category.)
ALL THE GOLD IN CALIFORNIA - Larry Gatlin
BLUE KENTUCKY GIRL - Johnny Mullins
EVERY WHICH WAY BUT LOOSE - Steve Dorff, Milton Brown, Snuff Garrett
IF I SAID YOU HAVE A BEAUTIFUL BODY WOULD YOU HOLD IT AGAINST ME - David Bellamy
YOU DECORATED MY LIFE - Bob Morrison, Debbie Hupp

GOSPEL PERFORMANCE - CONTEMPORARY OR INSPIRATIONAL (G-950)

(This category is for contemporary-flavored gospel recordings.) (All nominations are albums)
ALL THINGS ARE POSSIBLE - Dan Peek (MCA/Songbird)
FOLLOWING YOU - Andrus, Blackwood & Co. (Greentree)
HEED THE CALL - Imperials (Dayspring)
MY FATHER'S EYES - Amy Grant (Myrrh)
NEVER THE SAME - Evie Tornquist (Word)

GOSPEL PERFORMANCE - TRADITIONAL (G-951)
(All nominations are albums)
A CHORAL CONCERT OF LOVE - Dottie Rambo Choir (Heartwarming)
BREAKOUT - The Mercy River Boys (Canaan)
FEELINGS - Rex Nelon Singers (Canaan)
LIFT UP THE NAME OF JESUS - The Blackwood Brothers (Skylite)
YOU AIN'T HEARD NOTHING YET! - The Cathedral Quartet (Canaan)

SOUL GOSPEL PERFORMANCE - CONTEMPORARY (G-952)
CASSIETTA IN CONCERT - Cassietta George (Album) (Audio Arts)
GIVE ME SOMETHING TO HOLD ON TO - Myrna Summers (Album) (Savoy)
I'LL BE THINKING OF YOU - Andrae Crouch (Album) (Light)
MORE THAN MAGIC - Bili Thedford (Album) (Good News)
PUSH FOR EXCELLENCE - Rev. Jesse L. Jackson, Walter Hawkins & Family, Edwin Hawkins, Push Choir, Jackie Verdell, Dannibelle, Bili Thedford, Jessy Dixon, Andrae Crouch (Myrrh)
THANK YOU - Kevin Yancy directing the Fountain of Life Joy Choir (Single) (Gospel Roots)

SOUL GOSPEL PERFORMANCE - TRADITIONAL (G-953)
(All nominations are albums)
CHANGING TIMES - Mighty Clouds of Joy (Epic)
FOR THE WRONG I'VE DONE - Willie Banks & The Messengers (HSE)
IN GOD'S OWN TIME - James Cleveland & Triboro Mass Choir, Albert Jamison, Dir. (Savoy)
IT'S A NEW DAY - James Cleveland and the So. California Community Choir (Savoy)
TRY JESUS - Troy Ramey and The Soul Searchers (Nashboro)

INSPIRATIONAL PERFORMANCE (G-954)
(This category is for religious recordings by other than regular gospel recording artists.)
BAND AND BODYWORKS - Noel Paul Stookey (Album) (New World)
I SAW THE LIGHT - Willie Nelson & Leon Russell (Track) (Columbia)
I'LL SING THIS SONG FOR YOU - Mike Douglas (Album) (Word)
JUST THE WAY I AM - Pat Boone (Album) (Lamb & Lion)
YOU GAVE ME LOVE (WHEN NOBODY GAVE ME A PRAYER) - B. J. Thomas (Album) (Myrrh)

ETHNIC OR TRADITIONAL RECORDING (G-955)
(This category includes traditional blues and pure folk recordings.) (All nominations are albums)
THE CHIEFTAINS 7 - The Chieftains (Columbia)
ICE PICKIN' - Albert Collins (Alligator)
LAUGH YOUR BLUES AWAY - Uncle Dave Macon (Rounder)
LIVING CHICAGO BLUES, VOL. 1 - The Jimmy Johnson Blues Band, Eddie Shaw & The Wolf Gang, Left Hand Frank & His Blues Band (Alligator)
LIVING CHICAGO BLUES, VOL. 3 - Lonnie Brooks Blues Band, Pinetop Perkins & Sons of the Blues (Alligator)
MUDDY "MISSISSIPPI" WATERS LIVE - Muddy Waters (Blue Sky-CBS)
NEW ENGLAND TRADITIONAL FIDDLING - Paul F. Wells, Producer (John Edwards Memorial Foundation)
NEW ORLEANS JAZZ & HERITAGE FESTIVAL - Eubie Blake, Charles Mingus, Roosevelt Sykes, Clifton Chenier (Flying Fish)
SO MANY ROADS - Otis Rush (Delmark)

LATIN RECORDING (G-956)
(This category is for pure Latin music.) (All nominations are albums)
CROSS OVER - Fania All Stars (Columbia)
ETERNOS - Celia Cruz & Johnny Pacheco (Vaya)

IRAKERE - Irakere (Columbia)
TOUCHING YOU, TOUCHING ME - Airto Moreira (WB)

RECORDING FOR CHILDREN (G-957)
(This category is intended for recordings created specifically for children.) (All nominations are albums)
THE MUPPET MOVIE - Jim Henson, Creator - Paul Williams, Producer (Atlantic)
ANNE MURRAY SINGS FOR THE SESAME STREET GENERATION - Anne Murray (Sesame St.)
SESAME DISCO! - Jim Henson, Creator - Joe Raposo & Michael Delugg, Producers (Sesame St.)
THE STARS COME OUT ON SESAME STREET - Jim Henson, Creator - Jon Stone, Producer - Jim Timmens, Record Editor (Sesame St.)
YOU'RE IN LOVE, CHARLIE BROWN - Jymn Magon & Lee Mendelson, Producers (Charlie Brown)

COMEDY RECORDING (G-958)
(Either spoken word or musical performances are eligible here.)
COMEDY IS NOT PRETTY - Steve Martin (Album) (WB)
I NEED YOUR HELP BARRY MANILOW - Ray Stevens (Track) (WB)
REALITY. . .WHAT A CONCEPT - Robin Williams (Album) (Casablanca)
RUBBER BISCUIT - Blues Brothers (Track) (Atlantic)
WANTED - Richard Pryor (Album) (WB)

SPOKEN WORD, DOCUMENTARY OR DRAMA RECORDING (G-959)
(This category is for non-musical show albums including comedy show albums.)
APOCALYPSE NOW Original Motion Picture Soundtrack - (Elektra)
AGES OF MAN (READINGS FROM SHAKESPEARE) - Sir John Gielgud (Caedmon)
AN AMERICAN PRAYER - Jim Morrison (Elektra)
THE OX-BOW INCIDENT - Henry Fonda (Caedmon)
STARE WITH YOUR EARS - Ken Nordine (Snail)
ORSON WELLES/HELEN HAYES AT THEIR BEST - Orson Welles & Helen Hayes (Mark 56)

INSTRUMENTAL COMPOSITION (G-960)
(A Composer's Award for an original non-classical composition with or without lyrics which first gained recognition as an instrumental.)
AMBIANCE - Marian McPartland
ANGELA (THEME FROM "TAXI") - Bob James
CENTRAL PARK - Chick Corea
MAIN TITLE THEME FROM "SUPERMAN" - John Williams
RISE - Andy Armer, Randy Badazz

ORIGINAL SCORE - MOTION PICTURE OR A TELEVISION SPECIAL (G-961)
(A Composer's award for an original background score or original songs written specifically for the motion picture or television special.)
ALIEN - Jerry Goldsmith, Composer (RCA)
APOCALYPSE NOW - Carmine Coppola, Francis Coppola, Composers (Elektra)
ICE CASTLES - Alan Parsons, Eric Woolfson, Marvin Hamlisch, Composers - Carole Bayer Sager, Lyrics (Arista)
THE MUPPET MOVIE - Paul Williams & Kenny Ascher, Composers and Lyricists (Atlantic)
SUPERMAN - John Williams, Composer (WB)

CAST SHOW ALBUM (G-962)

(Awards to the Composer(s), Lyricist(s) and Album Producer. Original cast albums, albums by road casts, or working casts, including show revival casts, are eligible.)
BALLROOM - Billy Goldenberg, Comp - Alan & Marilyn Bergman, Lyrs - Larry Morton, Producer (Columbia)
THE GRAND TOUR - Jerry Herman, Comp/Lyr - Mike Berniker & Jerry Herman, Producers (Columbia)
I'M GETTING MY ACT TOGETHER AND TAKING IT ON THE ROAD - Gretchen Cryer & Nancy Ford, Comps - Edward Kleban, Producer (Columbia)
SWEENEY TODD - Stephen Sondheim, Comp/Lyr - Thomas Z. Shepard, Producer (RCA)
THEY'RE PLAYING OUR SONG - Marvin Hamlisch, Comp - Carole Bayer Sager, Lyr - Brooks Arthur, Carole Bayer Sager, Marvin Hamlisch, Producers (Casablanca)

JAZZ FUSION - VOCAL OR INSTRUMENTAL (G-963)

(This category is for any type of borderline jazz performance, rock, pop, R&B, classical, etc.) (All nominations are albums)
BETCHA - Stanley Turrentine (Elektra)
CHICK COREA/SECRET AGENT - Chick Corea Group (Polydor)
8:30 - Weather Report (ARC-CBS)
LIVIN' INSIDE YOUR LOVE - George Benson (WB)
THREE WORKS FOR JAZZ SOLOISTS & SYMPHONY ORCHESTRA - Don Sebesky with Jazz Quintet & Soloists and Symphony Orchestra (Gryphon)

JAZZ VOCAL (G-964)

(This category is for a soloist, duo or group.) (All nominations are albums)
FINE AND MELLOW - Ella Fitzerald (Pablo)
I LOVE BRAZIL - Sarah Vaughan (Pablo)
THE LIVE-LIEST - Eddie Jefferson (Muse)
PREZ AND JOE - Joe Williams (GNP/Crescendo)
SNEAKIN' AROUND - Helen Humes (Classic Jazz)

JAZZ - SOLOIST (G-965)

(This category is for a solo instrumental performance with or without a group or band.) (All nominations are albums)
MANHATTAN SYMPHONIE - Dexter Gordon (Columbia)
JOUSTS - Oscar Peterson (Pablo)
PAUL DESMOND - Paul Desmond (Artists House)
REFLECTORY - Pepper Adams (Muse)
WARM TENOR - Zoot Sims (Pablo)

JAZZ - GROUP (G-966)

(This category is for an instrumental group.) (All nominations are albums)
AFFINITY - Bill Evans/Toots Thielemans (WB)
ARNETT COBB & THE MUSE ALL STARS/LIVE AT SANDY'S - Arnett Cobb (Muse)
DUET - Gary Burton & Chick Corea (ECM/WB)
THE GIFTED ONES - Dizzy Gillespie/Count Basie (Pablo)
LOVE FOR SALE - The Great Jazz Trio (Hank Jones, Buster Williams, Tony Williams (Inner City)
WARM TENOR - Zoot Sims (Pablo)

JAZZ - BIG BAND (G-967)

(This category is primarily for a big band sound.) (All nominations are albums)
AT FARGO, 1940 LIVE - Duke Ellington (Book of the Month Club)
KOGUN - Toshiko Akiyoshi/Lew Tabackin Big Band (RCA)
NATURALLY - Mel Lewis & The Jazz Orchestra (Telarc)

NOTE SMOKING - Louie Bellson & The Explosion (Discwasher)
THAD JONES/MEL LEWIS & UMO - Thad Jones, Mel Lewis & UMO (RCA)

INSTRUMENTAL ARRANGEMENT (G-968)

(An Arranger's Award. This category is for a specific arrangement released for the first time during the eligibility year on either a single or an album track.)
SABOTAGE - John Serry - John Serry, Arr (Chrysalis)
LAZY AFTERNOON - Freddie Hubbard - Claus Ogerman, Arr (CBS)
SEBASTIAN'S THEME - Don Sebesky - Don Sebesky, Arr (Gryphon)
SOULFUL STRUT - George Benson - Claus Ogerman, Arr (WB)
WAVE - Harvey Mason - Jeremy Lubbock & Harvey Mason, Arrs (Arista)

ARRANGEMENT ACCOMPANYING VOCALIST(S) (G-969)

(An Arranger's Award. This category is for a specific arrangement released for the first time during the eligibility year on either a single or an album track.)
AFTER THE LOVE HAS GONE - Earth, Wind & Fire - Jerry Hey & David Foster, Arrs (ARC-CBS)
EVERYTHING MUST CHANGE - Benard Ighner - Byron Olson, Arr (Alfa)
I'LL NEVER LOVE THIS WAY AGAIN - Dionne Warwick - Artie Butler & Barry Manilow, Arrs (Arista)
ROUND MIDNIGHT - Richard Evans - Richard Evans, Arr (Horizon)
SEPTEMBER - Earth, Wind & Fire - Tom Tom 84, Arr (ARC-CBS)
WHAT A FOOL BELIEVES - The Doobie Brothers - Michael McDonald, Arr (WB)

ALBUM PACKAGE (G-970)

(An Art Director's Award. This category is for either classical or non-classical single-jacket or multiple pocket album packages.)
BREAKFAST IN AMERICA - Supertramp - Mike Doud & Mick Haggerty, Art Dir (A&M)
CHICAGO 13 - Chicago - Tony Lane, Art Dir (Columbia)
FEAR OF MUSIC - Talking Heads - John Gillespie, Art Dir (Sire)
IN THROUGH THE OUT DOOR - Led Zeppelin - Hipgnosis, Art Dir (Swan Song)
LOOK SHARP - Joe Jackson - Michael Ross, Art Dir (A&M)
MORNING DANCE - Spyro Gyra - Peter Corriston, Art Dir (Infinity)
NEAR PERFECT/PERFECT - Martin Mull - Ron Coro/Johnny Lee, Art Dirs (Elektra)
RAMSEY - Ramsey Lewis - John Berg, Art Dir (Columbia)
WITH SOUND REASON - Sonny Fortune - Lynne Dresse Breslin, Art Dir (Atlantic)

ALBUM NOTES (G-971)

(An Annotator's Award. This category is for original writing for a specific album. Either classical or non-classical albums qualify.)
BILLIE HOLIDAY (GIANTS OF JAZZ) - Melvin Maddocks, Ann (Time - Life)
DUKE ELLINGTON (GIANTS OF JAZZ) - Dan Morgenstern & Stanley Dance, Anns (Time - Life)
HOAGY CARMICHAEL - A LEGENDARY PERFORMER AND COMPOSER - Richard M. Sudhalter, Ann (RCA)
THE MAGICAL MUSIC OF WALT DISNEY - Dick Schory, Ann (Ovation)
CHARLIE PARKER: THE COMPLETE SAVOY SESSIONS - Bob Porter & James Patrick, Anns (Savoy)

HISTORICAL REISSUE (G-972)

(Grammy to the Reissue Album Producer(s).)
ONE NEVER KNOWS, DO ONE? THE BEST OF FATS WALLER - George Spitzer, Chick Crumpacker, Producers (Book of the Month Records)

BILLIE HOLIDAY (GIANTS OF JAZZ) - **Jerry Korn, Producer (Time - Life)**
DUKE ELLINGTON (GIANTS OF JAZZ) - Jerry Korn, Producer (Time - Life)
THE MAGICAL MUSIC OF WALT DISNEY - Dick Schory, Producer (Ovation)
A TRIBUTE TO E. POWER BIGGS - Andrew Kazdin, Producer (Columbia)

BEST ENGINEERED RECORDING (G-973)

(Non-Classical) (An Engineer's Award.) (All nominations are albums)
BREAKFAST IN AMERICA - Supertramp - Peter Henderson, Eng (A&M)
EVE - The Alan Parsons Project - Alan Parsons, Eng (Arista)
JUST FRIENDS - LA-4 - Phil Edwards, Eng (Concord Jazz)
RICKIE LEE JONES - Rickie Lee Jones - Lee Herschberg, Lloyd Clifft, Tom Knox, Roger Nichols, Engs (W.B.)
CORNERSTONE - Styx - Gary Loizzo, Eng (A&M)

PRODUCER OF THE YEAR (G-974)

(Non-Classical) (A Producer's Award for consistently outstanding creativity in producing.) Listed below are examples of producer's activities. (A) Album; (S) Single; (T) Track
LARRY BUTLER: "The Gambler" (S) & (A), "She Believes In Me" (S), "You Decorated My Life" (S), "Kenny" (A), - Kenny Rogers
MIKE CHAPMAN: "Stumblin' In" (S) - Suzie Quatro & Chris Norman; "My Sharona" (T), "Get The Knack" (A) - The Knack; "One Way Or Another" (S) - Blondie
QUINCY JONES: "Don't Stop 'Til You Get Enough" (S), "Rock With You" (T) - Michael Jackson; "Do You Love What You Feel" (S), "Master Jam" (A) - Rufus & Chaka
TED TEMPLEMAN: "Van Halen II" (A) - Van Halen; "What A Fool Believes" (S), "Minute By Minute" (S) & (A) - The Doobie Brothers
MAURICE WHITE: "Walking The Line" (S) - The Emotions; "After The Love Has Gone" (S), "I Am" (A), "September" (S) - Earth, Wind & Fire

CLASSICAL ALBUM (G-975)

(Grammys to the Artists, and to the Producer if other than the artist.) (Certificates to the Engineer(s) and Classical Orchestra Committee.)
BRAHMS: SYMPHONIES (4) COMPLETE - Sir Georg Solti cond. Chicago Symphony Orchestra - James Mallinson, Producer (London)
BRITTEN: PETER GRIMES - Colin Davis cond. Orchestra & Chorus of Royal Opera House, Covent Garden/Prin. Solos: Vickers, Harper, Summers - Vittorio Negri, Producer (Philips)
THE HOROWITZ CONCERTS 1978/79 - Vladimir Horowitz - John Pfeiffer, Producer (RCA)
MUSSORGSKY-RAVEL: PICTURES AT AN EXHIBITION; STRAVINSKY: THE FIREBIRD SUITE - Riccardo Muti cond. The Philadelphia Orchestra - Christopher Bishop, Producer (Angel)
SHOSTAKOVICH: LADY MACBETH OF MTSENSK - Mstislav Rostropovich cond. London Philharmonic/Ambrosian Opera Chorus/Prin. Solos: Vishnevskaya, Gedda - Suvi Raj Grubb, Producer (Angel)
WEBERN: THE COMPLETE WORKS OF ANTON WEBERN, VOLUME 1 - Pierre Boulez cond. Ensemble - Paul Myers, Producer (Columbia)

CLASSICAL PERFORMANCE ORCHESTRA - (G-976)

(Grammys to the Conductor and Producer. Certificate to the Classical Orchestra Committee.)
BRAHMS: SYMPHONIES (4) COMPLETE - Sir Georg Solti cond. Chicago Symphony - James Mallinson, Producer (London)
HOLST: THE PLANETS - Sir Georg Solti cond. London Philharmonic - James Mallinson, Producer (London)
IVES: THREE PLACES IN NEW ENGLAND - Dennis Russell Davies cond. St. Paul Chamber Orchestra - Tom Voegeli, Producer (Sound 80)

MAHLER: SYMPHONY NO. 4 IN G MAJOR - Andre Previn cond. Pittsburgh Symphony - Suvi Raj Grubb, Producer (Angel)
RACHMANINOFF: SYMPHONIES NOS. 2 IN E MINOR & 3 IN A MINOR - Leonard Slatkin cond. St Louis Symphony - Marc Aubort & Joanna Nickrenz, Producers (Vox Box)
SIBELIUS: FOUR LEGENDS FROM THE "KALEVALA" - Eugene Ormandy cond. The Philadelphia Orchestra - John Willan, Producer (Angel)
ZELENKA: ORCHESTRAL WORKS (COMPLETE) - Alexander Van Wijnkoop Cond. Camerata Bern - Dr. Andreas Holschneider, Producer (DG)

OPERA RECORDING (G-977)

(Grammys to the Conductor and Producer; special plaques to the Principal Soloists.
BRITTEN: PETER GRIMES - Colin Davis (cond. Orchestra & Chorus of the Royal Opera House, Covent Garden - Prin. Solos: Vickers, Harper, Summers) Vittorio Negri, Producer (Philips)
HINDEMITH: MATHIS DER MALER - Rafael Kubelik (cond. Bavarian Radio Symphony & Bavarian Radio Chorus - Prin. Solos: Fischer-Dieskau, King) - Friedrich Welz & John Willan, Producers (Angel)
SHOSTAKOVICH: LADY MACBETH OF MTSENSK - Mstislav Rostropovich (cond. London Philharmonic, Ambrosian Opera Chorus - Prin. Solos: Vishnevskaya, Gedda) Suvi Raj Grubb, Producer (Angel)
VERDI: OTELLO - James Levine (cond. National Philharmonic - Prin. Solos: Domingo, Scotto, Milnes) Richard Mohr, Producer (RCA)
VERDI: RIGOLETTO - Julius Rudel (cond. Philharmonia Orchestra & Ambrosian Opera Chorus - Prin. Solos: Sills, Kraus, Milnes) John Fraser, Producer (Angel)

CHORAL PERFORMANCE - OTHER THAN OPERA (G-978)

(Grammys to the Conductor and Choral Director)
AMERICAN MUSIC FOR CHORUS - John Oliver (cond. Tanglewood Festival Chorus) (DG)
BEETHOVEN: "CHORAL FANTASY", ELEGIAC SONG & "CALM SEA AND PROSPEROUS VOYAGE" - Jerzy Semkow, Cond.; Thomas Peck, Choral Dir. (St. Louis Symphony Chorus & Orchestra) (Candide)
BEETHOVEN: MISSA SOLEMNIS - Leonard Bernstein (cond. Radio Chorus of the N.O.S. Hilversum & Concertgebouworkest) (DG)
BERLIOZ: LA DAMNATION DE FAUST - Daniel Barenboim (cond. Chorus of Orchestre de Paris & Orchestre de Paris) (DG)
BERLIOZ: REQUIEM - Lorin Maazel, Cond.; Robert Page, Choral Dir. (Cleveland Orchestra & Chorus) (London)
BRAHMS: A GERMAN REQUIEM - Sir Georg Solti, Cond.; Margaret Hillis, Choral Dir. (Chicago Symphony & Chorus) (London)
BRITTEN: SPRING SYMPHONY - Andre Previn, Cond.; Richard Hickox, Chorus Master; Keith Walters, Choral Director (London Symphony Chorus/St. Clement Danes School Boys' Choir & London Symphony) (Angel)
STRAVINSKY: SYMPHONY OF PSALMS - Maurice Abravanel, Cond.: Newell B. Wright, Choral Dir. (Utah Chorale & Utah Symphony) (Angel)

CHAMBER MUSIC PERFORMANCE (G-979)

(Instrumental or Vocal.)
BERG: CHAMBER CONCERTO FOR PIANO & VIOLIN/FOUR PIECES FOR CLARINET & PIANO - Pierre Boulez, Daniel Barenboim, Pinchas Zukerman/Pay & Ensemble Inter-Contemporain (DG)
BOLLING: SUITE FOR VIOLIN & JAZZ PIANO - Pinchas Zukerman & Claude Bolling with Max Hediguer & Marcel Sabiani (Columbia)
COPLAND: APPALACHIAN SPRING - Davis cond. St. Paul Chamber Orchestra (Sound 80)
DEBUSSY: QUARTET IN G MINOR/RAVEL: QUARTET IN F - Tokyo Quartet (Columbia)
DOHNANYI: SERENADE, OP. 10/BEETHOVEN: SERENADE, OP. 8 - Itzhak Perlman, Lynn Harrell, Pinchas Zukerman (Columbia)
SHOSTAKOVICH: QUARTETS NOS. 5 & 6 - Fitzwilliam Quartet (L'Oiseau Lyre)
TELEMANN: 6 SONATAS FOR 2 FLUTES - Michael Debost & James Galway (Seraphim)
VIVALDI: FOUR FLUTE CONCERTOS - KOTO FLUTE - Ransom Wilson

& The New Koto Ensemble of Tokyo - Yoshikazu Fukumura, Conductor (Angel)

CLASSICAL PERFORMANCE - INSTRUMENTAL SOLOIST(S) (WITH ORCHESTRA) (G-980)

ANNIE'S SONG & OTHER GALWAY FAVORITES - James Galway (Gerhardt cond. National Philharmonic) (RCA)
BARTOK: CONCERTOS FOR PIANO NOS. 1 & 2 - Maurizio Pollini (Abbado cond. Chicago Symphony) (DG)
CHOPIN: CONCERTO FOR PIANO NO. 1 IN E MINOR - Krystian Zimerman (Giulini cond. Los Angeles Philharmonic) (DG)
HORN CONCERTOS BY JOSEPH HAYDN & MICHAEL HAYDN - Barry Tuckwell (English Chamber Orchestra) (Angel)
ISAAC STERN & JEAN-PIERRE RAMPAL PLAY VIVALDI & TELEMANN - Isaac Stern & Jean-Pierre Rampal (Jerusalem Music Center Chamber Orchestra) (Columbia)
MOZART: CONCERTOS FOR VIOLIN NO. 3 IN G MAJOR & NO. 5 IN A MAJOR - Anne Sophie Mutter (von Karajan cond. Berlin Philharmonic) (DG)
TRUMPET CONCERTOS BY HAYDN, TELEMANN, ALBINONI & MARCELLO - Maurice Andre (Lopez-Cobos cond. London Philharmonic) (Angel)

CLASSICAL PERFORMANCE - INSTRUMENTAL SOLOIST(S) (WITHOUT ORCHESTRA) (G-981)

BACH: GOLDBERG VARIATIONS - Rosalyn Tureck (Columbia)
BACH: TOCCATAS, VOLUME 1 - Glenn Gould (Columbia)
BOULEZ: SONATA FOR PIANO NO. 2 - Maurizio Pollini (DG)
DEBUSSY: ESTAMPES, IMAGES, BOOKS 1 & 2 - Paul Jacobs (Nonesuch)
FRANCK: PRELUDE, CHORALE & FUGUE FOR PIANO/BACH-BUSONI: CHACONNE/MOZART: RONDO IN A MINOR - Artur Rubinstein (RCA)
THE HOROWITZ CONCERTS 1978/79 - Vladimir Horowitz (RCA)
RZEWSKI: THE PEOPLE UNITED WILL NEVER BE DEFEATED - Ursula Oppens (Vanguard)
SCARLATTI: SONATAS (12) - Igor Kipnis (Angel)
VILLA-LOBOS: ETUDES (12) & SUITE POPULAIRE BRASILIENNE - Julian Bream (RCA)

CLASSICAL PERFORMANCE - VOCAL SOLOIST - (G-982)

FREDERICA VON STADE SONG RECITAL - Frederica von Stade (Martin Katz, Accomp.) (Columbia)
LIEDER BY SCHUBERT & RICHARD STRAUSS - Leontyne Price (David Garvey, Accomp.) (Angel)
MOZART: LIEDER - Elly Ameling (Dalton Baldwin, Accomp.) (Philips)
MUSSORGSKY: SONGS - Yevgeny Nesterenko (Shenderovich & Krainev, Accomps.) (Col./Mel.)
O SOLE MIO (Favorite Neapolitan Songs) - Luciano Pavarotti (Bologna Orchestra) (London)
SCHUBERT: LIEDER - Dietrich Fischer-Dieskau (Svjatoslav Richter, Accomp.) (DG)
RAVEL: CHANSONS MADECASSES - Jan de Gaetani (Dunkel, Anderson, Kalish, Accomps.) (Nonesuch)
VICTORIA DE LOS ANGELES IN CONCERT - Victoria de los Angeles (Gerald Moore, Accomp.) (Angel)

BEST ENGINEERED RECORDING - CLASSICAL (G-983)

(An Engineer's Award.)
BARTOK: CONCERTOS FOR PIANO NOS. 1 & 2 - Maurizio Pollini/Abbado cond. Chicago Symphony - Klaus Hiemann, Engineer (DG)
THE BERMUDA TRIANGLE - Isao Tomita - Isao Tomita, Engineer (RCA)
BRITTEN: PETER GRIMES - Davis cond. Royal Opera House, Covent Garden/Prin. Solos: Vickers, Harper, Summers - Vittorio Negri, Engineer (Philips)
COPLAND: APPALACHIAN SPRING/IVES: THREE PLACES IN NEW ENGLAND - Davis cond. St. Paul Chamber Orchestra - Tom Jung, Engineer (Sound 80)
HINDEMITH: CONCERT MUSIC FOR STRINGS & BRASS/SYMPHONIC METAMORPHOSIS ON THEMES BY WEBER - Ormandy cond. The

Philadelphia Orchestra - John Kurlander, Engineer (Angel)
MUSSORGSKY-RAVEL: PICTURES AT AN EXHIBITION - Maazel cond. The Cleveland Orchestra - Jack Renner, Engineer (Telarc)
PROKOFIEV: SCYTHIAN SUITE/LT. KIJE - Abbado cond. Chicago Symphony - Klaus Hiemann, Engineer (DG)
RACHMANINOFF: SYMPHONIES NOS. 2 & 3 - Slatkin cond. St Louis Symphony - Marc Aubort & Joanna Nickrenz, Engineers (Vox Box)
SIBELIUS: FOUR LEGENDS FROM THE "KALEVALA" - Ormandy cond. Philadelphia Orchestra - John Kurlander, Engineer (Angel)
SONDHEIM: SWEENEY TODD - Original Cast - Anthony Salvatore, Engineer (RCA)
STRAVINSKY: THE FIREBIRD SUITE/BORODIN: PRINCE IGOR - Shaw cond. Atlanta Symphony Orchestra & Chorus - Jack Renner, Engineer (Telarc)

CLASSICAL PRODUCER OF THE YEAR (G-984)

(A Producer's Award for consistently outstanding creativity in producing. Listed below are examples of producer's activities.)
MARC AUBORT & JOANNA NICKRENZ: BEETHOVEN: CHORAL FANTASY, ELEGIAC SONG, CALM SEAS & PROSPEROUS VOYAGE, RONDO IN B FLAT - Semkow & Peck/St. Louis Orchestra & Chorus (Candide); BEETHOVEN: QUINTET IN E-FLAT MAJOR FOR PIANO & WINDS - Simon, Woodhams, Silfies, Berry Pandolfi (Turnabout); BRAHMS: QUINTET IN B MINOR FOR CLARINET & STRINGS - Banes, Sant'Ambrogio, Silfies, Korman, Beiler (Turnabout); RACHMANIN-OFF: SYMPHONIES NOS. 2 & 3 - Slatkin cond. St. Louis Symphony (Vox Box)
ANDREW KAZDIN: BACH: TOCCATAS, VOLUME 1 - Glenn Gould (Columbia); LALO: SYMPHONIE ESPAGNOLE FOR VIOLIN & ORCHESTRA - Zukerman/Mehta cond. Los Angeles Philharmonic (Columbia); MANHATTAN (Music from the Film) - Graffman/Mehta cond. New York Philharmonic (Columbia); MENOTTI: THE TELEPHONE - Mester cond. Louisville Orchestra/Seibel, Orth (Louisville); SCHOENBERG: VERKLARTE NACHT - Boulez cond. New York Philharmonic (Columbia); TCHAIKOVSKY: CONCERTO FOR VIOLIN & ORCHESTRA IN D MAJOR - Stern/Rostropovich cond. National Symphony (Columbia)
JAMES MALLINSON: BERLIOZ: REQUIEM - Maazel cond. Cleveland Orchestra & Chorus (London); BRAHMS: SYMPHONIES (4) COMPLETE - Solti cond. Chicago Symphony (London); HOLST: THE PLANETS - Solti cond. London Philharmonic (London); NEW YEAR'S IN VIENNA - Boskovsky cond. Vienna Philharmonic (London); PUCCINI: TOSCA - Rescigno cond./Freni, Pavarotti (London); TCHAIKOVSKY: 1812 OVERTURE - Dorati cond. Detroit Symphony (London)
PAUL MYERS: BEETHOVEN: SYMPHONIES (9) - Maazel cond. Cleveland Orchestra (Columbia); FAURE: REQUIEM - Davis cond. Ambrosian Singers & Philharmonic Orchestra (Columbia); FREDERICA VON STADE SONG RECITAL - Frederica von Stade (Columbia); JOHN WILLIAMS PLAYS GUITAR MUSIC FORM ENGLAND, JAPAN, BRAZIL, VENEZUELA, ARGENTINA & MEXICO - John Williams (Columbia); PUCCINI: MADAME BUTTERFLY - Maazel cond./Scotto, Domingo (Columbia); WEBERN: COMPLETE WORKS - Boulez cond. Ensemble (Columbia)
VITTORIO NEGRI: BRITTEN: PETER GRIMES - Davis cond./Vickers, Harper, Summers (Philips); DVORAK: SYMPHONY NO. 8 IN G MAJOR - Davis cond. Concertgebouw Orchestra (Philips); STRAVINSKY: THE FIREBIRD (COMPLETE) - Davis cond. Concertgebouw Orchestra (Philips)
THOMAS Z. SHEPARD: SONDHEIM: SWEENEY TODD - Original Cast (RCA)
ROBERT WOODS: CHOPIN: PIANO MUSIC - Frager (Telarc); MUSSORGSKY-RAVEL: PICTURES AT AN EXHIBITION - Maazel cond. The Cleveland Orchestra (Telarc); STRAVINSKY: THE FIREBIRD SUITE - Shaw cond. Atlanta Symphony (Telarc)

1980 HALL OF FAME WINNERS (G-985)

BALLAD FOR AMERICANS (Album) - Paul Robeson - Victor #P20 - Released in 1940
IN A MIST - Bix Beiderbacke (Piano Solo) - Okeh # - Released in 1927
JELLY ROLL MORTON: THE SAGA OF MR. JELLY LORD (The Library

of Congress Recordings) (12 Albums) - Ferdinand "Jelly Roll" Morton - Circle Sound 1-12 - Released 1949-1950

1980

RECORD OF THE YEAR (G-986)

(Grammys to artist and producer if other than the artist. This category is for singles. An album track released as a single during the eligibility year is eligible provided that the track itself did not receive a previous nomination award.)

LADY - Kenny Rogers; Lionel Richie Jr, producer (Liberty/UA)
THE ROSE - Bette Midler; Paul A Rothchild, producer (Atlantic)
SAILING - Christopher Cross; Michael Omartian, producer (WB)
THEME FROM NEW YORK, NEW YORK - Frank Sinatra; Sonny Burke, producer (Reprise)
WOMAN IN LOVE - Barbra Streisand; Barry Gibb, Albhy Galuten and Karl Richardson, producers (Columbia)

ALBUM OF THE YEAR (G-987)

(Grammys to artist and producer if other than the artist. This category is for non-classical albums)

CHRISTOPHER CROSS - Christopher Cross; Michael Omartian, producer (WB)
GLASS HOUSES - Billy Joel; Phil Ramone, producer (Columbia)
GUILTY - Barbra Streisand; Barry Gibb, Albhy Galuten and Karl Richardson, producers (Columbia)
TRILOGY: PAST, PRESENT & FUTURE - Frank Sinatra; Sonny Burke, producer (Reprise)
THE WALL - Pink Floyd; Bob Ezrin, David Gilmour and Roger Waters, producers (Columbia)

SONG OF THE YEAR (G-988)

(A songwriter's award. Any song is eligible if a new recording of it has been released during the eligibility year, provided it was not a previous final nomination in a songwriting category.)

FAME - Michael Gore and Dean Pitchford, songwriters; MGM Affiliated Music Inc, publisher.
LADY - Lionel Richie Jr, songwriter: Brockman Music, publisher.
THEME FROM NEW YORK, NEW YORK - John Kander and Fred Ebb, songwriters; Unart Music Corp, publisher.
THE ROSE - Amanda McBroom, songwriter; Fox Fanfare Music Inc, publisher.
SAILING - Christopher Cross, songwriter; Pop 'N' Roll Music, publisher.
WOMAN IN LOVE - Barry Gibb and Robin Gibb, songwriters; Stigwood Music Inc, publisher.

NEW ARTIST (G-989)

(This category is for an artist or organized group whose first recording was released during the eligibility year.)

IRENE CARA - (RSO)
CHRISTOPHER CROSS - (WB)
ROBBIE DUPREE - (Electra)
AMY HOLLAND - (Capitol)
PRETENDERS - (Sire)

POP VOCAL - FEMALE (G-990)

(Solo performance. All nominations are singles.)

FAME - Irene Cara (RSO)
MAGIC - Olivia Newton-John (MCA)
ON THE RADIO - Donna Summer (Casablanca)
THE ROSE - Bette Midler (Atlantic)
WOMAN IN LOVE - Barbra Streisand (Columbia)

POP VOCAL - MALE (G-991)

(Solo Performance.)

CHRISTOPHER CROSS - Christopher Cross (WB - album)
LADY - Kenny Rogers (Liberty/UA - single)
LATE IN THE EVENING - Paul Simon (WB - single)
THEME FROM NEW YORK, NEW YORK - Frank Sinatra (Reprise - single)
THIS IS IT - Kenny Loggins (Columbia - track from Alive)

POP VOCAL - DUO OR GROUP WITH VOCAL (G-992)

(All recordings on which the group receives artist billing on the label are eligible even though the vocal may feature only one member of the group.)

AGAINST THE WIND - Bob Seger and The Silver Bullet Band (Capitol - track from Against The Wind)
BIGGEST PART OF ME - Ambrosia (WB - single)
DON'T FALL IN LOVE WITH A DREAMER - Kenny Rogers and Kim Carnes (UA - single)
GUILTY - Barbra Streisand and Barry Gibb (Columbia - track from Guilty)
HE'S SO SHY - Pointer Sisters (Planet - single)

POP INSTRUMENTAL (G-993)

(Recordings are for either pure instrumental or instrumentals with vocal coloring.)

BEYOND - Herb Alpert (A&M - single)
ONE ON ONE - Bob James and Earl Klugh (Columbia - album)
RAVEL'S BOLERO - Henry Mancini (WB - single)
SOUTH BAY STRUT - The Doobie Brothers (WB - track from One Step Closer)
YODA'S THEME - John Williams and London Symphony Orchestra (RSO - track from The Empire Strikes Back)

ROCK VOCAL - FEMALE (G-994)

(Solo Performance.)

BROKEN ENGLISH - Marianne Faithful (Island - album)
CRIMES OF PASSION - Pat Benatar (Chrysalis - album)
DREAMS - Grace Slick (RCA - album)
HOW CRUEL - Joan Armatrading (A&M - album)
HOW DO I MAKE YOU - Linda Ronstadt (Asylum - single)

ROCK VOCAL - MALE (G-995)

(Solo Perfomance.)

BOULEVARD - Jackson Browne (Asylum - single)
COMING UP (LIVE AT GLASGOW) - Paul McCartney (Columbia - single)
MEDLEY: DEVIL WITH THE BLUE DRESS/GOOD GOLLY MISS MOLLY/JENNY TAKE A RIDE - Bruce Springsteen (Asylum - track from No Nukes)
GLASS HOUSEs - Billy Joel (Columbia - album)
I'M ALRIGHT (THEME FROM CADDYSHACK) - Kenny Loggins (Columbia - single)

ROCK PERFORMANCE - DUO OR GROUP WITH VOCAL (G-996)

(All recordings on which the group receives artist billing on the label are eligible even though vocal may feature only one member of the group.)

AGAINST THE WIND - Bob Seger and The Silver Bullet Band (Capitol - album)
ANOTHER ONE BITES THE DUST - Queen (Elektra - single)
BRASS IN POCKET (I'M SPECIAL) - Pretenders (Sire - single)
CALL ME - Blondie (Chrysalis - single)
THE WALL - Pink Floyd (Columbia - album)

ROCK INSTRUMENTAL (G-997)

(All recordings are for either pure instrumentals or instrumentals with vocal coloring.)

BEACH GIRL - Jean-Luc Ponty (Atlantic - single)
DREGGS OF THE EARTH - Dixie Dregs (Arista - album)
PETER GUNN - Emerson, Lake & Palmer (Atlantic - single)
REGATTA DE BLANC - Police (A&M - track from Regatta De Blanc)
SPACE INVADER - Pretenders (Sire - track from Pretenders)

R&B VOCAL - FEMALE (G-998)

(Solo performance.)

CAN'T TURN YOU LOOSE - Aretha Franklin (Arista - track from Aretha)
LOVE LIVES FOREVER - Minnie Riperton (Capitol - album)
NEVER KNEW LOVE LIKE THIS BEFORE - Stephanie Mills (20th Century - single)
ROBERTA FLACK FEATURING DONNY HATHAWAY - Roberta Flack (Atlantic - album)
UPSIDE DOWN - Diana Ross (Motown - single)

R&B VOCAL - MALE (G-999)

(Solo performance.)

GIVE ME THE NIGHT - George Benson (WB/QWest - album)
LET'S GET SERIOUS - Jermaine Jackson (Motown - single)
MASTER BLASTER (JAMMIN) - Stevie Wonder (Motown/Tamla - single)
NEVER GIVIN' UP - Al Jarreau (WB - single)
ONE IN A MILLION YOU - Larry Graham (WB -album)

R&B PERFORMANCE - DUO OR GROUP WITH VOCAL (G-1000)

(All recordings on which the group receives artist billing on the label are eligible here even though the vocal may feature only one member of the group.)

ABOUT LOVE - Gladys Knight & The Pips (Columbia - album)
BACK TOGETHER AGAIN - Roberta Flack with Donny Hathaway (Atlantic - single)
CUPID/I'VE LOVED YOU FOR A LONG TIME - Spinners (Atlantic - single)
HEROES - Commodores (Motown - album)
SHINING STAR - Manhattans (Columbia - single)
TRIUMPH - Jacksons (Epic - album)

R&B INSTRUMENTAL (G-1001)

(All recordings are for either pure instrumentals or instrumentals with vocal coloring.)

ANYTHING YOU WANT - David Sanborn (WB - single)
NIGHT CRUISER - Deodato (WB - single)
OFF BROADWAY - George Benson (WB/QWest - track from Give Me The Night)
SMILIN' ON YA - Brothers Johnson (A&M - track from Light Up The Night)
WHEN I'M WRONG - B B King (MCA - track from Now Appearing At Ole Miss)

RHYTHM & BLUES SONG (G-1002)

(A songwriter's award. Any song is eligible if a new recording of it has been released during eligibility year, provided it was not a previous final nomination in a songwriting category.)

GIVE ME THE NIGHT - Rod Temperton, songwriter; Rodsongs, publisher.
LET'S GET SERIOUS - Lee Garrett and Stevie Wonder, songwriters; Jobete Music/Black Bull Music, publishers.
NEVER KNEW LOVE LIKE THIS BEFORE - Reggie Lucas and James Mtume, songwriters; Frozen Butterfly, publisher.
SHINING STAR - Leo Graham and Paul Richmond, songwriters; Content Music, publishers.
UPSIDE DOWN - Bernard Edwards and Nile Rodgers, songwriters; Chic, publisher.

COUNTRY VOCAL - FEMALE (G-1003)

(Solo performance.)

THE BEST OF STRANGERS - Barbara Mandrell (MCA - single)
COAL MINER'S DAUGHTER - Sissy Spacek (MCA -single)
COULD I HAVE THIS DANCE - Anne Murray (Capitol - single)
IF YOU EVER CHANGE YOUR MIND - Crystal Gayle (Columbia - single)
ROSES IN THE SNOW - Emmylou Harris (WB - album)

COUNTRY VOCAL - MALE (G-1004)

(Solo performance. All nominations are singles.)

DRIVIN' MY LIFE AWAY - Eddie Rabbitt (Elektra)
HE STOPPED LOVING HER TODAY - George Jones (Epic)
I WISH I WAS EIGHTEEN AGAIN - George Burns (Mercury)
LOOKIN' FOR LOVE - Johnny Lee (Full Moon/Asylum)
ON THE ROAD AGAIN - Willie Nelson (Columbia)

COUNTRY - DUO OR GROUP WITH VOCAL (G-1005)

(All recordings on which the group receives artist billing on the label are eligible here even though the vocal may feature only one member of the group. All nominations are singles.)

DREAM LOVER - Tanya Tucker and Glen Campbell (MCA)
HEART OF MINE - Oak Ridge Boys (MCA)
IN AMERICA - The Charlie Daniels Band (Epic)
TAKE ME TO YOUR LOVIN' PLACE - Larry Gatlin & The Gatlin Brothers Band (Columbia)
THAT LOVIN' YOU FEELIN' AGAIN - Roy Orbison and Emmylou Harris (WB)

COUNTRY INSTRUMENTAL (G-1006)

(All recordings are for either pure instrumental or instrumentals with vocal coloring.)

COTTON EYED JOE - Danny Davis & The Nashville Brass (RCA - single)
DALLAS - Floyd Cramer (RCA - album)
DANCE WITH ME - Chet Atkins (RCA - single)
THE LONG RIDERS - Ry Cooder (WB - album)
ORANGE BLOSSOM SPECIAL/HOEDOWN - Gilley's Urban Cowboy Band (Full Moon/Asylum - track from Urban Cowboy)

COUNTRY SONG (G-1007)

(A songwriter's award. Any song is eligible if a new recording of it has been released during the eligibility year, provided it was not a previous final nomination in a songwriting category.)

DRIVIN' MY LIFE AWAY - Eddie Rabbitt, Even Stevens & David Malloy, songwriters; Debdave Music/Briarpatch Music, publishers.
HE STOPPED LOVING HER TODAY - Bobby Braddock, Curly Putman, songwriters; Tree Int'l, publisher.
I BELIEVE IN YOU - Roger Cook and Sam Hogin, songwriters; Roger Cook Music/Cook House Music, publishers.
LOOKIN' FOR LOVE - Bob Morrison, Wanda Mallette, Patti Ryan, songwriters; Southern Nights, publisher.
ON THE ROAD AGAIN - Willie Nelson, songwriter; Willie Nelson Music, publisher.

GOSPEL PERFORMANCE - CONTEMPORARY OR INSPIRATIONAL (G-1008)
(This category is for contemporary-flavored gospel re-cordings.)
THE BUILDER - Michael & Stormie Omartian (Myrrh - album)
IT'S GONNA RAIN - Andrae Crouch (Light - single)
THE LORD'S PRAYER - Reba Rambo, Dony McGuire, B J Thomas, Andrae Crouch, The Archers, Walter & Tramaine Hawkins, Cynthia Clawson (Light - album)
NEVER ALONE - Amy Grant (Myrrh - album)
ONE MORE SONG FOR YOU - Imperials (Dayspring - album)

GOSPEL PERFORMANCE - TRADITIONAL (G-1008A)
(All nominations are albums.)
CROSSIN' OVER - The Rambos (Heartwarming)
IN HIS PRESENCE - Kenneth Copeland (KCP)
INTERCEDING - The Speers (Heartwarming)
MAKE A JOYFUL NOISE. . . - Lanny Wolfe Trio (Impact)
WE COME TO WORSHIP - Blackwood Brothers (Voice Box)
WORSHIP - Jimmy Swaggart (Jim)

SOUL GOSPEL PERFORMANCE - CONTEMPORARY (G-1009)
I CAN'T LET GO - Kristle Murden (Light - album)
I FEEL LIKE GOING ON - The Rance Allen Group (Stax - album)
REJOICE - Shirley Caesar (Word - album)
TRAMAINE - Tramaine Hawkins (Light - album)
YOU DON'T KNOW WHAT GOD HAS DONE FOR ME - The Dynamic Disciples (L Brown - single)

SOUL GOSPEL PERFORMANCE - TRADITIONAL (G-1010)
(All nominations are albums.)
AIN'T NO STOPPING US NOW - The Gospel Keynotes (Nashboro)
GOD CAN - Dorothy Norwood (Savoy)
HE CHOSE ME - O'Neal Twins (Savoy)
LORD, LET ME BE AN INSTRUMENT - James Cleveland & The Charles Fold Singers (Savoy)
PLEASE BE PATIENT WITH ME - Albertina Walker with James Cleveland (Savoy)
A PRAYING SPIRIT - James Cleveland & The Voices of Cornerstone (Savoy)

INSPIRATIONAL PERFORMANCE (G-1011)
(This category is for religious recordings by other than regular gospel recording artists.)
EVERYTHING ALWAYS WORKS OUT FOR THE BEST - B J Thomas (Songbird - single)
FAMILY BIBLE - Willie Nelson (Songbird - album)
JESUS IS LOVE - Commodores (Motown - track from Heroes)
SAVED - Bob Dylan (Columbia - album)
WITH MY SONG I WILL PRAISE HIM - Debby Boone (Lamb & Lion - album)

ETHNIC OR TRADITIONAL RECORDING (G-1012)
(This category includes traditional blues and pure folk recordings. All nominations are albums.)
ATLANTA BLUES: 1933 - Blind Willie McTell, Curley Weaver, Buddy Moss (John Edwards Memorial Foundation)
BOIL THE BREAKFAST EARLY - The Chieftains 9 (Columbia)
KIDNEY STEW IS FINE - Eddie "Cleanhead" Vinson (Delmark)
QUEEN IDA AND THE BON TEMPS ZYDECO BAND IN NEW ORLEANS - Queen Ida (GNP Crescendo)
RARE BLUES - Dr Isaiah Ross, Maxwell Street Jimmy, Big Joe William, Son House, Rev. Robert Wilkins, Little Brother Montgomery, Sunnyland Slim; produced by Norman Dayron (Takoma)

LATIN RECORDING (G-1013)
(Category is for pure Latin music. All nominations here are albums.)
DANCEMANIA '80 - Tito Puente (Tico)
HEY - Julio Iglesias (Discos CBS Int'l)
IRAKERE 2 - Irakere (Columbia)
LA ONDA VA BIEN - Cal Tjader Sextet (Concord Jazz)
RICAN/STRUCTION - Ray Barretto (Fania)

RECORDING FOR CHILDREN (G-1014)
(This category is intended for recordings created specifically for children. All nominations are albums.)
BIG BIRD'S BIRDTIME STORIES - The Sesame St Muppets & Cast; Jim Henson, Muppets creator; Jim Timmens, album producer (Sesame St)
CHRISTMAS EVE ON SESAME STREET - Muppets & Sesame St cast; Jim Henson, Muppets creator; Dulcy Singer and Jon Stone, album producers (Sesame St)
IN HARMONY/A SESAME STREET RECORD - The Doobie Bros, James Taylor, Carly Simon, Bette Midler, Muppets, Al Jarreau, Linda Ronstadt, Wendy Waldman, Libby Titus & Dr John, Livingston Taylor, George Benson & Pauline Wilson, Lucy Simon, Kate Taylor & The Simon/Taylor Family; Lucy Simon and David Levine, producers (Sesame St)
LOVE - Sesame St Muppets & Cast; Jim Henson, Muppets creator; Arthur Shimkin, album producer (Sesame St)
THE PEOPLE IN YOUR NEIGHBORHOOD - The Sesame Street Muppets; Jim Henson, Muppets creator; Jeffrey Moss, album producer (Sesame St)

COMEDY RECORDING (G-1015)
(Either spoken word or musical performances are eligible here. All nominations are albums.)
CONTRACTUAL OBLIGATION - Monty Python (Arista)
HOLY SMOKE - Richard Pryor (Laff)
LIVE AT ST DOUGLAS CONVENT - Father Guido Sarducci (WB)
LIVE FROM NEW YORK - Gilda Radner (WB)
NO RESPECT - Rodney Dangerfield (Casablanca)

SPOKEN WORD, DOCUMENTARY OR DRAMA RECORDING (G-1016)
(This category is for nonmusical show albums including comedy show albums. All nominations are albums.)
ADVENTURES OF LUKE SKYWALKER - The Empire Strikes Back original cast with narration; Pat Glasser, album producer (RSO)
A CURB IN THE SKY (JAMES THURBER) - Peter Ustinov (Caedmon)
GERTRUDE STEIN, GERTRUDE STEIN, GERTRUDE STEIN - Pat Carroll (Caedmon)
I SING BECAUSE I'M HAPPY, VOLUMES 1 & 2 - Mahalia Jackson (Folkways)
OBEDIENTLY YOURS/ORSON WELLES - Orson Welles (Mark 56)

INSTRUMENTAL COMPOSITION (G-1017)
(A composer's award for an original nonclassical composition with or without lyrics which first gained recognition as an instrumental.)
AN AMERICAN CONCERTO - Patrick Williams, composer; Keel One Music, publisher.
THE EMPIRE STRIKES BACK - John Williams, composer; Fox Fanfare Music Inc & Bantha Music, publishers.
GIVE IT ALL YOU GOT - Chuck Mangione, composer; Gates Music, publisher.
THE IMPERIAL MARCH (DARTH VADER'S THEME) - John Williams, composer; Fox Fanfare Music Inc & Bantha Music, publishers.
YODA'S THEME - John Williams, composer; Fox Fanfare Music Inc & Bantha Music, publishers.

ORIGINAL SCORE - MOTION PICTURE OR A TELEVISION SPECIAL (G-1018)

(A composer's/songwriter's award for an original background score or original songs written specifically for the motion picture or television special.)

THE EMPIRE STRIKES BACK - John Williams, composer (RSO)
FAME - Michael Gore , Anthony Evans, Paul McCrane, Dean Pitchford, Lesley Gore, Robert F Colesberry, songwriters (RSO)
ONE TRICK PONY - Paul Simon, songwriter (WB)
STEVIE WONDER'S JOURNEY THROUGH THE SECRET LIFE OF PLANTS - Stevie Wonder, Michael Sembello, Stephanie Andrews and Yvonne Wright, songwriters (Tamla)
URBAN COWBOY - J D Souther, Boz Scaggs, David Foster, Jerry Foster, Bill Rice, Brian Collins, Robby Campbell, Joe Walsh, Bob Morrison, Johnny Wilson, Dan Fogelberg, Bob Seger, Wayland Holyfield, Bob House, Wanda Mallette, Patti Ryan, songwriters (Full Moon/Asylum)

CAST SHOW ALBUM (G-1019)

(Awards to the composer(s), lyricist(s) and album producer. Original cast albums, albums by road casts, or working casts, including show revival casts, are eligible. Grammys to the composer(s) of new material and album producer. Awards certificates to composer(s) and lyricist(s) of previous released songs.)

BARNUM - Cy Coleman, composer; Michael Stewart, lyrics; Cy Coleman and Mike Berniker, producers (CBS Masterworks)
A DAY IN HOLLYWOOD/A NIGHT IN THE UKRAINE - Frank Lazarus, Jerry Herman, composers; Dick Vosburgh, Jerry Herman, lyrics; Hugh Fordin, producer (DRG)
EVITA - Premier American Recording - Andrew Lloyd Webber, composer; Tim Rice, lyrics; Andrew Lloyd Webber, Tim Rice, producers (MCA)
OKLAHOMA! - Richard Rodgers, composer; Oscar Hammerstein II, lyrics; Thomas Z Shepard, producer (RCA)
ONE MO' TIME - Songs by 27 different songwriters performed in early black vaudeville days. Carl Seltzer, producer (WB)

JAZZ FUSION PERFORMANCE - VOCAL OR INSTRUMENTAL (G-1020)

(This category is for any type of borderline jazz performance - rock, pop, r&b, classical, etc.)

AN AMERICAN CONCERTO - Patrick Williams (Columbia - album)
DREAM COME TRUE - Earl Klugh (UA - album)
BIRDLAND - Manhattan Transfer (Atlantic - single)
AMERICAN GARAGE - Pat Metheny (ECM - album)
CATCHING THE SUN - Spyro Gyra (MCA - album)
FUN AND GAMES - Chuck Mangione (A&M - album)

JAZZ VOCAL - FEMALE (G-1021)

(Solo performance. All nominations are albums.)
THE AUDIENCE WITH BETTY CARTER - Betty Carter (Betcar)
CHASIN' THE BIRD - Helen Merril (Inner City)
HELEN HUMES AND THE MUSE ALL STARS - Helen Humes (Muse)
A PERFECT MATCH/ELLA & BASIE - Ella Fitzgerald (Pablo)
SARAH VAUGHAN: DUKE ELLINGTON SONG BOOK ONE - Sarah Vaughan (Pablo)

JAZZ VOCAL - MALE (G-1022)

(Solo performance.)
MOODY'S MOOD - George Benson (WB/QWest - track from Give Me The Night)
SATISFACTION GUARANTEED - Mark Murphy (Muse - album)
SIDEWALKS OF NEW YORK - Slam Stewart (Stash - track from New York New York, Sounds Of The Apple)
STREET OF DREAMS - Bill Henderson (Discovery - album)
TORME/A NEW ALBUM - Mel Torme (Gryphon - album)

JAZZ - SOLOIST (G-1023)

(This category is for a solo instrumental performance with or without a group or band. All nominations are albums.)

CHASIN' THE BIRD - Pepper Adams (of the Helen Merrill Sextet) (Inner City)
CUNNINGBIRD - Jimmy Knepper (Steeplechase)
I REMEMBER YOU - Hank Jones (Classic Jazz)
I WILL SAY GOODBYE - Bill Evans (Fantasy)
THE PHIL WOODS QUARTET-VOLUME ONE - Phil Woods (Clean Cuts)

JAZZ - GROUP (G-1024)

(Category is for an instrumental group. All nominations are albums.)

BOBBY SHEW, OUTSTANDING IN HIS FIELD - Bobby Shew (Inner City)
I REMEMBER YOU - Hank Jones (Classic Jazz)
L A BOUND - Nick Brignola (Sea Breeze)
LIVE AT THE PUBLIC THEATRE - The Heath Brothers (CBS)
PHIL WOODS QUARTET-VOLUME ONE - Phil Woods (Clean Cuts)
WE WILL MEET AGAIN - Bill Evans (WB)

JAZZ - BIG BAND (G-1025)

(This category is primarily for a big band sound. All nominations are albums.)

BOB BROOKMEYER COMPOSER/ARRANGER - Mel Lewis & The Jazz Orchestra (Gryphon)
DYNAMITE! - Louis Bellson Big Band (Concord Jazz)
FAREWELL - Toshiko Akiyoshi-Lew Tabackin Big Band (Ascent)
LIVE AT CONCERTS BY THE SEA - Bob Florence Big Band (Trend)
ON THE ROAD - Count Basie and Orchestra (Pablo)
PRESENT PERFECT - Rob McConnell & The Boss Brass (Pausa)

INSTRUMENTAL ARRANGEMENT (G-1026)

(An instrumental arranger's award. This category is for a specific arrangement released for the first time during the eligibility year on either a single or an album track.)

DINORAH, DINORAH - George Benson - Quincy Jones and Jerry Hey, arrangers (WB - track from Give Me The Night)
FORGET THE WOMAN - Eddie Daniels - Jorge Calandrelli, arranger (CBS - track from Morning Thunder)
MARCOSINHO - Dave Valentin - Dave Grusin, arranger (GRP - track from The Hawk)
SKYLARK - Mel Lewis - Bob Brookmeyer, arranger (Gryphon - track from Bob Brookmeyer Composer/Arranger)
WAVE - Antonio Carlos Jobim - Claus Ogerman, arranger (WB - track from Terra Brasilis)

ARRANGEMENT ACCOMPANYING VOCALIST(S) (G-1027)

(An instrumental arranger's award. This category is for a specific arrangement released for the first time during the eligibility year on either a single or an album track.)
BIGGEST PART OF ME - Ambrosia - Joe Puerta, Burleigh Drummond, David Pack, arrangers (WB - single)
MONEY - The Flying Lizards - David Cunningham, arranger (Virgin - single)
SAILING - Christopher Cross - Michael Omartian, arranger (WB - single)
TANGERINE - The Singers Unlimited - Rob McConnell, arranger (Pausa - track from The Singers Unlimited with Rob McConnell & The Boss Brass)
THEME FROM NEW YORK, NEW YORK - Frank Sinatra - Don Costa, arranger (Reprise - single)

ARRANGEMENT FOR VOICES (G-1028)

(A vocal arranger's award. This category covers all voices on a recording, excluding a featured soloist, if any.)

BIGGEST PART OF ME - Ambrosia - Joe Puerta, Burleigh Drummond, David Pack, vocal arrangers (WB - single)

BIRDLAND - Manhattan Transfer - Janis Siegel, vocal arranger (Atlantic - track from Extensions)

GIVE ME THE NIGHT - George Benson - Rod Temperton, vocal arranger (WB/QWest - single)

SWEET GEORGIA BROWN - The Singers Unlimited - Gene Puerling, vocal arranger (Pausa - track from Friends)

TWILIGHT ZONE/TWILIGHT TONE - Manhattan Transfer - Alan Paul and Jay Graydon, vocal arrangers (Atlantic - track from Extensions)

ALBUM PACKAGE (G-1029)

(An art director's award. This category is for either classical or nonclassical single-jacket or multiple pocket album packages.)

AGAINST THE WIND - (Bob Seger & The Silver Bullet Band) - Roy Kohara, art director (Capitol)

CATS - (Cats) - Ron Coro/Johnny Lee, art directors (Elektra)

CHICAGO XIV - (Chicago) - John Berg, art director (Columbia)

ONE ON ONE - (Bob James & Earl Klugh) - Paula Scher, art director (Columbia)

TUSK - (Fleetwood Mac) - Vigon Nahas Vigon, art director (WB)

ALBUM NOTES (G-1030)

(An annotator's award. This category is for original writing for a specific album. Either classical or nonclassical albums qualify.)

ATLANTA BLUES: 1933 (Blind Willie McTell, Curley Weaver, Buddy Moss) - David Evans, Bruce Bastin, annotators (John Edwards Memorial Foundation)

CHICAGO CONCERT - 1956 (Louis Armstrong) - Dan Morgenstern, annotator (Columbia)

ELVIS ARON PRESLEY - Lorene Lortie, annotator (RCA)

LESTER YOUNG (Giants Of Jazz) - John McDonough and Richard M Sudhalter, annotators (Time/Life)

TRILOGY: PAST, PRESENT & FUTURE (Frank Sinatra) - David McClintock, annotator (Reprise)

HISTORICAL REISSUE ALBUM (G-1031)

(Grammy to the reissue album producer(s).)

FIRST EDITION/THE GOLDEN AGE OF BROADWAY - C E Crumpacker, producer (RCA Spec Prod)

SONGS OF THE DEPRESSION: HAPPY DAYS ARE HERE AGAIN - George Spitzer and Michael Brooks, producers (Book of the Month)

THE GUITARISTS (Giants Of Jazz) - Jerry Korn and Michael Brooks, producers (Time/Life)

SEGOVIA - THE EMI RECORDINGS 1927-39 - Keith Hardwick; producer (Angel)

EARLY HISTORY OF THE PHONOGRAPH RECORD - George Garabedian, producer (Mark 56)

BEST ENGINEERED RECORDING (G-1032)

CHRISTOPHER CROSS - (Christopher Cross) - Chet Himes, engineer (WB - album)

GIVE ME THE NIGHT - (George Benson) - Bruce Swedien, engineer (WB/QWest - track from Give Me The Night)

GROWING UP IN HOLLYWOOD TOWN - (Lincoln Mayorga & Amanda McBroom) - Bill Schnee, engineer (Sheffield Lab - album)

NEW BABY - (Don Randi and Quest) - Bill Schnee, engineer (Sheffield Lab album)

THE WALL - (Pink Floyd) - James Guthrie, engineer (Columbia)

PRODUCER OF THE YEAR (G-1033)

(A producer's award for consistently outstanding creativity in producing.)

QUINCY JONES

MICHAEL OMARTIAN

QUEEN AND MACK

PHIL RAMONE

STEVIE WONDER

CLASSICAL ALBUM (G-1034)

(Grammy to the artist, and to the producer if other than the artist. Certificates to the engineer(s) and orchestra if applicable.)

BARTOK: CONCERTO FOR VIOLIN & ORCHESTRA - Pinchas Zukerman/Zubin Mehta conducting Los Angeles Philharmonic; Andrew Kazdin, producer (Columbia)

BERG: CONCERTO FOR VIOLIN & ORCHESTRA/STRAVINSKY: CONCERTO IN D MAJOR FOR VIOLIN & ORCHESTRA - Itzhak Perlman/Seiji Ozawa conducting Boston Symphony; Rainer Brock, producer (DG)

BERG: LULU (COMPLETE VERSION) - Perre Boulez conducting Orchestre de l'Opera de Paris/Principal Soloists: Teresa Stratas, Yvonne Minton, Franz Mazura, Toni Blankenheim; Guenther Breest, Michael Horwarth, producers (DG)

BRUCKNER: SYMPHONY NO 6 IN A MAJOR - Sir Georg Solti conducting Chicago Symphony; Ray Minshull, producer (London)

RUGGLES: COMPLETE MUSIC - Michael Tilson Thomas conducting Buffalo Philharmonic; Steven Epstein, producer (Columbia)

CLASSICAL PERFORMANCE ORCHESTRA - (G-1035)

(Grammys to the conductor and producer. Certificate to the orchestra.)

BEETHOVEN: SYMPHONIES (9) - Leonard Bernstein conducting Vienna Philharmonic; Hanno Rinke, producer (DG)

BRUCKER: SYMPHONY NO 6 IN A MAJOR - Sir Georg Solti conducting Chicago Symphony; Ray Minshull, producer (London)

RESPIGHI: FESTE ROMANE/FOUNTAINS OF ROME - Michael Tilson Thomas conducting Los Angeles Philharmonic; Steven Epstein, producer (Columbia)

RUGGLES: COMPLETE MUSIC - Michael Tilson Thomas conducting Buffalo Philharmonic; Steven Epstein, producer (Columbia)

SHOSTAKOVICH: SYMPHONY NO 5 - Leonard Bernstein conducting New York Philharmonic; John McClure, producer (Columbia)

OPERA RECORDING (G-1036)

(Grammys to the conductor and producer; special plaques to the principal soloists.)

BARTOK: BLUEBEARD'S CASTLE - Sir Georg Solti conducting London Philharmonic/Principal Soloists: Sylvia Sass, Kolos Kovats; Christopher Raeburn, producer (London)

BERG: LULU (COMPLETE VERSION) - Pierre Boulez conducting Orchestre de l'Opera de Paris/Principal soloists; Teresa Stratas, Yvonne Minton, Franz Mazura, Toni Blankenheim; Guenther Breest, Michael Horwarth, producers (DG)

DEBUSSY: PELLEAS ET MELISANDE - Herbert von Karajan conducting Berlin Philharmonic/Principal Soloists: Frederica von Stade, Richard Stilwell; Michel Glotz, producer (Angel)

PUCCINI: LA BOHEME - James Levine conducting National Philharmonic/Ambrosian Chorus/Principal Soloists: Renata Scotto, Alfredo Kraus, Carol Neblett, Sherrill Milnes; John Mordler, producer (Angel)

WEILL: SILVERLAKE - Julius Rudel conducting New York City Opera Orchestra & Chorus/Principal Soloists: Joel Grey, William Neill, Elizabeth Hynes, Jack Harrold, Elaine Bonazzi; Eric Salzman, producer (Nonesuch)

CHORAL PERFORMANCE - OTHER THAN OPERA (G-1037)

BOITO: PROLOGUE TO MEFISTOFELE - Robert Shaw, conductor; The Atlanta Symphony Chorus & Orchestra (Telarc)

MENOTTI: THE UNICORN, THE GORGON AND THE MANTICORE - Thomas Hilbish, conductor; University of Michigan Chamber Choir & Chamber Ensemble (University of Michigan School of Music)

MOZART: REQUIEM - Carlo Maria Giulini, conductor; Norbert Balatsch, chorus master; Philharmonia Chorus & Orchestra (Angel)

PROKOFIEV: ALEXANDER NEVSKY - Claudio Abbado, conductor; London Symphony Chorus and Orchestra (DG)

SCHOENBERG: GURRELIDER - Seiji Ozawa, conductor; John Oliver, chorus master; Tanglewood Festival Chorus & Boston Symphony (Philips)

CHAMBER MUSIC PERFORMANCE (G-1038)

(Instrumental or vocal.)

BEETHOVEN: EARLY QUARTETS, OP 18 - Cleveland Quartet (RCA)

DEBUSSY: SONATA NO 3 IN G MINOR FOR VIOLIN & PIANO/FAURE: SONATA IN A MAJOR FOR VIOLIN & PIANO - Pinchas Zukerman, Marc Neikrug (Columbia)

MESSIAEN: QUARTET FOR THE END OF TIME - Daniel Barenboim, Luben Yordanoff, Albert Tetard, Claude Desurmont (DG)

MUSIC FOR TWO VIOLINS (MOSZKOWSKI: SUITE FOR TWO VIOLINS/SHOSTAKOVICH: DUETS/PROKOFIEV: SONATA FOR TWO VIOLINS) - Itzhak Perlman, Pinchas Zukerman (Angel)

SCHUBERT: QUARTET NO 15 IN G MAJOR, OP 161 - Juilliard Quartet (Columbia)

CLASSICAL PERFORMANCE - INSTRUMENTAL SOLOIST(S) (WITH ORCHESTRA) (G-1039)

BACH FOR TRUMPET - Maurice Andre; Maurice Andre conducting Franz Liszt Chamber Orchestra (Angel)

BARTOK: CONCERTO FOR VIOLIN & ORCHESTRA - Pinchas Zukerman; Zubin Mehta conducting Los Angeles Philharmonic (Columbia)

BERG: CONCERTO FOR VIOLIN & ORCHESTRA/STRAVINSKY: CONCERTO IN D MAJOR FOR VIOLIN & ORCHESTRA - Itzhak Perlman; Seiji Ozawa conducting Boston Symphony (DG).

BRAHMS: CONCERTO IN A MINOR FOR VIOLIN & CELLO ('DOUBLE CONCERTO') - Itzhak Perlman & Mstislav Rostropovich; Bernard Haitink conducting Concertgebouw Orchestra (Angel)

THE CLASSIC TRUMPET CONCERTI OF HAYDN & HUMMEL - Gerard Schwarz; Gerard Schwarz conducting Y Chamber Symphony of New York (Delos)

TELEMANN: CONCERTOS IN G & C FOR FLUTE & SUITE IN A MINOR - James Galway; I Solisti di Zagreb (RCA)

CLASSICAL PERFORMANCE - INSTRUMENTAL SOLOIST(S) (WITHOUT ORCHESTRA) (G-1040)

BACH: TOCCATAS, VOLUME II - Glenn Gould (Columbia)

BRAHMS: VARIATIONS AND FUGUE ON A THEME BY HANDEL - Rudolf Serkin (Columbia)

COPLAND: THE COMPLETE MUSIC FOR SOLO PIANO - Leo Smit (Columbia)

(JOPLIN) DIGITAL RAGTIME - Music Of Scott Joplin - Joshua Rifkin (Angel)

RACHMANINOFF: MUSIC FOR PIANO, VOLUME 7 (SONATAS NOS 1 & 2) - Ruth Laredo (Columbia)

THE SPANISH ALBUM - Itzhak Perlman (Angel)

CLASSICAL PERFORMANCE - VOCAL SOLOIST - (G-1041)

BERG: DER WEIN - Concert Aria - Jessye Norman; Pierre Boulez conducting New York Philharmonic (Columbia)

BERG: LULU SUITE - Judith Blegen; Pierre Boulez conducting New York Philharmonic (Columbia)

MAHLER: SONGS OF A WAYFARER & RUCKERT SONGS - Frederica von Stade; Andrew Davis conducting London Philharmonic (Columbia)

MOZART: SONGS - Elly Ameling; Jorg Demus, accompanist (Seraphim)

PRIMA DONNA, VOLUME 5 - Great Soprano Arias From Handel To

Britten - Leontyne Price; Henry Lewis conducting Philharmonic Orchestra (RCA)

(R) STRAUSS: FOUR LAST SONGS & ORCHESTRAL SONGS - Kiri Te Kanawa; Andrew Davis conducting London Symphony (Columbia)

BEST ENGINEERED RECORDING - CLASSICAL (G-1042)

ALMEIDA: FIRST CONCERTO FOR GUITAR & ORCHESTRA - Laurindo Almeida/Elmer Ramsey conducting Los Angeles Orchestra de Camera (Concord Concerto)

BACH: THE SIX BRANDENBURG CONCERTOS - Gerard Schwarz conducting Los Angeles Chamber Orchestra; Robert Norberg and Mitchell Tanenbaum, engineers (Angel)

BARTOK: CONCERTO FOR VIOLIN & ORCHESTRA - Pinchas Zukerman/Zubin Mehta conducting Los Angeles Philharmonic; Bud Graham and Ray Moore, engineers (Columbia)

BERG: LULU (COMPLETE VERSION) - Pierre Boulez conducting Orchestre de l'Opera de Paris/Principal soloists: Teresa Stratas, Yvonne Minton, Franz Mazura, Toni Blankenheim; Karl-August Naegler, engineer (DG)

BRAHMS: CONCERTO IN A MINOR FOR VIOLIN & CELLO ('DOUBLE CONCERTO') - Itzhak Perlman and Mstislav Rostropovich/ Bernard Haitink conducting Concertgebouw Orchestra; Michael Gray, engineer (Angel)

SHOSTAKOVICH: SYMPHONY NO 5 - Leonard Bernstein conducting New York Philharmonic; John McClure and Ed Michalski, engineers (Columbia)

CLASSICAL PRODUCER OF THE YEAR (G-1043)

STEVEN EPSTEIN - BEETHOVEN: SYMPHONY NO 6 ('PASTORALE'), Michael Tilson Thomas conducting English Chamber Orchestra (Columbia); DEBUSSY: SONATA NO 3 IN G MINOR VIOLIN & PIANO/ FAURE: SONATA IN A MAJOR FOR VIOLIN & PIANO, Pinchas Zukerman, Marc Neikrug (Columbia); MOZART: SERENADE NO 7 IN D MAJOR ('HAFFNER SERENADE'), Pinchas Zukerman/members of the Los Angeles Philharmonic (Columbia); RESPIGHI: FOUNTAINS OF ROME, Michael Tilson Thomas conducting Los Angeles Philharmonic (Columbia); RUGGLES: COMPLETE MUSIC, Michael Tilson Thomas conducting Buffalo Philharmonic (Columbia); SCHUBERT: QUARTET NO 15 IN G MAJOR, OP 161, Juilliard Quartet (Columbia)

ANDREW KAZDIN - BACH: TOCCATAS, VOLUME II, Glenn Gould (Columbia); BARTOK: CONCERTO FOR VIOLIN & ORCHESTRA, Pinchas Zukerman/Zubin Mehta conducting Los Angeles Philharmonic (Columbia); BERG: LULU SUITE & DER WEIN, Jessye Norman/Judith Blegen/Pierre Boulez conducting New York Philharmonic (Columbia); MUSSORGSKY: PICTURES AT AN EXHIBITION/RAVEL: LA VALSE, Zubin Mehta conducting New York Philharmonic (Columbia); STRAVINSKY: PETROUCHKA, Zubin Mehta conducting New York Philharmonic (Columbia)

JOHN McCLURE - HAYDN: MASS NO 10 IN B FLAT MAJOR (THERESIEN), Leonard Bernstein conducting London Symphony Orchestra & Chorus/Popp, Elias, Tear, Hudson (Columbia); PROKOFIEV: SYMPHONY NO 5, Leonard Bernstein conducting Israel Philharmonic (Columbia); SHOSTAKOVICH: SYMPHONY NO 5, Leonard Bernstein conducting New York Philharmonic (Columbia)

PAUL MYERS - ELGAR: SEA PICTURES, Yvonne Minton/Daniel Barenboim conducting London Philharmonic (Columbia); ITALIAN OPERA ARIAS, Frederica von Stade; Mario Bernardi conducting National Arts Centre Orchestra (Columbia); MAHLER: SONGS OF A WAYFARER, Frederica von Stade; Andrew Davis conducting London Philharmonic (Columbia); MOZART: DON GIOVANNI, Lorin Maazel conducting Orchestra & Chorus of the Paris Opera/Principal soloists: Teresa Berganza, Kiri Te Kanawa, Edda Moser, Jose Van Dam, Ruggero Raimondi (Columbia); (R) STRAUSS: DON JUAN, Lorin Maazel conducting Cleveland Orchestra (Columbia); (R) STRAUSS: FOUR LAST SONGS, Kiri Te Kanawa; Andrew Davis conducting London Symphony (Columbia)

ROBERT WOODS - BIZET: CARMEN SUITES 1 & 2/GRIEG; PEER GYNT SUITES 1 & 2, Leonard Slatkin conducting St Louis Symphony (Telarc); BOITO: PROLOGUE TO 'MEFISTOFELE', Robert Shaw conducting Atlanta Symphony Orchestra & Chorus/John Cheek (Telarc); CHAUSSON: CONCERTO, OP 21, Cleveland Orchestra String Quartet with Israela Margalit & Lorin Maazel (Telarc); FREDERICK FENNELL/THE CLEVELAND SYMPHONIC WINDS, selections com-

1979—22nd ANNUAL GRAMMY AWARDS—Emmylou Harris

1981—24th ANNUAL GRAMMY AWARDS—Yoko Lennon with son
Sean

1981—24th ANNUAL GRAMMY AWARDS—Rick Springfield

1982—25th ANNUAL GRAMMY AWARDS—TOTO

© N.A.R.A.S.

1982—25th ANNUAL GRAMMY AWARDS—Marvin Gaye and Jennifer
Holliday

© N.A.R.A.S.

posed by Grainger, Vaughan Williams, Arnaud (Telarc); SAINT-SAENS: SYMPHONY NO 3 ('ORGAN'), Eugene Ormandy conducting Philadelphia Orchestra/Michael Murray (Telarc); TCHAIKOVSKY: SYMPHONY NO 4 IN F MINOR, Lorin Maazel conducting The Cleveland Orchestra (Telarc)

1981 HALL OF FAME WINNERS (G-1044)

BEETHOVEN: QUARTETS FOR STRINGS COMPLETE (16) - Budapest String Quartet - Released in 1952 - Columbia Albums ML 4576 through 4587; also SL 172 through 174
BLACK AND TAN FANTASY - Duke Ellington & his Orchestra - Released in 1928 - Victor 21137
MAHLER: DAS LIED VON DER ERDE - Bruno Walter conducting the Vienna Philharmonic Orchestra; with Kathleen Ferrier and Julius Patzak - Released in 1952 - London Album LL 625/6
NOBODY - Bert Williams - Released in 1906 - Columbia 3423
OVER THE RAINBOW - Judy Garland - Released in 1939 - Decca 2672

1981

RECORD OF THE YEAR (G-1045)

BETTE DAVIS EYES - Kim Carnes; Val Garay, Producer (EMI-America)
ARTHUR'S THEME (BEST THAT YOU CAN DO) - Christopher Cross; Michael Omartian, Producer (WB)
ENDLESS LOVE - Diana Ross & Lionel Richie; Lionel Richie, Producer (Motown)
(JUST LIKE) STARTING OVER - John Lennon; John Lennon, Yoko Ono, Jack Douglas, Producers (Geffen/WB)
JUST THE TWO OF US - Bill Withers/Grover Washington, Jr.; Grover Washington, Jr & Ralph MacDonald, Producers (Elektra/Asylum)

ALBUM OF THE YEAR (G-1046)

DOUBLE FANTASY - John Lennon/Yoko Ono; John Lennon, Yoko Ono & Jack Douglas, Producers (Geffen/WB)
BREAKIN' AWAY - Al Jarreau; Jay Graydon, Producer (WB)
THE DUDE - Quincy Jones; Quincy Jones, Producer (A&M)
GAUCHO - Steely Dan; Gary Katz, Producer (MCA)
MISTAKEN IDENTITY - Kim Carnes; Val Garay, Producer (EMI-America)

SONG OF THE YEAR (G-1047)

(A Songwriter's Award. Any song is eligible if a new recording of it has been released commercially during the Eligibility Year, provided it did not receive a previous nomination or award in a songwriting category.)
BETTE DAVIS EYES - Donna Weiss & Jackie DeShannon
ARTHUR'S THEME (BEST THAT YOU CAN DO) - Peter Allen, Burt Bacharach, Carole Bayer Sager, Christopher Cross
ENDLESS LOVE - Lionel Richie
JUST THE TWO OF US - Bill Withers, William Salter, Ralph MacDonald
9 to 5 - Dolly Parton

NEW ARTIST (G-1048)

(This category is for an artist or organized group whose first recording was released during the Eligibility Year.)
SHEENA EASTON (EMI-America)
ADAM AND THE ANTS (Epic/CBS)
GO-GO'S (I.R.S.)
JAMES INGRAM (A&M)
LUTHER VANDROSS (Epic/CBS)

POP VOCAL - FEMALE (G-1049)

(Solo performance)
LENA HORNE: THE LADY AND HER MUSIC LIVE ON BROADWAY - Lena Horne (Album) (QWest/W.B.)
ANGEL OF THE MORNING - Juice Newton (Single) (Capitol)
BETTE DAVIS EYES - Kim Carnes (Single) (EMI-America)
FOR YOUR EYES ONLY - Sheena Easton (Single) (Liberty)
PHYSICAL - Olivia Newton-John (Single) (MCA)

POP VOCAL - MALE (G-1050)

(Solo performance)
BREAKIN' AWAY - Al Jarreau (Album) (WB)
ARTHUR'S THEME (BEST THAT YOU CAN DO) - Christopher Cross (Single) (WB)
DOUBLE FANTASY - John Lennon (Lennon Tracks Only) (Geffen/WB)
JUST ONCE - James Ingram (Track) (A&M)
JUST THE TWO OF US - Bill Withers (Track) (E/A)

POP VOCAL - DUO OR GROUP WITH VOCAL (G-1051)

(All recordings on which the group receives artist billing on the label are eligible here even though the vocal may feature only one member of the group.)
BOY FROM NEW YORK CITY - The Manhattan Transfer (Single) (Atlantic)
ENDLESS LOVE - Diana Ross & Lionel Richie (Single) (Motown)
GAUCHO - Steely Dan (Album) (MCA)
PRIVATE EYES - Daryl Hall & John Oates (Album) (RCA)
SLOW HAND - Pointer Sisters (Single) (E/A)

POP INSTRUMENTAL (G-1052)

(This category is for an orchestra, group or sololist, and is for either pure instrumentals or instrumentals with vocal coloring.)
THEME FROM HILL STREET BLUES - Mike Post featuring Larry Carlton (E/A) (Single)
HOOKED ON CLASSICS - Louis Clark conducting The Royal Philharmonic Orchestra (RCA) (Single)
LATE NIGHT GUITAR - Earl Klugh (Liberty) (Album)
RIT (Side 2 - Instrumentals) - Lee Ritenour (E/A) (Album)
VELAS - Quincy Jones (Track) (A&M)

ROCK VOCAL - FEMALE (G-1053)

(Solo performance)
FIRE AND ICE - Pat Benatar (Single) (Chrysalis)
COLD LOVE - Donna Summer (Track) (Geffen/WB)
EDGE OF SEVENTEEN - Stevie Nicks (Track) (Modern/Atl)
WALKING ON THIN ICE - Yoko Ono (Single) (Geffen/WB)
WHO'S FOOLIN' WHO - Lulu (Track) (Alfa)

ROCK VOCAL - MALE (G-1054)

(Solo peformance)
JESSIE'S GIRL - Rick Springfield (Single) (RCA)
DEDICATION - Gary U. S. Bonds (Album) (EMI-America)
THE RIVER - Bruce Springsteen (Album) (Col/CBS)
SUPER FREAK - (Single) (Gordy/Motown)
YOUNG TURKS - Rod Stewart (Single) (Warner Br)

ROCK PERFORMANCE - DUO OR GROUP WITH VOCAL (G-1055)

(All recordings on which the group receives artist billing on the label are eligible here even though the vocal may feature only one member of the group)

DON'T STAND SO CLOSE TO ME - The Police (Single) (A&M)
4 - Foreigner (Album) (Atlantic)
HI INFIDELITY - REO Speedwagon (Album) (Epic/CBS)
STOP DRAGGIN' MY HEART AROUND - Stevie Nicks with Tom Petty & The Heartbreakers (Single) (Modern/Atl)
TATTOO YOU - Rolling Stones (Album) (Rolling St/Atl)

ROCK INSTRUMENTAL (G-1056)

(This category is for an orchestra, group or soloist, and is for either pure instrumentals or instrumentals with vocal coloring)

BEHIND MY CAMEL - The Police (Track) (A&M)
COMPUTER WORLD - Kraftwerk (Track) (WB)
THE LEAGUE OF GENTLEMEN - Robert Fripp (Album) (Polygram/Polydor)
UNSUNG HEROES - The Dregs (Album) (Arista)
YYZ - Rush (Track) (Mercury)

R&B VOCAL - FEMALE (G-1057)

(Solo performance)

HOLD ON I'M COMIN' - Aretha Franklin (Track) (Arista)
IT MUST BE MAGIC - Teena Marie (Album) (Gordy/Motown))
RAZZAMATAZZ - Patti Austin (Track) (A&M)
STEPHANIE - Stephanie Mills (Album) (20th Century)
WHAT CHA' GONNA DO FOR ME - Chaka Khan (Album) (Warner Bros)

R&B VOCAL - MALE (G-1058)

(Solo performance)

ONE HUNDRED WAYS - James Ingram (Track) (A&M)
I CAN'T LIVE WITHOUT YOUR LOVE - Teddy Pendergrass (Single) (Phila Intl/CBS)
NEVER TOO MUCH - Luther Vandross (Album) (Epic/CBS)
SHE'S A BAD MAMA JAMA (SHE'S BUILT, SHE'S STACKED) - Carl Carlton (20th Century)
STREET SONGS - Rick James (Album) (Gordy/Motown)

R&B - DUO OR GROUP WITH VOCAL (G-1059)

(All recordings on which the group receives artist billing on the label are eligible here even though the vocal may feature only one member of the group)

THE DUDE - Quincy Jones (Album) (A&M)
BLACK & WHITE - Pointer Sisters (Album) (Planet/E/A)
THE CLARKE/DUKE PROJECT - Stanley Clarke & George Duke (Album) (Epic/CBS)
LADY (YOU BRING ME UP) - Commodores (Single) (Motown)
LET'S GROOVE - Earth, Wind & Fire (Single) (ARC/CBS)

R&B INSTRUMENTAL (G-1060)

(This category is for an orchestra, group or soloist, and is for either pure instrumentals or instrumentals with vocal coloring)

ALL I NEED IS YOU - David Sanborn (Single) (WB)
EAST ST. LOUIS MELODY - Noel Pointer (Track) (Liberty)
INHERIT THE WIND - Wilton Felder (Album) (MCA)
YOU'RE WELCOME, STOP ON BY - Ahmad Jamal (Track) (20th Century)
WINDS OF CHANGE (HENKA NON NAGARE) - Hiroshima (Track) (Arista)

RHYTHM & BLUES SONG (G-1061)

(A Songwriter's Award. Any song is eligible if a new recording of it has been released commercially during the Elibibility Year, provided it did not receive a previous nomination or award in a songwriting category)

JUST THE TWO OF US - Bill Withers, William Salter, Ralph MacDonald
AI NO CORRIDA - Chas Jankel & Kenny Young
LADY (YOU BRING ME UP) - Harold Hudson, William King & Shirley King
SHE'S A BAD MAMA JAMA (SHE'S BUILT, SHE'S STACKED) Leon Haywood
WHEN SHE WAS MY GIRL - Marc Blatte, Larry Gottlieb

COUNTRY VOCAL - FEMALE (G-1062)

(Solo performance)

9 to 5 - Dolly Parton (Single) (RCA)
I WAS COUNTRY WHEN COUNTRY WASN'T COOL - Barbara Mandrell (MCA) (Single)
QUEEN OF HEARTS - Juice Newton (Single) (Capital)
SEVEN YEAR ACHE - Rosanne Cash (Album) (Col/CBS)
SOMEBODY'S KNOCKIN' - Terri Gibbs (Album) (MCA)

COUNTRY VOCAL - MALE (G-1063)

(Solo performance)

(THERE'S) NO GETTIN' OVER ME - Ronnie Milsap (Single) (RCA)
I'M JUST AN OLD CHUNK OF COAL (BUT I'M GONNA BE A DIAMOND SOMEDAY) - John Anderson (Single) (WB)
SOMEWHERE OVER THE RAINBOW - Willie Nelson (Album) (Columbia)
STEP BY STEP - Eddie Rabbitt (Single) (E/A)
STILL DOIN' TIME - George Jones (Single) (Epic/CBS)

COUNTRY PERFORMANCE - DUO OR GROUP WITH VOCAL (G-1064)

(All recordings on which the group receives artist billing on the label are eligible here even though the vocal may feature only one member of the group)

ELVIRA - Oak Ridge Boys (Single) (MCA)
FEELS SO RIGHT - Alabama (Album) (RCA)
IF I NEEDED YOU - Emmylou Harris & Don Williams (Single) (WB)
WHAT ARE WE DOIN' IN LOVE - Dottie West & Kenny Rogers (Single) (Liberty)
YOU'RE THE REASON GOD MADE OKLAHOMA - David Frizzell & Shelly West (Single) (WB)

COUNTRY INSTRUMENTAL (G-1065)

(This category is for an orchestra, group or soloist, and is for either pure instrumentals or instrumentals with vocal coloring)

COUNTRY–AFTER ALL THESE YEARS - Chet Atkins (Album) (RCA)
INSTRUMENTAL MEDLEY: MOUNTAIN DEW, FIREBALL MAIL, OLD JOE CLARK, NIGHT TRAIN, UNCLE JOE'S BOOGIE - Barbara Mandrell (Track) (MCA)
REFLECTIONS - Chet Atkins & Doc Watson (Album) (RCA)
THE TEXAS FIDDLE COLLECTION - Johnny Gimble (Album) (CMH)
TRAVIS PICKIN' - Merle Travis (Album) (CMH)

COUNTRY SONG (G-1066)

(A Songwriter's Award. Any song is eligible if a new recording of it has been released commercially during the Eligibility Year, provided it did not receive a previous nomination or award in a songwriting category)

9 to 5 - Dolly Parton
ELVIRA - Dallas Frazier
I WAS COUNTRY WHEN COUNTRY WASN'T COOL - Kye Fleming &

Dennis W. Morgan
SOMEBODY'S KNOCKIN' - Ed Penney & Jerry Gillespie, Songwriters
YOU'RE THE REASON GOD MADE OKLAHOMA - Larry Collins & Sandy Pinkard

GOSPEL PERFORMANCE - CONTEMPORARY OR INSPIRATIONAL (G-1067)

(This category is for contemporary-flavored gospel recordings. All nominations are albums)

PRIORITY - Imperials (Dayspring/Word)
IN CONCERT - Amy Grant (Myrrh/Word)
FINEST HOUR - Cynthia Clawson (Triangle/Benson)
SPREADIN' LIKE WILDFIRE - The Archers (Songbird/MCA)
THIS AIN'T HOLLYWOOD - DeGarmo & Key (Lamb & Lion/Benson)

GOSPEL PERFORMANCE - TRADITIONAL (G-1068)

(All nominations are albums)

THE MASTERS V - J.D. Sumner/James Blackwood/Hovie Lister/ Rosie Rozell/Jake Hess (Skylite)
CAN'T STOP THE MUSIC - The Lanny Wolfe Trio (Impact/Benson)
ESCAPE TO THE LIGHT - Rusty Goodman (Canaan/Word)
GOIN' HIGHER - The Happy Goodman Family (Canaan/Word)
RAMBO REUNION - Rambos (Heartwarming/Benson)

SOUL GOSPEL PERFORMANCE - CONTEMPORARY (G-1069)

DON'T GIVE UP - Andrae Crouch (Album) (WB)
EDWIN HAWKINS LIVE - Edwin Hawkins (Album) (Myrrh/Word)
WALTER HAWKINS: THE HAWKINS FAMILY - Walter Hawkins (Album) (Light)
INTRODUCING THE WINANS - The Winans (Album) (Light/Lexicon)
THE LORD WILL MAKE A WAY - Al Green (Track) (Hi-Myrrh/Word)

SOUL GOSPEL PERFORMANCE - TRADITIONAL (G-1070)

(All nominations are albums)

THE LORD WILL MAKE A WAY - Al Green (Hi-Myrrh/Word)
CLOUDBUST - Mighty Clouds of Joy (Myrrh/Word)
DANIEL HAWKINS - Daniel Hawkins (Light/Lexicon)
GO - Shirley Caesar (Myrrh/Word)
WHERE IS YOUR FAITH - James Cleveland & So. California Comm Choir (Savoy)

INSPIRATIONAL PERFORMANCE (G-1071)

(This category is for religious recordings by other than regular gospel recording artists)

AMAZING GRACE - B.J. Thomas (Album) (Myrrh/Word)
I BELIEVE IN JESUS - Donna Summer (Track) (Geffen/WB)
I'M SO GLAD I'M STANDING HERE TODAY - Crusaders with Joe Cocker (Single) (MCA)
IN MY HEART - Barbara Mandrell (Track) (MCA)
MIRACLES - Don Williams (Single) (MCA)
SHOT OF LOVE - Bob Dylan (Album) (Columbia/CBS)

ETHNIC OR TRADITIONAL RECORDING (G-1072)

(This category includes traditional blues and pure folk recordings. All nominations are albums)

THERE MUST BE A BETTER WORLD SOMEWHERE - B.B. King (MCA)
BLUES DELUXE - (The Lonnie Brooks Blues Band, The Son Seals Blues Band, Mighty Joe Young, Muddy Waters, Koko Taylor & Her Blues Machine, Willie Dixon and The Chicago Blues Allstars) (XRT/Alligator)
FROM THE HEART OF A WOMAN - Koko Taylor (Alligator)
FROZEN ALIVE! - Albert Collins (Alligator)
LIVING CHICAGO BLUES VOL. IV - A.C. Reid and The Spark Plugs, Scotty and The Rib Tips, Lovie Lee with Carey Bell (Alligator)

LATIN RECORDING (G-1073)

(This category is for pure Latin music)

GUAJIRA PA' LA JEVA - Clare Fischer (Track) (Pausa)
BRAZILIAN SOUL - Laurindo Almeida & Charlie Byrd (Album) (Concord Jazz Picante)
EDDIE PALMIERI - Eddie Palmieri (Album) (Barbaro)
GOZAME! PERO YA. . . - Cal Tjader (Album) (Concord Jazz Picante)
"SUMMERTIME" - DIGITAL AT MONTREUX, 1980 - Dizzy Gillespie & Mongo Santamaria (Album) (Pablo Live)

RECORDING FOR CHILDREN (G-1074)

(This category is intended for recordings created specifically for children. All Nominations are albums)

SESAME COUNTRY - (The Muppets, Glen Campbell, Crystal Gayle, Loretta Lynn, Tanya Tucker) Jim Henson, Muppets Creator; Dennis Scott, Album Producer (Sesame St)
ANTS'HILLVANIA - (Pat Boone & Various Artists) Jimmy Owens, Carol Owens, Cherry Boone O'Neill, Writers; Dan Collins, Producer (Birdwing/Sparrow)
BIG BIRD DISCOVERS THE ORCHESTRA - (Big Bird, Voices and Orchestra) Jim Henson, Creator; Arthur Shimkin, Producer (Sesame St)
A CHIPMUNK CHRISTMAS - (The Chipmunks & Santa Claus) Janice Karman & Ross Bagdasarian, Writers & Producers (RCA)
THE FOX AND THE HOUND - (Songs & Dialog from the original motion picture soundtrack featuring Pearl Bailey, Jack Albertson & Mickey Rooney) Elena Engel, Album Producer (Disneyland)

COMEDY RECORDING (G-1075)

(Either spoken word or musical performances are eligible here)

REV. DU RITE - Richard Pryor (Album) (Laff)
AIRPLANE! (Comedy dialog from the original soundtrack) Lloyd Segal, Album Producer (Album) (Regency)
THE INQUISITION - Mel Brooks (Track) (WB)
MEL BROOKS' HISTORY OF THE WORLD PART I - Mel Brooks & Steve Barri, Album Producers (Album) (WB)
URBAN CHIPMUNK - (The Chipmunks) Larry Butler, Janice Karman & Ross Bagdasarian, Album Producers (Album) (RCA)

SPOKEN WORD, DOCUMENTARY OR DRAMA RECORDING (G-1076)

(This category is for non-musical show albums including comedy show albums)

DONOVAN'S BRAIN - Orson Welles (Album) (Radio)
JUSTICE HOLMES' DECISIONS - Read by E.G. Marshall, Introductory Commentary Read by Louis Nizer (Album) (Caedmon)
THE MC CARTNEY INTERVIEW (Originally recorded for Musician: Player & Listener Magazine) Paul McCartney; Vic Garbarini, Interviewer (Album) (Columbia)
'TWAS THE NIGHT BEFORE CHRISTMAS - Ed McMahon (Track) (Livingsong)
VLADIMIR NABOKOV: LOLITA - James Mason (Album) (Caedmon)

INSTRUMENTAL COMPOSITION (G-1077)

(A Composer's Award for an original non-classical composition)

THEME FROM HILL STREET BLUES - Mike Post
ALTERED STATES - John Corigliano
AS FALLS WICHITA, SO FALLS WICHITA FALLS - Pat Metheny & Lyle Mays
FOR AN UNFINISHED WOMAN - Gerry Mulligan
THE SLAVES - Jerry Goldsmith

ORIGINAL SCORE - MOTION PICTURE OR A TELEVISION SPECIAL (G-1078)

(A Composer's/Songwriter's Award for an original background score or original songs written specifically for the motion picture or television special. All nominations are for the Motion Picture Soundtrack)

RAIDERS OF THE LOST ARK - John Williams (Columbia/CBS)
THE ELEPHANT MAN - John Morris (20th Century Fox)
ENDLESS LOVE - Jonathan Tunick, Lionel Richie & Thomas McClary (Mercury/Polygram)
THE JAZZ SINGER - Neil Diamond, Gilbert Becaud, Alan Lindgren, Richard Bennett & Doug Rhone (Capitol)
9 TO 5 - Charles Fox & Dolly Parton (20th Century Fox)

CAST SHOW ALBUM (G-1079)

(Awards to the Composer(s), Lyricist(s) and Album Producer. Original cast albums, albums by road casts, or working casts including show revival casts, are eligible. Grammys to the Composer(s) of new material & Album Producer. Awards Certificates to Composer(s) & Lyricist(s) of previously released songs)

LENA HORNE: THE LADY AND HER MUSIC LIVE ON BROADWAY - Quincy Jones, Producer (Various Composers & Lyricists) (Qwest/WB)
DUKE ELLINGTON'S SOPHISTICATED LADIES - Thomas Z. Shepard, Producer (Duke Ellington & other composers & lyricists) (RCA)
42ND STREET - Thomas Z. Shepard, Producer (Harry Warren, Composer Al Dubin, Johnny Mercer & Mort Dixon, Lyricists) (RCA)
THE PIRATES OF PENZANCE - Peter Asher, Producer (William S. Gilbert, Lyricist; Arthur Sullivan, Composer) (E/A)
WOMAN OF THE YEAR - John Kander, Composer; Fred Ebb, Lyricist; John McClure, Producer (Arista)

VIDEO OF THE YEAR (G-1080)

(Videos - video cassettes and video discs - in any format are eligible if the programming has been created specifically for the home video market and commercially released for the first time during the Eligibility Year)

MICHAEL NESMITH IN ELEPHANT PARTS - Michael Nesmith (VHS) (Pacific Arts Video)
EAT TO THE BEAT - Blondie (VHS) (Chrysalis/WCI/RCA)
THE FIRST NATIONAL KIDISC - (Various) Video Producer: Bruce Seth Green (Videodisc) (OPA/MCA)
ONE-NIGHT STAND: A KEYBOARD EVENT - (Eubie Blake, Kenny Barron, Arthur Blythe, Ron Carter, Stanley Clarke, George Duke, Charles Earland, Rodney Franklin, Herbie Hancock, Sir Roland Hanna, Bobby Hutcherson, Bob James, Hubert Laws, Buddy Williams) Video Producer: Richard Namm (VHS) (CBS Video Enterprises)
PAUL SIMON - Paul Simon (Disc) (Pioneer Artists)

JAZZ FUSION PERFORMANCE, VOCAL OR INSTRUMENTAL (G-1081)

(This is for any type of borderline jazz performance; rock, pop, R&B, classical, etc)

WINELIGHT - Grover Washington, Jr (Album) (E/A)
APPLE JUICE - Tom Scott (Album) (Col/CBS)
AS FALLS WICHITA, SO FALLS WICHITA FALLS - Pat Metheny/Lyle Mays (Album) (ECM)
THE MAN WITH THE HORN - Miles Davis (Album) (Col/CBS)
NIGHT PASSAGE - Weather Report (Album) (ARC/CBS)

JAZZ VOCAL - FEMALE (G-1082)

(Solo performance) (All nominations are albums)

DIGITAL III AT MONTREUX - Ella Fitzgerald (Pablo Live)
HELEN - Helen Humes (Muse)
THE JANET LAWSON QUINTET - Janet Lawson (Inner City/Music Minus One)
NEVER MAKE YOUR MOVE TOO SOON - Ernestine Anderson (Concord Jazz)
SAVE YOUR LOVE FOR ME - Etta Jones (Muse)

JAZZ VOCAL - MALE (G-1083)

(Solo performance)

BLUE RONDO ALA TURK - Al Jarreau (Track) (WB)
HAVE NO FEAR, JOE TURNER IS HERE - Joe Turner (Album) (Pablo)
MEL TORME & FRIENDS RECORDED LIVE AT MARTY'S NEW YORK CITY - Mel Torme (Album) (Finesse/CBS)
MUSIC'S THE ONLY THING THAT'S ON MY MIND - Jimmy Rowles (Track) (Progressive)
JOHNNY HARTMAN ONCE IN EVERY LIFE - Johnny Hartman (Album) (Bee Hive)

JAZZ VOCAL - DUO OR GROUP (G-1084)

(This category is for a duo/group performance)

UNTIL I MET YOU (CORNER POCKET) - The Manhattan Transfer (Track) (Atlantic)
CLARE FISCHER & SALSA PICANTE PRESENT 2 ∎ 2 - Clare Fischer's 2 ∎ 2 (Album) (Pausa)
EAST OF SUEZ - Jackie & Roy (Album) (Concord Jazz)
NOW - The Hi-Lo's (Album) (Pausa)
SILLY HABITS - Mel Torme & Janis Ian (Track) (Finesse/CBS)

JAZZ INSTRUMENTAL - SOLOIST (G-1085)

(This category is for a solo instrumental performance with or without a group or band. All nominations are albums)

BYE BYE BLACKBIRD - John Coltrane (Pablo)
THE INCREDIBLE IRA SULLIVAN - Ira Sullivan (Stash)
THE MASTER. . .PEPPER ADAMS - Pepper Adams (Muse)
MUSIC'S THE ONLY THING ON MY MIND - Jimmy Rowles (Progressive)
SELF PORTRAIT - Pete Christlieb (Bosco 1)

JAZZ INSTRUMENTAL - GROUP (G-1086)

(This category is for an instrumental group. All nominations here are albums)

CHICK COREA AND GARY BURTON IN CONCERT, ZURICH, OCTOBER 28, 1979 - Chick Corea & Gary Burton (ECM)
LIVE AT THE VILLAGE VANGUARD - Red Rodney Featuring Ira Sullivan (Muse)
NONPAREIL - Al Cohn (Concord)
THE SWINGER - Zoot Sims (Pablo)
VIC DICKENSON QUINTET - Vic Dickenson (Storyville)

JAZZ INSTRUMENTAL - BIG BAND (G-1087)

(This category is primarily for a big band sound)

WALK ON THE WATER - Gerry Mulligan and his Orchestra (Album) (DRG)
BURNIN' (BLUES FOR BIRD) - Don Menza & His '80's Big Band (Track) (RealTime)
PANAMA FRANCIS AND THE SAVOY SULTANS-VOL II - Panama Francis and the Savoy Sultans (Album) (Classic Jazz)
TANUKI'S NIGHT OUT - Toshiko Akiyoshi - Lew Tabackin Big Band (Album) (Jazz America Marketing)
TRIBUTE - Rob McConnell & The Boss Brass (Album) (Pausa)

INSTRUMENTAL ARRANGEMENT (G-1088)

(An Instrumental Arranger's Award. This category is for an instrumental arrangement on an instrumental recording, released for the first time during the Eligibility Year on either a single or an album track)

VELAS - Quincy Jones (Track) Quincy Jones, Arranger; Johnny Mandel, Synthesizer & String Arranger (A&M)
A BIT BYAS'D - Toshiko Akiyoshi - Lew Tabackin Big Band (Track) Toshiko Akiyoshi, Arranger (Jazz America Marketing)
MOUNTAIN DANCE - Dave Grusin (Track) Dave Grusin, Arranger (GRP/Arista)
THE SLAVES - Jerry Goldsmith (Track) Jerry Goldsmith, Arranger (MCA)
SOUTH RAMPART STREET PARADE - John Williams, Boston Pops (Track) Billy May, Arranger (Philips)

ARRANGEMENT ACCOMPANYING VOCAL(S) (G-1089)

(An Instrumental Arranger's Award. This category is for an instrumental arrangement accompanying a solo vocalist, a vocal duo, vocal group or chorus, released for the first time during the Eligibility Year on either a single or an album track)

AI NO CORRIDA - Quincy Jones (Track) Quincy Jones & Jerry Hey
AND THE MELODY STILL LINGERS ON (NIGHT IN TUNISIA) - Chaka Khan (Track) Arif Mardin (WB)
DU, DU - 2 ▮ 2 - (Track) Clare Fischer (Pausa)
LIVING INSIDE MYSELF - Gino Vannelli (Track) Gino Vannelli, Joe Vannelli & Ross Vannelli (Arista)
WHAT IS HIP - Tower Of Power (Track) Greg Adams (Sheffield Lab)

ARRANGEMENT FOR VOICES (G-1090)

(A Vocal Arranger's Award. This category covers all voices on a recording, excluding a featured soloist, if any. It may include a cappella as well as voices with instrumental accompaniment)

A NIGHTINGALE SANG IN BERKELEY SQUARE - The Manhattan Transfer (Track) Gene Puerling (Atlantic)
DU, DU - 2 ▮ 2 - Clare Fischer (Track) (Pausa)
KAFKA - The Manhattan Transfer (Track) Bernard Kafka & Jay Graydon (Atlantic)
THE NIGHT WE CALLED IT A DAY - The Hi-Lo's (Track) Gene Puerling (Pausa)
(THE WORD OF) CONFIRMATION - The Manhattan Transfer (Track) Milcho Leviev (Atlantic)

ALBUM PACKAGE (G-1091)

(An Art Director's Award. This category is for either classical or non-classical single-jacket or multiple pocket album packages)

TATTOO YOU - Rolling Stones - Peter Carriston (Rolling Stones)
EAGLES LIVE - Eagles - Kosh (E/A)
POSITIVE TOUCH - Undertones - Bush Hollyhead (Harvest/Capitol)
SOCIAL STUDIES - Carla Bley - Carla Bley & Paul McDonough (ECM)
WORKING CLASS DOG - Rick Springfield - Mike Doud (RCA)

ALBUM NOTES (G-1092)

(An Album Notes Writer's Award. This category is for an original writing for a specific album. Either classical or non-classical albums qualify)

ERROLL GARNER: MASTER OF THE KEYBOARD - Dan Morgenstern (Book-of-the-Month Records)
FATS WALLER (GIANTS OF JAZZ) - David Thomson & Philip W. Payne (Time-Life)
JAMES P. JOHNSON (GIANTS OF JAZZ) - Dick Wellstood with Willa

Rouder & Frank Kappler (Time-Life)
THE MARIO LANZA COLLECTION - C. P. Crumpacker (RCA/Red Seal)
PEE WEE RUSSELL (GIANTS OF JAZZ) - John McDonough (Time-Life)

HISTORICAL ALBUM (G-1093)

(Grammys to the Reissue Album Producer(s) for a new album released during the Eligibility Year, whose predominant contents (over 50%) were recorded at least 25 years before the start of the Eligibility Year. Excluded are reissues of old albums that have no change in their sequence of tracks or packages)

HOAGY CARMICHAEL: FROM "STAR DUST" TO "OLE BUTTERMILK SKY" - George Spitzer & Michael Brooks (Book-of-the-Month)
BIRMINGHAM QUARTET ANTHOLOGY - (Various) Doug Seroff, Producer (Clanka/Lanka)
MILES DAVIS: CHRONICLE THE COMPLETE PRESTIGE RECORDINGS - Orrin Keepnews (Prestige)
THE QUINTET OF THE HOT CLUB OF FRANCE (1936-1937) (Django Reinhardt/Stephane Grappelli) - Kevin Yatarola (Inner City/Music Minus One)
THE SMITHSONIAN COLLECTION OF CLASSIC COUNTRY MUSIC - (Various) Bill C. Malone & Bill Bennett (Smithsonian)

BEST ENGINEERED RECORDING (G-1094)

(Non-Classical. All nominations are albums)

GAUCHO - Steely Dan - Roger Nichols, Elliot Scheiner, Bill Schnee & Jerry Garszza (MCA)
THE DUDE - Quincy Jones - Bruce Swedien (A&M)
ESCAPE - Journey - Mike Stone & Kevin Elson (Columbia/CBS)
TURN OF A FRIENDLY CARD - Alan Parsons Project - Alan Parsons (Arista)
ZENYATTA MONDATTA - Police - Nigel Gray (A&M)

PRODUCER OF THE YEAR (NON-CLASSICAL) (G-1095)

(A Producer's Award for consistently outstanding creativity in producing. Listed below are examples of producer's activities. (A)Album; (S)Single; (T)Track)

QUINCY JONES - "Ai No Corrida" (S), Quincy Jones; "The Dude" (A), Quincy Jones; "Every Home Should Have One" (A), Patti Austin; "Just Once" (featuring James Ingram) (S); "Lena Horne: The Lady and Her Music Live On Broadway" (A); "100 Ways" (Featuring James Ingram) (T)
VAL GARAY - "Bette Davis Eyes" (S), Kim Carnes; "Deep Inside My Heart" (S), Randy Meisner; "Draw of the Card" (T), Kim Carnes; "Mistaken Identity" (A), Kim Carnes; "One More Song" (A), Randy Meisner
ROBERT JOHN "MUTT" LANGE AND MICK JONES - "4" (A), Foreigner; "Urgent" (S), Foreigner; "Waiting For A Girl Like You" (S), Foreigner
ARIF MARDIN - "Love All the Hurt Away" (A), Aretha Franklin; "Love All the Hurt Away" (S), Aretha Franklin & George Benson; "What Cha' Gonna Do For Me" (A), Chaka Khan; "What Cha' Gonna Do For Me" (S), Chaka Khan
LIONEL RICHIE - "Endless Love" (S), Diana Ross & Lionel Richie; "I Don't Need You" (S), Kenny Rogers; "Share Your Love" (A), Kenny Rogers; "Through The Years" (T), Kenny Rogers

CLASSICAL ALBUM (G-1096)

(Grammys to the Artist, and to the Album Producer if other than the artist. Certificates to the Engineer(s) and Orchestra if applicable)

MAHLER: SYMPHONY NO. 2 IN C MINOR - Sir Georg Solti cond Chicago Symphony Orchestra & Chorus/Isobel Buchanan, Mira Zakai; James Mallinson, Producer (London)
THE HOROWITZ CONCERTS 1979/80 - Vladimir Horowitz - John Pfeiffer, Producer (RCA)
ISAAC STERN 60TH ANNIVERSARY CELEBRATION - Isaac Stern, Itz-

hak Perlman, Pinchas Zukerman/Zubin Mehta cond New York Philharmonic; Andrew Kazdin, Producer (CBS)
LIVE FROM LINCOLN CENTER - SUTHERLAND - HORNE - PAVAROTTI - Joan Sutherland, Marilyn Horne, Luciano Pavarotti/Richard Bonynge cond New York City Opera Orchestra; Ray Minshull, Producer (London)
THE UNKNOWN KURT WEILL - Teresa Stratas - Eric Salzman, Producer (Nonesuch)

CLASSICAL PERFORMANCE - ORCHESTRA (G-1097)

(Grammys to the Conductor and Album Producer. Certificate to the Classical Orchestra)

MAHLER: SYMPHONY NO. 2 IN C MINOR - Sir Georg Solti cond Chicago Symphony; James Mallinson, Producer (London)
GERSHWIN: PORGY & BESS (SYMPHONIC PICTURE)/CUBAN OVERTURE & SECOND RHAPSODY - Andre Previn cond London Symphony; Suvi Raj Grubb, Producer (Angel)
HOLST: THE PLANETS - Simon Rattle cond Philharmonia Orchestra; John Willan, Producer (Angel)
MAHLER: SYMPHONY NO. 10 (Deryck Cooke Final Version) - James Levine cond Philadelphia Orchestra; Jay David Saks, Producer (RCA)
(MOZART) THE SYMPHONIES: SALZBURG 1775-1783, VOL. 5 - Christopher Hogwood & Jaap Schroder, Conductors, Academy of Ancient Music; Morten Winding, Producer (L'Oiseau-Lyre)

OPERA RECORDING (G-1098)

(Grammys to the Conductor, Album Producer and Principal Soloists)

JANACEK: FROM THE HOUSE OF THE DEAD - Sir Charles Mackerras cond Vienna Philharmonic/Principal Soloists: Jiri Zahradnicek, Vaclav Zitek, Ivo Zidek; James Mallinson, Producer (London)
BERG: WOZZECK - Christoph von Dohnanyi cond Vienna Philharmonic & Vienna State Opera Chorus/Principal Solists: Eberhard Waechter, Anja Silja; Christopher Raeburn & Michael Haas, Producers (London)
KORNGOLD: VIOLANTA - Marek Janowski cond Munich Radio Orchestra/Bavarian Radio Chorus/Principal Soloists: Eva Marton, Siegfried Jerusalem, Walter Berry, Ruth Hesse; George Korngold, Producer (CBS)
MONTEVERDI: IL RITORNO D'ULISSE IN PATRIA - Raymond Leppard cond London Philharmonic/Glyndebourne Chorus/Principal Soloists: Frederica von Stade, Richard Stillwell; David Mottley, Producer (CBS)
PUCCINI: LE VILLI - Lorin Maazel cond National Philharmonic/Ambrosian Opera Chorus/Principal Soloists: Renata Scotto, Placido Domingo, Leo Nucci, Tito Gobbi; Paul Myers, Producer (CBS)
ROSSINI: L'ITALIANA IN ALGERI - Claudio Scimone cond I Solisti Veneti/Chorus of Prague/Principal Soloists: Marilyn Horne, Samuel Ramey, Kathleen Battle, Ernesto Palacio; Michel Gacin, Producer (RCA)
WAGNER: PARSIFAL - Herbert von Karajan cond Berlin Philharmonic/Chorus of Deutsche Oper Berlin/Principal Soloists: Peter Hofmann, Dunja Vejzovic, Kurt Moll, Jose van Dam, Siegmund Nimsgern, Victor von Halem; Guenther Breest, Producer (DG)

CHORAL PERFORMANCE - OTHER THAN OPERA (G-1099)

HAYDN: THE CREATION - Neville Marriner, Conductor - Chorus of Academy of St. Martin-in-the Fields & Academy of St. Martin-in-the-Fields (Philips)
ORFF: CARMINA BURANA - Robert Shaw, Conductor - Atlanta Symphony Chorus/Atlanta Boy Choir/Atlanta Symphony (Telarc)
ORFF: CARMINA BURANA - Richard Cooke, Choral Conductor - London Symphony Orchestra Chorus/Eduardo Mata, Conductor - London Symphony (RCA)
PROKOFIEV: IVAN THE TERRIBLE from MUSIC FROM THE FILMS - Thomas Peck, Choral Director - Saint Louis Symphony Chorus/Leonard Slatkin, Conductor - Saint Louis Symphony (Vox Cum Laude)
VERDI: REQUIEM - Richard Westenburg, Choral Conductor - Musica Sacra Chorus/Zubin Mehta, Conductor - New York Philharmonic (CBS)

CHAMBER MUSIC PERFORMANCE (G-1100)

(Instrumental or Vocal)

TCHAIKOVSKY: PIANO TRIO IN A MINOR - Itzhak Perlman, Lynn Harrell, Vladimir Ashkenazy (Angel)
BARTOK: DUOS FOR TWO VIOLINS - Itzhak Perlman & Pinchas Zukerman (Angel)
BARTOK: QUARTETS FOR STRINGS (6) COMPLETE - Toyko String Quartet (DG)
THE COMPLETE STRING QUARTETS OF BRAHMS & SCHUMANN - Guarneri Quartet (RCA)
OBOE QUARTETS (MOZART, J.C. BACH, KARL STAMITZ, WANHAL) - Ray Still, Itzhak Perlman, Pinchas Zukerman, Lynn Harrell (Angel)

CLASSICAL PERFORMANCE - INSTRUMENTAL SOLOIST(S) (WITH ORCHESTRA) (G-1101)

ISAAC STERN 50TH ANNIVERSARY CELEBRATION - Isaac Stern, Itzhak Perlman, Pinchas Zukerman (Zubin Mehta cond New York Philharmonic) (CBS)
CHOPIN: CONCERTO FOR PIANO NO. 1 IN E MINOR - Emanuel Ax (Eugene Ormandy cond Philadelphia Orchestra) (RCA)
CORIGLIANO: CONCERTO FOR CLARINET & ORCHESTRA - Stanley Drucker (Zubin Mehta cond New York Philharmonic) (New World)
FRENCH FLUTE CONCERTOS - James Galway (Charles Dutoit cond Royal Philharmonic) (RCA)
SIBELIUS: CONCERTO FOR VIOLIN IN D MINOR SAINT-SAENS: INTRODUCTION & RONDO CAPRICCIOSO - Dylana Jenson (Eugene Ormandy cond Philadelphia Orchestra) (RCA)

CLASSICAL PERFORMANCE - INSTRUMENTAL SOLOIST(S) (WITHOUT ORCHESTRA) (G-1102)

THE HOROWITZ CONCERTS 1979/80 - Vladimir Horowitz (RCA)
ARTUR RUBINSTEIN - SCHUMANN - RAVEL - DEBUSSY - ALBENIZ - Artur Rubinstein (RCA)
BARTOK: SONATA FOR PIANO (1926)/IMPROVISATIONS ON HUNGARIAN PEASANT SONGS/SUITE, OP. 14 - Murray Perahia (CBS)
ITZHAK PERLMAN PLAYS FRITZ KREISLER, ALBUM 3 - Itzhak Perlman (Samuel Sanders, Accompanist) (Angel)
VIRTUOSO VIOLIN - Pinchas Zukerman (Marc Neikrug, Accompanist) (CBS)

CLASSICAL PERFORMANCE - VOCAL SOLOIST (G-1103)

(Grammy to the vocal soloist. Certificate to accompanist or orchestra conductor, whichever is featured on the recording)

LIVE FROM LINCOLN CENTER - SUTHERLAND - HORNE - PAVAROTTI - Joan Sutherland, Marilyn Horne, Luciano Pavarotti (Richard Bonynge cond New York City Opera Orchestra) (London)
DEL TREDICI: FINAL ALICE - Barbara Hendricks (Sir Georg Solti cond Chicago Symphony) (London)
RAVEL: SHEHERAZADE/FROM CINQ MELODIES POPULAIRES GRECQUES/DEUX MELODIES HEBRAIQUES/CHANSONS MADECASSES - Frederica von Stade (Seiji Ozawa cond Boston Symphony) (CBS)
THINK ON ME - Elly Ameling (Dalton Baldwin, Accompanist) (CBS)
THE UNKNOWN KURT WEILL - Teresa Stratas (Richard Woitach, Accompanist) (Nonesuch)

BEST ENGINEERED RECORDING - CLASSICAL (G-1104)

ISAAC STERN 60TH ANNIVERSARY CELEBRATION - Isaac Stern, Itzhak Perlman, Pinchas Zukerman/Zubin Mehta cond New York Philharmonic; Bud Graham, Ray Moore & Andrew Kazdin, Engineers (CBS)
HOLST: THE PLANETS - Simon Rattle cond Philharmonia Orchestra/Ambrosian Singers; Michael Sheady, Engineer (Angel)
MAHLER: SYMPHONY NO. 10 - (Deryck Cooke Final Version) - James Levine cond Philadelphia Orchestra; Paul Goodman, Jules Bloomenthal, Sydney Davis & Don Morrison, Engineers (RCA)

ORFF: CARMINA BURANA - Eduardo Mata cond London Symphony/ Richard Cooke cond London Symphony Chorus/Hendricks, Aler, Hagegard; Michael Gray and Paul Goodman, Engineers (RCA)
ORFF: CARMINA BURANA/HINDEMITH: SYMPHONIC METAMORPHOSIS OF THEMES BY WEBER - Robert Shaw cond Atlanta Symphony Orchestra & Chorus/Atlanta Boys Choir/Blegen, Brown, Hagegard; Jack Renner, Jules Bloomenthal, Sydney Davis & Jim Wolvington, Engineers (Telarc)

1982 HALL OF FAME WINNERS (G-1106)

BIRTH OF THE COOL - Miles Davis (Album) (Capitol) Released in 1957
GOD BLESS AMERICA - Kate Smith (Victor) Released in 1939
I'LL NEVER SMILE AGAIN - Tommy Dorsey with Frank Sinatra & The Pied Pipers (Victor) Released in 1940
ROCK AROUND THE CLOCK - Bill Haley & The Comets (Decca) Released in 1955
SING, SING, SING - Benny Goodman (Original Recording) (Victor) Released in 1937

1982

CLASSICAL PRODUCER OF THE YEAR (G-1105)

(A Producer's Award for consistently outstanding creativity in producing. Listed below are examples of producer's activities)

JAMES MALLINSON: BRUCKNER: SYMPHONY NO. 5 - Sir Georg Solti cond Chicago Symphony (London); **DEL TREDICI: FINAL ALICE** - Barbara Hendricks/Sir Georg Solti cond Chicago Symphony (London); **JANACEK: FROM THE HOUSE OF THE DEAD** - Sir Charles Mackerras cond Vienna Philharmonic/Principal Soloists: Jiri Zahradnicek, Vaclav Zitek, Ivo Zidek (London); **MAHLER: SYMPHONY NO. 2 IN C MINOR** - Sir Georg Solti cond Chicago Symphony Orchestra & Chorus/Isobel Buchanan, Mira Zakai (London); **ROSSINI: WILLIAM TELL** - Riccardo Chailly cond National Philharmonic/Principal Soloists: Luciano Pavarotti, Mirella Freni, Sherrill Milnes (London); **STRAVINSKY: PETRUSHKA** - Antal Dorati cond Detroit Symphony (London)
STEVEN EPSTEIN: BEETHOVEN: SYMPHONY NO. 5 IN C MINOR (CBS); SCHUBERT: SYMPHONY NO. 8 IN D MINOR ("UNFINISHED") - Lorin Maazel cond Vienna Philharmonic (CBS); BIZET: L'ARLESIENNE SUITES NOS. 1 & 2/PETITE SUITES - Andrew Davis cond Toronto Symphony (CBS); BRAHMS: CONCERTO FOR PIANO NO. 1 Lazar Berman/Erich Leinsdorf cond Chicago Symphony (CBS); DVORAK: QUARTETS FOR PIANO & STRINGS NOS. 1 & 2 - Rudolf Firkusny/Members of Juilliard Quartet (CBS); TSCHAIKOVSKY: MANFRED SYMPHONY - Michael Tilson Thomas cond London Symphony (CBS); VIVALDI: THE FOUR SEASONS - Pinchas Zukerman/Pinchas Zukerman cond St. Paul Chamber Orchestra (CBS)
ANDREW KAZDIN: BERLIOZ: SYMPHONIE FANTASTIQUE - Lorin Maazel cond Cleveland Orchestra (CBS); CHOPIN: CONCERTO FOR PIANO NO. 1 - Murray Perahia/Zubin Mehta cond New York Philharmonic (CBS); CORIGLIANO: CONCERTO FOR CLARINET & ORCHESTRA/BARBER: THIRD ESSAY FOR ORCHESTRA - Stanley Drucker/Zubin Mehta cond New York Philharmonic (New World); ISAAC STERN 60TH ANNIVERSARY CELEBRATION - Isaac Stern, Itzhak Perlman, Pinchas Zukerman/Zubin Mehta cond New York Philharmonic Orchestra (CBS); TSCHAIKOVSKY: CONCERTO FOR PIANO NO. 1 - Emil Gilels/Zubin Mehta cond New York Philharmonic (CBS)
JAY DAVID SAKS: CHOPIN: CONCERTO FOR PIANO NO. 1 - Emanuel Ax/Eugene Ormandy cond Philadelphia Orchestra (RCA); MAHLER: SYMPHONY NO. 10 - (Deryck Cooke Final Version) - James Levine cond Philadelphia Orchestra (RCA); ORFF: CARMINA BURANA - Eduardo Mata cond London Symphony Orchestra and Chorus/Hendricks, Aler, Hagegard (RCA); SCHUMANN: SYMPHONIES(4) - James Levine cond Philadelphia Orchestra (RCA); SIBELIUS: CONCERTO FOR VIOLIN IN D MINOR - Dylana Jenson/Eugene Ormandy cond Philadelphia Orchestra (RCA); THE VILLAGE BAND - The Canadian Brass (RCA)
ROBERT WOODS: BEETHOVEN: CONCERTO FOR PIANO & ORCHESTRA NO. 5 IN E FLAT MAJOR - Rudolf Serkin/Seiji Ozawa cond Boston Symphony (Telarc); BEETHOVEN: SYMPHONY NO. 5 IN C MINOR - Seiji Ozawa cond Boston Symphony (Telarc); DVORAK: SYMPHONY NO. 9 IN E MINOR ("NEW WORLD") - Leonard Slatkin cond St. Louis Symphony (Telarc); ORFF: CARMINA BURANA/HINDEMITH: SYMPHONIC METAMORPHOSIS OF THEMES BY WEBER - Robert Shaw cond Atlanta Symphony Orchestra & Chorus/Atlanta Boy Choir/Blegen, Hagegard, Brown (Telarc); RAVEL: BOLERO/DAPHNIS ET CHLOE SUITE NO. 2/PAVANE POUR UNE INFANTE DEFUNTE - Leonard Slatkin cond St. Louis Symphony (Telarc); STRAVINSKY: THE RITE OF SPRING - Lorin Maazel cond Cleveland Orchestra (Telarc)

RECORD OF THE YEAR: (G-1107)

(Grammys to the artist, and to producer if other than the artist. This category is for singles. An album track released as a single during the awards year is eligible if it did not receive a previous nomination or award).

ROSANNA - Toto; Toto, producer (Columbia)
ALWAYS ON MY MIND - Willie Nelson; Chips Moman, producer (Columbia)
CHARIOTS OF FIRE - Vangelis; Vangelis, producer (Polydor)
EBONY & IVORY - Paul McCartney and Stevie Wonder; George Martin, producer (Columbia)
STEPPIN' OUT - Joe Jackson; David Kershenbaum and Joe Jackson, producers (A&M)

ALBUM OF THE YEAR: (G-1108)

(Grammys to the artist, and to producer if other than the artist. This category is for nonclassical albums.)

TOTO IV - Toto; Toto, album producer (CBS/Columbia)
AMERICAN FOOL - John Cougar; John Cougar Mellencamp and Don Gehman, album producers (Riva/Polygram)
THE NIGHTFLY - Donald Fagen; Gary Katz, album producer (WB)
THE NYLON CURTAIN - Billy Joel; Phil Ramone, album producer (CBS/Columbia)
TUG OF WAR - Paul McCartney; George Martin, album producer (Columbia)

SONG OF THE YEAR: (G-1109)

(A songwriter's award. Any song is eligible if a new recording of it has been released commercially during the eligibility year, provided it did not receive a previous nomination or award in a sonwriting category.)

ALWAYS ON MY MIND - Johnny Christopher, Mark James, Wayne Thompson, songwriters; Screen Gems, EMI Music Inc & Rose Bridge Music, publishers (CBS)
EBONY & IVORY - Paul McCartney, songwriter; MPL, publisher (CBS/Columbia)
EYE OF THE TIGER - Frankie Sullivan, Jim Peterik, songwriters; Holey Moley Music/Rude Music/WB Music/Easy Action Music, publishers (Scotti Bros/CBS)
I.G.Y. (WHAT A BEAUTIFUL WORLD) - Donald Fagen, songwriter; Freejunket Music, publisher (WB)
ROSANNA - David Paich, songwriter; Hudmar Publishing, publisher (CBS/Columbia)

NEW ARTIST: (G-1110)

(This category is for an artist or organized group whose first recording was released during the eligibility year.)

MEN AT WORK - (Columbia)
ASIA - (Geffen/WB)
JENNIFER HOLLIDAY - (Geffen/WB)
THE HUMAN LEAGUE - (A&M)
STRAY CATS - (EMI/America)

POP VOCAL–FEMALE: (G-1111)

(This category is for a solo performance.)

YOU SHOULD HEAR HOW SHE TALKS ABOUT YOU - Melissa Manchester (Arista)
GET CLOSER - Linda Ronstadt (Asylum-E/A)
GLORIA - Laura Branigan (Atlantic)
HEART ATTACK - Olivia Newton-John (MCA)
LOVE'S BEEN A LITTLE BIT HARD ON ME - Juice Newton (Capitol)

POP VOCAL–MALE: (G-1112)

(This category is for a solo performance.)

TRULY - Lionel Richie (Motown)
BLUE EYES - Elton John (Geffen/WB)
DON'T TALK TO STRANGERS - Rick Springfield (RCA)
I.G.Y. (WHAT A BEAUTIFUL WORLD) - Donald Fagen (WB)
I KEEP FORGETTING (EVERYTIME YOU'RE NEAR) - Michael McDonald (WB)
STEPPIN' OUT - Joe Jackson (A&M)

POP VOCAL–DUO OR GROUP WITH VOCAL: (G-1113)

(All recordings on which the group receives artist billing on the label are eligible here even though the vocal may feature only one member of the group.)

UP WHERE WE BELONG - Joe Cocker and Jennifer Warnes (Island)
EBONY & IVORY - Paul McCartney and Stevie Wonder (Columbia)
HARD TO SAY I'M SORRY - Chicago (Full Moon/WB)
MANEATER - Daryl Hall & John Oates (RCA)
ROSANNA - Toto (Columbia)

POP INSTRUMENTAL: (G-1114)

(Pure instrumentals, or instrumentals with vocal coloring, are eligible here.)

CHARIOTS OF FIRE (Theme) (Dance Version) - Ernie Watts (Qwest/WB)
AS WE SPEAK - David Sanborn (WB)
CRAZY FOR YOU - Earl Klugh (Liberty/Capitol)
E.T. (Music from the original motion picture soundtrack) - John Williams (MCA)
HOOKED ON CLASSICS - Louis Clark conducting The Royal Philharmonic Orchestra (RCA)

ROCK VOCAL–FEMALE: (G-1115)

(This category is for a solo performance.)

SHADOWS OF THE NIGHT - Pat Benatar (Chrysalis)
GET CLOSER - Linda Ronstadt (Asylum-E/A)
GREEN LIGHT - Bonnie Raitt (WB)
PROTECTION - Donna Summer (Geffen/WB)
VOYEUR - Kim Carnes (EMI/America)

ROCK VOCAL–MALE: (G-1116)

(This category is for a solo performance.)

HURTS SO GOOD - John Cougar (Riva/Polygram)
DIRTY LAUNDRY - Don Henley (Elektra)
I GET EXCITED - Rick Springfield (RCA)
SHOCK THE MONKEY - Peter Gabriel (Geffen/WB)
TONIGHT I'M YOURS - Rod Stewart (WB)

ROCK PERFORMANCE–DUO OR GROUP WITH VOCAL: (G-1117)

(All recordings on which the group receives artist billing on the label are eligible here even though the vocal may feature only one member of the group.)

EYE OF THE TIGER - Survivor (Scotti Bros/CBS)
ASIA - Asia (Geffen/WB)
CENTERFOLD - J Geils Band (EMI/America)

DON'T FIGHT IT - Kenny Loggins with Steve Perry (CBS/Columbia)
VALLEY GIRL - Frank & Moon Zappa (Barking Pumpkin)

ROCK INSTRUMENTAL: (G-1118)

(Pure instrumentals, or instrumentals with vocal coloring, are eligible here.)

D.N.A. - A Flock Of Seagulls (Jive/Arista)
DON'T STOP - Maynard Ferguson (Columbia)
INDUSTRY STANDARD - The Dregs (Arista)
REQUIEM - King Crimson (EB/WB)
SCANDINAVIA - Van Morrison (WB)

R&B VOCAL–FEMALE: (G-1119)

(This category is for a solo performance.)

AND I AM TELLING YOU I'M NOT GOING - Jennifer Holliday (Geffen/WB)
FORGET ME NOTS - Patrice Rushen (Elektra)
IT'S GONNA TAKE A MIRACLE - Deniece Williams (Columbia)
JUMP TO IT - Aretha Franklin (Arista)
LOVE IS IN CONTROL (FINGER ON THE TRIGGER) - Donna Summer (Geffen/WB)
MUSCLES - Diana Ross (RCA)

R&B VOCAL–MALE: (G-1120)

(This category is for a solo performance.)

SEXUAL HEALING - Marvin Gaye (Columbia/CBS)
DO I DO - Stevie Wonder (Tamla/Motown)
FOREVER, FOR ALWAYS, FOR LOVE - Luther Vandross (Epic/CBS)
THE OTHER WOMAN - Ray Parker Jr (Arista)
TURN YOUR LOVE AROUND - George Benson (WB)

R&B PERFORMANCE–DUO OR GROUP WITH VOCAL: (G-1121)

(All recordings on which the group receives artist billing on the label are eligible here even though the vocal may feature only one member of the group.)

LET IT WHIP - Dazz Band (Motown)
WANNA BE WITH YOU - Earth, Wind & Fire (ARC/CBS)
A PENNY FOR YOUR THOUGHTS - Tavares (RCA)
STREET LIFE - The Crusaders with BB King and Josie James (MCA)
WHAT'S THAT YOU'RE DOING - Paul McCartney and Stevie Wonder (Columbia)

R&B INSTRUMENTAL: (G-1122)

(Pure instrumentals, or instrumentals with vocal coloring, are eligible here.)

SEXUAL HEALING - Marvin Gaye (Columbia/CBS)
BOOGIE IN YOUR BUTT - Eddie Murphy (Columbia/CBS)
COME MORNING - Grover Washington Jr (Elektra)
NUMBER ONE - Patrice Rushen (Elektra/Asylum)
STRIPES - Spyro Gyra (MCA)

RHYTHM & BLUES SONG: (G-1123)

(A songwriter's award. Any song is eligible if a new recording of it has been released commercially during the eligibility year, provided it did not receive a previous nomination or award in a songwriting category.)

TURN YOUR LOVE AROUND - Jay Graydon, Steve Lukather, Bill Champlin, songwriters; Garden Rake Music, Rehtakul Veets Music, JSH Music, publishers.
DO I DO - Stevie Wonder, songwriter; Jobete Music Co & Black Bull Music, publishers.
IT'S GONNA TAKE A MIRACLE - Teddy Randazzo, Bobby Weinstein, Lou Stallman, songwriters; Vogue Music, publisher.
LET IT WHIP - Reggie Andrews, Leon "Ndugu" Chancler, songwriters; Ujima Music & MacVacalac Music, publishers.

SEXUAL HEALING - Marvin Gaye, O Brown, songwriters; April Music Inc, publisher.
THAT GIRL - Stevie Wonder, songwriter; Jobete Music & Black Bull Music, publishers.

COUNTRY VOCAL–FEMALE: (G-1124)

(This category is for a solo performance.)

BREAK IT TO ME GENTLY - Juice Newton (Capitol)
AIN'T NO MONEY - Rosanne Cash (Columbia)
CIMARRON - Emmylou Harris (WB)
I WILL ALWAYS LOVE YOU - Dolly Parton (RCA)
NOBODY - Sylvia (RCA)

COUNTRY VOCAL–MALE: (G-1125)

(This category is for a solo performance.)

ALWAYS ON MY MIND - Willie Nelson (Columbia/CBS)
HE GOT YOU - Ronnie Milsap (RCA)
HEARTBROKE - Ricky Skaggs (Epic/CBS)
LOVE WILL TURN YOU AROUND - Kenny Rogers (EMI/Liberty-Capitol)
SHE GOT THE GOLDMINE (I GOT THE SHAFT) - Jerry Reed (RCA)

COUNTRY–DUO OR GROUP WITH VOCAL: (G-1126)

(All recordings on which the group receives artist billing on the label are eligible here even though the vocal may feature only one member of the group.)

MOUNTAIN MUSIC - Alabama (RCA)
BOBBIE SUE - Oak Ridge Boys (MCA)
LOVE HURTS - Gram Parsons & Emmylou Harris (Sierra)
(SITTIN' ON) THE DOCK OF THE BAY - Waylon Jennings & Willie Nelson (RCA)
YOU PUT THE BLUE IN ME - The Whites (Elektra/Curb)

COUNTRY INSTRUMENTAL: (G-1127)

(Pure instrumentals, or instrumentals with vocal coloring, are eligible here.)

ALABAMA JUBILEE - Roy Clark (Churchill)
BELOW FREEZING - Doc & Merle Watson (Flying Fish)
FEUDIN' - Poco (MCA)
THE JOE MAPHIS FLAT-PICKING SPECTACULAR - Joe Maphis (CMH)
JUST HOOKED ON COUNTRY - Albert Coleman's Atlanta Pops Orchestra (Epic/CBS)

COUNTRY SONG: (G-1128)

(A songwriter's award. Any song is eligible if a new recording of it has been released commercially during the eligibility year, provided it did not receive a previous nomination or award in a songwriting category.)

ALWAYS ON MY MIND - Johnny Christopher, Wayne Thompson, Mark James, songwriters; Screen Gems, EMI Music Inc & Rose Bridge Music, publishers.
I'M GONNA HIRE A WINO TO DECORATE OUR HOME - D Blackwell, songwriter; Peso Music, Wallet Music, publishers.
NOBODY - Kye Fleming, Dennis W Morgan, songwriters; Tom Collins Music Corp, publisher.
RING ON HER FINGER, TIME ON HER HANDS - Don Goodman, Pam Rose, Mary Ann Kennedy, songwriters; Tree Publishing Co Inc, Love Wheel Music, publishers.
SHE GOT THE GOLDMINE (I GOT THE SHAFT) - Tim DuBois, songwriter; House of Gold Music Inc, publisher.

GOSPEL PERFORMANCE–CONTEMPORARY: (G-1129)

(This category is for contemporary-flavored gospel recordings.)

AGE TO AGE - Amy Grant (Myrrh/Word)
LADY LIVE - Reba Rambo (Light/Lexicon)
STAND BY THE POWER - Imperials (Dayspring/Word)
LIFT UP THE LORD - Sandi Patti (Impact/Benson)
MY TRIBUTE - Andrae Crouch (Light/Lexicon)

GOSPEL PERFORMANCE–TRADITIONAL: (G-1130)

I'M FOLLOWING YOU - Blackwood Brothers (Voice Box)
FEELING AT HOME - Rex Nelon Singers (Canaan/Word)
MAKIN' MY OWN PLACE - Dottie Rambo (Heart Warming/Benson)
O, WHAT A SAVIOR - The Masters V (Skylite-Sing)
SOMETHING SPECIAL - The Cathedrals (Canaan/Word)

SOUL GOSPEL PERFORMANCE–CONTEMPORARY: (G-1131)

HIGHER PLANE - Al Green (Myrrh/Word)
EDWIN HAWKINS LIVE WITH THE OAKLAND SYMPHONY ORCHESTRA - Edwin Hawkins (Myrrh/Word)
FINALLY - Andrae Crouch (Light-E/A)
MIRACLE MAN - Mighty Clouds of Joy (Myrrh/Word)
TOUCH ME, LORD - Larnelle Harris (Impact/Benson)

SOUL GOSPEL PERFORMANCE–TRADITIONAL: (G-1132)

PRECIOUS LORD - Al Green (Myrrh/Word)
HE BELIEVES IN ME - Ben Moore (Priority/CBS)
JESUS IS ALIVE AND WELL - Jessy Dixon (Light/Lexicon)
MIRACLE MAN - Might Clouds of Joy (Myrrh/Word)
WE NEED TO HEAR FROM YOU - Andrae Crouch (Light-E/A)

INSPIRATIONAL PERFORMANCE: (G-1133)

(This category is for religious recordings by other than regular gospel recording artists.)

HE SET MY LIFE TO MUSIC - Barbara Mandrell (MCA/Songbird)
CROSSFIRE - Kansas (Kirshner/CBS)
GOD BLESS AMERICA - Leontyne Price (RCA)
MIRACLE - B J Thomas (Myrrh/Word)
WOULD THEY LOVE HIM DOWN IN SHREVEPORT - Oak Ridge Boys (MCA)

TRADITIONAL BLUES: (G-1134)

(This category is for traditional blues recordings only.)

ALRIGHT AGAIN - Clarence Gatemouth Brown (Rounder)
GENUINE HOUSEROCKING MUSIC - Hound Dog Taylor and the HouseRockers (Alligator)
HE WAS A FRIEND OF MINE - Eddie 'Cleanhead' Vinson & Roomful of Blues (Muse)
THE NEW JOHNNY OTIS SHOW - Johnny Otis (Alligator)
SIPPIE - Sippie Wallace (Atlantic)

ETHNIC OR TRADITIONAL FOLK RECORDING: (G-1135)

(This category is for ethnic and traditional folk recordings only. All nominations here are albums.)

QUEEN IDA AND THE BON TEMPS ZYDECO BAND ON TOUR - Queen Ida (GNP Crescendo)
IN THE TRADITION - Boys of the Lough (Flying Fish)
LIVE IN AMERICA - The John Renbourn Group (Flying Fish)
METROPOLIS - Klezmorim (Flying Fish)
REGGAE SUNSPLASH '81 A TRIBUTE TO BOB MARLEY - Various (Elektra)
TENNESSEE: FOLK HERITAGE - THE MOUNTAINS - Various; album producer, Charles Wolfe (Tennessee Folklore Society)

LATIN RECORDING: (G-1136)

(This category is for pure Latin music. All nominations here are albums.)

MACHITO AND HIS SALSA BIG BAND '82 - Machito (Timeless)
CANCIONES DEL SOLAR DE LOS ABURIDOS - Willie Colon/Ruben Blades (Fania)
ESCENAS DE AMOR - Jose Feliciano (Motown Latino)
MOMENTOS - Julio Iglesias (Disco CBS International)
RHYTHM OF LIFE - Ray Barretto (Fania)

RECORDING FOR CHILDREN: (G-1137)

(This category is intended for recordings created specifically for children. All nominations here are albums.)

IN HARMONY 2 - Billy Joel, Bruce Springsteen, James Taylor, Kenny Loggins, Carly and Lucy Simon, Teddy Pendergrass, Crystal Gayle, Lou Rawls, Deniece Williams, Janis Ian, Dr John; Lucy Simon & David Levine, album producers (CBS)
ANIMALS AND OTHER THINGS - Candle with the Agapeland Singers; Tony Salerno, album producer (Birdwing/Sparrow)
BEST OF FRIENDS - The Smurfs; Frans Erkelens, album producer (Sessions/Starland)
THE CHIPMUNKS GO HOLLYWOOD - The Chipmunks; Janice Karman and Ross Bagdasarian, album producers (RCA)
HERE COMES GARFIELD - Lou Rawls and Desiree Goyette (CBS/Epic)
I AM GOD'S PROJECT - Birdwing Kids Korus; Billy Ray Hearn, Linda Gray, Frostie Gray, album producers (Birdwing/Sparrow)

COMEDY RECORDING: (G-1138)

(Either spoken word or musical performances are eligible here.)

LIVE ON THE SUNSET STRIP - Richard Pryor (Warner Bros.)
EDDIE MURPHY - Eddie Murphy (Columbia/CBS)
GREAT WHITE NORTH - Bob & Doug McKenzie (Mercury/Polygram)
A PLACE FOR MY STUFF - George Carlin (Atlantic)
THE STEVE MARTIN BROTHERS - Steve Martin (Warner Bros.)

SPOKEN WORD, DOCUMENTARY OR DRAMA RECORDING: (G-1139)

(This category is for nonmusical show albums including comdey show albums.)

RAIDERS OF THE LOST ARK: THE MOVIE ON RECORD - Actual dialog, music and sound effects; Tom Voegeli, album producer (Columbia)
CHARLES DICKENS' NICHOLAS NICKELBY - Read by Roger Rees (Caedmon)
FOUNDATION'S EDGE - Read by Isaac Asimov (Caedmon)
NO MAN'S ISLAND - Sir John Gielgud & Sir Ralph Richardson (Caedmon)
2010: ODYSSEY TWO - Read by Arthur C Clarke (Caedmon)

INSTRUMENTAL COMPOSITION: (G-1140)

(A composer's award for an original nonclassical composition with or without lyrics which first gained recognition as an instrumental.)

FLYING (THEME FROM E.T. - THE EXTRATERRESTRIAL) - John Williams, composer; MCA publisher.
ADVENTURE ON EARTH - John Williams, composer; MCA, publisher.
ARE YOU GOING WITH ME? - Pat Metheny & Lyle Mays, composers; Pat-Meth Music/Lyle Mays Inc, publishers.
DESIRE - Tom Scott, composer; Tomscot Music, publisher.
IN THE PRESENCE AND ABSENCE OF EACH OTHER PARTS 1, 2 & 3 - Claus Ogerman, composer; Gema/Ebony Musik Verlag, Gema, publishers.

ORIGINAL SCORE–MOTION PICTURE OR A TELEVISION SPECIAL: (G-1141)

(A composer's/songwriter's award for an original background score or original songs written specifically for the motion picture or television special.)

E.T. - THE EXTRATERRESTRIAL - John Williams, composer (MCA)
THE FRENCH LIEUTENANT'S WOMAN - Carl Davis, composer (DRG)
ON GOLDEN POND - Dave Grusin, composer (MCA)
RAGTIME - Randy Newman, composer (Elektra)
VICTOR/VICTORIA - Henry Mancini, composer; Leslie Bricusse, lyricist (MGM/Polygram)

CAST SHOW ALBUM: (G-1142)

(Awards to the composer(s), lyricist(s) of a new score and album producer. Original cast albums, albums by road casts, or working casts, including show revival casts, are eligible.)

DREAMGIRLS - Henry Krieger, composer; Tom Eyen, lyricist; David Foster, album producer (Geffen/WB)
CATS - Andrew Lloyd Webber, Richard Stilgoe & Trevor Nunn, composers; poems by T S Eliot; Andrew Lloyd Webber, album producer (Geffen/WB)
JOSEPH & THE AMAZING TECHNICOLOR DREAMCOAT - Andrew Lloyd Webber, composer; Tim Rice, lyricist; Tim Rice and Roger Watson, album producers (Chrysalis)
MERRILY WE ROLL ALONG - Stephen Sondheim, composer & lyricist; Thomas Z Shepard, producer (RCA)
NINE - Maury Yeston, composer & lyricist; Michael Berniker, producer (Columbia/CBS)

VIDEO OF THE YEAR: (G-1143)

(Videos (video cassettes and video disks) in any format are eligible if the programming has been created specifically for the home video market and released for sale to the public for the first time during the awards eligibility year.)

OLIVIA PHYSICAL - Olivia Newton-John (MCA Video)
FUN & GAMES - Various; Margaret Murphy, producer (OPA/RCA Video)
THE TALES OF HOFFMANN - The Royal Opera conducted by George Pretre with Placido Domingo (Pioneer Artists)
THE TUBES VIDEO - The Tubes (Pioneer Artists)
VISIONS: ELTON JOHN - Elton John (Embassy Home Entertainment)

JAZZ FUSION PERFORMANCE, VOCAL OR INSTRUMENTAL: (G-1144)

(This is for any type of borderline jazz performance-rock, pop, R&B, classical, etc.)

OFFRAMP - Pat Metheny Group (ECM/WB)
AS WE SPEAK - David Sanborn (WB)
DESIRE - Tom Scott (Elektra/Musician)
INCOGNITO - Spyro Gyra (MCA)
WEATHER REPORT - Weather Report (Columbia)

JAZZ VOCAL–FEMALE: (G-1145)

(This category is for a solo performance. All nominations here are albums.)

GERSHWIN LIVE - Sarah Vaughan (CBS)
A CLASSY PAIR - Ella Fitzgerald (Pablo Today)
ECHOES OF AN ERA - Chaka Khan (Elektra/Musician)
MAXINE SULLIVAN WITH THE IKE ISAACS QUARTET - Maxine Sullivan (Audiophile/Jazzology)
SMILIN' THROUGH - Cleo Laine (Finesse)

JAZZ VOCAL–MALE: (G-1146)

(This category is for a solo performance.)

AN EVENING WITH GEORGE SHEARING AND MEL TORME - Mel Torme (Concord Jazz)
BOP FOR KEROUAC - Mark Murphy (Muse)
THE DAVE FRISBERG SONGBOOK VOLUME I - Dave Frisberg (Omnisound Jazz)
8 TO 5 I LOSE - Joe Williams (Warner Bros.)
A TRIBUTE TO JOHNNY MERCER - Bill Henderson (Discovery)

JAZZ VOCAL–DUO OR GROUP: (G-1147)

(This category is for a duo/group performance.)

ROUTE 66 - The Manhattan Transfer (Atlantic)
EASY TO LOVE - The Singers Unlimited (Pausa)
HIGH STANDARDS - Jackie & Roy (Concord Jazz)
LOVE - Jon Hendricks & Company (Muse)
ONE NIGHT IN A DREAM - Clare Fischer and Salsa Picante with 2 ∎ 2 (Discovery)

JAZZ–SOLOIST: (G-1148)

(This category is for a solo instrumental performance with or without a group or band. All nominations here are albums.)

WE WANT MILES - Miles Davis (Columbia)
JIMMY ROWLES PLAYS DUKE ELLINGTON AND BILLY STRAYHORN - Jimmy Rowles (Columbia)
THE MAGNIFICENT TOMMY FLANAGAN - Tommy Flanagan (Progressive)
NIGHT AND DAY - Ira Sullivan (Muse)
WYNTON MARSALIS - Wynton Marsalis (Columbia)

JAZZ–GROUP: (G-1149)

(This category is for an instrumental group. All nominations here are albums)

MORE LIVE - Phil Woods Quartet (Adelphi)
DIZZY GILLESPIE - LIVE WITH THE MITCHELL-RUFF DUO - Dizzy Gillespie with the Mitchell-Ruff Duo (Book-of-the-Month)
GIANT STEPS - Tommy Flanagan Trio (Enja/London)
STRAIGHT AHEAD - Art Blakey and the Jazz Messengers (Concord Jazz)
A WORK OF ART - The Art Farmer Quartet (Concord Jazz)

JAZZ–BIG BAND: (G-1150)

(This category is primarily for a big band sound. All nominations here are albums.)

WARM BREEZE - Count Basie & His Orchestra (Pablo Today)
LIVE IN DIGITAL - Rob McConnell and The Boss Brass (Dark Orchid)
MAKE ME SMILE & OTHER NEW WORKS BY BOB BROOKMEYER - Mel Lewis & The Jazz Orchestra (Finesse)
WESTLAKE - Bob Florence Big Band (Discovery)
THE WOODY HERMAN BIG BAND LIVE AT THE CONCORD JAZZ FESTIVAL 1981 - The Woody Herman Big Band (Concord Jazz)

INSTRUMENTAL ARRANGEMENT: (G-1151)

(An instrumental arranger's award. This category is for an instrumental arrangement on an instrumental recording, released for the first time during the eligibility year on either a single or an album track.)

FLYING - John Williams; John Williams, arranger (MCA)
ARE YOU GOING WITH ME - Pat Metheny Group; Pat Metheny, Lyle Mays, arrangers; (ECM)
BALLADINA - Earl Klugh; Earl Klugh, Ronnie Foster, Claire Fischer, arrangers; (EMI/Liberty)
PAVANE POUR UNE INFANTE DEFUNTE - Claus Ogerman featuring Jan Akkerman; Claus Ogerman, arranger (Jazzman)
PAVANE - Les Hooper Big Band; Les Hooper, arranger (Jazz Hounds)

ARRANGEMENT ACCOMPANYING VOCAL(S): (G-1152)

(An instrumental arranger's award. This category is for an instrumental arrangement accompanying a solo vocalist, a vocal duo, vocal group or chorus, released for the first time during the eligibility year, either a single or an album track.)

ROSANNA - Toto; Jerry Hey, David Paich, instr. arrangers (Columbia)
DO I DO - Stevie Wonder; Stevie Wonder, Paul Riser, instr arrangers (Tamla/Motown)
EASY TO LOVE - The Singers Unlimited; Les Hooper, instr arranger (Pausa)
ONLY A MIRACLE - Kenny Loggins; Marty Paich instr arranger (Columbia)
I.G.Y. (WHAT A BEAUTIFUL WORLD) - Donald Fagen; Rob Mounsey, Donald Fagen, instr arrangers (Warner Bros.)

ARRANGEMENT FOR VOICES: (G-1153)

(A vocal arranger's award. This category covers all voices on a recording, excluding a featured soloist, if any. If may include a cappella as well as voices with instrumental accompaniment.)

ROSANNA - Toto; David Paich, vocal arranger (Columbia)
LULLABY OF BIRDLAND - The Singers Unlimited; Gene Puerling, vocal arranger (Pausa)
ONE NIGHT (IN A DREAM) - Clare Fischer & Salsa Picante with 2 ∎ 2; Clare Fischer, vocal arranger (Discovery)
ROUTE 66 - The Manhattan Transfer; Al Capps, vocal arranger (Warner Bros)
RUBY BABY - Donald Fagen; Donald Fagen, vocal arranger (Warner Bros)

ALBUM PACKAGE: (G-1154)

(An art director's award, classical or non-classical.)

GET CLOSER (Linda Ronstadt) - Kosh with Ron Larson, art directors (Elektra/Asylum)
NOTHING TO FEAR (Oingo Boingo) Jules Bates, art director (A&M)
ONGAKU-KAI LIVE IN JAPAN (The Crusaders) - George Osaki, art director (Crusaders/MCA)
VACATION (The Go-Go's) - Mick Haggerty & Ginger Canzoneri, art directors (IRS Records)
WE ARE ONE (Pieces of a Dream) - Denise Minobe, Ron Coro, art directors (Elektra)

ALBUM NOTES: (G-1155)

(A liner notes writer's award for original writing for a specific album, classical or nonclassical.)

BUNNY BERIGAN (GIANTS OF JAZZ) - (Bunny Berigan) John Chilton, Richard Sudhalter, annotators (Time Life)
AN EXPERIMENT IN MODERN MUSIC; PAUL WHITEMAN AT AEOLIAN HALL - (Paul Whiteman) Thornton Hagert, annotator (Smithsonian Collection)
DUKE ELLINGTON 1941 - (Duke Ellington & His Orchestra) Gary Giddins, annotator (Smithsonian Collection)
THE GREATEST COUNTRY MUSIC RECORDINGS OF ALL TIME - summary and glossary (Various) William Ivey, annotator (Franklin Mint Recording Soc)
60 YEARS OF COUNTRY MUSIC - (Various) William Ivey, Bob Pinson, annotators (RCA)
YOUNG BLOOD - (The Coasters) Robert Palmer, annotator (Atlantic/Deluxe)

HISTORICAL ALBUM: (G-1156)

(Grammy to the album producer(s) for a new album released during the eligibility year, whose predominant contents (over 50%) were recorded at least 25 years before the start of the eligibility year. Contents may include previously-released recordings, alternate takes and/or previously unreleased recordings in any combination. Excluded are reissues of old albums that have no change in their sequence of tracks or packages.)

THE TOMMY DORSEY/FRANK SINATRA SESSIONS VOLS 1, 2, 3 - (Tommy Dorsey and Frank Sinatra) Alan Dell, album producer (RCA)
BARTOK AT THE PIANO, 1920-1945 - (Bela Bartok) Dora Antal, album producer (Hungaroton)
BUNNY BERIGAN GIANTS OF JAZZ - (Bunny Berigan) Michael Brooks, album producer (Time Life)
AN EXPERIMENT IN MODERN MUSIC: PAUL WHITEMAN AT AEOLIAN HALL - (Paul Whiteman) Martin Williams, J R Taylor, album producers (RCA)
MINSTRELS & TUNESMITHS: THE COMMERCIAL ROOTS OF EARLY COUNTRY MUSIC - (Various) producer not listed (John Edwards Memorial Foundation)

ENGINEERED RECORDING (Nonclassical): (G-1157)

(An engineer's award.)

TOTO IV - (Toto) Al Schmitt, Tom Knox, Greg Ladanyi, David Paich, Steve Porcaro, Dick Gall, Bruce Heigh, engineers (Columbia)
AMERICAN FOOL - (John Cougar) George Tutko, Don Gehman, Mark Stebbeds, engineers (Riva/Polygram)
EYE IN THE SKY - (The Alan Parsons Project) Alan Parsons, engineer (Arista)
LOVE OVER GOLD - (Dire Straits) Neil Dorfsman, engineer (Warner Bros)
THE NIGHTFLY - (Donald Fagen) Roger Nichols, Daniel Lazerus, Elliot Scheiner, engineers (Warner Bros)

PRODUCER OF THE YEAR (Nonclasscial): (G-1158)

(A producer's award for consistently outstanding creativity in producing)

TOTO
JOHN COUGAR MELLENCAMP and DON GEHMAN
DAVID FOSTER
QUINCY JONES
GARY KATZ

CLASSICAL ALBUM: (G-1159)

(Grammy to the artist, and to the album producer if other than the artist. Certificates to the engineer(s), and the classical orchestra if applicable)

BACH: THE GOLDBERG VARIATIONS - Glenn Gould; Glenn Gould & Samuel Carter, album producers (CBS)
BERLIOZ: LA DAMNATION DE FAUST - Sir Georg Solti conducts Chicago Symphony Orchestra & Chorus/Frederica Von Stade, Kenneth Riegel, Jose Van Dam; James Mallinson, album producer (London)
DEBUSSY: LA MER/PRELUDE A L'APRES-MIDI D'UN FAUNE/DANSES SACREE ET PROFANE - Leonard Slatkin conducts Saint Louis Symphony; Frances Tietov, harp; Robert Woods, album producer (Telarc)
MAHLER: SYMPHONY NO 7 IN E MINOR (SONG OF THE NIGHT) - James Levine conducts Chicago Symphony; Thomas Z Shepard & Jay David Saks, album producers (RCA)
STAVINSKY: THE RECORDED LEGACY - Igor Stavinsky & Robert Craft conduct various orchestras, ensembles with various solo artists; John McClure, album producer (CBS)

CLASSICAL ORCHESTRAL RECORDING: (G-1160)

(Grammy to the conductor and album producer. Certificate to the classical orchestra)

MAHLER: SYMPHONY NO 7 IN E MINOR (SONG OF THE NIGHT) - James Levine conducts Chicago Symphony; Thomas Z Shepard & Jay David Saks, album producers (RCA)
DEBUSSY: LA MER/PRELUDE A L'APRES-MIDI D'UN FAUNE/DANSES SACREE ET PROFANE - Leonard Slatkin conducts Chicago Symphony; Robert Woods, album producer (Telarc)
HOLST: THE PLANETS - Herbert von Karajan conducts Berlin Philharmonic; Guenther Breest & Michel Glotz, album producers (DG)
MOZART: SYMPHONIES - VOLUME 1 (THE EARLY WORKS) - Christopher Hogwood conducts Academy of Ancient Music; Morton Winding, album producer (L'Oiseau-Lyre)
(R) STRAUSS: DEATH & TRANSFIGURATION/DON JUAN/SALOME - DANCE OF THE SEVEN VEILS - Eduardo Mata conducts Dallas Symphony; Jay David Saks, album producer (RCA)

OPERA RECORDING: (G-1161)

(Grammy to the conductor, album producer and principal soloists.)

WAGNER: DER RING DES NIBELUNGEN - Pierre Boulez conducts Bayreuth Festival Orchestra; Gwyneth Jones, Jeannine Altmeyer, Orton Wenkel, Peter Hofmann, Manfred Jung, Siegfried Jerusalem, Heinz Zednik, Donald McIntyre, Matti Salminen, Hermann Becht, principal soloists; Andrew Kazdin, album producer (Philips)
FAURE: PENELOPE - Charles Dutiot conducts Orchestre Philharmonique de Monte Carlo; Jessye Norman, Alain Vanzo, Philippe Huttenlocher, principal soloists; Pierre Tavoix, album producer (Erato)
JANACEK: THE CUNNING LITTLE VIXEN - Sir Charles Mackerras conducts Vienna Philharmonic Orchestra & Vienna State Opera Chorus; Lucia Popp, Eva Randova, Dalibor Jedlicka, principal soloists; James Mallinson, album producer (London)
PUCCINI: TOSCA - James Levine conducts Philharmonia Orchestra & Ambrosian Opera Chorus; Renata Scotto, Placido Domingo, Renato Bruson, principal soloists; John Willan, album producer (Angel)
PUCCINI: TURANDOT - Herbert von Karajan conducts Vienna Philharmonic Orchestra & Vienna State Opera Chorus & Vienna Boys' Choir; Placido Domingo, Katia Ricciarelli, Piero de Palma, Ruggero Raimondi, Barbara Hendricks, Gottfried Hornik, principal soloists; Guenther Breest & Michael Glotz, album producers (DG)
WEINBERGER: SCHWANDA, THE BAGPIPER - Heinz Wallberg conducts Munich Radio Orchestra & Bavarian Radio Chorus; Lucia Popp, Siegfried Jerusalem, Hermann Prey, Gwendolyn Killebrew, Sigmund Nimsgern, principal soloists; George Krongold, album producer (CBS)

CHORAL PERFORMANCE (OTHER THAN OPERA): (G-1162)

(This category is for vocal groups, with or without orchestra, of more than 14 voices. Grammy to the choral conductor and to the orchestra conductor if an orchestra is on the recording.)

BERLIOZ: LA DAMNATION DE FAUST - Margaret Hillis, chorus master, Chicago Symphony Orchestra Chorus; Sir George Solti, conductor, Chicago Symphony Orchestra (London)
BACH: CANTATAS - VOLUME 30 (NOS 120, 121, 122, 123) - Gerhard Schmidt-Gaden, choral conductor; Tolzer Knabenchor & Nikolaus Harnoncourt, conductors, Concentus Musicus Wien (Telefunken)
BRAHMS: GERMAN REQUIEM - Norbert Balatsch, chorus master, Vienna State Opera Chorus; Bernard Haitink, conductor, Vienna Philharmonic Orchestra; Gundula Janowitz, Tom Krause, soloists (Philips)
HAYDN: THE SEASONS - Laszlo Heltay, chorus master, Chorus of Academy of St Martin-in-the-Fields; Neville Marriner conducts Academy of St Martin-in-the-Fields; Dietrich Fischer-Dieskau, Edith Mathis, Siegfried Jerusalem, soloists (Philips)
JANACEK: GLAGOLITIC MASS - Nicholas Cleobury, chorus master, City of Birmingham Symphony Orchestra Chorus; Simon Rattle, conductor, City of Birmingham Symphony Orchestra (Angel)
POULENC: GLORIA FOR SOPRANO, CHOIR AND ORCHESTRA (G MAJOR) - Robert Shaw conducts Atlanta Symphony Orchestra Chorus

& Atlanta Symphony Orchestra; Sylvia McNair (Telarc)
RACHMANINOFF: THE BELLS & RUSSIAN SONGS (From album RACHMANINOFF ORCHESTRAL MUSIC) Thomas Peck, chorus master, Saint Louis Symphony Chorus; Leonard Slatkin, conducts Saint Louis Symphony Orchestra (Vox Cum Laude)

CHAMBER MUSIC PERFORMANCE: (G-1163)

(Grammy to the chamber orchestra conductor. Certificate to the orchestra.)

BRAHMS: THE SONATAS FOR CLARINET & PIANO, OP 120 - Richard Stoltzman and Richard Goode (London)
BACH: TRIO SONATAS (BWV 1038, 1039, 1079) - James Galway, Kung-Wha Chung, Phillip Moll and Moray Welsh (RCA)
BORODIN: QUARTET NO 2 IN D MAJOR/DOHNANYI: QUARTET NO 2 IN D-FLAT MAJOR, OP 15 - Guarneri Quartet (RCA)
BRAHMS: SONATAS FOR CELLO & PIANO NO 1 IN E MINOR, OP 38 & NO 2 IN F MAJOR, OP 99 - Lynn Harrell & Vladimir Ashkenazy (RCA)
BRAHMS: THE STRING SEXTETS (B-FLAT MAJOR, OP 18 & G MAJOR, OP 36) - The Cleveland Quartet with Pinchas Zuckerman and Bernard Greenhouse (RCA)

CLASSICAL PERFORMANCE - INSTRUMENTAL SOLOIST(S) (WITH ORCHESTRA): (G-1164)

ELGAR: CONCERTO FOR VIOLIN IN B MINOR - Itzhak Perlman; Daniel Barenboim conducts Chicago Symphony (DG)
BEETHOVEN: CONCERTO FOR PIANO NO 4 IN G MAJOR, OP 58 - Rudolf Serkin; Seiji Ozawa conducts Boston Symphony (Telarc)
MOZART: CONCERTO FOR PIANO NO 22 IN E-FLAT MAJOR, K 482 (ASHKENAZY PLAYS & CONDUCTS MOZART) - Vladimir Ashkenazy; Vladimir Ashkenazy conducts Philharmonia (London)
SCHUMANN: CONCERTO FOR PIANO IN A MINOR/RACHMANINOV: CONCERTO FOR PIANO NO 2 IN C MINOR, OP 18 - Alicia de Larrocha; Charles Dutoit conducts Royal Philharmonic (London)
VIVALDI: THE FOUR SEASONS - Joseph Silverstein; Seiji Ozawa conducts Boston Symphony (Telarc)

CLASSICAL PERFORMANCE - INSTRUMENTAL SOLOIST(S) (WITHOUT ORCHESTRA): (G-1165)

BACH: THE GOLDBERG VARIATIONS - Glenn Gould (CBS)
THE ALKAN PROJECT (ETUDES, OP 39 - IN ALL THE MINOR KEYS) - Ronald Smith (Arabesque)
BARBER: SONATA FOR PIANO OP 26/SOUVENIRS, OP 28/NOCTURNE, OP 33 - Ruth Laredo (Nonesuch)
GRANADOS: DANZAS ESPANOLAS - Alicia de Larrocha (London)
GROFE-TOMITA: GRAND CANYON SUITE/ANDERSON-TOMITA: SYNCOPATED CLOCK - Isao Tomita (RCA)
HOROWITZ AT THE MET (SCARLATTI, CHOPIN, LISZT, RACHMANINOFF) - Vladimir Horowitz (RCA)
SCHUMANN: HUMORESKE, OP 20/FANTASIESTUCKE OP 12 - Emanuel Ax (RCA)

CLASSICAL VOCAL SOLOIST PERFORMANCE: (G-1166)

(Grammy to the vocal soloist. Certificate to the solo accompanist or orchestra conductor, whichever is featured on the recording.)

VERDI: ARIAS (LEONTYNE PRICE SINGS VERDI) - Leontyne Price; Zubin Mehta conducts Israel Philharmonic (London)
BERLIOZ: LA MORT DE CLEOPATRE - Jessye Norman; Daniel Barenboim conducts Orchestre de Paris (DG)
FAURE: LA BONNE CHANSON/DEBUSSY: CHANSONS DE BILITIS & ARIETTES OUBLIEES - Elly Ameling; Dalton Baldwin, accompanist (CBS)
FREDERICA VON STADE LIVE! - Frederica Von Stade; Martin Katz, accompanist (CBS)
MOZART: CONCERT ARIAS (ANDROMEDA, IL BURBERO DI BUON CORE, ARTASERSE, IDOMENEO, CERERE PLACATA) - Kiri Te Kanawa; Gyorgy Fischer conducts Vienna Chamber Orchestra (London)

ENGINEERED RECORDING CLASSICAL: (G-1167)

(An engineer's award.)

MAHLER: SYMPHONY NO 7 IN E MINOR (SONG OF THE NIGHT) - James Levine conducts Chicago Symphony Orchestra; Paul Goodman, engineer (RCA)
BACH: THE GOLDBERG VARIATIONS; Glenn Gould - Stan Tonkel, John Johnson, Ray Moore, Martin Greenblatt, Bud Graham, engineers (CBS)
BERLIOZ: LA DAMNATION DE FAUST; Sir Georg Solti conducts Chicago Symphony Orchestra & Chorus; Frederica Von Stade, Kenneth Riegel, Jose Van Dam/James Lock & Simon Eadon, engineers (London)
DVORAK: SYMPHONY NO 9 IN E MINOR (FROM THE NEW WORLD); James Levine conducts Chicago Symphony Orchestra; Paul Goodman, engineer (RCA)
HOLST: THE PLANETS; Herbert von Karajan conducts Berlin Philharmonic; Gunter Hermanns, engineer (DG)

CLASSICAL PRODUCER OF THE YEAR: (G-1168)

(Grammy to the classical album producer.)

ROBERT WOODS - Beethoven: Concerto For Piano No 4 In G Major, Op 58: Rudolf Serkin; Seiji Ozawa conducts Boston Symphony (Telarc); Berlioz: Symphonie Fantastique: Lorin Maazel conducts The Cleveland Orchestra (Telarc); Debussy: La Mer/Prelude A L'Apres-Midi D'un Faune/Danses Sacree Et Profane: Leonard Slatkin conducts Saint Louis Symphony; Frances Tietov, soloist (Telarc); Poulenc: Gloria For Soprano, Choir & Orchestra (G Major)/Concerto In G Minor For Organ, Strings & Timpani: Robert Shaw conducts Atlanta Symphony Orchestra & Chorus; Sylvia McNair; Michael Murray (Telarc); Vivaldi: The Four Seasons: Seiji Ozawa conducts Boston Symphony; Joseph Silverstein (Telarc)
STEVEN EPSTEIN - Gershwin Live!: Sarah Vaughan/Michael Tilson Thomas conducts Los Angeles Philharmonic (CBS); Haydn: Trios & Divertisements: Jean-Pierre Rampal, Isaac Stern, Mstislav Rostropovich (CBS); Mozart: Concerto For Violin No 3 In G Major, K. 215 & No 5 In A Major, K 219 ("Turkish"): Pinchas Zukerman; Pinchas Zukerman conducts Saint Paul Chamber Orchestra (CBS); Tchaikovsky: Suites For Orchestra Nos 2 & 4: Michael Tilson Thomas conducts Philharmonic Orchestra (CBS); Tchaikovsky: Symphony No 5 In E Minor, Op 64: Lorin Maazel conducts The Cleveland Orchestra (CBS)
GLENN GOULD & SAMUEL CARTER - Bach: The Goldberg Variations: Glenn Gould (CBS); Haydn: The Six Last Sonatas For Piano: Glenn Gould (CBS)
JAMES MALLINSON - Berlioz: La Damnation De Faust: Sir George Solti conducts Chicago Symphony Orchestra & Chorus; Frederica Von Stade, Kenneth Riegel, Jose Van Dam, soloists (London); Bruckner: Symphony No 4 In E-Flat Major ("Romantic"): Sir George Solti conducts Chicago Symphony (London); Stravinsky: The Rite Of Spring: Antal Dorati conducts The Detroit Symphony (London)
JAY DAVID SAKS - Gershwin: An American In Paris/Cuban Overture/Porgy & Bess - A Symphonic Picture: Eduardo Mata conducts Dallas Symphony (RCA); Mozart: Symphony No 40 In G Minor & Symphony No 41 In C Major ("Jupiter"): James Levine conducts Chicago Symphony (RCA); Schumann: Humoreske, Op 20/Fantasiestucke, Op 12: Emanuel Ax (RCA); Sibelius: Symphony No 4 In A Minor/Tapiola: Eugene Ormandy conducts Philadelphia Orchestra (RCA); (R) Strauss: Death & Transfiguration/Don Juan/Salome - Dance Of The Seven Veils: Eduardo Mata conducts Dallas Symphony (RCA)

1983 HALL OF FAME WINNERS: (G-1169)

BACH: THE GOLDBERG VARIATIONS (Album) Glenn Gould (Columbia) 1956
EMPTY BED BLUES Bessie Smith (Columbia) 1928
IN THE MOOD Glenn Miller (Bluebird) 1939
PINETOP'S BOOGIE WOOGIE Pinetop Smith (Vocalion) 1928
YOUR CHEATING HEART Hank Williams (MGM) 1953

PULITZER PRIZE PLAYS

1917 None

1918 WHY MARRY? Jesse Lynch Williams

1919 None

1920 BEYOND THE HORIZON Eugene O'Neill

1921 MISS LULU BETT Zona Gale

1922 ANNA CHRISTIE Eugene O'Neill

1923 ICEBOUND Owen Davis

1924 HELL-BENT FOR HEAVEN Hatcher Hughes

1925 THEY KNEW WHAT THEY WANTED Sidney Howard

1926 CRAIG'S WIFE George Kelly

1927 IN ABRAHAM'S BOSOM Paul Green

1928 STRANGE INTERLUDE Eugene O'Neill

1929 STREET SCENE Elmer L. Rice

1930 THE GREEN PASTURES Marc Connelly

1931 ALISON'S HOUSE Susan Glaspell

1932 OF THEE I SING George S. Kaufman, Morrie Ryskind, Ira Gershwin. Music by George Gershwin

1933 BOTH YOUR HOUSES Maxwell Anderson

1934 MEN IN WHITE Sidney Kingsley

1935 THE OLD MAID Zoe Akins

1936 IDIOT'S DELIGHT Robert E. Sherwood

1937 YOU CAN'T TAKE IT WITH YOU Moss Hart and George S. Kaufman

1938 OUR TOWN Thornton Wilder

1939 ABE LINCOLN IN ILLINOIS Robert E. Sherwood

1940 THE TIME OF YOUR LIFE William Saroyan

1941 THERE SHALL BE NO NIGHT Robert E. Sherwood

1942 None

1943 THE SKIN OF OUR TEETH Thornton Wilder

1944 None SPECIAL CITATION Richard Rodgers and Oscar Hammerstein II for the musical OKLAHOMA!

1945 HARVEY Mary Chase

1946 STATE OF THE UNION Russel Crouse and Howard Lindsay

1947 None

1948 A STREETCAR NAMED DESIRE Tennessee Williams

1949 DEATH OF A SALESMAN Arthur Miller

1950 SOUTH PACIFIC Richard Rodgers, Oscar Hammerstein II and Joshua Logan

1951 None

1952 THE SHRIKE Joseph Kramm

1953 PICNIC William Inge

1954 THE TEAHOUSE OF THE AUGUST MOON John Patrick

1955 CAT ON A HOT TIN ROOF Tennessee Williams

1956 DIARY OF ANNE FRANK Albert Hackett and Frances Goodrich

1957 LONG DAY'S JOURNEY INTO NIGHT Eugene O'Neill

1958 LOOK HOMEWARD ANGEL Ketti Frings

1959 J.B. Archibald MacLeish

1960 FIORELLO! book by Jerome Weidman and George Abbott, music by Jerry Bock, lyrics by Sheldon Harnick

1961 ALL THE WAY HOME Tad Mosel

1962 HOW TO SUCCEED IN BUSINESS WITHOUT REALLY TRYING Frank Loesser and Abe Burrows

1963 None

1964 None

1965 THE SUBJECT WAS ROSES Frank D. Gilroy

1966 None

1967 A DELICATE BALANCE Edward Albee

1968 None

1969 THE GREAT WHITE HOPE Howard Sackler

1970 NO PLACE TO BE SOMEBODY Charles Gordone

1971 THE EFFECT OF GAMMA RAYS ON MAN-IN-THE-MOON MARIGOLDS Paul Zindel

1972 None

1973 THAT CHAMPIONSHIP SEASON Jason Miller

1974 None

1975 SEASCAPE Edward Albee

1976 A CHORUS LINE Michael Bennett, James Kirkwood, Nicholas Dante, Marvin Hamlisch, Edward Kleban

1977 THE SHADOW BOX Michael Cristofer

1978 THE GIN GAME D. L. Coburn

1979 BURIED CHILD Sam Shepard

1980 TALLEY'S FOLLY Lanford Wilson

1981 CRIMES OF THE HEART Beth Henley

1982 A SOLDIER'S PLAY Charles Fuller

1983 'NIGHT, MOTHER Marsha Norman

INDEX

Chandler, Michael (E-2005)

Chandler, Raymond (O-234) (O-270)

Chandler, Robert (E-762) (E-1081)

Chaney, Bob (E-1081)

Chaney, Edward (E-550)

Chaney, H. Lee (E-1292) (E-1405) (E-1406)

Chang (O-09)

Change of Heart (O-221)

Change Partners and Dance With Me (O-135)

Changing Room, The (T-521)

Channel 7 Australia (E-1807)

Channing, Carol (O-680) / (T-168) (T-280) (T-349) (T-438) (T-537)

Channing, Stockard (G-875)

Chaperot, Georges (O-288)

Chapin, Harry (G-584) (G-689)

Chaplin, Charles (O-02) (O-04) (O-08) (O-157) (O-158) (O-163) (O-288) (O-775) (O-789)

Chaplin, Saul (O-368) (O-406) (O-425) (O-464) (O-564) / (G-120)

Chaplin, Sydney (T-191) (T-348)

Chapman, Christopher (O-691) (O-692)

Chapman, Edward (G-206)

Chapman, Harold (G-214)

Chapman, Leonard (O-910) (O-993)

Chapman, Linda (O-967)

Chapman, Michael (O-938) / (E-1063)

Chapman, Mike (G-974)

Chapman, Ralph (O-591)

Chapter Two (T-617)

Charade (O-605)

Charbonneau, Ron (E-817)

Chariots of Fire (film) (O-950)

Chariots Of Fire (record) (G-1107)

Chariots of the Gods (O-753)

Charisse, Zan (T-558)

Charlap, Moose (G-332)

Charles Fold Singers (G-1010)

Charles, Glen (E-1437) (E-1541) (E-1569) (E-1691) (E-1718) (E-1840) (E-2009) (E-2037)

Charles, Jon (E-2049)

Charles, Les (E-1437) (E-1541) (E-1569) (E-1691) (E-1718) (E-1840) (E-2009) (E-2037)

Charles, Ray (singer) (G-64) (G-69) (G-70) (G-92) (G-94) (G-105) (G-130) (G-144) (G-145) (G-150) (G-179) (G-189) (G-239) (G-339) (G-340) (G-366) (G-376) (G-379) (G-465) (G-599) (G-741) (G-783) (G-883) (G-905) (G-940)

Charles, Ray Singers (G-75) (G-239) (G-369) (G-421) (G-461)

Charles, Ray (writer) (E-440) (E-721) (E-797) (E-1731)

Charleson, Leslie (E-1605) (E-1915) (E-2089)

Charlet, Francois (E-895) (E-1007)

Charlie and Algernon (T-681)

Charlie Brown and Charles Schulz (E-628)

Charlie Brown Celebration (E-1848)

Charlie Brown Christmas, A (E-412)

Charlie Brown Thanksgiving, A (E-903)

Charlie Brown's All Stars (E-470)

Charlie Daniels Band (G-1005)

Charlie/Papa Productions (O-888) (O-927)

Charman, Roy (O-848) (O-906) (O-964)

Charmoli, Nick (E-459)

Charmoli, Tony (E-99) (E-137) (E-867) (E-928) (E-939) (E-1141) (E-1158) (E-1253) (E-1367) (E-1396) (E-1566) (E-1715) (E-1717)

Charnin, Martin (E-634) (E-770) (E-787) (E-794) (E-860) / (T-600) (T-602) (T-699) (T-700) / (G-565) (G-863)

Charters Pour L'Enfer (Charters to Hell) (E-1806)

Chartoff, Robert (O-853) (O-931)

Chartoff-Winkler Productions (O-853) (O-931)

Charyk, Dr. Joseph V. (E-1087)

Chase (G-540)

Chase, Allan (E-966) (E-1091)

Chase, Borden (O-306)

Chase, Chevy (E-1130) (E-1145) (E-1235) (E-1245) (E-1360)

Chase, David (E-1324) (E-1439) (E-1542) (E-1572)

Chase, Ken (E-1296) (E-1513)

Chase, Mary (P-1945)

Chase of Death (O-333)

Chase, Stanley (E-1115) / (T-193)

Chase, Sylvia (E-1423) (E-1671) (E-1993)

Chase The Clouds Away (G-758)

Chatelain, Arthur B. (O-263)

Chatfield, Rocci (E-1382) (E-1487)

Chattanooga Choo Choo (O-185)

Chatterton, Ruth (O-13) (O-20)

Chayefsky, Paddy (O-439) (O-498) (O-763) (O-859) / (E-90) (E-124) / (T-259) (T-307)

Cheapest Way To Go, The (E-1827)

Checchi, Robert (E-654) (E-724) (E-798) (E-1058) (E-1059) (E-1163) (E-1280) (E-1391) (E-1395) (E-1421) (E-1501)

Checker, Chubby (G-128)

Checkmate (G-119)

Cheech & Chong (G-567) (G-613) (G-659) (G-707) (G-807)

Cheek to Cheek (O-81)

Cheers (E-2009)

Chegwidden, Ann (E-1014)

Chekhov, Michael (O-249)

Chekmayan, Ara (E-1833)

Chelsea Theatre Centre (T-599)

Chen, Tina (E-478)

Chenault Productions (O-655)

Chenier, Clifton (G-897) (G-955)

Chennault, Robert (E-1264) (E-1619) (E-1769) (E-1928)

Cher (E-768) (E-770) (E-838) (E-899) (E-1021) / (G-546)

Cherin, Milt (G-493) (G-721) (G-770) (G-820) (G-872)

Chermak, Cy (E-577) (E-631) (E-691)

Chernack, Jerry (E-1676) (E-1832)

Cherry Orchard, The (T-607)

Cherry, Wendell (T-716)

Chet Huntley Reporting (E-245)

Chetwynd, Lionel (O-821)

Chevalier, Maurice (O-19) (O-510) / (T-438)

Chevallier, Christian (G-778)

Chevry, Bernard (O-733)

Chevy Show, The (E-142)

Chew, Richard (O-844) (O-882)

Chewey, Michael V. (O-930)

Chianese, Francesco (E-2045)

Chiari, Mario (O-685)

Chicago (group) (G-452) (G-495) (G-505) (G-772) (G-773) (G-789) (G-1113)

Chicago (group album) (G-495)

Chicago (play) (T-580) (T-582) (T-583)

Chicago (play album) (G-760)

Chicago Blues Allstars, The (G-1072)

Chicago Brass Ensemble (G-486) (G-488)

Chicago Conspiracy Trial (E-620)

Chicago Democratic Convention Coverage (E-570)

Chicago Symphony (G-39) (G-78) (G-134) (G-161) (G-201) (G-260) (G-1034) (G-1035) (G-1097) (G-1103)

Chicago Symphony Orchestra And Chorus (G-1096)

Chicago X (G-773)

Chichester Palms (G-317)

Chicken, The (Le Poulet) (O-649)

Chico Buarque De Hollanda (G-364)

Chicos, Cathy (E-1382) (E-1487) (E-1614) (E-1766)

Chief Dan George (G-804)

Chieftains (G-955)

Chieftains 9, The (G-1012)

Chihara, Paul (E-1729)

Chikaya, Inoue (O-747)

Chilberg, John E. II (E-1500) (E-1725)

Child Beating (E-380)

Child, Julia (E-436) (E-812)

Child of our Time (E-199) (E-233)

Child Snatching (ABC News "20/20") (E-1671)

Children Are Waiting, The (E-678)

Hager, Louis Bush Associates (T-676)

Hager, Robert (E-1827)

Hagert, Thornton (G-1155)

Haggard, Merle (G-514) (G-517) (G-605) (G-609) (G-702)

Haggard, Merle and the Stranger (G-516)

Haggart, Jerome (E-1435) (E-1627)

Haggerty, Mick (G-730) (G-970) (G-1154)

Hagman, Larry (E-1553) (E-1702)

Hague, Albert (T-244)

Hahn, Edwin C (O-154)

Hahn, Ken (E-2063)

Hahn, Phil (E-543) (E-592) (E-793) (E-935) (E-1145)

Haid, Charles (E-1708) (E-1857)

Haigood, Harry (E-1018) (E-1534) (E-1668) (E-1822)

Haigood, W. (E-1822)

Hailey, Arthur (E-188)

Hailey, Oliver (E-1870)

Haimes, Ted (E-2000)

Haimsohn, George (G-480)

Haines, Fred (O-682)

Haines, Larry (E-1199) (E-1276) (E-1606) (E-1757) / (T-389) (T-445)

Haines-Stiles, Geoffrey (E-1698)

Hair (album) (G-437)

Hair (play) (T-449)

Haire, Chris (E-1890) (E-2063)

Haitian Refugees (NBC "Weekend") (E-1495)

Haitink, Bernard (G-573) (G-1162)

Hajos, Karl (O-238) (O-256)

Halas, John (O-607)

Halas and Batchelor Productions (O-607) (O-926)

Hale, Barbara (E-216) (E-277)

Hale, Joe (O-928)

Hale, John (O-723)

Hale, Lee (E-483) (E-559) (E-721) (E-1222) (E-1336)

Hale, Ron (E-1478) (E-1606)

Halee, Roy (G-409) (G-455) (G-495) (G-500) (G-629)

Haley, Alex (G-860)

Haley, Bill (G-1106)

Haley, Harold (E-518) (E-1000) (E-1495)

Haley, Jack Jr. (E-546) (E-1076) (E-1222) (E-1446) (E-1846)

Half A Sixpence (album) (G-282)

Half A Sixpence (play) (T-378)

Hall, Alexander (O-179)

Hall, Carol (G-904)

Hall, Charles D (O-132)

Hall, Conrad (O-641) (O-662) (O-683) (O-724) (O-841)

Hall, Daryl (G-1051) (G-1113)

Hall, David (O-114) (O-643)

Hall, Dean (E-1593) (E-1744) (E-1893)

Hall, Deirdre (E-1607)

Hall, Delores (T-596) / (G-850)

Hall, Delos (E-571) (E-1011)

Hall, Don Jr. (E-450) (E-662) (E-729) (E-1176) (E-1406)

Hall, Grayson (O-617)

Hall, Houston (E-723)

Hall, Jim (G-151) (G-288) (G-334) (G-638) (G-733) (G-784)

Hall, John (O-189)

Hall, Joyce C. (E-291)

Hall, Juanita (T-44)

Hall, Karen (E-2038)

Hall, Michael (E-1162)

Hall, Monty (E-1101)

Hall, Norman (E-882) (E-979) (E-1762) (E-1921) (E-2096)

Hall of Kings (E-487)

Hall, Peter (T-413) (T-503) (T-638) (T-657) (T-677)

Hall, Rich (E-1792)

Hall, Rick (G-684)

Hall, Sam (E-1614) (E-1766) (E-1925) (E-2101)

Hall, Sherwood III (G-15)

Hall, Tom T. (G-411) (G-430) (G-589) (G-651) (G-654) (G-731)

Halle, Roland (O-947) (O-967)

Halle/Ladue Inc (O-947)

Hallelujah, Baby! (album) (G-371)

Hallelujah, Baby! (play) (T-431)

Hallelujah Film (O-826) (O-922)

Hallenberger, Harry (O-181)

Haller, Ernest (O-147) (O-164) (O-253) (O-345) (O-579) (O-599)

Haller, Joseph (O-131)

Haller, Michael (E-944)

Halliday, Richard (T-263) (T-265)

Hallig, Klaus (E-1025) (E-1117) (E-1219)

Halligan, Dick (G-453) (G-499)

Hallinan, Eda Godel (E-1770)

Hallmark Hall of Fame (E-172) (E-381) (E-1220) (E-1871)

Halloway, Galon (E-1322)

Halloween Is Grinch Night (E-1332)

Halloween That Almost Wasn't, The (E-1550)

Halper, Bob (E-1819) (E-1980)

Halprin, Sol (O-261) (O-413)

Halsey, Richard (O-863)

Halston (T-624)

Ham, Al (O-667)

Haman,Richard Y. (E-1501)

Hambleton, T. Edward (T-263)

Hambling, Gerry (O-902) (O-941)

Hamel, Veronica (E-1705) (E-1854) (E-2023)

Hamill, Pete (G-731)

Hamilton, Alexander (E-378)

Hamilton, Arthur (O-750)

Hamilton, Fenton (O-736) (O-776)

Hamilton, George IV (G-256)

Hamilton, Joe (E-529) (E-579) (E-633) (E-693) (E-768) (E-770) (E-838) (E-840) (E-899) (E-901) (E-1113) (E-1215) (E-1218) (E-1326)

Hamilton, Joe Frank & Reynolds (G-540)

Hamilton, Murray (T-368)

Hamilton, Nancy (O-448)

Hamilton, Scott (E-2139)

Hamilton, William (G-173) (G-215)

Hamlet (film) (TV) (O-300)

Hamlet (TV) (E-208) (E-692)

Hamlisch, Marvin (O-770) (O-808) (O-809) (O-884) (O-885) (O-905) (O-924) (O-983) / (T-583) / (G-678) (G-691) (G-710) (G-760) (G-824) (G-861) (G-862) (G-961) (G-962) / (P-1976)

Hammer, Peter (E-1780) (E-1939)

Hammeras, Ralph (O-10) (O-32) (O-316)

Hammerman, Roy (E-885) (E-959) (E-1073) (E-1311) (E-1312) (E-1425) (E-1426) (E-1528) (E-1813)

Hammerstein, Jane Howard (E-1465)

Hammerstein, Oscar II (O-135) (O-185) (O-257) (O-275) (O-369) / (T-50) (T-51) (T-90) (T-175) (T-241) (T-263) / (G-88) (G-904) (G-1019) / (P-1944) (P-1950)

Hammerstein, William (T-206)

Hammett, Dashiell (O-216)

Hammond, Bob (E-1081)

Hammond, Jon (E-1818) (E-1979)

Hammond, Lawrence (E-1615) (E-1767) (E-1801) (E-1926) (E-1958) (E-2102) (E-2119)

Hammond, R (E-1984) (E-2157)

Hammons, Paul (E-1990) (E-2163) (E-2164)

Hamm's Beer (E-139)

Hamner, Earl Jr. (E-791) (E-861)

Hampden, Walter (E-36)

Hample, Stuart (E-575)

Hampshire, Susan (E-639) (E-700) (E-848)

Hampton, Christopher (T-480)

Hampton, John (E-1678)

Hampton, Lionel (E-1682)

Hampton, Orville H (O-619)

Han Productions (O-543)

Hanalis, Blanche (E-1362)

Hanan, Stephen (T-714)

Hance, Wiley F. (E-524) (E-628)

Hanchett, Willis (E-1768) (E-2103)

Hancock, Herbie (G-440) (G-527) (G-570) (G-691) (G-709) (G-710) (G-743) (G-794) (G-942) (G-1080)

Paramount Film Laboratory (O-299)

Paramount Music Dept. (O-80) (O-98)
(O-116) (O-337)

Paramount News Issue # 37 (O-278)

Paramount Set Construction Dept. (O-318)

Paramount Sound Dept. (O-33) (O-42)
(O-191) (O-263) (O-337) (O-356)
(O-408) (O-466) (O-486) (O-506)

Paramount Special Photographic Dept.
(O-375)

Paramount Still Dept. (O-299)

Paramount Studio Laboratory (O-191)

Paramount Technical Depts. (O-471)

Paramount Transparency Dept. (O-209)
(O-227) (O-299) (O-451) (O-471)

Paramount West Coast Laboratory (O-281)

Paravati, Don (E-1821)

Parc Films (O-748)

Parc-Madeleine-Beta Films Productions
(O-624)

Parent, Gail (E-543) (E-592) (E-717)
(E-865) (E-935) (E-1246)

Parent Trap (G-120)

Parichy, Dennis (T-664) (T-684)

Parinello, Bill (E-2157)

Paris Blues (album) (G-119)

Paris Blues (theme) (G-108)

Paris, Bobby (G-361) (G-362) (G-376)
(G-377)

Paris, George (E-1092)

Paris, Jerry (E-374) (E-427) (E-1363)
(E-1713)

Paris Opera Comique & National Theatre
Orch. (G-83)

Parish, Roger (E-730)

Parkening, Christopher (G-864)

Parker, Alan (O-897)

Parker, Art (E-1534) (E-1822)

Parker, Arthur Jeph (O-862) (O-920) /
(E-1501)

Parker, Charlie (G-685)

Parker, Chris (G-142) (G-820) (G-925)

Parker, Col. Tom (G-61)

Parker, Dorothy (O-112) (O-288) / (G-123)

Parker, Edward M. (E-1726)

Parker, Eleanor (O-340) (O-359) (O-435) /
(E-332)

Parker, Fess (E-66)

Parker, G. Ross (E-986)

Parker, James (E-885)

Parker, Jim (E-630) (E-690) (E-1840)

Parker, Larry (E-1665) (E-1825) (E-1989)
(E-2148)

Parker, Max (O-200)

Parker, Ray Jr (G-1120)

Parker, Rod (E-483) (E-835) (E-842)

Parker, Ross (T-241)

Parker, Tim (E-1665) (E-2148)

Parkes, Walter F (O-850)

Parkins, Barbara (E-416)

Parkins, Leroy (G-712)

Parks, Hildy (E-1446) (E-1548) (E-1843)
(E-2012) / (T-658)

Parks, Larry (O-265)

Parks, Peter D (O-970)

Parnell, Jack (E-942) (E-943)

Parr, Terry (E-1060)

Parrish, Robert (O-291) (O-329)

Parrondo, Gil (O-746) (O-766) (O-786)

Parry, Gordon (G-209) (G-398) (G-448)
(G-536) (G-580) (G-627) (G-673)
(G-770)

Parry, Les (E-896)

Parsons, Alan (G-634) (G-729) (G-779)
(G-915) (G-916) (G-961) (G-973)
(G-1094) (G-1157)

Parsons, Estelle (O-680) (O-701) / (T-440)
(T-473) (T-610)

Parsons, Gram (G-1126)

Parsons, Wayne (E-1593)

Partee, Mayo (E-1302)

Parton, Dolly (O-944) / (E-1354) / (G-472)
(G-513) (G-515) (G-555) (G-557)
(G-560) (G-604) (G-652) (G-698)
(G-746) (G-797) (G-837) (G-851)
(G-887) (G-1047) (G-1062) (G-1066)
(G-1078) (G-1124)

Partos, Frank (O-306)

Partridge Family, The (G-497)

Parts, Dean (G-696)

*Party With Betty Comden and Adolph Green,
A* (album) (G-48)

Partyka, John (E-2156)

Pasetta, Marty (E-928) (E-1221) (E-1254)
(E-1715) (E-1864) (E-2034)

Pass, Joe (G-686)

Pass That Peace Pipe (O-293)

Passas, Peter S. (E-1594)

Passport to Nowhere (O-296)

Password (E-325) (E-844) (E-968)

Password Plus (E-1911)

Pastic, George (O-830)

Pastoria, Andre (T-726)

Pastorius, Jaco (G-784) (G-785) (G-834)

Pat Garrett & Billy the Kid (G-662)

Pat Metheny Group (G-1144)

Patapoff, Al (E-2063)

Patches (G-511)

Patchett, Thomas M. (edit) (E-1175)

Patchett, Tom (wri) (E-865) (E-935)
(E-1213) (E-2009) (E-2032) (E-2037)

Patchke Productions (O-692)

Patel, Ishu (O-887)

Paterson, Neil (O-518)

Paterson Project, The (E-1995)

Patinkin, Mandy (T-654)

Patrick, George (E-163)

Patrick, Jack (O-270)

Patrick, James (G-971)

Patrick, John (T-130) / (P-1954)

Patriot, The (O-11)

Patrono, Carmelo (O-805)

Patterson, Alfred Nash (G-266) (G-359)

Patterson, James (E-1985) / (T-422)

Patterson, Kenneth (E-1653) (E-1893)
(E-2067) (E-2068)

Patterson, Sam (E-2161)

Patti, Sandi (G-1129)

Pattillo, Alan (E-1586)

Patton (O-737) (O-754)

Patzak, Julius (G-1044)

Paul, Alan (G-1028)

Paul, Billy (G-599)

Paul Bunyan (O-507)

Paul, Byron (E-466) (E-1215)

Paul, Charles (E-1615) (E-1768) (E-1927)
(E-2103)

Paul, Dave (E-1821)

Paul, Edward (O-238)

Paul Jacobs and the Nuclear Gang (E-1495)

Paul, Les (G-800) (G-881) (G-926)

Paul, M.B. (O-337)

Paul Robeson: Tribute To An Artist (O-927)

Paul, Sam (E-1693) (E-1842)

Paul, Stanley M. (E-1739)

Paul, Terry (G-544)

Paull, Lawrence G (O-980)

Paulos, Talley (E-1739)

Paulsen, Albert (E-365)

Paulsen, Bill (E-2065)

Paulsen, Pat (E-558)

Paunetto, Bobby (G-754)

Pavan, Marisa (O-437)

Pavarotti, Luciano (E-1651) (E-1696)
(E-2014) (E-2031) / (G-871) (G-924)
(G-982) (G-1096) (G-1103)

Pavarotti In Philadelphia: La Boheme
(E-2014)

Pavoncello (E-619)

Paw (O-523)

Pawlak, Chester (E-1081) (E-1322)

Paxinou, Katina (O-214)

Paxton, Gary S. (G-608) (G-802) (G-846)

Paxton, Glenn (E-1630)

Paxton, John (O-288)

Paycheck, Johnny (G-556) (G-888)

Payne, Ed (E-743) (E-1822)

Payne, Freda (G-550)

Payne, James (O-601) (O-664) (O-805)

Payne, Philip W. (G-1092)

Payne, Robert (E-1598)

Payne, Russ (G-729)

Payton-Wright, Pamela (E-1127)